CANADIAN
GLOBAL
ALMANAC
2002

WINTER AIR MASSES AND CIRCULATION

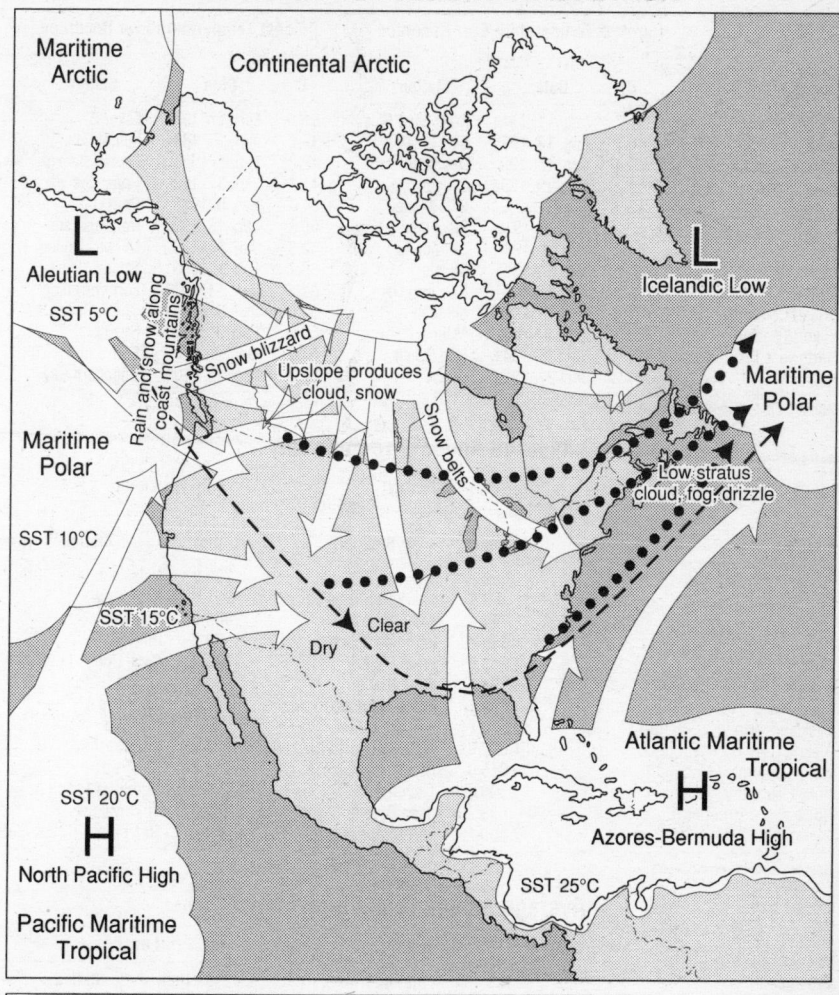

- – – – Polar jet stream
- •••• Primary storm tracks
- SST Sea Surface Temperature

Continental Arctic: very cold, dry, stable
Maritime Arctic: very unstable, clouds, frequent showers or flurries
Maritime Polar: milder, more stable than Arctic air
Pacific Maritime Tropical: stable in lower 1000m
Atlantic Maritime Tropical: warm and humid

Provincial Weather Facts

	Warmest Temperature Ever Recorded			Coldest Temperature Ever Recorded		
Province	°C	Date	Station	°C	Date	Station
Newfoundland	41.7	Aug. 11, 1914	Northwest River	-51.1	Feb. 17, 1973	Esker 2
P.E.I.	36.7	Aug. 19, 1935	Charlottetown	-37.2	Jan. 26, 1884	Kilmahumaig
New Brunswick	39.4	Aug. 18, 1935	Nepisiguit Falls	-47.2	Feb. 1, 1955	Sisson Dam
Nova Scotia	38.3	Aug. 19, 1935	Collegeville	-41.1	Jan. 31, 1920	Upper Stewiacke
Quebec	40.0	July 6, 1921	Ville Marie	-54.4	Feb. 5, 1923	Doucet
Ontario	42.2	July 20, 1919	Biscotasing	-58.3	Jan. 23, 1935	Iroquois Falls
Manitoba	44.4	July 11, 1936	St. Albans	-52.8	Jan. 9, 1899	Norway House
Saskatchewan	45.0	July 5, 1937	Midale	-56.7	Feb. 1, 1893	Prince Albert
Alberta	43.3	July 21, 1931	Bassano Dam	-61.1	Jan. 11, 1911	Fort Vermilion
British Columbia	44.4	July 16, 1941	Lillooet	-58.9	Jan. 31, 1947	Smith River
Yukon Territory	36.1	June 14, 1969	Mayo	-63.0	Feb. 3, 1947	Snag
Northwest Territories	39.4	July 18, 1941	Fort Smith	-57.2	Dec. 26, 1917	Fort Smith
Nunavut	33.9	July 22, 1973	Arviat	-57.8	Feb. 13, 1973	Shepherd Bay

Source: *Environment Canada*

Average Annual Precipitation

	Greatest		Least	
Province	mm	Station	mm	Station
Newfoundland	1 699.7	Burgeo	739.8	Nain
Prince Edward Island	1 169.4	Charlottetown A	921.0	Montague
New Brunswick	1 444.4	Saint John A	909.6	Upsalquitch Lake
Nova Scotia	1 630.7	Ingonish Beach	973.7	Pugwash
Quebec	1 559.8	Mont Logan	295.9	Cape Hopes Advance
Ontario	1 191.1	West Guilford	569.0	Kenora TCPL
Manitoba	696.1	Peace Gardens	402.3	Churchill A
Saskatchewan	530.1	Brabant Lake	287.9	Nashlyn
Alberta	1 072.0	Waterton Park HQ	270.8	Empress
British Columbia	6 655.0	Henderson Lake	205.6	Ashcroft
Yukon Territory	590.6	Tuchitua	135.9	Komakuk Beach A
Northwest Territories	663.2	Cape Dyer A	137.6	Tuktoyaktuk
Nunavut	355.1	Fort Simpson	61.0	Rea Point

Source: *Environment Canada*

Average Annual Bright Sunshine

	Greatest		Least	
Province	Hrs	Station	Hrs	Station
Newfoundland	1 572	Churchill Falls A	1 303	St. Shotts
Prince Edward Island	1 967	Tignish	1 817	East Baltic
New Brunswick	2 010	Chatham A	1 373	Summit Depot
Nova Scotia	1 969	Shearwater A	1 449	Sable Island
Quebec	2 054	Montreal Int'l. A	1 158	Mont Logan
Ontario	2 203	Thunder Bay A	1 635	New Liskeard
Manitoba	2 460	Delta U	1 828	Churchill A
Saskatchewan	2 537	Estevan A	2 073	Cree Lake
Alberta	2 490	Coronation A	1 724	Banff
British Columbia	2 244	Cranbrook A	949	Stewart A
Yukon Territory	1 844	Whitehorse A	1 789	Watson Lake A
Northwest Territories	2 277	Yellowknife A	1 899	Inuvik
Nunavut	2 091	Eureka	1 443	Mould Bay A

Source: *Environment Canada*

Average Annual Snowfall

	Greatest		Least	
Province	**cm**	**Station**	**cm**	**Station**
Newfoundland	322.8	Woody Point	91.6	St. Shotts
Prince Edward Island	330.6	Charlottetown A	173.3	Montague
New Brunswick	448.8	Dawson Settlement	176.2	Southwest Head
Nova Scotia	406.7	Cheticamp	104.1	Baccaro
Quebec	648.4	Mont Logan	161.6	Havre aux Maisons
Ontario	430.0	Searchmount	74.0	Lakeview MOE
Manitoba	332.7	Island Lake	94.9	Lundar
Saskatchewan	348.6	Collins Bay	58.0	Aylesbury
Alberta	642.9	Columbia Icefield	59.9	Empress
British Columbia	1 433.0	Glacier NP Mt. Fidelity	20.4	Carnation Creek
Yukon Territory	365.7	Keno Hill	60.1	Komakuk Beach A
Northwest Territories	234.5	Fort McPherson	65.2	Tuktoyaktuk
Nunavut	602.4	Cape Dyer A	28.6	Rea Point

Source: *Environment Canada*

	Highest Average Annual Wind Speed			Highest % of Calms	
Province	**km/hr**		**Station**	**%**	**Station**
Newfoundland	28.0	(W)	Bonavista	17.1	Wabush Lake A
Prince Edward Island	22.4	(SSW)	Summerside A	4.4	Summerside A
New Brunswick	22.4	(W)	Miscou Island (AUT)	11.8	Fredericton A
Nova Scotia	25.7	(W)	Sable Island	16.9	Greenwood A
Quebec	32.0	(NW)	Grindstone Island	20.4	Gaspé A
Ontario	21.0	(SW)	Bruce Ontario Hydro	30.2	White River
Manitoba	22.7	(WNW)	Churchill A	21.0	Norway House A
Saskatchewan	22.9	(W)	Swift Current A	12.8	La Ronge A
Alberta	21.5	(W)	Pincher Creek	39.7	High Level A
British Columbia	33.7	(NW)	Cape St. James	48.5	Quesnel A
Yukon Territory	14.1	(SSE)	Whitehorse A	57.5	Dawson A
Northwest Territories	19.9	(E)	Nicholson Peninsula	18.9	Fort Simpson
Nunavut	35.3	(NW)	Resolution Island	35.1	Eureka

Source: *Environment Canada*

"Coldest Days" (Wind Chill)

Province	**ET/WCF[1]**	**Location**	**Date**	**Temp (°C)**	**Wind (km/hr)**
Newfoundland	-71/2814	Wabush Lake	Jan. 20, 1975	-41	40
Prince Edward Island	-57/2450	Charlottetown	Jan. 18, 1982	-32	37
Nova Scotia	-53/2309	Sydney	Jan. 18, 1982	-25	59
New Brunswick	-61/2547	Charlo	Jan. 18, 1982	-31	54
Quebec	-77/3001	Nitchequon	Jan. 20, 1975	-42	56
Ontario	-70/2753	Thunder Bay	Jan. 10, 1982	-36	54
Manitoba	-76/2938	Churchill	Jan. 18, 1975	-41	56
Saskatchewan	-70/2757	Swift Current	Dec. 15, 1964	-34	89
Alberta	-68/2740	Red Deer	Dec. 15, 1964	-35	61
British Columbia	-69/2749	Old Glory Mtn.	Dec. 15, 1964	-36	58
Yukon Territory	-83/3152	Komakuk Beach	Feb. 12, 1975	-50	40
NWT/Nunavut	-92/3357	Pelly Bay	Jan. 13, 1975	-51	56

Source: *Environment Canada*

(1) ET is equivalent wind chill temperature in °C. WCF is wind chill factor in watts/square metre

Weather Summaries for 2000–2001

JULY 2000: Around suppertime on July 14, a powerful F3 tornado with spinning winds of 330 km/h slammed into the Green Acres campground at Pine Lake, Alberta, 60 km southeast of Red Deer. 12 people died and 140 were injured. Damage estimates were around $13 million.

On July 3, a huge downpour flooded the community of Vanguard, SK, southeast of Swift Current. More than 375 mm of rain—a year's worth—fell in less than six hours, one of the largest rainfall intensities ever recorded in Canada, drowning field crops and flooding roads and rail-lines. The thunderstorm produced more cloud-to-ground lightning strikes than that part of southern Saskatchewan would expect in two years.

Day-long torrential rains lashed parts of Ontario on numerous occasions, washing out roads, filling underpasses, cutting power and flooding basements. Heavy rainfalls might have hurt water quality: authorities tending to the Walkerton E. coli outbreak have suggested that heavy rains flushing cattle manure into the town's water supply might have been a factor. A rainstorm in Muskoka on July 31 dumped rain in excess of 150 mm over four to five hours. Southern Manitoba also had a few gully washers. The biggest deluge occurred on July 7, when a torrential downpour dumped a month's worth of rain, between 75 and 110 mm, in a few hours.

AUGUST 2000: The story was a summer that wasn't very hot. The Great Lakes/St. Lawrence had the most unseasonable temperatures in the country, about 0.5°C cooler than normal. Torrid days with maximum temperatures above 30°C generally numbered one or two, none in Hamilton and London—not the typical 10 or 12.

Nationally, it was the third wettest summer on record in 53 years—13% more precipitation than normal. In Montreal, between June 1 and October 31, it rained 19 out of 22 weekend days, including every long weekend. London had its wettest summer in 60 years. Business at marinas in the Great Lakes was down 25%, and park visitations in Quebec were off as much as 20%.

The wet conditions created an ideal breeding ground for insects and diseases like stem rot and blight on the farms. Virtually every major crop was affected by some type of virus, bacteria or fungi. In southern Quebec, sunshine between May and August totaled 1,000 hours, compared to the normal of 1,173. Grain corn producers in Ontario and Quebec reported production was 15% less than 1999. Ranchers and farmers in southern Alberta faced some of the driest weather in memory. At Lethbridge, a meager 68 mm fell between May and August, instead of over 200 mm of rain.

SEPTEMBER 2000: By Labour Day, forest fire managers knew they had just gone through the quietest season on record. Tinderbox conditions forced an early ban on campfires, but steady rains, cool temperatures and minimal lightning combined to produce very few fires.

Water levels on the upper Great Lakes continued to decline in 2000. Lakes Michigan-Huron were 1 m lower than three years ago and the lowest since 1964. Superior was at its lowest level since 1925. Lakes Erie and Ontario experienced a reprieve in their declines; however, scanty rains in September dropped year-end levels close to their low marks of a year ago.

On the last day of summer, parts of British Columbia and Alberta received their first snowfall of the season.

OCTOBER 2000: October began with record-low temperatures in the four western provinces. On the 6th, a low of -8.8°C in Winnipeg broke the previous record set in 1896; and the next day Regina's -13.1° was the city's new low previously set in 1884. One of the earliest snowstorms ever dumped 24 cm of snow on Yellowknife. In nearby Fort Providence, winds gusting up to 55 km/h from the northwest produced a tidal effect on the Mackenzie River. Ferry service was cancelled due to low water levels.

An active hurricane season in the Atlantic Ocean brought 14 named storms; eight of them became hurricanes; and three of those were major. Hurricane Michael tore into southern Newfoundland late on October 19 packing strong winds with gusts of 172 km/h at St. Lawrence, NF. Ten days later a huge snowstorm hit eastern Quebec and the Atlantic provinces. Some areas of Gaspe, PQ got more than 40 cm of snow, an October record for any Quebec station. A late-October storm battered Prince Edward Island, coastal New Brunswick and Newfoundland.

NOVEMBER 2000: Just before Halloween, the longest spell of dreary weather and sunless skies that residents of Atlantic Canada could ever remember began. St. John's, Charlotte-town, Sydney and Greenwood all set records for continuously overcast skies, between 400 and 500 hours, after a low-pressure system anchored south of Nova Scotia refused to budge. On Cape Breton Island, 19 days of rain, totalling nearly 400 mm, waterlogged residents and washed roads out. Flood damage exceeded $3 million.

On November 2, residents of southeastern Saskatchewan dug out from more than 65 cm of heavy, wet snow. The same storm and another system from Colorado a couple of days later dropped record rains totalling between 100 and 250 mm in southern Manitoba. Five municipalities in southeastern Manitoba declared local states of emergency.

On the 20th, residents of Fort Erie, ON tried to cope with 43 cm of local lake-effect snow that fell on the town. About that time, a record snowfall of 47.5 cm falling over four days closed Sudbury.

DECEMBER 2000: During the first week of December, cold Arctic air spread across western and central Canada bringing Alberta its coldest temperatures in about three years. In Northern Manitoba, the bitter cold combined with strong winds to produce a ferocious blizzard and wind chills below -70°C. With the sudden onslaught of winter, residents, cranked up their thermostats, consuming 50% more energy than the same time last year.

A mammoth storm struck Ontario and Quebec on December 11–12, dumping between 20 and 50 cm of snow. Two days later, a second storm left residents digging out from knee-deep drifts. From Windsor to Quebec City, schools, shops and services closed. In Sarnia, 60 cm with monstrous drifts caused the roof of a store to collapse, killing an employee. The storm continued eastward bringing heavy snows to northern New Brunswick and copious rains and strong winds to the rest of the Maritimes. At the other side of Canada, winter's clutches had reached British Columbia by mid-December. Up to 15 cm of snow blanketed some Vancouver suburbs and gale-force winds knocked down power lines in the Lower Mainland and on southern Vancouver Island. Hydro customers in Quebec also lost power when, on December 18, an intense winter storm packing hurricane-force winds tracked across the St. Lawrence River and the Saguenay and Lac St. Jean regions.

By the end of December, there was abundant snow on the ground from southern Saskatchewan to Newfoundland. Total snowfall records were set in many Ontario communities, including Waterloo (74.7 cm), Toronto (76.2 cm), Windsor (89.0 cm)—the most of any month, Sarnia (110.4 cm) and Mount Forest (143.6 cm).

JANUARY 2001: Across the west and north-west, temperatures were much warmer and precipitation much drier than normal in January. Snowpacks in southern BC were at or below their lowest levels in about 15 years, raising concerns about potential energy shortages, drought and forest fires beginning in the spring. In Yukon, unseasonably mild temperatures kept waterways open, spelling trouble for February's Yukon Quest sled dog race between Whitehorse and Fairbanks.

At Edmonton, it was the warmest January in over 100 years of records with the average temperature -2.7°, nearly 10 degrees warmer than normal. The city also set a record for the least amount of snowfall with less than 1 cm. The Alberta capital got more rain (1.8 mm) than snow. Residents of Saskatoon experi-enced their second warmest and second driest January in over 100 years.

Winter struck Atlantic Canada hard and often. Charlottetown received a total of 43 cm of snow during a storm on the 6th and 7th. The same storm dropped 53 cm of snow on Moncton. Another storm dumped a record 47.5 cm of snow in Halifax on the 21st. By the end of January, residents of St. John's had to deal with a snowfall total to date of over 3½ metres.

FEBRUARY 2001: Winter continued to pummel the Atlantic Provinces. On the 6th, a storm raked the region with strong winds and heavy snowfalls. Charlo, NB received 49 cm of snow. Another fierce storm pounded the area less than a week later.

In Ontario, generally warmer-than-normal conditions prevailed, despite temperature swings. Early in the month, residents of southwestern Ontario experienced temperatures around 12°C with a thunderstorm. However, just before the spring-like weather, they had a storm with 30 to 40 cm of snow falling in some places. In the Toronto area, tens of thousands of commuters were delayed as the storm hit just before morning rush hour. In Sudbury and Sault Ste. Marie, streets were slick and sidewalks impossible to navigate. The two cities were shut down and highways closed. The storm moved into Quebec, where traffic accidents took the lives of six people. Strong winds gusting as high as 120 km/h left 300,000 Quebecers without power. The storm also shut down Winterlude in Ottawa, when peak winds hit 85 km/h and windchills dipped to -21°C.

Below-normal temperatures and precipitation amounts were recorded throughout the Prairies. From November to February, Vancouver recorded 373 mm of precipitation, the lowest total for that period since 1976–77, and the second lowest since 1938 when records were first kept.

MARCH 2001: In southern Alberta, a shortage of rain and snow and a snowpack 30% below normal, combined with warmer-than-normal temperatures, forced officials to declare the opening of the fire season a month earlier than normal. Farmers faced another year of drought. Winter precipitation in most of Alberta was less than 40% of normal, breaking dryness records set in the 1930s.

Toronto set a record for consecutive number of days with a measurable snow cover—103 days from December 6 to March 18. Winter enthusiasts were ecstatic about the snow and ice conditions.

On March 22, a snowstorm brought traffic woes to southern Quebec when 20+ cm of snow fell. Several highways were closed. In the Trois-Rivières region the storm caused power blackouts, school closings and hundreds of traffic accidents.

On March 10 yet another storm dumped between 30 to 60 cm of snow on southern New Brunswick. Winds blowing between 60 and 70 km/h whipped up monster drifts. On March 31, New Brunswickers woke up to another fresh layer of snow between 20 and 30 cm. Moncton was the hardest hit (28 cm). Atlantic Canada had just over double the normal amount of snow on the ground for this time of the year.

APRIL 2001: On April 2–3, a spring blizzard paralyzed Cape Breton Island. Drifts of snow were so high and heavy that snowploughs got stuck. The storm continued into Newfoundland, dropping snowfall amounts of 20 to 40 cm across the Island. The fierce storm hit the same day a massive public-service strike started, which kept most snowplow drivers off the road. Many of the province's roads and highways were blocked for days, which led to food and fuel shortages in many small communities. On April 7, St. John's made history. By the end of the day, the city airport had recorded a seasonal snowfall total of 602.8 cm, breaking a record that had stood since the winter of 1881–82. In the Rockies, abundant spring snows were a godsend for ski resorts looking to extend the ski season and make up for a poor winter.

Particles of dust from Mongolia and western China began blowing across the lower Mainland of BC and into the interior on the Easter weekend. Winds transported the dust cloud 15,000 km after it was whipped up in a storm on the Gobi Desert during the first week of April.

On the 18th, winter's last gasp raked parts of the Maritimes with 20 cm of snow. The storm snarled traffic and closed schools throughout southern NB before moving on to PEI and Cape Breton. Fredericton got 10 cm of heavy, wet snow. Sydney, NS got rain, not snow. The city was again waterlogged after a torrential storm dumped 70 mm of rain, leaving roads knee deep in water, sewers backed up, basements flooded, and residents without heat and hot water.

MAY 2001: Summer came early to eastern Canada at least for a day or two. On May 1, the temperature in downtown Montreal soared to 31°C. In Ottawa it was the hottest May 1 on record when temperatures soared to 29.7°C, only a half a degree cooler than the hottest temperature recorded in all of 2000. The heat also brought smog to large portions of Ontario—the earliest on record for the province.

The dry weather continued across central Alberta. The lack of pasture and water forced some ranchers to move their herds or sell them. Water was being rationed in the irrigation districts for the first time during a spring season. Edmonton had just 38 mm of rain in the past seven months, well below anything recorded in the dustbowl 1930s. Drivers on Highway 2 between Red Deer and Calgary faced a rare blackout as the wind whipped topsoil off farmers' fields. The blinding wall of soil caused a 15-car pileup near Carstairs, about 70 km north of Calgary. Two hours later, conditions went from blackout to whiteout as a freak snowstorm pounded Calgary.

The number of forest fires in Saskatchewan this spring was nearly three times normal, owing to one of the driest spring seasons on record. North of Edmonton at Chisholm, AB, a huge forest fire burned out of control, fanned by high winds, high temperatures, low relative humidity and drought conditions.

A low pressure system that stalled south of Nova Scotia on May 14 brought prolonged rain with thundershowers to mainland Nova Scotia and southeastern sections of New Brunswick. Over the course of the event, there was a total recorded rainfall of 98.7 mm at Halifax—the highest daily rainfall recorded since records began in 1871. Moncton got a storm total of 98.2 mm, also a record.

Just as city residents were saying goodbye to the last of the snow from this year's record-breaking winter, a pea soup fog drifted into St. John's for a few days.

JUNE 2001: Firefighters in Alberta got welcome rain in early June, enabling them to extinguish the Chisholm forest fire. For farmers in southern Alberta, the "million dollar" rains came just in time to save the season's crop from total failure. Calgary received more than 100 mm of rain in June compared to a more typical amount of 76.9 mm and Edmonton got more than 85 mm of rain since May 28.

Across Ontario, a stationary cold dome that set up in late May hung over the province for more than a week bringing endless days of cool temperatures, rain and cloudy skies. Once the system moved on, tropical air blanketed the province, giving residents the first long spell of real summer-like weather in two years but also creating bouts of haze and smog. Poor air quality readings prompted smog alerts from Windsor to Timmins.

Around mid-June, temperatures soared above 30°C in the Maritimes. In Fredericton, the mercury climbed to a record 33°C on June 15 and this, combined with the excessive moisture in spring, insured hordes of mosquitoes in the heavily forested areas.

Vancouver and the Lower Mainland got much-needed rain in June—more than 50 mm—but it was not enough to ease water shortages arising from very dry conditions the past eight months.

During June severe thunderstorms caused problems. Lightning killed a teenage girl at a hostel north of Ottawa and injured about a dozen soccer players and bystanders in Montreal. It also damaged an apartment building in Regina. In the Lac-St. Jean region of Quebec, a F3 tornado struck the towns of Saint-Gedeon and Alma on June 19.

Seasonal Temperature and Precipitation in Canada

All figures are based on the thirty-year period 1961 to 1990 inclusive.
Airport station unless * designates city office station.

Station	January Average Temperature (°C) Mid Afternoon	Early Morning	Total Precipitation (mm)	April Average Temperature (°C) Mid Afternoon	Early Morning	Total Precipitation (mm)
Calgary, Alta.	-3.6	-15.7	12.2	10.6	-2.4	25.1
Charlottetown, PEI	-3.4	-12.2	106.3	6.3	-1.8	81.6
Churchill, Man.	-22.9	-30.9	17.3	-5.2	-14.8	22.6
Dawson, Yukon*	-27.1	-34.2	16.5	5.9	-9.7	9.4
Edmonton, Alta.	-8.7	-19.8	22.9	9.9	-2.7	21.8
Fredericton, NB	-4.0	-15.4	93.3	9.4	-1.4	83.4
Halifax, NS	-1.5	-10.3	146.9	8.0	-0.9	124.4
Hamilton, Ont.	-2.6	-10.0	61.3	11.3	1.2	74.3
Iqaluit, NT	-21.7	-30.0	21.8	-9.9	-19.6	28.4
Kitchener, Ont.*	-3.3	-11.4	54.3	11.2	0.4	72.6
London, Ont.	-2.8	-10.7	69.0	11.7	0.7	79.2
Moncton, NB	-3.7	-13.9	119.7	7.7	-2.0	100.9
Montreal, Que.	-5.8	-14.9	63.3	10.7	0.6	74.8
Ottawa, Ont.	-6.3	-15.5	58.0	10.8	0.3	69.0
Quebec, Que.	-7.7	-17.3	90.0	7.9	-1.5	75.5
Regina, Sask.	-11.0	-22.1	14.7	10.5	-2.4	20.4
Saint John, NB	-2.8	-13.6	128.3	7.9	-1.5	109.7
St. John's, Nfld	-0.7	-7.9	147.8	4.8	-2.2	110.4
Saskatoon, Sask.	-12.3	-22.9	15.9	10.0	-2.2	25.7
Sault Ste. Marie, Ont. . . .	-5.5	-15.4	74.4	8.5	-2.0	65.2
Toronto, Ont.	-2.5	-11.1	45.6	11.5	0.6	64.0
Vancouver, BC	5.7	0.1	149.8	12.7	4.9	75.4
Victoria, BC	6.5	0.3	141.1	12.9	3.8	41.9
Whitehorse, Yukon	-14.4	-23.2	16.9	5.7	-5.1	8.3
Windsor, Ont.	-1.3	-8.8	50.3	13.4	2.7	80.3
Winnipeg, Man.	-13.2	-23.6	19.3	9.8	-2.3	35.9
Yellowknife, NWT	-23.9	-32.2	14.9	-0.5	-12.0	10.3

▶

Watching the Weather

_C_anada, like most other countries, collects weather data on a daily basis, from stations across the country. To get representative figures, the Meteorological Service of Canada calculates averages for each place and date over a 30-year period; the averages are updated every decade.

Temperatures are measured using a device called a Stevenson screen, mounted 1.5 metres above the ground, which is usually a level, grassy surface. The maximum temperature is the highest recorded in a 24-hour period ending in the morning of the next day. The minimums are for a period of the same length, beginning the evening of the previous day.

Rain, drizzle, freezing rain, freezing drizzle and hail are measured using the standard Canadian rain gauge, a cylindrical container 40 centimetres high and 11.3 centimetres in diameter. The precipitation is funnelled into a plastic graduate cylinder, which is the measuring device. Snowfall is the measured depth of newly fallen snow, measured using a snow ruler.

Station	July Average Temperature (°C) Mid Afternoon	Early Morning	Total Precipitation (mm)	October Average Temperature (°C) Mid Afternoon	Early Morning	Total Precipitation (mm)
Calgary, Alta.	23.2	9.5	69.9	12.6	-1.2	15.5
Charlottetown, PEI	23.1	13.6	81.6	12.1	4.0	111.7
Churchill, Man. ...	16.9	6.8	50.7	1.4	-4.3	46.5
Dawson, Yukon* .	22.8	6.5	33.9	-0.5	-10.4	27.9
Edmonton, Alta. ..	22.5	9.4	101.0	11.3	-2.2	17.7
Fredericton, NB ...	25.6	12.9	84.5	13.1	1.5	93.1
Iqaluit, NT	11.6	3.7	58.2	-2.1	-7.8	42.4
Halifax, NS	23.4	13.2	96.8	13.0	4.0	128.9
Hamilton, Ont.	26.4	15.1	81.0	13.9	4.7	66.3
Kitchener, Ont.* ..	26.1	13.6	90.4	13.2	2.9	70.4
London, Ont.	26.4	14.2	76.7	14.2	3.9	76.4
Moncton, NB	24.4	12.5	102.6	12.7	2.1	106.4
Montreal, Que.	26.2	15.4	85.6	13.0	3.6	75.4
Ottawa, Ont.	26.4	15.1	88.1	12.8	3.0	74.8
Quebec, Que......	24.9	13.2	118.5	11.0	2.0	96.0
Regina, Sask.	26.3	11.9	58.9	11.9	-1.7	20.3
Saint John, NB ...	22.1	11.6	103.7	12.1	2.9	122.5
St. John's, Nfld ...	20.2	10.5	121.2	10.6	3.4	151.7
Saskatoon, Sask. .	25.4	11.7	58.0	11.1	-1.5	16.9
Sault Ste. Marie, Ont.	24.3	11.2	65.6	11.8	2.9	83.2
Toronto, Ont......	26.8	14.2	76.6	14.1	3.6	63.0
Vancouver, BC ...	21.7	12.7	36.1	13.5	6.4	115.3
Victoria, BC	21.8	10.7	17.6	14.1	5.3	74.4
Whitehorse, Yukon	20.3	7.6	39.3	4.3	-3.1	23.0
Windsor, Ont.	27.7	17.0	85.3	15.8	6.0	57.9
Winnipeg, Man. ..	26.1	13.4	72.0	11.3	0.1	29.5
Yellowknife, NWT .	20.8	12.0	35.2	1.3	-4.2	34.8

Source: *Environment Canada*

Preparing for the Worst

*T*he weather outside can be frightening, but if you plan ahead, it needn't be a disaster, according to the Meteorological Service of Canada, which suggests forethought can minimize the danger of weather emergencies.

If there's a severe weather watch, secure or put away loose objects like lawn furniture, listen for weather updates and watch the skies. Make sure everyone concerned knows where to go and what precautions to take. Have a plan: take a few minutes to choose the best shelter within your home or office in case of a severe weather incident like a tornado. (Choose a small interior room or stairwell, ideally with reinforced walls, on the lowest floor.) Beforehand, make up an emergency pack: battery-powered flashlight and radio, tools for emergency repair, food supplies, first aid, blankets and extra clothing.

Also, choose a meeting place where your family can gather after a severe storm, to ensure that you are all safe and accounted for. How does Environment Canada know when to warn you? Satellites and radar will spot the severe weather events, and members of local networks of CANWARN, a volunteer organization of ham radio operators also keep an eye out and report any signs.

For more information, take a look at the "Severe Weather Watcher Handbook" (www.msc-smc.ec.gc.ca/severe_weather).

Spring and Fall Frost Dates in Canada

Frost occurs whenever temperatures fall to 0°C or lower. All frost dates and values are based on the available data during the period 1951-1980.

Growing degree-day data are from the period 1961-90. Data reported from airport stations unless * designates city office station.

	1 in 10 Chance Last Spring Frost After Date	1 in 10 Chance First Fall Frost Before Date	Frost-free Period (days)	Growing Degree-Days Above 5°C[1]
Newfoundland				
Corner Brook*	June 10	Sept. 8	139	1 432
St. John's*	June 24	Sept. 19	131	1 262
Prince Edward Island				
Charlottetown	May 27	Oct. 6	151	1 636
Nova Scotia				
Halifax	May 28	Sept. 30	155	1 707
New Brunswick				
Fredericton	June 10	Sept. 13	126	1 760
Moncton	June 10	Sept. 14	124	1 649
Saint John	June 10	Sept. 18	139	1 499
Quebec				
Chicoutimi*	June 4	Sept. 18	135	1 575
Gaspé*	June 12	Sept. 11	123	1 336
Montreal	May 19	Sept. 26	157	2 079
Quebec	May 28	Sept. 14	137	1 688
Schefferville	June 27	Aug. 22	77	604
Ontario				
Kitchener*	May 25	Sept. 17	151	1 992
London	May 25	Sept. 23	147	2 121
Moosonee*	July 6	July 30	70	1 078
Ottawa	May 25	Sept. 21	147	2 045
St. Catharines*	May 18	Oct. 5	173	2 451
Sudbury	June 11	Sept. 11	128	1 680
Thunder Bay	June 13	Aug. 29	104	1 427
Timmins	June 23	Aug. 19	91	1 395
Toronto	May 25	Sept. 18	149	2 090
Windsor	May 10	Oct. 3	177	2 544
Manitoba				
Brandon	June 9	Aug. 31	108	1 652
Churchill	July 7	Aug. 20	76	562
Flin Flon	June 10	Sept. 2	115	1 379
Winnipeg	June 10	Sept. 11	121	1 802
Saskatchewan				
Prince Albert	June 21	Aug. 17	95	1 455
Regina	June 14	Aug. 27	109	1 723
Saskatoon	June 10	Sept. 1	117	1 658
Alberta				
Banff*	June 30	Aug. 6	89	1 124
Calgary	June 10	Aug. 27	112	1 435
Edmonton	June 14	Aug. 13	105	1 352
Fort McMurray	June 30	Aug. 2	84	1 352
Lethbridge	May 31	Sept. 2	124	1 779
Medicine Hat	May 27	Sept. 8	129	1 971
Peace River	June 23	Aug. 13	93	1 276
British Columbia				
Fort Nelson	June 7	Aug. 14	106	1 289
Kamloops	May 18	Sept. 19	149	2 259
Penticton	May 23	Sept. 14	148	2 163
Prince George	July 1	Aug. 11	85	1 238
Prince Rupert	May 25	Sept. 28	156	1 181
Vancouver	Apr. 21	Oct. 13	216	2 018
Victoria	Apr. 30	Oct. 17	201	1 864

▶

	1 in 10 Chance Last Spring Frost After Date	1 in 10 Chance First Fall Frost Before Date	Frost-free Period (days)	Growing Degree-Days Above 5°C[1]
▶ **Yukon**				
Dawson*	June 16	Aug. 6	91	1 015
Whitehorse	June 24	Aug. 13	82	871
Northwest Territories				
Yellowknife	June 9	Sept. 3	111	1 039
Nunavut				
Alert*	July 15	July 16	4	30
Iqaluit	July 12	July 26	59	177
Resolute	July 15	July 16	9	29

Source: *Environment Canada*
(1) Growing degree days represent the average total number of heat units (daily mean temp. -5°C) during the growing season

Plant Hardiness Zones in Canada

A plant's hardiness rating is related to its ability to survive in specific climate conditions. Plant hardiness zones were originally based on average minimum winter temperatures in a location, and first developed by the US Department of Agriculture (USDA).

The USDA created 11 zones, each of which have since been split into subzones a and b. Canada's Department of Agriculture and Agri-Food took the concept of hardiness further by including other factors besides minimum temperature in designating Canada's plant hardiness zones. They created a weighted equation that took into account such factors as the average minimum temperature of the coldest month; the average length of the frost-free period; average rainfall between June and November; the average maximum temperature in the hottest month; the amount of snow; and the maximum windspeeds in the last 30 years in any given area.

Canada's zones range from 0a in our coldest regions to 9a in our most temperate locations, and the minimum temperature equivalents are shown below. Canadian gardeners may find themselves in micro-climates that differ from the conditions the zone map indicates; however most should choose perennials based on the zone the garden is in and the hardiness rating of the plant. (A plant can survive in the zone it's rated for or a higher/warmer one.)

To find out what zone you're in, consult a local nursery or visit the map at http://res.agr.ca/CANSIS/SYSTEMS/online_maps.html

Hardiness Zone	Average Minimum Temperature (°C)
0a - 0b	-46 or colder
1a - 1b	-46 to -37
2a - 2b	-37 to -29
3a - 3b	-29 to -23
4a - 4b	-23 to -20

Hardiness Zone	Average Minimum Temperature (°C)
5a - 5b	-20 to -15
6a - 6b	-15 to -12
7a - 7b	-12 to -6
8a - 8b	-6 to -1
9a	-1 to 4 or warmer

Source: *Agriculture and Agri-Food Canada*

Historic Experimental Farm

The Central Experimental Farm, established in 1886 as the first of five experimental farms across Canada, was designated a National Historic Site more than 100 years later, in 1998. The farm, located in Ottawa, was called "a cultural landscape of national, historic and architectural significance" by the Historic Sites and Monuments Board of Canada.

Originally occupying 188 hectares, the Central Experimental Farm today covers more than 400 hectares in the middle of Ottawa and 28 of its buildings have been designated as heritage buildings. The farm includes administration areas, labs and model farm buildings; ornamental gardens; and experimental fields. The farm also houses the headquarters of Agriculture and Agri-Food Canada, the Canada Agriculture Museum, the Dominion Arboretum, the Fletcher Wildlife Garden, and the Tropical Greenhouse, which features more than 500 tropical plants. There is also a non-profit organization—Friends of the Farm—dedicated to the preservation, protection and enhancement of the Central Experimental Farm.

PROVINCES AND TERRITORIES

Latitude, Longitude, Elevation of Canadian Cities

City	Lat. N °	'	Long.W °	'	Elev. (m)	City	Lat. N °	'	Long.W °	'	Elev. (m)
Alert, NT*	82	30	62	22	31	Moose Jaw, Sask.	50	23	105	32	544
Brandon, Man.	49	51	99	57	409	Niagara Falls, Ont.	43	06	79	03	180
Brantford, Ont.	43	08	80	15	215	North Bay, Ont.	46	18	79	27	204
Burlington, Ont.	43	19	79	47	87	Ottawa, Ont.	45	26	75	41	56
Calgary, Alta.	51	02	114	03	1 045	Peterborough, Ont.	44	18	78	19	205
Charlottetown, PEI	46	14	63	07	9	Prince Rupert, BC	54	19	130	19	38
Churchill, Man.	58	45	94	10	29	Quebec, Que.	46	48	71	12	50
Dartmouth, NS	44	39	63	34	7	Regina, Sask.	50	27	104	36	577
Dawson, Yukon	64	03	139	26	369	Saint John, NB	45	16	66	03	8
Edmonton, Alta.	53	32	113	29	666	St. John's, Nfld	47	34	52	43	61
Fredericton, NB	45	57	66	38	9	Saskatoon, Sask.	52	07	106	39	484
Guelph, Ont.	43	32	80	14	325	Sault Ste. Marie, Ont.	46	30	84	20	180
Halifax, NS	44	38	63	34	18	Sherbrooke, Que.	45	24	71	53	191
Hamilton, Ont.	43	15	79	52	100	Sudbury, Ont.	46	29	80	59	347
Hull, Que.	45	25	75	42	56	Sydney, NS	46	08	60	11	62
Iqaluit, NT*	63	45	68	31	34	Thunder Bay, Ont.	48	22	89	14	188
Kingston, Ont.	44	13	76	28	80	Toronto, Ont.	43	39	79	23	91
Kitchener, Ont.	43	26	80	29	335	Trois-Rivières, Que.	46	21	72	33	35
LaSalle, Que.	45	25	73	39	34	Vancouver, BC	49	18	123	04	43
Laval, Que.	45	33	73	44	43	Victoria, BC	48	25	123	21	17
Lethbridge, Alta.	49	41	112	49	910	Whitehorse, Yukon	60	43	135	03	703
London, Ont.	42	59	81	14	251	Winnipeg, Man.	49	53	97	08	232
Moncton, NB	46	05	64	46	12	Yellowknife, NWT	62	28	114	22	205
Montreal, Que.	45	30	73	33	27						

Source: *Natural Resources Canada*   *Nunavut*

Area[1] of Canadian Provinces and Territories

(sq. km)

	Land	Water	Total	% of Total Area of Canada
Newfoundland and Labrador	373 872	31 340	405 212	4.06
Prince Edward Island	5 660	—	5 660	0.06
Nova Scotia	53 338	1 946	55 284	0.55
New Brunswick	71 450	1 458	72 908	0.73
Quebec	1 365 128	176 928	1 542 056	15.44
Ontario	917 741	158 654	1 076 395	10.78
Manitoba	553 556	94 241	647 797	6.49
Saskatchewan	591 670	59 366	651 036	6.52
Alberta	642 317	19 531	661 848	6.63
British Columbia	925 186	19 549	944 735	9.46
Yukon Territory	474 391	8 052	482 443	4.83
Northwest Territories	1 183 085	163 021	1 346 106	13.48
Nunavut	1 936 113	157 077	2 093 190	20.96
Canada	**9 093 507**	**891 163**	**9 984 670**	**100.00**

Source: *Natural Resources Canada*

(1) Calculated from the National Atlas of Canada 1:1000000 scale hydrology base. (—) = zero

Newfoundland

□ **CAPITAL:** St. John's, metro pop. (2000) 175 062. **Date entered Confederation:** Mar. 31, 1949.

□ **POPULATION (2000): 539 000**; Pop. density: 1.4 per sq. km.; **Pop. growth (1996–2000): -3.9%; Pop.** Urban (1996): 56.9%; **Official Languages** (1996): 96% English; 3.9% bilingual. **Net interprovincial migration** (2000): -3 534.

□ **VITAL STATISTICS:** Rates (per 1 000 pop., 1999-2000): **Birth:** 8.8; **Death:** 8.5; **Life expectancy at birth** (1996): male: 75; female: 81.

□ **GEOGRAPHY: Total area** 405 212 sq. km; **Land area** 373 872 sq. km; **Forested land** 142 000 sq. km; **Length of coastline** 23 232 km. **Climate:** ranges from subarctic in Labrador and northern tip of island to humid continental with cool summers and heavy precipitation. **Topography:** Island of Newfoundland: highlands of the Long Range Mtns. (elev. 900 m) along w. coast; barren and rocky central plateau descends to lowlands towards the n. east; coast is deeply indented with bays and fjords. Labrador: mountainous in the n.; rugged coast and interior plateau.

□ **ECONOMY: Gross Domestic Product** (1999): $12 110 million; **% change GDP** (1998–99): 7.8%; **Per capita GDP** (1999): $22 384. **Employment distrib.** (2000): goods-producing industries (agriculture, primary ind., mfg, construction) 22%; service-producing industries (transpt., trade, finance, service, pub. admin, unclassified) 78%. **Unemployment rate** (2000): 16.7%. **Principal industries:** mining, manufacturing, fishing, logging and forestry, electricity production, tourism.

□ **EDUCATION (1998–99): No. of schools:** 372 elem. and sec.; 3 post-sec. **Enrolment:** 98 129 elem. and sec.; 19 088 post-sec.

□ **INTERNATIONAL AIRPORTS:** Gander.

□ **NATIONAL PARKS:** Gros Morne, Terra Nova.

□ **PROVINCIAL DATA: Motto:** *Quaerite Prime Regnum Dei:* "Seek Ye First the Kingdom of God." **Flower:** Pitcher plant. **Bird:** Atlantic Puffin (unofficial). **Anthem:** Ode to Newfoundland. **Tartan:** Newfoundland Tartan.

□ **POLITICS: Premier:** Roger Grimes (Lib.). **Leaders, opposition parties:** Jack Harris (NDP), Danny Williams (Prog. Cons.). **Date of last general election:** Feb. 9, 1999. **Lt. Governor:** Hon. A.M. House.

Prince Edward Island

□ **CAPITAL:** Charlottetown, metro pop. (2000) 33 636. **Date entered Confederation:** July 1, 1873.

□ **POPULATION (2000): 139 000**; Pop. density: 24.6 per sq. km.; **Pop. growth (1996–2000): 2.2%; Pop.** Urban (1996): 44.2%; **Official Languages** (1996): 88.9% English; 0.1% French, 11.0% bilingual. **Net interprovincial migration** (2000): 255.

□ **VITAL STATISTICS:** Rates (per 1 000 pop., 1999-2000): **Birth:** 10.7; **Death:** 9.1; **Life expectancy at birth** (1996): male: 74; female: 81.

□ **GEOGRAPHY: Total area** 5 660 sq. km; **Land area** 5 660 sq. km; **Forested land** 3 000 sq. km; **Length of coastline** 1 076 km. **Climate:** humid continental with temperatures moderated by maritime location. **Topography:** flat through gently rolling hills; sharply indented coastline; many streams but only small rivers and lakes.

□ **ECONOMY: Gross Domestic Product** (1999): $2 994 million; **% change GDP** (1998–99): 5.0%; **Per capita GDP** (1999): $21 696. **Employment distrib.** (2000): goods-producing industries (agriculture, primary ind., mfg, construction) 27%; service-producing industries (transpt., trade, finance, service, pub. admin, unclassified) 73%. **Unemployment rate** (2000): 12.0%. **Principal industries:** agriculture, tourism, fishing, manufacturing.

□ **EDUCATION (1998–99): No. of schools:** 71 elem. and sec.; 3 post-sec. **Enrolment:** 24 441 elem. and sec.; 4 369 post-sec.

□ **INTERNATIONAL AIRPORTS:** none.

□ **NATIONAL PARKS:** Prince Edward Island (north shore).

□ **PROVINCIAL DATA: Motto:** *Parva Sub Ingenti:* "The small under the protection of the great." **Flower:** Lady's slipper. **Bird:** Blue Jay. **Tree:** Red Oak.

□ **POLITICS: Premier:** Pat Binns (Prog. Cons.) **Leaders, opposition parties:** Ron MacKinley (Lib.), Dr. H. Dickieson (NDP). **Date of last general election:** April 17, 2000. **Lt. Governor:** Hon. J. Léonce Bernard.

Nova Scotia

☐ **CAPITAL:** Halifax, metro pop. (2000) 355 996. **Date entered Confederation:** July 1, 1867.

☐ **POPULATION (2000):** 941 000; **Pop. density:** 17.6 per sq. km.; **Pop. growth** (1996–2000): 1.1%; **Pop.** Urban (1996): 54.8%; **Official Languages** (1996): 90.4% English; 0.2% French, 9.3% bilingual. **Net interprovincial migration** (2000): -208.

☐ **VITAL STATISTICS: Rates** (per 1 000 pop., 1999-2000): **Birth:** 9.9; **Death:** 9.4; **Life expectancy at birth** (1996): male: 75; female: 81.

☐ **GEOGRAPHY: Total area** 55 284 sq. km; **Land area** 53 338 sq. km; **Forested land** 41,000 sq. km; **Length of coastline** 6 014 km. **Climate:** humid continental with some moderating effects due to maritime location. **Topography:** Atlantic Uplands are segmented by river valleys; Cape Breton Is. rises from lowland in the s. to a high plateau; many rivers, lakes and jagged coastline.

☐ **ECONOMY: Gross Domestic Product** (1999): $22 407 million; **% change GDP** (1998–99): 6.1%; **Per capita GDP** (1999): $23 837. **Employment distrib.** (2000): goods-producing industries (agriculture, primary ind., mfg, construction) 22%; service-producing industries (transpt., trade, finance, service, pub. admin, unclassified) 78%. **Unemployment rate** (2000): 9.1%. **Principal industries:** manufacturing, fishing and trapping, mining, agriculture, pulp and paper.

☐ **EDUCATION (1998–99): No. of schools:** 512 elem. and sec.; 17 post-sec. **Enrolment:** 163 122 elem. and sec.; 37 066 post-sec.

☐ **INTERNATIONAL AIRPORTS:** Halifax

☐ **NATIONAL PARKS:** Cape Breton Highlands, Kejimkujik.

☐ **PROVINCIAL DATA: Motto:** *Munit Haec et Altera Vincit:* "One defends and the other conquers." **Flower:** Mayflower. **Bird:** Osprey. **Tree:** Red Spruce. **Gem:** Agate.

☐ **POLITICS: Premier:** Dr. John Hamm (Prog. Cons.). **Leaders, opposition parties:** Wayne Gaudet (Lib.), Darrel Dexter (NDP). **Date of last general election:** July 27, 1999. **Lt. Governor:** Hon. Myra A. Freeman.

New Brunswick

☐ **CAPITAL:** Fredericton, metro pop. (2000) 47 200. **Date entered Confederation:** July 1, 1867.

☐ **POPULATION (2000):** 756 000; **Pop. density:** 10.6 per sq. km.; **Pop. growth** (1996–2000): 0.4%; **Pop.** Urban (1996): 48.8%; **Official Languages** (1996): 57.3% English; 10.1% French, 32.6% bilingual. **Net interprovincial migration** (2000): 15.

☐ **VITAL STATISTICS: Rates** (per 1 000 pop., 1999-2000): **Birth:** 10.1; **Death:** 9.0; **Life expectancy at birth** (1996): male: 75; female: 81.

☐ **GEOGRAPHY: Total area** 72 908 sq. km; **Land area** 71 450 sq. km; **Forested land** 61,000 sq. km; **Length of coastline** 2 298 km. **Climate:** humid continental climate except along the shores where there is a marked maritime effect. **Topography:** northern upland; rolling central plateau; southern lowland plain with many rivers.

☐ **ECONOMY: Gross Domestic Product** (1999): $18 390 million; **% change GDP** (1998–99): 5.3%; **Per capita GDP** (1999): $24 358. **Employment distrib.** (2000): goods-producing industries (agriculture, primary ind., mfg, construction) 25%; service-producing industries (transpt., trade, finance, service, pub. admin, unclassified) 75%. **Unemployment rate** (2000): 10.0%. **Principal industries:** manufacturing, fishing, mining, forestry, pulp and paper, agriculture.

☐ **EDUCATION (1998–99): No. of schools:** 384 elem. and sec.; 10 post-sec. **Enrolment:** 130 801 elem. and sec.; 23 750 post-sec.

☐ **INTERNATIONAL AIRPORTS:** none.

☐ **NATIONAL PARKS:** Fundy, Kouchibouguac.

☐ **PROVINCIAL DATA: Motto:** *Spem Reduxit:* "Hope was restored." **Flower:** Purple Violet. **Bird:** Black- capped Chickadee. **Tree:** Balsam Fir.

☐ **POLITICS: Premier:** Bernard Lord (Prog. Cons.). **Leaders, opposition parties:** Bernard Richard (Lib.), Elizabeth Weir (NDP). **Date of last general election:** June 7, 1999. **Lt. Governor:** Hon. Marilyn Trenholme Counsell.

Quebec

□ **CAPITAL:** Quebec, metro pop. (2000) 689 654. **Date entered Confederation:** July 1, 1867.

□ **POPULATION (2000): 7 372 000; Pop. density:** 5.4 per sq. km.; **Pop. growth** (1996–2000): 1.3%; **Pop. Urban** (1996): 78.4%; **Official Languages** (1996): 56.1% English; 5.1% French, 37.8% bilingual. **Net interprovincial migration** (2000): -14 724.

□ **VITAL STATISTICS:** **Rates** (per 1 000 pop., 1999-2000): **Birth:** 10.0; **Death:** 7.1; **Life expectancy at birth** (1996): male: 75; female: 81.

□ **GEOGRAPHY: Total area** 1 542 056 sq. km; **Land area** 1 356 128 sq. km; **Forested land** 940 000 sq. km; **Length of coastline** 15 208 km. Climate: varies from subarctic to continental. **Topography:** lowlands along the St. Lawrence R. valley separate the Laurentian Mtns. to the n. and the Appalachian Mtns. to the s.; Canadian Shield landscape dominates north.

□ **ECONOMY: Gross Domestic Product** (1999): $204 062 million; **% change GDP** (1998–99): 5.4%; **Per capita GDP** (1999): $27 782. **Employment distrib.** (2000): goods-producing industries (agriculture, primary ind., mfg, construction) 26%; service-producing industries (transpt., trade, finance, service, pub. admin, unclassified) 74%. **Unemployment rate** (2000): 8.4%. **Principal industries:** manufacturing, electric power, mining, pulp and paper, transportation equipment.

□ **EDUCATION (1998–99): No. of schools:** 3 002 elem. and sec.; 96 post-sec. **Enrolment:** 1 125 066 elem. and sec.; 298 631 post-sec.

□ **INTERNATIONAL AIRPORTS:** Dorval; Mirabel.

□ **NATIONAL PARKS:** Forillon, La Mauricie, Mingan Archipelago, Saguenay-St. Lawrence Marine Park.

□ **PROVINCIAL DATA: Motto:** *Je me souviens:* "I remember." **Flower:** Lys blanc de jardin (White Garden (Madonna) Lily). **Bird:** Harfang des neiges (Snowy Owl).

□ **POLITICS: Premier:** Bernard Landry (Parti Québécois). **Leader, opposition parties:** Jean Charest (Lib.), Mario Dumont (A.D.). **Date of last general election:** Nov. 30, 1998. **Lt. Governor:** Hon. Lise Thibault.

Ontario

□ **CAPITAL:** Toronto, metro pop. (2000) 4 751 408. **Date entered Confederation:** July 1, 1867.

□ **POPULATION (2000): 11 669 000; Pop. density:** 12.7 per sq. km.; **Pop. growth** (1996–2000): 5.1%; **Pop. Urban** (1996): 83.3%; **Official Languages** (1996): 85.7% English; 0.4% French, 11.6% bilingual. **Net interprovincial migration** (2000): 21 940.

□ **VITAL STATISTICS:** **Rates** (per 1 000 pop., 1999-2000): **Birth:** 11.1; **Death:** 7.4; **Life expectancy at birth** (1996): male: 76; female: 81.

□ **GEOGRAPHY: Total area** 1 076 395 sq. km; **Land area** 917 741 sq. km; **Forested land** 807 000 sq. km; **Length of coastline** 1 324 km. Climate: ranges from humid continental in south to subarctic in far north; westerly winds bring winter storms; the Great Lakes moderate winter temperatures. **Topography:** Rugged, rocky Canadian Shield plateau is broken by lowlands around Great Lakes, St. Lawrence R. and Hudson Bay.

□ **ECONOMY: Gross Domestic Product** (1999): $396 775 million; **% change GDP** (1998–99): 6.5%; **Per capita GDP** (1999): $34 460. **Employment distrib.** (2000): goods-producing industries (agriculture, primary ind., mfg, construction) 27%; service-producing industries (transpt., trade, finance, service, pub. admin, unclassified) 73%. **Unemployment rate** (2000): 5.7%. **Principal industries:** manufacturing, construction, agriculture, forestry, mining.

□ **EDUCATION (1998–99): No. of schools:** 5 474 elem. and sec.; 61 post-sec. **Enrolment:** 2 128 642 elem. and sec.; 372 326 post-sec.

□ **INTERNATIONAL AIRPORTS:** Pearson (Toronto); Ottawa.

□ **NATIONAL PARKS:** Bruce Peninsula, Fathom Five Marine Park, Georgian Bay Islands, Point Pelee, Pukaskwa, St. Lawrence Islands.

□ **PROVINCIAL DATA: Motto:** *Ut Incepit Fidelis Sic Permanet:* "Loyal she began, loyal she remains." **Flower:** White trillium. **Bird:** Common Loon. **Tree:** Eastern White Pine. **Gem:** Amethyst.

□ **POLITICS: Premier:** Mike Harris (Prog. Cons.). **Leaders, opposition parties:** Dalton McGinty (Lib.); Howard Hampton (NDP). **Date of last general election:** June 21, 1999. **Lt. Governor:** Hon. Hilary Weston.

Manitoba

☐ **CAPITAL:** Winnipeg, metro pop. (2000) 681 146. **Date entered Confederation:** July 15, 1870.

☐ **POPULATION (2000): 1 148 000; Pop. density:** 2.1 per sq. km.; **Pop. growth** (1996–2000): 1.2%; **Pop.** Urban (1996): 71.8%; **Official Languages** (1996): 89.4% English; 0.1% French, 9.4% bilingual; 1.1% neither English nor French. **Net interprovincial migration** (2000): -2 410.

☐ **VITAL STATISTICS: Rates** (per 1 000 pop., 1999-2000): **Birth:** 12.4; **Death:** 9.0; **Life expectancy at birth** (1996): male: 75; female: 81.

☐ **GEOGRAPHY: Total area** 647 797 sq. km; **Land area** 553 556 sq. km; **Forested land** 349 000 sq. km; **Length of coastline** 990 km. **Climate:** continental with seasonal extremes. **Topography:** the land rises gradually south and west from Hudson Bay; flat plateau through south central region; countless lakes, streams and bogs.

☐ **ECONOMY: Gross Domestic Product** (1999): $30 995 million; **% change GDP** (1998–99): 3.4%; **Per capita GDP** (1999): $27 094. **Employment distrib.** (2000): goods-producing industries (agriculture, primary ind., mfg, construction) 26%; service-producing industries (transpt., trade, finance, service, pub. admin, unclassified) 74%. **Unemployment rate** (2000): 4.9%. **Principal industries:** manufacturing, agriculture, food industry, mining, construction.

☐ **EDUCATION (1998–99): No. of schools:** 858 elem. and sec.; 12 post-sec. **Enrolment:** 223 013 elem. and sec.; 25 064 post-sec.

☐ **INTERNATIONAL AIRPORTS:** Winnipeg.

☐ **NATIONAL PARKS:** Riding Mountain, Wapusk.

☐ **PROVINCIAL DATA: Motto:** Glorious and Free. **Flower:** Prairie Crocus. **Bird:** Great Gray Owl. **Tartan:** Manitoba Tartan.

☐ **POLITICS: Premier:** Gary Doer (NDP). **Leaders, opposition parties:** Suart Murray (Prog. Cons.), Jon Gerrard (Lib.). **Date of last general election:** Sept. 21, 1999. **Lt. Governor:** Hon. Peter M. Liba.

Saskatchewan

☐ **CAPITAL:** Regina, metro pop. (2000) 200 455. **Date entered Confederation:** Sept. 1, 1905.

☐ **POPULATION (2000): 1 023 000; Pop. density:** 1.7 per sq. km.; **Pop. growth** (1996–2000): 0.4%; **Pop.** Urban (1996): 63.3%; **Official Languages** (1996): 94.3% English; 5.2% bilingual; 0.5% neither English nor French. **Net interprovincial migration** (2000): -8 426.

☐ **VITAL STATISTICS: Rates** (per 1 000 pop., 1999-2000): **Birth:** 12.3; **Death:** 9.1; **Life expectancy at birth** (1996): male: 75; female: 82.

☐ **GEOGRAPHY: Total area** 651 036 sq. km; **Land area** 591 670 sq. km; **Forested land** 178 000 sq. km; **Climate:** continental, with cold winters and hot summers. **Topography:** gently rolling plains through south; higher, hilly plateaus in the s.w.; north is rugged Canadian Shield.

☐ **ECONOMY: Gross Domestic Product** (1999): $30 143 million; **% change GDP** (1998–99): 4.6%; **Per capita GDP** (1999): $29 322. **Employment distrib.** (2000): goods-producing industries (agriculture, primary ind., mfg, construction) 28%; service-producing industries (transpt., trade, finance, service, pub. admin, unclassified) 72%. **Unemployment rate** (2000): 5.2%. **Principal industries:** agriculture, mining, manufacturing, electric power, construction, chemical prod.

☐ **EDUCATION (1998–99): No. of schools:** 903 elem. and sec.; 8 post-sec. **Enrolment:** 209 768 elem. and sec.; 26 396 post-sec.

☐ **INTERNATIONAL AIRPORTS:** Saskatoon.

☐ **NATIONAL PARKS:** Grasslands, Prince Albert.

☐ **PROVINCIAL DATA: Motto:** *Multis E Gentibus Vires:* "from many peoples strength". **Flower:** Western Red Lily. **Bird:** Prairie sharp-tailed grouse. **Tree:** White Birch. **Tartan:** Saskatchewan Tartan.

☐ **POLITICS: Premier:** Lorne Calvert (NDP). **Leaders, opposition parties:** Elwin Hermanson (Sask.), Jim Melenchuk (Lib.). **Date of last general election:** Sept. 16, 1999. **Lt. Governor:** Hon. Lynda M. Haverstock.

Alberta

☐ **CAPITAL:** Edmonton, metro pop. (2000) 944 194. **Date entered Confederation:** Sept. 1, 1905.

☐ **POPULATION (2000): 2 997 000; Pop. density:** 4.7 per sq. km.; **Pop. growth** (1996–2000): 7.8%; **Pop.** Urban (1996): 79.5%; **Official Languages** (1996): 91.9% English; 0.1 French; 6.7% bilingual; 1.3% neither English nor French. **Net interprovincial migration** (2000): 21 951.

☐ **VITAL STATISTICS: Rates** (per 1 000 pop., 1999–2000): **Birth:** 12.7; **Death:** 6.1; **Life expectancy at birth** (1996): male: 76; female: 81.

☐ **GEOGRAPHY: Total area** 661 848 sq. km; **Land area** 642 317 sq. km; **Forested land** 349 000 sq. km. **Climate:** great variance in temperatures between regions and seasons; summer highs between 16°C and 32°C; winters as low as -45°C. **Topography:** Rocky Mtns. in s.w. to rolling prairie throughout southern region; far north is a forested plateau.

☐ **ECONOMY: Gross Domestic Product** (1999): $116 990 million; **% change GDP** (1998–99): 10.2%; **Per capita GDP** (1999): $39 457. **Employment distrib.** (2000): goods-producing industries (agriculture, primary ind., mfg, construction) 27%; service-producing industries (transpt., trade, finance, service, pub. admin, unclassified) 73%. **Unemployment rate** (2000): 5.0%. **Principal industries:** chemical products, mining, agriculture, food, manufacturing, construction, oil prod. and refinement.

☐ **EDUCATION (1998–99): No. of schools:** 1 862 elem. and sec.; 29 post-sec. **Enrolment:** 566 361 elem. and sec.; 85 509 post-sec.

☐ **INTERNATIONAL AIRPORTS:** Edmonton; Calgary.

☐ **NATIONAL PARKS:** Banff, Elk Island, Jasper, Waterton Lakes, Wood Buffalo (shared with Northwest Territories).

☐ **PROVINCIAL DATA: Motto:** *Fortis et Liber:* "Strong and free." **Flower:** Wild Rose. **Bird:** Great horned owl. **Tree:** Lodge pole pine. **Tartan:** Alberta Tartan. **Stone:** Petrified wood.

☐ **POLITICS: Premier:** Ralph Klein (Prog. Cons.). **Leaders, opposition parties:** Ken Nicol (Lib.), Raj Pannu (NDP). **Date of last general election:** March 12, 2001. **Lt. Governor:** Hon. Lois E. Hole.

British Columbia

☐ **CAPITAL:** Victoria, metro pop. (2000) 317 492. **Date entered Confederation:** July 20, 1871.

☐ **POPULATION (2000): 4 064 000; Pop. density:** 4.4 per sq. km.; **Pop. growth** (1996–2000): 4.7%; **Pop.** Urban (1996): 82.1%; **Official Languages** (1996): 90.6% English; 6.7% bilingual; 2.6% neither English nor French. **Net interprovincial migration** (2000): -14 123.

☐ **VITAL STATISTICS: Rates** (per 1 000 pop., 1999–2000): **Birth:** 10.3; **Death:** 7.5; **Life expectancy at birth** (1996): male: 76; female: 82.

☐ **GEOGRAPHY: Total area** 944 735 sq. km; **Land area** 925 186 sq. km; **Forested land** 633 000 sq. km; **Length of coastline** 22 898 km. **Climate:** maritime with mild temperatures and abundant rainfall in the coastal areas; continental climate with temperature extremes in the interior and northeast. **Topography:** mostly mountainous; deep river valleys and gorges, except for the n.e. area which is an extension of the Great Plains; indented coast with numerous bays and islands.

☐ **ECONOMY: Gross Domestic Product** (1999): $118 783 million; **% change GDP** (1998–99): 4.2%; **Per capita GDP** (1999): $29 526. **Employment distrib.** (2000): goods-producing industries (agriculture, primary ind., mfg, construction) 21%; service-producing industries (transpt., trade, finance, service, pub. admin, unclassified) 79%. **Unemployment rate** (2000): 7.2%. **Principal industries:** forestry, wood and paper, mining, tourism, agriculture, fishing, manufacturing.

☐ **EDUCATION (1998–99): No. of schools:** 2 080 elem. and sec.; 32 post-sec. **Enrolment:** 675 874 elem. and sec.; 91 166 post-sec.

☐ **INTERNATIONAL AIRPORTS:** Vancouver; Victoria.

☐ **NATIONAL PARKS:** Glacier, Kootenay, Mount Revelstoke, Pacific Rim, Gwaii Haanas (South Moresby), Yoho.

☐ **PROVINCIAL DATA: Motto:** *Splendor Sine Occasu:* "Splendor without Diminishment." **Flower:** Dogwood. **Bird:** Stellar's Jay.

☐ **POLITICS: Premier:** Gordon Campbell (Lib.). **Leader, opposition parties:** Joy MacPhail (NDP). **Date of last general election:** April 18, 2001. **Lt. Governor:** Hon. Iona Campagnolo.

Yukon Territory

☐ **CAPITAL:** Whitehorse, metro pop. (2000) 18 670. **Date entered Confederation:** June 13, 1898.

☐ **POPULATION (2000): 31 000; Pop. density:** 0.1 per sq. km.; **Pop. growth** (1996–2000): -3.1%; **Pop. Urban** (1996): 60.0%; **Official Languages** (1996): 89.2% English; 0.2% French; 10.5% bilingual; 0.2% neither English nor French. **Net interprovincial migration** (2000): -727.

☐ **VITAL STATISTICS: Rates** (per 1 000 pop., 1999-2000): **Birth:** 11.9; **Death:** 5.3; **Life expectancy at birth** (1996): male: 71; female: 84.

☐ **GEOGRAPHY: Total area** 482 443 sq. km; **Land area** 474 391 sq. km; **Forested land** 242 000 sq. km; **Length of coastline** 418 km. **Climate:** great variance in temperatures; warm summers, very cold winters; low precipitation. **Topography:** main feature is the Yukon plateau with 21 peaks exceeding 3 300 m; open tundra in the far north.

☐ **ECONOMY: Gross Domestic Product** (1999): $1 080 million; **% change GDP** (1998–99): -2.5%; **Per capita GDP** (1999): $34 839. **Unemployment rate** (2000): n.a. **Principal industries:** mining, tourism.

☐ **EDUCATION (1998–99): No. of schools:** 28 elem. and sec.; 1 post-sec. **Enrolment:** 6 199 elem. and sec.; 258 post-sec.

☐ **INTERNATIONAL AIRPORTS:** Whitehorse.

☐ **NATIONAL PARKS:** Ivvavik, Kluane, Vuntut.

☐ **PROVINCIAL DATA: Flower:** Fireweed. **Bird:** Common Raven.

☐ **POLITICS: Govt. Leader:** Pat Duncan (Lib). **Leader, opposition party:** Peter Jenkins (Yukon Party), Eric Fairclough (NDP). **Date of last general election:** April 17, 2000. **Commissioner:** Hon. Jack Cable.

Northwest Territories

☐ **CAPITAL:** Yellowknife, metro pop. (2000) 18 990. **Date entered Confederation:** July 15, 1870.

☐ **POPULATION (2000): 42 000; Pop. density:** 0.04 per sq. km.; **Pop. growth** (1996–2000): 0%; **Pop. Urban** (1996): 42.5%; **Official Languages** (1996): 87.1% English; 6.3% bilingual; 6.5% neither English nor French. **Net interprovincial migration** (2000): -113.

☐ **VITAL STATISTICS: Rates** (per 1 000 pop., 1999-2000): **Birth:** 18.2; **Death:** 3.8; **Life expectancy at birth** (1996): male: 70; female: 76.

☐ **GEOGRAPHY: Total area** 1 346 106 sq. km; **Land area** 1 183 085 sq. km; **Forested land** 615 000 sq. km; **Length of coastline** 14 734 km. **Climate:** extreme temperatures and low precipitation; arctic and sub-arctic. **Topography:** mostly tundra plains formed on the rocks of the Canadian Shield; the Mackenzie Lowland is a continuation of the Great Plains; the Mackenzie River Valley is forested.

☐ **ECONOMY: Gross Domestic Product** (1999): $2 167 million; **% change GDP** (1997–98): -1.3%; **Per capita GDP** (1999): $51 595. **Unemployment rate** (2000): n.a. **Principal industries:** construction, utilities, services, tourism.

☐ **EDUCATION (1998–99): No. of schools:** 89 elem. and sec.; 2 post-sec. **Enrolment:** 18 041 elem. and sec.; 269 post-sec.

☐ **INTERNATIONAL AIRPORTS:** none.

☐ **NATIONAL PARKS:** Aulavik, Nahanni, Tuktut Nogait, Wood Buffalo (shared with Alberta).

☐ **PROVINCIAL DATA: Flower:** Mountain Avens. **Bird:** Gyrfalcon. **Tree:** Jack pine.

☐ **POLITICS: Premier:** Stephen Kakfwi. **Date of last general election:** Dec. 6, 1999. **Commissioner:** Hon. Glenna F. Hansen.

Provinces on the Web

Newfoundland: http://www.gov.nf.ca
Prince Edward Island: http://www.gov.pe.ca
Nova Scotia: http://www.gov.ns.ca
New Brunswick: http://www.gov.nb.ca
Quebec: http://www.gouv.qc.ca
Ontario: http://www.gov.on.ca
Manitoba: http://www.gov.mb.ca

Saskatchewan: http://www.gov.sk.ca
Alberta: http://www.gov.ab.ca
British Columbia: http://www.gov.bc.ca
Nunavut: http://www.gov.nu.ca
Northwest Territories: http://www.gov.nt.ca
Yukon Territory: http://www.gov.yk.ca

Nunavut

☐ **CAPITAL:** Iqaluit, metro pop. (2000): 4 867. **Date became territory:** April 1, 1999.

☐ **POPULATION (2000):** 28 000; **Pop. density:** 0.01 per sq. km.; **Pop. growth** (1996–2000): 7.7%; **Pop. Urban** (1996): 25.4%; **Official Languages** (1996): 71.4% Inukitut; 23.6% English; 1.6% French. **Net interprovincial migration** (2000): 104.

☐ **VITAL STATISTICS:** Rates (per 1 000 pop., 1999-2000): **Birth:** 28.5; **Death:** 5.2; **Life expectancy at birth** (1996): male: 70; female: 76.

☐ **GEOGRAPHY: Total area:** 2 093 190 sq. km; **Land area:** 1 936 113 sq. km. **Lenth of costline:** 114 920 km. **Climate:** extreme temperatures and low precipitation; arctic. **Topography:** rocky tundra with stunted vegetation located above the treeline; snow-covered most of the year.

☐ **ECONOMY: Gross Domestic Product** (1999): 731 million; **% change GDP** (1998–99): n.a.%; **Per capita GDP** (1999): 27 074. **Unemployment rate** (1996): 15.4. **Principal industries:** mining, tourism, shrimp and scallop fishing, hunting and trapping, arts and crafts production.

☐ **EDUCATION (1999–2000 est.):** No. of schools: 42 elem. and sec.; 1 post-sec. **Enrolment:** 7 462 elem. and sec.; 167 post-sec.

☐ **INTERNATIONAL AIRPORTS:** Iqaluit Airport.

☐ **NATIONAL PARKS:** Auyuittuq, Quttinirpaaq (Ellesmere Island), Sirmilik.

☐ **PROVINCIAL DATA:** n.a.

☐ **POLITICS: Premier:** Paul Okalik. **Date of last general election:** Feb. 9, 1999. **Commissioner:** Hon. Peter Irniq.

CANADIAN CITIES

A census metropolitan area (CMA) is a very large urban area (known as the urban core) together with adjacent urban and rural areas (known as urban and rural fringes) that have a high degree of social and economic integration with the urban core. A CMA has an urban core population of a least 100 000 based on the previous census. Once an area becomes a CMA, it is retained as a CMA even if the population of its urban core declines below 100 000. All CMAs are subdivided into census tracts. A CMA may be consolidated with adjacent census agglomerations (CAs) if they are socially and economically integrated. This new grouping is known as a consolidated CMA and the component CMA and CA(s) are known as the primary census metropolitan area (PCMA) and primary census agglomeration(s) [PCA(s)]. A CMA may not be consolidated with another CMA.

Calgary, Alta

Year Incorporated: 1893. **Area:** 5 083 sq. km.

☐ **DEMOGRAPHICS: CMA Population** (2000): 952 960. **Pop. density:** 187.5 per sq. km. **Pop. growth** (1996–2000): 12.7%. **Immigrant pop.** (1996): 170 880, 20.8%. **Age Structure** (1996): Male pop.: under 25: 35.8%, over 65: 7.4%; Female pop.: under 25: 34.1%, over 65: 10.0%.

☐ **OFFICIAL LANGUAGES (1996):** 90.7% English; 0.1% French; 7.3% bilingual; 1.9% neither.

☐ **FAMILIES (1996): Avg. family size:** 3.2. **Lone-parent families:** 13.2% of families.

☐ **INCOME (1995): Avg. Employment Income:** $28 991. **Avg. Family Income:** $63 586. **Incidence of low income:** 19.8%.

☐ **LABOUR FORCE (2000): Employed (000s):** 545.6. **Unemployed (000s):** 25.9. **Unemployment rate:** 4.5%. **Participation rate:** 74.9%. **Employment rate:** 71.5%.

☐ **CLIMATE: Avg. day/night temps.:** -3.6°/-15.7° (Jan.); 23.2°/9.5° (July). **Avg. annual sunshine:** 2 395 h. **Avg. annual precip.:** 398.8 mm. **Avg. annual snowfall:** 135.4 cm.

Chicoutimi–Jonquière, Que.

Year Incorporated: 1976. **Area:** 1 723 sq. km.

☐ **DEMOGRAPHICS: CMA Population** (2000): 160 130. **Pop. density:** 92.9 per sq. km. **Pop. growth** (1996–2000): -1.7%. **Immigrant pop.** (1996): 1 165, 0.7%. **Age Structure** (1996): Male pop.: under 25: 36.3%, over 65: 8.8%; Female pop.: under 25: 33.0%, over 65: 12.6%.

☐ **OFFICIAL LANGUAGES (1996):** 0.1% English; 82.5% French; 17.4% bilingual.

☐ **FAMILIES (1996): Avg. family size:** 3.1. **Lone-parent families:** 15.0% of families.

☐ **INCOME (1995): Avg. Employment Income:** $25 127. **Avg. Family Income:** $46 656. **Incidence of low income:** 20.7%.

☐ **LABOUR FORCE (2000):** Employed (000s): 67.4. Unemployed (000s): 7.3. Unemployment rate: 9.8%. Participation rate: 56.6%. Employment rate: 51.5%.

☐ **CLIMATE:** Avg. day/night temps.: -10.2°/-21.5° (Jan.); 24.2°/11.8° (July). Avg. annual sunshine: 1 676 h. Avg. annual precip.: 929.7 mm. Avg. annual snowfall: 345 cm.

Edmonton, Alta

Year Incorporated: 1904. **Area:** 9 537 sq. km.

☐ **DEMOGRAPHICS: CMA Population** (2000): 944 194. **Pop. density:** 99.0 per sq. km. **Pop. growth** (1996–2000): 6.7%. **Immigrant pop.** (1996): 158 370, 18.4%. **Age Structure** (1996): Male pop.: under 25: 37.0%, over 65: 8.4%; Female pop.: under 25: 35.1%, over 65: 11.1%.

☐ **OFFICIAL LANGUAGES (1996):** 90.9% English; 0.1% French; 7.5% bilingual; 1.6% neither.

☐ **FAMILIES (1996):** Avg. family size: 3.2. Lone-parent families: 15.0% of families.

☐ **INCOME (1995):** Avg. Employment Income: $25 974. Avg. Family Income: $56 090. Incidence of low income: 21.3%.

☐ **LABOUR FORCE (2000):** Employed (000s): 488.9. Unemployed (000s): 28.5. Unemployment rate: 5.5%. Participation rate: 70.2%. Employment rate: 66.4%.

☐ **CLIMATE:** Avg. day/night temps.: -8.7°/-19.8° (Jan.); 22.5°/9.4° (July). Avg. annual sunshine: 2 303 h. Avg. annual precip.: 465.8 mm. Avg. annual snowfall: 127.1 cm.

Halifax, NS

Year Incorporated: 1841. **Area:** 2 503 sq. km.

☐ **DEMOGRAPHICS: CMA Population** (2000): 355 996. **Pop. density:** 142.2 per sq. km. **Pop. growth** (1996–2000): 4.3%. **Immigrant pop.** (1996): 23 635, 7.1%. **Age Structure** (1996): Male pop.: under 25: 35.0%, over 65: 8.3%; Female pop.: under 25: 32.4%, over 65: 11.8%.

☐ **OFFICIAL LANGUAGES (1996):** 88.9% English; 0.1% French; 10.7% bilingual; 0.3% neither.

☐ **FAMILIES (1996):** Avg. family size: 3.1. Lone-parent families: 15.9% of families.

☐ **INCOME (1995):** Avg. Employment Income: $25 419. Avg. Family Income: $54 241. Incidence of low income: 17.8%.

☐ **LABOUR FORCE (2000):** Employed (000s): 184.0. Unemployed (000s): 11.7. Unemployment

rate: 6.0%. Participation rate: 70.6%. Employment rate: 66.4%.

☐ **CLIMATE:** Avg. day/night temps.: -1.5°/-10.3° (Jan.); 23.4°/13.2° (July). Avg. annual sunshine: 1 949 h. Avg. annual precip.: 1 473.5 mm. Avg. annual snowfall: 261.4 cm.

Hamilton, Ont.

Year Incorporated: 1846. **Area:** 1 359 sq. km.

☐ **DEMOGRAPHICS: CMA Population** (2000): 671 679. **Pop. density:** 494.2 per sq. km. **Pop. growth** (1996–2000): 4.5%. **Immigrant pop.** (1996): 145 660, 23.3%. **Age Structure** (1996): Male pop.: under 25: 34.2%, over 65: 12.0%; Female pop.: under 25: 31.3%, over 65: 15.7%.

☐ **OFFICIAL LANGUAGES (1996):** 91.7% English; 0.1% French; 6.8% bilingual; 1.5% neither.

☐ **FAMILIES (1996):** Avg. family size: 3.1. Lone-parent families: 14.3% of families.

☐ **INCOME (1995):** Avg. Employment Income: $29 455. Avg. Family Income: $60 899. Incidence of low income: 19.0%.

☐ **LABOUR FORCE (2000):** Employed (000s): 345.3. Unemployed (000s): 18.1. Unemployment rate: 5.0%. Participation rate: 67.2%. Employment rate: 63.8%.

☐ **CLIMATE:** Avg. day/night temps.: -2.6°/-10.0° (Jan.); 26.4°/15.1° (July). Avg. annual sunshine: 2 079 h. Avg. annual precip.: 890.4 mm. Avg. annual snowfall: 152.4 cm.

Kitchener, Ont.

Year Incorporated: 1912. **Area:** 824 sq. km.

☐ **DEMOGRAPHICS: CMA Population** (2000): 421 764. **Pop. density:** 511.8 per sq. km. **Pop. growth** (1996–2000): 6.7%. **Immigrant pop.** (1996): 82 760, 21.6%. **Age Structure** (1996): Male pop.: under 25: 37.0%, over 65: 8.9%; Female pop.: under 25: 34.5%, over 65: 12.8%.

☐ **OFFICIAL LANGUAGES (1996):** 91.4% English; 0.1% French; 6.9% bilingual; 1.6% neither.

☐ **FAMILIES (1996):** Avg. family size: 3.2. Lone-parent families: 13.7% of families.

☐ **INCOME (1995):** Avg. Employment Income: $27 893. Avg. Family Income: $59 658. Incidence of low income: 14.6%.

☐ **LABOUR FORCE (2000):** Employed (000s): 223.5. Unemployed (000s): 13.2. Unemployment rate: 5.6%. Participation rate: 70.8%. Employment rate: 66.9%.

☐ **CLIMATE:** **Avg. day/night temps.:** -3.3°/-11.4° (Jan.); 26.1°/13.6° (July). **Avg. annual sunshine:** 1 969 h. **Avg. annual precip.:** 917.0 mm. **Avg. annual snowfall:** 158.0 cm.

London, Ont.

Year Incorporated: 1855. **Area:** 2 105 sq. km.

☐ **DEMOGRAPHICS:** **CMA Population** (2000): 421 296. **Pop. density:** 200.1 per sq. km. **Pop. growth** (1996–2000): 2.7%. **Immigrant pop.** (1996): 75 975, 19.1%. **Age Structure** (1996): Male pop.: under 25: 35.9%, over 65: 10.6%; Female pop.: under 25: 32.6%, over 65: 14.5%.

☐ **OFFICIAL LANGUAGES (1996):** 92.2% English; 6.6% bilingual; 1.1% neither.

☐ **FAMILIES (1996):** **Avg. family size:** 3.1. **Lone-parent families:** 15.5% of families.

☐ **INCOME (1995):** **Avg. Employment Income:** $27 289. **Avg. Family Income:** $58 671. **Incidence of low income:** 17.3%.

☐ **LABOUR FORCE (2000):** **Employed (000s):** 218.1. **Unemployed (000s):** 13.8. **Unemployment rate:** 6.0%. **Participation rate:** 68.9%. **Employment rate:** 64.8%.

☐ **CLIMATE:** **Avg. day/night temps.:** -2.8°/-10.7° (Jan.); 26.4°/14.2° (July). **Avg. annual sunshine:** 1 858 h. **Avg. annual precip.:** 955.1 mm. **Avg. annual snowfall:** 212.3 cm.

Montreal, Que.

Year Incorporated: 1832. **Area:** 4 024 sq. km.

☐ **DEMOGRAPHICS:** **CMA Population** (2000): 3 480 342. **Pop. density:** 864.9 per sq. km. **Pop. growth** (1996–2000): 2.6%. **Immigrant pop.** (1996): 586 470, 17.6%. **Age Structure** (1996): Male pop.: under 25: 33.3%, over 65: 9.8%; Female pop.: under 25: 30.3%, ,over 65: 14.1%.

☐ **OFFICIAL LANGUAGES (1996):** 8.5% English; 39.8% French; 49.7% bilingual; 1.9% neither.

☐ **FAMILIES (1996):** **Avg. family size:** 3.1. **Lone-parent families:** 17.4% of families.

☐ **INCOME (1995):** **Avg. Employment Income:** $26 918. **Avg. Family Income:** $52 795. **Incidence of low income:** 27.3%.

☐ **LABOUR FORCE (2000):** **Employed (000s):** 1 689.9. **Unemployed (000s):** 141.1. **Unemployment rate:** 7.7%. **Participation rate:** 65.4%. **Employment rate:** 60.4%.

☐ **CLIMATE:** **Avg. day/night temps.:** -5.8°/-14.9° (Jan.); 26.2°/15.4° (July). **Avg. annual sunshine:** 2 015 h. **Avg. annual precip.:** 939.7 mm. **Avg. annual snowfall:** 214.2 cm.

Oshawa, Ont.

Year Incorporated: 1924. **Area:** 894 sq. km.

☐ **DEMOGRAPHICS:** **CMA Population** (2000): 297 869. **Pop. density:** 333.2 per sq. km. **Pop. growth** (1996–2000): 7.5%. **Immigrant pop.** (1996) 44 105, 16.4%. **Age Structure** (1996): Male pop.: under 25: 37.6%, over 65: 8.4%; Female pop.: under 25: 35.1%, over 65: 11.2%.

☐ **OFFICIAL LANGUAGES (1996):** 92.8% English; 0.1% French; 6.7% bilingual; 0.5% neither.

☐ **FAMILIES (1996):** **Avg. family size:** 3.2. **Lone-parent families:** 14.1% of families.

☐ **INCOME (1995):** **Avg. Employment Income:** $31 332. **Avg. Family Income:** $62 101. **Incidence of low income:** 12.4%.

☐ **LABOUR FORCE (2000):** **Employed (000s):** 148.6. **Unemployed (000s):** 9.0. **Unemployment rate:** 5.7%. **Participation rate:** 68.3%. **Employment rate:** 64.4%.

☐ **CLIMATE:** **Avg. day/night temps.:** -1.7°/-9.9° (Jan.); 25.2°/15.3° (July). **Avg. annual sunshine:** 2 025 h. **Avg. annual precip.:** 880.3 mm. **Avg. annual snowfall:** 125.7 cm.

Ottawa-Hull, Ont/Que

Year Incorporated: 1854 (Ottawa). **Area:** 5 686 sq. km.

☐ **DEMOGRAPHICS:** **CMA Population** (2000): 1 080 986. **Pop. density:** 190.1 per sq. km. **Pop. growth** (1996–2000): 4.2%. **Immigrant pop.** (1996): 161 885, 16.0%. **Age Structure** (1996): Male pop.: under 25: 35.1%, over 65: 8.4%; Female pop.: under 25: 32.3%, over 65: 11.9%.

☐ **OFFICIAL LANGUAGES (1996):** 45.8% English; 9.0% French; 44.0% bilingual.

☐ **FAMILIES (1996):** **Avg. family size:** 3.1. **Lone-parent families:** 15.6% of families.

☐ **INCOME (1995):** **Avg. Employment Income:** $30 633. **Avg. Family Income:** $64 243. **Incidence of low income:** 18.9%.

☐ **LABOUR FORCE (2000):** **Employed (000s):** 567.0. **Unemployed (000s):** 33.4. **Unemployment rate:** 5.6%. **Participation rate:** 69.9%. **Employment rate:** 66.0%.

☐ **CLIMATE:** **Avg. day/night temps.:** -6.3°/-15.5° (Jan.); 26.4°/15.1° (July). **Avg. annual sunshine:** 2 054 h. **Avg. annual precip.:** 910.5 mm. **Avg. annual snowfall:** 221.5 cm.

Quebec, Que.

Year Incorporated: 1832. **Area:** 3 150 sq. km.

☐ **DEMOGRAPHICS: CMA Population** (2000): 689 654. **Pop. density:** 218.9 per sq. km. **Pop. growth** (1996–2000): 0.9%. **Immigrant pop.** (1996): 17 390, 2.6%. **Age Structure** (1996): Male pop.: under 25: 33.1%, over 65: 9.1%; Female pop.: under 25: 30.0%, over 65: 14.0%.

☐ **OFFICIAL LANGUAGES (1996):** 0.2% English; 69.6% French; 30.0% bilingual; 0.2% neither.

☐ **FAMILIES (1996):** **Avg. family size**: 3.0. **Lone-parent families**: 16.1% of families.

☐ **INCOME (1995):** **Avg. Employment Income:** $26 039. **Avg. Family Income:** $52 570. **Incidence of low income:** 22.8%.

☐ **LABOUR FORCE (2000): Employed (000s):** 326.6. **Unemployed (000s):** 28.5. **Unemployment rate:** 8.0%. **Participation rate:** 62.9%. **Employment rate:** 57.9%.

☐ **CLIMATE: Avg. day/night temps.:** -7.7°/-17.3° (Jan.); 24.9°/13.2° (July). **Avg. annual sunshine:** 1 910 h. **Avg. annual precip.:** 1 207.7 mm. **Avg. annual snowfall:** 337.0 cm.

Regina, Sask.

Year Incorporated: 1903. **Area:** 3 422 sq. km.

☐ **DEMOGRAPHICS: CMA Population** (2000): 200 455. **Pop. density:** 58.6 per sq. km. **Pop. growth** (1996–2000): 0.5%. **Immigrant pop.** (1996): 15 230, 7.9%. **Age Structure** (1996): Male pop.: under 25: 38.5%, over 65: 9.8%; Female pop.: under 25: 35.5%, over 65: 13.6%.

☐ **OFFICIAL LANGUAGES (1996):** 93.9% English; 0.1% French; 5.6% bilingual; 0.4% neither.

☐ **FAMILIES (1996):** **Avg. family size**: 3.2. **Lone-parent families**: 16.6% of families.

☐ **INCOME (1995):** **Avg. Employment Income:** $25 918. **Avg. Family Income:** $56 844. **Incidence of low income:** 17.6%.

☐ **LABOUR FORCE (2000): Employed (000s):** 104.4. **Unemployed (000s):** 5.3. **Unemployment rate:** 4.8%. **Participation rate:** 70.3%. **Employment rate:** 66.9%.

☐ **CLIMATE: Avg. day/night temps.:** -11.0°/-22.1° (Jan.); 26.3°/11.9° (July). **Avg. annual sunshine:** 2 365 h. **Avg. annual precip.:** 364.0 mm. **Avg. annual snowfall:** 107.4 cm.

St. Catharines–Niagara, Ont.

Year Incorporated: 1876. **Area:** 1 400 sq. km.

☐ **DEMOGRAPHICS: CMA Population** (2000): 389 965. **Pop. density:** 278.5 per sq. km. **Pop. growth** (1996–2000): 1.9%. **Immigrant pop.** (1996): 67 290, 18.1%. **Age Structure** (1996): Male pop.: under 25: 33.8%, over 65: 14.2%; Female pop.: under 25: 30.2%, over 65: 18.3%.

☐ **OFFICIAL LANGUAGES (1996):** 90.8% English; 0.2% French; 8.3% bilingual; 0.7% neither.

☐ **FAMILIES (1996):** **Avg. family size**: 3.0. **Lone-parent families**: 14.8% of families.

☐ **INCOME (1995):** **Avg. Employment Income:** $25 749. **Avg. Family Income:** $53 674. **Incidence of low income:** 16.1%.

☐ **LABOUR FORCE (2000): Employed (000s):** 193.2. **Unemployed (000s):** 12.3. **Unemployment rate:** 6.0%. **Participation rate:** 64.6%. **Employment rate:** 60.8%.

☐ **CLIMATE: Avg. day/night temps.:** -1.3°/-8.4° (Jan.); 27.2°/15.8° (July). **Avg. annual sunshine:** 2 079 h. **Avg. annual precip.:** 953.1 mm. **Avg. annual snowfall:** 163.7 cm.

Saint John, NB

Year Incorporated: 1785. **Area:** 3 509 sq. km.

☐ **DEMOGRAPHICS: CMA Population** (2000): 127 713. **Pop. density:** 36.4 per sq. km. **Pop. growth** (1996–2000): -0.2%. **Immigrant pop.** (1996): 4 915, 3.9%. **Age Structure** (1996): Male pop.: under 25: 36.4%, over 65: 10.4%; Female pop.: under 25: 32.9%, over 65: 14.7%.

☐ **OFFICIAL LANGUAGES (1996):** 87.5% English; 0.1% French; 12.3% bilingual; 0.1% neither.

☐ **FAMILIES (1996):** **Avg. family size**: 3.1. **Lone-parent families**: 16.9% of families.

☐ **INCOME (1995):** **Avg. Employment Income:** $24 201. **Avg. Family Income:** $49 138. **Incidence of low income:** 20.0%.

☐ **LABOUR FORCE (2000): Employed (000s):** 61.0. **Unemployed (000s):** 4.8. **Unemployment rate:** 7.3%. **Participation rate:** 65.4%. **Employment rate:** 60.6%.

☐ **CLIMATE: Avg. day/night temps.:** -2.8°/-13.6° (Jan.); 22.1°/11.6° (July). **Avg. annual sunshine:** 1 894 h. **Avg. annual precip.:** 1 432.8 mm. **Avg. annual snowfall:** 283.2 cm.

St. John's, Nfld

Year Incorporated: 1888. **Area:** 790 sq. km.

☐ **DEMOGRAPHICS: CMA Population** (2000): 175 062. **Pop. density:** 221.6 per sq. km. **Pop. growth** (1996–2000): -1.1%. **Immigrant pop.** (1996): 5 065, 2.9%. **Age Structure** (1996): Male pop.: under 25: 37.4%, over 65: 8.2%; Female pop.: under 25: 34.4%, over 65: 11.7%.

☐ **OFFICIAL LANGUAGES (1996):** 94.5% English; 0% French; 5.4% bilingual; 0.1% neither.

☐ **FAMILIES (1996):** Avg. family size: 3.2. Lone-parent families: 16.8% of families.

☐ **INCOME (1995):** Avg. Employment Income: $24 717. Avg. Family Income: $52 054. Incidence of low income: 19.5%.

☐ **LABOUR FORCE (2000):** Employed (000s): 84.3. Unemployed (000s): 8.7. Unemployment rate: 9.4. Participation rate: 65.7%. Employment rate: 59.5%.

☐ **CLIMATE:** Avg. day/night temps.: -0.7°/-7.9° (Jan.); 20.2°/10.5° (July). Avg. annual sunshine: 1 527 h. Avg. annual precip.: 1 481.7 mm. Avg. annual snowfall: 322.1 cm.

Saskatoon, Sask.

Year Incorporated: 1906. **Area:** 5 322 sq. km.

☐ **DEMOGRAPHICS: CMA Population** (2000): 232 600. **Pop. density:** 43.7 per sq. km. **Pop. growth** (1996–2000): 2.9%. **Immigrant pop.** (1996): 16 455, 7.5%. **Age Structure** (1996): Male pop.: under 25: 39.5%, over 65: 9.4%; Female pop.: under 25: 37.0%, over 65: 12.8%.

☐ **OFFICIAL LANGUAGES (1996):** 92.9% English; 0.0% French; 6.5% bilingual; 0.5% neither.

☐ **FAMILIES (1996):** Avg. family size: 3.2. Lone-parent families: 15.9% of families.

☐ **INCOME (1995):** Avg. Employment Income: $24 033. Avg. Family Income: $53 196. Incidence of low income: 21.4%.

☐ **LABOUR FORCE (2000):** Employed (000s): 116.7. Unemployed (000s): 6.9. Unemployment rate: 5.6%. Participation rate: 68.5%. Employment rate: 64.7%.

☐ **CLIMATE:** Avg. day/night temps.: -12.3°/-22.9° (Jan.); 25.4°/11.7° (July). Avg. annual sunshine: 2 381 h. Avg. annual precip.: 347.2 mm. Avg. annual snowfall: 105.4 cm.

Sherbrooke, Que.

Year Incorporated: 1875. **Area:** 980 sq. km.

☐ **DEMOGRAPHICS: CMA Population** (2000): 152 897. **Pop. density:** 156.0 per sq. km. **Pop. growth** (1996–2000): 1.9%. **Immigrant pop.** (1996): 6 225, 4.2%. **Age Structure** (1996): Male pop.: under 25: 35.7%, over 65: 9.6%; Female pop.: under 25: 32.5%, over 65: 14.7%.

☐ **OFFICIAL LANGUAGES (1996):** 1.9% English; 58.8% French; 39.1% bilingual; 0.3% neither.

☐ **FAMILIES (1996):** Avg. family size: 3.0. Lone-parent families: 17.0% of families.

☐ **INCOME (1995):** Avg. Employment Income: $23 410. Avg. Family Income: $47 198. Incidence of low income: 22.8%.

☐ **LABOUR FORCE (2000):** Employed (000s): 73.1. Unemployed (000s): 6.4. Unemployment rate: 8.0%. Participation rate: 63.9%. Employment rate: 58.7%.

☐ **CLIMATE:** Avg. day/night temps.: -5.6°/-17.7° (Jan.); 24.7°/11.2° (July). Avg. annual sunshine 1 901 h. Avg. annual precip.: 1 108.9 mm. Avg. annual snowfall: 288.2 cm.

Sudbury, Ont.

Year Incorporated: 1930. **Area:** 2 612 sq. km.

☐ **DEMOGRAPHICS: CMA Population** (2000): 157 132. **Pop. density:** 60.2 per sq. km. **Pop. growth** (1996–2000): -4.8%. **Immigrant pop.** (1991): 12 840, 8.1%. **Age Structure** (1996): Male pop.: under 25: 35.8%, over 65: 10.4%; Female pop.: under 25: 33.5%, over 65: 13.0%.

☐ **OFFICIAL LANGUAGES (1996):** 58.0% English; 1.5% French; 40.1% bilingual; 0.3% neither.

☐ **FAMILIES (1996):** Avg. family size: 3.1. Lone-parent families: 15.2% of families.

☐ **INCOME (1995):** Avg. Employment Income: $28 345. Avg. Family Income: $57 109. Incidence of low income: 17.3%.

☐ **LABOUR FORCE (2000):** Employed (000s): 76.0. Unemployed (000s): 6.7. Unemployment rate: 8.1%. Participation rate: 64.0%. Employment rate: 58.8%.

☐ **CLIMATE:** Avg. day/night temps.: -8.5°/-18.7° (Jan.); 24.8°/13.3° (July). Avg. annual sunshine: 1 960 h. Avg. annual precip.: 871.8 mm. Avg. annual snowfall: 266.6 cm.

Thunder Bay, Ont.

Year Incorporated: 1970. **Area:** 2 295 sq. km.

☐ **DEMOGRAPHICS: CMA Population** (2000): 126 343. **Pop. density:** 55.1 per sq. km. **Pop. growth** (1996–2000): -2.1%. **Immigrant pop.** (1996): 15 275, 12.2%. **Age Structure** (1996): Male pop.: under 25: 34.3%, over 65: 12.2%; Female pop.: under 25: 32.0%, over 65: 15.9%.

☐ **OFFICIAL LANGUAGES (1996):** 91.7% English; 0.1% French; 7.4% bilingual; 0.7% neither.

☐ **FAMILIES (1996):** Avg. family size: 3.1. Lone-parent families: 16.0% of families.

☐ **INCOME (1995):** Avg. Employment Income: $27 649. Avg. Family Income: $58 731. Incidence of low income: 14.5%.

☐ **LABOUR FORCE (2000):** Employed (000s): 61.2. Unemployed (000s): 4.1. Unemployment rate: 6.3%. Participation rate: 64.2%. Employment rate: 60.1%.

☐ **CLIMATE:** Avg. day/night temps.: -8.9°/-21.3° (Jan.); 24.4°/11.0° (July). Avg. annual sunshine: 2 183 h. Avg. annual precip.: 703.5 mm. Avg. annual snowfall: 195.5 cm.

Toronto, Ont.

Year Incorporated: 1834. **Area:** 5 568 sq. km.

☐ **DEMOGRAPHICS: CMA Population** (2000): 4 751 408. **Pop. density:** 853.3 per sq. km. **Pop. growth** (1996–2000): 7.9%. **Immigrant pop.** (1996): 1 772 905, 41.6%. **Age Structure** (1996): Male pop.: under 25: 34.7%, over 65: 9.5%; Female pop.: under 25: 31.6%, over 65: 12.4%.

☐ **OFFICIAL LANGUAGES (1996):** 87.4% English; 0.1% French; 8.0% bilingual; 4.5% neither.

☐ **FAMILIES (1996):** Avg. family size: 3.3. Lone-parent families: 15.5% of families.

☐ **INCOME (1995):** Avg. Employment Income: $31 264. Avg. Family Income: $64 044. Incidence of low income: 21.1%.

☐ **LABOUR FORCE (2000):** Employed (000s): 2 499.8. Unemployed (000s): 144.7. Unemployment rate: 5.5%. Participation rate: 68.7%. Employment rate: 65.0%.

☐ **CLIMATE:** Avg. day/night temps.: -2.5°/-11.1° (Jan.); 26.8°/14.2° (July). Avg. annual sunshine: 2 038 h. Avg. annual precip.: 780.8 mm. Avg. annual snowfall: 124.2 cm.

Trois–Rivières, Que.

Year Incorporated: 1857. **Area:** 872 sq. km.

☐ **DEMOGRAPHICS: CMA Population** (2000): 141 785. **Pop. density:** 162.6 per sq. km. **Pop. growth** (1996–2000): -0.3%. **Immigrant pop.** (1996): 2 220, 1.6%. **Age Structure** (1996): Male pop.: under 25: 33.2%, over 65: 10.5%; Female pop.: under 25: 30.1%, over 65: 15.6%.

☐ **OFFICIAL LANGUAGES (1996):** 0.1% English; 75.4% French; 24.4% bilingual.

☐ **FAMILIES (1996):** Avg. family size: 3.0. Lone-parent families: 16.1% of families.

☐ **INCOME (1995):** Avg. Employment Income:

$24 763. Avg. Family Income: $47 242. Incidence of low income: 23.4%.

☐ **LABOUR FORCE (2000):** Employed (000s): 62.1. Unemployed (000s): 7.3. Unemployment rate: 10.5%. Participation rate: 59.6%. Employment rate: 53.4%.

☐ **CLIMATE:** Avg. day/night temps.: -7.5°/-17.7° (Jan.); 25.6°/14.1° (July). Avg. annual sunshine: 1 910 h. Avg. annual precip.: 1 046.7 mm. Avg. annual snowfall: 242.0 cm.

Vancouver, BC

Year Incorporated: 1886. **Area:** 2 821 sq. km.

☐ **DEMOGRAPHICS: CMA Population** (2000): 2 048 823. **Pop. density:** 726.3 per sq. km. **Pop. growth** (1996–2000): 7.1%. **Immigrant pop.** (1996) 633 740, 34.6%. **Age Structure** (1996): Male pop.: under 25: 32.8%, over 65: 10.1%; Female pop.: under 25: 30.6%, over 65: 13.5%.

☐ **OFFICIAL LANGUAGES (1996):** 87.9% English; 0.1% French; 7.4% bilingual; 4.7% neither.

☐ **FAMILIES (1996):** Avg. family size: 3.2. Lone-parent families: 13.9% of families.

☐ **INCOME (1995):** Avg. Employment Income: $29 122. Avg. Family Income: $60 438. Incidence of low income: 23.3%.

☐ **LABOUR FORCE (2000):** Employed (000s): 1 044.5. Unemployed (000s): 65.3. Unemployment rate: 5.9%. Participation rate: 65.9%. Employment rate: 62.1%.

☐ **CLIMATE:** Avg. day/night temps.: 5.7°/0.1° (Jan.); 21.7°/12.7° (July). Avg. annual sunshine: 1 919 h. Avg. annual precip.: 1 167.4 mm. Avg. annual snowfall: 54.9 cm.

Victoria, BC

Year Incorporated: 1862. **Area:** 633 sq. km.

☐ **DEMOGRAPHICS: CMA Population** (2000): 317 492. **Pop. density:** 501.6 per sq. km. **Pop. growth** (1996–2000): 0.2%. **Immigrant pop.** (1996): 57 795, 19.0%. **Age Structure** (1996): Male pop.: under 25: 30.7%, over 65: 15.1%; Female pop.: under 25: 27.6%, over 65: 20.4%.

☐ **OFFICIAL LANGUAGES (1996):** 90.6% English; 0.0% French; 8.6% bilingual; 0.7% neither.

☐ **FAMILIES (1996):** Avg. family size: 2.9. Lone-parent families: 14.1% of families.

☐ **INCOME (1995):** Avg. Employment Income: $27 038. Avg. Family Income: $59 585. Incidence of low income: 15.4%.

☐ **LABOUR FORCE (2000):** Employed (000s): 153.6. Unemployed (000s): 11.1. **Unemployment rate:** 6.7%. **Participation rate:** 64.2%. **Employment rate:** 59.9%.

☐ **CLIMATE:** Avg. day/night temps.: 6.5°/0.3° (Jan.); 21.8°/10.7° (July). **Avg. annual sunshine:** 2 082 h. **Avg. annual precip.:** 857.9 mm. **Avg. annual snowfall:** 46.9 cm.

Windsor, Ont.

Year Incorporated: 1892. Area: 862 sq. km.

☐ **DEMOGRAPHICS: CMA Population** (2000): 304 390. **Pop. density:** 353.1 per sq. km. **Pop. growth** (1996–2000): 5.9%. **Immigrant pop.** (1996): 56 990, 20.4%. **Age Structure** (1996): Male pop.: under 25: 35.7%, over 65: 10.8%; Female pop.: under 25: 32.9%, over 65: 15.0%.

☐ **OFFICIAL LANGUAGES (1996):** 87.8% English; 0.2% French; 10.5% bilingual; 1.5% neither.

☐ **FAMILIES (1996):** Avg. family size: 3.2. **Lone-parent families**: 16.0% of families.

☐ **INCOME (1995):** Avg. **Employment Income:** $30 048. **Avg. Family Income:** $62 244. **Incidence of low income:** 15.7%.

☐ **LABOUR FORCE (2000):** Employed (000s): 154.2. Unemployed (000s): 8.8. **Unemployment rate:** 5.4%. **Participation rate:** 66.6%. **Employment rate:** 63.0%.

☐ **CLIMATE:** Avg. day/night temps.: -1.3°/-8.8° (Jan.); 27.7°/17.0° (July). **Avg. annual sunshine:** 2 045 h. **Avg. annual precip.:** 901.6 mm. **Avg. annual snowfall:** 123.3 cm

Winnipeg, Man.

Year Incorporated: 1873. Area: 4 078 sq. km.

☐ **DEMOGRAPHICS: CMA Population** (2000): 681 146. **Pop. density:** 167.0 per sq. km. **Pop. growth** (1996–2000): 0.3%. **Immigrant pop.** (1996): 111 690, 16.7%. **Age Structure** (1996): Male pop.: under 25: 35.4%, over 65: 10.9%; Female pop.: under 25: 32.5%, over 65: 15.6%.

☐ **OFFICIAL LANGUAGES (1996):** 87.9% English; 0.1% French; 10.9% bilingual; 1.1% neither.

☐ **FAMILIES (1996):** Avg. family size: 3.1. **Lone-parent families**: 15.8% of families.

☐ **INCOME (1995):** Avg. **Employment Income:** $30 048. **Avg. Family Income:** $62 244. **Incidence of low income:** 15.7%.

☐ **LABOUR FORCE (2000):** Employed (000s): 351.9. Unemployed (000s): 19.6. **Unemployment rate:** 5.3%. **Participation rate:** 69.2%. **Employment rate:** 65.6%.

☐ **CLIMATE:** Avg. day/night temps.: -13.2°/-23.6° (Jan.); 26.1°/13.4° (July). **Avg. annual sunshine:** 2 377 h. **Avg. annual precip.:** 504.4 mm. **Avg. annual snowfall:** 114.8 cm.

NATIONAL PARKS

Canada's national parks are protected by law to preserve representative natural areas throughout the country. The parks are maintained to enhance public understanding, appreciation and enjoyment of the country's natural heritage, and increasingly, park management efforts are being directed to protect Canada's wide variety of ecosystems for the long term.

In 1988, the National Parks Act was amended to ensure that each park's management plan would maintain the ecological integrity of the area, that is, that the structure and function of the existing ecosystem would not be harmed by human activity. This amendment was made as it became increasingly clear that many ecological features, such as grizzly bear populations, require very large areas and very long time lines if they are to survive, if not thrive. The host of modern environmental stresses also affect protected areas and their inhabitants, and mere protection is not enough; a co-operative parks management structure—including public, corporate, environmental and Aboriginal interest groups—and an ecosystem management approach is the preferred management model to minimize damage.

The goal of the national parks policy is to create at least one national park in each of Canada's 39 natural regions. Thirty-nine national parks and national park reserves currently exist, however, 14 more national parks are needed. Once completed, the parks system will preserve just over 3 percent of the country's land mass. For more information, visit parkscanada.pch.gc.ca ▶

Park	Location	Size (sq. km)	Year est.	Description
Aulavik	northern portion of Banks Is., NWT	12 200	(1992)[1]	Thomsen River forms core of a park marked by deep river canyons and desert-like badlands. Area supports high concentration of musk oxen. The Thomsen River is Canada's most northerly navigable river.
Auyuittuq[2]	Cumberland Peninsula, Baffin Is., NT	21 469	1976	Located on the Arctic Circle; this is an isolated and very rugged wilderness area with mountains, fjords, tundra and permafrost. Park protects part of Northern Davis Strait Natural Region and portions of Baffin Island Shelf Marine region. Contains prehistoric and historic resources from ancient Thule settlements.
Banff	Banff, Alta.	6 641	1885	Our first national park is noted for ice-capped peaks, canyons, glaciers, hot springs, and hoodoos (rock pillars, often in fantastic shapes). Wildlife includes bighorn sheep, black and grizzly bears, elk and caribou. Banff is part of UNESCO's Rocky Mountain Parks World Heritage Site.
Bruce Peninsula, including Fathom Five National Marine Park	299 km northwest of Toronto, between Lake Huron and Georgian Bay	154	(1987)[1]	This park was created to protect the Niagara Escarpment and the limestone cliffs on Georgian Bay; contains mixed forests, wetlands and limestone cliffs. Fathom Five National Marine Park includes 19 islands, over 20 shipwrecks, clear water and distinctive underwater geological features.
Cape Breton Highlands	across northern Cape Breton Is., NS	948	1936	The scenic Cabot Trail is characterized by a rugged shoreline with plunging cliffs.
Elk Island	45 km east of Edmonton, Alta.	194	1913	A large population of plains and wood bison, elk and moose inhabit the rolling woodlands and lakes. Other wildlife include bear, beaver and coyote.
Forillon	northeast tip of Gaspé Peninsula, Que.	244	1970	Protects parts of the Notre-Dame and Mégantic mountains and some of the Gulf of St. Lawrence marine area. Features a rich variety of seabirds and animals, limestone cliffs, Arctic-alpine plants and the highest mountains in eastern Canada.
Fundy	southeastern shore on the Bay of Fundy, NB	206	1948	The giant tides of the Bay of Fundy, among the highest in the world, and a bold, irregular coastline.
Georgian Bay Islands	160 km northwest of Toronto, Ont.	25	1929	59 glacier swept islands are home to endangered species, limestone cliffs, caves and archaeological sites. This area was the inspiration for many of the Group of Seven artists.

Park	Location	Size (sq. km)	Year est.	Description
Glacier	45 km east of Revelstoke, BC	1 349	1886	Protects a section of the Columbia Mountains Natural Region that includes habitats for grizzly bear and mountain caribou. Steep angular mountains, deep valleys, icefields, glaciers, waterfalls, avalanche paths and high precipitation characterise the area.
Grasslands	100 km south of Swift Current, Sask.	906	(1975)[1]	Unique natural habitat of short-grass prairie; blacktailed prairie dogs, pronghorn antelope and the prairie falcon are found.
Gros Morne	west coast of Nfld	1 805	(1970)[1]	Park is dominated by a coastal lowland and an alpine plateau that each boast a variety of land mammals, bird species, fish and trees, ferns and flowers. The park has been declared a UNESCO World Heritage Site because of its spectacular geology.
Gwaii Haanas (South Moresby)[2] including Gwaii Haanas, National Marine Conservation Area	southern part of Queen Charlotte Islands, BC	1 495	(1987)[1]	Canada's "Galapagos," home to 39 unique plants, an estimated 750,000 seabirds come to nest, and animals such as black bear, pine marten, deer mice, shrews and weasels. Geography features deep fjords, rugged mountains, and one of the finest old-growth temperate rainforest left on Pacific coast.
Ivvavik	northern tip of Yukon	10 168	1984	Migration route for Porcupine caribou herd; major North American waterfowl area; home to grizzly, black and polar bears. Contains unique non-glaciated landscape.
Jasper	340 km west of Edmonton, Alta.	10 878	1907	Contains the largest icefield in the Canadian Rockies—Columbia Icefield—and preserves the headwaters of major rivers, particularly the Athabasca.
Kejimkujik	central southwestern NS	404	1974	Gently rolling country with many lakes and rivers; provides good canoeing and camping. The earliest inhabitants—Maritime Archaic Indians—arrived about 4,500 years ago.
Kluane[2]	southwest corner of Yukon	22 013	1976	Features Mount Logan, Canada's highest peak, Kluane Lake (Yukon's largest), grizzly bears, dall sheep and whitewater rivers.
Kootenay	1 km east of Radium Hot Springs, BC	1 406	1920	The park contains Rocky Mountain wilderness and is part of UNESCO's Rocky Mountain Parks World Heritage Site. Hot springs, alpine lakes, canyons, glaciers, two river valleys; home to bighorn sheep, mountain goats.
Kouchibouguac	eastern NB	239	1979	Swimming, sunbathing on the beaches and dunes; cycling, hiking trails; windsurfing.
La Mauricie	55 km north of Trois-Rivières, Que.	536	1977	Hilly terrain at the edge of the Canadian Shield with transitional forest vegetation from evergreens to deciduous. Beaver, moose and the common loon; an area filled with brooks, lakes and waterfalls.
Mingan Archipelago[2]	N of Anticosti Is. along the St. Lawrence shore, QC	151	1984	This is a limestone environment that is home to diversified plant species, nesting seabirds and whales, seals and porpoises.

Park	Location	Size (sq. km)	Year est.	Description
Mount Revelstoke	Revelstoke, BC	260	1914	Columbia Mountain ranges. Park is characterised by deep snow accumulation and high annual precipitation. Contains three ecoregions: Interior Alpine Tundra, Interior Sub-alpine Tundra and Interior Cedar Hemlock. Each is packed with their own variety of vegetation and wildlife.
Nahanni[2]	southwestern NWT	4 765	1976	The wild and spectacular South Nahanni river passes through this long, narrow park. The route contains four canyons; the river plunges from twice the height of Niagara Falls at Virginia Falls. Park contains sulphur hotsprings, alpine tundra and vast forests, plus numerous species of birds, mammals and fish.
Pacific Rim [2]	west coast of Vancouver Island	500	(1970)[1]	3 sections—Long Beach, Broken Group Islands and West Coast Trail—offer rainforest, beaches and scenic, rugged hiking. Park contains native archaeological sites that indicate settlement for at least 4,300 years.
Point Pelee	southernmost point of Ont.	15	1918	Extensive marshlands and beaches provide refuge for many migratory birds and butterflies. The temperate climate allows over 70 species of tree to survive, as well as a huge variety of reptiles, birds, amphibians, insects and spiders.
Prince Albert	200 km north of Saskatoon, Sask.	3 875	1927	Mixture of forest land and lakes, home to woodland caribou, bison and a pelican colony. Archaeological digs indicate that the area has been inhabited by Aboriginal cultures for at least 6,000 years.
Prince Edward Island	north shore of PEI	22	1937	40 km of fine saltwater beaches, sand dunes, high coastal cliffs, marshes, ponds and wood-lands. Green Gables in located in this park.
Pukaskwa	northeastern shore of Lake Superior	1 878	(1971)[1]	Hilly terrain is characterised by ridges and cliffs, and lakes on rocky shores with shallow soil. Park interior features spruce, fir, cedar, aspen and birch. Wildlife includes moose, wolves, black bears and woodland caribou. This park is also the site of rare Arctic plants.
Quttinirpaaq (Ellesmere Island)	northern tip of Canada	37 775	1988	Vast isolated high Arctic wilderness park. Mountains, glaciers, musk-oxen, Peary's caribou. Fragile permafrost environments. Historic sites and artifacts from early Arctic explorers
Riding Mountain	270 km northwest of Winnipeg, Man.	2 973	1929	Wildlife—wolf, elk, moose, black bear and beaver—abound.
Saguenay-St. Lawrence Marine Park	At the confluence of the Saguenay Fjord and St. Lawrence estuary; access through L'Anse-Saint-Jean, on the north shore of the St. Lawrence near Tadoussac		1988	A rich diversity of marine life; whales, seals, plants and birds of all kinds

▶

► Park	Location	Size (sq. km)	Year est.	Description
Sirmilik[2]	northern Baffin Is., incl Bylot Is. and Borden Penin	22 200	(1992)	Mountains, snowfields, glaciers, tundra. Sparse vegetation: 50 bird species incl. murres, kittiwakes, snow geese. Caribou, wolf, Artic fox, lemming, seals, whales, walrus, polar bear
St. Lawrence Islands	Thousand Islands	8	1904	Park includes over 21 islands and 90 islets between Kingston and Brockville, with 100 acres on the mainland at Mallorytown Landing. The area features Thousand Islands landscape and the St. Lawrence River. The Great Lakes moderate the climate, allowing many animals and plants to exist further north than might otherwise be possible.
Terra Nova	east coast of Nfld on Bonavista Bay	400	1957	Rolling forested hills are remnants of the ancient Appalachian Mountains. Rugged cliffs and sheltered inlets are featured on the coast; the interior has spongy bogs, rolling hills covered with forest and inland ponds.
Tuktut Nogait	east of Inuvik in NWT	16 340	1996	Spectacular river canyons and cliffs dotted by hundreds of archaeological sites. Park protects calving grounds of Bluenose caribou and one of the highest concentrations of birds of prey in North America.
Vuntut	Old Crow Flats, northern Yukon	4 345	(1993)[1]	Yukon's most important waterfowl habitat and home to porcupine caribou, grizzly bear, moose, muskrat and several species of fish. Vertebrate fossils found at over 56 sites within park. The area is only 300 m in elevation and features over 2,000 shallow lakes.
Wapusk	northeast corner of Manitoba	11 475	1996	This region of flat inland expanse of tundra, eskers and permafrost includes one of the world's largest known polar bear denning areas.
Waterton Lakes	southwest corner of Alta.	505	1895	Officially renamed the Waterton-Glacier International Peace Park in 1932; the world's first park established by two governments. Protects transition from prairie grasslands to Rocky Mountains and a rich variety of wildlife.
Wood Buffalo	straddles the Alta.-NWT border	44 802	1922	Canada's largest national park is also a UNESCO World Heritage Site. Home to the largest free-roaming herd of bison; only site of naturally nesting whooping cranes, peregrine falcons and red-sided garter snakes. Geography features sinkholes, underground rivers, caves and sunken valleys.
Yoho	25 km east of Golden, BC	1 313	1886	Contains several of the highest peaks in the Rocky Mountains, icefields, waterfalls and a varied plant and animal life.

Source: *Canadian Heritage, Parks Canada*

(1) Park created by federal/provincial/territorial agreement rather than federal enactment and administered by special legislation. (2) Park reserve, set aside for national park and under jurisdiction of National Parks Act, but lands, fish and wildlife are subject to future settlement of native land claims.

THE PEOPLE

POPULATION

Population of Provinces and Territories[1]
(thousands)

	Canada	Nfld	PEI	NS	NB	Que	Ont	Man	Sask	Alta	BC	YT	NWT	NVT
1861[2] ...	3 230	n.a.	81	331	252	1 112	1 396	*	n.a.	n.a.	52	*	7	n.a.
1871 ...	3 689	n.a.	94	388	286	1 192	1 621	25	n.a.	n.a.	36	*	48	n.a.
1881 ...	4 325	n.a.	109	441	321	1 360	1 927	62	n.a.	n.a.	49	*	56	n.a.
1891 ...	4 833	n.a.	109	450	321	1 489	2 114	153	*	*	98	*	99	n.a.
1901 ...	5 371	n.a.	103	460	331	1 649	2 183	255	91	73	179	27	20	n.a.
1911 ...	7 207	n.a.	94	492	352	2 006	2 527	461	492	374	393	9	7	n.a.
1921 ...	8 788	n.a.	89	524	388	2 361	2 934	610	758	588	525	4	8	n.a.
1931 ...	10 377	n.a.	88	513	408	2 875	3 432	700	922	732	694	4	9	n.a.
1941 ...	11 507	n.a.	95	578	457	3 332	3 788	730	896	796	818	5	12	n.a.
1951 ...	14 009	361	98	643	516	4 056	4 598	777	832	940	1 165	9	16	n.a.
1961 ...	18 238	458	105	737	598	5 259	6 236	922	925	1 332	1 629	15	23	n.a.
1971 ...	21 962	531	113	797	643	6 137	7 849	999	932	1 666	2 241	19	36	n.a.
1981 ...	24 820	575	124	855	706	6 548	8 811	1 036	976	2 294	2 824	24	48	n.a.
1986 ...	26 101	577	128	889	725	6 708	9 438	1 092	1 029	2 431	3 004	25	55	n.a.
1991[3] ...	28 031	580	130	915	746	7 065	10 428	1 110	1 003	2 593	3 373	29	39	22
1996[3] ...	29 672	561	136	931	753	7 274	11 101	1 134	1 019	2 781	3 882	32	42	26
2000[4] ...	30 750	539	139	941	756	7 372	11 669	1 148	1 023	2 997	4 064	31	42	28
2001[4] ...	31 081	534	139	943	757	7 411	11 874	1 150	1 016	3 064	4 096	29	40	28

Source: © *Census of Canada, Statistics Canada*

(n.a.) Not applicable. (*) Included with the Northwest Territories. (1) As of July 1 in non-census years. Includes data from incompletely enumerated population. Totals may not add up due to rounding. (2) Pre-Confederation. (3) Final postcensal estimates. (4) Updated intercensal estimates.

Age Structure of the Population[1]

	Total (000s)	% Under 5 Years	% 5–19 Years	% 20–44 Years	% 45–64 Years	% 65+ Years
1851	2 436	18.51	37.81	31.65	9.40	2.67
1861	3 230	16.81	37.21	32.66	10.15	3.03
1871	3 689	14.67	38.03	32.58	11.14	3.66
1881	4 325	13.85	36.02	33.94	12.14	4.12
1891	4 833	12.64	34.49	35.40	12.91	4.55
1901	5 371	12.03	32.73	36.19	14.00	5.05
1911	7 207	12.35	30.15	38.81	14.06	4.66
1921	8 788	12.05	31.51	36.63	15.02	4.78
1931	10 377	10.36	31.29	36.07	16.74	5.55
1941	11 507	9.14	28.39	37.19	18.61	6.67
1951	14 009	12.29	25.60	36.63	17.74	7.75
1961	18 238	12.37	29.44	33.19	17.37	7.63
1971	21 568	8.42	30.97	33.87	18.66	8.09
1981	24 343	7.32	24.70	39.14	19.13	9.70
1991	27 297	6.99	20.42	41.33	19.66	11.61
1996	29 672	6.62	20.35	39.63	21.32	12.07
2000[2]	30 750	5.78	20.05	38.31	23.34	12.52

Source: © *Census of Canada, Statistics Canada*
(1) As of July 1 each year. Percentages may not add to 100 due to rounding. (2) Preliminary intercensal estimates.

Male and Female Population by Age Group

(thousands)

		Total Population	Under 5 Years	5–9 Years	10–14 Years	15–24 Years	25–34 Years	35–44 Years	45–54 Years	55–64 Years	65 Years and Over
1851	MALE	1 250	233	173	152	248	168	116	78	46	35
	FEMALE ...	1 186	218	173	146	252	161	103	67	38	30
1861	MALE	1 660	277	218	203	341	232	156	107	70	54
	FEMALE ...	1 570	266	211	196	337	222	141	92	59	44
1871	MALE	1 869	276	264	243	374	249	175	132	86	74
	FEMALE ...	1 820	265	255	233	385	256	171	120	73	61
1881	MALE	2 189	304	284	262	455	302	217	161	111	94
	FEMALE ...	2 136	295	278	251	464	301	212	153	100	84
1891	MALE	2 460	309	300	282	504	366	263	191	131	115
	FEMALE ...	2 373	302	292	272	499	354	246	180	122	105
1901	MALE	2 752	326	313	297	543	412	331	234	157	139
	FEMALE ...	2 620	320	306	285	530	386	299	214	148	133
1911	MALE	3 822	450	396	356	745	687	475	334	209	171
	FEMALE ...	3 385	440	389	346	653	535	388	286	184	165
1921	MALE	4 530	534	529	462	757	693	630	434	276	215
	FEMALE ...	4 258	525	521	452	761	650	532	366	246	206
1931	MALE	5 375	543	573	543	990	778	707	590	356	295
	FEMALE ...	5 002	531	560	531	962	717	627	485	306	281
1941	MALE	5 901	534	529	556	1 083	920	745	649	494	391
	FEMALE ...	5 606	518	517	545	1 069	891	691	579	421	377
1951	MALE	7 089	879	714	575	1 070	1 066	950	728	557	551
	FEMALE ...	6 921	843	684	556	1 077	1 108	919	679	520	535
1961	MALE	9 219	1 154	1 064	948	1 316	1 258	1 191	959	655	674
	FEMALE ...	9 019	1 102	1 016	908	1 301	1 222	1 199	920	635	717
1971	MALE	10 795	930	1 152	1 181	2 016	1 462	1 286	1 132	854	782
	FEMALE ...	10 773	887	1 102	1 129	1 988	1 428	1 241	1 160	877	963
1981	MALE	12 068	914	912	985	2 356	2 106	1 497	1 256	1 031	1 011
	FEMALE ...	12 275	869	865	936	2 303	2 110	1 471	1 242	1 128	1 350
1991	MALE	13 455	976	978	963	1 944	2 420	2 176	1 487	1 180	1 330
	FEMALE ...	13 842	931	930	915	1 887	2 446	2 196	1 479	1 220	1 840
1996	MALE	14 692	1 007	1 033	1 031	2 059	2 400	2 502	1 891	1 253	1 515
	FEMALE ...	14 980	958	984	978	1 965	2 346	2 499	1 897	1 286	2 067
2000[1]	MALE	15 223	911	1 048	1 052	2 128	2 222	2 666	2 176	1 384	1 645
	FEMALE ...	15 517	866	996	998	2 025	2 171	2 640	2 189	1 427	2 204

Source: © *Census of Canada, Statistics Canada* (1) Updated intercensal population estimates as of July 1, 2000.

Canadian Population Projections[1] by Age Group

(thousands)

	Total Population	Under 5 Years	5–9 Years	10–14 Years	15–24 Years	25–34 Years	35–44 Years	45–54 Years	55–64 Years	65 Yrs and Over
2006										
MALE	15 947.4	841.4	918.4	1 075.8	2 213.4	2 228.3	2 519.7	2 509.1	1 796.5	1 844.8
FEMALE ...	16 281.2	798.8	872.0	1 020.6	2 109.6	2 167.4	2 482.9	2 517.5	1 855.3	2 457.3
2011										
MALE	16 511.6	855.1	880.0	957.7	2 261.3	2 311.7	2 343.3	2 667.9	2 129.3	2 105.4
FEMALE ...	16 850.2	811.3	835.9	905.9	2 155.0	2 244.8	2 305.2	2 651.2	2 200.4	2 740.6
2016										
MALE	17 044.8	877.0	893.6	919.8	2 155.4	2 383.3	2 369.6	2 536.7	2 388.1	2 521.0
FEMALE ...	17 375.0	831.7	848.2	870.3	2 051.3	2 313.1	2 321.5	2 505.9	2 451.9	3 181.1
2021										
MALE	17 531.4	890.6	915.2	933.2	2 003.3	2 430.3	2 449.2	2 374.1	2 545.9	2 989.7
FEMALE ...	17 850.4	844.3	868.4	882.4	1 904.5	2 356.1	2 394.2	2 337.4	2 582.0	3 681.1
2026										
MALE	17 939.6	880.9	928.6	954.5	1 979.9	2 327.9	2 517.4	2 403.3	2 431.6	3 515.5
FEMALE ...	18 250.9	834.9	880.8	902.2	1 881.7	2 254.8	2 458.2	2 354.3	2 446.4	4 237.5

Source: © *Statistics Canada* (1) Figures represent the medium-growth projection and are based on 2000 population estimates. Due to rounding, the totals may not always add up to the sum of the figures.

Canadian Population by Country of Birth

	1931	1951	1971	1991	1996*
Total Population	10 376 786	14 009 429	21 568 310	27 296 855	28 846 760
Total Foreign Born	2 307 525[11]	2 059 911[11]	3 295 530[11]	4 342 885[11]	4 971 070[11]
Afghanistan[1]	—	—	—	5 545	10 915
Africa—Other	—	—	—	26 355	43 160
Algeria[1]	—	—	—	3 900	8 005
Argentina[1]	—	—	—	11 110	11 740
Asia—Other	6 310	6 740	52 795	24 310	47 940
Australia	3 565	4 161	14 335	13 955	14 660
Austria[2]	37 391	37 598	40 450	26 680	24 600
Barbados[3]	—	—	—	14 825	15 225
Belgium	17 033	17 251	25 770	22 480	21 805
Brazil[1]	—	—	—	7 330	9 360
Cambodia[1]	—	—	—	17 960	19 355
Caribbean & Bermuda—Other	—	—	—	25 995	36 965
Central America—Other	—	—	—	5 745	9 025
Chile[1]	—	—	—	22 870	23 880
China	42 037	24 166	57 150	157 405	231 055
Colombia[1]	—	—	—	7 865	9 465
Czech and Slovak Federal . . . Republic, former [12]	22 835	29 546	43 100	42 615	41 225
Denmark[14]	17 217	15 679	28 045	—	—
Ecuador[1]	—	—	—	8 015	9 640
Egypt[1]	—	—	—	28 020	33 930
El Salvador[1]	—	—	—	28 295	39 020
Ethiopia, former[1]	—	—	—	11 060	18 595
Europe—Other[5]	10 657	10 858	87 255	8 665	7 980
Fiji[3]	—	—	—	15 995	20 580
Finland[14]	30 354	22 035	24 930	—	—
France	16 756	15 650	51 655	55 159	62 600
Germany[6]	39 163	42 693	211 060	180 525	181 650
Ghana[1]	—	—	—	6 675	13 085
Greece	5 579	8 594	78 780	83 680	79 695
Guatemala[1]	—	—	—	8 920	13 270
Guyana[3]	—	—	—	66 060	77 700
Haiti[1]	—	—	—	39 880	49 395
Hong Kong[3]	—	—	—	152 405	241 095
Hungary	28 523	32 929	68 495	57 010	54 225
India[3,7]	4 672	3 934	43 645	173 675	235 930
Indonesia	—	—	—	7 610	8 515
Iran[1]	—	—	—	30 710	47 405
Iraq[1]	—	—	—	7 165	16 795
Ireland	—	24 110	38 490	28 405	28 940
Israel (and Palestine/ . . . . West Bank/Gaza Strip)[1]	—	—	—	16 770	20 390
Italy	42 578	57 789	385 755	351 615	332 110
Jamaica[3]	—	—	—	102 440	115 800
Japan	12 261	6 239	9 485	12 280	14 990
Kenya[3]	—	—	—	16 585	18 005
Korea[4,13]	—	—	—	33 170	46 025
Laos[4]	—	—	—	14 445	14 765
Lebanon[1]	—	—	—	54 600	63 130
Malaysia[4]	—	—	—	16 100	19 460
Malta[3]	—	—	—	10 185	9 445
Mexico[1]	—	—	—	19 400	27 480
Morocco[1]	—	—	—	16 790	20 435
Netherlands	10 736	41 457	133 525	129 615	124 545
Nicaragua[1]	—	—	—	6 460	8 545
Norway[14]	32 679	22 969	16 350	—	—
Oceania—Other[15]	—	—	—	16 305	13 780 ▶

	1931	1951	1971	1991	1996
▶ Pakistan[7]	—	—	—	25 180	39 245
Peru[1]	—	—	—	11 480	15 235
Philippines[4]	—	—	—	123 295	184 550
Poland[8]	171 169	164 474	160 040	184 695	193 375
Portugal[8]	—	—	—	161 180	158 815
Romania[9]	40 322	19 733	24 405	33 785	46 400
Scandanavia	—	—	—	54 980	50 145
Singapore[1]	—	—	—	6 285	7 970
Somalia[1]	—	—	—	5 290	16 740
South America—Other	—	—	—	15 840	19 445
South Africa[3]	2 235	2 057	—	24 730	28 465
Spain[8]	—	—	—	11 170	11 240
Sri Lanka[4]	—	—	—	25 435	67 425
Syria[1]	—	—	—	11 005	13 105
Sweden[14]	34 415	22 635	14 110	—	—
Switzerland[8]	6 076	6 414	13 895	16 330	19 310
Taiwan[4]	—	—	—	17 770	49 290
Tanzania[1]	—	—	—	17 820	18 130
Thailand[1]	—	—	—	5 815	7 710
Trinidad/Tobago[3]	—	—	—	49 385	62 020
Turkey[8]	—	—	—	12 180	14 430
Uganda[1]	—	—	—	8 960	10 755
USSR, former[10]	133 869	188 292	160 120	99 355	108 390
United Kingdom	1 138 942	912 482	933 040	717 750	655 535
UK possessions/ dependencies[5]	35 416	10 415	112 120	—	—
United States	344 574	282 010	309 640	249 075	244 695
Viet Nam[4]	—	—	—	113 595	139 325
Yugoslavia, former[8]	17 110	20 912	78 285	88 815	121 975

Source: © *Statistics Canada, Census of Canada**   (—) Not reported.

*Statistics Canada will release data from the 2001 Census in Spring, 2002. (1) Included in "Other countries" until 1986 Census. (2) Includes Hungary (Austria-Hungary) in 1911 Census. (3) British possessions/dependencies (see UK possessions) during various census years could include African, Asian, Caribbean, Mediterranean and Pacific possessions, as well as any territory in British North America prior to Confederation with Canada (in the case of Newfoundland, this was not until 1949); many not reported separately until 1986 Census. (4) Included in "Asia—Other" until 1986 Census. (5) More detailed breakdown given in subsequent census data. (6) Total for Germany includes both East and West Germany. (7) Totals for India before 1986 include Pakistan. (8) Where not reported, included in "Europe—Other." (9) For 1911 Census, also includes Bulgaria. (10) Includes Russia. (11) Totals include those where country unknown or not noted: 1931: 3 051; 1951: 6 089; 1971: 78 805; 1991: 65; 1996: 20. (12) Includes Czech and Slovak Federal Republics. (13) Includes North and South Korea. (14) After 1986, reported as Scandanavia. (15) Includes New Zealand.

What Does Population Density Tell Us?

*C*anada's largest cities (Toronto, Vancouver and Montreal) attract the lion's share of newcomers. In 1999, 190,001 immigrants arrived in Canada; 70.8% headed to one of those three cities. (Nearly 44% went to Toronto.) But while these cities appear to be crowded—sprawling into nearby land and stretching resources to the limit—population density figures indicate that our country is fairly empty.

Canada's population density (total population divided by total area) is 3.1 persons per sq. km. Compared to more densely populated countries—the Netherlands, with 387.5 residents per sq. km, Japan (335.3), Belgium (334.5) or the U.K. (242)—Canada is thinly populated. If Canada had the same population density as the Netherlands, there would be around 1,858,626,070 of us.

Could Canada support such a population? While the country has abundant natural resources, a lot of the land within our borders is barely habitable. The Arctic tundra and much of the Canadian Shield have delicate ecosystems that can only support the tiny, hardy vegetation and nomadic wildlife that speckle their territory. As in Australia (pop. density 2.5), another country with big cities and large tracts of inhospitable desert, this figure can be misleading.

Top 15 Ethnic Origins in Canada, 1996[1]

Ethnic origin as defined in the Census refers to the ethnic or cultural group(s) to which an individual's ancestors belonged. In other words, it refers to the ancestral roots of the population—not place of birth, citizenship or nationality.

In the 1996 Census, respondents were given four blank spaces to indicate single or multiple ethnic origins. Over 35 percent of them (10.2 million) reported more than one ethnic origin, reflecting intermarriage among those who have been in Canada for several generations.

The table below shows the 15 most commonly cited ethnic origins, either as the sole ethnic origin or as part of a mixed heritage.

	Total Responses	Single Ethnic Origin	Multiple Ethnic Origins
Total population	28 528 125	18 303 625	10 224 495
Canadian	8 806 275	5 326 995	3 479 285
English	6 832 095	2 048 275	4 783 820
French	5 597 845	2 665 250	2 932 595
Scottish	4 260 840	642 970	3 617 870
Irish	3 767 610	504 030	3 263 580
German	2 757 140	726 145	2 030 990
Italian	1 207 475	729 455	478 025
Aboriginal	1 101 955	477 630	624 330
Ukrainian	1 026 475	331 680	694 790
Chinese	921 585	800 470	121 115
Dutch	916 215	313 880	602 335
Polish	786 735	265 930	520 805
South Asian	723 345	590 145	133 200
Jewish	351 705	195 810	155 900
Norwegian	346 310	47 805	298 500

Source: © *Census of Canada, Statistics Canada*   (1) Data from the Census 2001 will be released in Spring 2002.

Visible Minority Population by Group, 1996[1]

The 1996 Census also gathered information on the number of people in Canada who are members of a visible minority, as defined by the Employment Equity Act: "persons, other than Aboriginal peoples, who are non-Caucasian in race or non-white in colour." According to the 1996 Census, these groups accounted for 11.2 percent of the population (3,197,480 people).

The visible minorities are represented by the following groups:

	Total Number	% of Total Population[2]
Total visible minority population	3 197 480	11.2
Chinese	860 150	3.0
South Asian	670 585	2.4
Black	573 860	2.0
Arab/West Asian	244 665	0.9
Filipino..................	234 200	0.8

	Total Number	% of Total Population[2]
Latin American	176 975	0.6
Southeast Asian	172 765	0.6
Japanese	68 135	0.2
Korean	64 835	0.2
Visible minority not included elsewhere.....	69 745	0.2
Multiple visible minority	61 570	0.2

Source: © *Census of Canada, Statistics Canada*
(1) Data from the Census 2001 will be released in Spring 2002. (2) Total population in 1996 was 28 528 125.

Canadian Population by Mother Tongue[1]

As Canada's population has become more diverse, so have the mother tongues reported at census time. The table below shows all languages reported to be the mother tongue of 10,000 Canadians or more in the 1996 Census, with historical comparisons.

(thousands of persons and percent of total population)

	1941	%	1951	%	1961	%	1971	%	1991	%	1996	%
Total Population .	11 507		14 009		18 238		21 568		27 297		28 847	
English	6 448	56.0	8 281	59.1	10 661	58.5	12 974	60.2	16 170	59.2	16 891	58.6
French	3 355	29.2	4 069	29.0	5 123	28.1	5 794	26.9	6 503	23.8	6 637	23.0
Chinese	34	0.3	28	0.2	49	0.3	95	0.4	499	1.8	716	2.5
Italian	80	0.7	92	0.7	340	1.9	538	2.5	511	1.9	485	1.7
German	322	2.8	329	2.3	564	3.1	561	2.6	466	1.7	450	1.6
Spanish	1	...	2	...	7	...	24	0.1	177	0.6	213	0.7
Polish	129	1.1	129	0.9	162	0.9	135	0.6	190	0.7	213	0.7
Portugese	n.a.		n.a.		18	0.1	87	0.4	212	0.8	211	0.7
Punjabi	n.a.		n.a.		n.a.		n.a.	n.a.	136	0.5	202	0.7
Ukranian	313	2.7	352	2.5	361	2.0	310	1.4	187	0.7.	163	0.6
Arabic	8	0.1	5	...	13	0.1	29	0.1	100	0.4	149	0.5
Dutch	53	0.5	88	0.6	170	0.9	145	0.7	139	0.5	134	0.5
Tagalog (Philipino)	n.a.		n.a.		n.a.		n.a.		100	0.4	133	0.5
Greek	9	0.1	8	0.1	40	0.2	104	0.5	126	0.5	121	0.4
Vietnamese ...	n.a.		n.a.		n.a.		n.a.		79	0.3	107	0.4
Hungarian	46	0.4	42	0.3	86	0.5	87	0.4	80	0.3	77	0.3
Cree	n.a.		n.a.		n.a.		n.a.		74	0.3	77	0.3
Tamil	n.a.		n.a.		n.a.		n.a.		31	0.1	67	0.2
Persian (Farsi) .	n.a.		n.a.		n.a.		n.a.		41	0.2	60	0.2
Russian	52	0.5	39	0.3	43	0.2	32	0.1	35	0.1	58	0.2
Korean	n.a.		n.a.		n.a.		n.a.		36	0.1	55	0.2
Croatian	n.a.		n.a.		n.a.		n.a.		40	0.1	50	0.2
Gujarati	n.a.		n.a.		n.a.		n.a.		38	0.1	45	0.2
Hindi	n.a.		n.a.		n.a.		n.a.		35	0.1	43	0.2
Urdu	n.a.		n.a.		n.a.		n.a.		25	0.1	40	0.1
Romanian	n.a.		n.a.		n.a.		n.a.		22	0.1	36	0.1
Creoles	n.a.		n.a.		n.a.		n.a.		28	0.1	35	0.1
Japanese	22	0.2	18	0.1	18	0.1	17	0.1	30	0.1	34	0.1
Serbian	n.a.		n.a.		n.a.		n.a.		11	...	29	0.1
Inuktitut	n.a.		n.a.		n.a.		n.a.		24	0.1	27	0.1
Armenian	n.a.		n.a.		n.a.		n.a.		26	0.1	26	0.1
Czech[2]	38	0.3	46	0.3	51	0.3	45	0.2	27	0.1	25	0.1
Finnish	37	0.3	32	0.2	45	0.2	37	0.2	28	0.1	25	0.1
Somali	n.a.		n.a.		n.a.		n.a.		—		25	0.1
Ojibway	n.a.		n.a.		n.a.		n.a.		22	0.1	23	0.1
Yiddish	130	1.1	104	0.7	82	0.4	50	0.2	25	0.1	21	0.1
Danish	19	0.2	16	0.1	35	0.2	27	0.1	22	0.1	20	0.1
Macedonian ...	n.a.		n.a.		n.a.		n.a.		15	0.1	19	0.1
Serbo-Croatian .	n.a.		n.a.		n.a.		n.a.		5	...	18	0.1
Slovak	n.a.		n.a.		n.a.		n.a.		18	0.1	18	0.1
Bengali	n.a.		n.a.		n.a.		n.a.		8	...	16	0.1
Khmer	n.a.		n.a.		n.a.		n.a.		14	...	15	0.1
Slovenian	n.a.		n.a.		n.a.		n.a.		9	...	14	...
Hebrew	n.a.		n.a.		n.a.		n.a.		12	...	13	...
Lao	n.a.		n.a.		n.a.		n.a.		12	...	13	...
Turkish	n.a.		n.a.		n.a.		n.a.		9	...	12	...
Estonian	n.a.		n.a.		n.a.		n.a.		12	...	11	...
Norwegian	60	0.5	44	0.3	40	0.2	27	0.1	13	...	10	...
Swedish	50	0.4	36	0.3	33	0.2	22	0.1	12	...	10	...
Latvian	n.a.		n.a.		n.a.		n.a.		10	...	10	...
Lithuanian	n.a.		n.a.		n.a.		n.a.		11	...	9	...

Source: © *Census of Canada, Statistics Canada*   (n.a.) Not available/not collected. (...) Too small to be included.
(1) The language first spoken in childhood and still understood. (2) Prior to 1996, includes Slovak.

Native Population of Canada

	1991				1996[2]			
	Total Population with Aboriginal Origins[1,4]	Native Indian	Métis	Inuit	Total Aboriginal Population[3]	Native Indian	Métis	Inuit
Canada	1 002 675	783 980	212 650	49 255	799 010	554 290	210 190	41 080
Newfoundland	13 110	5 845	1 605	6 460	14 205	5 430	4 685	4 265
Prince Edward Island ..	1 880	1 665	185	75	950	825	120	15
Nova Scotia	21 885	19 950	1 590	770	12 380	11 340	860	210
New Brunswick	12 815	11 835	975	450	10 250	9 180	975	120
Quebec	137 615	112 590	19 480	8 480	71 415	47 600	16 075	8 300
Ontario	243 550	220 135	26 905	5 250	141 525	118 830	22 790	1 300
Manitoba	116 200	76 370	45 575	900	128 685	82 990	46 195	360
Saskatchewan	96 580	69 385	32 840	540	111 245	75 205	36 535	190
Alberta	148 220	99 650	56 310	2 825	122 840	72 645	50 745	795
British Columbia	169 035	149 570	22 295	1 990	139 655	113 315	26 750	815
Yukon	6 390	5 870	565	170	6 175	5 530	565	110
Northwest Territories ..	35 390	11 100	4 310	21 355	39 690	11 400	3 895	24 600
Nunavut[5]	n.a.	n.a.	n.a.	n.a.	20 690	90	80	20 490

Source: © *Census of Canada*   (n.a.) Not applicable.
(1) The 1991 Census question on ethnic or cultural origins gathered information on the number of people who reported North American Indian, Métis or Inuit origin as either a single response or in combination with other origins. (2) The numbers shown may exceed the total population as 6 400 respondents counted themselves as belonging to more than one group. (3) The 1996 data examined the responses to both an ancestry and an identity question, and the resulting information is a compilation of the two. The identity question included a more direct inquiry into whether the person considered him or herself to have an Aboriginal identity in addition to an Aboriginal ancestry. (4) In the 1991 Census, 78 reserves were incompletely enumerated, representing 37 000 individuals. (5) Data from the 1996 Census was used to create a profile for Nunavut.

Status Indian Population[1], 2000

	Number of Bands	On Reserve	On Crown Land	Off Reserve	Total Indian Population
Canada	612	368 556	23 437	283 506	675 499
Atlantic Provinces	31	17 053	22	9 322	26 397
Quebec	39	43 046	1 228	19 041	63 315
Ontario	126	76 872	1 474	75 600	153 946
Manitoba	62	68 357	1 737	37 052	107 146
Saskatchewan	70	52 291	1 802	52 018	106 111
Alberta	44	53 641	2 904	28 828	85 373
British Columbia	198	56 359	442	53 728	110 529
Yukon Territory	16	699	3 173	3 761	7 633
Northwest Territories	26	238	10 655	4 156	15 049

Source: *Indian and Northern Affairs Canada*
(1) Status Indians are those individuals registered with the Indian and Northern Affairs Canada under the *Indian Act*.

Largest Native Bands in Canada, 2000

Band, Province	Population[1]	Band, Province	Population[1]
Six Nations of the Grand River[2], Ontario ..	20 876	Lac La Ronge, Saskatchewan	7 126
Mohawks of Akwesasne, Ontario	9 500	Peguis, Manitoba	7 077
Blood, Alberta	9 051	Mohawks of the Bay of Quinte	7 046
Kahnawake, Quebec	8 888	Peter Ballantyne Cree Nation, Saskatchewan	6 901
Saddle Lake, Alberta	7 648	Wikwemikong, Ontario	6 479

Source: *Indian and Northern Affairs Canada*
(1) Registered Indian population as of December 31, 2000. (2) This Six Nations Band consists of the following 13 registry groups: Bay of Quinte Mohawk, Bearfoot Onondaga, Deleware, Konadaha Seneca, Lower Cayuga, Lower Mohawk, Niharondasa Seneca, Oneida, Onondaga Clear Sky, Tuscarora, Upper Cayuga, Upper Mohawk, Walker Mohawk.

Canadian Urban and Rural Population

(thousands)

Year	Urban Total	Urban %	Rural Non-Farm	%	+ Rural Farm	%	= Rural Total	%
1871	722	19.6	n.a.	n.a.	n.a.	n.a.	2 967	80.4
1881	1 110	25.7	n.a.	n.a.	n.a.	n.a.	3 215	74.3
1891	1 537	31.8	n.a.	n.a.	n.a.	n.a.	3 296	68.2
1901	2 014	37.5	n.a.	n.a.	n.a.	n.a.	3 357	62.5
1911	3 273	45.4	n.a.	n.a.	n.a.	n.a.	3 934	54.6
1921	4 352	49.5	n.a.	n.a.	n.a.	n.a.	4 436	50.5
1931	5 469	52.7	1 670	16.1	3 238	31.2	4 908	47.3
1941	6 271	54.5	2 123	18.4	3 113	27.1	5 236	45.5
1951	8 817	62.9	2 423	17.3	2 769	19.8	5 192	37.1
1956	10 715	66.6	2 734	17.0	2 632	16.4	5 366	33.4
1961	12 700	69.6	3 465	19.0	2 073	11.4	5 538	30.4
1966	14 727	73.6	3 374	16.9	1 914	9.6	5 288	26.4
1971	16 410	76.1	3 738	17.3	1 420	6.6	5 158	23.9
1976	17 367	75.5	4 591	20.0	1 035	4.5	5 626	24.5
1981	18 436	75.7	4 867	20.0	1 040	4.3	5 907	24.3
1986	19 352	76.5	5 067	20.0	890	3.5	5 957	23.5
1991	20 907	76.6	5 583	20.5	807	3.0	6 390	23.4
1996	22 461	77.9	n.a.	n.a.	n.a.	n.a.	6 386	22.1

Source: © *Census of Canada, Statistics Canada*
(n.a.) Not available.

Definitions: Urban: persons living in a built-up area having a population of 1 000 or more, and a population density of 400 or more per sq. km; **Rural:** persons living outside "urban areas"; **Rural Farm:** persons living in rural areas who are members of households of farm operators; **Rural Non-Farm:** persons living in rural areas who are not members of households of farm operators.

Urban and Rural Population by Province

Province	1951 Rural	1951 Urban	1991 Rural	1991 Urban	1996 Rural	1996 Urban
Canada	5 174 555	8 473 458	6 389 724	20 907 135	6 385 551	22 461 210
Newfoundland[1]	n.a.	n.a.	264 023	304 451	237 973	313 819
Prince Edward Island	73 744	24 685	77 952	51 813	75 097	59 460
Nova Scotia	297 753	344 831	418 434	481 508	411 424	497 858
New Brunswick	300 686	215 011	378 686	345 214	377 712	360 421
Quebec	1 358 363	2 697 318	1 544 752	5 351 211	1 541 170	5 597 625
Ontario	1 346 443	3 251 099	1 831 043	8 253 842	1 794 832	8 958 741
Manitoba	336 961	439 580	304 767	787 175	313 835	800 063
Saskatchewan	579 258	252 470	365 531	623 397	363 059	627 178
Alberta	489 826	449 675	514 660	2 030 893	554 011	2 142 815
British Columbia	371 739	793 471	641 922	2 640 139	667 112	3 057 388
Yukon Territory	6 502	2 594	11 462	16 335	12 319	18 447
Northwest Territories	13 280[2]	2 724[2]	36 492[2]	21 157[2]	19 073	20 176
Nunavut[3]	n.a.	n.a.	n.a.	n.a.	17 934	7 219

Source: © *Census of Canada, Statistics Canada*
(1) Newfoundland joined confederation in 1949, and urban/rural split in population was not included in 1951 census data. (2) Includes Nunavut. (3) Nunavut became a province in 1999, but data from the 1996 Census was used to create a profile.

2001 Census Data Release Dates

Population and Dwelling Counts	*Spring 2002*	*Aboriginal/Citizenship/Immigration*	*January 2003*
Age and Sex	*July 2002*	*Employment questions*	*February 2003*
Marital Status	*October 2002*	*Education questions*	*March 2003*
Language/Mobility/Migration	*December 2002*	*Socio-economic questions*	*May 2003*

Population of Canadian Towns and Cities

(more than 5,000 inhabitants)

Town or city classification is made according to the official designations adopted by provincial or federal authority. *Indicates a city or *ville* in Quebec; all others are towns.

	POPULATION		AREA
	1991	1996	(sq. km)

■ NEWFOUNDLAND

	POPULATION		AREA
	1991	1996	(sq. km)
Bay Roberts	5 474	5 472	24.15
Carbonear	5 259	5 168	11.81
Channel-Port aux Basques	5 644	5 243	37.83
Clarenville	4 473	5 335	139.98
Conception Bay South	17 590	19 265	59.40
Corner Brook*	22 410	21 893	147.55
Deer Lake	5 161	5 222	71.75
Gander	10 339	10 364	101.16
Grand Falls-Windsor	14 693	14 160	56.66
Happy Valley-Goose Bay	8 610	8 655	306.42
Labrador City	9 061	8 455	6.47
Marystown	6 739	6 742	59.27
Mount Pearl*	23 676	25 519	15.06
Paradise	7 358	7 960	27.83
Placentia	5 515	5 013	58.00
Portugal Cove-St. Philip's	5 459	5 773	56.43
St. John's*	104 659	101 936	431.75
Stephenville	7 621	7 764	34.80
Torbay	4 707	5 230	36.04

■ PRINCE EDWARD ISLAND

	1991	1996	(sq. km)
Charlottetown*	31 541	32 531	42.64
Stratford	5 427	5 869	22.14
Summerside*	13 636	14 525	27.71

■ NOVA SCOTIA

	1991	1996	(sq. km)
Amherst	9 742	9 669	16.65
Bedford	11 618	13 638	39.79
Bridgewater	7 248	7 351	13.35
Dartmouth*	67 798	65 629	58.57
Halifax*	114 455	113 910	79.22
Kentville	5 506	5 551	17.12
New Glasgow	9 905	9 812	10.36
Truro	11 683	11 938	38.09
Yarmouth	7 781	7 568	11.14

■ NEW BRUNSWICK

	1991	1996	(sq. km)
Bathurst*	14 409	13 815	90.94
Campbellton*	8 699	8 404	17.30
Dieppe	10 650	12 497	51.62
Edmunston*	10 835	11 033	34.58
Fredericton*	46 466	46 507	129.58
Grand Falls (Grand-Sault)	6 083	6 133	17.73
Miramichi	21 165	19 241	175.07

	POPULATION		AREA
	1991	1996	(sq. km)
Moncton*	56 823	59 313	142.37
Oromocto	9 325	9 194	22.08
Quispamsis	8 446	8 839	39.98
Riverview	16 270	16 653	34.26
Sackville	5 494	5 393	74.42
Saint John*	74 969	72 494	322.88
Woodstock	4 782	5 092	14.08

■ QUEBEC

	1991	1996	(sq. km)
Alma*	25 910	26 127	109.27
Amos*	13 783	13 632	428.72
Amqui*	6 518	6 800	120.82
Anjou*	37 207	37 308	13.64
Asbestos*	6 487	6 271	13.47
Aylmer*	32 244	34 901	91.21
Baie-Comeau*	26 012	25 554	352.27
Beaconsfield*	19 616	19 414	10.64
Beauharnois*	6 449	6 435	40.44
Beauport*	69 158	72 920	71.32
Bécancour*	10 911	11 489	434.29
Beloeil*	18 516	19 294	24.01
Bernieres-Saint-Nicholas	14 431	15 594	94.12
Blainville*	22 679	29 603	55.20
Boisbriand*	21 124	25 227	27.32
Bois-des-Filion*	6 337	7 124	3.92
Boucherville*	33 796	34 989	69.33
Brossard*	64 793	65 927	44.98
Buckingham*	10 548	11 678	14.59
Candiac*	10 765	11 805	16.54
Cap-de-la-Madeleine*	33 716	33 438	17.30
Cap-Rouge*	14 105	14 163	6.39
Carignan*	5 386	5 614	62.35
Chambly*	15 893	19 716	25.06
Charlemagne*	5 598	5 739	1.76
Charlesbourg*	70 792	70 942	67.53
Charny*	10 239	10 661	8.80
Chateauguay*	39 833	41 423	35.40
Chibougamau*	8 855	8 664	754.08
Chicoutimi*	62 670	63 061	156.66
Coaticook*	6 637	6 653	12.60
Cote-Saint-Luc*	30 126	29 705	7.40
Cowansville*	11 986	12 051	49.12
Delson*	6 063	6 703	7.15
Deux-Montagnes*	13 035	15 953	6.05
Dolbeau*	8 181	8 310	46.32 ▶

	POPULATION		AREA		POPULATION		AREA
	1991	1996	(sq. km)		1991	1996	(sq. km)
Dollard-des-Ormeaux*	46 922	47 826	15.05	Mont-Saint-Hilaire*	12 267	13 064	43.39
Donnacona*	5 659	5 739	20.12	Montmagny*	11 861	11 885	125.77
Dorval*	17 249	17 572	20.76	Montréal*	1 017 669	1 016 376	177.10
Drummondville*	43 171	44 882	70.25	Montréal-Nord*	85 516	81 581	11.03
Farnham*	6 146	6 044	25.07	Montréal-Ouest*	5 180	5 254	1.63
Fleurimont*	14 727	16 262	34.77	Outremont*	22 935	22 571	3.68
Gaspé*	16 402	16 517	1 105.11	Pierrefonds*	48 735	52 986	24.39
Gatineau*	92 284	100 702	140.62	Pincourt*	9 749	10 023	9.24
Granby*	42 804	43 316	72.73	Plessisville*	6 952	6 810	4.34
Grand-Mere*	14 287	14 223	70.79	Point-Claire*	27 647	28 435	19.19
Greenfield Park*	17 652	17 337	4.58	Port-Cartier*	7 383	7 070	87.34
Hampstead*	7 219	6 986	1.77	Québec*	167 517	167 264	88.86
Hull*	60 707	62 339	37.35	Repentigny*	49 630	53 824	24.42
Iberville*	9 352	9 635	4.90	Rimouski*	30 873	31 773	76.02
Joliette*	17 396	17 541	22.52	Riviere-du-Loup*	14 017	14 721	16.94
Jonquiere*	57 933	56 503	209.62	Roberval*	11 628	11 640	147.24
Kirkland*	17 495	18 678	10.34	Rock Forest*	14 551	16 604	51.34
L'Ancienne-L'orette*	15 242	15 895	7.87	Rosemere*	11 198	12 025	10.20
L'Assomption*	10 817	11 366	66.44	Rouyn-Noranda*	28 958	28 819	210.79
L'Ile Bizard*	11 352	13 038	22.69	Roxboro*	5 879	5 950	2.23
L'Ile Perrot*	8 065	9 178	4.92	Saint-Antoine*	10 232	10 806	9.90
La Baie*	20 995	21 057	261.69	Saint-Basile-le-Grand*	10 127	11 771	34.84
La Plaine*	10 576	14 413	39.70	Saint-Bruno-de-Montarville*	23 849	23 714	41.79
La Prairie*	15 237	17 128	43.33	Saint-Constant*	18 424	21 993	57.32
La Sarre*	8 513	8 345	148.30	Saint-Emile*	6 916	9 889	8.77
La Tuque*	12 577	12 102	599.07	Saint-Eustache*	37 278	39 848	70.03
Lac-Mégantic*	5 852	5 864	20.97	Saint-Félicien*	9 340	9 599	168.56
Lachenaie*	15 052	18 489	42.75	Saint-Georges*	19 583	20 057	24.94
Lachine*	35 266	35 171	17.38	Saint-Hubert*	74 093	77 042	63.05
Lachute*	11 730	11 493	96.24	Saint-Hyacinthe*	39 292	38 981	36.63
LaSalle*	73 804	72 029	16.42	Saint-Jean-Chrysostome*	12 717	16 161	82.90
Laval*	314 398	330 393	245.40	Saint-Jean-sur-Richelieu*	37 607	36 435	47.42
Le Gardeur*	13 814	16 853	44.00	Saint-Jérome*	23 384	23 916	15.79
LeMoyne*	5 412	5 052	0.96	Saint-Lambert*	20 976	20 971	6.43
Lévis*	39 417	40 407	44.0	Saint-Laurent*	72 402	74 240	46.17
Longueuil*	129 808	127 997	42.85	Saint-Leonard*	73 120	71 327	12.93
Loretteville*	14 219	14 168	6.94	Saint-Louis-de-France	6 747	7 327	61.54
Lorraine*	8 410	8 876	5.46	Saint-Luc*	15 008	18 371	51.20
Louiseville*	8 000	7 911	62.57	Saint-Raymond*	8 126	8 773	671.22
Magog*	14 034	14 050	15.28	Saint-Rédempteur*	5 862	6 358	3.46
Marieville*	5 128	5 510	3.42	Saint-Rémi*	5 768	5 707	79.67
Mascouche*	25 828	28 097	107.95	Saint-Romuald*	9 830	10 604	18.34
Masson-Angers*	5 753	7 989	55.60	Saint-Timothée*	8 292	8 495	68.02
Matane*	12 756	12 364	24.35	Sainte-Agathe-des-Monts*	5 452	5 669	15.58
Mercier*	8 227	9 059	45.89	Sainte-Anne-des-Monts*	5 652	5 617	106.06
Mirabel*	17 971	22 689	492.20	Sainte-Anne-des-Plaines*	10 787	12 908	92.23
Mistassini*	6 842	6 904	248.50	Sainte-Catherine*	9 805	13 724	9.06
Mont-Joli*	6 265	6 267	9.59	Sainte-Foy*	71 133	72 330	83.86
Mont-Laurier*	7 862	8 007	82.05	Sainte-Julie*	20 632	24 030	47.91
Mont-Royal*	18 212	18 282	7.43	Sainte-Marie*	10 513	10 966	105.31 ▶

	POPULATION		AREA
	1991	1996	(sq. km)
Sainte-Marthe-sur-le-Lac* ..	7 410	8 295	9.01
Sainte-Thérèse*	24 158	23 477	10.09
Salaberry-de-Valleyfield* ...	27 598	26 600	27.47
Sept-Îles*	24 848	25 224	298.93
Shawinigan*	19 931	18 678	26.27
Shawinigan-Sud*	11 584	11 804	51.52
Sherbrooke*	76 431	76 786	57.77
Sillery*	12 519	12 003	6.73
Sorel*	24 253	23 248	38.04
Terrebonne*	39 700	42 214	73.21
Thetford Mines*	18 251	17 635	33.91
Tracy*	13 181	12 773	19.11
Trois-Rivières*	49 426	48 419	77.81
Trois-Rivières-Ouest*	20 076	22 886	28.75
Val-Bélair*	17 181	20 176	68.52
Val d'Or*	23 842	24 285	1 206.60
Vanier*	10 833	11 174	4.66
Varennes*	14 758	18 842	93.96
Vaudreuil-Dorion*	17 109	18 466	73.13
Verdun*	61 307	59 714	8.15
Victoriaville*	36 392	38 174	83.49
Westmount*	20 239	20 420	3.96

■ **ONTARIO**

	POPULATION		AREA
	1991	1996	(sq. km)
Ajax	57 350	64 430	67.70
Amherstburg	8 921	10 245	11.26
Ancaster	21 988	23 403	174.55
Arnprior	6 679	7 113	13.63
Aurora	29 454	34 857	49.16
Aylmer	6 244	7 018	5.85
Barrie*	62 278	79 191	76.79
Belleville*	37 243	37 083	29.13
Bracebridge	12 308	13 223	632.09
Bradford-West Gwillimbury .	17 702	20 213	197.26
Brampton*	234 445	268 251	265.04
Brantford*	81 997	84 764	71.22
Brockville*	21 582	21 752	20.25
Burlington*	129 575	136 976	177.40
Caledon	34 965	39 893	686.16
Cambridge*	92 772	101 429	115.64
Carleton Place	7 432	8 450	7.30
Chatham*	43 632	43 409	30.86
Clarington	49 479	60 615	607.79
Cobourg	15 079	16 027	15.89
Collingwood	14 382	15 596	33.60
Cornwall*	47 137	47 403	63.49
Dryden	6 505	6 711	16.86
Dundas	21 868	23 125	24.20
Dunnville	12 131	12 471	302.92
East Gwillimbury	18 637	19 770	245.14
Elliot Lake*	14 089	13 588	756.79

	POPULATION		AREA
	1991	1996	(sq. km)
Espanola	5 527	5 454	17.66
Essex	6 759	6 785	6.48
Etobicoke*	309 993	328 718	123.93
Fergus	7 940	8 884	7.23
Flamborough	29 616	34 037	489.90
Fort Erie	26 006	27 183	168.30
Fort Frances	8 891	8 790	26.05
Gananoque	5 209	5 219	9.01
Georgina	29 746	34 777	286.27
Gloucester*	101 677	104 022	293.86
Goderich	7 452	7 553	6.97
Gravenhurst	9 988	10 030	524.06
Grimsby	18 520	19 585	68.12
Guelph*	88 444	95 821	87.12
Haldimand	20 573	22 128	638.15
Halton Hills	36 816	42 390	275.86
Hamilton*	318 499	322 352	122.99
Hanover	6 711	6 844	6.49
Hawkesbury	9 713	10 162	8.71
Hearst	6 079	6 049	96.85
Huntsville	14 997	15 918	700.90
Ingersoll	9 378	9 849	10.21
Innisfil	21 249	24 711	284.10
Iroquois Falls	5 999	5 714	689.94
Kanata*	37 344	47 909	132.21
Kapuskasing	10 344	10 036	83.92
Kenora	9 782	10 063	15.33
Kincardine	6 601	6 620	10.25
Kingston*	56 597	55 947	29.64
Kingsville	5 716	5 991	4.27
Kirkland Lake	10 440	9 905	270.01
Kitchener*	168 282	178 420	135.15
LaSalle	16 628	20 566	65.61
Leamington	14 140	16 188	10.63
Lincoln	17 149	18 801	163.43
Lindsay	16 696	17 638	15.19
Listowel	5 404	5 467	6.19
London*	311 620	325 646	437.99
Markham	153 811	173 383	211.53
Midland	14 485	15 035	21.75
Milton	32 075	32 104	367.20
Mississauga*	463 388	544 382	273.86
Nanticoke*	22 727	23 485	674.72
Napanee	5 179	5 450	4.41
Nepean*	107 627	115 100	217.00
New Liskeard	5 431	5 112	6.42
New Tecumseth	20 344	22 902	274.83
Newmarket	45 474	57 125	35.91
Niagara Falls*	75 399	76 917	212.02
Niagara-on-the-Lake	12 945	13 238	131.11
Nickel Centre	12 332	13 017	378.36 ▶

	POPULATION 1991	1996	AREA (sq. km)
North Bay*	55 405	54 332	312.88
North York*	563 270	589 653	176.87
Oakville	114 670	128 405	138.18
Onaping Falls	5 402	5 277	228.98
Orangeville	17 921	21 498	14.07
Orillia*	25 925	27 846	28.55
Oshawa*	129 344	134 364	143.41
Ottawa*	313 987	323 340	110.15
Owen Sound*	21 674	21 390	23.69
Paris	8 600	8 987	13.64
Parry Sound	6 125	6 326	14.98
Pelham	13 328	14 343	124.52
Pembroke*	13 997	14 177	15.33
Penetanguishene	6 862	7 291	12.58
Perth	5 576	5 886	9.18
Peterborough*	68 379	69 535	53.99
Pickering*	68 631	78 989	226.52
Port Colborne*	18 766	18 451	122.82
Port Elgin	6 857	7 041	5.92
Port Hope	11 505	11 698	13.00
Rayside-Balfour	15 039	16 050	328.21
Renfrew	8 134	8 125	12.25
Richmond Hill	80 142	101 725	99.42
Rockland	6 771	8 070	8.49
Sarnia*	74 167	72 738	163.73
Sault Ste. Marie*	81 476	80 054	221.52
Scarborough*	524 598	558 960	187.70
Simcoe	15 539	15 380	40.51
Smiths Falls	9 439	9 131	8.20
St. Catharines*	129 300	130 926	94.43
St. Marys	5 496	5 952	12.14
St. Thomas*	30 332	32 275	32.22
Stoney Creek*	49 968	54 318	98.60
Stratford*	27 666	28 987	20.33
Strathroy	10 566	11 852	13.89
Sturgeon Falls	5 837	6 162	5.79
Sudbury*	92 884	92 059	262.73
Tecumseh	10 495	12 828	6.17
Thorold*	17 542	17 883	84.54
Thunder Bay*	113 496	113 662	322.87
Tillsonburg	12 019	13 211	21.99
Timmins*	47 461	47 499	3 004.39
Toronto*	635 395	653 734	97.15
Trenton*	16 908	17 179	11.68
Valley East	21 939	23 537	518.03
Vanier*	18 150	17 247	2.93
Vaughan*	111 359	132 549	275.34
Walden	9 805	10 292	718.62
Wallaceburg	11 846	11 772	10.71
Wasaga Beach	6 457	8 698	55.62

	POPULATION 1991	1996	AREA (sq. km)
Waterloo*	71 181	77 949	64.43
Welland*	47 914	48 411	81.23
Whitby	61 281	73 794	142.99
Whitchurch-Stouffville	18 357	19 835	206.85
Windsor*	191 435	197 694	120.29
Woodstock*	30 075	32 086	24.78
York*	139 819	146 534	23.18

■ MANITOBA

Brandon*	38 575	39 175	74.85
Dauphin	8 453	8 266	11.94
Flin Flon* (part in Man. balance in Sask.)	7 119	6 572	11.55
Morden	5 273	5 689	12.44
Portage La Prairie*	13 186	13 077	24.03
Selkirk	9 815	9 881	24.71
Steinbach	8 213	8 478	25.24
The Pas	6 166	5 945	28.46
Thompson*	14 977	14 385	16.85
Winkler	6 397	7 241	16.33
Winnipeg*	615 215	618 477	464.13

■ SASKATCHEWAN

Estevan*	10 240	10 752	17.67
Humboldt	4 989	5 074	11.92
Lloydminster*(part in Sask)	7 241	7 636	17.37
Melfort*	5 628	5 759	14.66
Melville*	4 905	4 646	15.41
Moose Jaw*	33 593	32 973	46.64
North Battleford*	14 348	14 051	35.48
Prince Albert*	34 181	34 777	64.98
Regina*	179 183	180 400	114.06
Saskatoon*	186 067	193 647	136.79
Swift Current*	14 824	14 890	22.87
Weyburn*	9 673	9 723	14.04
Yorkton*	15 315	15 154	23.82

■ ALBERTA

Airdrie*	12 456	15 946	21.02
Banff	5 688	6 098	4.86
Beaumont	5 042	5 810	5.59
Bonnyville	5 132	5 100	14.39
Brooks	9 433	10 093	15.81
Calgary*	710 795	768 082	716.79
Camrose*	13 420	13 728	26.10
Canmore	5 681	8 354	67.08
Coaldale	5 310	5 731	7.06
Cochrane	5 267	7 424	16.09
Crowsnest Pass	6 680	6 356	379.19
Drayton Valley	5 983	5 883	7.95
Drumheller*	6 263	6 587	26.24

	POPULATION		AREA
	1991	**1996**	**(sq. km)**
Edmonton*	616 741	616 306	670.08
Edson	7 323	7 399	25.89
Fort Saskatchewan*	12 092	12 408	45.10
Grande Prairie*	28 271	31 140	41.83
High River	6 269	7 359	11.58
Hinton	9 046	9 961	22.27
Innisfail	5 700	6 116	9.82
Lacombe	6 934	8 018	12.45
Leduc*	13 970	14 305	25.49
Lethbridge*	60 974	63 053	119.90
Lloydminster (part)*	10 042	11 317	23.93
Medicine Hat*	43 625	46 783	112.96
Morinville	6 104	6 226	12.32
Okotoks	6 723	8 510	15.76
Olds	5 549	5 815	10.14
Peace River	6 717	6 536	21.20
Ponoka	5 861	6 149	10.07
Red Deer*	58 145	60 075	58.18
Rocky Mountain House	5 641	5 805	10.82
Slave Lake	5 607	6 553	18.00
Spruce Grove	12 908	14 271	25.57
St. Albert*	42 146	46 888	33.97
Stettler	4 947	5 220	9 35
Stony Plain	7 226	8 274	26.51
Sylvan Lake	4 210	5 178	8.18
Taber	6 664	7 214	15.66
Vegreville	5 138	5 337	13.86
Wainwright	4 732	5 079	8.16
Wetaskiwin*	10 657	10 959	16.45
Whitecourt	6 938	7 783	25.40

■ BRITISH COLUMBIA

Abbotsford	86 928	105 403	343.85
Burnaby	158 858	179 209	88.45
Castlegar*	6 579	7 027	16.16
Colwood*	13 468	13 848	17.87
Comox	9 477	11 069	14.47
Coquitlam*	84 021	101 820	123.36
Courtenay*	11 698	17 335	15.49
Cranbrook*	16 447	18 131	17.18
Dawson Creek*	10 981	11 125	20.30

	POPULATION		AREA
	1991	**1996**	**(sq. km)**
Fort St. John*	14 156	15 021	21.73
Kamloops*	67 057	76 394	296.06
Kelowna*	75 953	89 442	212.57
Kimberley*	6 531	6 738	58.19
Ladysmith	4 875	6 456	7.53
Langley*	19 765	22 523	10.18
Merritt*	6 898	7 631	23.74
Nanaimo*	60 129	70 130	88.19
Nelson*	8 849	9 585	7.71
New Westminster*	43 585	49 350	15.38
North Vancouver*	38 436	41 475	10.77
Parksville	7 381	9 472	15.93
Penticton*	27 258	30 987	40.80
Port Alberni*	18 523	18 468	17.81
Port Coquitlam*	36 773	46 682	28.76
Port Moody*	17 756	20 847	26.21
Prince George*	69 653	75 150	315.94
Prince Rupert*	16 620	16 714	53.56
Qualicum Beach	5 137	6 728	11.14
Quesnel*	8 208	8 468	23.00
Revelstoke*	7 729	8 047	34.09
Richmond*	126 624	148 867	124.20
Sidney	10 082	10 701	5.02
Smithers	5 029	5 624	13.63
Surrey*	245 173	304 477	301.76
Terrace*	11 433	12 779	19.21
Trail*	7 921	7 696	18.74
Vancouver*	471 844	514 008	113.09
Vernon*	27 722	31 817	75.09
Victoria*	71 228	73 504	18.78
View Royal	5 996	6 441	15.42
White Rock*	16 314	17 210	5.05
Williams Lake*	10 395	10 472	23.45

■ YUKON TERRITORY

Whitehorse*	17 925	19 157	413.48

■ NORTHWEST TERRITORIES

Yellowknife*	15 179	17 275	102.38

■ NUNAVUT

Iqaluit	n.a.	4 220	n.a.

Source: © _Census of Canada, Statistics Canada_   *Indicates a city or _ville_ in Quebec; all others are towns.

What's an Urban Area?

S_tatistics Canada defines an urban area as a minimum population of 1,000 and a population density of at least 400 people per square kilometre, based on the previous census. All territory outside of these areas is considered rural._

Statistics Canada occasionally redefines an urban land area, reflecting either urban growth or municipal reorganization. For example, while the land area shown for most cities is the same for both the 1991 and 1996 census, St. John's quadrupled and Charlottetown went from 6.99 to 42.64 sq. km.

Population of Census Metropolitan Areas[1] in Canada

Statistics Canada defines a census metropolitan area (CMA) as a very large urban area, together with neighbouring urban and rural areas that have a high degree of economic and social integration with that large urban area. The urban area itself (or urbanized core) must have a population of at least 100,000 based on the previous census. For a more detailed look at these cities, see "Canadian Cities" pages 31–37.

CMA	Population (000s)					Land Area (sq. km)
	1976	1986	1996[2]	1999[3]	2000[4]	1996
Calgary, Alta.	469 917	671 453	845 493	925 578	952 960	5 083.28
Chicoutimi, Que.	128 643	158 468	162 949	161 980	160 130	1 723.31
Edmonton, Alta.	554 228	774 026	885 123	928 308	944 194	9 536.63
Halifax, N.S.	267 991	295 922	341 463	352 396	355 996	2 503.10
Hamilton, Ont.	529 371	557 029	642 729	664 499	671 679	1 358.50
Kitchener, Ont.	272 158	311 195	395 208	415 097	421 764	823.64
London, Ont..	270 383	342 302	410 407	418 536	421 296	2 105.07
Montreal, Que.	2 802 485	2 921 357	3 393 739	3 447 237	3 480 342	4 024.21
Oshawa, Ont.	135 196	203 543	277 073	292 486	297 869	894.19
Ottawa-Hull, Ont.-Que.	693 288	819 263	1 037 853	1 068 059	1 080 986	5 686.45
Quebec, Que.	542 158	603 267	683 741	688 297	689 654	3 149.65
Regina, Sask.	151 191	186 521	199 527	199 998	200 455	3 421.58
St. Catharines-Niagara, Ont.	301 921	343 258	382 813	388 480	389 965	1 399.80
St. John's, Nfld.	143 390	161 901	177 054	175 532	175 062	789.66
Saint John, N.B.	112 974	121 265	128 029	127 762	127 713	3 509.34
Saskatoon, Sask.	133 750	200 665	225 963	230 910	232 600	5 322.09
Sherbrooke, Que.	104 505	129 960	150 098	152 548	152 897	979.94
Sudbury, Ont.	157 030	148 877	165 009	159 341	157 132	2 612.11
Thunder Bay, Ont.	119 253	122 217	129 089	127 063	126 343	2 295.27
Toronto, Ont.	2 803 101	3 431 981	4 403 092	4 665 727	4 751 408	5 867.73
Trois Rivières, Que.	98 583	128 888	142 234	141 918	141 785	871.91
Vancouver, B.C.	1 166 348	1 380 729	1 912 120	2 027 899	2 048 823	2 820.66
Victoria, B.C..	218 250	255 225	316 828	316 933	317 492	633.44
Windsor, Ont..	247 582	253 988	287 486	300 079	304 390	861.66
Winnipeg, Man.	578 217	625 304	679 174	680 014	681 146	4 077.64

Source: © *Census of Canada, Statistics Canada*

(1) Total land area considered to be part of CMA varied from census to census. (2) Final postcensal estimate. (3) Updated postcensal estimate. (4) Preliminary estimate.

FOCUS ON...

Counting Canada's People

It will take over 37,000 persons to do the census of Canada's population of roughly 31 million persons. It will also take time to do the job thoroughly, that is from May 15, 2001 known as Census Day, to Spring 2002 when the first set of data will be released and beyond as the data is refined. The census counted the population and collected important information about the social and economic situation of the people living in the various regions of Canada. In addition to the data gathered about the people themselves, however, numerous other tidbits of information have emerged about how the Census 2001 was done and about the process of carrying out the actual exercise. Here are some of these facts and figures involved in counting Canada's people.

The census provides a statistical portrait of Canada's people. Every five years Statistics Canada conducts a census which enumerates everyone living in Canada: that is Canadian citizens, both native-born and naturalized, landed immigrants and non-permanent residents, such as students and those claiming refugee status. The Census also counts citizens and landed immigrants who are temporarily outside Canada on Census Day, for example military and civilian personnel stationed outside Canada and their families, as well as persons aboard merchant ships of the Canadian government. People in prisons are counted, and those who live in other institutions such as hospitals and residences for senior citizens. The census counts persons alive at midnight between May 14 and 15, 2001. This means that a child born on May 15 will not be counted until the next census in 2006.

Collecting the data

Some 34,000 census representatives throughout Canada delivered the census questionnaires to every household, that is across the 9.2 million square kilometers of Canadian territory, so that everyone could be included.

About 2,800 census commissioners trained and supervised these census representatives, who had to pass a written test and a reliability check after completing at least 19 hours of training.

Each census representative had a designated geographic area to cover, called an enumeration area (EA). A large urban EA had a maximum of about 650 dwellings. In fact, an EA could be just one apartment building. A rural EA had a minimum of approximately 125 dwellings and could cover an area of many square kilometers. Roughly 43,000 EAs were covered in the 2001 Census. For the 1996 Census there were 50,000 EAs. This means that the EAs are now larger and with more households than in 1996. Census representatives therefore had larger assignments, and more time to drop off questionnaires: 10 days as compared with 6 days in 1996.

Everyone took part and "counted themselves in" when they mailed back their completed forms, and roughly 13.2 million questionnaires are collected. Not everyone received the same questionnaire. Four out of five households (80%) received the short census questionnaire that contained seven questions on basic topics such as relationship to person 1, age, sex, marital status, and mother tongue. One in five households (20%) received the long form which contained the seven questions from the short form plus 52 additional questions on topics such as religion, education, ethnicity, mobility, and new questions on birthplace of parents and language spoken at work.

The census taking began before the official census date on May 15. In remote areas of the north such as Baffin Island, the census was conducted in February and March, to enumerate inhabitants before they migrated to hunting and fishing camps for the summer. In those areas, the census was conducted by personal interview. In addition, there was preparation time well before the actual census day. In fact, the countdown for the

2001 Census began more than five years ago with the first planning meeting in December 1995. Some of the information gathered in a census cannot be provided by other means, so in that early planning period Statistics Canada consults with the public and major data users about their needs for information through the census database. In this manner, the census content is put through a rigorous testing and review process to ensure that the questions asked on census day take account of new information requirements and cover emerging social and economic issues.

After the roughly 13.2 million questionnaires were collected, the next step in the census operations was the Processing phase. It began about one month after Census Day–translating the responses from approximately 11.8 million households into meaningful data. Data are keyed, in a process requiring about 5 billion key strokes. The job of entering this enormous volume of data from the census questionnaires is contracted out to the Canada Customs and Revenue Agency (CCRA), formerly Revenue Canada, since they are equipped to handle masses of data on an annual basis each time they do our income tax returns. CCRA performs the work at the seven regional tax centers across the country: St. John's, Summerside, Shawinigan, Jonquière, Sudbury, Winnipeg and Surrey, and at the main CCRA office in Ottawa. As the data are key-entered, they are transmitted across dedicated lines to the Ottawa office, then the data are transferred to cartridges and transported by bonded carrier to Statistics Canada on a daily basis, to be loaded on the mainframe computer in Ottawa.

Despite the use of computers in processing, census operations still consume enormous volumes of paper. One area alone, the respondent's guide to accompany the short-form questionnaire, consumed some 215,460 kg of paper. This guide is no longer printed.

Number Crunching

Editing and imputation is a very important activity in the processing phase. This is done during two periods, August 2001 through April 2002 to prepare the first set of data of reports for publication and through October 2002 for the second set. The data collected in any survey or census contain omissions or inconsistencies. These errors can be the result of respondents missing a question, or they can be due to errors generated during processing.

The editing process detects errors, and the imputations process corrects them. The edit and imputation activity is very important because these statistics must be accurate. The edited census data are used to produce population estimates. These estimates are then used to make the allocation of transfer payments from the federal government to the provinces and territories, and from the provincial/territorial governments to municipalities. In 2001 approximately 40 billion dollars will be transferred. Even a small error in the estimates could lead to the misallocation of millions of dollars. At a level that affects Canadians more directly, consistent estimates are essential to users, particularly those counts that are used as official estimates for administrative purposes, such as for planning the social programs of Old Age Security and the Child Tax Benefit, or to plan a variety of services such as day-care centres, schools and senior citizens' homes.

Time and Money

A census of population is a major undertaking. It involves significant numbers of skilled human resources, computer equipment and software, processing time, and volumes of paper, just to mention the major resources needed. For the Census 1986 about 42,000 people carried out the enumeration and other field activities at a total cost of roughly $150 million. By Census 1991 the project budget was $265 million. As the number crunching continues for the 2001 census, preparations for Census 2006 are underway. Planners are aware that they have to balance new data requirements, such as questions related to environmental concerns, with cost limitations; and the overall costs must be consistent with the relevant cost per household of the two previous censuses in 1991 and 1996.

Source: *Statistics Canada, Newsletter produced by the Census Communications Project.*

VITAL STATISTICS

Births in Canada

	Live Births	Birth Rate[1]		Live Births	Birth Rate[1]
1921	264 879	29.3	1961	475 700	26.1
1922	259 825	28.3	1962	469 693	25.3
1923	247 404	26.7	1963	465 767	24.6
1924	251 351	26.7	1964	452 915	23.5
1925	249 365	26.1	1965	418 595	21.3
1926	240 015	24.7	1966	387 710	19.4
1927	241 149	24.3	1967	370 894	18.2
1928	243 616	24.1	1968	364 310	17.6
1929	242 226	23.5	1969	369 647	17.6
1930	250 335	23.9	1970	371 988	17.5
1931	247 205	23.2	1971	362 187	16.8
1932	242 698	22.5	1972	347 319	15.9
1933	229 791	21.0	1973	343 373	15.5
1934	228 296	20.7	1974	350 650	15.4
1935	228 396	20.5	1975	359 323	15.8
1936	227 980	20.3	1976	359 987	15.7
1937	227 869	20.1	1977	361 400	15.5
1938	237 091	20.7	1978	358 852	15.3
1939	237 991	20.6	1979	366 064	15.9
1940	252 577	21.6	1980	370 709	15.5
1941	263 993	22.4	1981	371 346	15.3
1942	281 569	23.5	1982	373 082	15.0
1943	292 943	24.2	1983	373 689	15.0
1944	293 967	24.0	1984	377 031	15.0
1945	300 587	24.3	1985	375 727	14.8
1946	343 504	27.2	1986	372 913	14.2
1947	372 589	28.9	1987	369 742	13.9
1948	359 860	27.3	1988	376 795	14.0
1949	367 092	27.3	1989	392 625	14.4
1950	372 009	27.1	1990	405 417	14.6
1951	381 092	27.2	1991	402 528	14.4
1952	403 559	27.9	1992	398 642	14.0
1953	417 884	28.1	1993	388 394	13.5
1954	436 198	28.5	1994	385 112	13.3
1955	442 937	28.2	1995	378 011	12.9
1956	450 739	28.0	1996	366 200	12.3
1957	469 093	28.2	1997	348 598	11.6
1958	470 118	27.5	1998[2]	342 418	11.3
1959	479 275	27.4	1999[3]	335 627	11.0[4]
1960	478 551	26.8	1999–00[3]	333 954	10.9[4]

Source: © *Statistics Canada*
(1) Per 1 000 population (2) Final data for Births from 1989 to 1998. (3) Updated data at July 16, 2001. (4) From July 1 of one year to June 30 of the next year.

Births by Province, 1999–2000[1]

	Births	Birth Rate[2]		Births	Birth Rate[2]
Canada	333 954	10.9	Manitoba	14 239	12.4
Newfoundland	4 724	8.8	Saskatchewan	12 632	12.3
Prince Edward Island	1 473	10.7	Alberta	37 775	12.7
Nova Scotia	9 314	9.9	British Columbia	41 667	10.3
New Brunswick	7 659	10.1	Yukon	368	11.9
Quebec	73 536	10.0	Northwest Territories	758	18.2
Ontario	129 030	11.1	Nunavut	779	28.5

Source: © *Statistics Canada*   (1) From July 1 to June 30. Updated data at July 16. (2) Rate per 1 000 population.

Expected Years of Life Remaining by Age, 1991

Age	Male % Dying[1]	Male Years of Life Remaining	Female % Dying[1]	Female Years of Life Remaining	Age	Male % Dying[1]	Male Years of Life Remaining	Female % Dying[1]	Female Years of Life Remaining
0	0.71	74.55	0.58	80.89	56	0.84	22.53	0.48	27.42
1	0.05	74.08	0.05	80.36	57	0.93	21.71	0.52	26.55
2	0.04	73.12	0.03	79.40	58	1.03	20.91	0.57	25.69
3	0.03	72.15	0.02	78.42	59	1.15	20.12	0.62	24.83
4	0.03	71.18	0.02	77.44	60	1.13	19.35	0.68	23.98
5	0.02	70.19	0.01	76.46	61	1.41	18.59	0.74	23.15
6	0.02	69.21	0.01	75.47	62	1.56	17.85	0.81	22.31
7	0.02	68.22	0.01	74.48	63	1.71	17.13	0.89	21.49
8	0.01	67.23	0.01	73.48	64	1.87	16.42	0.97	20.68
9	0.01	66.24	0.01	72.49	65	2.04	15.72	1.06	19.88
10	0.02	65.25	0.01	71.50	66	2.23	15.04	1.16	19.09
11	0.02	64.26	0.01	70.51	67	2.44	14.37	1.28	18.31
12	0.02	63.27	0.02	69.52	68	2.68	13.72	1.40	17.54
13	0.03	62.28	0.02	68.53	69	2.93	13.08	1.53	16.78
14	0.05	61.30	0.02	67.54	70	3.20	12.46	1.67	16.03
15	0.07	60.33	0.03	66.56	71	3.50	11.85	1.84	15.30
16	0.08	59.37	0.03	65.58	72	3.84	11.27	2.04	14.57
17	0.09	58.42	0.04	64.60	73	4.22	10.70	2.26	13.87
18	0.10	57.47	0.04	63.62	74	4.62	10.15	2.51	13.18
19	0.11	56.53	0.04	62.64	75	5.06	9.61	2.78	12.50
20	0.11	55.58	0.04	61.67	76	5.54	9.10	3.09	11.85
21	0.11	54.64	0.04	60.69	77	6.08	8.60	3.45	11.21
22	0.11	53.70	0.04	59.71	78	6.67	8.13	3.84	10.59
23	0.12	52.77	0.04	58.73	79	7.31	7.67	4.27	9.99
24	0.12	51.83	0.04	57.75	80	7.99	7.24	4.74	9.42
25	0.11	50.89	0.04	56.77	81	8.73	6.82	5.27	8.86
26	0.11	49.94	0.04	55.80	82	9.53	6.43	5.87	8.32
27	0.11	49.00	0.04	54.82	83	10.39	6.05	6.53	7.81
28	0.12	48.05	0.04	53.84	84	11.31	5.70	7.25	7.32
29	0.12	47.11	0.05	52.86	85	12.28	5.36	8.03	6.85
30	0.12	46.17	0.05	51.89	86	13.32	5.04	8.90	6.41
31	0.13	45.22	0.05	50.91	87	14.43	4.74	9.85	5.99
32	0.13	44.28	0.05	49.94	88	15.60	4.45	10.90	5.59
33	0.14	43.34	0.06	48.96	89	16.84	4.18	12.02	5.21
34	0.14	42.39	0.06	47.99	90	18.15	3.93	13.22	4.85
35	0.15	41.45	0.07	47.02	91	19.52	3.69	14.53	4.51
36	0.16	40.51	0.07	46.05	92	20.98	3.46	15.96	4.20
37	0.16	39.58	0.08	45.09	93	22.52	3.25	17.49	3.90
38	0.17	38.64	0.09	44.12	94	24.12	3.05	19.13	3.62
39	0.18	37.71	0.09	43.16	95	25.80	2.86	20.87	3.35
40	0.19	36.77	0.10	42.20	96	27.57	2.68	22.74	3.11
41	0.20	35.84	0.11	41.24	97	29.42	2.51	24.74	2.87
42	0.21	34.91	0.12	40.28	98	31.36	2.35	26.88	2.66
43	0.23	33.98	0.13	39.33	99	33.37	2.20	29.13	2.45
44	0.25	33.06	0.15	38.38	100	35.48	2.05	31.52	2.25
45	0.28	32.14	0.17	37.44	101	37.67	1.90	34.05	2.05
46	0.31	31.23	0.19	36.50	102	39.96	1.74	36.75	1.85
47	0.34	30.32	0.21	35.57	103	42.34	1.56	39.59	1.64
48	0.37	29.42	0.23	34.64	104	44.82	1.34	42.58	1.39
49	0.41	28.53	0.25	33.72	105	47.38	1.03	45.73	1.04
50	0.45	27.65	0.27	32.80	106	100.00	0.50	100.00	0.50
51	0.50	26.77	0.30	31.89					
52	0.55	25.90	0.33	30.98					
53	0.61	25.04	0.36	30.08					
54	0.68	24.19	0.40	29.19					
55	0.75	23.35	0.43	28.30					

Source: © *Census of Canada, Statistics Canada*

(1) Represents the percentage of the population that will die before reaching the next age; in some cases totals do not equal 100 percent due to rounding.

Canadian Health Indicators, 1999

The table below contains approximately 100 of the indicators most commonly used to measure health, and the factors that determine the health of Canadians. Use this table to gain a general picture of the health of Canadians only. Caution should be used in drawing any conclusions from this information due to different methods of collecting data for each category. As well, estimates are not age-standardized, unless otherwise noted. For example, "Injuries" includes people of all ages with injuries while "Work injuries" covers only those age 15 and over.

Well-being

Excellent health (self-rated)	25%
High self-esteem	49%

Function

Long-term activity limitation	16%
Disability days (past 2 weeks)	0.85
Very good health (functional status)	88%

Injuries

Injuries (admissions/10 000 pop.)	72.2
Work injuries (per 1 000 workers)	27.6
Traffic deaths (per 100 000 pop.)	10
Traffic injuries (per 100 000 pop.)	762

Miscellaneous Conditions

Low birth weight rate	5.8%
Stillbirths (per 10 000 births)	65.4
Overweight (age 20 to 64)	29%

Mental Health

Depression (probable)	4%
High chronic stress	26%
Psychiatric hospitalization rate	709.1
High work stress	4%

Sexually Transmitted Diseases

HIV positive tests	41 049
Gonorrhea (per 100 000 pop.)	16.8
Chlamydia (per 100 000 pop.)	114.8

Vaccine-Preventable Diseases

Measles (per 100 000 pop.)	1.1
Whooping cough (per 100 000 pop.)	18.0

Enteric, Foodborne and Waterborne Diseases

Campylobacter (per 100 000 pop.)	42.7
Salmonella (per 100 000 pop.)	22.0
Giardia (per 100 000 pop.)	20.3
Hepatitis A (per 100 000 pop.)	8.7
E. coli 0157 (per 100 000 pop.)	4.1

Cancer (new cases per 100 000 population)

Women	346
Men	501

Cancer (deaths per 100 000 population)

Women	151
Men	232

Chronic Conditions

Arthritis/Rheumatism	14%
Asthma	7%
Back problems	14%
Food allergies	7%
Non-food allergies	22%

Deaths (per 100 000 population)

Total	653
Cancer (all)	185
Lung cancer	49
Breast cancer (women only)	29
Cardiovascular disease	226
Coronary heart disease	133
Stroke	47
Respiratory (all)	58
Pneumonia/Influenza	22
Accidents (all)	43
Suicide (all)	13
Infant mortality (per 1 000 live births)	5.6
Perinatal mortality rate (per 1 000 births)	6.7
Early neonatal mortality rate (per 1 000 live births)	3.3
Therapeutic abortions (per 100 live births)	18.7

Potential Years of Life Lost (per 100 000 population)

Total	3 804
Cancer	1 098
Accidents	746
Suicide	417
Respiratory	113
Heart disease	491
Stroke	91
Other	848

Personal Health Practices

Current smoker	28%
Regular drinker	53%
14+ drinks per week	9%
5+ drinks per occasion	42%
Driving after drinking (1+ times)	10%
Currently use cannabis	7%
1+ illicit drugs, lifetime	24%
Physically active	21%
Walk to work	7%
Always use bicycle helmet	29%
Always insist on seatbelt use	86%
Took actions to improve health	47%

Health-Care Services

Influenza vaccination, ever	26%
Pap smear test, ever (women, age 18+)	87%
Screening mammogram, past 2 years (age 50–69)	54%
Blood pressure test, past year	71%
HIV/AIDS test, ever	15%
Visits to health professional (1+)	93%
Visits to a physician (1+)	81%
Visits to a dentist, past year	62%
Dental insurance	55%
Eye examination, past year	42%
Insurance for corrective lenses	47%
1+ medications used, past two days	63%
Insurance for prescription medicines	61%
Unmet health-care needs	5%
Emergency visits (per 1 000 pop.)	433.1
Hospital (average days of stay)	1.1
Health expenditures (% of GDP)	9.2%
Per capita health expenditures	$2,512.72

Sources: © *Statistics Canada; Health Canada*

Chronic Conditions by Age and Region[1], 1998–99

(percentage)

	Canada	Atlantic	Quebec	Ontario	Prairies	British Columbia
45-64						
Arthritis/Rheumatism	**19.9**	25.7[2]	14.8[2]	21.4	23.0[2]	18.3
Hypertension	**16.2**	19.4[2]	15.0	17.2	16.3	13.9
Heart disease	**4.8**	6.1	4.6	6.1[2]	3.8	2.3[2]
Diabetes	**5.1**	5.9	4.1	5.7	5.8	4.4
Migraine headaches	**7.5**	7.1	6.7	7.5	8.0	8.9
Asthma	**5.8**	5.4	5.7	6.2	4.5[2]	6.6
Bronchitis/Emphysema	**2.4**	3.4[2]	2.1	2.3	2.5	2.6
Activity limitation	**16.2**	20.4[2]	13.2[2]	16.7	17.4	16.9
65+						
Arthritis/Rheumatism	**41.5**	44.5	34.3[2]	45.4[2]	44.1	38.8
Hypertension	**35.6**	41.0[2]	35.3	37.9	31.3[2]	31.4
Heart disease	**17.4**	19.7	14.6	18.8	16.1	19.0
Diabetes	**11.6**	12.7	11.8	12.5	9.6	10.7
Migraine headaches	**3.3**	2.9	3.1	3.2	2.9	4.7
Asthma	**5.7**	7.5	4.5	6.0	6.8	4.9
Bronchitis/Emphysema	**5.8**	6.2	6.4	5.6	4.6	6.5
Activity limitation	**29.1**	32.3	22.9[2]	31.4	30.4	29.8

Sources: © *Health Reports; Statistics Canada*
(1) Prevalence of chronic conditions or long-term activity limitation. Data collected from 1978–79 Canada Health Survey; and 1998–99 National Population Health Survey, cross sectional sample. (2) Significantly different from national average.

Who's Still Smoking?

*S*tatistics Canada reported that 23% of the population over the age of 12 smoked in 1998/99. While the percentage was spread evenly across the age groups after age 20: 12-14 (3%); 15-19 (22%); 20-44 (28%); 45-64 (23%); and over 65 (11%), there was some variation among the provinces (and between genders).

	Total	Male	Female
Newfoundland	25%	28%	21%
Prince Edward Island	28%	33%	23%
Nova Scotia	26%	28%	23%
New Brunswick	25%	24%	25%
Quebec	27%	28%	25%
Ontario	21%	22%	20%
Manitoba	22%	24%	20%
Saskatchewan	24%	25%	23%
Alberta	24%	28%	20%
British Columbia	19%	20%	18%

There was also some variation among workers, with 28% of full-time workers smoking daily (about 33% of those smokers consumed more than 25 cigarettes a day). It was noted, however, that there had been a general decline in smoking since 1978/79, and that after 1986 there was a decline in the amount smoked, except among those in outdoor, blue-collar occupations. 60% of full-time workers now face smoking restrictions in their place of work.

Expected Years of Life Remaining by Sex

	At Birth		At Age 20		At Age 40		At Age 60		At Age 80	
	Male	Female	Male	Female	Male	Female	Male	Female	Male	Female
1921[1]	n.a.	n.a.	49.1	49.2	32.2	33.0	16.6	17.1	6.0	6.1
1931	60.0	62.1	49.1	49.8	32.0	33.0	16.3	17.2	5.6	5.9
1941	63.0	66.3	49.6	51.8	31.9	34.0	16.1	17.6	5.5	6.0
1951	66.3	70.8	50.8	54.4	32.5	35.6	16.5	18.6	5.8	6.4
1956	67.6	72.9	51.2	55.8	32.7	36.7	16.5	19.3	5.9	6.8
1961	68.4	74.2	51.5	56.7	33.0	37.5	16.7	19.9	6.1	6.9
1966	68.8	75.2	51.5	57.4	33.0	38.2	16.8	20.6	6.4	7.3
1971	69.3	76.4	51.7	58.2	33.2	39.0	17.0	21.4	6.4	7.9
1976	70.2	77.5	52.1	59.0	33.6	39.7	17.2	22.0	6.4	8.2
1981	71.9	79.0	53.4	60.1	34.7	40.7	18.0	22.9	6.9	8.8
1986	73.0	79.7	54.3	60.7	35.5	41.2	18.4	23.2	6.9	8.9
1991	74.6	80.9	55.6	61.7	36.8	42.2	19.4	24.0	7.2	9.4

Source: © *Census Canada, Statistics Canada*   (n.a.) Not available. (1) Excludes Quebec.

Deaths in Canada

	Deaths	Death Rates[1]		Deaths	Death Rates[1]		Deaths	Death Rates[1]
1921[2]	104 531	11.6	1974	166 794	7.3	1988	190 011	7.1
1926[2]	111 055	11.4	1975	167 404	7.2	1989	190 965	7.0
1931[3]	108 446	10.2	1976	167 009	7.1	1990	191 973	6.9
1936[3]	111 111	9.9	1977	167 498	7.0	1991	195 568	7.0
1941[3]	118 797	10.1	1978	168 179	7.0	1992	196 535	6.9
1946	118 785	9.4	1979	168 183	6.9	1993	204 912	7.1
1951	125 823	9.0	1980	171 473	7.0	1994	207 077	7.1
1956	131 961	8.2	1981	171 029	6.9	1995	210 733	7.2
1961	140 985	7.7	1982	174 413	6.9	1996	212 859	7.2
1966	149 863	7.5	1983	174 484	6.9	1997	215 669	7.2
			1984	175 727	6.8	1998	219 834	7.3
1971	157 272	7.3	1985	181 323	7.0	1999[4]	225 123	7.4
1972	62 413	7.4	1986	184 224	7.0	1999–00[5]	229 138	7.5
1973	164 039	7.4	1987	184 953	7.0			

Source: © *Statistics Canada*
(1) Per 1 000 population. (2) Excludes Que., Nfld., Yukon and N.W.T. (3) Excludes Nfld., Yukon and N.W.T. (4) Updated data. (5) From July 1 to June 30.

Deaths by Province, 1999-2000[1]

	Deaths	Death Rate[2]		Deaths	Death Rate[2]
Canada	**229 138**	**7.5**	Manitoba	10 344	9.0
Newfoundland	4 599	8.5	Saskatchewan	9 320	9.1
Prince Edward Island	1 255	9.1	Alberta	18 276	6.1
Nova Scotia	8 829	9.4	British Columbia	30 418	7.5
New Brunswick	6 788	9.0	Yukon	163	5.3
Quebec	52 527	7.1	Northwest Territories	160	3.8
Ontario	86 318	7.4	Nunavut	141	5.2

Source: © *Statistics Canada*
(1) From July 1 to June 30. Updated data at July 16. (2) Rate per 1 000 population.

Leading Causes of Male Death

	1977		1998	
	No. of Deaths	Rate[1]	No. of Deaths	Rate[1]
All Causes	96 872	875.5	113 006	754.3
Diseases of the Circulatory System	45 760	413.6	39 942	266.6
Ischaemic Heart Disease	31 180	281.8	23 692	158.1
Stroke	7 160	64.7	6 488	43.3
Cancer	20 378	184.2	32 392	216.2
Lung	6 142	55.5	10 016	66.9
Prostate	1 833	16.6	3 664	24.5
Respiratory Diseases	6 828	61.7	11 379	76.0
Other Chronic Airway Obstructions	2 584	23.4	4 639	31.0
Pneumonia and Influenza	2 764	25.0	4 112	27.4
External Causes of Injury and Poisoning	11 366	102.7	8 885	59.3
Suicide	2 459	22.2	2 925	19.5
Motor Vehicle Accidents	3 831	34.6	2 016	13.5
Diseases of the Digestive System	3 742	33.8	4 020	26.8
Chronic Liver Disease and Cirrhosis	1 924	17.4	1 435	9.6
Noninfective Enteritis and Colitis	n.a.	n.a.	439	2.8
Endocrine Diseases	1 616	14.6	3 622	24.2
Diabetes Mellitus	1 289	11.7	2 885	19.3
Fluid, Electrolyte and Acid-Base Balance	85	0.8	198	1.3
Diseases of the Nervous System	1 023	9.3	2 946	19.7
Alzheimer's Disease	n.a.	n.a.	896	6.0
Parkinson's Disease	n.a.	n.a.	722	4.8
Mental Disorders	763	6.9	2 413	16.I
Senile and Presenile Dementia	n.a.	n.a.	898	6.0
Psychoses, including Alcoholic	154	1.4	563	3.0
All Other Causes	5 396	48.8	7 407	49.4

Source: © *Statistics Canada*

(1) Per 100 000 population by gender.

Leading Causes of Female Death

	1977		1998	
	No. of Deaths	Rate[1]	No. of Deaths	Rate[1]
All Causes	70 626	644.3	105 083	688.4
Diseases of the Circulatory System	35 714	325.8	39 447	258.4
Ischaemic Heart Disease	20 228	184.6	19 337	126.7
Stroke	8 362	76.3	9 166	59.9
Cancer	16 041	146.5	28 205	184.8
Lung	1 519	13.9	6 249	40.9
Breast	3 321	30.3	4 875	31.9
Respiratory Diseases	4 005	36.5	10 454	68.5
Pneumonia and Influenza	2 392	21.8	4 990	32.7
Other Chronic Airway Obstructions	2 213	20.2	3 121	20.4
External Causes of Injury and Poisoning	4 635	43.4	4 377	28.7
Accidental Falls	829	7.6	1 491	9.8
Motor Vehicle Accidents	1 424	13.0	931	6.1
Endocrine Diseases	2 103	19.2	4 007	26.2
Diabetes Mellitus	1 721	15.7	731	4.8
Fluid, Electrolyte and Acid-Base Balance	98	0.9	683	4.5
Diseases of the Digestive System	2 388	21.8	3 806	24.9
Chronic Liver Disease and Cirrhosis	838	7.7	2 871	18.8
Noninfective Enteritis and Colitis	n.a.	n.a.	328	2.1
Diseases of the Nervous System	786	7.2	3 645	23.9
Alzheimer's Disease	n.a.	n.a.	1 916	12.5
Parkinson's Disease	n.a.	n.a.	564	3.7
Mental Disorders	382	3.57	3 863	25.3
Senile and Presenile Dementia	n.a.	n.a.	1 893	12.4
Psychoses, including Alcoholic	161	1.47	161	1.1
All Other Causes	4 572	41.71	7 279	47.7

Source: © *Statistics Canada*

(1) Per 100 000 population by gender.

MIGRATION

How to Become a Canadian Citizen

To become a Canadian citizen, you must be at least 18 years of age, a permanent resident and in Canada legally.

If you are a permanent resident, you must have lived in Canada for at least three of the four years before the date of your application. If you lived in Canada before becoming a permanent resident, that time is counted at half the rate if it was during the four years before your application date.

You must be able to speak and understand spoken English or French, or be able to read and write in simple English or French.

If you are between 18 and 59 years of age, you must learn about Canada before becoming a citizen. When you apply for citizenship, you'll be sent a free publication called *A Look at Canada* on which your citizenship test will be based.

Children under 18 don't need to meet the three-year residency requirement; however, you must already be a Canadian citizen or be applying to become one. Children don't write a citizenship test.

Who Doesn't Qualify

Not everyone can become a Canadian citizen. You cannot become a citizen if

- you were convicted of an indictable offence in the past three years
- you are under a deportation order
- you were in prison, on parole or on probation in the past four years
- you have been charged with an indictable offence
- you are now charged with an offence under the Citizenship Act
- your Canadian citizenship has been revoked in the past five years
- you are under investigation for war crimes or crimes against humanity

Applying

1. **Get the correct application form.** It should be the "Application for Citizenship." Each child for whom you are applying needs a separate form.

2. **Read the form.** The cost to process your forms isn't refundable, so be sure you are ready to become a citizen and fill the form out carefully. The current fee for citizenship for adults is $200, and the fee for children under 18 is $100.

3. **Complete the application and attach necessary documents.** Photocopies of documents are acceptable, but you may need to bring the original when you take the test. The application form comes with detailed instructions.

4. **Mail the completed application.** Check that you have included all documentation and filled in the application completely.

5. **Prepare for your test.** Read the book *A Look at Canada* that will be sent to you. You may want to take a citizenship class if one is being held near you. A notice detailing the date and time of your citizenship test will be sent to you. The test may be oral or written.

6. **Take the oath.** Once you have met all the requirements, you will receive a notice detailing when and where the citizenship ceremony will take place.

Call Centres and Citizenship Offices

You can get more information on any of the topics discussed here by contacting one of the call centres listed below.

Montreal: (514) 496-1010
Toronto: (416) 973-4444
Vancouver: (604) 666-2171
Toll-free: 1-888-242-2100

Case Processing Centre

P.O. Box 7000
Sydney, NS B1P 6V6

Source: *Citizenship and Immigration Canada*

Canadian Immigration Totals

1853*	29 464	1890	75 067	1927	158 886	1964	112 606
1854*	37 263	1891	82 165	1928	166 783	1965	146 758
1855*	25 296	1892	30 996	1929	164 993	1966	194 743
1856*	22 544	1893	29 633	1930	104 806	1967	222 876
1857*	33 854	1894	20 829	1931	27 530	1968	183 974
1858*	12 339	1895	18 790	1932	20 591	1969	164 531
1859*	6 300	1896	16 835	1933	14 382	1970	147 713
1860*	6 276	1897	21 716	1934	12 476	1971	121 900
1861*	13 589	1898	31 900	1935	11 277	1972	122 006
1862*	18 294	1899	44 543	1936	11 643	1973	184 200
1863*	21 000	1900	41 681	1937	15 101	1974	218 465
1864*	24 779	1901	55 747	1938	17 244	1975	187 881
1865*	18 958	1902	89 102	1939	16 994	1976	149 429
1866*	11 427	1903	138 660	1940	11 324	1977	114 914
1867	10 666	1904	131 252	1941	9 329	1978	86 313
1868	12 765	1905	141 465	1942	7 576	1979	112 093
1869	18 630	1906	211 653	1943	8 504	1980	143 136
1870	24 706	1907	272 409	1944	12 801	1981	128 639
1871	27 773	1908	143 326	1945	22 722	1982	121 176
1872	36 578	1909	173 694	1946	71 719	1983	89 188
1873	50 050	1910	286 839	1947	64 127	1984	88 273
1874	39 373	1911	331 288	1948	125 414	1985	84 333
1875	27 382	1912	375 756	1949	95 217	1986	99 326
1876	25 633	1913	400 870	1950	73 912	1987	152 001
1877	27 082	1914	150 484	1951	194 391	1988	161 500
1878	29 807	1915	36 665	1952	164 498	1989	191 497
1879	40 492	1916	55 914	1953	168 868	1990	216 398
1880	38 505	1917	72 910	1954	154 227	1991	232 751
1881	47 991	1918	41 845	1955	109 946	1992	254 820
1882	112 458	1919	107 698	1956	164 857	1993	256 739
1883	133 624	1920	138 824	1957	282 164	1994	224 373
1884	103 824	1921	91 728	1958	124 851	1995	212 860
1885	79 169	1922	64 224	1959	106 928	1996	226 044
1886	69 152	1923	133 729	1960	104 111	1997	216 024
1887	84 526	1924	124 164	1961	71 689	1998	174 191
1888	88 766	1925	84 907	1962	74 586	1999	190 001
1889	91 600	1926	135 982	1963	93 151	2000[1]	227 363

Source: *Citizenship and Immigration Canada*

(*) Pre-Confederation. (1) Preliminary figure.

New Canadians in Search of a New Home

*T*oronto continues to be Canada's top magnet for immigrants, absorbing 98,376 applicants and dependants in 1997; 75,799 in 1998; and 83,267 in 1999. In comparison, Vancouver attracted 41,263 (1997); 29,616 (1998) and 27,785 (1999); and Montreal drew 22,741 (1997), 20,866 (1998) and 23,522 (1999). Where did they come from?

In 1997, China's takeover of Hong Kong resulted in a spike in immigrants from that region in all three cities: Hong Kong was the #2 source of new Canadians. Toronto welcomed 10,037; Vancouver took in 8,171 and Montreal received 1,381. Since 1997 immigration from Hong Kong has dropped sharply, while newcomers from the People's Republic of China became the prime source of newcomers in Toronto and Vancouver in the next two years, and held down second spot in Montreal in 1999. How significant is this source ranking? In 1999, in Vancouver, the top ten source countries represented 75% of newcomers; the top two (China and Taiwan) were the source of 38.9% new residents. In Toronto, the top ten countries supplied 57% of the new population, and in Montreal, 52% came from just ten countries.

(Based on data from Citizenship and Immigration Canada)

Immigration to Canada[1]

	Total Immigrants	United States	Asia[2]	Europe	Caribbean[3]	South America	Africa	Oceania
1956	164 857	9 777	3 537	145 554	1 351	1 551	1 079	1 924
1957	282 164	11 008	3 244	257 540	1 586	2 376	2 970	3 345
1958	124 851	10 846	4 223	102 279	1 519	2 168	1 355	2 344
1959	106 928	11 338	5 368	84 517	1 529	1 750	843	1 512
1960	104 111	11 247	4 002	82 922	1 542	1 823	833	1 657
1961	71 689	11 516	2 706	52 132	1 454	1 301	1 088	1 432
1962	74 586	11 643	2 593	53 790	1 842	1 103	2 171	1 384
1963	93 151	11 736	3 553	69 069	2 611	1 779	2 431	1 692
1964	112 606	12 565	6 121	82 798	2 467	2 257	3 874	2 303
1965	146 758	15 143	11 215	108 285	3 420	2 471	3 196	2 711
1966	194 743	17 514	13 835	148 410	4 357	2 604	3 661	4 057
1967	222 876	19 038	20 740	159 979	9 004	3 090	4 608	6 168
1968	183 974	20 422	21 686	120 702	8 129	2 693	5 204	4 815
1969	161 531	22 785	23 319	88 363	13 908	4 767	3 297	4 411
1970	147 713	24 424	21 170	75 609	13 371	4 943	2 863	4 385
1971	121 900	24 366	22 171	52 031	11 653	5 058	2 841	2 902
1972	122 006	22 618	23 325	51 293	9 218	4 309	8 308	2 143
1973	184 200	25 242	43 193	71 883	20 704	11 057	8 307	2 671
1974	218 465	26 541	50 566	88 694	25 276	12 528	10 450	2 594
1975	187 881	20 155	47 382	72 898	19 483	13 270	9 867	2 174
1976	149 429	17 315	44 328	49 903	16 198	10 628	7 752	1 886
1977	114 914	12 888	31 368	40 748	13 187	7 840	6 372	1 545
1978	86 313	9 945	24 007	30 075	9 240	6 782	4 261	1 233
1979	112 096	9 617	50 540	32 858	7 060	5 898	3 958	1 395
1980	143 117	9 926	71 602	41 168	8 141	5 433	4 330	2 497
1981	128 618	10 559	48 831	46 299	9 625	6 163	4 889	2 253
1982	121 147	9 360	41 686	46 156	10 317	6 871	4 513	2 119
1983	89 157	7 381	36 906	24 312	10 864	4 816	3 659	1 213
1984	88 239	6 922	41 920	20 901	9 706	4 085	3 552	1 151
1985	84 302	6 669	38 597	18 859	11 143	4 356	3 545	1 128
1986	99 219	7 275	41 600	22 709	14 947	6 686	4 770	1 227
1987	152 098	7 967	67 337	37 563	18 100	10 801	8 501	1 827
1988	161 929	6 537	81 136	40 689	15 108	7 255	9 380	1 822
1989	192 001	6 931	93 261	52 105	16 764	8 685	12 199	2 041
1990	213 334	6 057	111 195	51 667	19 459	8 888	13 426	2 642
1991	232 020	20 122[4]	120 736	48 232	12 978	10 632	16 175	3 145[5]
1992	253 345	20 123[4]	139 546	44 933	14 993	10 415	19 669	3 666[5]
1993	255 935	8 025	147 378	46 622	24 315	9 588	16 922	3 085[5]
1994	223 912	6 242	141 600	38 652	13 486	7 919	13 708	2 305[5]
1995	212 463[6]	5 199	128 534	41 127	13 352	7 485	14 560	1 873[5]
1996	226 050[6]	5 896	143 956	40 009	12 958	6 115	14 836	2 058[5]
1997	216 050	5 053	138 018	38 580	8 195	5 682	14 473	2 024
1998	174 191	4 781	101 297	38 482	6 341	4 964	13 672	1 639
1999	190 001[8]	5 545	113 934	38 990	6 758	5 609	15 695	532
2000[7]	227 363[8]	5 832	140 988	42 950	7 149	6 784	19 828	696

Source: *Citizenship and Immigration Canada*

(1) By country of last permanent residence. (2) Includes China and Hong Kong. (3) Includes Central America, Greenland and St. Pierre & Miquelon for 1956–76; except for 1991, 1992 when North and Central America were included with U.S. figures (4) Includes North and Central America. (5) Includes Australia and other islands. (6) Includes those whose country of last permanent residence was not stated. (7) Preliminary numbers. (8) Includes those whose last permanent residence was North and Central America and those not stated.

Current Anti-terrorism Clauses

*T*he 2000 report on Minister's Permits to allow people to come to Canada or remain lists inadmissible classes. These include persons there are reasonable grounds to believe will engage in subversion against democracy (as we define it) or against institutions in Canada or elsewhere, or who will engage in terrorism, or are members of an organization that will engage in such activities.

Immigration by Province of Intended Destination

	Total immigrants[1]	Nfld	PEI	NS	NB	Que	Ont	Man	Sask	Alta	BC	YT	NWT
1956 ...	164 857	426	112	1 639	852	31 396	90 662	5 796	2 202	9 959	17 812	n.a.	n.a.
1960 ...	104 111	306	83	1 210	634	23 774	54 491	4 337	2 087	6 949	10 120	n.a.	n.a.
1965 ...	146 758	604	137	1 612	1 074	30 346	79 702	3 948	2 649	8 049	18 502	n.a.	n.a.
1970 ...	147 713	630	185	2 007	1 070	23 261	80 732	5 826	1 709	10 405	21 683	n.a.	n.a.
1975 ...	187 881	1106	235	2 124	2 093	28 042	98 471	7 134	2 837	16 277	29 272	n.a.	n.a.
1980 ...	143 117	541	190	1 616	1 207	22 538	62 257	7 683	3 603	18 839	24 437	n.a.	n.a.
1981 ...	128 618	483	128	1 405	990	21 182	55 032	5 370	2 402	19 330	22 095	n.a.	n.a.
1982 ...	121 147	406	165	1 256	751	21 336	53 049	4 931	2 125	17 949	18 999	n.a.	n.a.
1983 ...	89 157	275	105	833	554	16 374	40 036	3 978	1 735	10 688	14 447	n.a.	n.a.
1984 ...	88 239	299	109	1 034	600	14 641	41 527	3 903	2 150	10 670	13 190	n.a.	n.a.
1985 ...	84 302	325	113	974	609	14 884	40 730	3 415	1 905	9 001	12 239	n.a.	n.a.
1986 ...	99 219	274	168	1 097	641	19 459	49 630	3 749	1 860	9 673	12 552	49	67
1987 ...	152 098	458	159	1 227	642	26 822	84 807	4 799	2 119	11 975	18 913	80	72
1988 ...	161 929	408	153	1 299	679	25 789	88 996	5 009	2 223	14 025	23 204	68	76
1989 ...	192 001	468	159	1 473	905	34 171	104 799	6 138	2 142	16 211	25 335	100	100
1990 ...	214 230	546	176	1 563	842	40 842	113 438	6 637	2 361	18 994	28 723	83	75
1991 ...	232 020	641	150	1 504	685	52 155	119 257	5 659	2 455	17 043	32 263	84	124
1992 ...	253 345	787	151	2 359	754	48 597	138 453	5 084	2 511	17 696	36 709	133	111
1993 ...	255 935	807	165	3 021	702	44 964	134 420	4 874	2 403	18 580	45 724	104	171
1995 ...	212 463	585	167	3 581	639	27 182	115 681	3 603	1 949	14 329	44 541	108	91
1996 ...	226 072	585	154	3 225	717	29 802	119 072	3 928	1 824	13 896	52 026	87	92
1997[2] ...	216 048	431	150	2 873	631	27 905	117 431	3 799	1 759	12 976	47 880	86	101
1998[2] ...	174 190	412	136	2 059	750	26 645	92 220	3 015	1 578	11 214	35 998	62	63
1999[2,3] ...	190 001	424	137	1 608	670	291 999	104 146	3 720	1 725	12 083	36 084	76	59
2000[2,3] ...	227 363	414	188	1 596	763	32 462	133 586	4 620	1 872	14 287	37 357	61	77

Source: *Citizenship and Immigration Canada*
(1) Includes those whose destination was not stated. (2) Preliminary figures. (3) Nine immigrants reported Nunavut as their destination for 1999 and seven for 2000.

Persons Granted Canadian Citizenship[1]

1920	3 004	1941	15 594	1962	72 082	1983	90 328
1921	10 507	1942	14 213	1963	69 468	1984	109 504
1922	10 360	1943	12 533	1964	64 334	1985	126 466
1923	7 589	1944	12 827	1965	63 844	1986	103 800
1924	7 659	1945	13 562	1966	60 852	1987	73 638
1925	13 288	1946	9 047	1967	59 968	1988	58 810
1926	15 403	1947	15 335	1968	60 055	1989	87 478
1927	16 917	1948	11 410	1969	59 900	1990	104 267
1928	13 466	1949	11 991[2]	1970	57 556	1991	118 630
1929	13 099	1950	10 441	1971	63 669	1992	115 757
1930	21 221	1951	10 301	1972	80 866	1993	150 543
1931	21 392	1952	10 888	1973	104 697	1994	217 320
1932	32 517	1953	13 562	1974	130 278	1995	227 720
1933	23 613	1954	19 545	1975	137 507	1996	166 627
1934	21 908	1955	58 711	1976	117 276	1997	154 624
1935	20 903	1956	55 404	1977	123 655	1998	134 485
1936	30 679	1957	95 462	1978	223 214	1999	189 945
1937	31 744	1958	84 183	1979	156 699	2000	214 569
1938	27 455	1959	71 280	1980	118 590		
1939	21 418	1960	62 378	1981	94 457		
1940	18 207	1961	56 476	1982	87 468		

Source: *Citizenship and Immigration Canada*

(1) For fiscal year ending Mar 31 for 1920 to 1951; calendar years 1952 onwards. (2) Does not include approx 359 000 Newfoundlanders who became Canadian citizens when Newfoundland became Canada's 10th province in 1949.

Refugees to Canada[1]

1961 .... 1 813	**1971** 614	**1981** 15 058	**1991** 35 891
1962 .... 1 733	**1972** 5 204	**1982** 17 000	**1992** 36 943
1963 .... 2 024	**1973** 2 381	**1983** 14 062	**1993** 24 835
1964 .... 2 279	**1974** 1 656	**1984** 15 553	**1994** 19 739
1965 .... 2 131	**1975** 6 109	**1985** 17 000	**1995** 27 753
1966 .... 2 058	**1976** 5 576	**1986** 19 485	**1996** 28 352
1967 .... 1 499	**1977** 3 670	**1987** 21 950	**1997** 24 221
1968 .... 9 971	**1978** 3 038	**1988** 27 230	**1998** 22 787
1969 .... 3 604	**1979** 27 894	**1989** 37 361	**1999** 24 397
1970 .... 1 361	**1980** 40 638	**1990** 36 093	**2000** 30 072

Source: *Refugees Branch, Citizenship and Immigration Canada*
(1) Includes persons admitted from abroad as Convention Refugees or members of Designated Classes, as well as persons recognized in Canada as Convention Refugees or members of the special Backlog Clearance Designated Class. Does not include special humanitarian movements of other persons.

Refugees by Province of Destination[1]

	Total[2]	Nfld	PEI	NS	NB	Que	Ont	Man	Sask	Alta	BC	YT	NWT
1981	14 997	28	11	119	76	3 257	5 544	822	657	2 751	1 722	6	4
1982	16 991	40	28	161	47	3 200	7 013	1 031	644	3 112	1 706	7	2
1983	14 062	11	17	89	61	2 184	6 100	844	574	2 488	1 692	0	2
1984	15 553	40	20	175	85	2 228	6 900	1 032	773	2 446	1 848	1	5
1985	17 000	55	33	206	165	1 906	8 301	1 131	749	2 529	1 919	1	5
1986	19 485	77	43	253	170	2 530	9 580	1 350	777	2 677	2 018	5	5
1987	21 921	87	45	241	192	3 216	11 026	1 366	791	2 673	2 277	3	4
1988	27 230	93	18	290	208	3 690	14 716	1 653	806	3 265	2 453	7	1
1989	37 361	94	49	329	194	5 137	21 585	1 929	815	4 535	2 679	9	6
1990	36 093	94	50	361	182	5 085	20 644	2 325	776	4 118	2 447	6	5
1991	35 891	265	40	337	211	6 284	21 342	1 579	706	2 738	2 382	4	3
1992	36 943	220	28	176	95	7 111	22 894	1 048	568	2 428	2 374	1	0
1993	24 835	243	41	189	100	5 776	14 433	692	375	1 649	1 325	1	11
1994	19 739	225	64	173	137	4 430	10 485	582	515	1 606	1 520	2	0
1995	27 753	208	61	223	179	6 122	16 413	663	575	1 447	1 854	8	0
1996	28 352	173	72	232	189	8 909	13 937	683	547	1 341	2 264	2	3
1997	24 221	133	63	211	150	7 686	11 646	621	558	1 156	1 996	1	0
1998	22 787	113	58	235	162	6 227	11 496	655	532	1 275	2 033	0	1
1999	24 397	148	66	259	152	7 339	11 967	779	509	1 286	1 892	0	0
2000	30 072	140	109	269	267	8 046	15 117	1 025	649	1 867	2 587	0	1

Source: © *Refugees Branch, Citizenship and Immigration Canada* (1) Includes Refugees Resettled from Abroad, their Dependants and inland Determination where destination is known. (2) Shows only those whose destination was identified.

Canadian Emigration by Province[1]

(number of persons moving from Canada)

	Canada	Nfld	PEI	NS	NB	Que	Ont	Man	Sask	Alta	BC	YT	NWT	NVT
1976–81	278 228	1 812	434	2 509	4 643	46 110	131 672	9 873	4 982	37 891	37 773	384	145	n.a.
1981–86	277 579	2 274	483	2 413	4 651	43 062	125 735	9 305	5 778	42 666	40 540	363	309	n.a.
1986–91	212 532	1 378	283	2 860	4 366	28 496	91 635	10 799	4 527	35 105	32 446	254	383	n.a.
1991–96	229 136	1 353	379	4 228	4 744	30 938	97 178	11 047	4 875	38 639	35 036	332	387	n.a.
1996–97[2]	48 970	208	27	493	192	9 365	24 987	1 288	774	5 563	5 919	48	64	42
1998–99[2]	58 787	262	34	592	182	11 048	30 048	1 563	906	6 728	7 234	64	79	47
1999–00[3]	62 131	278	37	622	204	11 647	31 616	1 653	969	7 147	7 749	71	87	51

Source: © *Statistics Canada* (n.a.) Not applicable. (1) Year end June 30. (2) Revised data. (3) Preliminary data.

Where Canadians Move Within Canada

When Canadians move from one province to another, it tends to be related to economic conditions. During 1977–81 the resource boom in Alberta caused an influx from other provinces. Falling oil prices in the early 1980s led to a reversal as Canadians moved east, especially to Ontario.

By the late '80s, BC was the choice location. In 1999 and 2000, Ontario and Alberta were on top again. The table shows net interprovincial migration—the number of persons moving into a province minus the number of persons moving out.

	Nfld	PEI	NS	NB	Que	Ont	Man	Sask	Alta	BC	YT	NWT	NVT[1]
1977–81	-21 086	-1 451	-8 185	-13 680	-156 817	-60 890	-42 115	-11 729	190 719	131 176	-2 363	-3 579	n.a.
1982–86	-14 117	811	7 442	835	-67 235	165 460	-2 395	-7 057	-82 737	3 226	-2 393	-1 840	n.a.
1987–91	-11 355	-65	-607	-2 063	-45 406	28 876	-39 533	-69 397	-13 198	154 126	871	-2 249	n.a.
1992–95	-18 730	1 826	-5 454	-3 015	-37 711	-32 592	-18 977	-19 418	242	135 036	-129	-1 078	n.a.
1996[2]	-8 380	315	-246	-1 263	-14 711	-5 942	-2 638	-1 160	13 902	20 665	168	-710	n.a.
1997[3]	-9 279	-466	-3 555	-1 688	-17 789	5 149	-7 008	-3 288	33 834	5 554	-433	-1 231	n.a.
1998[3]	-7 972	-76	-1 491	-2 847	-15 674	11 118	-2 801	-327	43 381	-20 984	-1 455	-852	-20
1999[3]	-2 865	669	1 440	80	-13 553	16 624	-1 435	-6 230	13 985	-8 129	-577	14	-23
2000[4]	-3 534	255	-208	15	-14 724	21 940	-2 410	-8 426	21 951	-14 123	-727	-113	104

Source: © *Statistics Canada*   (n.a.) Not applicable. (1) Nunavut became a territory in 1999. (2) Updated postcensal estimates. (3) Updated data. (4) Preliminary data.

Population Growth Components

(thousands)

Population growth is made up of natural increase (births minus deaths) plus net migration (immigration minus emigration). As the birth rate in Canada falls and the death rate continues to rise, the role of immigration becomes an increasingly important factor in population growth. By 2030, natural increase is expected to be close to zero, and immigration will become our sole source of population growth.

	Total Population Growth	Natural Increase		Net Migration	
		Births	Deaths	Immigration	Emigration
1851–1861	**793**	1 281	670	352	170
1861–1871	**459**	1 370	760	260	411
1871–1881	**636**	1 480	790	350	404
1881–1891	**508**	1 524	870	680	826
1891–1901	**538**	1 548	880	250	380
1901–11	**1 836**	1 925	900	1 550	739
1911–21	**1 581**	2 340	1 070	1 400	1 089
1921–31	**1 589**	2 415	1 055	1 200	971
1931–41	**1 130**	2 294	1 072	149	241
1941–51	**2 141**	3 186	1 214	548	379
1951–56	**2 072**	2 106	633	783	184
1956–61	**2 157**	2 362	687	760	278
1961–66	**1 777**	2 249	731	539	280
1966–71	**1 553**	1 856	766	890	427
1971–76	**1 492**	1 755	824	1 053	492
1976–81	**1 382**	1 820	843	771	366
1981–86	**1 304**	1 872	885	677	360
1986–91	**1 907**	1 933	946	1 199	279
1991–96	**1 848**	1 935	1 027	1 170	230
1997	**321**	349	216	216	50
1998	**237**	343	220	174	58
1999[1]	**254**	336	227	190	61[2]
2000[2]	**266**	331	232	227	60

Source: © *Statistics Canada*   (n.a.) Not applicable. (1) Updated data. (2) Preliminary data.

FOCUS ON...

Social Trends

Changes in Canadian Families

The average Canadian family is getting smaller. At the beginning of the new century there were over eight million families in Canada, and the average size was just over 3.0, including 1.2 children. In the 1980s and 1990s, families had 3.1 members; 3.7 was the average family size in the 1970s.

Not only is the size of the family changing, but its nature as well. More families now consist of single-parent families and step-family units. Divorces, conjugal arrangements and childbearing decisions of lone mothers have transformed the composition of families. In 1999, there were 69,672 divorces registered in Canada, representing a steady increase from previous years. In 2000, the country's 8.2 million families included about 1.3 million lone-parent families (families made up of a single, never married or divorced parent. This represented a steady rise in the number of lone parent families during the two previous decades. In 1981, about 1 in 10 families was headed by a lone parent, compared with about 1 in 6 in 1997. In addition, research shows the development of the "blended family" and stepfamily arrangements, in which lone parents enter new unions, sometimes with partners who also have children from earlier unions.

Changes in the Age Distribution of the Population

Over the last 20 years the age distribution of the population has changed significantly. Most noticeable is the difference in the proportions made up by senior citizens and children and youth. In 1981, the nearly one third (32 percent) were in the under-20 age group. At the other end of the scale, seniors 65 years and over represented close to 10 percent of the population. By 2000, senior citizens accounted for an estimated 12.52 percent of the population of 30.7 million, and children and youth had declined relatively to just over 25 percent of the population. The middle group, age 20-64, increased steadily both in numbers and in relative size. Over the twenty-year period the group increased from

over 58 percent to roughly 62 percent of the population. This changing age distribution has wide-ranging implications for policy, planning, and public and commercial services provided, as well as overall needs, employment and spending patterns.

Changes in Average Family Income

Average family income has been increasing in the 1990s. In 1998 the overall after-tax average income in an "economic family" of two persons or more was $49,626. An economic family refers to a group of individuals sharing a common dwelling unit who are related by blood, marriage (including common-law relationships) or adoption. When government transfers are added to this after tax income, the "average market income" was $55, 224.

Included in this average are those families classified as low-income families. In 1998, 9.1 percent of economic families were so classified. In lone parent families, where the average after-tax income was $26,279, 38.1 percent fell within the low-income group.

Changes in Education

The educational levels of the Canadian population show steady improvement over the last 20 years. The proportion of those with less education is declining. For example in 1981, roughly 21 percent of the population had less than grade 9 education, and 28 percent had some post secondary education. By 1999, those with post secondary education had increased to about 37 percent, and those with lower levels of education had fallen to just about 11 percent of the population.

Trends in Debt and Bankruptcies

Although average incomes have been increasing, it is clear that spending has been increasing at a faster pace, so that number of consumers claiming and registering bankruptcy has also increased. The number of personal (consumer) bankruptcies reported in 2000 was 75,137; over 60 percent of these were registered in Ontario and Quebec.

SOCIAL TRENDS

Marriages and Divorces in Canada

	Marriages				Divorces		
	Total	Rate[1]	Average Age at Marriage		Total	Rate[1]	Average Length of Marriage[2]
			Brides[3]	Grooms[3]			
1925.	66 378	6.9	25.3	29.8	550	0.1	n.a.
1930.	73 341	7.0	25.0	29.2	875	0.1	n.a.
1935.	78 908	7.1	25.0	29.0	1 431	0.1	n.a.
1940.	125 797	10.8	25.2	28.9	2 416	0.2	n.a.
1945.	111 376	9.0	25.5	29.0	5 101	0.4	n.a.
1950.	125 083	9.1	25.3	28.5	5 386	0.4	n.a.
1955.	128 029	8.2	25.1	28.0	6 053	0.4	n.a.
1960.	130 338	7.3	24.7	27.7	6 980	0.4	n.a.
1965.	145 519	7.4	24.5	27.2	8 974	0.5	n.a.
1970.	188 428	8.8	24.9	27.3	29 775	1.4	n.a.
1975.	197 585	8.5	22.0	24.4	50 611	2.2	11.1
1980.	191 069	7.8	22.8	25.0	62 019	2.6	11.5
1985.	184 096	7.1	24.1	26.2	61 980	2.4	11.6
1986.	175 518	6.7	24.3	26.5	78 160	3.1	11.5
1987.	182 151	6.9	24.7	26.9	90 985	3.6	11.4
1988.	187 728	7.0	25.0	27.1	83 507	3.1	11.3
1989.	190 640	7.0	25.2	27.3	80 998	3.0	11.2
1990.	187 737	6.8	25.5	27.4	78 463	2.8	11.1
1991.	172 251	6.1	25.7	27.7	77 020	2.7	11.0
1992.	164 573	5.8	26.0	28.0	79 034	2.8	10.9
1993.	159 316	5.6	26.8	28.7	78 226	2.7	10.7
1994.	159 959	5.5	26.9	28.8	78 880	2.7	10.7
1995.	160 251	5.5	27.1	29.0	77 636	2.6	10.7
1996.	156 692	5.3	27.3	29.3	71 528	2.4	10.8
1997.	153 306	5.1	26.8	28.8	67 408	2.2	n.a.
1998[4]	153 190	5.0	n.a.	n.a.	68 073	2.3	n.a.
1999[4]	153 380	5.0	n.a.	n.a.	69 672	2.3	n.a.

Source: © *Statistics Canada*   (n.a.) Not available.
(1) Rate per 1 000 population. (2) Refers to the average length (in years) of those marriages ending in divorce during the year stated. (3) Data after 1975 represents average age of bride and groom at first marriage. (4) Updated data.

Marriages and Divorces by Province

	Marriages				Divorces			
	1998		1999[3]		1998		1999[3]	
	Total	Rate[1]	Total	Rate[1]	Total	Rate[2]	Total	Rate[2]
Canada.	153 190	5.1	153 380	5.0	69 088	2.2	69 672	2.3
Newfoundland	3 117	5.7	3 043	5.6	944	1.7	938	1.7
Prince Edward Island ...	866	6.3	866	6.3	279	2.0	282	2.0
Nova Scotia	5 125	5.5	5 102	5.4	1 933	2.1	1 943	2.1
New Brunswick.	4 044	5.4	4 013	5.3	1 473	2.0	1 476	2.0
Quebec.	23 746	3.2	23 884	3.2	16 916	2.3	16 970	2.3
Ontario	64 536	5.7	64 533	5.6	25 149	2.2	25 436	2.2
Manitoba	6 218	5.5	6 211	5.4	2 443	2.1	2 448	2.1
Saskatchewan.	5 730	5.6	5 752	5.6	2 246	2.2	2 253	2.2
Alberta	17 651	6.1	17 986	6.1	7 668	2.6	7 815	2.6
British Columbia.	21 788	5.5	21 630	5.4	9 827	2.5	9 904	2.5
Yukon Territory.	161	5.1	153	4.9	117	3.7	114	3.7
Northwest Territories ...	142	3.5	141	3.4	55	1.3	59	1.4
Nunavut	66	2.5	66	2.4	38	1.4	34	1.3

Source: © *Statistics Canada*   (1) Rate per 1 000 population. (2) Rate per 100 marriages. (3) Updated data.

Marital Status of the Canadian Population[1], 2000

Age Group	Total Population Male (000s)	Total Population Female (000s)	Single Male (%)	Single Female (%)	Married Male (%)	Married Female (%)	Widowed Male (%)	Widowed Female (%)	Divorced Male (%)	Divorced Female (%)
Total Population 15+	15 232.9	15 517.2	46.2	39.4	47.3	47.2	1.8	8.0	4.0	5.4
15–19	1 064.0	1 007.6	99.5	87.4	0.7	2.7	...	...	...	...
20–24	1 063.6	1 017.6	86.4	74.4	13.4	25.2	...	...	...	0.4
25–29	1 067.9	1 041.8	59.2	43.6	39.6	56.5	...	0.2	1.1	1.8
30–34	1 154.1	1 120.1	37.0	24.4	59.9	71.2	...	0.3	3.0	4.2
35–39	1 359.8	1 335.8	25.1	16.8	69.2	75.9	0.2	0.6	5.2	6.7
40–44	1 308.7	1 304.6	17.5	14.1	67.3	77.0	0.3	1.1	6.4	9.4
45–49	1 157.3	1 162.6	12.4	9.6	78.2	75.8	0.6	2.1	8.9	11.8
50–54	1 018.1	1 028.0	7.9	7.3	80.8	75.7	0.9	3.9	9.6	12.9
55–59	769.5	785.7	6.9	6.0	82.2	73.7	1.7	7.7	9.2	12.6
60–64	614.1	641.0	4.6	4.1	62.3	53.3	2.4	10.9	6.2	8.0
65–69	546.5	590.4	6.1	5.3	81.3	62.8	5.6	23.5	7.0	8.3
70–74	454.3	544.0	6.1	5.5	78.9	52.0	9.6	36.3	5.5	6.2
75–79	333.7	470.9	3.1	5.9	75.1	40.0	18.3	50.6	3.9	4.3
80–84	184.9	309.7	5.2	6.9	68.0	25.2	24.1	65.0	2.8	2.8
85–89	81.5	191.0	7.5	8.2	63.4	13.5	40.2	77.8	2.3	1.6
90+	35.0	88.6	6.2	11.1	35.0	3.5	54.3	95.4	1.6	0.9

Source: © *Statistics Canada*   (...) Less than 0.1 percent. (1) As of July 1.

Age-specific Fertility Rate

(per 1,000 women)

Age-specific fertility rates are calculated by dividing the number of live births in each age group by the total female population (in thousands) in each age group. Trends in the last ten years indicate that while women aged 25–29 are the most likely to give birth (although at a declining rate), births in the younger age groups are generally declining, while the fertility rates among women 30 and over hold steady or show modest increases.

	1986	1991	1995	1996	1997
15–19 years[1]	23.01	25.98	24.49	22.34	20.19
20–24 years	78.74	77.50	70.53	67.28	64.07
25–29 years	119.01	120.33	109.69	105.82	103.88
30–34 years	72.52	83.63	86.77	85.51	84.44
35–39 years	22.30	28.27	31.26	32.22	32.52
40–44 years	3.15	3.88	4.83	5.06	5.19
45–49 years[2]	0.13	0.17	0.19	0.20	0.20

Source: © *Statistics Canada*

(1) Births to women aged 14 and under are included in the 15–19 age group. (2) Births to women aged 50 and over are included in the 45–49 age group.

Fewer are Retiring Early

*A*ccording to Statistics Canada, the early retirement (before 60) trend peaked in 1997. In 1990, fewer than 30% of those retiring were under 60; by 1997, 46% of retirees were. That rate has declined, to about 40% in 2000. Why? Public sector downsizing was over by 1997. 65% of public sector retirees were under 60 in 1997, nearly double the early retirement rate in the private sector.

Lone-Parent Families by Province[1], 2000

Province	Lone-Parent Families	Average Family Size	Male Parent	Average Family Size	Female Parent	Average Family Size
Canada	1 290 774	2.5	213 207	2.4	1 077 567	2.6
Newfoundland	22 202	2.4	3 226	2.4	18 976	2.4
Prince Edward Island	6 017	2.6	1 035	2.6	4 982	2.6
Nova Scotia	44 688	2.5	6 596	2.3	38 092	2.6
New Brunswick	32 131	2.5	5 172	2.3	26 959	2.5
Quebec	342 600	2.5	63 811	2.3	278 789	2.5
Ontario	492 965	2.6	73 778	2.4	419 187	2.6
Manitoba	44 570	2.6	7 168	2.5	37 402	2.7
Saskatchewan	39 577	2.7	6 094	2.6	33 483	2.7
Alberta	105 370	2.6	19 227	2.4	86 143	2.6
British Columbia	160 654	2.6	27 100	2.4	133 554	2.6

Source: © *Statistics Canada*

(1) Preliminary intercensal estimates as of July 1.

Lone-Parent Families by Age[1], 2000

	Total Families	Size of Families		
		2 Members	3 Members	4 or more Members
Headed by Male Parent	**213 207**	**145 444**	**53 149**	**14 614**
Age 15–24	1 924	1 649	214	61
25–34	20 684	14 208	5 201	1 275
35–44	67 649	40 811	20 905	5 933
45–54	70 432	46 496	18 752	5 184
55–64	25 239	19 109	4 932	1 198
65+	27 279	23 171	3 145	963
Headed by Female Parent	**1 077 567**	**624 015**	**327 100**	**126 452**
Age 15–24	66 604	48 580	15 146	2 878
25–34	229 287	111 820	80 532	36 935
35–44	348 152	153 712	134 698	59 742
45–54	232 101	140 939	70 330	20 832
55–64	78 268	62 160	13 061	3 047
65+	123 155	106 804	13 333	3 018

Source: © *Statistics Canada*

(1) Preliminary intercensal estimates as of July 1.

Census Families[1] in Private Households

	1991	1996
Total families	**7 355 730**	**7 837 865**
Total husband-wife families	6 402 090	6 700 360
Families of married couples	5 682 815	5 779 720
Families of common-law couples	719 275	920 640
Total lone-parent families	953 640	1 137 510
Male parent	165 240	192 275
Female parent	788 395	945 230
Total persons in families	**22 568 125**	**23 907 975**
Average number of persons per family	3.1	3.1
Total persons not in families	4 163 580	4 482 710

Source: © *Census of Canada, Statistics Canada*

(1) A married or common-law couple living together, with or without never-married sons or daughters; or a lone parent living with at least one never-married son or daughter. Census families in private households exclude families living in institutions or other types of collective dwellings.

Composition of Canadian Families

(thousands)

	1971		1981		1991		1996	
	No. of Families	%	No. of Families	%	No. of Families	%	No. of Families	%
Total families[1]	5 071	100.0	6 325	100.0	7 356	100.0	7 838	100.0
Without children at home	1 545	30.5	2 013	31.8	2 580	35.1	2 730	35.0
With children at home	3 526	69.5	4 312	68.2	4 776	64.9	5 108	65.2
With one child	1 045	20.6	1 580	25.0	1 945	26.4	2 106	27.0
two children	1 077	21.2	1 648	26.1	1 927	26.2	2 047	26.1
three children	677	13.4	730	11.5	691	9.4	729	9.3
four children	367	7.2	243	3.8	165	2.2	175	2.2
five children or more..........	360	7.1	112	1.8	48	0.5	51	0.6
Lone parent families	471	9.3	653	10.3	955	13.0	1 137	14.5
lone female parent	371	7.3	541	8.6	786	10.7	945	12.1
lone male parent	100	2.0	112	1.8	168	2.3	192	2.5

Source: © *Census of Canada, Statistics Canada*

(1) Based on the census family definition: a husband and wife (without children or with children who never married) or a parent with one or more children who never married, living together in the same home.

Size of Families in Canada

(thousands)

	1971		1981		1991		1996	
	No. of Families	Avg. Size	No. of Families	Avg. Size	No. of Families	Avg. Size	No. of Families	Avg. Size
Canada	5 071	3.7	6 325	3.3	7 356	3.1	7 838	3.1
Newfoundland	108	4.4	135	3.8	151	3.3	156	3.1
Prince Edward Island	24	4.0	30	3.5	34	3.2	36	3.2
Nova Scotia	181	3.8	216	3.3	245	3.1	254	3.0
New Brunswick	140	4.0	177	3.4	198	3.1	207	3.0
Quebec	1 357	3.9	1 672	3.3	1 883	3.0	1 950	3.0
Ontario	1 882	3.6	2 279	3.2	2 727	3.1	2 933	3.1
Manitoba	236	3.6	262	3.2	286	3.1	293	3.1
Saskatchewan	216	3.7	246	3.3	258	3.2	260	3.1
Alberta	382	3.7	566	3.3	668	3.1	718	3.1
British Columbia	534	3.5	728	3.1	888	3.0	1 008	3.0
Yukon	11[1]	4.3[1]	6	3.3	7	3.1	8	3.1
Northwest Territories	11[1]	4.3[1]	9	4.0	13	3.7	15	3.6

Source: © *Census of Canada, Statistics Canada* /   (1) Includes both the Yukon and Northwest Territories.

Estimates of Family Size by Province, 2000[1]

Statistics Canada estimates that the size of Canadian families has continued to drop during the 1990s.

Compare these estimates with the chart above:

	No. of Families (000's)	Avg. Size		No. of Families (000's)	Avg. Size
Canada............	8 194 349	3.0	Ontario	3 112 598	3.1
Newfoundland	155 333	3.0	Manitoba	298 480	3.1
Prince Edward Island ...	37 629	3.1	Saskatchewan	267 761	3.1
Nova Scotia	257 873	3.0	Alberta	792 314	3.1
New Brunswick........	215 099	3.0	British Columbia.......	1 060 360	3.0
Quebec..............	1 996 902	3.0			

Source: © *Statistics Canada*   (1) Preliminary intercensal estimates as of July 1.

Average Time Spent on Activities, by Gender[1], 1998

Activity	Average hours spent per day by Participants in that Activity		Percent Participating	
	Men	**Women**	**Men**	**Women**
Paid work and related activities/unpaid work ...	**8.0**	**7.9**	**97**	**99**
Paid work and related activities	8.8	7.7	51	36
Paid work	8.2	7.1	50	35
Activities related to paid work	0.7	0.5	9	6
Travel	0.9	0.8	45	32
Unpaid work	**3.2**	**4.6**	**87**	**96**
Household work and related activities	2.8	4.3	85	95
Cooking/washing up	0.7	1.3	63	85
House cleaning and laundry	1.5	1.8	22	59
Maintenance and repair	2.7	2.0	9	4
Other household work	1.6	1.1	27	33
Shopping for goods and services	1.8	1.9	38	47
Primary child care	1.8	2.4	16	24
Civic and volunteer activities	2.0	1.9	17	19
Education and related activities	**6.0**	**6.3**	**9**	**9**
Sleep, meals and other personal activities	**10.2**	**10.6**	**100**	**100**
Night sleep	8.0	8.2	100	100
Meals (excluding restaurant meals)	1.2	1.2	92	91
Other personal activities	1.2	1.4	94	96
Free time	**6.1**	**5.7**	**97**	**97**
Socializing	3.0	2.8	62	70
Restaurant meals	1.6	1.5	20	18
Socializing (in homes)	2.5	2.3	49	61
Other socializing	2.7	2.6	12	12
Television, reading and other passive leisure	3.3	3.1	87	84
Watching television	3.0	2.7	80	75
Reading books, magazines, newspapers	1.3	1.4	30	34
Other passive leisure	1.1	1.1	9	9
Sports, movies and other entertainment events	2.6	2.8	6	6
Active leisure	2.6	2.2	41	39
Active sports	2.3	1.7	26	22
Other active leisure	2.4	2.1	21	22

Source: © *Statistics Canada*   (1) Average over a seven-day week by Canadians over the age of 15.

Most Popular Sports Played by Active Canadians, 1998

	% Active Population[1]	% Active Males	% Active Female
Golf	7.4	11.1	3.9
Hockey (ice)	6.2	12.0	0.5
Baseball	5.5	8.0	3.1
Swimming	4.6	3.6	5.6
Basketball	3.2	4.6	1.9
Volleyball	3.1	3.3	2.8
Soccer	3.0	4.6	1.5
Tennis	2.7	3.6	1.8
Skiing, downhill/alpine	2.7	2.9	2.6
Cycling	2.5	3.0	2.0
Skiing, cross-country/nordic	2.1	1.7	2.5
Weightlifting	1.8	2.5	1.1
Badminton	1.7	1.7	1.7
Football	1.6	2.9	0.3
Curling	1.3	1.5	1.1

Source: © *Statistics Canada*   (1) Population aged 15 years and older.

Average Household Expenditure, including Budget Share

(dollars)

In the latest update, 17,000 private households in all the provinces and territories were surveyed from January to March 2000 to capture detailed information on household spending habits, and the data was compared to previous years. Results showed that Canadian households spent an average of $53,470 in 1999, on everything from furniture to entertainment. While the budget share of each item was mostly unchanged from previous years, overall spending increased 4% over 1998 and 7% over 1997 levels. There were higher increases in some spending areas. In particular, slightly more was spent on automobile purchases, home heating bills, food and personal taxes. Consumer spending on transportation rose about 8% in 1999, a big increase given the 2% growth the year before.

What sparked some of the bigger increases? Gas prices rose 9% between 1998 and 1999, and more car and truck purchases were made in 1999. Spending on driving lessons, registration fees and licences also rose. Increases in the price of natural gas pushed heating fuel costs up 7%. The 10% increase in spending on entertainment was largely due to an increase in spending on cable and satellite services, along with more spending on movies and live sports events. On the tax front, households paid an average of $11,590 in personal taxes (including sales tax). That's $740 more than in 1998, but the jump is explained by a corresponding increase in average household income. The $6,100 spent on food in 1999 is up 3% from 1998. The increase in spending on clothing (6%) was mostly due to more spending on women's and girl's wear.

	Average expenditure 1997 $ current (not adjusted for inflation)	Share of budget %	Average expenditure 1998 $ current (not adjusted for inflation)	Share of budget % (not adjusted for inflation)	Average expenditure 1999 $ current (not adjusted for inflation)	Share of budget %
Total expenditure	$49 920		$51 200		$53 470	
Personal taxes	10 590	21	10 820	21	11 560	22
Shelter	9 820	20	10 080	20	10 240	19
Transportation	6 250	13	6 390	12	6 880	13
Food	5 720	11	5 910	12	6 100	11
Recreation	2 780	6	2 920	6	2 960	6
Personal insurance payments and pension contributions	2 750	6	2 760	5	2 840	5
Household operation	2 280	5	2 350	5	2 410	5
Clothing	2 170	4	2 200	4	2 330	4
Household furnishings and equipment	1 330	3	1 480	3	1 480	3
Gifts of money and contributions	1 250	3	1 150	2	1 360	3
Health care	1 150	2	1 190	2	1 260	2
Tobacco products and alcoholic beverages	1 150	2	1 210	2	1 180	2
Miscellaneous expenditures	800	2	810	2	860	2
Education	680	1	710	1	760	1
Personal care	660	1	690	1	710	1
Reading materials and other printed matter	270	1	280	1	270	1
Games of chance expense (net)	250	0.5	250	0.5	270	0.5

Source: © *Statistics Canada*

Average Household[1] Expenditure by Province/Territory

(dollars)

The average spending costs shown opposite can be further broken down to show definite regional differences with those in the Northwest Territories and Yukoners paying a premium for their lifestyles. Alberta and Ontario were the next most expensive when it comes to maintaining a household. Households in Newfoundland and Labrador once again had the lowest average household spending.

	1998 $ current (not adjusted for inflation)	1999 $ current (not adjusted for inflation)
Newfoundland and Labrador	41 080	42 510
Prince Edward Island	42 560	45 400
Nova Scotia	43 280	45 850
New Brunswick	41 350	44 730
Quebec	44 090	46 870
Ontario.	56 700	58 780
Manitoba	46 630	49 410
Saskatchewan	45 000	46 900
Alberta.	56 560	59 210
British Columbia	53 920	54 970
Yukon	59 010	60 080
Northwest Territories.	72 060	79 680
Nunavut	44 840	46 830

Source: © *Statistics Canada*   (1) A family or group of unrelated persons living in a dwelling.

Average Household Expenditure by Metropolitan Area

(dollars)

Given the statistics above on household spending by province it is no surprise that households in Yellowknife took top honours as the most expensive however Toronto ($65 810) and Calgary ($65 010) beat Whitehorse by a wide margin.

1999 Rank		1998 $ current (not adjusted for inflation)	1999 $ current (not adjusted for inflation)
1.	Yellowknife	81 950	93 830
2.	Toronto.	60 490	65 810
3.	Calgary	63 700	65 010
4.	Whitehorse	61 580	62 880
5.	Ottawa.	61 780	61 170
6.	Vancouver.	58 600	60 600
7.	Edmonton	61 220	58 380
8.	Regina.	54 620	56 200
9.	Winnipeg.	49 020	53 060
10.	Victoria	51 180	52 440
11.	Halifax.	50 640	52 420
12.	Montréal	46 490	2 020
13.	St. John's	53 780	51 940
14.	Saskatoon.	47 640	49 540
15.	Québec	45 770	48 200
16.	Saint John.	43 600	47 410
17.	Charlottetown-Summerside	44 000	43 030

Source: © *Statistics Canada*

Average Assets and Debts held by Family Units, by Province

	Canada		Newfoundland		Prince Edward Island	
Number of family units	12 215 629		198 630		54 205	
	% of Families[1]	$ Average	% of Families[1]	$ Average	% of Families[1]	$ Average
ASSETS	**100.0**	**237 163**	**100.0**	**114 687**	**100.0**	**194 919**
Financial assets	93.0	74 774	80.8	37 801	92.0	54 450
Within registered plans	61.0	56 442	42.0	34 112	52.2	60 380
RRSPs & LIRAs[2]	54.9	51 189	39.1	32 658	45.4	57 255
Other registered plans[3]	14.7	42 967	x	x	x	x
Outside registered plans	90.0	39 047	79.5	20 424	88.5	21 016
Deposits in fin inst	87.9	14 970	78.1	7 657	84.6	8 060
Mutual & investmt funds	30.0	53 928	19.4	15 407	30.4	28 732
Other financial assets[4]	8.9	64 948	x	x	x	x
Non-financial assets	100.0	138 593	100.0	77 755	100.0	102 550
Principal residence	60.4	149 661	73.2	66 440	67.2	92 108
Other real estate	16.5	116 999	17.0	42 225	x	x
Vehicles	77.2	13 329	77.1	10 616	84.0	11 913
Other non-financial assets[5]	100.0	18 689	100.0	13 767	100.0	19 184
Equity in business	18.7	155 610	x	x	x	x
DEBTS	**68.0**	**55 155**	**75.3**	**29 332**	**74.5**	**31 853**
Mortgages	35.1	82 844	25.1	46 332	31.8	49 491
Principal residence	32.7	76 116	24.2	42 237	30.5	47 139
Other real estate	4.7	88 550	x	x	x	x
Line of credit	15.9	13 542	x	x	x	x
Cr card & installmt debt[6]	38.5	3 033	52.6	2 614	48.2	2 628
Student loans	11.8	10 361	19.8	15 831	x	x
Vehicle loans	21.2	11 226	31.7	10 130	28.0	9 253
Other debt	16.3	9 301	19.4	8 562	32.1	5 950
NET WORTH[7]	**99.9**	**199 789**	**100.0**	**92 612**	**100.0**	**171 189**

	Nova Scotia		New Brunswick		Quebec	
Number of family units	376 191		300 177		3 115 360	
	% of Families[1]	$ Average	% of Families[1]	$ Average	% of Families[1]	$ Average
ASSETS	**100.0**	**154 005**	**100.0**	**182 705**	**100.0**	**149 587**
Financial assets	86.4	55 194	92.9	58 226	86.4	42 063
Within registered plans	54.0	43 020	57.2	49 632	48.0	41 585
RRSPs & LIRAs[2]	49.2	38 335	50.9	44 856	43.8	38 378
Other registered plans[3]	13.6	32 174	12.1	45 716	11.9	26 146
Outside registered plans	81.3	30 045	90.5	28 423	83.7	19 595
Deposits in fin inst	78.1	10 598	89.4	11 491	81.2	10 670
Mutual & investmt funds	30.4	31 983	21.8	49 374	23.3	27 992
Other financial assets[4]	9.9	65 025	6.3	74 464	x	x
Non-financial assets	100.0	94 340	100.0	101 815	100.0	91 874
Principal residence	64.4	87 382	55.4	109 481	70.2	78 715
Other real estate	19.4	50 615	16.8	101 942	19.7	52 090
Vehicles	76.9	12 122	72.8	11 740	82.2	12 779
Other non-financial assets[5]	100.0	18 928	100.0	15 522	100.0	15 871
Equity in business	14.1	84 989	14.4	186 422	x	x
DEBTS	**74.5**	**34 523**	**65.1**	**42 297**	**72.8**	**30 796**
Mortgages	32.4	51 732	32.6	65 594	33.1	40 762
Principal residence	30.3	49 829	29.9	55 532	31.6	38 376
Other real estate	x	x	5.2	93 151	x	x
Line of credit	17.4	10 559	15.8	7 082	12.0	9 759
Cr card & installmt debt[6]	45.6	2 626	33.8	2 081	49.0	2 373
Student loans	13.7	11 178	11.9	7 971	18.3	10 137
Vehicle loans	29.4	10 601	21.1	9 696	32.2	10 533
Other debt	18.3	6 816	15.4	8 496	15.2	9 041
NET WORTH[7]	**99.8**	**128 502**	**100.0**	**155 261**	**100.0**	**127 155** ▶

	Ontario		Manitoba		Saskatchewan	
Number of family units	4 480 409		446 152		401 649	
	% of Families[1]	$ Average	% of Families[1]	$ Average	% of Families[1]	$ Average
ASSETS	**100.0**	**264 348**	**100.0**	**190 268**	**100.0**	**224 291**
Financial assets	94.6	87 690	92.2	70 312	94.5	72 337
Within registered plans	64.9	62 377	62.9	52 422	63.3	51 155
RRSPs & LIRAs[2]	58.5	55 119	55.3	47 802	56.2	47 644
Other registered plans[3]	17.0	48 485	17.1	38 271	16.8	33 345
Outside registered plans	91.3	46 451	87.7	36 342	91.2	39 416
Deposits in fin inst	89.6	17 893	84.1	16 227	88.6	19 311
Mutual & investmt funds	34.0	65 386	33.4	43 895	34.2	41 637
Other financial assets[4]	8.3	50 412	9.8	36 364	16.4	28 118
Non-financial assets	100.0	160 277	100.0	96 467	100.0	104 626
Principal residence	60.5	181 395	64.1	91 348	69.1	82 091
Other real estate	16.3	128 634	17.7	57 351	18.0	90 831
Vehicles	76.7	13 062	78.8	13 079	84.3	15 595
Other non-financial assets[5]	100.0	19 513	100.0	17 504	100.0	18 337
Equity in business	19.6	108 038	17.3	167 572	28.9	177 529
DEBTS	**68.0**	**63 579**	**62.9**	**37 604**	**66.2**	**38 418**
Mortgages	36.3	94 406	33.0	51 196	30.6	48 616
Principal residence	34.1	88 689	31.2	49 201	29.2	45 424
Other real estate	4.5	88 417	x	x	x	x
Line of credit	16.1	16 978	12.4	8 556	16.2	11 090
Cr card & installmt debt[6]	39.9	3 373	33.5	3 069	38.6	2 690
Student loans	12.2	11 680	x	x	11.4	11 309
Vehicle loans	19.4	11 529	21.5	11 201	26.9	12 839
Other debt	13.9	9 078	18.3	8 447	19.7	15 068
NET WORTH[7]	**99.9**	**221 233**	**100.0**	**166 628**	**100.0**	**198 911**

	Alberta		British Columbia	
Number of family units	1 157 207		1 685 649	
	% of Families[1]	$ Average	% of Families[1]	$ Average
ASSETS	**100.0**	**278 016**	**100.0**	**302 934**
Financial assets	93.2	79 624	92.8	82 775
Within registered plans	63.4	55 611	61.0	60 882
RRSPs & LIRAs[2]	58.7	53 703	54.7	56 644
Other registered plans[3]	14.2	26 533	14.1	43 822
Outside registered plans	89.4	43 553	90.4	43 882
Deposits in financial institutions	86.1	15 771	87.5	14 231
Mutual funds & investment funds stocks & bonds				
(saving & other)	33.2	42 022	33.3	53 280
Other financial assets[4]	12.9	88 595	11.2	84 493
Non-financial assets	100.0	146 583	100.0	189 208
Principal residence	66.4	135 917	57.7	225 202
Other real estate	16.2	126 108	14.3	183 179
Vehicles	84.3	15 870	78.6	15 087
Other non-financial assets[5]	100.0	22 513	100.0	21 140
Equity in business	25.1	228 367	20.9	176 758
DEBTS	**71.9**	**58 441**	**69.1**	**74 860**
Mortgages	41.0	78 108	36.4	115 849
Principal residence	38.1	72 687	33.4	107 152
Other real estate	5.7	76 536	5.8	108 932
Line of credit	17.2	14 543	16.4	18 547
Credit card & installment debt[6]	39.7	3 379	38.3	3 814
Student loans	11.0	9 242	9.7	10 433
Vehicle loans	23.1	13 032	18.2	12 278
Other debt	18.1	11 688	20.3	9 034
NET WORTH[7]	**99.9**	**236 198**	**99.9**	**251 517**

Source: © *Statistics Canada*

x Data unavailable, not applicable or confidential.

(1) Family units: economic families (a group of two or more persons who live in the same dwelling & are related to each other by blood marriage common law or adoption) & unattached individuals (a person living either alone or with others to whom he or she is unrelated). (2) Registered Retirement Savings Plans (RRSPs) & Locked-in Retirement Accounts (LIRAs). (3) Plans other than RRSPs or LIRAs e.g. Registered Retirement Income Funds (RRIFs) Deferred Profit Sharing Plans (DPSPs) & Registered Education Savings Plans (RESPs). (4) Includes treasury bills mortgage-backed securities money held in trust annuities money owed to the respondent & other miscellaneous financial assets including shares of privately held companies not held within registered plans. (5) The value of the contents of the respondent's principal residence valuables & collectibles copyrights & patents etc. (6) Includes major credit cards & retail store cards gasoline station cards etc. Installment debt is the total amount owing on deferred payment or installment plans where the purchased item is to be paid for over a period of time. (7) Net worth = assets less debts.

EDUCATION

Canadian Population[1] by Highest Level of Schooling

(percentage)

	1976	1981	1986	1991	1996	1999
Less than grade 9	25.4	20.7	17.7	14.3	12.4	11.0
Grades 9 to 13	44.1	43.7	42.5	42.6	40.4	37.7[2]
Some postsecondary education	24.1	27.6	30.2	31.7	33.9	36.6[3]
University degree	6.4	8.0	9.6	11.4	13.3	14.8

Source: © *Census of Canada, Statistics Canada*   (1) Over the age of 15. (2) "Some secondary", and "Graduated from high school" data categories added together. (3) "Some post secondary" and "Post secondary certificate or diploma" data categories added together.

Canadian Population[1] by Highest Level of Schooling and Province, 1996

(percentage)

	Elementary–Secondary Schooling Only	Post secondary, Non-university Education	University Without a Degree	University With a Degree
Canada	**52.8**	**24.2**	**9.7**	**13.3**
Newfoundland	58.2	23.0	10.7	8.1
Prince Edward Island	55.4	22.5	11.5	10.6
Nova Scotia	52.8	23.8	11.2	12.2
New Brunswick	58.3	21.6	9.9	10.2
Quebec	57.5	22.3	8.0	12.2
Ontario	51.1	24.6	9.4	14.9
Manitoba	55.9	21.0	11.5	11.6
Saskatchewan	56.8	21.6	11.8	9.8
Alberta	48.7	27.8	10.2	13.3
British Columbia	47.5	27.0	11.9	13.6
Yukon Territory	40.0	33.5	12.0	14.5
Northwest Territories	53.3	28.7	7.5	10.5

Source: © *Census of Canada, Statistics Canada*   (1) Over the age of 15.

Elementary-Secondary Enrolment by School Type and Province

(thousands)

	Canada	Nfld	PEI	NS	NB	Que	Ont [1]	Man	Sask	Alta	BC	YK	NWT
1994–95	5 362.82	114.4	24.5	168.5	138.3	1 137.6	2 140.1	221.7	212.7	544.6	638.1	5.8	16.3
1995–96	5 430.82	110.9	24.7	168.0	136.8	1 138.7	2 189.0	223.0	213.0	548.5	654.4	6.1	17.6
1996–97	5 414.62	106.5	24.8	167.2	135.3	1 137.1	2 161.5	223.8	212.9	553.7	667.1	6.4	18.0
1997–98	5 386.32	102.1	24.7	164.7	133.2	1 130.0	2 131.9	224.1	211.1	563.2	677.3	6.4	17.5
1998–99	5 369.72	98.1	24.4	163.1	130.8	1 125.1	2 128.6	223.0	208.8	566.2	675.9	6.2	18.0
Public	4 999.3	97.6	24.1	159.0	129.1	1 014.9	2 022.4	192.5	193.6	530.1	611.6	6.2	18.0
Private	297.8	0.4	0.2	2.5	0.8	102.6	90.6	14.1	2.6	24.7	59.3	...	...
Federal	71.0[2]	...	0.0	1.6	0.9	6.9	14.9	16.2	13.6	11.4	5.0	...	...
Visually and hearing impaired	1.5	0.1	...	...	...	0.6	0.6	0.2	...[3]	0.1	...[3]	...	...

Source: © *Statistics Canada*   (...) Nil or zero.
(1) Includes correctional institutions and hospital schools. Check previous years show as exclusion. this is for Ontario only. (2) Includes DND schools overseas. (3) The "Visually and hearing impaired" category for Saskatchewan and British Columbia is included with the "Public" category.

Postsecondary Enrolment, 1998–99

	Full-time	Part-time
Community college..........................	**403 516**	**91 439**
Career programs.............................	298 898	55 249
University transfer programs...................	104 618	36 190
University..................................	**580 376**	**245 985**
Undergraduate programs....................	500 951	206 595
Bachelor's and first professional..............	470 039	101 120
Other undergraduate........................	30 912	105 475
Graduate programs.........................	79 425	39 390
Master's...................................	44 794	26 499
Doctoral...................................	23 809	2 798
Other graduate.............................	10 822	10 093
Total Enrolment............................	**983 892**	**337 424**

Source: © *Statistics Canada*

University Graduates by Field of Study, 1998

Field of Study	Bachelor's/ First Professional Degree	Diploma and Certificate	Men	Women	Total Undergraduate
Education	19 374	2 386	6 355	15 405	21 760
Fine/applied arts	4 276	425	1 504	3 197	4 701
Humanities	14 721	2 687	6 111	11 297	17 408
Social Sciences	47 760	8 259	22 269	34 250	56 519
Agricultural/biological sciences ..	10 079	671	4 043	6 707	10 750
Engineering/applied sciences	9 255	674	7 824	2 105	9 929
Health professions	8 620	1 497	2 590	7 527	10 117
Mathematics/physical sciences .	7 239	565	5 361	2 443	7 804
Other	3 537	1 657	1 723	3 471	5 194
TOTAL	124 861	18 821	57 780	86 402	144 182

Field of Study	Masters	Doctoral	Graduate Diploma and Certificate	Men	Women	Total Graduate
Education	3 330	367	499	1 210	2 986	4 196
Fine/applied arts	490	35	30	231	324	555
Humanities	2 742	482	184	1 478	1 930	3 408
Social Sciences	9 219	737	1 044	5 724	5 276	11 000
Agricultural/biological sciences ..	972	437	50	736	723	1 459
Engineering/applied sciences	2 182	679	40	2 297	604	2 901
Health professions	1 625	509	407	924	1 617	2 541
Mathematics/physical sciences .	1 398	695	95	1 514	674	2 188
Other	68	35	43	54	92	146
TOTAL	22 026	3 976	2 392	14 168	14 226	28 394

Source: © *Statistics Canada*   (n.a.) Not available.

(1) Estimate. (2) Revised.

Education Expenditures in Canada

(millions of dollars)

	1976	1981	1986	1991	1996	1999
Total	$15 099.7	$25 373.1	$36 610.8	$53 144.3	$58 125.1[2]	$61 865.1[2]
Elementary–Secondary	10 070.9	16 703.2	22 968.0	33 444.9	36 744.7	37 498.9[1]
Vocational	959.9	1 601.2	3 275.1	4 573.8	5 301.8[2]	6 229.6[1]
College	1 081.5	2 088.1	2 999.0	3 870.7	4 477.9[2]	5 261.7[1]
University	2 987.5	4 980.7	7 368.7	11 254.8	11 600.7[2]	12 874.9[1]
Spending as a % of GDP	7.6	7.1	7.3	7.9	7.1	n.a.
Elementary–Secondary pupil-educator ratio	18.1	17.0	16.5	15.5	16.3[1,2]	16.6[1]

Source: © *Statistics Canada*   (n.a.) Not available.
(1) Estimated. (2) Revised.

How We Compare: Education Spending by G7 Countries, 1998

(percentage)

	Canada	United States	France	United Kingdom	Germany	Italy	Japan
Social and Economic Context							
Education Attainment							
Lower secondary or less	20	14	39	18	16	56	20
Secondary graduate or higher	39	35	21	24	23	9	18
Labour force participation by education attainment							
Secondary graduate or higher							
Men	78	86	64	70	89	43	80
Women	79	87	58	50	79	40	80
Costs and school processes							
Public expenditure on education as a percentage of total public expenditures	11.6	15.3	10.6	11.0	9.2	8.9	10.1
Public expenditure on education as a percentage of GDP	5.4	5.2	5.8	4.6	4.5	4.6	3.6
Participation rate in formal education	82	74	88	70	88	70	...
Educational Outcomes							
Ratio of secondary school graduates to population	72	74	87	...	93	...	96
Unemployment rate by level of education attainment							
All levels							
Men	8	4	9	6	9	7	3
Women	8	4	13	4	11	13	3
Secondary graduate or higher							
Men	12	8	14	14	18	8	5
Women	12	9	17	7	15	16	3

Source: © *Statistics Canada*

CRIME AND JUSTICE

Rates[1] of Criminal Code Incidents in Canada

	1989	1990	1991	1992	1993	1994
Population[2](000)	27 286.2	27 700.6	28 030.9	28 376.6	28 703.1	29 036.0
Violent crime rate	911	973	1 059	1 084	1 081	1 046
Annual % change.	5.0	6.8	8.9	2.3	−0.3	−3.2
Property crime rate	5 289	5 611	6 160	5 902	5 571	5 250
Annual % change.	−2.8	6.1	9.8	−4.2	−5.6	−5.8
Other criminal code rate	2 691	2 900	3 122	3 051	2 879	2 817
Annual % change.	3.0	7.8	7.7	−2.3	−5.6	−2.2
Total[3] criminal code rate	8 891	9 484	10 342	10 036	9 531	9 114
Annual % change.	−0.3	6.7	9.0	−3.0	−5.0	−4.4
	1995	**1996**	**1997**	**1998**	**1999**	**2000**
Population[2](000)	29 353.9	29 671.9	29 987.2	30 246.9	30 491.3	30 750.1
Violent crime rate	1 007	1 000	990	979	955	982
Annual % change.	−3.7	−0.7	−1.0	−1.1	−2.4	2.8
Property crime rate	5 283	5 264	4 867	4 556	4 266	4 070
Annual % change.	0.6	−0.4	−7.5	−6.4	−6.4	−4.5
Other criminal code rate	2 702	2 650	2 596	2 602	2 512	2 603
Annual % change.	−4.1	−1.9	−2.1	0.3	−3.5	3.7
Total[3] criminal code rate	8 993	8 914	8 453	8 137	7 733	7 655
Annual % change.	−1.3	−0.9	−5.2	−3.7	−5.0	−1.0

Source: *Uniform Crime Reporting Survey, Canadian Centre for Justice Statistics, © Statistics Canada*
(1) Rates are calculated per 100 000 people. (2) Population estimates as of July 1. (3) Does not include traffic violations.

Persons Charged by Gender and Age, 2000

(percentage)

	Age Group[1] by Gender				Total by Age Group[1]	
	Adults		Youth		Adults	Youth
	Male	**Female**	**Male**	**Female**		
Homicide[2]	90	10	88	12	92	8
Attempted murder.	89	11	89	11	91	9
Assaults	84	16	71	29	85	15
Sexual assaults	98	2	96	4	82	18
Other sexual offences	97	3	96	4	83	17
Abduction	55	45	25	75	96	4
Robbery	91	9	85	15	66	34
Total Violent crime	**85**	**15**	**75**	**25**	**84**	**16**
Break and enter.	93	7	91	9	63	37
Motor vehicle theft	92	8	85	15	59	41
Fraud	70	30	63	37	92	8
Theft over $5,000	77	23	85	15	87	13
Theft $5,000 and under	71	29	66	34	73	27
Total Property crime	**78**	**22**	**77**	**23**	**73**	**27**
Mischief	88	12	88	12	67	33
Arson	81	19	86	14	52	48
Prostitution.	49	51	14	86	98	2
Offensive weapons	93	7	93	7	78	22
Total Criminal Code	**82**	**18**	**77**	**23**	**79**	**21**
Impaired driving[3]	88	12	87	13	99	1
Cannabis Offences	87	13	87	13	83	17
Cocaine Offences	82	18	79	21	95	5
Other Drugs Offences	83	17	83	17	85	15

Source: *© Statistics Canada, Uniform Crime Report Survey, Canadian Centre for Justice statistics*
(1) Adults are defined as people age 18 and over, Youth between the ages of 12 and 17. (2) Data based on Homicide Survey.
(3) Includes impaired operation of a vehicle causing death, causing bodily harm, alcohol rate over 80 mg., failure/refusal to provide a breath/blood sample. Dated based on Incident-based survey.

Selected Criminal Code Incidents by Province, 2000

	Canada	Nfld	PEI	NS	NB	Que	Ont
Population	30 750 087	538 823	138 928	940 996	756 598	7 372 448	11 669 344
Homicide							
Number	542	6	3	15	10	148	155
Rate[1]	1.8	1.1	2.2	1.6	1.3	2.0	1.3
Annual % change in rate[2]...	−0.1	201.1	197.2	15.2	10.8	7.7	−5.6
Sexual Assault							
Number	24 049	572	105	750	771	3 424	8 825
Rate[1]	78	106	76	80	102	46	76
Annual % change in rate[2]...	0.0	−0.3	−0.9	−16.2	−0.8	−0.6	5.3
Assault							
Number	233 517	4 057	824	7 580	5 646	37 442	79 913
Rate[1]	759	753	593	808	746	508	685
Annual % change in rate[2]...	4.6	1.7	5.7	−0.9	−2.4	13.8	4.6
Robbery							
Number	27 012	57	14	521	166	7 642	8 396
Rate[1]	88	11	10	55	22	104	72
Annual % change in rate[2]...	−6.8	−10.6	−27.0	25.0	2.2	−8.1	−5.0
Total violent crime							
Number	**301 875**	**4 849**	**999**	**9 319**	**7 089**	**52 911**	**103 540**
Rate[1]	**982**	**900**	**719**	**990**	**937**	**718**	**887**
Annual % change in rate[2] ..	**2.8**	**1.3**	**4.7**	**−1.6**	**−2.1**	**7.8**	**4.1**
Breaking and Entering							
Number	293 416	3 519	809	7 673	5 209	79 984	85 408
Rate[1]	954	653	582	815	688	1 085	732
Annual % change in rate[2]...	−8.5	−7.1	−10.5	−15.4	−5.1	−6.2	−8.9
Motor Vehicle Theft							
Number	160 268	642	218	2 864	1 556	42 458	48 284
Rate[1]	521	119	157	304	206	576	414
Annual % change in rate[2]...	−1.5	21.8	13.1	−1.4	−4.9	−1.7	−4.8
Other Theft							
Number	683 997	7 349	2 655	18 730	11 972	126 441	219 392
Rate[1]	2 224	1 364	1 911	1 990	1 582	1 715	1 880
Annual % change in rate[2]...	−3.2	1.0	−0.9	−12.0	1.5	1.3	−4.6
Total property crime							
Number	**1 251 667**	**12 991**	**4 129**	**33 652**	**21 760**	**269 124**	**394 786**
Rate[1]	**4 070**	**2 411**	**2 972**	**3 576**	**2 876**	**3 650**	**3 383**
Annual % change in rate[2] ..	**−4.5**	**−1.4**	**−4.8**	**−11.0**	**−3.7**	**−1.9**	**−5.3**
Offensive weapons							
Number	15 306	176	33	502	346	1 150	6 279
Rate[1]	50	33	24	53	46	16	54
Annual % change in rate[2]...	−5.2	36.9	12.7	6.6	−10.6	0.9	−5.7
Mischief							
Number	326 369	5 230	1 703	11 430	7 138	54 605	101 373
Rate[1]	1 061	971	1 226	1 215	943	741	869
Annual % change in rate[2]...	3.6	10.9	−5.4	−8.2	−3.1	6.3	2.9
Total other criminal code							
Number	**800 384**	**12 932**	**4 161**	**28 272**	**20 471**	**122 307**	**250 907**
Rate[1]	**2 603**	**2 400**	**2 995**	**3 004**	**2 706**	**1 659**	**2 150**
Annual % change in rate[2] ..	**3.7**	**7.5**	**−6.3**	**−9.2**	**−5.9**	**6.8**	**3.5**
TOTAL CRIMINAL CODE[3]							
Number	**2 353 926**	**30 772**	**9 289**	**71 243**	**49 320**	**444 342**	**749 233**
Rate[1]	**7 655**	**5 711**	**6 686**	**7 571**	**6 519**	**6 027**	**6 421**
Annual % change in rate[2] ..	**−1.0**	**2.6**	**−4.5**	**−9.1**	**−4.4**	**1.5**	**−1.3** ▶

	Man	Sask	Alta	BC	YK	NWT[4]	NVT[4]
Population	1 147 880	1 023 636	2 997 236	4 063 760	30 663	42 083	27 692
Homicide							
Number	30	26	58	85	2	1	3
Rate[1]	2.6	2.5	1.9	2.1	6.5	2.4	10.8
Annual % change in rate[2]	14.9	100.4	–6.1	–23.4	102.7	–2.3	46.3
Sexual Assault							
Number	1 365	1 525	2 497	3 727	86	181	221
Rate[1]	119	149	83	92	280	430	798
Annual % change in rate[2]	4.0	11.1	–9.2	–5.6	–3.1	–12.5	5.6
Assault							
Number	14 930	13 627	25 071	40 616	842	1 648	1 321
Rate[1]	1 301	1 331	836	999	2 746	3 916	4 770
Annual % change in rate[2]	8.1	5.5	1.7	–0.2	5.8	–3.4	15.5
Robbery							
Number	1 845	919	2 532	4 877	13	18	12
Rate[1]	161	90	84	120	42	43	43
Annual % change in rate[2]	–7.6	3.8	–1.6	–13.9	–12.1	–7.4	67.2
Total violent crime							
Number	**18 805**	**17 025**	**31 830**	**50 819**	**1 020**	**1 987**	**1 682**
Rate[1]	**1 638**	**1 663**	**1 062**	**1 251**	**3 326**	**4 722**	**6 074**
Annual % change in rate[2]	**4.1**	**4.4**	**–0.1**	**–2.5**	**6.4**	**–4.9**	**15.7**
Breaking and Entering							
Number	14 184	15 815	26 781	51 839	774	817	604
Rate[1]	1 236	1 545	894	1 276	2 524	1 941	2 181
Annual % change in rate[2]	–7.2	–6.1	–9.7	–11.5	40.1	–9.5	18.0
Motor Vehicle Theft							
Number	11 797	7 635	14 893	29 266	245	211	199
Rate[1]	1 028	746	497	720	799	501	719
Annual % change in rate[2]	9.5	8.1	–1.0	–2.4	8.9	–8.4	14.8
Other Theft							
Number	27 638	30 361	75 663	160 802	1 291	1 207	406
Rate[1]	2 408	2 966	2 524	3 957	4 210	2 868	1 791
Annual % change in rate[2]	–4.1	7.3	–6.5	–4.4	9.2	5.0	9.9
Total property crime							
Number	**57 008**	**60 088**	**133 447**	**258 410**	**2 502**	**2 394**	**1 376**
Rate[1]	**4 966**	**5 870**	**4 452**	**6 359**	**8 160**	**5 689**	**4 969**
Annual % change in rate[2]	**–2.4**	**1.8**	**–7.0**	**–6.0**	**14.7**	**–1.6**	**14.1**
Offensive weapons							
Number	1 063	701	1 622	3 261	78	56	39
Rate[1]	93	68	54	80	254	133	141
Annual % change in rate[2]	–9.1	–17.7	–3.9	–6.0	34.0	–18.3	–7.2
Mischief							
Number	22 218	19 512	40 464	57 156	1 120	3 108	1 312
Rate[1]	1 936	1 906	1 350	1 406	3 653	7 385	4 738
Annual % change in rate[2]	–3.1	16.2	5.1	2.5	41.4	11.2	21.7
Total other criminal code							
Number	**47 271**	**53 193**	**99 146**	**148 073**	**3 696**	**7 145**	**2 810**
Rate[1]	**4 118**	**5 196**	**3 308**	**3 644**	**12 054**	**16 978**	**10 147**
Annual % change in rate[2]	**5.0**	**7.8**	**3.0**	**2.8**	**29.8**	**25.0**	**19.4**
TOTAL CRIMINAL CODE[3]							
Number	**123 084**	**130 306**	**264 423**	**457 302**	**7 218**	**11 526**	**5 868**
Rate[1]	**10 723**	**12 730**	**8 822**	**11 253**	**23 540**	**27 389**	**21 190**
Annual % change in rate[2]	**1.3**	**4.5**	**–2.7**	**–2.9**	**20.5**	**12.6**	**17.1**

Source: © *Statistics Canada, Uniform Crime Reporting Survey, Canadian Centre for Justice Statistics*
(1) Rates are calculated on the basis of 100 000 population. Population estimates at July 1. (2) In comparison to the previous year. Percent change based on unrounded rates. (3) Without traffic offences.

Rate of Homicide Offences, by Province

(rate per 100,000 population)

	1995	1996	1997	1998	1999
Canada	**2.00**	**2.14**	**1.95**	**1.84**	**1.76**
Newfoundland	0.88	1.25	1.26	1.28	0.37
Prince Edward Island	0.74	0.73	0.00	0.73	0.72
Nova Scotia	1.83	1.93	2.57	2.56	1.38
New Brunswick	1.86	1.20	1.06	0.66	1.19
Quebec	1.86	2.12	1.81	1.87	1.85
Ontario	1.65	1.68	1.58	1.37	1.40
Manitoba	2.39	3.97	2.73	2.90	2.27
Saskatchewan	2.07	3.14	2.45	3.22	1.26
Alberta	2.19	1.91	2.15	2.20	2.06
British Columbia	3.17	3.22	2.93	2.25	2.73
Yukon	12.95	0.00	3.10	9.50	3.26
Northwest Territories incl. Nunavut	4.51	5.92	4.42	7.41	x
Northwest Territories	x	x	x	x	2.40
Nunavut	x	x	x	x	7.40

Source: © *Statistics Canada*　　　　　　　　　x Data unavailable, not applicable or confidential.

Location of Homicide Offences

	1993	1994	1995	1996	1997
All locations	**627**	**596**	**588**	**635**	**581**
Victim's residence	290	274	271	303	312
Suspect's residence	63	36	60	57	56
Other private place or work place	99	108	95	100	82
Correctional institution	6	7	3	7	4
Public place	129	132	129	126	101
Other	24	23	17	21	20
Not known	16	16	13	21	6

Source: © *Statistics Canada*

Youth Court Sentencing in Canada

	1995–1996	1996–1997	1997–1998	1998–1999	1999–2000
			(Number of cases)		
All sentences	**72 945**	**74 797**	**74 527**	**71 961**	**68 184**
Secure custody	10 850	11 772	12 199	12 312	11 610
Open custody	13 462	13 506	13 470	12 857	11 605
Probation	35 783	37 960	35 913	34 451	33 028
Fine	4 226	3 574	4 295	4 081	4 062
Community service order	5 020	4 594	5 256	4 988	4 750
Absolute discharge	2 094	1 464	1 160	1 130	1 094
Other sentences[1]	1 510	1 927	2 234	2 142	2 035

Source: © *Statistics Canada*

(1) Includes restitution, prohibition, compensations, pay purchaser, and other sentences such as essays, apologies, counseling programs and conditional discharges.

The National Anthem: O Canada

The music of *O Canada* was composed by Calixa Lavallée and the lyrics were written in French by Adolphe-Basile Routhier in Quebec City. Originally called *Chant National*, it was first performed at a banquet in Quebec City on June 24, 1880. The anthem grew in popularity in Quebec but was not heard in English until the early 1900s. There have been several English versions of the work, the most popular of which was written in 1908 by Robert Stanley Weir. In 1967 a Special Joint Committee of the Senate and the House of Commons was formed to recommend official versions of Canada's National and Royal Anthems. With a few minor changes, the official English version of *O Canada* is based on Weir's lyrics. On June 27, 1980 the House of Commons passed Bill C-36 designating both the music and lyrics of *O Canada* as Canada's national anthem. It was proclaimed July 1, 1980.

O Canada

O Canada! Terre de nos aïeux,

Ton front est ceint de fleurons glorieux!

Car ton bras sait porter l'épée,

Il sait porter la croix!

Ton histoire est une épopée

Des plus brillants exploits,

Et ta valeur, de foi trempée,

Protégera nos foyers et nos droits,

Protégera nos foyers et nos droits.

O Canada

O Canada! Our home and native land!

True patriot love in all thy sons command.

With glowing hearts we see thee rise,

The True North strong and free!

From far and wide, O Canada,

We stand on guard for thee.

God keep our land glorious and free!

O Canada, we stand on guard for thee.

O Canada, we stand on guard for thee!

The National Flag

The National Flag was adopted by Parliament Dec. 15, 1964 and proclaimed by Queen Elizabeth II. It was inaugurated on Feb. 15, 1965.

It is a red flag of the proportions two by length and one by width, containing in its centre a white square, the width of the flag, bearing a single, red, stylized maple leaf. The maple leaf has been looked upon as an emblem of Canada since the early 1700s. Red and white were declared Canada's official colours by King George V on Nov. 21, 1921.

The National Flag is to be flown daily at all federal government buildings, airports and military bases and establishments within and outside Canada. When flown with other flags, it should be given a place of honour.

The National Coat of Arms

The creation of coats of arms dates back to the Middle Ages. Centuries ago few could read, nor did they have access to print material, pictures or the other means we now use to identify people. Heraldry was developed as a form of picture-writing, used in the Middle Ages to create visual emblems that identified individuals or members of a community or nation, particularly on the field of battle.

Over time, the development of such symbols became quite sophisticated; a coat of arms could identify not only the individual but tell if his father was still alive, his birth order, whether or not he was married and the prestige of his branch of the family. In war, the device was painted on a shield; in peace, it would be embroidered on a coat or banner. Because of its significance, heraldry came to be carefully regulated; colleges of arms controlled the grant and use of them.

At the time of Confederation, Canada did not have a coat of arms and used the Royal Arms of the United Kingdom to identify the offices of the Government of Canada. By 1868, however, a Great Seal was required and the government adopted a design that was also used as the Arms of Canada. The design showed the emblems of the original four provinces of the federation—Nova Scotia, New Brunswick, Quebec and Ontario—on a shield. When new provinces joined the federation, their emblems were added to the shield and the design became fragmented and confusing as the provinces multiplied. In 1919, the governor general convened a special committee to study the question of a Canadian coat of arms; a request for a grant of arms was later submitted to the sovereign.

Canada's Coat of Arms was granted by a royal proclamation of King George V on Nov. 21, 1921. Although simplified in 1957 and augmented in 1994, the coat of arms we have now is faithful to that original design.

The most important part of the design is the shield, which shows the emblems of the four founding peoples (English, Scottish, Irish and French) with an added sprig of distinctly Canadian maple leaves. The shield is supported on one side by the lion of England holding the Royal Union flag and the unicorn of Scotland holding a banner of royalist France on the other. A royal helmet and mantle sit above the shield, with a crest showing a royal lion holding a maple leaf on top of the helmet. (The crest is the symbol used on the Governor General's standard.) The imperial crown above the crest represents the monarch as Canada's head of state.

Below the shield is Canada's motto, "A Mari usque ad Mare" (from sea to sea) which is based on a verse from Psalm 72 of the Bible: "He shall have dominion from sea to sea and from the river unto the ends of the earth." Around the shield is a ribbon with the motto of the Order of Canada: "Desiderantes Meliorem Patriam" (They desire a better country). The floral emblems of the four founding nations are found at the base of the design: the English rose, the Scottish thistle, the French fleur-de-lis and the shamrock of Ireland.

Canada's coat of arms represents national sovereignty and is used on federal government property such as buildings, official seals, money, passports, proclamations and publications as well as badges of some members of the armed forces. This national symbol is protected from unauthorized commercial use by the *Trade Marks Act*.

CANADIAN HISTORY

■ Exploration and First Settlements

The first people who came to North America arrived during the last Ice Age which began about 80,000 years ago and ended about 12,000 years ago. These Native People were hunters who crosssed from Asia via a land bridge that is now submerged beneath the Bering Sea. Although there is continuing debate among archeologists as to how early humans might have settled in what is now Canada, the earliest accepted occupation site is at the Bluefish Caves in the Yukon; artifacts at least 12,000 to 17,000 years old have been found there. As the glaciers of the Ice Age retreated, human settlements spread across Canada and gradually, these first Canadians developed lifestyles based on the environments in which they lived. They obtained their food by hunting, fishing, gathering, and in the case of Eastern Woodland tribes, by farming. By the time explorers from Europe reached Canada, the Native People had well developed trading patterns, arts and crafts, languages, writing, religious beliefs, laws and government.

There has been much conjecture as to who the first Europeans to come to Canada were. The claim that an Irish monk, St. Brendan, arrived about the year 550 has not been proven. However, the theory that Vikings settled in Newfoundland was confirmed by archeological excavations at L'Anse aux Meadows during the 1960s and 1970s.

A burst of European exploration didn't take place until the Age of Discovery in the 15th and 16th centuries. Explorers found what they called a New World while in search of a route to the Far East. In 1497, Giovanni Caboto (John Cabot), an Italian sailing for England, landed on the Canadian coast, likely in Cape Breton or Newfoundland, and claimed the land for Henry VII. Although Cabot probably died on a second expedition in 1498, his voyages helped open up the rich fishing grounds of the Grand Banks.

European navigators and fishermen continued to visit the shores of Canada, but the first serious exploration of the area was undertaken by Jacques Cartier, who discovered the Gulf of St. Lawrence while searching for a passage to Asia, in 1534. The next year he travelled up the St. Lawrence River as far as the native settlements of Stadacona (Quebec) and Hochelaga (Montreal). On this voyage, Cartier picked up the Iroquoian word for village, Kanata (thought to be the origin of "Canada"), and used it to apply to the whole region he had discovered. Cartier's discoveries gave France a claim to Canada and led to the first French settlements.

In 1541–42, Cartier and the Sieur de Roberval established a short-lived settlement at Charlesbourg-Royal just above Quebec. In 1605, the Sieur de Monts and Samuel de Champlain established the colony of Port Royal in what is now Nova Scotia. Champlain went on to establish a settlement at Quebec in 1608, to explore the interior and to draw maps of New France. Champlain also started a fur-trading network (mostly in beaver pelts) with the Algonquins and the Hurons who inhabited the St. Lawrence and Great Lakes regions. This trade relationship became a military alliance as Champlain supported these groups against the Iroquois. This enmity between the French and the Iroquois prevailed throughout most of the history of New France.

Circa 1000 **Leif Ericsson** and other **Vikings** visit Labrador and Newfoundland.

1497 **John Cabot** (Giovanni Caboto) claims Cape Breton Island (or possibly Newfoundland or Labrador) for Henry VII of England (June 24).

1498 **Cabot** makes his second voyage to North America.

1534 **Jacques Cartier** visits the Strait of Belle Isle (Newfoundland), and charts the Gulf of St Lawrence (landing in Gaspé July 14).

1535 **Cartier** sails up the St Lawrence River to **Quebec** and **Montreal**.

1541 Cartier and the Sieur de Roberval found Charlesbourg-Royal, the **first French settlement** in America.

1577 **Martin Frobisher** of England makes the first of his three attempts to find a northwest passage, sailing as far as Hudson Strait.

1600 King Henry IV of France grants a **fur-trading monopoly** in the Gulf of St Lawrence to a group of French merchants.

1605 **Samuel de Champlain** and the Sieur de Monts found Port Royal (Annapolis, NS).

1608 **Champlain** founds Quebec.

1609 Champlain supports the Algonquins against the Iroquois at Lake Champlain.

1610 **Étienne Brûlé** goes to live among the Huron and eventually becomes the first European to see Lakes Ontario, Huron and Superior. **Henry Hudson** explores Hudson Bay.

1617 Louis Hébert, the **first habitant (farmer),** arrives in Quebec.

1625 Jesuits arrive in Quebec to begin missionary work among the Indians.

1627 The **Company of One Hundred Associates** is founded (Apr. 29) to establish a French empire in North America.

■ The Growth of New France (1627-1660)

The economic foundation of New France was the fur trade. In fact, the French kings were content to let fur-trading companies run the colony. Although these companies expanded the territory's boundaries, they failed to encourage settlement. One of King Louis XIII's most able advisers, Cardinal Richelieu, tried to remedy this problem by granting a fur-trading monopoly to the Company of One Hundred Associates in 1627, on condition that it bring out several hundred settlers each year. However, war between England and France broke out and Quebec was captured in 1629. Even after peace was restored in 1633, the Company of One Hundred Associates failed to honor its commitment to bring out settlers.

Despite the lack of settlers, the colony was expanding in other ways. As governor, Champlain encouraged the expansion of the fur trade. The Jesuits had arrived in 1625 and were vigorously pursuing their missionary work among the Hurons.

Champlain died in 1635, just two years after the colony was restored to France. No leader possessing his vision or drive emerged to replace him. Next, despite their conviction, the French missionaries made few converts among the native people. Even Sainte-Marie among the Hurons, their central mission-post, was abandoned in 1649 in the face of invasion by the Iroquois, who dispersed the Hurons and disrupted the French fur-trading network. Finally, the security of the centre of the fur trade, Montreal (founded in 1642), and the rest of the colony was threatened by the wars against the Iroquois. When the wars were renewed in 1659-1660, after a brief peace, there were still only about 3,000 French settlers in the colony. Clearly, the French king would have to act to secure France's foothold in North America.

1629 **David Kirke** captures Quebec for Britain (July 19).

1632 The **Treaty of Saint-Germain-en-Laye** returns Quebec to France.

1634–40 The **Huron nation** is reduced by half from European diseases (smallpox epidemic, 1639).

1637 **Kirke** is named first governor of Newfoundland.

1642 **Montreal** is founded (May 18) by the Sieur **de Maisonneuve**.

1649 The Jesuit Father **Jean de Brébeuf** is martyred by the **Iroquois** at St-Ignace (Mar. 16). The Iroquois disperse the Huron nation (1648–49).

1659 **François de Laval,** later to become Canada's first bishop, arrives in Quebec (June).

1660 **Adam Dollard des Ormeaux** makes his last stand against the Iroquois at Long Sault (May). The small party of French fights so well that the Iroquois decide not to attack Montreal.

■ Royal Government in New France (1663-1700)

In 1663 King Louis XIV made New France a crown colony. Regular troops were sent out and undertook a successful campaign against the Iroquois, which resulted in the signing of a peace treaty in 1667. Several hundred of these regulars stayed on as settlers, thereby adding to the security of the colony. A system of government headed by a governor, an intendant and a bishop was instituted. The governor, who was the king's representative, was charged with defence. The intendant was responsible for industry, trade and administrative affairs. The bishop looked after religious matters, which included education. In theory, this system provided for a clear separation of powers; but, in practice, there were frequent disputes among the three officials. Still, this system survived intact for the remainder of the colony's history, and it provided New France with some remarkably dynamic officials. Two of these arrived in the first years of the Royal Government.

The first intendant of New France, Jean Talon (1665–1672), introduced innovative measures, including awards for early marriage, to boost the population. As well, he tried to build a diversified economy on the St. Lawrence by promoting crafts, farming and local industry. Few subsequent officials in New France shared Talon's concern for settlement or economic diversity. Most were more interested in profits from the fur trade. Count Frontenac, governor for all but seven years between 1672 and 1698, threw his support behind the fur trade, not only raising profits but also encouraging exploration. Under his rule, French adventurers explored the Mississippi River from its upper reaches to the Gulf of Mexico, greatly expanding the fur-trading boundaries of New France. Frontenac gained more fame when he withstood the attack of an English army which besieged Quebec in 1690.

But Frontenac had not only exceeded his powers in promoting territorial expansion, he had also undermined the security of the colony. With its limited population, New France now found itself competing for the fur trade with the more populous English colonies around them. In the north, there was rivalry with the Hudson's Bay Company, founded in 1670. To the south, there was border warfare between French fur traders and their Indian allies, and the English with their Iroquois allies. New France fared well in the limited warfare of the 1680s and 1690s; but in the 18th century there was a series of major wars which resulted in disaster for the colony.

1663 Quebec becomes a **royal province**.

1665 The Carignan-Salières regiment is sent from France to Quebec to deal with the Iroquois. **Jean Talon** becomes Quebec's intendant.

1666 Canada's **first census** counts 3,215 non-native inhabitants in 668 families.

1670 The **Hudson's Bay Company** is formed and granted trade rights over all territory draining into Hudson Bay (May 2).

1672 Count **Frontenac** becomes Governor of Quebec.

1673 **Marquette** and **Jolliet** explore the Mississippi to its junction with the Arkansas.

1674 **Laval** becomes first Bishop of Quebec.

1678–79 Dulhut explores the headwaters of the Mississippi.

1682 **La Salle** explores the Mississippi to its mouth.

1686 **De Troyes** and **D'Iberville** capture the English posts of Moose Fort (June 20), Rupert House (July 3) and Fort Albany (July 26) on James Bay.

1689 The Iroquois kill many French settlers at Lachine.

1690 **Sir William Phips captures Port Royal** (May 11). Frontenac repels Phips's attack on Quebec (Oct.).

1697 The **Treaty of Ryswick** restores the status quo in the struggle between England and France. All captured territory is returned.

■ **The Collapse of New France (1701-1763)**

In the early years of the 18th century, New France stretched from Hudson Bay to the Gulf of Mexico, and from Newfoundland to the Great Lakes. Its population was thinly scattered in the north, south and west but its fur-trading posts in these regions gave legitimacy to its territorial claims. In the Atlantic region, there were several hundred colonists in Newfoundland and another 1,500 in Acadia. The heartland of New France was the settlement of about 20,000 colonists in Montreal, Quebec and in the small communities along the St. Lawrence. The prosperity of the French settlements was to be hurt by long periods of war.

The first of these was the war of the Spanish Succession fought between France and Austria (and their allies) between 1701-1714. Although the British failed to capture their main objective in the North American campaign, the fortress city of Quebec, they made other gains at the bargaining table. In the Treaty of Utrecht, which ended the conflict, France gave up claims to the Hudson Bay territory, all of Acadia except Cape Breton, and Newfoundland.

During a 30-year period of peace, New France enjoyed limited prosperity. The populaton grew, farm yields increased, some industry was established and furs were still exported. But military expenditure necessary to protect the colony was turning it into a financial burden for France. Much of that expenditure went into the huge fortress of Louisbourg, built on Cape Breton Island to protect the offshore fisheries and guard the St. Lawrence.

Prussia, France, Spain, Naples, Bavaria and Saxony fought Austria and England when the war of Austrian Succession broke out in 1740 and Louisbourg was a natural target. The fortress fell to the British, although it was returned to France at the war's end in 1748. The British established their own military and naval base at Halifax in 1749.

The fragile peace was broken in 1754, when fighting broke out between the English and French colonists in the Ohio Valley. Within two years, Britain and France were officially at war again in what became known as the Seven Years' War. Despite some early victories, the French suffered the loss of Louisbourg in 1758. In the following year, General Wolfe defeated General Montcalm on the Plains of Abraham above the St. Lawrence at Quebec. Although Montreal did not fall until the next year, the loss of Quebec was an irreversible setback. The British army occupied New France, and in 1763 the treaty ending the Seven Years' War confirmed British sovereignty.

New France had fallen because of decisive military defeats at Louisbourg and Quebec, but more significant was the inability of France to supply its colony in the face of British naval supremacy. The British were now masters in North America.

1701 The **War of the Spanish Succession** begins in Europe; the conflict spreads to North America the following year.

1710 Francis Nicholson captures Port Royal for England.

1713 The **Treaty of Utrecht** confirms British possession of Hudson Bay, Newfoundland and Acadia (except Cape Breton Island). France starts building Fort **Louisbourg**.

1739 La Vérendrye expedition explores Lake Winnipeg.

1740 The **War of the Austrian Succession** pits Britain against France; the European conflict spreads to North America (**King George's War**) in **1744**.

1745 Massachusetts Governor William Shirley takes the French fortress of **Louisbourg**.

1748 Louisbourg is returned to France by the **Treaty of Aix-la-Chapelle**.

1749 Britain founds **Halifax** to counter the French presence at Louisbourg.

1752 Canada's **first newspaper**, the Halifax *Gazette*, appears (Mar. 25).

1753 **George Washington**'s military expedition to the Monogahela is defeated by the French.

1754 Beginning of **French and Indian War** in America. Although war is not officially declared for another two years, this marks the final phase in the struggle between France and Britain in North America.

1755 Britain expels the **Acadians** from Nova Scotia, scattering them throughout her other North American colonies.

1756 Beginning of the **Seven Years' War** in Europe pits Britain against France. The Marquis **de Montcalm** assumes command of French troops in North America.

1758 The British under Generals Amherst and Wolfe take Louisbourg.

1759 **Wolfe takes Quebec**, defeating Montcalm on the Plains of Abraham (Sept. 13). Both generals are killed.

1760 General **James Murray** is appointed military governor of Quebec; he becomes civil governor in **1764**.

■ The First Years of British Rule (1763-1812)

The British had been active on the continent during their search for a northwest passage to the far east; however, their victory over the French encouraged a shift from exploration and fur trading to settlement and the strengthening of British customs in the new territory.

In 1763 a Royal Proclamation was imposed by the British government on the newly-acquired territories of New France. The intent of this proclamation was clear. By encouraging the establishment of Protestant schools, by promoting the Church of England, and by stipulating that an assembly be elected, the proclamation aimed at Anglicization. The intent was most visible in the matter of the assembly. Although the French inhabitants were in the majority, under British law no Roman Catholic could hold office. If an assembly were elected, a few hundred British settlers would control about 65,000 Canadiens.

Fortunately for the French in Canada, James Murray, the governor of Quebec from 1760 to 1768, felt that the loyalty of the French colonists could more likely be gained by fair treatment. Murray refused to call elections for the assembly, and allowed French legal practices to continue. Murray's sympathies provoked a storm of protest from the British colonists in Quebec and he was recalled. But his successor, Guy Carleton, also realized that the Royal Proclamation of 1763 would only alienate the recently-defeated colonists. Carleton saw that even if Anglicization were carried out, few colonists from the Thirteen Colonies in America or immigrants from Britain would be lured to the rugged colony of Quebec. Consequently, Carleton advised the government in London to replace the proclamation with more liberal legislation.

The result was the Quebec Act of 1774, which dropped the assembly in favour of an appointed council on which Catholics might serve. As well, the French system of civil law and the seigneurial system of land tenure were both guaranteed. Finally, the Quebec Act expanded the borders of the colony to include the rich lands of the Ohio Valley. The British had acted to win the support of the Canadiens. In doing so, however, the British government angered the citizens of the Thirteen Colonies, who resented the special treatment given to their former enemies. These English colonists were especially upset over the loss of the Ohio Valley, a region into which they expected to expand.

The Quebec Act was not the only cause for complaint in the Thirteen Colonies. Protests over British taxation policies and trade restriction led to talk of revolution. That talk led to action, and in 1775 an invading American army took Montreal. Quebec held out against the American siege until relieved by British forces. Although there was some sympathy for the American cause in both Quebec and Nova Scotia, it was not a strong enough sentiment to cause these two colonies to join the revolution.

During and immediately after the American Revolution, some American colonists who wished to retain their British ties fled from the newly-created United States into the Maritimes and Quebec. The arrival of about 30,000 of these Loyalists in Nova Scotia resulted in the creation of a new colony, New Brunswick, in 1784. Similarly, the influx of 10,000 Loyalists into Quebec led to division of the colony, and in 1791, the western part of the colony became Upper Canada. The remainder of the old colony was known as Lower Canada.

Despite these changes, fur trading remained an important economic activity in the interior of British North America. In fact, there was keen rivalry for furs between the Hudson's Bay Company and the newly-formed (1784) North West Company based in Montreal which led to a flurry of western exploration. Alexander Mackenzie, a partner in the North West Company, explored a river (now known as the Mackenzie) to its mouth on the Beaufort Sea in 1789, and found a route to the Pacific via the Fraser and Bella Coola Rivers in 1793. Two other North West Company employees, Simon Fraser and David Thompson, also carried out voyages of discovery. Fraser followed the river named after him to the Pacific in 1808, and Thompson travelled down the Columbia River to the coast in 1811. These voyages, along with the earlier coastal explorations of James Cook in 1778 and George Vancouver in 1792-1795, helped establish Britain's claim to the northwest part of the continent.

1763 France cedes its North American possessions to Britain by the **Treaty of Paris.** A Royal Proclamation imposes British institutions on Quebec (Oct.). This proclamation also serves as the cornerstone for relations between Canadian aboriginal peoples and the Canadian government, preserving land for their use and giving the government exclusive right to negotiate treaties.

1768 Guy Carleton succeeds Murray as governor of Quebec.

1769 Frances Brooke publishes *The History of Emily Montague*, a novel with descriptions of geography, climate and social culture in the New World.

1774 The **Quebec Act** provides for British criminal law but restores French civil law and guarantees religious freedom for Roman Catholic colonists.

1775 Americans under Montgomery capture Montreal (Nov.) and attack Quebec (Dec. 31).

1776 Under Carleton, Quebec withstands American siege until the appearance of a British fleet (May 6).

1778 Captain **James Cook** anchors in Nootka Sound, Vancouver Island (Mar. 29–Apr. 26).

1783 The American Revolutionary War ends; the border between Canada and the US is accepted between the Atlantic Ocean and Lake of the Woods.

1784 **United Empire Loyalists** arrive in Canada. The province of **New Brunswick** is created. The **North West Company** is formed.

1789 **Alexander Mackenzie** journeys to the Beaufort Sea, following what would later be named the Mackenzie River.

1791 **Constitutional Act** divides Quebec into Upper and Lower Canada.

1792 **George Vancouver** begins his explorations of the Pacific coast.

1793 **Alexander Mackenzie** reaches the **Pacific**.

1794 **Jay's Treaty** (Nov. 19) between the US and Britain promises British evacuation of the Ohio Valley forts. The treaty's appointment of officials to settle boundary disputes marks the beginning of international arbitration through its provisions for boundary settlements.

1797 **David Thompson** joins the North West Company as a surveyor and mapmaker.

1806 *Le Canadien*, Quebec nationalist newspaper, is founded.

1808 **Simon Fraser**, a North West Company employee, travels the river named after him to the Pacific.

1811 **David Thompson** charts the Columbia River to the Pacific coast.

■ The War of 1812

Although the British and Americans signed a peace treaty in 1783 to end the American War of Independence, there was still friction between them. One source of conflict was the British fur-trading posts in the Ohio Valley which now belonged to the United States. Although Britain surrendered these posts in 1796 as stipulated by Jay's Treaty (1794), there were still American complaints that the British were arming the local native people. At the same time there was growing American resentment over British interference with shipping. The British, who were at war with France, claimed the right to search American ships for cargoes bound for the enemy. In the process, the British often forced American sailors on these ships to join the British navy. Resentment grew among Americans until June

1812, when the United States declared war on Britain.

In the first year of the war, the Americans under General William Hull crossed the Detroit River to invade Upper Canada. Hull expected Canadian sympathizers to flock to his cause but he was disappointed. Without fighting a major battle, he retreated to Detroit. British General Isaac Brock and the Shawnees, under Chief Tecumseh, moved against Detroit and General Hull surrendered. This British and Canadian victory was followed by a victory at Queenston Heights on the Niagara River. Brock was killed in this battle which nevertheless gave confidence to the defenders of the British colonies.

In 1813, the Americans carried out a successful raid on York (now Toronto), and also gained a foothold in the Niagara district. But by the summer of that year the Americans had been pushed back across the Niagara River by British victories at Stoney Creek and Beaver Dam. Meanwhile, the Americans were building up a large fleet on the Great Lakes, and in September 1813 the Americans won control of Lake Erie at the Battle of Put-in-Bay. This victory prompted the British under General Proctor to abandon Fort Malden on the Detroit River. However, the American General Harrison caught the retreating forces at Moraviantown on the Thames River and defeated Proctor. Tecumseh was killed in this battle. In the east, a two-pronged attack on Montreal was repulsed. The American invaders were defeated on the Chateauguay River and at Crysler's Farm near Cornwall in the fall of 1813.

In 1814, the Americans again invaded the Niagara district but were halted at the Battle of Lundy's Lane. From Halifax, British forces attacked targets in Maine, and occupied most of that state. Another attack from Halifax was launched on the American capital, Washington. The British raiders burned the government buildings there in retaliation for the destruction of York the previous year. Despite these successes, a major British offensive against Plattsburgh on Lake Champlain failed. By now the war was in stalemate and both sides were tired. British and American negotiators signed the Treaty of Ghent in Dec. 1814, to end the war.

In the aftermath of the war, the two sides made an effort to settle outstanding differences. The Rush-Bagot Agreement of 1817 provided for naval disarmament on the Great

Lakes. In the following year Britain and the United States agreed to accept the 49th parallel as the international boundary from the Lake of the Woods to the Rocky Mountains. In addition, they agreed to the joint occupation of the Oregon Territory for 10 years.

1812 The US declares war on Britain (June 18), beginning the **War of 1812**. Americans under General William Hull invade Canada from Detroit (July 11). The Red River settlement is begun in Canada's northwest (Aug.–Oct.). Battle of Queenston Heights (Oct. 13): Canadian victory. British **General Isaac Brock** is killed in this battle.

1813 Americans burn York (Apr. 27). Battle of Stoney Creek (June 5): Canadian victory. Battle of Beaver Dams (June 23): Canadian victory; **Laura Secord**, driving a cow, passes American sentries and walks 32 km through dense bush to warn of American attack. Battle of Put-in-Bay, Lake Erie (Sept. 10): American victory. Battle of Moraviantown (Oct. 5): American victory; the Indian Chief **Tecumseh** is killed. Battle of Chateauguay (Oct. 25): Canadian victory. Battle of Crysler's Farm (Nov. 11): Canadian victory.

1814 Battle of Chippewa (July 5): American victory. Battle of Lundy's Lane (July 25): Canadian victory. A British naval force takes Washington (Aug. 24). Battle of Lake Champlain (Sept. 6–11): American victory. The **Treaty of Ghent** ends the War of 1812 (Dec. 24).

■ **Rebellion and Reform (1814-1839)**

In the years after the War of 1812, there was considerable growth in British North America. The population increased as immigrants from both the United States and Britain arrived to take up land that was free or inexpensive. The economy became more diversified as lumbering, farming and shipbuilding developed in the Canadas and in the Maritimes. Finally, a sense of nationalism began to grow in parts of British North America. This feeling arose partly out of postwar patriotism and partly out of the shared experiences of a demanding colonial life.

As the colonies became more populous, political interest increased. In both the Canadas and the Maritimes friction between ruling elites and the ordinary colonists developed and was partially fueled by the form of government in each colony. British governors or lieutenant-governors picked their own officials, including the members of legislative or executive councils. There were elected assemblies in each colony, but their powers were limited. Legislation might pass in the assembly but be turned down by the legislative council. The assemblies, the voice of the people, found themselves frustrated by the power of appointed officials.

By the mid-1830s, economic distress increased the discontent that had been building during the 1820s. In Lower Canada, where cultural prejudice against the Canadiens added to the tension, Louis Joseph Papineau emerged as leader of the radical Patriote Party. When the colonial authorities would not grant the reforms called for by Papineau and his followers, rebellion broke out in November 1837. But loyalist forces quickly defeated the badly-organized and poorly-led rebels. Papineau and other leaders fled to the United States.

In Upper Canada, the reform movement was able to gain a majority in the assembly in several elections. Still, the reformers could not turn their program into legislation because of Tory control of the Legislative Council. When an anti-reform lieutenant-governor, Sir Francis Bond Head, took over in 1836, some reformers became more radical. Their leader was William Lyon Mackenzie, a newspaper editor and member of the assembly. The Tories won the election of 1836, when Head directly intervened in the campaign. Mackenzie and his followers, spurred on by events in Lower Canada, took up arms in early December of 1837. Mackenzie's disorganization, and lack of widespread support among the colonists, doomed the rebellion. After a skirmish north of Toronto the main body of rebels fled. An uprising in the western districts of Upper Canada was equally unsuccessful. Throughout the following year some rebels and American sympathizers mounted raids on Upper Canada from the United States, but these received no popular support.

In the aftermath of the rebellions came political change. The British government sent out Lord Durham to act as Governor General of British North America and investigate the rebellion. The Durham Report of 1839 contained two main recommendations: the first called for the union of Upper and Lower Canada as a first step in the eventual assimilation of the French Canadians; the second recommended the granting of responsible government (in which the executive is responsible to the assembly), a key demand of reformers.

1816 Agents of the North West Company kill Robert Semple, governor of the Hudson's Bay Company's Red River colony, and 21 others at White Oaks (June 19).

1817 The **Rush-Bagot** agreement limits the number of battleships on the Great Lakes.

1818 The **49th parallel** is accepted as **Canada's border** with the US from Lake of the Woods to the Rocky Mountains.

1821 The Hudson's Bay Company and the North West Company are amalgamated as the HBC.

1829 The **Lachine** and **Welland Canals** are completed.

1835 **William Lyon Mackenzie** becomes the first mayor of Toronto.

1836 Opening of Canada's **first railway line**, from St. Johns, Que., to La Prairie, Que.

1837 Unsuccessful **rebellions** in Upper and Lower Canada are led by Mackenzie and Louis-Joseph Papineau.

1839 **Lord Durham's Report** recommends union of Upper and Lower Canada and the establishment of responsible government.

■ The Road to Confederation (1840-1867)

The middle years of the 19th century were both satisfying and disturbing for British North Americans. Immigrants from Europe streamed into the colonies, more land was cleared and towns grew. Local industries were started while lumbering and shipbuilding activities increased. Montreal and Toronto became commercial centres and the ports of the Maritimes were prosperous, fuelled by ship building and trade. Transportation improved as roads, canals and, by the 1850s, railways were built. Some British North Americans looked beyond their borders and began to think of a federation of British colonies that included not only Canada and the Maritimes, but the Red River settlement and the colonies in British Columbia.

Despite the prosperity, there were reasons to consider such an alliance. Until the mid-1840s, the colonies had enjoyed a preferential trading relationship whereby Britain reduced tariffs on colonial products. This advantage was lost in 1846 when Britain adopted free trade. At first, the colonies found some advantage in entering into a limited free trade arrangement with the United States. But the Americans allowed this Reciprocity Treaty of 1854 to lapse in 1866. British North Americans would have to look to themselves as trading partners.

There was also concern in British North America about the United States. That country seemed intent on fulfilling its "Manifest Destiny" to take over North America. The threat was especially clear during and after the American Civil War (1861-65). During the war, the Northern States were angered by British support for the South, and after the war, there was a fear that the large Northern army might march into British territory.

As well, there was a serious political problem in the colony of Canada. The union of Upper and Lower Canada in 1841 had resulted in the creation of a single legislature for the new colony, Canada. By the 1860s, however, this legislature was barely functioning. No single party could gain enough support from both Francophones and Anglophones to gain a majority. There had been 12 different governments in 15 years, and Canadian politicians were desperate for a solution.

Three powerful figures in Canada's legislature, John A. Macdonald, George Brown and George-Étienne Cartier formed a coalition and proposed a larger union of British North America as a way to end the political deadlock. In addition, this proposal would solve the problem of trade and provide security against the American threat. Meanwhile, on the east coast there was interest in a union too, a union of the Maritimes. A conference had been called for Charlottetown in September 1864 to discuss that topic. When the leaders of the new Canadian coalition heard of this meeting, they asked for an invitation. At Charlottetown the British North American delegates decided on a federation of all the colonies. A second conference at Quebec in October 1864 resulted in a plan for federal union. A federal government would control defence, trade and other matters of national interest. Provincial governments would have power over local matters such as roads and education. The final details were hammered out at another conference in London, England, in 1866.

The British government, which supported this colonial initiative, passed the British North America Act in March of 1867. On July 1, 1867, the provinces of Nova Scotia, New Brunswick, Ontario (formerly Canada West) and Quebec (formerly Canada East), became the Dominion of Canada.

1841 The **Act of Union** unites Upper and Lower Canada.

1842 The Ashburton-Webster Treaty settles the Maine-New Brunswick border dispute.

1843 **Fort Victoria** is built to bolster Britain's claim to Vancouver Island.

1846 Great Britain ends a preferential trading policy with the British North American colonies and enters into a **limited free trade agreement** with the United States.

1848 **Responsible government** is achieved in the Canadas and in the Maritimes, thanks to the work of **Robert Baldwin** and **Joseph Howe**.

1849 The boundary of the 49th parallel is extended to the Pacific Ocean. The province of Canada adopts both English and French as official languages. All bills of the United Canada Parliament, now Quebec and Ontario, are given assent in both English and French.

1851 Britain transfers control of the colonial postal system to Canada.

1854 The **Reciprocity Treaty** between Canada and the US is signed (June 6).

1857 **Ottawa** is named **Canada's capital** by Queen Victoria.

1860 Cornerstone of the **Parliament Buildings** is laid (Sept. 1).

1861 The **Grand Trunk Railway** through the length of the Province of Canada is completed.

1864 The **Charlottetown Conference** (Sept. 1–9) takes the first steps toward **Confederation**. The **Quebec Conference** (Oct. 10–27) sets out the basis for union.

1866 The **London Conference** (Dec. 4) passes resolutions which are redrafted to become the **British North America Act**. First raid into Canada by the **Fenians**, a radical Irish-American anti-British group, takes place (June 2). The American government allows the **Reciprocity Treaty of 1854** to lapse.

1867 Confederation. Britain's North American colonies are united by means of the **BNA Act** to become the **Dominion of Canada** (July 1). **Sir John A. Macdonald** is Canada's first prime minister. The BNA Act, now the **Constitution Act, 1867**, confirms the practice of **official bilingualism**, guaranteeing the use of French and English in the debates of the House of Commons and in the Senate, in federal courts and in publications of federal statutes. The provincial legislature, statutes and courts of Quebec are also made bilingual.

■ The Nation Expands (1867-1885)

Soon after the Confederation of Ontario, Quebec, New Brunswick and Nova Scotia in 1867, the new nation of Canada began to acquire more territory. In 1869, guided by the national vision of Prime Minister John A. Macdonald, the federal government bought Rupert's Land from the Hudson's Bay Company. This was a huge territory which included most of modern Manitoba, as well as parts of Saskatchewan, Alberta and the Northwest Territories. The few Ontario immigrants in the Red River Settlement there welcomed this move; but the far more numerous Métis (descendants of French fur traders and native people) were suspicious, especially because they had not been consulted beforehand. When newly-appointed Lieutenant-Governor William McDougall tried to enter the settlement before the territory had officially been transferred to Canada, the Métis turned him back. In the absence of a legitimate government, the Métis, under their leader Louis Riel, seized Fort Garry on the Red River and proclaimed a provisional government. The Métis demanded the right to vote, land laws, the official use of both French and English, and the provision of both Roman Catholic and Protestant schools. The Métis list of rights became the terms for negotiating Manitoba's entry into Confederation in 1870.

In the same year, representatives from the colony of British Columbia arrived in Ottawa to discuss union. With the promise from Ottawa to build a transcontinental railway, British Columbia entered Confederation in 1871. Canada now stretched from sea to sea, but the work of nation building was still not complete.

In 1868, Nova Scotia elected an anti-Confederation provincial government and sent a delegation, led by veteran politician Joseph

Howe, to London to seek a repeal of the union. But Britain was unsympathetic, and in 1869 Macdonald seized the opportunity to offer Nova Scotia better terms and Howe a cabinet position. With the Nova Scotia situation resolved, Macdonald turned his attention to Prince Edward Island. The Islanders were more attracted to the idea of union after an expensive railway project nearly bankrupted the colony. Macdonald agreed to assume the colony's debts, offered a cash subsidy and promised a steamer service to the mainland. In 1873, Prince Edward Island agreed to the terms and became Canada's 7th province.

In the 1870s and 1880s railways were built to link the provinces of the new nation. The Intercolonial Railway, joining central Canada to the Maritimes, was completed in 1876, but construction of a rail link to British Columbia ran into several delays. First, Macdonald's government was defeated in 1873 over charges of corruption associated with the railway project. The new prime minister, Alexander Mackenzie, refused to fund railway projects because the country was in the midst of a depression. However, after Macdonald's re-election in 1878, railway building began in earnest. In February 1881, the Canadian Pacific Railway Company (CPR) was incorporated, and in November 1885 the last spike was driven at Craigellachie in British Columbia to complete the link to the Pacific.

Even before it was fully completed, the CPR was used to carry troops to quell a rebellion in the spring of 1885. Trouble had started several years earlier when settlers in the North-West Territory (modern Alberta and Saskatchewan) complained to the government about land titles, shipping rates, and their lack of an elected government. Among those who complained were the Métis, some of whom had moved farther west after the Red River troubles of 1870. When the federal government was slow to respond, the Métis, again under Louis Riel, rose up in March 1885 against the territorial council appointed by Ottawa. By late April, 5,000 Canadian soldiers, who had travelled by the new railway, were on the march against Riel and his Métis and native followers. At the Battle of Batoche in May, the forces of General Middleton defeated the rebels. Riel was found guilty of treason by an English-speaking jury and executed.

1868 Confederationist **Thomas D'Arcy McGee** is **assassinated** by a Fenian in Canada's first political assassination.

1869 Canada purchases Rupert's Land from the Hudson's Bay Company for £300,000.

1870 **Louis Riel** leads the Métis in resisting Canadian authority in Canada's northwest. The Métis negotiate with the Canadian government over the right to vote, land laws, the official use of both French and English and the provision of Roman Catholic and Protestant schools. The Manitoba Act creates the province of **Manitoba**.

1871 **British Columbia** joins Confederation upon the promise from Ottawa to build a **transcontinental railway**.

1872 Macdonald's Conservatives win federal re-election.

1873 **Prince Edward Island** joins Confederation. A period of economic depression begins. The North-West Mounted Police are formed. **Alexander Mackenzie** becomes Canada's second prime minister after **Macdonald resigns** over the **Pacific Scandal**.

1874 Liberals win federal election.

1875 The **Supreme Court of Canada** is established.

1876 The **Intercolonial Railway** linking central Canada and the Maritimes is completed (July 1). The **Indian Act of 1876** defines special status for aboriginal people living on land reserves and sets out land regulations. Status Indians have no vote in Canadian elections and are exempted from taxation.

1878 Conservatives under Macdonald win federal election.

1879 Macdonald introduces **protective tariffs** as part of his **National Policy**.

1880 **Emily Stowe** receives her medical licence after practising medicine in Toronto since her graduation from a New York medical school in 1867.

1881 The **Canadian Pacific Railway** is incorporated.

1884 **Riel returns** to Canada.

1885 Métis and the NWMP clash at Duck Lake (Mar. 26). The Métis are defeated at Batoche (May 9–12). The **last spike of the transcontinental railway** is driven at Craigellachie in Eagle Pass, BC, by Donald

Smith (Nov. 7). **Louis Riel** is **hanged** in Regina (Nov. 16).

1887 Conservatives win federal election. Liberals choose **Wilfrid Laurier** as leader. The **first provincial premiers' conference** takes place in Quebec City.

1889 The **Dominion Women's Enfranchisement Association** is created to campaign for female voting rights in Canada.

1890 Manitoba Liberals under Thomas Greenway halt public funding of Catholic schools in Manitoba (Mar.).

1891 Conservatives win federal election. **Sir John A. Macdonald dies**. **Sir John Abbott** takes office as prime minister (June 16).

1892 Abbott resigns (Nov. 24). **Sir John Thompson** becomes prime minister (Dec. 5). He establishes the **Canadian Criminal Code**.

1894 Thompson dies (Dec. 12). **Sir Mackenzie Bowell** is asked by the governor general, the Earl of Aberdeen, to form the fourth Conservative government since 1891.

■ The Laurier Era (1896-1911)

Conservative Prime Minister John A. Macdonald died in 1891, soon after winning a federal election. The Conservatives could not find a suitable successor and by 1896 there had been four prime ministers—John Abbott, John Thompson, Mackenzie Bowell and Charles Tupper. During this period, the Conservatives had to deal with a crisis over school legislation introduced in Manitoba. The Manitoba legislature had replaced the dual school system (both Protestant and Catholic schools) which had been guaranteed in the terms of union, with a single Protestant system. Francophone Catholics across Canada were already bitter about Louis Riel's execution. Now the Manitoba schools legislation convinced them that English Protestant Canadians wanted to stamp out French Catholic rights. Extremists on both sides inflamed the issue, and the Conservatives' inability to settle the matter hurt them in the election of 1896. The Liberals, under Wilfrid Laurier, formed a government.

Laurier settled the Manitoba school question by adopting a compromise approach. Religious instruction would be allowed within the single system, and instruction in French could take place where numbers warranted. The issue died down, but Laurier remained sensitive to the tensions between Anglophone Protestants and Francophone Catholics. Many English Canadians were swept up in a great wave of pro-imperial sentiment associated with the Diamond Jubilee of Queen Victoria. In Britain the event was seen as an opportunity to strengthen ties within the British Empire. Laurier acknowledged Canada's support for the Empire, but resisted proposals for a closer relationship with Britain and the other colonies. The prime minister did not wish to yield Canadian autonomy, nor did he wish to lose support in French Canada. The issue of Canada's role in the Empire came to a head in 1899 during the Boer War when the South African Republic (Transvaal) and the Orange Free State fought against Britain. Once again steering a middle course, Laurier agreed to equip and transport Canadian volunteers to South Africa, but sent no official troops. Although this compromise did not satisfy all Canadians, it avoided a bitter dispute. For a time, imperial issues were forgotten, as Canadians enjoyed boom times after the turn of the century.

Laurier summed up the nation's mood when he declared that the "twentieth century is Canada's century." Impressive growth in both industrial and agricultural production provided support for his words. Canada's prospects appealed to immigrants who flocked to the industrial cities and to the farmland of the Prairies. Many of them were attracted by an extensive government advertising campaign and by the lure of free land in the west. As a result of this influx, two new provinces, Alberta and Saskatchewan, were created in 1905. The immigrant tide boosted Canada's population from 5,371,315 in 1901 to 7,206,643 in 1911. The mood of the country was so confident that two new transcontinental railway building projects got under way in the early years of the century.

The international scene, however, was not so bright. In 1903, the British sided with the Americans in the Alaska Boundary Dispute, a disagreement over the international boundary near the Klondike gold fields. Canadians were dismayed, but Britain was less concerned about the Canadian claim than for the need to maintain good relations with the United States. Tension in Europe was increasing and Britain found itself outside of the complicated system of alliances which had developed there. This same concern led both the British government and the Canadian pro-imperialists to pressure

Laurier into providing money to build British warships. Again, Laurier staked out a middle position by introducing a Naval Service Act which created a Canadian navy that could help Britain where the need arose.

Laurier's compromise on naval policy satisfied neither side. Some French Canadians supported the views of Quebec nationalist Henri Bourassa who claimed Laurier had betrayed his people. Anglophone pro-imperialists complained that Laurier's "tin pot navy" was not enough. Canada's naval policy became an issue in the 1911 election, as did the Liberal plan for free trade with the United States. Conservative leader Robert Borden was able to use both to characterize Laurier as not only disloyal to Britain but favoring annexation to the United States. The Conservatives won the election. Borden became prime minister and Laurier stayed on as leader of the Opposition, continuing to advocate conciliatory policies when the interests of French and English Canadians clashed.

1896 The economic depression ends. Bowell resigns, calling his cabinet a "nest of traitors" (Apr. 27). **Sir Charles Tupper** leads an interim government until the Liberals under Laurier win federal election on **Manitoba Schools Question** (June 23). Canada's minister of the interior, **Clifford Sifton,** develops an immigration plan that will bring farmers from central and eastern Europe to settle on the Prairies. Gold is discovered in the Klondike (Aug. 16).

1897 **Gold Rush** begins in the Klondike. **Clara Brett Martin** is the first woman admitted to the bar of Ontario.

1898 Yukon becomes a separate entity from the Northwest Territories. **Kit Coleman,** the first female Canadian war correspondent, covers the Spanish-American War for a Toronto newspaper.

1899 The first **Canadian troops** ever sent overseas are dispatched to the **Boer War** (Oct. 30).

1901 Marconi receives the **first transatlantic radio message** at St. John's, Newfoundland.

1903 Canada loses the **Alaska Boundary Dispute** when British tribunal representative Lord Alverstone sides with the US (Oct. 20). In northern Ontario, Fred LaRose throws hammer at what he thinks are fox's eyes and hits world's richest silver vein.

1904 Liberals win federal election.

1905 The provinces of **Alberta** and **Saskatchewan** are formed.

1907 The **National Council of Women** calls for "equal pay for equal work."

1908 Liberals win federal election.

1909 The Department of External Affairs is formed. John McCurdy's Silver Dart is first heavier-than-air machine to achieve powered flight in Canada at Baddeck, NS. University of Toronto wins **first Grey Cup** football match.

1910 Laurier creates a Canadian navy via the Naval Service Bill.

1911 **Robert Borden** and the Conservatives win federal election, defeating Laurier on the reciprocity issue.

■ **Canada and the First World War (1914-1918)**

In August 1914, Britain declared war on Germany and Austria–Hungary. The declaration automatically applied to Canada, as part of the British Empire. At first, there was an enthusiastic response, especially among recent British immigrants. When the minister of militia, Sam Hughes, called for 25,000 volunteers, nearly 33,000 appeared. In 1915, when the government asked the Canadian public to buy $50 million in war bonds, they bought $100 million. But enthusiasm for war began to fade as the casualties mounted and the realities of trench warfare became known.

Canadian troops sailed for Europe in October 1914 and, after training in Britain, went into action at Ypres, Belgium, in April 1915. There they gained a reputation for courage, holding their positions in the face of a poison gas attack, a new weapon at the time. Canadians took part in the costly battles at St. Eloi and Mont Sorrel in 1916. By the Battle of the Somme, in late summer of 1916, Canada had four army divisions in France; in the spring of 1917, all four were deployed in the attack on Vimy Ridge, which resulted in the first real Canadian victory of the war. But by now it was clear that every battle would result in terrible losses. At Passchendaele in October 1917, the Canadians sustained more than 15,000 casualties.

Voluntary recruitment could not keep pace with the high casualty rates. Prime Minister Borden was forced to consider conscription to draft soldiers into the army and took the question to the electorate in 1917, unleashing one of the most bitterly fought campaigns in Canadian history. In Quebec, Henri Bourassa rallied anti-conscription supporters and argued that Canada had done enough. In Ontario, Borden's supporters condemned French-Canadian anti-conscriptionists as traitors. For his part Borden introduced the Wartime Elections Act to help secure victory. This act removed the right to vote from enemy aliens, even though some were Canadian citizens. It also gave the right to vote to women relatives of soldiers. In the election Borden won in every province except Quebec where he was soundly rejected. Conscription had created a deep division between Quebec and the rest of Canada and once in practice, it had little impact on the course of the war. When the first 400,000 conscripts were called up, 90% of them appealed for exemption, and by the war's end only about 24,000 conscripts had reached the front.

While the conscription crisis raged at home, Canadian soldiers played a major role in the events leading to an Allied victory. They took part in the successful battle at Amiens in August 1918 and helped to roll the Germans back to Mons by November. The Canadians were still fighting at Mons when the armistice was signed Nov. 11, 1918.

Canadians also served with distinction in other theatres of war. By 1918, Canadians made up almost 25% of the pilots in Britain's Royal Flying Corps. Other Canadians served in the Royal Navy or on coastal patrol in Canada's own small navy. Some served in forestry corps overseas and others operated the railways behind the British lines. Some, including women, served as ambulance drivers at the front. Many Canadian women also played key roles as nurses overseas and in the munitions factories in Canada.

Canada's war effort won the country a place in the Imperial War Cabinet during the war, and a seat in the League of Nations afterwards. There were other benefits, too. Women's contributions to the war effort helped them win the right to vote in federal elections and in provincial elections in seven of the provinces by 1919. Yet these advances came at a terrible cost. Overseas, 68,300 Canadians had died. At home, bitterness over the conscription issue had created a division between French and English Canadians that would be remembered for decades.

1914 CP ship *Empress of Ireland* sinks in the St Lawrence in 14 minutes after being rammed in fog, with the loss of 1,014 lives (May 29). **Canada is automatically at war** with Germany when Britain declares war (Aug. 4). The first Canadian troops leave for England (Oct. 3). Parliament passes the **War Measures Act**, allowing suspension of civil rights during periods of emergency. European immigration to Canada increases. Over one million settlers come between 1911 and 1913, bringing total immigration to three million since 1891.

1915 Canadians face German gas attack at **Ypres,** Belgium (Apr. 22). John McCrae writes "In Flanders Fields."

1916 **Nellie McClung** succeeds in persuading the Manitoba government to grant women the right to vote and to hold office (Jan.). The Parliament Buildings are destroyed by fire (Feb. 3). Canadian troops fight in the Battle of the **Somme** (July to Nov.); 24,713 Canadians and Newfoundlanders are killed. The unreliable, Canadian-made Ross rifle is withdrawn from war service (Aug.). **Emily Gowan Murphy** is the first woman magistrate appointed within the British Empire.

1917 **Income tax** is introduced as a "temporary wartime measure." Prime Minister Sir Robert Borden sits as a member of the Imperial War Cabinet (Feb. 23), giving Canada a voice in war policy. The Military Service Bill is introduced (June 11), leading to the **Conscription Crisis** between Quebec and English Canada. Unionist government under Borden wins federal election, in which **women vote** for the first time. **Louise McKinney** is elected to the Alberta legislature, the first woman in the British Commonwealth to hold such office. Canadians capture **Vimy Ridge,** France (Apr. 9–12). Canadians take **Passchendaele,** Belgium, (Nov. 7) in one of the war's worst battles; of the 20,000 Canadian troops sent into the two-week battle, 15,654 are killed or wounded. Explosion of a munitions ship in **Halifax harbour** wipes out two square miles (5.2 sq. km) of Halifax, killing almost 2,000 and injuring 9,000 (Dec. 6).

1918 Canadians break through German trenches at Amiens (Aug. 8), "the black day of the German army." The period from this date until the end of the war becomes known as "Canada's Hundred Days." Armistice ends war (Nov. 11).

■ Canada in the 1920s

As the soldiers returned home, many expected to find a Canada ready to reward them for their sacrifices. What they found was a nation in the midst of painful postwar readjustment. Industry had to convert to peacetime production, but interest rates were so high investment capital was scarce. Jobs were hard to find and wages were low, and tariffs on imported goods kept prices high. By 1921, 300,000 men and women—more than 15% of the work force—were unemployed. Farmers, especially on the Prairies, also suffered. During the war, the west had become the world's breadbasket: wheat prices had soared and many farmers had borrowed heavily to expand their production. But with the war's end, world markets collapsed; wheat prices fell by almost half within two years.

These conditions, along with resentment over wartime profiteering by big business, created unrest. The One Big Union movement, centred in western Canada, attempted to create a single union to represent all workers. The Winnipeg General Strike of 1919 grew out of the organizers' efforts and the general discontent. Although the Winnipeg workers were striking over such issues as the right to collective bargaining, better wages and improved working conditions, the opponents of the general strike characterized it as a communist conspiracy by raising the spectre of a revolution similar to the one in Russia two years earlier. The federal government sided with the anti-strike forces. Immigration laws were amended to deport "alien" labour radicals, the strike leaders were arrested and the Royal North West Mounted Police fired into a rioting crowd on June 21, 1919—"Bloody Sunday"—killing 1 and wounding 30. The six-week strike was over and so was the growth of labor unions. In 1919 alone there were more than 400 strikes, but after the Winnipeg General Strike, the federal government and most governments at the provincial level opposed union activities. Throughout the 1920s there was a decline in union membership.

The reasons for unrest and discontent varied from region to region in the 1920s. The government takeover of five financially troubled railways had led to the creation of the Canadian National Railways in 1919 and railway rates in the Maritimes were raised 40% to bring them up to central Canadian levels. Angry over the rail rates and feeling that Ottawa was making decisions on the basis of central Canada's interests, many Maritimers protested by forming the Maritimes Rights movement, aimed at winning transportation concessions and federal subsidies. At the same time it promoted regional rights and pride.

Canadian farmers, resentful over low prices for farm products, high rail rates and high prices for manufactured goods, formed the United Farmers' movement. United Farmers' parties won provincial elections in Ontario in 1919, in Alberta in 1921, and in Manitoba in 1922. At the federal level, the Progressive Party embraced some of the program of the United Farmers' movement. The Progressives called for free trade, nationalization (especially in the case of railways) and more direct democracy (such as the use of a referendum to decide a controversial issue). Although they were a new party, the Progressives were to play an important role in politics in the 1920s.

The election of 1921 marked new directions in Canadian politics. Both major parties had new leaders: Arthur Meighen had replaced Borden as prime minister; William Lyon Mackenzie King had taken over as Liberal leader after Laurier's death. Of even greater significance was that for the first time, Canadians could vote for one of three parties at the federal level: the Liberals, the Conservatives or the Progressives. The Liberals won the 1921 election, but the Progressives finished second and formed the opposition. Their position in the House of Commons was even more important after the 1925 election in which the Conservatives under Meighen won the most seats, but King remained in power by claiming the support of the Progressives. After 1925 the Progressives declined, and many of their supporters voted Liberal in King's 1926 election victory. But the influence of the Progressive movement was felt as King's government, anxious to keep their support, passed Canada's first Old Age Pension Act in 1927.

In foreign affairs, King made sure that Canada played a cautious role in the League of Nations, because he feared that Canada would be drawn into international disputes. In imperial matters, his insistence on autonomy contributed to a redefinition of the empire at the Imperial Conference of 1926. There it was acknowledged that Canada and the other British dominions were autonomous even in their external affairs. As a result, by 1929, Canada had diplomatic posts in Washington, Paris and Tokyo and Britain had a high commissioner in Ottawa. The Governor General became a symbolic representative of the Crown rather than a representative of the British government.

At home, there were many signs that good times had finally come to Canada. World markets for Canadian manufactured goods had revived, and wheat prices were soaring to new levels. New mining and lumbering areas were developed. By 1928, more than a billion dollars' worth of products were being extracted from the newly-developed primary industries of the Canadian Shield. Immigrants poured into Canada by the hundreds of thousands to provide labour in the growing industrial cities. Cars, radios, telephones, electrical appliances and other consumer goods were being bought, especially by middle-class Canadians, often using credit plans. Credit was also used to buy shares on the stock market, as the country became increasingly optimistic about its future. On both sides of the Canadian-American border, the Roaring Twenties were in full swing and there seemed no end in sight to the good times.

1919 Alcock and Brown take off from St. John's, Nfld, (June 14) on the first successful flight across the Atlantic to Cliften, Ireland. A **general strike paralyzes Winnipeg** (May–June), where an armed charge by the RCMP kills one person and injures 30 (June 21).

1920 **Canada joins** the **League of Nations** at its inception (Jan. 10). The flow of emigrants from the British Isles and Europe resumes, many going to urban centres. Federal legislation makes **women eligible** to sit in the **House of Commons**. The Northwest Mounted Police became the Royal Canadian Mounted Police (RCMP).

1921 Liberals under **Mackenzie King** defeat Conservatives under Arthur Meighen in federal election; the Progressive Party comes in second. **Agnes Macphail** becomes the first woman elected to Parliament. The world's

fastest fishing schooner, the ***Bluenose,*** is launched at Lunenburg, NS. (Mar. 26). **Postwar economic depression** puts 300,000 men and women out of work—more than 15% of the work force.

1922 Canada declines to rally to Britain's side during the Chanak Crisis. Sir Frederick **Banting**, Dr Charles **Best**, Dr J.J.R. MacLeod and J.B. Collip share Nobel Prize for the **discovery of insulin**.

1923 The Canadian Northern and Canadian Transcontinental are merged to form the **Canadian National Railways**. Canada signs the Halibut Treaty with the US without a corroborating British signature. Mackenzie King leads opposition to a common imperial policy ("one voice for the empire") at an Imperial Conference in London.

1924 The Saskatchewan Wheat Pool begins operations.

1925 Although Conservatives win more seats in federal election, Mackenzie King's Liberals remain in power with the support of the Progressives.

1926 King's Liberals win federal election. An Imperial Conference defines British dominions as autonomous (Balfour Report).

1927 Britain's Privy Council awards Labrador to Newfoundland instead of to Quebec (Mar. 1). The Diamond Jubilee of Confederation (July 1) is marked by Canada's first coast-to-coast radio network broadcast. King's government, with the support of the Progressive Party, passes Canada's first **Old Age Pension Act**.

1928 The Supreme Court of Canada rules that, according to the British North America Act, women are not "persons" who could hold public office. This decision is reversed by British Privy Council in 1929.

■ The Great Depression (1929-1939)

In 1929, Canadians looked with confidence toward the next decade and that confidence made the effects of the Great Depression of the 1930s even more bitter. The Depression was worldwide, but the effects were especially felt in Canada because about a third of the nation's gross national product was based on exports. The first signs of Canadian economic collapse appeared in October 1929 when wheat prices began to fall. In the same month the stock market collapsed, ruining thousands of shareholders, some of whom, on paper at least, had been millionaires. By 1930, the number of unemployed had doubled and the Conservatives, under R.B. Bennett, won the 1930 federal election decisively as voters hoped a change in government would bring a change in fortune. However by 1933, one in five Canadians was unemployed.

Western Canada was hardest hit in "The Dirty Thirties" because of its reliance on wheat. The Prairie provinces also suffered from a drought which led to crop failure during these hard times. The combined results were devastating. In Saskatchewan, provincial income fell by 90% and two-thirds of the province's population had to go on welfare. In the 1930s, welfare, or "relief" as it was then known, became a burden for municipal and provincial governments across the country. By 1935, 10% of Canadians were on relief.

Bennett's government did not intervene to rebuild the economy. In the 1930s, politicians, economists and business leaders assumed that the Depression, like other downswings in the business cycle, would soon be followed by a recovery. Their experience, and most economic theory at the time, did not encourage them to consider major government spending as a way to stimulate a depressed economy.

One of the few federally financed programs created involved sending single unemployed men to camps where they did manual work in return for their keep and a small allowance. Working in isolated conditions, often at meaningless tasks, did nothing to satisfy the men and those in the British Columbia camps took action. In 1935, about 1,500 camp inmates decided to present their complaints directly to Bennett in Ottawa. They began the "On to Ottawa" trek by taking over freight trains heading east. By the time they reached Regina, there were about 2,000 protesters and the railway refused to provide further transportation. Representatives of the Trekkers met with Prime Minister Bennett in Ottawa, but the talks were inconclusive. When the delegation returned to Regina, Bennett decided to arrest the protest leaders. On July 1, there was a bloody riot in Regina involving the Trekkers, local police and the RCMP, which left one policeman dead and several dozen rioters, constables and local citizens injured. The Trek was over and the protesters returned home over the next few days; but Bennett's handling of the affair hurt his image. In the election of

1935, the people turned to King again, in the hope that this time he could deal with the Depression.

After 1935, economic conditions began to improve slowly, yet federal politicians did little to speed this recovery. The failure of the Liberals and the Conservatives to deal with the Depression led to the rise of reform parties. A socialist party, the Co-operative Commonwealth Federation (CCF) won seven seats in the 1935 election and elected members to several provincial legislatures. Other new parties appeared at the provincial level. In Alberta, the Social Credit Party promised $25 prosperity certificates to each resident; but the plan fell flat because the province did not have the power to issue currency. In Quebec, Maurice Duplessis established the Union Nationale and promised economic reform. But the Union Nationale, like the other parties, could not end the Depression, the effects of which faded only with the outbreak of World War II in 1939.

1929 The **Great Depression** begins.

1930 **Cairine Wilson** is appointed Canada's first woman senator (Feb. 20). The Canadian Federation of Business and Professional Women's Clubs is organized. Conservatives under **R.B. Bennett** win federal election (Aug. 7).

1931 The **Statute of Westminster** (Dec. 11) grants Canada full legislative authority domestically and in external affairs. The Governor General becomes a representative of the Crown.

1932 Ottawa Agreements provide for preferential trade between Canada and other Commonwealth nations. The **Co-operative Commonwealth Federation** (**CCF**) is founded at Calgary.

1933 One in five Canadians is unemployed.

1934 The Bank of Canada is formed. The **Dionne quintuplets** are born in Callander, Ont.

1935 Ten % of Canadians rely on welfare or "relief." The **On to Ottawa Trek** by young men from government work camps ends in a riot at Regina (July 1). Liberals under Mackenzie King win federal election. The CCF win seven seats. Social Credit claims 17. **William Aberhart** leads Social Credit into office in Alberta. The Canadian Wheat Board is created.

1936 Union Nationale under **Maurice Duplessis** wins its first election in Quebec.

1937 The **Rowell-Sirois Commission** is appointed to investigate the financial relationship between the federal government and the provinces. First regular flight of **Trans Canada Air Lines** (Sept. 1).

1938 Franklin D. Roosevelt becomes first US President in office to visit Canada, meeting Mackenzie King at Kingston.

■ Canada in World War II (1939-1945)

While most Canadians focused attention on the effects of the Depression at home, events in Europe during the 1930s were moving the world closer to another global conflict. After taking over Austria and Czechoslovakia (present-day Czech and Slovak republics), Germany invaded Poland in 1939; Britain and France responded by declaring war. Following Britain's action, King quickly summoned Parliament. On Sept. 10, one week after Britain had entered the conflict, the Canadian Parliament declared war on Germany and its allies.

Parliamentary support for the war declaration was based in part on King's known preference for a limited Canadian role and his assurance that there would be no conscription. Initially, only one Canadian division was sent to Britain. But by 1940, France had fallen and Britain faced invasion. King abandoned the concept of limited participation and decided to dispatch more troops. By late 1942, Canada had five divisions overseas. Canadian soldiers first saw action in December 1941 during the unsuccessful defence of Hong Kong. In August 1942, 5,000 Canadians took part in the disastrous raid on the French port of Dieppe, suffering casualties of 2,200 killed or captured. Despite these setbacks, the Canadian army played a major role in defeating enemy forces in Italy and took part in the Allied landings at Normandy in June of 1944. After taking key targets in France, Canadian soldiers moved northward to liberate Holland in 1945.

Canadians contributed to the war effort in other important ways. The Royal Canadian Navy grew from six destroyers and less than 2,000 personnel in 1939 to 471 warships, 99,688 men and 6,500 women by the war's end in 1945. The navy helped win the Battle of the Atlantic against German submarines by providing protection to the convoys of merchant ships carrying essential supplies from North America to Britain. (Despite the protection German U-boats sank 5,150 merchant ships.) Canadians also fought in the air as members of Britain's Royal Air Force, and, in increasing numbers throughout the war, in the Royal Canadian Air Force (RCAF). By 1945, there were 48 RCAF squadrons overseas. Other members of the RCAF were involved in the British Commonwealth Air Training Plan. Operating from Canadian airfields, this plan trained 131,000 aircrew from around the Commonwealth.

Canada also produced a wide variety of munitions, and provided important food supplies to the Allied war effort. Much of Canada's war production went directly to Britain, so did more than $3 billion in financial assistance.

While the contributions of Canadian men and women to the war effort were significant, the conflict raised disturbing issues at home. In reversing his earlier stand against conscription, Prime Minister King called for a national plebiscite on the issue in 1942. In all provinces except Quebec the electorate voted for conscription; relations between Quebec and the rest of Canada were strained, although not as severely as in World War I.

In a move that would later become controversial, Japanese–Canadians were interned and their property was confiscated in the name of national security after the Japanese attack on Pearl Harbor in 1941. The interned included Japanese–Canadians who had fought for Canada in World War I and more than 40 years later the Canadian government would officially apologize to the interned and their families.

By the war's end, more than a million Canadians had served in the armed forces and more than 42,000 had died. Canada's war effort enhanced its international image. At the same time, Canada had developed closer ties with the United States as the country's interests shifted away from Britain and Europe.

1939 **Canada declares war** on Germany (Sept. 10) after remaining neutral for a week following the British declaration. Quebec Premier Maurice Duplessis, who opposed Quebec participation in the war, is defeated by the provincial Liberals on that issue (Oct. 26).

1940 **Unemployment insurance** is **introduced**. Liberals win federal election (Mar.

26). The Permanent Joint Board of Defence is formed between Canada and the US. **Thérèse Casgrain** wins women in Quebec the right to vote and to hold provincial office.

1941 Canadians are captured when Hong Kong falls to Japanese (Dec. 25); about 500 of the POWs subsequently die in Japanese camps. Immigration has changed Canadian demographic structure. Canadians of British ancestry now make up 49.7% of the population, of French descent 30.3% and of other ethnic backgrounds 20%.

1942 In the Canadian army's first European war action, many soldiers are captured or killed in the disastrous **Dieppe** raid (Aug. 19). Canadians of Japanese descent are moved inland from the coast of British Columbia as "security risks"; their property is confiscated. A national plebiscite releases Mackenzie King from his pledge of no conscription but reveals deep divisions between Quebec and the rest of Canada.

1943 Canadians participate in the invasion of Sicily (July 10). Canadians win the Battle of Ortona (Dec. 20–28). **Ernest C. Manning** wins first of nine successive elections for the Social Credit in Alberta.

1944 Canadian troops push further inland than any other Allied unit on D-Day (June 6). Canadian forces fight as a separate army (July 23). Saskatchewan elects Tommy Douglas's CCF, the first socialist government in North America. Maurice Duplessis regains office for the Union Nationale in Quebec.

1945 War in Europe ends (May 8). One million Canadians fought in WW II; 42,042 were killed. Canadians killed while fighting for other Allied forces numbered 4,500. Liberals win federal election (June 11). First **family allowance payments** are **made** (June 20). Canada joins the **United Nations** (June 26). Igor Gouzenko defects from the Soviet Embassy in Ottawa (Sept. 5) and reveals the existence in Canada of a Soviet spy network. Canada's first nuclear reactor begins operations at Chalk River, Ontario.

■ Postwar Canada: 1945-1968

In the years following World War II, Canadians enjoyed a standard of living that was in stark contrast to the Depression years. The economy had boomed during the war and the gross national product had doubled. The war had prompted development in new industries which continued to expand in peacetime. Consumer spending had increased dramatically during the war, and continued to rise with the postwar baby boom. This boom, along with large numbers of European immigrants, resulted in a 40% population increase between the war's end and 1958. In Canada's quickly growing cities and suburbs, home ownership was made easier by the National Housing Act, designed to make mortgages easier to obtain. This example of government involvement in the economy was characteristic of the times. By 1945, unemployment insurance and family allowance legislation had been passed and other social welfare measures were being discussed.

Prime Minister King retired in 1948, and was followed as Liberal leader by Louis St. Laurent. One of St. Laurent's first achievements was the entry of Newfoundland into Confederation in 1949. In 1951, his government increased old age pensions and, in 1957, introduced a hospital insurance plan. St. Laurent negotiated with the United States to build the St. Lawrence Seaway, an impressive feat of engineering completed in 1959. In 1956, however, the government used closure (a limit on debate) to cut off the parliamentary debate concerning the building of the trans-Canada pipeline for oil and gas. In the election the following year, the Conservatives under John Diefenbaker won a minority victory. In 1958, Diefenbaker called another election to consolidate his position. This time the Conservatives swept the country, winning 208 of 265 seats.

Western agriculture found huge new markets when the government arranged wheat sales to China. In 1960, Diefenbaker's government introduced the Bill of Rights to protect the rights of all Canadians, and granted Native Canadians the right to vote in federal elections.

Despite continuing popular support for the British Commonwealth, the government of Canada signed the North American Air Defence Agreement (NORAD) with the United States to increase security during a time of international tension. But it could not deal with an economic recession that led to a devalued dollar and high unemployment. Also, the prime minister dealt Canada's fledgling aircraft industry a serious blow when he cancelled production of the Canadian-made Avro Arrow fighter jet, and his refusal to allow nuclear warheads on the American missiles based in Canada earned him the emnity of the US government. In the election of 1962, his government was returned to power, but in a minority situation that forced another election in 1963. The 1963 election also resulted in a minority government, but this time, the Liberals, under Lester B. Pearson, were in power.

As prime minister, Pearson, a career diplomat, concentrated on domestic matters. His government relied on the support of the New Democratic Party (formerly the CCF) to hold a majority in the House of Commons, and the partnership produced legislation that broadened social welfare by introducing Medicare, the Canada Pension Plan and the Canada Assistance Plan. Canadian nationalism was heightened with the adoption of the maple leaf flag in 1965, and in the same year another federal election produced a Liberal government one seat short of a clear majority. The opening of the world's fair, Expo in Montreal, in Canada's centennial year, 1967, marked a year of celebration across the country.

During the 1960s, Pearson was sensitive to growing nationalism in Quebec. His government established a Royal Commission on Bilingualism and Biculturalism in 1963, to demonstrate that Quebec's interests could be served by federalism, and he encouraged some of those closely associated with the Quiet Revolution to run for federal office. Quebec had been transformed from traditional to modern attitudes towards education, social reform and industrialization, a movement known as the Quiet Revolution, under Premier Jean Lesage. The Quebec government was implementing the ideas of the Quiet Revolution, and championed provincial rights with its slogan *maîtres chez nous* (masters in our own house). This sentiment took centre stage during Centennial celebrations. Visiting French President Charles de Gaulle ended a Montreal speech with the cry *"Vive le Québec libre!"* ("Long live free Quebec") which set off a storm of diplomatic protest and delighted local nationalists. Despite growing nationalist sentiment, many Quebeckers, including Pierre Trudeau, went to Ottawa. Trudeau was elected to the House of Commons in 1965, and was named minister of justice in 1967. In 1968, following Pearson's retirement, Trudeau became Liberal leader.

1947 Imperial Oil discovers the **Leduc oil field** (Feb. 13).

1948 **Louis St. Laurent** succeeds Mackenzie King as prime minister (Nov. 15).

1949 Under Premier **Joey Smallwood**, **Newfoundland** becomes Canada's 10th province (Mar. 31). Canada joins NATO. Canadian appeals to Britain's Judicial Committee of the Privy Council are abolished: Canada's Supreme Court becomes final court of appeal. Liberals under St Laurent defeat Conservatives under George Drew in federal election (June 3).

1950 The Korean War begins (June 25); Canadian troops participate in the conflict as part of a United Nations force.

1951 The midcentury census reports Canada's population as 14,009,429. **Postwar immigration** to Canada exceeds 100,000 annually during the 1950s, primarily moving from central and eastern Europe to hold manufacturing jobs in urban centres. The Massey Royal Commission reports that Canadian cultural life is dominated by American influences. Revisions to the **Indian Act**, beginning in 1951, limit its coverage of aboriginal people. Indian women married to non-Indian men are excluded from the act. This provision was removed in 1985 after much protest of discrimination. **Charlotte Whitton**, the first woman to be mayor of a major Canadian city, is elected in Ottawa.

1952 **Vincent Massey** becomes the first native-born Governor General of Canada. Canada's **first television** stations begin broadcasting in Montreal (Sept. 6) and Toronto (Sept. 8). **W.A.C. Bennett** begins **Social Credit**'s administration in British Columbia.

1953 Canada's National Library is established in Ottawa (Jan. 1). The Stratford Festival opens (July 13). The **Korean War ends** (July 27); total Canadian casualties are 314 killed and 1,211 wounded. Liberals under St Laurent defeat Conservatives under Drew in federal election (Aug. 10).

1954 An economic slump interrupts the postwar boom. Canada's **first subway** opens in Toronto (Mar. 30). Roger Bannister and John Landy run the "miracle mile" at the British Empire Games in Vancouver (Aug.), the first to run a mile in less than four minutes. Sixteen-year-old Marilyn Bell becomes the first person to swim Lake Ontario (Sept. 9).

Hurricane Hazel hits Toronto, killing 83 people (Oct. 15). The Geneva Conference on the Far East invites Canada to join India and Poland in **supervising peace in Indochina**. This peacekeeping commitment continues for nearly 20 years to 1973.

1955 The Canadian Labour Congress is formed. The suspension of Montreal Canadiens' hockey star Maurice (Rocket) Richard leads to rioting in Montreal (Mar. 17).

1956 The Liberals use closure to limit the **Pipeline Debate** (May 8–June 6), a manoeuvre that contributes to their electoral defeat the following year.

1957 Conservatives under **John Diefenbaker** win federal election (June 10) and form minority government. Ellen Fairclough becomes the first woman federal cabinet minister. The Canada Council is created to help foster Canadian cultural life. **Lester B. Pearson wins Nobel Prize** (Oct. 12) for his role in resolving the Suez Crisis. Canadian supply and services troops are sent to work with a multinational UN force around the **Gulf of Aqaba**. They stay until 1967 and return there in 1973.

1958 Conservatives under Diefenbaker win 208 seats in federal election (Mar. 31). Coal mine disaster at Springhill, NS, results in death of 74 miners.

1959 The **Avro Arrow** project is terminated, with a loss of almost 14,000 jobs (Feb. 20). The **St. Lawrence Seaway** is **opened** (June 26).

1960 Liberals under **Jean Lesage** win provincial election in Quebec (June 22), inaugurating the **Quiet Revolution**. A **Canadian Bill of Rights** is approved by Parliament. Native people get the right to vote in federal elections. During the 1960s French is recognized as a language of instruction in elementary and secondary schools in New Brunswick, Ontario and Manitoba. It is recognized subsequently in other provincial jurisdictions.

1961 The **New Democratic Party** replaces the CCF.

1962 Conservatives are reduced to minority status in federal election (June 18). Social

Credit wins 30 seats and NDP take 19 to control the balance of power in the House of Commons. The Saskatchewan NDP introduces the first Canadian **Medicare** plan (July 1), and is opposed by a doctors' strike. **Trans-Canada Highway** officially opens (Sept. 3). Canadian-made satellite *Alouette* is launched (Sept. 29), making Canada the third nation in space. Canada's last execution, the double hanging of Ronald Turpin and Arthur Lucas, takes place (Dec. 11), at the Don Jail in Toronto.

1963 Liberals under Pearson win federal election (Apr. 8), and form a minority government. The Quebec separatist group **Front de libération du Québec (FLQ)** sets off a series of bombs in Montreal (Apr.–May). A TCA flight crashes in Quebec, killing all 118 people aboard (Nov. 29). The **Royal Commission on Bilingualism and Biculturalism** begins its work.

1964 Canadians get social insurance cards (Apr.). Canada ends difficult peacekeeping duties in the Congo (Zaïre) after four years of service with heavy casualties. Canadian troops join UN forces in Cyprus.

1965 Canada gets a new flag (Feb. 15). The **Autopact** between Canada and the US is signed. Canadian Roman Catholic Churches begin to celebrate mass in English (Mar. 7). Liberals win federal election (Nov. 8) to continue as a minority government. Failure of an Ontario Hydro relay device at Queenston plunges eastern North America into a power blackout (Nov. 9).

1966 The Munsinger Affair becomes Canada's first major parliamentary sex scandal (Mar. 4). The **Canada Pension Plan** is established. The CBC begins colour television broadcasting (Oct. 1).

1967 The Canadian army, navy and air forces are **unified** to become the Canadian **Armed Forces** (Apr. 25). Montreal hosts a world's fair, **Expo 67** (opened Apr. 27). Canada celebrates its **Centennial** (July 1). French President Charles **de Gaulle** delivers his "Vive le Québec Libre" speech in Montreal (July 24). The federal Department of Manpower and Immigration establishes the **"points system"** for immigrants. Patterns shift in the 1960s from European to Third World immigration as humanitarian objectives and family reunification policies increase multicultural immigration.

■ The Trudeau Years (1968-1984)

The Liberals won a majority victory in the election of 1968. Trudeau was a strong federalist, determined to show that Ottawa could promote the rights of French Canada. The Official Languages Act of 1969 recognized both English and French as official languages, and required federal institutions to provide services in both languages. Although the legislation was supported by all parties, it was not universally popular, even in Quebec.

In the October Crisis of 1970 separatist extremists belonging to the FLQ (Front de libération du Québec) kidnapped British Trade Commissioner James Cross, and killed Quebec cabinet minister Pierre Laporte. Trudeau used the War Measures Act to apply emergency measures of arrest, detention and martial law. This move was generally accepted but was criticized by advocates of civil rights, especially since the FLQ had little real support and the Act was in effect across the country.

In his early years in power, Trudeau attempted to concentrate decision-making in Ottawa, and his newly created Prime Minister's Office led to western Canadian accusations of an eastern-dominated federal government. At the same time opposition parties charged that Trudeau was undermining both the power of the cabinet and of Parliament. The Liberals were almost defeated in the election of 1972, but retained office through a minority government that saw the New Democrats, under David Lewis, hold the balance of power. During this period the Foreign Investment Review Agency was set up (1973) to protect the Canadian economy against foreign domination; business critics claimed that it discouraged investment.

By 1974, the Liberals had regained a majority; their agenda was dominated by an economy battered by inflation. The government tried a variety of economic measures, including a three-year imposition of wage and price controls under the Anti-Inflation Act of 1975. Although the controls may have had some effect, world conditions, especially the international oil crisis, kept inflation high.

In 1976, the separatist Parti Québécois under René Lévesque defeated the provincial Liberals, led by Robert Bourassa in the Quebec election. This election fueled public uncertainty over the future of Quebec (and Canada), while continuing inflation and western alienation also undermined Liberal support. In the 1979 election, the Liberals lost, and Conservative leader Joe Clark took office as head of a minority government. Clark's government was short-lived as it suffered defeat in the House of Commons that same year.

The Liberals won the election of 1980, and Trudeau, lured out of planned retirement by the sudden election, embarked on an eventful term of office. He and members of his government actively campaigned on the victorious NO side in the 1980 Quebec referendum on sovereignty association. The Liberals brought in the National Energy Program in the same year, again attempting to regulate ownership and control in part of the economy, and again succeeding in alienating foreign and local business interests. Resistance to the NEP, particularly in the west, was deep and persistent.

Then, after a long (18 months) and difficult campaign waged in Parliament, at federal-provincial meetings and in the media, Trudeau succeeded in getting an agreement on patriating the Canadian constitution amongst all provinces except Quebec. Patriation officially took place when Queen Elizabeth II proclaimed the new Constitution Act in Ottawa on Apr. 17, 1982. The Charter of Rights and Freedoms was also proclaimed, entrenching bilingualism in the federal jurisdiction and providing for minority language education rights across Canada.

By 1984 the country was mired in a recession and in no mood for the international interest Trudeau was pursuing; he retired and John Turner became Liberal leader and prime minister for a brief period. The Liberal government was at the end of its mandate and parliament was dissolved. After nearly 16 years of Liberal government, the voters were eager for a change.

1968 **Pierre Elliott Trudeau** succeeds Pearson as prime minister (Apr. 6), and leads Liberals to majority in federal election (June 25). A Royal Commission on the Status of Women is appointed. Canadian divorce law is reformed.

1969 Saturday postal deliveries end. Abortion law is liberalized (May). English and

French become **official languages** of federal administration (July 9). New Brunswick declares official bilingualism. The breathalizer comes into use as a test for alcohol-impaired drivers (Dec. 1).

1970 The FLQ kidnaps British trade commissioner James Cross (Oct. 5), precipitating the **October Crisis**. Quebec labour and immigration minister Pierre Laporte is kidnapped (Oct. 10), and found murdered (Oct. 17). The federal government invokes the **War Measures Act** (Oct. 16), leading to the arrest of 465 people.

1971 A policy of **multiculturalism** is adopted by the federal government. Canadian Gerhard Herzberg wins the Nobel Prize in chemistry for his studies of chemical reactions that help produce smog.

1972 Canada defeats the USSR in the first hockey series between the Soviets and Canadian professionals (Aug.–Sept.). Liberals win federal election with 109 seats to the Conservatives 107, with the NDP holding the balance of power at 31 (Oct. 30).

1973 The separatist Parti Québécois becomes the official Opposition in Quebec. Canadian troops are sent to the Middle East and serve with the United Nations Emergency Task Force there until 1979.

1974 Liberals under Trudeau win federal election and form majority government (July 8). **Pauline McGibbon** becomes the first female lieutenant-governor (Ontario) in the British Commonwealth.

1975 The **CN Tower**, the world's tallest free-standing structure at 553.339 metres, is completed in Toronto (Apr. 2). Federal government announces (July 18) its intention to screen foreign investment in Canada, via the Foreign Investment Review Agency (FIRA). Television cameras are allowed inside the House of Commons for the first time. Federal government imposes **wage and price controls** in an effort to fight inflation (Oct. 14). **Grace Hartman** is elected president of the Canadian Union of Public Employees.

1976 Canada announces 200-nautical-mile coastal fishing zone (June 4). **Death penalty** is **abolished** in a free vote (130–124) in Parliament (July 14). Montreal hosts **Olympic Games** (July 17–31). Team Canada wins the first **Canada Cup** hockey series (Sept. 15).

The **Parti Québécois** under René Lévesque wins provincial election in Quebec (Nov. 15).

1977 Quebec government pases Bill 101, restricting English-language schooling to children whose mother or father had attended English elementary school in Quebec (Aug. 26). Highway signs in most of Canada become metric (Sept. 6).

1978 **Soviet nuclear-powered satellite crashes** in Canadian north (Jan. 24). Sun Life Assurance Co. announces a head office move from Montreal to Toronto because of language laws and political instability in Quebec. **Hilda Watson**, first woman to lead a political party in Canada, wins leadership of Yukon Progressive Conservative party.

1979 Conservatives under **Joe Clark** win federal election (May 22). Canada's first gold bullion coin, the Maple Leaf, goes on sale (Sept. 5). Supreme Court of Canada declares Manitoba and Quebec legislation creating unilingual courts and legislatures unconstitutional (Dec. 13). Federal Conservatives lose non-confidence vote on budget (Dec. 13), forcing the government's resignation. **Antonine Maillet** wins the prestigious French literary prize, the Prix Goncourt, for her novel *Pélagie-la-Charette*.

1980 Canada's ambassador to Iran, Ken Taylor, arranges the successful **escape of six American Embassy staff** from Tehran while their colleagues are held hostage (Jan. 28). Liberals win federal election (Feb. 18). Canada boycotts the Olympic Games in Moscow because of the Soviet invasion of Afghanistan. **Jeanne Sauvé** becomes the first female Speaker of the House of Commons (Apr. 14). **Quebec votes "no"** to "sovereignty-association" in a **referendum** (May 22). **"O Canada"** becomes Canada's national anthem (June 27). The Supreme Court awards Rosa Becker half the assets accumulated during a 19-year common-law relationship. **National Energy Program** is created to encourage oil self-sufficiency, increase Canadian ownership in the oil industry and obtain a larger share of Canadian energy revenues.

1981 Quebec bans public signs in English (Sept. 23). The federal government and every province except Quebec reach agreement on a method for patriating Canada's constitution (Nov. 5). The 1981 census indicates significant increases in the percentage of new Canadians from Asia, the Caribbean and Latin America.

1982 Bertha Wilson becomes Canada's first woman to be appointed a justice of the Supreme Court (Mar. 4). The Quebec Court of Appeal rejects the Quebec government's claim of veto power over constitutional change (Apr. 7). Canada gains a new **Constitution** and **Charter of Rights and Freedoms** (Apr. 17). Canada's GNP falls 4.8% in the worst recession since the Great Depression of the 1930s.

1983 Canadian pay-TV channels begin operation (Feb. 1). **Jeanne Sauvé** is Canada's first woman to be appointed Governor General (Dec. 23). Canada approves a US plan to test unarmed **cruise missiles** in western Canada beginning in 1984.

■ Mulroney in Power (1984-1993)

In the 1984 general election, the Conservatives, under Brian Mulroney, won a decisive victory, taking 211 of 282 seats in the House of Commons, including 58 seats in Quebec, a former Liberal stronghold. In contrast to the previous government, the Conservatives sought to strengthen ties with the United States and took steps to attract more foreign investment to Canada. The recession of the early 80s was over and business and government were both ready to expand.

One of the goals of the Mulroney government was to amend the Constitution Act of 1982 to obtain the support of Quebec. The prime minister and 10 provincial premiers reached an agreement, which became known as the Meech Lake Accord, on such an amendment in 1987; the agreement was to be taken to provincial legislatures and to parliament for approval by June 23, 1990. Also in 1987, the government negotiated a Canada-US free trade agreement (FTA) which provided for the elimination of all cross-border tariffs over 10 years. But the deal was rejected by both opposition parties and Liberal leader John Turner announced that the Liberal-dominated Senate would not approve free trade unless the Conservatives obtained public support in a general election. Mulroney called an election for November 1988. The campaign that followed was fractious; emotions ran high and there were wide fluctuations in public opinion. Anti-FTA sentiment was split between the opposition parties and the Conservatives won

a second majority government. The FTA was approved in December and took effect Jan. 1, 1989.

As the deadline for ratification of the Meech Lake Accord approached, its confirmation became increasingly uncertain. Provincial governments had changed in the interim and both Manitoba and Newfoundland indicated that they had reservations about the agreement. Despite a last-minute first ministers' conference and a great deal of political pressure, the Manitoba legislature failed to ratify the accord and Newfoundland withdrew its consent; the deal lapsed on June 23, 1990. The following years were marked by numerous federal-provincial conferences, a variety of proposals and pressure from Quebec to include recognition of its distinct society. In August 1992 a new federal-provincial agreement was reached (the Charlottetown Accord) in time to be considered in a referendum Quebec Premier Robert Bourassa had pledged to hold on the future of Quebec. The other provinces also took part in a national referendum on the terms of the accord, which included not only recognition of Quebec as a distinct society, but also provisions to transfer mining, forestry, telecommunications and many other jurisdictions to the provinces. Canadians from all walks of life grappled with the issues raised by the terms of the Charlottetown Accord and the question dominated national media, (aside from the sports pages which were distracted by the prospect of a Canadian team, the Toronto Blue Jays, winning the 1992 World Series). The referendum was held on Oct. 26, 1992 and the deal was rejected by 54.8% of the voters.

The Conservatives' second term of office was also marked by the introduction of the Goods and Services Tax (GST), a tax designed to replace the manufacturers' tax and spread the tax burden more evenly across the economy. This tax was deeply unpopular and the Liberal-appointed members of the Senate vowed to block its passage in the upper chamber. Mulroney responded by temporarily increasing the number of senators to 112, with new appointees who would support the measure. The tax was the subject of heated debate and much protest across the country as Canadians transferred their frustration over the endless constitutional discussion, the now faltering economy and disappointment over the results of FTA to the government.

The GST took effect on Jan. 1, 1991, and the Conservative government continued to pursue wider trade agreements by joining the US and Mexico in negotiations for a North American Free Trade Agreement that would supersede the FTA. Amid much controversy, the deal was signed in December and the government's popularity continued to plumb the depths of the popularity polls. In February, Mulroney announced his decision to step aside as leader; Kim Campbell became the new leader of the Conservatives and the country's first female prime minister after a June leadership convention. As the Conservative mandate drew to a close, Campbell attempted to present herself as a brand-new prime minister at the head of a brand-new government. In the election in October 1993, Canadian voters made it clear they did not accept this stance: the Liberals under Jean Chrétien won a lopsided victory in an election that changed the political map of the country. The new government took office with a record number of rookie MPs, the Loyal Opposition was made up of members of the separatist Bloc Québécois, with the Reform Party from western Canada nearly matching the BQ's number of seats. The Conservatives elected only two members and the NDP also fared poorly at the hands of the electorate.

1984 Trudeau is succeeded as prime minister by **John Turner** (June 30). Conservatives under **Brian Mulroney** win federal election with 211 seats, the largest majority in Canada's history (Sept. 4). The **Pope visits Canada** (Sept. 9–20). **Marc Garneau** becomes the first Canadian in space, aboard US space shuttle *Challenger* (Oct. 5). Council for the Northwest Territories recognizes the use of **aboriginal languages** as well as English and French.

1985 The voyage through the Northwest Passage of US icebreaker *Polar Sea* challenges Canada's **Arctic sovereignty**. Prime Minister Mulroney and US President Reagan declare mutual support for **Star Wars research** and **free trade** between the two nations at "Shamrock Summit" (Mar. 18) in Quebec City. The Quebec provincial Liberals under Robert Bourassa defeat the Parti Québécois (Dec. 2).

1986 The Canadian dollar hits a then all-time low of 70.20 cents US (Jan. 31). The **Expo 86** world's fair is held in Vancouver (May 2–Oct. 13). Canada joins other Commonwealth nations (Aug. 5) in adopting **economic sanctions against South Africa** because of its apartheid policy. Canada receives a United Nations award (Oct. 6) for providing a haven for world refugees. Canadian John Polanyi shares the Nobel Prize for chemistry.

1987 The Bank of Canada rate drops to a 13-year low of 7.49% (Jan. 28); 6-month residential mortgages are as low as 7.5%. The **Meech Lake Accord**, proposing major constitutional amendments, is agreed to by Prime Minister Brian Mulroney and the 10 provincial premiers (Apr. 30). Ontario passes the first **pay equity legislation** for the private sector enacted in North America (June). A free vote in Parliament on restoration of **capital punishment** defeats the proposal 148–127 (June). A **free trade** agreement between Canada and the United States is set out (Oct. 3). **Stock prices tumble** (Oct. 19) in Canada and throughout the world. The founding assembly of the **Reform Party of Canada** is held (Nov.).

1988 Canada is left without an **abortion law** (Jan. 28) when the Supreme Court rules that existing legislation is unconstitutional. Canadian sprinter **Ben Johnson** sets a world record and wins a gold medal at the Summer Olympics in Seoul (Sept. 24) but is stripped of both (Sept. 26) after testing positive for steroids. Yukon Territory passes language legislation recognizing the use of aboriginal languages. Brian Mulroney's Progressive Conservatives win a second consecutive majority in the **federal election** (Nov. 21), after a bitter campaign fought over the free trade agreement with the US. Quebec's **French-only sign law** is struck down by the Supreme Court (Dec. 15) but is re-instated by Quebec (Dec. 21) using the "notwithstanding" clause in the Charter of Rights and Freedoms. Free trade legislation passes the House of Commons (Dec. 24) and the Senate (Dec. 30). The "Kamloops Amendment" to the Indian Act grants band councils jurisdiction over all reserve land, including the power to impose taxes.

1989 The Free Trade Agreement takes effect (Jan. 1). The federal government announces a new **goods and services tax** (GST) to take effect in January 1991. Audrey McLaughlin becomes Canada's **first female national party leader** as the NDP chooses a successor to Ed Broadbent (Dec. 2).

1990 Revisions to the Criminal Code provide choice of language in criminal hearings (Jan.). Several Quebec Conservative MPs, led by cabinet minister Lucien Bouchard (May 21), leave the government to form the pro-independence **Bloc Québécois**. The **Meech Lake Accord dies** when both Newfoundland and Manitoba fail to ratify the constitutional agreement by the deadline (June 23). Manitoba MLA **Elijah Harper** refuses the unanimous consent required for debate and a vote on the Meech Lake Accord because the accord does not provide special status for aboriginal peoples as it does for Quebec. Jean Chrétien becomes leader of the federal Liberal party. A land dispute leads to a 78-day armed confrontation between Mohawk warriors and government forces at the Kanesatake reserve near **Oka**, Que. **Canada sends warships** to the Persian Gulf as part of the multinational force being assembled to force Iraq to withdraw from occupied Kuwait. Brian Mulroney's Conservative government stacks the Senate (Sept. 27) with new appointees to ensure passage of the federal **goods and services tax (GST)**, which takes effect Jan. 1.

1991 Canadian military personnel participate with the Allied forces in the assault against Iraq beginning Jan. 16 (the **Gulf War**). Prime Minister Brian Mulroney and US President George Bush sign an **acid rain accord** with the goal of ending acid rain within 10 years. **Rita Johnston** succeeds BC Premier **William Vander Zalm** as premier, the first woman to enter the provincial premier's office in Canada. Mulroney's government announces a **new constitutional reform package** promising aboriginal self-government within 10 years and guaranteeing aboriginal representation in an elected Senate. **Gun control** is passed, imposing tougher controls and banning imported military assault weapons. **Yukon First Nations** sign umbrella agreement on land claims and self-government; an agreement is reached on creation of Nunavut.

1992 A year-long crisis in the Atlantic **fisheries** results in a two-year shutdown of the cod fishery (July 2), a five-year ban on commercial salmon fishing in Newfoundland (Mar. 6) and international negotiations to protect the fish stocks. **Gwich'in Indians** sign a deal with Ottawa, giving them title to nearly 24,000 sq. km of land in the NWT and Yukon (Apr. 22).

The details of the North American Free Trade Agreement (**NAFTA**) are announced Aug. 12. Prime Minister Mulroney signs the deal on Dec. 17. Negotiations on constitutional reform occur throughout the year, and the **Charlottetown Accord**, which wins Quebec's approval, is announced Aug. 19. Proposals include Senate reform, an enlarged House of Commons and self-government for native people. On Oct. 26, a national referendum is held on the accord; the rejectionists claim victory.

1993 The **Sahtu Tribe** of the Great Bear Lake region in the NWT settles a land claim to 41,437 sq. km; the **Cree** in northern Quebec win compensation from Hydro-Quebec for damage done around James Bay. On Jan. 19 Canadian troops begin the planned pull-out from NATO bases. On Feb. 24 Prime Minister Mulroney announces his resignation, to take effect in June. Four members of the **Canadian Airborne Regiment**, in Somalia since January on a peacekeeping mission, are charged in the death of a Somali civilian. NAFTA legislation passes in the House of Commons on May 27. Yukon's 14 First Nations sign the **Umbrella Final Agreement** in Whitehorse on May 29; the settlement includes 41,400 sq. km of land and $280 million. Defence Minister **Kim Campbell** takes over the Conservative government after a second ballot victory at the leadership convention on June 25. On Oct. 25, the Liberal Party wins a decisive victory in a federal election that sees the emergence of **two new parties**—the Bloc Québécois and the Reform party—and the near demise of the Progressive Conservatives. The cod moratorium of 1992 is extended to include the Gulf of St. Lawrence and is slated to last until the end of the decade.

1994 Most of the country west of the Rockies endures the coldest winter since the 1950s. **Cigarette taxes** are cut federally and provincially in an effort to curb a black market in cigarettes. The Liberals first budget forecasts cuts in defence spending, UI benefits, tax deductions and foreign aid and freezes transfer payments and public sector salaries. The **Canada Pension Plan** posts a deficit for the first time in 28 years. Members of the **Saskatchewan Wheat Pool** vote to transform the organization, formed in 1924, into a public company. The prime minister and provincial premiers sign an agreement to end trade barriers among the provinces. The Inuit of Quebec sign a self-government deal with the Quebec government. **Canadian troops leave CFB Lahr**, officially ending 27 years of Canadian service for NATO in Europe. The **Algonquins** of Gold Lake, Ont., sign an agreement to begin negotiating an 8.5-million-acre land claim in southern Canada. Canadian sports fans are left hockey-less until the new year by a labour dispute and **NHL lock-out**.

1995 The Canadian Airborne Regiment is disbanded in January after a new scandal compounds damage done by the **Somalia Affair**. Federal fisheries officials seize the Spanish fishing vessel *Estai* in March, in a battle over fishing rights on the Grand Banks. A settlement of the dispute in April gives the **North Atlantic Fishing Organization** greater powers; in the same month, Canada loses its triple A bond rating courtesy of Moody's Investors Service of New York. BC's Fraser River salmon run is shut down in August, because fish stocks are too low. In September, Newfoundland voters approve a proposal to shift control of education from the church to the province. In October, **Alexa McDonough** is elected leader of the federal NDP. On Oct. 30, after a bruising campaign that sees federal Opposition Leader Bouchard take over the YES side, the **proposal that Quebec separate from Canada** to form a sovereign state is narrowly defeated in a referendum—49.4% Yes, and 50.6% against.

1996 The Mint unveiled the new $2 coin (Feb. 19). On May 29, Canada and the US signed a **softwood lumber agreement** after 15 years of controversy. On July 9, the **Innu** of Davis Inlet agreed to relocate to Sango Bay. On July 20-21, **devastating floods** hit the Saguenay valley in Quebec. On Oct. 2, former Quebec premier **Robert Bourassa** died. On Oct. 8, Gen. Jean Boyle resigned as head of Canada's armed forces after controversial evidence arose at the **Somalia inquiry**. On Nov. 18, Canada and Chile signed a free trade deal. In December, Canada signed a $4 billion contract with China for two **CANDU** reactors.

1997 The federal government announced an out-of-court settlement with Brian Mulroney in his libel suit over the **Airbus investigation** (Jan. 6). Voters in Alberta gave Premier **Ralph Klein** another majority (Mar. 11). On Mar. 6, the federal government's **anti-smoking bill**, which limited tobacco company funding of arts and sports activities, was passed in the House of Commons. Census data

taken in 1996 and released on Apr. 15 revealed that Quebec's share of Canada's population had fallen below 25% for the first time since 1867. Premier **Gary Filmon** declared an emergency in southern Manitoba as the **Red River** flooded across the US border (Apr. 22). An independent auditor confirmed that the gold in samples from the **Bre-X claim** in Indonesia was "negligible" (May 4). The **Confederation Bridge** officially opened to traffic between PEI and the mainland (May 31). The federal Liberals won re-election but with a reduced majority; the Reform party became the Opposition (June 2). **Phil Fontaine** was elected national chief of the Assembly of First Nations (July 30). Casting ballots in a second referendum on creating secular schools, Newfoundland voters supported the change (Sept. 2). A judge ruled that the **Red Cross** was negligent in the tainted blood scandal (Oct. 8). A bus crash in Quebec killed 43 in the worst road accident in Canadian history (Oct. 13). **Saskatchewan Conservatives** voted to mothball their party for at least two provincial elections (Nov. 9). The annual **APEC conference** was held in Vancouver (Nov. 21–25); the RCMP pepper-sprayed student demonstrators. Canada agreed to the **Kyoto Convention** on greenhouse gas emissions (Dec. 11).

1998 An **ice storm** crippled Quebec and eastern Ontario, leaving one million people without power and food (Jan. 6). Ottawa apologized to Canada's aboriginals for past mistreatment (Jan. 7). On Feb. 17, **Ontario Hydro** reported a loss of $6.32 billion in 1997–the largest business loss in Canadian history. By Feb. 22, Canadian athletes at the **Nagano Winter Olympics** had won a record 15 medals. On Mar. 27, federal Conservative leader **Jean Charest** said he would run for leader of Quebec's Liberal party. On the same day, federal and provincial governments announced $1.1 billion in compensation for victims who contracted hepatitis C from tainted blood in 1986–90. Ottawa and Washington agreed to save Pacific salmon. The **Nisga'a** people and the BC government signed a historic land claim treaty (July 15). The Supreme Court of Canada ruled on **Quebec's proposed secession from Canada:** Canada–Quebec talks must begin after a majority in Quebec votes for independence in a referendum with an unambiguous question (Aug. 20). On Sept. 1, a new blood collection agency replaced the Canadian Red Cross. **Swissair Flight 111** crashed off the coast of Nova Scotia, killing all 229 passengers (Sept. 2). Ten thousand gun owners met on Parliament Hill to protest firearm registration (Sept. 22). Canada won a seat on the UN Security Council (Oct. 8). Canada's first diamond mine opened in NWT (Oct. 14). Statistics Canada reported that inflation had sunk to 1960s levels (Oct. 21). The *National Post* published its first edition (Oct. 27). Ontario passed the **Energy Competition Act** to end Ontario Hydro's monopoly on power provision in 2001 (Oct. 29). Former Prime Minister **Joe Clark** was elected leader of the federal Conservative party (Nov. 14). Canada pledged $100 million in hurricane relief to Central America over four years (Nov. 15). The Saskatchewan Court of Appeal ruled that **Robert Latimer** must serve at least 10 years in prison for the 1993 killing of his disabled daughter (Nov. 23). **Environment Canada** declared 1998 the warmest year globally in 130–140 years (Nov. 30). On Dec. 1, federal Justice Minister **Anne McLellan** officially launched Canada's new gun control law three years after Parliament had passed the bill. Statistics Canada reported that the national jobless rate fell to 8% in November–the lowest level this decade (Dec. 4). Nova Scotia Labour Minister **Russell MacKinnon** reneged on a pledge to compensate Westray miners (Dec. 8). Finance Minister Paul Martin prohibited Canadian **bank mergers**, saying they would concentrate economic power in the hands of fewer bankers and reduce competition (Dec. 14).

1999 Toronto's task force on homelessness reported that the fastest growing groups of **homeless people** were youths under age 18 and families with children (Jan. 14). The next day, snowfall in Toronto surpassed 120 cm for January and broke an 1871 record for snowfall in one month. Statistics Canada said the number of self-employed and part-time workers steadily grew in the 1990s (Jan. 27). Ottawa pulled the plug on the **Cape Breton Development Corp.**, announcing the closure of the Phalen coal mine by the year 2000 while putting a second mine up for sale (Jan. 28). At the **World Economic Forum** in Davos, Switzerland, Prime Minister Chrétien rejected the idea of a Canadian–US dollar (Jan. 29). Prime Minister Chrétien got nine premiers to agree to a **social union accord**

after promising more health-care funding for the provinces but failed to secure Quebec's signature (Feb. 4). Voters in the eastern Arctic elected 19 members to the first assembly of **Nunavut** (Feb. 15) before the new territory appeared on the map. In his federal budget address, Finance Minister Paul Martin promised an $11.5 billion boost in **health-care transfers** to the provinces over the next five years (Feb. 16). **Ralph Klein** declared future Alberta budget surpluses will be split 75% for debt payment and 25% for new spending (Feb. 16). The *Free Press* of Regina and Saskatoon declared bankruptcy (Feb. 17). In Ottawa, **Kurds** hurled a gasoline bomb at a police line outside the Turkish Embassy, setting one officer ablaze (Feb. 17); in Montreal, police and about 100 Kurds clashed outside the Israeli consulate (Feb. 22). Ottawa and all provinces except Nova Scotia offered $1.5 billion in relief to 45,000 farm families facing financial hardship caused by falling international grain and hog markets (Feb. 24). Senator **Eric Berntson** became the 15th Conservative convicted in Saskatchewan's long-running expense fraud scandal (Feb. 25). Health Minister **Allan Rock** approved medical studies on the benefits of **marijuana** use (Mar. 3). The Liberal government moved to bar federal Crown corporations from donating to political parties (Mar. 5). The **Canadian Wheat Board** and the **Canadian Pacific Railway** settled their dispute over who was to blame for the disastrous 1996–97 grain shipping season (Mar. 8). Canada's four **stock exchanges** announced major reforms, including the merger of the Vancouver and Alberta exchanges (Mar. 15). Canadian **CF-18 fighter-bombers** began taking part in NATO air strikes against **Yugoslavia** (Mar. 24); in Toronto, Serbs threw rocks, paint and Molotov cocktails at the US consulate and police (Mar. 24–25). In Manitoba, an inquiry led by **Alfred Monnin** reported that senior Tories illegally recruited and backed supposedly independent aboriginal candidates in the 1995 provincial election to split popular support for the NDP (Mar. 29). For the first time in Canada, **Mohawks** on Quebec's Kahnawake reserve won the right to collect tax-like levies from non-natives on reserves (Mar. 30). MPs from all federal parties endorsed Canadian participation in NATO's air war against **Yugoslavia** (Mar. 31). **Nunavut** became Canada's newest territory; **Paul Okalik** became its first premier (Apr. 1).

Ontario sold **Highway 407** to a Quebec-led consortium for $3.1 billion in the biggest privatization in Canadian history to date (Apr. 13). Statistics Canada reported that the average household was no richer than it was 20 years ago (Apr. 14). **Wayne Gretzky** played his last professional hockey game (Apr. 18). The Supreme Court of Canada said the courts put too many offenders behind bars, making Canada's incarceration rate one of the highest in the world (Apr. 23). Prime Minister Chrétien announced the departure of 800 soldiers to **Macedonia** to join a larger NATO force for training exercises (Apr. 27). BC Premier **Glen Clark** signed the **Nisga'a Treaty** after invoking closure on debate (Apr. 27); the treaty gave the Nisga'a about 2,000 sq. km of land, fishing and hunting rights and some self-government. A 14-year-old killed one student and wounded another in shootings at the W.R. Myers High School in **Taber**, Alta (Apr. 28). Newfoundland's legislature unanimously voted to change the province's official name to Newfoundland and Labrador (Apr. 29). After a two-year probe, the RCMP said that crimes occurred at **Bre-X Minerals Ltd**, but lack of evidence prevented the laying of charges (May 12). Ottawa approved the construction of a dry storage site for used nuclear fuel at Ontario's **Bruce Nuclear Power Development** (May 14). **David Milgaard**, who spent 22 years in prison for a murder he did not commit, got a record $10 million in compensation from the Saskatchewan and federal governments (May 17). The Canadian Radio-television and Telecommunications Commission said it would not regulate the Internet or impose Canadian content rules (May 17). The Supreme Court of Canada ruled that the **Ontario Family Law Act**'s definition of spouse—which applies only to heterosexual couples—is unconstitutional because it discriminates against gays; the court also opened band elections to off-reserve natives for the first time (May 20). Ottawa unanimously passed a law giving victims more voice in the criminal justice system (May 28). Ottawa agreed to liberalize trade with five Andean countries (May 31). The House of Commons passed a Reform party motion that said marriage is a union between man and woman (June 8). The federal NDP disciplined **Svend Robinson** (June 9) for presenting a petition in the House of Commons that called for the removal of God from the Constitution (June 8).

Health Canada opened a new high-security lab in Winnipeg to study the deadliest human and animal diseases in the world (June 11). BC's NDP government repaid some of the money ($118,000) stolen from charities during the bingo scandal of 1983–84 (June 11). Defence Minister **Art Eggleton** announced the departure of another 500 peacekeepers to **Kosovo** (June 11), two days after Western generals and Yugoslavia signed a peace accord. The Supreme Court of Canada ruled that children's organisations can be liable for sexual abuse if their workplaces make employees' sex crimes easier to commit (June 17). US forestry giant **Weyerhaeuser Co.** announced its intention to buy **MacMillan Bloedel Ltd** for $3.6 billion (June 20). In Toronto, a fire in a **Bell Canada** switching room knocked out bank machines and 100,000 telephone lines for a day (July 16). The **Coast Guard** intercepted a cargo ship filled with 123 Chinese **illegal immigrants** off Vancouver Island (July 20). Statistics Canada reported that Canada's crime rate fell for the seventh year in a row and hit a 19-year low (July 21). **Quebec nurses** ended a four-week strike for higher pay (July 26). Canadian goaltender **Steve Vézina** tested positive for banned stimulants at the **Pan American Games**; his roller hockey team was stripped of its gold medals (Aug. 1). The **World Trade Organization** gave Canada 90 days to scrap or radically change Technology Partnerships Canada, Ottawa's biggest high-technology development program (Aug. 2). **Toronto-Dominion Bank** announced plans to buy **Canada Trust** for $7.85 billion (Aug. 3). In Winnipeg, the Pan American Games closed after Canadian athletes won 196 medals, 64 of them gold. Five Cuban athletes defected (Aug. 8). Explosions rocked an oil recycling plant in Calgary (Aug. 9). A second cargo ship dumped 131 Chinese illegal immigrants in the Queen Charlotte Islands (Aug. 11). After 130 years, **Eaton's** filed for bankruptcy protection and announced plans to close its stores (Aug. 20). BC Premier **Glen Clark** resigned following the revelation that he was under criminal investigation for awarding a casino license to a friend (Aug. 21). The NDP met for a national convention in Ottawa; **Alexa McDonough** won support for a policy of balanced budgets and moderate tax cuts (Aug. 27–29). The Canadian Forces, RCMP and Coast Guard rescued Chinese immigrants aboard a third ship near Vancouver Island (Aug. 31). The Aboriginal Peoples Television

Network aired for the first time (Sept. 1). Seven people died in a **63-vehicle crash** on Ontario's Highway 401 (Sept. 3). A BC court sentenced **Dave Stupich**, a provincial finance minister in the 1980s, to two years in prison for stealing hundreds of thousands of dollars from an NDP fundraising society in Nanaimo (Sept. 3). A three-day meeting of the world's Francophone leaders ended in Moncton, NB (Sept. 5). The owners of Toronto's **Maple Leaf Gardens** put the 68-year-old hockey arena up for sale (Sept. 8). Prime Minister Chrétien said Canada would send up to 600 peacekeepers to **East Timor** (Sept. 12). Cape Breton's Phalen coal mine shut down ahead of schedule; 400 workers lost their jobs (Sept. 13). **Louise Arbour** was sworn in as the newest justice on the Supreme Court of Canada (Sept. 15). **Donald Marshall** won a victory in the Supreme Court of Canada defending historic Mi'kmaq fishing rights (Sept. 17). On Oct. 3, non-natives, angry that aboriginals had been allowed to fish off-season, destroyed native lobster traps in **Miramichi Bay** off the coast of northeastern New Brunswick. (The Supreme Court of Canada judgment on Sept. 17, 1999, ruled that terms of a 1760 Mi'kmaq treaty allow East Coast natives to earn a moderate livelihood from hunting, fishing and gathering was valid.) On Oct. 10, Fisheries Minister **Herb Dhaliwal** announced future limits on native fishing. On Oct. 13, the **World Trade Organization** ruled that the 1965 Canada-US auto pact violated rules that call for freer global trade. A Quebec judge struck down **language law** provisions requiring French predominance on commercial signs. The judge ruled (Oct. 20) that a sign outside an antiques store in Knowlton, Que., did not violate the law even though its French and English lettering were of equal size. On Oct. 29, Ottawa agreed to pay **$3.6 billion in back pay** to thousands of mostly female workers to compensate for wage gaps between men and women. The Federal Court had upheld a Human Rights Tribunal ordering the payment. On Nov. 7, a labour dispute shut down West Coast ports for everything but bulk grain shipments for a week, costing the **Port of Vancouver** alone $90 million a day. On Nov. 23, **Wayne Gretzky** was inducted into the Hockey Hall of Fame. On Nov. 23, the federal government vowed to step up efforts to counter **tobacco research and marketing**. Health Canada released 1,200 pages of industry documents showing Canadian-based Imperial Tobacco Ltd. assessed smokers as young as nine and "fortified" products to increase their addictive qualities. On Dec. 3, the jobless rate was reported at 6.9%, the lowest in 18 years. **Air Canada** gained control of **Canadian Airlines** on Dec. 8 and reached a release agreement with AMR Corp., Canadian's largest shareholder. **Merchant mariners** and the federal government reached a deal (Dec. 15) on compensation for civilian seamen who served aboard cargo ships during the Second World War.

2000 On Jan. 12, **Beverley McLachlin** was sworn in as chief justice of the Supreme Court of Canada—the first woman to hold the office. On Jan. 13, Ottawa announced it would pay $1 billion over the next two years to help farmers through the latest crisis in agricultural prices, but critics said the promised aid wasn't enough. On Jan. 14, a shipment of **weapons-grade plutonium** from the US arrived at a Chalk River, Ont., lab by helicopter, thwarting protesters' plans to block highways along its route. On Jan. 27, the Reform party opened the convention destined to create the **Canadian Alliance**. Human Resources Minister **Jane Stewart** spent much of January trying to play down reports that her department had misspent $1 billion on dubious projects. On Jan. 31, Ottawa approved the $8 billion takeover of **Canada Trust** by **Toronto Dominion Bank**. More than 1,500 **students** demonstrated on Parliament Hill on Feb. 2 to protest the lack of money for university students and high debt loads. On Feb. 3, the Toronto police union called off a fundraising campaign aimed at financing bids to defeat politicians the union leadership didn't like. BC Attorney General **Ujjal Dosanjh**'s first ballot win (Feb. 20) at the NDP convention set the stage for him to become Canada's first Indo-Canadian premier four days later. On Mar. 2, the Alberta government tabled a bill to allow **for-profit clinics** to compete with public hospitals; the move set off a protest by people who thought the bill would undermine universal health care. On Mar. 15, the House of Commons voted overwhelmingly in favour of legislation to clarify the rules if Quebec, or any other province, holds a referendum on secession. After months of debate and political manoeuvring aimed at scuttling the bill, the Bloc Québécois failed to neutralize Ottawa's clarity and it passed 208–55. On Apr. 2, the BC government passed an emergency law to end a week-long **school strike** and reopened the schools for 350,000 students. On Apr. 11, the federal government's **same-sex bill** ended its turbulent passage through the Commons as MPs voted overwhelmingly for the proposed legislation. The bill gives same-sex pairs the same social and tax benefits as heterosexual couples. On Apr. 13, **Nisga'a leaders** smiled and fought tears as a land-claim treaty started 113 years ago by their ancestors cleared its last Parliamentary hurdle. The BC First Nation received self-government powers and $253 million in cash and economic funding. Ottawa will kick in $255 million toward the deal that will cost a total of $487 million. In late May, seven deaths in **Walkerton**, Ont., were blamed on the worst *E. coli* outbreak in Canadian history. The contamination by the deadly bacteria was traced to the town's water supply; local officials were accused of failing to alert townspeople to the danger. As the controversy grew, the Ontario Ministry of Environment and government cutbacks were also drawn into the debate over responsibility for the outbreak. Alberta's controversial Bill 11, authorizing some private health care services, was given royal assent on May 31; critics of the bill claimed that its inclusion of provisions for private health care would make Canada's health care system open to globalization. On June 4 in Windsor, Ont., **anti-globalization protesters** were blasted with pepper spray and arrested as police riot squads braced for the opening of the annual general assembly of the Organization of American States. Human Resources Development Minister Jane Stewart announced that the **"Big Brother" database**, a set of e-files cross-referencing up to 2,000 bits of information about each Canadian, would be dismantled, citing the potential for invasion of privacy. On June 15, the Supreme Court upheld the five-year-old **Firearms Act** that requires every gun owner to get a licence and register every firearm by the end of 2000. Baton-wielding riot police dodged bricks, paint bombs and Molotov cocktails on June 15 as more than 1,000 **anti-poverty protesters** attempted to storm the Ontario legislature to protest the policies of the Harris government. Preston Manning placed second to **Stockwell Day** on June 24 as the Canadian

Alliance voted for its first leader. Manning was defeated two weeks later in a second ballot. On July 5, federal agriculture minister Lyle Vanclief declared that Canada's **agriculture ministers** signed a $5.5 billion-dollar deal to take some of the uncertainty out of the farming business. **Matthew Coon Come**, a Cree leader from northern Quebec, unseated Phil Fontaine as national chief of the Assembly of First Nations on July 12. On July 15, a **tornado** hit Pine Lake, Alta, killing 10 people and injuring more than 130. Ninety **Chinese migrants** who arrived in BC by boat in 1999 were returned to China on July 27 to face jail and fines. A new multimedia colossus was created July 31 as **CanWest Global Communications Corp.** announced a $3.5 billion takeover of all the major Canadian newspapers held by Conrad Black's **Hollinger Inc.** On July 31, Ontario's highest court declared the law banning possession of **marijuana** unconstitutional and gave Ottawa one year to amend it. The Ontario Court of Appeal ruled that Canada's marijuana law fails to recognize that people who suffer from chronic illnesses can use pot as medicine. On Aug. 3, armed Canadian soldiers dropped from helicopters to take charge of the American cargo ship **GTS Katie**, loaded with Canadian military equipment, which was refusing to complete its delivery because of a dispute over payment. The ship was escorted off the coast of Newfoundland to port in Quebec by two warships. Victims of Canada's tainted blood tragedy agreed to a $79-million compensation plan on Aug. 30. The people infected by **hepatitis C** and **HIV** were infected before 1986 or after 1990, making them ineligible for the $1.5 billion federal-provincial compensation package announced two years earlier. Premiers struck a **health care deal** on Sept. 11 with Prime Minister Jean Chrétien that will raise federal transfers to $18.3 billion next year. The provinces wanted federal transfer payments restored to 1994 levels of $18.7 billion, which they said would cost $4.2 billion annually. On Sept. 11, Canadian Alliance leader Stockwell Day and PC leader Joe Clark won seats in **federal by-elections.** Former Ontario premier **Bob Rae** tried to mediate an agreement between Mi'kmaq fishermen from the **Burnt Church** First Nation and the federal Fisheries and Oceans Department over control of the lobster fishery in Miramichi Bay, but gave up when he concluded the two sides were too far apart. On Sept. 23, three non-natives were arrested after shots were fired at fishing boats. **Michel Auger**, Quebec's leading crime reporter, was shot five times in the back on Sept. 13, the day after publication of his latest exposé on organized crime. He survived. On Sept. 13, Groupe Videotron Ltee. agreed to be taken over by **Quebecor Inc.** for $5.4 billion. Finance Minister **Paul Martin** announced Sept. 20 that the surplus for 1999–2000 was $12.3 billion, with a $11.4 billion surplus in the first four months of the latest fiscal year. Saskatchewan's NDP premier Roy Romanow, Canada's longest-serving premier, announced his intention to leave politics on Sept. 25. On Sept. 28, former prime minister **Pierre Trudeau** died at the age of 80; his body was brought to Ottawa to lie in state on Sept. 30 and his state funeral was held at Montreal's Notre-Dame Basilica on Oct. 3. Brian Tobin announced he was stepping down as Newfoundland premier to run for the Liberals in the upcoming federal election (Oct. 16). On Oct. 22 Prime Minister Jean Chretien called a general election for Nov. 27. On Oct. 27, RCMP arrested two men charged in connection with the 15-year-long investigation of the Air India Flight 182 bombing in 1985. NASDAQ Canada, the tech-oriented stock exchange, commenced trading in Montreal on Nov. 21. Margaret Atwood won the Booker Prize for her novel *The Blind Assassin* (Nov. 7). On Nov. 27 the Liberals won the general election with a healthy majority with 173 seats; the CA took 66 to become the Official Opposition, the BQ claimed 37, NDP 13 and the PC party triumphed in just 12 ridings. Canadian astronaut Marc Garneau lifted off on his third space mission on board the space shuttle *Endeavour* on Nov. 30. His mission was to take and install solar panels on the International Space Station. He returned to Earth on Dec. 11. An Alberta judge ruled a law prohibiting the cultivation of marijuana unconstitutional because it didn't allow for medical use of the drug (Dec. 11). Justice Darlene Acton threw out a charge relating to growing and using pot to alleviate MS.On Dec. 15, the Supreme Court upheld the authority of **Canada Customs** to seize imported sexually obscene publications but shifted responsibility for proving obscenity in court from importers to custom officials.

Fathers of Confederation

Union of the British North American colonies into the Dominion of Canada was discussed and its terms negotiated at three confederation conferences held at Charlottetown (C), Sept. 1, 1864; Quebec (Q), Oct. 10, 1864; and London (L), Dec. 4, 1866. The names of delegates are followed by the provinces they represented; Canada refers to what are now the provinces of Ontario and Quebec.

Adams G. Archibald, NS	C,Q,L
George Brown, Canada	C,Q
Alexander Campbell, Canada	C,Q
Frederick B.T. Carter, Nfld	Q
George-Étienne Cartier, Canada	C,Q,L
Edward B. Chandler, NB	C,Q
Jean-Charles Chapais, Canada	Q
James Cockburn, Canada	Q
George H. Coles, PEI	C,Q
Robert B. Dickey, NS	Q
Charles Fisher, NB	Q,L
Alexander T. Galt, Canada	C,Q,L
John Hamilton Gray, NB	C,Q
John Hamilton Gray, PEI	C,Q
Thomas Heath Haviland, PEI	Q
William A. Henry, NS	C,Q,L
William P. Howland, Canada	L
John M. Johnson, NB	C,Q,L
Hector L. Langevin, Canada	C,Q,L
Jonathan McCully, NS	C,Q,L
A.A. Macdonald, PEI	C,Q
John A. Macdonald, Canada	C,Q,L
William McDougall, Canada	C,Q,L
Thomas D'Arcy McGee, Canada	C,Q
Peter Mitchell, NB	Q,L
Oliver Mowat, Canada	Q
Edward Palmer, PEI	C,Q
William H. Pope, PEI	C,Q
John W. Ritchie, NS	L
J. Ambrose Shea, Nfld	Q
William H. Steeves, NB	C,Q
Sir Étienne-Paschal Taché, Canada	Q
Samuel Leonard Tilley, NB	C,Q,L
Charles Tupper, NS	C,Q,L
Edward Whelan, PEI	Q
R.D. Wilmot, NB	L

Canadian Disasters

Aug. 29, 1583: Canada's first recorded marine disaster took 85 lives when the *Delight* was wrecked on Sable Island.

1710: Ships arriving in Quebec City from the West Indies brought a cargo that included yellow fever. The resulting epidemic killed a number of people, including six nurses, 12 priests and the ship's crew.

Aug. 23, 1711: As many as 950 drowned when ships attached to the British fleet preparing to attack Quebec were grounded and sank on the rocks of Ile-aux-Oeufs.

1746: Typhus broke out on a flotilla of French warships sailing for Port Royal in Acadia. Of the 3,150 soldiers aboard, 1,270 died at sea; another 1,130 died in the Bedford Basin while waiting for an army from Quebec. Typhus then spread to the Mi'kmaq population.

Oct. 5, 1825: The Miramichi fire, north of New Brunswick's Miramichi River, destroyed the towns of Newcastle and Douglastown, and killed between 200–500 people.

1832–34: Cholera swept through Lower Canada when diseased Irish and English immigrants arrived in Quebec City. In Montreal, it killed at least 947 people between June 10–27, 1832.

Despite attempts by the authorities to quarantine infected immigrants on Grosse Île in the St Lawrence River, between 1833–34, the cholera killed about 3,800 people in Quebec City and 1,900 more in Montreal.

May 17, 1841: On this date, several large boulders from Cap Diamant tumbled down the precipitous cliffs above the Lower Town of Quebec City and demolished eight houses, killing 32 people.

1847: Ireland's potato famine prompted tens of thousands of Irish to sail for North America. Typhus killed about 5,000 immigrants at sea; at Grosse Île, medical inspectors buried at least 5,424 people throughout the year. From Grosse Île, some ships went to Pointe Saint-Charles, Montreal, where another 6,000 Irish immigrants died and were buried. The epidemic also spread to the population of Montreal and Quebec City.

1847–48: Under the command of Sir John Franklin, a British naval officer, 129 men perished of starvation and cold when their ships, *HMS Terror* and *HMS Erebus*, became trapped in pack ice west of King William Island in the Arctic archipelago. Franklin had been searching for the Northwest Passage.

Oct. 27, 1854: In one of the earliest Canadian train disasters, a gravel train running near Baptiste Creek, 24 km west of Chatham, Ont., was hit by an express train on the same line. In the collision, 52 persons were killed and 48 seriously injured.

June 29, 1864: Near St-Hilaire, Que., a passenger train was unable to stop for an open drawbridge at the Beloeil bridge on the Richelieu River. The train plunged through the opening onto passing barges, killing 99 and injuring 100 people.

Apr. 1, 1873: Sailing from Liverpool to New York, the steamer *Atlantic* struck Meager's Rock off the coast of Nova Scotia and sank with the loss of 535 people.

May 13, 1873: Sixty men died when a fire and subsequent explosion in a coal mine at Westville, Pictou County, NS, trapped firemen and workers. The mine was eventually sealed to starve the fire of oxygen and it was two years before all the bodies were recovered.

Aug. 25, 1873: The Great Nova Scotia Cyclone swept over Cape Breton Island. The hurricane destroyed 1,200 vessels and 900 buildings, demolished dikes, wharves and bridges and claimed 500 lives.

1885: A smallpox epidemic swept through Montreal killing 3,164 people—2,117 of whom were children. The catastrophe prompted city authorities to vaccinate the population, but some doctors said vaccination merely spread the disease. On Sept. 18, terrified rioters ransacked the home of the chief medical vaccinator, pharmacies, magistrates' homes and city hall.

May 3, 1887: An explosion at the Number One mine in Nanaimo, BC owned by the Vancouver Coal Mining and Land Company, killed 148 miners.

Jan. 24, 1888: Seventy-seven men lost their lives in a fire in the Number Five Mine at Wellington, just outside of Nanaimo, BC.

Feb. 21, 1891: In the first of several major disasters in the coal mines of Springhill, NS, 125 men were killed in an explosion.

May 26, 1896: Fifty-five people were killed when a bridge at Point Ellice in Victoria, BC, collapsed while a streetcar was passing over it. The bridge was too weak to support the weight of a recently built tramline.

Sept. 19, 1899: A massive rockslide from the cliffs above Quebec City's Lower Town demolished most of Champlain St, killing 45 people.

Apr. 29, 1903: Parts of the town of Frank, Alta, were obliterated by a sudden landslide when over 90 million tonnes of limestone came crashing down Turtle Mountain, crossed the four-km-wide valley floor and rolled up the other side of the valley. Approximately 75 people were killed. The landslide also sealed a mine entrance at the foot of the mountain and trapped 17 miners inside. The men were able to escape by digging a new tunnel to the surface.

Aug. 29, 1907: The Quebec Bridge, 11 km north of Quebec City, was the largest cantilevered bridge in the world at the time. As the bridge was nearing completion, the southern cantilever span collapsed, killing 75 workmen.

Aug. 2, 1908: A fire in BC's Kootenay Valley caused $5 million in damages and killed 70 people.

Mar. 5, 1910: Sixty-two train men and labourers died 2 km west of Rogers Pass, BC, when their engine was hit by an avalanche and hurtled 500 m into Bear Creek. Over 600 volunteers used pick axes and shovels to dig through 10 m of snow in the search for survivors.

June 30, 1912: The worst tornado in Canadian history swept through Regina, Sask., killing 28 residents, injuring hundreds and causing $75 million damage (est. 1990 dollars).

Nov. 7–13, 1913 Thirty-four ships sank and 270 sailors drowned when a storm swept over Lake Erie and Lake Ontario. Winds reached speeds of 140 km/h. Days later, one ship was found afloat with its dead crew lashed to the mast.

Apr. 1, 1914: Seventy-seven sealers froze to death on the ice during a storm off the southeast coast of Labrador. At the storm's height, from Mar. 31 to Apr. 2, the temperature fell to –23°C and winds reached 64 km/h.

May 29, 1914: The Canadian Pacific liner *Empress of Ireland* collided with a Norwegian coal ship in the St Lawrence River near Rimouski, Que., and sank in only 14 minutes with the loss of 1,014 lives. This was one of the worst naval disasters in history, with the eighth largest loss of life for a naval accident.

June 19, 1914: The worst coal mine disaster in Canadian history occurred at Hillcrest, Alta, when dust explosions killed 189 men.

July 29, 1916: A forest fire in northern Ontario, thought to have been started by lightning and locomotive sparks, engulfed the towns of Cochrane and Matheson, killing at least 233 persons.

Sept. 11, 1916: The Quebec Bridge was the scene of further tragedy when a new centre span being hoisted into position fell into the river below. Thirteen men were killed, bringing the loss of life during construction of the bridge to 88.

Dec. 6, 1917: Halifax was the scene of Canada's worst single disaster when a French munitions ship filled with explosives collided with a freighter in Halifax harbour. The French ship, the *Mont Blanc*, was split to the waterline; fuel oil spilled over its explosive cargo and started a fire in the hold. The crew abandoned ship without attempting to extinguish the fire.

In the explosion that followed, the *Mont Blanc* was tossed more than 1,000 m into the air. The explosion levelled homes and businesses in a large part of the city and set off explosives stockpiled on shore. The blast, heard as far away as Prince Edward Island, is thought to be the largest-ever accidental explosion, and the largest non-nuclear blast in history. More than 1,600 people were killed, 9,000 injured, and 6,000 left homeless. Property damage was estimated at $35 million.

Oct. 23, 1918: The Canadian Pacific steamship *Princess Sophia* ran onto Vanderbilt Reef while sailing from Alaska to Vancouver. The ship sank two days later on Oct. 25. All 343 aboard were drowned.

Jan. 9, 1927: A small fire that broke out in Montreal's Laurier Palace Theatre was quickly extinguished, but in the panic that ensued 12 people were crushed to death and 64 were asphyxiated, including many children.

Aug. 24–25, 1927: A hurricane struck Newfoundland, killing 56 people at sea. Throughout Atlantic Canada, the storm washed out roads, flooded houses, and swamped boats.

Apr. 14, 1928: The 18-gun sloop *Acorn* sank near Halifax with 115 men on board.

Nov. 18, 1929: Newfoundland's Burin Peninsula was struck by a 4.5-m tidal wave. Property damage was extensive and 27 were killed.

June 26, 1930: A store of dynamite blew up when lightning struck the bow of the *John B. King*, a drillship on the St Lawrence River. The explosion killed 30 people and injured 11 others.

1933–37: Throughout these years, the Prairies received only 60 percent of normal rainfall. The region turned into a dustbowl: Farmers lost thousands of animals to starvation and suffocation, crops withered, and 250,000 people left the Prairies to seek better lives elsewhere.

July 5–17, 1936: During an intense heat wave, 1,180 Canadians died in Manitoba and Ontario. Temperatures exceeding 44°C killed large numbers of infants and seniors; drowning killed about 400 people who went swimming to escape the heat.

Dec. 12, 1942: An arsonist set fire to the Knights of Columbus hostel in St John's. Because the hostel had no emergency lighting, the doors opened inwards and exits were restricted, 99 people died and another 100 were seriously injured.

May–June 1948: BC's worst flood of the century occurred when the Fraser River overflowed. The water destroyed 2,300 homes and forced 16,000 people to flee. Ten people drowned. For three weeks, Vancouver had no rail connection with the rest of Canada.

Sept. 17, 1949: Seven hundred people were aboard the Great Lakes excursion ship *Noronic* when it caught fire and burned at its pier in Toronto harbour. The ship's fire hydrants were dry and no alarm was sent to the city fire department until 15 minutes after the blaze was discovered. In the meantime, the single exit became blocked by fire and 118 lives were lost.

Spring 1950: The Red River flooded, forcing the evacuation of 100,000 people from southern Manitoba and damaging 5,000 homes. The provincial government responded by building the Winnipeg Floodway to forestall future floods.

Oct. 15, 1954: During the worst inland storm in Canadian history, Hurricane Hazel, over 10 cm of rain fell in Toronto in 12 hours. At that time, many houses in Toronto were built on low-lying flood plains. The storm and resulting floods caused 83 deaths and widespread property damage.

Nov. 1, 1956: A second major tragedy struck the coal mines at Springhill, NS, when an accident killed 39 men.

Dec. 9, 1956: A DC-4 North Star flown by Trans-Canada Airways (later Air Canada) crashed into the east face of Mount Slesse, killing all 62 on board.

June 17, 1958: Design errors in Vancouver's Second Narrows Bridge caused one section to collapse. The accident killed 18 men, including the two engineers that an investigation later determined were responsible for the errors.

Oct. 23, 1958: A third mining accident in Springhill, NS, killed 75 when a tunnel collapsed.

June 20, 1959: More than 30 fishermen drowned and 22 salmon boats sank near Esuminac, NB, when a storm suddenly struck the Gulf of St Lawrence.

Nov. 19, 1963: A Trans Canada Airlines DC-8F crashed after takeoff from Dorval in Montreal, killing 118.

July 5, 1970: At Toronto International Airport, an Air Canada DC-8 lost one starboard engine during a landing attempt. During the pilot's effort to take off and land again, the remaining starboard engine fell off. The aircraft crashed, killing all 109 persons aboard.

May 4, 1971: During a prolonged rainstorm in St-Jean-Vianney, Que., a giant sinkhole appeared in the ground. The hole swallowed 40 houses, several cars and a bus, and 31 people were killed.

Nov. 10, 1975: The 218-m ore carrier *Edmund Fitzgerald*, based in Sault Ste Marie, broke apart during a storm on Lake Superior and sank in 156 m of water with all 29 members of the crew aboard. Two days later only two rubber rafts and some life preservers from the ship were found.

June 21, 1977: A fire that broke out in the cell block of the city police headquarters of St John, NB, was so hot that the locks on several cell doors were fused. Twenty prisoners were killed and 12 police officers who attempted to rescue the prisoners were injured.

Feb. 11, 1978: A Pacific Western Airlines aircraft crashed at Cranbrook, BC, killing 43 people.

Aug. 4, 1978: The brakes on a chartered bus failed near Eastman, Que. The bus plunged into a lake, and 41 passengers were killed.

Dec. 31, 1979: Forty-four persons were killed during New Year's Eve celebrations at a social club in Chapais, Que., in a fire caused by a man playing with a lighter who set decorations ablaze.

Feb. 15, 1982: The ocean drilling rig *Ocean Ranger* overturned and sank during a storm while operating 265 km east of Newfoundland, killing 84 men. Inadequate safety procedures and equipment were later blamed for the accident.

May 31, 1985: A midafternoon tornado struck Barrie, Ont., killing 12, including four children. Property damage was in the hundreds of millions of dollars.

Dec. 12, 1985: In the worst air crash in Canada, an Arrow Airlines DC-8, after refueling in Gander en route to Hopkinsville, Ky., crashed seconds after takeoff, killing 256 passengers and crew.

Feb. 8, 1986: A 16-unit VIA Rail passenger train slammed head-on into a 118-unit CN freight train near Hinton, Alta. Twenty-six people were killed and dozens were seriously injured.

July 31, 1987: A tornado touched down in Edmonton, Alta, killing 26 people, injuring 250 others and causing an estimated $250 million damage.

Mar. 10, 1989: An Air Ontario jet crashed immediately after takeoff from Dryden, Ont., killing 24 people.

Feb. 12, 1990: One of the worst tire fires in North America broke out near Hagersville,

Ont., spewing oil and toxic smoke. The dump, which stored 14 million tires for recycling, burned for 16 days; the blaze was extinguished at a cost of $1.5 million.

May 9, 1992: Twenty-six miners died underground in the Westray coal mine near Plymouth, NS, after a methane gas explosion. Fifteen bodies were recovered but the bodies of the remaining victims could not be reached in the debris.

July 16, 1993: Nineteen people died when a truck towing tanks of diesel fuel collided with a van carrying senior citizens near Lac-Bouchette, Que.

July 19-20, 1996: Ten people died in the Lac-St-Jean Saguenay Region when flash floods from overflowing dams and reservoirs wiped out communities along the Saguenay River.

April–May 1997: Manitoba's Red River flooded 2,000 square km of valley land when water rose 12 m above winter levels—the highest for the river in the 20th century. Thousands of volunteers and soldiers fought the flood for days. Damage estimates reached half a billion dollars.

Oct. 13, 1997: Forty-four passengers were killed when the brakes failed on their sightseeing bus; the vehicle missed a turn at the bottom of a steep hill and crashed into a ravine in Les Eboulements, 110 km northeast of Quebec City.

Jan. 4–9, 1998: One of the most destructive ice storms in Canadian history struck Quebec and Eastern Ontario causing hardship for 4 million people and costing $3 billion. Losses included 130 transmission towers, 120,000 km of power and phone lines, and millions of trees. Power outages lasted up to four weeks.

Sept. 2, 1998: All 229 passengers were killed when a Swissair MD-11 en route from New York to Geneva crashed in the Atlantic near Peggy's Cove, NS. The accident was the second worst in Canadian aviation history.

May 2000: At least seven people died and up to 2,000 people fell ill after drinking tap water infected by *E. coli* bacteria in Walkerton, Ont.

Prime Ministers of Canada

■ Sir John A. Macdonald

Canada's first prime minister, Sir John A. Macdonald, was born in Glasgow, Scotland, Jan. 11, 1815. At age five he came to Canada with his parents who settled at Kingston, Upper Canada.

Called to the bar in 1836, Macdonald practised law in Kingston and then in Toronto. He established a reputation as a corporate lawyer, company director and businessman.

He was elected to the Legislative Assembly of the Province of Canada in 1844 and was re- elected in 1848, 1851, 1854, 1857, 1861 and 1863. In 1864, he joined a coalition with George Brown, leader of the Upper Canadian reformers, dedicated to bringing about Confederation. That same year, Macdonald was a delegate to the Charlottetown and Quebec Conferences, and became the principal author of the Confederation resolutions agreed upon in Quebec. He was chairman of the London Conference (1866–67) and played a pivotal role in bringing about Confederation.

Macdonald became Canada's first prime minister when the Conservative party won a majority of seats in Parliament following the first post-Confederation general election in 1867. Though he was re-elected in 1872, Macdonald's second administration was marred by the "Pacific Scandal" in 1873, when the Liberal opposition charged that his government had awarded the CPR contract to Sir Hugh Allan in return for political contributions. An investigation into these charges was held, and the government resigned on Nov. 5, 1873.

Macdonald's Liberal-Conservatives were re-elected Sept. 17, 1878, and Macdonald remained prime minister until his death in Ottawa on June 6, 1891.

During his first administration, the Dominion of Canada expanded to include the provinces of British Columbia, Prince Edward Island and the newly created Manitoba.

The building of the transcontinental railway is the most memorable feature of his second administration, but other accomplishments include the establishment of the "National Policy"—a system of tariff protection to aid the development of Canadian industries (1879)—and the increased settlement of the Western provinces that followed the construction of the railway.

■ Alexander Mackenzie

Alexander Mackenzie was born on Jan. 28, 1822 near Dunkeld, Perthshire, Scotland. He left school and became a stonemason at the age of 14.

He emigrated to Canada in 1842 and became a contractor at Lambton, Ontario, and then editor of the *Lambton Shield*. From 1866–74, he was a major in the 27th Lambton Battalion Volunteer Infantry.

In 1861, Mackenzie was elected to the Legislative Assembly of the Province of Canada, where he gave his support to the Confederation plan. When George Brown was defeated in the 1867 election, Mackenzie became *de facto* leader of the Opposition, though it was not until after the 1872 elections that he formally accepted this title.

It was Mackenzie who led the attack on the Macdonald administration over the "Pacific Scandal"; when Macdonald resigned on Nov. 5, 1873, Mackenzie became prime minister.

During his 5-year term of office, Mackenzie introduced changes to election laws that included the secret ballot and universal male suffrage. The Supreme Court of Canada was established under Mackenzie's rule, and Wilfrid Laurier was brought into Mackenzie's cabinet.

Severe economic depression plagued Canada during the Mackenzie years, and in 1878, his Liberal party was routed at the polls.

Mackenzie retained his own seat, however, and was still a member of Parliament when he died Apr. 17, 1892, in Toronto.

■ Sir John Abbott

Sir John Joseph Caldwell Abbott was born Mar. 12, 1821, at St. Andrews, Lower Canada—the first prime minister to be born on Canadian soil.

After taking his law degree from University of McGill College, he was admitted to the bar

in 1847 and practised law in Montreal. From 1855–80 he was dean of the Faculty of Law, McGill University.

Abbott was elected to the Legislative Assembly of the Province of Canada in 1857, re-elected in 1861 and 1863, and sat until Confederation. He was then elected to the House of Commons in 1867, 1872 and 1874. He was last elected in 1882 and appointed to the Senate on May 12, 1887.

When Sir John A. Macdonald died in 1891, Abbott—though a senator—inherited the Conservative leadership. The three other leading Conservatives—Langevin, Tupper and Thompson—were unwilling or unable to assume the post. Abbott held the office of prime minister from June 16, 1891, until his resignation on Nov. 24, 1892. He died in Montreal on Oct. 30, 1893.

■ Sir John Thompson

Sir John Sparrow David Thompson was born in Halifax, NS, on Nov. 10, 1845.

Thompson was called to the Nova Scotia bar in 1865, and was instrumental in founding Dalhousie Law School in 1883, where he eventually became a lecturer.

In May 1882, Thompson became premier of Nova Scotia, but when his government was defeated two months later, he retired from politics and became a judge of the Supreme Court of Nova Scotia.

Prime Minister Macdonald coaxed Thompson back into politics, making him Minister of

Justice in 1885. When Macdonald died in 1891, Thompson declined the leadership, fearing that his conversion to Roman Catholicism in 1870 would hinder his party's fortunes. However, the following year, Thompson changed his mind, and on Dec. 5, 1892, he became prime minister.

Though prime minister for just over 2 years, Thompson was largely responsible for the establishment of the Criminal Code and penetentiary reforms. He very nearly succeeded in bringing Newfoundland into Confederation in 1894, and successfully negotiated fisheries clauses in the Treaty of Washington.

He died while still in office on Dec. 12, 1894.

■ Sir Mackenzie Bowell

Mackenzie Bowell was born at Rickinghall, Suffolk, England, on Dec. 27, 1823, and came to Canada in 1832. In 1834, he became an

apprentice printer at Belleville, Upper Canada and was later editor and proprietor of the Belleville *Intelligencer*. He served in the militia of the United Province of Canada during the American Civil War and the Fenian raids of 1866.

Bowell was elected to the House of Commons in 1867 for Hastings North, Ont., and was re-elected in 1872, 1874, 1878, 1887 and 1891.

As spokesman for the Orange Association of British America, Bowell was instrumental in having Louis Riel expelled from the Commons in 1874.

On Dec. 5, 1892, Bowell was appointed to the Senate and, after Thompson's death in 1894, was invited by the Governor General to form a government.

Perhaps the thorniest problem facing Prime Minister Bowell was the Manitoba Schools question. In 1890, Manitoba legislation had withdrawn school privileges from the Roman Catholic and primarily French minority in that province. By the time Bowell assumed office, attempts were being made to restore those lost school privileges by federal remedial legislation. Bowell was not equal to the political challenges facing him; he lost control of his cabinet ministers, several of whom eventually called for his resignation. Bowell denounced this cabinet rebellion as a "nest of traitors," but eventually he resigned on Apr. 27, 1896. He died in Belleville, Ont., on Dec. 10, 1917, at age 93.

■ Sir Charles Tupper

Charles Tupper was born at Amherst, NS, July 2, 1821. He took a degree in medicine at Edinburgh University. At the age of 22, he began practising medicine in Amherst and became the first president of the Canadian Medical Association (1867–70).

The 1855 election that brought him to the Legislative Assembly of Nova Scotia was declared void on Feb. 24, 1857. He was subsequently re-elected in a by-election that same year and was elected again in 1859 and 1863.

Tupper was active in the Confederation movement, and was a delegate to the

Charlottetown, Quebec and London Conferences. He was elected to the House of Commons in 1867 and re-elected 1870, 1872, 1874, 1878 and 1882. He resigned in 1884 and served as High Commissioner for Canada in the United Kingdom from May 28 of that year to Jan. 26, 1887. In 1887, he was re-elected to the House of Commons, but resigned the following year and again served as High Commissioner from May 23, 1888, to Jan. 14, 1896.

In 1896, following the rebellion of Bowell's cabinet, Tupper became *de facto* leader of the administration until Bowell formally resigned on Apr. 27, 1896. At that time, the Governor General invited Tupper to form the government. Parliament was dissolved shortly thereafter and in the election that followed on June 23, Tupper's Conservatives were defeated. Tupper stayed on as leader of the Opposition until Feb. 5, 1901, then retired from public life. He died Oct. 30, 1915 at Bexley Heath, Kent, England.

■ Sir Wilfrid Laurier

Wilfrid Laurier was born at St-Lin, Canada East, Nov. 20, 1841. He first attended College de l'Assomption and then took his degree from McGill University.

He was called to the bar of Lower Canada in 1865. He practised law at Montreal and at Arthabaskaville, Que.

First elected to the Legislative Assembly of Quebec in 1871, Laurier resigned in Jan. 1874 and later that year was elected to the House of Commons. He became leader of the Liberal Opposition in June 1887. Then, following the 1896 election that gave his party a 23-seat majority, Laurier became Canada's first French-speaking prime minister on July 11, 1896. The Liberals retained power in 1900 and won a landslide election victory in 1904.

Immigration increased during his time in office as Clifford Sifton, Laurier's minister of the interior from 1896–1905, mounted a powerful campaign to attract immigrants from Britain, the United States and Europe. In 1905, Laurier created the provinces of Alberta and Saskatchewan and established the boundaries of Manitoba. During Laurier's years in power the Canadian West became a major world wheat producer. In 1909, Laurier established the External Affairs Department.

His government's controversial support for the creation of a Canadian navy, and his unpopular attempt to enter into a reciprocal trade agreement with the United States (an agreement that would have reduced or eliminated duties on many imported goods) spelled trouble for Laurier in 1911. His party was

defeated in the Sept. 21 election. He remained an Opposition M.P. until his death on Feb. 17, 1919, in Ottawa.

■ Sir Robert Borden

Robert Laird Borden was born at Grand Pré, NS, June 26, 1854. At age 14 he gave up formal schooling to become an assistant master in classical studies. He taught classics and mathematics in New Jersey in 1873, before returning to Nova Scotia to study law. He was admitted to the Nova Scotia bar in 1878 and practised first in Halifax, then in Kentville, NS.

Borden was elected to the House of Commons in 1896 and 1900 and became leader of the Conservative party on Feb. 6, 1901. He served as leader of the Opposition until 1911, when he led his party to victory in the Sept. 21 election.

Borden was prime minister throughout World War I, and during the war years his government was accused of scandal over British munitions contracts and its staunch support of the Ross Rifle—a weapon known to jam in battle. Borden's government introduced the first federal income tax, nationalized Canadian railways and introduced conscription in 1917.

In the election of Dec. 17, 1917, Borden led a re-organized Union Government made up of

Conservatives and pro-conscription Liberals to victory. Borden headed the Canadian delegation at the Paris Peace Conference in 1919, where the autonomy of Canada and other dominions within the British Commonwealth was successfully established. He resigned on July 10, 1920, and died in Ottawa June 10, 1937.

■ **Arthur Meighen**

Arthur Meighen was born at Anderson, Ont., June 16, 1874. Following his graduation from university in 1896, Meighen taught high school for a year, then moved to Winnipeg in 1898 to study law. He was called to the Manitoba bar in 1902, and practised at Portage La Prairie.

He was first elected to the House of Commons in 1908, re-elected in 1911, 1913 and 1917, defeated in 1921, and re-elected in 1922 and 1925.

Meighen first achieved national prominence in 1913 when he helped devise a closure rule which permitted the government to end debate on a bill which was to effect a $35-million contribution to the British navy. Prior to closure, the bill had been obstructed by a fierce and protracted Opposition party blockade.

Prime Minister Borden appointed Meighen his solicitor general on Oct. 2, 1915, and

Meighen held this post for two years. A strong supporter of conscription, Meighen essentially drafted Canada's 1917 conscription bill, and put it into operation. He was also the chief draughtsman of the Wartime Elections Act.

When Borden resigned on July 10, 1920, Meighen succeeded him as prime minister. In the general election of Dec. 6, 1921, Meighen's party was defeated. Though his Conservatives won the most seats in the election of Oct. 29, 1925, the Liberals were able to stay in power with the support of Progressive and Labour members.

Following the resignation of William Lyon Mackenzie King's government on June 28, 1926, the Governor General invited Meighen to form a new ministry. This government was less than three months old, however, when it was defeated in the House of Commons (by only one vote) and Canadians again went to the polls.

Following a Liberal victory in the election of Sept. 14, 1926, Meighen resigned as Conservative leader in the House of Commons. He was appointed to the Senate on Feb. 3, 1932, during Richard Bennett's ministry and became government leader in the Senate. Then, following King's victory in 1935, he became Senate Opposition leader.

On Nov. 12, 1941, he once again became leader of the Conservative party, but failed in his bid to win a seat in the Commons in a federal by-election on Feb. 2, 1942. Following this defeat, he retired from politics and resumed his law practice in Toronto where he died Aug. 5, 1960.

■ Mackenzie King

William Lyon Mackenzie King, grandson of William Lyon Mackenzie, was born in Kitchener (then called Berlin) on Dec. 17, 1874.

He took his B.A. and law degrees from the University of Toronto and also studied at the University of Chicago and Harvard University.

He served as deputy minister of labour from 1900–08.

He was first elected to the House of Commons in 1908, and succeeded Laurier as leader of the Liberal party in 1919. King became prime minister when the Liberals won the general election of Dec. 6, 1921.

Though Meighen's Conservatives won a majority of seats in the general election of Oct. 29, 1925, King stayed in office with the help of Progressive and Labour members who supported his proposed tariff reductions and old-age pension legislation. King had lost his York North seat in the 1925 election but returned to the House of Commons as the member for Prince Albert, Sask., following a by-election on Feb. 15, 1926. King's government was shaken in 1926 by the revelation that the customs department was tainted with corruption and incompetence. In the furor that followed, King lost the support of many members of Parliament and, although never technically defeated in the House of Commons, decided that he could no longer hold his minority government. He appealed to Governor General Lord Byng to dissolve Parliament, even though the government had not been defeated. Byng refused. King subsequently resigned on June 28, 1926, and the Governor General invited Arthur Meighen to form a government which was subsequently defeated in the House of Commons.

In the general election of Sept. 14, 1926, King's Liberals regained power and held it until 1930. But the disastrous fall in the price of wheat and other Canadian exports in 1929 soured Canadians on their government, and King was defeated by R.B. Bennett's Conservatives in the election of July 28, 1930.

Five years later, King was back in the prime minister's office, following the Liberal victory in the general election of Oct. 14, 1935. In the coming years, King, an ardent supporter of Canada's autonomy within the British Commonwealth, was faced with the issue of Canada's participation in an impending European war. To soothe French-Canadian concerns over Canadian support of Great Britain, King promised there would be no conscription; Canada declared war in September 1939. Later, however, heavy casualties in France and Italy in 1944 prompted King to break his promise and send conscripts overseas.

King's government began introducing postwar recovery legislation even before peace was declared. These measures included recon-

struction plans and social security schemes such as mother's allowances.

King resigned as prime minister on Nov. 15, 1948, supporting Louis St Laurent as his successor. In poor health in his final years, King died July 22, 1950, at Kingsmere, his estate in Wright County, Que.

■ Richard Bennett

Richard Bedford Bennett was born at Hopewell, NB, July 3, 1870. Bennett studied law at Dalhousie University. He read and practised law in Chatham, NB, from 1893–97, before moving to Calgary where he entered a legal partnership with Senator James A. Lougheed.

Bennett was first elected to the House of Commons in 1911. He served as minister of justice in Arthur Meighen's 1921 cabinet, and minister of finance and minister of mines in Meighen's 1926 government.

Bennett was chosen to replace Meighen as Conservative leader at the party convention in

Winnipeg in 1927. He became prime minister following the Conservative victory in the election of July 28, 1930.

Bennett had the task of governing Canada during the worst years of the Depression. Virtually every measure his government attempted ended in failure. High unemployment levels continued despite Bennett's efforts to reduce them. Negotiations for a reciprocity treaty with the United States did not succeed. A plan of preferential tariffs agreed to in 1930 at the Imperial Conference did little to ease Canada's economic woes.

Then, in 1935, near the end of his term, Bennett took an unexpected step to the political left. He proclaimed that "the old order is gone" and that it was time for a new economic system. That new system was to include a state-planned economy, new unemployment and health insurance legislation and old-age pension laws.

In the election of Oct. 14, 1935, Bennett's Conservatives suffered a devastating defeat, winning just 39 seats. Bennett remained in Opposition until 1937, when he retired to England. There he was given the title Viscount Bennett of Mickelham, Hopewell and Calgary.

Despite the overwhelming problems of the Great Depression, Bennett's term saw the creation of the Canadian Radio Broadcasting Corporation (the predecessor to the CBC) and the Bank of Canada. As well, it was during Bennett's tenure that the Statute of

Westminster gave Canada increased autonomy in 1931.

Bennett died June 27, 1947.

■ Louis St Laurent

Louis Stephen St Laurent was born at Compton, Que., Feb. 1, 1882. Called to the Quebec bar in 1905, he practised law in Quebec City, and became Professor of Law at Université Laval. He was elected president of the Canadian Bar Association in 1930.

St Laurent became justice minister in Mackenzie King's cabinet on Dec. 10, 1941. On Feb. 9, 1942, he was elected to the House of Commons in a by-election for Quebec East.

Originally planning to hold his cabinet post only during the war, St Laurent was persuaded to stay on. On Dec. 10, 1946, he became secretary of state for external affairs. A firm believer in collective security, St Laurent was one of the architects of the North Atlantic Treaty Organization (NATO). On Aug. 7, 1948, he accepted his party's nomination to be King's successor, and on Nov. 15 became prime minister.

While in power St Laurent ended the practice of appealing court cases to the Judicial Committee of the Privy Council in England, and made the Supreme Court of Canada the final Canadian court of appeal. He won the acceptance of a new apportionment of taxes in 1956 and, in negotiation with President Truman, laid the foundation for a US–Canada agreement to develop the St Lawrence Seaway.

In 1958, he retired and returned to Quebec City to practise law. He died July 25, 1973.

■ John Diefenbaker

John George Diefenbaker was born at Neustadt, Ont., Sept. 18, 1895. He received his B.A. from the University of Saskatchewan in 1915 and his M.A. one year later.

After the outbreak of World War I, he joined the Canadian Officers' Training Corps, and served overseas as a lieutenant with the 105th 'Saskatoon Fusiliers' Regiment from 1916 to 1917.

Returning to Saskatchewan, he took his law degree from the University of Saskatchewan in 1919 and established a law practice at Wakaw. He later moved to Prince Albert.

After several unsuccessful attempts to gain a seat, first in the federal, then in Saskatchewan's provincial parliament, Diefenbaker was finally elected to the House of Commons in 1940. He was a candidate for leadership of the Progressive Conservative Party at the 1942 and 1948 conventions, but did not win the nomination until Dec. 14, 1956.

The PCs won the election of June 10, 1957 by a slim margin, and on June 21, John Diefenbaker officially became prime minister. A year later, he called an election, hoping to turn his Conservative minority government into a clear majority. He was overwhelmingly successful, winning 208 of the 265 seats in the Mar. 31, 1958, election. He fared less well in the 1962 election, when only 116 PCs were elected, and in the general election of 1963, a Liberal victory relegated Diefenbaker to the role of Opposition leader. Diefenbaker remained Conservative leader until Sept. 1967, when he was replaced by Robert Stanfield.

The Diefenbaker years (1957–63) saw the passage of the Canadian Bill of Rights, a "roads-to- resources" program to encourage the development of northern resources, legislation providing support for agriculture, encouragement of technical training and improved health and welfare programs. Regional development was emphasized by significant public works such as construction of the South Saskatchewan Dam, and simultaneous translation was introduced in the House of Commons.

Diefenbaker died Aug. 16, 1979, at his home in Rockliffe Park, Ottawa.

■ Lester Pearson

Lester Bowles Pearson was born at Newtonbrook, Ont., on Apr. 23, 1897. He took his B.A. at the University of Toronto and his M.A. at Oxford University.

After serving overseas in World War I, he became a history professor at the University of Toronto, where he taught from 1924–1928. He joined Canada's foreign service in 1928, became Canada's ambassador to the UN in 1945, was appointed under-secretary of state for external affairs in 1946 and accepted the invitations of King and St Laurent to become minister of external affairs in Sept. 1948.

In 1956, following the Anglo-French-Israeli invasion of Egypt, Pearson's work at the United Nations helped establish a UN Emergency Force which kept peace on the Israeli–Egyptian border for the next decade. His settlement of the Suez crisis brought him the Nobel Peace Prize in 1957—the only time a Canadian has been so honoured.

Pearson was chosen leader of the Liberal party Jan. 15, 1958. In the general election of

Apr. 8, 1963, the Liberals won 129 seats in the House of Commons, and Pearson became the leader of a minority government.

In the 1965 election, the Liberals made slight gains, but were still short of a majority. Pearson announced his resignation in Dec. 1967 and, in Apr. 1968, was succeeded by Pierre Trudeau.

Under Pearson, the old age pension was extended and a national health plan created. He secured the adoption of a national flag and established the Royal Commission on Bilingualism and Biculturalism.

Though he retired in 1968, his international reputation prompted the World Bank to commission him to prepare a report on international aid programs.

He died in Ottawa, Dec. 27, 1972.

■ Pierre Trudeau

Pierre Elliott Trudeau was born in Montreal on Oct. 18, 1919. He attended the University of Montreal, Harvard University, Université de Paris and the London School of Economics. He was called to the Quebec bar in 1943. From 1949–51, he was a member of the Privy Council staff in Ottawa. In 1950, he co-founded the magazine _Cité Libre_. From 1952–62, he practised law and was a journalist and broadcaster in Montreal. From 1962–65, he was a law professor at the University of Montreal.

First elected to the House of Commons in 1965, Trudeau was named justice minister in Lester Pearson's cabinet in 1967. The following year, he won the Liberal leadership and became prime minister Apr. 19, 1968. In the general election of the same year, the Liberals won a solid majority.

During his first four years in power, Trudeau faced the "FLQ Crisis"—the kidnapping of British diplomat James Cross and Quebec cabinet minister Pierre Laporte by the radical separatist organization Front de libération du Québec. (Laporte was later murdered.) In response he invoked the War Measures Act, a statute giving the state broad powers of arrest and detention.

In the general election of 1972, Trudeau returned to power with a minority government. In 1974, he regained a majority.

In the general election of 1979, the Progressive Conservatives under Joe Clark won a narrow victory and were able to form a minority government. Trudeau announced his intention to retire, but when the Clark government fell later that year, Trudeau led the Liberals in the election and won a majority on Feb. 18, 1980.

Trudeau's final term in office was devoted to constitutional reform which, for the first time, allowed Canada's Parliament to amend the constitution without appeal to the UK government. A constitutionally-entrenched Charter of Rights and Freedoms was also introduced.

Trudeau's introduction of a National Energy Program led to bitter disputes between the federal government and the energy-producing provinces, particularly Alberta. The NEP was aimed at increasing Canadian control of the oil industry, promoting energy self-sufficiency and generating more federal revenues in the energy sector.

During his final year as prime minister Trudeau launched a world peace initiative, visiting more than 40 world leaders to appeal for peace and an end to the nuclear arms race.

In June of 1984, Trudeau resigned. He was succeeded by John Turner and left politics, eventually joining a Montreal law firm.

Trudeau died Sept. 28, 2000 at his home in Montreal.

■ Joe Clark

Charles Joseph "Joe" Clark was born at High River, Alta., on June 5, 1939. He was educated at the University of Alberta.

Clark was first elected to the House of Commons in 1972. In 1976 he became leader of the Progressive Conservative party and, in the general election of 1979, won enough seats to form a minority government. At 39, Clark was Canada's youngest prime minister. But his minority government fell in Dec. 1979 on a vote of non-confidence on its proposed budget. In the Feb. 1980 election that followed, the Liberals returned to power.

At a national general meeting of the Cons-

ervative party in Jan. 1983, Clark received the support of only two-thirds of the delegates and called for a national party leadership convention. In June 1983, Clark lost the leadership to Brian Mulroney on the 4th ballot. He remained an MP and, when Mulroney became prime minister in 1984, Clark joined the cabinet as secretary of state for external affairs.

In 1991, he was appointed as minister responsible for constitutional affairs and given the task of succeeding where the Meech Lake Accord had failed. Late 1991 and the first half of 1992 were marked by weeks of cross-country constitutional negotiations under Clark's guidance. In August 1992 the Charlottetown Accord—an agreement to amend the Constitution Act of 1982—was agreed upon by all first ministers. The text of the agreement was presented to Canadians and a national referendum was held on Oct. 26, 1992, on the issue of whether or not to approve the deal. The agreement was rejected by the majority of voters across the country.

Clark left federal politics after the 1993 election. In 1998, he re-entered public life when Jean Charest vacated the federal Conservative leadership to run in Quebec's provincial election. On Nov. 14, 1998, Clark was re-elected federal Conservative leader.

■ John Turner

John Napier Turner was born at Richmond, Surrey, England on June 7, 1929. He attended the University of British Columbia, Oxford University and Université de Paris. He was called to the bar in England in 1953 and the bar in Quebec in 1954. He lectured for a time in the Faculty of Commerce at Sir George Williams University.

First elected to the House of Commons in 1962, Turner entered Lester Pearson's cabinet in 1965. He became minister of consumer and corporate affairs in 1967. In 1968, he was a candidate for the Liberal leadership, finishing 3rd on the final ballot.

In 1968, Turner was appointed minister of justice in Pierre Trudeau's cabinet. In 1972, he became minister of finance, a post he held until his resignation in Sept. 1975. In Feb. 1976 he left politics and joined a Toronto law firm.

Turner remained in private practice until Trudeau's retirement in 1984, when he successfully ran for leader of the Liberal party and became prime minister on June 30, though he did not have a seat in the House of Commons. He dissolved Parliament July 9, and in the ensuing general election the Liberals were overwhelmingly defeated by the Progressive Conservatives.

As leader of the Opposition, Turner used the Liberal majority in the Senate to block passage of the Conservatives' free trade legislation and force an election on the issue in 1988. The Conservatives won the election and were able to form another majority government.

Early in 1989, Turner announced plans to step down as leader; in June 1990, he was succeeded by Jean Chrétien.

■ Brian Mulroney

Martin Brian Mulroney was born at Baie Comeau, Que., Mar. 20, 1939. He attended St. Francis Xavier University and Université Laval. Called to the bar of Quebec in 1965, Mulroney practised law in Montreal. In 1976, he joined the Iron Ore Company of Canada as executive vice-president and was elected company president the following year.

Mulroney made an unsuccessful bid for the Progressive Conservative party leadership in 1976. In 1983 he ran again, defeating the incumbent leader, Joe Clark, on the 4th ballot.

A by-election for the Maritime riding of Central Nova brought Mulroney into

Parliament as leader of the Opposition. In the general election of 1984, he led the Conservatives to victory, winning the largest number of seats (211) in Canadian history.

Mulroney's major initiatives between 1984 and 1988 were the Meech Lake Accord—a package of constitutional changes designed to end Quebec's boycott of the 1982 constitutional reform—and the negotiation of a free trade agreement with the United States.

In 1988, with free trade the central election issue, Mulroney won a second majority government. The free trade agreement subsequently received final approval and took effect in 1989.

His term from 1988 to 1993 was marked by intense negotiations to bring about a new constitutional agreement to replace the Meech Lake Accord which was not ratified by all provinces by the June 1990 deadline. Agreement was reached amongst federal and provincial officials in what became known as the Charlottetown Accord, but the proposals were rejected in a national referendum held on Oct. 26, 1992.

The Conservatives under Mulroney continued their free trade initiative and finalized a North American free trade deal (NAFTA) with the US and Mexico.

Mulroney announced his intention to retire in February 1993 and on June 25, 1993 he was replaced by Kim Campbell, newly-elected leader of the Conservative party.

■ Kim Campbell

Avril Phaedra (Kim) Campbell was born Mar. 10, 1947 in Port Alberni, BC. She attended the University of British Columbia, earning an honours degree in political science.

After an academic career in BC, she studied law at UBC. In September 1985, she joined BC Premier William Bennett's office as a policy advisor. In May 1986, Campbell ran in the provincial election and won a seat in the legislature, representing Vancouver/Point Grey. She served in the provincial legislature until October 1988 when she resigned her seat to contest the federal riding of Vancouver Centre. An ardent defender of free trade, Campbell joined Prime Minister Mulroney's cabinet with the Indian Affairs and Northern Development portfolio.

In 1990 Campbell became the first woman promoted to the Attorney General and Justice post. In January of 1993 she became Canada's first female defence minister and a candidate in the Conservative leadership contest that year. On June 13, 1993, she was elected leader on the second ballot; on June 25, she was sworn in as Canada's first female prime minister. In the election of Oct. 1993, however, the Conservatives lost all but two seats in the House of Commons. Campbell's tenure as prime minister ended on Nov. 4; she stepped down as federal Conservative leader on Dec. 14, 1993.

■ Jean Chrétien

Jean Chrétien was born in Shawinigan, Quebec, on Jan. 11, 1934. He studied law at Laval University and was called to the bar of Quebec in 1958.

Chrétien was first elected to the House of Commons in 1963 and after re-election in 1965 served as parliamentary secretary to the prime minister (1965) and the finance minister (1966). He became minister of national revenue in 1968; after the June 1968 election, he became responsible for Indian affairs and northern development. In 1974, he was appointed president of the treasury board; in 1976, he served as minister of industry, trade and commerce. In 1977, he was named finance minister; in 1980 he became justice minister and attorney general and also served as minister of state for social development. Chrétien played an important role in patriating the Constitution. In 1982, he became minister of energy, mines and resources; in 1984, he became deputy prime minister and secretary of state for external affairs.

In 1984, Chrétien ran second to John Turner in the Liberal leadership race; in the 1984 election, Chrétien kept his seat in the House of Commons. In 1986, when Liberals confirmed Turner's leadership at a party convention, Chrétien resigned his seat to practice law.

In 1990, Turner resigned as Liberal leader

after losing a second election to the Conservatives, and Chrétien won the Liberal leadership. He subsequently won a by-election in Beausejour and took his seat in the House of Commons as leader of the Opposition.

Chrétien inherited a party that was disorganized and almost bankrupt. His support for the Charlottetown Accord in 1992 cost him support among Quebec's nationalists. Nonetheless, in the election of Oct. 25, 1993, Chrétien led the Liberals to victory over the ruling Conservatives. He was re-elected in his old riding of Saint-Maurice and was sworn in as Canada's 20th prime minister.

The new government inherited a troubled economy. In 1993, Canada suffered from high unemployment, a large national debt and an alarming annual deficit. Chrétien chose to limit or cut federal programs, including subsidies to the provinces, and to eliminate the national deficit. Chrétien also chose to keep the Goods and Services Tax, despite an election pledge to abolish it.

In his first term, Chrétien also struggled with Quebec's separatists. In 1993, the federal Liberals won only 20 seats in Quebec compared to the 54 seats won by the Bloc Québécois. In the Quebec referendum of Oct. 30, 1995, the federalists sustained the barest margin of victory over the separatists, and Chrétien's role in the federalist campaign was criticized.

In foreign policy, Chrétien stressed international trade. He led a series of well-publicized "Team Canada" missions around the globe and endorsed the North American Free Trade Agreement (NAFTA), which came into force on Jan. 1, 1994. Chrétien also established a cordial relationship with US President Bill Clinton.

In the election of June 2, 1997, Chrétien led his party to another victory, but the number of Liberal seats in the House of Commons fell from 177 to 155. The government continued the economic policies of its first term and, in 1998, the government declared a budget surplus for the first time in 25 years. In 1999, the Chrétien government committed Canadian troops to NATO's war against the Serbs in the Balkans.

In the election of Nov. 27, 2000, Chrétien led the Liberals to a third consecutive victory at the polls.

GOVERNMENT OF CANADA

Canada is an independent, self-governing democracy whose form of government is a constitutional monarchy. There are three types of government power: legislative, executive and judicial. In Canada the legislative and executive powers are joined, while the judiciary remains separate. The executive proposes legislation, presents budgets and implements laws; the legislature adopts laws and votes on recommendations for taxes or other revenue; the judiciary interprets the laws.

■ The Monarchy

The Queen (crowned Queen Elizabeth II on June 2, 1953) is Canada's official head of state through which the entire authority of the government is set in motion and in whose name laws are enacted. The Queen's role is set out in the Constitution Act, (formerly the British North America Act, 1867), and that same act gives the monarch ultimate authority over Canada's armed forces.

In practice, however, the Queen has little or no part to play in Canadian government. She appoints the Governor General, but does so only on the prime minister's recommendation. Once appointed, it is the Governor General who performs the monarch's duties, and these duties have been mainly ceremonial for many years. Only during royal visits does the Queen carry out those functions normally performed in her name by the Governor General, such as the opening of Parliament.

■ The Governor General

The Governor General is selected by the prime minister and formally appointed by the Queen to act as her representative in Canada. The appointment is usually for five years but has sometimes been extended to seven.

Bills passed in the House of Commons and Senate do not become law until the Governor General has given them royal assent. The Governor General executes all orders-in-council and other state documents, appoints all superior court judges (on the advice of Cabinet) and summons, prorogues and dis-

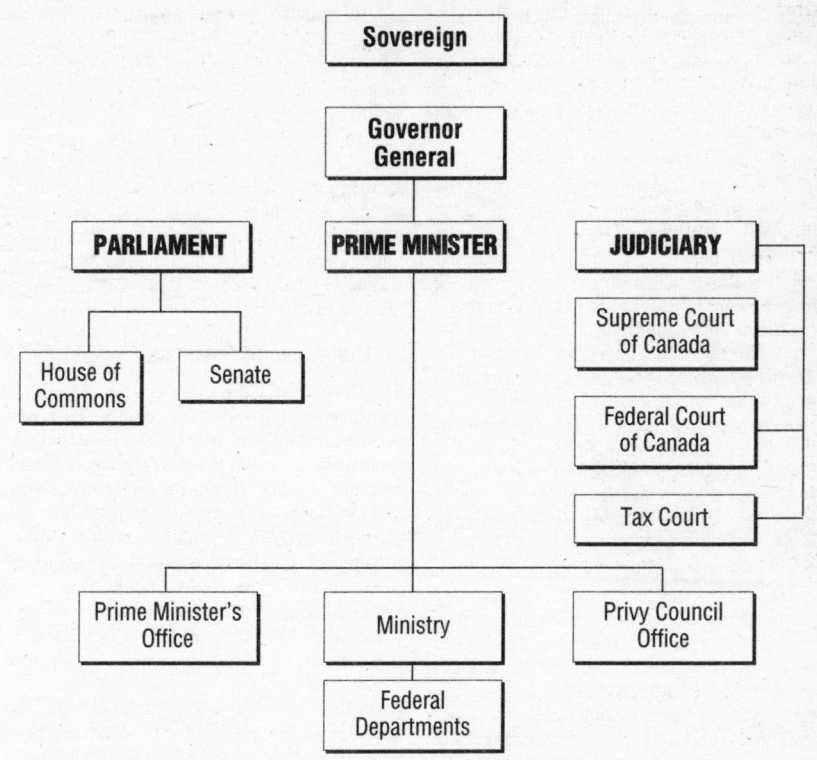

Sovereign → Governor General → PARLIAMENT (House of Commons, Senate), PRIME MINISTER, JUDICIARY (Supreme Court of Canada, Federal Court of Canada, Tax Court) → Prime Minister's Office, Ministry (Federal Departments), Privy Council Office

solves Parliament (on the advice of the prime minister). Also, the Governor General invites the leader of the political party with the most support in the House of Commons to form a government. Thus, that leader becomes prime minister.

The Imperial Conferences of 1926 and 1930 established that the Governor General was not the representative or agent of the British government and should act only on the advice of the Canadian prime minister and Cabinet. Therefore, the Governor General is obliged to respect the principle of responsible government and to follow the wishes of Canada's elected representatives. Because of this, the role of the Governor General has become largely symbolic, with duties that are chiefly ceremonial.

Three members of the royal family have held the post: the Marquess of Lorne (1878–83), the Duke of Connaught (1911–16) and the Earl of Athlone (1940–46).

The first Canadian Governor General was Vincent Massey (1952–59).

The Legislature

Canada's legislature or Parliament consists of the Queen, an upper house, known as the Senate, and the House of Commons. Senators are appointed by the Governor General on the advice of the prime minister; the seats in the Senate are distributed on a regional basis; originally, there were 72 senators, but through the years the Senate has increased as the number of provinces and the population have grown. In 1975 the Senate was increased to 104 members; in 1990 Prime Minister Brian Mulroney employed a never-before-used section of the Constitution Act to increase the number temporarily to 112. The House of Commons is an elected assembly in which each member represents one of 301 electoral districts distributed according to population.

■ The Senate

The Senate is the Upper House of the

Canadian Parliament through which all legislation must pass before it becomes law. Its members, appointed by the Governor General on the recommendation of the prime minister, hold office until age 75. (If appointed before June 1965 they hold office for life).

After 1999, there were 105 Senate seats apportioned on a regional basis: 24 from the Maritime provinces (Nova Scotia, 10; New Brunswick, 10; Prince Edward Island, 4); 24 from Quebec; 24 from Ontario; 24 from the Western provinces (Manitoba, 6; Saskatchewan, 6; Alberta, 6; British Columbia, 6); 6 from Newfoundland; 1 each from the Yukon, Northwest Territories and Nunavut.

To be eligible for Senate appointment, a person must be a Canadian citizen, at least 30 years old, a resident of the province for which he or she is appointed, possess land in that province with an unencumbered value of $4,000 and have a net estate of $4,000. A Senator for Quebec must either be resident in the division for which he or she is appointed, or have property qualification there.

A Speaker of the Senate, who is appointed by the Governor General on the prime minister's advice, presides over the Upper House's proceedings. By custom, the appointment to the Speaker's chair alternates between anglophone and francophone members. The Speaker decides questions of privilege and points of order. The Speaker also represents the Senate when receiving parliamentary and foreign dignitaries.

Technically, the Senate's legislative powers are equal to those of the House of Commons with two restrictions: first, on certain constitutional amendments, the Senate may delay resolutions of the House of Commons for up to 180 days, but cannot defeat them; second, the Senate cannot initiate money bills.

In practice, however, the Senate's chief role is to provide technical reviews of legislation proposed in the House of Commons rather than to initiate political action. These reviews are done by Senate committees, which inspect each bill clause-by-clause and hear evidence from groups or individuals who may be affected by the proposed legislation.

Historically, the Senate rarely used its powers to impede legislation originating from the elected House of Commons. From 1984 to 1990, however, the Liberal-dominated Senate attempted several times to stall or block legislation approved by the Conservative majority in the House of Commons. In 1990, when the Senate blocked his government's goods and services tax, Mulroney temporarily increased the size of the Senate and added eight new Conservatives, ensuring that the measure would be made law.

In recent years, there have been repeated calls, especially from the West, for constitutional reform which would include an elected Senate with more representation from the Western provinces and Newfoundland. Plans for discussions leading to a Senate overhaul are now part of other constitutional discussions.

■ The House of Commons

The House of Commons is Canada's 301-member elected federal assembly. Its members are chosen in general elections held at least once every five years. By-elections are held if a member dies or resigns between general elections.

All bills governing matters within federal jurisdiction must be passed by a majority of members of Parliament to become law.

Members of Parliament usually belong to a political party and will normally vote with that party on any proposed legislation. Occasionally, members will break with their party on a vote and will sometimes leave the party they were affiliated with when elected to sit as independents or to join another political party within the House. Members of Parliament can also be elected as independent candidates who do not belong to a political party.

The **prime minister** is the leader of the political party able to command the support of a majority of the members of the House of Commons. If no party holds a clear majority of seats, a "minority government" is formed, usually led by the party with the most seats in Parliament, provided it has enough support from the other parties to enable it to pass legislation.

When the House of Commons is in session it convenes at two o'clock daily and 11 o'clock on Fridays when the Speaker of the House takes the chair. After the mace is laid on the table in front of the Speaker and the daily prayer is read, business commences. Members of the government sit to the Speaker's right and the Opposition sits on the left. The leaders of other opposition parties sit on the left farther away from the Speaker's chair.

The Speaker of the House, who is elected

from and by the members after a general election, presides over the legislature. This official decides all procedural questions and maintains order. The Speaker is impartial at all times, enforcing the House's rules without regard to party loyalty. The Speaker also chairs the Board of Internal Economy, which controls the House of Commons staff and its annual budget of $235 million. Some Speakers resign their party membership and run as independents in subsequent elections to maintain their impartial standing in the House.

An important feature of Parliament is the daily question period at which time members question Cabinet ministers about their policies and actions. But most of Parliament's time is spent discussing proposed legislation introduced as "bills." Any member may introduce a bill, although this is usually done by a member of Cabinet. After readings in the House and detailed examination in committee, the bill will go for "third reading" in the House and if passed, will be forwarded to the Senate.

The Leader of the Government in the House of Commons—who is a Cabinet minister but not the prime minister—shepherds the government's bills through the legislature. The House Leader of the Government works with the Leader of the Government in the Senate to coordinate the smooth passage of bills there. The House Leader of the Government also keeps Opposition members informed about all legislative matters.

Before a vote on a bill occurs, the party whips—who are drawn from their respective caucuses—ensure that their party's members appear in the legislature or at committee meetings to vote. Party whips rely more on persuasion than coercion to ensure member attendance; occasionally whips offer minor rewards (e.g., trips and committee memberships) to party colleagues to ensure that they vote. In 2001, the Liberal government appointed the first woman—Marlene Catterall of Ontario West—to the post of Chief Government Whip in the House of Commons.

When a major piece of legislation introduced by the government is defeated in the House of Commons, the government is obliged to resign. The Governor General may then call on the leader of the Opposition to form a government but, in most cases, will call a general election so that the electorate can decide which party has the most public support for its policies.

The Executive

■ The Prime Minister

The prime minister is the pre-eminent figure in Canadian politics. The power and authority of the office come from the fact that the prime minister is the leader of the party (or group of parties) that has control of, if not a clear majority of seats in the House of Commons, at least more seats than any of the other parties. The prime minister is an elected member of parliament as well as national party leader and as such has a mandate to govern via programs and policies and to speak on behalf of Canada.

The prime minister has control over appointments, including appointing (and shifting) cabinet members, senior staff in the public service and parliamentary secretaries; and appointing senators, judges, lieutenant governors, privy councillors, provincial administrators, and speakers of the senate. In addition, the prime minister recommends to the monarchy the appointment of the governor general. The prime minister has the authority to dissolve parliament and can therefore control the timing of an election. The prime minister also controls the organization of government, including the power to: create or shut down crown corporations; create, modify or merge cabinet portfolios and bureaucratic agencies; and appoint royal commissions.

■ The Cabinet

The Cabinet is a group of government ministers who, chosen and led by the prime minister, determine executive policies and are responsible for them to the House of Commons. Cabinet members are usually given responsibility for heading specific areas of the government such as finance or foreign policy and will introduce legislation pertaining to them in the House of Commons. They will also explain or defend government actions when questioned in the House.

Cabinet ministers are generally chosen from members of the government's party in the House of Commons, although Senators are sometimes appointed to provide Cabinet representation from all parts of the country. When Senators join the Cabinet they do not usually head a government department because a Senator is constitutionally forbidden to introduce tax or "money bill" legislation.

There are five categories of cabinet ministers:

1. Department Ministers who assume responsibility for running one or more government departments.

2. Ministers with special parliamentary responsibilities.

3. Ministers without portfolios who do not have responsibility for running a department and are often appointed to balance regional representation in the Cabinet.

4. Ministers of state for designated purposes who formulate and develop new policies outside normal departmental responsibilities.

5. Other ministers of state who may assist departmental ministers, though the departmental minister remains legally responsible for the duties and functions performed by the minister of state.

■ The Privy Council Office

The Privy Council Office is directed by the senior member of the public service, the Clerk of the Privy Council, who also serves as the Secretary to the Cabinet. As part of the executive branch of government, the Office staffs the Cabinet secretariat and provides services to ensure the smooth functioning of the Cabinet and Cabinet meetings. In its advisory capacity, the Privy Council Office advises the Prime Minister on government appointments, relations with Parliament and the Monarchy, the roles and responsibilities of ministers and the organization of government. The Office assists in the co-ordination of policy, ensuring that new proposals are compatible both with existing policy and the government's objectives. During a transition period between governments, the Privy Council Office assists in the winding down of outgoing administrations and the startup of the newly-elected government.

The Privy Council Office's primary responsibilities are to ensure the smooth functioning of the machinery of government and the decision-making process, provide support to the Cabinet, monitor developments throughout the government, and act as a broker to resolve governmental problems.

■ The Treasury Board

The Treasury Board is a committee of the Privy Council that reviews planned expenditures and programs proposed by the various government departments, and assigns priorities to each. The Board is responsible for preparing a long-range and comprehensive fiscal plan that projects government income and expenses for up to four years; it also prepares operational plans for departmental programs. The Board's estimates of the costs of existing programs, major statutory payments (such as transfer payments) and public debt charges form the basis of the Main Estimates, which are tabled by the first of March each year for review by various House committees.

The Treasury Board is also responsible for administrative policy; organization of the public service; and financial, expenditure and personnel management. In 1988, the Board was also given responsibility for the policies and programs of the Official Languages Act. The Board's Secretariat negotiates collective agreements with the federal public service, acting as employer on the government's behalf.

■ Departments

Legislation and government policies are administered through departments, departmental branches and corporations, corporations owned or controlled by the government, special boards and various commissions and advisory bodies. Departments and departmental corporations are accountable to a Cabinet minister and ultimately to Parliament; they perform research, administrative, advisory, supervisory or regulatory roles. Crown corporations usually operate in a competitive or commercial environment and some are accountable to Parliament through a minister as well.

The Canadian Judiciary

■ The Supreme Court of Canada

The Supreme Court of Canada is Canada's highest court of law. It was created by federal statute in 1875. Originally, Supreme Court decisions could be appealed to a special tribunal in England, but such appeals were abolished for criminal cases in 1933 and for civil cases in 1949. Since then, the Supreme Court of Canada has been the court of last resort for every case—criminal or civil—commenced in a Canadian court.

The Supreme Court has jurisdiction to hear appeals from the courts of appeal of each province, as well as from the Federal Court of Canada. The Court is also empowered to consider questions referred to it by the federal cabinet, and to rule on the legality of bills submitted by the government.

The Constitution Act, 1982, with its new Canadian Charter of Rights and Freedoms, has expanded the role of the courts in general, and of the Supreme Court in particular. Though it has always been within the power of Canadian courts to declare laws or other government actions invalid, this power had narrow limits prior to 1982. Legislation could only be struck down if the government introducing it had exceeded its legislative authority as defined in the Constitution Act, 1867 (the BNA Act). In other words, the federal government was not permitted to legislate on matters within provincial legislative authority, and the provincial governments were not permitted to legislate on matters within federal legislative authority. As long as the legislation satisfied that test, it was valid.

But since the Constitution Act became law in 1982, the courts have had the power to strike down legislation or invalidate other government actions if they infringe or deny any of the fundamental rights and freedoms recognized by the Charter of Rights and Freedoms. This new power has made Supreme Court judges the watchdogs of Parliament and, ultimately, the guardians of our constitutionally-guaranteed rights. As the highest court in the land, it is the Supreme Court of Canada that has the final word on whether laws violate the Constitution.

The Supreme Court consists of 9 judges, including the Chief Justice. Three of the judges must be appointed from Quebec. By convention (although it is not legally required) 3 have usually been appointed from Ontario, 2 from the West and one from Atlantic Canada. All judges are appointed and paid by the federal government, and may hold office until age 75.

■ Federal Court of Canada

This Court consists of a trial division and a court of appeal and has jurisdiction over a small range of specialized areas such as admiralty law, income tax, patents and customs. Once called the Exchequer Court, the Federal Court is administered by the federal government.

■ Appellate Courts

When a decision of the provincial superior courts is to be appealed, these courts hear the appeal and decide upon it. An appeal is not a new trial; there are rarely any witnesses called and the judges do not rehear the whole case. Instead, they examine written transcripts of the trial and listen to legal arguments presented by the parties' lawyers. The appellate courts are provincial institutions and are called either the Court of Appeal, the Supreme Court Appeal Division or Appellate Division; the judges are appointed by the federal government.

■ Superior Court of Original Jurisdiction

This is the highest court at the provincial level, with jurisdiction to hear all civil and criminal cases, unless a statute specifically says otherwise. The name of the superior court differs among provinces. It can be called either the Court of Queen's Bench, the High Court of Justice or the Supreme Court Trial Division. The judges of these courts are appointed and paid by the federal government.

■ District or County Courts

These trial courts hear all but the most serious criminal matters and civil matters up to a certain dollar value. The judges of these courts are also appointed by the federal government.

■ Provincial Courts

This is the lowest rung of the judicial ladder. The jurisdiction of the provincial courts is limited by statute to the less serious criminal matters and civil cases involving relatively small sums of money. These judges are appointed and paid by the province in which they serve.

■ Federal and Provincial Legislative Authority

Because Canada is a federal state, legislative powers are divided between 2 levels of government: federal and provincial. (Municipal governments only exercise powers delegated to them by the provincial government).

Each level of government has a distinct sphere of authority. With a few exceptions, neither level is permitted to encroach on the legislative authority of the other.

The Constitution Act, 1867 (formerly called the British North America Act, 1867), lists the classes of subject over which the federal and provincial governments have exclusive authority. The federal government, in addition to a general power to make laws for the "peace, order and good government of Canada," has exclusive power in a number of areas including criminal law, unemployment insurance, postal service, regulation of trade, external relations, money and banking, transportation, citizenship, Indian affairs and defence. Matters exclusively within provincial legislative authority include property and civil rights, administration of justice, education, health and welfare, municipal institutions and matters of a merely local or private nature.

Many of the subject classes set out in the Constitution Act, 1867, are broadly worded, and considerable debate has arisen over which level of government has authority to pass certain laws. Confusion has also arisen over the proper distribution of powers to regulate matters that could not have been foreseen by the Fathers of Confederation, such as air travel, radio and television broadcasting, etc. These difficulties have led to long political debates and frequently to court challenges which arise when a person adversely affected by a particular law claims that the law is invalid because it is *ultra vires*—beyond the powers of the level of government that enacted it. Prior to the passing of the Constitution Act, 1982, only statutes found to be *ultra vires* could be declared inoperative by the Constitution. Now, there is an additional restraint on the federal parliament and the provincial legislatures to comply with constitutional provisions, including the Canadian Charter of Rights and Freedoms.

■ The Provincial Governments

Canada's provinces have a system of government which parallels that of the federal government in several ways. A premier, like the prime minister, leads the government by virtue of being leader of the party with the most support in the provincial legislature and forms a Cabinet from the elected members of the governing party. Members of a provincial legislature, like members of the federal Parliament, represent constituencies and approve legislation within their constitutional jurisdiction. A lieutenant-governor, like the Governor General, gives royal assent to the laws passed by the legislature.

The major difference between the provincial and federal systems is that the provinces have no equivalent body to Canada's Senate.

■ Government in the Yukon, Northwest Territories and Nunavut

The Yukon, Northwest Territories and Nunavut are governed by elected representatives. Although the administration of each territory is technically in the hands of a commissioner appointed by the federal government, in practice, the commissioners' role has become much like that of the provincial lieutenant-governors' in that they follow the wishes of the territories elected representatives when exercising their authority.

In the Northwest Territories, the legislature consists of 14 elected members who run for office as independents rather than as members of political parties. This assembly selects the territory's political executives: a premier, who must win more than 50 per cent of the vote, and five other cabinet ministers.

In Nunavut, the legislature consists of 19 elected members who also run for office as independents rather than as members of political parties. The territory's executive, which is drawn from this assembly, consists of a premier and seven cabinet ministers.

Yukon has a 17-member legislative assembly which features political parties. The leader of the party supported by a majority of the assembly's elected representatives is named government leader. Executive power is in the hands of an executive council, which functions like a provincial cabinet. Its members are appointed by Yukon's commissioner on the advice of the government leader.

In the territories, the elected bodies have jurisdiction over such areas as education, housing, social services and renewable resources.

In 1990, the Northwest Territories established six aboriginal languages (Dogrib, Chipewyan, Gwich'in, Cree, Slavey and Inuktitut) as Official Languages, in addition to English and French.

■ Mechanics of Government

Formation of Government: General elections to choose House of Commons members occur at least every five years. But they may take place more often if the prime minister decides to call an election or if the governing party loses the support of the majority of members of the House.

Following an election, the Governor General calls upon the leader of the party with the greatest House of Commons support to become prime minister. This is almost always the leader of the party with the most seats in the House but, under unusual circumstances, it could be the leader of another party which is able to gain majority support in Parliament.

The prime minister selects the cabinet, usually from members of his party in the House of Commons. Formally, the prime minister and cabinet act as advisors to the Governor General. In practice, however, they wield executive power and the Governor General's role is mainly ceremonial.

Passage of Legislation: To become law, proposed legislation (known as bills) must be passed by a majority of members in both the House of Commons and the Senate and must then be given royal assent by the Governor General. Most bills are introduced by members of the government in the House of Commons. Typically, a bill is given three "readings" in the House. The first reading is simply to introduce the bill. The second reading is accompanied by debate on the principle of the bill. The bill is then voted on and, if approved, is sent to a House committee composed of representatives of all parties to be considered clause-by-clause. The committee prepares a report and submits it to the House of Commons along with any proposed amendments. These amendments, plus any others moved by any member of Parliament, are debated and usually voted on. A motion is then brought for the bill to be given third reading. If the vote is favorable, the bill is then introduced in the Senate where it undergoes a similar process. After a bill has been approved by both Houses, the Governor General gives it royal assent in a ceremony that takes place in the Senate chamber.

Defeat of a Government: Between elections, a government can be forced to resign if it is defeated in a vote on a major government bill. When this happens the government is considered to have lost the support of the majority of Parliament's elected representatives. This typically occurs only when the party in power has formed a minority government—that is, if it holds more seats than any other single party but fewer seats than the combined Opposition parties. This last happened federally in 1979 when a minority Conservative government, elected earlier that year, introduced a budget which was defeated by the combined votes of the Liberal and New Democratic Party members in the House. Parliament was dissolved, an election was called and the Liberals regained power.

■ The Constitution of Canada

Canada's constitution consists of written documents and unwritten conventions. The written constitution is embodied in the Constitution Acts 1867–1982. The 1867 legislation (originally titled the British North America Act) was a British statute that established a federal state with a Parliament modelled on the British system. That Act assembled the colonies of Nova Scotia, New Brunswick and Canada (Ontario and Quebec) into the "Dominion of Canada," created a federal government in Ottawa, and divided the powers of government between Ottawa and the provinces.

The BNA Act gave Ottawa broad jurisdiction over internal matters, including unlimited powers of taxation, while allowing the provinces only a narrow field of local control. In general, the Canadian constitution of the late 19th century was a centralist document.

Under the BNA Act, Britain still had the power to veto Canadian laws or to enact statutes affecting Canada. But the British had no desire to raise revenue in Canada, for example, or to tax Canadians directly. This approach extended to trade and tariffs. Gradually, the practice was established that where money was involved, even in trade treaties, Canada would determine its own policy.

The same was not true of political foreign policy. When Britain declared war on Germany in 1914, Canada, as part of the British Empire, was automatically at war. During this period, British courts also interpreted Canadian statutes, especially those involving the division of power between Ottawa and the provinces. Through this process, the constitution's strong centralist thrust was altered to give more authority to the provinces.

The constitution was also adjusted more directly, through amendments. But because the BNA Act was a British statute, Canada could make formal changes to it only with the consent of the British Parliament. Ottawa tended to seek such amendments only when they did not affect provincial powers or when the provinces agreed with the changes. This process worked at least some of the time: 29 times, in fact, between 1870 and 1975. In 1940, for example, unemployment insurance became a federal responsibility through an amendment to the BNA Act.

In 1931, Britain attempted to tidy up relations with Canada and other self-governing dominions within the Commonwealth by passing the Statute of Westminster. The Statute ceded full powers over foreign affairs and trade to Canada. But because the federal and provincial governments could not agree on a method for amending the BNA Act at home, the British Parliament retained ultimate power over Canada's constitution. Until 1949, British courts continued to review Canadian constitutional cases.

From 1927 until 1982, a succession of federal governments attempted to resolve the problem of getting the provinces to agree to an amending formula. These negotiations failed as the provinces used them as a means to gain concessions from Ottawa.

The catalyst in constitutional discussions during the late 20th century has been the province of Quebec, where provincial governments since 1960 have sought to expand the province's jurisdiction. To protect French culture, the Quebec government requested more powers, over culture itself, and over the economy and social institutions.

Ottawa resisted the move under prime ministers Lester Pearson and Pierre Trudeau. Trudeau argued that without a strong central power a country as sprawling and diverse as Canada would be fatally weakened and might disintegrate.

In lengthy negotiations with the provinces, Trudeau was unable to gain agreement on an amending formula, even when he offered increased powers in return. In 1976, the election of the separatist Parti Québécois in Quebec made constitutional compromise even more unlikely and the matter was set aside.

After Quebec's 1980 referendum on the question of sovereignty association was won by the "No" side, constitutional renewal was back on the agenda. However, federal-provincial discussions became mired in disagreement through the summer of 1980. In September, Trudeau announced that the federal government, with the support of only Ontario and New Brunswick, would ask the British parliament to amend the BNA Act to patriate the constitution and establish a Charter of Rights and Freedoms to protect individual liberties. The Charter would also protect minority rights in education and the mobility rights of Canadian citizens, and change the name of the constitution: the BNA Act became the Constitution Act, 1982.

It took 18 months to get the new amendments approved by the Canadian Parliament, resolve the concerns of eight provincial governments, and get the act through the British Parliament. But, in April 1982, the Constitution Act was proclaimed—although the consent of the Quebec government was never given.

The Constitution Act, 1982, consolidated all the previous BNA Acts and added an amending formula and a Charter of Rights and Freedoms. The Charter, which provided for basic democratic rights, also contained a "notwithstanding" clause that allowed Parliament or any provincial legislature to over-ride its provisions.

The amending formula provided for two types of constitutional change: the division of powers between the federal and provincial governments could be modified with the consent of the federal Parliament and seven provincial legislatures in provinces totalling more than 50 percent of the Canadian population; matters such as the composition of the Supreme Court or the status of English or French, however, required unanimous consent. It also stipulated that no amendment could take longer than three years to be ratified by Ottawa and all 10 provinces.

Government of Canada Primary Internet Site

The Canada Site is the official website of the Canadian government. It provides access to information and services about Canada and Canadian governments. The starting point is http://canada.gc.ca/main_e.html, and the information appears in French and English. Across the top of the site, the following web links appear in red:

WHAT'S NEW: This link connects you to an archive of press releases, advisories and reports about politics, health, science, technology, agriculture, business and other issues. The information is organized by date, archive and website. You can find news bulletins in the *Canada Gazette, The Wire* and Statistics Canada's *The Daily*. Web links to calendars list forthcoming government-sponsored events across Canada.

ABOUT CANADA: This links you to sites on Canada's geography, history, institutions, economy, environment, culture and people. "Symbols," for example, connects you to a Department of Canadian Heritage site on national, provincial and historical flags and emblems. Other sites include information on museums, libraries, sports and parks.

ABOUT GOVERNMENT: "Government at a Glance" provides an overview of Canada's federal system including websites for the Queen, the Governor General, Parliament and the Supreme Court. "Other Governments" connects you to the official websites of the provinces, territories, municipalities and international organizations. "Frequently Requested Acts" provides access to federal laws (e.g., the Immigration Act).

PUBLICATIONS: This link connects you to Canadian Government Publishing. You can find specialized books and CD-ROMs listed by subject or title. You can check for recent releases and order them online. (Some publications are free!) The site lists public libraries that carry federal government publications. The "Canadian Library Gateway" allows you to browse through library websites and catalogues across Canada.

E-SERVICES AND FORMS: This connects you to "Interactive Forum," a web page featuring links to questionnaires, notices, e-mail forums and interactive databases. "Shop On-line" links you to sites that allow you to buy videos from the National Film Board or clothing from the Musical Ride Boutique. E-Services and Forms also provides links to commonly requested government forms (e.g., GST/HST remittance forms).

The centre of the Canada Site's home page also features three "Information and Service Gateways":

CANADIANS: This link connects you to a range of public services and information sites for consumers, job seekers, seniors, aboriginals, youth, rural dwellers, new immigrants and Canadians living abroad.

CANADIAN BUSINESS: This links you to sites on business start-ups, taxation, federal regulations, financing, business statistics and analysis, mergers, acquisitions and bankruptcy. Other links connect you to sites on human resource management, exports and imports, technology, research and development. One site advises you on selling goods or services to the government.

NON-CANADIANS: The last gateway links you to "Canada International," a site of interest to tourists, immigrants and foreign investors. Several links connect you to pages that explain Canadian foreign policy and culture to non-Canadians.

A red-and-gold bar on the Canada Site's home page provides more web links, including one to the official website of Prime Minister Jean Chrétien. "Government Contacts" connects you to a search engine at "Government of Canada Employees Directory" and the websites of elected officials at "Members of Parliament." You can even find postal codes through "Postal Code Lookup."

The Canada Site: a world of information at the click of a mouse!

If You're Not on the Internet...

*T*he Government of Canada provides a toll-free telephone inquiry service called 1 (800) O Canada. Operators at **1 (800) 622-6232** will direct callers to a service that will supply the needed information.

FOCUS ON...

Canada's Virtual War Memorials

"Memorials to Canada's War Dead" is part of the official website of Veterans' Affairs Canada. The site commemorates the more than 116,000 Canadians and Newfoundlanders who died in past wars. The site provides information on military campaigns, soldiers and the monuments erected in their memory. Text appears in French and English.

Begin your tour at http://www.vac-acc.gc.ca At the home page, choose "Memorials" and then click your mouse on the following web links:

The Canadian Virtual War Memorial: This link connects you to the Canadian registry of war dead for the First and Second World Wars. A search engine helps you locate information on individual soldiers and the places where they are buried. In some cases, you can see photos and memorabilia that belonged to the soldiers.

Type a name into the search engine. A search for Charles McElwee, for example, turns up one result: a Charles McElwee died on Sept. 2, 1918. Clicking on the surname *McElwee*, however, yields more data about this soldier: He was a corporal serving with the 44th Battalion of the Canadian Infantry (New Brunswick Regiment). His service number was 234434. He was the son of John and Mary McElwee of Donegal, Ireland. Corporal McElwee was 33 when he was killed.

The web page also declares where Corporal McElwee is buried: Vis-en-Artois British Cemetery in Harcourt, France. The web page provides a gravesite number (VI. E. 19) and directions if you plan to visit the cemetery. Clicking on another web link allows you to see a map of the cemetery.

Books Of Remembrance: This link allows you to see individual pages of the six Books of Remembrance. The books record the names of Canada's war dead and are kept in the Peace Tower on Parliament Hill. Three books record the names of Canadian soldiers who died fighting in World War I, World War II and the Korean War. A fourth book records the names of Canadians who died fighting in Britain's colonial wars (i.e., the Nile Expedition and the South African War). A fifth book records the names of Newfoundland's war dead before 1949. The sixth book records the names of merchant mariners who died at sea.

Memorials in Canada: This link connects you to sites on Canada's major monuments, such as the National War Memorial, the Newfoundland National Memorial, the Commonwealth Air Forces Ottawa Memorial, the Halifax Memorial and the Victoria Memorial. Most sites feature photos and text describing the monuments' history and design.

First World War Memorials in Europe: This link connects you to sites on Canada's and Newfoundland's monuments in France and Belgium. The sites commemorate some of the fiercest battles of the war: Beaumont-Hamel, Passchendaele, Sanctuary Wood, Vimy Ridge and others. The text describes the roles our soldiers played and the horrific casualties they suffered. The larger monuments are featured in aerial photos.

Second World War Memorials in Europe: This link connects you to sites about monuments in Western Europe. Although fewer in number than the WWI sites, these web pages also commemorate costly struggles, such as the siege of Monte Cassino (1944), the air war over Malta and the battles in Northwestern Europe (1944–45) following the invasion of Normandy. These monuments commemorate British Commonwealth, rather than exclusively Canadian, sacrifices.

Memorials in Asia and Africa: This link connects you to sites featuring more British Commonwealth monuments where Canadians fought and died: El Alamein (Egypt), Singapore and Pusan (Korea). Although located on the sites of major battles, these monuments commemorate all the Allied soldiers who died in the region throughout the war. The cemetery at Sai Wan Bay commemorates the valiant but doomed Allied defence of Hong Kong in 1941.

Other Sites and Memorials: This link connects you to numerous smaller monuments, including those commemorating Canadian prisoners of war who were murdered by German SS troops in Northwestern Europe in 1944.

"Memorials to Canada's War Dead" is a useful website for students, researchers—and those who simply want to remember.

FOCUS ON...

Canada's Charter of Rights and Freedoms—20 Years Later

On April 17, 1982, the Canadian government patriated the Constitution and introduced a new Canadian Charter of Rights and Freedoms. Queen Elizabeth II and Prime Minister Pierre Trudeau signed the documents into law during a ceremony in Ottawa. The act had major consequences for both the Supreme Court and Canadian governments.

First, the passage of the Constitution Act enhanced the independence of the Supreme Court. The Act requires that any change to the court cannot occur without a constitutional amendment. Changes to the court's composition, for example, require the consent of both Houses of Parliament and every provincial legislature. Changes to the court's decisions require the consent of Parliament and seven provincial legislatures representing at least 50 percent of Canada's population. This degree of consensus ensures the court's independence from Parliament.

Second, the Constitution included the new Canadian Charter of Rights and Freedoms. The Charter aims at protecting the citizen against the state and minorities against parliamentary majorities. The Charter guarantees fundamental freedoms, democratic rights, mobility rights, legal rights, equality rights and language rights. While the inclusion of these rights in the Constitution seemed like a radical step, in 1993, retired Chief Justice Brian Dickson noted that "it is extremely important to recognize that [the advent of the Charter] is one with deep roots in our nation's history…"

Before 1982, the court had ruled on the division of powers between the federal and provincial governments and had struck down laws that violated the division. After 1982, the court also ruled on whether federal and provincial laws were compatible with the Charter—adding the concept of a government's obligation to respect human rights as it exercised power. Thus the court gained the power to strike down laws that violated, for example, freedom of speech or association.

The federal Bill of Rights (1960) which preceded the Charter began the process of formally protecting individual rights, but included only federal laws and was not constitutionally entrenched. In the 22 years following its passage, the court ruled on only 34 cases related to that law. In the 15 years following the Charter's passage, the court ruled on 352 Charter-related cases, in many cases upholding claims and striking down provisions in federal and provincial laws. The court's Charter decisions serve to establish the precedents and interpretations of many of our Charter rights.

The Supreme Court's tendency to uphold individual rights in applying the Charter has led to criticisms that the justices are making policy rather than merely interpreting the law. The justices themselves have countered that (a) the court still respects the tradition of Parliamentary supremacy; (b) Parliament, not the court, made the justices the interpreters of the Charter; and (c) if Parliament strongly objects to a Supreme Court ruling, Parliament can invoke Section 33 of the Charter (the "notwithstanding" clause) to override the decision.

Before the signing of the 1982 Charter, Canadian constitutional scholar William Lederman suggested that "…independent courts and democratic legislatures have been, are, and will be partners and not rivals as preliminary decision-makers in a very complex total process, with heavy demands being made on both institutions." Retired Chief Justice Brian Dickson further noted that "there was more to the adoption of the Charter than simply providing the courts with new responsibilities. The advent of the Charter also reflected a decision on the part of government to subject *itself* to new responsibilities. The focus of the Charter is, after all, government activity, at the federal and provincial levels. …The more successful in crafting laws consistent with this country's values, the less often courts will have to remind a government of its duties."

Text of the Canadian Charter of Rights and Freedoms

Whereas Canada is founded upon principles that recognize the supremacy of God and the rule of law:

Guarantee of Rights and Freedoms

1 The Canadian Charter of Rights and Freedoms guarantees the rights and freedoms set out in it subject only to such reasonable limits prescribed by law as can be demonstrably justified in a free and democratic society.

Fundamental Freedoms

2 Everyone has the following fundamental freedoms: (a) freedom of conscience and religion; (b) freedom of thought, belief, opinion and expression, including freedom of the press and other media of communication; (c) freedom of peaceful assembly; and (d) freedom of association.

Democratic Rights

3 Every citizen of Canada has the right to vote in an election of members of the House of Commons or of a legislative assembly and to be qualified for membership therein.

4 (1) No House of Commons and no legislative assembly shall continue for longer than five years from the date fixed for the return of the writs at a general election of its members. (2) In time of real or apprehended war, invasion or insurrection, a House of Commons may be continued by Parliament and a legislative assembly may be continued by the legislature beyond five years if such continuation is not opposed by the votes of more than one-third of the members of the House of Commons or the legislative assembly, as the case may be.

5 There shall be a sitting of Parliament and of each legislature at least once every twelve months.

Mobility Rights

6 (1) Every citizen of Canada has the right to enter, remain in and leave Canada. (2) Every citizen of Canada and every person who has the status of a permanent resident of Canada has the right (a) to move to and take up residence in any province; and (b) to pursue the gaining of a livelihood in any province. (3) The rights specified in subsection (2) are subject to (a) any laws or practices of general application in force in a province other than those that discriminate among persons primarily on the basis of province of present or previous residence; and (b) any laws providing for reasonable residency requirements as a qualification for the receipt of publicly provided social services. (4) Subsections (2) and (3) do not preclude any law, program or activity that has as its object the amelioration in a province of conditions of individuals in that province who are socially or economically disadvantaged if the rate of employment in that province is below the rate of employment in Canada.

Legal Rights

7 Everyone has the right to life, liberty and security of the person and the right not to be deprived thereof except in accordance with the principles of fundamental justice.

8 Everyone has the right to be secure against unreasonable search or seizure.

9 Everyone has the right not to be arbitrarily detained or imprisoned.

10 Everyone has the right on arrest or detention (a) to be informed promptly of the reasons therefor; (b) to retain and instruct counsel without delay and to be informed of that right; and (c) to have the validity of the detention determined by way of *habeas corpus* and to be released if the detention is not lawful.

11 Any person charged with an offence has the right (a) to be informed without unreasonable delay of the specific offence; (b) to be tried within a reasonable time; (c) not to be compelled to be a witness in proceedings against that person in respect of the offence; (d) to be presumed innocent until proven guilty according to law in a fair and public hearing by an independent

and impartial tribunal; (e) not to be denied reasonable bail without just cause; (f) except in the case of an offence under military law tried before a military tribunal, to the benefit of trial by jury where the maximum punishment for the offence is imprisonment for five years or a more severe punishment; (g) not to be found guilty on account of any act or omission unless, at the time of the act or omission, it constituted an offence under Canadian or international law or was criminal according to the general principles of law recognized by the community of nations; (h) if finally acquitted of the offence, not to be tried for it again and, if finally found guilty and punished for the offence, not to be tried or punished for it again; and (i) if found guilty of the offence and if the punishment for the offence has been varied between the time of commission and the time of sentencing, to the benefit of the lesser punishment.

12 Everyone has the right not to be subjected to any cruel and unusual treatment or punishment.

13 A witness who testifies in any proceedings has the right not to have any incriminating evidence so given used to incriminate that witness in any other proceedings, except in a prosecution for perjury or for the giving of contradictory evidence.

14 A party or witness in any proceedings who does not understand or speak the language in which the proceedings are conducted or who is deaf has the right to the assistance of an interpreter.

■ Equality Rights

15 (1) Every individual is equal before and under the law and has the right to the equal protection and equal benefit of the law without discrimination and, in particular, without discrimination based on race, national or ethnic origin, colour, religion, sex, age or mental or physical disability. (2) Subsection (1) does not preclude any law, program or activity that has as its object the amelioration of conditions of disadvantaged individuals or groups including those that are disadvantaged because of race, national or ethnic origin, colour, religion, sex, age or mental or physical disability.

■ Official Languages of Canada

16 (1) English and French are the official languages of Canada and have equality of status and equal rights and privileges as to their use in all institutions of the Parliament and government of Canada. (2) English and French are the official languages of New Brunswick and have equality of status and equal rights and privileges as to their use in all institutions of the legislature and government of New Brunswick. (3) Nothing in this Charter limits the authority of Parliament or a legislature to advance the equality of status or use of English and French.

17 (1) Everyone has the right to use English or French in any debates and other proceedings of Parliament. (2) Everyone has the right to use English or French in any debates and other proceedings of the legislature of New Brunswick.

18 (1) The statutes, records and journals of Parliament shall be printed and published in English and French and both language versions are equally authoritative. (2) The statutes, records and journals of the legislature of New Brunswick shall be printed and published in English and French and both language versions are equally authoritative.

19 (1) Either English or French may be used by any person in, or in any pleading in or process issuing from, any court established by Parliament. (2) Either English or French may be used by any person in, or in any pleading in or process issuing from, any court of New Brunswick.

20 (1) Any member of the public in Canada has the right to communicate with, and to receive available services from, any head or central office of an institution of the Parliament or government of Canada in English or French, and has the same right with respect to any other office of any such institution where (a) there is a significant demand for communications with and services from that office in such language; or (b) due to the nature of the office, it is reasonable that communications with and services from that office be available in both English and French. (2) Any member of the public in New Brunswick has the right to communicate with, and to receive available services from, any office of an institution of the legislature or government of New Brunswick in English or French.

21 Nothing in sections 16 to 20 abrogates or derogates from any right, privilege or obligation with respect to the English and French languages, or either of them, that exists or is continued by virtue of any other provision of the Constitution of Canada.

22 Nothing in sections 16 to 20 abrogates or derogates from any legal or customary right or privilege acquired or enjoyed either before or after the coming into force of this Charter with respect to any language that is not English or French.

■ Minority Language Educational Rights

23 (1) Citizens of Canada (a) whose first language learned and still understood is that of the English or French linguistic minority population of the province in which they reside, or (b) who have received their primary school instruction in Canada in English or French and reside in a province where the language in which they received that instruction is the language of the English or French linguistic minority population of the province, have the right to have their children receive primary and secondary school instruction in that language in that province. (2) Citizens of Canada of whom any child has received or is receiving primary or secondary school instruction in English or French in Canada, have the right to have all their children receive primary and secondary school instruction in the same language. (3) The right of citizens of Canada under subsections (1) and (2) to have their children receive primary and secondary school instruction in the language of the English or French linguistic minority population of a province (a) applies wherever in the province the number of children of citizens who have such a right is sufficient to warrant the provision to them out of public funds of minority language instruction; and (b) includes, where the number of those children so warrants, the right to have them receive that instruction in minority language educational facilities provided out of public funds.

■ Enforcement

24. (1) Anyone whose rights or freedoms, as guaranteed by this Charter, have been infringed or denied may apply to a court of competent jurisdiction to obtain such remedy as the court considers appropriate and just in the circumstances. (2) Where, in proceedings under subsection (1), a court concludes that evidence was obtained in a manner that infringed or denied any rights or freedoms guaranteed by this Charter, the evidence shall be excluded if it is established that, having regard to all the circumstances, the admission of it in the proceedings would bring the administration of justice into disrepute.

■ General

25 The guarantee in this Charter of certain rights and freedoms shall not be construed so as to abrogate or derogate from any aboriginal, treaty or other rights or freedoms that pertain to the aboriginal peoples of Canada including (a) any rights or freedoms that have been recognized by the Royal Proclamation of October 7, 1763; and (b) any rights or freedoms that now exist by way of land claims agreements or may be so acquired. (SI/84-102)

26 The guarantee in this Charter of certain rights and freedoms shall not be construed as denying the existence of any other rights or freedoms that exist in Canada.

27 This Charter shall be interpreted in a manner consistent with the preservation and enhancement of the multicultural heritage of Canadians.

28 Notwithstanding anything in this Charter, the rights and freedoms referred to in it are guaranteed equally to male and female persons.

29 Nothing in this Charter abrogates or derogates from any rights or privileges guaranteed by or under the Constitution of Canada in respect of denominational, separate or dissentient schools.

30 A reference in this Charter to a province or to the legislative assembly or legislature or a province shall be deemed to include a reference to the Yukon Territory and the Northwest Territories, or to the appropriate legislative authority thereof, as the case may be.

31 Nothing in this Charter extends the legislative powers of any body or authority.

■ Application of Charter

32 (1) This Charter applies (a) to the Parliament and government of Canada in respect of all matters within the authority of Parliament including all matters relating to the Yukon Territory and Northwest Territories; and (b) to the legislature and government of each province in respect of all matters within the authority of the legislature of each province. (2) Notwithstanding subsection (1), section 15 shall not have effect until three years after this section comes into force.

33 (1) Parliament or the legislature of a province may expressly declare in an Act of Parliament or of the legislature, as the case may be, that the Act or a provision thereof shall operate notwithstanding a provision included in section 2 or sections 7 to 15 of this Charter. (2) An Act or a provision of an Act in respect of which a declaration made under this section is in effect shall have such operation as it would have but for the provision of this Charter referred to in the declaration. (3) A declaration made under subsection (1) shall cease to have effect five years after it comes into force or on such earlier date as may be specified in the declaration. (4) Parliament or the legislature of a province may re-enact a declaration made under subsection (1). (5) Subsection (3) applies in respect of a re-enactment made under subsection (4).

■ Citation

34 This Part may be cited as the Canadian Charter of Rights and Freedoms.

Canadian Orders and Decorations

For more information on Canada's orders and decorations, see the website of the Governor General of Canada at http://www.gg.ca/honour_e.html and the website of Veterans Affairs Canada at http://www.vacacc.gc.ca/general/sub.cfm?source=collections/cmdp/mainmenu.

☐ National Orders

■ The Order of Canada

History Creation of the Order of Canada was announced by Prime Minister Lester B. Pearson in 1967. It was instituted on the centennial of Canadian Confederation, July 1, 1967.

Basis of Award To honour Canadians for outstanding achievement and service to their country or humanity. Appointments are announced twice annually, around July 1 and Jan. 1. Investitures occur three times a year, in February, April and October when the awards are given by the Governor General.

Eligibility Every living Canadian is eligible to become a member. Federal and provincial politicians and judges are ineligible while in office.

Membership There are three categories of membership. The first is Companion of the Order of Canada (C.C.). No more than 15 companions may be appointed in any one year, and no more than 165 living companions may hold the order at one time.

The second is Officer of the Order of Canada (O.C.). No more than 52 appointments may be made annually.

The third is Member of the Order of Canada (C.M.)., which recognizes service in a locality or a field of activity. No more than 106 appointments may be made annually.

Badge A stylized snowflake bearing the crown with a ribbon in the same proportions of white and red which appear on the Canadian flag and the Latin motto *Desiderantes Meliorem Patriam*—"They Desire a Better Country." Worn at the neck by companions and officers and on the left breast by members.

■ The Order of Military Merit

History The Order of Military Merit was instituted on July 1, 1972.

Basis of Award To recognize exceptional service and conspicuous merit by regular and reserve members of Canada's Armed Forces.

Appointments are made by the Governor General on the recommendation of the Chief of Defence Staff.

Eligibility Active members of the Canadian Armed Forces, regular and reserve. A formula limits the number of annual appointments per year to one-tenth of one per cent of the average number of persons who were members of the Armed Forces during the previous year.

Membership There are three categories of membership. The first is Commander of the Order of Military Merit (C.M.M.). Six percent of annual appointments go to this category of membership.

The second is Officer of the Order of Military Merit (O.M.M.). Thirty percent of annual appointments go to this category of membership.

The third is Member of the Order of Military Merit (M.M.M.). The balance of annual appointments go to this category of membership.

Badge In the form of an enamelled blue cross having expanded arms, with a blue ribbon edged in gold. Bears the words "Merit Merite Canada." Worn at the neck by commanders and on the left breast by officers and members.

☐ Medals for Military Valour

The Military Valour Decorations, consisting of the Victoria Cross (Canadian), the Star of Military Valour and the Medal of Military Valour, enable Canada to recognize members of the Canadian Forces, or members of an allied armed force serving with the Canadian Forces, for deeds of military valour.

■ Victoria Cross (V.C.) (Canadian)

History Approved by Queen Elizabeth II on Feb. 2, 1993. The British Victoria Cross was created by Queen Victoria in 1856 and was awarded to Canadians in all wars until 1945. There have been 93 Canadian recipients of the British V.C. and none of the Canadian version.

Basis of Award In recognition of "the most conspicuous bravery, a daring or pre-eminent act of valour or self-sacrifice or extreme devotion to duty, in the presence of the enemy." The V.C. will be awarded by the Governor General on the advice of the Military Valour Advisory Committee. It is the highest in the order of precedence in Canadian honours.

Eligibility Members of the Canadian Forces or a member of an allied armed force that is serving with or in conjunction with the Canadian Forces on or after Jan. 1, 1993. The V.C. may be awarded posthumously.

Badge The Cross is a bronze straight armed cross, suspended from a crimson ribbon. The face has, in the middle of the cross, a lion

guardant standing on the Royal Crown, with the Latin inscription *Pro Valore*—"For Valour". The date of the act for which the decoration is bestowed is engraved in a raised circle on the reverse.

■ The Star of Military Valour (S.M.V.)

History Approved by Queen Elizabeth II on Feb. 2, 1993.

Basis of Award Awarded for distinguished and valiant service in the presence of the enemy.

Eligibility Members of the Canadian Forces or a member of an allied armed force that is serving with or in conjunction with the Canadian Forces on or after Jan. 1, 1993. The S.M.V. may be awarded posthumously.

Badge A gold star with four points with a maple leaf in each of the angles, on the face of which a gold maple leaf is superimposed in the centre of a sanguine field surrounded by a silver wreath of laurel and on the reverse of which the Royal Cypher and Crown and the Latin inscription *Pro Valore*—"For Valour" shall appear. The Star shall be worn, suspended from a crimson ribbon with two white stripes, immediately after any order and before the Star of Courage.

■ The Medal of Military Valour (M.M.V.)

History Approved by Queen Elizabeth II on Feb. 2, 1993.

Basis of Award Awarded for an act of valour or devotion to duty in the presence of the enemy.

Eligibility Members of the Canadian Forces or a member of an allied armed force that is serving with or in conjunction with the Canadian Forces on or after Jan. 1, 1993. The M.M.V. may be awarded posthumously.

Badge A circular gold medal, on the face of which there shall be a maple leaf surrounded by a wreath of laurel and on the reverse of which the Royal Cypher and Crown and the Latin inscription *Pro Valore*—"For Valour" will appear. The medal shall be worn, from a crimson ribbon with three white stripes, immediately after the Meritorious Service Cross and before the Medal of Bravery.

☐ Decorations for Bravery

The Decorations for Bravery, consisting of the Cross of Valour, the Star of Courage and the Medal of Bravery honour those who have risked their lives to save or protect others. These three Canadian decorations replaced the following non-combatant Commonwealth medals: the George Cross, the George Medal and the Queen's Gallantry Medal, respectively.

■ The Cross of Valour (C.V.)

History Created in 1972, the Cross of Valour takes precedence before all orders and other decorations except the Victoria Cross.

Basis of Award Awarded for acts of the most conspicuous courage in circumstances of extreme peril.

Eligibility May be awarded to civilians or members of the Armed Forces. Only 19 have been awarded. May be awarded posthumously.

Badge A gold cross bearing the words "Valour Vaillance."

■ The Star of Courage (S.C.)

History Created in 1972.

Basis of Award Awarded for acts of conspicuous courage in circumstances of great peril.

Eligibility May be awarded to civilians or members of the Armed Forces. May be awarded posthumously.

Badge A four-pointed silver star with the word "Courage."

■ The Medal of Bravery (M.B.)

History Created in 1972.

Basis of Award Awarded for acts of bravery in hazardous circumstances.

Eligibility May be awarded to civilians or members of the Armed Forces. May be awarded posthumously.

Badge A circular silver medal with the words "Bravery Bravoure."

■ The Meritorious Service Cross (M.S.C.) (military and civilian)

History Military division created in 1984; civilian division created in 1991.

Basis of Award *Military division*: awarded in recognition of a military deed or activity that has been performed in an outstandingly professional manner, according to a rare high standard that brings considerable benefit or great honour to the Canadian Forces. *Civilian division*: awarded in recognition of the performance of a deed or activity performed in an outstandingly professional manner or according to an uncommonly high standard that brings considerable benefit or great honour to Canada.

Eligibility A member of the Canadian and allied forces, persons serving in conjunction with the Canadian Forces or other persons, Canadian and foreigners.

Badge A Greek cross of silver, ends splayed and convexed, ensigned with the Royal Crown. On the face appear a maple leaf within a circle and a laurel wreath between the arms. Recipients are entitled to use the letters "M.S.C." after their names.

■ The Meritorious Service Medal (M.S.M.) (military and civilian)

History Created in 1991.

Basis of Award *Military division*: awarded in recognition of a military deed or activity that has been performed in a highly professional manner or is of a very high standard that brings benefit or honour to the Canadian Forces. *Civilian division*: awarded in recognition of the performance of a deed or activity performed in a highly professional manner or of a very high standard that brings benefit or honour to Canada.

Eligibility A member of the Canadian and allied forces, persons serving in conjunction with the Canadian Forces or other persons, Canadian and foreigners.

Badge A circular medal of silver ensigned with the Royal Crown. On the face appears the design of the cross. On the reverse appears the Royal Cypher and, within a double circle, the words "Meritorious Service Méritoire." Recipients are entitled to use the letters "M.S.M." after their names.

□ Other Notable Awards

The Governor General also bestows these awards.

■ The Academic Medal

Created in 1873. Awarded for academic excellence. Medals are distributed in March to colleges and universities and in April to high schools.

■ The Governor General's Caring Canadian Award

Created in 1996. Awarded to unpaid volunteers for their extraordinary contributions, performed behind the scenes and for several years, in support of family, community or humanitarian causes.

Governors General of Canada

Name	Date Appointed	Assumed Office	Term
Sir Charles Stanley, Viscount Monck	June 1, 1867	July 1, 1867	1867–69
Sir John Young, Baron Lisgar	Dec. 29, 1868	Feb. 2, 1869	1869–72
Frederick Temple Hamilton Blackwood, Earl of Dufferin	May 22, 1872	June 25, 1872	1872–78
John Douglas Sutherland Campbell, Marquess of Lorne	Oct. 5, 1878	Nov. 20, 1878	1878–83
Henry Charles Keith Petty-Fitzmaurice, Marquess of Lansdowne	Aug. 18, 1883	Oct. 23, 1883	1883–88
Frederick Arthur Stanley, Baron Stanley of Preston	May 1, 1888	June 11, 1888	1888–93
John Campbell Hamilton-Gordon, Earl of Aberdeen	May 22, 1893	Nov. 18, 1893	1893–98
Gilbert John Elliott Murray-Kynynmound, Earl of Minto	July 30, 1898	Nov. 12, 1898	1898–1904
Albert Henry George Grey, Earl Grey	Sept. 26, 1904	Dec. 10, 1904	1904–11
His Royal Highness The Prince Arthur, Field Marshal Duke of Connaught	Mar. 21, 1911	Oct. 13, 1911	1911–16
Victor Christian William Cavendish, Duke of Devonshire	Aug. 19, 1916	Nov. 11, 1916	1916–21
Julian Byng, General Baron Byng of Vimy and of Thorpe	Aug. 2, 1921	Aug. 11, 1921	1921–26
Freeman Freeman-Thomas, Baron Willingdon of Ratton	Aug. 5, 1926	Nov. 2, 1926	1926–31
Vere Brabazon Ponsonby, Earl of Bessborough	Feb. 9, 1931	Apr. 4, 1931	1931–35
John Buchan, Baron Tweedsmuir	Aug. 10, 1935	Nov. 2, 935	1935–40
Alexander George Cambridge, Major General Earl of Athlone	Apr. 3, 1940	June 21, 1940	1940–46
Sir Harold George Alexander, Field Marshal Viscount Alexander of Tunis	Aug. 1, 1945	Apr. 18, 1946	1946–52
The Right Honourable Vincent Massey	Jan. 24, 1952	Feb. 22, 1952	1952–59
General the Right Honourable Georges P. Vanier	Aug. 1, 1959	Sept. 15, 1959	1959–67
The Right Honourable Daniel Roland Michener	Mar. 25, 1967	Apr. 15, 1967	1967–74
The Right Honourable Jules Léger	Oct. 5, 1973	Jan. 14, 1974	1974–79
The Right Honourable Edward Richard Schreyer	Dec. 7, 1978	Jan. 22, 1979	1979–83
The Right Honourable Jeanne Sauvé	Dec. 23, 1983	May 14, 1984	1984–90
The Right Honourable Ramon John Hnatyshyn	Oct. 6, 1989	Jan. 21, 1990	1990–95
The Right Honourable Roméo LeBlanc	Nov. 22, 1994	Feb. 8, 1995	1995–99
The Right Honourable Adrienne Clarkson	Sept. 8, 1999	Oct. 7, 1999	1999–

Prime Ministers of Canada

Prime Minister	Party	Term(s)	Born	P.M. at age	Died
Sir John A. Macdonald	Conservative	July 1, 1867–Nov. 5, 1873 Oct. 9, 1878–June 6, 1891	Jan. 11, 1815	52	June 6, 1891
Alexander Mackenzie	Liberal	Nov. 5, 1873–Oct. 9, 1878	Jan. 28, 1822	51	Apr. 17, 1892
Sir John Abbott	Conservative	June 15, 1891–Nov. 24, 1892	Mar. 12, 1821	70	Oct. 30, 1893
Sir John Thompson	Conservative	Nov. 25, 1892–Dec. 12, 1894	Nov. 10, 1845	48	Dec. 12, 1894
Sir Mackenzie Bowell	Conservative	Dec. 13, 1894–Apr. 27, 1896	Dec. 27, 1823	70	Dec. 10, 1917
Sir Charles Tupper	Conservative	Apr. 27, 1896–July 8, 1896	July 2, 1821	74	Oct. 30, 1915
Sir Wilfrid Laurier	Liberal	July 11, 1896–Oct. 6, 1911	Nov. 20, 1841	54	Feb. 17, 1919
Sir Robert Borden	Conservative/ Unionist	Oct. 10, 1911–Oct. 12, 1917 Oct. 12, 1917–July 10, 1920	June 26, 1854	57	June 10, 1937
Arthur Meighen	Unionist/ Conservative	July 10, 1920–Dec. 29, 1921 June 29, 1926–Sept. 25, 1926	June 16, 1874	46	Aug. 5, 1960
Mackenzie King	Liberal	Dec. 29, 1921–June 28, 1926 Sept. 25, 1926–Aug. 6, 1930 Oct. 23, 1935–Nov. 15, 1948	Dec. 17, 1874	47	July 22, 1950
Richard B. Bennett	Conservative	Aug. 7, 1930–Oct. 23, 1935	July 3, 1870	60	June 27, 1947
Louis St. Laurent	Liberal	Nov. 15, 1948–June 21, 1957	Feb. 1, 1882	66	July 25, 1973
John Diefenbaker	Prog. Cons.	June 21, 1957–Apr. 22, 1963	Sept. 18, 1895	61	Aug. 16, 1979
Lester Pearson	Liberal	Apr. 22, 1963–Apr. 20, 1968	Apr. 23, 1897	65	Dec. 27, 1972
Pierre Trudeau	Liberal	Apr. 20, 1968–June 4, 1979 Mar. 3, 1980–June 30, 1984	Oct. 18, 1919	48	Sept. 28, 2000
Joe Clark	Prog. Cons.	June 4, 1979–Mar. 3, 1980	June 5, 1939	39	
John Turner	Liberal	June 30, 1984–Sept. 17, 1984	June 7, 1929	55	
Brian Mulroney	Prog. Cons.	Sept. 17, 1984–June 25, 1993	Mar. 20, 1939	45	
Kim Campbell	Prog. Cons.	June 25, 1993–Nov. 4, 1993	Mar. 10, 1947	46	
Jean Chrétien	Liberal	Nov. 4, 1993–	Jan. 11, 1934	59	

Canadian Cabinet Ministers and Secretaries of State

(as of October 2001)

Cabinet ministers are the most powerful elected officials in government. They are sworn to the Privy Council and are bound by collective responsibility. They work with their staffs to set policies for their ministries and present (or defend) those policies in the House of Commons. They shepherd their bills through various readings and committees before having their bills voted into law.

Secretaries of state, although sworn to the Privy Council and bound by collective responsibility as well, are not members of the Cabinet. Secretaries of state are assigned to support specific Cabinet ministers; they also get smaller staffs and less pay than Cabinet ministers. Prime Minister Jean Chrétien introduced the distinction between these "senior" and "junior" officials on Nov. 4, 1993.

For Cabinet updates after October 2001, visit www.cdgbooks.com and look for Almanac FastFacts.

■ The Cabinet

The Prime Minister of Canada
The Right Hon. Jean Chrétien
(Saint-Maurice, Quebec)
Telephone: (613) 992-4211
Fax: (613) 941-6900
E-mail: pm@pm.gc.ca

The Deputy Prime Minister of Canada
The Hon. Herbert Eser Gray
(Windsor West, Ontario)
Telephone: (613) 995-7548
Fax: (613) 995-3259
E-mail: Gray.H@parl.gc.ca

The Leader of the Government in the Senate
Represents the Cabinet in the Senate.
The Hon. Sharon Carstairs
(Manitoba)
Telephone: (613) 947-7123
Fax: (613) 947-7125

The Minister of Agriculture and Agri-Food
Responsible for nearly all aspects of production, processing, marketing and protection of crops and livestock, including research and technology; soil conservation; food processing and inspection; and trade policies and support programs.
The Hon. Lyle Vanclief
(Prince Edward–Hastings, Ontario)
Telephone: (613) 992-5321
Fax: (613) 996-8652
E-mail: Vanclief.L@parl.gc.ca

The Minister of Canadian Heritage
Responsible for both Canada's natural heritage (parks) and our historic and cultural heritage, including the arts, sports and multiculturalism.
The Hon. Sheila M. Copps
(Hamilton East, Ontario)
Telephone: (613) 995-2772
Fax: (613) 994-1267
E-mail: Copps.S@parl.gc.ca

The Minister of Citizenship and Immigration
Administers policies and procedures for citizenship and immigration.
The Hon. Elinor Caplan
(Thornhill, Ontario)
Telephone: (613) 992-0253
Fax: (613) 992-0887
E-mail: Caplan.E@parl.gc.ca

The Minister of the Environment
Protects and conserves Canada's air and water; monitors climate and pollution.
The Hon. David Anderson
(Victoria, British Columbia)
Telephone: (613) 996-2358
Fax: (613) 952-1458
E-mail: Anderson.D@parl.gc.ca

The Minister of Finance
Provides the federal government with an annual budget; provides research and advice on financial issues; regularly monitors the performance of Canada's economy.
The Hon. Paul Martin
(LaSalle–Émard, Quebec)
Telephone: (613) 992-4284
Fax: (613) 992-4291
E-mail: Martin.P@parl.gc.ca

▶

The Minister of Fisheries and Oceans
Manages Canada's resources in the water, particularly in the ocean, when outside other jurisdictions; oversees public harbours and coastal and inland fisheries.
The Hon. Harbance Singh Dhaliwal
(Vancouver South–Burnaby, British Columbia)
Telephone: (613) 995-7052
Fax: (613) 995-2962

The Minister of Foreign Affairs
Creates foreign policy; promotes and protects Canada's interests abroad; manages Canadian embassies and diplomatic staff; ensures Canadian citizens abroad receive fair treatment under foreign laws.
The Hon. John Paul Manley
(Ottawa South, Ontario)
Telephone: (613) 995-7052
Fax: (613) 995-2962

The Minister of Health
Provides funding and policies for a national health care system; sets and enforces health standards.
The Hon. Allan Rock
(Etobicoke Centre, Ontario)
Telephone: (613) 947-5000
Fax: (613) 947-4276
E-mail: Rock.A@parl.gc.ca

The Minister of Human Resources Development
Fosters an educated and mobile workforce; provides income as necessary for seniors, the unemployed and the disabled.
The Hon. Jane Stewart
(Brant, Ontario)
Telephone: (613) 992-3118
Fax: (613) 943-5790
E-mail: Stewart.J@parl.gc.ca

The Minister of Indian Affairs and Northern Development
Meets the federal government's treaty obligations to Inuit and First Nations people, including the provision of basic services; negotiates and oversees claims settlements.
The Hon. Robert Daniel Nault
(Kenora–Rainy River, Ontario)
Telephone: (613) 996-1161
Fax: (613) 996-1759
E-mail: Nault.R@parl.gc.ca

The Minister of Industry
Drafts major federal bills and programs for consumer and business groups; provides policy advice, business services and industrial information.
The Hon. Brian V. Tobin
(Bonavista–Trinity–Conception, Newfoundland)
Telephone: (613) 992-4133
Fax: (613) 992-7277

The Minister for International Cooperation
Administers economic and technical aid to the developing world through CIDA.
The Hon. Maria Minna
(Beaches–East York, Ontario)
Telephone: (613) 992-2115
Fax: (613) 996-7942
E-mail: Minna.M@parl.gc.ca

The Minister for International Trade
Takes part in international trade talks and institutions to promote Canadian business abroad and to resolve trade disputes.
The Hon. Pierre S. Pettigrew
(Papineau–Saint-Denis, Quebec)
Telephone: (613) 995-8872
Fax: (613) 995-9926
E-mail: Pettigrew.P@parl.gc.ca

The Minister of Justice and Attorney General of Canada
Provides legal services to all government departments and agencies; supervises the administration of justice.
The Hon. Anne McLellan
(Edmonton West, Alberta)
Telephone: (613) 992-4524
Fax: (613) 943-0044
E-mail: McLellan.A@parl.gc.ca

The Minister of Labour
Enforces the labour code including health and safety in the workplace; promotes fairness and cooperation between labour and management; provides mediation and conciliation in labour disputes.
The Hon. Claudette Bradshaw
(Moncton–Riverview–Dieppe, New Brunswick)
Telephone: (613) 992-8072
Fax: (613) 992-8083
E-mail: Bradshaw.C@parl.gc.ca

The Minister of National Defence
Administers Canada's armed forces, defends citizens at home and meets Canada's military obligations abroad.
The Hon. Arthur C. Eggleton
(York Centre, Ontario)
Telephone: (613) 941-6339
Fax: (613) 941-2421
E-mail: Eggleton.A@parl.gc.ca

The Minister of National Revenue and Secretary of State (Economic Development Agency of Canada for the Regions of Quebec)
Administers the Customs and Excise Acts as well as import and export taxes and permits.
The Hon. Martin Cauchon
(Outremont, Quebec)
Telephone: (613) 995-7691
Fax: (613) 995-0114

►

The Minister of Natural Resources and Minister responsible for Canadian Wheat Board
Proposes and plans national policies for energy, mines and resources (renewable and nonrenewable); researches conservation and development strategies.
The Hon. Ralph E. Goodale
(Wascana, Saskatchewan)
Telephone: (613) 996-2007
Fax: (613) 996-4516

The Minister of Public Works and Government Services
Buys services to support the daily operation of government; provides office space and maintains public buildings; provides telecommunications and information services; prepares public audits and disburses public monies.
The Hon. Alfonso Gagliano
(Saint-Léonard–Saint Michel, Quebec)
Telephone: (613) 995-9420
Fax: (613) 992-8523
E-mail: Gagliano.A@parl.gc.ca

The Minister of State and Leader of the Government in the House of Commons
Plans and manages the government's legislative agenda in its pre-parliamentary and parliamentary stages; maintains relations with the Opposition.
The Hon. Don Boudria
(Glengarry–Prescott–Russell, Ontario)
Telephone: (613) 996-2907
Fax: (613) 996-9123
E-mail: Boudria.D@parl.gc.ca

The Minister of Transport
Oversees national policies to ensure competitive, safe and environmentally sustainable transportation.
The Hon. David Michael Collenette
(Don Valley East, Ontario)
Telephone: (613) 995-4988
Fax: (613) 995-1686
E-mail: Collenette.D@parl.gc.ca

The Minister of Veterans Affairs and Secretary of State (Francophonie) (Western Economic Diversification)
Provides Canadian combat veterans and their families with benefits; preserves the memory veterans' sacrifices and achievements.
The Hon. Ronald Duhamel
(Saint Boniface, Manitoba)
Telephone: (613) 995-0579
Fax: (613) 996-7571
E-mail: Duhamel.R@parl.gc.ca

The President of the Queen's Privy Council for Canada and Minister of Intergovernmental Affairs
Manages federal-provincial relations; provides legal advice on constitutional issues and national unity.
The Hon. Stéphane Dion
(Saint-Laurent–Cartierville, Quebec)
Telephone: (613) 996-5789
Fax: (613) 996-6562

The President of the Treasury Board and Minister responsible for Infrastructure
Functions as the government's chief employer and general manager; responsible for finances, personnel and administration.
The Hon. Lucienne Robillard
(Westmount–Ville Marie, Quebec)
Telephone: (613) 996-7267
Fax: (613) 995-8632
E-mail: Robillard.L@parl.gc.ca

The Solicitor General of Canada
Responsible for prisons, the RCMP, CSIS, parole boards and everything within Parliament's jurisdiction that is not legally assigned somewhere else.
The Hon. Lawrence MacAuley
(Cardigan, Prince Edward Island)
Telephone: (613) 995-9325
Fax: (613) 995-2754
E-mail: MacAulay.L@parl.gc.ca

■ Secretaries of State

Secretary of State (Amateur Sport)
The Hon. Denis Coderre
(Bourassa, Quebec)
Telephone: (613) 995-6108
Fax: (613) 995-9755
E-mail: Coderre.D@parl.gc.ca

Secretary of State (Asia-Pacific)
The Hon. Rey Pagtakhan
(Winnipeg North–St. Paul, Manitoba)
Telephone: (613) 992-7148
Fax: (613) 996-9125
E-mail: Pagtakhan.R@parl.gc.ca

Secretary of State (Atlantic Canada Opportunities Agency)
The Hon. Robert Thibault
(West Nova, Nova Scotia)
Telephone: (613) 995-5711
Fax: (613) 996-9857
E-mail: Thibault.R@parl.gc.ca

Secretary of State (Children and Youth)
The Hon. Ethel Blondin-Andrew
(Western Arctic, Northwest Territories)
Telephone: (613) 992-4587
Fax: (613) 992-7411
E-mail: Blondin-Andrew.E@parl.gc.ca

Secretary of State (Federal Economic Development Initiative for Northern Ontario) (Rural Development)
The Hon. Andrew Mitchell
(Parry Sound–Muskoka, Ontario)
Telephone: (613) 996-3434
Fax: (613) 991-2147
E-mail: Mitchell.A@parl.gc.ca

Secretary of State (International Financial Institutions)
The Hon. James Scott Peterson
(Willowdale, Ontario)
Telephone: (613) 992-4964
Fax: (613) 992-1158
E-mail: Peterson.J@parl.gc.ca

Secretary of State (Latin America and Africa)
The Hon. David Kilgour
(Edmonton Southeast, Alberta)
Telephone: (613) 995-8695
Fax: (613) 995-6465
E-mail: Kilgour.D@parl.gc.ca

Secretary of State (Multiculturalism) (Status of Women)
The Hon. Hedy Fry
(Vancouver Centre, British Columbia)
Telephone: (613) 992-3213
Fax: (613) 995-0056
E-mail: Fry.H@parl.gc.ca

Secretary of State (Science, Research and Development)
The Hon. Gilbert Normand
(Bellechasse–Etchemins–Montmagny–L'Islet, Quebec)
Telephone: (613) 992-2289
Fax: (613) 992-6864
E-mail: Normand.G@parl.gc.ca

Deputy Prime Ministers of Canada

(as of October 2001)

The title of deputy prime minister is strictly honorary. It is conferred at the prime minister's discretion on a member of the Cabinet. The title has no standing in law and carries no formal duties or tasks. Deputy prime ministers, however, often have other Cabinet portfolios.

Prime Minister Pierre Trudeau named the first deputy prime minister during a press interview after the nomination of his Cabinet on Sept. 16, 1977.

Since then only Prime Minister Joe Clark (1979–80) has not named a deputy prime minister.

In 1984, Prime Minister Brian Mulroney began the practice of appointing the deputy prime minister by "instrument of advice." An instrument of advice is a private letter written by the prime minister to the Crown. Since 1984, all deputy prime ministers have been appointed by this method.

Deputy Prime Minister	Date Appointed	Term Ended	Designated by Prime Minister
Allan J. MacEachen	Sept. 16, 1977	June 3, 1979	Pierre Trudeau
Allan J. MacEachen	Mar. 3, 1980	June 29, 1984	Pierre Trudeau
Jean Chrétien	June 30, 1984	Sept. 16, 1984	John Turner
Erik Nielsen	Sept. 17, 1984	June 29, 1986	Brian Mulroney
Donald Mazankowski	June 30, 1986	June 24, 1993	Brian Mulroney
Jean J. Charest	June 25, 1993	Nov. 3, 1993	Kim Campbell
Sheila M. Copps	Nov. 4, 1993	Apr. 30, 1996	Jean Chrétien
Sheila M. Copps	June 19, 1996	June 10, 1997	Jean Chrétien
Herbert E. Gray	June 11, 1997		Jean Chrétien

Source: Library of Parliament, Information and Documentation Branch

FOCUS ON...

The Opposition

The legislatures in Canada, including the House of Commons in Ottawa and the provincial bodies across the country, are divided into government and opposition benches. The role of the government representatives is clear—providing vocal support for government policies as they are put forward and favourable votes when the time comes to formally approve the measures. The role of the Opposition is also clear—giving voice to dissenting opinions. No policy is perfect, and no policy can serve all members of a society. One of the key roles of the Opposition is to ensure that the voices of those who disagree, either on principle or due to their circumstances, are heard.

Canadian society's commitment to the right of those opposed to be heard is embedded in the institution of public debate in the legislatures across the land. The daily Question Period when the House is in session is another facet of the right to publicly disagree. Opposition members are also players in the committee system (see page 160) where legislation is refined or issues are investigated. While at no time are opposition members allowed to outnumber (and thus outvote) the government members in committee, the views of opposition members are sought and the members are expected to participate.

In the federal election of November 2000, five political parties won enough votes to be represented in the House of Commons, but four of them did not have enough seats to form a majority government: the Canadian Alliance, the Bloc Québécois, the New Democratic Party and the Progressive Conservative party. Together, they form the opposition to the Liberal government in Ottawa for the current government's term of office—a maximum of five years.

The expression of opposition is based on either party ideology: the right, the left and the Quebec sovereignists, by definition of party goals and objectives, represent a different view than that of the traditionally centrist Liberals; or on the needs of the constituents they represent. Urban and rural citizens often have different (and perhaps conflicting) goals and needs, as do citizens from the various geographic or economic regions.

The opposition parties organize themselves much the same way the government does. They set up shadow cabinets that mirror the governing cabinet in order to better review and mount challenges to proposed policies. (These shadow cabinets also serve as training grounds for future ministers should their party be the next to form a government.) It is the members of the shadow cabinet who often lead the opposition charges in debate on issues related to their expertise. They and their party's leader are most often the ones to rise during discussion. The opposition parties are granted office space, research staff and other resources at the taxpayers' expense to support their work as advocates for those opposed. These resources are allocated in proportion to the size of the party's representation. Federally, the minimum requirement for "official party" status (which means entitlement to a share of the resources) is 12 members in the House. The opposition party with the largest number of seats is given the title of "Her Majesty's Loyal Opposition" and, as the official opposition, gets first choice of resources and debating opportunities.

The effectiveness of the opposition is directly related to the number of members it has on hand. A government with a large majority faces very little opposition, raising concerns about checks and balances on the its power—the provincial government elected in New Brunswick in 1987 faced no opposition during its term of office; the opposition to the current provincial government in BC is very small. When a government majority is very small, or when the total number of opposition members outnumbers the government side, it is more likely to pay attention to opinions expressed from across the floor and more likely to find compromises to make contentious policies more acceptable.

FOCUS ON...

Parliamentary Committees

In Parliament, much of the work of our appointed and elected representatives is performed in small, specialized committees. The committee system serves two basic purposes. The first is investigative. If the government wishes to look into an issue (e.g., a crisis in aboriginal housing or the proper disposal of nuclear waste), the government will direct the appropriate committee to research the issue and report on it. This type of committee also scrutinizes budgets.

The second purpose is legislative. After a bill has passed second reading in the Commons, the appropriate committee examines the bill, clause by clause. The committee may hear advice from civil servants, private citizens and the cabinet minister sponsoring the bill. After a detailed discussion, the committee can amend the bill before returning it to the Commons for third reading and a vote. The same process can apply in the Senate.

At present, the Senate has one special and 15 standing committees. The House of Commons has two special and 17 standing committees. Senators and MPs cooperate in three more joint committees. If the occasion merits it, Parliament can create still more committees, or committees can delegate responsibilities to subcommittees.

Most committees share a similar structure. Most are chaired by one person, although joint committees of the Senate and House of Commons are co-chaired. Most committees have one vice-chair, although some have two. Most committees have between 7 and 15 additional members. Each Senate committee has members from all parties represented in the Senate; each committee of the House of Commons has members from all parties represented in the House of Commons.

In the Senate, members from any party can chair committees. A committee's members are drawn equally from the four geographic regions of Canada (i.e., the West, Ontario, Quebec, and the Atlantic provinces). In addition, party representation on a committee is proportionate to the number of seats that the party has in the Senate.

In the House of Commons, committees are chaired by a member of the governing party. (The exception is the Standing Committee on Public Accounts; by tradition since 1958, this committee is chaired by a member of the Official Opposition.) The chair and vice-chairs of each committee are elected by committee members drawn from the majority party. Party representation on a committee is proportionate to the number of seats that each party has in the House of Commons.

To fulfill their roles, committees can demand documents and summon witnesses. They can also administer oaths and affirmations. Although committees lack the power to punish absentee witnesses, the House can hold such persons in contempt and order their arrest for the duration of the parliamentary session. Committees can also delegate powers to subcommittees, except the power to report to the House.

In general, custom governs the procedure of committee meetings. The rules allow greater time for discussion than in the Commons and the Senate to ensure an informal airing of views. Any member can try to amend bills before the committee.

■ Standing Committees

In the Senate and the House of Commons, standing committees are the most common type. Standing committees are established at the start of a parliamentary session and last for the session's duration (i.e., up to five years). They may be directed by the government to investigate an issue, or they may initiate their own investigations. After due consideration, standing committees report back to the appropriate House.

In the House of Commons, standing committees focus more on budget estimates and inquiries; they focus less on studying bills. Some standing committees also report on Crown corporations.

Standing Committees of the House of Commons

(as of October 2001)

Standing Committee on	Chair (Party)	No. of Subcommittees	Clerk's Telephone
Aboriginal Affairs, Northern Development and Natural Resources	Nancy Karetak-Lindell (Lib.)	1	(613) 996-1173
Agriculture and Agri-Food	Charles Hubbard (Lib.)	—	(613) 947-6732
Canadian Heritage	Clifford Lincoln (Lib.)	—	(613) 947-6729
Citizenship and Immigration	Joe Fontana (Lib.)	—	(613) 995-8525
Environment and Sustainable Development	Charles Caccia (Lib.)	—	(613) 992-5023
Finance	Maurizio Bevilacqua (Lib.)	1	(613) 992-9753 (613) 947-6728
Fisheries and Oceans	Wayne Easter (Lib.)	2	(613) 996-3105
Foreign Affairs and International Trade	Bill Graham (Lib.)	3	(613) 996-1540
Health	Bonnie Brown (Lib.)	—	(613) 996-1483
Human Resources Development and the Status of Persons with Disabilities	Peter Adams (Lib.)	3	(613) 996-1542
Industry, Science and Technology	Susan Whelan (Lib.)	1	(613) 996-7938
Justice and Human Rights	Andy Scott (Lib.)	—	(613) 996-1553 (613) 995-8013
Liaison	Bill Graham (Lib.)	1	(613) 992-3156
National Defence and Veterans' Affairs	David Pratt (Lib.)	1	(613) 995-9461
Procedure and House Affairs	Derek Lee (Lib.)	3	(613) 996-0506
Public Accounts	John Williams (CA)	1	(613) 996-1175
Transport and Government Operations	Ovid Jackson (Lib.)	1	(613) 996-4663

Lib.—Liberal; CA—Canadian Alliance

Special Committees of the House of Commons

(as of October 2001)

In both Houses of Parliament, special committees are created to study issues that are not routinely discussed in Parliament, such as drug abuse. Special committees are created when the need arises and usually last about six months. Committee members hire research staff, travel and hear witnesses. Special committees cease to exist after they table their final reports in the House. Sometimes these committees are called task forces.

Special Committee on	Chair (Party)	No. of Subcommittees	Clerk's Telephone
Modernization and Improvement of the Procedures of the House of Commons	Bob Kilger (Lib.)	—	(613) 996-1478
Non-Medical Use of Drugs	Paddy Torsney (Lib.)	—	(613) 947-0007

■ Legislative Committees

In the House of Commons, legislative committees are created solely to examine bills after second reading. Legislative committees usually have no more than seven members, and the Speaker of the House appoints their chairs. Legislative committees cease to exist after reporting back to the appropriate members of the House of Commons. These committees were first established by Prime Minister Brian Mulroney in 1984 to ease the workloads of standing committees.

■ Joint Committees

Joint committees are made up of both senators and members of the House of Commons. Most joint committees are standing committees, but special joint committees can be established too. Joint committees work on matters that affect both Houses of Parliament. For example, the Standing Joint Committee on the Library of Parliament helps ensure the smooth operation of the library.

Source: *Library of Parliament, Information and Documentation Branch*

Members of Canada's Senate

(12 vacancies as of Oct. 1, 2001)

The Governor General appoints senators under the Great Seal of Canada on the prime minister's advice.

To be eligible for the Senate, a candidate must be a Canadian citizen and at least 30 years old. A candidate must also live in the region the appointment represents—either Ontario, Quebec, the West, the Maritimes or a territory. He or she must own land in that region with an unencumbered value of at least $4,000 and have a net estate worth at least $4,000. A senator from Quebec must either live in or have land in Quebec. A senator must retire at age 75.

Senator	Birthdate	Date Appointed	Appointed by	Province
Willie Adams	June 22, 1934	Apr. 5, 1977	Trudeau	Nunavut
Raynell Andreychuk	Aug. 14, 1944	Mar. 11, 1993	Mulroney	Sask.
W. David Angus	July 21, 1937	June 10, 1993	Mulroney	Que.
Norm Atkins	June 27, 1934	July 2, 1986	Mulroney	Ont.
Jack Austin	Mar. 2, 1932	Aug. 19, 1975	Trudeau	BC
Lise Bacon	Aug. 25, 1934	Sept. 15, 1994	Chrétien	Que.
Tommy Banks	Dec. 17, 1936	Apr. 7, 2000	Chrétien	Alta
Gérald Beaudoin	Apr. 15, 1929	Sept. 26, 1988	Mulroney	Que.
Roch Bolduc	Sept. 10, 1928	Sept. 26, 1988	Mulroney	Que.
John G. Bryden	Aug. 25, 1937	Nov. 23, 1994	Chrétien	NB
John Buchanan	Apr. 22, 1931	Sept. 12, 1990	Mulroney	NS
Catherine Callbeck	July 25, 1939	Sept. 23, 1997	Chrétien	PEI
Pat Carney	May 26, 1935	Aug. 30, 1990	Mulroney	BC
Sharon Carstairs	Apr. 26, 1942	Sept. 15, 1994	Chrétien	Man.
Thelma Chalifoux	Feb. 8, 1929	Nov. 26, 1997	Chrétien	Alta
Ione Christensen	Oct. 10, 1933	Sept. 2, 1999	Chrétien	YT
Ethel Cochrane	Sept. 23, 1937	Nov. 17, 1986	Mulroney	Nfld
Gérald J. Comeau	Feb. 1, 1946	Aug. 30, 1990	Mulroney	NS
Joan Cook	Oct. 6, 1934	Mar. 6, 1998	Chrétien	Nfld
Anne C. Cools	Aug. 12, 1943	Jan. 13, 1984	Trudeau	Ont.
Eymard Corbin	Aug. 2, 1934	July 9, 1984	Turner	NB
Jane Marie Cordy	July 2, 1950	June 9, 2000	Chrétien	NB
Pierre De Bané	Aug. 2, 1938	June 29, 1984	Chrétien	NS
Consiglio Di Nino	Jan. 24, 1938	Aug. 30, 1990	Mulroney	Ont.
C. William Doody	Feb. 26, 1931	Oct. 3, 1979	Clark	Nfld
John Trevor Eyton	July 12, 1934	Sept. 23, 1990	Mulroney	Ont.
Joyce Fairbairn	Nov. 6, 1939	June 29, 1984	Trudeau	Alta
Marisa Ferretti Barth	Apr. 28, 1931	Sept. 23, 1997	Chrétien	Que.
Sheila Finestone	Jan. 28, 1927	Aug. 11, 1999	Chrétien	Que.
Isobel Finnerty	July 15, 1930	Sept. 2, 1999	Chrétien	Ont.
D. Ross Fitzpatrick	Feb. 4, 1933	Mar. 6, 1998	Chrétien	BC
John Michael Forrestall	Sept. 23, 1932	Sept. 27, 1990	Mulroney	NS
Joan Fraser	Nov. 12, 1944	Sept. 17, 1998	Chrétien	Que.
George Furey	May 12, 1948	Aug.11, 1999	Chrétien	Nfld
Jean-Robert Gauthier	Oct. 22, 1929	Nov. 23, 1994	Chrétien	Ont.
Aurélien Gill	Aug. 26, 1933	Sept. 17, 1998	Chrétien	Que.
Jerahmiel S. Grafstein	Jan. 2, 1935	Jan. 13, 1984	Trudeau	Ont.
B. Alasdair Graham	May 21, 1929	Apr. 27, 1972	Trudeau	NS
Leonard J. Gustafson	Nov. 10, 1933	May 26, 1993	Mulroney	Sask.
Daniel Hays	Apr. 24, 1939	June 29, 1984	Trudeau	Alta
Céline Hervieux-Payette	Apr. 22, 1941	Mar. 21, 1995	Chrétien	Que.
Elizabeth Hubley	Sept. 8, 1942	Mar. 8, 2001	Chrétien	PEI
Mobina S.B. Jaffer	Aug. 20, 1949	June 13, 2001	Chrétien	BC
Janis Johnson	Apr. 27, 1946	Sept. 27, 1990	Mulroney	Man.
Serge Joyal	Feb. 1, 1945	Nov. 26, 1997	Chrétien	Que.

▶

▶ James Francis Kelleher	Oct. 2, 1930	Sept. 23, 1990	Mulroney	Ont.
Colin Kenny	Dec. 10, 1943	June 29, 1984	Trudeau	Ont.
Wilbert Joseph Keon	May 17, 1935	Sept. 27, 1990	Mulroney	Ont.[1]
Noel A. Kinsella	Nov. 28, 1939	Sept. 12, 1990	Mulroney	NB
Michael Kirby	Aug. 5, 1941	Jan. 13, 1984	Trudeau	NS
E. Leo Kolber	Jan. 18, 1929	Dec. 23, 1983	Trudeau	Que.
Richard H. Kroft	May 22, 1938	June 11, 1998	Chrétien	Man.
Laurier L. LaPierre	Nov. 21. 1929	June 13, 2001	Chrétien	Ont.
Jean Lapointe	Dec. 6, 1935	June 13, 2001	Chrétien	Que.
Edward M. Lawson	Sept. 24. 1929	Oct. 7, 1970	Trudeau	BC
Marjory LeBreton	July 4, 1940	June 18, 1993	Mulroney	Ont.
Viola Léger	June 29, 1930	June 13, 2001	Chrétien	NB
Rose-Marie Losier-Cool	June 18, 1937	Mar. 21. 1995	Chrétien	NB
John Lynch-Staunton	June 19, 1930	Sept. 23, 1990	Mulroney	Que.
Shirley Maheu	Oct. 7, 1931	Feb. 1, 1996	Chrétien	Que.
Frank Mahovlich	Jan. 10, 1938	June 11, 1998	Chrétien	Ont.
Michael Arthur Meighen	Mar. 25, 1939	Sept. 27, 1990	Mulroney	Ont.[1]
Lorna Milne	Dec. 13, 1934	Sept. 22, 1995	Chrétien	Ont.
Wilfred P. Moore	Jan. 14, 1942	Sept. 26, 1996	Chrétien	NS
Yves Morin	Nov. 28, 1929	Mar. 8, 2001	Chrétien	Que.
Lowell Murray	Sept. 26, 1936	Sept. 13, 1979	Clark	Ont.
Pierre Claude Nolin	Oct. 30, 1950	June 18, 1993	Mulroney	Que.
Donald H. Oliver	Nov. 16, 1938	Sept. 7, 1990	Mulroney	NS
Landon Pearson	Nov. 16, 1930	Sept. 15, 1994	Chrétien	Ont.
Lucie Pépin	Sept. 7, 1936	Apr. 8, 1997	Chrétien	Que.
P. Michael Pitfield	June 18, 1937	Dec. 22, 1982	Trudeau	Ont.
Marie-Paule Poulin	June 21, 1945	Sept. 21, 1995	Chrétien	Ont.
Vivienne Poy	May 15, 1941	Sept. 17, 1998	Chrétien	Ont.
Marcel Prud'homme	Nov. 30, 1934	May 26, 1993	Mulroney	Que.
Jean-Claude Rivest	Jan. 27, 1943	Mar. 11, 1993	Mulroney	Que.
Brenda Mary Robertson	May 23, 1929	Dec. 21, 1984	Mulroney	NB
Fernand Robichaud	Dec. 2, 1939	Sept. 23, 1997	Chrétien	NB
Douglas Roche	June 14, 1929	Sept. 17, 1998	Chrétien	Alta.
William Rompkey	May 13, 1936	Sept. 22, 1995	Chrétien	Nfld
Eileen Rossiter	July 14, 1929	Nov. 17, 1986	Mulroney	PEI
Gerry St. Germain	Nov. 6, 1937	June 23, 1993	Mulroney	BC
Raymond C. Setlakwe	July 3, 1928	June 20, 2000	Chrétien	Que.
Nick G. Sibbeston	Nov. 21, 1943	Sept. 2, 1999	Chrétien	NWT
Herbert O. Sparrow	Jan. 4, 1930	Feb. 9, 1968	Pearson	Sask.
Mira Spivak	July 12, 1934	Nov. 17, 1986	Mulroney	Man.
Peter A. Stollery	Nov. 29, 1935	July 2, 1981	Trudeau	Ont.
Terrance R. Stratton	Mar. 16, 1938	Mar. 25, 1993	Mulroney	Man.
Nicholas W. Taylor	Nov. 17, 1927	Mar. 7, 1996	Chrétien	Alta.
David Tkachuk	Feb. 18, 1945	June 8, 1993	Mulroney	Sask.
James Tunney	June 16, 1927	Mar. 8, 2001	Chrétien	Ont.
Charlie Watt	June 29, 1944	Jan. 16, 1984	Trudeau	Que.
John (Jack) Wiebe	May 31, 1936	Apr. 7. 2000	Chrétien	Sask.
The Very Rev. Lois Wilson	Apr. 8, 1927	June 11, 1998	Chrétien	Ont.

(1) Represents region rather than a province.

Senate Changes

*A*s of Oct. 1, 2001, four senators are slated to retire in 2002: Sheila Finestone on Jan. 28, the Very Rev. Lois Wilson on Apr. 8, James Tunney on June 16, and Nicholas W. Taylor on Nov. 17. Tunney was appointed to the Senate in 2001.

Members of Parliament

(as of October 2001)

Correspondence to Members of Parliament should be addressed individually and may be sent postage free to the following address: (Name of MP), House of Commons, Ottawa, Ontario, K1A 0A6. For general information, call (613) 992-4793.

To contact a government department or minister's office via the Internet, go to http://canada.gc.ca/main_e.html (the website for the Government of Canada) and access "About Government."

In the event of a post-publication election, visit www.cdgbooks.com and look for Almanac FastFacts for an updated list of MPs.

■ Newfoundland

Riding	Member (year of birth)	Party	Occupation	First Elected[1]
Bonavista/Trinity/Conception	Brian Tobin (1954)	Lib.	Politician	1980
Burin/St. George's	Bill Matthews (1947)	Lib.	Politician	1997
Gander/Grand Falls	George S. Baker (1942)	Lib.	M.P.	1974
Humber/St. Barbe/Baie Verte	Gerry Byrne (1966)	Lib.	Civil Servant	1996*
Labrador	Lawrence O'Brien (1951)	Lib.	Civil Servant	1996*
St. John's East	Norman Doyle (1945)	PC	Politician	1997
St. John's West	Loyola Hearn (1943)	PC	Teacher	2000

■ Prince Edward Island

Riding	Member (year of birth)	Party	Occupation	First Elected[1]
Cardigan	Lawrence MacAulay (1946)	Lib.	M.P.	1988
Egmont	Joe McGuire (1944)	Lib.	M.P.	1988
Hillsborough	Shawn Murphy (1951)	Lib.	Lawyer	2000
Malpeque	Wayne Easter (1949)	Lib.	Farmer	1993

■ Nova Scotia

Riding	Member (year of birth)	Party	Occupation	First Elected[1]
Bras d'Or/Cape Breton	Rodger Cuzner (1955)	Lib.	Event Organizer	2000
Cumberland/Colchester	Bill Casey (1945)	PC	Financial Advisor	1997
Dartmouth	Wendy Lill (1950)	NDP	Social Worker	1997
Halifax	Alexa McDonough (1945)	NDP	Social Worker	1997
Halifax West	Geoff Regan (1959)	Lib.	Lawyer	2000
Kings/Hants	Scott Brison (1967)	PC	Sales Manager	2000
Pictou/Antigonish/Guysborough	Peter Mackay (1965)	PC	Crown Attorney	1997
Sackville/Musquodoboit Valley/ Eastern Shore	Peter Stoffer (1956)	NDP	Customer Serv.	1997
South Shore	Gerald Keddy (1953)	PC	Businessman	1997
Sydney/Victoria	Mark Eyking (1960)	Lib.	Farmer	2000
West Nova	Robert Thibault (1959)	Lib.	City Admin.	2000

■ New Brunswick

Riding	Member (year of birth)	Party	Occupation	First Elected[1]
Acadie/Bathurst	Yvon Godin (1955)	NDP	Staff Reprsntative	1997
Beauséjour/Petitcodiac	Dominic LeBlanc (1967)	Lib.	Lawyer	2000
Fredericton	Andy Scott (1955)	Lib.	Public Servant	1993
Fundy/Royal	John Herron (1967)	PC	Manager	1997
Madawaska/Restigouche	Jeannot Castonguay (1944)	Lib.	Doctor	2000
Miramichi	Charles Hubbard (1940)	Lib.	School Principal	1993
Moncton/Riverview/Dieppe	Claudette Bradshaw (1949)	Lib.	Public Servant	1997
New Brunswick Southwest	Greg Thompson (1947)	PC	Educator	1997
Saint John	Elsie Wayne (1932)	PC	Retired	1993
Tobique/Mactaguac	Andy Savoy (1963)	Lib.	Engineer	2000

▶

▶ ■ **Quebec**

Riding	Member (year of birth)	Party	Occupation	First Elected[1]
Abitibi/Baie-James/Nunavik	Guy St-Julien (1940)	Lib.	Lawyer	1997
Ahuntsic	Eleni Bakopanos (1954)	Lib.	Political Admin.	1993
Anjou/Rivière-des-Prairies	Yvon Charbonneau (1940)	Lib.	Politician	1997
Argenteuil/Papineau/Mirabel	Mario Laframboise (1957)	BQ	Notary	2000
Bas-Richelieu/Nicolet/Bécancour	Louis Plamondon (1943)	BQ	Businessman	1984
Beauce	Claude Drouin (1956)	Lib.	Civil Servant	1997
Beauharnois/Salaberry	Serge Marcil (1944)	Lib.	Businessman	2000
Beauport/Montmorency/ Côte-de-Beaupré/Île-d'Orléans	Michel Guimond (1953)	BQ	Lawyer	1993
Bellechasse/Etchemins/Montmagny/L'Islet	Gilbert Normand (1943)	Lib.	Doctor	1997
Berthier/Montcalm	Michel Bellehumeur (1963)	BQ	Lawyer	1993
Bonaventure/Gaspé/ Îles-de-la-Madeleine/Pabok	Georges Farrah (1957)	Lib.	Administrator	2000
Bourassa	Denis Coderre (1963)	Lib.	Editor	1997
Brome/Missisquoi	Denis Paradis (1949)	Lib.	Lawyer	1995
Brossard/La Prairie	Jacques Saada (1947)	Lib.	Teacher	1997
Chambly	Ghislain Lebel (1946)	BQ	Notary Public	1993
Champlain	Marcel Gagnon (1936)	BQ.	Businessman	2000
Charlesbourg-Jacques Cartier	Richard Marceau (1970)	BQ	Lawyer	1997
Charlevoix	Gérard Asselin (1950)	BQ	Foreman	1993
Châteauguay	Robert Lanctot (1963)	BQ	Lawyer	2000
Chicoutimi-Le Fjord	André Harvey (1941)	Lib.	School Com.	1997
Compton/Stanstead	David Price (1945)	Lib.	Mayor	1997
Drummond	Pauline Picard (1947)	BQ	Admin. Assistant	1993
Frontenac/Mégantic	Gerard Binet (1955)	Lib.	Businessman	2000
Gatineau	Mark Assad (1940)	Lib.	Professor	1988
Hochelaga/Maisonneuve	Réal Ménard (1962)	BQ	Political Attaché	1993
Hull/Aylmer	Marcel Proulx (1946)	Lib.	Administrator	1999
Joliette	Pierre Paquette (1955)	BQ	Professor	2000
Jonquière	Jocelyne Girard-Bujold (1943)	BQ	Businesswoman	1997
Kamouraska/Rivière-du-Loup/ Témiscouata/Les Basques	Paul Crête (1943)	BQ	Personnel Dir.	1993
Lac-Saint-Jean-Saguenay	Stéphan Tremblay (1973)	BQ	Bush Pilot	1996*
Lac-Saint-Louis	Clifford Lincoln (1928)	Lib.	Consultant	1993
LaSalle/Émard	Paul Martin (1938)	Lib.	M.P.	1988
Laurentides	Monique Guay (1959)	BQ	Businesswoman	1993
Laurier/Sainte-Marie	Gilles Duceppe (1947)	BQ	M.P.	1990*
Laval Centre	Madeleine Dalphond-Guiral (1938)	BQ	Professor	1993
Laval-Est	Carole-Marie Allard (1949)	Lib.	Author	2000
Laval-Ouest	Raymonde Folco (1940)	Lib.	Commissioner	1997
Lévis-et-Chutes-de-la-Chaudière	Antoine Dubé (1947)	BQ	Administrator	1993
Longueuil	Caroline St. Hilaire (1969)	BQ	Author agent	1997
Lotbinière—L'Érable	Odina Desrochers (1951)	BQ	Civil servant	1997
Louis-Hébert	Helene Scherrer (1950)	Lib.	Event Organizer	2000
Manicouagan	Ghislain Fournier (1938)	BQ	Businessman	1997
Matapédia/Matane	Jean-Yves Roy (1949)	BQ	Teacher	2000
Mercier	Francine Lalonde (1940)	BQ	Lecturer	1993
Mont-Royal	Irwin Cotler (1940)	Lib.	Professor	1999
Notre-Dame-de-Grace-Lachine	Marlene Jennings (1951)	Lib.	Public Servant	
Outremont	Martin Cauchon (1962)	Lib.	Lawyer	1993
Papineau/Saint-Denis	Pierre Pettigrew (1951)	Lib.	Businessman	1996*
Pierrefonds/Dollard	Bernard Patry (1943)	Lib.	Doctor	1993
Pontiac/Gatineau/Labelle	Robert Bertrand (1953)	Lib.	Insurance Agent	1993
Portneuf	Claude Duplain (1954)	Lib.	Contractor	2000
Québec	Christiane Gagnon (1948)	BQ	Real Estate Agent	1993
Québec-Est	Jean Guy Carignan (1941)	Lib.	Administrator	2000
Repentigny	Benoît Sauvageau (1963)	BQ	Teacher	1997
Richmond/Arthabaska	André Bachand (1951)	PC	Educator	1997
Rimouski-Neigette-et-la-Mitis	Suzanne Tremblay (1937)	BQ	Professor	1993

▶

▶ Rivière-des-Mille-Îles . . . . Gilles–A. Perron (1940) . . . . BQ   Pol. Advisor   1997
Roberval . . . . Michel Gauthier (1950) . . . . BQ   Administrator   1993
Rosemont—Petite-Patrie . . . . Bernard Bigras (1970) . . . . BQ   Civil Servant   1997
Saint-Bruno/Saint-Hubert . . . . Pierrette Venne (1945) . . . . BQ   Notary Public   1988
Saint-Hyacinthe/Bagot . . . . Yvan Loubier (1959) . . . . BQ   Economist   1993
Saint-Léonard/Saint-Michel . . . . Alfonso Gagliano (1942) . . . . Lib.   CGA   1984
Saint-Jean . . . . Claude Bachand (1951) . . . . BQ   Educator   1993
Saint-Lambert . . . . Yolande Thibeault (1939) . . . . Lib.   Director (DRO)   1997
Saint-Laurent/Cartierville . . . . Stéphane Dion (1955) . . . . Lib.   Professor   1996*
Saint-Maurice . . . . Jean Chrétien (1934) . . . . Lib.   Lawyer   1963
Shefford . . . . Diane St-Jacques (1953) . . . . Lib.   P.R.   1997
Sherbrooke . . . . Serge Cardin (1950) . . . . BQ   Accountant   1998*
Témiscamingue . . . . Pierre Brien (1970) . . . . BQ   Economist   1993
Terrebonne/Blainville . . . . Diane Bourgeois (1949) . . . . BQ   Teacher   2000
Trois-Rivières . . . . Yves Rocheleau (1944) . . . . BQ   Consultant   1993
Vaudreuil/Soulanges . . . . Nick Discepola (1949) . . . . Lib.   Mayor   1993
Verchères/Les-Patriotes . . . . Stéphane Bergeron (1965) . . . . BQ   Political Attaché   1993
Verdun/St-Henri/St-Paul/Pt St-Charles . . Raymond Lavigne (1945) . . . . Lib.   Consultant   1993
Westmount/Ville-Marie . . . . Lucienne Robillard (1945) . . . . Lib.   Politician   1995

■ Ontario

Riding	Member (year of birth)	Party	Occupation	First Elected[1]
Algoma/Manitoulin	Brent St. Denis (1950)	Lib.	Parl. Assistant	1993
Ancaster-Dundas-Flamborough -Aldershot	John Bryden (1943)	Lib.	Journalist	1993
Barrie/Simcoe/Bradford	Aileen Carroll (1944)	Lib.	Businesswoman	1997
Beaches/East York	Maria Minna (1948)	Lib.	Consultant	1993
Bramalea/Gore/Malton/Springdale	Gurbax Singh Malhi (1949)	Lib.	Real Estate Agent	1993
Brampton Centre	Sarkis Assadourian (1948)	Lib.	Businessman	1993
Brampton West/Mississauga	Colleen Beaumier (1944)	Lib.	Businesswoman	1993
Brant	Jane Stewart (1955)	Lib.	Human Resources	1993
Bruce/Grey/Owen Sound	Ovid L. Jackson (1939)	Lib.	Teacher	1993
Burlington	Paddy Torsney (1962)	Lib.	Consultant	1993
Cambridge	Janko Peric (1949)	Lib.	Welder	1993
Chatham/Kent/Essex	Jerry Pickard (1940)	Lib.	Teacher	1997
Davenport	Charles Caccia (1930)	Lib.	Economist	1968
Don Valley East	David Collenette (1946)	Lib.	Mgmt. Consultant	1993
Don Valley West	John Godfrey (1942)	Lib.	Journalist	1993
Dufferin/Peel/Wellington/Grey	Murray Calder (1951)	Lib.	Poultry Producer	1993
Durham	Alex Shepherd (1946)	Lib.	C.A.	1993
Eglinton/Lawrence	Joseph Volpe (1947)	Lib.	Educator	1988
Elgin/Middlesex/London	Gar Knutson (1956)	Lib.	Manager	1993
Erie/Lincoln	John Maloney (1945)	Lib.	Lawyer	1993
Essex	Susan Whelan (1963)	Lib.	Lawyer	1993
Etobicoke Centre	Allan Rock (1947)	Lib.	Lawyer	1993
Etobicoke/Lakeshore	Jean Augustine (1937)	Lib.	School Principal	1993
Etobicoke North	Roy Cullen (1944)	Lib.	Accountant	1996*
Glengarry/Prescott/Russell	Don Boudria (1949)	Lib.	Civil Servant	1984
Guelph/Wellington	Brenda Chamberlain (1952)	Lib.	Exec. Director	1993
Haldimand/Norfolk/Brant	Bob Speller (1956)	Lib.	M.P.	1988
Haliburton/Victoria/Brock	John O'Reilly (1940)	Lib.	Real Estate Broker	1993
Halton	Julian Reed (1936)	Lib.	Farmer	1993
Hamilton East	Sheila Copps (1952)	Lib.	M.P.	1984
Hamilton Mountain	Beth Phinney (1938)	Lib.	M.P.	1988
Hamilton West	Stan Keyes (1953)	Lib.	M.P.	1988
Hastings/Frontenac/Lennox & Addington	Larry McCormick (1940)	Lib.	Consultant	1993
Huron/Bruce	Paul Steckle (1942)	Lib.	Businessman	1993
Kenora/Rainy River	Robert D. Nault (1955)	Lib.	M.P.	1988
Kingston & the Islands	Peter Milliken (1946)	Lib.	Lawyer	1988
Kitchener Centre	Karen Redman (1953)	Lib.	Councillor	1997
Kitchener/Waterloo	Andrew Telegdi (1946)	Lib.	Mun. Politician	1993
Lambton/Kent/Middlesex	Rose-Marie Ur (1946)	Lib.	Farmer	1993
Lanark/Carleton	Scott Reid (1964)	CA	Author	2000

▶

▶ Leeds/Grenville	Joe Jordan (1958)	Lib.	Professor	1997
London/Fanshawe	Pat O'Brien (1948)	Lib.	Teacher	1993
London North Centre	Joe Fontana (1950)	Lib.	Businessman	1988
London West	Sue Barnes (1952)	Lib.	Lawyer	1993
Markham	John McCallum (1950)	Lib.	Economist	2000
Mississauga Centre	Carolyn Parrish (1946)	Lib.	Public Servant	1993
Mississauga East	Albina Guarnieri (1953)	Lib.	M.P.	1988
Mississauga South	Paul Szabo (1948)	Lib.	Chartered Acct.	1993
Mississauga West	Steve Mahoney (1947)	Lib.	Bus./Politician	1997
Nepean/Carleton	David Pratt (1955)	Lib.	Mun. Politician	1997
Niagara Centre	Tony Tirabassi (1957)	Lib.	Sales Rep.	2000
Niagara Falls	Gary Pillitteri (1936)	Lib.	Farmer	1993
Nickel Belt	Raymond Bonin (1942)	Lib.	Professor	1993
Nipissing	Bob Wood (1940)	Lib.	M.P.	1988
Northumberland	Paul Macklin (1944)	Lib.	Lawyer	2000
Oak Ridges	Bryon Wilfert (1952)	Lib.	Teacher	1997
Oakville	M.A. Bonnie Brown (1941)	Lib.	Social Worker	1993
Oshawa	Ivan Grose (1928)	Lib.	Businessman	1993
Ottawa Centre	Mac Harb (1953)	Lib.	M.P.	1988
Ottawa-Orleans	Eugène Bellemare (1932)	Lib.	M.P.	1988
Ottawa South	John Manley (1950)	Lib.	Lawyer	1988
Ottawa/Vanier	Mauril Bélanger (1955)	Lib.	M.P.	1995
Ottawa West/Nepean	Marlene Catterall (1939)	Lib.	M.P.	1988
Oxford	John Finlay (1929)	Lib.	Retired	1993
Parkdale/High Park	Sarmite Bulte (1953)	Lib.	Lawyer	1997
Parry Sound/Muskoka	Andy Mitchell (1953)	Lib.	Bank Manager	1993
Perth/Middlesex	John Richardson (1932)	Lib.	Self-employed	1993
Peterborough	Peter Adams (1936)	Lib.	Professor	1993
Pickering/Ajax/Uxbridge	Dan McTeague (1962)	Lib.	Media Relations	1993
Prince Edward/Hastings	Lyle Vanclief (1943)	Lib.	Agrologist	1988
Renfrew/Nipissing/Pembroke	Cheryl Gallant (1960)	CA	Office Manager	2000
Sarnia/Lambton	Roger Gallaway (1948)	Lib.	Lawyer	1993
Sault Ste. Marie	Carmen Provenzano (1942)	Lib.	Lawyer	1997
Scarborough/Agincourt	Jim Karygiannis (1955)	Lib.	Engineer	1988
Scarborough Centre	John Cannis (1951)	Lib.	HR Consultant	1993
Scarborough East	John McKay (1948)	Lib.	Lawyer	1997
Scarborough/Rouge River	Derek Lee (1948)	Lib.	Lawyer	1988
Scarborough Southwest	Tom Wappel (1950)	Lib.	M.P.	1988
Simcoe North	Paul DeVillers (1946)	Lib.	Lawyer	1993
Simcoe/Grey	Paul Bonwick (1964)	Lib.	Businessman	1997
St. Catharines	Walt Lastewka (1940)	Lib.	Plant Manager	1993
St. Paul's	Carolyn Bennett (1950)	Lib.	Doctor	1997
Stoney Creek	Tony Valeri (1957)	Lib.	Insurance	1993
Stormont/Dundas/Charlottenburgh	Bob Kilger (1944)	Lib.	Businessman	1988
Sudbury	Diane Marleau (1943)	Lib.	M.P.	1988
Thornhill	Elinor Caplan (1944)	Lib.	Provincial Politician	1997
Thunder Bay/Atikokan	Stan Dromisky (1931)	Lib.	Retired	1993
Thunder Bay/Superior North	Joe Comuzzi (1933)	Lib.	M.P.	1988
Timiskaming/Cochrane	Benoît Serré (1951)	Lib.	Businessman	1993
Timmins/James Bay	Réginald Bélair (1949)	Lib.	M.P.	1997
Toronto Centre/Rosedale	Bill Graham (1939)	Lib.	Lawyer	1993
Toronto/Danforth	Dennis Mills (1946)	Lib.	Businessman	1988
Trinity/Spadina	Tony Ianno (1957)	Lib.	Businessman	1993
Vaughan/King/Aurora	Maurizio Bevilacqua (1960)	Lib.	Consultant	1988
Waterloo/Wellington	Lynn Myers (1951)	Lib.	Mayor	1997
Whitby/Ajax	Judi Longfield (1947)	Lib.	Exec. Assistant	1997
Willowdale	Jim Peterson (1941)	Lib.	Lawyer	1988
Windsor/St. Clair	Joe Comartin (1947)	NDP	Director	2000
Windsor West	Herb Gray (1931)	Lib.	Lawyer	1962
York Centre	Arthur C. Eggleton (1943)	Lib.	Consultant	1993
York North	Karen Kraft Sloan (1952)	Lib.	Consultant	1993
York South/Weston	Alan Tonks (1943)	Lib.	Teacher	2000
York West	Judy Sgro (1944)	Lib.	Politician	1999 ▶

▶ ■ Manitoba

Riding	Member (year of birth)	Party	Occupation	First Elected[1]
Brandon/Souris	Rick Borotsik (1950)	PC	Mayor	1997
Charleswood St. James/Assiniboia	John Harvard (1938)	Lib.	Broadcaster	1988
Churchill	Bev Desjarlais (1955)	NDP	School Trustee	1997
Dauphin/Swan River	Inky Mark (1947)	CA	Mayor	1997
Portage/Lisgar	Brian Pallister (1954)	CA	Financial Analyst	2000
Provencher	Vic Toews (1952)	CA	Lawyer	2000
Saint Boniface	Ronald J. Duhamel (n.a.)	Lib.	M.P.	1988
Selkirk/Interlake	Howard Hilstrom (1947)	CA	RCMP Officer	1997
Winnipeg Centre	Pat Martin (1955)	NDP	Union Official	1997
Winnipeg North-St. Paul	Rey Pagtakhan (1935)	Lib.	Physician	1988
Winnipeg North Centre	Judy Wasylycia-Leis (1951)	NDP	Provincial Politician	1997
Winnipeg South	Reg Alcock (1948)	Lib.	Politician	1993
Winnipeg South Centre	Anita Neville (1942)	Lib.	Economist	2000
Winnipeg/Transcona	Bill Blaikie (1951)	NDP	Clergyman	1979

■ Saskatchewan

Riding	Member (year of birth)	Party	Occupation	First Elected[1]
Battlefords-Lloydminster	Gerry Ritz (1951)	CA	Rancher	1997
Blackstrap	Lynne Yelich (1953)	CA	Administrator	2000
Churchill River	Rick Laliberte (1958)	Lib.	Education	1997
Cypress Hills-Grasslands	David Anderson (1957)	CA	Farmer	2000
Palliser	Dick Proctor (1941)	NDP	Journalist	1997
Prince Albert	Brian Fitzpatrick (1945)	CA	Lawyer	2000
Regina-Lumsden-Lake Centre	Larry Spencer (1941)	CA	Minister	2000
Regina-Qu'Appelle	Lorne Nystrom (1947)	NDP	Politician	1968
Saskatoon-Humboldt	Jim Pankiw (1966)	CA	Chiropractor	1997
Souris-Moose Mountain	Roy Bailey (1928)	CA	School Supt.	1997
Saskatoon-Rosetown-Biggar	Carol Skelton (1945)	CA	Rancher	2000
Saskatoon-Wanuskewin	Maurice Vellacott (1955)	CA	Minister	1997
Wascana	Ralph E. Goodale (1949)	Lib.	Business Exec.	1993
Yorkton-Melville	Garry Breitkreuz (1945)	CA	Teacher	1993

■ Alberta

Riding	Member (year of birth)	Party	Occupation	First Elected[1]
Athabasca	David Chatters (1946)	CA	Farmer	1993
Calgary Centre	Joe Clark (1939)	PC	Politician	1972
Calgary East	Deepak Obhrai (1950)	CA	Entrepreneur	1997
Calgary Northeast	Art Hanger (1943)	CA	Police Officer	1993
Calgary/Nose Hill	Diane Ablonczy (1949)	CA	Lawyer	1993
Calgary Southeast	Jason Kenney (1968)	CA	Exec. Director	1997
Calgary Southwest	Preston Manning (1942)	CA	Consultant	1993
Calgary West	Rob Anders (1972)	CA	Lobbyist	1997
Crowfoot	Kevin Sorenson ((1958)	CA	Farmer	2000
Edmonton Centre-East	Peter Goldring (1944)	CA	Businessman	1997
Edmonton North	Deborah Grey (1952)	CA	Teacher	1989*
Edmonton Southeast	David Kilgour (1941)	Lib.	M.P.	1979
Edmonton/Strathcona	Rahim Jaffer (1971)	CA	Entrepreneur	1997
Edmonton Southwest	James Rajotte (1970)	CA	Researcher	2000
Edmonton West	Anne McLellan (1950)	Lib.	Professor	1993
Elk Island	Ken Epp (1939)	CA	Instructor	1993
Lakeland	Leon E. Benoit (1950)	CA	Civ.servant/ Farmer	1993
Lethbridge	Rick Casson (1943)	CA	Manager/Printer	1997
Macleod	Grant Hill (1943)	CA	Physician	1993
Medicine Hat	Monte Solberg (1958)	CA	Businessman	1993
Peace River	Charlie Penson (1942)	CA	Farmer	1993

▶

▶ Red Deer	Bob Mills (1941)	CA	Businessman	1993
St Albert	John Williams (1946)	CA	Accountant	1993
Wetaskiwin	Dale Johnston (1941)	CA	Farmer	1993
Wild Rose	Myron Thompson (1936)	CA	Retired	1993
Yellowhead	Bob Merrifield (1953)	CA	Businessman	2000

■ British Columbia

Riding	Member (year of birth)	Party	Occupation	First Elected[1]
Burnaby/Douglas	Svend J. Robinson (1952)	NDP	M.P.	1979
Cariboo/Chilcotin	Philip Mayfield (1937)	CA	Ord. Minister	1993
Delta/South Richmond	John Cummins (1942)	CA	Teacher	1993
Dewdney/Alouette	Grant McNally (1962)	CA	Teacher	1997
Esquimalt/Juan de Fuca	Keith Martin (1960)	CA	Physician	1993
Fraser Valley	Chuck Strahl (1957)	CA	Logging Cont.	1993
Kamloops/Thompson/Highland Valleys	Betty Hinton (1950)	CA	Businesswoman	2000
Kelowna	Werner Schmidt (1932)	CA	Businessman	1993
Kootenay/Boundary/Okanagan	Jim Gouk (1946)	CA	Real Estate Agt.	1993
Kootenay-Columbia	Jim Abbott (1942)	CA	Businessman	1993
Langley/Abbotsford	Randy White (1948)	CA	CMA	1993
Nanaimo/Alberni	James D. Lunney (1951)	CA	Chiropractor	2000
Nanaimo/Cowichan	Reed Elley (1945)	CA	Minister	1997
New Westminster/Coquitlam/Burnaby	Paul E. Forseth (1946)	CA	Probation Officer	1993
North Vancouver	Ted White (1949)	CA	Company Pres.	1993
Okanagan/Coquihalla	Stockwell Day (1950)	CA	Politician	2000
Okanagan/Shuswap	Darrel Stinson (1945)	CA	Mining	1993
Port Moody/Coquitlam/Port Coquitlam	James Moore (1976)	CA	Broadcaster	2000
Prince George/Bulkley Valley	Richard M. Harris (1944)	CA	Retired	1993
Prince George/Peace River	Jay Hill (1952)	CA	Farmer	1993
Richmond	Joe Peschisolido (1963)	CA	Lawyer	2000
Saanich/Gulf Islands	Gary Lunn (1957)	CA	Lawyer	1997
Skeena	Andy Burton (1942)	CA	Property Manager	2000
South Surrey/White Rock/Langley	Val Meredith (1949)	CA	Businesswoman	1993
Surrey Central	Gurmant Grewal (1957)	CA	Real Estate Agt.	1997
Surrey North	Chuck Cadman (1948)	CA	Elec. Eng. Tech.	1997
Vancouver Centre	Hedy Fry (1941)	Lib.	Physician	1993
Vancouver East	Elizabeth Davies (1953)	NDP	Councillor	1997
Vancouver Island North	John Duncan (1948)	CA	Forester	1993
Vancouver Kingsway	Sophia Leung (1934)	Lib.	Social Worker	1997
Vancouver Quadra	Stephen Owen (1948)	Lib.	Lawyer	2000
Vancouver South/Burnaby	Harbance Singh Dhaliwal (1952)	Lib.	Businessman	1993
Victoria	David Anderson (1937)	Lib.	Env. Consultant	1968
West Vancouver/Sunshine Coast	John Reynolds (1942)	CA	Businessman	1997

■ Yukon

Riding	Member (year of birth)	Party	Occupation	First Elected[1]
Yukon	Larry Bagnell (1949)	Lib.	Exec. Director	2000

■ Northwest Territiories

Riding	Member (year of birth)	Party	Occupation	First Elected[1]
Western Arctic	Ethel Blondin-Andrew (1951)	Lib.	Politician	1988

■ Nunavut

Riding	Member (year of birth)	Party	Occupation	First Elected[1]
Nunavut	Nancy Karetak-Lindell (1957)	Lib.	Businessperson	1997

(1) General election unless * indicating by-election. (n.a.) not available. PC—Progressive Conservative; Lib.—Liberal; NDP—New Democratic Party; CA—Canadian Alliance.

Salaries of Federal Political Figures

(as of October 2001)

The **GOVERNOR GENERAL** receives $105 700 per year.
All **LIEUTENANT–GOVERNORS** receive $100 100 per year (taxable).
SENATORS .... $106 400 plus 64 travel points[2] per year.[3]

The following senators receive as *extra* salary on top of their Senate salaries:

Leader of the Government	$63 096 plus $2 122 car allowance
Leader of the Opposition...	$30 200
Speaker of the Senate	$46 200 plus $3 000 residence allowance and $1 061 car allowance
Speaker pro tempore	$19 100
Deputy Leader of the Government..............................	$30 200
Deputy Leader of the Opposition	$19 100
Government Whip	$9 400
Opposition Whip	$5 700
Chairs of Standing Committees[4]	$9 400
Vice-Chairs of Standing Committees[4].........................	$4 900

MEMBERS OF PARLIAMENT—$69 100 plus $22 800 tax-free expense allowance[1] and 64 travel points[2] per year.[3]

The following members of Parliament receive as *extra* salary on top of their MP salaries:

Prime Minister	$75 100 plus $2 122 car allowance
Cabinet Ministers......................................	$50 000 plus $2 122 car allowance
Speaker of the House......................	$52 700 plus $1 061 car allowance and $3 000 rent allowance
Secretaries of State	$37 500
Deputy Speaker..	$27 500 plus $1 500 rent allowance
Official Opposition Leader	$52 700 plus $2 122 car allowance
Other Opposition Party Leaders..................	$31 600
Official Opposition House Leader	$25 300
Other House Leaders	$10 800
Government and Official Opposition Whips...	$13 900
Other Party Whips....................................	$7 900
Government and Opposition Deputy Whips ..	$7 900
Deputy Chairman, Committees of the Whole House	$11 200
Assistant Deputy Chairman, Committees of the Whole House ...	$11 200
Parliamentary Secretaries	$11 200

(1) MPs representing large rural districts listed in Schedule III of the Canada Elections Act receive an annual tax-free expense allowance of $27,700; MPs from Nunavut and the Western Arctic receive annual tax-free expense allowances of $29,700 each. (2) One travel point represents a business-class return air trip anywhere in Canada and can be used by representatives or their spouses or a designated family member. (3) Members and senators who travel in Canada on official business and are at least 100 km from their principal residences may claim up to $12,000 in food, accommodation, and incidental expenses. (4) Excludes the Standing Joint Committee on the Library of Parliament.

■ SENATORS' OFFICE BUDGET

Each senator is entitled to a budget of $125,000 per fiscal year for research and office expenses. The expenses must be incurred while the senator fulfills his or her parliamentary role.

■ SENATORS' PENSION PLAN

Senators must contribute 7 percent of their basic salaries (and may contribute up to 9 percent extra) to their pensions. Senators must serve at least six years to be eligible for a monthly pension for life. Senators who retire with fewer than six years' service get their pension contributions returned. Retirement benefits are indexed to the cost of living after age 60. No senator may collect pension benefits before age 55.

The maximum basic pension equals 75 percent of a senator's average best five years after 25 years of service (accrued at 3 percent annually). There is no maximum to extra salary pension, and the amount is accrued at 4 percent annually. After a senator dies, the surviving spouse is entitled to three fifths of the senator's pension; up to three dependent children are entitled to a further one tenth each of the deceased senator's pension.

■ MEMBERS' OFFICE BUDGET

Each of the 301 elected members has an office in both Ottawa and his or her riding, with staff to assist constituents with problems they may encounter when dealing with federal government departments and agencies. Each member's office budget covers staff salaries in Ottawa and constituency offices as well as individuals or firms hired under contract. The budget is also intended to cover the costs of renting, equipping and maintaining constituency offices as well as covering the costs of travel within the constituency and within the member's province.

A member's office budget is set at $214,800, $218,000 or $221,400 according to the size of the constituency and its number of urban and/or rural polling divisions.

Geographic and Elector Supplement: Members receive supplements to the main office budget if they represent large constituencies with over 70,000 voters (e.g., the riding of York North) and/or geographic boundaries over 8,000 sq. km (e.g., the riding of Nunavut). These annual budgetary supplements cover the additional staff, operating and travel expenses required to serve the riding. Based on constituency characteristics, these supplements range from $6,630 to $39,850 and may change after each general election as the riding demographics change. A member may have more than one constituency office should he or she so desire, and many do.

Other Services: To help meet the needs and requests of their constituents, members are also given access to printing, translation, mail and other support services that help them respond to the thousands of letters and requests they receive. (Canadians may write to members of Parliament free of charge from anywhere in Canada.) The services also allow members to keep the public up-to-date on the

events in Ottawa through a parliamentary report generally known as a "householder." Finally, members are provided with desks, computers, photocopiers and other office supplies and equipment required to run an efficient office in Ottawa.

■ MEMBERS' PENSION PLAN

Members' pensions are provided for by law under the Members of Parliament Retiring Allowances Act and, like many pension plans, members must make a financial contribution. Specifically, members must contribute 9 percent of their annual sessional allowance (salary) of $68,200. For members who are receiving additional salaries for extra duties such as ministers, whips or parliamentary secretaries, they have the option to contribute up to 9 percent of these salaries as well. The Act also provides that, upon ceasing to be a member of the House of Commons, a former member who retired prior to 1995 is immediately entitled to an annual pension after a minimum of six years of service. This pension is payable at the rate of 4 percent per year of service (i.e., a minimum of 24 percent: 6 x 4 percent) up to a maximum of 75 percent (18.75 years of service) of the average of the best consecutive six years of earnings. Members who serve less than six years must withdraw their contributions.

Indexing of a former member of the House of Commons' pension begins only when he or she reaches the age of 60, except for extraordinary situations such as disability. Survivors' benefits are payable to spouses and dependent children. If a former member in receipt of a pension is re-elected to the House of Commons or becomes a senator, the pension allowance is suspended for the period in office. In 1995 the pension plan was amended to allow members to opt out; eliminate "double dipping" (drawing more than one pension after holding several positions); and provide that a former member cannot receive a pension until they are at least 55 years old.

Source: *Public Information Office, House of Commons*

Supreme Court Justices of Canada

(as of October 2001)

Name	Date of Birth	Date Appointed	Appointed from
The Rt. Hon. Madam Justice Beverley McLachlin	Sept. 7, 1943	Mar. 30, 1989[1]	Supreme Court of BC
The Hon. Madam Justice Louise Arbour	Feb. 10, 1947	June 10, 1999	Ontario Court of Appeal
The Hon. Mr. Justice Michel Bastarache	June 10, 1947	Oct. 1, 1997	NB Court of Appeal
The Hon. Mr. Justice William Ian Corneil Binnie	Apr. 14, 1939	Jan. 8, 1998	Private law practice
The Hon. Mr. Justice Charles Doherty Gonthier	Aug. 1, 1928	Feb. 1, 1989	Quebec Court of Appeal
The Hon. Mr. Justice Frank Iacobucci	June 29, 1937	Jan. 7, 1991	Federal Court of Canada
The Hon. Madam Justice Claire L'Heureux-Dubé	Sept. 7, 1927	Apr. 15, 1987	Quebec Court of Appeal
The Hon. Mr. Justice Louis LeBel	Nov. 30, 1939	Jan. 7, 2000	Quebec Court of Appeal
The Hon. Mr. Justice John Charles Major	Feb. 20, 1931	Nov. 13, 1992	Alberta Court of Appeal

Source: *Supreme Court of Canada*   (1) Appointed Chief Justice Jan. 7, 2000

Chief Justices of the Supreme Court of Canada

Name	Date of Birth	Date Appointed Chief Justice	Term Ended
The Hon. Sir William Buell Richards	May 2, 1815	Sept. 30, 1875	Jan. 10, 1879
The Hon. Sir William Johnston Ritchie	Oct. 28, 1813	Jan. 11, 1879	Sept. 25, 1892
The Rt. Hon. Sir Samuel Henry Strong	Aug. 13, 1825	Dec. 13, 1892	Nov. 18, 1902
The Rt. Hon. Sir Henri-Elzéar Taschereau	Oct. 7, 1836	Nov. 21, 1902	May 2, 1906
The Rt. Hon. Sir Charles Fitzpatrick	Dec. 19, 1853	June 4, 1906	Oct. 21, 1918
The Rt. Hon. Sir Louis Henry Davies	May 6, 1845	Oct. 23, 1918	May 1, 1924
The Rt. Hon. Francis Alexander Anglin	Apr. 2, 1865	Sept. 16, 1924	Feb. 28, 1933
The Rt. Hon. Sir Lyman Poore Duff	Jan. 7, 1865	Mar. 17, 1933	Jan. 7, 1944
The Rt. Hon. Thibaudeau Rinfret	June 22, 1879	Jan. 8, 1944	June 22, 1954
The Hon. Patrick Kerwin	Oct. 25, 1889	July 1, 1954	Feb. 2, 1963
The Rt. Hon. Robert Taschereau	Sept. 10, 1896	Apr. 22, 1963	Sept. 1, 1967
The Rt. Hon. John Robert Cartwright	Mar. 23, 1895	Sept. 1, 1967	Mar. 23, 1970
The Rt. Hon. Joseph Honoré Gérald Fauteux	Oct. 22, 1900	Mar. 23, 1970	Dec. 23, 1973
The Rt. Hon. Bora Laskin	Oct. 5, 1912	Dec. 27, 1973	Mar. 26, 1984
The Rt. Hon. Robert George Brian Dickson	May 25, 1916	Apr. 18, 1984	June 30, 1990
The Rt. Hon. Antonio Lamer	Jul. 8, 1933	July 1, 1990	Jan. 6, 2000
The Rt. Hon. Beverley McLachlin	Sept. 7, 1943	Jan. 7, 2000–	

Source: *Supreme Court of Canada and Canadian Parliamentary Guide*

Contacting the Supreme Court

*F**or information on the Supreme Court of Canada, turn to page 141. Visit the court's website at http://www.scc-csc.gc.ca for more information on judges, history, recent decisions, tours and news. You may also write to the Supreme Court of Canada, 301 Wellington Street, Ottawa, Ontario, K1A 0J1. Phone (613) 995-4330 or e-mail reception@scc-csc.gc.ca*

FOCUS ON...

Key Decisions of the Supreme Court of Canada

The Persons Case (1928): The court unanimously decided that women were not "persons" qualified for appointment to the Canadian Senate. In 1929, the British Privy Council overturned the decision on appeal, declaring the exclusion of women from public office "a relic of days more barbarous than ours."

Alberta Press Act Reference (1938): The court struck down an Alberta bill that would have required newspapers, when called upon by government officials, to publish the government's rebuttal of criticism that had appeared in the newspapers. The decision blocked one form of government interference with press freedom.

Saumur v City of Quebec (1953): The court narrowly upheld the province's right to authorize municipal bans on street pamphleteering. (The ban had been challenged by Jehovah's Witnesses who were distributing leaflets.) However, one majority judge declared that a Quebec law guaranteeing religious freedom prevented the authorities from banning the distribution of *religious* pamphlets. Thus the court attempted to protect this form of religious expression.

Roncarelli v Duplessis (1959): The court ruled that Maurice Duplessis, former premier and attorney general of Quebec, committed a civil wrong when he revoked the liquor licence of Roncarelli, a restaurateur, in 1946. Duplessis had revoked the licence, and had ruined Roncarelli's business, because Roncarelli had aided Jehovah's Witnesses who had been arrested for pamphleteering. The court ordered Duplessis to pay damages.

R. v Drybones (1970): The court used a clause declaring equality before the law in the Bill of Rights to strike down part of the Indian Act that made it an offence for a Native person to be drunk when off a reserve. The court decided that if a federal law cannot be applied without infringing on a citizen's rights, the law must be suspended until Parliament declares that the law still applies—regardless of the Bill of Rights. Then the court ruled that Drybones, an aboriginal man found drunk while away from his reserve, had been punished for his race under a law whose penalty differed for other Canadians.

R. v Kienapple (1975): The court abolished the practice of sentencing defendants twice for offences that amounted to being the same act.

CUPE Local 963 v New Brunswick Liquor Corp. (1979): The court affirmed the growing role of administrative tribunals and established when the courts can interfere with the tribunals' decisions.

Patriation Reference (1981): The court ruled that the federal government could patriate the constitution (then known as the British North America Act) without the consent of the provinces; however, the court also said that the federal government would violate a political tradition if it patriated the constitution without first securing "a substantial degree" of provincial consent.

The Bill 101 Case (1984): The court struck down two sections of Quebec's Bill 101 (The Charter of the French Language) that dealt with anglophone schooling. The sections attempted to make French the language of instruction in elementary schools for anglophones who had moved to Quebec from elsewhere in Canada. The court declared that this was incompatible with minority-language education guarantees in the Canadian Charter of Rights and Freedoms.

R. v Big M Drug Mart (1985): The court struck down the Lord's Day Act, a federal law passed in 1907 that banned business activities on Sundays. The court declared that, by forcing all members of society to observe the Christian Sabbath, the law infringed on the religious freedoms of non-Christian minorities; therefore, the Act was incompatible with the religious freedom guarantees in the Canadian Charter of Rights and Freedoms. Big M Drug Mart had been charged with selling merchandise on Sundays.

R. v Oakes (1986): The court struck down a section of the Narcotic Control Act that conflicted with the presumption of innocence of accused persons—a presumption guaranteed in the Canadian Charter of Rights and Freedoms. The court also established a two-step test to see whether laws measure up to Charter guarantees. First, the government must prove the existence of a purpose important and urgent enough to justify the suppression of a right; second, the government's legislative methods must be reasonable, fair and proportionate to the goal.

The Ford Case (1988): The court struck down two more sections of Quebec's Bill 101. The provisions attempted to impose the exclusive use of French on public and commercial signs in Quebec. The court decided that these provisions violated the freedom of expression guarantees in the Canadian Charter of Rights and Freedoms, although the *predominant* use of French on such signs could be legally justified.

Daigle v Tremblay (1989): The court declared that fetuses have no constitutional rights; constitutional rights begin at the time of live birth. The court also decided that the father of a fetus may not use a court injunction to prevent the mother from exercising her right of choice to have an abortion. Tremblay had tried to stop his partner, Daigle, from aborting their unborn child.

R. v Stinchcombe (1990): The court unanimously affirmed that the Crown must reveal all its evidence against an accused to the defence so the defence can properly defend the accused. This responsibility of the Crown, which had existed in common law, became obligatory rather than merely voluntary. The ruling also required police and prosecutors to disclose all their evidence before the accused chose a mode of trial or entered a plea.

R. v Sparrow (1990): The court affirmed the rights of aboriginal peoples in the Constitution Act and declared that these rights must be interpreted broadly. The authorities had charged Sparrow, an aboriginal man, with breaking a federal fishing law. Sparrow successfully argued that the right to fish was protected by treaty and the Constitution. The court also established criteria for interpreting aboriginal rights in the Constitution.

R. v Stillman (1997): The court decided that the common-law power to conduct a search incidental to an arrest excluded the right to seize body substances by force. The police had subjected a suspect, Stillman, to an intrusive body search without consent. The court ruled that such searches must meet three requirements to be legal: the arrest must be legal, the search must be incidental, and the search must be conducted in a reasonable way.

Delgamuukw v British Columbia (1997): The court defined the content and extent of aboriginal title to ancestral lands. The court required aboriginals seeking such title to prove that they occupied the territory before Canada's declaration of sovereignty. The court also decided to consider admitting oral history as evidence.

R. v Caslake (1998): The court decided that a police search made for purposes of inventory, conforming to police policy but without a search warrant or permission, is an abusive search. Caslake had been arrested for possessing narcotics; an RCMP search of Caslake's van several hours after the arrest—which led to the seizure of more narcotics—prompted the dispute over "abusive searches" in court.

Quebec Secession Reference (1998): The court ruled unanimously that a unilateral declaration of independence by a province (i.e., Quebec) would be illegal according to the Canadian Constitution and international law. However, a constitutional amendment would make secession possible. The court also said that if a clear majority of Quebeckers voted for secession in a referendum, the rest of Canada would be obliged to negotiate the terms of independence. The negotiations would have to respect democracy, federalism, the rule of law and the protection of minorities.

Vriend v Alberta (1998): The court unanimously declared that Alberta's failure to include sexual orientation as an illegal form of discrimination in its Individual Rights Protection Act violated the Canadian Charter of Rights and Freedoms. The court ruled that Vriend, a homosexual, had been wrongfully dismissed from his job at an Edmonton college after he acknowledged his sexual orientation to his employer.

Lieutenant-Governors and Commissioners

(as of October 2001)

On the advice of the prime minister, the governor general of Canada appoints 10 provincial lieutenant-governors and three territorial commissioners. Lieutenant-governors and commissioners represent the monarch and perform the same duties at the provincial and territorial levels that the governor general performs at the federal level. They open, prorogue and dissolve legislatures and give royal assent to legislation and orders-in-council.

Lieutenant-governors and commissioners are paid by the federal government and usually serve terms of five years.

Province or Territory	Lieutenant-Governor/ Commissioner	Birthdate	Date Sworn in
Newfoundland	Hon. Arthur M. House	Aug. 10, 1926	Feb. 5, 1997
Prince Edward Island	Hon. J. Léonce Bernard	May 23, 1943	May 28, 2001
Nova Scotia	Hon. Myra A. Freeman	May 17, 1949	May 17, 2000
New Brunswick	Hon. Marilyn T. Counsell	Oct. 22, 1933	Apr. 18, 1997
Quebec	Hon. Lise Thibault	Apr. 2, 1939	Jan. 30, 1997
Ontario	Hon. Hilary Weston	Jan. 12, 1942	Jan. 24, 1997
Manitoba	Hon. Peter M. Liba	May 10, 1940	Mar. 2, 1999
Saskatchewan	Hon. Lynda M. Haverstock	Sept. 16, 1948	Feb. 21, 2000
Alberta	Hon. Lois Elsa Hole	1933	Feb. 10, 2000
British Columbia	Hon. Iona Campagnolo	Oct. 18, 1932	Sept. 25, 2001
Nunavut	Hon. Peter Irniq	1947	Apr. 1, 2000
Northwest Territories	Hon. Glenna F. Hansen	Aug. 10, 1956	Mar. 31, 2000
Yukon	Hon. Jack Cable	Aug. 17, 1934	Sept. 30, 2000

n.a. not available

Provincial Premiers: A Historical Listing

(as of October 2001)

■ Newfoundland

Premier	Term	Party	Elected or sworn in
Joseph R. Smallwood	1949–72	Liberal	Apr. 1, 1949
Frank D. Moores	1972–79	Conservative	Jan. 18, 1972
A. Brian Peckford	1979–89	Conservative	Mar. 26, 1979
Tom Rideout	1989	Conservative	Mar. 22, 1989
Clyde Wells	1989–96	Liberal	May 5, 1989
Brian Tobin	1996–2000	Liberal	Jan. 26, 1996
Beaton Tulk	2000–01	Liberal	Oct. 16, 2000
Roger Grimes	2001–	Liberal	Feb. 13, 2001

■ Prince Edward Island

Premier	Term	Party	Elected or sworn in
C. Pope	1873	Conservative	Apr., 1873
L. C. Owen	1873–76	Conservative	Sept., 1873
L. H. Davies	1876–79	Liberal (Coalition)	Aug.,1876
W. W. Sullivan	1879–89	Conservative	Apr. 25, 1879
N. McLeod	1889–91	Conservative	Nov., 1889
F. Peters	1891–97	Liberal	Apr. 27, 1891
A. B. Warburton	1897–98	Liberal	Oct., 1897
D. Farquharson	1898–1901	Liberal	Aug., 1898
A. Peters	1901–08	Liberal	Dec. 29, 1901
F. L. Haszard	1908–11	Liberal	Feb. 1, 1908
H. James Palmer	1911	Liberal	May 16, 1911
John A. Mathieson	1911–17	Conservative	Dec. 2, 1911
Aubin Arsenault	1917–19	Conservative	June, 21, 1917
J. H. Bell	1919–23	Liberal	Sept. 9, 1919
James D. Stewart	1923–27	Conservative	Sept. 5, 1923
Albert C. Saunders	1927–30	Liberal	Aug. 12, 1927
Walter M. Lea	1930–31	Liberal	May 20, 1930

▶

▶

James D. Stewart	1931–33	Conservative	Aug. 29, 1931
William J. P. MacMillan	1933–35	Conservative	Oct. 14, 1933
Walter M. Lea	1935–36	Liberal	Aug. 15, 1935
Thane A. Campbell	1936–43	Liberal	Jan. 14, 1936
J. Walter Jones	1943–53	Liberal	May 11, 1943
Alexander W. Matheson	1953–59	Liberal	May 25, 1953
Walter Shaw	1959–66	Prog. Conservative	Sept. 16, 1959
Alexander B. Campbell	1966–78	Liberal	July 28, 1966
William Bennett Campbell	1978–79	Liberal	Sept. 18, 1978
J. Angus MacLean	1979–81	Prog. Conservative	May 3, 1979
James M. Lee	1981–86	Prog. Conservative	Nov. 17, 1981
Joseph A. Ghiz	1986–93	Liberal	May 2, 1986
Catherine Callbeck	1993–96	Liberal	Jan. 25, 1993
Keith Milligan	1996	Liberal	Oct. 10, 1996
Patrick Binns	1996–	Prog. Conservative	Nov. 27, 1996

■ Nova Scotia

Premier	Term	Party	Elected or sworn in
H. Blanchard	1867	Conservative	July 4, 1867
William Annand	1867–75	Liberal	Nov. 7, 1867
P. C. Hill	1875–78	Liberal	May 11, 1875
S. H. Holmes	1878–82	Conservative	Oct. 22, 1878
John S. D. Thompson	1882	Conservative	May 25, 1882
W. T. Pipes	1882–84	Liberal	Aug. 3, 1882
W. S. Fielding	1884–96	Liberal	July 28, 1884
George H. Murray	1896–1923	Liberal	July 20, 1896
E. H. Armstrong	1923–25	Liberal	Jan. 24, 1923
E. N. Rhodes	1925–30	Conservative	July 16, 1925
Col. Gordon S. Harrington	1930–33	Conservative	Aug. 11, 1930
Angus L. Macdonald	1933–40	Liberal	Sept. 5, 1933
A. S. MacMillan	1940–45	Liberal	July 10, 1940
Angus L. Macdonald	1945–54	Liberal	Sept. 8, 1945
Harold Connolly	1954	Liberal	Apr. 13, 1954
Henry D. Hicks	1954–56	Liberal	Sept. 30, 1954
Robert L. Stanfield	1956–67	Prog. Conservative	Nov. 20, 1956
George Smith	1967–70	Prog. Conservative	Sept. 13, 1967
Gerald A. Regan	1970–78	Liberal	Oct. 28, 1970
John Buchanan	1978–90	Prog. Conservative	Oct. 5, 1978
Roger Bacon	1990–91	Prog. Conservative	Sept. 12, 1990
Donald Cameron	1991–93	Prog. Conservative	Feb. 9, 1991
John Savage	1993–97	Liberal	June 11, 1993
Russell MacLellan	1997–99	Liberal	July 18, 1997
John Hamm	1999–	Prog. Conservative	July 27, 1999

■ New Brunswick

Premier	Term	Party	Elected or sworn in
Andrew Wetmore	1867–70	Confederation Party	1867
G.E. King	1870–71	Conservative	1870
George Hatheway	1871–72	Conservative	1871
G.E. King	1872–78	Conservative	1872
James Fraser	1878–82	Conservative	1878
D. L. Hanington	1882–83	Conservative	1882
Andrew Blair	1883–96	Liberal	1883
James Mitchell	1896–97	Liberal	July, 1896
Henry Emmerson	1897–1900	Liberal	Oct. 29, 1897
L. J. Tweedie	1900–07	Liberal	Aug. 31, 1900
William Pugsley	1907	Liberal	Mar. 6, 1907
Clifford Robinson	1907–08	Liberal	May 31, 1907
John Douglas Hazen	1908–11	Conservative	Mar. 24, 1908
James K. Flemming	1911–14	Conservative	Oct. 16, 1911
George J. Clark	1914–17	Conservative	Dec. 17, 1914
James Murray	1917	Conservative	Feb. 1, 1917
Walter E. Foster	1917–23	Liberal	Apr. 4, 1917
Peter Veniot	1923–25	Liberal	Feb. 28, 1923
John B. M. Baxter	1925–31	Conservative	Sept. 14, 1925

▶

▶ Charles D. Richards .... 1931–33 Conservative May 19, 1931
Leonard Tilley .... 1933–35 Conservative June 1, 1933
Allison Dysart .... 1935–40 Liberal July 16, 1935
John McNair .... 1940–52 Liberal Mar. 13, 1940
Hugh J. Flemming .... 1952–60 Prog. Conservative Oct. 8, 1952
Louis J. Robichaud .... 1960–70 Liberal July 12, 1960
Richard Hatfield .... 1970–87 Prog. Conservative Nov. 12, 1970
Frank McKenna .... 1987–97 Liberal Oct. 27, 1987
Ray Frenette (interim) .... 1997–98 Liberal Oct 14, 1997
Camille Thériault .... 1998–99 Liberal May 14, 1998
Bernard Lord .... 1999– Prog. Conservative June 21, 1999

■ Quebec

Premier	Term	Party	Elected or sworn in
Pierre-Joseph-Olivier Chauveau	1867–73	Conservative	July 15, 1867
Gédéon Ouimet	1873–74	Conservative	Feb. 26, 1873
Charles E. Boucher deBoucherville	1874–78	Conservative	Sept. 22, 1874
Henri Joly	1878–79	Liberal	Mar. 8, 1878
J. Adolphe Chapleau	1879–82	Conservative	Oct. 31, 1879
J. Alfred Mousseau	1882–84	Conservative	July 31, 1882
John J. Ross	1884–87	Conservative	Jan. 23, 1884
L. Olivier Taillon	1887	Conservative	Jan. 25, 1887
Honoré Mercier	1887–91	Liberal	Jan. 27, 1887
Charles E. Boucher deBoucherville	1891–92	Conservative	Dec. 21, 1891
L. Olivier Taillon	1892–96	Conservative	Dec. 16, 1892
Edmund J. Flynn	1896–97	Conservative	May 11, 1896
F. Gabriel Marchand	1897–1900	Liberal	May 24, 1897
S. Napoléon Parent	1900–05	Liberal	Oct. 3, 1900
Lomer Gouin	1905–20	Liberal	Mar. 23, 1905
L. Alexandre Taschereau	1920–36	Liberal	July 9, 1920
Adélard Godbout	1936	Liberal	June 11, 1936
Maurice Duplessis	1936–39	Union Nationale	Aug. 26, 1936
Adélard Godbout	1939–44	Liberal	Nov. 8, 1939
Maurice Duplessis	1944–59	Union Nationale	Aug. 30, 1944
Paul Sauvé	1959–60	Union Nationale	Sept. 11, 1959
Antonio Barrette	1960	Union Nationale	Jan. 8, 1960
Jean Lesage	1960–66	Liberal	July 5, 1960
Daniel Johnson	1966–68	Union Nationale	June 16, 1966
Jean-Jacques Bertrand	1968–70	Union Nationale	Oct. 2, 1968
Robert Bourassa	1970–76	Liberal	May 12, 1970
René Lévesque	1976–85	Parti Québécois	Nov. 25, 1976
Pierre-Marc Johnson	1985	Parti Québécois	Oct. 3, 1985
Robert Bourassa	1985–94	Liberal	Dec. 12, 1985
Daniel Johnson	1994–94	Liberal	Jan. 11, 1994
Jacques Parizeau	1994–96	Parti Québécois	Sept. 26, 1994
Lucien Bouchard	1996–2001	Parti Québécois	Jan. 29, 1996
Bernard Landry	2001–	Parti Québécois	Mar. 8, 2001

■ Ontario

Premier	Term	Party	Elected or sworn in
J.S. Macdonald	1867–71	Coalition	July 16, 1867
Edward Blake	1871–72	Liberal	Dec. 20, 1871
Oliver Mowat	1872–96	Liberal	Oct. 25, 1872
Arthur S. Hardy	1896–99	Liberal	July 25, 1896
George William Ross	1899–1905	Liberal	Oct. 21, 1899
Sir James P. Whitney	1905–14	Conservative	Feb. 8, 1905
Sir William Hearst	1914–19	Conservative	Oct. 2, 1914
Ernest C. Drury	1919–23	United Farmers of Ontario	Nov. 14, 1919
George Howard Ferguson	1923–30	Conservative	July 16, 1923
George Stewart Henry	1930–34	Conservative	Dec. 15, 1930
Mitchell F. Hepburn	1934–42	Liberal	July 10, 1934
Gordon Daniel Conant	1942–43	Liberal	Oct. 21, 1942
Harry C. Nixon	1943	Liberal	May 18, 1943
George Drew	1943–48	Prog. Conservative	Aug. 17, 1943
Thomas L. Kennedy	1948–49	Prog. Conservative	Oct. 19, 1948 ▶

▶ Leslie M. Frost	1949–61	Prog. Conservative	May 4, 1949
John P. Robarts	1961–71	Prog. Conservative	Nov. 8, 1961
William G. Davis	1971–85	Prog. Conservative	Mar. 1, 1971
Frank Miller	1985	Prog. Conservative	Feb. 8, 1985
David Peterson	1985–90	Liberal	June 26, 1985
Bob Rae	1990–95	New Democratic	Oct. 1, 1990
Mike Harris	1995–	Prog. Conservative	June 28, 1995

■ Manitoba

Premier	Term	Party	Elected or sworn in
A. Boyd	1870–71	n.a.	Sept. 16, 1870
M. A. Girard	1871–72	Conservative	Dec. 14, 1871
H. H. Clarke	1872–74	n.a.	Mar. 14, 1872
M. A. Girard	1874	Conservative	July 8, 1874
R. A. Davis	1874–78	n.a.	Dec. 3, 1874
John Norquay	1878–87	Conservative	Oct. 16, 1878
D. H. Harrison	1887–88	Conservative	Dec. 26, 1887
T. Greenway	1888–1900	Liberal	Jan. 19, 1888
H. J. Macdonald	1900	Conservative	Jan. 8, 1900
Sir R. P. Roblin	1900–15	Conservative	Oct. 29, 1900
T. C. Norris	1915–22	Liberal	May 12, 1915
John Bracken	1922–43	Coalition[1]	Aug. 8, 1922
S. S. Garson	1943–48	Coalition	Jan. 8, 1943
D. L. Campbell	1948–58	Conservative	Nov. 11, 1948
Duff Roblin	1958–67	Prog. Conservative	June 16, 1958
Walter Weir	1967–69	Prog. Conservative	Nov. 25, 1967
Edward Schreyer	1969–77	New Democratic	July 15, 1969
Sterling Lyon	1977–81	Prog. Conservative	Nov. 24, 1977
Howard Pawley	1981–88	New Democratic	Nov. 30, 1981
Gary Filmon	1988–99	Prog. Conservative	Apr. 26, 1988
Gary Doer	1999–	New Democratic	Oct. 5, 1999

■ Saskatchewan

Premier	Term	Party	Elected or sworn in
Walter Scott	1905–16	Liberal	Sept. 5, 1905
W. M. Martin	1916–22	Liberal	Oct. 20, 1916
C. A. Dunning	1922–26	Liberal	Apr. 5, 1922
J. G. Gardiner	1926–29	Liberal	Feb. 26, 1926
J. T. M. Anderson	1929–34	Conservative	Sept. 9, 1929
J. G. Gardiner	1934–35	Liberal	July 19, 1934
W. J. Patterson	1935–44	Liberal	Nov. 1, 1935
Tommy Douglas	1944–61	C.C.F.[2]	July 10, 1944
W. S. Lloyd	1961–64	C.C.F.—N.D.P.	Nov. 7, 1961
W. Ross Thatcher	1964–71	Liberal	May 22, 1964
Allan E. Blakeney	1971–82	New Democratic	June 30, 1971
Grant Devine	1982–91	Prog. Conservative	May 8, 1982
Roy Romanow	1991–2001	New Democratic	Nov. 1, 1991
Lorne Calvert	2001–	New Democratic	Feb. 8, 2001

■ Alberta

Premier	Term	Party	Elected or sworn in
Alex Rutherford	1905–10	Liberal	Sept. 2, 1905
A. L. Sifton	1910–17	Liberal	May 26, 1910
Charles Stewart	1917–21	Liberal	Oct. 30, 1917
Herbert Greenfield	1921–25	United Farmers of Alberta	Aug. 13, 1921
John E. Brownlee	1925–34	United Farmers of Alberta	Nov. 23, 1925
Richard G. Reid	1934–35	United Farmers of Alberta	July 10, 1934
William Aberhart	1935–43	Social Credit	Sept. 3, 1935
E. C. Manning	1943–68	Social Credit	May 31, 1943
Harry Strom	1968–71	Social Credit	Dec. 12, 1968
Peter Lougheed	1971–85	Prog. Conservative	Sept. 10, 1971
Don Getty	1985–92	Prog. Conservative	Nov. 1, 1985
Ralph P. Klein	1992–	Prog. Conservative	Dec. 14, 1992

▶ ■ British Columbia

Premier	Term	Party	Elected or sworn in
J. F. McCreight	1871–72	n.a.	Nov. 13, 1871
Amor De Cosmos	1872–74	n.a.	Dec. 23, 1872
G. A. Walkem	1874–76	n.a.	Feb. 11, 1874
A. C. Elliott	1876–78	n.a.	Feb. 1, 1876
G. A. Walkem	1878–82	n.a.	June 25, 1878
Robert Beaven	1882–83	n.a.	June 13, 1882
William Smithe	1883–87	n.a.	Jan. 29, 1883
A. E. B. Davie	1887–89	n.a.	May 1, 1887
John Robson	1889–92	n.a.	Aug. 2, 1889
Theodore Davie	1892–95	n.a.	July 2, 1892
J. H. Turner	1895–98	n.a.	Mar. 4, 1895
C. A. Semlin	1898–1900	n.a.	Aug. 15, 1898
Joseph Martin	1900	n.a.	Feb. 28, 1900
James Dunsmuir	1900–02	n.a.	June 15, 1900
E. G. Prior	1902–03	n.a.	Nov. 21, 1902
Richard McBride	1903–15	Conservative	June 1, 1903
William J. Bowser	1915–16	Conservative	Dec. 15, 1915
Harlan C. Brewster	1916–18	Liberal	Nov. 23, 1916
John Oliver	1918–27	Liberal	Mar. 6, 1918
John D. MacLean	1927–28	Liberal	Aug. 20, 1927
Simon F. Tolmie	1928–33	Conservative	Aug. 21, 1928
T. D. Pattullo	1933–41	Liberal	Nov. 15, 1933
John Hart	1941–47	Liberal[3]	Dec. 9, 1941
Byron Johnson	1947–52	Liberal[3]	Dec. 29, 1947
W. A. C. Bennett	1952–72	Social Credit	Aug. 1, 1952
David Barrett	1972–75	New Democratic	Sept. 15, 1972
William R. Bennett	1975–86	Social Credit	Dec. 22, 1975
Bill Vander Zalm	1986–91	Social Credit	Aug. 6, 1986
Rita Johnston	1991–91	Social Credit	Apr. 2, 1991
Michael Harcourt	1991–96	New Democratic	Nov. 5, 1991
Glen Clark	1996–99	New Democratic	Feb. 22, 1996
Dan Miller	1999–2000	New Democratic	Aug. 25, 1999
Ujjal Dosanjh	2000–01	New Democratic	Feb. 24, 2000
Gordon Campbell	2001–	Liberal	June 5, 2001

■ Nunavut

Premier	Term	Party	Elected or sworn in
Paul Okalik	1999–	n.a.	Apr. 1, 1999

■ Northwest Territories

Premier	Term	Party	Elected or sworn in
George Braden	1980–83	n.a.	July 25, 1980
Richard Nerysoo	1984–85	n.a.	Jan. 12, 1984
Nick Sibbeston	1985–87	n.a.	Nov. 5, 1985
Dennis Patterson	1987–91	n.a.	Nov. 12, 1987
Nellie Cournoyea	1991–95	n.a.	Nov. 13, 1991
Don Morin	1995–98	n.a.	Nov. 20, 1995
James L. Antoine	1998–2000	n.a.	Dec. 10, 1998
Stephen Kakfwi	2000–	n.a.	Jan. 19, 2000

■ Yukon

Government Leader	Term	Party	Elected or sworn in
Chris Pearson	1978–85	Prog. Conservative	
Willard Phelps	1985	Prog. Conservative	Mar. 20, 1985
Tony Penikett	1985–92[4]	New Democratic	May 29, 1985
John Ostashek	1992–96	Yukon Party	Nov. 7, 1992
Piers McDonald	1996–2000	New Democratic	Oct. 19, 1996
Pat Duncan	2000–	Liberal.	May 6, 2000

Source: *Historical Statistics of Canada; Provincial Archives*

(1) United Farmer/Progressive, 1922–27; Coalition, 1927–37; Liberal—Progressive, 1937–43. (2) Co-operative Commonwealth Federation. (3) Coalition. (4) From 1989–92, Government Leader was designated Premier. (n.a.) not available.

Cabinets of the Provinces and Territories

(as of October 2001)

■ Newfoundland and Labrador

Ministry or Portfolio	Minister
Premier	Roger Grimes
Deputy Premier; Industry, Trade and Rural Development	Beaton Tulk
Education	Judy Foote
Environment	Ralph Wiseman
Fisheries and Aquaculture	Gerry Reid
Forest Resources and Agrifoods	Rick Woodford
Finance; Treasury Board	Joan Marie Aylward
Government Services and Lands	Walter Noel
Health and Community Services (Acting); Human Resources and Employment; Strategic Social Plan	Gerald Smith
Intergovernmental Affairs; Government House Leader	Tom Lush
Justice and Attorney General	Kelvin Parsons
Labour	Anna Thistle
Labrador and Aboriginal Affairs	Ernest McLean
Mines and Energy	Lloyd Matthews
Municipal and Provincial Affairs	Oliver Langdon
Tourism, Culture and Recreation	Kevin Aylward
Works, Services and Transportation	Percy Barrett
Youth Services and Postsecondary Education; Status of Women	Sandra Kelly

■ New Brunswick

Ministry or Portfolio	Minister
Premier; Intergovernmental Affairs	Bernard Lord
Deputy Premier; Supply and Services	Dale Graham
Agriculture, Fisheries and Aquaculture; La Francophonie	Paul Robichaud
Attorney General; Justice; Aboriginal Affairs	Bradley Green
Business New Brunswick	Joan MacAlpine
Education; Culture and Sport	Elvy Robichaud
Environment and Local Government	Kim Jardine
Family and Community Services	Percy Mockler
Finance	Norman Betts
Health and Wellness	Dennis Furlong
Investment and Exports; Service New Brunswick	Peter Mesheau
Natural Resources and Energy	Jeannot Volpé
Public Safety	Milton Sherwood
Training and Employment Development	Norman McFarlane
Transportation; Status of Women	Margaret-Ann Blaney

■ Nova Scotia

Ministry or Portfolio	Minister
Premier; Intergovernmental Affairs	John F. Hamm
Agriculture and Fisheries; Natural Resources	Ernest L. Fage
Attorney General; Justice	Michael G. Baker
Community Services; Disabled Persons	Peter G. Christie
Economic Development	Gordon D. Balser
Education; Technology and Science; Status of Women	Jane S. Purves
Environment and Labour	David Morse
Finance; Acadian Affairs	Neil J. LeBlanc
Health	Jamie A. Muir
Service Nova Scotia and Municipal Relations	Angus MacIsaac
Tourism and Culture; Sport and Recreation	Rodney J. MacDonald
Transportation and Public Works; Treasury and Policy Board; Communications Nova Scotia; Government House Leader	Ronald S. Russell

■ Prince Edward Island

Ministry or Portfolio	Minister
Premier; Intergovernmental Affairs	Patrick G. Binns
Agriculture and Forestry	P. Mitchell Murphy
Attorney General; Education	Jeff Lantz
Community and Cultural Affairs	Gail Shea

▶

▶ Development and Technology . . . . Michael Currie
Fisheries, Aquaculture and Environment . . . . Chester Gillan
Health and Social Services . . . . Jamie Ballem
Provincial Treasurer . . . . Patricia J. Mella
Tourism . . . . Greg Deighan
Transportation and Public Works . . . . Don MacKinnon

■ Quebec

Ministry or Portfolio*	Minister
Premier	Bernard Landry
Deputy Premier; Min. of State for the Economy and Finance; Finance; Research, Science and Technology	Pauline Marois
Min. of State for Administration and Public Service; Administration and Public Service; Treasury	Sylvain Simard
Min. of State for Child and Family Welfare; Child and Family Welfare; Seniors; Status of Women	Linda Goupil
Min. of State for Culture and Communications; Charter of the French Language; Culture and Communications; Information Highway	Diane Lemieux
Min. of State for Education and Youth; Education	Francois Legault
Min. of State for Health and Social Services; Health and Social Services	Rémy Trudel
Min. of State for International Relations; International Relations; La Francophonie	Louise Beaudoin
Min. of State for Labour, Employment and Social Solidarity; Employment and Social Solidarity; Labour	Jean Rochon
Min. of State for Municipal Affairs and Greater Montreal; Municipal Affairs and Greater Montreal	Louise Harel
Min. of State for Regions; Industry and Trade; Recreation and Sport; Regions	Gilles Baril
Agriculture, Fisheries and Food	Maxime Arseneau
Canadian Intergovernmental Affairs; Citizens and Immigration; Relations with French-speaking and Acadian Communities	Joseph Facal
Electoral Reform; Native Affairs; Transport; Wildlife and Parks	Guy Chevrette
Elimination of Poverty and Exclusion	Nicole Léger
Environment	André Boisclair
Government House Leader; Natural Resources; Parliamentary Reform	Jacques Brassard
Health, Social Services and Youth Protection	Agnès Maltais
Justice	Paul Bégin
National Capital Region	Rosaire Bertrand
Public Security	Serge Ménard
Research, Science and Technology	David Cliche
Revenue	Guy Julien
Tourism, Recreation and Sport	Richard Legendre
Transport and Maritime Policy	Jacques Baril
Sec. of State: Municipal Infrastructures	Claude Boucher
Sec. of State: Reception and Integration of Immigrants	André Boulerice
Sec. of State: Regional Resources	Lucie Papineau
Sec. of State: Status of Women	Jocelyne Caron

■ Ontario

Ministry or Portfolio	Minister
Premier	Michael D. Harris
Deputy Premier; Finance	Jim Flaherty
Agriculture, Food and Rural Affairs	Brian Coburn
Attorney General; Native Affairs	David Young
Citizenship; Seniors	Cam Jackson
Community and Social Services; Children; Francophone Affairs	John Baird
Consumer and Business Services	Norman W. Sterling
Correctional Services	Rob Sampson
Economic Development and Trade	Robert Runciman
Education; Government House Leader	Janet Ecker
Energy, Science and Technology	Jim Wilson
Environment	Elizabeth Witmer
Health (Assoc. Min.)	Helen Johns
Health and Long-term Care	Tony Clement
Intergovernmental Affairs	Brenda Elliott
Labour	Chris Stockwell
Management Board of Cabinet	David Tsubouchi
Municipal Affairs and Housing	Chris Hodgson
Natural Resources	John Snobelen

▶ Northern Development and Mines .... Dan Newman
Solicitor General .... David Turnbull
Tourism, Culture and Recreation .... Tim Hudak
Training, Colleges and Universities; Women's Issues .... Dianne Cunningham
Transportation .... Brad Clark
Without Portfolio .... Gary Stewart

■ Manitoba

Ministry or Portfolio	Minister
Premier; Federal-Provincial Relations	Gary Albert Doer
Deputy Premier; Intergovernmental Affairs	Jean Myfanwy Friesen
Aboriginal and Northern Affairs	Eric Robinson
Advanced Education; Status of Women; Seniors	Diane McGifford
Agriculture and Food	Rosann Wowchuk
Conservation	Oscar Lathlin
Consumer and Corporate Affairs	Scott Smith
Culture, Heritage and Tourism; Sport	Ron Lemieux
Education, Training and Youth	Drew Caldwell
Family Services and Housing; Persons with Disabilities	Tim Sale
Finance; French Language Services	Gregory F. Selinger
Health; Sport	David Walter Chomiak
Industry, Trade and Mines	MaryAnn Mihychuk
Justice and Attorney General; Constitutional Affairs; Government House Leader	Gord Mackintosh
Labour and Immigration; Multiculturalism	Becky Barrett
Transportation and Government Services; Gaming	Steve Ashton

■ Saskatchewan

Ministry or Portfolio	Minister
Premier	Lorne Calvert
Deputy Premier; Agriculture and Food	Clay Serby
Aboriginal Affairs	Pat Lorje
Crown Investments Corporation; Energy and Mines	Maynard Sonntag
Culture, Youth and Recreation; Information Highway	Joanne Crofford
Economic and Co-operative Development; Government House Leader	Eldon Lautermilch
Education	Jim Melenchuk
Environment and Resource Management	Buckley Belanger
Finance	Eric Cline
Health; Seniors	John Nilson
Highways and Transportation; Rural Revitalization	Patricia Atkinson
Justice and Attorney General; Intergovernmental Affairs	Chris Axworthy
Labour; Gaming	Kim Trew
Municipal Affairs and Housing	Ron Osika
Northern Affairs	Keith Goulet
Post-secondary Education and Skills Training	Glenn Hagel
Saskatchewan Property Management Corporation; Status of Women	Doreen Hamilton
Social Services; Disability Issues	Harry Van Mulligen

■ Alberta

Ministry or Portfolio	Minister
Premier	Ralph Klein
Aboriginal Affairs and Northern Development	Pearl Calahasen
Agriculture, Food and Rural Development	Shirley McClellan
Children's Services	Iris Evans
Community Development	Gene Zwozdesky
Economic Development	Mark Norris
Energy	Murray Smith
Environment	Lorne Taylor
Finance	Patricia Nelson
Gaming	Ron Stevens
Government Services	David Coutts
Health and Wellness	Gary Mar
Human Resources and Employment	Clint Dunford
Infrastructure	Ty Lund
Innovation and Science	Victor Doerksen
International and Intergovernmental Relations	Halvar Jonson
Justice and Attorney General	David Hancock
Learning	Lyle Oberg
Municipal Affairs	Guy Boutilier

▶

Revenue	Greg Melchin
Seniors	Stan Woloshyn
Solicitor General	Heather Forsyth
Sustainable Resource Development	Mike Cardinal
Transportation	Ed Stelmach

■ British Columbia

Ministry or Portfolio*	Minister
Premier	Gordon Campbell
Deputy Premier; Education	Christy Clark
Min. of State for Community Charter	Ted Nebbeling
Min. of State for Deregulation	Kevin Falcon
Min. of State for Early Childhood Development	Linda Reid
Min. of State for Intergovernmental Relations	Greg Halsey-Brandt
Min. of State for Intermediate, Long Term and Home Care	Katherine Whittred
Min. of State for Mental Health	Gulzar Cheema
Min. of State for Women's Equality	Lynn Stephens
Advanced Education	Shirley Bond
Agriculture Food and Fisheries	John van Dongen
Attorney General; Treaty Negotiations	Geoff Plant
Children and Family Development	Gordon Hogg
Community, Aboriginal and Women's Services	George Abbott
Competition, Science and Enterprise	Rick Thorpe
Energy and Mines	Richard Neufeld
Finance	Gary Collins
Forests	Michael de Jong
Health Planning	Sindi Hawkins
Health Services	Colin Hansen
Human Resources	Murray Coell
Management Services	Sandy Santori
Provincial Revenue	Bill Barisoff
Public Safety and Solicitor General	Rich Coleman
Skills Development and Labour	Graham Bruce
Sustainable Resource Management	Stan Hagen
Transportation	Judith Reid
Water, Land and Air Protection	Joyce Murray

■ Yukon Territory

Ministry or Portfolio	Minister
Premier; Finance; Land Claims and Devolution	Pat Duncan
Community and Transportation Services; Justice	Pam Buckway
Economic Development	Scott Kent
Education; Public Service Commission; Renewable Resources	Dale Eftoda
Government Services; Yukon Housing Corporation	Wayne Jim
Health and Social Services; Yukon Development Corporation	Don Roberts
Tourism; Women's Directorate	Sue Edelman

■ Northwest Territories

Ministry or Portfolio	Minister
Premier; Intergovernmental Affairs; NWT Power Corporation	Stephen Kakfwi
Deputy Premier; Health and Social Services; Seniors; Status of Women	Jane Groenewegen
Aboriginal Affairs; Justice	James L. Antoine
Education, Culture and Employment	Jake Ootes
Finance; Resources, Wildlife and Economic Development	Joe Handley
Municipal and Community Affairs; NWT Housing Corporation; Youth	Roger T. Allen
Public Works and Services; Transportation	Vince Steen

■ Nunavut

Ministry or Portfolio	Minister
Premier; Executive and Intergovernmental Affairs; Justice	Paul Okalik
Community Government and Transportation	Jack Anawak
Culture, Language, Elders and Youth	Peter Kattuk
Education	Peter Kilabuk
Finance and Administration; Human Resources	Kelvin Ng
Health and Social Services	Edward Picco
Public Works and Services	Manitok Thompson
Sustainable Development	Olayuk Akesuk

* In the Cabinets of B.C. and Quebec, a distinction exists between ministers of state and ministers. Ministers of state are indicated;

POLITICS AND ELECTIONS

Federal Political Parties in Parliament

Five parties occupy seats in the House of Commons:

Bloc Québécois: Founded in 1991, the BQ consists of Quebec MPs who left the Progressive Conservative and Liberal parties after the failure of the Meech Lake Accord. The BQ promotes sovereignty for Quebec.

Canadian Reform Conservative Alliance: Founded in Ottawa in 2000, the CRCA replaced the populist Reform party. It seeks to reduce the size, scope and cost of government and to decentralize the federal system. Reform was founded in Winnipeg in 1987.

Liberal Party: Rooted in the movement for responsible government in the 19th century, the Liberal party ruled Canada throughout most of the 20th century. Since the 1930s, Liberals have projected an image of competence and compromise while staying close to the political centre.

New Democratic Party: Founded in Ottawa in 1961, the NDP united the Canadian Labour Congress and the Co-operative Commonwealth Federation (CCF). The NDP promotes the public ownership of key industries and the redistribution of wealth. Its predecessor, the CCF, was founded in Calgary in 1932.

Progressive Conservative Party: The Conservative party first defined itself in the election of 1878 as the party of the National Policy, protectionism and a strong central government. In 1942, after a series of defeats, the party allied itself with the Progressive Party, supporters of free trade, nationalization and direct democracy.

Registered Federal Political Parties

(as of October 2001)

Federal political parties can only be registered at election time, when they qualify for registration by fielding at least 50 candidates by the nomination deadline in a forthcoming election. In between elections, parties can be founded and organized, and can apply for registration to the chief electoral officer.

Bloc Québécois—Ste 307, 3750 Crémazie Blvd E, Montreal, QC H2A 1B6; Tel: (514) 526-3000; Fax: (514) 526-2868. Leader: Gilles Duceppe. Website: http://www.blocquebecois.org

Canadian Action Party—Ste 302, 99 Atlantic Ave, Toronto, ON M6K 3J8; Tel: (416) 535-4144; Fax: (416) 535-6325. Leader: The Hon. Paul Hellyer. Website: http://www.canadianactionparty.ca

Canadian Reform Conservative Alliance—600–833 4th Ave SW, Calgary, AB T2P 0K5; Tel.: (403) 269-1990; Fax: (403) 266-6748. Leader: Stockwell Day. Website: http://www.canadian alliance.ca

Communist Party of Canada—290A Danforth Ave, Toronto, ON M4K 1N6; Tel: (416) 469-2446; Fax: (416) 469-4063. Leader: Miguel Figueroa. Website: http://www.communist-party.ca

The Green Party—244 Gerrard St E, Toronto, ON M5A 2G2; Tel.: (416) 929-2397; Fax (416) 929-7709. Leader: Chris Bradshaw. Website: http://green.ca

Liberal Party of Canada—Ste 400, 81 Metcalfe St, Ottawa, ON K1P 6M8; Tel: (613) 237-0740; Fax: (613) 235-7208. Leader: The Right Hon. Jean Chrétien. Website: http://www.liberal.ca

Marijuana Party—Ste 100, 810 Rachel St E, Montreal, QC H2J 2H6; Tel.: (514) 528-1768; Fax: (514) 527-8723. Leader: Marc-Boris St-Maurice. Website: http://www.marijuanaparty.com

Marxist-Leninist Party of Canada—Ste 200, 396 Cooper St, Ottawa, ON K2P 2H7; Tel: (613) 565-6446; Fax: (613) 565-8787. Leader: Sandra Smith. Website: http://www.cpcml.ca

Natural Law Party of Canada—500 Wilbrod St, Ottawa, ON K1N 6N2; Tel: (613) 565-8517; Fax: (613) 565-1596. Leader: Dr. Neil Paterson. Website: http://www.natural-law.ca

New Democratic Party—Ste 802, 85 Albert St, Ottawa, ON K1P 6A4; Tel: (613) 236-3613; Fax: (613) 230-9950. Leader: Alexa McDonough. Website: http://www.ndp.ca

Progressive Conservative Party of Canada—Ste 806, 141 Laurier Ave W, Ottawa, ON K1P 5J3; Tel: (613) 238-6111; Fax: (613) 238-7429. Leader: The Right Hon. Joe Clark. Website: http://www.pcparty.ca

Source: *Elections Canada*

Federal Election Results, 1867–2000

🍁 1867–1904

	1867	1872	1874	1878	1882	1887	1891	1896	1900	1904
Canada										
Conservative	101	103	73	137	139	123	123	89	80	75
Liberal	80	97	133	69	71	92	92	117	133	139
Other	—	—	—	—	—	—	—	7	—	—
Prince Edward Island[1]										
Conservative	—	—	—	5	4	—	2	3	2	3
Liberal	—	—	6	1	2	6	4	2	3	1
Nova Scotia										
Conservative	3	11	4	14	15	14	16	10	5	
Liberal	16	10	17	7	6	7	5	10	15	18
New Brunswick										
Conservative	7	7	5	5	10	10	13	9	5	6
Liberal	8	9	11	11	6	6	3	5	9	7
Quebec										
Conservative	45	38	32	45	48	33	30	16	7	11
Liberal	20	27	33	20	17	32	35	49	58	54
Other	—	—	—	—	—	—	—	5	—	—
Ontario										
Conservative	46	38	24	59	54	52	48	44	55	48
Liberal	36	50	64	29	37	40	44	43	37	38
Other	—	—	—	—	—	—	—	5	—	—
Manitoba[2]										
Conservative	—	3	2	3	2	4	4	4	4	3
Liberal	—	1	2	1	3	1	1	2	3	7
Other	—	—	—	—	—	—	—	1	—	—
British Columbia[3]										
Conservative	—	6	6	6	6	6	6	2	2	—
Liberal	—	—	—	—	—	—	—	4	4	7
Yukon[4]										
Conservative	—	—	—	—	—	—	—	—	—	1
Northwest Territories[2]										
Conservative	—	—	—	—	—	4	4	1	—	3
Liberal	—	—	—	—	—	—	—	2	4	7
Other	—	—	—	—	—	—	—	1	—	—

🍁 1908–1940

	1908	1911	1917[7]	1921	1925	1926	1930	1935	1940
Canada									
Conservative	85	133	153	50	116	91	137	39	39
Liberal	133	86	82	117	101	116	88	171	178
Progressive	—	—	—	64	25	—	2	—	—
CCF	—	—	—	—	—	—	—	7	8
Social Credit	—	—	—	—	—	—	—	17	10
Other	3	2	—	4	3	38	18	11	10
Prince Edward Island									
Conservative	1	2	2	—	2	1	3	—	—
Liberal	3	2	2	4	2	3	1	4	4
Nova Scotia									
Conservative	6	9	12	—	11	12	10	—	1
Liberal	12	9	4	16	3	2	4	12	10
CCF	—	—	—	—	—	—	—	—	1

▶

(1) Entered Confederation July 1, 1873. (2) Entered Confederation July 15, 1870. (3) Entered Confederation July 20, 1871. (4) Entered Confederation June 13, 1898. (5) Entered Confederation Mar. 31, 1949. (6) Entered Confederation Sept. 1, 1905. (7) For the 1917 election, Conservative refers to "Unionists," a coalition of Conservatives and pro-conscription Liberals; Liberals, for the 1917 election, are sometimes called "Laurier Liberals" because of their support for Laurier's anti-conscription stand. (8) The New Democratic Party (NDP) replaced the Co-operative Commonwealth Federation (CCF) in 1961. (9) From 1908–1949 shared one representative. In 1953, the number was increased to two. (10) The Canadian Reform Conservative Alliance (or Canadian Alliance) replaced the Reform party in 2000. (11) Nunavut's first federal election occurred in 2000.

❦ 1908–1940

	1908	1911	1917[7]	1921	1925	1926	1930	1935	1940
New Brunswick									
Conservative	2	5	7	5	10	7	10	1	5
Liberal	11	8	4	5	1	4	1	9	5
Other	—	—	—	1	—	—	—	—	—
Quebec									
Conservative	11	27	3	—	4	4	24	5	—
Liberal	53	37	62	65	60	60	40	55	61
Other	1	1	—	—	1	1	1	5	4
Ontario									
Conservative	48	72	74	37	68	53	59	25	25
Liberal	36	36	8	21	12	23	22	56	55
Progressive	—	—	—	24	2	4	—	—	—
Other	2	1	—	—	—	2	1	1	2
Manitoba									
Conservative	8	8	14	—	7	—	11	1	1
Liberal	2	2	1	2	1	4	1	12	14
CCF	—	—	—	—	—	—	—	2	1
Progressive	—	—	—	12	7	4	—	—	—
Other	—	—	—	1	2	9	5	2	1
Saskatchewan[6]									
Conservative	1	1	16	—	—	—	8	1	2
Liberal	9	9	—	1	15	16	11	16	12
CCF	—	—	—	—	—	—	—	2	5
Progressive	—	—	—	15	6	5	2	—	—
Social Credit	—	—	—	—	—	—	—	2	—
Other	—	—	—	—	—	—	—	—	2
Alberta[6]									
Conservative	3	1	11	—	3	1	4	1	—
Liberal	4	6	1	—	4	3	3	1	7
Progressive	—	—	—	10	9	—	—	—	—
Social Credit	—	—	—	—	—	—	—	15	10
United Farmers of Alta	—	—	—	—	—	11	9	—	—
Other	—	—	—	2	—	1	—	—	—
British Columbia									
Conservative	5	7	13	7	10	12	7	5	4
Liberal	2	—	—	3	3	1	5	6	10
CCF	—	—	—	—	—	—	—	3	1
Progressive	—	—	—	2	1	—	—	—	—
Social Credit	—	—	—	—	—	—	—	—	—
Other	—	—	—	1	—	1	2	2	1
Yukon and Northwest Territories[9]									
Conservative	—	1	—	1	1	1	1	—	1
Liberal	1	—	—	—	—	—	—	—	—
Other	—	—	—	—	—	—	—	1	—

❦ 1945–1968

	1945	1949	1953	1957	1958	1962	1963	1965	1968
Canada									
Conservative	67	41	51	112	208	116	95	97	72
Liberal	125	190	170	105	48	99	129	131	155
NDP (CCF)[8]	28	13	23	25	8	19	17	21	22
Social Credit	13	10	15	19	—	30	24	5	14
Other	12	8	6	4	1	1	—	11	15
Newfoundland[5]									
Conservative	—	2	—	2	2	1	—	—	6
Liberal	—	5	7	5	5	6	7	7	1
NDP (CCF)	—	—	—	—	—	—	—	—	—
Prince Edward Island									
Conservative	1	1	1	4	4	4	2	4	4
Liberal	3	3	3	—	—	—	2	—	—

❦ 1945–1968

	1945	1949	1953	1957	1958	1962	1963	1965	1968
Nova Scotia									
Conservative	3	2	1	10	12	9	7	10	10
Liberal	8	10	10	2	—	2	5	2	1
NDP (CCF)	1	1	1	—	—	1	—	—	—
New Brunswick									
Conservative	3	2	3	5	7	4	4	4	5
Liberal	7	7	7	5	3	6	6	6	5
Other	—	1	—	—	—	—	—	—	—
Quebec									
Conservative	1	2	4	9	50	14	8	8	4
Liberal	54	66	66	63	25	35	47	56	56
NDP (CCF)	—	—	—	—	—	—	—	—	—
Social Credit	—	—	—	—	—	26	20	—	—
Other	10	5	5	3	—	—	—	11	14
Ontario									
Conservative	48	25	33	61	67	35	27	25	17
Liberal	34	56	50	20	14	43	52	51	64
NDP (CCF)	—	—	—	3	3	6	6	9	6
Other	—	2	2	1	1	1	—	—	1
Manitoba									
Conservative	2	1	3	8	14	11	10	10	5
Liberal	10	12	8	1	—	1	2	1	5
NDP (CCF)	5	3	3	5	—	2	2	3	3
Saskatchewan									
Conservative	1	1	1	3	16	16	17	17	5
Liberal	2	14	5	4	—	1	—	—	2
NDP (CCF)	18	5	11	10	1	—	—	—	6
Alberta									
Conservative	2	2	2	3	17	15	14	15	15
Liberal	2	5	4	1	—	—	1	—	4
NDP (CCF)	—	—	—	—	—	—	—	—	—
Social Credit	13	10	11	13	—	2	2	2	—
British Columbia									
Conservative	5	3	3	7	18	6	4	3	—
Liberal	5	11	8	2	—	4	7	7	16
NDP (CCF)	4	3	7	7	4	10	9	9	7
Social Credit	—	—	4	6	—	2	2	3	—
Other	2	1	—	—	—	—	—	—	—
Yukon[9]									
Conservative	1	—	—	—	1	1	1	1	1
Liberal	—	1	2	1	—	—	—	—	—
NDP (CCF)	—	—	—	—	—	—	—	—	—
Northwest Territories[9]									
Conservative	n.a.	n.a.	n.a.	—	—	—	1	—	—
Liberal	n.a.	n.a.	n.a.	1	1	1	—	1	1
NDP (CCF)	n.a.	n.a.	n.a.	—	—	—	—	—	—

❦ 1972–2000

	1972	1974	1979	1980	1984	1988	1993	1997	2000
Canada									
Bloc Québécois	—	—	—	—	—	—	54	44	38
Conservative	107	95	136	103	211	169	2	20	12
Liberal	109	141	114	147	40	83	177	155	172
NDP	31	16	26	32	30	43	9	21	13
Reform/Canadian Alliance[10]	—	—	—	—	—	—	52	60	66
Social Credit	15	11	6	—	—	—	—	—	—
Other	2	1	—	—	1	—	1	1	—
Newfoundland									
Conservative	4	3	2	2	4	2	—	3	2
Liberal	3	4	4	5	3	5	7	4	5
NDP	—	—	1	—	—	—	—	—	—
Prince Edward Island									
Conservative	3	3	4	2	3	—	—	—	—
Liberal	1	1	—	2	1	4	4	4	4
NDP									—

▶

❦ 1972–2000

	1972	1974	1979	1980	1984	1988	1993	1997	2000
Nova Scotia									
Conservative	10	8	8	6	9	5	—	5	4
Liberal	1	2	2	5	2	6	11	—	4
NDP	—	1	1	—	—	—	—	6	—
New Brunswick									
Conservative	5	3	4	3	9	5	1	5	3
Liberal	5	6	6	7	1	5	9	3	6
NDP	—	—	—	—	—	—	—	2	1
Other	—	1	—	—	—	—	—	—	—
Quebec									
Bloc Québécois	—	—	—	—	—	—	54	44	38
Conservative	2	3	2	1	58	63	1	5	1
Liberal	56	60	67	74	17	12	19	26	36
NDP	—	—	—	—	—	—	—	—	—
Social Credit	15	11	6	—	—	—	—	—	—
Other	1	—	—	—	—	—	1	—	—
Ontario									
Conservative	40	25	57	38	67	46	—	1	—
Liberal	36	55	32	52	14	43	98	101	100
NDP	11	8	6	5	13	10	—	—	1
Reform/Canadian Alliance[10]	—	—	—	—	—	—	1	—	2
Other	1	—	—	—	1	—	—	1	—
Manitoba									
Conservative	8	9	7	5	9	7	—	1	1
Liberal	2	2	2	2	1	5	12	6	5
NDP	3	2	5	7	4	2	1	4	4
Reform/Canadian Alliance[10]	—	—	—	—	—	—	1	3	4
Saskatchewan									
Conservative	7	8	10	7	9	4	—	—	—
Liberal	1	3	—	—	—	—	5	1	2
NDP	5	2	4	7	5	10	5	5	2
Reform/Canadian Alliance[10]	—	—	—	—	—	—	4	8	10
Alberta									
Conservative	19	19	21	21	21	25	—	—	1
Liberal	—	—	—	—	—	—	4	2	2
NDP	—	—	—	—	—	1	—	—	—
Reform/Canadian Alliance[10]	—	—	—	—	—	—	22	24	23
British Columbia									
Conservative	8	13	19	16	19	12	—	—	—
Liberal	4	8	1	—	1	1	6	6	5
NDP	11	2	8	12	8	19	2	3	2
Reform/Canadian Alliance[10]	—	—	—	—	—	—	24	25	27
Yukon									
Conservative	1	1	1	1	1	—	—	—	—
Liberal	—	—	—	—	—	—	—	—	1
NDP	—	—	—	—	—	1	1	1	—
Northwest Territories									
Conservative	—	—	1	1	2	—	—	—	—
Liberal	—	—	—	—	—	2	2	2	1
NDP	1	1	1	1	—	—	—	—•	—
Nunavut[11]									
Conservative									—
Liberal									1
NDP									—

Minority Party election results

*I**n the federal election of 2000, six of the eleven political parties that ran candidates for seats in the House of Commons failed to elect a single person. Of these six parties, the most popular was The Green Party of Canada which won 104,402 votes. The other parties, ranked in descending order of popularity, were the Marijuana Party (66,258 votes); the Canadian Action Party (27,103 votes); the Natural Law Party of Canada (16,577 votes); the Marxist-Leninist Party of Canada (12,068 votes); and the Communist Party of Canada (8,776 votes).*

Source: *Elections Canada*

Federal Election 2000: Total Votes by Province and Party

	Bloc Québécois	Canadian Alliance	Liberal	New Democrat	Progressive Conservative	Other[1]
Newfoundland*	—	8 837	103 103	29 993	79 157	8 408
Prince Edward Island	—	3 719	35 021	6 714	28 610	400
Nova Scotia	—	41 752	158 870	104 277	126 557	3 813
New Brunswick	—	60 277	159 803	44 778	116 980	1 174
Quebec	1 377 727	212 874	1 529 642	63 611	192 153	80 891
Ontario	—	1 051 209	2 292 075	368 709	642 438	98 174
Manitoba	—	148 293	158 713	101 741	70 635	8 450
Saskatchewan	—	207 004	89 697	113 626	20 855	2 515
Alberta	—	739 514	263 008	68 363	169 093	16 021
British Columbia	—	797 518	446 624	182 993	117 614	69 972
Yukon	—	3 659	4 293	4 223	991	53
Northwest Territories	—	2 273	5 855	3 430	1 282	—
Nunavut	—	—	5 327	1 410	633	349
Total votes cast	**1 377 727**	**3 276 929**	**5 252 031**	**1 093 868**	**1 566 998**	**290 220**

Source: *Elections Canada.* (1) Includes Canadian Action, Communist, Green, Marijuana, Marxist-Leninist, Natural Law, and Independent

Federal Election 2000: % of Popular Vote by Province and Party

	Bloc Québécois	Canadian Alliance	Liberal	New Democrat	Progressive Conservative	Other[1]
Newfoundland	—	3.9	44.9	13.1	34.5	3.7
Prince Edward Island	—	5.0	47.0	9.0	38.4	0.5
Nova Scotia	—	9.6	36.5	24.0	29.1	0.9
New Brunswick	—	15.7	41.7	11.7	30.5	0.3
Quebec	39.9	6.2	44.2	1.8	5.6	2.3
Ontario	—	23.6	51.5	8.3	14.4	2.2
Manitoba	—	30.4	32.5	20.9	14.5	1.7
Saskatchewan	—	47.7	20.7	26.2	4.8	0.6
Alberta	—	58.9	20.9	5.4	13.5	1.3
British Columbia	—	49.4	27.7	11.3	7.3	4.3
Yukon	—	27.7	32.5	31.9	7.5	0.4
Northwest-Territories	—	17.7	45.6	26.7	10.0	—
Nunavut	—	—	69.0	18.3	8.2	4.5
Canada	**10.7**	**25.5**	**40.8**	**8.5**	**12.2**	**2.3**
Total seats	**38**	**66**	**172**	**13**	**12**	**0**

Source: *Elections Canada.* (1) Includes Canadian Action, Communist, Green, Marijuana, Marxist-Leninist, Natural Law, and Independent

Voter Turnout at Canada's Federal Elections, 1867–2000

(percentage of eligible voters casting votes)

	Voter turnout[1]		Voter turnout[1]		Voter turnout[1]		Voter turnout[1]		Voter turnout[1]
1867	73%	1900	79%	1930	76%	1958	81%	1979	76%
1872	70	1904	84	1935	75	1962	80	1980	69
1874	75	1908	79	1940	71	1963	80	1984	75
1878	71	1911	72	1945	76	1965	76	1988	76
1882	72	1917	90	1949	75	1968	76	1993	70
1887	70	1921	71	1953	68	1972	77	1997	67
1891	65	1925	69	1957	75	1974	71	2000	61
1896	61	1926	70						

Source: *Elections Canada*

[1]Percentage of actual votes to eligible voters. In many early general elections, several electoral districts were won by acclamation; hence, no eligible voters nor actual votes were recorded. Furthermore, in some of the more remote districts, votes were cast but no voters' lists had been prepared.

FOCUS ON...

Choosing a Party Leader

How do Canada's political parties choose a leader? As in the United Kingdom and unlike the U.S., Canadian voters do not choose their leaders directly. Instead, the party with the most members elected forms the government and that party's leader becomes the country's (or province's) leader.

Party leaders are chosen, usually at conventions called for that purpose, and only party members are allowed to vote for the leader. The actual process of choosing is usually explained in the party's constitution (the document that outlines the purpose of the party, conditions of membership, how the party will be organized and managed, and how it chooses its leader). The mechanics of the process vary.

Canadian Reform Conservative Alliance

The Alliance's constitution [clause 10(c)] provides that: "In the event that National Council has called a leadership election, such election shall respect the principle that each eligible member of the Alliance shall have the right to one vote in the election of the Leader."

Those who have been members for a minimum of seven days are eligible.

Liberal Party of Canada

In the Liberals' constitution, members of the party vote by ballot for their preferred leader and their choice of delegate to represent them at a National Leadership convention. (The delegates may or may not have declared their support for a particular leadership candidate; they may have chosen to stand as undeclared delegates.) The elected delegates attend the convention and must support the chosen candidate on the first ballot. Clause 17(11) notes that there will be successive ballots as the lowest candidates are taken out of the race, but makes no directive on how delegates must vote on those ballots.

Members for a minimum of 90 days or "immediate past members" are eligible to vote. "Immediate past members" must renew their memberships.

New Democratic Party

The NDP constitution stipulates that the Party "shall meet in Convention at least once every other calendar year" [Article V.1.(1)] and that "The Leader, President, Associate Presidents and Treasurer shall be elected at each Federal Convention." (VII.3). Each federal constituency can send one delegate for every 50 members (up to four delegates for the first 200 members and one delegate per 100 members after that) to the Convention. Provincial parties and other affiliated local groups or contributory organizations are also allowed to send representation, based on their proportionate membership or support.

"Members in good standing" have paid their fees and are eligible to vote in the leadership election.

Progressive Conservative Party of Canada

The PC party also uses delegates to choose the party leader. Clause 11.4.4 states "The leadership selection process shall be based on the objective that all Members should be encouraged and be able to participate in the [leadership selection] process through their constituency associations"

Each Constituency Member "is entitled to cast one (1) ballot in that Constituency Member's constituency association in the election for the Leader. It shall be a preferential ballot on which the Constituency Member shall rank the candidates in order of preference." Clause 11.4.6.3 goes on to explain that "The percentage of votes cast by such Constituency members in each constituency association for each candidate for Leader shall be applied to the selection-votes from each constituency association and the selection-votes determined in that manner will be allocated to each candidate."

The candidate receiving more than 50% of all allocated selection-votes becomes leader. Should this process not produce a clear winner on the first vote, subsequent counts will look at the runners-up on the preferential ballots.

"Members in good standing" have paid their dues at least 14 days before voting in the leadership selection process.

Federal Political Party Leaders

■ Progressive Conservative[1] Party

Leader	Term
Sir John A. Macdonald	1854–June 6, 1891
Sir J.J.C. Abbott	June 16, 1891–Dec. 5, 1892
Sir John Thompson	Dec. 5, 1892–Dec. 12, 1894
Sir Mackenzie Bowell	Dec. 21, 1894–Apr. 27, 1896
Sir Charles Tupper	May 1, 1896–Feb. 5, 1901
Sir Robert Borden	Feb. 6, 1901–July 10, 1920
Arthur Meighen	July 10, 1920–Oct. 11, 1926
Hugh Guthrie[2]	Oct. 11, 1926–Oct. 12, 1927
R.B. Bennett	Oct. 12, 1927–July 7, 1938
R.J. Manion	July 7, 1938–May 13, 1940
R.B. Hanson[2]	May 13, 1940–Nov. 12, 1941
Arthur Meighen	Nov. 12, 1941–Dec. 11, 1942
John Bracken	Dec. 11, 1942–Oct. 2, 1948
George A. Drew	Oct. 2, 1948–Dec. 14, 1956
John G. Diefenbaker	Dec. 14, 1956–Sept. 9, 1967
Robert L. Stanfield	Sept. 9, 1967–Feb. 22, 1976
Joe Clark	Feb. 22, 1976–Feb. 8, 1983
Erik Nielsen[2]	Feb. 9, 1983–June 11, 1983
Brian Mulroney	June 11, 1983–June 13, 1993
Kim Campbell	June 13, 1993–Dec. 13, 1993
Jean Charest	Dec. 14, 1993–Apr. 3, 1998
Elsie Wayne	Apr. 6, 1998–Nov. 13, 1998
Joe Clark	Nov. 14, 1998–

■ Liberal Party

Leader	Term
Robert Baldwin	1804–1858
Louis-H. Lafontaine	1807–1864
George Brown	1867–1872
Alexander Mackenzie	Mar. 6, 1873–Apr. 27, 1880
Edward Blake	May 4, 1880–June 2, 1887
Sir Wilfrid Laurier	June 1887–Feb. 17, 1919
Daniel D. McKenzie[2]	Feb. 1919–Aug. 1919
W.L. Mackenzie King	Aug. 7, 1919–Aug. 7, 1948
Louis St. Laurent	Aug. 7, 1948–Jan. 16, 1958
Lester B. Pearson	Jan. 16, 1958–Apr. 2, 1968
Pierre E. Trudeau	Apr. 6, 1968–June 16, 1984
John N. Turner	June 16, 1984–June 23, 1990
Jean Chrétien	June 23, 1990–

■ New Democratic Party[3]

Leader	Term
James S. Woodsworth	Aug. 1932–July 1942
M.J. Coldwell	July 1942–Aug. 1960
Hazen Argue	Aug. 1960–Aug. 1961
Tommy Douglas	Aug. 1961–Apr. 1971
David Lewis	Apr. 24, 1971–July 7, 1975
Ed Broadbent	July 7, 1975–Dec. 2, 1989
Audrey McLaughlin	Dec. 2, 1989–Oct. 1995
Alexa McDonough	Oct. 14, 1995–

■ Bloc Québécois

Leader	Term
Lucien Bouchard	June 15, 1991–Jan. 18, 1996
Michel Gauthier	Feb. 17, 1996–Mar. 15, 1997
Gilles Duceppe	Mar. 16, 1997–

■ Canadian Reform Conservative Alliance[4]

Leader	Term
E. Preston Manning	Nov. 1, 1987–July 8, 2000
Stockwell Day	July 8, 2000–

(1) Name changed from Conservative to Progressive Conservative Dec. 1942. (2) Interim leader appointed to fill a vacancy until a party leadership convention could be held. (3) Prior to Aug. 1961 party was called the Co-operative Commonwealth Federation (CCF). (4) Before Jan. 2000, party was called the Reform Party of Canada

Provincial Election Results

■ Newfoundland and Labrador

	1971	1972	1975	1979	1982	1985	1989	1993	1996	1999
Liberal	20	9	16	19	8	15	31	35	37	32
Progressive Conservative	21	33	30	33	44	36	21	16	9	14
New Democratic	—	—	—	—	—	1	—	1	1	2
Other	1	—	5	—	—	—	—	—	1	—
Size of legislature	42	42	51	52	52	52	52	52	48	48

■ Prince Edward Island

	1970	1974	1978	1979	1982	1985	1989	1993	1996	2000
Liberal	27	26	17	11	14	21	30	31	8	1
Progressive Conservative	5	6	15	21	18	11	2	1	18	26
New Democratic	—	—	—	—	—	—	—	—	1	—
Size of legislature	32	32	32	32	32	32	32	32	27	27

■ Nova Scotia

	1967	1970	1974	1978	1981	1984	1988	1993	1998	1999
Liberal	6	23	31	17	13	6	21	40	19	11
New Democratic[1]	—	2	3	4	1	3	2	3	19	11
Progressive Conservative[2]	40	21	12	31	37	42	28	9	14	30
Other	—	—	—	—	1	1	1	—	—	—
Size of legislature	46	46	46	52	52	52	52	52	52	52

■ New Brunswick

	1963	1967	1970	1974	1978	1982	1987	1991	1995	1999
Liberal	332	32	26	25	28	18	58	46	48	10
Progressive Conservative[3]	20	26	32	33	30	39	—	3	6	44
New Democratic	—	—	—	—	—	1	—	1	1	1
Confederation of Regions	—	—	—	—	—	—	—	8	—	—
Size of legislature	52	58	58	58	58	58	58	58	55	55

■ Quebec

	1962	1966	1970	1973	1976	1981	1985	1989	1994	1998
Crédit Social	—	—	12	2	1	—	—	—	—	—
Equality	—	—	—	—	—	—	—	4	—	—
Liberal	63	50	72	102	26	42	99	92	47	48
Parti Québécois[4]	—	—	7	6	71	80	23	29	77	76
Union Nationale	31	56	17	—	11	—	—	—	—	—
Other	1	2	—	—	1	—	—	—	1	1
Size of legislature	95	108	108	110	110	122	122	125	125	125

■ Ontario

	1967	1971	1975	1977	1981	1985	1987	1990	1995	1999
Liberal	28	20	36	34	34	48	95	36	30	35
New Democratic[5]	20	19	38	33	21	25	19	74	17	9
Progressive Conservative[3]	69	78	51	58	70	52	16	20	82	59
Independent	—	—	—	—	—	—	—	—	1	—
Size of legislature	117	117	125	125	125	125	130	130	130	103

■ Manitoba

	1966	1969	1973	1977	1981	1986	1988	1990	1995	1999
Liberal	14	4	5	1	—	1	20	7	3	1
New Democratic[5]	11	28	31	23	34	30	12	20	23	32
Progressive Conservative[6]	31	22	21	33	23	26	25	30	31	24
Other	1	3	—	—	—	—	—	—	—	—
Size of legislature	57	57	57	57	57	57	57	57	57	57

■ Saskatchewan

	1964	1967	1971	1975	1978	1982	1986	1991	1995	1999
Liberal	33	35	15	15	—	—	1	1	11	4
New Democratic[7]	25	24	45	39	44	8	25	55	42	29
Progressive Conservative[8]	1	—	—	7	17	56	38	10	5	—
Saskatchewan Party	—	—	—	—	—	—	—	—	—	25
Size of legislature	59	59	60	61	61	64	64	66	58	58

■ Alberta

	1967	1971	1975	1979	1982	1986	1989	1993	1997	2001
Liberal	3	—	—	—	—	4	8	32[9]	18	7
New Democratic[1]	—	1	1	1	2	16	16	—	22	2
Progressive Conservative[6]	6	49	69	74	75	61	59	51	63	74
Social Credit	55	24	4	4	—	—	—	—	—	—
Other	1	1	1	—	2	2	—	—	—	—
Size of legislature	65	75	75	79	79	83	83	83	83	83

■ British Columbia

	1966	1969	1972	1975	1979	1983	1986	1991	1996	2001
Liberal	6	5	5	1	—	—	—	17	33	77
New Democratic[5]	16	12	38	18	26	21	22	51	39	2
Progressive Conservative[6]	—	—	2	1	—	—	—	—	—	—
Social Credit	33	38	10	35	31	35	47	7	—	—
Other	—	—	—	—	—	1	—	—	3	—
Size of legislature	55	55	55	55	57	57	69	75	75	79

■ Yukon

	1978	1982	1985	1989	1992	1996	2000
Liberal	2	—	2	—	1	3	10
New Democratic	1	6	8	9	6	11	6
Progressive Conservative	11	10	6	7	—	—	—
Yukon Party	—	—	—	—	7	3	1
Independent	2	—	—	—	3	—	—
Size of Legislature	16	16	16	16	17	17	17

(1) Known as the Co-operative Commonwealth Federation until 1962. (2) Known as the Conservative Party until 1946. (3) Known as the Conservative Party until 1943. (4) Formed in 1968. (5) Known as the Co-operative Commonwealth Federation until 1961. (6) Known as the Conservative Party until 1944. (7) Known as the Co-operative Commonwealth Federation until 1967. (8) Known as the Conservative Party until 1945. (9) One Alberta Liberal became an independent.

Provincial Party Leaders[1]

(as of October 2001)

■ Newfoundland and Labrador

Progressive Conservative Party		Liberal Party		New Democratic Party	
Tom Rideout	1989–91	Stephen Neary	1984–85	Peter Fenwick	1981–89
Len Simms	1991–95	Leo Barry	1985–87	Cle Newhook	1989–92
Lynn Verge	1995–96	Clyde Wells	1987–96	Jack Harris	1992–
Loyola Sullivan	1996–98	Brian Tobin	1996–2000		
Ed Byrne	1998–2001	Beaton Tulk	2000–01		
Danny Williams	2001–	Roger Grimes	2001–		

■ Prince Edward Island

Progressive Conservative Party		Liberal Party		New Democratic Party	
James M. Lee	1981–87	Bennett Campbell	1978–81	Douglas Murray	1979–81
Leone Bagnall	1987–88	Joseph Ghiz	1981–93	David Burke	1982–83
Melbourne Gass	1988–90	Catherine Callbeck	1993-96	Jim Mayne	1983–89
Pat Mella	1990–96	Keith Milligan	1996–99	Larry Duchesne	1991–95
Patrick Binns	1996–	Wayne Carew	1999–2000	Herb Dickieson	1995–
		Ron MacKinley	2000–		

■ Nova Scotia

Progressive Conservative Party[2]		Liberal Party		New Democratic Party[3]	
George I. Smith	1967–71	Vincent J. MacLean	1985	Jeremy Akerman	1968–80
John M. Buchanan	1971–90	J. William Gillis	1985–86	Alexa McDonough	1980–94
Donald Cameron	1991–93	Vincent J. MacLean	1986–92	John Holme	1994–96
Terence R.B. Donahoe	1993–95	John Savage	1992–97	Robert Chisholm	1996–2000
Dr. John Hamm	1995–	Russell MacLellan	1997–2000	Helen MacDonald	2000–01
		Wayne Gaudet	2000–	Darrel Dexter	2001–

■ New Brunswick

Progressive Conservative Party		Liberal Party		New Democratic Party	
Richard B. Hatfield	1969–87	Joe Daigle	1978–82	Elizabeth Weir	1988–
Malcolm MacLeod	1987–89	Doug Young	1982–83		
Barbara Baird Filliter	1989–91	Frank McKenna	1985–97		
Dennis Cochrane	1991–95	Ray Frenette	1997–98		
Bernard Valcourt	1995–97	Camille Theriault	1998–2001		
Bernard Lord	1997–	Bernard Richard	2001–		

■ Quebec

Parti Québécois		Parti Libéral		Action démocratique	
René Lévesque	1968–85	Robert Bourassa	1970–77	Mario Dumont	1994–
Pierre-Marc Johnson	1985–88	Claude Ryan	1978–82		
Jacques Parizeau	1988–96	Robert Bourassa	1983–94		
Lucien Bouchard	1996–2001	Daniel Johnson	1994–98		
Bernard Landry	2001–	Jean Charest	1998–		

■ Ontario

Progressive Conservative Party		Liberal Party		New Democratic Party[4]	
Frank Miller	1985	Stuart Smith	1977–81	Stephen H. Lewis	1970–78
Larry Grossman	1985–87	David Peterson	1982–90	Michael Cassidy	1978–82
Andrew Brandt	1987–90	Lyn McLeod	1992–96	Bob Rae	1982–96
Mike Harris	1990–	Dalton McGinty	1996–	Howard Hampton	1996–

■ Manitoba

Progressive Conservative Party	Liberal Party	New Democratic Party [4]
Sidney Spivak 1971–75	Paul Edwards 1993–96	A. Russell Paulley 1960–69
Sterling Lyon 1975–83	Ginny Hasselfield 1996–98	Edward R. Schreyer 1969–79
Gary Filmon 1983–2000	Neil Gaudry 1998	Howard R. Pawley 1979–88
Bonnie Mitchelson 2000	Jon Gerrard 1998–	Gary Doer 1988–
Stuart Murray 2000–		

■ Saskatchewan

Progressive Conservative Party	Liberal Party	New Democratic Party [4]
Party inactive as of Nov. 9, 1997	Ron Osika (interim) 1996	Tommy Douglas 1944–61
	Jim Melenchuk. 1996–	Woodrow Lloyd 1961–70
Saskatchewan Party		Allan Blakeney 1970–78
Ken Karwetz 1997–98		Roy Romanow 1987–2001
Elwin Hermanson 1998–		Lorne Calvert 2001–

■ Alberta

Progressive Conservative Party	Liberal Party	New Democratic Party [4]
Milt Harradance 1962–64	Laurence Decore 1988–94	W. Grant Notley 1968–84
Peter Lougheed 1965–85	Betty Hewes (interim) 1994	Ray Martin 1984–94
Donald R. Getty 1985–92	Grant Mitchell 1994–98	Ross Harvey. 1994–96
Ralph P. Klein 1992–	Nancy MacBeth 1998–2001	Pam Barrett 1996–2000
	Ken Nicol 2001–	Raj Pannu 2000–

■ British Columbia

Reform Party of British Columbia	New Democratic Party	Liberal
Ron Gamble 1993–95	Bob Skelly 1984–87	Jevington Blair Tothill .. 1979–81
Jack Weisgerber 1995–97	Michael Harcourt 1987–96	Shirley McLoughlin 1981–83
Wilf Hanni 1997-98	Glen Clark 1996–99	Arthur Lee 1984–87
Bill Vander Zalm 1998–2001	Dan Miller. 1999–2000	Gordon Wilson 1987–93
	Ujjal Dosanjh 2000–01	Gordon Campbell 1993–
	Joy MacPhail 2001–	

■ Yukon

Progressive Conservative Party	Liberal Party	New Democratic Party
Willard Phelps 1985–91	Ron Veale 1980–85	Fred Berger 1978–81
Chris Young 1991	Roger Coles 1985–92	Tony Penikett 1981–95
Yukon Party	Paul Theriault 1992–95	Piers McDonald 1995–2000
John Ostashek 1991–2000	Ken Taylor 1995–98	Trevor Harding 2000
Peter Jenkins 2000–	Pat Duncan 1998–	Eric Fairclough 2001–

(1) Includes up to 5 most recent leaders of the major parties; for years no leader is listed, the leadership was vacant or there was an interim leader.

(2) Known as the Conservative Party until 1946.

(3) Known as the Co-operative Commonwealth Federation until 1962.

(4) Known as the Co-operative Commonwealth Federation until 1961.

DEFENCE

Canadian security policy is based on three elements: defence and collective security, arms control and disarmament, and the peaceful resolution of disputes. The Department of National Defence and the Canadian Forces support this policy by their contributions to strategic deterrence, conventional defence, sovereignty, peacekeeping and arms control.

In addition, the Department of National Defence provides special support to other government departments in areas such as search and rescue, fisheries patrols, enforcement of drug prohibitions, disaster relief, and aid to civil powers in law enforcement. These tasks are carried out both in emergencies and where it complements military surveillance and control responsibilities.

The Defence Department's website can be found at http://www.dnd.ca.

Canadian Regular Armed Forces Strength

Canada has an all-volunteer Armed Forces which, since 1968, has been a single body composed of what had been a separate army, navy and air force.

	Navy	Army	Air Force	Total Armed Forces		Navy	Army	Air Force	Total Armed Forces
1914	379	3 000	—	3 379	1951	11 082	34 986	22 359	68 427
1915	1 255	81 195	—	82 450	1952	13 505	49 278	32 611	95 394
1916	1 557	274 194	—	275 751	1953	15 546	48 458	40 423	104 427
1917	2 220	304 585	—	306 805	1955	19 207	49 409	49 461	118 077
1918	4 792	326 258	—	331 050	1960	20 675	47 185	51 737	119 597
1919	5 495	228 292	—	233 787	1965	19 756	46 264	48 144	114 164
1920	1 048	4 684	—	5 732	1970	—	—	—	93 353
1925	496	3 410	384	4 290	1975	—	—	—	79 817
1930	783	3 510	844	5 137	1980	—	—	—	80 166
1935	860	3 509	794	5 163	1985	—	—	—	83 740
1939	1 585	4 169	2 191	7 945	1990	—	—	—	87 976
1940	6 135	76 678	9 483	92 296	1991	—	—	—	87 319
1941	17 036	194 774	48 743	260 553	1992	—	—	—	84 792
1942	32 067	311 118	111 223	454 408	1993	—	—	—	78 376
1943	56 259	460 387	176 307	692 953	1994	—	—	—	75 949
1944	81 582	495 804	210 089	787 475	1995	—	—	—	72 079
1945	92 529	494 258	174 254	761 041	1996	—	—	—	61 336
1950	9 259	20 652	17 274	47 185	1997	—	—	—	60 320
					1998	—	—	—	60 942
					1999	—	—	—	58,567
					2000	—	—	—	56 706

Source: *Department of National Defence*

Senior Canadian Military Personnel

(as of Oct. 1, 2001)

Chief of the Defence Staff	Gen. Ray R. Henault
Vice-Chief of the Defence Staff	Lt.-Gen. George MacDonald
Deputy Chief of the Defence Staff	Vice-Admiral Greg R. Maddison
Chief of the Land Staff	Lt.-Gen. Mike Jeffery
Chief of the Maritime Staff	Vice-Admiral Ron D. Buck
Chief of the Air Staff	Lt.-Gen. Lloyd C. Campbell
Canadian Military Representative, North Atlantic Treaty Organization	Vice-Admiral J.A. King
Deputy Commander-in-Chief, North American Aerospace Defence	Lt.-Gen. K.R. Pennie
Commander, Canadian Defence Liaison Staff (London)	Brig.-Gen. Bill Richard
Commander, Canadian Defence Liaison Staff (Washington)	Rear Admiral Ian D. Mack

Source: *Department of National Defence*

Canadian Military Ranks

Army/Air Force	Navy
General Officers: General, Lieutenant-General, Major- General, Brigadier-General	**Flag Officers**: Admiral, Vice-Admiral, Rear Admiral, Commodore
Senior Officers: Colonel, Lieutenant-Colonel, Major	**Senior Officers**: Captain (N), Commander, Lieutenant-Commander
Junior Officers: Captain, Lieutenant, Second Lieutenant, Officer Cadet	**Junior Officers**: Lieutenant (N), Sub-Lieutenant, Acting Sub-Lieutenant, Officer Cadet
Non-commissioned Members: Chief Warrant Officer, Master Warrant Officer, Warrant Officer, Sergeant, Master Corporal, Corporal, Private	**Non-commissioned Members**: Chief Petty Officer 1st class, Chief Petty Officer 2nd class, Petty Officer 1st class, Petty Officer 2nd class, Master Seaman, Leading Seaman, Able Seaman

Source: *Department of National Defence*

Canadian Forces Units in Canada

National Defence Headquarters in Ottawa oversees a network of military installations across Canada. These installations are classified differently.

Canadian Forces Bases (CFBs), which are designated by the defence minister, support either land, air or naval units. Canadian Forces Stations (CFSs) are smaller than bases. Stations have fewer resources and personnel; they are organized for operations and lack support capability.

Area Support Units (ASUs) provide food, fuel, maintenance and transportation for nearby operational units. Forward Operating Locations (FOLs) are unmanned airstrips stocked with aviation fuel for use in emergencies. All FOLs are in the Arctic.

Source: *Department of National Defence*

Air Force Bases:
CFB Bagotville (Que.)
CFB Cold Lake (Alta)
CFB Comox (BC)
CFB Gander (Nfld)
CFB Goose Bay (Nfld)
CFB Greenwood (NS)
CFB Moose Jaw (Sask.)
CFB North Bay (Ont.)
CFB Shearwater (NS)
CFB Trenton (Ont.)
CFB Winnipeg (Man.)

Land Force Bases:
CFB Edmonton (Alta)
CFB Gagetown (NB)
CFB Kingston (Ont.)
CFB Montreal (Que.)
CFB Petawawa (Ont.)
CFB Shilo (Man.)
CFB Suffield (Alta)

Naval Bases:
CFB Esquimalt (BC)
CFB Halifax (NS)

Training Base:
CFB Borden (Ont.)

Other Units and Locations:
ASU Longue-Pointe (Que.)
ASU Saint-Jean (Que.)
ASU Valcartier (Que.)
CFS Alert (Nunavut)
FOL Inuvik (NWT)
FOL Iqaluit (Nunavut)
FOL Rankin Inlet (Nunavut)

Source: *Department of National Defence*   Note: as of October 2001

Distant Early Warning Line Clean-up

On Aug. 31, 2001, Canada's military and the Inuit of Nunavut signed the latest in a series of agreements aimed at cleaning up contaminated radar sites in Canada's Arctic.

The radar sites, which were built by the US government, dot the 66th parallel from the Yukon to Baffin Island. Beginning in the 1950s, soldiers dumped lead, PCBs, oil and gas into the soil.

Canada's military will spend $320 million cleaning up 21 of the 42 sites in Canada. Work should finish by 2008. The US government will contribute another US$100 million over 10 years to clean up four other bases.

Canadian Participation in UN Peacekeeping Missions 1947–2001

Location	Year	Mission (Canadian participation)
Korea	1947–48	Supervising elections (2)
India, Pakistan	1949–96	Supervising a ceasefire between India and Pakistan (39)
Korea	1950–53	Supervising the Armistice Agreement (6 146)
Cambodia, Laos, Vietnam	1954–74	Supervising the withdrawal of French forces (133)
Egypt (Sinai)	1956–67	Supervising the withdrawal of French, British and Israeli forces (1 007)
Lebanon	1958	Preventing infiltration across Lebanese borders (77)
Congo	1960–64	Keeping law and order (421)
West New Guinea (now West Irian)	1962–63	Maintaining peace and security (13)
Yemen	1963–64	Observing the withdrawal of Egyptian troops (36)
Dominican Republic	1965–66	Observing the withdrawal of OAS troops (1)
India, Pakistan	1965–66	Supervising a border ceasefire (112)
Nigeria	1968–70	Observing a ceasefire (2)
Egypt (Sinai)	1973–79	Supervising the redeployment of Israeli and Egyptian forces (1 145)
South Vietnam	1973	Supervising a truce (248)
Southern Lebanon	1978	Confirming the withdrawal of Israeli forces (117)
Afghanistan	1988–90	Confirming the withdrawal of Soviet troops (5)
Iran, Iraq	1988–91	Supervising a ceasefire and the withdrawal of forces (525)
Namibia	1989–90	Aiding the transition to independence (301)
Central America	1989–92	Verifying compliance with the Esquipulas Agreement (174)
Haiti	1990–91	Observing the 1990 elections (11)
Afghanistan, Pakistan	1990–92	Providing military advice (1)
Persian Gulf	1990–91	Securing the liberation of Kuwait
Iraq, Kuwait	1991	Monitoring the demilitarized pre-war boundary at the end of the Persian Gulf War (5)
Western Sahara	1991–94	Monitoring a ceasefire; supervising a referendum (34)
Angola	1991–93	Monitoring a ceasefire (15)
Former Yugoslavia and neighbouring states	1991–94	Monitoring a ceasefire (15); reporting on breaches of the Geneva Convention (7)
El Salvador	1991–94	Investigating human rights abuses; monitoring the progress of military reform (55)
El Salvador	1992–95	Investigating human rights abuses; developing a process for military reform and elections (55)
Red Sea	1992	Participating in a naval embargo of Iraq after the Gulf War (250)
Cambodia	1992–93	Monitoring a ceasefire; establishing landmine awareness; monitoring disarmament (240)
Yugoslavia	1992–95	Observing patrols; clearing landmines; building shelters (2 400)
Somalia	1992–93	Providing headquarters staff (12)
Somalia, Kenya	1992–93	Distributing relief supplies (1 250)
Somalia	1993–95	Providing relief and political reconciliation (9)
Haiti	1993–94	Enforcing an embargo (250)
Mozambique	1993–95	Providing security, removing landmines; verifying a ceasefire (4)
Rwanda, Uganda	1993–94	Monitoring the border to enforce a military embargo (3)
Rwanda	1993–96	Providing security for refugees; distributing relief supplies (112)
Yugoslavia	1993–95	Enforcing a no-fly zone (13)
Dominican Republic	1994	Monitoring the DR-Haitian border; providing technical advice to the UN for enforcing a Haitian trade embargo (15)
Haiti	1994–96	Providing security and stability for the training of Haiti's military and police and for elections (500)

▶ Haiti	1996–97	Professionalizing the Haitian police (5)
Central African Republic	1998–99	Providing security, police training, advice and technical support (55)
Central Europe	1998–99	Taking part in OSCE military inspections in Macedonia and Slovakia and military evaluations in Estonia and Moldova
Kosovo	1999	Supporting CF-18 fighter jets in Italy (260); supporting land forces in Macedonia (800); coordinating humanitarian aid in Albania (10)
Mozambique	1999	Clearing landmines (3)
East Timor	1999–2000	Securing peace and order; supporting a UN mission (650)
Eritrea, Ethiopia	2000–01	Preserving a ceasefire (450)

Source: *Department of National Defence*

Current Canadian Participation in UN Peacekeeping

Location	Year	Mission (Canadian participation)
Korea	1953–	Supervising the armistice between North and South (1)
Middle East	1954–	Supervising a 1949 armistice between Israel and Egypt, Lebanon, Jordan and Syria (11)
Cyprus	1964–	Maintaining a ceasefire since 1974 (3)
Israel, Syria	1974–	Supervising a ceasefire at Golan Heights (190)
Egypt (Sinai)	1986–	Supervising the 1979 Camp David Accord (28)
Iraq, Kuwait	1991–	Enforcing UN restrictions on Iraq's trade at sea (236); monitoring the Iraqi-Kuwaiti border (2)
Bosnia-Herzegovina	1995–	Enforcing the Dayton Peace Accords (1 641)
Croatia	1996–	Monitoring the demilitarized zone in Prevlaka (1)
Guatemala	1997–	Monitoring the Comprehensive Agreement on Human Rights (1)
Democratic Republic of Congo	1999–	Investigating ceasefire violations (6)
Kosovo	1999–	Participating in UN interim administration (2)
Sierra Leone	2000–	Monitoring the disarming and demobilizing of combatants (5); reorganizing the government's military (9)
Eritrea, Ethiopia	2001–	Monitoring a ceasefire (6)

Source: *Department of National Defence*

Humanitarian Missions

Canadian Forces have taken part in numerous humanitarian missions since 1947. Recent efforts have included hurricane disaster relief in Florida and the Caribbean; relief after the 1998 mudslides in Sarno, Italy; and aid to Turkish residents following the August 1999 earthquake.

Aid was brought to		Aid was brought to	
1947	Japan	1989	Monserrat
1948	British Columbia	1989–90–91	Northern Ontario
1960	Congo, Chile	1991	Iraq
1965	Zambia	1992	Bahamas, Florida
1967	India	1992–93	Somalia, CIS
1970	Peru	1992–96	Sarajevo
1971	Pakistan	1993–95	Somalia
1973	West Africa, Newfoundland	1994, 1996	Rwanda
1973–79	Nicaragua	1996	Haiti
1974–89	Manitoba	1996	Quebec (Saguenay floods)
1974	Saskatchewan	1997	Manitoba
1979	St. Vincent	1998	Quebec, Ont., NB, Italy, Carribbean
1983	Grenada		
1988–91	Ethiopia	1999	Turkey

Source: *Department of National Defence*

THE ECONOMY

Understanding the Economy: A Glossary of Terms

Appreciation: the increase in the value of a currency relative to other currencies under free market conditions.

Balance of payments: a measure of all yearly business transactions between one country and the rest of the world. It is the difference between the value of exports and imports, as well as the difference between investment money coming into and leaving the country.

Balanced budget: when a government's budget is balanced, all revenues equal expenditures in a budget year. There is no surplus or deficit, but a national debt may still exist.

Bank of Canada: the sole money-issuing bank in Canada, acting as banker to all other financial institutions and the government. It is responsible for Canada's banking system, sets interest rates and regulates the money supply.

Bank rate: the interest rate at which the Bank of Canada lends money to the chartered banks.

Cartel: a group of companies in a specific industry that band together to restrict output and increase prices to get higher profits. In Canada, cartels are illegal. The best known international cartel is the Organization of Petroleum Exporting Countries (OPEC).

Constant dollars: dollars in a specified base year used to adjust for the effects of inflation.

Consumer price index: an indexed measure of the average prices of household goods to show inflationary trends; compiled monthly by Statistics Canada.

Cost of living: the cost of maintaining a particular standard of living measured in terms of purchased goods and services. The rise in the cost of living is the same as the rate of inflation.

Current dollars: cost of an asset in today's prices.

Deficit spending: the practice whereby a government goes into debt to finance some expenditures.

Deflation: a decline in general price levels, often caused by a reduction in the supply of money or credit.

Depreciation: the decrease in the value of a currency relative to other currencies under free market conditions. This differs from devaluation.

Depression: a long period of little business activity when prices are low, unemployment is high, and purchasing power decreases sharply.

Devaluation: the official lowering of the value of a nation's currency relative to foreign currencies.

Disposable income: income after taxes available to persons for spending and saving.

Equalization payments: transfers of tax revenues from the Canadian government to provinces with a high proportion of lower-income earners as compensation for their lower per capita tax revenues.

Exchange rate: the price of one country's currency relative to another country's currency.

Fiscal policy: the deliberate use of government budget measures (i.e., tax and spending policies) to alleviate economic problems such as low GNP, high unemployment and inflation.

Free trade: a system whereby the free movement of all goods and services, investment money and workers between countries is neither restricted nor encouraged by governments.

Gross domestic product (GDP): the value of all goods and services produced in a country.

Gross national product (GNP): the value of all goods and services produced by citizens of a country both inside and outside the country.

Inflation: a steady rise in the average level of prices in an economy.

Less developed countries (LDCs): also known as Third World countries, these are countries considered economically underdeveloped relative to the western industrialized nations.

Minimum wage: a minimum hourly wage as set by federal or provincial legislation.

Monetary policy: the government's manipulation of interest rates and the money supply to achieve economic growth, employment and price stability.

Money supply: the amount of money in an economy, with money defined as all currency in circulation and in chequing accounts.

National debt: the debt of the central government; in Canada's case, the federal government.

Per capita GNP: also known as per capita income, it is the nation's gross national product divided by its population.

Prime interest rate: the rate charged by chartered banks on short-term loans to large commercial customers with the best credit ratings.

Protectionism: government policies designed to restrict imports to protect domestic industries. These policies include customs duties (tariffs) and restrictions on the quantity of imports (quotas). ▶

▶ **Real GNP:** gross national product adjusted for inflation.

Recession: not as severe or as long-lasting as a depression but with the same general characteristics: a decline in real GNP for two consecutive quarters, with resulting unemployment and widespread softening in many sectors of the economy.

Stagflation: a high inflation rate combined with a high unemployment rate.

Supply-side economics: a school of thinking that states that an economy can prosper through policies affecting costs of production—that is, by giving production incentives to labour and greater financial rewards to investors.

Trade balance: the difference between the value of exports and imports.

Transfer payments: government payments to the provinces where no productive return is provided, such as old age pensions, unemployment insurance and welfare.

Wage-price controls: legislation whereby the government sets wage, salary and price increases to curb inflation.

Wage-price spiral: inflation brought about by increased wages that increase costs to the producers, who in turn increase prices. The increase in prices would cause labour to bargain for higher wages, resulting in a spiralling inflation.

ECONOMIC INDICATORS

Canadian Gross Domestic Product

(millions of dollars)

Gross domestic product is the unduplicated value of production originating within Canada, regardless of the ownership of the factors of production.

There are three ways to measure the GDP: *Income Based Approach*: adding up all incomes earned in current production; *Expenditure Based Approach*: adding up all sales of current production to final users; or *Value Added Approach*: summing the difference between an industry's total revenue and the costs of materials and services purchased by that company.

In addition, there are two ways to express GDP: at Market Prices or at Factor Cost. At *Market Prices*: GDP is expressed in terms of the prices actually paid by the purchaser of the product or service–including indirect taxes, but excluding subsidies. GDP at *Factor Cost* reflects the costs of the factors of production—expressed in terms of the expenses of the producer rather than the purchase price—again, including subsidies but not indirect taxes.

The costs themselves are then expressed either in Current Dollars—the prices in effect at the time that the data is for, or in Constant Dollars—also known as "real dollars". These are dollar figures adjusted for inflation growth in the economy. Constant Dollars allow us to compare data from different time period (trends). The table below shows Expenditure-based real GDP at market prices.

Expenditure-Based GDP at 1997 Prices

(millions of dollars)

	1992	1996	1997	1998	1999	2000
PERSONAL	446 415	490 157	512 856	528 320	546 451	566 229
GOVERNMENT						
Current	178 875	173 201	171 883	174 947	179 555	183 562
Investment						
Gross fixed capital	21 160	20 773	20 104	19 917	22 371	24 064
Inventories	-67	-3	5	-25	-3	23
BUSINESS						
Investment	119 865	130 974	154 737	159 072	169 712	180 913
Residential construction	42 885	40 236	43 519	41 982	44 222	45 399
Business investment	76 895	90 734	111 218	117 084	125 478	135 613
Non-residential	33 180	37 275	43 872	44 063	44 873	47 274
Machinery and equipment	43 815	53 465	67 346	73 037	80 703	88 550
Final domestic demand	766 507	815 098	859 580	882 250	918 038	954 600
Inventory change	-9 190	2 558	8 175	5 409	4 630	9 157
Non-farm	-7 727	1 522	9 174	5 165	3 623	8 721
Farm[1]	-1 603	846	-999	-73	616	-16
Exports	224 857	321 787	348 604	379 514	417 093	448 812
Imports	224 920	289 968	331 271	347 417	372 935	403 126
Statistical discrepancy	-1 650	-634	-71	146	159	510
GDP at market prices	**757 954**	**848 667**	**885 022**	**919 770**	**966 362**	**1 009 182**
Annual % change	0.9	1.6	4.3	3.9	5.1	4.4

Source: © *Statistics Canada*   (1) Includes grain in commercial channels.

Canadian Consumer Price Index by Year

(1992 = 100)

Year	Index	Year	Index	Year	Index	Year	Index
1915	7.3	1961	18.7	1975	34.5	1989	89.0
1920	13.5	1962	18.9	1976	37.1	1990	93.3
1925	10.9	1963	19.2	1977	40.0	1991	98.5
1930	10.9	1964	19.6	1978	43.6	1992	100.0
1935	8.7	1965	20.0	1979	47.6	1993	101.8
1940	9.5	1966	20.8	1980	52.4	1994	102.0
1945	10.9	1967	21.5	1981	58.9	1995	104.2
1950	14.9	1968	22.4	1982	65.3	1996	105.9
1955	16.8	1969	23.4	1983	69.1	1997	107.6
1956	17.1	1970	24.2	1984	72.1	1998	108.6
1957	17.6	1971	24.9	1985	75.0	1999	110.5
1958	18.0	1972	26.1	1986	78.1	2000	113.5
1959	18.3	1973	28.1	1987	81.5	2001[1]	117.5
1960	18.5	1974	31.1	1988	84.8		

Source: © *Statistics Canada*   (1) As of June 2001.

Canadian Consumer Price Index by Item

(1992 = 100)

This table shows the relative costs, as far back as 1950, of categories of purchases made by Canadian consumers. To compare 1997 costs with those of another year, divide the 1997 index by the index for the year you wish to compare it with; then multiply that by your actual cost in the year for which you are making the comparison.

Example: you spent $65 per week on family food purchases in 1985. To calculate what that would be in today's dollars, divide the 2000 food index (112.2) by the 1985 food index (78.8). Now multiply the result by $65. The answer, $92.55, is what you now must spend to buy the same package of groceries that cost $65 in 1985.

	All Items	Food	Housing	Clothing and Footwear	Transportation	Health and Personal Care	Recreation and Education	Tobacco and Alcohol
1950	14.9	14.2	n.a.	n.a.	14.8	12.0	15.7	11.3
1955	16.8	15.5	n.a.	n.a.	16.6	14.9	18.9	11.8
1960	18.5	16.9	n.a.	n.a.	19.7	18.2	22.3	12.7
1965	20.0	18.8	n.a.	n.a.	20.7	20.6	23.8	13.4
1970	24.2	22.3	n.a.	n.a.	24.6	25.5	29.6	16.2
1975	34.5	36.4	n.a.	n.a.	33.1	34.6	39.3	20.6
1980	52.4	58.6	50.2	n.a.	51.4	51.8	53.0	30.4
1985	75.0	78.8	74.7	74.8	79.6	73.1	72.9	52.9
1986	78.1	82.8	76.8	76.8	82.1	76.1	76.6	59.2
1987	81.5	86.4	80.3	79.8	85.1	80.0	80.4	63.1
1988	84.8	88.7	84.0	84.2	86.7	83.5	84.9	67.8
1989	89.0	92.0	88.9	87.6	91.2	87.1	88.8	74.1
1990	93.3	95.8	93.9	90.0	96.3	91.4	92.5	80.6
1991	98.5	100.4	98.2	99.0	98.0	97.8	98.9	94.4
1992	100.0	100.0	100.0	100.0	100.0	100.0	100.0	100.0
1993	101.8	101.7	101.4	101.0	103.2	102.7	102.4	101.6
1994	102.0	102.1	101.8	101.6	107.8	103.6	105.5	85.0
1995	104.2	104.5	102.9	101.6	113.4	103.5	109.5	84.9
1996	105.9	105.9	103.1	101.3	117.8	104.1	112.1	86.6
1997	107.6	107.6	103.3	102.7	121.5	105.9	114.9	89.3
1998	108.6	109.3	103.7	103.9	120.5	108.1	117.5	92.6
1999	110.5	110.7	105.1	105.3	124.5	110.2	119.6	94.5
2000	113.5	112.2	108.8	105.5	130.7	112.0	122.5	97.6

Source: © *Statistics Canada*

Canadian Inflation Rate by Year

This table shows annual inflation rates, as measured by the percentage change in the Consumer Price Index (CPI) from one year to the next. The CPI, determined monthly by Statistics Canada, is a "weighted" average of the cost of a package of goods and services — such as food, clothing, housing and health care — normally purchased by Canadian households. Weighted average means that some items are given more importance according to the proportion of household income spent on them.

Prices increase for several reasons: rising production costs, limited availability of the commodity, unfavourable exchange rates pushing up import prices, excessive consumer demand and too much currency in the economy.

Year	Rate	Year	Rate	Year	Rate	Year	Rate
1915	1.4	1958	2.3	1973	7.7	1988	4.0
1920	16.4	1959	1.7	1974	10.7	1989	5.0
1925	1.9	1960	1.1	1975	10.9	1990	4.8
1930	-0.9	1961	1.1	1976	7.5	1991	5.6
1935	1.2	1962	1.1	1977	7.8	1992	1.5
1940	3.3	1963	1.6	1978	9.0	1993	1.8
1945	0.9	1964	2.1	1979	9.2	1994	0.2
1950	2.8	1965	2.0	1980	10.1	1995	2.2
1951	10.1	1966	4.0	1981	12.4	1996	1.6
1952	3.0	1967	3.4	1982	10.9	1997	1.6
1953	-1.2	1968	4.2	1983	5.8	1998	0.9
1954	0.6	1969	4.5	1984	4.3	1999	1.7
1955	0.0	1970	3.4	1985	4.0	2000	2.7
1956	1.8	1971	2.9	1986	4.1	2001[1]	3.3
1957	2.9	1972	4.8	1987	4.4		

Source: © *Statistics Canada*   (1) As of June 2001.

Canadian Interest Rates

(average annual)

	Bank Rate	Prime Rate	Savings Rate[1]	Conventional 5 Year Mortgage	Govt of Canada Average Bond Yield (10 yrs and over)
1985	9.65	10.58	6.08	12.13	11.04
1986	9.21	10.52	6.02	11.21	9.52
1987	8.40	9.52	4.81	11.17	9.95
1988	9.69	10.83	5.69	11.65	10.22
1989	12.29	13.33	8.08	12.06	9.92
1990	13.05	14.06	8.77	13.35	10.85
1991	9.03	9.94	4.48	11.13	9.76
1992	6.78	7.48	2.27	9.51	8.77
1993	5.09	6.10	0.77	8.78	7.85
1994	5.79	7.25	0.50	9.53	8.63
1995	7.31	8.65	0.50	9.16	8.28
1996	4.53	6.06	0.50	7.93	7.50
1997	3.52	4.96	0.50	7.07	6.42
1998	5.10	6.60	0.10	6.93	5.47
1999	4.92	6.44	0.10	8.53	5.89
2000	5.77	7.27	0.10	8.75	5.94
2001[2]	4.75	6.25	0.10	7.75	5.97

Source: *Bank of Canada*   (1) Non-chequable savings deposit. (2) As of June 2001.

1992 = 100

*A*ll indexes measuring changes over time must have a specified time base. The time base is the reference point against which all levels are compared. Without a common time base, the indexes are meaningless. When quoting an index figure, the time base should always be included [e.g., all-items CPI in 1985 was 75.0 (1992 = 100)].

As of January, 1998, the time base changed from 1986 to 1992. All constant dollar series were converted to 1992 dollars during the process, including historical tables for CPI.

Foreign Currency Exchange Rates

	Canadian Dollars in US Dollars			Foreign Currency Units Per Canadian Dollar (annual averages)				
	High	Low	Average	British Pound	French Franc	German Mark	Swiss Franc	Japanese Yen
1975	1.0095	0.9615	0.9830	0.4426	4.2070	2.4131	2.5368	291.5452
1976	1.0389	0.9588	1.0141	0.5615	4.8379	2.5510	2.5336	300.5711
1977	0.9985	0.8963	0.9403	0.5385	4.6189	2.1805	2.2502	251.2563
1978	0.9170	0.8363	0.8770	0.4568	3.9448	1.7572	1.5547	182.4818
1979	0.8778	0.8320	0.8536	0.4023	3.6311	1.5640	1.4192	186.0465
1980	0.8767	0.8249	0.8554	0.3677	3.6088	1.5518	1.4314	192.9385
1981	0.8506	0.8031	0.8340	0.4117	4.3346	1.8804	1.6335	183.4862
1982	0.8446	0.7680	0.8103	0.4634	5.3050	1.9662	1.6418	201.3693
1983	0.8208	0.7990	0.8114	0.5352	6.1576	2.0687	1.7027	192.6782
1984	0.8038	0.7486	0.7723	0.5780	6.7250	2.1911	1.8093	183.2509
1985	0.7587	0.7107	0.7325	0.5649	6.5232	2.1381	1.7809	173.4004
1986	0.7332	0.6913	0.7197	0.4905	4.9751	1.5564	1.2872	120.5400
1987	0.7721	0.7248	0.7541	0.4603	4.5290	1.3543	1.1230	108.8376
1988	0.8444	0.7688	0.8124	0.4560	4.8263	1.4229	1.1844	104.0150
1989	0.8652	0.8254	0.8445	0.5151	5.3821	1.5863	1.3801	116.1980
1990	0.8859	0.8275	0.8570	0.4806	4.6577	1.3824	1.1862	123.6094
1991	0.8934	0.8573	0.8728	0.4932	4.9044	1.4422	1.2458	117.3709
1992	0.8771	0.7729	0.8276	0.4694	4.3706	1.2892	1.1592	104.7120
1993	0.8065	0.7416	0.7753	0.5162	4.3879	1.2814	1.1449	85.8369
1994	0.7642	0.7097	0.7321	0.4778	4.0502	1.1843	0.9976	74.6826
1995	0.7533	0.7009	0.7285	0.4614	3.6311	1.0426	0.8596	68.0272
1996	0.7212	0.7526	0.7334	0.4699	3.7495	1.1028	0.9049	79.6813
1997	0.6945	0.7493	0.7223	0.4409	4.2105	1.2509	1.0473	87.3362
1998	0.6311	0.7123	0.6743	0.4067	3.9683	1.1834	0.9748	87.7963
1999	0.6462	0.6935	0.6730	0.4160	4.1391	1.2343	1.0100	76.2777
2000[1]	0.6693	0.6776	0.6742	0.4317	4.8852	1.4567	1.4567	72.9395
2001[2]	0.6523	0.6557	0.6526	0.4493	4.8972	1.4603	1.1289	81.6327

Source: *Bank of Canada*   (1) As of May 3, 2000. (2) As of July 31, 2001.

Construction in Canada—Building Permits

(millions of dollars)

	Total	Annual % Change	Residential	Non-Residential Total	Industrial	Commercial	Institutional and Government
1955	1 805	18.6	1 031	774	196	254	311
1960	2 025	-14.9	944	1 080	184	433	460
1965	3 810	16.6	1 757	2 053	430	783	840
1970	4 700	-4.0	2 312	2 389	498	807	1 084
1975	10 598	14.2	6 129	4 469	876	2 251	1 342
1980	15 452	9.2	7 468	7 984	1 911	4 322	1 751
1985	19 524	25.9	10 883	8 641	1 885	4 640	2 116
1986	24 690	26.5	14 219	10 471	1 899	6 152	2 420
1987	30 981	25.5	18 832	12 148	2 806	7 039	2 303
1988	34 829	12.4	20 119	14 710	3 046	8 756	2 908
1989	39 318	12.9	21 268	18 050	5 492	9 666	2 892
1990	32 131	-18.3	17 424	14 706	3 393	7 975	3 338
1991	28 468	-11.4	16 632	11 836	2 120	5 906	3 811
1992	26 995	-5.2	17 161	9 834	1 643	4 918	3 273
1993	25 586	-5.2	16 433	9 154	1 756	4 268	3 130
1994	27 637	8.0	17 590	10 047	2 250	4 993	2 803
1995	24 595	-11.0	13 242	11 353	2 823	5 441	3 089
1996	26 155	6.4	15 718	10 347	2 643	5 567	2 227
1997	30 838	17.9	18 317	12 521	3 455	6 520	2 546
1998	33 341	8.1	17 945	15 395	4 261	8 115	3 019
1999	35 736	7.2	19 957	15 779	3 630	8 463	3 686
2000	36 950	3.4	20 342	16 608	3 976	8 907	3 726

Source: © *Statistics Canada*

Annual Bankruptcies in Canada

	Personal	Business	Total		Personal	Business	Total
1970	2 732	2 927	5 659	1989	29 202	8 664	37 866
1975	8 335	2 958	11 293	1990	42 782	11 642	54 424
1980	21 025	6 595	27 620	1991	62 277	13 496	75 773
1981	23 036	8 055	31 091	1992	61 822	14 317	76 139
1982	30 643	10 765	41 408	1993	54 456	12 527	66 983
1983	26 822	10 260	37 082	1994	53 802	11 810	65 612
1984	22 022	9 578	31 600	1995	65 432	13 258	78 690
1985	19 752	8 663	28 415	1996	79 631	14 229	93 860
1986	21 765	8 502	30 267	1997	85 297	12 200	97 497
1987	24 384	7 659	32 043	1998	75 465	10 791	86 256
1988	25 817	8 031	33 848	1999	72 997	10 026	83 023
				2000	75 137	10 055	85 192

Source: *Bankruptcy Branch, Industry Canada*

Business Bankruptcies by Province[1], 2000

	Total Bankruptcies	Total Assets ($)	Total Liabilities ($)	Total Deficiency ($)
Canada	10 055	1 943 015 526	4 487 688 581	2 544 673 055
Newfoundland	120	9 028 005	24 871 198	15 843 193
Nova Scotia	352	27 290 169	64 282 088	36 991 918
Prince Edward Island	26	733 342	2 706 176	1 972 834
New Brunswick	225	18 672 966	54 921 296	36 248 330
Quebec	3 011	279 901 388	751 640 636	471 739 248
Ontario	2 928	337 642 376	1 526 473 659	1 188 831 284
Manitoba	253	28 558 940	50 179 874	21 620 935
Saskatchewan	438	55 068 999	94 111 353	39 042 354
Alberta	1 710	1 045 043 157	1 451 544 661	406 501 504
British Columbia	980	140 662 490	464 856 467	324 193 977
Yukon	4	98 194	380 061	281 867
Northwest Territories	8	315 500	1 721 111	1 405 611
Nunavut	0	0	0	0

Sources: *Bankruptcy Branch, Industry Canada*   (1) Total business bankruptcies reported in the calendar year.

Consumer Bankruptcies by Province[1], 2000

	Total Bankruptcies	Total Assets ($)	Total Liabilities ($)	Total Deficiency ($)
Canada	75 137	2 477 450 800	4 090 505 791	1 613 054 991
Newfoundland	1 556	51 889 563	70 802 863	18 913 300
Nova Scotia	2 815	85 478 707	120 594 185	34 115 479
Prince Edward Island	182	6 133 191	8 582 708	2 449 517
New Brunswick	1 393	48 367 475	65 300 987	16 933 512
Quebec	23 159	516 426 284	1 107 799 995	591 373 711
Ontario	23 588	765 949 059	1 389 705 834	623 756 775
Manitoba	2 475	72 139 284	107 235 039	35 095 755
Saskatchewan	1 833	64 732 147	76 723 770	11 991 624
Alberta	8 847	395 370 028	445 749 637	50 379 609
British Columbia	9 184	465 444 118	691 798 628	226 354 511
Yukon	40	1 397 626	1 940 707	543 081
Northwest Territories	64	2 751 812	3 685 108	933 296
Nunavut	0	0	0	0

Sources: *Bankruptcy Branch, Industry Canada*   (1) Total consumer bankruptcies reported in the calendar year.

Canadian Unemployment Rates[1]

	1980	1985	1990	1995	1996	1997	1998	1999	2000
Canada	**7.5**	**10.7**	**8.1**	**9.4**	**9.6**	**9.1**	**8.3**	**7.6**	**6.8**
Newfoundland	13.1	20.8	16.9	18.1	19.3	18.6	18.0	16.9	16.7
Prince Edward Island	10.5	13.5	14.6	15.0	14.7	15.4	13.8	14.4	12.0
Nova Scotia	9.7	13.6	10.5	12.1	12.3	12.1	10.5	9.6	9.1
New Brunswick	11.1	15.3	12.1	11.2	11.6	12.7	12.2	10.2	10.0
Quebec	10.0	12.2	10.4	11.4	11.9	11.4	10.3	9.3	8.4
Ontario	6.8	8.1	6.2	8.7	9.0	8.4	7.2	6.3	5.7
Manitoba	5.5	8.4	7.3	7.2	7.2	6.5	5.5	5.6	4.9
Saskatchewan	4.2	8.3	7.0	6.6	6.6	5.9	5.7	6.1	5.2
Alberta	3.8	10.0	6.8	7.8	6.9	5.8	5.6	5.7	5.0
British Columbia	6.6	14.5	8.6	8.4	8.7	8.4	8.8	8.3	7.2

Source: © *Statistics Canada*   (1) Percentage of labour force.

FEDERAL GOVERNMENT SPENDING

Statement of Assets and Liabilities

as at March 31, 2000 (millions of dollars)

	1999	2000
Assets		
Current Assets		
Cash	9 306	13 025
Cash in transit	5 432	5 386
Less outstanding cheques and warrants	(4 045)	(3 900)
Accounts receivable[1]	4 580	4 353
FOREIGN EXCHANGE ACCOUNTS	34 668	41 494
Loans, Investments and Advances		
Enterprise Crown corporations[2]	11 052	10 562
National governments including developing countries and international organizations	7 555	7 316
Provincial and territorial governments and other loans, investments and advances	3 100	2 944
Portfolio investments	1 241	1 240
Less allowance for valuation	(9 412)	(8 266)
Total Assets	**63 477**	**74 154**
Accumulated Deficit	**576 824**	**564 526**
Liabilities		
Current Liabilities and Allowances		
Accounts payable and accrued liabilities	24 509	20 551
Interest and matured debt	9 791	8 353
Allowance for employee benefits	6 926	7 924
Allowance for loan guarantees and for borrowings of Crown corporations ...	4 090	3 920
INTEREST-BEARING DEBT		
Unmatured debt payable in Canadian currency		
Marketable bonds	295 752	293 927
Treasury bills	96 950	99 850
Canada savings bonds	27 662	26 489
Bonds for Canada Pension Plan	4 063	3 552
Unmatured debt payable in foreign currencies	36 000	32 588
Public sector pensions	122 407	128 346
Canada Pension Plan (net of securities)	5 427	6 217
Other pension and other accounts	6 724	6 963
Total Liabilities	**640 301**	**638 680**

Source: *Public Works and Government Services Canada (Receiver General)*
(1) Net of allowance for doubtful accounts of $2,432 million in 1999; $2,261 million in 2000. (2) Also includes other government business enterprises.

Statement of Revenue and Expenditure

for the Year Ended March 31, 2000

(net, millions of dollars)

	1999	2000
Revenue		
Tax revenue		
Income tax		
Personal	72 488	79 378
Corporation	21 575	23 170
Other income tax revenues	2 901	3 499
Employment insurance premiums	19 363	18 512
Excise tax and duties		
Goods and services tax	20 684	22 790
Energy taxes	4 716	4 757
Customs import duties	2 359	2 105
Other excise taxes and duties	3 640	3 234
Non-tax Revenue		
Return on investments	4 991	5 251
Other non-tax revenue	2 954	3 012
Total Revenue	**155 671**	**165 708**
Expenditure		
Transfer payments		
Old age security benefits, guaranteed income supplements and spouse's allowances	22 781	23 410
Other levels of government	25 523	23 243
Employment insurance benefits[1]	11 884	11 301
Other transfer payments	18 735	18 535
Crown Corporation expenditures	3 497	2 953
Other program expenditures		
National Defence	8 781	10 201
All other departments and agencies	20 192	22 120
Public debt charges	41 394	41 647
Total Expenditure	**152 787**	**153 410**
Surplus	**2 884**	**12 298**

Source: *Public Works and Government Services Canada (Receiver General)*

(1) Employment insurance benefits exclude administration costs of $1 360 million in 1999.

Government Debt

*W**hat's the difference between a debt and a deficit? A deficit is the shortfall between income and expenditures in a given year. Debt is the accumulated deficits of the past years' budgets.*
Some people may erroneously interchange the two terms, but there is a big difference. Along with debt comes a corresponding interest charge on the money owed. If not for this debt charge, the federal government could have had a significant surplus of government revenue over expenditure in the 1990s. However, the federal government had to deal with the results of their over-spending in the 1970s, high interest rates in the 1980s, and the recession of the early 1990s.*

In the 1990s, Canadians became increasingly concerned about the size of the government debt. In 1991, the accumulated federal debt was $390.8 billion, but within four years it had risen to $545.7 billion. It wasn't until 1998, that the federal government was able to make a dent in the debt.

Although the government began restructuring in order to reduce government spending, it wasn't until the recession ended, and government revenue began rising sharply through increased tax income, that the government made any significant headway in reducing debt. By the fiscal year 1999/2000, the federal government was able to report a surplus of almost $2.8 billion, its third consecutive surplus, and the discussion concerning paying down the debt began.

Federal Ministry Spending

(millions of dollars)

Department	1987-88	1997-98	1998-99	1999-2000
Agriculture and Agri-Food	3 386.6	1 911.7	1 580.0	2 411.2
Canada Customs and Revenue Agency	1 328.5	2 441.9	2 757.2	2 935.2
Canadian Heritage (Communications)	1 706.5	2 619.6	2 722.4	2 908.9
Citizenship and Immigration	—	748.8	789.2	943.8
Consumer and Corporate Affairs	533.7	—[1]	—[1]	—[1]
Energy, Mines & Resources	1 335.8	—[2]	—[2]	—[1]
Environment	784.9	557.9	574.4	731.4
Finance	35 973.6	64 439.9	70 497.3	70 739.4
Fisheries and Oceans	608.5	1 151.5	1 333.7	1 379.0
Foreign Affairs and International Trade (External Affairs)	3 172.8	3 363.8	3 443.3	3 584.5
Governor General (and Lieutenant-Governors)	8.1	11.2	13.0	15.3
Health	—	1 884.3	2 270.4	3 211.3
Human Resources Development	—	24 943.5	25 961.9	26 159.5
Indian and Northern Affairs	2 824.1	4 555.9	4 926.1	4 698.2
Industry	—	4 523.2	4 030.8	4 773.3
Justice	567.9	828.1	986.5	1 069.9
Labour	222.7	—[3]	—[3]	—[3]
Manpower/Employment and Immigration	4 622.5	—[3]	—[3]	—[3]
National Defence	10 650.4	10 187.3	10 256.5	11 521.7
National Health and Welfare	28 973.6	—[4]	—[4]	—[4]
Natural Resources	—	753.3	782.5	918.5
Parliament	225.2	296.5	316.0	324.0
Post Office	—	—	—	—
Privy Council	88.2	339.4	237.4	264.3
Public Works and Government Services	2 925.1	3 757.0	3 929.1	3 824.1
Regional Economic (Industrial) Expansion	1 425.7	—[1]	—[1]	—[1]
Science and Technology	799.2	—[1]	—[1]	—[1]
Secretary of State	3 382.7	—[5]	—[5]	—[5]
Solicitor General	1 905.3	2 738.0	2 766.7	3 007.8
Supply & Services	768.8	—[6]	—[6]	—[6]
Transport	4 758.6	2 256.4	1 094.4	927.2
Treasury Board	417.8	1 150.6	998.5	1 136.4
Urban Affairs and Housing	—	—	—	—
Veterans Affairs	1 611.7	1 934.7	1 996.8	2 076.6
Total	**115 110.5**	**141 298.8**	**144 264.0**	**149 561.4**

Source: *Public Accounts of Canada*

(1) See Industry.

(2) See Natural Resources.

(3) Responsibilities moved to Human Resources Development.

(4) See Health.

(5) Split between Canadian Heritage and Human Resources Development.

(6) See Public Works.

Federal Government Annual Surplus or Deficit

Fiscal Year Ending March 31 (millions of dollars)

	Surplus or Deficit[1]	% of GDP[2]		Surplus or Deficit[1]	% of GDP[2]		Surplus or Deficit[1]	% of GDP[2]
1960	-600	1.7[3]	1974	-1 999	1.6	1988	-28 201	5.1
1961	-529	1.4[3]	1975	-2 009	1.3	1989	-28 951	4.8
1962	-948	2.3	1976	-5 737	3.3	1990	-28 996	4.4
1963	-833	1.9	1977	-6 297	3.2	1991	-30 618	4.7
1964	-1 169	2.5	1978	-10 426	4.8	1992	-34 643	5.1
1965	-315	0.6	1979	-12 617	5.2	1993	-41 021	5.8
1966	-303	0.5	1980	-11 501	4.2	1994	-42 012	5.6
1967	-187	0.3	1981	-13 522	4.4	1995	-37 462	4.8
1968	-711	1.0	1982	-14 872	4.2	1996	-28 617	3.6
1969	-400	0.5	1983	-27 816	7.4	1997	-8 897	1.0
1970	332	0.4	1984	-32 399	8.0	1998	3 478	0.4
1971	-780	0.9	1985	-38 324	8.7	1999	2 884	0.3
1972	-1 542	1.6	1986	-34 404	7.2	2000	12 298	1.2
1973	-1 675	1.5	1987	-30 733	6.0			

Source: *Public Accounts of Canada*

(1) A minus (-) sign indicates a deficit. (2) GDP (Gross Domestic Product) represents the value (in current dollars) of all goods and services produced in Canada.

Per Capita Accumulated Federal Debt[1]

	(millions of dollars)		(dollars)	
	Net Debt	Interest on Debt	Net Debt Per Capita	Interest Per Capita
1940	3 271	139	288	12
1945	11 298	409	936	34
1950	11 645	440	849	32
1955	11 263	478	718	30
1960	12 089	736	677	41
1965	15 504	1 012	789	52
1970	16 943	1 676	796	79
1975	19 276	3 164	849	139
1980	72 159	8 494	2 853	353
1985	199 092	22 445	7 911	892
1986	233 496	25 441	9 210	1 003
1987	264 101	26 658	10 306	1 040
1988	292 184	29 028	11 276	1 120
1989	320 918	33 183	12 240	1 266
1990	357 811	38 820	13 484	1 472
1991	388 429	42 537	14 424	1 590
1992	423 072	41 020	15 469	1 499
1993	466 198	38 825	16 301	1 356
1994	508 210	37 982	17 381	1 299
1995	545 672	42 046	18 435	1 420
1996	574 289	46 905	19 908	1 626
1997	583 186	44 973	19 247	1 484
1998	579 708	40 931	19 166	1 353
1999	576 824	41 394	18 918	1 358
2000	564 526	41 647	18 358	1 354

Source: *Public Accounts of Canada*

(1) As of Mar. 31, on a public accounts basis.

Annual Federal Government Expenditure

(millions of dollars)[1]

	Total Expenditure	Expenditure on Goods & Services	Transfer Payments[2]	Interest on Public Debt
1965	8 556	3 093	4 411	1 052
1970	15 058	4 922	8 274	1 862
1975	35 364	9 369	22 290	3 705
1980	60 846	15 335	35 614	9 897
1985	112 362	26 701	60 923	24 738
1986	114 476	27 335	60 925	26 216
1987	120 669	28 434	64 352	27 883
1988	129 012	29 950	67 351	31 711
1989	138 561	31 904	69 233	37 424
1990	151 590	35 067	74 643	41 880
1991	161 314	35 910	84 351	41 053
1992	164 547	36 498	88 491	39 558
1993	167 301	37 690	90 392	39 219
1994	166 003	37 912	87 934	40 157
1995	172 500	37 887	88 359	46 254
1996[3]	166 086	36 610	84 124	45 352
1997[3]	160 069	35 019	81 643	43 407
1998[3]	163 149	35 988	83 392	43 769
1999[3]	171 536	37 991	90 218	43 327
2000	178 857	42 800	91 001	44 156

Source: © *Statistics Canada*
(1) Expressed in constant dollars, 1992 = 100. (2) Includes payments to persons, businesses, non-residents, and provinces and local administrations. (3) Revised data.

Interest on Public Debt

(millions of dollars)[1]

	Mun.	Prov.	Fed.	Total		Mun.	Prov.	Fed.	Total
1965	330	306	1 052	1 688	1985	3 298	12 549	24 738	40 585
1966	373	359	1 151	1 883	1986	3 313	13 693	26 216	43 222
1967	430	435	1 245	2 110	1987	3 340	15 056	27 883	46 279
1968	476	548	1 409	2 433	1988	3 365	15 730	31 711	50 806
1969	517	710	1 589	2 816	1989	3 495	17 366	37 424	58 285
1970	591	856	1 862	3 309	1990	3 722	18 684	41 880	64 286
1971	728	1 049	1 974	3 751	1991	3 886	19 587	41 053	64 526
1972	748	1 243	2 253	4 244	1992	4 089	21 594	39 558	65 241
1973	858	1 534	2 518	4 910	1993	4 295	23 337	39 219	66 851
1974	846	1 681	2 961	5 488	1994	4 219	25 221	40 157	69 597
1975	942	1 992	3 705	6 639	1995	4 316	26 957	46 254	77 527
1976	1 220	2 503	4 519	8 242	1996	4 176	26 756	45 352	76 284
1977	1 443	2 888	5 101	9 432	1997[2]	3 949	26 679	43 407	74 035
1978	1 638	3 693	6 410	11 741	1998[2]	3 590	27 747	43 769	75 106
1979	1 781	4 196	8 080	14 057	1999[2]	3 479	28 298	43 327	75 104
1980	1 986	5 150	9 897	17 033	2000	3 367	28 878	44 156	76 401
1981	2 257	6 534	13 739	22 530					
1982	2 544	8 200	16 675	27 419					
1983	2 837	9 558	17 463	29 858					
1984	3 015	11 126	21 006	35 147					

Source: © *Statistics Canada*   (1) Expressed in constant dollars, 1992 = 100. (2) Revised data.

Employment Insurance

On July 1, 1996 the Employment Insurance (EI) Act replaced the Unemployment Insurance and the National Training Act. The EI program consists of two parts(Income Benefits (Part 1) and Active Re-employment Benefits (Part 2).

EI Income Benefits provide temporary income support for claimants while they look for work. Under the EI program every hour of work, including part-time, counts towards determining eligibility. There is also a Family Income Supplement that increases benefits for low-income claimants with children.

Active Re-employment Benefits provide assistance to unemployed workers returning to work through a set of active re-employment benefits and support measures. Targeted wage subsidies, self-employment assistance and job creation partnerships are available in all provinces and territories. Skills loans and grants are being implemented with the agreement of provinces and territories.

Eligibility

Most claimants require 420 to 700 insured hours of employment within the last 52 weeks, depending on the local unemployment rate. The higher the unemployment rate, the fewer hours of work are required. Claimants who are entering the workforce for the first time or re-entering after a two-year absence will require 910 hours of work. To qualify for special benefits (sickness, maternity, parental) all claimants require 700 hours regardless of where they live.

Source: *Human Resources Development Canada*

Income Benefits

Claimants will receive 55% of their average weekly-insured earnings to a maximum of $413 per week. Claimants in receipt of the Family Income Supplement are exempt from the reduction of the benefit rate.

Claim Period

A claim for benefits lasts a maximum of 1 year, or until all benefits have been collected, whichever occurs first. The number of weeks of benefits a claimant is entitled to is determined by the unemployment rate in their region and the number of insured hours used to establish the claim. The more insured hours used the more weeks of benefits, the higher the unemployment rate the more weeks of benefits.

Special Benefits

Claimants who are unable to work due to illness or injury are also entitled to benefits. A maximum of 15 weeks of sick benefits can be paid per claim. Claimants who are off work on maternity leave are entitled to a maximum of 15 weeks of benefits. A claimant off work caring for a newly born or adopted child can collect 35 weeks parental benefits. A claimant cannot collect more than a total of 50 weeks of special benefits (sick, maternity, parental) per claim.

Effective December 31, 2000 the Government of Canada increased the duration of parental benefits to 35 weeks for biological and adoptive parents. A maximum of 50 weeks of combined maternity, parental and sickness benefits are available. Presently, claimants must accumulate 600 hours of insured employment ($3,760 for fishers) to receive maternity and parental benefits.

Additional information on Employment Insurance can be obtained at http://www.hrdc-drhc.gc.ca/ae-ei/employment_insurance.shtml

Employment Insurance Program Payments

	Claims[1,2] (000s)	Benefit Payments ($000)[3]	Weeks Paid (000s)[4]	Maximum Weekly Payment	Average Weekly Payment[4]
1945	296.4	$ 14 576	1 224	$ 14.40	$ 11.91
1950	1 150.2	98 994	6 980	21.00	14.18
1955	1 929.8	228 860	12 375	30.00	18.49
1960	2 700.4	481 836	21 592	36.00	22.32
1965	1 628.2	312 110	12 718	36.00	24.54
1970	2 260.8	695 222	19 817	53.00	35.08
1975	2 857.2	3 146 497	37 327	123.00	84.64
1980	2 762.2	4 393 308	36 333	174.00	120.92
1985	3 312.4	10 266 888	59 788	276.00	171.05
1990	3 259.0	13 189 000	57 052	384.00	231.18
1995	3 095.8	13 748 243	50 462	448.00	260.14
1996	2 972.5	13 069 982	47 932	413.00	259.26
1997	2 766.7	12 018 601	40 933	413.00	254.13
1998	2 842.2	11 995 880	39 102	413.00	258.60
1999	2 692.3	11 830 162	36 789	413.00	264.50
2000	2 566.9	11 154 439	34 482	413.00	269.28

Source: *Human Resources Development Canada*
(1) Refers to the program in place prior to July 1, 1996. (2) Initial and renewal. (3) The Total Benefit Payments include all payments under the EI Act. In addition to Employment Insurance benefits there are labour support measures. The EI benefit payments for 2000 were $9 285 233 000. (4) The weeks paid and the average weekly payment are for EI benefits.

Canada and Quebec Pension Plans[1]

The Canada Pension Plan and the Quebec Pension Plan were instituted in 1966 to provide benefits to Canadians who have contributed to the plan during their working lives. Both plans pay a monthly retirement benefit in addition to a one-time death benefit, survivor benefits for the spouse and dependent children of a deceased contributor and benefits to the severely disabled and their families. Same-sex common-law partners now have the same benefits and obligations as opposite-sex common-law partners according to the CPP.

Payments to the plan are made by all workers between the ages of 18 and the time they claim retirement (between the ages of 60 and 70). Payments are based on a contribution rate which in 2001 was 8.6 percent of "pensionable earnings." Employers and employees share this payment equally; self-employed persons must pay the entire amount themselves.

The contribution rate is scheduled to increase steadily, targeted to reach 9.9 percent in 2003. Contributions are not paid if income falls below an annual minimum ($3,500 in 2001) or on income above an annual maximum ($38,300 in 2001).

Retirement benefits from the plan are based on lifetime earnings and generally amount to 25 per-cent of average annual employment income to a maximum, adjusted for inflation. The maximum monthly benefit at age 65 in 2001 was $775.

Spouses in a continuing marriage, and partners in a common-law relationship, may apply to receive an equal share of the retirement pension earned by both parties during their life together.

A provision that allows divorced couples to divide CPP credits earned during marriage was introduced in 1978. On January 1, 1987, the provision was expanded to include legally separated married spouses and those living in a common-law union. In March 1991, a further amendment allowed those previously denied a division due to a property waiver to have their situation remedied.

Since January 1987, Canadians eligible for benefits who retire before age 65 can receive pensions beginning as early as age 60. Those who begin collecting at 60 receive 70 percent of the amount they would be entitled to at age 65. For each month past age 60 that a person delays retirement an additional half a percentage point is added—so that someone retiring at age 61 would receive 76 percent of their full (age 65) pension while someone postponing retirement to age 70 would receive 130 percent.

The federal government administers the Canada Pension Plan, while the Quebec government's Régie des rentes (pension board) administers the Quebec Pension Plan. Essentially, the rules and benefits are similar for both plans.

Sources: *Human Resources Development Canada; Régie des rentes du Québec*
(1) The figures and dates mentioned above apply to the Canada Pension Plan. Some of these figures are slightly different for the Quebec Pension Plan.

Canada and Quebec Pension Plans Payments

	Canada Pension				Quebec Pension Plan			
	Benefi-ciaries[1]	Benefits paid[2] ($000)	Contrib-utors[3] (000s)	Avg. monthly retirement payments[1]	Benefi-ciaries[1]	Benefits paid[2] ($000s)	Contrib-utors[3] (000s)	Avg. monthly retirement payments[1]
1971	251 853	89 236	6 755	23	101 294	43 507	2 242	37
1976	774 890	587 834	7 561	67	262 308	266 181	2 736	109
1981	1 274 306	2 010 924	8 626	144	432 552	811 177	2 923	191
1986	1 764 604	4 887 134	8 932	247	657 624	2 067 293	2 949	274
1991	2 584 986	10 541 912	9 630	342	837 043	3 469 425	3 100	319
1992	2 713 692	11 792 756	9 429	363	873 984	3 848 675	3 039	338
1993	2 845 059	13 199 084	9 399	370	908 608	4 114 525	3 020	346
1994	2 988 911	14 402 175	9 595	380	950 767	4 393 671	3 046	352
1995	3 116 453	15 256 542	9 726	384	999 591	4 638 239	3 070	349
1996	3 212 847	15 969 269	9 800	393	1 051 157	4 954 834	3 066	353
1997	3 281 603	16 675 314	10 061	400	1 087 965	5 191 214	3 120	358
1998	3 365 808	17 536 907	10 385	409	1 118 874	5 458 377	3 272	364
1999	3 437 649	18 184 939	10 642	412	1 150 140	5 664 279	3 338	367
2000	3 514 482	18 754 816	n.a.	418	1 185 909	5 917 146	3 365	372
2001[4]	3 585 896	19 485 371	n.a.	428	1 212 700	6 273 537	3 422	380

Source: *Human Resources Development Canada and the Régie des rentes du Québec*   (n.a.) Not available.
Note: From 1971 to 1978, data are for calendar years; from 1981 to 1988, data are for fiscal years ending Mar. 31.
(1) As of March. (2) For fiscal years ending Mar. 31. (3) Calendar years. (4) Estimated.

Old Age Security, Guaranteed Income Supplement and Spouse's Allowance

The Old Age Security (OAS) program, introduced in 1952, provides pensions to persons 65 years and older who meet Canadian residence requirements. Full pensions ($436.55 per month as of July 2001) are paid to persons who have lived in Canada for 40 years since the age of 18. Partial pensions, introduced in 1977, are based on the number of years a pensioner has lived in Canada. A minimum of 10 years residence in Canada after age 18 is required.

The Guaranteed Income Supplement (GIS) was introduced in 1967 to assist those with little or no income other than their OAS pension. The amount of income supplement depends upon the pensioner's income, marital status and spouse's/common-law partner's income. Same-sex common-law partners now have the same benefits and obligations as opposite sex common-law partners.

Generally, the maximum GIS payment is reduced by $1 for every $2 of other monthly income a pensioner has above his/her Old Age Security pension. For example, in July 2001 a single pensioner with no personal income received a basic OAS pension of $436.55 per month and an income supplement of $518.82 per month. If this person had a private pension of $400 per month, the GIS would be reduced $200 to $318.82 per month.

Spousal allowance (SPA) benefits are payable to low-income persons aged 60 to 64 whose spouses have died, or whose spouse/common-law partner receives the Guaranteed Income Supplement. Like the Guaranteed Income Supplement, the amount of the benefit is dependent on income and marital status. The maximum benefit payable in July 2001 was $855.05 for survivors, and $774.49 for spouses/common-law partners of OAS pensioners receiving the GIS.

Source: *Human Resources Development Canada*

Old Age Security Program Payments

	Number of Recipients[1] (000s)			Net Payments[2] ($000 000)			Average Yearly[3] Payment per Pensioner		
	OAS	GIS	SPA	OAS	GIS	SPA	OAS	GIS	SPA
1961	905	n.a.	n.a.	$ 592	n.a.	n.a.	n.a.	n.a.	n.a.
1966	1 106	n.a.	n.a.	927	n.a.	n.a.	n.a.	n.a.	n.a.
1971	1 720	860	n.a.	1 627	$ 280	n.a.	$ 956	$ 340	n.a.
1976	1 957	1 087	54	2 976	923	$ 35	1 537	863	$1 788
1981	2 303	1 245	85	5 322	1 918	178	2 338	1 592	2 168
1986	2 652	1 330	142	8 858	3 319	348	3 385	2 555	3 105
1991	3 099	1 346	121	12 705	3 976	450	4 153	3 009	3 759
1992	3 180	1 329	116	13 808	4 139	446	4 386	3 171	3 927
1993	3 264	1 331	113	14 421	4 250	435	4 464	3 268	3 964
1994	3 341	1 355	112	15 027	4 446	429	4 542	3 372	3 984
1995	3 420	1 377	112	15 478	4 604	429	4 570	3 422	3 942
1996	3 500	1 368	106	15 999	4 628	408	4 615	3 464	3 980
1997	3 564	1 376	103	16 576	4 639	396	4 678	3 452	3 951
1998	3 635	1 376	100	17 114	4 729	389	4 745	3 466	3 934
1999	3 694	1 382	99	17 564	4 805	383	4 785	3 532	3 944
2000	3 755	1 375	98	18 087	4 936	391	4 848	3 601	4 041
2001	3 828	1 371	95	18 833	5 038	388	4 958	3 701	4 105

Source: *Human Resources Development Canada*   (n.a.) Not available or not applicable.

OAS = Old Age Security; GIS = Guaranteed Income Supplement; SPA = Spouse's Allowance.

(1) As of March. (2) For fiscal years ending Mar. 31. (3) For fiscal years ending Mar. 31, using annual average number of recipients.

FOREIGN TRADE

Canadian Balance of International Payments

(millions of dollars)

The balance of payments statement provides information about a country's economic transactions with non-residents for a specified time frame. Canada produces balance of payments statistics on a quarterly basis. It is structured under two broad accounts: the Current Account and the Capital and Financial Account.

The current account measures revenues and expenditures arising from transactions in goods and services, investment income and current transfers. The capital and financial account comprises the capital account (capital transfers and non-produced, non-financial assets), and the financial account (transactions in financial instruments). The financial account provides information about the financing and investing activities of Canadian residents with non-residents.

	Current Account			Capital Account[3]			
	Receipts[1]	Payments	Balance[2]	Canadian Assets	Canadian Liabilities	Financial Account[4]	Total Capital and Financial Account[4]
1971	23 167	24 214	-1 046	-1 888	3 993	2 105	2 352
1972	26 428	27 813	-2 385	-2 216	5 769	3 553	3 834
1973	32 999	35 054	-2 055	-5 988	8 448	2 460	2 805
1974	42 098	46 573	-4 475	-3 209	8 016	4 808	5 346
1975	43 038	51 357	-8 319	-1 954	10 354	8 400	8 895
1976	48 067	55 611	-7 544	-6 303	16 311	10 008	10 531
1977	56 058	63 465	-7 407	-4 356	12 841	8 485	8 941
1978	66 872	76 222	-9 350	-10 021	21 603	11 582	11 714
1979	84 918	94 750	-9 832	-12 064	22 697	10 633	11 177
1980	98 419	105 540	-7 120	-21 411	27 894	6 483	6 979
1981	108 933	123 927	-14 994	-22 459	41 250	18 791	19 423
1982	112 362	110 060	2 302	-9 656	8 070	-1 586	-28
1983	115 409	118 541	-3 132	-9 973	15 141	5 168	6 506
1984	143 435	145 109	-1 673	-12 633	20 228	7 594	8 967
1985	151 338	159 166	-7 828	-7 352	19 556	12 204	13 659
1986	155 323	170 836	-15 514	-20 153	35 746	15 593	17 416
1987	162 736	180 542	-17 806	-17 716	34 868	17 152	20 869
1988	181 791	200 120	-18 328	-17 602	30 599	12 997	17 817
1989	186 280	212 091	-25 812	-19 745	41 882	22 137	27 617
1990	194 972	218 107	-23 135	-19 699	38 664	18 965	25 167
1991	188 719	214 348	-25 629	-15 128	34 509	19 381	25 791
1992	205 455	230 815	-25 360	-14 411	27 727	13 316	21 890
1993	235 576	263 670	-28 093	-26 943	50 706	23 763	34 467
1994	285 601	303 331	-17 730	-49 029	56 550	7 520	17 762
1995	330 978	337 078	-6 099	-38 394	32 905	-5 489	1 294
1996	351 038	346 438	4 600	-73 306	53 116	-20 191	-12 234
1997[5]	385 415	396 812	-11 397	-62 546	70 803	8 256	15 764
1998[5]	412 624	424 901	-12 277	-67 307	67 339	32	4 964
1999[5]	456 100	454 410	1 690	-45 313	28 256	-17 057	-12 009
2000	526 229	499 334	26 894	-134 903	114 477	-20 426	-15 164

Source: © *Statistics Canada*

(1) Money received for Canadian exports of goods and services. (2) Receipts minus payments. (3) Net flows. (4) The difference between the Financial Account and Total Capital and Financial Account is the net on Capital Account (not shown). For example, in 1999 the Financial Account was -17 057 and Total Capital and Financial Account was -12 009. Therefore, the net on the Capital Account would be 5 048. (5) Revised data.

Canadian Trade Balance[1]

(millions of dollars)

	1996	1997	1998	1999	2000
Total[2]	43 253	25 126	20 077	34 756	55 521
Australia	-274	-200	-320	-259	-365
Belgium	720	662	563	947	1 081
Brazil	295	373	5	-331	-449
Chile	73	67	-21	-61	-112
China[3]	-1 916	-3 934	-5 157	-6 264	-7 648
Colombia	216	159	107	-25	-25
Cuba	-109	11	148	91	-78
Egypt	136	157	123	145	132
El Salvador	-16	-23	1	-23	-130
France[4]	-1 651	-3 468	-3 192	-3 427	-2 273
Germany	-1 486	-2 666	-3 366	-4 533	-4 623
Hong Kong	137	488	174	-187	-136
Hungary	1	18	1	-42	-117
India	-251	-252	-479	-563	-693
Iran	324	222	110	428	534
Israel	-27	-63	-188	-147	-282
Italy[5]	-1 346	-1 529	-1 902	-2 155	-1 935
Jamaica	-147	-170	-158	-104	-98
Japan	772	-1 383	-5 370	-6 615	-7 522
Kenya	15	20	5	30	7
Malaysia	-1 036	-1 292	-1 516	-1 637	-2 080
Mexico	-4 776	-5 744	-6 215	-7 927	-10 064
Morocco	113	135	106	69	142
Netherlands	741	642	705	333	164
New Zealand	-94	-71	-174	-165	-327
Nigeria	-268	-416	-246	-270	-398
Peru	49	177	17	23	16
Philippines	-261	-299	-694	-751	-1 016
Poland	36	19	35	-24	-119
Romania	52	-3	-66	-64	-48
Russia	-117	-242	-443	-428	-467
Saudi Arabia	-12	-90	-78	-133	-588
Singapore	-620	-627	-755	-875	-1 031
South Africa	-206	-127	-196	-238	-266
Spain	-164	-190	-255	-224	-286
Sweden	-921	-916	-1 001	-1 095	-1 424
Switzerland	2	-499	-183	-771	-883
Taiwan (Taipei)	-1 434	-1 853	-2 849	-3 450	-3 820
Turkey	113	141	-24	-36	-33
United Kingdom	-1 868	-2 630	-1 902	-3 321	-7 264
United States[6]	66 225	59 475	66 346	92 594	129 642
Venezuela	-104	-19	-137	-493	-775

Source: © *Statistics Canada*
(1) The trade balance is the value of merchandise exports minus the value of merchandise imports; (2) Total includes countries not shown. (3) China figure includes Mongolia. (4) France figures include Monaco and Andorra. (5) Italy figures include Vatican City State. (6) U.S. figures include Puerto Rico and the US Virgin Islands.

Canadian Imports by Country

(millions of dollars)

	1996 $	1996 %	1997 $	1997 %	1998 $	1998 %	1999 $	1999 %	2000 $	2000 %
Total[1]	232 566	100.00	272 946	100.00	298 367	100.00	320 261	100.00	356 660	100.00
Australia	1 291	0.56	1 186	0.43	1 295	0.43	1 220	0.38	1 550	0.43
Belgium.	818	0.35	846	0.31	959	0.32	932	0.29	978	0.27
Brazil.	1 134	0.49	1 320	0.48	1 377	0.46	1 374	0.43	1 499	0.42
Chile	342	0.15	326	0.12	360	0.12	422	0.13	555	0.16
China[2]	4 931	2.12	6 341	2.32	7 655	2.57	8 927	2.79	11 280	3.16
Colombia.	297	0.13	314	0.12	364	0.12	280	0.09	332	0.09
Cuba	401	0.17	353	0.13	333	0.11	305	0.10	409	0.11
Egypt.	20	0.01	29	0.01	35	0.01	40	0.01	37	0.01
El Salvador . . .	28	0.01	45	0.02	33	0.01	36	0.01	153	0.04
France[3]	3 402	1.46	5 137	1.88	4 877	1.63	5 313	1.66	4 164	1.17
Germany	4 824	2.07	5 401	1.98	6 081	2.04	6 947	2.17	7 774	2.18
Hong Kong . . .	1142	0.49	1 263	0.46	1 252	0.42	1 304	0.41	1 449	0.41
Hungary	48	0.02	75	0.03	95	0.03	100	0.03	157	0.04
India	604	0.26	743	0.27	899	0.30	1 018	0.32	1 231	0.35
Iran	238	0.10	506	0.19	154	0.05	112	0.03	123	0.03
Israel.	267	0.11	315	0.12	417	0.14	443	0.14	597	0.17
Italy[4]	2 719	1.17	3 070	1.12	3 437	1.15	3 599	1.12	3 665	1.03
Jamaica.	239	0.10	258	0.09	256	0.09	201	0.06	198	0.06
Japan	10 439	4.49	12 551	4.60	14 006	4.69	15 033	4.69	16 601	4.65
Kenya	19	0.01	18	0.01	19	0.01	13	0.00	13	0.00
Malaysia	1 579	0.68	1 991	0.73	1 997	0.67	2 057	0.64	2 486	0.70
Mexico	6 035	2.59	7 022	2.57	7 681	2.57	9 540	2.98	12 096	3.39
Morocco	82	0.04	66	0.02	88	0.03	109	0.03	98	0.03
Netherlands. . .	927	0.40	1 059	0.39	1 164	0.39	1 224	0.38	1 267	0.36
New Zealand . .	322	0.14	369	0.14	384	0.13	371	0.12	519	0.15
Nigeria.	311	0.13	521	0.19	301	0.10	299	0.09	462	0.13
Peru	126	0.05	135	0.05	171	0.06	150	0.05	189	0.05
Philippines . . .	553	0.24	726	0.27	958	0.32	1 047	0.33	1 404	0.39
Poland.	144	0.06	147	0.05	171	0.06	185	0.06	273	0.08
Romania	50	0.02	69	0.03	121	0.04	99	0.03	102	0.03
Russia.	449	0.19	621	0.23	731	0.25	607	0.19	668	0.19
Saudi Arabia . .	651	0.28	648	0.24	394	0.13	429	0.13	916	0.26
Singapore	1 192	0.51	1 174	0.43	1 180	0.40	1 252	0.39	1 398	0.39
South Africa . .	439	0.19	497	0.18	514	0.17	487	0.15	508	0.14
Spain.	687	0.30	786	0.29	834	0.28	854	0.27	942	0.26
Sweden	1 201	0.52	1 316	0.48	1 368	0.46	1 486	0.46	1 772	0.50
Switzerland . . .	938	0.40	929	0.34	1 111	0.37	1 256	0.39	1 408	0.39
Taiwan (Taipei)	2 852	1.23	3 475	1.27	4 030	1.35	4 592	1.43	4 972	1.39
Turkey.	152	0.07	194	0.07	250	0.08	251	0.08	293	0.08
United Kingdom (U.K.)	5 908	2.54	6 499	2.38	6 314	2.12	8 114	2.53	12 995	3.64
United States[5] .	156 953	67.49	184 414	67.56	203 563	68.23	215 482	67.28	229 513	64.35
Venezuela	726	0.31	972	0.36	842	0.28	1 017	0.32	1 411	0.40

Source: © *Statistics Canada*

(1) Total includes countries not shown. (2) China figure includes Mongolia. (3) France figures include Monaco and Andorra.
(4) Italy figures include Vatican City State. (5) U.S. figures include Puerto Rico and the US Virgin Islands.

Canadian Exports by Country

(millions of dollars)

	1996 $	1996 %	1997 $	1997 %	1998 $	1998 %	1999 $	1999 %	2000 $	2000 %
Total[1]	275 819	100.00	298 072	100.00	318 444	100.00	355 017	100.00	412 181	100.00
Australia	1 017	0.37	986	0.33	975	0.31	961	0.27	1 185	0.29
Belgium......	1 539	0.56	1 508	0.51	1 522	0.48	1 878	0.53	2 059	0.50
Brazil........	1 429	0.52	1 693	0.57	1 382	0.43	1 043	0.29	1 051	0.25
Chile	416	0.15	392	0.13	340	0.11	360	0.10	444	0.11
China[2]	3 015	1.09	2 407	0.81	2 498	0.78	2 663	0.75	3 632	0.88
Colombia.....	512	0.19	473	0.16	471	0.15	255	0.07	307	0.07
Cuba........	292	0.11	364	0.12	481	0.15	397	0.11	331	0.08
Egypt........	156	0.06	186	0.06	158	0.05	185	0.05	168	0.04
El Salvador ...	11	0.00	22	0.01	34	0.01	14	0.00	22	0.01
France[3]	1 752	0.64	1 669	0.56	1 684	0.53	1 886	0.53	1 890	0.46
Germany	3 338	1.21	2 735	0.92	2 715	0.85	2 414	0.68	3 152	0.76
Hong Kong ...	1 279	0.46	1 751	0.59	1 426	0.45	1 117	0.31	1 313	0.32
Hungary	49	0.02	93	0.03	96	0.03	58	0.02	39	0.01
India	353	0.13	491	0.16	420	0.13	455	0.13	538	0.13
Iran	562	0.20	728	0.24	264	0.08	539	0.15	656	0.16
Israel........	240	0.09	252	0.08	229	0.07	295	0.08	315	0.08
Italy[4]	1 372	0.50	1 540	0.52	1 535	0.48	1 444	0.41	1 731	0.42
Jamaica......	92	0.03	88	0.03	98	0.03	97	0.03	100	0.02
Japan	11 210	4.06	11 167	3.75	8 635	2.71	8 418	2.37	9 079	2.20
Kenya	34	0.01	38	0.01	24	0.01	43	0.01	21	0.01
Malaysia	543	0.20	699	0.23	481	0.15	421	0.12	406	0.10
Mexico	1 259	0.46	1 277	0.43	1 467	0.46	1 612	0.45	2 032	0.49
Morocco	195	0.07	200	0.07	194	0.06	177	0.05	239	0.06
Netherlands...	1 668	0.60	1 701	0.57	1 869	0.59	1 557	0.44	1 431	0.35
New Zealand ..	228	0.08	298	0.10	209	0.07	206	0.06	192	0.05
Nigeria.......	43	0.02	104	0.03	55	0.02	29	0.01	63	0.02
Peru	175	0.06	312	0.10	188	0.06	173	0.05	205	0.05
Philippines ...	292	0.11	427	0.14	264	0.08	296	0.08	387	0.09
Poland.......	180	0.07	166	0.06	206	0.06	161	0.05	155	0.04
Romania	103	0.04	66	0.02	56	0.02	35	0.01	54	0.01
Russia.......	332	0.12	379	0.13	288	0.09	180	0.05	201	0.05
Saudi Arabia ..	639	0.23	558	0.19	316	0.10	296	0.08	328	0.08
Singapore	573	0.21	547	0.18	424	0.13	378	0.11	368	0.09
South Africa ..	234	0.08	371	0.12	318	0.10	250	0.07	242	0.06
Spain........	524	0.19	597	0.20	579	0.18	630	0.18	656	0.16
Sweden......	280	0.10	399	0.13	367	0.12	391	0.11	348	0.08
Switzerland ...	941	0.34	430	0.14	928	0.29	485	0.14	525	0.13
Taiwan (Taipei)	1 418	0.51	1 622	0.54	1 181	0.37	1 142	0.32	1 153	0.28
Turkey.......	265	0.10	335	0.11	226	0.07	215	0.06	260	0.06
United Kingdom	4 040	1.46	3 869	1.30	4 412	1.39	4 793	1.35	5 730	1.39
United States[5] .	223 177	80.91	243 888	81.82	269 909	84.76	308 076	86.78	359 155	87.14
Venezuela	622	0.23	954	0.32	705	0.22	524	0.15	636	0.15

Source: © *Statistics Canada*

(1) Total includes countries not shown. (2) China figure includes Mongolia. (3) France figures include Monaco and Andorra.
(4) Italy figures include Vatican City State. (5) U.S. figures include Puerto Rico and the US Virgin Islands.

Foreign Investment in Canada

(millions of dollars)

	Total	United States	United Kingdom	Other EU[1]	Japan	Other OECD[2]	All Other
1926	1 782	1 403	336	—	—	—	43
1930	2 427	1 993	392	—	—	—	42
1935	2 284	1 870	373	—	—	—	41
1940	2 477	2 064	362	—	—	—	51
1945	2 831	2 422	348	—	—	—	61
1950	4 098	3 549	468	—	—	—	81
1955	8 010	6 778	905	—	—	—	327
1960	13 583	11 210	1 550	553	—	—	270
1965	17 864	14 408	2 107	968	10	240	131
1970	27 374	22 054	2 641	1 617	103	580	379
1975	38 728	30 506	3 830	2 520	257	987	628
1980	64 708	50 368	5 773	5 168	605	1 524	1 270
1985	90 358	67 874	8 643	6 774	2 250	2 562	2 255
1990	130 932	84 089	17 185	14 339	5 222	5 871	4 227
1991	135 234	86 396	16 224	14 908	5 596	6 803	5 308
1992	137 918	88 161	16 799	15 056	5 962	6 913	5 027
1993	141 493	90 600	15 872	15 732	6 249	7 312	5 727
1994	154 594	102 629	14 693	16 824	6 587	7 989	5 873
1995	168 167	112 948	14 097	21 778	6 987	5 827	6 529
1996[3]	182 126	121 943	14 292	24 406	7 873	6 748	6 865
1997[3]	198 241	132 794	15 751	25 483	8 136	8 878	7 197
1998[3]	221 647	149 476	17 135	30 806	8 352	8 896	6 982
1999[3]	246 780	171 483	14 089	35 542	8 245	10 000	7 422
2000	291 520	185 238	19 268	58 653	8 442	9 229	9 689

Source: © Statistics Canada

(1) Other European Union countries (EU) include Belgium, Denmark, Germany, France, Greece, Ireland, Italy, Luxembourg, Netherlands, Portugal, Spain; from January 1995, Austria, Finland and Sweden. (2) Other OECD countries include Australia, Iceland, New Zealand, Norway, Switzerland and Turkey; from July 1994, Mexico; from December 1995, Czech Republic; from May 1996, Hungary, from November 1996, Poland; and up to December 1994, Austria, Finland and Sweden. (3) Revised data.

Foreign Investment in Canada by Industry

(millions of dollars)

	Total	Wood & Paper	Energy & Metallic Minerals	Machinery & Transportation Equipment	Finance & Insurance	Services & Retailing	Other Industries
1991	135 234	7 902	31 706	18 212	25 939	10 363	41 112
1992	137 918	8 895	30 062	18 496	26 873	10 807	42 785
1993	141 493	9 109	30 846	20 641	26 685	11 010	43 203
1994	154 594	9 598	29 959	24 638	28 119	14 417	47 864
1995	168 167	10 010	29 061	25 305	29 086	16 885	57 820
1996[1]	182 126	10 206	31 799	25 366	33 506	18 852	62 399
1997[1]	198 241	12 517	33 943	27 901	39 653	19 607	64 620
1998[1]	221 647	13 841	38 342	29 278	44 387	21 273	74 548
1999[1]	246 780	15 542	41 342	29 741	48 411	23 301	88 443
2000	291 520	15 318	50 584	42 750	49 662	24 349	108 837

Source: © Statistics Canada   (1) Revised data.

Canadian Investment Abroad

(millions of dollars)

	Total	United States	United Kingdom	Other EU[1]	Japan	Other OECD[2]	All Other
1920	212	132	1	—	1	—	78
1925	246	144	1	—	1	—	100
1930	443	260	14	—	1	—	168
1935	485	266	46	—	—	—	173
1940	681	412	58	—	1	—	210
1945	720	455	54	—	2	—	209
1950	1 043	814	73	—	—	—	156
1955	1 835	1 362	145	—	6	—	322
1960	2 600	1 716	277	46	15	—	546
1965	3 655	2 178	510	125	28	44	769
1970	6 520	3 518	636	304	48	142	1 871
1975	11 091	5 975	1 105	633	74	699	2 605
1980	28 413	17 849	3 080	1 377	109	1 370	4 628
1985	60 292	41 851	4 865	2 868	276	2 293	8 139
1990	98 402	60 049	13 527	7 098	917	3 996	12 815
1991	109 068	63 379	15 262	8 505	2 182	3 548	16 192
1992	111 691	64 502	12 271	9 071	2 521	3 957	19 370
1993	122 427	67 677	12 907	11 478	2 845	4 355	23 165
1994	146 315	77 987	15 038	15 620	3 485	6 635	27 551
1995	161 237	84 562	16 412	18 106	2 739	7 166	32 251
1996[3]	181 238	93 939	17 825	19 192	2 676	8 392	39 215
1997[3]	213 583	107 144	22 322	22 219	2 985	9 318	49 596
1998[3]	255 648	128 534	24 803	28 999	3 270	11 584	58 758
1999[3]	270 181	135 593	25 090	27 325	3 948	12 482	65 743
2000	301 357	154 033	25 301	31 222	5 502	15 316	69 984

Source: © *Statistics Canada*
(1) Other European Union countries (EU) include Belgium, Denmark, Germany, France, Greece, Ireland, Italy, Luxembourg, Netherlands, Portugal, Spain; from January 1995, Austria, Finland and Sweden. (2) Other OECD countries include Australia, Iceland, New Zealand, Norway, Switzerland and Turkey; from July 1994, Mexico; from December 1995, Czech Republic; from May 1996, Hungary, from November 1996, Poland; and up to December 1994, Austria, Finland and Sweden. (3) Revised data.

Canadian Investment Abroad by Industry

(millions of dollars)

	Total	Wood & Paper	Energy & Metallic Minerals	Machinery & Transportation Equipment	Finance & Insurance	Services & Retailing	Other Industries
1991	109 068	3 473	22 051	2 794	32 443	10 043	38 264
1992	111 691	3 576	24 198	3 188	32 140	10 263	38 326
1993	122 427	3 727	27 008	4 030	37 353	10 423	39 887
1994	146 315	4 358	32 189	4 681	44 725	12 066	48 297
1995	161 237	5 340	37 219	5 207	48 932	17 892	46 646
1996[1]	181 238	4 710	44 703	5 867	58 098	19 724	48 138
1997[1]	213 583	6 154	52 875	7 678	70 131	21 760	54 985
1998[1]	255 648	7 054	57 762	11 731	80 884	31 395	66 821
1999[1]	270 181	7 322	58 668	10 550	97 429	30 277	65 935
2000	301 367	7 759	63 898	16 285	103 767	32 676	76 972

Source: © *Statistics Canada*   (1) Revised data.

BUSINESS

Mining in Canada

(millions of dollars)

	1950	1960	1970	1980	1990	1998	1999
Total Value[1]	1 045.5	2 492.5	5 722.1	31 841.8	40 778.4	44 315.1	53 466.0
METALS							
Cadmium.............	1.9	3.3	15.3	7.6	11.6	1.3	0.7
Cobalt	1.0	6.7	10.2	134.7	49.6	167.7	114.0
Copper..............	123.2	264.8	779.2	1 859.6	2 428.9	1 693.2	1 361.3
Gold................	168.9	157.2	88.1	1 165.4	2 407.6	2 322.4	2 132.5
Iron Ore..............	23.4	175.1	588.6	1 700.9	1 258.8	1 584.1	1 419.7
Lead	47.9	43.9	123.1	273.7	279.3	118.0	117.4
Nickel	112.1	295.6	830.2	1 497.4	2 027.9	1 419.4	1 562.9
Platinum metals........	10.3	28.9	43.6	159.1	189.4	222.9	250.9
Silver................	18.8	30.2	81.9	828.8	249.7	293.5	296.5
Uranium	n.a.	269.9	n.a.	702.0	887.9	0.0	502.5
Zinc.................	98.0	108.6	398.9	858.2	2 272.6	1 487.0	1 533.3
NON-METALS							
Asbestos	65.9	121.4	208.1	618.5	272.1	167.2	162.5
Gypsum..............	6.7	9.5	14.2	39.5	80.1	88.0	101.2
Potash..............	—	178.7	108.7	1 020.7	964.9	1 667.0	1 775.8
Salt	7.1	19.4	36.1	122.8	240.9	399.5	391.5
Sulphur (elemental).....	2.2	4.3	28.4	444.1	368.9	54.3	63.1
STRUCTURAL MATERIALS							
Cement	35.9	93.3	155.7	581.4	991.4	1 126.9	1 232.1
Sand and gravel........	36.4	111.2	133.6	508.4	817.3	819.9	861.7
Stone	25.9	60.6	87.9	341.2	663.4	646.2	732.4

Source: © *Statistics Canada*
(1) Total includes metals, non-metals, structural materials and fuels that are not shown.

Mining by Province, 1999

(millions of dollars)

	Nfld	PEI	NS	NB	Que	Ont	Man	Sask	Alta	BC	YT	NWT	NVT
METALS:													
Copper	–	–	–	24.8	293.8	491.9	122.1	0.4	–	428.4	–	–	-
Gold	18.9	–	–	3.0	506.7	1 030.1	110.9	23.0	0.1	337.0	61.3	41.5	-
Iron Ore	883.0	–	–	–	...	...	–	–	–	...	–	–	-
Lead	–	–	–	54.8	–	–	–	–	–	30.1	-	-	32.4
Nickel	–	–	–	–	175.9	1 115.7	271.4	–	–	–	-	–	-
Zinc	–	–	–	456.3	281.7	140.1	140.9	0.5	–	200.4	-	-	313.4
NON-METALS:													
Asbestos ...	–	–	–	–	162.4	–	–	–	–	–	–	–	-
STRUCTURAL MATERIALS:													
Cement	...	–	...	–	229.9	510.5	–	–	...	171.6	–	–	-
Sand & Gravel	17.9	1.4	10.8	...	64.6	321.7	...	...	196.1	163.4	2.1	2.2	-
Stone	16.6	–	42.1	22.6	211.0	360.2	22.5	–	4.9	47.9	–	4.6	-

Source: © *Statistics Canada*   (…) Sample too small.

Agriculture in Canada

(millions of dollars)[1]

	1950	1960	1970	1980	1990	1999	2000[2]
Total value of agricultural products ..	2 135.8	2 811.7	4 250.9	15 958.8	21 997.9	30 311.4	32 767.2
Barley	45.8	69.4	144.7	553.6	545.2	448.0	568.9
Canola..............	n.a	14.8	96.7	673.6	789.6	1 824.7	1 580.1
Cattle...............	421.8	469.7	858.9	3 221.4	3 627.1	5 543.0	5 925.6
Corn	7.2	10.1	49.4	467.5	521.5	707.3	682.6
Dairy products	328.2	486.5	678.9	2 015.5	3 154.8	3 923.2	4 023.5
Eggs	86.9	137.8	172.8	407.0	482.3	482.4	500.5
Fruits................	33.6	52.1	91.8	137.3	348.1	546.5	540.6
Ginseng.............	n.a.	n.a.	n.a.	n.a.	30.5	50.1	58.2
Honey	n.a	n.a.	n.a.	44.8	45.0	73.9	70.7
Maple products	8.9	9.5	8.1	34.1	70.8	153.9	150.3
Nurseries............	n.a.	n.a.	n.a.	276.2	913.6	1 319.9	1 615.4
Oats................	42.6	23.9	20.9	53.5	81.0	203.6	199.9
Pigs................	286.9	266.8	484.5	1 404.2	2 021.2	2 397.9	3 380.3
Potatoes	29.9	67.4	90.1	211.9	399.0	714.8	673.3
Poultry	80.1	135.5	262.7	670.2	1 201.6	1 572.4	1 616.2
Sheep	1.3	0.4	0.3	2.9	2.3	4.0	5.4
Soybeans	n.a.	10.0	23.7	183.3	256.6	612.2	677.5
Sugar Beets...........	13.5	12.8	15.1	73.5	42.9	30.5	33.0
Tobacco	56.7	96.4	154.8	212.5	281.1	361.0	365.3
Vegetables...........	43.8	68.1	125.1	360.1	706.5	1 098.5	1 199.8
Wheat	377.5	442.7	570.1	2 774.5	2 351.5	1 795.5	1 915.5

Source: © *Statistics Canada*
(1) Not adjusted for inflation. (2) Farm Cash Receipts from Farming Operations.

Canadian Agriculture by Province, 2000

(thousands of dollars)

	Nfld	PEI	NS	NB	Que	Ont	Man	Sask	Alta	BC
Barley........	...	4 821	436	1 658	18 192	7 065	41 608	221 762	165 936	2 499
Calves	295	408	2 405	2 158	214 071	81 438	106 387	236 634	11 185	65 099
Canola.......	...	...	...	...	3 371	10 066	291 676	737 361	529 159	8 486
Cattle	2 125	25 507	30 277	26 574	216 353	931 440	390 454	730 712	3 327 582	242 438
Corn........	...	...	223	...	252 224	407 353	22 100	...	658	...
Dairy products .	25 946	50 987	90 368	69 041	1 546 513	1 319 954	154 029	110 974	318 454	336 977
Eggs.........	9 880	3 123	21 766	13 445	85 157	197 134	48 871	19 947	38 404	64 926
Fruits	925	3800	46 760	14 860	92 400	201401	1 995	850	1610	176 104
Ginseng	...	...	...	...	...	28 548	...	...	...	29 670
Hogs	2 257	29 571	35 011	30 873	1 019 215	829 994	672 623	213 738	500 552	47 690
Honey	140	1 582	380	4 859	7 958	12 011	16 587	20 585	6 243	
Maple products	...	...	1 494	3 219	128 062	17 540	...	...	...	...
Nurseries.....	8 636	1 934	35 147	42 947	156 634	826 336	35 530	18 288	105 186	384 764
Potatoes......	1 212	154 941	10 137	77 594	94 156	65 365	95 400	27 120	113 228	33 876
Poultry.......	14 634	5 466	66 537	44 156	443 385	543 311	74 534	47 530	139 552	249 556
Sheep........	9	9	50	14	809	3 724	108	64	263	347
Soybeans.....	...	589	...	...	93 711	583 159	...	...	...	...
Sugar beets ...	...	...	...	...	...	...	...	...	32 899	...
Tobacco	...	...	...	...	20 368	344 962	...	...	...	
Vegetables....	2 931	11 317	19 582	8 844	239 225	612 171	26 242	2 407	54 908	224 194
Wheat	...	2 101	761	323	7 598	63 223	352 300	1 228 600	706 130	10 388

Source: © *Statistics Canada*

(...) Too small to be included.

Fuel Production in Canada

(millions of dollars)

	1950	1960	1970	1980	1990	1998	1999
Total fuels	201.2	565.9	1 717.7	17 943.9	22 989.9	27 770.1	36 422.1
Coal.	110.1	74.7	86.1	932.0	1 823.7	1 793.2	1 484.4
Natural gas.	6.4	52.2	315.1	6 148.8	5 692.0	11 196.0	13 696.4
Natural gas by-products[1] . .	n.a.	16.1	160.1	1 825.1	2 370.8	1 790.6	2 347.3
Petroleum, crude	84.6	422.9	1 156.5	9 037.9	13 103.4	12 990.3	18 894.0

Source: © *Statistics Canada*
(1) Incl. butane, propane and pentane plus.

Fuel Production by Province, 1999

(millions of dollars)

	Nfld	PEI	NS	NB	Que	Ont	Man	Sask	Alta	BC	YT	NWT
Total fuels	979.6	–	165.6	21.6	–	86.1	97.5	3 711.8	28 356.2	2 745.2	27.1	231.4
Coal	–	–	101.1	21.6	–	–	–	127.3	429.7	804.8	–	–
Natural gas . . .	–	–	–	–	–	44.0	–	546.0	11 632.6	1 435.0	27.1	11.7
Natural gas by-products[1] .	–	–	–	–	–	–	–	6.5	2 289.1	51.7	–	–
Crude oil and equivalent	979.6	–	64.5	–	–	42.1	97.5	3 032.1	14 004.8	453.7	–	219.6

Source: © *Statistics Canada*
(1) Incl. butane, propane and pentane plus.

Primary Energy Supply

(annual petajoules)[1]

	Petroleum	Natural Gas[2]	Coal	Hydro-electricity	Nuclear Energy[3]	Steam & Biomass	Total
1988	3 878	3 465	1 614	1 096	281	516	11 222
1989	3 769	3 654	1 718	1 039	271	507	11 337
1990	3 765	3 732	1 673	1 058	248	477	11 343
1991	3 765	3 980	1 748	1 099	288	482	11 763
1992	3 932	4 415	1 554	1 128	274	483	12 218
1993	4 117	4 901	1 651	1 154	319	471	13 098
1994	4 300	5 353	1 735	1 176	366	548	13 979
1995	4 458	5 648	1 801	1 198	332	554	14 573
1996	4 591	5 852	1 832	1 268	315	552	14 999
1997	4 843	5 953	1 897	1 250	280	554	15 381
1998	5 022	6 125	1 651	1 183	243	571	15 402
1999	4 779	6 189	1 589	1 232	250	609	15 288

Source: © *Statistics Canada*
(1) A petajoule is one quadrillion joules (10^{15}).
(2) Incl. butane, propane and pentane plus.
(3) 3.6 MJ/kwh.

Television Operating Revenues and Expenses[1]

	1996		1997		1998		1999	
	Private Broadcasters[2]	Cable[3]	Private Broadcasters[2]	Cable[3]	Private Broadcasters[2]	Cable[3]	Private Broadcasters[2]	Cable[3]
Revenues	1 581 024	1 903 555	1 703 298	1 964 993	1 821 868	1 995 895	1 873 902	2 028 130
Expenses								
Program	861 944	85 541	917 540	85 175	1 053 939	83 245	1 022 363	81 584
Technical services .	75 946	422 808	73 837	640 524	77 818	644 951	76 816	723 581
Sales and promotion	172 057	69 815	187 962	61 692	202 504	70 067	210 686	67 517
Administration and general	199 434	395 040	200 014	393 285	226 493	449 276	216 631	454 715
Depreciation	58 835	324 139	59 716	367 443	60 352	396 660	68 035	443 289
Interest expense ..	102 126	409 366	84 945	488 897	80 231	478 216	84 468	428 687
Net profit after income tax	30 168	132 396	85 340	151 978	52 986	294 804	95 387	-129 913
Total subscribers ..		7 867		7 946		7 994		8 041

Source: © *Statistics Canada*   (1) Figures in thousands. (2) Excludes cable TV, pay TV and non-commercial broadcasting stations operated by religious groups, educational institutions and provincial governments. (3) Includes all cable TV systems licensed to operate in Canada by the CRTC. Master antenna TV and pay TV (such as First Choice or Superchannel) are not included.

Telecommunications Carriers Operating Revenue, 2000

Wired	2000 ($000)	1999–2000 % change	Wireless	2000 ($000)	1999–2000 % change
Carrier services	3 120 157	-3.2	Carrier services	469 963	
Voice services			Local telephony		
Local telephony	7 066 327	4.7	Fixed (recurrent services)	2 312 134	
Long distance telephony	5 458 473	-6.1	Air time (measured services)	1 032 419	
Calling features	998 414	6.0	Other local telephony	219 998	
Connection	388 287	9.3	Total local telephony	3 564 551	16.1
Total voice services	13 911 501	0.4	Long distance telephony		
Data and high speed services			Air time	411 263	
Narrowband packet-switched	920 861		Other long distance telephony	18 436	
High speed switched[1]	900 137		Total long distance telephony	429 699	11.2
Total data and high speed services	1 820 998		Messaging – paging	204 872	
Non-switched services (private lines)			Dispatch services (RCC)	63 506	
Narrowband	908 384		Other telecommunications services	346 068	
High speed	123 263		Other operating revenue	343 109	-7.7
Total non-switched services (private lines)	1 031 647				
Other telecommunications services	1 255 478		**Total operating revenue**	**5 583 060**	**19.9**
Other operating revenues	2 452 484	3.9			
Total operating revenue[2]	**24 324 530**	**7.1**	**Revenue performance($)**[2]		
			Operating revenue per capita	181.73	18.9
Revenue performance($)[3]			Local revenue per subscriber	452.10	-9.0
Operating revenue per capita	791.91	6.2	Average revenue per local minute (cents)	21.07	-20.1
Voice services per PSTN[4] line	701.08	-0.9	Long distance revenue		
Local revenue per PSTN[4] line	356.09	2.5	per subscriber	54.44	-12.8
Long distance revenue per PSTN[4] line	275.11	-8.0	Average revenue per long distance minute (cents)	22.04	-27.1
Average revenue per long distance minute (cents)	11.73	-20.9	Paging revenue per subscriber	144.70	-2.7
Advanced services ratio (%)[5]	21.30	65.1			

Source: © *Statistics Canada*   (1) Wideband and broadband circuit- and packet-switched services. (2) Does not include undercoverage estimate. (3) Calculations do not include undercoverage estimates, and where applicable are based on voice-grade equivalent (VGE) PSTN lines. (4) PSTN – Public Switched Telephone Network. (5) Ratio of operating revenues from new services compared to traditional telecommunications services (%).

Transportation and Storage Industries

(Gross Domestic Product, $millions)[1]

	1996	1997	1998	1999	2000
Transportation and storage industries total	31 214	32 645	33 505	34 924	36 522
Transportation Industries	26 939	28 232	28 992	30 415	32 045
Air	3 693	3 830	3 878	3 845	3 936
Railway	4 109	4 634	4 513	4 739	5 012
Water	2 216	2 289	2 321	2 386	2 631
Truck......................	10 052	10 630	11 394	12 479	13 330
Public passenger transit systems	3 102	3 189	3 252	3 306	3 437
Other transport and services.....	3 767	3 660	3 634	3 660	3 699
Pipeline transport	4 666	4 561	4 535	4 561	4 599
Storage and warehousing industries	861	943	961	983	1 065

Source: © *Statistics Canada* (1) At 1992 prices.

Trucking Operating Revenues[1]

(millions of dollars)

	1995	1996	1997	1998	1999
Total Operating Revenues	**12 054.9**	**12 763.9**	**14 224.1**	**14 885.8**	**16 943.4**
Domestic movements					
Intraprovincial...............	5 277.7	5 414.2	6 431.4	6 891.3	7 123.7
Interprovincial..............	3 496.3	3 640.5	3 498.4	3 568.1	4 037.3
Total domestic movements.....	8 774.1	9 054.7	9 929.9	10 459.4	11 161.0
International movements					
Into Canada................	1 457.0	1 605.1	1 873.3	1 917.0	2 806.7
Out of Canada	1 532.4	1 779.5	2 027.3	2 139.2	2 611.4
Total international movements ..	2 989.2	3 384.6	3 900.6	3 056.1	5 348.1
Total transportation revenues	11 763.3	12 439.5	13 849.7	14 562.1	16 579.4
Other revenues	291.6	324.4	374.6	323.7	363.9

Source: © *Statistics Canada* (1) For-hire carriers, revenues by type of movement.

Major Canadian Airlines

	Total Operating Revenues ($thousands)	Total Operating Expenses ($thousands)	Total Passengers (thousands)	Total Passenger Kilometres (thousands)	Total Goods Transported (thousands of kilograms)	Total Goods Tonne-kilometres (thousands)
1985	4 653 924	4 564 665	23 281	47 169 986	403 403	1 169 013
1986	4 889 763	4 599 049	23 188	49 124 261	379 238	1 155 488
1987	4 980 699	4 796 049	23 799	48 628 014	380 907	1 210 285
1988	5 453 507	5 262 624	24 097	54 279 293	403 806	1 323 315
1989	5 608 588	5 535 479	22 482	53 178 429	442 675	1 445 191
1990	5 660 477	5 765 017	21 236	50 091 785	435 224	1 487 833
1991	5 514 264	5 845 917	21 000	43 626 433	390 819	1 315 448
1992	5 498 189	5 820 218	21 261	45 414 285	392 514	1 331 586
1993	5 601 108	5 739 512	21 947	44 806 137	419 838	1 463 995
1994	5 529 198	5 356 713	19 126	45 281 336	395 674	1 537 977
1995	6 114 883	5 932 592	21 428	51 798 045	386 560	1 728 762
1996	6 322 113	6 369 399	23 164	57 016 000	405 975	1 882 803
1997	7 128 654	6 694 766	24 363	62 479 000	449 828	2 058 953
1998	7 463 998	7 382 909	24 571	64 426 000	431 150	2 340 594
1999	8 237 466	7 906 199	24 047	65 711 000	451 801	2 016 503
2000..........	9 194 576	9 350 994	24 480	68 517 000	407 876	1 934 683

Source: © *Statistics Canada*

Manufacturing in Canada, 1998

(millions of dollars)

	Value of Shipments of Goods Manufactured	Value Added	% Change of Goods Shipped 1997–98
All industries[1]	441 142.2	179 172.7	3.4
Food industries	51 465.9	17 313.8	1.9
Beverage and tobacco	11 190.5	7 098.5	10.2
Textile mills	4 075.3	1 872.2	8.1
Textile product mills	2 295.3	953.1	4.9
Clothing	6 967.8	3 588.1	0.3
Leather and allied products	944.1	457.9	-5.7
Wood products	25 994.3	9 716.9	0.1
Paper	29 790.1	13 405.6	0.1
Printing and related support activities	9 341.7	5 028.9	4.2
Petroleum and coal products	16 324.5	1 894.0	-22.0
Chemical	31 374.1	14 370.7	-3.4
Plastics and rubber products	17 361.1	8 041.7	5.2
Non-metallic mineral products	8 930.2	4 844.9	5.2
Primary metal products	29 596.7	12 064.8	3.0
Fabricated metal products	22 849.9	10 891.8	8.4
Machinery	23 097.0	11 781.8	5.8
Computer and electronic products	25 356.0	11 204.8	9.5
Electrical equipment, appliance and parts	8 486.5	3 820.0	5.0
Transportation equipment	101 063.6	33 161.6	8.9
Furniture and related products	9 013.0	4 674.8	14.2
Miscellaneous manufacturing	5 625.1	2 986.9	7.5

Source: © *Statistics Canada* (1) Industry classification has changed from SIC to NAIC.

Manufacturing Establishments by Employment Size, 1998

	Total	1 to 49 Employees	%	50 to 99 Employees	%	100 to 199 Employees	%	200 Employees and more	%
All industries	32 151	23 987	74.6	3 979	12.4	2 499	7.8	1 683	5.2
Food industries	3 669	2 783	75.9	418	11.4	257	7.0	211	5.8
Beverage and tobacco	235	135	57.4	40	17.0	26	11.1	34	14.5
Textile mills	399	241	60.4	72	18.0	50	12.5	36	9.0
Textile product mills	456	366	80.3	51	11.2	21	4.6	15	3.3
Clothing	1 537	1 106	72.0	231	15.0	121	7.9	79	5.1
Leather and allied products	203	147	72.4	23	11.3	21	10.3	12	5.9
Wood products	2 330	1 641	70.4	306	13.1	259	11.1	124	5.3
Paper	669	297	44.4	117	17.5	126	18.8	129	19.3
Printing and related support activities	2 917	2 542	87.1	223	7.6	110	3.8	42	1.4
Petroleum and coal products	193	151	78.2	17	8.8	9	4.7	16	8.3
Chemical	1 349	962	71.3	171	12.7	129	9.6	87	6.4
Plastics and rubber products	1 503	892	59.3	289	19.2	219	14.6	103	6.9
Non-metallic mineral products	1608	1 381	85.9	126	7.8	72	4.5	29	1.8
Primary metal products	482	233	48.3	81	16.8	65	13.5	103	21.4
Fabricated metal products	4 545	3 647	80.2	576	12.7	230	5.1	92	2.0
Machinery	2 833	2 036	71.9	449	15.8	241	8.5	107	3.8
Computer and electronic products	1 084	748	69.0	154	14.2	85	7.8	97	8.9
Electrical equipment, appliance and parts	650	420	64.6	108	16.6	70	10.8	52	8.0
Transportation equipment	1 404	825	58.8	179	12.7	181	12.9	219	15.6
Furniture and related products	1 832	1 415	77.2	219	12.0	135	7.4	63	3.4
Miscellaneous manufacturing	2 253	2 019	89.6	129	5.7	72	3.2	33	1.5

Source: © *Statistics Canada*

Value of Manufacturing[1] by Province, 1998

(millions of dollars)

	Newfoundland	Prince Edward Island	Nova Scotia	New Brunswick	Quebec
All industries[1]	1 700.9	935.5	6 538.1	8 133.8	104 479.5
Food industries	717.0	635.9	1 728.6	1 590.3	11 691.7
Beverage and tobacco	133.9	n.a.	165.1	n.a.	3 282.6
Textile mills	n.a.	1.4.	n.a.	n.a.	2 581.3
Textile product mills	n.a.	n.a.	n.a.	12.3	962.1
Clothing	n.a.	n.a.	n.a.	n.a.	4 237.1
Leather and allied products	n.a.	n.a.	8.2.	n.a.	468.1
Wood products	38.1	n.a.	367.5	1 131.7	6 673.6
Paper	n.a.	4.8	756.2	2 072.0	10 388.7
Printing and related support activities	4.7	n.a.	n.a.	n.a.	2 667.4
Petroleum and coal products	n.a.	32.0	n.a.	n.a.	3 406.8
Chemical	n.a.	n.a.	n.a.	n.a.	6 526.4
Plastics and rubber products	n.a.	5.9	773.7	n.a.	4 037.5
Non-metallic mineral products	9.8	24.5	114.8	n.a.	1 818.2
Primary metal products	n.a.	n.a.	n.a.	n.a.	10 632.8
Fabricated metal products	28.2	15.3	206.7	194.0	4 583.5
Machinery	14.0	22.0	n.a.	n.a.	4 342.0
Computer and electronic products	n.a.	94.9	n.a.	n.a.	8 509.4
Electrical equipment, appliance and parts	n.a.	n.a.	n.a.	n.a.	2 228.6
Transportation equipment	n.a.	10.7	930.7	n.a.	11 216.6
Furniture and related products	n.a.	n.a.	n.a.	n.a.	2 345.7
Miscellaneous manufacturing	11.1	n.a.	n.a.	n.a.	1 879.4

	Ontario	Manitoba	Saskatchewan	Alberta	British Columbia
All industries[1]	238 276.8	10 371.7	6 079.1	32 840.9	31 756.0
Food industries	21 063.4	2 136.5	1 665.4	6 660 4	3 576.5
Beverage and tobacco	5 440.7	n.a.	88.1	n.a.	874.8
Textile mills	1 220.7	n.a.	n.a.	n.a.	n.a.
Textile product mills	1 043.6	n.a.	n.a.	37.1	104.9
Clothing	1 793.6	368.3	25.0	141.8	317.3
Leather and allied products	435.7	n.a.	n.a.	n.a.	10.0
Wood products	4 597.3	421.0	313.9	2 215.2	10 191.6
Paper	8 974.5	n.a.	n.a.	1 356.6	4 913.0
Printing and related support activities	4 784.9	393.1	113.2	571.8	674.5
Petroleum and coal products	5 488.0	n.a.	n.a.	3 271.5	729.4
Chemical	16 493.2	464.8	519.6	6 215.4	884.8
Plastics and rubber products	10 483.3	389.6	59.0	732.2	747.5
Non-metallic mineral products	4 374.7	n.a.	95.2	1 065.5	1 029.9
Primary metal products	15 245.9	n.a.	n.a.	937.9	n.a.
Fabricated metal products	13 295.8	543.6	316.3	2 176.5	1 418.9
Machinery	12 964.1	1 347.3	543.1	2 261.1	1 421.3
Computer and electronic products	13 036.0	n.a.	56.3	2 238.2	1 112.2
Electrical equipment, appliance and parts	5 150.7	172.1	324.3	185.8	357.4
Transportation equipment	84 941.8	1 626.9	226.9	524.3	1 366.5
Furniture and related products	4 582.7	484.3	32.2	714.1	459.1
Miscellaneous manufacturing	2 686.1	186.1	40.5	336.3	335.4

Source: © *Statistics Canada*

(n.a.) Not reported.

(1) Industry classification has changed from SIC to NAIC.

Retail Merchandising in Canada

(millions of dollars)[1]

	1996	1997	1998	1999	2000
Total	**220 870**	**237 837**	**246 641**	**260 691**	**277 033**
Total excl. motor vehicles	**165 367**	**175 089**	**182 183**	**191 314**	**203 929**
Supermarkets and grocery stores	48 918	51 655	53 346	54 500	56 592
All other food stores	4 417	4 294	4 318	4 389	4 498
General merchandise stores	24 009	26 183	27 956	29 990	31 297
Service stations	16 774	16 928	16 187	18 001	22 364
Automotive parts and services	12 133	13 628	14 336	14 938	15 583
Shoe stores	1 683	1 650	1 671	1 626	1 770
Clothing stores – men's	1 516	1 570	1 582	1 536	1 531
Clothing Stores – women's	4 203	4 335	4 406	4 505	4 627
Other	5 522	5 830	6 259	6 667	7 350
Furniture and appliance stores	8 469	9 306	10 107	11 082	12 276
Other household furnishings stores	2 079	2 300	2 429	2 572	2 883
Drug stores	12 107	12 298	12 944	13 335	13 499
Other semi-durable goods stores	7 519	8 188	8 218	8 493	8 721
Other durable goods stores	5 551	6 008	6 750	7 060	7 460
Other	10 469	10 897	11 675	12 621	13 478
Volume (1992 $)	200 367	221 036	228 715	237 453	248 857
% Change	1.5	5.6	3.5	3.8	4.6

Source: © Statistics Canada   (1) Retail sales estimates exclude the Goods and Services Tax (GST).

Retail Merchandising by Province, 2000[1]

(millions of dollars)

	Nfld	PEI	NS	NB	Que	Ont
Supermarkets, grocery and other food stores	1 149.0	311.8	2 061.1	1 720.5	14 319.0	17 930.1
General merchandise and all other stores	970.3	235.5	1 844.9	1 373.7	11 383.6	25 673.3
Motor vehicle, recreational vehicle, automotive parts and gas stations	1 808.7	473.1	3 297.3	2 862.2	25 912.7	43 255.4
Shoe stores	13.2	–	26.7	25.6	557.4	609.7
Clothing stores	143.8	33.3	311.4	256.6	3 389.5	5 477.8
Household goods	156.9	53.0	321.5	274.6	3 731.6	5 813.6
Drug stores	249.4	76.0	539.9	348.4	2 810.1	5 544.0

	Man	Sask	Alta	BC	YT/NWT/NVT
Supermarkets, grocery and other food stores	2 231.7	1 931.2	6 696.5	8 019.7	221.7
General merchandise and all other stores	2 027.5	1 809.0	7 112.7	8 177.8	346.6
Motor vehicle, recreational vehicle, automotive parts and gas stations	3 876.1	3 263.6	12 829.9	13 201.8	–
Shoe stores	49.6	26.3	154.3	214.3	–
Clothing stores	368.8	312.1	1 505.1	1 666.8	–
Household goods	443.4	357.6	1 932.5	2 050.1	23.8
Drug stores	315.1	371.8	1 303.6	1 907.2	–

Source: © Statistics Canada   (1) Some data may be incomplete or unavailable.

FOCUS ON...

Canada... Wired

Canadians lead the world in home Internet use. A study quoted on CANOE (CANadian Online Explorer) reported in May 2001 that the average wired Canadian spends more than 15 hours online, at home, each month—about 3 minutes a day. In the sample survey for April 2001, Canadians were online nearly an hour a month more than their counterparts in the United States, the next closest country. (Coincidentally, Canadians also talk on the phone more than anyone else in the world.) The top five countries online—based on minutes used per month—were Canada (932), United States (876), Germany (710), Japan (707) and Brazil (621). In Canada, women spent the most time online; top usage, nearly 22 hours during the month, was by women in the 45–49 age group. In a later survey it was revealed that 14 million Canadians used the Web during June, with six million of us surfing on the average day.

A survey by Statistics Canada confirmed high usage of the Internet by Canadians. More than half of all Canadians over the age of 15—and nine out of 10 teens—used the Internet at least once in 2000. This was a three-fold increase over the rate in 1994, when only 18 percent of people reported using the Internet. In contrast, a government study in France reported that only one household in five is connected to the Internet. Moreover, few French homeowners planned to get hooked up in the near future.

What the Statistics Showed

Internet use varied by age. Canadians using the Internet were generally younger (almost all teens were online), and tended to be in higher income brackets and have a higher level of education than those who did not use it. Internet use was highest in Alberta and British Columbia where about 61 percent of residents logged on at least once during the year.

The Internet was used for a wide variety of purposes, from research for high school and college studies, to connecting with friends and family overseas, filing income taxes, making travel arrangements and shopping for best buys.

Shopping but Not Ready to Buy

The Statistics Canada survey found that while surfing is popular, e-commerce has not caught on among Canadians. Although there is much use of the Internet for e-commerce searching, similar to traditional window-shopping, the actual commitment of placing orders and making purchases on the Internet was low. Most users expressed concern about security. Only 28 percent of users said they had purchased something online during 2000.

In spite of such hesitancy, Canada ranked fourth in e-readiness—a measure of the countries best prepared to conduct electronic commerce. *The Economist Intelligence Unit*, a service sponsored by the publication *The Economist*, said the United States was the most "e-ready" country in the world, followed by Australia and the United Kingdom. The research group looked at, among other things, the telecommunications infrastructure, the security of credit card transactions, regulatory frameworks and computer literacy in each country to come up with its rankings. The EIU defines e-readiness as the "extent to which a country's business environment promotes Internet-based commercial opportunities."

Beyond Surfing

The federal government, largely through Industry Canada, has set itself the goal of bringing broadband access to every Canadian by 2004. This means universal access to a high-speed communications network. What else does this mean?

It could mean radical changes in the way we receive our education, healthcare services and government services. It could mean connecting the scattered population of the second biggest country in the world in ways that were unimagined even a generation ago. Canada could become a virtual nation where businesses in small communities have the same chance at success as those in big cities, and where citizens in far-flung communities have the same access to the rich array of services available elsewhere. Stay tuned.

Internet Use and Web Site Presence

	% of Enterprises that use the Internet			% of Enterprises with a Web site		
	1999	2000	1999–2000 % change	1999	2000	1999–2000 % change
All private sector	**52.8**	**63.4**	**10.6**	**21.7**	**25.7**	**4.0**
Forestry, logging and support activities	32.8	42.3	9.5	5.7	4.7	-1.0
Mining and oil and gas extraction	60.6	78.0	17.4	27.6	22.6	-5.0
Utilities	82.4	80.8	-1.7	27.3	31.3	4.0
Manufacturing	63.7	77.5	13.8	31.7	38.0	6.3
Wholesale trade	63.0	75.3	12.3	26.1	34.3	8.2
Retail trade	40.5	52.7	12.2	16.0	22.9	6.9
Transportation and warehousing	43.8	57.5	13.7	17.6	12.9	-4.8
Information and cultural industries	89.1	92.7	3.6	61.7	54.5	-7.2
Finance and insurance	65.9	75.9	10.0	27.2	34.4	7.2
Real estate and rental and leasing	46.3	51.2	4.9	18.4	21.9	3.5
Professional, scientific and technical services	77.5	84.0	6.5	27.6	30.0	2.4
Management of companies and enterprises	47.0	52.9	5.9	9.9	16.9	7.0
Administration and support, waste management and remediation services	55.4	75.0	19.6	29.5	32.7	3.2
Educational services (private sector)	74.5	89.2	14.7	44.0	69.7	25.7
Health care and social assistance (private sector)	46.2	61.7	15.5	10.0	15.6	5.6
Arts, entertainment and recreation	51.0	69.2	18.2	29.7	36.0	6.3
Accommodation and food services	32.0	44.0	12.0	17.4	18.5	1.1
Other services (except public administration)	44.5	51.8	7.3	19.3	22.3	3.0

Source: © *Statistics Canada*

Internet Purchases and Sales

	% of Enterprises that Use the Internet to Buy Goods or Services			% of Enterprises that Use the Internet to Sell Goods or Services		
	1999	2000	1999–2000 % change	1999	2000	1999–2000 % change
All private sector	**13.8**	**18.2**	**4.4**	**10.1**	**6.4**	**-3.7**
Forestry, logging and support activities	7.4	4.5	-2.9	1.1	1.6	0.5
Mining and oil and gas extraction	19.3	20.4	1.1	7.1	0.4	-6.7
Utilities	24.7	25.5	0.8	9.2	4.6	-4.6
Manufacturing	18.9	21.3	2.4	14.9	8.2	-6.7
Wholesale trade	13.9	22.9	9.0	13.6	13.5	-0.1
Retail trade	10.8	13.5	2.7	10.9	8.7	-2.2
Transportation and warehousing	10.7	15.0	4.3	10.1	2.0	-8.2
Information and cultural industries	49.6	52.7	3.1	20.1	18.9	-1.2
Finance and insurance	12.7	20.2	7.5	14.7	7.3	-7.4
Real estate and rental and leasing	8.2	8.8	0.6	9.5	4.8	-4.7
Professional, scientific and technical services	30.0	35.8	5.8	11.5	7.2	-4.4
Management of companies and enterprises	12.9	8.5	-4.4	8.0	1.4	-6.6
Administration and support, waste management and remediation services	13.4	22.5	9.1	17.3	6.4	-10.9
Educational services (private sector)	27.2	41.0	13.8	17.3	15.6	-1.7
Health care and social assistance (private sector)	9.5	14.4	4.9	3.1	1.3	-1.8
Arts, entertainment and recreation	12.1	15.9	3.8	10.1	5.3	-4.8
Accommodation and food services	3.9	10.1	6.2	7.9	5.1	-2.8
Other services (except public administration)	6.5	10.5	4.0	3.7	3.5	-0.2

Source: © *Statistics Canada*

New Vehicle Sales in Canada

New motor vehicle sales grew slightly (3 percent) in 2000, after a year of strong growth (7.9 percent) in 1999. While sales of passenger cars increased in 2000, the market share of North American made cars dropped slightly.

New passenger car sales have been slowing since the end of 1999, after a period of growth that started in the fall of 1998. There were a total of 1,587 units sold in 2000, compared to 1,542 in the previous year.

(thousands of units)

	Total units sold	Total commercial vehicles	Total passenger cars	Passenger cars manufactured in North America	% of total passenger cars	Passenger cars manufactured overseas	% of total passenger cars
1953	466	103	363	337	93	26	7
1954	384	72	312	292	94	20	6
1955	463	78	385	363	94	23	6
1956	495	91	404	370	92	34	8
1957	460	76	384	333	87	50	13
1958	450	69	381	302	79	78	21
1959	500	78	423	310	73	113	27
1960	522	75	446	321	72	126	28
1961	515	75	440	339	77	102	23
1962	577	82	495	420	85	74	15
1963	648	98	550	499	91	51	9
1964	723	108	614	549	89	65	11
1965	828	122	706	631	89	75	11
1966	831	133	698	630	90	68	10
1967	812	136	677	603	89	74	11
1968	887	148	739	636	86	104	14
1969	920	157	763	641	84	122	16
1970	773	134	640	496	78	144	22
1971	935	159	776	588	76	187	24
1972	1 062	207	855	651	76	204	24
1973	1 230	256	973	784	81	190	19
1974	1 249	306	943	796	84	147	16
1975	1 328	328	1 000	844	84	156	16
1976	1 281	343	939	785	84	153	16
1977	1 349	355	994	802	81	192	19
1978	1 365	377	987	816	83	171	17
1979	1 396	393	1 003	862	86	141	14
1980	1 268	332	936	742	79	194	21
1981	1 191	286	906	649	72	256	28
1982 ...	925	207	718	494	69	224	31
1983	1 079	238	841	623	74	218	26
1984	1 283	312	971	724	75	247	25
1985	1 528	393	1 135	795	70	340	30
1986	1 523	422	1 102	765	69	337	31
1987	1 530	469	1 061	698	66	364	34
1988	1 564	508	1 056	724	69	332	31
1989	1 481	496	985	671	68	313	32
1990	1 318	433	885	579	65	306	35
1991	1 288	415	873	573	66	300	34
1992	1 227	429	798	503	63	295	37
1993	1 193	454	739	494	67	245	33
1994	1 260	511	749	573	77	175	23
1995	1 167	496	670	553	83	117	17
1996	1 205	544	661	573	87	88	13
1997	1 424	685	739	629	85	110	15
1998....	1 428	688	741	591	80	150	20
1999....	1 542	736	806	625	78	181	22
2000.....	1 587	738	849	641	75	208	25

Source: © *Statistics Canada*

Operating Profits by Major Industry

(millions of dollars)

Some industries have fared better than others when it comes to making profits in the last fifteen years—or perhaps just not quite as badly. While businesses in industries such as food, computers and electronics, and communications have experienced a measure of stability when it comes to making profits, others—such as wood and paper, construction, metals, motor vehicles and transportation—have come through much more volatile times.

The year 2000 saw a growth in profits for most major industries, although the difference in growth varied

dramatically for some industries and fell for three. Agriculture again saw a sharp rise in profit (124.2 percent), more than double the amount from the previous year. Education, in contrast, experienced a drastic drop of 44.8 percent, in contrast to their sharp rise in profits in 1999. Most other industries experienced a profit, ranging from an increase of 28.2 percent to 3.2 percent. The Accommodation and Food industry experienced the worst drop in profit, falling by more than 100 percent.

	Agriculture & Other Primary	Utilities	Manufacturing	Construction	Transportation	Trade	Finance, Insurance & Real Estate
1996[1]	13 533	1 712	33 392	4 645	3 719	7 743	45 670
1997[1]	12 287	1 679	37 269	3 513	4 832	8 731	57 000
1998[1]	5 478	1 624	35 654	5 778	4 017	9 870	53 096
1999[1]	11 013	2 167	46 582	3 859	4 068	15 910	58 301
2000	24 693	2 335	53 263	4 002	5 089	17 389	67 157

	Health & Social	Managerial & Related	Professional & Related	Educational	Information & Recreation	Accommodation & Food	Other Services
1996[1]	1 023	6 998	725	79	6 193	2 094	817
1997[1]	825	10 070	767	76	7 468	1 930	953
1998[1]	1 387	9 251	1 196	74	7 655	3 969	1 011
1999[1]	1 664	10 345	1 093	268	7 423	4 304	1 323
2000	1 457	11 200	1 128	148	8 193	-17	1 696

Source: © *Statistics Canada*   (1) Revised data.

Establishments by Industry and Employment Size, 2000[1,2]

	Total	Employment Size			
		0 to 4[3] Employees	5 to 49 Employees	50 to 99 Employees	100 Employees and more
All industries	2 024 508	1 586 749	383 062	31 081	23 616
Goods-producing sector	545 600	447 881	82 320	8 234	7 165
Primary industries	209 644	191 573	16 600	865	606
Agriculture	165 859	156 224	9 254	264	117
Other primary	43 785	35 349	7 346	601	489
Fishing and trapping	9 607	7 978	1 546	60	23
Logging and forestry	20 134	16 517	3 263	226	128
Mining quarrying and oil wells	14 044	10 854	2 537	315	338
Utilities	4 926	3 282	1 350	123	171
Manufacturing	105 209	66 080	28 893	5 028	5 208
Non-durables manufacturing	47 112	31 264	11 862	1 867	2 119
Durables manufacturing	58 097	34 816	17 031	3 161	3 089
Construction	225 821	186 946	35 477	2 218	1 180
Services-producing sector	1 478 908	1 138 868	300 742	22 847	16 451
Transportation, storage and communication	102 160	86 266	13 498	1 304	1 092
Trade	375 492	260 522	104 047	6 878	4 045
Wholesale trade	132 640	93 384	35 096	2 716	1 444
Retail trade	242 852	167 138	68 951	4 162	2 601
Finance, insurance and real estate	301 519	267 137	30 349	2 431	1 602
Community business and personal services	691 937	522 558	149 062	11 659	8 658
Amusement & recreational services	42 582	33 265	8 123	686	508
Educational services	15 301	10 105	3 794	433	969
Health and social services	92 989	58 505	30 139	1 878	2 467
Business and personal services	541 065	420 683	107 006	8 662	4 714
Public administration	7 800	2 385	3 786	575	1 054

Source: © *Statistics Canada*   (1) Based on the 1980 Standard Industrial Classification. (2) As of December 31. (3) The "0-4" category includes establishments with an "indeterminate" employment status. Such establishments do not maintain employee payrolls but may have a workforce that consists of contracted workers, part-time employees, family members or business owners.

LABOUR

Provincial Labour Force by Industry, 1990

(thousands)

	Canada	Nfld	PEI	NS	NB	Que	Ont	Man	Sask	Alta	BC
All industries	14 240.9	249.5	64.2	432.0	341.2	3 504.3	5 533.0	555.6	488.6	1 372.1	1 700.3
Agriculture	468.5	1.5	6.5	8.5	6.8	72.5	116.7	40.9	84.7	97.2	33.2
Primary industries[1]	343.2	19.0	3.4	20.5	15.5	57.1	63.1	9.0	14.5	79.5	61.5
Utilities	145.8	3.6	0.2	3.2	4.1	32.8	64.6	5.9	4.5	13.5	13.4
Construction.	953.6	17.5	5.5	32.4	26.4	213.4	369.8	27.8	27.9	96.6	136.2
Manufacturing	2 227.7	27.1	5.8	48.8	42.3	665.5	1 059.8	61.2	26.3	101.3	189.6
Trade[2].	2 221.3	41.5	9.2	76.3	59.4	549.8	822.5	87.2	74.9	220.5	279.9
Transportation & warehousing . .	688.0	12.2	2.7	22.4	17.1	163.8	245.4	35.4	20.7	70.3	97.8
Finance, insurance, real estate & leasing	880.2	8.5	2.1	23.4	13.7	193.4	402.5	31.2	23.5	77.0	104.9
Services[3]	601.8	6.0	1.4	11.2	8.4	121.5	270.8	18.4	11.3	60.7	92.2
Management, admin. & other support .	350.2	4.2	0.9	8.4	7.0	80.4	149.6	12.2	8.8	37.5	41.2
Educational services	877.2	19.2	3.6	29.4	22.5	211.3	333.9	37.6	32.1	94.8	92.8
Health care & social assistance	1 325.6	27.2	6.2	43.2	35.6	340.7	486.7	60.5	51.9	120.6	153.0
Information, culture & recreation	550.4	7.5	2.2	15.1	11.6	124.8	225.0	20.5	17.4	52.1	74.4
Accommodation & food services . . .	859.1	13.6	5.0	26.0	20.1	204.1	311.2	36.8	28.3	84.2	129.8
Other services	655.6	12.2	3.7	20.9	18.9	173.2	231.3	27.0	22.6	64.3	81.5
Public administration[4]	870.1	19.4	5.1	34.3	24.5	218.5	321.5	35.5	31.9	86.4	93.1
Unclassified industries	222.5	9.4	0.6	8.1	7.2	81.6	58.6	8.6	7.5	15.5	25.5

Source: © *Statistics Canada* (1) Primary industries include fishing, trapping, forestry, mining, oil and gas extractions. (2) Trade is the sales and distribution network of merchandise. Includes wholesale and retail. (3) Services refers to professional, scientific and technical occupations in which a service is provided but no goods are produced. (4) Includes municipal, provincial and federal levels.

Provincial Employment by Industry, 1990

(thousands)

	Canada	Nfld	PEI	NS	NB	Que	Ont	Man	Sask	Alta	BC
All industries	13 084.0	207.4	54.8	386.5	299.8	3 141.4	5 191.3	515.2	454.3	1 278.5	1 554.9
Agriculture	446.8	1.2	5.4	7.4	5.5	67.1	112.6	40.0	83.0	95.3	29.2
Primary industries[1]	305.7	16.8	2.6	18.0	13.1	48.1	58.6	8.3	12.8	74.9	52.4
Utilities	142.5	3.3	0.2	3.0	4.1	32.0	63.4	5.7	4.4	13.4	13.0
Construction.	817.2	11.6	3.9	25.9	20.3	177.6	327.1	23.7	23.3	84.3	119.6
Manufacturing	2 052.5	21.1	4.6	43.7	37.4	599.3	994.4	56.6	24.8	94.4	176.2
Trade[2].	2 076.8	36.7	8.4	71.3	54.3	505.7	777.1	81.6	71.0	207.3	263.4
Transportation & warehousing. . . .	647.2	10.9	2.4	20.2	16.0	153.4	233.9	33.9	19.2	66.5	90.8
Finance, insurance, real estate & leasing	848.1	8.1	1.9	22.4	12.8	183.7	392.0	30.2	22.8	74.2	100.0
Services[3]	573.7	5.3	1.2	10.3	7.8	112.6	262.4	17.5	10.5	58.0	88.1
Management, admin. & other support .	310.8	3.3	0.8	6.9	5.9	69.7	134.6	11.0	8.0	34.0	36.5
Educational services	846.1	18.1	3.4	27.8	21.4	203.2	324.9	35.9	30.9	91.5	88.8
Health care & social assistance	1 284.7	25.3	5.8	41.5	33.6	328.3	476.7	58.7	50.6	116.3	147.9
Information, culture & recreation	514.5	6.8	2.0	13.8	10.6	113.3	214.5	19.7	16.3	49.3	68.4
Accommodation & food services . . .	772.7	11.5	4.1	23.1	17.4	179.7	287.2	33.2	25.3	75.6	115.6
Other services	611.7	10.0	3.3	19.4	17.3	159.5	219.2	25.4	21.0	60.8	75.9
Public administration[4]	832.9	17.3	4.6	31.9	22.5	208.0	312.8	33.8	30.3	82.7	89.0
Unclassified industries	—	—	—	—	—	—	—	—	—	—	—

Source: © *Statistics Canada* (1) Primary industries include fishing, trapping, forestry, mining, oil and gas extractions. (2) Trade is the sales and distribution network of merchandise. Includes wholesale and retail. (3) Services refers to professional, scientific and technical occupations in which a service is provided but no goods are produced. (4) Includes municipal, provincial and federal levels.

Provincial Labour Force by Industry, 2000

(thousands)

	Canada	Nfld	PEI	NS	NB	Que	Ont	Man	Sask	Alta	BC
All Industries	15 999.2	245.6	73.3	461.6	371.7	3 753.2	6 227.9	583.2	511.7	1 671.4	2 099.7
Agriculture	391.9	1.9	5.5	7.8	7.1	66.3	102.3	33.7	63.2	70.6	33.4
Primary industries[1]	314.6	17.8	3.6	17.3	15.8	48.5	37.8	7.0	17.2	87.8	61.8
Utilities	119.0	1.9	0	2.9	4.7	27.0	47.5	6.8	3.7	12.8	11.7
Construction.	896.4	15.4	4.9	30.0	24.5	156.9	343.2	31.2	27.0	128.3	125.3
Manufacturing	2 392.8	21.3	7.6	47.5	46.4	669.1	1 135.6	73.5	30.3	145.9	215.6
Trade[2].	2 423.3	40.6	10.5	78.9	58.1	580.7	909.7	84.5	79.3	262.6	318.3
Transportation & warehousing . . .	811.6	13.1	2.8	21.5	20.9	182.8	286.9	36.0	28.9	99.1	119.7
Finance, insurance, real estate &leasing	889.8	8.1	2.3	22.9	13.2	187.0	395.0	30.2	27.3	81.4	122.4
Services[3]	978.7	7.6	2.1	17.9	11.8	209.7	436.4	24.5	17.3	111.2	140.0
Management, admin. & other support . .	595.8	6.2	2.3	19.1	14.6	122.2	266.2	17.9	11.3	57.2	78.8
Educational services	1 006.7	17.3	4.4	33.5	24.8	227.4	379.0	40.6	37.2	103.0	139.6
Health care & social assistance	1 558.0	31.0	7.8	51.8	41.6	387.2	555.8	70.5	55.3	151.3	205.8
Information, culture & recreation	706.1	8.0	2.9	18.4	13.5	155.6	296.4	21.5	19.1	66.2	104.5
Accommodation & food services	1 032.9	13.9	5.8	30.1	24.5	225.3	364.0	38.8	35.3	121.3	174.0
Other services[4]	726.2	12.8	3.7	23.6	18.0	174.5	260.9	25.1	24.6	79.4	103.7
Public administration[4]	783.7	17.6	6.1	26.5	24.0	212.6	280.1	34.0	27.4	63.6	91.8
Unclassified	371.8	11.1	0.9	11.7	8.1	120.5	131.2	7.3	7.3	20.1	53.4

Source: © *Statistics Canada* (1) Primary industries include fishing, trapping, forestry, mining, oil and gas extractions. (2) Trade is the sales and distribution network of merchandise. Includes wholesale and retail. (3) Services refers to professional, scientific and technical occupations in which a service is provided but no goods are produced. (4) Includes municipal, provincial and federal levels.

Provincial Employment by Industry, 2000

(thousands)

	Canada	Nfld	PEI	NS	NB	Que	Ont	Man	Sask	Alta	BC
All industries	14 909.7	204.6	64.5	419.5	334.4	3 437.7	5 872.1	554.4	485.0	1 588.2	1 949.1
Agriculture	372.6	1.1	5.4	6.9	6.1	61.7	97.6	33.3	62.1	69.3	29.7
Primary industries[1]	283.0	15.2	2.7	15	13.2	40.6	35.2	6.6	15.9	83.3	55.4
Utilities	116.4	1.8	0	2.8	4.3	26.8	46.4	6.8	3.6	12.5	11.3
Construction.	815.6	10.9	3.8	24.6	19.6	139.7	323.6	28.5	24.0	128.3	112.5
Manufacturing	2 280.2	16.0	6.5	43.5	41.1	629.0	1 098.7	70.8	29.2	140.1	205.4
Trade[2].	2 318.1	37.0	9.9	75.4	55.1	552.6	874.3	81.6	76.3	252.6	303.2
Transportation & warehousing . . .	779.8	11.4	2.5	20.6	19.8	172.9	278.2	35.0	28.1	97.0	114.4
Finance, insurance, real estate & leasing	867.0	7.6	2.2	22.2	12.7	182.2	385.3	29.7	26.6	79.0	119.5
Services[3]	945.9	7.0	2.0	17.1	11.3	200.2	423.5	23.5	16.7	108.3	136.4
Management, admin. & other support . .	546.2	4.8	2.0	17.3	13.1	111.7	245.6	16.4	10.4	53.1	71.9
Educational services	974.8	16.1	4.2	32.3	23.2	220.0	369.0	39.3	36.0	99.9	134.9
Health care & social assistance	1 526.4	29.3	7.6	50.8	40.4	378.8	544.4	69.6	54.6	148.7	202.1
Information, culture and recreation . . .	665.5	7.0	2.5	16.7	12.4	145.3	282.1	20.1	18.0	62.3	99.3
Accommodation & food services . .	960.6	12.1	5.0	27.0	22.4	202.9	342.6	36.5	33.1	115.0	164
Other services	695.8	11.1	3.3	22.0	16.9	167.1	251.7	23.8	23.8	76.9	99.3
Public administration[4]	761.7	16.1	5.6	25.4	22.9	206.2	274.0	33.1	26.7	61.9	89.7
Unclassified											

Source: © *Statistics Canada* (1) Primary industries include fishing, trapping, forestry, mining, oil and gas extractions. (2) Trade is the sales and distribution network of merchandise. Includes wholesale and retail. (3) Services refers to professional, scientific and technical occupations in which a service is provided but no goods are produced. (4) Includes municipal, provincial and federal levels.

Canadian Labour Force by Province, 2000

(thousands)

	Population 15 Years and Over	Labour Force[1]	Participation Rate[2]	Employed	Employment Population Ratio[3]	Un-employed	% Un-employed
Canada	24 284.9	15 999.2	65.9	14 909.7	61.4	1 089.6	6.8
Newfoundland	439.9	245.6	55.8	204.6	46.5	41.0	16.7
Prince Edward Island . . .	109.5	73.3	66.9	64.5	58.9	8.8	12.0
Nova Scotia	747.7	461.6	61.7	419.5	56.1	42.0	9.1
New Brunswick	603.5	371.7	61.6	334.4	55.4	37.3	10.0
Quebec	5 935.9	3 753.2	63.2	3 437.7	57.9	315.5	8.4
Ontario	9 274.4	6 227.9	67.2	5 872.1	63.3	355.7	5.7
Manitoba	858.5	583.2	67.9	554.4	64.6	28.7	4.9
Saskatchewan	763.7	511.7	67.0	485.0	63.5	26.7	5.2
Alberta	2 315.1	1 671.4	72.2	1 588.2	68.6	83.1	5.0
British Columbia	3 236.6	2 099.7	64.9	1 949.1	60.2	150.6	7.2

Source: © *Statistics Canada*

(1) The labour force consists of employed workers, and those who are unemployed but actively seeking work. (2) Participation rate is the percent of the total population aged 15 and over that makes up the labour force. (3) The percent of the total population aged 15 and over that is employed.

Labour Force by Age, 2000

(thousands)

	Population 15 Years and Over	Labour Force[1]	Participation Rate[2]	Employed	Employment Population Ratio[3]	Un-employed	% Un-employed
Males	11 927.8	8 649.2	72.5	8 049.3	67.5	600.0	6.9
15 - 19 years	1 039.9	538.8	51.8	444.5	42.7	94.3	17.5
20 - 24 years	1 037.3	829.2	79.9	733.6	70.7	95.6	11.5
25 - 34 years	2 160.0	1 979.6	183.2	1 850.1	171.2	129.6	13.1
35 - 44 years	2 610.3	2 412.0	184.9	2 276.8	174.5	135.2	11.2
45 - 54 years	2 144.1	1 906.3	177.7	1 809.9	168.6	96.3	10.1
55 - 59 years	759.7	554.0	72.9	524.2	69.0	29.8	5.4
60 - 64 years	605.6	279.4	46.1	264.1	43.6	15.3	5.5
65 - 69 years	535.7	86.3	16.1	83.4	15.6	2.9	3.4
70 years and over	1 035.2	63.6	6.1	62.7	6.1	0	0
Females	12 357.0	7 350.0	59.5	6 860.4	55.5	489.6	6.7
15 - 19 years	989.9	512.8	51.8	435.5	44.0	77.4	15.1
20 - 24 years	1 001.6	739.7	73.9	675.6	67.5	64.0	8.7
25 - 34 years	2 142.6	1 708.0	159.4	1 599.4	149.3	108.7	12.7
35 - 44 years	2 614.2	2 097.0	160.4	1 977.3	151.2	119.6	11.4
45 - 54 years	2 169.1	1 637.1	150.4	1 551.4	142.5	85.7	10.5
55 - 59 years	778.2	415.3	53.4	392.3	50.4	23.0	5.5
60 - 64 years	633.4	172.4	27.2	163.0	25.7	9.3	5.4
65 - 69 years	580.0	42.1	7.3	40.5	7.0	1.5	3.6
70 years and over	1 448.0	25.7	1.8	25.3	1.7	0	0

Source: © *Statistics Canada*

(1) The labour force consists of employed workers, and those who are unemployed but actively seeking work. (2) Participation rate is the percent of the total population aged 15 and over that makes up the labour force. (3) The percent of the total population aged 15 and over that is employed.

Average Weekly Earnings

(dollars)

	1996[1]	1997[1]	1998[1]	1999[1]	2000
Average weekly earnings	611.12	623.23	632.02	638.69	653.55
Goods producing industries	762.45	782.10	795.70	803.33	820.92
Forestry	745.69	786.46	760.59	765.63	803.21
Mining	1 035.14	1 047.19	1 094.54	1 101.04	1 137.37
Manufacturing	733.82	752.42	769.90	780.19	794.52
Construction	767.56	786.91	781.44	782.63	808.06
Services-producing industries	566.69	576.00	582.84	588.75	602.17
Transportation, communication and other utilities	670.75	690.16	704.89	716.21	728.02
Trade	492.29	507.18	523.84	530.08	535.65
Finance, insurance & real estate	760.24	791.81	811.26	815.55	836.32
Health & education	536.76	545.48	543.00	544.56	562.89
Professional, management & related	770.68	801.82	808.31	827.84	866.08
Public administration	725.35	725.14	725.45	737.52	747.63
Accommodation & food	262.96	259.65	255.53	259.80	273.13

Source: © *Statistics Canada*

(1) Revised series.

Labour Income[1]

(millions of dollars)

	1970	1975	1980	1985	1990
Total labour income[2]	215 562	299 915	351 781	368 916	428 291
Agriculture, fishing and trapping	1 809	2 345	2 746	3 115	3 081
Forestry	2 356	2 890	3 333	2 669	2 913
Mines	4 788	6 296	9 206	9 635	8 638
Manufacturing	52 797	63 076	71 172	69 459	71 550
Construction	14 024	24 279	23 009	19 076	26 504
Transportation, communication and other utilities	22 492	28 897	34 427	34 962	36 738
Trade	28 537	39 722	44 190	44 403	55 094
Finance, insurance and real estate	11 093	17 304	22 972	25 476	32 272
Services	49 162	70 146	85 129	95 690	116 982
Public administration	15 258	2 2677	25 751	28 403	31 202

	1996	1997	1998	1999[3]	2000
Total labour income[2]	428 792	453 103	474 571	502 400	536 578
Agriculture, fishing & trapping	3 511	3 720	3 846	6 870[4]	7 199[4]
Forestry	3 007	3 053	2 984	3 013	...
Mining	8 375	9 296	9 802	8 323	8 820
Manufacturing	68 677	72 488	77 562	78 970	84 434
Construction	20 231	22 962	24 335	27 062	29 562
Transportation, communication and other utilities	34 571	35 761	37 332	24 823[5]	26 218[5]
Trade	53 113	57 491	60 633	61 907	64 903
Finance, insurance & real estate	31 838	35 900	38 137	41 493	43 749
Services	122 154	127 580	134 867	109 233[6]	119 395[6]
Public administration	30 244	29 786	29 692	31 091	33 956

Source: © *Statistics Canada*

(1) Figures adjusted for inflation. (2) Total includes income categories not shown. (3) Revised data. (4) Includes Forestry. (5) Transportation only. (6) Health, Professional and Personal Services.

Employment in Manufacturing by Sector, 1998

	Number of Manufacturing Establishments	Number of Production and Related Workers	Person Hours Paid
All industries..........................	**32 151**	**1 461 312**	**3 071 660**
Food.................................	3 664	154 509	310 151
Beverage and tobacco products...........	234	15 588	32 544
Textile mills	399	22 971	50 805
Textile products mills....................	456	15 225	31 880
Clothing..............................	1 536	74 170	158 781
Leather and allied products	203	9 562	18 458
Wood products	2 326	105 905	221 590
Paper................................	669	77 603	159 094
Printing and related support activities	2 914	61 099	127 155
Petroleum and coal products.............	192	6 676	14 366
Chemical	1 346	57 026	121 859
Plastics and rubber products..............	1 500	93 661	197 525
Non-metallic mineral products............	1 606	38 698	82 642
Primary metal	482	73 918	151 828
Fabricated metal products	4 543	140 115	302 858
Machinery	2 833	115 631	246 507
Computer and electronic products.........	1 084	62 966	131 159
Electronic equipment, appliance and parts...	650	35 440	72 977
Transportation equipment	1 404	188 739	404 119
Furniture and related products............	1 830	69 381	149 464
Miscellaneous manufacturing	2 280	42 429	85 898

Source: © *Statistics Canada*

Employment in Manufacturing by Labour

(thousands)

	Labour Force	Employment	Full-time Employment	Part-time Employment	Unemployed	Unemployment Rate
1987	2 193.7	2 039.8	1 970.3	69.6	153.9	7.0
1988	2 246.3	2 104.3	2 025.2	79.1	142.0	6.3
1989	2 272.6	2 129.7	2 044.4	85.3	142.9	6.3
1990	2 227.7	2 052.5	1 978.2	74.4	175.2	7.9
1991	2 101.7	1 891.8	1 814.9	76.9	209.9	10.0
1992	2 011.6	1 821.5	1 740.5	81.0	190.2	9.5
1993	1 957.3	1 786.4	1 707.6	78.8	170.9	8.7
1994	1 962.6	1 820.3	1 741.9	78.4	142.3	7.3
1995	2 037.1	1 905.5	1 821.8	83.7	131.6	6.5
1996	2 079.7	1 931.1	1 842.5	88.6	148.5	7.1
1997	2 143.6	2 022.4	1 937.9	84.5	121.2	5.7
1998	2 248.0	2 113.8	2 028.7	85.0	134.2	6.0
1999	2 344.8	2 217.4	2 135.3	82.1	127.4	5.4
2000	2 392.8	2 280.2	2 202.1	78.1	112.6	4.7

Source: © *Statistics Canada*

Employment in Retail by Sector, 2000

	Total Number of Employees (000s)	Number of Employees Paid by the Hour	Average Weekly Hours
All Retail	1 443.9	1 036.1	26.1
Food & beverage stores	374.2	305.2	24.4
Grocery stores	313.9	256.6	24.4
Motor vehicle & parts dealers	150.2	68.1	36.7
Automobile dealers	116.6	50.6	37.5
Gasoline stations	77.6	57.9	26.9
Automotive parts, accessories & tire stores	21.2	12.1	33.2
Florists	10.1	6.9	25.2
Office supplies, stationery & gift stores	29.3	19.9	26.9
Used merchandise stores	8.9	6.3	27.2
Other miscellaneous store retailers	24.0	16.6	26.8
Electronic shopping & mail-order houses	9.0	6.5	30.8
Vending machine operators	6.1	4.4	28.2
Direct selling establishments	23.0	13.9	31.7

Source: © *Statistics Canada*

Employment in Retail by Labour

(thousands)

	Labour Force	Employment	Full-time Employment	Part-time Employment	Unemployed	Unemployment Rate
1987	1 679.6	1 571.6	1 082.3	489.3	107.9	6.4
1988	1 733.3	1 624.7	1 112.7	512.0	108.6	6.3
1989	1 738.4	1 631.0	1 128.7	502.4	107.4	6.2
1990	1 765.7	1 649.0	1 129.1	519.9	116.7	6.6
1991	1 783.3	1 642.3	1 105.2	537.1	141.0	7.9
1992	1 771.0	1 632.4	1 106.9	525.5	138.7	7.8
1993	1 760.2	1 623.8	1 084.6	539.2	136.4	7.7
1994	1 771.2	1 649.9	1 101.2	548.6	121.4	6.9
1995	1 775.5	1 663.1	1 128.5	534.7	112.4	6.3
1996	1 770.7	1 661.3	1 112.3	549.1	109.4	6.2
1997	1 773.7	1 673.3	1 128.0	545.3	100.4	5.7
1998	1 789.8	1 695.5	1 145.8	549.7	94.4	5.3
1999	1 798.7	1 712.2	1 136.4	575.7	86.6	4.8
2000	1 854.2	1 769.9	1 198.4	571.5	84.3	4.5

Source: © *Statistics Canada*

PERSONAL FINANCE

What's a Dollar Worth?[1]

This table shows how many current (2000) dollars it would take to equal the purchasing power of a single dollar in earlier years. For example, if you spent $30 a week on groceries in 1985 and want to know what that would be by today's standards, multiply

$30 times the relative value of a 1985 dollar ($1.57) and you have your answer: $47.10. The relative value of a dollar for the years listed was calculated according to changes in the cost of living in Canada as measured by the Consumer Price Index (CPI).

CPI by Year	Rate	2001 Relative Value	CPI by Year	Rate	2001 Relative Value	CPI by Year	Rate	2001 Relative Value	CPI by Year	Rate	2001 Relative Value
1915	7.3	16.10	1961	18.7	6.28	1975	34.5	3.41	1989	89.2	1.32
1920	13.5	8.70	1962	18.9	6.22	1976	37.1	3.17	1990	93.1	1.26
1925	10.9	10.78	1963	19.2	6.12	1977	40.0	2.94	1991	98.9	1.19
1930	10.9	10.78	1964	19.6	5.99	1978	43.6	2.69	1992	100.0	1.18
1935	8.7	13.51	1965	20.0	5.88	1979	47.6	2.47	1993	101.6	1.16
1940	9.5	12.37	1966	20.8	5.65	1980	52.1	2.26	1994	101.6	1.16
1945	10.9	10.78	1967	21.5	5.47	1981	58.9	1.99	1995	104.4	1.13
1950	14.9	7.89	1968	22.4	5.25	1982	65.3	1.80	1996	105.9	1.11
1955	16.8	6.99	1969	23.4	5.02	1983	69.2	1.70	1997	107.7	1.09
1956	17.1	6.87	1970	24.2	4.86	1984	72.1	1.63	1998	108.8	1.08
1957	17.6	6.68	1971	24.9	4.72	1985	75.0	1.57	1999	110.5	1.06
1958	18.0	6.53	1972	26.1	4.50	1986	77.8	1.51	2000	113.7	1.03
1959	18.3	6.42	1973	28.1	4.18	1987	81.5	1.44	2001	117.5	1.00
1960	18.5	6.35	1974	31.1	3.78	1988	84.7	1.39			

Source: © *Statistics Canada* (1) Based on Consumer Price Index as of June 2001.

Credit Summary

(millions of dollars)[1]

Year	Household Credit			Business Credit
	Consumer	Mortgage	Total	
1975	21 746	40 269	62 014	90 702
1976	25 234	48 067	73 302	100 988
1977	29 039	58 538	87 577	113 704
1978	33 362	69 767	103 129	128 391
1979	38 465	81 333	119 798	151 757
1980	42 738	90 543	133 281	180 064
1981	47 464	96 475	143 939	221 426
1982	47 168	97 668	144 836	252 141
1983	47 285	101 932	149 217	257 123
1984	50 191	110 383	160 574	269 664
1985	55 729	117 945	173 673	291 568
1986	62 433	132 801	195 233	317 637
1987	69 929	155 329	225 258	346 740
1988	80 098	182 346	262 445	384 719
1989	89 843	210 578	300 421	428 837
1990	98 656	240 447	339 103	471 198
1991	101 218	259 896	361 114	487 624
1992	102 296	282 976	385 272	495 599
1993	104 683	305 250	409 933	498 961
1994	112 624	325 171	437 795	522 786
1995	120 873	337 274	458 146	548 196
1996[2]	128 388	353 570	481 959	576 235
1997[2]	141 324	372 415	513 739	627 192
1998[2]	156 273	390 206	546 479	695 457
1999[2]	167 979	407 750	575 729	735 979
2000	187 824	426 424	614 248	787 449

Source: © *Statistics Canada* (1) Not adjusted for inflation. (2) Revised data.

Total Individual Income, 1999

(millions of dollars)

	Median Income[1] ($)	1998–99 % change		Median Income[1] ($)	1998–99 % change
St. John's	44 800	-1.2	Kitchener	58 400	2.0
Halifax	51 700	1.5	London	54 400	0.5
Saint John	46 100	2.8	Windsor	62 400	2.6
Chicoutimi-Jonquière	47 800	0.9	Sudbury	52 400	-0.3
Quebec	50 500	1.3	Thunder Bay	55 000	0.3
Sherbrooke	45 100	1.5	Winnipeg	50 600	0.3
Trois-Rivières	43 900	1.1	Regina	54 800	0.0
Montreal	47 600	1.1	Saskatoon	49 800	0.1
Ottawa-Hull	60 000	2.2	Calgary	57 800	-1.0
Oshawa	62 500	2.4	Edmonton	53 100	-0.7
Toronto	53 400	1.4	Vancouver	48 100	-0.8
Hamilton	57 900	0.9	Victoria	52 700	-0.2
St. Catharines–Niagara	51 700	1.3			

Source: © *Statistics Canada* (1) Data primarily based on income tax returns filed in Spring 2000.

Note: Median income corresponds exactly to the mid-point of income distribution. It is not affected by extreme income values as is average income.

Minimum Hourly Wage by Province

On December 18, 1996, the minimum hourly wage provisions of the Canada Labour Code were amended to align the federal minimum wage with the provincial and territorial general adult minimum wage rates. Minimum wage rates may not apply to registered apprentices who are paid according to a provincial apprenticeship act, to certain employees who are being trained on the job or special types of employees in some provinces (see table).

If an employee is paid through a system based on something besides hours (such as mileage), the employee's pay, if divided by the hours worked, must be equivalent to the appropriate provincial or territorial minimum wage.

	Adult Minimum Wage Rate ($)	Date Effective	Other Categories of Workers	Different Minimum Wage Rates ($)
Newfoundland	5.50	October 1999	–	–
Prince Edward Island	5.80[1]	January 2000	–	–
Nova Scotia	5.80	October 2001	For inexperienced workers	5.35
New Brunswick	5.90	July 2001	–	–
Quebec	7.00	February 2001	For workers receiving gratuities	6.25
Ontario	6.85	January 1995	For students;	6.40
			For liquor servers	5.95
Manitoba	6.25	April 2001	–	–
Saskatchewan	6.00	January 1999	–	–
Alberta	5.90	October 1999	–	–
British Columbia	8.00	November 2001	–	–
Yukon	7.20	October 1998	–	–
Northwest Territories	6.50	April 1991	Beyond the NWT Highway System;	7.00
			Youth	6.00
			For Youth beyond the NWT Highway System	6.50
Nunavut	6.50	April 1999	In areas distant from the highway system	7.00
			Employees under 16	6.00
			Employees under 16 in areas distant from the highway system	6.50

Sources: *HRDC; provincial labour departments* (1) $6.00 as of January 2002.

Note: For workers in federal jurisdiction industries, the federal minimum wage is aligned with the general adult minimum wage rates in each provincial and territorial jurisdiction.

Canadian Income Tax

Income tax was introduced in 1917 as a temporary measure to finance Canada's participation in World War I. The law introducing the tax (the Income War Tax Act) was shorter and much simpler than our current legislation. It imposed tax at graduated rates, ranging from 4 percent on the first $1,500 to 25 percent for income over $100,000.

This "temporary" tax was not repealed when the war ended. But on Jan. 1, 1949, the federal government removed "war" from the title and gave the statute the name it has today—the Income Tax Act. This act has been amended many times—most notably in 1972 when a major overhaul of the tax system broadened the tax base and introduced a tax on capital gains. This is still the basis of our federal income tax laws today.

In 1988, all personal exemptions and many deductions were changed to non-refundable tax credits. Unlike deductions, which reduce taxable income, credits are used to reduce the amount of tax payable. The term "non-refundable" refers to the fact that, although you can use these credits to reduce or eliminate your federal tax payable, any unused portion is not refundable to you. In some cases, however, you may be able to transfer the unused portion of the credits to someone else.

Because the credits are calculated by multiplying eligible amounts by 17 percent—the same as the lowest personal tax rate—the change makes no difference to those whose income falls within the lowest tax bracket. But it increases taxes for most of those with higher incomes.

Source: *Revenue Canada*

For the 2001 tax year, the federal income tax rates for individual income are: 16 percent on income up to $30,754; $4,921 plus 22 percent on the next $30,755 up to $61,509; $11,687 plus 26 percent on the next $38,491 up to $100,000; and $21,694 plus 29 percent on income in excess of $100,000. There is a maximum total tax for the first three brackets of $21,695, but no maximum tax for the over $100,000 bracket.

Provincial Income Tax

In previous years, all provinces and territories except Quebec computed income tax as a percentage of basic federal tax ("tax-on-tax" system). In 2000, five provinces switched to the "tax-on-income" system, with the other provinces and three territories following suit for the 2001 tax year. All jurisdictions, except for Quebec, continue to use the federal definition of taxable income. However, under a tax-on-income system, provinces set their own rates, brackets and credits.

Filing Tax Returns

Though corporations must file tax returns each year, individuals need only file if they owe taxes or if they are eligible to claim tax credits such as the Child Tax Credit, or the Goods and Services Tax Credit. Persons owing money must file a return by April 30 of the year following the taxation year. Failure to do so makes the taxpayer liable to a late-filing penalty of 5 percent of unpaid tax plus an additional penalty of 1 percent per month on the amount outstanding, to a maximum of 12 months, plus interest on amounts owing.

Federal Income Tax Rates on Individual Income, 2001

The federal components of personal income tax rates apply to all taxpayers.

Federal Tax Brackets, Marginal Rates and Minimum Amounts of Tax

Basic Federal Tax Brackets	Other than Quebec		Quebec	
	Marginal Rate	Minimum Federal Tax Payable	Marginal Rate[2]	Minimum Federal Tax Payable
$0 to $30 754	16%	$0[1]	13.36%	$0[1]
$30 755 to $61 509	22%	$4 921	18.37%	$4 109
$61 510 to $100 000	26%	$11 687	21.71%	$9 759
over $100 000[3]	29%	$21 694	24.22%	$18 114

Source: © *PricewaterhouseCoopers*

(1) The basic personal credit eliminates federal tax for taxable income below $7,412. (2) Marginal rates for the federal component of personal tax are adjusted by a factor of 83.5 percent in Quebec: 13.36 percent = 16 percent x 83.5 percent; 18.37 = 22 percent x 83.5 percent; 21.71 percent = 26 percent x 83.5 percent; 24.215 percent = 83.5 percent x 29 percent. The federal surtax is not affected. The 83.5 percent factor is what remains after the 16.5 percent abatement. (3) Starting in 2001, the federal surtax was replaced by the $100,000 bracket.

Individual Provincial Income Tax Rates, 2001

For 2001, all provinces and territories compute income tax as "tax-on-income" systems. All jurisdictions, except for Quebec, continued to use the federal definition of taxable income. However, under a tax-on-income system, provinces set their own rates, brackets and credits.

Five provinces have surtaxes, calculated as a percentage of provincial tax. Alberta, Manitoba and Saskatchewan have eliminated their flat taxes, while several provinces have eliminated their surtaxes.

	Basic Tax Credit Amount	Basic Brackets and Rates					Provincial Surtax[1] On Provincial Tax Above:	Reduction for Low Incomes
Nfld	$7 410	$0 to $29 589 10.57%	$29 590 to $59 179 16.16%	over $59 180 18.02%			$7 032 9% of tax	No
PEI	$7 412	$0 to $30 753 9.8%	$30 754 to $61 508 13.8%	over $61 509 16.7%			$5 200 10% of tax	Yes
N. Scotia	$7 231	$0 to $29 589 9.77%	$29 590 to $59 179 14.95%	over $59 180 16.67%			$10 000 10% of tax	No
N. Brunswick	$7 412	$0 to $30 753 9.68%	$30 754 to $61 508 14.82%	$61 509 to $99 999 16.52%	over $100 000 17.84%		n.a.	Yes
Quebec[2]	$7 201	$0 to $25 999 17%	$26 000 to $51 999 21.25%	over $52 000 24.5%			n.a.	Yes
Ontario	$7 426	$0 to $30 813 6.2%	$30 814 to $61 628 9.24%	over $61 629 11.16%			$3 560 20% of tax $4 491 +36% of tax	Yes
Manitoba	$7 358	$0 to $30 543 10.9%	$30 544 to $61 088 16.2%	over $61 089 17.4%			n.a.	Yes
Sask.	$8 000	$0 to $29 999 11.5%	$30 000 to $59 999 13.5%	over $60 000 16%			n.a.	Yes
Alberta	$12 900	on taxable income 10%						Yes
B.C.	$8 000	$0 to $30 483 7.3%	$30 484 to $60 968 10.5%	$60 969 to $69 999 13.7%	$70 000 to $84 999 15.7%	over $85 000 16.7%	n.a.	No
Yukon	$7 412	$0 to $30 753 7.36%	$30 754 to $61 508 10.12%	$61 509 to $99 999 11.96%	over $100 000 13.34%		$6 000 5% of tax	No
NWT & NVT	$7 412	$0 to $30 753 7.2%	$30 754 to $61 508 9.9%	$61 509 to $99 999 11.7%	over $100 000 13.05%		n.a.	No
Non-residents	n.a.	$0 to $30 753 7.68%	$30 754 to $61 508 10.56%	$61 509 to $99 999 12.48%	over $100 000 13.92%		n.a.	No

Source: © *PricewaterhouseCoopers*   (n.a.) Not applicable.

Note: Basic tax is calculated as 48% of the federal tax, so the marginal rates are the same percentage of basic federal rates. Basic personal credits eliminate tax on taxable income up to the amounts listed in this table. The territories do not have their own basic credit, but in effect use the federal amount of $7,412.

(1) Surtax rates are the percentage of provincial tax above the basic provincial tax thresholds.

(2) Quebec's basic amount is $10,406 under the simplified tax system.

Personal Tax Credits, 2001

(dollars)

	Federal Amount[13]	Federal Credit[14]	Quebec Credit[15]
Basic	7 412	1 186	1 224
Spouse[1]	6 294	1 007	1 224
Age 65[2]	3 619	579	456[16]
Disability[3]	6 000	960	456
Infirm dependant[4]	3 500	560	1 224
Care giver[5]			550
Dependant[6]			
–1st	–	–	539
–Children (Additional)	–	–	498
Single parent	–	–	270
Living alone	–	–	218[16]
Pension income[7]	1 000	160	207[16]
CPP/QPP[8]	1 496	239	310
Employment Insurance (EI).	877	140	182
Education (per month)[9]			
–Full-time	400	64	342
–Part-time	120	19	342
CREDITS AS PERCENTAGE OF ACTUAL PAYMENT			
Dividends[10]	–[13]	13.33%[14]	10.83%
Charitable donations[11]			
First $200	–[13]	16%[14]	20.75%
Over $200	–[13]	29%[14]	20.75%
Tuition[12]	–[13]	16%[14]	20.75%

Source: © PricewaterhouseCoopers   (1) The spousal and equivalent credits are reduced when the income of the spouse or qualifying dependent exceeds $629. Any net income of the spouse reduces the Quebec spouse credit. (2) The age credit is reduced if income exceeds $26,941. (3) Basic credit for individuals with severe and prolonged impairment. The under 18 supplement is reduced if childcare and attendant care expenses claimed for child exceed $2,050. (4) Reduced if dependent's income exceeds $4,966. Any income reduces the Quebec infirm dependant credit. (5) For providers of in-home care for an adult relative (reduced if relative's income exceeds $11,953). The caregiver credit for Quebec is refundable. (6) Quebec's childcare credit is refundable and depends on net family income, and ranges from 26% to 75% of the expense. To qualify for the additional credit for children, children must be full-time students or under 19 years of age at the end of the year. (7) Maximum pension credit is $160. (8) For employees, the maximum credit is $379; self-employed persons deduct half of CPP/QPP premiums paid for their own coverage and claim a credit for half of these premiums. (9) The education credit is $64/month for full-time students, $19/month for part-time students. Quebec's maximum education credit is $342 per term (maximum two terms per year) for a supporting Quebec parent, which is not transferable. (10) Credits for taxable Canadian dividends apply to the grossed-up amount (125 percent) of dividends. (11) Eligible donations are limited to 75% of net income. (12) Tuition credit is available only if at least $100 in fees is paid to an institution. (13) Provinces use their own amounts to determine credits. (14) Maximum dollar value of credits that are based on prescribed amounts. Provinces have their own maximum dollar value of credits. (15) Under Quebec's simplified tax regime, some credits shown are not available and are replaced by a $2,625 lump-sum amount. (16) The total of Quebec's age, pension and living alone credits is reduced if net family income exceeds $26,000.

Individual Tax Tables, 2001

This table shows the combined federal and provincial (or territorial) income taxes, including surtaxes and flat taxes, payable on the assumption that only the basic personal tax credit is available, and that all income is either interest or ordinary income (such as salary).

Amount of combined federal and provincial/territorial income tax

Taxable Income	$20 000	$30 000	$40 000	$50 000	$60 000	$70 000	$80 000	$90 000	$100 000
Newfoundland	3 345	6 025	9 796	13 612	17 465	21 968	26 533	31 097	35 661
PEI	3 248	5 828	9 332	12 912	16 605	20 933	25 370	29 807	34 244
Nova Scotia	3 212	5 860	9 510	13 205	16 914	21 120	25 395	29 829	34 263
New Brunswick	3 233	5 801	9 399	13 081	16 673	20 929	25 181	29 433	33 685
Quebec[1]	3 884	7 090	11 014	14 976	19 198	23 769	28 390	33 011	37 632
Ontario	2 794	5 014	8 068	11 192	14 433	18 541	22 882	27 223	31 564
Manitoba	3 367	6 082	9 828	13 648	17 468	21 735	26 075	30 415	34 755
Saskatchewan	3 394	6 144	9 649	13 199	16 749	20 889	25 089	29 289	33 489
Alberta	2 649	5 324	8 479	11 679	14 879	18 419	22 019	25 619	29 219
British Columbia	2 890	5 220	8 409	11 659	14 909	18 788	22 958	27 178	31 448
Yukon	2 941	5 277	8 423	11 635	14 847	18 554	22 403	26 258	30 114
NWT & Nunavut	2 920	5 240	8 365	11 555	14 745	18 427	22 197	25 967	29 737

Source: © PricewaterhouseCoopers   (1) In some situations, the calculation of taxable income for federal and Quebec purposes may be different, and the amounts shown may require adjustments.

Taxable Income by Age and Gender, 1998

	Number of Taxable Returns Filed		Total Income Assessed ($thousands)		Average Income Assessed	
	Male	Female	Male	Female	Male	Female
Under 20	134 950	86 170	1 916 207	1 168 165	14 199	13 556
20-24	535 100	408 310	11 337 534	7 313 455	21 188	17 912
25-29	730 380	604 540	23 094 503	15 557 819	31 620	25 735
30-34	859 470	709 380	35 129 906	21 615 985	40 874	30 472
35-39	1 030 840	833 160	48 600 486	26 823 308	47 146	32 195
40-44	958 280	835 580	50 794 601	28 423 733	53 006	34 017
45-49	845 220	743 650	47 365 329	25 991 452	56 039	34 951
50-54	749 910	617 700	43 730 776	21 247 856	58 315	34 398
55-59	553 620	431 650	30 878 684	13 636 857	55 776	31 592
60-64	448 760	322 910	21 037 605	9 162 374	46 879	28 374
65-69	398 700	285 870	16 743 928	8 106 019	41 996	28 356
70-74	322 950	276 260	12 693 231	7 837 320	39 304	28 369
75 and over	401 020	452 110	14 657 529	13 280 014	36 551	29 373
Total	**7 970 050**	**6 607 490**	**358 046 999**	**200 168 148**	**44 924**	**30 294**

Source: © *Canada Customs and Revenue Agency*

Income Taxes Collected, 1998

(millions of dollars)

	Number of Returns	Total Income Assessed	Taxable Income Assessed	Net Federal Tax	Net Provincial Tax	Total Tax Paid
Canada	14 577 540.0	$558 215.0	$504 906.0	$78 587.0	$31 142.0	$109 729.0
Newfoundland/Labrador	222 440.0	6 750.0	6 171.0	825.0	565.0	1 390.0
Prince Edward Island	65 080.0	1 922.0	1 747.0	226.0	135.0	362.0
Nova Scotia	424 800.0	14 208.0	13 006.0	1 838.0	1 012.0	2 850.0
New Brunswick	342 410.0	10 707.0	9 842.0	1 324.0	796.0	2 120.0
Quebec	3 547 340.0	122 117.0	111 240.0	16 205.0	23.0	16 228.0
Ontario	5 570 240.0	233 371.0	211 000.0	34 581.0	16 154.0	50 735.0
Manitoba	545 360.0	18 579.0	16 774.0	2 399.0	1 526.0	3 925.0
Saskatchewan	474 570.0	15 765.0	14 093.0	1 960.0	1 312.0	3 272.0
Alberta	1 453 370.0	60 597.0	54 587.0	8 982.0	4 146.0	13 127.0
British Columbia	1 880 710.0	71 890.0	64 506.0	9 853.0	5 314.0	15 167.0
Yukon	14 280.0	568.0	461.0	68.0	34.0	102.0
Northwest Territories	18 490.0	842.0	702.0	116.0	51.0	167.0
Nunavut	7 240.0	331.0	269.0	45.0	20.0	65.0
Outside Canada	11 210.0	568.0	507.0	166.0	56.0	221.0

Source: *Canada Customs and Revenue Agency*

Mortgage Rates by Year[1]

	One-Year	Three-Year	Five-Year		One-Year	Three-Year	Five-Year
1980	13.98	n.a.	14.52	1990	13.40	13.38	13.35
1981	1812	18.33	18.38	1991	10.08	10.90	11.13
1982	16.85	17.83	18.04	1992	7.87	8.95	9.51
1983	10.98	12.52	13.23	1993	6.91	8.10	8.78
1984	12.00	13.21	13.58	1994[2]	7.83	8.99	9.53
1985	10.31	11.54	12.12	1995[2]	8.38	8.82	9.16
1986	10.15	10.88	11.21	1996[2]	6.19	7.37	7.93
1987	9.85	10.69	11.17	1997[2]	5.54	n.a.	7.07
1988	10.83	11.42	11.65	1998[2]	6.50	n.a.	6.93
1989	12.85	12.15	12.06	1999[2]	6.80	n.a.	7.56
				2000	7.85	n.a.	8.35

Source: © *Bank of Canada, CMHC, Statistics Canada.* (n.a.) Not available.

(1) Average typical mortgage rates. (2) 1-Year and 5-Year figures revised.

Average Resale Value of Canadian Homes[1]

The average resale value of Canadian homes increased by more than $6,000 between 1999 and 2000; 3.8% was the average growth. However, while there was growth in housing value in all the major cities, the growth was far from even. Halifax-Dartmouth led the pack with an 8% jump in value, followed by Ottawa (6.7%), Toronto (6.5%) and Calgary (6.1%). Great Vancouver's housing prices recovered from a slow growth period the previous year with a 5.3% increase (compared to .9% the year before), while Victoria saw only a tiny increase of 0.6%.

	1980	1985	1990	1995	1999	2000
Canada	**66 951**	**80 122**	**139 922**	**150 321**	**158 030**	**164 091**
Calgary	93 977	80 462	128 484	132 114	166 110	176 305
Edmonton........................	84 623	74 309	101 040	110 329	118 871	124 203
Halifax-Dartmouth.................	53 161	79 350	97 238	103 011	118 522	128 003
Hamilton-Burlington & District	54 835	72 973	165 742	141 109	158 162	164 168
Mississauga	80 341	99 675	224 449	180 295	213 150	224 393
Montreal..........................	49 419	70 564	111 956	109 929	119 689	125 333
Ottawa-Carleton	63 177	107 640	141 562	143 127	149 626	159 623
Regina...........................	48 628	61 403	71 054	76 629	90 181	94 518
Saint John........................	45 170	57 088	78 041	83 498	88 731	93 697
St. John's	53 247	66 642	88 939	89 655	95 606	100 763
Toronto[2]	75 621	109 094	254 890	203 028	228 372	243 249
Greater Vancouver	100 065	112 852	226 385	307 747	281 163	295 978
Victoria	85 066	88 451	160 743	210 669	249 930[3]	251 398[3]
Winnipeg.........................	50 491	62 478	81 740	82 994	n.a.	n.a.

Source: *The Canadian Real Estate Association; Victoria Real Estate Board* (n.a.) Not available.

(1) Average price of all homes sold on the Multiple Listing Service in constant dollars.
(2) Includes Mississauga, Brampton, Durham, Orangeville and York Region figures.
(3) Figures from Victoria Real Estate Board; based on single family homes.

The Effect of Interest Rate Changes on Mortgage Payments

The table below shows the monthly mortgage payment (principal and interest) for each $1,000 of mortgage debt. To calculate your payment at a given interest rate, choose the corresponding amount in the amortization column you select and multiply the amount by the number of thousands of dollars of debt. For example, if you want to know the cost per month to carry an $85,000 mortgage amortized over 25 years at 7.00 percent, multiply 7 by 85 and the result, $595, is your monthly payment. If the same mortgage was coming up for renewal at 8.00 percent, the new payment amount would be $648.66 (7.63 x 85) or $53.56 more each month.

Monthly Payments for Each $1 000 of Mortgage

Interest Rate (%)	Amortization Period							
	1 Year	2 Years	3 Years	5 Years	10 Years	15 Years	20 Years	25 Years
4.00	$85.13	$43.41	$29.51	$18.40	$10.11	$7.38	$6.04	$5.26
4.25	85.25	43.52	29.62	18.51	10.23	7.50	6.17	5.40
4.50	85.36	43.63	29.73	18.62	10.34	7.63	6.30	5.53
4.75	85.47	43.74	29.84	18.74	10.46	7.75	6.44	5.67
5.00	85.58	43.85	29.95	18.85	10.58	7.88	6.57	5.82
5.25	85.70	43.96	30.06	18.96	10.70	8.01	6.71	5.95
5.50	85.81	44.07	30.17	19.07	10.82	8.14	6.84	6.10
5.75	85.92	44.18	30.28	19.19	10.94	8.27	6.98	6.25
6.00	86.03	44.29	30.39	19.30	11.07	8.40	7.12	6.40
6.25	86.14	44.40	30.50	19.41	11.19	8.53	7.26	6.55
6.50	86.26	44.51	30.61	19.53	11.31	8.66	7.41	6.70
6.75	86.37	44.62	30.72	19.64	11.43	8.80	7.55	6.85
7.00	86.48	44.73	30.83	19.75	11.56	8.93	7.69	7.00
7.25	86.59	44.84	30.94	19.87	11.68	9.07	7.84	7.16
7.50	86.70	44.95	31.05	19.98	11.81	9.21	7.99	7.32
7.75	86.82	45.06	31.16	20.10	11.94	9.34	8.13	7.47
8.00	86.93	45.17	31.28	20.21	12.06	9.48	8.28	7.63
8.25	87.04	45.28	31.39	20.33	12.19	9.62	8.43	7.79
8.50	87.15	45.39	31.50	20.45	12.32	9.76	8.59	7.95
8.75	87.26	45.50	31.61	20.56	12.45	9.90	8.74	8.12
9.00	87.38	45.61	31.72	20.68	12.58	10.05	8.89	8.28
9.25	87.49	45.72	31.84	20.80	12.71	10.19	9.05	8.44
9.50	87.60	45.83	31.95	20.91	12.84	10.33	9.20	8.61
9.75	87.71	45.94	32.06	21.03	12.97	10.48	9.36	8.78
10.00	87.82	46.05	32.17	21.15	13.10	10.62	9.52	8.94
10.25	87.93	46.16	32.28	21.27	13.24	10.77	9.68	9.11
10.50	88.04	46.27	32.40	21.38	13.37	10.92	9.83	9.28
10.75	88.16	46.38	32.51	21.50	13.50	11.06	10.00	9.45
11.00	88.27	46.49	32.62	21.62	13.64	11.21	10.16	9.63
11.25	88.38	46.61	32.74	21.74	13.77	11.36	10.32	9.80
11.50	88.49	46.72	32.85	21.86	13.91	11.51	10.48	9.97
11.75	88.60	46.83	32.96	21.98	14.04	11.66	10.65	10.14
12.00	88.71	46.94	33.08	22.10	14.18	11.82	10.81	10.32
12.25	88.82	47.05	33.19	22.22	14.32	11.97	10.98	10.49
12.50	88.94	47.16	33.30	22.34	14.46	12.12	11.14	10.67
12.75	89.05	47.27	33.42	22.46	14.59	12.28	11.31	10.85
13.00	89.18	47.38	33.53	22.58	14.73	12.43	11.48	11.02

Source: *The Royal Bank of Canada*

Housing Affordability Table

The table below shows how expensive a home an individual or family could likely afford, using various income levels and mortgage interest rates—assuming a down-payment of 25 percent of the purchase price. As income rises, housing becomes more affordable, but it becomes less affordable as interest rates increase.

For example, most couples with a combined annual income of $60,000 would qualify for a mortgage on a home costing $192,170 at an 8 percent interest rate—provided they had a down-payment of $38,094 (25 percent of the purchase price). But at a 10 percent interest rate, the same couple earning the same income could only afford a $163,967 home.

The table assumes that mortgage payments, property taxes, heating costs and 50 percent of condominium fees should not exceed 32 percent of gross income (net income if self-employed). Most lending institutions use this percentage when calculating how large a mortgage you can afford. For this table, we have established annual costs of $2,400 for taxes and $2,400 for taxes and $2,400 for heating. Most lenders will also require that you total debt service ratio (mortgage payments, property taxes, heating cots 50 percent of condo fees and any other liabilities such as car loans or other debts) does not exceed 40 percent of gross income.

Mortgage Interest Rate (%)[1]	Annual Income							
	$30 000	**$40 000**	**$50 000**	**$60 000**	**$70 000**	**$80 000**	**$90 000**	**$100 000**
4.00	25 348	109 838	194 332	278 823	363 314	439 357	506 951	574 546
4.25	24 707	107 062	189 420	271 776	354 132	428 252	494 138	560 024
4.50	24 090	104 391	184 693	264 993	345 294	417 564	481 806	546 048
4.75	23 497	101 818	180 142	258 464	336 785	407 275	469 934	532 593
5.00	22 925	99 341	175 760	252 176	328 592	397 367	458 501	519 636
5.25	22 374	96 955	171 538	246 119	320 700	387 823	447 489	507 155
5.50	21 844	94 658	167 471	240 283	313 095	378 627	436 878	495 129
5.75	21 333	92 440	163 550	234 658	305 766	369 764	426 652	483 539
6.00	20 840	90 334	159 771	229 236	298 701	361 220	416 793	472 386
6.25	20 364	88 244	156 127	224 007	291 887	352 980	407 285	461 591
6.50	19 906	86 257	152 611	218 863	185 315	345 032	398 115	451 197
6.75	19 463	84 340	149 219	214 096	278 973	337 363	389 265	441 169
7.00	19 036	82 490	145 946	209 399	272 853	329 962	380 726	431 490
7.25	18 624	80 704	142 785	204 865	256 945	322 817	372 482	422 147
7.50	18 226	78 979	139 733	200 486	261 239	315 917	364 520	413 124
7.75	17 842	77 313	136 785	196 257	255 728	309 252	356 830	404 408
8.00	17 470	75 703	133 937	192 170	250 403	302 813	349 400	395 987
8.25	17 111	74 147	131 184	188 220	245 256	296 589	342 219	387 848
8.50	16 764	72 643	128 523	184 402	240 281	290 572	335 276	379 981
8.75	16 428	71 188	125 950	180 170	235 470	284 754	328 583	372 372
9.00	16 103	69 781	123 461	177 138	230 816	279 127	322 070	365 013
9.25	15 789	68 420	121 052	173 683	226 314	273 682	315 787	357 893
9.50	15 485	67 103	118 722	170 339	221 958	268 413	309 707	351 002
9.75	15 191	65 827	116 465	167 102	217 738	263 312	303 822	344 332
10.00	14 906	64 593	114 281	163 967	213 654	258 372	296 122	337 873
10.25	14 630	63 397	112 165	160 932	209 698	253 588	292 602	331 616
10.50	14 363	62 238	110 115	157 990	205 865	248 953	287 254	325 555
10.75	14 104	61 115	108 128	155 139	202 151	244 462	282 072	319 682
11.00	13 852	60 027	106 202	152 376	198 550	240 108	277 048	313 988
11.25	13 609	58 971	104 335	149 697	195 060	235 886	272 177	308 468
11.50	13 373	57 948	102 524	147 099	191 674	231 792	267 453	303 114
11.75	13 144	56 955	100 767	144 579	188 390	227 820	262 870	297 920
12.00	12 921	55 991	99 063	142 133	185 203	223 966	258 423	292 880
12.25	12 705	55 058	97 408	139 759	182 110	220 225	254 107	287 988
12.50	14 496	54 148	95 802	137 454	179 196	216 594	249 917	283 239
12.75	12 292	53 267	94 242	135 216	176 190	213 067	245 847	278 627
13.00	12 095	52 410	92 727	133 042	173 358	209 642	241 895	274 148

Source: *The Royal Bank of Canada*

(1) Compounded semi-annually. Mortgage payments based on a 25-year amortization.

Personal Income and Savings

	Total Personal Income ($millions)	Annual % Change in Personal Income	Total Personal Disposable Income ($millions)	Total Personal Saving ($millions)	Personal Saving Rate
1965	$ 41 881	9.8	$ 37 113	$ 2 306	6.2
1970	67 840	8.3	55 295	3 537	6.4
1971	74 531	9.9	60 462	4 222	7.0
1972	84 423	13.3	68 838	5 902	8.6
1973	98 528	16.7	80 373	8 324	10.4
1974	117 905	19.7	95 304	11 166	11.7
1975	136 921	16.1	111 258	14 052	12.6
1976	156 372	14.2	126 157	15 543	12.3
1977	173 286	10.8	139 752	16 536	11.8
1978	193 519	11.7	158 055	20 292	12.8
1979	217 974	12.6	178 544	23 792	13.3
1980	248 188	13.9	203 161	28 960	14.3
1981	289 797	16.8	235 056	37 349	15.9
1982	320 241	10.5	259 065	48 039	18.5
1983	337 138	5.3	270 794	40 963	15.1
1984	365 056	8.3	294 145	44 020	15.0
1985	395 166	8.2	317 392	44 390	14.0
1986	423 088	7.1	334 854	39 244	11.7
1987	454 736	7.5	356 134	35 928	10.1
1988	499 206	9.8	388 639	40 903	10.5
1989	542 295	8.6	425 566	47 744	11.2
1990	581 741	7.3	449 644	50 030	11.1
1991	600 658	3.3	464 289	52 832	11.4
1992	616 055	2.6	475 645	53 381	11.2
1993	627 885	1.9	486 641	48 618	10.0
1994	640 275	2.0	493 625	39 345	8.0
1995	666 390	4.0	511 378	37 608	7.4
1996	687 738	2.3	529 818	37 136	7.0
1997	715 999	4.1	548 355	26 635	4.9
1998	747 178	4.4	569 410	25 015	4.4
1999	783 322	4.8	597 710	24 939	4.2
2000	830 757	6.1	631 023	24 542	3.9

Source: © *Statistics Canada*   (1) As of June 2000.

Income Growth

*W*hile the year 2000 showed a 6.1% change in personal income, the growth was not even across the country. From east to west, the figures for percentage change were: Newfoundland, 4.4; Prince Edward Island, 5.1; Nova Scotia, 4.7; New Brunswick, 4.9; Quebec, 5.7; Ontario, 6.4; Manitoba, 7.0; Saskatchewan, 4.4, Alberta, 7.3; British Columbia, 5.3; Yukon, 3.0; Northwest Territories, 8.5; and Nunavut, 6.4. What fuelled the growth? According to Statistics Canada, labour income grew through both employment gains and an increase in average earnings. Alberta's income growth was in construction, commercial services and manufacturing industries, while employees in Ontario and Quebec received increases courtesy of federal pay equity payments.

Farm income in 2000 suffered from continued weak grain and oilseed prices. This was particularly noticeable in Manitoba and Saskatchewan, however farm aid programs and better livestock revenues helped the situation. Personal disposable income in Alberta and Ontario was also increased by tax cuts.

The growth was matched by an increase in consumer spending. Alberta's shoppers pushed retail sales up 8.9%.

RRSP Contributions by Taxpayers, 1998

Total Income Class	Number of Taxpayers	Average Income per Return	Number of Taxpayers with RRSP Room	Average Amount of RRSP Room Available	Number of Taxpayers Making RRSP Contributions	Average Amount of RRSP Contribution
Taxpayers under age 45						
Under $10 000	3 717 100	$4 207.50	2 634 700	$4 837.79	106 660	$988.69
$10 000 – $20 000	2 384 980	$14 602.91	2 236 570	$8 892.73	448 540	$1 480.74
$20 000 – $30 000	1 798 390	$24 915.90	1 771 330	$14 986.03	696 790	$2 045.99
$30 000 – $40 000	1 397 760	$34 710.54	1 383 880	$19 367.92	760 200	$2 751.34
$40 000 – $50 000	904 470	$44 506.52	900 500	$21 607.25	575 210	$3 565.29
$50 000 – $60 000	547 040	$54 608.99	543 960	$22 442.05	387 150	$4 406.72
$60 000 – $80 000	492 400	$67 896.19	488 830	$23 134.61	374 990	$5 833.66
$80 000 – $100 000	146 430	$88 230.51	144 920	$23 144.65	122 720	$8 274.08
$100 000 and over	163 520	$195 236.55	155 120	$20 854.83	135 350	$12 174.04
TOTAL	11 552 110	$25 293.88	10 259 810	$13 211.39	3 607 600	$3 574.23
By Gender						
Males	5 707 010	$31 424.09	5 171 940	$15 689.16	1 983 720	$4 083.27
Females	5 845 100	$19 308.50	5 087 870	$10 692.68	1 623 890	$2 952.37
Taxpayers aged 45–65						
Under $10 000	1 438 900	$4 489.22	1 025 480	$7 239.73	64 680	$1 275.26
$10 000 – $20 000	1 076 490	$14 651.12	972 310	$11 281.21	234 440	$2 026.02
$20 000 – $30 000	929 180	$25 064.19	896 750	$15 485.55	360 880	$2 636.69
$30 000 – $40 000	841 910	$34 747.77	818 370	$17 542.68	434 350	$3 259.40
$40 000 – $50 000	604 400	$44 750.53	588 560	$18 908.58	362 050	$4 081.25
$50 000 – $60 000	453 890	$54 804.42	444 270	$18 309.44	304 200	$4 543.07
$60 000 – $80 000	476 490	$68 119.20	468 900	$18 249.37	353 570	$5 923.32
$80 000 – $100 000	170 120	$88 425.12	163 970	$16 631.96	134 060	$8 306.31
$100 000 and over	220 100	$219 942.25	194 040	$16 801.45	161 010	$13 139.01
TOTAL	6 211 460	$35 838.22	5 572 640	$14 435.47	2 409 240	$4 610.46
By Gender						
Males	3 160 510	$46 702.73	2 923 140	$17 048.22	1 331 670	$5 388.23
Females	3 050 950	$24 583.55	2 649 500	$11 552.89	1 077 570	$3 649.29
Taxpayers aged 65+						
Under $10 000	484 680	$6 602.55	130 880	$4 273.05	2 010	$994.03
$10 000 – $20 000	1 734 070	$14 048.22	587 050	$5 290.81	20 740	$1 549.04
$20 000 – $30 000	641 430	$24 490.02	334 430	$6 062.77	27 880	$2 265.93
$30 000 – $40 000	329 200	$34 340.72	183 270	$6 523.13	26 110	$3 066.49
$40 000 – $50 000	169 550	$44 445.54	97 130	$7 398.15	20 050	$4 042.19
$50 000 – $60 000	90 630	$54 477.39	54 040	$8 268.26	11 710	$5 644.49
$60 000 – $80 000	78 250	$68 219.34	47 290	$9 303.64	13 160	$7 123.94
$80 000 – $100 000	31 590	$88 863.41	19 980	$11 414.01	6 820	$10 020.97
$100 000 and over	58 870	$252 399.78	42 850	$18 088.91	15 850	$18 076.40
TOTAL	3 618 260	$24 888.06	1 496 900	$6 344.33	144 320	$5 356.93
By Gender						
Males	1 621 290	$31 016.79	892 520	$7 262.35	97 300	$5 261.69
Females	1 996 970	$19 912.30	604 380	$4 988.63	47 020	$5 554.02

Source: *Canada Customs and Revenue Agency*

Home Buyers' Plan Use by Taxpayers, 1998

Total Income Class	Number of Taxpayers	Average Income per Return	Number Participating in Home Buyers' Plan	Average Balance in Home Buyers' Plan	Number of Taxpayers Making Repayments	Average Home Buyers' Plan Repayment
Taxpayers under age 45						
Under $10 000	3 717 100	$4 207.50	36 910	$6 669.87	10 910	$947.66
$10 000 – $20 000	2 384 980	$14 602.91	51 720	$6 668.91	17 170	$617.76
$20 000 – $30 000	1 798 390	$24 915.90	93 070	$7 316.90	31 080	$598.81
$30 000 – $40 000	1 397 760	$34 710.54	114 940	$7 992.49	46 550	$646.49
$40 000 – $50 000	904 470	$44 506.52	98 280	$8 390.11	42 420	$727.44
$50 000 – $60 000	547 040	$54 608.99	60 960	$8 936.63	30 410	$828.81
$60 000 – $80 000	492 400	$67 896.19	59 000	$9 734.69	33 720	$996.38
$80 000 – $100 000	146 430	$88 230.51	16 860	$9 940.04	10 410	$1 094.33
$100 000 and over	163 520	$195 236.55	15 910	$11 598.87	10 680	$1 822.66
TOTAL	11 552 110	$25 293.88	547 650	$8 192.41	233 330	$815.02
By Gender						
Males	5 707 010	$31 424.09	302 890	$8 619.24	129 800	$845.19
Females	5 845 100	$19 308.50	244 750	$7 664.51	103 530	$777.20
Taxpayers aged 45–65						
Under $10 000	1 438 900	$4 489.22	11 340	$9 903.17	3 520	$880.40
$10 000 – $20 000	1 076 490	$14 651.12	14 360	$9 327.99	6 410	$727.77
$20 000 – $30 000	929 180	$25 064.19	22 090	$9 473.70	8 270	$1 704.72
$30 000 – $40 000	841 910	$34 747.77	26 390	$10 015.50	13 350	$981.50
$40 000 – $50 000	604 400	$44 750.53	24 090	$10 093.81	12 690	$1 010.95
$50 000 – $60 000	453 890	$54 804.42	15 960	$10 639.35	8 980	$1 034.74
$60 000 – $80 000	476 490	$68 119.20	15 030	$11 029.74	9 570	$1 070.53
$80 000 – $100 000	170 120	$88 425.12	5 640	$11 818.79	3 760	$1 429.26
$100 000 and over	220 100	$219 942.25	4 730	$13 166.81	3 580	$1 867.60
TOTAL	6 211 460	$35 838.22	139 650	$10 222.07	70 130	$1 132.05
By Gender						
Males	3 160 510	$46 702.73	75 930	$10 744.62	37 740	$1 116.30
Females	3 050 950	$24 583.55	63 710	$9 600.89	32 380	$1 150.77
Taxpayers aged 65+						
Under $10 000	484 680	$6 602.55	770	$13 594.81	160	$681.25
$10 000 – $20 000	1 734 070	$14 048.22	2 070	$11 923.19	180	$983.33
$20 000 – $30 000	641 430	$24 490.02	1 700	$12 898.82	580	$1 108.62
$30 000 – $40 000	329 200	$34 340.72	1 190	$11 068.07	770	$2 133.77
$40 000 – $50 000	169 550	$44 445.54	810	$13 881.48	490	$2 038.78
$50 000 – $60 000	90 630	$54 477.39	360	$14 294.44	260	$3 234.62
$60 000 – $80 000	78 250	$68 219.34	410	$12 092.68	130	$938.46
$80 000 – $100 000	31 590	$88 863.41	110	$11 863.64	50	$4 300.00
$100 000 and over	58 870	$252 399.78	140	$15 764.29	80	$3 037.50
TOTAL	3 618 260	$24 888.06	7 560	$12 580.56	2 710	$1 842.44
By Gender						
Males	1 621 290	$31 016.79	4 570	$12 407.66	1 740	$2 052.30
Females	1 996 970	$19 912.30	2 990	$12 844.82	980	$1 452.04

Source: *Canada Customs and Revenue Agency*

INVESTMENT

Investment: A Glossary of Terms

Annual report: A report issued by a company to its shareholders at the end of the fiscal year. It contains a report on company operations and formal financial statements.

Bankers' acceptance: A commercial draft backed by the guarantee of a bank. The bankers' acceptance promises repayment on a certain date, usually not more than 90 days ahead, and bears a rate of return competitive with other chartered bank securities.

Bear market: A market in which prices are falling.

Bid and ask: The bid price is the highest price anyone is willing to pay to buy a stock; the ask is the lowest price anyone will accept to sell a stock. Together, the bid and ask prices are a quote.

Blue chip stocks: Stocks with good investment qualities, usually common shares of well-established companies with good earnings records and long-time dividend payments.

Board lot: A unit of trading. Board lots on the Toronto Stock Exchange are: under 10 cents each—1000 shares; between 10 cents and 99 cents each—500 shares; at and above $1 each—100 shares.

Bond: A written promise or IOU by the issuer to repay a fixed amount of borrowed money on a specified date, and to pay a set annual rate of interest in the meantime, generally at semi-annual intervals. Bonds are usually considered a safe investment because the borrower (whether a company or the government) must make interest payments before its money is spent on anything else.

Bull market: A market in which prices are rising.

Call: An option to buy a fixed amount of a certain stock at a specified price within a specified time.

Canada Savings Bonds: These are issued each fall, and are popular with small investors because they come in denominations starting at $100. They are not traded. They have a term of several years and a minimum guaranteed rate of interest. However, the government sets an effective rate during the issuing period each year, and adjusts it when necessary to conform with interest rate trends. Interest can be awarded yearly or compounded, depending upon the type of bond.

Capital gain or loss: Profit or loss resulting from the sale of an asset, such as a security. The gain or loss is the difference between the buying and selling price of the security with commissions figured in.

Commercial paper: Short-term negotiable securities issued by corporations that call for the payment of a specific amount of money at a given time.

Common shares: Securities issued by the company that represent part-ownership in the company. Common shares sometimes carry a voting privilege and entitle the holder to a share in the company's profits, usually issued in the form of dividends.

Convertible bond: A corporate bond (see below) that may be converted into a stated number of shares of the corporation's common stock. Its price tends to fluctuate with the price of the stock, as well as with changes in interest rates.

Corporate bonds: Evidence of debt by a corporation. The bond bears interest much like a government bond, and matures at a certain date in the future. Considered safer than the common or preferred stock of the same company.

Day order: An order to buy or sell a security valid only for the day the order is given.

Dividend: A portion of a company's profit paid to the common and preferred shareholders. The amount is decided upon by the company's board of directors, and may be paid in cash or stock.

Equities: Common and preferred stocks that represent a share in the ownership of a company.

Ex-dividend: Without dividend. The buyer of shares quoted ex-dividend is not entitled to receive an already declared dividend. When shares are un-dividend, the purchaser will receive the declared dividend.

Floor trader: A brokerage-firm employee who works on the stock exchange trading floor, and is responsible for executing buy and sell orders on behalf of the firm and its clients.

Futures: Contracts to buy or sell specific quantities of a commodity or financial instrument with delivery delayed until some agreed-upon time in the future.

Government of Canada bonds: These bear a fixed rate of interest and a maturation date in the future, and are traded on the market, with the price rising and falling in response to interest rate trends. ▶

▶ Long-term government bonds are considered a safe investment. Provinces and municipalities may also issue long-term bonds.

Index: Statistical measure of the state of the stock market or economy, based on the performance of stocks or other components. Examples are the TSE 300 Composite Index and the Toronto 35 Index.

Limit order: An order to buy or sell securities in which the client has specified the price. The order can be executed only at the specified price or a better one.

Liquidity: The measure of how quickly an investor can turn securities into cash. A security is liquid if it can be bought and sold quickly with small price changes between transactions.

Long: A term signifying ownership of securities. "I am long 100 XYZ" means that the speaker owns 100 shares of XYZ.

Margin: The amount paid by clients when they use credit to buy a security, the balance being loaned by their brokers.

Market order: An order to buy a security immediately at the best possible price.

Money market: Part of the capital market established for short-term borrowing and lending of funds. Money market dealers conduct business over the telephone, and trade securities such as short-term (three years and less) government bonds, government treasury bills and commercial paper.

Mutual fund: A portfolio, or selection, of professionally bought and managed stocks in which the investor pools money with thousands of others. A share price is based on net asset value, or the value of all the investments owned by the fund, less any debt, divided by the total number of shares. The major advantage is less risk—an investment is spread out over many stocks, and if one or two do badly, the remainder may shield the investor from the losses. Bond funds are mutual funds that deal in the bond market exclusively. Money market mutual funds concentrate on debt instruments sold on the money market. Equity mutual funds place their investments in the common shares of companies.

Odd lot: A number of shares less than a board lot.

Open order: An order to buy or sell a security at a specified price, valid until executed or cancelled.

Over-the-counter: The over-the-counter (OTC) or unlisted market is the market maintained by securities dealers for issues not listed on a stock exchange.

Penny stock: Low-priced, often speculative issues selling at less than $1 a share.

Preferred shares: Shares that carry dividends at fixed rates that must be paid before any dividends are paid to common shareholders.

Price/earnings ratio: A common stock's current market price divided by the company's annual per share earnings.

Prospectus: A legal document describing securities being offered for sale to the public. It must be prepared in accordance with provincial securities commission regulations.

Put: An option to sell a fixed amount of a certain stock at a specified price within a specified time.

Registered representative: A salesperson or broker employed by an investment firm. Salespersons must be registered with the provincial securities commission.

Right: A temporary privilege granted to existing common shareholders to purchase additional shares directly from the company at a stated price.

Settlement date: The date on which a securities buyer must pay for a purchase or a seller must deliver the securities sold. In general, settlement must be made on or before the third business day following the transaction date.

Short sale: The sale of shares that the seller does not own. The seller is speculating that the stock price will fall, in the hope of later purchasing the same number of securities at a lower price, thereby making a profit. Sellers must advise their brokers when they are selling short.

Stock yield: The percentage of the dividend paid in relation to the price of the stock. For example, a stock selling at $40 a share with an annual dividend of $2 a share yields 5 percent.

Transfer agent: A trust company appointed by a company to keep a record of the names, addresses and numbers of shares held by its shareholders. Transfer agents are often responsible for distributing dividend cheques.

Underwriting: The purchase for resale of a new issue of securities by an investment dealer or group of dealers.

Warrant: A certificate giving the holder the right to purchase securities at a stipulated price within a specified period of time. They are often detachable and may be traded separately.

Government of Canada Average Bond Yields

Year	1 to 3 Years	3 to 5 Years	5 to 10 Years	10 Years and Over
1981	15.97	15.68	15.29	15.22
1985	10.12	10.39	10.78	11.04
1990	11.65	11.19	10.82	10.85
1995	7.26	7.63	7.93	9.49
1996[1]	5.35	6.21	6.88	7.50
1997[1]	4.68	5.33	5.87	6.42
1998[1]	5.09	5.13	5.26	5.47
1999[1]	5.36	5.55	5.56	5.69
2000[2]	5.91	5.99	5.96	5.89

Source: *Bank of Canada*   (1) Revised data. (2) Preliminary data.

RRSP Contributors and Contributions

	Nfld	PEI	NS	NB	Que	Ont	Man	Sask	Alta	BC	YT	NWT[2]	NVT[2]
Contributors (000)													
1997	65.9	21.4	145.2	108.5	1 444.5	2 425.2	230.5	211.6	654.6	835.8	6.1	7.4	2.1
1998	64.4	20.8	142.4	104.8	1 415.5	2 445.6	231.1	202.3	659.1	820.9	5.8	7.0	2.0
1999	65.5	21.1	145.2	108.1	1 457 0	2 479.6	231.4	197.2	664.3	822.6	5.9	7.1	2.1
Contributions ($000,000)													
1997[1]	276.8	96.2	622.1	439.6	6 102.9	11 393.3	873.9	825.3	2 955.8	3 778.4	29.2	39.3	12.3
1998[1]	266.1	80.8	578.3	394.1	5 555.3	11 423.9	867.7	762.3	2 952.7	3 675.5	26.4	36.7	11.5
1999	274.0	81.0	587.4	418.2	5 889.7	11 911.3	882.9	758.6	3 109.2	3 800.6	26.3	36.9	13.1

Source: © *Statistics Canada*

(1) Current dollars. (2) Data for the Northwest Territories and Nunavut are based on the current boundaries created when Nunavut became a new territory in April 1999.

Toronto Stock Exchange Activity

	Toronto Stock Exchange	
Year	Combined volume (millions)	Value of shares traded ($millions)
1970	523	3 654
1975	470	4 089
1980	2 009	29 514
1985	3 298	44 196
1990	5 660	64 009
1995	15 758	207 665
1996	22 341	301 299
1997	25 670	423 170
1998	26 800	493 212
1999	29 300	529 000
2000	40 800	944 300

Restructuring of Canada's stock exchanges was completed in the spring of 2000, with Bourse de Montréal (formerly the Montreal Stock Exchange) officially becoming the country's only financial derivatives exchange. The final transfer of the options market from the Toronto Stock Exchange took place on March 27, 2000. Shortly after, the Bourse demutualized and became a for-profit company owned by shareholders. As of September 28, 2001 the Bourse ceased to operate as an equity stock exchange and all its junior stocks were transferred to the Canadian Venture Exchange (CDNX).

Under the new structure, the TSE is the senior equities exchange, the CDNX handles junior stocks and the Bourse trades options and derivatives. The TSE has also demutualized.

Sources: © *Montreal Stock Exchange; Toronto Stock Exchange*

Global Superlatives

Largest continent	Asia	44 485 900 sq. km
Smallest continent	Australia	7 682 300 sq. km
Largest ocean	Pacific	166 241 000 sq. km
Smallest ocean	Arctic	9 485 000 sq. km
Deepest point of any ocean	Mariana Trench, Pacific Ocean	10 924 m
Largest sea	South China Sea	2 974 600 sq. km
Largest lake	Caspian Sea, Russian Fed., Kazakhstan, Turkmenistan, Iran, Azerbaijan	371 000 sq. km
Deepest lake	Lake Baykal, Russia	1 620 m
Largest freshwater lake	Lake Superior, North America	82 100 sq. km
Highest major lake	Lake Titicaca, Bolivia-Peru, South America	3 809 m
Lowest major lake	Caspian Sea, Russian Fed., Kazakhstan, Turkmenistan, Iran, Azerbaijan	-28 m
Largest island	Greenland, Denmark	2 175 600 sq. km
Longest reef	Great Barrier Reef, Australia-Papua New Guinea	2 027 km
Longest river	Nile, Africa	6 671 km
Largest nation	Russia	17 075 272 sq. km
Smallest nation	Vatican City	.44 ha. km
Most populous nation	People's Republic of China (July 1999 est)	pop. 1 246 871 951
Oldest city	Damascus, Syria	continuously inhabited since c. 2500 B.C.
Highest point	Mount Everest, Nepal-Tibet	8 848 m
Lowest point	Dead Sea, Israel-Jordan	-400 m
Highest city	La Paz, Bolivia	3 636 m
Coldest city	Norilsk, Russia	average temp. -10.9°C
Hottest city	Djibouti, Djibouti	average temp. 30°C
Coldest place	Plateau Station, Antarctica	-56.7°C
Hottest place	Dalol, Danakil Depression, Ethiopia	35°C avg.
Coldest recorded temperature	Vostok, Antarctica (Australian territory), July 21, 1983	-89.2°C
Hottest recorded temperature (shade)	Al-Aziziyah, Libya, Sept. 13, 1922	58°C
Wettest spot	Mount Waialeale, Kauai, Hawaii	avg. ann. rainfall of 16 800 mm
Driest spot	Atacama Desert, Chile	avg. ann. precipitation barely measurable
Greatest snowfall in 24 hrs	Silver Lake, Colorado, U.S., Apr. 14–15, 1921	193 cm
Greatest rainfall in 24 hrs	Cilaos, Reunion Island, Indian Ocean, Mar. 15–16, 1952	1 870 mm
Largest desert	Sahara, Africa	9 million sq. km
Largest waterfall (by volume)	Khone, Kampuchea-Laos	11 610 cu. m/sec.
Tallest waterfall	Angel Falls, Venezuela	807 m
Largest gorge	Grand Canyon, Colorado River, Arizona	349 km long; 6–20 km wide; 1.6 km deep
Deepest gorge	Colca River Canyon, Peru	3 223 m
Oldest tree	a bristlecone pine, Wheeler's Peak, Nevada	approx. age of 5 100 yrs.
Greatest tides	Bay of Fundy, Nova Scotia	14.5 m
Most devastating volcanic eruption	Tambora, Sumbawa, Indonesia, Apr. 5–7, 1815	92 000 deaths
Longest bridge	Confederation, linking New Brunswick and Prince Edward Island (main span 11 km); bridge between the tip of Florida and Key West is also 11 km.	12.9 km
Largest man-made lake	Owen Falls, Uganda	2 700 000 cu. m
Longest street	Yonge Street, from Toronto, Ont. to Rainy River (at. Man. border)	1 896.2 km
Tallest building	Sears Tower, Chicago, Illinois	110 storeys, 443 m
Tallest free-standing structure	CN Tower, Toronto, Ont.	553.34 m
Most common language	Mandarin	approx. 750 million speakers

GEOGRAPHY

The Continents

Continent	Total Area (sq. km)	% of Earth's Land	Population	% of World Total
Asia	44 485 900	30.0	3 292 337 000	62.4
Africa	30 269 680	20.4	702 013 000	13.2
North and Central America	24 235 280	16.3	441 826 000	8.4
South America	17 820 770	12.0	309 634 000	5.9
Antarctica	13 209 000	8.9	uninhabited	
Europe	10 530 750	7.1	504 925 000	9.6
Oceania	7 830 682	5.3	27 752 000	.5

Source: *National Geographic Atlas of the World (1990), FAO Production Yearbook (1993)*

Highest and Lowest Points on Each Continent

Continent	Highest Point (metres)		Lowest Point (metres)	
Asia	Everest	8 848	Dead Sea	-400
South America	Aconcagua	6 960	Valdés Peninsula	-40
North America	McKinley (Denali)	6 194	Death Valley	-86
Africa	Kilimanjaro	5 895	Lake Assal	-156
Europe	El'brus	5 642	Caspian Sea	-28
Antarctica	Vinson Massif	4 897	—	-2 538
Australia	Kosciusko	2 228	Lake Eyre	-16

Source: *National Geographic Atlas of the World (1990)*

World's Highest Cities

City	Altitude[1]	City	Altitude[1]
Cerro de Pasco, Peru	4 259 m	Cuaco, Peru	3 400 m
Potosi, Bolivia	4 200 m	Quito, Ecuador	2 811 m
Shigatse, Tibet	3 939 m	Sucre, Bolivia	2 790 m
La Paz, Bolivia	3 665 m	Toluca de Lerdo, Mexico	2 680 m
Lhasa, Tibet	3 606 m	Addis Ababa, Ethiopia	2 450 m

Source: *Global Atlas, Gage Educational Publishing Co., South American Handbook.*
(1) Estimates vary, depending on source.

Oceans' Area and Depth

Ocean	Area (sq. km)	% of Earth's Water Area	Deepest Point	Depth (metres)
Pacific	166 241 000	46.0	Mariana Trench	10 924
Atlantic	86 557 000	23.9	Puerto Rico Trench	8 605
Indian	73 427 000	20.3	Java Trench	7 258
Arctic	9 485 000	2.6	Eurasia Basin	5 122

Source: *National Geographic Atlas of the World (1990)*

Major Seas of the World

Sea	Area (sq. km)	Average Depth (metres)	Sea	Area (sq. km)	Average Depth (metres)
South China	2 974 600	1 464	Sea of Japan	1 012 900	1 667
Caribbean	2 515 900	2 575	Hudson Bay	730 100	93
Mediterranean	2 510 000	1 501	East China	664 600	189
Bering	2 261 100	1 491	Andaman	564 900	1 118
Gulf of Mexico	1 507 600	1 615	Black	507 900	1 191
Sea of Okhotsk	1 392 100	973	Red	453 000	538

Source: *National Geographic Atlas of the World (1990)*

Largest Lakes of the World

Lake	Location	Area sq. mi.	Area sq. km
Caspian (Sea)	Iran/Caspian Sea, Russian Fed., Kazakhstan, Turkmenistan, Iran, Azerbaijan	146 100	378 400
Superior	Canada/U.S.	31 760	82 260
Aral (Sea)	Kazakhstan-Uzbekistan	24 750	64 100
Victoria	Kenya/Tanzania/Uganda	24 300	62 940
Huron	Canada/U.S.	23 000	59 580
Michigan	U.S.	22 400	58 020
20 Tanganyika	Burundi/Tanzania/Zaire/Zambia	12 350	32 000
Baykal	Russia	12 160	31 500
Great Bear	**NWT, Canada**	**12 030**	**31 150**
Great Slave	**NWT, Canada**	**11 030**	**28 570**

Source: *World Facts and Figures, 1989; Victor Showers; John Wiley & Sons, Inc.*

Major Islands of the World

Island	Area (sq. km)	Island	Area (sq. km)
Greenland (Denmark)	2 175 600	Sumatra (Indonesia)	427 300
New Guinea (independent)	792 500	Honshu (Japan)	227 400
Borneo (Indonesia)	725 500	Great Britain (independent)	218 100
Madagascar (independent)	587 000	**Victoria (Canada)**	**217 300**
Baffin (Canada)	**507 500**	**Ellesmere (Canada)**	**196 200**

Source: *National Geographic Atlas of the World (1990)*

Highest Waterfalls in the World

Fall/Country	Height[1] (m)	Fall/Country	Height[1] (m)
Angel, Venezuela	807	Pilao, Brazil	524
Monge, Norway	774	Montoya, Venezuela	505
Itatinga, Brazil	628	Ribbon, United States	491
Ormeli, Norway	563	Great, Guyana	488
Tusse, Norway	533	Vestre Mardals, Norway	468

Source: *World Facts and Figures, 1989; Victor Showers; John Wiley & Sons Inc.*

(1) Height of the greatest individual leap.

Highest Mountains by Continent

Peak	Mountain Range or System	Location	Elevation[1] ft	Elevation[1] m	First Ascent
■ Africa					
Kibo	n.a.	Tanganyika, Tanzania	19 340	5 890	1889
Mawensi	n.a.	Tanganyika, Tanzania	17 100	5 210	1912
Batian	n.a.	Kenya	17 050	5 200	1899
Nelion	n.a.	Kenya	17 020	5 190	1929
Margherita	Ruwenzori	Uganda/D. Rep. of Congo	16 760	5 110	1906
Alexandra	Ruwenzori	Uganda/D. Rep. of Congo	16 700	5 090	1906
Albert	Ruwenzori	Dem. Rep. of Congo	16 690	5 090	1932
Savoia	Ruwenzori	Uganda	16 330	4 980	1906
Elena	Ruwenzori	Uganda	16 300	4 970	1906
Elizabeth	Ruwenzori	Uganda	16 170	4 930	1953
■ Antarctica					
—	Sentinel	Antarctica	16 860	5140	1966
Tyree	Sentinel	Antarctica	16 290	4970	1967
Shinn	Sentinel	Antarctica	15 750	4800	1966
Gardner	Sentinel	Antarctica	15 370	4690	1966
Epperly	Sentinel	Antarctica	15 100	4600	n.a.
Kirkpatrick	Queen Alexandra	Antarctica	14 850	4530	n.a.
Elizabeth	Queen Alexandra	Antarctica	14 700	4480	n.a.
Markham	Queen Elizabeth	Antarctica	14 290	4360	n.a.
Bell	Queen Alexandra	Antarctica	14 120	4300	n.a.
Mackellar	Queen Alexandra	Antarctica	14 100	4300	n.a.
■ Asia					
Everest (alt Qomolangma, Chumulangma)	Nepal Himalaya	China/Nepal	29 030	8 850	1953
K2 (alt Chogori, Dapsang, Godwin Austen	Karakoram	Pakistan-held Kashmir	28 250	8 610	1954
Kangchenjunga (alt Kanchenjunga): highest peak	Nepal Himalaya	India/Nepal	28 170	8 590	1955
Lhotse (alt E1, Luozi, Lotzu)	Nepal Himalaya	China/Nepal	27 890	8 500	1956
Kangchenjunga: S peak	Nepal Himalaya	India/Nepal	27 800	8 470	n.a.
Makalu I	Nepal Himalaya	China/Nepal	27 790	8 470	1955
Kangchenjunga: W peak	Nepal Himalaya	India/Nepal	27 620	8 420	1973
Lhotse Shar (alt Lhotse: E peak)	Nepal Himalaya	China/Nepal	27 500	8 380	1970
Dhaulagiri I (alt Daulagiri I)	Nepal Himalaya	Nepal	26 810	8 170	1960
Cho Oyu (alt Zhuoaoyu, Choaoyu): highest peak	Nepal Himalaya	China/Nepal	26 750	8 150	1954
■ Europe					
Elbrus (for Elborus): W peak	Caucasus (off Kavkaz)	Russia	18 480	5630	1874
Elbrus: E peak	Caucasus	Russia	18 360	5 590	1829
Shkhara: E peak	Caucasus	Georgia/Russia	17 060	5 200	1888
Dykh(-Tau): W peak	Caucasus	Russia	17 050	5 200	1888
Dykh(-Tau): E peak	Caucasus	Russia	16 900	5 150	1938
Koshtan(-Tau)	Caucasus	Russia	16 880	5 140	1888
Shkhara: W peak	Caucasus	Georgia/Russia	16 880	5 140	n.a.
Pushkina	Caucasus	Russia	16 730	5 100	1938
Dzhangi(-Tau): NW peak	Caucasus	Georgia	16 570	5 050	1903
Kazbek: E peak	Caucasus	Georgia	16 560	5 050	1868 ▶

▶ ■ **North America**

McKinley: S peak	Alaska	Alaska, U.S.	20 320	6 190	1913
Logan: central peak	Saint Elias	Yukon, Canada	19 520	5 959	1925
Logan: W peak	Saint Elias	Yukon, Canada	19 470	5 930	1925
McKinley: N peak	Alaska	Alaska, U.S.	19 470	5 930	1910
Logan: E peak	Saint Elias	Yukon, Canada	19 420	5 920	1957
Citlaltepetl (alt Orizaba)	Neovolcanica	Puebla-Veracruz, Mexico	18 410	5 610	1848
Logan: N peak	Saint Elias	Yukon, Canada	18 270	5 570	1959
Saint Elias	Saint Elias	Canada/U.S.	18 010	5 490	1897
Popocatepetl	Neovolcanica	Puebla, Mexico	17 930	5 460	1520
Foraker	Alaska	Alaska, U.S.	17 400	5 300	1934

■ **Oceania**

Jaya (for Carstensz, Djaja, Sukarno)	Sudirman (for Nassau)	Irian Jaya, Indonesia	16 500	5 030	1936
Daam	Jayawijaya (for Djajawidjaja, Orange)	Irian Jaya, Indonesia	16 150	4 920	n.a.
Pilimsit (for Idenburg)	Sudirman	Irian Jaya, Indonesia	15 750	4 800	1962
Trikora (for Wilhelmina)	Jayawijaya	Irian Jaya, Indonesia	15 580	4 750	1913
Mandala (for Juliana)	Jayawijaya	Irian Jaya, Indonesia	15 420	4 700	1959
Wilhelm	Bismarck	Papua New Guinea	15 400	4 690	n.a.
Wisnumurti (for Jan Pieterszoon Coen)	Jayawijaya	Irian Jaya, Indonesia	15 080	4 590	n.a.
Yamin (for Prins Hendrik)	Jayawijaya	Irian Jaya, Indonesia	14 860	4 530	n.a.
Kubor	Kubor	Papua New Guinea	14 300	4 360	n.a.
Herbert	Bismarck	Papua New Guinea	14 000	4 270	n.a.

■ **South America**

Aconcagua	Andes	Mendoza, Argentina	22 840	6 960	1897
Ojos del Salado: SE peak	Andes	Argentina/Chile	22 560	6 870	1937
Bonete	Andes	La Rioja, Argentina	22 550	6 870	1913
Pissis	Andes	Catamarca, La Rioja, Argentina	22 240	6 780	1937
Huascaran: S peak	Blanca (Andes)	Peru	22 210	6 770	1932
Mercedario	Andes	San Juan, Argentina	22 210	6 770	1934
Llullaillaco	Andes	Argentina/Chile	22 100[1]	6 730	bef 1550
Libertador (for Cachi: N peak)	Andes	Salta, Argentina	22 050	6 720	1950
Ojos del Salado: NW peak	Andes	Argentina/Chile	22 050	6 720	1937
Tupungato	Andes	Argentina/Chile	21 900	6 670	1897

Source: *World Facts and Figures, 1989; Victor Showers; John Wiley & Sons, Inc.*

(1) Rounded figures except from some Canadian peaks from Energy, Mines and Resources Canada. n.a. not available or not applicable.

Longest Rivers in the World

		Length	
River	**Outflow and Location**	**mi.**	**km**
Nile-Kagera-Ruvuvu-Luvironza...................	Mediterranean Sea, Egypt	4 140	6 670
Amazon-Ucayali-Tambo-Ene-Apurimac	Atlantic Ocean, Amapa-Para, Brazil	4 080	6 570
Yangtze.............................	East China Sea, Jiangsu, China	3 720	5 980
Mississippi-Missouri-Jefferson-Beaverhead-Red Rock	Gulf of Mexico, Louisiana, U.S.	3 710	5 970
Yenisey-Angara-Selenga-Ider......................	Yenisey Gulf of Kara Sea, Russia	3 650	5 870
Amur-Argun-Kerulen	Tatar Strait, Russia	3 590	5 780
Ob-Irtysh	Gulf of Ob of Kara Sea, Russia	3 360	5 410
Plata-Parana-Grande	Atlantic Ocean, Argentina-Uruguay	3 030	4 880
Huang	Gulf of Chihli of Yellow Sea, Shandong, China	3 010	4 840
Congo-Lualaba	Atlantic Ocean, Angola-Dem. Rep. of Congo	2 880	4 630

Source: *World Facts and Figures, 1989; Victor Showers; John Wiley & Sons, Inc.*

WORLD POPULATION

The 30 Largest Countries by Population, 1950

(millions)

Rank	Country	Population	Rank	Country	Population
1	China	555	16	Viet Nam	30
2	India	358	17	Spain	28
3	United States of America	158	18	Mexico	28
4	Russian Federation	102	19	Poland	25
5	Japan	84	20	Egypt	22
6	Indonesia	80	21	Philippines	21
7	Germany	68	22	Turkey	21
8	Brazil	54	23	Republic of Korea	20
9	United Kingdom	51	24	Thailand	20
10	Italy	47	25	Ethiopia	18
11	France	42	26	Myanmar	18
12	Bangladesh	42	27	Argentina	17
13	Pakistan	40	28	Iran (Islamic Republic of)	17
14	Ukraine	37	29	Romania	16
15	Nigeria	33	**30**	**Canada**	**14**

Source: *World Population Prospects: The 1996 Revision, Population Division of the United Nations*

The 30 Largest Countries by Population, 2001

(millions)

Rank	Country	Population	Rank	Country	Population
1	China (mainland)	1 273.3	16	Turkey	66.3
2	India	1 033.0	17	Iran	66.1
3	United States	284.5	18	Ethiopia	65.4
4	Indonesia	206.1	19	Thailand	62.4
5	Brazil	171.8	20	United Kingdom	60.0
6	Pakistan	145.0	21	France	59.2
7	Russia	144.4	22	Italy	57.8
8	Bangladesh	133.5	23	Democratic Republic of the Congo	53.6
9	Japan	127.1	24	Ukraine	49.1
10	Nigeria	126.6	25	South Korea	48.8
11	Mexico	99.6	26	Myanmar	47.8
12	Germany	82.2	27	South Africa	43.6
13	Vietnam	78.7	28	Colombia	43.1
14	Philippines	77.2	29	Spain	39.8
15	Egypt	69.8	30	Poland	38.6

Source: *Based on UN Population Reference Bureau Data Sheet*

The 30 Largest Countries by Population, 2050 (projection)

(millions)

Rank	Country	Population	Rank	Country	Population
1	India	1 363.0	16	Iran	88.4
2	China (mainland)	1 431.0	17	Turkey	85.2
3	United States	346.0	18	Tanzania	59.8
4	Pakistan	251.9	19	Uganda	48.0
5	Indonesia	272.0	20	Thailand	72.1
6	Nigeria	204.5	21	Colombia	59.7
7	Brazil	219.0	22	Yemen	39.6
8	Bangladesh	180.5	23	Germany	80.0
9	Democratic Republic of the Congo	106.0	24	Myanmar	60.2
10	Ethiopia	117.6	25	Afghanistan	45.9
11	Mexico	130.9	26	France	64.2
12	Philippines	107.8	27	United Kingdom	64.1
13	Russia	136.9	28	Sudan	49.6
14	Vietnam	104.1	29	Saudi Arabia	40.9
15	Egypt	96.2	30	Argentina	47.2

Source: *Based on UN Population Reference Bureau Data Sheet*

Population Projections by Region and for Selected Countries

(millions)

Region and Country	2025	2050	Region and Country	2025	2050
WORLD TOTAL	7 818	9 036	Gabon	1.4	1.8
More Developed[1]	1 248	1 242	Sao Tome and Principe	0.3	0.5
Less Developed[2]	6 570	7 794	**Southern Africa**	42	41
AFRICA	1 268	1 800	Botswana	1.2	1.2
Sub-Saharan Africa	1 067	1 560	Lesotho	2.4	2.8
Northern Africa	251	304	Namibia	2	2.5
Algeria	43.2	51.5	South Africa	35.1	32.5
Egypt	96.2	114.7	Swaziland	1.4	2
Libya	8.3	10.8	**NORTH AMERICA**	382	450
Morocco	40.5	48.4	Canada	36	36.6
Sudan	49.6	63.5	United States	346	413.5
Tunisia	12.5	14.2	**LATIN AMERICA AND THE CARIBBEAN**	697	815
Western Sahara	0.4	0.6	**Central America**	190	228
Western Africa	393	581	Belize	0.4	0.6
Benin	11.7	18.1	Costa Rica	5	5.6
Burkina Faso	21.6	34.3	El Salvador	9.3	12.4
Cape Verde	0.5	0.4	Guatemala	22.1	31.5
Côte d'Ivoire	25.6	35.7	Honduras	9.8	12.2
Gambia	2.7	4.2	Mexico	130.9	149.7
Ghana	26.5	32	Nicaragua	8.6	11.6
Guinea	12.6	18.1	Panama	3.8	4.3
Guinea-Bissau	2.2	3.3	**Caribbean**	46	50
Liberia	6	10	Antigua and Barbuda	0.1	0.1
Mali	21.6	36.4	Bahamas	0.4	0.5
Mauritania	5.4	8.5	Barbados	0.3	0.3
Niger	18.8	28.5	Cuba	11.9	11
Nigeria	204.5	303.6	Dominica	0.1	0.1
Senegal	16.5	22.7	Dominican Republic	12.1	14.9
Sierra Leone	9.9	15.7	Grenada	0.1	0.1
Togo	7.6	9.7	Guadeloupe	0.5	0.6
Eastern Africa	398	574	Haiti	9.6	11.9
Burundi	10.5	16.1	Jamaica	3.3	3.9
Comoros	1.1	1.8	Martinique	0.4	0.4
Djibouti	0.8	1.1	Netherlands Antilles	0.2	0.3
Eritrea	8.3	13.3	Puerto Rico	4.2	4.2
Ethiopia	117.6	172.7	St. Kitts-Nevis	0.05	0.1
Kenya	33.3	37.4	Saint Lucia	0.2	0.2
Madagascar	30.8	47	St. Vincent and the Grenadines	0.1	0.1
Malawi	17.1	22.2	Trinidad and Tobago	1.4	1.4
Mauritius	1.4	1.5	**SOUTH AMERICA**	462	537
Mayotte	0.4	0.6	Argentina	47.2	54.5
Mozambique	21.6	22.9	Bolivia	13.2	17.1
Reunion	0.9	1	Brazil	219	247.2
Rwanda	8	8.9	Chile	18.6	19.3
Seychelles	0.1	0.1	Colombia	59.7	71.5
Somalia	14.9	25.5	Ecuador	18.7	24.7
Tanzania	59.8	88.3	French Guiana	0.3	0.4
Uganda	48	84.1	Guyana	0.6	0.5
Zambia	14.3	20.3	Paraguay	9.7	14.4
Zimbabwe	9.5	9.3	Peru	35.5	42.3
Middle Africa	183	300	Suriname	0.5	0.4
Angola	20.5	29.6	Uruguay	4	4.5
Cameroon	24.7	34.7	Venezuela	34.8	40.2
Central African Republic	4.9	6.4	**ASIA**	4 714	5 262
Chad	18.2	33.3	**Asia (Excl. China)**	3 283	3 893
Congo	6.3	10.7	**Western Asia**	299	400
Congo, Dem. Rep. of	106	181.9	Armenia	4.1	3.8
Equatorial Guinea	0.9	1.4	Azerbaijan	9.8	11.5

▶ Bahrain	1.7	2.9
Cyprus	1	1
Georgia	4.8	4.2
Iraq	40.3	53.6
Israel	8.9	10.6
Jordan	8.7	11.8
Kuwait	4.2	6.4
Lebanon	5.4	5.8
Oman	4.9	7.6
Palestinian Territory	7.4	11.2
Qatar	0.8	0.9
Saudi Arabia	40.9	60.3
Syria	27.1	35.2
Turkey	85.2	97.2
United Arab Emirates	4.5	5.1
Yemen	39.6	71.1
South Central Asia	**2 061**	**2 503**
Afghanistan	45.9	67.2
Bangladesh	180.5	208.6
Bhutan	1.4	2
India	1 363.00	1 628.00
Iran	88.4	100.2
Kazakhstan	14.7	14
Kyrgyzstan	6.5	7.5
Maldives	0.5	0.8
Nepal	37	49.5
Pakistan	251.9	345.4
Sri Lanka	22.7	23.2
Tajikistan	7.7	8.7
Turkmenistan	6.5	7
Uzbekistan	34.1	40.4
Southeast Asia	**685**	**775**
Brunei	0.5	0.6
Cambodia	16.4	18.1
East Timor	1.2	1.4
Indonesia	272	304.8
Laos	9	9.2
Malaysia	33.7	43.9
Myanmar	60.2	68.5
Philippines	107.8	129.2
Singapore	8	10.4
Thailand	72.1	71.9
Vietnam	104.1	117.2
East Asia	**1 669**	**1 584**
China	1 431.00	1 369.00
China, Hong Kong SAR[3]	8.4	7.4
China, Macao SAR[3]	0.6	0.8
Japan	120.9	100.5
Korea, North	25.7	26.4
Korea, South	53.3	51.1
Mongolia	3.4	3.9
Taiwan	25.2	25.2
EUROPE	**717**	**662**
Northern Europe	**102**	**101**
Denmark	5.8	6.2
Estonia	1.2	0.9
Finland	5.3	4.8
Iceland	0.3	0.3
Ireland	4.5	4.5
Latvia	2.2	1.8
Lithuania	3.5	3.1
Norway	5	5.2
Sweden	9.4	9.5
United Kingdom	64.1	64.2
Western Europe	**189**	**180**
Austria	8.3	8.2
Belgium	10.3	10
France	64.2	65.1
Germany	80	70.3
Liechtenstein	0.04	0.04
Luxembourg	0.6	0.6
Monaco	0.04	0.04
Netherlands	17.7	18
Switzerland	7.6	7.4
Eastern Europe	**287**	**259**
Belarus	9.4	8.5
Bulgaria	6.6	5.3
Czech Republic	10.3	9.4
Hungary	9.2	8
Moldova	4.5	4.2
Poland	38.6	33.9
Romania	21.6	19.3
Russia	136.9	127.7
Slovakia	5.2	4.7
Ukraine	45.1	38.4
Southern Europe	**139**	**122**
Albania	4.5	5.2
Andorra	0.1	0.1
Bosnia-Herzegovina	3.6	3.4
Croatia	4.4	3.9
Greece	10.4	9.7
Italy	55	46
Macedonia[4]	2.2	2.1
Malta	0.4	0.4
Portugal	9.3	8.2
San Marino	0.03	0.03
Slovenia	2	1.7
Spain	36.7	30.8
Yugoslavia	10.7	10.2
OCEANIA	**40**	**46**
Australia	23.2	25
Federated States of Micronesia	0.2	0.2
Fiji	1	0.9
French Polynesia	0.3	0.4
Guam	0.2	0.3
Kiribati	0.2	0.2
Marshall Islands	0.2	0.3
Nauru	0.02	0.02
New Caledonia	0.3	0.3
New Zealand	4.6	5
Palau	0.03	0.03
Papua-New Guinea	8.3	11.3
Solomon Islands	0.9	1.5
Tonga	0.2	0.2
Tuvalu	0.02	0.02
Vanuatu	0.3	0.3
Western Samoa	0.2	0.2

Source: © *United Nations Population Reference Bureau*
(1) More developed regions comprise Northern America, Japan, Europe, Australia-New Zealand. (2) Less developed regions comprise all regions of Africa, Latin America, Asia (excluding Japan), and Melanesia, Micronesia and Polynesia. (3) Special Administrative Region. (4) The former Yugoslav Republic.

United Nations

The first United Nations declaration was signed by 22 Allied governments on Jan. 1, 1942, and was an alliance against Germany, Italy and Japan. This anti-Axis coalition was converted into an international body in 1945 when 51 nations signed a United Nations Charter to form an organization that would "save succeeding generations from the scourge of war." The Charter was drawn up at the Conference on International Organization held in San Francisco from Apr. 25 to June 26, 1945, and took effect Oct. 24, 1945. UN membership has since grown to 189.

The UN has six parts, with the General Assembly—the central organ—acting as the main deliberative body. General Assembly meetings have been held at UN Headquarters in New York since 1946. The International Court of Justice in The Hague, Netherlands, is the only major UN organ not based in New York. Specialized agencies are located throughout the world.

General information on the UN may be requested from the Public Inquiries Unit, Dept. of Public Information, Room GA-057A, United Nations, New York, NY 10017; or the United Nations Association in Canada, 900-130 Slater St., Ottawa, Ont., K1P 6E2, or obtained from the UN website at http://www.un.org

■ Structure of the United Nations

General Assembly The General Assembly is the UN's forum for discussing issues, reviewing UN activities and setting the agenda for initiatives. All member states are represented, and each is entitled to one vote. Resolutions require a majority vote before adoption. A president, 21 vice-presidents and six committee chairs head the Assembly, which sits from mid-September to mid-December or as required for the rest of the year. The six committees study issues relating to: disarmament and security; economy and finance; social, humanitarian and cultural issues; UN administrative and budgetary matters; legal issues; and political and security issues and report back to a plenary session of the Assembly.

The General Assembly sets UN policies, admits new members on recommendation of the Security Council, approves the budget and receives reports from all other UN bodies.

Security Council The Security Council has the power to act for the maintenance of peace and security. It can enforce military action or economic sanctions, and it can send peace-keeping units (the Blue Berets) to troubled areas. The Security Council may also try to negotiate a ceasefire in the case of conflicts.

The Council has 15 members, five permanent and 10 elected by the General Assembly for two-year terms. Decisions require nine affirmative votes, but all permanent members have the right to veto. The permanent members are: China, France, the United Kingdom, the United States and the Russian Federation. Canada served its sixth term as a non-permanent member of the Council (from Jan. 1, 1999 to Dec. 31, 2000). The Security Council is permanently in session and representatives are on call 24 hours a day.

Economic and Social Council The Economic and Social Council co-ordinates the economic and social work of the UN and its related agencies. The Council's 54 members hold two month-long sessions each year: one in New York, the other in Geneva. Each member is elected by the General Assembly for a three-year term.

Trusteeship Council The council, created to oversee the independence of trust territories, is now in abeyance.

International Court of Justice (World Court) The Security Council elects 15 judges to the Court for nine-year terms. No two members may be from the same nation. The Court, located in The Hague, only sits in judgement on disputes between states. Both member and non-member states may submit grievances (border disputes, resource access, breach of treaty, etc.).

Countries can opt out of any proceeding, unless required to participate by treaty provisions. But after agreeing to become a party in a case, a nation must comply with the Court's decision, enforced by the Security Council.

Secretariat The Secretariat administers the programs and policies laid out by other UN bodies. The Secretary General is the Chief Administrative Officer of the Secretariat, which administers the work of the UN as directed by the General Assembly, Security Council and other organs.

Glossary of United Nations Acronyms

FAO: Food and Agriculture Organization

IAEA: International Atomic Energy Agency

IBRD: International Bank for Reconstruction and Development

ICAO: International Civil Aviation Organization

IDA: International Development Association

IFAD: International Fund for Agricultural Development

IFC: International Finance Corporation

ILO: International Labour Organization

IMF: International Monetary Fund

INSTRAW: International Research and Training Institute for the Advancement of Women

ITU: International Telecommunications Union

MICAH: International Civilian Support Mission in Haiti

MINUGUA: United Nations Mission for the Verification of Human Rights in Guatemala

MINURSO: United Nations Mission for the Referendum in Western Sahara

MONUC: United Nations Mission in the Democratic Republic of the Congo

UNAMSIL: United Nations Mission in Sierra Leone

UNCHS/HABITAT: United Nations Centre for Human Settlements

UNCTAD: United Nations Conference on Trade and Development

UNDOF: United Nations Disengagement Observer Force

UNDP: United Nations Development Programme

UNEP: United Nations Environment Programme

UNESCO: United Nations Educational, Scientific and Cultural Organization

UNFICYP: United Nations Peacekeeping Force in Cyprus

UNFPA: United Nations Population Fund

UNHCR: Office of the United Nations High Commissioner for Refugees

UNICEF: United Nations Children's Fund

UNIDO: United Nations Industrial Development Organization

UNIFIL: United Nations Interim Force in Lebanon

UNIKOM: United Nations Iraq-Kuwait Observation Mission

UNITAR: United Nations Institute for Training and Research

UNMEE: United Nations Mission in Ethiopia and Eritrea

UNMIBH: United Nations Mission in Bosnia and Herzegovina

UNMIK: United Nations Interim Administration Mission in Kosovo

UNMOGIP: United Nations Military Observer Group in India and Pakistan

UNMOP: United Nations Mission of Observers in Prevlaka

UNOCHA: United Nations Office for the Coordination of Humanitarian Affairs

UNOMIG: United Nations Mission of Observers in Georgia

UNRWA: United Nations Relief and Works Agency for Palestine Refugees in the Near East

UNSMIH: United Nations Support Mission in Haiti

UNTAET: United Nations Transitional Administration in East Timor

UNTSO: United Nations Truce Supervision Organization

UNU: United Nations University

UNV: United Nations Volunteers

UPU: Universal Postal Union

WFP: World Food Programme

WHO: World Health Organization

WIPO: World Intellectual Property Organization

WMO: World Meteorological Organization

WTO: World Trade Organization (formerly General Agreement on Tariffs and Trade)

■ Functional Commissions

Commission for Social Development

Commission of Sustainable Development

Commission on Human Rights

Commission on Narcotic Drugs

Commission on the Status of Women

Population Commission

Statistical Commission

■ Regional Commissions

ECA: Economic Commission for Africa

ECE: Economic Commission for Europe

ECLAC: Economic Commission for Latin America and the Caribbean

ESCAP: Economic and Social Commission for Asia and the Pacific

ESCWA: Economic and Social Commission for Western Asia

The United Nations System

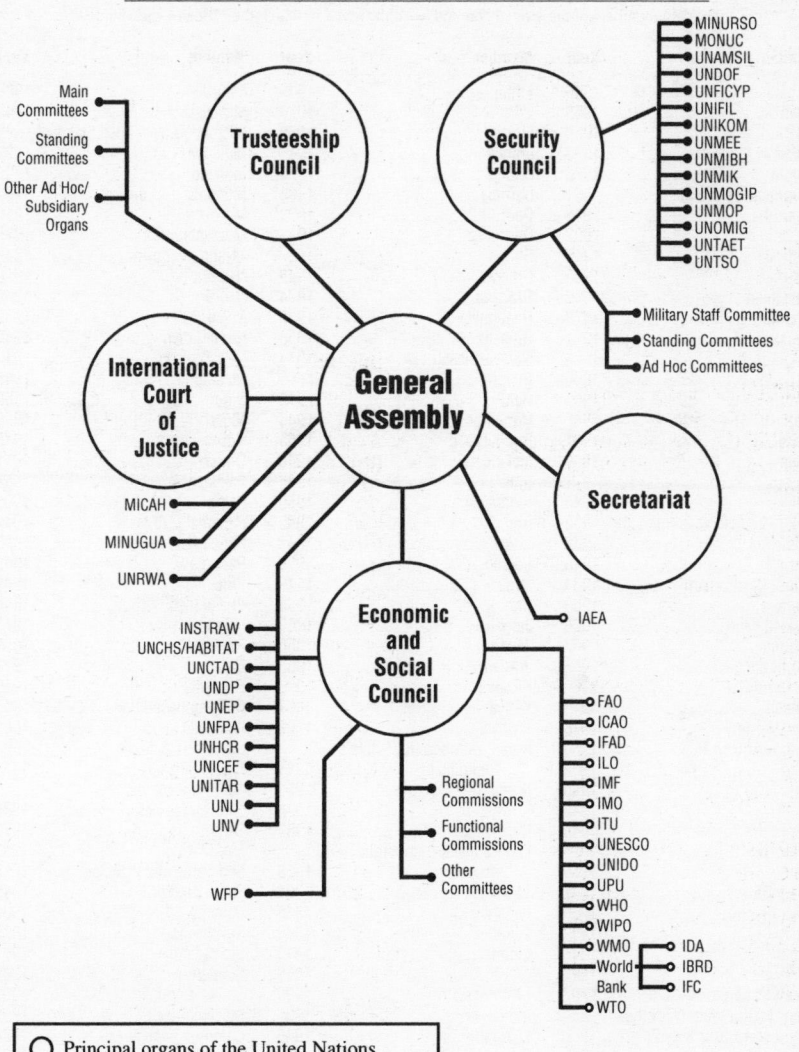

Trusteeship Council

Security Council

- MINURSO
- MONUC
- UNAMSIL
- UNDOF
- UNFICYP
- UNIFIL
- UNIKOM
- UNMEE
- UNMIBH
- UNMIK
- UNMOGIP
- UNMOP
- UNOMIG
- UNTAET
- UNTSO

Main Committees
Standing Committees
Other Ad Hoc/ Subsidiary Organs

- Military Staff Committee
- Standing Committees
- Ad Hoc Committees

International Court of Justice

General Assembly

Secretariat

MICAH
MINUGUA
UNRWA

IAEA

INSTRAW
UNCHS/HABITAT
UNCTAD
UNDP
UNEP
UNFPA
UNHCR
UNICEF
UNITAR
UNU
UNV

Economic and Social Council

Regional Commissions
Functional Commissions
Other Committees

WFP

- FAO
- ICAO
- IFAD
- ILO
- IMF
- IMO
- ITU
- UNESCO
- UNIDO
- UPU
- WHO
- WIPO
- WMO
- World Bank
- WTO

- IDA
- IBRD
- IFC

○ Principal organs of the United Nations

• United Nations programmes and organs

○ Specialized agencies and other autonomous organizations within the system

N.B. The establishment of an International Criminal Court was approved in July 1998 at a UN conference but has yet to be ratified and therefore is not included on this chart.

United Nations Association in Canada – August 2001

Roster of the United Nations

(As of October 2001)

The 189 members of the United Nations, with the years in which they became members.

Member	Year	Member	Year	Member	Year
Afghanistan	1946	Ethiopia	1945	Mauritius	1968
Albania	1955	Fiji	1970	Mexico	1945
Algeria	1962	Finland	1955	Micronesia, Federated States of	1991
Andorra	1993	France	1945	Moldova	1992
Angola	1976	Gabon	1960	Monaco	1993
Antigua and Barbuda	1981	Gambia	1965	Mongolia	1961
Argentina	1945	Georgia	1992	Morocco	1956
Armenia	1992	Germany	1973	Mozambique	1975
Australia	1945	Ghana	1957	Myanmar (Burma)	1948
Austria	1955	Greece	1945	Namibia	1990
Azerbaijan	1992	Grenada	1974	Nauru	1999
Bahamas	1973	Guatemala	1945	Nepal	1955
Bahrain	1971	Guinea	1958	Netherlands	1945
Bangladesh	1974	Guinea-Bissau	1974	New Zealand	1945
Barbados	1966	Guyana	1966	Nicaragua	1945
Belarus	1945	Haiti	1945	Niger	1960
Belgium	1945	Honduras	1945	Nigeria	1960
Belize	1981	Hungary	1955	Norway	1945
Benin	1960	Iceland	1946	Oman	1971
Bhutan	1971	India	1945	Pakistan	1947
Bolivia	1945	Indonesia	1950	Palau	1995
Bosnia and Herzegovina	1992	Iran	1945	Panama	1945
Botswana	1966	Iraq	1945	Papua New Guinea	1975
Brazil	1945	Ireland	1955	Paraguay	1945
Brunei Darussalam	1984	Israel	1949	Peru	1945
Bulgaria	1955	Italy	1955	Philippines	1945
Burkina Faso	1960	Jamaica	1962	Poland	1945
Burundi	1962	Japan	1956	Portugal	1955
Cambodia	1955	Jordan	1955	Qatar	1971
Cameroon	1960	Kazakhstan	1992	Romania	1955
Canada	1945	Kenya	1963	Russian Federation	1945
Cape Verde	1975	Kiribati	1999	Rwanda	1962
Central African Rep.	1960	Korea, Democratic People's		Saint Kitts & Nevis	1983
Chad	1960	Republic of	1991	Saint Lucia	1979
Chile	1945	Korea, Republic of	1991	Saint Vincent and the	
China	1945	Kuwait	1963	Grenadines	1980
Colombia	1945	Kyrgyzstan	1992	Samoa	1976
Comoros	1975	Lao People's Democratic		San Marino	1992
Congo	1960	Republic	1955	Sao Tome and Principe	1975
Costa Rica	1945	Latvia	1991	Saudi Arabia	1945
Côte d'Ivoire	1960	Lebanon	1945	Senegal	1960
Croatia	1992	Lesotho	1966	Seychelles	1976
Cuba	1945	Liberia	1945	Sierra Leone	1961
Cyprus	1960	Libya	1955	Singapore	1965
Czech Republic	1993	Liechtenstein	1990	Slovak Republic	1993
Democratic Republic of the		Lithuania	1991	Slovenia	1992
Congo (formerly Zaïre)	1960	Luxembourg	1945	Solomon Islands	1978
Denmark	1945	Macedonia, Former Yugoslav		Somalia	1960
Djibouti	1977	Republic of	1993	South Africa	1945
Dominica	1978	Madagascar	1960	Spain	1955
Dominican Rep.	1945	Malawi	1964	Sri Lanka	1955
Ecuador	1945	Malaysia	1957	Sudan	1956
Egypt	1945	Maldives	1965	Suriname	1975
El Salvador	1945	Mali	1960	Swaziland	1968
Equatorial Guinea	1968	Malta	1964	Sweden	1946
Eritrea	1993	Marshall Islands	1991	Syria	1945
Estonia	1991	Mauritania	1961	Tajikistan	1992

Member	Year	Member	Year	Member	Year
Tanzania, United Rep. of	1961	Tuvalu	2000	Vanuatu	1981
Thailand	1946	Uganda	1962	Vietnam	1977
Togo	1960	Ukraine	1945	Venezuela	1945
Tonga	1999	United Arab Emirates	1971	Yemen	1947
Trinidad & Tobago	1962	United Kingdom	1945	Yugoslavia, Federal Republic of,	
Tunisia	1956	United States of America	1945	(Serbia and Montenegro)	1945
Turkey	1945	Uruguay	1945	Zambia	1964
Turkmenistan	1992	Uzbekistan	1992	Zimbabwe	1980

Source: *United Nations Association   http://www.un.org*

United Nations Secretaries-General

The Secretary-General, heading the Secretariat, is responsible for the UN's administration and for alerting the Security Council to any threats to international peace and security, and acts as spokesperson for the UN. The Secretary-General is elected by the General Assembly on the recommendation of the Security Council and cannot be from one of the five permanent members of the Security Council.

Secretary, Nation	Date Installed
Trygve Lie, Norway	Feb. 1946
Dag Hammarskjold, Sweden	Apr. 1953
U Thant, Burma	Nov. 1961
Kurt Waldheim, Austria	Dec. 1971

Secretary, Nation	Date Installed
Javier Perez de Cuellar, Peru	Dec. 1981
Boutros Boutros-Ghali, Egypt	Jan. 1992
Kofi Annan, Ghana	Jan. 1997
	(to Dec. 31, 2006)

Source: *United Nations Association*

Canadian Ambassadors to the United Nations

Ambassador	Date Appointed
Andrew McNaughton	Jan. 1948
John Holmes	Jan. 1950
Gerald Riddell	June 1950
David Johnson	Oct. 1951
Robert MacKay	June 1955
Charles Ritchie	Nov. 1957
Paul Tremblay	May 1962
George Ignatieff	Mar. 1966
Yvon Beaulne	Jan. 1969

Ambassador	Date Appointed
Saul Forbes Rae	June 1972
William Barton	May 1976
Michel Dupuy	Mar. 1980
Gérard Pelletier	Aug. 1981
Stephen H. Lewis	Oct. 1984
Yves Fortier	July 1988
Louise Fréchette	Jan. 1992
Robert K. Fowler	Jan. 1995
Paul Heinbecker	June 2000

Source: *Dept. of Foreign Affairs*

Seeking Canadian Consular Help Abroad

While travelling outside Canada, you might need aid. Canada keeps more than 270 offices worldwide where consular officials can help.

Consular officials can replace passports; advise you on getting visas and information about local laws and customs; contact your relatives or friends to ask for emergency funds; and help during natural disasters, medical crises and civil uprisings.

If you are arrested, consular officials can tell your relatives or friends and try to ensure fair treatment under local laws. Consular officials can also tell your family about accidents or deaths.

There may be a fee for service.

Wide demand has led to the restriction of these services: transferring funds or paying local bills; storing personal items; searching for lost items; aiding job searches; getting visas; and getting local licences.

Canadian government offices abroad offer 24-hour help; during non-office hours, your phone calls go to an officer in Ottawa. You may also call (collect) the Department of Foreign Affairs and International Trade at (613) 996-8885.

Other International Organizations in the News

Arab League
(also known as League of Arab States)
Midan Attahrir, Tahrir Square,
P.O. Box 11642, Cairo, Egypt
Website: http://www.leagueofarabstates.org
Established: 22 March 1945
Aim: to promote economic, social, political, and military cooperation among member states
Members: (22) Algeria, Bahrain, Comoros, Djibouti, Egypt, Iraq, Jordan, Kuwait, Lebanon, Libya, Mauritania, Morocco, Oman, Palestine, Qatar, Saudi Arabia, Somalia, Sudan, Syria, Tunisia, United Arab Emirates, Yemen

Arctic Council
Arctic Council Secretariat
Ministry for Foreign Affairs
Unit for Northern Dimension
P.O. Box 176, FIN-00161 Helsinki
Finland
Website: http://www.arctic-council.org
Established: 19 September 1996
Aim: to promote sustainable development and environmental protection through circumpolar cooperation
Members: (8) Canada, Denmark-Greenland-Faroe Islands, Finland, Iceland, Norway, Russia, Sweden and the USA; plus 6 international aboriginal organizations with permanent participant status

Association of Southeast Asian Nations (ASEAN)
Jalan Sisingamangaraja 70A, Kebayoran Baru,
P.O. Box 2072, Jakarta 12110, Indonesia
Website: http://www.aseansec.org
Established: 9 August 1967
Aim: to encourage regional economic, social and cultural cooperation among member states
Members: (10) Brunei Darussalam, Cambodia, Indonesia, Laos, Malaysia, Myanmar, Philippines, Singapore, Thailand, Vietnam

Commonwealth
Commonwealth Secretariat, Marlborough House, Pall Mall, London SWIY 5HX, United Kingdom
Website:
http://www.thecommonwealth.org/home.htm
Established: 11 December 1931
Aim: to promote democracy and cooperation among former members of the British Empire.
Members: 54 including Canada

International Civil Aviation Organization (ICAO)
999 University St., Montreal QC H3C 5H7, Canada
Website: http://www.icao.int
Established: 7 December 1944
Aim: to promote international cooperation in civil aviation; a UN specialized agency
Members: 187 including Canada

International Criminal Police Organization (Interpol)
General Secretariat
200, quai Charles de Gaulle
69006 Lyon
France
Website: http://www.interpol.int
Established: 13 June 1956
Aim: to promote international cooperation among police authorities in fighting crime
Members: 178 countries including Canada

International Federation of Red Cross and Red Crescent Societies (formerly Red Cross)
P.O. Box 372, CH-1211, Geneva 19, Switzerland
Website: http://www.ifrc.org
Established: 1919
Aim: to promote humanitarianism, prepare for disaster relief, provide relief after disasters, and promote health in communities
Members: 176 national societies worldwide, including Canada

International Monetary Fund (IMF)
700 19th Street NW, Washington, DC 20431, USA
Website:
http://www.imf.org/external/index.htm
Established: 22 July 1944
Aim: to promote world monetary stability and economic development; a UN special-ized agency
Members: 183 including Canada

International Olympic Committee (IOC)
Chateau de Vidy, CP 356, 1007 Lausanne Switzerland
Website: http://www.olympic.org
Established: 23 June 1894
Aim: to promote the Olympic ideals and administer the Olympic games: 2002 Winter Olympics in Salt Lake City, United States;

2004 Summer Olympics in Athens, Greece
Members: 199 National Olympic Committees
including Canada

International Organization for Standardization (ISO)

CP 56, 1 rue de Varembe, CH-1211
Geneva 20, Switzerland
Website: http://www.iso.ch
Established: 23 February 1947
Aim: to promote the development of
international standards to aid the
international exchange of goods and services
Members: 92 member bodies, including
Canada; 37 correspondent members

International Organization of Francophones (also known as La Francophonie)

Cabinet du Secrétaire général de l'OIF
28, rue de Bourgogne
75007 Paris, France
Website: http://www.francophonie.org
Established: 20 March 1970
Aim: to promote peace, democracy and
French culture throughout the French-
speaking world
Members: 51 including Canada;
plus 4 observers

Inter-Parliamentary Union (IPU)

CP 438, 1211 Geneva 19, Switzerland
Website: http://www.ipu.org
Established: 30 June 1889
Aim: to promote dialogue and cooperation
among parliamentarians
Members: 141 national parliaments,
including Canada's; five associate
(international) parliaments

Liberal International

1 Whitehall Place, London SW1A 2HD
United Kingdom
Website: http://www.worldlib.org
Established: 10-14 April 1947
Aim: to strengthen ties among liberal parties
and governments worldwide
Members: 88 political parties, including
Canada's

Organization of African Unity (OAU)

P.O. Box 3243, Addis Ababa, Ethiopia
Website: http://www.oau-oua.org
Established: 25 May 1963
Aim: to promote the unity of African states,
defend members' sovereignty and coordinate
socio-economic policies
Members: 52 states plus Western Sahara

Organization of American States (OAS)

Corner of 17th St. and Constitution Ave.
NW, Washington, DC 20006, USA
Website: http://www.oas.org
Established: 30 April 1948
Aim: to promote regional peace and security
as well as economic and social development
Members: 35 including Canada; plus 50
observers including the European Union.
Cuba, although still a member of the OAS,
has been barred from participating by a
resolution passed in 1962.

Organization of Petroleum Exporting Countries (OPEC)

Obere Donaustrasse 93, A-1020 Vienna,
Austria
Website: http://www.opec.org
Established: 14 September 1960
Aim: to coordinate petroleum policies
Members: (11) Algeria, Indonesia, Iran, Iraq,
Kuwait, Libya, Nigeria, Qatar, Saudi Arabia,
United Arab Emirates, Venezuela

Socialist International

Maritime House, Old Town, Clapham, London
SW4 0JW United Kingdom
Website: http://www.socialistinternational.org
Established: 30 June–3 July 1951 (in its
present form)
Aim: to strengthen ties among social democratic,
socialist and labour parties
Members: 89 full member parties; 25 consul-
tative parties; plus other organizations

World Council of Churches (WCC)

P.O. Box 2100, 1211, Geneva 2, Switzerland
Website: http://www.wcc-coe.org
Established: 23 August 1948
Aim: to promote the visible unity of
Christianity
Members: 342 Christian churches in 120
countries including Canada

WWF-International

Avenue du Mont-Blanc, CH-1196, Gland,
Switzerland
Website: http:www.panda.org/home.cfm
Established: 11 September 1961
Aim: to save wildlife and their habitats from
extinction around the world
Members: offices in 40 countries including
Canada; five associate organizations

The European Union (EU)

The European Union (EU) represents a unique relationship among 15 democratic nations, with the aim of constructing a united Europe. The EU is more than an international organization but not a full-blown federation. It is the world's largest trading entity, accounting for well over 20 percent of world trade. Its population totals about 376 million people.

The European Union originated as the European Coal and Steel Community (ECSC). Formed in 1951 by France, West Germany, Italy, the Netherlands, Belgium and Luxembourg, it became operational in 1952.

The ECSC boosted internal trade in coal and steel by 129 percent in five years. Its success spurred the Six to apply the same approach to the entire economy. In 1957, the same six countries formed the European Economic Community (EEC), creating a common market for all sectors of the economy. The EEC committed the Six to dismantle trade barriers and to allow the free movement of goods, services, capital and people. At the same time, the Six formed the European Atomic Energy Community (Euratom) to further the use of nuclear energy for peaceful purposes.

In 1967, the institutions of the ECSC, Euratom and the EEC were merged. In 1973, Denmark, Ireland and the United Kingdom became members, as did Greece in 1981, Spain and Portugal in 1986 and Austria, Finland and Sweden in 1995.

From its inception, the European Community (EC) has tried to reduce the gap in living standards between the various Member States, supporting the poorer regions. To that end, the EC uses the following instruments: the European Regional Development Fund, the European Social Fund, the European Agricultural Guidance and Guarantee Fund and the Cohesion Fund.

Part of the Single European Act, which came into force in 1987, was the Europe 1992 project. This aimed at completing the common market and creating a single internal market by dismantling the remaining physical, technical and fiscal barriers among the Member States.

The Maastricht Treaty on European Union, signed in 1992, came into effect in November 1993. This Treaty created a European Union of three pillars. The first pillar is the European Community with its joint supranational institutions. The two new pillars are intergovernmental cooperation in foreign and security policy as well as intergovernmental cooperation in justice and home affairs. While this cooperation is intergovernmental, the European Commission is fully associated with all activities.

The Maastricht Treaty committed the Member States to create an economic and monetary Union, including the establishment of a European Central Bank in Frankfurt. In January 1999, the Euro was introduced as the new single European currency. In January 2002, the Euro coins and banknotes will be in circulation. The Treaty also committed the 15 to political union, by developing a common foreign and security policy.

The Treaty gave the regions a part to play in the Community by setting up a Committee of the Regions. It also introduced the principle of "subsidiarity," by which the EC deals only with matters it is better equipped to deal with than the Member States.

In 1997, the 15 agreed to revise the Maastricht Treaty by drawing up a new Treaty of Amsterdam. Coming into force in May 1999, the Treaty of Amsterdam contains four major objectives. They are to:
• put citizens' rights at the heart of the Union;
• ensure that citizens can move freely within the Union;
• strengthen the Union's objectives in foreign policy; and
• make the Union's institutions and decision-making process more effective.

At the European Council in Nice in December 2000, the Heads of State and Government of the 15 Member States concluded the Intergovernmental Conference on institutional reform by agreeing on the draft of a new treaty. This will amend the Maastricht Treaty on European Union, the Treaties establishing the European Communities and the Protocol on Enlargement of the European Union. The amendments will come into force when all the Member States ratify the Treaty of Nice in accordance with their respective constitutional rules.

The Treaty of Nice prepares the EU for the accession of countries that have applied for EU membership. The Treaty of Nice will allow qualified-majority voting for decisions on 30 articles of the Treaty that previously required unanimity, thus reducing the number of cases in which Member States can impose their veto and thereby aiding EU decision-making on enlargement. The new Treaty changes, from the year 2005, the weighting of votes in the Council and reallocates the number of seats among the Member States in the European Parliament.

As of mid-2001, 13 countries had applied for membership. Accession negotiations are being held with Estonia, Hungary, Poland, the Czech Republic, Slovenia, Cyprus, Bulgaria, Latvia, Lithuania, Romania, Slovakia and Malta. Negotiations have not started with Turkey. The basic principle of the negotiations is that all applicants must accept existing EU law.

■ INSTITUTIONS OF THE EU

The European Union creates its own laws and policies through the following institutions:

The European Commission proposes legislation, implements policy and enforces the treaties. It has investigative powers and can take legal action. It also represents the EU in trade negotiations. The Commission is headed by 20 commissioners: France, Germany, Italy, Spain and the UK each appoint two commissioners while the other Member States appoint one commissioner each. The commissioners are appointed for five years.

The European Parliament is directly elected by the citizens of the Union. Its 626 members debate issues, question the Commission and Council, and scrutinize proposed legislation. It can dismiss the Commission and has final approval over the EC budget. Elections take place every five years. Presently and until 2004, the number of MPs from each country are Germany 99; UK 87; France 87; Italy 87; Spain 64; Netherlands 31; Belgium 25; Portugal 25; Greece 25; Sweden 22; Austria 21; Denmark 16; Finland 16; Ireland 15; and Luxembourg 6. MPs sit according to political affiliation and not nationality.

The Council of the European Union is composed of ministers from the 15 member countries. The Council acts on Commission proposals and is the final decision-making body. Participation changes according to the agenda. Agricultural ministers, for instance, decide on agricultural matters and economic and finance ministers on economic and monetary matters. Ministers represent and defend the interests of their countries while seeking agreements that promote the Union's goals. The presidency of the Council rotates among the Member States every six months. In one of the EC's most important reforms, the Single European Act provided for majority voting in the Council in certain areas that previously required unanimity.

The European Council consists of the heads of state or government of the EU Member States and the Commission president. The group meets at least twice a year to define major internal and foreign policy orientations. The European Council does not legislate, but its written conclusions provide guidance.

The Court of Justice is the EC's supreme court. It interprets EC law and its rulings are binding—also on Member States. The court has 15 judges assisted by 9 advocates-general. Both groups are appointed for six years by mutual consent of the Member States.

The Court of Auditors audits the accounts of the EC and EC bodies.

The Committee of the Regions and the **Economic and Social Committee** must be consulted by the Commission and the Council on policies and proposals for legislation.

The European Central Bank governs monetary policy.

Members of the European Union

(As of October 2001)

Member	Year Joined	Member	Year Joined
Austria	1995	Italy	1952
Belgium	1952	Luxembourg	1952
Denmark	1973	Netherlands	1952
Finland	1995	Portugal	1986
France	1952	Spain	1986
Germany	1952	Sweden	1995
Greece	1981	United Kingdom	1973
Ireland	1973		

Source: *Commission of the European Communities*
For Internet information, visit: http://europa.eu.int and http://www.delcan.cec.eu.int

FOCUS ON...

The Euro in 2002

Since January 1, 1999, Austria, Belgium, Finland, France, Germany, Ireland, Italy, Luxembourg, the Netherlands, Portugal and Spain have been participants in the common currency of the European Union. On January 1, 2001, Greece also joined the euro zone. The transition to a common currency began behind the scenes—the euro first became the currency for government and commercial finance. The year 2002 is when the countries' citizens will become part of the process; the participating nations will be replacing their currency with euro notes and coins. (The governments of Denmark and the United Kingdom have chosen not to be part of this common currency; Sweden participated initially, but its economic divergence has led it to step aside.)

As of January 1, 2002, euro coins and notes will be in circulation at the same time as the old national currencies. However, it is expected that most cash transactions will be in euro by mid-January and most member countries plan to have all their old currency out of circulation by the end of February. (The conversion of the euro zone's 3.5 million vending machines may take a little longer.) The buying power of local salaries, pensions or savings will not be affected by the conversion; the same volume of goods and services will be available for a corresponding amount of euro.

■ How will the euro work?

One euro is equal to 100 euro cents; each country's currency will be exchanged at a fixed rate, established in January of 1999. (See the table below for rates.) The new currency will be available in 8 denominations of euro coin and 7 euro notes. The coins have a common face representing a map of the European Union, with national symbols, chosen by each participating Member State on the reverse. Coinage will bear the national symbol of the Member State where it originated; the coins will circulate freely throughout the euro zone as legal tender regardless of their origin. The coins will be in

denominations of 2 euro, 1 euro, 50 euro cents, 20 euro cents, 10 euro cents, 5 euro cents, 2 euro cents and 1 euro cent. The notes will be in denominations of 5, 10, 20, 50, 100, 200 and 500 euro. The notes are in different sizes, and colours used include green, yellow, blue, mauve and orange. The banknotes have incorporated the most advanced safety features in order to make counterfeiting as difficult as possible, as have the coins.

Regulations governing the changeover ensure that contracts will continue to be in force and any rounding up or down in conversions from national currencies will be fair.

■ Why a common currency?

The various nations of Europe have been involved in economic cooperation for centuries, with the most recent formal organization beginning in 1951 (see European Union, pages 268–69). As the integration of the economies in the European Union continued, and free flow of goods, services and labour increased, it was felt that the participants would benefit from a common currency that replaced the 15 currencies that flourished throughout the region. Currency changes and fluctuations made it difficult for businesses and consumers alike to judge competitive products, the performance of a company or the soundness of investments. Conversions from one currency to another cost all participants both time and money.

■ How can 12 different countries share a common currency?

The establishment of a common currency is a long-term project. A common currency within the European Union has been under discussion since 1960, and it's been an official objective since 1969. The plan for its creation was tabled in 1970, and it was estimated that it would take 10 years to implement. Political controversy, oil crises, economic policy divergence and currency weaknesses slowed progress, although Germany, Denmark and the Benelux countries did manage to tie their currencies in the 1970s. In 1979, the European Monetary System (EMS) was created in an effort to restart the process. The Exchange Rate Mechanism (ERM) and the ECU (European Currency Unit) were created, to set an average of the participating currencies and to test the concept of stable but adjustable central exchange rates.

The turning point for the process was the 1991 Maastricht Treaty. By that date, the EMS was judged a success—1979-85 exchange rate volatility had been reduced to half of the previous decade's levels; between 1986-89, volatility was cut in half again. The necessary convergence of inflation rates, long-term interest rates and deficit management was beginning to emerge. While the EMS was judged a success, member states retained their currencies and control of national monetary policies. The goal of a common currency would require further harmonization. The Economic and Monetary Union (EMU) replaces the EMS with a European Central Bank which sets a single monetary policy and requires closer convergence of economic and fiscal policies; and, of course, the majority of participants in the EMU use a common currency.

The Maastricht Treaty set out the economic preconditions necessary for participation in the EMU. These conditions relate to the achievement of agreed-upon levels of performance on inflation, public deficits and debts, exchange rates and interest rates. Achievement of these levels ensures both stability and a relative equality of the economies to be united, and these preconditions will continue to be benchmarks in the years ahead.

What are these conditions?

• Annual government deficits must not be more than 3% of GDP, and stock of government debt must not exceed 60% of GDP;
• The annual benchmark for inflation is set by the three best performing Member States in terms of price stability for the previous year; Member States cannot exceed this benchmark by more than 1.5%;
• The Member State's currency had to stay within the normal fluctuation margins of the EMS for at least two years;
• The benchmark for long-term interest rates is based on the average of the three lowest rates among Member States; long-term interest rates cannot exceed this benchmark by more than 2%.

The economies of some of the participants were better able to meet these standards than others were. In 1993, the EU established the Cohesion Fund to help the economies of Greece, Ireland, Spain and Portugal. The fund makes money available to those Member States with a GDP less than 90% of the average EU GDP for investment in environment and transport infrastructure projects. This fund has been renewed until 2006, with the goal to further reduce economic and social disparities. The economies of those using the fund will be reviewed in 2003 to reassess eligibility for access; it is expected that by 2003, Ireland will no longer qualify.

■ Are the countries not using the euro still part of the EU?

Those not taking part in the euro zone (United Kingdom, Denmark and Sweden) remain full members of the EU and thus have the same rights and responsibilities as other Member States. They will continue to participate in the implementation of economic policy. They retain an autonomous monetary policy, but are required to meet the same economic targets and guidelines as other Member States. They are not subject to sanctions should their economy's performance deviate too widely from the established norms. Their central banks will still be part of the European System of Central Banks.

Euro Conversion Rates (established January 1, 1999)
1 EURO = 40.3399 Belgian franc
= 1.95583 German mark
= 340.750 Greek drachma
= 166.386 Spanish peseta
= 6.55957 French franc
= .787564 Irish pound
= 1936.27 Italian lira
= 40.3399 Luxembourg franc
= 2.20371 Dutch guilder
= 13.7603 Austrian schilling
= 200.482 Portuguese escudo
= 5.94573 Finnish markkaa

A Euro currency converter allowing the conversion of any of the currency units of the 12 Member States is posted at the official Euro web site, at http://europa.eu

Asia-Pacific Economic Cooperation (APEC)

APEC is an association of 21 Asia-Pacific countries. It promotes economic cooperation, freer trade and greater prosperity throughout the Pacific basin. APEC's members include wealthy countries (e.g., the United States) and poor countries (e.g., Vietnam). Members include capitalist and socialist economies. In 1999, trade among APEC countries amounted to almost 44 percent of global trade; the combined gross domestic product of APEC's members was valued at US$18 trillion.

APEC was established in 1989 at a conference of trade and foreign ministers in Canberra, Australia. The 12 founding states included Canada. APEC's members agreed to meet annually for informal talks in different member countries. They also agreed to hold alternate ministerial meetings in APEC countries that belonged to the Association of Southeast Asian Nations (ASEAN).

In the first years, talks were held at the ministerial level. In 1990, Singapore hosted the second meeting of ministers which created seven working groups. These groups focussed on trade and investment data, trade promotion, investment and technology transfer, human resource development, regional energy cooperation, marine resource conservation and telecommunications.

In 1991, APEC's members met in Seoul, Korea. They committed themselves to private enterprise and "open regionalism." China, Hong Kong and Taiwan participated for the first time. Three new working groups were created: fisheries, tourism and transportation. In 1992 in Bangkok, Thailand, the ministers decided to create a permanent Secretariat in Singapore and a central fund to cover APEC's administration.

In 1993, the United States hosted ministerial talks in Seattle and, for the first time, the political leaders of APEC's member states met for separate talks on Blake Island. The resulting "Economic Vision Statement" recognized the interdependence of Asia-Pacific economies and the need for freer trade. The talks also produced a Committee on Trade and Investment to increase cooperation in the exchange of goods, services and investment according to the principles of the World Trade Organization.

Separate meetings of APEC's political leaders became annual events. In 1994, after a ministerial meeting in Jakarta, Indonesia, APEC's leaders issued the "Bogor Declaration of Common Resolve." This statement set the goals of total free trade and investment within the region by 2010 for APEC's industrialized economies and by 2020 for its developing economies. The 1995 meetings in Osaka, Japan, and the 1996 meetings in the Philippines discussed how to accomplish these goals. At Osaka, APEC created a Business Advisory Council (ABAC) to enlist more support from private businesses.

The 1997 conferences took place in Vancouver amidst a financial crisis in Southeast Asia. APEC conferees identified 15 economic sectors for early trade liberalization: environmental goods and services, fish, toys, forest products, gems and jewellery, medical equipment, chemicals, energy, food, natural and synthetic rubber, telecommunications, fertilizers, automobiles, oilseeds and civil aircraft. APEC also aimed at streamlining customs procedures by 2002.

In 1998, APEC participants met in Kuala Lumpur, Malaysia. The United States and Japan proposed a US$10 billion aid package to ease the financial crisis which, APEC leaders acknowledged, had spread beyond the Asia-Pacific region. The 1999 summit was in Auckland, New Zealand; the 2000 summit was in Brunei Darussalam.

The executive director of the APEC Secretariat is Zhang Yan of China; he was appointed to the post on January 1, 2001.

Member Economies (date of membership)	
Australia (1989)	Papua New Guinea (1993)
Brunei Darussalam (1989)	People's Republic of China (1991)
Canada (1989)	Peru (1998)
Chile (1994)	Philippines (1989)
Chinese Taipei (1991)	Russia (1998)
Hong Kong (1991)	Singapore (1989)
Indonesia (1989)	South Korea (1989)
Japan (1989)	Thailand (1989)
Malaysia (1989)	United States (1989)
Mexico (1993)	Vietnam (1998)
New Zealand (1989)	

For more information about APEC, visit the official websites at http://www.apecsec.org.sg and http://dfait-maeci.gc.ca/canada-apec/menu-e.asp

Organization for Economic Co-operation and Development (OECD)

The Organization for Economic Co-operation and Development was launched in 1961 to foster economic growth among the world's major industrialized market economies. The OECD replaced the Organization for European Economic Co-operation (OEEC), which was created in 1948 to administer American Marshall Plan aid to the devastated economies of Western Europe after World War II. Twenty European and North American countries joined the OECD at its inception; today the organization has 30 member states.

The OECD offers, through its many committees and working groups, opportunities for government officials to talk to one another about economic and social policy. These groups meet two-to-four times a year and consist of senior policy-makers. They propose trade and investment policies aimed at reducing conflict among the OECD's member states and at helping the economies of non-member countries to develop.

The OECD has been variously described as a think tank, a monitoring agency and a rich man's club. Its members include the wealthiest countries on earth, which produce approximately two thirds of the world's goods and services. Member states proclaim their commitment to "the principles of the market economy, pluralist democracy and respect for human rights." A few non-member countries also participate in the OECD; often this participation precedes full membership. In 2000, Slovakia became the latest country to accept OECD membership.

OECD headquarters are located on the western edge of Paris at the Château de la Muette, and the Secretariat there helps the flow of information and analysis among member countries. Parts of the OECD Secretariat collect data, monitor trends, analyse and forecast economic developments, while other divisions study social changes, trade patterns, agriculture, taxation, technology or the environment. The work is done in consultation with policy-makers from the member governments which use the data, and it also supports international discussion at committee level.

Among the numerous directorates, the most well-known is the Economics Department which publishes the *OECD Economic Outlook* twice a year, in June and December. That publication evaluates trends in the recent past and forecasts economic conditions for the coming 12 months. The economy of each member country (and many non-members) is monitored by the Country Studies Branch and that data is published annually in an *Economic Survey*.

The Statistics Directorate collects and compares economic statistics from across the OECD. The figures appear in electronic and printed form in *Main Economic Indicators*. This monthly journal also publishes statistics on Eastern Europe's newly emerging market economies.

Other directorates focus on environmental issues, aid to developing countries, public management (how governments go about their business), trade, market development, science and technology as it relates to industry, social policy (including education, unemployment and migration), agriculture, energy (including nuclear), and how cities and regions grow and develop.

For more information about the OECD, visit the website at http://www.oecd.org/

Members (date of membership)

Australia (1971)	Luxembourg (1961)
Austria (1961)	Mexico (1994)
Belgium (1961)	Netherlands (1961)
Canada (1961)	New Zealand (1973)
Czech Republic (1995)	Norway (1961)
Denmark (1961)	Poland (1996)
Finland (1969)	Portugal (1961)
France (1961)	Slovakia (2000)
Germany (1961)	South Korea (1996)
Greece (1961)	Spain (1961)
Hungary (1996)	Sweden (1961)
Iceland (1961)	Switzerland (1961)
Ireland (1961)	Turkey (1961)
Italy (1961)	United Kingdom (1961)
Japan (1964)	United States (1961)

The World Trade Organization (WTO)

The World Trade Organization (WTO) was established on January 1, 1995. It was the result of eight years of global trade negotiations, collectively known as the Uruguay Round, among 125 nations. The result of those negotiations–a 22,000-page 385-pound agreement–was signed in Marrakech, Morocco, on April 15, 1994. It created the WTO and established the framework for global commerce.

The WTO is now the only international body dealing with the rules of trade among nations. It succeeds the General Agreement on Tariffs and Trade (GATT) which was established provisionally after the Second World War in the wake of other new institutions dedicated to international economic cooperation–including the forerunners to the World Bank and the International Montary Fund.

■ Promoting fair competition

The WTO is not a true "free trade" institution because it permits tariffs and, in limited circumstances, other forms of economic protection. But the WTO does oversee a system of rules dedicated to open, fair and undistorted competition. All WTO agreements are founded on the basic principles of non-discrimination, freer trade, predictable policy-making, encouragement of competition and providing for less developed countries.

The rules on non-discrimination are designed to secure fair trade conditions; so too are the rules on dumping and subsidies. Previous GATT rules established which governments could impose compensating duties on these two forms of "unfair" competition, but GATT's rules only dealt with goods. WTO agreements have extended and clarified GATT's rules to include services and intellectual property.

At the beginning of the 21st century, the WTO describes its six main functions as administering WTO trade agreements; providing forums for trade talks; handling trade disputes; monitoring national trade policies; providing technical aid and training for developing countries; and cooperating with other international organizations.

■ The structure of the WTO

The WTO has 142 member countries, 32 observer countries and seven observer organizations to the General Council. As of July 27, 2001, Moldova was the last country to join; most observer nations are waiting for full membership.

The WTO's highest authority is the Ministerial Conference. It consists of representatives of all WTO members, and it must meet at least once every two years. It decides on all matters that affect any of the trade agreements.

The General Council directs the daily work of the WTO. It consists of all WTO members and reports to the Ministerial Conference. The General Council works regularly for the Conference and convenes two more bodies: the Dispute Settlement Body and the Trade Policy Review Body. The latter regularly reviews the trade policies of individual WTO members. Numerous other councils, committees, working parties and negotiating groups are responsible for specific areas or agreements.

Mike Moore, a New Zealander, is the Director-General of the WTO. His three-year term began on September 1, 1999. He will be succeeded by Dr. Supachai Panitchpakdi of Thailand in 2002.

For more information on the WTO, visit the website at http://www.wto.org or write to the World Trade Organization at 154 rue de Lausanne, CH-1211 Geneva 21, Switzerland.

Source: *Information and Media Relations Division, WTO; http://www.DFAIT-maeci.gc.ca*

North Atlantic Treaty Organization (NATO)

The North Atlantic Treaty Organization (NATO) is a political and military alliance, created in Washington on April 4, 1949, when 12 states in Europe and North America signed the North Atlantic Treaty. NATO defends the peace and freedom of its members through collective security without sacrificing members' sovereignty. Headquarters is in Brussels, Belgium.

NATO was created to defend Western and Southern Europe from a perceived threat of invasion by the Soviet Union following World War II. Western leaders began negotiating in 1948, after a Soviet attempt to deny Western access to West Berlin.

Today 19 countries belong, including the original 12: Belgium, Canada, Denmark, France, Iceland, Italy, Luxembourg, the Netherlands, Norway, Portugal, the United Kingdom and the United States, plus Greece and Turkey (1952), Germany (joined as West Germany, 1955) and Spain (1982). On March 12, 1999, NATO admitted its newest members—former members of the Soviet-led Warsaw Pact—Hungary, Poland and the Czech Republic.

The highest authority within NATO is the North Atlantic Council (NAC). It consists of Permanent Representatives, who act as ambassadors for their respective countries, and is directed by a Secretary General. Meetings are weekly; the NAC also convenes less frequent meetings of Foreign or Defence Ministers or Heads of State. Discussions cover political, economic, military and scientific issues. The NAC reaches decisions only after all member states have been consulted. It cannot impose decisions on any of its members, although members can block the wishes of others by withholding consent.

The NAC can create subordinate committees and planning groups. The most important are the Defence Planning Committee and the Nuclear Planning Group. The Defence Planning Committee, which consists of Permanent Representatives and Defence Ministers, deals with collective defence planning. The Nuclear Planning Group, which consists of Defence Ministers, deals with nuclear weapons issues. Both are chaired by the NAC's Secretary General. This post is currently held by Lord George Robertson, who took office on October 14, 1999, and who had previously served as the UK's Secretary of State for Defence.

At the Rome Summit in 1991, NATO outlined a new strategy for Europe in response to the collapse of the Soviet Union: cooperation with the ex-Warsaw Pact states, reduced dependence on nuclear weapons, reductions in the size and readiness of military forces, improvements in military flexibility, greater use of multinational military units and a new focus on peacekeeping.

Also concurrent with the disintegration of the Soviet Union, NATO created a number of mechanisms for consultation and co-operation with former Warsaw Pact states, including the North Atlantic Cooperation Council (NACC) (1991), the Partnership for Peace program (1994) and the Euro-Atlantic Partnership Council (1997). The goal of these organisations was peaceful progress toward a new security environment in Europe. Despite these efforts, the political and economic transformation of many of the former Soviet republics destabilized the area as regional ethnic and political rivalries emerged.

In 1995, NATO first sent land troops outside NATO territory when 60 000 personnel went into Bosnia and Herzegovina under United Nations' authority to enforce the Dayton Peace Accord, negotiated to end armed conflict in the former Yugoslavia. NATO forces and troops from 19 non-NATO countries, including Russia, worked together during the mission, first as part of the Implementation Force (IFOR) and then as Stabilisation Force (SFOR), which is ongoing.

On March 23, 1999, the NAC authorised air strikes by NATO forces against targets in the Federal Republic of Yugoslavia in an effort to end that country's campaign against ethnic Albanians in Kosovo. The air strike campaign continued until June 10when the withdrawal of Yugoslav forces from the Kosovo region began. As of June 12, 1999, NATO forces joined a UN-mandated peacekeeping force (Kosovo Force or KFOR), to enforce the withdrawal agreement.

For more information about NATO, visit the websites at http://www.nato.int

HISTORY IN HEADLINES

■ Ancient History 5000 BC to AD 476

5000–3501: The earliest known cities are in Mesopotamia—in southwest Asia between the Tigris and Euphrates Rivers—a plain rendered fertile by canals; the Egyptian calendar is regulated by the sun and moon; Sumerian writing exists, in southern Mesopotamia on clay tablets, consisting of 2,000 pictograph signs; the Neolithic period in western Europe is characterized by polished stone weapons and tools and agriculturally-based settlements; Cretan ships appear in the Mediter-ranean Sea; copper alloys are used, and there is smelting of gold and silver in Sumer and Egypt; harps and flutes are played in Egypt; painted pottery appears along the Mediter-ranean; coloured ceramic ware from Russia reaches China.

3500–2001: The Middle Eastern Bronze Age begins (c. 3500 BC); the height of Sumerian civilization (in the region of the Euphrates River valley) is noted for having a numerical system, irrigated agriculture, poetry, potters' wheels, linen, wheeled vehicles, wedge-shaped (cuneiform) script, barley, bread, beer, use of metal coins as legal tender, oil-burning lamps, brick temples and medicine; the dynasty of Pharoahs as god-kings in Egypt begins (2200–525 BC); the Great Sphynx of Gizeh is built; wrestling is the first highly developed sport; glass beads are worn in Egypt; the bow and arrow is first used in warfare; the Yao dynasty is the first recorded in China (2500–2300); the Indus civilization begins in India; the earliest Egyptian mummies are made; equinoxes and solstices are calculated in China; the first library is in Egypt.

2000–1501: The Egyptian height of power and achievement (18th dynasty) features an irrigation system, contraceptives, bathrooms with a water supply, an alphabet of 24 signs, and the oldest form of a novel (*Story of Sinuhe*); the Persian empire begins (1750–1550); the first legal system and laws of a kingdom are set up by Hammurabi, king of Babylonia; the first of seven periods of Chinese literature begins; Stonehenge is built; Abraham, the patriarch of the Jewish religion, lives (c. 1800); Babylonia uses geometry as the basis for astronomical measurements, and describes the signs of the Zodiac; religious dances are performed in Crete.

1500–1001: The Israelites, led by Moses, leave bondage in Egypt (eventually settling in Canaan in 1250), and receive the Ten Commandments and the world's first monotheistic belief at Mt Sinai; the decline of Egyptian power begins (1200–1090); Troy is destroyed during the Trojan War (1193–83) over Helen of Sparta (Greek legend); the Iron Age begins in the Mediterranean area (1000); obelisk structures are used as sundials in Egypt; the first Chinese dictionary is written; silk fabrics appear in China; leprosy spreads in India and Egypt; Phoenicia is the dominant trading power in the Mediterranean; the Mexican Sun Pyramid is built in Teotihuacan.

1000–901: Asiatic and Greek civilizations are linked by Phoenician trading; David is the king of the united kingdom of Judah and Israel (1000–960) with Jerusalem as its capital; David is succeeded by his son Solomon who presides over the height of Israel's ancient civilization (960–25); classical paganism reigns in Greece; pantheistic belief reigns in India (teaching reincarnation and the caste system); the Chou dynasty's rational philosophy reigns in China; Pinto Indians build huts in southwest North America; brush and ink painting appears in China; gold vessels and jewellery are made in northern Europe; the Hebrew alphabet and literature are developed; the Germanic peoples begin to migrate en masse.

900–601: Carthage is founded as a trading centre (813); *Iliad* and *Odyssey* are written and credited to the poet Homer (c. 800); according to legend, Rome is founded by the twins Romulus and Remus (753); the first recorded Olympic Games are held in Greece (776), and every four years thereafter during ancient times; the earliest record of music is a hymn on a Sumerian tablet; arts and crafts flourish in Asia Minor and Greece; a canal between the Nile River and the Red Sea is started under Pharoah Nechos; Etruscan art forms emerge in Tuscany; the Assyrians destroy Babylon and divert the Euphrates River to cover the site of the city; the Babylonians and their allies later destroy the Assyrian empire, which is then divided among the conquerors; the Acropolis, a fortified hill and religious centre, is built in Athens; limestone and marble are used in the construction of Greek temples; flutes and lyres accompany song; Greek choral and lyric poetry use strophe and antistrophe; Zoroaster, a religious teacher and prophet of ancient Persia, lives (c. 628–c. 551).

600–451: The Mayan civilization flourishes in Mexico; Nebuchadnezzer builds what may be the terraced Hanging Gardens of Babylon (600); Babylonian troops destroy the Jewish Temple at Jerusalem and take many Jews as slaves; Jews write the early books of the Bible during the Babylonian Captivity; Siddhartha Gautama, who becomes Buddha, the "enlightened" Indian philosopher and religious teacher, is born (563): at age 29 he renounces world luxuries and searches for enlightenment, which he attains at age 35 while meditating under a pipal tree at Bodh Gaya, and he teaches monks to continue his work; Confucius, the Chinese philosopher and teacher, is born (551); his moral and religious system governs China and is contained in the sayings of *Analects*; Cyrus II the Great of Persia conquers Babylon and surrounding areas and transforms Persia into a vast empire (c. 540): he frees the Jews from Babylon (536) and aids their return to Israel; Darius I divides the Persian empire into 20 provinces and introduces reforms including a common currency, regular taxes and a standing army; Solon's laws are adopted in Athens; Milo of Crotona, a legendary athlete, is crowned six times at the Olympic Games (536); Chinese feudal structure begins to weaken during Chou dynasty (c. 500–451); Greek cities are freed from Persian domination when the Greeks in Cyprus win the Persian Wars (490–49); the marble temple of Apollo is built at Delphi (478); the statue of Zeus, the centrepiece of the temple of Olympia, is built (460); Aeschylus writes *Prometheus Bound* (460); the *Fables of Aesop* is written by a former Phrygian slave.

450–301: The Greek Periclean Age unfolds with the philosophers Socrates and (his pupil) Plato, the dramatists Sophocles and Euripides and historians Thucydides and Herodotus; the beginning of the Indian empire is centred at Magadha (the "cradle of Buddhism"); the Torah becomes the moral code of the Jewish people; Celtic settlements begin in the British Isles; the Spartans use chemicals in warfare (charcoal, sulphur and pitch); the Parthenon, the masterpiece of Greek architecture, is built (447–32); the population of Greece reaches two million citizens and one million slaves; indigenous Indian civilization ends in Mexico; the Peloponnesian Wars between Athens and Sparta (431–04) end when the Spartan navy destroys the Athenian navy at Aegospotami: this leads to the decline of Athens as a great power; the first horoscopes are developed in Mesopotamia (c. 410); Socrates is put to death for state offences (399); Brennus leads the Gauls from northern Italy to sack Rome (390); Rome is rebuilt (387) and city walls are built around it (377); Plato, a Greek philosopher, founds the most influential school in the world, the Academy (c. 387); the use of catapults as weapons of war begins; Aristotle, the Greek philosopher, is born (384); Alexander the Great, son of Philip II of Macedon, is born (356); Shung-tse founds Chinese monist philosophy (the doctrine that the universe can be explained by one principle) (350); Corinth becomes a trading centre (338); Philip II is assassinated (336); Alexander succeeds his father and conquers Persia, Jerusalem and Tyre, extending his empire to the Indus River in India where his generals force him to turn back; Alexander dies in Babylon (323) and his empire is divided among his generals who fight civil wars for a time (beginning in 321); the Hellenistic period of Greek arts begins (330–20) and the leading Greek schools of thought are: Stoics, Epicureans and Cynics; Euclid writes *Elements*, a standard work on geometry (323); Alexandria is the centre of Greek learning.

300–151: The Mexican sun temple Atetello is built at Teotihuacan (300); accurate star maps are compiled by Chinese astronomers (c. 300); full equality between patricians and plebeians is mandated in Rome (287); Archi-medes, the Greek mathematician, is born (287); the practical end of the history of Babylon coincides with Babylonian re-establishment in the new city of Seleucia (275); Manetho, the high priest of Egypt, writes a history of Egypt in Greek (275); the Colossus at Rhodes is completed (275); the Lighthouse of Pharos is completed at Alexandria (275); the First Punic War between the Cartha-ginians and the Romans (264–41) arises out of a dispute involving the Sicilian cities of Messana and Syracuse: the Romans win naval battles at Mylae (260) and Cape Ecnomus (256) but lose in Africa (255); a Roman victory of the Aegadian Isles (241) brings a peace treaty that gives Sicily to Rome, but Rome reneges on the treaty and invades Sardinia and Corsica; the leap year is introduced into the Egyptian calendar (239); the Greeks and Romans play ball games, roll dice and play board games; the death of Sun-tsi marks the end of Chinese classical philosophy; the Great Wall of China (2,400 km long) is built to keep out invaders (215); the Second Punic War (218–01) opens when Hannibal and the Carthaginians conquer the Spanish city Saguntum, a Roman ally, and Rome declares war: Hannibal successfully invades Italy from the north (217) and makes an alliance with Philip V of Macedon (216), but is later defeated by the Romans at Zama (202) in Africa; Carthage surrenders its war fleet to Rome as well as its Spanish province; the Second Macedonian War (200–197) ends with the Romans under Flamius defeating Philip V of Macedon; the use of gears leads to the invention of the ox-driven water wheel for irrigation (200); an inscription is engraved on the Rosetta Stone (c. 200); Antiochus IV of Syria persecutes the Jews in Israel and desecrates their Temple of Jerusalem (168); the Jews revolt under Judas Maccabeus and repel the Syrians, then rededicate (Chanukah) the Temple (165); the inventor of trigonometry, Hipparchus of Nicaea, is born (160).

150–1 BC: During the Third Punic War (149–46) the Romans destroy Corinth and massacre the inhabitants of Carthage (due to alleged breach of treaty); the Roman Empire now consists of seven provinces; the Venus of Milo is sculpted (140); Cicero, the greatest Roman orator, is born (106); the first Chinese ships reach the east coast of India (100); the greatest of Roman poets, Virgil, is born (70): he pens the epic *Aeneid*; Horace, the lyric poet, is born (65); Julius Caesar, Roman military commander, organizes the First Trium-virate (60) with Pompey, commander-in-chief of the army, and Marcus Crassus; Caesar conquers the northern Gauls (55) and the Britons; Caesar and Pompey battle for control of Rome after Caesar crosses the Rubicon River and provokes a civil war; Caesar emerges victorious (48); the Julian calendar and leap year are adopted in Rome (46); Cleopatra, the last queen of Egypt, orders the death of Pompey; Caesar, now the dictator of Rome, is murdered by a group headed by Brutus and Cassius Longinus (44); Mark Antony, Octavian and Lepidus form the Second Triumvirate and defeat Brutus and Cassius at Phillipi (42); Mark Antony returns to Egypt (38) where he and Cleopatra commit suicide after being defeated by Octavian at Actium (31); Octavian, retitled Augustus, is a virtual emperor of Rome

(30–AD 14); Herod the Great is appointed king of Judea by the Romans (c. 40); the probable date of the birth of Jesus, the Jewish son of Mary, in Bethlehem (AD 4).

AD 1–150: Jesus, who is revered as the Son of God by his followers, the Christians, preaches for three years in Galilee (c. 30); in the third year of his preaching, Jesus is crucified in Jerusalem by Roman authorities at the request of local political and religious leaders; Caligula becomes emperor of Rome (37) and is known for his ruthlessness and insanity: he is assassinated by the Praetorian Guard (42) and is succeeded by Claudius I, who consolidates and reinvigorates the empire despite a paralysis (dies in 54); the apostle Paul sets out on his missionary travels (45) and spreads Christianity; Nero, emperor of Rome, is the first to persecute the Christians, for allegedly burning half of Rome (64); the Gospels according to Matthew, Mark and John are written; Jews revolt against Rome and the Romans destroy the second Temple at Jerusalem and enslave many inhabitants (70); 1,000 Jewish Zealots hold off the 15,000-member Roman legion for three years on the mountaintop fortress of Masada, and the Zealots commit suicide to escape capture (73); under Emperor Trajan, the Roman Empire reaches its greatest geographical extent when he conquers Dacia and much of Parthia (98–116); paper is made by the Chinese, though not for writing (by 100); Hadrian's Wall is built as the northern boundary and defence line of the Roman Empire (122–26); the medical authority up to the 16th century, Greek physician and writer Galen, (c. 130–200) demonstrates that arteries carry blood (not air) and establishes the importance of the spinal cord by correlating earlier medical knowledge with his discoveries based on experiments and animal dissection; the earliest known Sanskrit inscriptions are made in India (150).

151–300: Ptolemy, a Greco-Egyptian thinker, compiles *Almagest*, the 13-volume work on ancient astronomy (earth-centred universe), mathematics, geography and science, which is influential to the 16th century; the oldest known Maya monuments are built (c. 164); the period of Neo-Platonism, the last of the Greek philosophies, begins (c. 200); silkworms are exported from Korea to China and then to Japan (c. 200); citizenship is granted to every freeborn subject in the Roman Empire (212); Afghanistan is invaded by the Huns (200); the

Goths invade Asia Minor and the Balkan Peninsula (220); the end of the Han dynasty in China is followed by four centuries of division (220); the southern part of India breaks into several kingdoms; Rome celebrates its 1,000th anniversary (248); persecution of Christians increases and martyrs are revered as saints (c. 250); the first book of algebra is written by Diophantus of Alexandria (c. 250); the Goths attack the Black Sea area (257) as well as Athens, Sparta and Corinth (268); Pappus of Alex-andria documents use of cogwheel, lever, pulley, screw and wedge (c. 285); Rome is partitioned into a western and an eastern empire; five distinct German dukedoms emerge (Saxons, Franks, Alemanni, Thuringians and Goths) (c. 300).

301–400: Constantine the Great reunites the western and eastern Roman Empires and becomes sole emperor (310–37); Constantine establishes toleration of Christianity with the Edict of Milan (313); the seat of the Roman Empire is moved to Constantinople (c. 331); the Basilican Church of St Peter is erected (330); Emperor Constantine is baptized on his deathbed (337) and is succeeded by his three sons, who again split Rome into two empires; the Huns invade Europe (360) and Russia (376); books begin to replace scrolls (360); Lo-Tsun, a Chinese monk, founds the Caves of the Thousand Buddhas in Kansu (360); Theodosius the Great becomes the last emperor of a united Roman Empire (392); Alaric, king of the Visigoths, invades Greece (396) and plunders Athens and the Balkans (398); the first definite records of Japanese history appear (400), although legend claims Japan was founded in 660 BC.

401–76: The Visigoths invade Italy (401); Alaric sacks Rome (410); Roman legions withdraw from Britain to defend Italy from the Visigoths (410); barbarians settle in Roman provinces (425); Attila becomes ruler of the Huns (433); St Augustine, Christian theologian, writes *The City of God* (411); alchemy begins with the search for the Philosopher's Stone and the Elixir of Life as chief objects; pre-Inca culture develops in Peru; Venice is founded by refugees from Attila's Huns (452); the Vandals sack Rome (455) and destroy the Roman fleet at Cartegena (460); the Huns leave Europe (470); the Mayan civilization flourishes in southern Mexico (c. 470); the first Shinto religious shrines are built in Japan (478): they deal primarily with nature and

ancestor worship; the German barbarian Odoacer takes Ravenna and deposes Emperor Romulus Augustulus, thereby ending the Western Roman Empire (476); Aryabhata, Hindu astronomer and mathematician, studies powers and roots of numbers (b. 476).

■ Middle or Dark Ages: 477–1450

477–529: Chi dynasty in southern China (479–502); Clovis, leader of the Franks (since 481), converts to Christianity (496); the first schism between the Western and Eastern Churches occurs when Pope Felix III excommunicates Patriarch Acacius of Constantinople (484–519); Armenian Church separates from Byzantium and Rome (491); the Moshica culture of the Chimic Indians flowers in Peru with agriculture, pottery and textiles; the Vatican Palace in Rome is first planned (500); Tamo carries tea from India to China (c. 500); Clovis kills Alaric II and annexes the Visigoth kingdom of Toulouse (507), and Clovis's realm is divided among his four sons upon his death (511); Emperor Wu-Ti converts to Buddhism and encourages the new religion in central China (517); Justinian I becomes the Byzantine Emperor (527): he is known for heavy taxes, public works and codifying Roman law; the Saxon kingdoms of Essex and Middlesex appear; Chosroes I is king of Persia (531–79) and encourages culture and art.

530–99: Arthur, the semi-legendary king of the Britons, is first mentioned at the Battle of Mt Badon (c. 540); the earliest Chinese roll paintings appear in Tun-huang (landscapes); war breaks out between Persia and the Byzantine Empire (539–62); St Gildas writes the first important source of early British history, *De excido et conquestu Brittaniae* (542); disastrous earthquakes occur around the world (543); the plague of Constantinople, imported by rats from Egypt and Syria, spreads throughout Europe and reaches Britain (547); the Golden Era of Byzantine art begins (550); Poles settle in western Galacia, Ukrainians in eastern Galacia (550); chess begins in India (c. 550); Buddhism is introduced into Japan by Emperor Shotoko Taishi (c.552–621), and the first Buddhist monastery in Japan is founded (587); Japanese prehistory ends and the Asuka period begins; Justinian sends missionaries to China and Ceylon to smuggle out silkworms and the European silk industry becomes a Byzantine state monopoly (553); Mohammed, the founder of Islam, is born (570); war is renewed between Persia and the Byzantine Empire (572–91), and again when Chosroes II ascends the throne of Persia (590–628); the plague ends after killing half the population of Europe (542–94); first verified account of decimal number system in India (595); probably the first English school is established at Canterbury (598); the authoritative Talmud Babli, a compilation of Jewish Oral Law with rabbinical interpretations, is compiled (c. 6th century).

600–749: Books printed in China (600); Czechs and Slovaks take up land in Bohemia and Moravia, Yugoslavs in Serbia (c. 600); smallpox spreads from India, via China and Asia Minor, to southern Europe; the oldest surviving wooden building in the world, the Horyuji temple and hospital, is completed in Japan (607); Mohammed experiences a religious vision on Mt Hira (610); "burning water" (petroleum) is used in Japan (615); orchestras are formed in China (619); porcelain is produced in China (620); the Hegira is named after Mohammed's flight from hostile Mecca to Yathrib (later renamed Medina), and is year one in the Muslim calendar (622); an encyclopedia of arts and sciences is written by Isidore of Seville (622); Shaka Trinity, the famous altarpiece of the Kondo in Japan, is built by Tori (623); Mohammed begins to dictate the Koran (the sacred book of Islam) in Arabic (625); the Byzantines decisively defeat the Persians at Nineveh (627); Mohammed captures Mecca and writes letters to world leaders explaining the Muslim faith (628); cotton is introduced in Arab countries (630); Buddhism becomes the state religion in Tibet (632); Medina is the seat of the first caliph (religious and political leader of Muslims) who is Abu Bekr, Mohammed's father-in-law; the Arabs attack Persia (633); Damascus is the new capital of the caliphs (635–70); Jerusalem is conquered by the Arabs (637); the book-copying industry of the west is destroyed by the Arabs and the Alexandrian school ceases to be the centre of Western culture (641); the Arabs under Omar destroy the Persian Empire: the caliphs rule the area (until 1258), and Islam replaces the religion of Zoroaster; the Eastern Roman Empire is weakened by the Arab conquest of Egypt, Mesopotamia and Syria (642); the Dome of the Rock, a Muslim mosque, is begun in Jerusalem (643); the Muslim fleet destroys the Byzantine fleet at Lycia (655);

Croats and Serbs settle in Bosnia (650); Chinese artists invent lamp-black ink and wood block printing (c. 650); Caliphs organize first news service (650); Japanese Buddhism and Shintoism are reconciled by the Korean-born priest Gyogi (c. 668–749); the Byzantines use "Greek Fire," a missile weapon of sulphur, rock, salt, resin and petroleum, against the Arabs at the siege of Constantinople (671–78); glass windows appear in English churches (674); the first Arab coinage is introduced (695); the Arabs destroy Carthage (697); Greek, instead of Latin, becomes the official language of the Eastern Roman Empire (700); the Arabs conquer Algiers (700) and virtually eliminate Christianity in northern Africa; mass migration of European peoples is followed by their subjection at the hands of property owners; China's population grows rapidly (700) and the first large urban developments appear there; the Great Mosque of Damascus is built (705); Buddhist monasteries in Japan become centres of civilization (710); the first written history of Japan, *Kojiki*, is compiled (712); the Lombard kingdom in northern Italy reaches its height (c. 600–c. 799); the Muslim empire now extends from the Pyrenees to China, with Damascus as its capital (715); the earliest Islamic paintings appear (715); Caliph Omar II grants tax exemption to all Muslim believers (717); the Chinese capital Ch'ang-an is the largest city in the world and Constantinople is the second largest (725); Casa Grande, a North American Indian fort and large irrigation works, is built in Arizona (725); Charles Martel (mayor of the Frankish court) wins victory over the Arabs in the battle of Tours and halts their westward advance (732); first printed newspaper published in Beijing (748).

750–849: Pueblos are built in southwest North America (750–900); Spain, under Arab influence, excels in mathematics, optics and chemistry (c. 750); Kiev, Russia, becomes known as a trading centre (750); the Turkish Empire is founded by a Tartar tribe in Armenia (760); Charlemagne becomes ruler of the Franks after the death of his father (Pepin the Short, son of Charles Martel) (768) and brother Carloman (771); Arabic learning flourishes under Harun-al-Rashid (790), peaks during reign of Caliph Mamun (813–33); the Byzantine Empress Irene overthrows her son Constantine (797), an act heralded by the Greek Church; Charlemagne is crowned Holy Roman Emperor (Western Empire) at Rome (800); the earliest records of Persian poetry and literature appear (800); the Vikings dominate Ireland (802); Arabic numerals are created under Indian influence (814); the Arabs conquer Crete, proceed as far as the Greek isles (826) and begin their conquest of Italy and Sardinia (827); Prince Mimir founds the Great Moravian Empire (830) from a confederation of Slavs in Bohemia, Moravia, Slovakia, Hungary and Transylvania; the Treaty of Verdun divides the Frankish Empire into France, Germany and Italy (843); paper currency in China creates inflation and state bankruptcy (845); Abu Tamman writes *Hamasa*, a collection of Arabian legends, proverbs and heroic stories (845); the Arabs sack Rome (846), damage the Vatican and destroy the Venetian fleet.

850–99: Salerno University is founded (850); the discovery of coffee is credited to Arabia (850); Jews settling in Germany develop the Yiddish language (c. 850); the first important Japanese painter, Kudara Kuwanari, dies (853); Norse pirates enter the Mediterranean and sack the coast up to Asia Minor (859); Iceland is discovered by the Northmen (861); Russian Northmen sack parts of France (861) and attack Constantinople (865); Basil I, the Byzantine Emperor, compiles the Basilican code (reforming finance and law and restoring the prestige of the military), and begins the Macedonian dynasty (867); Alfred the Great, king of England, recaptures London from the Danes (878); Emperor Charles III becomes king of France and once more unites the empire of Charlemagne (884), he is deposed (887) and there is a final separation of Germany and France; England's King Alfred establishes a regular militia and navy, extends the power of the king's courts and institutes fairs and markets (890).

900–99: The Vikings discover Greenland (900); the Mayans relinquish their settlements in the lowlands of Mexico and emigrate to the Yucatan peninsula (900); England is divided into shires with county courts in order to safeguard the civil rights of the inhabitants (900); the Arabian tales *A Thousand and One Nights* is begun (900); castles become the seats of the European nobility (900); Cordoba, Spain, is the seat of Arab learning, science, commerce and industry (930); Yenching becomes new capital city of China, later known as Beijing (938); revolts against imperial rule in Japan set off a period of civil war (939–1185); the Arab

empire creates advanced postal and news services (942); the earliest record of the existence of a London bridge (963); a Chinese encyclopedia of 1,000 volumes is begun (978–84); the rule of nobles in Rome ends (980); Venice and Genoa carry on a flourishing trade between Asia and Western Europe (983); systematic musical notation develops (990); canonization of Christian saints begins.

1000–99: The heroic poem *Beowulf* is written in Old English by an unknown author (1000); Leif Ericsson, son of Eric the Red, sails to North America (1000); the Chinese invent gunpowder (1000); Mayan culture on the Yucatan peninsula achieves its zenith (1000); Sridhara, Indian mathematician, describes the importance of zero (1000); the Holy Sepulchre in Jerusalem is sacked by Muslims (1009); Danes under Canute control England (1016); Canute conquers Norway (1028); Jaroslav the Wise, Prince of Kiev (1020–54), codifies Russian law and builds cities, schools and churches; Byzantine power begins to decline (1025); Canute dies (1035) and his kingdom of England, Norway and Denmark is divided among his three sons; after murdering Duncan of Scotland, Macbeth becomes king (1040) and is later murdered by Malcolm (1057); time values are given to musical notes (1050); the separation of the Roman and Eastern Churches becomes permanent (1054); Westminster Abbey is consecrated (1065); William of Normandy is crowned William the Conqueror, of England (1066); the comet, later known as Halley's comet, appears (1066); She-tsung, Emperor of China, nationalizes agricultural production and distribution (1068); Constantine the African brings Greek medicine to the Western world (1071); the original Tower of London is built (1078); the Domesday Book, a survey of assessment for tax purposes, is compiled (1086); the start of the First Crusade (1096) is proclaimed by Pope Urban II to recapture the Holy Land from the Turks; Crusaders take Jerusalem (1099).

1100–99: Middle English supercedes Old English (1100); Islamic science begins to decline; secular music first appears; Robert of Normandy is appeased after invading England in the Treaty of Alton (1101); colonization of eastern Germany begins (1105); the earliest record of a miracle play is from Dunstable, England (1110): based on Scriptures and the lives of saints, they are widely performed until the 16th century; Bologna University founded

(1119); the earliest account of a mariner's compass is by Alexander Neckham (1125); the Second Crusade begins (1146) and fails one year later; Paris University is founded (1150); Bologna Medical School is founded (1150); the first recorded fire and plague insurance is in Iceland (1151); the Japanese clans Taira and Minamoto fight each other (1156); Eric of Sweden conquers Finland (1157); Thomas à Becket is elected Archbishop of Canterbury (1162) in an effort to curb church power, but he later quarrels with King Henry II over growing royal power; Becket is murdered by Norman knights (1170) and buried at Canterbury; jails are ordered erected in all English counties and boroughs (1166); Oxford University is founded (1167); rules for the canonization of saints are established by Pope Alexander III (1170); first authenticated influenza epidemics occur (1173); the Campanile ("Leaning Tower") of Pisa is built (1174); Walter Map organizes the Arthurian legends in their present form (1176); all Jews are banished from France (1182); the Third Crusade (1189–93) fails to recapture Jerusalem from the Muslims; Moses Maimonides, Jewish philosopher, introduces Aristotle to modern western philosophy when he attempts to reconcile Aristotle's theories with those of Jewish philosophy in *Guide to the Perplexed* (1190), and he is also credited with organizing all Jewish law for the layman as well as religious educators.

1200–49: Cambridge University founded (1200); Islam takes root in India; the Fourth Crusade begins with crusaders from Venice fighting Constantinople and establishing a Latin Kingdom of Jerusalem (1204); St Francis of Assisi issues the first rules of his brotherhood of educators and missionaries, the Franciscans (1209); in the Children's Crusade (1212), thousands of children from Europe leave for the Holy Land, but most are either sold as slaves or die of hunger or disease; Genghis Khan becomes chief prince of the Mongols (1206) and conquers most of the Chinese empire of north China (1213–15) as well as Turkistan, Afghanistan and Trans-oxania (1218–24), and he raids Persia and Eastern Europe; Genghis Khan's empire is divided among his descendants upon his death (1227); the Council of St Albans is the precursor to the British Parliament (1213); King John puts his seal on England's Magna Carta at Runnymede under compulsion by the barons (1215): it

defines the limitations of royal power and sets out basic civil rights; the Fifth Crusade fails in Egypt (1217–21); the oldest national flag in the world, Danneborg, is adopted by Denmark (1218); the form of the sonnet develops in Italian poetry (1221); Thomas Aquinas (1225–74) theorizes philosophical proofs for the existence of God and reconciles Greek ideas with Christian theology; the Sixth Crusade is led by Emperor Frederick II (1228); crusaders bring back leprosy to Europe (1230), and they secure a temporary truce with the Muslims; three later crusades against Muslims in the 13th century fail; coal is mined for the first time in Newcastle, England (1233); the Inquisition begins as the pope makes Dominicans responsible for putting an end to heresy (1233); Alexander Nevski made Grand Duke of Novgorod (1236).

1250–99: Kublai Khan becomes governor of China (1251) and ruler of the Mongol peoples (1259–94); he fails to conquer Japan (1274), southeast Asia and Indonesia, but he defeats the Sung dynasty of China (1279); instruments of torture are first used in the Inquisition (1252); the Sorbonne is founded by Robert de Sorbon as the Paris School of Theology (1254); the House of Commons is established in England (1258); Mongols control Baghdad, end caliphate (1258); Roger Bacon writes *"De computo naturali"* (1264); the glass mirror is invented (1278); Marco Polo, the Venetian explorer, journeys to China (1271–95) and is in the diplomatic service of Kublai Khan (1275–92); Florence, Italy, is the leading European city in commerce and finance (c. 1282); the Teutonic Order, a German military and religious order, conquers Prussia (1283) after killing the native "heathens" and replacing them with Germans; spectacles (eyeglasses) are invented (1290); the crusades end and the Knights of St John of Jerusalem settle in Cyprus (1291).

1300–99: Trade fairs at Bruges, Antwerp, Lyons and Geneva (c. 1300); Edward I of England standardizes the yard and the acre (1305); Dante composes his *Divina Commedia* (1307–21); mechanical clocks are driven by weights in Europe; Salic Law, excluding women from succession to the throne, is adopted in France (1317); No plays originate in Japan (1325); the Aztecs establish Mexico City (1327); the sawmill is invented (1328); weaving at York first documented (1331); the Hundred Years War between

France and England begins (1337) as a dispute over lands held by the English crown in France: it later becomes a dispute over the French crown itself; the first scientific weather forecasts are attempted by William Merlee of Oxford (1337); the Black Death (bubonic plague) devastates Europe, killing about 75 million people, more than one-third of the population (1347–51); Boccaccio writes *Decameron* (1348–53), which is intended to be a diversion from the horrors of the plague; Timur the Lame (Tamerlaine) begins his conquest of Asia (1363); the Aztecs of Mexico build their capital, Tenochtitlan (1364); the Mongol Yüan dynasty in China is overthrown by the national Ming dynasty (1368–1644); the building of the Bastille begins in Paris (1369); "Robin Hood," the legendary hero who robbed the rich to help the poor, appears in English ballads and literature; the Great Schism in the Catholic Church begins (1378–1417) when, after the death of Pope Gregory XI, two popes are elected, one each at Rome and Avignon; Venice wins its Hundred Years War against Genoa (1256–1381); Briton John Wyclif calls for the reform of church practices (1379); he is condemned as a heretic (1380, 1382) and inspires the first English translation of the Latin Bible, the Wyclif Bible; Chaucer writes *The Canterbury Tales*; the rival southern and northern courts of Japan's divided imperial family reunite after 50 years of strife; Denmark, Sweden and Norway unite under Queen Margaret of Denmark (1397) in the Union of Kalmar.

1400–39: Russia's greatest icon painter, Andrei Rublex, creates *Trinity* (1411); England and France sign a perpetual peace treaty upon the marriage of Henry V and Catherine of Valois (1420); Joan of Arc and her French followers defeat the British at Orleans (1429) and march triumphantly to Paris: she is then taken prisoner by the Burgundians (1430) and condemned and executed (1431) in a political inquisition and trial; complete suits of metal armor plate replace chain mail in Europe (1430); China shuts out the western world and bans voyages there (1433) because Confucian doctrine sees little merit in trade; the Portugese find the way round Cape Bojador (on the west coast of Africa) under Henry the Navigator (1434); the Greek (Eastern or Byzantine) Church unites with the Roman church (1439) in order to save itself from the Turkish threat; Montezuma becomes ruler of the Aztecs in Mexico (1440) and begins to conquer surrounding tribes.

■ **Renaissance: 1440–1650**

1440–69: The rise of the Italian city-states heralds the Renaissance (1440–50), and the richest families (such as the Medici) vie with each other as patrons of art and learning (mainly in Florence); the first oil painter, Jan van Eyck, dies in Flanders (1441); France defeats England at Castillion, ending the Hundred Years War (1453), and the English give up everything except Calais, thus ending English rule in France; Zimbabwe, the great African kingdom, declines after 200 years of expansion (1450) because of food shortages; Constantinople, the old capital of the Byzantine empire, falls to the Ottomans (1453); a treaty unites rival Italian city-states (1454), requiring them to protect each other from outside aggression; Ming porcelain pottery appears in Europe (1460); the Bible is printed mechanically with metal type faces and oil-based ink by Johann Gutenberg (1455); the Wars of the Roses begin in England (1455) as a struggle for the throne between the houses of York and Lancaster, and end (1485) when Henry VII of the house of Lancaster prevails over Richard III; Plato's writings are translated into Latin at the Platonic Academy in Florence (1469).

1470–99: Music sheets, maps and posters are mechanically printed (1470s); Vlad the Impaler dies in Transylvania (1477) and the mass murderer becomes the source for Dracula legends; Peruvian-centred Inca rule expands to include the entire Andean region (3,200 sq. km) under Pachacuti, and his son Topa Inca (1470), and it is characterized by terracing, irrigation, pantheistic religion with human sacrifice, advanced metalwork, tapestry making and construction; the Spanish Catholic Inquisition begins (1478); King Ferdinand V of Aragón and Queen Isabella I of Castile unite their crowns in Spain to ward off Alfonso V of Portugal (1479); Ivan the Great declares Russian independence (1480) from the Mongols when he refuses to continue paying them tribute; the first European manual of navigation and nautical almanac is prepared in Portugal by mathematical experts (1484) who calculate the latitude of the sun, based on the work of the Jewish astronomer Abraham Zacuto; the spread of witchcraft and heresy in Germany is attacked by Pope Innocent VIII (1484) and he authorizes Dominican inquisitors to torture and burn witches; the publication of an encyclopedia of witchcraft, *Malleus Maleficarum* (1486), adds to witch hunt hysteria; the Genoese seaman Christopher Columbus secures the sponsorship of Queen Isabella of Spain (1486) for his expedition to discover a western route to Asia (he sets sail with his three ships: Santa María, Pinta and Niña in 1492); the Aztecs of Mexico inaugurate the Great Temple of Tenochtitlan (1487) when they ritually sacrifice the hearts of 20,000 people; the Portugese explorer Bartholomew Dias rounds the Cape of Good Hope off South Africa (1488); Leonardo da Vinci is in his prime in Italy (1488) as an artist, scientist, inventor and philosopher, with inventions centuries ahead of their time (e.g., he conceives of flying machines and an apparatus to enable humans to breathe under water); the Great Wall of China is rebuilt by Ming emperors as a defence against attacks by northern Barbarians (1488); the first terrestrial globe is made by Martin Behaim, a German (1492); Jews are ordered by Spain's Catholic rulers to choose between expulsion or forced conversion (1492), and the rulers change the options to conversion or death (1498); Spain conquers Granada (1492), the last Muslim kingdom in Spain; Spain and Portugal sign a treaty dividing lands discovered in the new world, but Spain benefits the most from the treaty (1494); French armies in Italy bring a virus later identified as syphilis to Naples and the epidemic spreads through Europe (1495); Columbus brings tobacco back from the new world (1496); the Chinese invent a toothbrush (1498); Vasco da Gama discovers a sea route round the Cape of Good Hope to India via the Indian Ocean (1498); the Italian navigator Amerigo Vespucci explores the northeast coast of South America (1499) and reports cannibals (1502); Portugal's Pedro Cabral discovers the east coast of Brazil and observes natives using stone to cut wood (1499).

1500–25: The discovery of plays and poems by Hroswitha of Gandersheim, a 10th-century saxoness, makes her the first European playwright since the Classical Age (1500); King Ferdinand of Spain sanctions a system of levying tribute payments from Indians in the new world and using Indians as forced labour (1501); Shi'ism becomes the state religion in Persia (1502) and Sunni Muslim dissenters are executed there; a hand-held timepiece, made

possible by the invention of the coiled mainspring, is constructed by German locksmith Peter Henlein (1502); *David*, a 13-foot statue, is completed by Michelangelo Buon-arrotti (1504) in Florence, Italy; Leonardo da Vinci paints the *Mona Lisa* (1505); Venice dominates Mediterranean trade (c. 1507); a map calls the new world "America" after Amerigo Vespucci (1507) and shows it as a distinct continent; the first great German artist, Albrecht Dürer (painter/engraver), creates his *Adam and Eve* oil painting (1507); Michelangelo paints the ceiling of the Sistine Chapel (1508–12); Sebastion Cabot sails around Cuba, proving it is an island (1508) and later reaches Hudson Bay in search of a northwest passage; the first African slaves are brought to the Americas (Cuba) (1510); Erasmus, the Dutch humanist, writes the satirical *In Praise of Folly* (1511); Juan Ponce de Léon claims Florida for Spain (1513) while searching for the Fountain of Youth; Niccolo Machiavelli writes *The Prince* (1513) which discusses the uses and abuses of power; Vasco Núñez de Balboa discovers the "South Sea," or Pacific Ocean, for Spain (1513); Spain orders new world natives to convert to Christianity under threat of enslavement or death (1514); Henry VIII of England puts forth measures to protect peasants from enclosure—the dividing and closing off of common land (1515); Sir Thomas More writes *Utopia*, which depicts an ideal state (1516); Martin Luther, a German Augustinian monk, writes his *95 Theses*, attacking the Catholic church's sale of indulgences granting the forgiveness of sins (1517) and nails it to the door of the Wittenberg church; English sailors complain to King Henry VIII about the growing number of French cod fishermen in Newfoundland (1517); the rule of Suleiman I the Magnificent sees the Ottoman Turks reach the zenith of their empire with the conquest of Egypt, Syria and Hungary (1520); Ferdinand Magellan begins a three-year voyage to circumnavigate the globe (1519); Hernando Cortes lands at Vera Cruz, Mexico, where Montezuma II and the Aztecs surrender (1519); chocolate is introduced to Europe from Mexico (1520); Nicholas Copernicus publishes his "Commentariolus" stating his theory that the earth revolves around the sun (1521); Martin Luther translates the Bible into German (1522).

1526–49: Lutheran German troops sack and burn Rome (1527); Hippocrates' ancient idea of the four humours governing bodily health is first disputed (1528); Henry VIII separates from the Church of Rome and becomes head of the English Church (1534) after he is refused an annulment of his first marriage; the Jesuit order of missionaries is founded by Ignatius Loyola (1534); Jacques Cartier searches for riches in North America along the St Lawrence River (1535); John Calvin, the French leader of the Protestant Refor-mation in Geneva, theorizes the concepts of predestination and God's omniscience (1536); the first mechanical artificial limbs appear for crippled war veterans (1539); the founder of the Sikh religion, Guru Nanak, dies in India (1539); Henry VIII becomes King of Ireland and Head of the Irish Church (1541); John Knox leads the Calvinist Reformation in Scotland (1541); oil is discovered in North America by the Spaniards (1543); Portugese traders are the first to sell guns to Japan (1543); Nostradamus, the French astrologer, begins making predictions (1547); Ivan IV (the Terrible) is crowned the first czar of Russia (1547): he calls the first national assembly (1549).

1550–99: Jesuit missionaries protect natives in the new world from slavery (1551); Ivan the Terrible defeats the Mongols (1552), and conquers as far as the Caspian Sea (1556); Lady Jane Grey is executed for treason in England by Queen Mary Tudor (1554), who becomes known as "Bloody Mary" after persecuting Protestants (1555); Mary restores papal authority in England and Wales (1554); Charles V relinquishes the Holy Roman Empire and Spain to his brother and son, and goes to a monastery (1556); an influenza epidemic hits Europe (1557); Elizabeth I becomes Queen of England (1558) and rejects papal power in England (1559); the Huguenot (Calvinist French Protestant) conspiracy occurs at Amboise: liberty of worship is promised in France (1560); the Edict of Orleans suspends persecution of Huguenots (1561); the Peace of Amboise ends the first War of Religion in France and the Huguenots are granted limited toleration (1563); Andreas Vesalius, the Flemish founder of modern anatomy, dies (1564); Nobunaga deposes the Japanese shogunate and centralizes the government (1567); the Iroquois Confederacy of five North American nations (Mohawk, Oneida, Onondaga, Cayuga, Seneca) is founded (c. 1570); Huguenots are massacred on St Bartholomew's Day in Paris (1572); the Dutch War of Independence begins (1572); the Union of Utrecht is the foundation of the Dutch Republic (1579); William of Orange accepts the sovereignty of northern Nether-lands and is assassinated (1584); the first English colony in Newfoundland is founded (1582); Elizabeth of England orders Mary Queen of Scots beheaded for treason (1587); Christopher Marlowe completes *Dr. Faustus* (1588); the first Spanish Armada leaves for England and is defeated by the English under Charles Howard (1588); Sir Francis Drake, with 18,000 men, fails to take Lisbon for England (1589); William Shakespeare completes the play *Romeo and Juliet* (1594); the Second Spanish Armada leaves for England but is scattered by storms (1597); an English Act of Parliament calls for convicted criminals to serve their terms in the colonies (1597).

1600–49: France boasts the largest population in central Europe, with 16 million persons (1600); William Shakespeare completes *Hamlet* (1600); Dutch opticians invent the telescope (1600); the first modern public company is founded, the Dutch East India Company (1602); Guy Fawkes is arrested and accused of trying to blow up the House of Lords during James I's state opening of Parliament (The Gunpowder Plot, 1605); Fawkes is sentenced to death (1606); the first English settlement on the American mainland is founded at Jamestown, Virginia (1607); Shakespeare writes his *Sonnets* (1609); the first cheques appear in Netherlands as "cash letters" (1608); the *King James Bible* is published (1611); Peter Paul Rubens paints *Descent from the Cross* (1611); the North American Indian princess Pocahantas marries English colonist John Rolfe (1614); Galileo Galilei, Italian astronomer, faces the Inquisition for the first time for renouncing the Ptolemaic system of the earth-centred universe and embracing the Copernican sun-centred system (1615); the Thirty Years War begins in Prague as Protestants rebel against Catholic oppression (1618); slavery in North America begins when the first Africans are brought to Virginia (1619) and the triangular slave trade starts (British goods are sent to west Africa and are traded for slaves, who are traded for agricultural staples in the new world, which are sent back to Britain); pilgrims arriving on the *Mayflower* found Plymouth Colony, Massachusetts (1620); patent law is created in England to protect inventors (1623); construction begins on the Taj Mahal mausoleum in

Agra, North India (1628); Charles I dissolves the English Parliament for 11 years (1629); Cardinal Richelieu, chief minister of Louis XIII of France, rules France (1630–42); Galileo is forced by the Inquisition to cease promulgating the theories of Copernicus (1633); Japan forbids foreign books, Christianity and any European contacts (1637); René Descartes, called the father of modern philosophy, writes *Discourse on Method* (1637); the Ming dynasty in China ends and the Manchu dynasty takes power (1644–1912); Charles I of England, after a long struggle for power with Parliament (English Civil War 1642–48), is beheaded by Oliver Cromwell for treason (1649).

1650–99: Bishop James Ussher dates the creation of the world at Oct. 23, 4004 BC (1650); the wholesale massacre of North American Indians by European settlers begins (1650); Thomas Hobbes writes *Leviathan*, a defence of absolute monarchy in England (1651); Oliver Cromwell becomes Lord Protector in England, dissolves Parliament, divides England into 11 districts, prohibits Anglican services (1653) and readmits Jews to England after 365 years (1655); Blaise Pascal (French) develops the basic laws of probability (1654); the Portugese drive the Dutch out of Brazil (1654); the first London opera house opens (1656); Dutch peasants (Boers) first settle in South Africa (1660); the Royal Society is founded in London to promote scientific discussion among great thinkers (1660); the earliest condemnation of industrial pollution, *The Inconvenience of the Air and Smoke of London Dissipated*, is written by John Evelyn (1661); Louis XIV (the Sun King) begins to build the palace at Versailles (1662); Jean Baptiste Colbert forms the North American colony of New France with Quebec as its capital (1663); the British annex New Netherlands from the Dutch and rename the main city New York (1664); Isaac Newton begins to experiment with gravity and develops calculus (1664–66); the cell is named and described by Briton Robert Hooke (1665); the French army uses the first hand grenades (1667); Portugal gains independence from Spain through the Treaty of Lisbon (1668); microorganisms are discovered by Anton van Leeuwenhoek (Dutch, 1669) who later observes bacteria (1683) for the first time; the Hudson's Bay Company is incorporated by a British royal charter to trade in the region of North America defined by those rivers which drain into Hudson Bay (1670); Dutch philosopher Baruch Spinoza writes *Ethics* (1675); the poems of Bashu (a pseudonym) popularize Japanese haiku poetry (1675); the *Declaration of the People of Virgina* by Nathaniel Bacon lends support to rebellion against authorities in the colonies (1676); Roman Catholics are excluded from both houses of Parliament in England (1678); the Habeas Corpus Amendment Act in England protects citizens from unjust imprisonment (1679); the French colonial empire of North America, reaching from Quebec to the mouth of the Mississippi River, is organized (1680); the large dodo bird with small, flightless wings becomes extinct (1680); Sir Isaac Newton writes *Principles of Natural Philo-sophy* (1687), which discusses universal gravitation; the Glorious Revolution establishes the constitutional monarchy in England (1688–89) and William of Orange III and Mary II ascend the throne; Peter the Great becomes Czar of Russia (1689); John Locke writes *Essay Concerning Human Understanding* and *Two Treatises on Civil Government* (1690).

1700–49: The War of the Spanish Succession to the childless Charles II, Hapsburg king of Spain, is fought (1701–14) between the French Bourbons and Austrian Hapsburgs; rebellion occurs in Astrakhan against Czar Peter's westernization of Russia (1705); England and Scotland form Great Britain (1707); the Peace of Utrecht is signed between Spain and England: Spain cedes Gibraltar and Minorca to England (1713) and Philip of France retains the Spanish crown; D.G. Fahrenheit constructs a mercury thermometer with a temperature scale (1714); George F. Handel writes *Water Music* for King George I (1717); Daniel Defoe writes *The Life and Strange Surprising Adventures of Robinson Crusoe* (1719); the German composer and virtuoso organist J.S. Bach composes *The Brandenburg Concertos* (1721); Johnathan Swift writes *Gulliver's Travels* (1726); Benjamin Franklin, American statesman, scientist, printer and writer, writes *Poor Richard's Almanack* (1732); John Kay patents the fly shuttle loom, which revolutionizes weaving (1733); Alexander Pope, poet and English verse satirist, writes *Essay on Man* (1733); the modern classification system of plants and animals is introduced by Carolus Linnaeus (Swedish, 1735); Alaska is discovered by Victor Behring (1740); Frederick the Great introduces freedom of the press and freedom of worship in Prussia (1740); sign language for the deaf is created by Rodriguez Pereire (1749).

■ Industrial Revolution: 1750–1850

1750–99: Benjamin Franklin experimented with static electricity and invented the lightning conductor (1752); in the Seven Years War (1756–63) Britain declares war on France and, in the North American colonies, the French drive the British from the Great Lakes area (1756); the French lose Quebec to the British (1759) during the battle on the Plains of Abraham; Voltaire writes the philosophical novel *Candide* (1759); Catherine II (the Great) becomes czarina of Russia (1762); Swiss-French philosopher Jean Jacques Rousseau writes *Social Contract* (1762) which discusses his theory of "natural man"; the Peace of Paris (1763) ends the war between England and France and gives Canada to England; eight-year-old Mozart writes his first symphony (1764); the spinning jenny, which spins up to 120 threads at once is invented by Briton James Hargreaves (1764); the British Parliament passes the Stamp Act for taxing American colonies: Virginia and New York challenge the right of Britain to taxation without representation (1766); the Mason-Dixon Line is drawn by English surveyors between Pennsylvania and Maryland (1767) and is later the boundary between "slave" and "free" states; Daniel Rutherford and Joseph Priestley independently discover nitrogen (1772); the Bolshoi Ballet is founded in Russia (1773); during the Boston Tea Party American colonists protesting British taxes dress as Indians and dump the cargo of three tea ships in the Boston, Mass., harbor (1773); James Watt, Scottish inventor, perfects the steam engine (1775); the American Revolution begins (1775); the Second Continental Congress assembles at Philadelphia and appoints George Washing-ton commander-in-chief of the American forces; the Americans proclaim the *Declara-tion of Independence* (July 4, 1776); Edward Gibbon writes *Decline and Fall of the Roman Empire* (1776); Adam Smith completes *Wealth of Nations* (1776); after the American victory in the Saratoga Campaign (1777) France entered into an alliance with the Americans (1778); Washington's army suffers at Valley Forge (1778); Hawaii is discovered by James Cook

(1778); Franz Mesmer practices mesmerism (hypnotism) (1778); Spain joins the American War of Indepen-dence against Britain (1779); the Dutch support the American side (1780); Sir William Herschel discovers Uranus (1781); British General Cornwallis surrenders to the Ameri-cans (Oct. 1781) at the end of the Yorktown Campaign, and the Treaty of Paris recognizes American independence (1783); John Wesley writes the *Deed of Declaration,* the charter of Wesleyan Methodism (1784); the British colony of Australia is founded (1788); the French Revolution begins (1789); a Paris mob opposing the monarchy storms the Bastille jail; French royalists begin to emigrate; the French revolutionaries proclaim the Decrees of Aug. 4 and the *Declaration of the Rights of Man and of the Citizen;* the government limits the monarchy's power, abolishes the French feudal system, extends religious tolerance to Jews and protestants and reorganizes the Catholic Church; A.L. Lavoisier completes the *Table of Thirty-One Chemical Elements* (1790); the Constitutional Act divides Britain's Canadian colony into Upper Can-ada (English-speaking) and Lower Canada (French-speaking) (1791); Thomas Paine writes *The Rights of Man* in defence of the French Revolution (1791); the French King Louis XVI and Queen Marie Antoinette are beheaded for treason (Jan., 1793); the Reign of Terror (guillotine executions of prisoners) under the Jacobin government ends with the execution of Maximilien Robespierre; Robert Burns' *Auld Lang Syne* is published (1794); Edward Jenner discovers a smallpox vaccine (1796).

1800–09: Ottawa is founded (1800); Eli Whitney makes muskets with interchangeable parts (1800); the Library of Congress is established in Washington, DC by Thomas Jefferson (1800); the first battery is produced from zinc and copper plates by Alessandro Volto (1800); William Herschel discovers the existence of infrared solar rays (1800); the first submarine *Nautilus* is made by American civil engineer Robert Fulton (1801); the atomic theory of chemistry is put forth by John Dalton (1802); the US buys land from France in the Louisiana Purchase (1803); Henry Shrapnel invents the shell used in warfare (1803); Napoleon crowns himself emperor of the French empire (1804) and king of Italy (1805); modern Egypt is established when Mehemet Ali becomes Pasha (1805); morphine is isolated by F.W.A. Satürner (1805); Napoleon wins his greatest victory, at Austerlitz, over the Austrians and Russians allied against him (1805); the American frigate *Chesapeake* is stopped and boarded by British naval officers looking for deserters, almost causing a war (1807); Ludwig van Beethoven, the great German composer who brought together Classical and Romantic styles, performs his *Fifth Symphony* (written for Napoleon) and *Sixth Symphony* (1808); the first part of J.W. von Goethe's *Faust* is published (1808); Washington Irving writes *Rip van Winkle* (1809).

1810–19: Simón Bolívar becomes a leading figure in South American politics (1810) and liberates Greater Colombia (Panama, Venezuela, Ecuador and Colombia) (1819) and Peru (1824) from Spanish rule; a machine for spinning flax is invented by Philippe Girard (1812); German folklorist Jakob Grimm completes *Grimm's Fairy Tales* (1812–15); Napoleon Bonaparte's first military setback is in the Peninsular War (1808–14); and he later retreats from an unsuccessful invasion of Russia; the War of 1812 (1812–14) between Britain and the United States is foreshadowed by the battle at Tippecanoe (1811); Jane Austen writes *Pride and Prejudice* (1813), depicting English country life and mores; Austria, Russia and Prussia form an alliance against Napoleon and defeat him at Leipzig (1813) and recapture Paris (1814); Napoleon abdicates and is exiled to Elba Island; the War of 1812 continues in North America as the British capture Washington, DC (1814) but the Americans win battles at Fort McHenry, Thames (killing Tecumseh, an Indian ally of the British) and at Plattsburgh (1814); the British initiate peace in the Treaty of Ghent (1814) but this news travels too slowly to stop the Battle of New Orleans (1815), won by the Americans; Napoleon escapes from exile and returns to march on Paris; he is defeated at Waterloo (1815), abdicates again and is banished to St Helena Island; the German Confederation, dominated by Austria and Prussia, is created to replace the Holy Roman Empire (1815); Argentina declares its independence from Spain (1816); the classical economist David Ricardo (British) writes *The Principles of Political Economy and Taxation* (1817), discussing the determination of wage and value; Georg Hegel writes his all-embracing *Encyclopedia of the Philosophical Sciences* (1817); Mary Wollstonecraft Shelley writes

Frankenstein (1818); Lord Byron begins *Don Juan* (1818–23); Chile proclaims its independence from Spain (1818); electromagnetism is discovered by Danish physicist Hans C. Oersted (1819); Greater Colombia (including Panama, Venezuela, Ecuador and Colombia) declares independence from Spain (1819).

1820–29: Andre Ampere (French) writes *Laws of Electrodynamic Action* (1820); Liberia is founded by the Washington Colonization Society, for the repatriation of black slaves (1820); Sir Walter Scott writes *Ivanhoe* (1820); John Keats writes *Ode to a Nightingale* (1820); an electric recording device for sound reproduction is invented by Sir Charles Wheatstone (1821); Peru and Guatemala declare their independence from Spain (1821); the Reign of Terror begins between the Greeks and the Turks (1821); Franz Liszt, the Hungarian pianist who revolutionizes Romantic music and invents the symphonic poem, makes his debut at age 11 in Vienna (1822); Brazil declares itself independent from Portugal (1822); the Monroe Doctrine closes the American continent to colonial settlement by European powers (1823); Spanish are defeated and Paris independence recognized (1824); Simón Bolívar creates his namesake, Bolivia (1825); the first steam-powered railroads carrying freight and passengers, operated by the the Stockton and Darlington Railway, run in England (1825); the Erie Canal opens, linking the Hudson River and the Great Lakes (1825); the first major American author, James Fenimore Cooper, writes *The Last of the Mohicans* (1826); Felix Mendelssohn composes the Overture to *A Midsummer Night's Dream* (1826); the great cholera epidemic begins in India (1826) and spreads from Russia into Central Europe; J. J. Audubon writes *Birds of North America* (1827); Noah Webster writes the *American Dictionary of the English Language* (1828); Uruguay declares independence from Brazil (1828); the Peace of Adrianople ends the Russo-Turkish war and Turkey acknowledges the independence of Greece (1829); Frederic Chopin, the Polish pianist, debuts in Vienna (1829); Venezuela withdraws from Greater Colombia and becomes independent (1829).

1830–39: Charles Lyell of Scotland divides the geological system into three groups: Eocene, Miocene and Pliocene (1830); Ecuador declares independence (1830); mass demonstrations in Swiss cities lead to liberal reforms

(1831); Charles Darwin sails on the HMS *Beagle* as a naturalist, surveying South America, New Zealand and Australia (1831–36); the leading anti-slavery leader in the United States, W. L. Garrison, begins publishing *The Liberator* in Boston (1831); the wealthy middle classes emerging from the Industrial Revolution are enfranchised in Britain, doubling the number of voters (1832); the New England anti-slavery society is founded in Boston (1832); slavery is abolished in the British Empire (1833); the Spanish Inquisition, begun during the 13th century, is finally abolished (1834); France's leading writer, Victor Hugo, writes *The Hunchback of Notre Dame* (1834); the Poor Law Amendment Act decrees that no able-bodied person (displaced by the Industrial Revolution) in Great Britain shall receive assistance unless he or she enters a workhouse (1834); Hans Christian Anderson writes his first stories for children (1835); the American writer Ralph Waldo Emerson writes *Nature* (1836); the People's Charter initiates Britain's first national working-class movement, calling for universal suffrage for men and voting by ballot (1836); the Dutch (Afrikaner) farmers begin "The Great Trek" of emigration across the Orange and Vaal Rivers, South Africa (1836); the first botanical textbook, *The Elements of Botany*, is written by American Asa Gray (1836); Victoria becomes Queen of Great Britain (1837); citizens stage unsuccessful rebellions in Lower and Upper Canada (1837); Louis Braille invents his reading system for the blind (1837); Charles Dickens's *Oliver Twist,* a critique of British industrial society, is a bestseller (1838); the first bicycle is invented by a Scot, Kirkpatrick Macmillan (1839); the cell-growth theory is put forth by Theodor Schwann (1839); ozone is discovered by Christian Schönbein, a German-Swiss chemist (1839); American Charles Goodyear develops the process of vulcanization, making the commercial use of rubber possible (1839); a photograph produced on a silver-coated copperplate treated with iodine vapor, the daguerreotype, is invented by Louis Daguerre and J. Niepce (French) (1839); the First Opium War between Britain and China begins (1839).

1840–49: New Zealand becomes a British colony (1840); philosopher Thomas Carlyle writes *On Heroes, Hero-Worship and the Heroic in History* in support of strong government (1841); the father of the guided tour,

Thomas Cook (British), arranges his first trip (1841); showman P.T. Barnum gains fame after opening his American Museum of freak exhibitions (1841); the Webster-Ashburton Treaty between Britain and the US settles American border disputes with Canada (1842); the Treaty of Nanking ends the Opium War between Britain and China and confirms the cession of Hong Kong to Great Britain (1842); riots and strikes erupt in northern England's industrial areas (1842); Richard Wagner (German) finishes the opera *The Flying Dutchman* (1843); the amount of work required to produce a unit of heat, the joule, is determined by English physicist James P. Joule (1843); American social reformer Dorothea Dix reports on the shocking conditions in prisons and asylums, influencing the establishment of state hospitals for the insane in Europe and North America (1843); Samuel Morse's telegraph is used for the first time between Baltimore and Washington (1844); US troops are victorious over the Mexicans at Palo Alto (1846), Congress formally declares war, US forces take Santa Fe and annex New Mexico; the Smithsonian Institution, a research and educational centre, is founded in Washington, DC (1846); ether is first used as an anaesthetic by dentist W.T. Morton (1846); sisters Charlotte and Emily Brontë publish *Jane Eyre* and *Wuthering Heights* respectively (1847); US forces capture Mexico City (1847) and the Treaty of Guadalupe Hidalgo ends the Mexican-US war (1848), the US acquires Texas and much of the surrounding territory in return for $15 million; gold discoveries in California lead to the first gold rush (1848); a revolt in Paris causes Louis Philippe to abdicate (1848); a revolution in Vienna brings Metternich's resignation (1848); revolutions in Venice, Berlin, Milan, Rome and Parma (1848); the first Public Health Act is introduced in Britain (1848); the first women's rights convention, organized by Elizabeth Stanton and Lucretia Mott, is held in Seneca Falls, New York (1848); the *Communist Manifesto* is issued by Germans Karl Marx and Friedrick Engels (1848), championing the working class and establishing socialist theory.

1850–59: Harriet Beecher Stowe writes her anti-slavery novel *Uncle Tom's Cabin* (1852); the Transvaal is granted self-government (1852); the Crimean War (1853–56) begins when Russia occupies Moldavia and Walachia and Turkey declares war, the Russians destroy the Turkish fleet off Sinope, and England, France and Sardinia join Turkey's fight; after a long siege the Russian base Sevastopol falls to the allied forces (1855), and after the allied victory at Balaklava, Russia recognizes the integrity of Turkey (1856); English nurse Florence Nightingale founds modern nursing while tending soldiers during the Crimean War (1853–56); the first hypodermic syringe is used by Alexander Wood (1853); Samuel Colt revolutionizes the manufacture of small arms (1853); Commander Matthew Perry negotiates the first American-Japanese treaty, permitting US ships to use two Japanese ports (1854); the Elgin Reciprocity Treaty between Great Britain and the US implements free trade between Canada and the US (1854); steel making becomes inexpensive when Henry Bessemer introduces a converter into his process for making steel (1855); pure cocaine is extracted from coca leaves (1856); Gustave Flaubert, the French master of realistic novels, writes *Madame Bovary* (1856); Louis Pasteur discovers that fermentation is caused by micro-organisms (1857), and later invents pasteurization and discovers a vaccine for rabies; the first Neanderthal skeleton is found in a cave in Neander Valley (near Düsseldorf, Germany); the Indian Mutiny against British rule (1857) causes the British siege and capture of Delhi; the British Royal Navy destroys the Chinese fleet, and Britain and France take Canton (1857); Guiseppe Garibaldi forms the Italian National Association for the unification of Italy (1857); the Treaty of Tientsin ends the Anglo-Chinese war (1858); Charles Darwin writes *On the Origin of Species by Natural Selection*, explaining his theory of evolution (1859); the German National Association is formed to unite Germany under Prussia (1859); John Stuart Mill (British) writes his essay *On Liberty* (1859).

■ Modern Era

1860–64: Garibaldi and his redshirts sail from Genoa to take Palermo and Naples; Victor Emmanuel II (King of Sardinia) invades the Papal States and defeats the Papal troops, Garibaldi proclaims Emmanuel II king of Italy (1860); Anglo-French troops defeat the Chinese at Pa-li-Chau (1860) and sign the Treaty of Peking; the first Food and Drugs Act is enacted in Britain (1860); Lenoir constructs the first internal-combustion engine (1860); a

primitive form of typewriter is created by American Christopher L. Sholes (1860); hundreds of thousands of Irish and British citizens flee their homelands following the potato famine (by 1860); Russian troops fire at anti-Russian demonstrators in Poland during the Warsaw Massacre (1861); the first machine-chilled cold storage unit is built by T. S. Mort (1861); Krupp begins arms production in Essen, Germany (1861); the Archaeopteryx, the skeleton linking reptiles and birds, is discovered at Solnhofen, Germany (1861); the American Civil War (1861–65) begins after Abraham Lincoln, who views slavery as evil, is elected president; South Carolina secedes in protest, followed by 10 other southern states, to form the Confederacy fighting for states' rights and opposing the abolition of slavery; Lincoln issues the Emancipation Proclamation (1862) calling for the freeing of black slaves in Confederate territory; the Red Cross voluntary relief organization is proposed by Jean Henri Dunant, a Swiss humanist (1862); the first form of a machine gun is invented by the American Richard Gatling (1862); Otto von Bismarck becomes the prime minister of Prussia (1862) and begins his system of alliances and alignments that result in German preeminence in Europe; Victor Hugo writes *Les Miserables* (1862); Leo Tolstoy writes *War and Peace* (1864); the Geneva Convention establishes the neutrality of battlefield medical facilities (1864); liberalism, socialism and rationalism are condemned in *Syllabus Errorum*, issued by Pope Pius IX (1864); Cheyenne and Arapahoe Indians are massacred at Sand Creek, Colorado (1864); the First International Workingmen's Association is founded by Karl Marx in London and New York (1864); Confederate forces surrender finally at Appomattox, Virginia (1865) marking the end of the war and victory for the Union; slavery in the US is abolished by the Thirteenth Amendment; US Pres. Lincoln is assassinated by the actor John Wilkes Booth (1865).

1865–69: Lewis Carroll (British) writes *Alice's Adventures in Wonderland* (1865); Joseph Lister initiates antiseptic surgery by using carbolic acid on a compound wound (1865); line geometry is invented by German mathematician Julius Plücker (1865); Gregor Mendel, an Austrian monk, describes his Law of Heredity (1865); Bismarck, the Prussian foreign minister, provoked the brief Austro-Prussian War by invading the duchies of Schleswig-Holstein and overrunning the German states allied with Austria; after seven weeks a peace settlement gave Schleswig-Holstein, Hanover, Hesse, Nasau and Frankfurt to Prussia and excluded Austria from influence in German affairs (1866); *Crime and Punishment* by Feodor Dosto-evsky is published (1866); Alfred Nobel invents dynamite (1866); Johann Strauss popularizes the Viennese waltz with Blue Danube (1866); the underwater torpedo is invented by Robert Whitehead, an English engineer (1866); the fundamental law of biogenetics, *General Morphology,* is published by Ernst Haeckel (1866); Claude Monet, a French founder of Impressionism, paints *Camille* (1866); Russia sells Alaska to the US for $7.2 million (1867); Karl Marx writes *Das Kapital,* volume I (1867); the British North America Act establishes the Dominion of Canada and John A. Macdonald becomes prime minister (1867); Louisa May Alcott describes Victorian American life in *Little Women* (1868); a skeleton of Cro Magnon man from the Upper Paleolithic age (the first Homo sapiens in Europe, successor to the Neanderthal man) is found in France by Louis Lartet (1868); the first regular Trades Union Congress is held at Manchester, England (1868); Dmitri Mendeleyev formulates his periodic law for the classification of the elements (1869); John Stuart Mill writes *On the Subjection of Women* (1869); the major early treatise on eugenics, *Hereditary Genius,* is published by Francis Galton (1869); J.W. Hyatt invents celluloid (plastic) (1869); the First Nihilist Congress is held at Basel, Switzerland (1869); the strategically important Suez Canal opens (1869); the doctrine of papal infallibility is established by Pope Pius IX during Vatican Council I (1869–79).

1870–79: US industrialist John D. Rockefeller founds the Standard Oil Company (1870); T.H. Huxley, English biologist and educator, writes the *Theory of Biogenesis* (1870); the Franco-Prussian War begins (1870) and France under Napoleon III capitulates; William I, king of Prussia, is proclaimed the German Emperor at Versailles, and in the Peace of Frankfurt France cedes Alsace-Lorraine to Germany (1871); the Italian Law of Guarantees allows the Pope possession of the Vatican (1871); labour unions become legal in Britain (1871); Charles Darwin writes *The Descent of Man* (1871); the Great Fire ravages Chicago (1871);

explorer Sir Henry M. Stanley is sent to find David Livingstone in Africa (1871); the first modern luxury liner, SS *Oceanic,* is launched (1871); Civil War in Spain ends with the Carlists' defeat (1872); the Three Emperors League is established in Berlin as an alliance between Germany, Russia and Austria-Hungary (1872); colour photographs are first developed (1873); James C. Maxwell writes *Electricity and Magnetism* (1873); Willhelm Wundt, known for the experimental method, writes *Physiological Psychology* (1873); under the direction of Benjamin Disraeli as prime minister, Britain expands its imperial power by annexing the Fiji islands (1874); Johannes Brahms composes the *Hungarian Dances* (1874); Johann Strauss II performs the operetta *Die Fledermaus* in Vienna (1874); Bosnia and Herzegovina rebel against Turkish rule (1875): Turkish sultan promises reforms (1875); Mary Baker Eddy writes *Science and Health* (1875) and she founds the Christian Science movement (1879); Georges Bizet performs *Carmen* in Paris (1875); British Queen Victoria is crowned empress of India (1876); Britain annexes the Transvaal (1877); US General George Custer is killed along with his cavalry by Cheyenne Indians in the Battle of the Little Bighorn (1876); Alexander Graham Bell constructs a telephone (1876); first national lawn tennis championship played at Wimbledon (1877); German historian Heinrich Treitschke begins a racial anti-semite movement (1878); Gilbert and Sullivan write *HMS Pinafore* (1878); British troops are massacred by Zulus in Isand-hlwana, Africa (1879); the British occupy the Khyber Pass near Afghanistan and are massacred in Kabul (1879); Norwegian Henrik Ibsen completes the play *A Doll's House* (1879); Chile invades Bolivia and its ally Peru after Bolivia cancels a Chilean company's contract to exploit Bolivia's nitrate deposits (1879).

1880–84: Auguste Rodin sculpts *The Thinker* (1880); France annexes Tahiti (1880); Transvaal declares its independence from Britain and the Boers establish a republic after a brief war with Britain (1880–81); the first practical electrical lights are independently made by Thomas Edison and J.W. Swan (1880); the malaria parasite is discovered by Charles Laveran (1880); the first large steel furnace is developed by American steel baron Andrew Carnegie (1880); the Vatican opens its archives to scholars (1881); the first Japanese political parties are founded (1881); violent government-condoned attacks (po-groms) are carried out against Russian Jews (1881–1917) causing large-scale Jewish emigration to North America; the Federation of Organized Trades and Labor Unions of the US and Canada is formed (1881); Germany, Austria and Italy form an alliance (1882); the three-mile limit for territorial waters is agreed upon at the Hague Convention (1882); Peter I. Tchaikovsky composes the *1812 Overture* (1882); psychoanalysis begins when Joseph Breuer (Austrian) uses hypnosis to treat hysteria (1882); Thomas Edison designs the first hydroelectric plant in Wisconsin (1882); the Orient Express train between Paris and Istanbul makes its first run (1883); *On the Size of Atoms* is published by British scientist William Thomson, later Lord Kelvin (1883); peace is restored between Peru and Chile (1883); Friedrich Nietzsche (German philosopher) begins *Thus Spake Zarathustra* (1884–91); gold is discovered in the Transvaal (1884) and this leads to the rise of Johannesburg; a truce is signed between Bolivia and Chile, with Bolivia forced to cede its only coastal territory to Chile (1884); the *Oxford English Dictionary* begins publication (1884–1928); the Berlin Conference of 14 nations on African affairs is held (1884).

1885–89: Karl Benz builds the single-cylinder engine for motor cars (1885); the individuality of fingerprints is proved by Sir Francis Galton (1885); the first Indian National Congress meets (1886); the Statue of Liberty is presented to the US by France (1886); steam is first used to sterilize surgical instruments by Ernst von Bergmann (1886); Irish politician Charles Parnell, the Fenians, and British Prime Min. William Gladstone try unsuccessfully to pass the first Irish Home Rule Bill to give Ireland control over domestic affairs (1886); Sir Arthur Conan Doyle writes the first Sherlock Holmes story, *A Study in Scarlet* (1887); William II (the Kaiser) becomes emperor of Germany (1888); Vincent Van Gogh paints the series of sunflowers (1888) and later, *Starry Night*; the electric motor is first constructed by Nikola A. Tesla and manufactured by George Westinghouse (1888); radio waves are discovered to be of the same family as light waves by the independently working Heinrich Hertz and Oliver Lodge (1888); Kodak box camera produced by George Eastman (1888); "Jack the Ripper" murders six women in London (1888);

Alexander G. Eiffel designs the Eiffel Tower for the Paris World Exhibition (1889).

1890–94: The first Japanese general election is held (1890); German Chancellor Bismarck dismissed by Emperor William II (1890); the first moving picture shows appear in New York (1890); Oscar Wilde writes *The Picture of Dorian Gray* (1890); antitoxins are discovered by Emil von Behring (1890); the first entirely steel-framed building is erected in Chicago (1890); the Triple Alliance between Austria, Germany and Italy is renewed for 12 years (1891); Briton Thomas Hardy writes *Tess of the D'Ubervilles* (1891); Henri Toulouse-Lautrec produces his first music hall posters (1891); *Experiments in Aero-dynamics* is published by Samuel P. Langley (1891); the All-Deutschland Verband (Pan-Germany League) is founded (1891); Russia experiences widespread famine (1891); an earthquake in Japan kills ten thousand people (1891); the Java Man (*Pithecanthropus homo erectus*) is discovered by Dutch anthropologist Eugène Dubois, in Java (1891); Paul Gauguin (French) paints *By the Sea* in Tahiti (1892); Rudolph Diesel (German) patents his internal-combustion engine (1892); Tchai-kovsky performs his *The Nutcracker* ballet score in St Petersburg (1892); Karl Benz constructs his four-wheel car (1893); Jewish French army captain Alfred Dreyfus is arrested under controversy and convicted of spying for Germany (1894); Rudyard Kipling writes *The Jungle Book* (1894); after Japan sends troops to Seoul, Korea, Japan declares war on China and defeats the Chinese at Port Arthur (1894); Emil Berliner develops a horizontal gramophone disc, replacing the record cylinder for sound reproduction (1894).

1895–99: The Chinese-Japanese war ends with Japan victorious: Formosa and Port Arthur are first ceded to Japan and later returned to China for payment (1895); H.G. Wells writes *The Time Machine* (1895); William B. Yeats writes *Poems* (1895); x-rays are discovered by William Röntgen (1895); Marchese Marconi invents radio telegraphy (1895); the principle of rocket reaction propulsion is developed by Konstantin Isiolkovski (1895); the first modern Olympics is held in Athens, Greece (1896); Anton Chekhov (Russian) writes *The Sea Gull* (1896); five annual Nobel prizes are established by Alfred Nobel for persons who have contributed the most in the fields of physics, physiology and medicine, chemistry, literature and peace (1896); Wilfrid Laurier becomes the first French Canadian prime minister of Canada (1896–1911); the Klondike gold rush in Bonanza Creek, Canada, begins (1896); Edmond Rostand writes *Cyrano de Bergerac* (1897); Queen Victoria celebrates her Diamond Jubilee (1897); French writer Emile Zola writes an open letter, *J' accuse*, condemning the Dreyfus espionage trial and he is imprisoned (1898), Col. Henry admits forging documents in the case (1898), and Captain Dreyfus is pardoned after a retrial (1899)—the case polarized French politics for a decade; the US declares war on Spain over Cuba and destroys the Spanish fleet at Manila (1898); Spain cedes Cuba, Puerto Rico, Guam and the Philippines to the US for $20 million at the Treaty of Paris; Chinese Boxers, an anti-Western organization, is formed (1898); the Boer War begins as the South African Republic (Transvaal) and the Orange Free State unite against the British (1898); Marie and Pierre Curie discover radium and polonium (1898); German Count Ferdinand von Zeppelin builds his airship (1898); photographs using artificial light are first taken (1898); Marchese Marconi invents the radio (1899).

1900: The Boer War continues and Canadian troops set sail for South Africa to fight for England in their first foreign war; Boxer rebellion against Western influence, supported by the Dowager Empress Tzu-hsi, continues in China against Christian missionaries and foreigners; Sigmund Freud, the founder of psychoanalysis (Austrian), completes *The Interpretation of Dreams*; Wilhelm Wundt writes *Comparative Psychology*; Shintoism is reinstated in Japan to counter Buddhist influence; Commonwealth of Australia is created; Max Planck formulates the quantum theory; human speech is first transmitted via radio waves by the Canadian-born scientist R.A. Fessenden; Holland's senate creates an international arbitration court at The Hague; millions are reported starving in India; botanist Hugo de Vries rediscovers Gregor Mendel's laws of heredity after 30 years; 10,000 Ashanti natives attack a British force of 400 at Cape Coast, Ghana, and are defeated.

1901: Queen Victoria dies and is succeeded by her son Edward VII; the Dutch Boers begin organized guerrilla warfare against the British; the Cuba Convention makes Cuba a US protectorate; US Pres. William McKinley is assassinated and is succeeded by Theodore Roosevelt; a treaty is signed to build the Panama Canal

under US supervision; the hormone adrenaline is first isolated; Walter Nernst postulates the "third law of thermodynamics"; John Pierpont Morgan organizes the US Steel Corp., the first billion-dollar corporation; the Peace of Peking ends the Boxer uprising and China is forced to pay an indemnity of $333 million to the Allies to amend commercial treaties in favor of foreign nationals and to allow foreign troops to be posted in Peking; French physicist Henri Becquerel determines that atoms have internal structure; there are racial riots in New Orleans when American black leader Booker T. Washington is invited to the White House; the Trans-Siberian railroad reaches Port Arthur on the east coast of Russia; oil drilling begins in Persia (Iran).

1902: An Anglo-Japanese treaty recognizes the independence of China and Korea; the Treaty of Vereeniging ends the Boer War and the Orange Free State becomes a British colony; the Triple Alliance between Ger-many, Austria and Italy is renewed for another six years; the US acquires perpetual control over the Panama Canal; the Colonial Conference meets in London; the Committee of Imperial Defence meets in London for the first time; Jean Sibelius, Finnish composer and conductor, completes *Symphony No. 2*; Egypt's Aswan Dam is opened.

1903: The "Entente Cordiale" between England and France is established to counter German imperialism; the Russian Social Democratic Party splits into Mensheviks (led by Plechanoff) and Bolsheviks (led by Vladimir Lenin and Leon Trotsky); *The Conduction of Electricity through Gases* is published by Joseph John Thomson; Briton George Bernard Shaw writes *Man and Superman*; Orville and Wilbur Wright successfully fly a powered airplane near Kitty Hawk, North Carolina; the electrocardiograph, which records heart action, is invented by William Einthoven; Briton Emmeline Pankhurst founds the National Women's Social and Political Union and campaigns for women's right to vote; Albert I, Prince of Monaco, founds the International Peace Institute; Henry Ford founds the Ford Motor Company.

1904: The Russo-Japanese War breaks out over Korea and Manchuria; the Japanese besiege Port Arthur and occupy Seoul; the Russian fleet is partially destroyed off Port Arthur; the Russians are defeated at Mukden and Toushima Straits; Max Weber writes *The Protestant Ethic and the Birth of Capitalism*; the first performance of Giacomo Puccini's opera *Madame Butterfly* in Milan; the first radio transmission of music is at Graz, Austria; the general theory of radioactivity is postulated by Ernest Rutherford and Frederick Soddy; W.C. Gorgas eradicates yellow fever in the Panama Canal Zone; silicones are discovered by F.S. Kipping.

1905: Albert Einstein publishes four papers detailing his special theory of relativity, the relationship between mass and energy, the Brownian theory of motion and another formulating the photon theory of light; the Russian city of Port Arthur surrenders to the Japanese; in Russia troops fire at peaceful protest marchers heading for the czar's Winter Palace in St Petersburg, and the event becomes known as "Bloody Sunday"; Wil-liam II of Germany and Nicholas II of Russia sign the Treaty of Bjorko for mutual help in Europe; the Treaty of Portsmouth ends the Russo-Japanese War; a general strike in Russia in response to Bloody Sunday includes a sailors' mutiny on the battleship *Potemkin* and the creation of the first workers soviet in St Petersburg; Czar Nicholas establishes a constitutional government (the Imperial Duma); the Norwegian Parliament decides to separate from Sweden; the Anglo-Japanese alliance is renewed for 10 years; the Sinn Fein nationalist party is formed in Ireland; George Santayana writes his philosophical work *The Life of Reason*.

1906: Reform laws are proposed in Russia and the Imperial Duma is dissolved by the czar to end the radical change; the All India Muslim League is founded by Aga Khan; the term "allergy" is introduced by Clemens von Pirquet; the position of the magnetic North Pole is determined by Norwegian explorer Roald Amundsen; night-shift work for women is forbidden in many countries; the San Francisco earthquake kills 700 people and causes $400 million in property loss; Transvaal and Orange River colonies are granted self-government.

1907: The second Russian Duma meets in March; its radical proposals lead to its dissolution five months later; the US prohibits Japanese immigration; Lenin leaves Russia and founds the newspaper *The Proletarian*; Grigori Rasputin, a Russian mystic, gains influence with the royal family when he treats the hemo-philiac son of Nicholas II; New Zealand becomes a dominion within the British Empire; Baden-Powell forms the Boy Scout movement; Korea becomes a Japanese protectorate; Russian artist Marc Chagall paints *Peasant Women*; Gustav Mahler (Austrian) composes *Symphony No. 8*; Ivan Pavlov (Russian) studies conditioned reflexes in dogs; the SS *Lusitania* beats the SS *Mauritania* in a race from Ireland to New York.

1908: Austria occupies Bosnia and Herzegovina; Bulgaria declares independence from Turkey; Isadora Duncan emerges as a popular modern dancer; the Zeppelin airship crashes near Echterdingen; General Motors Corporation is formed in the US; Henry Ford designs the inexpensive, standardized Model T automobile while pioneering assembly line techniques for autos; an earthquake in Sicily and Calabria kills 150,000; American Gertrude Stein writes *Three Lives*; French writer Anatole France completes the political satire *Penguin Island*; Canadian Lucy Maud Montgomery writes *Anne of Green Gables*.

1909: Turkey and Serbia acknowledge Austrian control of Bosnia and Herzegovina; sultan of Turkey is deposed and replaced by his brother; Ezra Pound writes *Exultations*; the first newsreels appear and director D.W. Griffith features Canadian-born Mary Pickford, who becomes the first film star; Sergei Diaghilev presents his *Ballets Russes*, revolutionizing dance, in Paris; Bériot flies from Calais to Dover in 37 minutes, Farman makes the first 100-mile flight; W.E. Du Bois cofounds the National Negro Committee which becomes the National Association for the Advancement of Colored People in 1910; Girl Guides organized in Britain; Thomas Hunt Morgan begins research in genetics; US explorer Robert E. Peary reaches the North Pole.

1910: The Union of South Africa becomes a dominion within the British Empire with Louis Botha as premier; China abolishes slavery; Japan takes over Korea; Montenegro becomes an independent kingdom; Portugal becomes a republic after a revolution ends the monarchy; Albania rebels against Turkish rule; Roger Fry arranges the Post-Impressionist Exhibition in London with works by Cezanne, van Gogh and Matisse; Igor Stravinsky performs his ballet score *The Firebird* in Paris; the South American tango is the dance craze in Europe and North America; the first deep-sea research expedition is undertaken by Murray and Hjort; the five-day work week is instituted in the US, making the "week-end" possible.

1911: US-Japanese and Anglo-Japanese commercial treaties are signed; Diaz surrenders power in Mexico but revolutions continue; the Kaiser's Hamburg speech promises Germany's "Place in the Sun"; war erupts between Turkey and Italy and aircraft are first used for offensive measures; a revolution in Central China is followed by the fall of the Manchu dynasty (in power since 1644) and the proclamation of a Chinese Republic; Sun Yat-sen is elected president and he appoints Chiang Kai-shek as his military adviser; Russian premier, Peter Stolypin, is assassinated; Roald Amundsen reaches the South Pole; Marie Curie is the first person to win a second Noble Prize, in chemistry; Rutherford formulates his theory of atomic structure.

1912: British dock workers, coal miners and transport workers strike; the German-Austro-Italian alliance is renewed again; Lenin becomes editor of *Pravda*; Sun Yat-sen founds Kuomintang (Chinese National Party); Montenegro declares war against Turkey and Bulgaria, Greece and Serbia mobilize; Carl Jung writes *The Theory of Psychoanalysis*; the term "vitamin" is coined by Polish chemist Kasimir Funk; Stefansson and Anderson explore Arctic Canada; Wilson's cloud chamber (particle detector) photographs lead to the detection of protons and electrons; the Royal Flying Corps (later RAF) is established in Britain; SS *Titanic* sinks on its first voyage after colliding with an iceberg: 1,513 people drown.

1913: The London Peace Treaty ending the First Balkan War is signed and Turkey loses all possessions in Europe except E. Thrace; the Second Balkan War breaks out as Bulgaria attacks Serbia and Greece; Russia declares war on Bulgaria, Bulgaria and Turkey settle a peace treaty and Turkey regains Thrace, Serbia invades Albania; Greece and Turkey make peace; police crack down on suffragette demonstrations led by Emmeline Pankhurst in London; Maxim Gorki, the father of Soviet literature, writes *My Childhood*; Charlie Chaplin first stars in movies; Niels Bohr formulates his theory of atomic structure; Albert Schweitzer, medical missionary, opens his famous hospital in Lambaréné, French Congo.

1914: Archduke Francis Ferdinand, heir to the Austrian throne, is assassinated in Sarajevo (capital of the Austro-Hungarian province of Bosnia) by a Serbian nationalist (June 28); Austria-Hungary challenges Serbia and declares war (July 28); Russia and France support Serbia and mobilize troops; Austria's ally Germany declares war on Russia and France in response; the members of the Triple Entente (Britain, France, Russia) declare war on Turkey after Turks attack Russia; Germany, Austria-Hungary and the Ottoman Empire (Turkey) form alliance of Central Powers, they are opposed by UK, members of British Empire, France, Russia, Belgium, Japan and Serbia (Allied Powers); Germany invades Belgium, attacks France, and establishes the Eastern Front against the Russians at Tannenberg and the Masurian Lakes; on the Western Front the Germans are held in check after battles at Marne River, France (Sept. 6); the First Battle of Ypres, Belgium, is waged to prevent the Germans from cutting British supply lines to France; Austria-Hungary fails in three attacks on Serbia and, after the Russians capture the province of Galicia, retreats to its own territory; by Nov. 14, 1914 there is a deadlock along the Western Front (stretching 720 km across Belgium and northeast France to the Swiss border) that remains throughout the war; Irish writer James Joyce writes *Dubliners* (1914); John B. Watson writes *Behavior: an Introduction to Comparative Psychology* (1914); the first successful heart surgery is performed on a dog by Dr. Alexis Carrel (1914); the Panama Canal opens (1914); millions of immigrants leave southern and eastern Europe between 1905 and 1914.

1915: The Allied Gallipoli Campaign to neutralize Turkey fails and Australian and New Zealand troops suffer heavy losses; the first German submarine (U-boat) attack is at Le Havre; the German blockade of England begins; at the Second Battle of Ypres, Canadian forces hold off the German advance while under heavy fire and attacks from chlorine gas and newly-introduced flame throwers; Italy joins the Allied Powers, declares war on Austria-Hungary (May 23) and an Italian Front soon opens; a German submarine sinks the *Lusitania* (May 7); the first Zeppelin air attack takes place on London; Ottoman-controlled Mesopotamia (now Iraq) surrenders to Britain; Italians fight Austria-Hungary in continuous battles at Isonzo (1915–17); Germans invade

Warsaw and Brest-Litovsk; Allied troops land at Salonika; the first fighter airplane is constructed by Hugo Junkers; Henry Ford develops a farm tractor; the dysentery bacillus is isolated by British chemist James Kendall; the first book advocating birth control, by American Margaret Sanger, is published, and the author is sent to jail.

1916: Germany stages a Zeppelin raid on Paris and declares war on Portugal; Portugal and Rumania later join the Allied Powers; in the Middle East, T.E. Lawrence leads an Arab revolt against Turkey; heavy casualties occur at Verdun (Feb. 21); British and German fleets clash at the Battle of Jutland (May 31–June 1); the 1st Newfoundland Regiment is annihilated along with 624,000 Allied troops during the offensive at the Somme (launched July 1); HMS *Hampshire* is sunk; Italy declares war on Germany; the Germans first use gas masks and steel helmets; peace notes are exchanged between Germany and the Allies; Lloyd George becomes British prime minister; blood for transfusion is first refrigerated; the theory of shell shock is put forth by F.W. Mott; an underwater ultrasonic source for submarine detection is built by Paul Langevin; Britain initiates daylight-saving time; US purchases the Virgin Islands for $25 million.

1917: The United States enters the war on the Allied side (Apr. 6); Germans withdraw on the Western Front; the Russian Black Sea fleet mutinies at Sebastopol; there is revolution in Russia in Feb. and the Czar abdicates (Mar. 16); Kerensky becomes Russian premier and continues the war effort; Canadian forces seize Vimy Ridge in northern France; Germany stages air attacks on England; Greece joins the Allies (July); China declares war on Germany and Austria; the British-led offensive at the Third Battle of Ypres (Passchendaele) fails (July 31); the Italian army is defeated at Caporetto by Austria-Hungary; Kerensky's government is overthrown in Petrograd in Oct. and Lenin is appointed Chief Commissar, Trotsky becomes Commissar for Foreign Affairs and Russia seeks peace with Germany; the first tank battle is at Cambrai; starvation sweeps Germany; Finland declares independence from Russia; the Allies execute dancer Mata Hari as a spy; Lord Arthur Balfour, the British Foreign Secretary, issues the Balfour Declaration stating British support for a Jewish national homeland in Palestine; women are arrested for suffrage activities in the US.

1918: Russia, the Ukraine and the Central Powers conclude the Treaties of Brest-Litovsk: the first one establishes the independence of the Ukraine, the second strips Russia of its Baltic and Polish possessions; Turks surrender to British at Jerusalem; US Pres. Wilson puts forth Fourteen Points for world peace (including a proposal for a League of Nations); Rumania signs a peace treaty with the Central Powers; Germany launches three final offensives on the Western Front (Mar. 21); Germans bomb Paris; the Second Battle of the Marne (July 15–Aug. 6) is won by the Allies; the Allies win victories on all fronts in the fall; Japanese push into Siberia; Germany and Austria agree to retreat to their own territory before an armistice is signed; the Hungarian premier is assassinated; the Turkish and Austro-Hungarian empires and Bulgaria surrender to the Allies (Nov. 3); the German fleet mutinies at Kiel and the emperor flees; an armistice between the Allies and Germany is signed (Nov. 11); Germany agrees to the provisions of the Treaty of Versailles after the Allies threaten to invade; Emperor Charles of Austria loses the throne; the map of Europe is reshaped: Austria becomes a republic and the Serbo-Croatian-Slovene Kingdom of Yugoslavia is proclaimed, Poland and Czechoslovakia are created; Iceland becomes independent state; the Russian Revolution continues as Bolshevik workers take over government buildings, the Winter Palace and later Moscow and other cities; civil war between the Bolshevik (Red) and anti-Bolshevik (White) continues (until 1920); British, French and American troops intervene against the Reds; the British government abandons Home Rule for Ireland; ex-Czar Nicholas II and family are executed by Russian revolutionaries; Hsu-Shih-Chang becomes president of the Chinese Republic; women over 30 get the vote in Britain; controversy rages over the psychology of Freud and Jung; the true dimensions of the Milky Way are discovered by Harlow Shapley, an American astronomer.

1919: US Pres. Woodrow Wilson heads the first League of Nations meeting in Paris; the Peace Conference opens at Versailles; Benito Mussolini founds the Fasci del Combattimento in Italy; socialist governments are founded in Austria and Budapest, Hungary; the Treaty of Versailles is signed with Germany; the final treaty exacts heavy financial penalties on Germany, restricts the German army and navy, blames Germany for provoking the war and establishes the League of Nations; US refusal to ratify the treaty excludes it from League membership; the Allied peace treaty with Austria is signed at St Germain; the Treaty of Neuilly with Bulgaria is signed; the International Labor Congress in Washington endorses the eight-hour workday; the Red (Soviet) forces win successive battles in the Russian civil war; Soviets attack Finland; the first nonstop flight across the Atlantic is made from Newfound-land to Ireland by J.W. Alcock and A. Whitten Brown; Lady Astor is elected to Britain's Parliament, becoming the first female MP.

1920: The League of Nations is founded in Paris and establishes headquarters in Geneva; Russian civil war ends with Soviet victory; Great Britain gains control of Palestine from the Turks; The Hague becomes the International Court of Justice; the Little Entente between Czechoslovakia, Yugoslavia and Rumania is formed; the Treaty of Trianon is signed with Hungary; the Treaty of Sevres is signed with the Ottoman Empire; the 19th Amendment gives American women the vote; 200,000 Chinese die in an earthquake in Kansu province; the world population is 1.8 billion; Britain establishes separate parliaments for Northern and Southern Ireland; Adolph Hitler founds the Nazi party in Munich, Germany, and announces his 25-point program, blaming Germany's war defeat on Jews and Communists; Mohandas (Mahatma) Ghandi becomes India's leader in its struggle for independence from Britain; Prohibition goes into effect in the US, banning the sale and consumption of alcoholic beverages; a worldwide influenza epidemic, which began in 1918, leaves 22 million dead.

1921: The first Indian Parliament meets; German reparations payments totalling $33.3 million are fixed by the Allies at a Paris conference; Hitler's storm troopers (SA) begin to terrorize ideological opponents; Mackenzie King is elected prime minister of Canada; British Broadcasting Company is founded (changed to the British Broadcasting Corporation in 1927); the Spanish prime minister and Japanese premier are assassinated; founder of Portuguese republic is murdered; ex-emperor Charles stages two failed coup attempts to regain Hungarian throne; Britain and Ireland sign a peace treaty; German mark falls and rapid inflation plagues the economy;

coal is successfully hydrogenated into oil by Friedrich Bergius; the tuberculosis vaccine (B-C-G) is developed by Albert Calmette and Camille Guerin; the chromosome theory of heredity is put forth by American biologist Thomas Morgan; Albert Einstein wins Nobel Prize for Physics; Ku Klux Klan members terrorize blacks and black sympathizers in the southern US; one of the founders of modern aeronautics, Hermann J. Oberth, writes *The Rocket into Interplanetary Space*.

1922: Gandhi is sentenced to six years imprisonment for civil disobedience; German reconstruction minister Walter Rathenau is assassinated by German nationalists; the Arab Congress at Nablus rejects the British control of Palestine; Austria denounces "Anschluss" (union with Germany); Mussolini stages the March on Rome and forms a Fascist government; Irish Free State is proclaimed; the tomb of Tutankhamen is discovered by Lord Carnarvaron and Howard Carter; a self-winding wristwatch is invented by John Harwood (patented in 1924); a stock market "boom" begins in the US; Soviet states form the USSR; insulin, prepared by Canadian physicians Frederick Banting, Charles Best and John Macleod, is first given to diabetic patients.

1923: An earthquake kills 120,000 people in Tokyo and Yokohama; Adolph Hitler tries (and fails) to overthrow the German government ("Beer Hall Putsch"); Greek army overthrows monarch; Jewish philosopher Martin Buber writes the theological *I and Thou*; the theory of acids and bases is postulated by J.N. Brönsted; Lee de Forest demonstrates the process for motion pictures with sound; the first commercial airline, Aeroflot, is founded in the USSR.

1924: Ramsay MacDonald forms the first Labour government in Britain; Adolph Hitler writes *Mein Kampf* during an eight-month jail term; R.C. Andrews discovers skulls and skeletons of Mesozoic dinosaurs in the Gobi desert; Winston Churchill, having switched from the Liberals to the Conservatives, is named Chancellor of the Exchequer in Britain; in Russia, Lenin dies and Stalin, Zinoviev and Kamenev ally against Trotsky; the "Zinoviev letter," purported to be calling for a communist revolution in Britain, is published by the British Foreign Office; Greece becomes a republic; elections are held in Italy and Mussolini wins support of 65% of the electorate; leader of Italian socialists is murdered; Albanian Republic is founded; Sigmund Freud begins *Collected Writings* (12 vols. 1924–39); Ghandi fasts for 21 days, protesting feuding between Hindus and Muslims in India; British astronomer Arthur Eddington discovers that the luminosity of a star is approximately related to its mass; insecticides are used for the first time; a patent application for iconoscope (television) is filed by Russian-American inventor V.K. Zworkin; Danish polar explorer Knud Rasmussen completes the longest dog-sled journey ever made across the North American Arctic; British Imperial Airways begins commercial air flights.

1925: Locarno Conference creates a series of treaties between Germany, France, Belgium, Poland, UK, Italy and Czechoslovakia that set up a demilitarized zone in the Rhineland and confirmed borders between Belgium, France and Germany; Mrs Nellie Tayloe Ross of Wyoming becomes the first woman governor in the US; the United Church of Canada is founded; recognizable human features are transmitted by television by Scottish inventor John Logie Baird; Walter P. Chrysler founds the Chrysler Corporation; the (Franz) Fischer and (Hans) Tropsch synthesis leads to the industrial development of synthetic oil; Heisenberg, Bohr and Jordan develop quantum mechanics for atoms; the presence of cosmic rays in the upper atmosphere is discovered by US physicist Robert Andrews Millikan; the "flapper" era takes hold; an international convention condemns the illegal narcotics trade.

1926: Fascist youth organizations appear: "Balilla" in Italy and "Hitlerjugend" in Germany; Josef Pilsudski successfully stages a coup d'état in Poland and begins a military dictatorship; commerce in Britain is stopped by a general strike; Trotsky is expelled from Moscow; Hirohito succeeds his father Taisho as Emperor of Japan; Robert H. Goddard fires the first liquid fuel rocket; vitamin B is isolated by B. Jansen and W. Donath; Kodak produces the first 16mm movie film; British Imperial Chemical Industries (ICI) begins operations; H.L. Mencken writes *Notes on Democracy*; Turkish reforms include the abolition of polygamy, modernization of female attire and adoption of Latin alphabet (1926–28).

1927: The Allied military control of Germany ends; an economic conference in Geneva is attended by 52 nations; the economic system in Germany collapses ("Black Friday"); Trotsky expelled from the Communist Party in the USSR; Nazis on trial in Austria for political murder are acquitted and socialists riot in Venice to protest; the first film with sound, a "talkie," *The Jazz Singer*, stars Al Jolson; Lev Theremin invents the earliest electronic musical instrument; Charles Lindbergh flies the monoplane *Spirit of St Louis* in the first solo transatlantic flight, nonstop from New York to Paris in 33.5 hours; Canadian forests are the first sprayed with insecticides by airplanes; the first vehicular tunnel, the Holland Tunnel, links New York and New Jersey.

1928: The Supreme Court of Canada rules that women may not hold public office because they are not "persons" as defined by the British North America Act, but the British Privy Council overturns the decision in a landmark Commonwealth case in 1929; the Kellogg-Briand Pact outlawing war is signed by 65 states; Josef Stalin emerges as leader of Soviet Union; the first economic five-year plan begins in the USSR; Chiang Kai-Shek is elected president of China; over-production of coffee leads to the collapse of Brazil's economy; penicillin is discovered by Alexander Fleming (Scottish); American anthropologist Margaret Mead writes *Coming of Age in Samoa;* the first colour motion pictures are exhibited by George Eastman in Rochester, New York; J.L. Baird presents colour television; Mickey Mouse makes his Disney debut.

1929: The US Stock Exchange collapses on Oct. 28, Black Friday; the Great Depression, a world economic crisis, begins and is primarily caused by easy credit and stock market overspeculation, overproduction of goods and tariff and war-debt policies; six Chicago-area gangsters are machine-gunned to death in the St Valentine's Day Massacre; a dictatorship is established in Serbo-Croat-Slovene kingdom by the monarch and the country's name is changed to Yugoslavia; Trotsky is exiled from USSR; talks on Indian sovereignty begin betweeen Indian leaders and the Viceroy; the Lateran Treaty establishes the independence of Vatican City; precise timekeeping is made possible with the quartz-crystal clocks by W.A. Morrison; the airship *Graf Zeppelin* flies around the world in 21 days.

1930: Austria and Italy sign a treaty of friendship; Britain, the US, Japan, France and Italy sign a treaty on naval disarmament; right-wing coalition comes to power in Germany, Nazis later capture 107 more seats in an election; right-wing government is formed in Poland; Catholic-Fascist units are established in Austria; revolution in Argentina brings new military dictatorship to power; the planet Pluto is discovered by C.W. Tombaugh at Lowell Observatory; a yellow fever vaccine is developed by South African microbiologist Max Theiler; photoflash bulb is introduced; the word "technocracy," meaning the domination of technology, comes into use.

1931: A financial crisis in central Europe is caused by the collapse of Austria's Credit-Anstalt; all German banks close following the bankruptcy of the German Danatbank; Britain abandons the gold standard; Fascist party is formed in Britain; the Statute of Westminster established the British Commonwealth of Nations as a free association of autonomous nations sharing a common allegiance to the British crown, and declared that British Parliament could no longer legislate for any member states unless requested to do so; US Pres. Hoover proposes a one-year moratorium for reparations and war debts; the first trans-African railroad line is completed, Benguella-Katanga; the northern face of the Matterhorn is climbed for the first time by Franz and Toni Schmid.

1932: The Indian National Congress, a nationalist party dedicated to home rule, is declared illegal and its leader, Mahatma Gandhi, is arrested; the US criticizes Japanese aggression in Manchuria; the Nazis sweep the German Reichstag (Parliament) elections while WWI hero Hindenburg wins the Presidential election; Hitler refuses Hinden-burg's offer to become Vice Chancellor, and the Austrian-born Hitler receives German citizenship; Franklin D. Roosevelt wins the US presidential election and proposes domestic reform programs to provide recovery and relief from the Great Depression ("New Deal"); the USSR suffers famine; Zuider Zee, a huge dam and drainage project in Holland, is completed; Amelia Earheart is the first woman to fly solo across the Atlantic; Japan conquers world markets by undercutting prices; about 30 million people are unemployed worldwide; the neutron is discovered by James Chadwick; vitamin D is discovered.

1933: Reichstag building is burned in Berlin and Hitler uses the event to justify banning opposition parties and labour unions; Hitler is appointed German Chancellor and granted dictatorial powers with the Enabling Law; Nazi Hermann Goering is named Prussian prime minister; Parliamentary government is suspended in Austria; starvation spreads in USSR; Paul Joseph Goebbels is named Hitler's Minister of Propaganda; Japan withdraws from the League of Nations; the first concentration camps are built by the Nazis in Germany to hold Jews and ideological opponents; books by non-Nazi and Jewish authors are burned in Germany; Germans begin to boycott and restrict Jewish services; an anti-Nazi treatise, *Judaism-Christendom-Germanism*, is published by Cardinal von Faulhaber in Munich; Assyrian Christians are massacred in Iraq; US goes off the gold standard and tries to stimulate its economy by creating The Tennessee Valley Authority to construct dams and generate electricity.

1934: A revolution in Austria overturns the Social Democrats and Austrian Chancellor is assassinated by the Nazis; a general strike takes place in France; the USSR is admitted to the League of Nations; Winston Churchill warns the British Parliament of the German air menace; Hitler oversees purge of his associates and many are executed; a national vote grants him the title Führer (leader); Stalin's purge of the Soviet Communist party begins and he reportedly oversees the murder of millions of people; German scientist Albert Einstein is persecuted by the Nazis for being Jewish and he flees, settling in the US; Japan renounces the Washington treaties of 1922 and 1930; Mao Tse-tung, leader of the Chinese Communists, heads the Long March.

1935: Nazis repudiate the Treaty of Versailles and reintroduce compulsory military service; the autonomous territory of Saarland votes for reunion with Germany; an Anglo-German Naval Agreement is concluded; Nazis implement the Nuremburg Laws against Jews, stripping them of civic rights and forbidding intermarriage with non-Jews; Mussolini invades Ethiopia, and the League of Nations retaliates by imposing sanctions; the Chaco War, a bitter conflict between Paraguay and Bolivia begun in 1932 and fought over oil-rich but otherwise barren territory, ended after 100,000 lives were lost and both sides were exhausted (treaty not concluded until 1938); radar equipment to detect aircraft is built by Robert Watson Watt; oil pipelines between Iraq, Haifa and Tripoli open; Persia changes its name to Iran.

1936: King George V of England dies and is succeeded by Edward VIII; German troops occupy the Rhineland and Hitler wins the German elections with 99 percent of the vote; Italy, Austria and Hungary sign the Rome Pact; Britain, France and the US sign the London Naval Convention; an Austro-German convention acknowledges Austrian independence; the Spanish Civil War begins and Francisco Franco is appointed Chief of State by the Nationalist insurgents against the government's Loyalist republicans; Franco begins the siege of Madrid, rebels take Malaga and destroy Guernica and Gijon and Franco begins a naval blockade (1937); Heinrich Himmler is appointed head of the Gestapo, responsible for Nazi concentration camps (1936–45); King Edward VIII abdicates in order to marry American divorcee Wallis Simpson; Mussolini and Hitler proclaim the Rome-Berlin Axis; the Anti-Comintern Pact is signed by Germany and Japan; Chiang Kai-shek declares war on Japan; Dr Alexis Carrel develops an artificial heart; the airship *Hindenburg* burns at Lakehurst, New Jersey, after a transatlantic flight; black American athlete Jesse Owens upsets the Nazis when he wins four gold medals at the Olympic Games in Berlin.

1937: Poland refuses to return Danzig to Germany; the first worldwide radio broadcast is heard when George VI is crowned King of Great Britain; Roosevelt signs a US Neutrality Act, intended to keep the US out of a possible European war; Trotsky, exiled from Russia in 1929, is forced to leave Norway and settles in Mexico; aggressive Japanese war policy begins when Prince Konoye is named the Japanese premier, and the Japanese seize major Chinese cities (Beijing, Tianjin, Shanghai, Nanjing and Hangzhou), forcing Chiang Kai-shek and the Communists, under Mao Tse-tung and Chou En-lai, to unite; the Chinese government makes Chungking its capital; the Royal Commission on Palestine recommends the establishment of Arab and Jewish states; Stalin initiates a purge of Soviet generals and show trials of political leaders; Britain signs naval agreements with Germany and the USSR; Germany guarantees Belgian sovereignty; Italy joins the Anti-Comintern Pact and withdraws from the League of Nations; Japanese planes sink US gunboat in Chinese waters; Amelia Earheart disappears during a Pacific flight.

1938: Germany annexes Austria, "Anschluss" (Mar.); France calls up reservists; Great Britain, France and Italy agree to let Germany absorb the Sudetenland, Czechoslovakia, in a policy of appeasement (Munich Pact, Sept.) and Germany promises to cease its aggressive expansion; British foreign minister Anthony Eden resigns in protest against the appeasement policy and Winston Churchill also voices opposition; Franco begins an offensive against the Spanish Loyalists in Catalonia; anti-Jewish legislation is enacted in Italy; Kristallnacht, or "Night of Broken Glass," is a large-scale pogrom by the Nazis against German Jews; the US and Germany recall their respective ambassadors; Japan withdraws from the League of Nations and sets up a puppet Chinese government in Nanking; Howard Hughes flies around the world in less than four days.

1939: US Pres. Roosevelt demands assurances from Hitler and Mussolini that they have no plans to attack other states; Germany breaks the Munich Pact and occupies Bohemia and Moravia; Slovakia is placed under "protection"; Italy invades Albania; Germany renounces the nonaggression pact with Poland and naval agreement with England, and concludes a 10-year alliance with Italy and a nonaggression pact with the USSR, secretly dividing Poland; Germany stages a surprise (blitzkrieg) invasion of Poland, and annexes Danzig (Sept. 1); Britain and France declare war on Germany (Sept. 3); the Allied powers are Britain and France and the Axis powers are led by Germany; Canada declares war (Sept. 10); US Pres. Roosevelt announces US neutrality; Soviets invade Poland from the east (Sept. 17); Germans overrun western Poland and reach Brest-Litovsk and Warsaw; France masses troops along the Maginot Line on the eastern frontier of France and Germany sends troops to its parallel Siegfried Line; the British Expeditionary Force is sent to France; the USSR invades Finland and is expelled from the League of Nations; Japan occupies Hainan and blockades the British at Tientsin; the US renounces the Japanese trade agreement of 1911; the Spanish Civil War ends with Franco's Nationalists (supported by Hitler and Mussolini) victorious over the Loyalists (supported by the USSR); Spain joins the Anti-Comintern Pact and leaves the League of Nations; England and Poland sign a treaty of mutual assistance; women and children are first evacuated from London; the first helicopter is built by Russian-American Igor Sikorsky; the US economy booms from arms sales to Europe.

1940: Food rationing begins in Britain; Finland surrenders (Mar.) and signs a peace treaty with the USSR; Germany invades Norway and Denmark (Apr. 9); Winston Churchill becomes British prime minister (May 10); Norway falls (June); Germany invades Belgium, Luxembourg and the Netherlands (May 10); Holland and Belgium surrender to Germany and 340,000 Allied forces are trapped in Belgium, but most are evacuated from Dunkirk, a French seaport on the English channel (May 29 to June 3); Italy declares war on France and Britain; Germans attack France from the north and enter Paris (June 14); France concludes an armistice with Germany; southern France remains unoccupied until 1942 and is ruled by the Vichy government; USSR seizes Estonia, Latvia and Lithuania (summer); the Royal Navy sinks the French fleet in Oran; the Royal Air Force begins night bombing of Germany; the Battle of Britain in Aug. is the first battle fought completely in the air; Hitler begins bombing England (all-night blitzes) throughout fall and winter; Japan, Germany and Italy sign a military and economic pact; US destroyers are sold to Britain; Germany intensifies U-boat warfare; Italian forces attempt to take Egypt and Libya in order to cut off British access to Middle East oil and the Suez Canal; the British Eighth Army opens an offensive in North Africa and defeats the Italian forces; Trotsky is murdered in Mexico; Batista becomes president of Cuba; wall paintings dating to about 20,000 BC are discovered in France, the Lascaux caves; a giant cyclotron is built at the University of California for producing mesotrons from atomic nuclei.

1941: The British invade Ethiopia and defeat the Italians (by May); Germany opens a counter-offensive in North Africa to aid Italy; German General Rommel regains Libya and Egypt; Germans launch an airborne invasion against Crete, thereby securing an important base in the Mediterranean (by the end of May); England sinks the German battleship *Bismarck* in an effort to protect vital US shipments to Great Britain; Allies develop radar and sonar to track U-boats; German air raids over London continue; US freezes German and Italian assets in that country; Germans invade Russia (Operation Barbarossa, June 22); Churchill and Roosevelt sign the Atlantic charter (Aug. 14); German troops surround Leningrad and Moscow (Nov.), but an early, harsh winter saves the USSR; Marshal Timoshenko

launches the Russian counter-offensive; the US ambassador to Japan warns Pres. Roosevelt of possible Japanese attack; Japanese bomb Pearl Harbor (Dec. 7) and the US and Britain declare war on Japan (Dec. 8); China declares war on the Axis (Dec. 9); Japan invades the Philippines; Germany and Italy declare war on the US; the US declares war on Germany and Italy; British Hong Kong surrenders to the Japanese; Henry Moore draws refugees in London air raid shelters while an official war artist; Dmitri Shostakovich writes *Symphony No. 7* during the German siege of Leningrad; German dramatist Bertolt Brecht writes *Mother Courage and Her Children* while in exile from the Nazis.

1942: Hitler's Final Solution, the systematic murder of Jews in the Nazi gas chambers (Holocaust) is in full force at death camps such as Auschwitz and Dachau; the 26 Allied nations agree not to make separate treaties with the Axis powers; Rommel breaks through British lines and reaches El Alamein (320 km from the Suez Canal); Montgomery (British Eighth Army) scores the first decisive defeat of Rommel at El Alamein; Germans reach Stalingrad, Russia; 400,000 American troops land in French North Africa; Rommel, in full retreat, loses Tobruk and Benghazi; Japan invades Burma, the Dutch East Indies, and captures Singapore; the British bomb Cologne and Lübeck; the US and Canada intern residents of Japanese heritage in camps; many American and Philippine prisoners die in the Japanese-forced Bataan Death March; Americans bomb Tokyo; Americans begin successful island-hopping strategy against Japan and win the battles of the Coral Sea and Midway; French navy loses in Toulon; British and Indian troops advance in Burma; Fermi achieves the first controlled nuclear chain reaction when he splits the atom; the Manhattan Project of intensive US atomic research begins; the first electronic brain or automatic computer is developed in the US; a recorder using plastic magnetic recording tape is invented by German engineers; Gandhi demands independence from Britain and is arrested.

1943: German troops surrender at Stalingrad (Feb. 2) and begin to withdraw from the Caucasus; Churchill and Roosevelt meet in Casablanca; the Japanese are driven from Guadalcanal by US troops; the British Eighth Army reaches Tripoli; Axis powers surrender in North Africa (Tunisia, May 13); Russians destroy the German army southwest of Stalingrad; Russians recapture Rostov and Kharkov; the Royal Air Force raids Berlin; US planes sink the 22-ship Japanese convoy in the Battle of the Bismarck Sea; British and US armies in Africa link up and Rommel retreats; an armed Jewish uprising begins in the overcrowded Warsaw ghetto, but it is crushed by German troops (1943–44) who massacre Jewish inhabitants; the RAF bombs Ruhr dams; US forces land in New Guinea; US recaptures Aleutians; Allies land in Sicily (July 10); Churchill, Roosevelt and Mackenzie King meet in Quebec; US troops bomb Ploesti oil fields in Rumania and enter Messina; Allies land in Salerno Bay and invade Italy, which surrenders unconditionally (Sept. 8); Russians take Kiev; Chinese Gen. and Mme Chiang Kai-shek meet with Roosevelt and Churchill in Cairo and pledge to liberate Korea after Japan is defeated; Churchill, Stalin and Roosevelt hold the Teheran Conference; Allied round-the-clock bombing of Germany begins; the first fully electronic computer is used by the British government to crack German military codes; penicillin is used to treat chronic diseases; Bengal is swept by famine; rationing of selected foods begins in the US; major US cities are troubled by race riots.

1944: Germany continues air raids on London; Russian offensives continue in the Ukraine and Crimea; Allies bomb Berlin; Monte Cassino and Rome are liberated by the Allies June 4; D-day landings in Normandy (France, June 6): over 700 ships and 4,000 landing craft are involved and Canadian troops lead the trek from the Normandy beaches; Germans drop first flying bomb (V-1) on London; southern Japan is bombed by the US; US troops take Saipan; Russians capture 100,000 Germans at Minsk; German officers unsuccessfully attempt to assassinate Hitler; Russians reach Brest-Litovsk; Amer-icans capture Guam from the Japanese; the British Eighth Army takes Florence; creation of a United Nations is discussed at the Dunbarton Oaks conference in Washington; Charles De Gaulle leads the Free French into Paris (Aug. 25); Allies liberate Belgium; the first V-2 rockets land in Britain; Churchill and Roosevelt meet in Quebec; Americans cross the German frontier near Trier; British airborne forces land at Eindhoven and Arnheim but have to withdraw; US troops land in the Philippines; Russians and Yugoslavs enter Belgrade; Russian Army

occupies Hungary; Japanese suffer heavy losses in Battle of Leyte Gulf; Battle of the Bulge (Ardennes Forest) results in Allied victory; France regains Lorraine; Rommel commits suicide; Vietnam, under Ho Chi Minh, declares independence from France; American playwright Tennessee Williams completes *The Glass Menagerie*; quinine is synthesized; Richard Strauss completes the opera *Die Liebe der Danae* in Austria but its performance is cancelled when the Nazis shut down the theatres; French playwright Jean-Paul Sartre writes the existentialist work *Being and Nothingness*.

1945: Britain begins major offensive in Burma; Russians take Warsaw, Cracow and reach Oder River; Churchill, Roosevelt and Stalin meet at the Yalta Conference; Americans enter Manila; Russians take Budapest; British troops reach the Rhine; US air raids on Tokyo, Cologne and Danzig; Okinawa is captured; the British Second Army crosses the Rhine; the last German V-2 rocket falls on Britain; Franklin D. Roosevelt dies and is succeeded by Harry S. Truman; Russians reach Berlin; Bologna is captured; US and Soviet troops meet at Torgau and both liberate Nazi death camps, finding gas chambers and crematoriums; anti-Axis coalition agrees to set up new international body to replace ineffective League of Nations; new United Nations charter drawn up at conference in San Francisco (Apr.–June); Bremen, Genoa, Verona and Venice are captured by the Allies; the Allies cross the Elbe; Mussolini is killed by Italian partisans; Hitler commits suicide (Apr. 30); the German army on the Italian front surrenders; Berlin surrenders to the Russians (May 2) and Germany capitulates to the Allies (May 7); V-E Day (Victory in Europe) ends the war in Europe (May 8); Germany is divided into four zones by the Allies and the three-power occupation of Berlin begins; Churchill, Truman and Stalin meet at Potsdam; Clement Attlee replaces Churchill as prime minister of Great Britain in a Labour landslide; the first atomic bomb is detonated near Alamogordo, New Mexico after being developed by J. Robert Oppenheimer, Enrico Fermi and others (July 16); the Soviet Union declares war on Japan and occupied Manchuria; the US drops atomic bombs on Hiroshima (Aug. 6) and Nagasaki (Aug. 9); Japan surrenders and World War II ends; war dead are estimated at 35 million plus victims of Nazi concentration camps; the Nuremburg trials of Nazi war criminals begin; the League of Nations holds its final meeting in Geneva and turns over its assets to the UN (Oct.); Charles De Gaulle is elected president of the French provisional government; Tito is chief of state of the newly created Federal People's Republic of Yugoslavia; Nationalists and Communists resume civil war in north China; the Arab League is founded to oppose the creation of a Jewish state; Shintoism is abolished in Japan; vitamin A is synthesized; black markets for food, clothing and cigarettes develop in Europe; the UN World Bank (International Bank for Reconstruction and Development) is founded with authorized share capital of $27 billion.

1946: Albania, Bulgaria, Hungary and Transjordan become sovereign states; the UN General Assembly holds its first session in London (Jan. 7), electing Trygve Lie of Norway as its first Secretary-General, and its permanent headquarters is made in New York; Juan Perón is elected president of Argentina; a Peace Conference of 21 nations is held in Paris; 12 leading Nazis are sentenced to death following the Nuremburg trials and others get life imprisonment; power in Japan is transferred from the Emperor to an elected assembly; the UN Atomic Energy Commission is formed to monitor member nations; after a referendum in Italy, the king abdicates, Italy becomes a republic and de Gasperi becomes head of state; xerography (photocopying) is invented by Chester Carl-son; Dr Benjamin Spock writes *Baby and Child Care*, the "baby boom" reference book.

1947: British coal industry is nationalized; *The Diary of Anne Frank* is published by Anne's father, the only member of the German-Jewish Frank family to survive the Holocaust; Burma proclaims its independence; Paris Peace treaties signed; the Dead Sea Scrolls, dating from about 22 BC to AD 100, are discovered in Wadi Qumran, Palestine; American Chuck Yeager flies the first airplane at supersonic speeds; the transistor is invented by Bell Telephone Laboratory scientists; the UN divides Palestine, which is under British mandate, into a Jewish and an Arab state (Nov. 1947) and the British withdraw six months later; India gains independence from Great Britain and is partitioned into India and East and West Pakistan.

1948: Gandhi is assassinated by a Hindu opposing his tolerance of Muslims; a Communist coup d'état takes place in Czechoslovakia (Feb. 25); the Marshall Plan providing $17 billion in aid for Europe is passed by the US Congress; Winston Churchill chairs the Hague Congress for European unity; the Jewish state of Israel is proclaimed with Chaim Weizmann as president and David Ben-Gurion as premier (May 14); neighbouring Arab states declare war (1948–49) on Israel but by the end of the conflict Israel succeeds in increasing its territory; the Berlin airlift by the west begins after the USSR imposes a land and water blockade (1948–Sept. 1949); bread rationing ends in Britain; the World Council of Churches is organized in Amsterdam; American biologist Alfred C. Kinsey writes *Sexual Behavior in the Human Male*; the first World Health Assembly meets in Geneva; the first port radar system is installed in Liverpool, England.

1949: Tianjin, China, falls to the Communists, Chiang Kai-shek resigns as president of China, and removes his Nationalist forces to Formosa; the Communist People's Republic is proclaimed under Mao Tse-tung, with Chou En-lai as premier; the North Atlantic Treaty establishing a defence alliance (NATO) is signed by all parties (Belgium, Canada, Denmark, France, Iceland, Italy, Luxembourg, the Netherlands, Norway, Portugal, UK and US) in Washington; the Berlin blockade by the Soviet Union is lifted; the German Federal Republic (West Ger-many) comes into being with Bonn as its capital and Konrad Adenauer as Chancellor; republic of Eire is proclaimed with its capital in Dublin; Transjordan is renamed the Hashemite Kingdom of Jordan; the state of Vietnam, under Ho Chi Minh, is established at Saigon; civil war looms in Korea; the apartheid program of official racial discrimination is established in South Africa; the Democratic Republic is established in East Germany with Pieck as president; India becomes a federal republic with Pandit Nehru as prime minister; Indonesia gains sovereignty from Holland; the USSR tests its first atomic bomb; the US launches a guided missile to a height of 400 km, the highest altitude yet; George Orwell publishes *Nineteen Eighty-Four*.

1950: Communist China and Russia sign a treaty of friendship and mutual assistance, Britain also recognizes Communist China; 18 protesters are killed in anti-apartheid riots in South Africa; Vietnam, Laos and Cambodia gain independence from France; North Korea invades South Korea, capturing Seoul and forcing Pres. Syngman Rhee to flee; US Atomic Energy Commission begins work on hydrogen bomb; UN forces under Gen. Douglas MacArthur land in South Korea and push north of the 38th parallel, prompting Communist China to enter the war; US recognizes Vietnam, sends military supplies and instructors and signs pact for military assistance with Vietnam, Laos, Cambodia and France.

1951: North Korean forces reach the 38th parallel and capture Seoul: attempts to negotiate peace fail; Gen. MacArthur is replaced as commander in Korea for threatening massive retaliation against China; Winston Churchill forms the government in Britain; Remington Rand produces UNIVAC, the first large-scale, general-purpose computer; electricity is produced from atomic energy in the US; heart-lung machine devised by J. Andre-Thomas; penicillin and streptomycin available in US.

1952: Dwight D. Eisenhower is elected US president; Britain produces an atomic bomb; Elizabeth II becomes Queen of England; Egypt rocked by anti-British riots: premier resigns and the army seizes power; Mau-maus rebel in Kenya and government declares a state of emergency; first hydrogen bomb at Eniwetok Atoll in the Pacific; British Overseas Airways introduces the world's first jet passenger service from London to Rome; the first pocket-sized transistor radio is marketed by Sony in Japan.

1953: An armistice ending the Korean War is signed at Panmunjom; Soviet leader Joseph Stalin dies and is replaced by Malenkov; Sweden's Dag Hammarskjöld is elected UN secretary-general; the Soviet Union explodes a hydrogen bomb; Yugoslavia proclaims a new constitution and Marshall Tito becomes president; Egyptian generals establish a dictatorship and proclaim a republic; rebels from Vietnam attack Laos; Fidel Castro begins a campaign to overthrow Cuban dictator Fulgencio Batista; Ethel and Julius Rosenberg are executed after being convicted of passing American atomic secrets to the Soviet Union; Edmund Hillary and Tenzing Norgay become the first to scale Mt Everest; the first successful open heart surgery is performed in the US; researchers associate lung cancer with cigarette smoking.

1954: Vietnamese Communists defeat the French at Dien Bien Phu; racial segregation in public schools is banned by the US Supreme Court; Gammal Abdel Nasser becomes leader in Egypt; the US Senate censures Sen. Joseph McCarthy for launching a Communist witch-hunt; Canada and the US plan a joint radar defence system in the north (Distant Early Warning, DEW Line); the US *Nautilus* becomes the first nuclear-powered submarine; Dr Jonas Salk begins inoculating children against polio; the oral contraceptive pill is introduced in the US; the first successful kidney transplant is performed in the US; Roger Bannister becomes the first to run a mile in less than four minutes.

1955: Churchill resigns in Britain and is succeeded by Anthony Eden; Bulganin succeeds Malenkov as Soviet premier; eight east-European Communist bloc countries adopt the Warsaw Pact mutual defence treaty; West Germany joins NATO; border clashes between Israel and Jordan increase; Juan Perón is ousted by a military coup in Argentina; the first optical fibres are produced in Britain.

1956: Nasser elected Egyptian president; Egypt seizes control of the Suez Canal; Israeli troops invade Egypt and push towards the canal; British and French forces invade Egypt; a United Nations force arrives in Egypt, prompting a cease-fire; UN truce proposals for dispute between Jordan and Israel accepted; Soviet Communist leader Nikita Khrushchev denounces Joseph Stalin's "cult of personality"; Soviet tanks and troops crush an anti-Communist rebellion in Hungary; Sudan becomes a democratic republic; Pakistan becomes an Islamic republic; Martin Luther King, Jr, leads the campaign against racial segregation in the US South; trans-atlantic telephone service begins; the first computer programming language (FORTRAN) is developed in the US.

1957: Israeli troops withdraw from Egypt and the Gaza Strip comes under UN jurisdiction; UN reopens the Suez Canal; the space race begins as the USSR launches the first earth-orbiting satellite *Sputnik 1*; Belgium, France, Italy, Luxembourg, the Netherlands and West Germany sign the Rome Treaty to extend the common market established for the steel industry to all sectors of the economy; Pres. Eisenhower warns that the US will oppose Communist takeovers in the Middle East; Harold Macmillan leads the new Conserva-tive government in Britain; John Diefenbaker becomes Canada's prime minister.

1958: Nikita Khrushchev becomes Soviet premier; Charles De Gaulle is elected president of France; Pope Pius XII dies and is succeeded by John XXIII; the first US space satellite, *Explorer I*, is launched; scientists in the USSR send two dogs into space and return them safely; Egypt and Syria form the United Arab Republic; Iraq's King Faisal is assassinated in a military coup; Alaska becomes the 49th US state.

1959: Fidel Castro overthrows Fulgencio Batista and establishes a Communist government in Cuba, expropriating sugar mills owned by the US; Soviet Prem. Khrushchev visits the US; American Vice-Pres. Richard Nixon visits the Soviet Union and has the "kitchen debate" with Khrushchev; the USSR sends a space probe to the moon and photographs its hidden side; the St Lawrence Seaway opens; the first commercial photocopier is introduced; the Dalai Lama flees Tibet; Hawaii becomes the 50th state of the US.

1960: An American U-2 spy plane is shot down over the USSR, prompting Soviet Prem. Nikita Khrushchev to cancel a Soviet-American summit meeting; 50 South African black protesters are massacred at Sharpeville; the Congo (Zaïre) gains independence from Belgium, sparking political instability and UN intervention; Cyprus becomes independent and Archbishop Makarios wins the first presidential election; Israeli agents capture former Gestapo chief Adolf Eichmann in Argentina and smuggle him to Israel for trial; Germany bans Neo-Nazi political groups; John F. Kennedy is elected US president; the first weather and communications satellites are launched in the US; the first heart pacemaker is developed.

1961: Soviet Major Yuri Gagarin becomes the first man in space; US breaks off diplomatic ties with Cuba; the US-backed Bay of Pigs invasion by Cuban exiles fails to topple Cuba's Fidel Castro; astronaut Alan Shepard becomes the first American in space with a sub-orbital flight; East Germany builds the Berlin Wall to stop its citizens from moving to the West; Kuwait becomes independent from Britain, which sends troops to counter Iraqi annexation threats; UN Sec.-Gen. Dag Hammarskjöld dies in a plane crash over Northern Rhodesia; UK applies for membership in the Common Market; the silicon chip is patented by Texas Instruments in the US.

1962: Fearing nuclear war, many North Americans build fallout shelters; John Glenn becomes the first American to orbit the earth; US establishes a military council in South Vietnam; the discovery of Soviet missile bases in Cuba leads to a US naval blockade; the Cuban Missile Crisis ends when Soviet leader Khrushchev agrees to dismantle the bases; UN troops quell rebellion in the Congo's Katanga province; Algeria, Uganda and Jamaica gain independence; the UN votes in favor of economic sanctions against South Africa; Pope John XXIII opens the Second Vatican Council which will modernize the Catholic church; the TV satellite *Telstar* is launched in the US.

1963: US Pres. John Kennedy is assassinated in Dallas and Lyndon Johnson succeeds him; the US, Soviet Union and Britain ban nuclear tests in the atmosphere; South Vietnamese leader Ngo Dinh Diem is assassinated following a military coup; US sends financial aid to South Vietnam; Zanzibar and Kenya gain independence; Dr. Martin Luther King leads the March on Washington seeking equality for US blacks; the "hot line" emergency communications link is established between the White House and the Kremlin; UK application to Common Market rejected after French opposition; British government rocked by the Profumo affair and the scandal forces the resignation of a senior minister; Pope John XXIII dies and is succeeded by Paul VI; archaeologists find the remains of a thousand-year-old Viking settlement in Newfoundland; the first liver and lung transplants are performed; Valentina Tereshkova becomes the first female astronaut.

1964: Harold Wilson becomes prime minister in Britain; Communist China announces it has developed an atomic bomb; the US escalates its military involvement in Vietnam following a reported North Vietnamese attack on US destroyers in the Gulf of Tonkin; the Palestine Liberation Organization (PLO) is formed; Zambia, Malta and Malawi become independent; the sultan of Zanzibar is banished and the country is declared a republic; Zanzibar unites with Tanganyika to form Tanzania; Northern Rhodesia declares independence and adopts the name Zambia; Leonid Brezhnev and Alexei Kosygin become Soviet leaders after Khrushchev is deposed; the first word processor is developed by IBM; the Beatles appear on the Ed Sullivan Show as "Beatlemania" sweeps North America.

1965: Ferdinand Marcos is elected president of the Philippines; Gambia and Rhodesia declare independence from Britain; Rhodesia's declaration is met by an oil embargo; a massive power failure blacks out most of the northeast US and eastern Canada; Pope Paul VI reaffirms the Catholic Church's opposition to birth control; a Soviet cosmonaut is the first to leave a spacecraft and "float" in space; two US Gemini capsules rendezvous in space.

1966: China's Red Guards demonstrate against western influences as Mao launches the Cultural Revolution; Indira Gandhi becomes India's prime minister; floods destroy art treasures in Florence, Italy; De Gaulle asks that NATO forces leave France; South African Pres. Hendrik Verwoerd is stabbed to death during a Parliamentary session; Lesotho and Guyana become independent; civilian protests against the Vietnam War escalate in the US; government in Ghana overthrown by military coup; an artificial heart is successfully implanted for the first time by Dr Michael De Bakey in Houston; the Soviet Union lands an unmanned spacecraft on the moon.

1967: Israel defeats Egypt, Syria and Jordan in the Six Day War and occupies the Sinai Peninsula, Golan Heights, Gaza Strip and the east bank of the Suez Canal; Expo 67 world fair opens in Montreal; a Soviet cosmonaut becomes the first reported casualty of the space race; US manned space flights are suspended after astronauts Grissom, White and Chaffee die in Apollo capsule fire; race riots erupt in US cities during the "long hot summer"; Canada celebrates its centennial; Dr Christiaan Barnard of South Africa performs the world's first successful human heart transplant: the patient survives for 18 days.

1968: The US intelligence ship *Pueblo* is captured by North Korea; US civil rights leader Martin Luther King is assassinated in Memphis; presidential candidate Robert Kennedy is assassinated in Los Angeles; Soviet troops crush liberal reform in Czechoslovakia; a treaty limiting military use of outer space is signed by 62 nations; university student protest movement spreads worldwide; Richard Nixon is elected US president; Pierre Trudeau becomes prime minister in Canada; peace talks between the US and North Vietnam begin in Paris; British colony of Mauritius becomes independent; Pope Paul

VI issues an encyclical banning artificial birth control; three US astronauts circle the moon and return to Earth; *Surveyor 7*, uncrewed, lands on moon.

1969: US astronaut Neil Armstrong becomes the first man to walk on the moon as *Apollo 11* lands on the lunar surface; Yasir Arafat becomes PLO chairman; North Vietnamese leader Ho Chi Minh dies at age 79; the International Red Cross estimates that 1.5 million Biafrans have died, mostly by starvation, in the civil war with Nigeria; the US begins withdrawal of troops from Vietnam; Golda Meir becomes Israeli prime minister; the Concorde supersonic airliner makes its first flight; *Mariner* space probes transmit pictures of Mars back to earth.

1970: An earthquake kills about 30,000 people in Peru; US National Guardsmen kill four Kent State University students during anti-war protests at the campus and two students are killed at Jackson State following similar demonstrations; the first complete synthesis of a gene is announced by University of Wisconsin scientists; Arab commandos hijack three jets bound for New York from Europe; the civil wars in Nigeria end when Biafra capitulates to the federal government; the Front de Libération du Québec (FLQ) kidnaps British trade commissioner James Cross, and kidnaps and murders Quebec cabinet minister Pierre Laporte; the Canadian federal government responds to this "October Crisis" by invoking the War Measures Act, temporarily suspending civil liberties in Canada; Israel and United Arab Republic declare a 99-day truce in latest conflict; Gambia becomes a republic; a cyclone and tidal wave hit the offshore islands in the Ganges Delta of East Pakistan, leaving at least 168,000 people dead and about 1 million homeless.

1971: US planes bomb Cambodia, attacking Vietcong supply routes; fighting in Indochina spreads to Laos and Cambodia; the US conducts large-scale bombing raids against North Vietnam; mainland China is admitted to the United Nations; women are granted the right to vote in Switzerland; violence in Northern Ireland escalates after Britain introduces policies of internment without trial; India fights with the Bengali rebels against Pakistan; the US and USSR sign a treaty banning nuclear weapons on the ocean floor; Algeria seizes majority control of all French oil and gas interests within its borders but promises restitution; Idi Amin takes control over Uganda; Mao Zedong's heir-apparent, Lin Piao, dies in a mysterious air crash; the USSR soft-lands a space capsule on Mars; a Los Angeles earthquake kills 60 people and causes $1 billion in damage; the hormone that controls human growth is synthesized by Dr. Choh Hao Li at the University of California.

1972: The world's largest diamond (969.8 carats) is unearthed in Sierra Leone; US Pres. Richard Nixon meets Mao Zedong in China; Britain imposes direct rule on Northern Ireland and 467 people are killed in violence between Catholics and Protestants; Ceylon becomes a republic and changes its name to Sri Lanka; Philippine Pres. Ferdinand Marcos assumes near-dictatorial powers; a Soviet spacecraft soft-lands on Venus; more than 70 nations sign a treaty prohibiting the stockpiling of biological weapons; the US conducts its heaviest B-52 bombing raids of the war against North Vietnam but continues to withdraw troops, despite lack of progress at Paris peace talks; Arab terrorists massacre 11 Israeli Olympic athletes in a stand-off with West German police at the summer Olympic games in Munich; Richard Leakey and Glynn Isaac discover a 2.5-million-year-old human skull in northern Kenya; a US federal grand jury indicts seven persons, including two former White House aids, on charges of conspiracy to break into the Democratic national headquarters (in the Watergate building) in Washington, DC; Richard Nixon is reelected as US president.

1973: A cease-fire agreement, intended to end the Vietnam war, is signed in Paris; fighting in the Middle East between Israeli and Arab forces (Yom Kippur War) is resolved by a shaky ceasefire; Arab oil-producing states cut petroleum exports to the US, western Europe and Japan because of their support of Israel; the US Senate begins televised hearings on the Watergate scandal and it is revealed that Pres. Nixon had secretly taped all conversations in his White House office; US vice-president resigns in an unrelated scandal; US combat involvement in Indochina officially ends as American planes halt their bombing of Cambodia; typhoon "Nora" leaves 800,000 Filipinos homeless on the island of Luzon; Great Britain, Ireland and Denmark formally join the Common Market; the Bahamas are granted independence from Britain after three

centuries of colonial rule; Chilean Marxist Pres. Salvadore Allende is overthrown by a CIA-backed military junta which claims Allende commits suicide; Shah of Iran nationalizes foreign-owned oil companies.

1974: Oil-producing nations boost their prices and worldwide inflation accelerates as economic growth slows to near zero in most industrialized nations; the government of China launches a new "Cultural Revolution" program aimed at condemning both the Chinese philosopher Confucius and former Defence Minister Lin Piao; West German Chancellor Willy Brandt resigns after a scandal involving an East German spy; the Tower of London and the British Houses of Parliament are bombed by the Irish Republican Army; Soviet Nobel prize-winning author Aleksandr Solzhenitsyn is stripped of his citizenship and exiled; Portuguese dictatorship ended by military coup and democratic reforms are initiated; rebels supported by Greece overthrow government in Cyprus: Turkish forces invade and take over much of the island; India explodes a nuclear device; Syria and Israel agree to the boundaries of a demilitarized zone in the Golan Heights and they begin troop withdrawals from the region; US Pres. Richard Nixon resigns to avoid impeachment by Congress for his coverup of the Watergate scandal; Gerald Ford is sworn in to replace Nixon; the US and Soviet Union reach a tentative agreement to limit the numbers of strategic offensive nuclear weapons and delivery vehicles; severe drought threatens millions in Africa; scientists warn of the effects of chloroflourocarbons (CFCs) on the ozone layer.

1975: Portugal's new constitution grants most power to the military; Angola, Cape Verde, Sâo Tomé and Principe and Mozambique gain independence from Portugal; Turkish Cypriots declare the establishment of a separate state in the northern half of the island; US evacuates as North Vietnam seizes Saigon; Egypt reopens the Suez Canal, which had been closed since the 1967 Arab-Israeli war; a UN Security Council resolution calling for the imposition of an arms embargo against South Africa is vetoed by the US, Great Britain and France; Generalissimo Franco, Spain's chief of state, dies and is replaced by King Juan Carlos I; Peru's president is ousted in a military coup and replaced by a general; a democratic republic is proclaimed in Laos; Papua

New Guinea and Surinam become independent; civil war breaks out in Beirut between Christians and Muslims; rebels in Eritrea provoke battles with Ethiopian government.

1976: Chinese Prem. Chou En-lai and Communist Chinese leader Mao Zedong die within months of each other; riots against apartheid take place in the all-black township of Soweto outside of Johannesburg and spread to Cape Town in black townships and white areas; first reports surface that Libyan leader Col. Moammar Qaddafi is financing, training and arming a widespread terrorist network; the Parti Québécois wins power in Quebec's provincial election, raising the possibility of Quebec's secession from Canada; worldwide earthquakes kill an estimated 780,000 people; the Gang of Four (Mao Zedong's widow and three others) unsuccessfully attempt a coup in China; Venezuela nationalizes petroleum industry; president of Argentina overthrown by military junta; Spanish Sahara released from Spain's jurisdiction and divided between Morocco and Mauritania; North and South Vietnam reunited under Communist government; a military coup in Thailand topples the government; 9,000 refugees flee Angolan civil war.

1977: Cambodian refugees report economic and social disaster following the Communists' capture of Phnom Penh; Egypt severs diplomatic relations with Syria, Iraq, Libya, Algeria and South Yemen for attempting to disrupt its peace overtures to Israel; over 570 die in the world's worst aviation disaster when two Boeing 747s collide on the runway on the Canary Island of Tenerife; black South African leader Steven Biko dies in jail; French territories of Afars and Issa unite to form independent Republic of Djibouti; government of Pakistan is overthrown and martial law is imposed; Leonid Brezhnev becomes USSR president and Communist Party chief; Somalia-backed Eritrean guerrillas are stopped by Ethiopian army; Thailand government seized by military junta; Rhodesia's white government announces it will begin negotiations with black majority; cyclone in India leaves 20,000 dead and 2 million homeless; US unmanned spacecrafts *Voyager I* and *II* begin journeys to explore the outer solar system; the neutron bomb, which causes great loss of life but little property damage, is developed in the US.

1978: A Soviet-supported military junta takes power in Afghanistan and Soviet troops occupy the country; Lebanon is torn by Christian and Muslim militia activity as well as Palestinian guerrilla activity, and Arab League intervenes to restore peace; Israeli forces withdraw; Syria declares a unilateral cease-fire in and around Beirut, Lebanon; Egyptian Pres. Anwar Sadat and Israeli Prem. Menachem Begin sign peace accords, mediated by US Pres. Jimmy Carter; Shah Mohammed Riza Pahlevi of Iran imposes martial law to suppress anti-government demonstrations; leftist Sandinista guerrillas attempt to overthrow the government of Nicaraguan Pres. Anastasio Somoza; US establishes full diplomatic relations with Communist China; the first peaceful transfer of power takes place in Dominican Republic; Zaïre invaded by secessionist rebels: defence aid comes from other African nations, and France and Belgium after the massacre of Europeans; military junta seizes power in Honduras; army seizes government power in Bolivia; former Italian Prem. Aldo Moro is kidnapped and murdered by the Red Brigades, a revolutionary terrorist group; John Paul II (Karol Wojtyla) of Poland becomes the first non-Italian Pope in four centuries; the first "test-tube baby" (human baby conceived outside the womb) is born in England.

1979: Armed Islamic revolutionary followers of Ayatollah Khomeini overthrow the government of Iran and the Shah flees; students demanding the Shah's return to stand trial seize hostages at US embassy; a malfunction in the cooling system of a nuclear reactor at Three Mile Island in Pennsylvania, US, closes down the reactor and radiation escapes into the air; Conservative Margaret Thatcher becomes Britain's first female prime minister; a black government is formally installed in Rhodesia and its name is changed to Zimbabwe; China and the US establish formal commercial relations for the first time since 1949; Vietnamese army invades Cambodia and installs new government; St Lucia, St Vincent and the Grenadines become independent; coup in Grenada replaces government leader; president of Uganda, Idi Amin, overthrown; Egypt is expelled from Arab League after signing Camp David peace treaty; first elections for European Parliament held; the US-USSR SALT (Strategic Arms Limitation Treaty) Agreement is signed in Vienna; Iran nationalizes remaining privately-owned industries without compensation; sharp oil price increases contribute to high inflation worldwide; South Korean Pres. Park Chung Hee and his chief body guard are assassinated by a government official; emperor of Central African Empire overthrown; president of El Salvador is ousted by military coup.

1980: Soviet dissident Andrei Sakharov, a Nobel prize-winning physicist, is arrested in Moscow; human interferon, a promising natural disease-fighting substance, is made by gene splicing; Mt St Helens erupts in Washington, in a blast that sends debris 20 km up into the atmosphere and is heard over 300 km away; in a political comeback, Indira Gandhi wins a landslide victory in India's parliamentary elections; Soviet war in Afghanistan escalates as the US imposes an embargo on the sale of grain and high technology to the Soviet Union in response to the continued occupation of Afghanistan, and 50 nations boycott the Moscow Olympics in protest; Roman Catholic Archbishop Oscar Arnulfo Romero, an El Salvadoran reformer, is assassinated while saying mass; some 10,800 Cubans seek asylum in Peru's Cuban embassy and more than 125,000 Cubans escape by boat to the US; Liberian Pres. William Tolbert, Jr, is killed in a coup; military coup in Turkey unseats government; Zimbabwe gains independence from Britain; 350 Bengalis are massacred by native tribal people in India; black guerrillas successfully bomb two South African petroleum plants and a refinery; mass labour strikes in Poland force the government to allow independent trade unions, including Solidarity, led by Lech Walesa; 20 terrorist bomb attacks take place in France; the Iran-Iraq war begins when Iraqi fighter-bombers attack Iranian airfields and lay siege to its southwestern cities; 3,000 are killed in earthquakes centred in southern Italy; 20,000 die in two strong earthquakes in Algeria; *Voyager I* sends back the first pictures of Saturn; wreck of the *Titanic* found in North Atlantic.

1981: Aquired Immune Deficiency Syndrome (AIDS) is first recognized, in the US; in El Salvador, heavy fighting occurs between the government and leftist insurgents; the world's first reusable spacecraft, the Space Shuttle *Columbia*, is sent into space; clashes between Syrian troops and Christian militiamen in Lebanon are followed by Israeli bombing in

support of Christian forces; artificial bone and skin are developed in the US; Pope John Paul II is shot and seriously wounded outside the Vatican by a Turkish terrorist; Israel is condemned worldwide after Israeli warplanes destroy an Iraqi atomic reactor near Baghdad; Irish prisoners in Belfast stage hunger strikes to force the British government to grant political prisoner status to Irish nationalist inmates, and some die; South African troops invade Angola in pursuit of guerrillas; Belize, formerly British Honduras, becomes independent from Britain; Pres. Anwar el-Sadat of Egypt is assassinated by Muslim extremists during a military parade; Israel formally annexes the Golan Heights; a five-day war between Ecuador and Peru erupts over a border dispute; Greece joins the European Community; Italian government rocked by revelation that nearly 1,000 key government, army and business leaders support a secret outlawed Masonic lodge; president of Bangladesh assassinated; Iranian president, prime minister and 29 others killed in bomb attack; 5,000 die when Indonesian ferry sinks in Java Sea; martial law is instituted in Poland in the face of continued labour unrest; the personal computer is introduced by IBM in the US.

1982: Argentina moves to reclaim Malvinas (the Falkland Islands) from UK by invading the territory; Britain defeats Argentina in the subsequent war; Canada gains the power to amend its own constitution from Britain; Israel withdraws from the Sinai and turns it over to Egypt, fulfilling their 1979 peace treaty; Israel invades Lebanon and the PLO leadership leaves Lebanon under UN protection; Lebanese Christian militiamen massacre Palestinians in refugee camps and Israel is accused of indirectly aiding the attack; Iran invades Iraq, but Iraq claims to have killed 27,000 Iranians in 18 days of battle; a series of IRA bombs explode in London, killing nine and wounding 51; western nations debate a proposed Soviet oil pipeline to western Europe; Lech Walesa, former leader of Solidarity, the outlawed Polish labour union, is freed after 11 months of imprisonment; military coups in Bangladesh and Guatemala force changes in government; Soviet leader Leonid Brezhnev dies and Yuri Andropov succeeds him; in Cambodia, support for Khmer Rouge grows as coalition against Vietnamese-backed government joined by Prince Sihanouk; up to 1,200 Afghan civilians and

Soviet soldiers die in a tunnel explosion caused by the collision of two trucks; the first permanent artificial heart is transplanted into Dr Barney B. Clark, 61, in Utah; Mexican volcano, El Chichón, erupts, blasting debris into the stratosphere.

1983: Klaus Barbie, former chief of the German Gestapo in Lyons, France, during WW II is deported to France from Bolivia to face charges of "crimes against humanity"; Soviet citizens and diplomats accused of espionage are expelled from France, Spain, the US and Britain; the US government is accused of having illegally aided Nicaraguan rebels; anti-government protests increase in Chile, governed by Gen. Pinochet; Ethiopia appeals for aid to 4 million victims of drought and famine; Sri Lankan Sinhalese and Tamil forces clash, killing hundreds and destroying the homes of thousands of others; 1,200 die in an earthquake in Turkey; martial law is formally lifted in Poland; the Organization of Petroleum Exporting Countries (OPEC) agrees to cut crude oil prices for the first time in its 23-year-history; all 269 people aboard are killed when the Soviet Union shoots down a South Korean airliner, claiming that the plane had been on a spying mission and strayed into Soviet airspace; Benigno Aquino, opponent of Philippine Pres. Marcos, returns to Manila and is assassinated; 241 US Marines and sailors and 40 French paratroopers, members of a multinational peacekeeping force in Lebanon, are killed by suicide terrorists; the US and France support Chad's government against Libyan-supported guerrillas; Israeli withdrawal from Lebanon is followed by full-scale fighting between Lebanese ethnic and religious groups; US-led forces invade the small island of Grenada; US Cruise missiles in Europe are deployed in Britain despite Soviet and civilian opposition; white South Africans approve a new constitution granting limited political participation for persons of mixed race and Asians, but not for blacks, in a new tricameral legislature; Yasir Arafat and PLO guerrillas are evacuated from Lebanon to Tunis, under UN sponsorship; riots in Assam, India claim 5,000 lives and 300,000 refugees flee; the compact disc is introduced; after an 11-year journey, the *Pioneer 10* spacecraft leaves the solar system.

1984: Cholesterol is linked to heart disease following a 10-year study by US researchers; the Apple Macintosh with mouse enters the personal computer market; Konstantin Chernenko becomes Soviet leader following the death of Yuri Andropov; US astronauts fly free of the space shuttle *Challenger*, the first humans to do so without a tether; US and UN forces are withdrawn from Lebanon; French and American researchers, working separately, report that they have identified viruses which appear to be the cause of AIDS; Saudi, Greek and Swiss tankers are attacked by both Iran and Iraq in the Persian Gulf and Saudi Arabia shoots down two Iranian jets; hundreds die during a battle for the Golden Temple in Amritsar between Sikh militants and police in India; Indian Prime Min. Indira Gandhi is slain by two of her Sikh bodyguards in New Delhi and widespread violence follows; Daniel Ortega, Sandinista leader, wins in Nicaraguan elections; the international community sends aid to starving Ethiopians; in a secret operation, Israel airlifts 25,000 Ethiopian Jews (Falashas) out of the Sudan; Britain and China finalize an agreement on Hong Kong's future, guaranteeing its capitalist system for 50 years after it is turned over to China in 1997; a Union Carbide chemical plant leak kills 2,500 in Bhopal, India; the European Space Agency launches the largest telecommunications satellite in the world.

1985: South African police kill 18 blacks commemorating the Sharpville massacre in 1960, 19 more are killed while participating in a funeral procession and later the government declares a state of emergency; Daniel Ortega becomes president of Nicaragua; US president urges military aid to Nicaraguan opposition forces but only humanitarian aid is approved; Mikhail Gorbachev succeeds Konstantin Chernenko as Soviet leader and he opens disarmament talks with the US; Iraq turns back an Iranian offensive, allegedly killing 30,000 to 50,000 Iranians; Shiite Muslim hijackers release hostages after 17 days of captivity in Beirut, having demanded the release of hundreds of Shiites detained by Israeli forces; Argentine president imposes drastic economic measures to cut 1,010 percent inflation rate; top French officials are linked to the bombing of a ship owned by Greenpeace; two leading Soviet KGB officials defect to Britain and the US, where both name Soviet spies in the two countries; a cyclone and tidal waves hit Bangladesh, killing 10,000; a Mexican earthquake kills more than 7,000 and causes widespread destruction, leaving thousands homeless; border dispute between Mali and Burkina Faso leads to war but is eventually referred to International Court of Justice; Nicaragua suspends civil rights; four Palestinians seize the Italian cruise ship *Achille Lauro* off the coast of Egypt, murdering a wheelchair-bound American; Reagan and Gorbachev meet at the first superpower summit in six years; 95 Colombians die when 60 rebels seize the Palace of Justice in Bogotá and take more than 300 persons hostage; 60 die when Arab gunmen hijack an Egyptian jetliner, in an act allegedly backed by Libya's leader Col. Muammar Qaddafi; a Colombian volcanic eruption kills 20,000 people; Guatemala elects its first civilian president following three decades of military rule; Uruguay's military government replaced by civilian government; Sudanese and Ugandan presidents ousted by military coups; terrorists kill 20 people at two airports (in Rome and Vienna), both at the ticket counters of El Al, Israel's national airline; Live Aid rock concert in London, UK and Philadelphia, US raises over $60 million for African famine relief.

1986: Portugal and Spain join the European Community; Jean-Claude Duvalier, Haiti's "president for life," flees to France in the face of nationwide protest; Portugal elects its first civilian president in 60 years; Gorbachev calls for "radical reform" of Soviet economy and reshapes the leadership of the Communist party; Philippine Pres. Ferdinand Marcos flees to the US after allegations of electoral fraud; his opponent, Corazon Aquino, succeeds Marcos as president; Swedish Prime Min. Olof Palme is assassinated; former UN secretary general Kurt Waldheim is elected president of Austria; US planes bomb Libya citing retaliatory measures after missile attacks; radiation is spread following the meltdown of the Chernobyl nuclear power plant in the USSR; South African forces attack alleged African National Congress (ANC) bases in neighbouring Botswana, Zambia and Zim-babwe; the *New York Times* first links Panama's General Manuel Noriega with drug and arms trafficking; US president acknowledges a secret and illegal arms deal with Iran: the "Iran-Contra Affair" involving the US sale of arms in exchange for hostages is first reported in a Lebanese newspaper; The US space shuttle *Challenger* explodes one minute after liftoff and all seven crew members die instantly; *Voyager 2* spacecraft passes Uranus.

1987: Soviet leader Mikhail Gorbachev begins a campaign for openness (glasnost) and reconstruction (perestroika); Tamil separatists kill hundreds of Sri Lankans, mostly Sinhalese, and clash with government forces; German pilot Mathias Rust, 19, embarrasses Soviets when he lands his single-engine Cessna in Red Square, Moscow; Moscow's Communist Party chief, Boris Yeltsin, is dismissed after criticizing Soviet leader Gorbachev; South Africa withdraws its troops from Angola; an Iraqi warplane's missile kills 37 US sailors in the Persian Gulf, and the US escorts Kuwaiti oil tankers despite danger posed by the Iran-Iraq war; 402 Iranian pilgrims to Mecca die in battles with Saudi police; 24 nations sign a treaty to protect the ozone layer; Portugal and China agree that the Portuguese colony of Macao will be returned to China in 1999; stock market prices plunge worldwide; the Palestinian intifadah (uprising) begins against Israeli authorities in the Gaza Strip and West Bank, and thousands of protesters are imprisoned; Syrian troops enter Beirut in an attempt to bring a cease-fire; Lebanese prime minister dies in a bomb attack; a military coup ousts coalition government in Chad; 2,000 die in the Philippines when a ferry sinks.

1988: Nicaraguan contras and the Sandinista government reach a cease-fire agreement; the US and Soviet Union sign a treaty on intermediate-range nuclear forces (INF); Soviet troops begin to pull out of Afghanistan after a nine-year occupation; nationalist groups in Soviet-controlled Azerbaijan and Armenia clash; Colombian drug cartels defy government attempts to bring them to justice, and fight among themselves; a US navy warship accidentally shoots down a commercial Iranian airliner over the Persian Gulf, killing all 290 persons aboard; the Soviet communist party backs Gorbachev's plan for perestroika; Canadian and US governments ratify a free trade agreement, to take effect Jan. 1, 1989; Iran and Iraq agree on a cease-fire to end their eight-year war; Iraq uses poison gas on its Kurdish minority and razes Kurdish villages; Libya and Chad formally end their war; Thailand and Laos do battle in a brief border dispute; Ethiopia and Somalia end 11 years of disputes over borders with a peace treaty; Solidarity supporters stage widespread strikes in Poland; Vietnamese troops leave Kampuchea; a military coup in Burma causes a change in leadership; Yugoslavia's inflation rate tops 250%, ethnic Albanians in Kosovo province demand freedom from Serbian rule; Benazir Bhutto, daughter of a former Pakistani president, becomes prime minister of Pakistan; 270 people die when a bomb blows up a Pan Am jetliner over Lockerbie, Scotland; 25,000 Armenians die during an earthquake.

1989: Iran's Ayatollah Khomeini calls for the execution of UK author Salman Rushdie for blaspheming the prophet Mohammed; the Soviet Union holds historic multicandidate parliamentary elections and Boris Yeltsin emerges as Russian leader; Japanese Prime Min. Noboru Takeshita is toppled by financial scandal, Emperor Hirohito dies and is succeeded by his son; Chinese students lead more than one million in demonstrations for democratic reforms, but spreading unrest is checked by a government crackdown in Tiananmen Square that is suspected to have killed thousands; Hungary opens its border with Austria and moves toward political and economic reform; anti-Communist forces continue to battle the government in Afghanistan; fighting between Christians and Muslims in Beirut intensifies; 90 people die in ethnic violence in Soviet Uzbekistan; Poles participate in their first open election in 40 years and Solidarity wins a solid victory; the three Baltic states (Estonia, Latvia and Lithuania) protest Soviet domination; a Colombian presidential candidate is slain, prompting a renewed crackdown on illegal drug traffickers; thousands of East Germans flee to West Germany and the East German government proposes political reforms; Vietnamese forces withdraw from Cambodia; East German communist leader Erich Honecker is removed from power, he is later charged with corruption; thousands demonstrate in Czechoslovakia and force the communist government to resign, Vaclav Havel is elected president; the spaceship *Atlantis* is launched on a journey to Jupiter; East Germany opens the Berlin wall after 28 years and lifts visa and emigration restrictions; Panama's General Noriega annuls presidential elections after an opposition party victory, the US invades Panama and Noriega goes into hiding; Romanian Pres. Nicolae Ceausescu is overthrown and executed with his wife for genocide, abuse of power and theft; 80 nations sign an agreement to limit production of chorofluorocarbons (CFCs) to protect the ozone layer; Paraguay's president is toppled

by a military coup; the Exxon *Valdez* runs aground in Alaska and spills thousands of litres of oil; *Voyager 2* spacecraft reaches Neptune.

1990: Panama's Manuel Noriega surrenders to US authorities; violence erupts in Soviet Azerbaijan as Azerbaijanis attack Armenians; Bulgaria and Yugoslavia switch to multiparty systems; Violeta Chamorro defeats Sandinista leader Daniel Ortega to become the Nicaraguan president; South African government lifts restrictions on opposition organizations and declares amnesty for political prisoners, black leader Nelson Mandela is freed after 27 years in prison; the US, France, Great Britain and the Soviet Union reach agreement on a reunited Germany; Lithuania proclaims its sovereignty and Soviet troops move in; Namibia gains independence from South Africa; newly-released Soviet documents prove Soviet secret police killed 15,000 Polish military officers in the Katyn forest massacre of 1940; the $1.5-billion Hubble Space Tele-scope is sent into space, but flawed light-gathering mirrors distort transmissions; Iran's worst earthquake kills 40,000; more than 1,400 Muslim pilgrims to Mecca suffocate in a stampede in an overcrowded tunnel; the Ukraine declares its sovereignty within the Soviet Union; the two Germanys reunite, merging their economic, legal and political systems; Czechoslovakia and Romania hold their first free elections in the postwar era (Aug. 2); Iraq invades Kuwait over disagreements regarding oil production levels and appears ready to invade Saudi Arabia; the UN passes sweeping trade and financial sanctions against Iraq, and aid and troops pour into Saudi Arabia; civil war in black South African townships kills hundreds; the first human gene therapy for disease is done by blood transfusion; South Africa bans racial discrimination in public places; following a political challenge from within her own party, British Prime Min. Margaret Thatcher resigns and is succeeded by John Major; Mozambique adopts a constitution allowing for a multiparty democracy; civil war in Chad ends with overthrow of president; a military coup in Bangladesh unseats the president; Soviet Pres. Mikhail Gorbachev proposes Union Treaty to restructure Soviet Union; Helmut Kohl elected Chancellor of Unified Germany; Lech Walesa elected president of Poland; African National Congress (ANC) holds first conference in South Africa in 31 years; Rev. Jean-Bertrand Aristide elected president of Haiti; Edward Shevardnadze resigns as Soviet foreign minister; Slovenia and Croatia initiate secession from Yugoslavian republic.

1991: Iraq ignores Jan. 15 deadline for withdrawal from Kuwait and Allied forces (including the US, Canada, Britain, France, Italy, Japan, Pakistan and members of the Arab League) launch a six-week air attack; Soviets suppress independence movements in Baltic republics; US and Italy begin rescue of foreigners trapped in Somalian civil war; limited integration of schools begins in South Africa and sweeping reforms of apartheid law are proposed; Allies launch ground assault on Iraqi forces and informal cease-fire follows; 1,200 killed in major earthquake in Pakistan and Afghanistan; Lithuanians vote to secede from Soviet Union; Estonia and Latvia vote for independence from the Soviet Union; violent protests held in Belgrade to topple Yugoslavian government; Kuwaiti government forced to resign in wake of failure to establish post-war order; UN cease-fire formally ends Gulf War (Apr.) and Kurds flee from Iraq; Soviet republic of Georgia votes for independence; cease-fire declared in Angola's 16-year civil war; Rajiv Ghandi assassinated during Indian national election campaign; Boris Yeltsin elected president of Russia; Mt Pinatubo volcano erupts in Philippines; Population Registration Act repealed in South Africa; fighting between Yugoslav military and Slovenian nationalists escalates; Soviet hardliners attempt a coup against Mikhail Gorbachev: its failure results in the dissolution of the Communist party; rebels oust Haitian Pres. Jean-Bertrand Aristide; Serbia and Croatia reach political settlement but civil war continues; peace accord signed in El Salvador, paving the way to end of 11-year civil war; failed coup in Soviet Union speeds disintegration of the country as Lithuania, Estonia and Latvia act to enforce their independence; civil war in Croatia escalates; warring factions in Cambodia sign peace accord; talks on new constitution begin in South Africa; rebels fighting in Somalia claim to have taken over Mogadishu and deposed the president; Gorbachev resigns as USSR formally dissolved and Commonwealth of Independent States (CIS) created; fighting escalates in

Somalia; Slovenia and Croatia recognized as independent states by Germany; Islamic Salvation Front leads in Algerian elections; by year-end, cholera epidemic has killed 3,500 in Latin America and 12,500 in Africa.

1992: A Jan. military coup in Algeria gives power to a committee which cancels elections in progress; in June the Algerian president is assassinated and the defense minister assumes power. Brazil is the site of the Earth Summit (June), which sees 100 world leaders and 30,000 participants gather in Rio de Janeiro to discuss worldwide environmental protection; the country is rocked by political unrest in Aug., which results in the end of the presidency of President Fernando Collor de Mello over an influence-peddling and bribery scandal. The European Community's Maastricht Treaty is first rejected by Denmark (June), then ratified by Irish (June) and French (Sept.) voters, and the Italian senate (Sept.). Czechoslovakia's president, Vaclav Havel, resigns on July 20 and the Parliament of Slovakia declares its sovereignty. An earthquake on Oct. 12 leaves 300 dead and thousands injured in Egypt. The Uruguay round of the GATT (General Agreement on Tariffs and Trade) negotiations remains stalled over the issue of farm subsidies. Germany is plagued by riots and firebombings staged by right-wing extremists attacking foreign-born workers and refugees. Israel's national election results in a victory for the Labour Party and its leader, Yitzhak Rabin; in Aug., Rabin begins to hint that compromise in the area of peace and territorial disputes might be possible. Italy continues an anti-Mafia crackdown despite the assassination of two prominent judges and a police investigator. A ruptured petrol pipeline in Mexico's working-class district of Guadalajara is blamed for an explosion that kills 200 and injures nearly 1,500 in Apr. Peru's president, Alberto Fujimori, suspends sections of the country's constitution in Apr. and seizes power, citing a need to root out corruption and combat the combined forces of the Shining Path guerrillas and various drug barons. Russia's first experiments with free markets trigger soaring inflation and shortages. Civil war in Somalia brings 4.5 million of its people to the brink of starvation; by Aug. the UN brings in forces to ensure that food is distributed to the hungry, but is unable to restore order. The government in South Africa continues to work towards a power-sharing agreement with the black majority after receiving nearly 70% support in a Mar. whites-only referendum; in Sept. troops from the Ciskei homeland open fire on ANC supporters massed at the border and talks on democratic reform are again delayed. Citizens in Thailand take to the streets in a series of demonstrations that eventually force constitutional reforms and democratic elections. In the United Kingdom, the scandals of the royal family threaten the credibility of the monarchy; uncertainty over the fate of the Maastricht Treaty and pressure on UK currency force a withdrawal from the European Monetary System in Sept. and a devaluation of the UK pound. In the United States, riots in Los Angeles in late Apr./early May leave 42 dead; the US state of Florida is devastated by Hurricane Andrew (Aug.) which does an estimated $15 billion damage; on Oct. 12, the *Pioneer* spacecraft plunges into the scorching atmosphere surrounding the planet Venus and ends a 14-year space mission; in Nov., the Democrats, under Bill Clinton and Al Gore, are elected to a four-year term. Yugoslavia continues to disintegrate: the UN Security Council deploys peacekeepers in Jan.; Croatia and Slovenia are given diplomatic recognition by the European community as well as 20 other countries (including Canada); by Feb., Serbia and Montenegro reach agreement on a common state retaining the Yugoslav flag, anthem and joint parliament; in Mar., citizens of the republic of Bosnia-Hercegovina vote for independence; however, ethnic fighting over Bosnian territory escalates throughout the year amid charges of ethnic cleansing and atrocities, and a series of cease-fires that rarely hold for more than a few days; on Sept. 22, Yugoslavia (Serbia and Montenegro) is expelled from the UN General Assembly.

1993: Both sides in the Bosnia-Hercegovina conflict reject peace plans to settle the conflict. In Burundi an abortive Oct. coup leaves the President and 6 ministers dead before the army decides to back the existing government and order is restored. Despite opposition and active interference by the Khmer Rouge, 90% of registered voters cast their ballots in Cambodia's national election in May. One of the longest civil wars in Africa ends when the separation of Eritrea from Ethiopia is approved in a referendum. After 7 years of negotiation, the latest version of the GATT agreement is approved by 117

countries in late Dec. German military forces took part in missions outside its borders for the first time since WWII; the German parliament bows to right-wing pressures and places limits on their liberal immigration laws. Neither the OAS nor the UN is able to restore Haiti's deposed president Jean-Bertrand Aristide to power despite intense negotiations and increased blockades. On Sept 13, PLO leader Yasser Arafat and Israeli Prime Min. Yitzak Rabin meet in Washington to sign a peace agreement secretly negotiated in Norway; the agreement grants Palestinian autonomy over certain lands and recognized Israel's right to exist. The results of the June election in Nigeria are nullified by the long-time dictator, despite protests which include a 3-day general strike. A battle for power in the Russian parliament sees Pres. Boris Yeltsin strip Vice-Pres. Rutskoi of his powers and dissolve parliament to call Dec. elections; parliamentarians respond by barricading themselves in the building which is then surrounded by government troops; the seige is lifted when the insurgents surrender on Oct. 4; a new parliament is elected in Dec. and a new constitution is approved. Slovakia and the Czech republic declare independence on Jan 1. UK Prime Min. John Major and his Irish counterpart announce a tentative peace plan for Northern Ireland that would allow the people to decide their own fate. US troops in Somalia hands the mission to re-establish order over to a UN force made up of personnel from 20 countries and announces they will pull out at the end of Mar. 1994. In Sept. an agreement is reached in South Africa that paves the way for a multi-party transitional council that includes blacks; in Oct. the United Nations lifts economic sanctions; in Nov. a new constitution is approved and national all-race elections are scheduled; white rule ends officially in Dec. In the United States, a standoff outside the compound of a religious group in Waco Texas ends in tragedy when authorities stormed the area and the buildings erupt in flames. (Apr.); a rainy summer leads to record-breaking floods in nine states along the Mississippi River and in Oct. brush fires devaste six counties in California; in Nov. Pres. Clinton secures approval for NAFTA in the House of Representatives.

1994: Islamic fundamentalists in Algeria continue their fight to oust the government, targetting foreigners, journalists, and intellectuals. In Feb. a Bosnian Serb mortar attack on a Sarajevo marketplace kills 66, injures 200 and prompts NATO to threaten punitive bombing if Serb guns are not pulled back from the city; in Aug. the Bosnian Serb rejection of a peace plan moves the government of Serbia to sever relations; in Dec. Bosnian Serbs kidnap UN peace keepers and use them as human shields to halt NATO airstrikes. In Brazil, radical steps are taken to curb inflation; the currency (cruzeiro) is scrapped and replaced by the real, and severe budget cuts are instituted. Increasing numbers of Cuban citizens flee the country in the face of the effects of the trade embargo. A car ferry enroute from Estonia to Finland sinks, killing over 900 passengers and crew. Throughout the year German officials seize illegal shipments of plutonium apparently smuggled out of the former Soviet Union. A US-led force lands in Haiti on Sept. 19, and president-in-exile Jean Bertrand Aristide returns to Haiti in Oct. In Jan. a heavily-armed Jewish settler enters a mosque in Hebron on the West Bank and opens fire on Muslim worshippers; 40 Palestinians die and more than 250 are wounded in the riots that follow; throughout the year Islamic fundamentalists use suicide bombing in an effort to derail the peace talks. In May, Yasser Arafat and Israeli Prime Min. Rabin sign the peace accord that inaugurates Palestinian self-rule on the Gaza Strip and in Jericho; the PLO begins to create a government structure for the areas; in July, Jordan and Israel sign an agreement to normalize relations. Japan suffers a year of political uncertainty as a series of prime ministers are unable to maintain a coalition government. A string of comet fragments known as Shoemaker-Levy 9 collide with Jupiter between July 16-22, causing massive explosions in the planet's atmosphere. The government of North Korea reluctantly agrees to allows nuclear inspectors to visit the majority of their nuclear sites. Ruler Kim Il Sung dies as negotiations end; his son and successor Kim Jong Il appears to have a tenuous grip on power. A New Year's day rebellion in Mexico sets the stage for a turbulent year—Zapatista rebels in the southern state of Chiapas demand land reforms; in Mar. Luis Colosio, the leading candidate in the national election, was gunned down at an outdoor rally; in Dec., the peso loses 40% of its value over 8 days and trade allies move to prop up the economy. Workers try to bring down the military government in Nigeria by staging a general strike that drags on for six weeks. In Northern Ireland, the political wing of the IRA announces a "complete cessation of military operations" in Sept., paving the way for peace talks. In Oct., economic reforms lead to a steep plunge in the value of the ruble and widespread protests over unemployment; a leaky pipeline spills a massive quantity of oil onto the fragile permafrost and into surrounding rivers; in Dec., 40,000 Russian troops invade the rebel area of Chechnya to end the region's drive for independence. Plagued by racially motivated skirmishes at the beginning of the year, Rwanda dissolves into an ethnic blood bath after the death of the president in a plane crash; tens of thousands of Rwandans, mostly Tutsi, die at the hands of the rival Hutus in a killing spree that lasts for months; Tutsi-led forces eventually regain control of the country and thousands more flee to refugee camps in neighbouring countries to escape feared reprisals. In Somalia, factional fighting reignites as both the US and the UN withdraw the forces policing the area. All race elections are held for the first time in Apr. 26-28, and Nelson Mandela is elected president; South Africa is given full membership to the United Nations in June. In the US, California is rocked by a major earthquake in Jan., in Feb., Aldrich Ames, a mid-level officer in the CIA, is exposed as a spy operating for Moscow since the mid-1980s. By June, the US dollar was in a record-breaking dive.

1995: The Algerian civil war continued, with Muslim extremists stepping up attacks on foreigners, collaborators, journalists, women who adopted modern ways of life and the families of government officials. In the Atlantic region, a harsh hurricane season brought death and destruction to the Caribbean in the latter part of the year. In the Bosnian war, the blockade of Sarajevo continued for much of the year as truces failed to hold. In May NATO launched two days of airstrikes to break the impasse and Bosnian Serbs seized nearly 400 UN peace keepers; the hostages were slowly freed throughout May and June. In July Bosnian Serbs overran the UN safe areas of Srebrenica and Zepa and cleared the territory of Muslims. By August, NATO had resumed airstrikes in response to the shelling of a marketplace in

Sarajevo. The bombing missions continued in Sept. to force the Bosnian Serbs to withdraw from positions around Sarajevo; a ceasefire was finally inaugurated in October. In November, negotiators for all sides in the Bosnian conflict met at the Wright-Patterson Air Force Base outside Dayton, Ohio, for a three-week effort to hammer out a workable peace plan. By Dec. US and British military personnel were arriving in Bosnia to implement the agreement. Burmese officials freed political dissident Aung San Suu Kyi from house arrest in July. In Burundi, murders by members of rival factions raised fears of Rwandan-style massacres; thousands of Rwandan refugees fled to Tanzania to escape the violence. The UN's Fourth World Conference on Women was held in China in September. In Croatia, Pres. Tudjman allowed the UN peacekeeping mandate to lapse; in August, Croatian troops regained the territory in Krajina that had been lost to Croatian Serbs in 1991. France conducted three nuclear tests around the Muroroa Atoll in the South Pacific during the year, despite international protests and local demonstrations. Haitians went to the polls on Dec. 17 in the first election since exiled Pres. Jean-Bertrand Aristide was returned to power. In Ireland, a bitter campaign over the issue of lifting the ban on divorce ended in narrow approval for liberalizing the laws in November. Israel and the Palestinians struggled with the peace process throughout the year, postponing deadlines as suicide bomb attacks in Israel threatened to derail the process altogether. In October, Israeli forces began to withdraw from parts of the West Bank in accordance with an agreement on Palestinian self rule. On Nov. 4, a 25-year-old militant Jewish law student shot and killed Israeli Prime Min. Yitzak Rabin. On Jan. 17, the port of Kobe in Japan was struck by an earthquake measuring 7.2 on the Richter scale; 5,000 residents were killed, 25,000 were injured and 300,000 were left homeless. Also, in Japan a March nerve-gas attack during Monday morning rush hour in a Tokyo subway left 10 dead and 5,500 injured; two more incidents took place in April in Yokohama; police traced the attacks to a religious cult known as Aum Shinrikyo and arrested its leader Shoko Asahara. The Galileo space probe arrived at Jupiter in December after a 3.7 billion km trip that took six years. Mexico spent the early part of the year grappling with a financial crisis that saw

the peso fall to record lows; the US engineered a financial bail-out that was conditional upon stringent austerity measures and the reform of the country's electoral process; loan repayments began in October, ahead of schedule. In November, the military government in Nigeria condemned environmentalist and activist Ken Saro-Wiwa and eight others to death; the sentence was carried out on Nov. 10. Peru and Ecuador engaged in a month-long border war in the early part of the year. In Poland, long-time president Lech Walesa was defeated by a former communist who promised to continue western-style reforms in November. Throughout the year Russia was unable to subdue guerrillas in the breakaway republic of Chechnya; bombing raids on the capital of Grozny reduced the city to rubble. A 7.5 (Richter scale) earthquake struck the Sakhalin Island in Russia's far east in May, killing nearly 2,000. UN forces pulled out of Somalia after a two-year attempt to restore order amid drought, starvation and clan warfare. Sri Lanka's civil war with Tamil rebels continued as the Tamils refused to consider peace proposals. In Singapore, at the 232-year-old Barings Bank, a rogue trader's speculation on the currency market cost the bank more than $1 billion; Barings collapsed. In the US, on the anniversary of the FBI attack on the Branch Davidians in Waco, Texas, a bomb exploded outside a government building in Oklahoma City. One hundred and sixty-eight were killed and over 400 injured; police arrested Timothy McVeigh, a Gulf War veteran linked to American militia groups. On Oct. 16, Nation of Islam minister Louis Farrakhan rallied nearly a million black men in Washington.

1996: The Algerian civil war continued throughout the year. In Bosnia, prisoners were exchanged, residents were evacuated and Sarajevo was handed over to the Muslim-Croat federation. Bosnian Serb leader Radovan Karadzic withdrew from public life in July. In Sept. elections were held for the Serb Republic and the Muslim-Croat Federation. Bulgaria's currency collapsed in May; hyperinflation paralysed the economy. Rwandan refugees were forcibly repatriated in mid-July; days later the Tutsi-dominated army seized power in a coup. Borders closed as Rwanda's neighbours proclaimed sanctions. On Aug. 3, top generals of the Khmer Rouge opened amnesty negotiations with the Cambodian government to end decades of bloodshed. Hurricane Bertha hit the Caribbean islands and eastern US in July. In May, unrest in Tibet increased as Chinese authorities forbade demonstrations supporting the Dalai Lama. On July 29, the Chinese tested an underground nuclear device and then declared a moratorium on future testing. On Feb. 24, Cuban fighter planes shot down two civilian US aircraft for violating Cuban air space. An Arab summit held in Cairo in June called for Israeli withdrawal from Palestinian territory, including Arab Jerusalem. France's former Pres. Francois Mitterand died Jan. 8. France conducted a nuclear test on Jan. 27; on Jan. 29, Pres. Chirac announced a permanent end to nuclear tests and cancelled the last two. Yassir Arafat was sworn in as president of the Palestinian Council's executive in Feb.; on Apr. 24 the PLO revoked the charter clauses that called for the destruction of Israel and the waging of war against the Jewish state. In Israel, a May election resulted in victory for Benjamin Netanyahu and the Likud party. In Sept., an archaeological tunnel bordering on Islam's third-holiest site, the Al Aqsa Mosque, was opened, touching off a wave of violent protest. The Bank of Tokyo and Mitsubishi Bank merged on Apr. 1 to create the world's largest bank. On May 13, the World Food Programme and the FAO issued a joint alert over food shortages in N. Korea. In S. Korea, two former presidents were convicted of accepting bribes during their tenures. In Sept., a N. Korean submarine ran aground in S. Korea; most crew members died on S. Korean soil. On Apr. 6, the Liberian capital city of Monrovia was torn by factional fighting; UN troops took control of Monrovia on Apr. 21. In Nov., Pakistan's president dismissed Prime Min. Benazir Bhutto's government and called for elections in the wake of corruption allegations. In Peru, Tupac Amaru guerrillas took diplomats hostage for several months. In June, Russian Pres. Yeltsin narrowly won elections, and a run-off election in July confirmed the victory. In Rwanda, clashes between Hutu and Tutsi soldiers occurred in Jan.; by Nov. thousands of displaced Hutus (many of whom had been away since 1994) were returning home from Zaire. Serbian Pres. Milosevic ordered the results of local elections annulled in Nov. when opposition parties won; outraged

citizens protested well into 1997. On Mar. 29, leaders of Sierra Leone's military government transferred power to a democratically elected government. South Africa's main political parties agreed on a new constitution on May 8; on May 9, F.W. de Klerk took his National Party out of the government coalition. In Spain, Basque separatists detonated four bombs during July, killing at least 35 and prompting demonstrations against the ETA. In the UK, the IRA ended a 17-month cease-fire in Feb. with three bombings; attacks continued through June. On Mar. 13, a gunman killed 16 kindergarten children and their teacher in Dunblane, Scotland, before killing himself. A "mad-cow disease" scare prompted the banning of British beef by the EC and the eventual destruction of thousands of cattle and embryos to contain the problem. Northern Ireland's July marching season saw renewed violence. On Apr. 3, an arrest was made in the 17-year-old Unabomber case. The Summer Olympics opened in Atlanta on Jul. 19. US Pres. Clinton was re-elected in November.

1997: In Afghanistan's civil war, the Taliban took control of Kabul and other key cities; by year-end they had imposed strict Islamic rule in many areas. In Algeria, over 2,000 were killed in nearly 50 massacres as suspected Islamic terrorists continued their war against the government; a June election gave the military-backed regime a clear majority. The worst flooding of the century hit Central Europe in July, leaving hundreds dead as dams broke and power failed. In Bulgaria, anti-government strikes and political paralysis in Jan. led to economic collapse. In Cambodia, in July, Second Prime Min. Hun Sen seized control of Phnom Penh. Chinese premier Deng Xiaoping died on Feb. 19. In Nov., Egyptian terrorists killed 68 people in Luxor. On July 1, the British colony of Hong Kong returned to China, ending a 99-year lease agreement. In late Oct., Hong Kong's stock market dropped over 10% in four days; global markets followed suit. Indonesia's slash-and-burn farming techniques and a delayed rainy season blanketed much of the country with smoke and threatened the health of more than 20 million people. Iraqi leader Saddam Hussein confronted the U.S. in Nov. by barring American members of a UN weapons-inspection team; Allied mobilization prompted Hussein to allow the inspectors to continue their duties. In Japan, Yamichi Securities, one of the largest brokerages in the country, shut down on Nov. 24 amid the collapse of stock prices and a payoff scandal; the closure left US$24 billion in debts. In Dec., representatives from 150 nations met in Japan to devise controls on greenhouse gases to slow ozone damage and global warming. Liberia's former rebel Charles Taylor, a key figure in the country's seven-year civil war, won 75% of the presidential vote and a legislative majority in the country's general election on July 24. In Pakistan, the Muslim League defeated former Prime Min. Bhutto's party in national elections on Feb. 3. In Russia, Pres. Boris Yeltsin was hospitalized on Jan. 8 with double pneumonia; the Duma began discussing Yeltsin's impeachment. On Apr. 14, the World Bank agreed to loan US$6 billion over two years if Russia's economic reforms continued. Serbian protesters continued to demand that the results of the Nov. election be respected; by Feb., parliament recognized the election results and allowed the victors to take office. In Sierra Leone, in June, the third military coup in six years ended the fledgling civilian government. In Thailand, an economic crisis in Mar. forced the government to halt trading in all bank and financial stocks. The crisis continued as the government propped up the baht, and Asian neighbours offered loans to help maintain foreign currency reserves. The Philippines, Malaysia and Indonesia devalued their currency, and the IMF offered aid throughout the region in exchange for economic reforms. The Turkish army wiped out Kurdish camps in Northern Iraq. In Scotland, embryologist Ian Wilmut and four colleagues at Roslin Institute near Edinburgh revealed that they had cloned a sheep. In Nevada, British pilot Andy Green broke the sound barrier on Oct. 13 by driving a jet-propelled automobile at 1,229.775 kph. In the UK, Tony Blair and the Labour Party ended 18 years of Conservative rule on May 1 in general elections. Historic peace talks in Northern Ireland began on Oct. 7 as all parties, including Sinn Fein, tried to end violence. British Prime Min. Tony Blair and Sinn Fein leader Gerry Adams met at Downing Street on Dec. 11 to discuss Northern Ireland's peace–the first such meeting since the 1920s. Viewers around the world watched pictures sent back from Mars by the Pathfinder mission in July. On Oct. 6, the space shuttle Atlantis docked with the Mir space station. On Mars, Pathfinder fell silent. On Oct. 15, the space probe Cassini was launched for Saturn. In Zaire, Pres. Mobutu fled from an advancing rebel army on May 16; rebel troops subsequently entered Kinshasa, Laurent Kabila took power, and the country was renamed Democratic Republic of the Congo.

1998: In Jan., China ordered the slaughter of over one million poultry in Hong Kong to end the threat of the chicken flu. In Iran, Pres. Khatami called on the US on Jan. 7 to resume formal relations with his country for the first time since 1979. An earthquake measuring 6.2 on the Richter scale killed 50 and left 540,000 homeless in China's Hebei province. The last US shuttle to Mir was launched Jan. 22 to aid the aging space station. Pope John Paul II visited Catholics and Fidel Castro in Cuba from Jan. 21-25. US Pres. Clinton gave a deposition in the Paula Jones case (Jan. 17) and denied his sexual relationship with Monica Lewinsky (Jan. 26). On Jan. 29, tobacco executives acknowledged that smoking endangered health and agreed to a US$368.5 billion settlement in exchange for immunity from further lawsuits. In Feb., an earthquake in Afghanistan destroyed 15,000 homes and killed an estimated 5,000 people. In Bangladesh, a 22-year-old war in the southeastern part of the country ended when tribal fighters surrendered their weapons for more autonomy for their Buddhist culture. On Mar. 23, Russian Pres.Yeltsin fired Prime Min. Viktor Chernomyrdin and his entire cabinet; Yeltsin then appointed Sergei Kiriyenko as acting prime min. In Mar., in Sri Lanka, suicide bombers using boats packed with explosives rammed a navy convoy transporting troops to the Jaffna peninsula; two vessels went down and at least 40 soldiers died. On Mar. 24, two boys, aged 11 and 13, gunned down four classmates and a teacher in a shooting that wounded 10 others in Jonesboro, Arkansas. The drug company Pfizer released Viagra in the US. On Mar. 24, fighting erupted again between ethnic Albanians in Kosovo and Serbian police. Earlier in the month, a 10-day police action against the Kosovar Liberation Front caused 100 deaths of mostly elderly people, women and children. On Apr. 10, after 22 months of talks, the governments of

Ireland and Britain and representatives of the warring factions agreed to permit a referendum on the future of Northern Ireland and the creation of a self-governing Northern Ireland assembly. While the IRA retained its initial ceasefire, dissident groups began a campaign of violence. On Apr. 15, Pol Pot, the Khmer Rouge leader responsible for killing more than two million Cambodians in the 1970s, died. On Apr. 19, 34 leaders from the Western Hemisphere met in Santiago, Chile, to begin talks for a free-trade zone that would include all countries in the hemisphere except Cuba. On May 10, Sinn Fein members voted to support the Easter peace agreement and allow its members to sit in Northern Ireland's new assembly. By the end of the month, most Irish in the north and south supported the Easter pact. On May 12, Suharto's troops fired on student protesters in Indonesia; on May 18, a few hundred students occupied the parliament buildings and thousands of others massed outside. On May 21, Suharto resigned. On May 22, the military peacefully cleared the parliament buildings of 2,000 student occupiers. In May, India and Pakistan exchanged artillery fire along the Kashmiri border. On May 11, India exploded three nuclear devices in underground tests. Two more were detonated on May 13. On May 28, Pakistan announced the successful underground test of five nuclear devices. Ethnic turmoil exploded in Kosovo, an Albanian-dominated province in Yugoslavia, and spilled into Albania. In June, Ethiopia and Eritrea fought a border war. NATO warplanes flew over Kosovo to end Serbia's four-month battle with insurgents that had created 65,000 refugees. In July, monsoons in Bangladesh stranded eight million people near the country's capital. David Trimble, leader of the Ulster Unionist Party, was selected first minister of the new Northern Ireland assembly. Former Italian prime min. Silvio Berlusconi was sentenced for bribing tax inspectors. In Nigeria, Gen. Abubakar released hundreds of prisoners and abolished three discredited electoral bodies. On July 17, Papua New Guinea was devastated by tidal waves that killed at least 3,000 people and left another 3,000 missing. In Russia, as economic woes mounted, the IMF and other foreign lenders offered a US$22.6 billion rescue package on July 13. The remains of Tsar Nicholas and his family were interred in St. Petersburg on July 17. By mid-July, UN officials said 2.4 million Sudanese faced starvation because of a two-year-drought and a 15-year civil war. In Florida more than 120,000 people were evacuated from the paths of wildfires. In mid-July, 110 were killed in Kosovo as Kosovar separatists tried to enter the territory from Albania and clashed with the Yugoslav army. Yugoslavia's army tried to recapture the southern territory from rebels on July 24; it ended in early Aug. In the United States, the Dow Jones nosedived in late July; by Aug. 7, it had lost 10% of its value. Stock markets around the world followed suit. On Aug. 7, a car bomb exploded outside the US embassy in Kenya; 263 were killed and over 4,500 were injured. A second car bomb exploded outside the US embassy in Tanzania. Monica Lewinsky, a former White House intern, testified before a grand jury that she had sex with US Pres. Clinton between Nov. 1995 and May 1997–a relationship Clinton had denied. On Aug. 15, an IRA splinter group that refused to support the ceasefire in Northern Ireland detonated a car bomb in Omagh that killed 29 and injured over 220; all supporters of peace condemned the bombing. On Aug. 15, the Iraqi national assembly voted to suspend co-operation with the UN weapons inspectors to protest over eight years of economic sanctions. On Aug. 20, the US military fired missiles at the camp of suspected terrorist Osama bin Laden in retaliation for the bombing of its embassies in Africa. China suffered its worst flood season in 50 years; 3,600 were killed and over 1.4 million were displaced. By Aug. 27, massive flooding in northern and eastern India stranded some 1.5 million people. In Russia, Pres. Yeltsin fired his entire cabinet and reappointed Viktor Chernomyrdin as acting prime min. On Aug. 23, the Duma refused to confirm the appointment; on Aug. 29, Yeltsin agreed to give up some powers for the confirmation. Later, Pres. Yeltsin proposed and the Duma confirmed Yevgeni Primakov as prime min. In Sept., Hurricane Georges hit the Dominican Republic, Haiti and other islands killing over 200 people and leaving hundreds of thousands homeless. In Liberia, civil war flared up in the capital; thousands fled during the fighting. Floods in the southern part of Mexico left 1.2 million without homes or food. On Sept. 11, US Pres. Clinton admitted his affair with Lewinsky; the admission prompted calls for his impeachment because he had lied to the public. Special Prosecutor Kenneth Starr delivered his report on Clinton to the US Congress on the same day; his report was posted on the Internet. On Sept. 27, one of Europe's longest serving leaders, German Pres. Helmut Kohl, was defeated at the polls by Social Democrat Gerhard Schroeder. On Oct. 16, John Hume and David Trimble won the 1998 Nobel Peace Prize for their efforts in N. Ireland. On Oct. 29, South African Pres. Mandela received the report of the Truth and Reconciliation Commission on crimes committed during apartheid. On Oct. 16, British authorities arrested Chile's former dictator Augusto Pinochet in London. On Oct. 8, the US House of Representatives asked its judiciary committee to begin an impeachment inquiry against Pres. Clinton for his role in the Monica Lewinsky affair. On Oct. 15, Pres. Clinton began talks with Israeli Prime Min. Binyamin Netanyahu and Palestinian Pres. Yasser Arafat in Wye, Md.; the talks broke a 19-month impasse in Israeli-Palestinian relations over the West Bank. Yugoslav Pres. Milosevic and the West negotiated Yugoslavia's troop withdrawal from Kosovo. On Nov. 1, Hurricane Mitch ended after six days of devastation in Central America, killing more than 10,000 people and leaving about two million homeless. On Nov. 22, 11 EU governments launched "The New European Way," a manifesto for a socialist Europe. On Nov. 6, the USA agreed to send US$600 million in food and food credits to Russia after a poor harvest; the EU agreed to send another US$500 million in food aid. On Nov. 7, US Sen. John Glenn, 77, the oldest person to enter space, and the crew of the US space shuttle *Discovery* returned to earth after nine days in orbit. On Nov. 13, Pres. Clinton agreed to pay US$850,000 to Paula Jones to settle her sexual harassment suit. On Nov. 19, Independent Prosecutor Kenneth Starr appeared before the house judiciary committee to present his case against Pres. Clinton in the Lewinsky affair. On Nov. 6, the first unarmed international peacekeepers arrived in Kosovo under the command of the Organisation for Security and Co-operation in Europe (OSCE). In Algeria, terrorist violence surged across the country before Ramadan. On Dec. 16-20, the US and UK carried out air strikes to "degrade" Iraqi Pres. Saddam Hussein's military forces; the

attacks, prompted by Iraq's refusal to cooperate with UN weapons inspectors, lacked the support of the UN Security Council. On Dec. 6, South African Pres. Mandela ruled out a general amnesty for crimes committed during apartheid but repeated that amnesties were possible for those who applied for them. On Dec. 18, the US House of Representatives approved two articles of impeachment against Pres. Clinton.

1999: On Jan. 1, the euro, the new European single currency, was launched in 11 countries. On Jan. 3, an American rocket carrying the *Polar Lander* spacecraft took off for Mars. On Jan. 23-24, the International Olympic Committee in Switzerland, facing allegations of corruption in its selection of host cities, suspended six of its members. In late Jan., four IOC members resigned. On Jan. 19, US Pres. Clinton delivered his sixth State of the Union Address, concentrating on social security, education and health care. In Feb., Queensland, Australia, suffered its worst floods in a century. On Feb. 6-23, under threat of NATO air strikes, Yugoslavian Serbs and Albanian Kosovars met in France for unsuccessful talks aimed at ending the fighting in Kosovo. On Feb. 14, about 200,000 ultra-Orthodox Jews prayed near the Supreme Court in Jerusalem to protest the court's alleged religious persecution of them. On Feb. 15, Turkish authorities captured Abdullah Ocalan, leader of the Kurdistan Workers' Party in Kenya; Ocalan's return to Turkey sparked Kurdish protests around the world. On Feb. 22, George Robertson, the UK's secretary of state for defence, said the British army had destroyed its stock of two million landmines. On Feb. 12, the US Senate acquitted Pres. Clinton of perjury and obstruction charges stemming from the Paula Jones sexual harassment case and the Lewinsky scandal. On Mar. 16, the executive 20-member European Commission resigned en masse after an independent committee set up by the European Parliament found the commission guilty of fraud, nepotism and mismanagement. US and UK aircraft hammered Iraqi air defences while patrolling "no-fly zones." Periodic air strikes continued throughout 1999. On Mar. 9-11, Iranian Pres. Mohammad Khatami became the first Iranian leader to visit the West since 1979 during a visit to Italy. On Mar. 12,

NATO admitted three former Warsaw Pact states as members: Poland, Hungary and the Czech Republic. On Mar. 30, Russian Pres. Yeltsin condemned NATO air strikes against Yugoslavia. On Mar. 24, after the failure of peace talks in Paris, NATO launched air strikes against Yugoslavia to force Pres. Milosevic to compromise over Kosovo. Serbian forces in Kosovo stepped up the "ethnic cleansing" of Albanian Kosovars, creating tens of thousands of refugees. On Apr. 1, British Prime Min. Blair and Irish Prime Min. Bertie Ahern published the Hillsborough Declaration, aimed at disarming terrorists and bringing Sinn Fein into the power-sharing executive. On Apr. 15, former Pakistani Prime Min. Benazir Bhutto was convicted in absentia of corruption and sentenced to five years in prison. On Apr. 15, US astronomers announced the first discovery of a solar system outside our own orbiting the star Upsilon Andromeda. On Apr. 12, US Pres. Clinton became the first sitting president to be found in contempt of court when a judge declared that Clinton had lied in a 1998 deposition in the Paula Jones case. On Apr. 20, two student gunmen attacked a high school in Littleton, Col., killing 13 people before killing themselves. On May 26, for the first time since 1971, Indian fighter jets attacked Islamic guerrillas in Jammu and Kashmir. On May 27-28, Pakistan shot down three Indian aircraft during border fighting. On May 8, N. Korean officials said thousands of people had died from famine since 1995. On May 12, Russian Pres. Yeltsin dismissed the government of Prime Min. Primakov; Sergei Stepashin became prime min. On May 17, US Sec. of State Madeleine Albright announced food aid for N. Korea. Throughout May, NATO air forces hit targets in Serbia and Montenegro; on May 7, NATO mistakenly bombed the Chinese Embassy in Belgrade, prompting anti-NATO protests in China. On June 4, more than 70,000 people in Hong Kong commemorated the 1989 massacre in Tiananmen Square in Beijing. On June 15, the North and South Korean navies fought a battle in the Yellow Sea. On June 5, Pope John Paul II spoke to 700,000 people near Gdansk, Poland. On June 2, South Africa's ANC won landslide victories in national elections; on June 16, Pres. Thabo Mbeki was sworn into office. On June 6, the space shuttle *Discovery*, carrying Canadian Julie

Payette, returned to earth after a 10-day mission. On June 29, a Turkish court sentenced Abdullah Öcalan to death for leading the Kurdish rebellion. On June 19, UK's Prince Edward and Sophie Rhys-Jones wed at Windsor. On June 12, Gov. George W. Bush, Jr., of Tex. declared his bid for the Republican presidential nomination. On June 16, US V. Pres. Al Gore declared his second bid for the Democratic presidential nomination. On June 3, Yugoslav Pres. Milosevic accepted NATO's peace terms. On June 10, NATO's bombing campaign stopped. On June 11-13, NATO K-FOR and Russian troops entered Kosovo as peacekeepers. By June 20, Yugoslav troops had left Kosovo. In July, floods in Bangladesh displaced almost one million people. In China, the flooding of the Yangtze River and its tributaries displaced 1.84 million people. On July 21, Chinese police arrested about 30,000 members of Falun Gong in 30 cities. On July 8-12, FARC attacked 15 towns in Colombia; about 200 people died. Following the collapse of a ceasefire signed by six African states, the rebel Congolese Rally for Democracy launched a new offensive in the Democratic Republic of Congo and drove tens of thousands of refugees into Tanzania. On July 15, Indonesian officials confirmed the victory of the Indonesian Democratic Party in the June 7 parliamentary elections, the first held in 44 years. On July 7, Sierra Leone's government agreed to share power with the rebel Revolutionary United Front, ending an eight-year war. On Aug. 9, Berlin replaced Bonn as Germany's capital. On Aug. 30, East Timorese voted overwhelmingly for independence from Indonesia. On Aug. 15, more than 10,000 Catholics and Protestants united in Omagh, N. Ireland, to mark the anniversary of Ulster's worst IRA bombing. On Aug. 8, Russian troops launched attacks on Islamic rebels in Dagestan. On Aug. 9, Russian Pres. Yeltsin dismissed Prime Min. Stepashin's cabinet and appointed Vladimir Putin as prime min. On Aug. 17, an earthquake shook Izmit in Turkey; at least 12,000 people died, 30,000 people were injured and 200,000 were left homeless. On Aug. 19, up to 150,000 people in Belgrade peacefully demanded the resignation of Yugoslav Pres. Milosevic. On Sept. 1, 1.5 million unionized workers in Colombia ended a two-day strike to protest the government's austerity measures. In East Timor, pro-Jakarta militias stepped up attacks on East Timor's civilians. By mid-month, the Indonesian army had withdrawn at least 3,500 troops from East Timor while 8,000 UN troops under Australian command prepared to arrive. A series of bombings in Moscow and other Russian cities killed more than 200 people; authorities blamed Islamic rebels from Dagestan. On Sept. 15-17, Hurricane Floyd battered the US east coast, forcing three million people to flee and killing at least six. A supercyclone, the worst in the Bay of Bengal in three decades, hit India on Oct. 29, killing 10,000 and leaving 15 million homeless. In Mexico, rains caused flooding and mudslides that killed 450 and left 315,000 homeless in several southern states. In Pakistan, Gen. Pervez Musharraf seized power Oct. 12 in a bloodless coup. In N. Ireland, peace talks reached an agreement that allows for a government of Sinn Fein and Ulster Unionists, despite the IRA's refusal to decommission its arsenal. On Nov. 29, Protestant and Catholic adversaries joined forces to form the Ulster Assembly. On Nov. 5, a US federal judge declared Microsoft Corp. a monopoly, ruling that aggressive actions by Bill Gates's software empire to protect its technology dominance were hurting consumers. On Nov. 7, the space shuttle *Discovery* returned from a ten-day mission that included a return to space by John Glenn. On Nov. 30, protesters disrupted a World Trade Organization meeting in Seattle. Thousands of protesters faced pepper spray-equipped anti-riot officers, backed by armoured cars and mounted police. Russian military gave the residents of the Chechnyan capital Grozny until Dec. 11 to evacuate the area; they launched an all-out assault on the city to capture it the next day. European Union leaders wrapped up a successful summit in Finland on Dec. 11, endowing the EU with new military powers, preparing a move eastward that will almost double its membership. France bore the brunt of two storms that hit Western Europe in late December. On Dec. 26 winds up to 220 km/h killed 60 people. On the 27th another storm caused 120 deaths across Europe, including 70 in France, and left millions without electricity. Portugal handed over Macau to China, ending 442 years of colonial rule. Control of the Panama Canal was transferred from the US to Panama on Dec. 31. Russian Pres. Boris Yeltsin announced that he was stepping down on Dec. 31 and handing presidential powers to Prime Min. Vladimir Putin. In Sri Lanka, Pres. Kumaratunga was injured Dec. 18 in one of two bomb blasts that killed at least 18 people and injured 150 others at election rallies. The Mars Polar Lander slammed into Mars on Dec. 3; NASA was unable to make contact. In Venezuela, flooding and mudslides reached a crisis on Dec. 15 when 30,000 were killed, 35,000 homes were destroyed and 400,000 left homeless.

2000 In Algeria, a six-month amnesty ended and the government claimed that 6,000 Islamic guerrillas had surrendered; the government vowed to fight on against the estimated 1,500 at large. On Jan. 21, thousands of protesters stormed Ecuador's national palace after a rebellion led by Indians and backed by the military forced the unpopular president to flee. In Spain, one million people gathered in Madrid on Jan. 22 to protest a car-bomb attack blamed on Basque separatists. On Feb. 6, acting Russian Pres. Vladimir Putin announced that Russian troops had captured the last rebel stronghold in Grozny. When it became clear on Feb. 11 that the IRA would not meet any conditions set for the Feb. 12 decommissioning of weapons, Britain resumed direct control over N. Ireland, stripping power from the province's new Protestant-Catholic administration in an effort to save the coalition. On Mar. 26 Vladimir Putin was elected Russian president. More than 900 members of a religious cult were found dead in Uganda on Mar. 17 and the following days in one of the world's largest mass murders. On Mar. 17, Smith & Wesson agreed to install locks on its weapons to make them more childproof. In exchange, governments dropped lawsuits seeking damages for gun violence. On Mar. 12, Pope John Paul II asked God's forgiveness for the sins of Roman Catholics through the ages, including wrongs inflicted on Jews, women and minorities. A drought in Ethiopia left more than eight million people short of food and seeking international assistance. In Japan, 16,000 were evacuated from villages on Hakkaido as Mount Usu sent ash and rocks into the air and mudslides down its slopes after a series of earth tremors. The lower house of the Russian parliament ratified the START II treaty between the US and Russia; the agreement calls for cutting the number of nuclear warheads on ballistic missiles to 3,500 each by 2007. (The US approved the treaty in 1996.) By Apr. 5, technology stocks on the New York stock markets had suffered record drops sending the NASDAQ from a US$6.71 trillion high on Mar. 10 to US$5.61 trillion on Apr. 4. On Apr. 6, Celera Genomics said it had decoded all of the DNA pieces that make up the genetic pattern of a single human being. Zimbabwean Pres. Robert Mugabe sought to shore up his flagging popularity among the landless poor by backing squatters as they took over commercial farm property. In Iran, despite the reform policies of the government, the conservative judiciary ordered 16 pro-reform journals shut down. South Lebanon was in chaos May 22 after units of an Israeli-allied militia abandoned their positions and Shiite Muslim guerrillas rushed to reclaim villages held by Israeli forces for two decades. In N. Ireland, the IRA agreed to international monitoring of arms dumps as a way around the impasse over weapons decommissioning which has derailed the Ulster Assembly. In June, the Brazilian government banned the sale of firearms. In Chechnya, the day after a suicide bomb attack in Alkhan-Yurt, Russian Pres. Putin established direct presidential rule over the region. Ethiopia announced the end of its two-year war with Eritrea; however, the Eritreans vowed to fight on until all disputed territory was returned to them. On June 28, Elian Gonzalez returned to Cuba with his father, seven months after the boy was rescued at sea near Florida and taken to the US. In July, over 13,000 Japanese people suffered from food poisoning caused by contaminated milk products. In Mexico, Vicente Fox was elected president on July 2; his election ended 71 years of rule by the Institutional Revolutionary Party. The US and Vietnamese governments signed an agreement to lower trade barriers and increase US investment in Vietnam. The US House of Representatives voted to end restrictions on travel to Cuba as well as limits on the sale of food and medicine, but the measure was expected to encounter trouble in the Senate. In August, Malaysia's show trial of former deputy prime minister Anwar Ibrahim ended with a conviction on sodomy charges and a nine-year sentence. In Korea, 100 families were reunited in Seoul and Pyongyang 50 years after Korea was split in two during the run-up to the Korean War. On Aug. 14, the Russian nuclear sub Kursk with 118 sailors onboard sank in the Barents Sea, apparently after an explosion blew a hole in its starboard side. On Aug. 13, after almost a decade of chaos, more than 2,000 Somali clan leaders and citizens met in Djibouti to form a central Somali government. On Aug. 1, Zimbabwe's government confirmed plans to confiscate more than half of all white-owned farmland and redistribute it to 500,000 poor black families. Trade unions called for a general strike to protest. The Dutch Parliament voted Sept. 12 to give same-sex couples the right to marriage, adoption and divorce—approving legislation by a margin of more than three to one. On Sept. 17, Colombia's National Liberation Army kidnapped 55 people; the last hostages were not released until November. The Serbian presidential election on Sept. 24 was marred by corruption and ballot irregularities. Despite official attempts to downplay the results, it was clear that Pres. Slobodan Milosevic's opposition had won the vote. Milosevic called for a run-off vote on Oct. 8, while the opposition called for him to step down. In the United States, Chase Manhattan Corp. reached a deal Sept. 13 to buy J.P. Morgan & Co. for about US$36 billion, combining two Wall Street institutions. On Sept. 20, federal prosecutors concluded there was insufficient evidence that President Bill Clinton or his wife Hillary committed a crime in Whitewater. The conclusion ended the six-year investigation four months before the president left office. Israeli-Palestinian animosity was fuelled by an Oct. 12 visit to a disputed holy site by Ariel Sharon; violence culminated in the murder to two Israeli soldiers after the death of a Palestinian child and a military retaliation by Israel further destabilized the region. Also on Oct. 12 a terrorist bomb exploded on the USS Cole in the harbour at Aden, Yemen, killing 17 sailors. On Nov. 7, the US presidential election ended in a stalemate, with disputed votes in Palm Beach, Florida as the tie-breaker; the matter was not settled until Dec. 13, when George W. Bush was declared the winner. On Nov. 28, the Dutch parliament voted to allow euthanasia and physician-assisted suicide in special cases. On Dec. 10, Israeli Prime Min. Barak announced his resignation.

THE STATISTICS SHOWN ARE INTENDED TO PRESENT an informative and comparative picture of the various nations of the world and their dependent territories. All data, including the geographic, population and government data, are taken from the latest available sources. The economic and finance/trade data indicate the size of the national economies and the amount of economic activity in the respective countries; the population, health and education data, and communications and transportation data give some evidence of the quality of life and the state of the infrastructure in each nation.

All dollar amounts are in US dollars. International dollar price weights have been used instead of an official currency exchange rate in an attempt to make more equitable comparisons.

The "Total Fertility Rate" figure represents the number of children born per woman, and indicates the potential for population growth. A high total fertility rate will have an impact on a nation's workforce —women's participation may be limited; it may also have an impact on the amount of education available and the level of education achieved in the general population.

The information contained in this section reflects data available up to and including October 1, 2001. Sources used for information include:

CIA World Fact Book 2000 • "Compendium of Statistics: Illiteracy" (UNESCO) • "Facts on File" • Demographic Yearbook (UN) • Encyclopedia Britannica • Direction of Trade Statistics (International Monetary Fund) • Foreign Affairs Canada • Government Finance Statistics Monthly (International Monetary Fund) • "Human Development Report" (UN Development Programme) • International Financial Statistics Yearbook (International Monetary Fund) • International Financial Statistics (monthly IMF update) • "Keesing's Record of World Events" • Monthly Bulletin of Statistics (UN Statistical Division) • "Population and Vital Statistics Report" (UN Dept. of International Economic and Social Affairs) • Statesman's Yearbook (Macmillan) • UNESCO Statistical Yearbook • World Bank Atlas (World Bank) • World Book Encyclopedia • World Culture Report (UNESCO) • World Debt Tables • "World Development Report" (World Bank) • "World Motor Vehicle Data" (Motor Vehicle Manufacturers Assoc. of the US Inc.) • "World Population" (UNESCO) • "World Population Data Sheet" (Population Reference Bureau Inc.) • World Resources (World Resources Institute) • World Statistics Pocketbook • "World Tables" (Johns Hopkins UP) • Worldwide Government Directory with International Organizations (Belmont Publications) • Year Book of Labour Statistics (International Labour Office, Geneva).

Afghanistan

Long-Form Name: Islamic State of Afghanistan; note: the self-proclaimed Taliban government refers to the country as Islamic Emirate of Afghanistan
Capital: Kabul

■ GEOGRAPHY

Area: 652,000 sq. km
Coastline: none: landlocked
Climate: arid to semi-arid; cold winters and hot summers, considerable snowfall
Environment: damaging earthquakes occur in Hindu Kush mountains; poor soil, flooding, desertification, overgrazing, deforestation (largely due to logging for building materials and fuel), pollution, soil degradation.

Afghanistan is presently (2001) in the second year of its worst drought ever
Terrain: mostly rugged mountains; plains in north and southwest
Land Use: 12% arable land; no permanent crops; 46% meadows and pastures; 3% forest and woodland; 39% other, includes about 30,000 sq. km of irrigated farmland
Location: SW Asia (Middle East)

■ PEOPLE

Population: 25,838,797 (July 2000 est.)
Nationality: Afghan
Age Structure: 0-14 yrs: 42.37%; 15-64: 54.86%; 65+: 2.77% (2000 est.)
Population Growth Rate: 3.54% (2000 est.)
Net Migration: 11.54 migrants/1,000 population (2000 est.)

Ethnic Groups: 38% Pathan, 25% Tajik, 6% Uzbek, 19% Hazara; minor ethnic groups include Charar Aimaks, Turkoman, Baloch and others

Languages: 35% Pushtu (official), 50% Afghan Persian (Dari), 11% Turkic languages (primarily Uzbek and Turmen), 4% thirty minor languages (primarily Balochi and Pahai); much bilingualism

Religions: Islam (84% Sunni Muslim, 15% Shi'a Muslim), 1% other

Birth Rate: 41.82/1,000 population (2000 est.)

Death Rate: 18.01/1,000 population (2000 est.)

Infant Mortality: 149.28 deaths/1,000 live births (2000 est.)

Life Expectancy at Birth: 46.62 years male, 45.10 years female (2000 est.)

Total Fertility Rate: 5.87 children born/woman (2000 est.)

Literacy: 31.5% (1999 est.)

■ GOVERNMENT

Leader(s): Taliban Supreme Leader: Mullah Mohammad Omar Mujahid

Government Type: transitional government: a six-member council appointed by the Taliban movement of Muslim fundamentalists

Administrative Divisions: 30 provinces (relayat, sing. & pl.)

Nationhood: Aug. 19, 1919 (from UK)

National Holiday: Victory of the Muslim Nation, Apr. 28; Remembrance Day for Martyrs and Disabled, May 4; Independence Day, August 19

■ ECONOMY

Overview: a poor country, largely dependent on farming (wheat) and livestock (sheep and goats); the economy is adversely affected by political and military disruptions; much of the population continues to suffer from insufficient food, clothing, housing and medical care; inflation remains a serious problem; government efforts to encourage foreign investment have failed

GDP: US$21 billion, per capita US$800; real growth rate n.a. (1999 est.)

Inflation: n.a., but considerable

Industries: accounts for 28.5% of GDP; small-scale production of textiles, soap, furniture, shoes, fertilizer and cement; handwoven carpets; natural gas, oil, coal, copper

Labour Force: 8 million; 68% agriculture and animal husbandry, 16% industry, 16% services and other

Unemployment: n.a.

Agriculture: largely subsistence farming and nomadic animal husbandry; cash products— wheat, fruit, nuts, karakul pelts, wool, mutton, barley, corn; production is limited due to the shortage of modern machinery, high-grade seed and fertilizer. Accounts for 53% of GDP.

Natural Resources: natural gas, crude oil, copper, coal, salt, talc, barites, sulphur, lead, zinc, iron ore, slate, precious and semi-precious stones, especially lapis lazuli, amethysts, rubies

■ FINANCE/TRADE

Currency: afghani (Af) = 100 puls

International Reserves Excluding Gold: n.a.

Gold Reserves: n.a.

Budget: n.a.

Defence Expenditures: n.a.

Education Expenditures: n.a.

External Debt: n.a.

Exports: US$30 million (2000); commodities: natural gas 55%, fruit and nuts 24%, handwoven carpets, wool, cotton, hides; partners: FSU, Pakistan, Iran, Germany, India, UK, Belgium, Luxembourg, Czech and Slovak Republics

Imports: US$273 million (2000); commodities: food and petroleum products, most consumer goods; partners: former Soviet Union, Pakistan, Iran, Japan, Singapore, India, South Korea, Germany

■ COMMUNICATIONS

Daily Newspapers: 12

Televisions: 13/1,000 inhabitants (1997)

Radios: 132/1,000 inhabitants (1997)

Telephones: 1.0 lines/1,000 inhabitants (1999)

■ TRANSPORTATION

Motor Vehicles: 67,000; 35,000 passenger cars (1997 est.)

Roads: 21,000 km; 2,793 km paved

Railway: 9.6 km from Kushka (Turkmenistan) to Towraghondi, and 15.0 km from Termez (Uzbekistan) to Kheyrabad

Air Traffic: 90,000 passengers carried (1997)

Airports: 46; 14 have paved runways (1999 est.)

Canadian Embassy: c/o Canadian High Commission, Diplomatic Sector G-5, Islamabad; mailing address: GPO Box 1042, Islamabad, Pakistan. Tel: (011-92-51) 227-91-00. Fax: (011-92-51) 227-91-10. Email: isbad@dfait-maeci.gc.ca

Embassy in Canada: c/o High Commission for the Islamic Republic of Pakistan, Burnside Building, 151 Slater St, Ste 608, Ottawa ON K1P 5H3. Tel: (613) 238-7881. Fax: (613) 238-7296. Email: parepottawa@sprint.ca

Albania

Long-Form Name: Republic of Albania
Capital: Tirana

■ GEOGRAPHY

Area: 28,748 sq. km
Coastline: 362 km
Climate: mild temperate; cool, cloudy, wet winters; hot, clear, dry summers; interior is cooler and wetter, with severe winters
Environment: subject to destructive earthquakes; soil erosion; water pollution; tsunami occur along southwestern coast; deforestation and water pollution are still current issues
Terrain: mostly mountains and hills; small plains along coast
Land Use: 21% arable land; 5% permanent crops; 15% meadows and pastures; 38% forest and woodland, including 30% scrub forest; 21% other, includes 3,410 sq. km irrigated
Location: SE Europe, bordering on Adriatic Sea

■ PEOPLE

Population: 3,490,435 (July 2000 est.)
Nationality: Albanian
Age Structure: 0-14 yrs: 30%; 15-64: 63%; 65+: 7% (2000 est.)
Population Growth Rate: 0.26% (2000 est.)
Net Migration: -10.36 migrants/1,000 population (2000 est.)
Ethnic Groups: 95% Albanian, 3% Greek, 2% others (Vlachs, Gypsies, Serbs and Bulgarians)
Languages: Albanian (Tosk is official dialect, also Gheg dialect), Greek
Religions: 70% Muslim, 20% Albanian Orthodox, 10% Roman Catholic
Birth Rate: 19.47/1,000 population (2000 est.)
Death Rate: 6.50/1,000 population (2000 est.)
Infant Mortality: 41.33 deaths/1,000 live births (2000 est.)
Life Expectancy at Birth: 68.75 years male, 74.59 years female (2000 est.)
Total Fertility Rate: 2.37 children born/woman (2000 est.)
Literacy: 83.5% (1998)

■ GOVERNMENT

Leader(s): Pres. Rexhep Mejdani, Prime Min. Ilir Meta
Parliamentary elections held Jun 23, 2001
Government Type: in transition to democracy
Administrative Divisions: 36 districts (rrethe, sing. —rreth) and 1 municipality (bashki)
Nationhood: Nov. 28, 1912 (from Ottoman Empire); People's Socialist Republic of Albania declared Jan. 11, 1946
National Holiday: Independence Day, Nov. 28

■ ECONOMY

Overview: the poorest country in Europe, it is a Stalinist-type economy (central planning and state ownership of the means of production); though largely self-sufficient in food until 1990, the recent break-up of cooperative farms and the general economic decline has forced Albania to rely increasingly on foreign aid; the government has taken strong measures to restore public order and to revive economic activity and trade
GDP: US$5.6 billion, per capita US$1,650; real growth rate 8% (1999 est.)
Inflation: 0.05% (as of year-end 2000)
Industries: accounts for 25% of GDP; food processing, textiles and clothing, lumber, oil, cement, chemicals, basic metals, hydroelectricity; most industries produce at only fraction of past levels
Labour Force: 2 million (1999); 24.1% agriculture, 35.3% industry, 15.9% service
Unemployment: officially 14% (Oct. 1997), but likely to be as high as 28%
Agriculture: accounts for 54% of GDP; arable land per capita among lowest in Europe; one-half of workforce engaged in farming; produces wide range of temperate-zone crops and livestock; claims self-sufficiency in grain output; 80% of all arable land is now in private ownership
Natural Resources: crude oil, natural gas, coal, chromium, copper, timber, nickel, petroleum

■ FINANCE/TRADE

Currency: lek (L) = 100 quintars
International Reserves Excluding Gold: US$727 million (Dec. 2000)
Gold Reserves: US$0.112 million fine troy ounces (Dec. 2000)
Budget: revenues US$393 million; expenditures US$676 million, including capital expenditures of US$n.a. (1997)
Defence Expenditures: 3.52% of central government expenditures (1998)
Education Expenditures: 1.94% of central government expenditures (1998)
External Debt: US$975 million (1999)
Exports: US$258 million (2000); commodities: asphalt, bitumen, petroleum products, metals and metallic ores, electricity, oil, vegetables, fruit, tobacco; partners: Italy, Yugoslavia, Germany, Greece, Czech and Slovak Republics, Poland, Romania, Bulgaria, Hungary
Imports: US$995 million (2000); commodities: machinery, machine tools, iron and steel products, textiles, chemicals, pharmaceuticals; partners: Italy, Yugoslavia, Germany, Czech and Slovak Republics, Romania, Poland, Hungary, Bulgaria

■ COMMUNICATIONS
Daily Newspapers: 5
Televisions: 109/1,000 inhabitants (1998)
Radios: 217/1,000 inhabitants (1997)
Telephones: 36 lines/1000 persons (1999)

■ TRANSPORTATION
Motor Vehicles: n.a.
Roads: 18,000 km; 5,400 km paved
Railway: 670 km
Air Traffic: 55,000 passengers carried (1997)
Airports: 10; 3 have paved runways (1999 est.)

Canadian Embassy: The Office of the Canadian Embassy, Rruga Brigada VIII, Pallat 2, Apt. 1, Tirana, Albania, Postal Address: P.O. Box 47, Tirana, Albania. Tel: (011-355-42) 57275. Fax: (011-355-42) 57273. Email: trana@dfait-maeci.gc.ca
Embassy in Canada: Embassy of the Republic of Albania, 130 Albert St, Ste 302, Ottawa ON K1P 5G4. Tel: (613) 236-4114. Fax: (613) 236-0804. Email: embassyrepublicofalbania@on.aivn.com

---

Algeria

Long-Form Name: Democratic and Popular Republic of Algeria
Capital: Algiers

■ GEOGRAPHY
Area: 2,381,740 sq. km
Coastline: 998 km
Climate: arid to semi-arid; mild, wet winters with hot, dry summers along coast; drier with cold winters and hot summers on high plateau; sirocco is a hot, dust/sand-laden wind especially common in summer
Environment: mountainous areas subject to severe earthquakes; desertification; industrial and domestic pollution and soil erosion contribute to environmental problems
Terrain: mostly high plateau and desert; some mountains; narrow, discontinuous coastal plain
Land Use: 3% arable land; 0% permanent crops; 13% meadows and pastures; 2% forest and woodland; 82% other; cattle, sheep and goat grazing on grassland and shrub regions, includes 5,550 sq. km irrigated
Location: N Africa, bordering on Mediterranean Sea

■ PEOPLE
Population: 31,193,917 (July 2000 est.)
Nationality: Algerian
Age Structure: 0-14 yrs: 35%; 15-64: 61%; 65+: 4% (2000 est.)

Population Growth Rate: 1.74% (2000 est.)
Net Migration: -0.47migrants/1,000 population (2000 est.)
Ethnic Groups: 99% Arab-Berber, less than 1% European
Languages: Arabic (official), French, Berber dialects
Religions: 99% Sunni Muslim (state religion); 1% Christian and Jewish
Birth Rate: 23.14/1,000 population (2000 est.)
Death Rate: 5.30/1,000 population (2000 est.)
Infant Mortality: 41.97 deaths/1,000 live births (2000 est.)
Life Expectancy at Birth: 68.34 years male, 71.02 years female (2000 est.)
Total Fertility Rate: 2.80 children born/woman (2000 est.)
Literacy: 65% (1998 est.)

■ GOVERNMENT
Leader(s): Pres. Abdelaziz Bouteflika, Prime Min. Ali Benflis
Government Type: republic
Administrative Divisions: 48 provinces (wilayas, sing. —wilaya)
Nationhood: July 5, 1962 (from France)
National Holiday: Anniversary of the Revolution, Nov. 1

■ ECONOMY
Overview: the economy is largely based on the exploitation of oil and natural gas products; dropping oil and gas prices have contributed to Algeria's most serious social and economic crisis since independence; recently, reforms have been implemented to combat social and economic problems
GDP: US$147.6 billion, per capita US$4,700; real growth rate 3.9% (1999 est.)
Inflation: 2.65% (year-end 1999)
Industries: petroleum, light industries, natural gas, mining, electrical, petrochemical, food processing. Accounts for 51% of GDP
Labour Force: 10 million (1999 est.); 11% industry, 14% agriculture, 75% services
Unemployment: 30% (1999 estimate)
Agriculture: accounts for 12% of GDP and employs 22% of labour force; products include wheat, barley, grapes, oats, olives, fruit, livestock; must import more than one-third of its food
Natural Resources: crude oil, natural gas, iron ore, phosphates, uranium, lead, zinc

■ FINANCE/TRADE
Currency: dinar (DA) = 100 centimes
International Reserves Excluding Gold: US$12.393 billion (Jan. 2001)

Gold Reserves: US$5.583 million fine troy ounces (Jan. 2001)
Budget: revenues US$15.5 billion; expenditures US$15.1 billion, including capital expenditures US$n.a. (1999 est.)
Defence Expenditures: 17.38% of central government expenditure (1999)
Education Expenditures: 24.38% of central government expenditure (1999)
External Debt: US$28.015 billion (1999)
Exports: US$17.175 billion (2000); commodities: petroleum and natural gas 98%; partners: Netherlands, Czech and Slovak Republics, Romania, Italy, France, US
Imports: US$10.459 billion (2000); commodities: capital goods 35%, consumer goods 36%, food 20%; partners: France 25%, Italy 8%, Germany 8%, US 6–7%

■ COMMUNICATIONS

Daily Newspapers: 5
Televisions: 105/1,000 inhabitants (1998)
Radios: 241/1,000 inhabitants (1997)
Telephones: 52 lines/1,000 inhabitants (1999)

■ TRANSPORTATION

Motor Vehicles: 930,000; 500,000 passenger cars (1997 est.)
Roads: 104,000 km; 71,656 km paved
Railway: 4,820 km
Air Traffic: 3,518,000 passengers carried (1997)
Airports: 137; 51 have paved runways (1999 est.)

Canadian Embassy: The Canadian Embassy, 18 Mustapha Khalef St, Ben Aknoun, Algiers, Algeria; mailing address: P.O. Box 48, Alger-Gare, 1600 Alger, Algeria. Tel: (011-213) 21914951. Fax: (011-213) 21914973. Email: alger@dfait-maeci.gc.ca
Embassy in Canada: Embassy of the People's Democratic Republic of Algeria, 435 Daly Ave, Ottawa ON K1N 6H3. Tel: (613) 789-8505. Fax: (613) 789-1406. Email: ambalgott@sympatico.ca

American Samoa

Long-Form Name: Territory of American Samoa
Capital: Pago Pago (on Tutuila Island)

■ GEOGRAPHY

Area: 199 sq. km
Climate: tropical maritime, plentiful rainfall, temperatures consistent throughout the year
Land Use: 5% arable land, 10% permanent crops, 0% meadows and pastures, 70% forest and woodland, 15% other; n.a. km irrigated
Location: S Pacific Ocean, E of Australia and New Zealand

■ PEOPLE

Population: 65,446 (July 2000 est.)
Nationality: American Samoan; nationals of the United States
Ethnic Groups: Samoan (Polynesian) 89%, Caucasian 2%, Tongan 4%, other 5%
Languages: Samoan (a Polynesian dialect), English

■ GOVERNMENT

Colony Territory of: Dependent Territory of the United States
Leader(s): Pres. George W. Bush; Gov. Tauese P. Sunia
Government Type: US dependency with democratically elected governor: unorganized unincorporated territory
National Holiday: Territorial Flag Day, Apr. 17

■ ECONOMY

Overview: agriculture: taro, bread-fruit, yams, bananas, coconuts; livestock includes pigs, goats, poultry; industries: fish (tuna) canning; economic activity is closely tied to US; tourism is slowly developing

■ FINANCE/TRADE

Currency: American dollar (US$) = 100 cents
Canadian Embassy: n.a.
Representative to Canada: c/o Embassy of the United States of America, 490 Sussex Dr, Ottawa ON K1N 1G8. Tel: (613) 238-5335. Fax: (613) 688-3097. Email inquiries are not accepted

Andorra

Long-Form Name: Principality of Andorra
Capital: Andorra-la-Vella

■ GEOGRAPHY

Area: 468 sq. km
Coastline: none: landlocked
Climate: temperate; snowy, cold winters and warm, dry summers
Environment: deforestation, overgrazing, soil erosion; avalanches are a natural hazard
Terrain: rugged mountains separated by narrow valleys
Land Use: 4% arable land; 0% permanent crops; 45% meadows and pastures; 35% forest and woodland; 16% other; n.a. km irrigated
Location: SW Europe

■ PEOPLE

Population: 66,824 (July 2000 est.)

Nationality: Andorran
Age Structure: 0-14 yrs: 15%; 15-64: 72%; 65+: 13% (2000 est.)
Population Growth Rate: 1.22% (2000 est.)
Net Migration: 6.9 migrants/1,000 population (2000 est.)
Ethnic Groups: Catalan stock; 43% Spanish, 33% Andorran, 11% Portuguese, 7% French, 6% other
Languages: Catalan (official); many also speak some French and Spanish
Religions: predominantly Roman Catholic
Birth Rate: 10.58/1,000 population (2000 est.)
Death Rate: 5.27/1,000 population (2000 est.)
Infant Mortality: 4.08 deaths/1,000 live births (2000 est.)
Life Expectancy at Birth: 80.56 years male, 86.56 years female (2000 est.)
Total Fertility Rate: 1.25 children born/woman (2000 est.)
Literacy: 100%

■ GOVERNMENT

Leader(s): Co-Heads of State Jacques Chirac (France) and Joan Marti Alanis (Spain), Prem. Marc Forné Molné
Government Type: parliamentary democracy; retains as its heads of state a co-principality of president of France and Spanish bishop of Seo de Urgel, who are represented locally by officials called veguers
Administrative Divisions: 7 parishes (parroquies, sing. —parroquia)
Nationhood: 1278 (from France and Spain)
National Holiday: Mare de Deu de Meritxell, Sept. 8

■ ECONOMY

Overview: tourism is the backbone of the economy, due to its duty-free status and year-round resorts; most food is imported due to a scarcity of arable land
GDP: n.a.
Inflation: n.a.
Industries: tourism (particularly skiing), sheep, timber, tobacco, banking
Labour Force: 30,787 salaried employees (1998)
Unemployment: 0%
Agriculture: sheep raising, small quantities of tobacco, rye, wheat, barley, buckwheat, maize, oats and some vegetables, especially potatoes
Natural Resources: hydroelectricity, mineral water, timber, iron ore, lead

■ FINANCE/TRADE

Currency: French Franc = 100 centimes, Spanish peseta (F Ptas) = 100 centimos
International Reserves Excluding Gold: n.a.
Gold Reserves: n.a.
Budget: revenues US$385 million; expenditures US$342 million, including capital expenditures of US$n.a. (1997)
Defence Expenditures: defence is the responsibility of Spain and France
Education Expenditures: n.a.
External Debt: n.a.
Exports: exact figures for 2000 unavailable; commodities: electricity, tobacco products, furniture; partners: France, Spain
Imports: exact figures for 2000 unavailable; commodities: consumer goods, food; partners: France, Spain, US

■ COMMUNICATIONS

Daily Newspapers: 3
Televisions: 404/1,000 inhabitants (1997 est.)
Radios: 239/1,000 inhabitants (1997 est.)
Telephones: 447 lines/1,000 inhabitants (1999)

■ TRANSPORTATION

Motor Vehicles: 36,000; 35,500 passenger cars (1997 est.)
Roads: 269 km; 198 km paved
Railway: none
Air Traffic: n.a.
Airports: none
Canadian Embassy: The Canadian Embassy to Andorra, Apartado 587, 28080, Madrid, Spain. Tel: (011-34) 91-423-3252. Fax: (011-34) 91-423-3251, or (011-34) 91-423-3252. Email: mdrid@dfait-maeci.gc.ca
Embassy in Canada: c/o Embassy of the Principality of Andorra , 2 United Nations Plaza, 25th Fl, New York NY 10017, USA. Tel: (212) 750-8064. Fax: (212) 750-6630. Email: n.a.

Angola

Long-Form Name: Republic of Angola
Capital: Luanda

■ GEOGRAPHY

Area: 1,246,700 sq. km
Coastline: 1,600 km
Climate: semi-arid in south and along coast to Luanda; north has cool, dry season (May to October) and hot, rainy season (Nov. to Apr.)
Environment: locally heavy rainfall causes periodic flooding on plateau; desertification, especially on coastal plain, soil erosion and water pollution; deforestation
Terrain: narrow coastal plain rises abruptly to vast interior plain
Land Use: 2% arable land; 0% permanent crops; 23% meadows and pastures; 43% forest and

woodland; 32% other, includes 750 sq. km
irrigated
Location: SW Africa

■ PEOPLE

Population: 10,145,267 (July 2000 est.)
Nationality: Angolan
Age Structure: 0-14 yrs: 43%; 15-64: 54%; 65+:
3% (2000 est.)
Population Growth Rate: 2.15% (2000 est.)
Net Migration: -0.34% migrants/1,000 population
(2000 est.)
Ethnic Groups: 37% Ovimbundu, 25%
Kimbundu, 13% Bakongo, 2% Mestiço, 1%
European, 22% other
Languages: Portuguese (official); Bantu dialects
spoken include Ovimbundu, Kimbundu,
Bakongo and Chokwe
Religions: 38% Roman Catholic, 15%
Protestant, 47% Animist (indigenous beliefs)
Birth Rate: 46.89/1,000 population (2000 est.)
Death Rate: 25.01/1,000 population (2000 est.)
Infant Mortality: 195.78 deaths/1,000 live births
(2000 est.)
Life Expectancy at Birth: 37.11 years male, 39.56
years female (2000 est.)
Total Fertility Rate: 6.52 children born/woman
(2000 est.)
Literacy: 42% (1998 est.)

■ GOVERNMENT

Leader(s): Pres. José Eduardo dos Santos
Government Type: transitional government,
nominally a democracy with strong presidential
system
Administrative Divisions: 18 provinces
(provincias, sing. —provincia)
Nationhood: Nov. 11, 1975 (from Portugal)
National Holiday: Independence Day, Nov. 11

■ ECONOMY

Overview: subsistence agriculture is the main
livelihood of the population, but oil production
is the most lucrative activity; recent internal war
has weakened the economy, and food must be
imported
GDP: US$11.6 billion, per capita US$1,030; real
growth rate 4.0% (1999 est.)
Inflation: 325.03% (year-end 2000)
Industries: accounts for 53% of GDP; petroleum,
mining (phosphate rock, uranium, gold, iron ore,
bauxite, feldspar, diamonds), fish processing,
brewing, tobacco, sugar, textiles, cement, food
processing, building construction
Labour Force: 6 million economically active
(1999); 74% agriculture, 10% industry, 16%
services
Unemployment: extensive unemployment and

underemployment affects more than half the
population (1999 est.)
Agriculture: accounts for 13% of GDP; cash
crops—coffee, sisal, corn, cotton, sugar,
manioc, tobacco; food crops—cassava, corn,
vegetables, plantains, bananas and other local
foodstuffs
Natural Resources: petroleum, diamonds, iron
ore, phosphates, copper, feldspar, gold, bauxite,
uranium

■ FINANCE/TRADE

Currency: new kwanza (Kz) = 100 lwei
International Reserves Excluding Gold: US$1.029
billion (Dec. 2000)
Gold Reserves: n.a.
Budget: n.a.
Defence Expenditures: 25% of GDP (1997-98)
Education Expenditures: n.a.
External Debt: US$10.871 billion (1999)
Exports: US$4.940 billion (2000); commodities:
oil, coffee, diamonds, sisal, fish and fish
products, timber, cotton; partners: US, former
USSR countries, Cuba, Portugal, Brazil
Imports: US$1.550 billion (2000); commodities:
capital equipment (machinery and electrical
equipment), food, vehicles and spare parts,
textiles and clothing, medicines, substantial
military deliveries; partners: US, former USSR
countries, Cuba, Portugal, Brazil

■ COMMUNICATIONS

Daily Newspapers: 5
Televisions: 14/1,000 inhabitants (1998)
Radios: 54/1,000 inhabitants (1997)
Telephones: 8.0 lines/1,000 inhabitants (1999)

■ TRANSPORTATION

Motor Vehicles: 225,000; 200,000 passenger cars
(1997 est.)
Roads: 76,626 km; 19,156 km paved
Railway: 2,952 km
Air Traffic: 555,000 passengers carried (1997)
Airports: 249; 32 have paved runways (1999 est.)

Canadian Embassy: Consulate of Canada, Rua
Rei Katyavala 113, Luanda, Angola. Tel: (011-
244-2) 348-371. Fax: (011-244-2) 34-94-94.
Email: consul.can@angonet.org
Embassy in Canada: Embassy of the Republic of
Angola, 75 Albert St, Ste 900, Ottawa ON K1P
5E7. Tel: (613) 234-1152. Fax: (613) 234-1179.
Email: n.a.

Anguilla

Long-Form Name: Anguilla
Capital: The Valley

■ GEOGRAPHY

Area: 91 sq. km
Climate: dry and sunny, tropical with moderating northeast trade winds
Land Use: mostly rock, with sparse scrub, few trees, some commercial salt ponds; low rainfall limits agricultural potential
Location: West Indies, E of Puerto Rico

■ PEOPLE

Population: 11,797 (July 2000 est.)
Nationality: Anguillan
Ethnic Groups: of English ancestry, black/mixed-black African
Languages: English (official)

■ GOVERNMENT

Colony Territory of: Dependent Territory of the United Kingdom
Leader(s): Head of State: Queen Elizabeth II
Government Type: dependent territory of the U.K.
National Holiday: Anguilla Day, May 30

■ ECONOMY

Overview: agriculture: pigeon peas, corn, sweet potatoes; fishing; livestock includes sheep, goats, cattle, poultry; main trading partner: U.K.; there are few natural resources and the economy depends heavily on tourism

■ FINANCE/TRADE

Currency: Eastern Caribbean dollar (EC$) = 100 cents
Canadian Embassy: c/o The Canadian High Commission, Macdonald House 1, Grosvenor Square, London W1K 4AB, England, UK. Tel: (011-44-20) 7258-6600. Fax: (011-44-20) 7258-6333. Email: Ldn@dfait-maeci-gc.ca
Representative to Canada: c/o British High Commission, 80 Elgin St, Ottawa ON K1P 5K7. Tel: (613) 237-1530. Fax: (613) 237-7980. Email should be sent using the appropriate form at the British High Commission's website at http://www.britain-in-canada.org

Antigua and Barbuda

Long-Form Name: Antigua and Barbuda
Capital: Saint John's (on Antigua)

■ GEOGRAPHY

Area: 442 sq. km; includes Redonda (1.3 sq. km)
Coastline: 153 km
Climate: tropical marine; little seasonal temperature variation
Environment: subject to hurricanes and tropical storms (July to Oct.); insufficient freshwater resources are decreased further by clear-cutting of trees, which promotes rain run-off; occasional long periods of drought; deeply indented coastline provides many natural harbours
Terrain: mostly low-lying limestone and coral islands with some higher volcanic areas
Land Use: 18% arable land; 0% permanent crops; 9% meadows and pastures; 11% forest and woodland; 62% other; n.a. km irrigated
Location: Caribbean islands, SE of Puerto Rico

■ PEOPLE

Population: 66,422 (July 2000 est.)
Nationality: Antiguan, Barbudan
Age Structure: 0-14 yrs: 28%; 15-64: 67%; 65+: 5% (2000 est.)
Population Growth Rate: 0.73% (2000 est.)
Net Migration: -6.32 migrants/1,000 population (2000 est.)
Ethnic Groups: almost entirely of black African origin; some of British, Portuguese, Lebanese and Syrian origin
Languages: English (official), local dialects
Religions: Anglican (predominant), other Protestant sects, some Roman Catholic
Birth Rate: 19.60/1,000 population (2000 est.)
Death Rate: 5.99/1,000 population (2000 est.)
Infant Mortality: 23.05 deaths/1,000 live births (2000 est.)
Life Expectancy at Birth: 68.19 years male, 72.84 years female (2000 est.)
Total Fertility Rate: 1.92 children born/woman (2000 est.)
Literacy: 95% (1997)

■ GOVERNMENT

Leader(s): Head of State: Queen Elizabeth II, Gov. Gen. James B. Carlisle, Prime Min. Lester Bird
Government Type: parliamentary democracy
Administrative Divisions: 6 parishes, 2 dependencies
Nationhood: Nov. 1, 1981 (from UK)
National Holiday: Independence Day, Nov. 1

■ ECONOMY

Overview: tourism is the backbone of this service-oriented economy, therefore economic downturns, particularly in the US, can have adverse effects. A labour shortage is plaguing some sectors of the economy; agriculture is a minor but growing sector of the economy
GDP: US$524 million, per capita US$8,200; real growth rate 2.8% (1999 est.)
Inflation: n.a.
Industries: accounts for 12.5% of GDP; tourism, construction, light manufacturing (clothing, alcohol, household appliances)

Labour Force: 30,000; 82% commerce and services, 11% agriculture, 7% industry
Unemployment: 7% (1999 est.)
Agriculture: accounts for 4% of GDP; expanding output of cotton, fruit, vegetables and livestock; other crops—bananas, coconuts, sugar cane, cucumbers, mangoes; not self-sufficient in food
Natural Resources: negligible; pleasant climate and beautiful beaches foster tourism

■ FINANCE/TRADE

Currency: East Caribbean dollar ($EC) = 100 cents
International Reserves Excluding Gold: US$64 million (Dec. 2000)
Gold Reserves: n.a.
Budget: revenues US$122.6 million; expenditures US$141.2 million, including capital expenditures US$17.3 million (1997 est.)
Defence Expenditures: n.a.
Education Expenditures: n.a.
External Debt: US$357 million (1998)
Exports: US$39 million (2000); commodities: petroleum products 46%, manufactures 23%, food and live animals 4%, machinery and transport equipment 17%; partners: Trinidad and Tobago 2%, Barbados 15%, US 0.3%, others 26%
Imports: US$410 million (2000); commodities: food and live animals, machinery and transport equipment, manufactures, chemicals, oil; partners: US 27%, UK 16%, OECS 3%, Canada 4%, other 50%

■ COMMUNICATIONS

Daily Newspapers: 1
Televisions: 467/1,000 inhabitants (1997 est.)
Radios: 541/1,000 inhabitants (1997 est.)
Telephones: 489 lines/1,000 inhabitants (1999)

■ TRANSPORTATION

Motor Vehicles: 14,800; 13,400 passenger cars (1997 est.)
Roads: 250 km ; n.a. km paved
Railway: 77 km
Air Traffic: 1,250,000 passengers carried (1997)
Airports: 3; 2 have paved runways (1999 est.)
Canadian Embassy: c/o The Canadian High Commission, Bishop's Court Hill, St. Michael; mailing address: P.O. Box 404, Bridgetown, Barbados. Tel: 1-246-429-3550. Fax: 1-246-429-3780. Email: bdgtn@dfait-maeci-gc.ca
Embassy in Canada: c/o High Commission for the countries of the Organization of Eastern Caribbean States, 130 Albert St, Ste 700, Ottawa ON K1P 5G4. Tel: (613) 236-8952. Fax: (613) 236-3042. Email: echcc@travel-net.com

Argentina

Long-Form Name: Argentine Republic
Capital: Buenos Aires

■ GEOGRAPHY

Area: 2,766,890 sq. km
Coastline: 4,989 km
Climate: mostly temperate; arid in southeast; subantarctic in southwest
Environment: Tucamán and Mendoza areas in Andes subject to earthquakes; pamperos are violent windstorms that can strike the Pampas and northeast; irrigated soil degradation; desertification; air and water pollution in Buenos Aires; erosion is a current problem
Terrain: rich plains of the Pampas in northern half, flat to rolling plateau of Patagonia in south, rugged Andes along western border
Land Use: 9% arable land; 1% permanent crops; 52% meadows and pastures; 19% forest and woodland; 19% other, includes 17,000 sq. km irrigated
Location: SE South America

■ PEOPLE

Population: 36,955,182 (July 2000 est.)
Nationality: Argentine or Argentinian
Age Structure: 0-14 yrs: 27%; 15-64: 63%; 65+: 10% (2000 est.)
Population Growth Rate: 1.16% (2000 est.)
Net Migration: 0.65 migrants/1,000 population (2000 est.)
Ethnic Groups: 97% white (mostly Spanish and Italian), 3% mestizo, Indian, or other nonwhite groups
Languages: Spanish (official), English, Italian, German, French
Religions: 90% nominally Roman Catholic (less than 20% practising), 2% Protestant, 2% Jewish, 6% other
Birth Rate: 18.59/1,000 population (2000 est.)
Death Rate: 7.59/1,000 population (2000 est.)
Infant Mortality: 18.31 deaths/1,000 live births (2000 est.)
Life Expectancy at Birth: 71.67 years male, 78.61 years female (2000 est.)
Total Fertility Rate: 2.47 children born/woman (2000 est.)
Literacy: 97% (1998)

■ GOVERNMENT

Leader(s): Pres. Fernando De La Rua
Government Type: republic
Administrative Divisions: 23 provinces (provincias, sing. — provincia) and 1 federal district (distrito federal)
Nationhood: July 9, 1816 (from Spain)

National Holiday: Revolution Day, May 25

■ ECONOMY

Overview: though the country possesses abundant natural resources and a diversified industrial base, burgeoning debt is weakening the economy; high unemployment rates have been a persistent problem, largely because of rigid labour laws
GDP: US$367 billion, per capita US$10,000; real growth rate -3.0% (1999 est.)
Inflation: -0.94% (year-end 2000)
Industries: accounts for 29% of GDP; food processing (especially meat packing), motor vehicles, consumer durables, textiles, chemicals and petrochemicals, printing, metallurgy, steel
Labour Force: 15 million (1999); 13% agriculture, 34% industry, 53% services
Unemployment: 14% (Dec. 1999)
Agriculture: accounts for 7% of GNP (including fishing); produces abundant food for both domestic consumption and exports; among world's top five exporters of grain and beef; principal crops—wheat, corn, sorghum, soybeans, sugar beets, peanuts, grapes
Natural Resources: fertile plains of the Pampas, lead, zinc, tin, copper, iron ore, manganese, crude oil, uranium

■ FINANCE/TRADE

Currency: nuevo peso argentino = 100 centavos
International Reserves Excluding Gold: US$24.865 billion (Jan. 2001)
Gold Reserves: US$0.019 million fine troy ounces (Jan. 2001)
Budget: revenues US$44 billion; expenditures US$48 billion, including capital expenditures of US$n.a. (2000 est.)
Defence Expenditures: 1.3% of GDP (1999)
Education Expenditures: 5.80% of total govt. expenditure (1998)
External Debt: US$147.881 billion (1999)
Exports: US$27.074 billion (2000); commodities: meat, wheat, corn, oil seed, hides, wool; partners: US 14%, former USSR countries, Italy, Brazil, Japan, Netherlands
Imports: US$25.428 billion (2000); commodities: machinery and equipment, metals, chemicals, fuels and lubricants, agricultural products; partners: US 25%, Brazil, Germany, Bolivia, Japan, Italy, Netherlands

■ COMMUNICATIONS

Daily Newspapers: 181
Televisions: 289/1,000 inhabitants (1998)
Radios: 681/1,000 inhabitants (1997)
Telephones: 201 lines/1,000 inhabitants (1999)

■ TRANSPORTATION

Motor Vehicles: 6,100,000; 4,800,000 passenger cars (1997 est.)
Roads: 215,434 km; 63,553 km paved
Railway: 38,326 km
Air Traffic: 8,600,000 passengers carried (1997)
Airports: 1,359; 142 have paved runways (1999 est.)

Canadian Embassy: The Canadian Embassy, 2828 Tagle, 1425 Buenos Aires; mailing address: Casilla de Correo C1000WAP, Buenos Aires, Argentina. Tel: (011-54-1) 4805-3032. Fax: (011-54-1) 4806-1209. Email: bairs@dfait-maeci-gc.ca
Embassy in Canada: Embassy of the Argentine Republic, Royal Bank Centre, 90 Sparks St, Ste 910, Ottawa ON K1P 5B4. Tel: (613) 236-2351. Fax: (613) 235-2659. Email: n.a.

Armenia

Long-Form Name: Republic of Armenia
Capital: Yerevan

■ GEOGRAPHY

Area: 29,800 sq. km
Coastline: none: landlocked
Climate: severe winters; hot summers; dry year-round
Environment: prone to earthquakes; little land suitable for cultivation; air and water pollution; deforestation and drought; soil pollution is a current problem
Terrain: rugged highlands; 70% is mountains; little forest land; fast-flowing rivers; Aras River Valley has good soil
Land Use: 17% arable, 3% permanent crops, 24% meadows and pasture, 15% forests and woodland, 41% other, includes 2,870 sq. km irrigated; most farmland lies in the Aras Valley; animal herding predominant in the highlands
Location: SW Asia

■ PEOPLE

Population: 3,344,336 (July 2000 est.)
Nationality: Armenian
Age Structure: 0-14 yrs: 24%; 15-64: 66%; 65+: 10% (2000 est.)
Population Growth Rate: -0.28% (2000 est.)
Net Migration: -4.23 migrants/1,000 population (2000 est.)
Ethnic Groups: 93% Armenians, 2% Russians, 3% Azerbaijanis, 2% other, predominantly Kurds
Languages: Armenian (official), Azerbaijan, Russian

Religions: predominantly Armenian Orthodox
Birth Rate: 10.97/1,000 population (2000 est.)
Death Rate: 9.53/1,000 population (2000 est.)
Infant Mortality: 41.48 deaths/1,000 live births (2000 est.)
Life Expectancy at Birth: 61.98 years male, 71.04 years female (2000 est.)
Total Fertility Rate: 1.47 children born/woman (2000 est.)
Literacy: 98% (1998)

■ GOVERNMENT

Leader(s): Pres. Robert Kocharian, Prime Min. Andranik Markaryan
Government Type: republic
Administrative Divisions: 10 provinces (marzer, sing. —marz) and 1 city (k'aghak'ner, sing. —k'aghak')
Nationhood: Sept. 23, 1991 (from Soviet Union)
National Holiday: Referendum Day, Sept. 21

■ ECONOMY

Overview: predominantly manufacturing and agriculture; much of Armenia's population remains heavily dependent on remittances from relatives abroad
GDP: US$9.9 billion, per capita US$2,900; real growth rate 5% (1999 est.)
Inflation: -0.81% per month (year-end 2000)
Industries: accounts for 25% of GDP; electrical equipment and machinery, chemicals, machine tools, vehicles, textiles
Labour Force: 2 million (1999); 42% industry and construction, 18% agriculture and forestry, 40% other (1998)
Unemployment: 20% (1998 est.)
Agriculture: accounts for approximately 40% of GDP; fruit, grapes, vegetables, tobacco, grains, beetroot, potatoes, geranium oil, cattle and sheep herding
Natural Resources: marble, precious metals, iron, tufa, small deposits of gold, copper, molybdenum, zinc, alumina

■ FINANCE/TRADE

Currency: dram = 100 luma
International Reserves Excluding Gold: US$295 million (Jan. 2001)
Gold Reserves: US$0.045 million fine troy ounces (Jan. 2001)
Budget: revenues US$360 million; expenditures US$566 million, including capital expenditures of US$n.a (1999 est.)
Defence Expenditures: 4% of GDP (1999)
Education Expenditures: 2.0% of GNP (1997)
External Debt: US$932 million (1999)
Exports: US$270 million (2000); commodities include cotton, fruit, olives, pomegranates, machine tools, instruments, shoes

Imports: US$841 million (2000); commodities include machinery, energy, consumer goods

■ COMMUNICATIONS

Daily Newspapers: 11
Televisions: 218/1,000 inhabitants (1998)
Radios: 224/1,000 inhabitants (1997)
Telephones: 155 lines/1,000 persons (1999)

■ TRANSPORTATION

Motor Vehicles: n.a.
Roads: 15,998 km; n.a. km paved
Railway: 825 km (does not include industrial lines)
Air Traffic: 368,000 passengers carried (1997)
Airports: 11; 5 have paved runways
Canadian Embassy: The Consulate of Canada, #21, 25 Demirjian St, Yerevan, Armenia. Tel: (011-810-3749) 401-238. Fax: (011-810-3741) 56-79-03; mailing address: c/o Starokonyushenny Per 23, Moscow 121002, Russian Federation. Email: aemin@freenet.am
Embassy in Canada: Embassy of the Republic of Armenia, 7 Delaware Ave, Ottawa ON K2P 0Z2. Tel: (613) 234-3710.. Fax: (613) 234-3444. Email: erac@ican.net

Aruba

Long-Form Name: Aruba
Capital: Oranjestad

■ GEOGRAPHY

Area: 193 sq. km
Climate: tropical marine; little seasonal temperature variation
Land Use: 7% arable land; 0% permanent crops; 0% meadows and pastures; 0% forest and woodland; 93% other; 0.01 sq. km irrigated
Location: Caribbean island, off N coast of South America

■ PEOPLE

Population: 69,539 (July 2000 est.)
Nationality: Aruban
Ethnic Groups: 80% mixed European/Caribbean Indian
Languages: Dutch (official), Papiamento (a Spanish, Portuguese, Dutch, English dialect), English (widely spoken), Spanish

■ GOVERNMENT

Colony Territory of: Dependent Territory of the Netherlands
Leader(s): Head of State: Queen Beatrix (Netherlands); Gov. Gen. Olindo Koolman; Prime Min. Jan Hendrik Eman
Government Type: part of the Dutch realm;

parliamentary democracy; autonomy in internal affairs obtained in 1986
National Holiday: Flag Day, Mar. 18

■ ECONOMY

Overview: tourism is the mainstay; banking and oil refinery are also important

■ FINANCE/TRADE

Currency: Aruban florin (Af) = 100 cents

Canadian Embassy: c/o The Canadian Embassy, Sophialaan 7, 2514JP, The Hague, Netherlands. Tel.: (011-31-70) 311-1600. Fax: (011-31-70) 311-1620. Email: hague@dfait-maeci.gc.ca
Representative to Canada: c/o Embassy of the Kingdom of the Netherlands, 350 Albert St, Ste 2020, Ottawa ON K1R 1A4. Tel: (613) 237-5030. Fax: (613) 237-6471. Email: nlgovott@netcom.ca

Australia

Long-Form Name: Commonwealth of Australia
Capital: Canberra

■ GEOGRAPHY

Area: 7,686,850 sq. km; includes Macquarie Island
Coastline: 25,760 km
Climate: generally arid to semi-arid; temperate in south and east; tropical in north
Environment: subject to severe droughts and floods; cyclones along coast; limited fresh water availability; soil degradation; regular, tropical, invigorating, sea breeze known as "the Doctor" occurs along west coast in summer; desertification. Shipping activities and tourism are threatening the Great Barrier Reef
Terrain: mostly low plateau with deserts; fertile plain in southeast
Land Use: 6% arable land; negligible permanent crops; 54% meadows and pastures; 19% forest and woodland; 21% other, includes 21,070 sq. km irrigated
Location: continent of the eastern hemisphere, SE of Asia and S. of the equator; divides Indian and Pacific Oceans

■ PEOPLE

Population: 19,169,083 (July 2000 est.)
Nationality: Australian
Age Structure: 0-14 yrs: 21%; 15-64: 67%; 65+: 12% (2000 est.)
Population Growth Rate: 1.02% (2000 est.)
Net Migration: 4.26 migrants/1,000 population (2000 est.)
Ethnic Groups: 92% Caucasian, 7% Asian, 1% Aboriginal and other

Languages: English, native languages
Religions: 26.1% Anglican, 26% Roman Catholic, 24.3% other Christian; most of the rest do not profess a religion
Birth Rate: 13.08/1,000 population (2000 est.)
Death Rate: 7.12/1,000 population (2000 est.)
Infant Mortality: 5.04 deaths/1,000 live births (2000 est.)
Life Expectancy at Birth: 76.90 years male, 82.74 years female (2000 est.)
Total Fertility Rate: 1.79 children born/woman (2000 est.)
Literacy: 100% (1998)

■ GOVERNMENT

Leader(s): Head of State: Queen Elizabeth II/Gov. Gen. Peter Hollingsworth, Prime Min. John Howard
Government Type: federal parliamentary state
Administrative Divisions: 6 states, 2 territories; dependent areas inc.: Ashmore and Cartier Islands (uninhabited), Australian Antarctic Territory (uninhabited except for scientific staff), Cocos (Keeling) Islands, Coral Sea Islands Territory (uninhabited), Christmas Island, Heard and McDonald Islands (uninhabited), Norfolk Island
Nationhood: Jan. 1, 1901 (federation of UK colonies)
National Holiday: Australia Day, Jan. 26

■ ECONOMY

Overview: successful Western-style capitalist economy and a major exporter of natural resources and agricultural products; is looking to increase exports of manufactured goods
GDP: US$416.2 billion, per capita US$22,200; real growth rate 4.3% (1999 est.)
Inflation: 4.48% (year-end 2000)
Industries: accounts for 26% of GDP; mining, industrial and transportation equipment, food processing, chemicals, steel, motor vehicles
Labour Force: 10 million (1999); 27.5% community, social and business services, 25.5% trade and tourism, 14.2% manufacturing
Unemployment: 7.2% (Jan. 2001)
Agriculture: accounts for 3% of GDP and 30% of export revenues; world's largest exporter of beef and wool, second largest for mutton, and among top wheat exporters; major crops—wheat, barley, sugar cane, fruit; livestock—cattle, sheep, poultry
Natural Resources: bauxite, coal, iron ore, copper, tin, silver, uranium, nickel, tungsten, mineral sands, lead, zinc, diamonds, natural gas, crude oil

■ FINANCE/TRADE

Currency: dollar ($A) = 100 cents

International Reserves Excluding Gold: US$16.655 billion (Jan. 2001)
Gold Reserves: US$2.563 million fine troy ounces (Jan. 2001)
Budget: revenues US$90.73 billion; expenditures US$89.04 billion, including capital expenditures US$n.a. (1998–99 est.)
Defence Expenditures: 7.0% of central government expenditure (1998)
Education Expenditures: 7.64% of govt. expenditure (1998)
External Debt: US$222 billion (June 1999)
Exports: US$63.874 billion (2000); commodities: wheat, barley, beef, lamb, dairy products, wool, coal, iron ore; partners: Japan 26%, US 11%, New Zealand 6%, S Korea 4%, Singapore 4%, former USSR countries 3%
Imports: US$71.538 billion (2000); commodities: manufactured raw materials, capital equipment, consumer goods; partners: US 22%, Japan 22%, UK 7%, Germany 6%, New Zealand 4%

■ COMMUNICATIONS

Daily Newspapers: 65
Televisions: 639/1,000 inhabitants (1998)
Radios: 1,376/1,000 inhabitants (1997)
Telephones: 520 lines/1,000 inhabitants (1999)

■ TRANSPORTATION

Motor Vehicles: 10,900,000; 9,000,000 passenger cars (1997 est.)
Roads: 913,000 km; 353,331 km paved
Railway: 33,819 km
Air Traffic: 30,954,000 passengers carried (1997)
Airports: 408; 265 have paved runways (1999 est.)
Canadian Embassy: The Canadian High Commission, Commonwealth Ave, Canberra A.C.T. 2600, Australia. Tel: (011-61-2) 6270-4000. Fax: (011-61-2) 6273-3285. Email: cnbra@dfait-maeci.gc.ca
Embassy in Canada: Australian High Commission, 50 O'Connor St, Ste 710, Ottawa ON K1P 6L2. Tel: (613) 236-0841. Fax: (613) 236-4376. Email: n.a.

Austria

Long-Form Name: Republic of Austria
Capital: Vienna

■ GEOGRAPHY

Area: 83,858 sq. km
Coastline: none: landlocked
Climate: temperate; continental, cloudy; cold winter with frequent rain in lowlands and snow in mountains; cool summers with occasional showers

Environment: because of steep slopes, poor soils and cold temperatures, population is concentrated on eastern lowlands; air and soil pollution is due to emissions by coal, and oil-fired power stations and industrial plants
Terrain: mostly mountains with Alps in west and south; flat, with gentle slopes along eastern and northern margins
Land Use: 17% arable land; 1% permanent crops; 23% meadows and pastures; 39% forest and woodland; 20% other, includes 40 sq. km irrigated
Location: C Europe

■ PEOPLE

Population: 8,131,111 (July 2000 est.)
Nationality: Austrian
Age Structure: 0-14 yrs: 17%; 15-64: 68%; 65+: 15% (2000 est.)
Population Growth Rate: +0.25% (2000 est.)
Net Migration: +2.46 migrants/1,000 population (2000 est.)
Ethnic Groups: 98% German, 2% Croatian, Slovene and others
Languages: German (official); Slovene, Hungarian, and a Croatian dialect also spoken
Religions: 85% Roman Catholic, 6% Protestant, 9% other
Birth Rate: 9.90/1,000 population (2000 est.)
Death Rate: 9.91/1,000 population (2000 est.)
Infant Mortality: 4.50 deaths/1,000 live births (2000 est.)
Life Expectancy at Birth: 74.52 years male, 80.99 years female (2000 est.)
Total Fertility Rate: 1.39 children born/woman (2000 est.)
Literacy: 100% (1998 est.)

■ GOVERNMENT

Leader(s): Chanc. Wolfgang Schuessel, Pres. Thomas Klestil
Government Type: federal republic
Administrative Divisions: 9 states (bundeslaender, sing. — bundesland)
Nationhood: Nov. 12, 1918 (from Austro-Hungarian Empire)
National Holiday: National Day, Oct. 26

■ ECONOMY

Overview: prosperous, Western capitalist economy, as well as substantial welfare benefits and extensive nationalized industry; unemployment is a continuing problem
GDP: US$190.6 billion, per capita US$23,400; real growth rate 2% (1999 est.)
Inflation: 2.35% (year-end 2000)
Industries: accounts for 32.4% of GDP; foods, iron and steel, machines, textiles, chemicals, electrical, paper and pulp, tourism, mining

Labour Force: 4 million (1999); 25.1% manufacture, 24.5% community, social and business services, 19.5% trade and tourism; an estimated 200,000 Austrians are employed in other European countries; foreign labourers in Austria number 177,840, about 6% of labour force

Unemployment: 7.7% (Jan. 2001)

Agriculture: accounts for 1.3% of GDP (including forestry); principal crops and animals—grains, fruit, potatoes, sugar beets, sawn wood, cattle, pigs, poultry; 80–90% self-sufficient in food

Natural Resources: iron ore, crude oil, timber, magnesite, lead, coal, lignite, copper, hydroelectricity

■ FINANCE/TRADE

Currency: schilling (S) = 100 groschen; Euro (EUR) as of March 1, 2002

International Reserves Excluding Gold: US$13.140 billion (Jan. 2001)

Gold Reserves: US$12.137 million fine troy ounces (Jan. 2001)

Budget: revenues US$54 billion; expenditures US$59.5 billion, capital expenditures US$n.a. (1999 est.)

Defence Expenditures: 0.82% of GDP (1999 est.)

Education Expenditures: 9.21% of total govt. expenditure (1997)

External Debt: US$31.7 billion (1998)

Exports: US$59.011 billion (2000); commodities: machinery and equipment, iron and steel, lumber, textiles, paper products, chemicals; partners: Germany 35%, Italy 10%, Eastern Europe 9%, Switzerland 7%, US 4%, OPEC 3%

Imports: US$63.501 billion (2000); commodities: petroleum, foodstuffs, machinery and equipment, vehicles, chemicals, textiles and clothing, pharmaceuticals; partners: Germany 44%, Italy 9%, Eastern Europe 6%, Switzerland 5%, US 4%, former Soviet Union 2%

■ COMMUNICATIONS

Daily Newspapers: 17

Televisions: 516/1,000 inhabitants (1998)

Radios: 753/1,000 inhabitants (1997)

Telephones: 472 lines/1,000 inhabitants (1999)

■ TRANSPORTATION

Motor Vehicles: 5,000,000; 4,000,000 passenger cars (1997 est.)

Roads: 200,000 km, all paved

Railway: 6,123 km

Air Traffic: 5,154,000 passengers carried (1997)

Airports: 55; 22 have paved runways (1999 est.)

Canadian Embassy: The Canadian Embassy, Laurenzerberg 2 A-1010 Vienna, Austria. Tel: (011-43-1) 531-38-3000. Fax: (011-43-1) 531-38-3321. Email: vienn@dfait-maeci.gc.ca

Embassy in Canada: Embassy of the Republic of Austria, 445 Wilbrod St, Ottawa ON K1N 6M7. Tel: (613) 789-1444. Fax: (613) 789-3431. Email: embassy@austro.org

Azerbaijan

Long-Form Name: Azerbaijani Republic

Capital: Baku (or Baki)

■ GEOGRAPHY

Area: 86,600 sq. km

Coastline: none; landlocked. Inland coastline (Caspian Sea) approximately 800 km

Climate: Alpine to subtropical; dry, semi-arid steppe subject to drought

Environment: severe air and water pollution render Aspheron Peninsula, including Baku and Sumgait, the "most ecologically devastated area in the world," according to local scientists

Terrain: fertile central lowlands; large flat Kura-Aras Lowland; Caucasus Mountains in north; western uplands

Land Use: 18% arable, 5% permanent crops, 11% forests and woodland, 25% meadows and pastures, 41% other (includes 10,000 sq. km irrigated); grazing land in the Caucasus Mountains; farming in lowlands

Location: SW Asia, bordering on Caspian Sea

■ PEOPLE

Population: 7,748,163 (July 2000 est.)

Nationality: Azerbaijani

Age Structure: 0-14 yrs: 30%; 15-64: 63%; 65+: 7% (2000 est.)

Population Growth Rate: 0.27% (2000 est.)

Net Migration: -5.92 migrants/1,000 population (2000 est.)

Ethnic Groups: 90% Azerbaijani, 2.5% Russians, 2% Armenians, 3.2% Daghestanis, 2.3% other

Languages: Azerbaijani (official), Armenian, Russian, 6% other

Religions: Muslim 93.4%, Russian Orthodox 2.3%, Armenian Orthodox 2.3%, other 1.8%

Birth Rate: 18.08/1,000 population (2000 est.)

Death Rate: 9.47/1,000 population (2000 est.)

Infant Mortality: 83.41 deaths/1,000 live births (2000 est.)

Life Expectancy at Birth: 58.51 years male, 67.45 years female (2000 est.)

Total Fertility Rate: 2.19 children born/woman (2000 est.)

Literacy: 96.3% (1997)

■ GOVERNMENT

Leader(s): Pres. Haydar Aliyev, Prem. Artur Rasizade

Government Type: republic
Administrative Divisions: 59 (rayonlar, sing. — rayon), 11 cities (saharlar, sing. — sahar), 1 autonomous republic (muxtar respublika, rayons)
Nationhood: Aug. 30, 1991 (from Soviet Union)
National Holiday: Independence Day, May 28

■ ECONOMY

Overview: cotton and refining industries are most prominent; Azerbaijan is least industrially developed of the Transcaucasian States
GDP: US$14 billion, per capita US$1,770; real growth rate 7% (1999 est.)
Inflation: 1.77% (year-end 2000)
Industries: accounts for 18% of GDP; oil extraction and refining, steel, cement, textiles, chemicals, petrochemicals
Labour Force: 4 million (1999); 32% agriculture and forestry, 26% industry and construction, 42% other
Unemployment: 20% (1999 est.)
Agriculture: accounts for 22% of GDP; cotton, grain, grapes, tea, citrus fruit, vegetables, sheep and horse breeding
Natural Resources: oil reserves, minerals, iron, aluminum

■ FINANCE/TRADE

Currency: manat = 100 gopik
International Reserves Excluding Gold: US$905 million (Jan. 2001)
Gold Reserves: none (Jan. 2001)
Budget: n.a.
Defence Expenditures: 10.8% of central government expenditure (1997)
Education Expenditures: 3.2 % of central government expenditure (1999)
External Debt: US$1.036 billion (1999)
Exports: US$879 million (2000) to outside the successor states of the former USSR; oil and gas and related equipment, textiles, cotton. partners: European and successor states of the former USSR
Imports: US$788 million (2000) from outside the successor states of the former USSR; machinery and parts, foodstuffs, textiles, consumer durables

■ COMMUNICATIONS

Daily Newspapers: 6
Televisions: 254/1,000 inhabitants (1998)
Radios: 23/1,000 inhabitants (1997)
Telephones: 95 lines/1,000 persons (1999)

■ TRANSPORTATION

Motor Vehicles: n.a.
Roads: 24,981 km; 23,057 km hard-surfaced
Railway: 2,125 km (does not include industrial lines)
Air Traffic: 982,000 passengers carried (1997)
Airports: 69; 29 have paved runways

Canadian Embassy: c/o The Canadian Embassy, Nenehatun Caddesi No. 75, Gaziosmanpasa 06700, Ankara, Turkey. Tel: (011-90-312) 459-9200. Fax: (011-90-312) 459-9361. Email: ankra@dfait-maeci.gc.ca
Embassy in Canada: Embassy of the Republic of Azerbaijan, 927 15th St NW, Ste 700, Washington DC 20005, USA. Tel: (202) 842-0001. Fax: (202) 842-0004. Email: azerbaijan@mcimail.com

Bahamas

Long-Form Name: Commonwealth of The Bahamas
Capital: Nassau

■ GEOGRAPHY

Area: 13,940 sq. km
Coastline: 3,542 km
Climate: tropical marine; moderated by warm waters of Gulf Stream
Environment: subject to hurricanes and other tropical storms that cause extensive flood and wind damage; coral reef decay is a current issue
Terrain: long, flat coral islands with some low, rounded hills
Land Use: 1% arable land; 0% permanent crops; 0% meadows and pastures; 32% forest and woodland; 67% other; n.a. km irrigated
Location: Caribbean islands, E of Florida

■ PEOPLE

Population: 294,982 (July 2000 est.)
Nationality: Bahamian
Age Structure: 0-14 yrs: 30%; 15-64: 64%; 65+: 6% (2000 est.)
Population Growth Rate: 1.01% (2000 est.)
Net Migration: -2.67 migrants/1,000 population (2000 est.)
Ethnic Groups: 85% black, 12% white, 3% Asian and Hispanic
Languages: English; some Creole among Haitian immigrants
Religions: 32% Baptist, 20% Anglican, 19% Roman Catholic, smaller groups of other Protestants, Greek Orthodox and Jews
Birth Rate: 19.54/1,000 population (2000 est.)
Death Rate: 6.81/1,000 population (2000 est.)
Infant Mortality: 16.99 deaths/1,000 live births (2000 est.)
Life Expectancy at Birth: 68.25 years male, 73.94 years female (2000 est.)

Total Fertility Rate: 2.33 children born/woman (2000 est.)
Literacy: 95.8% (1997)

■ GOVERNMENT

Leader(s): Head of State: Queen Elizabeth II/Gov. Gen. Orville Turnquest. Prime Min. Hubert Alexander Ingraham
Government Type: constitutional parliamentary democracy
Administrative Divisions: 21 districts
Nationhood: July 10, 1973 (from UK)
National Holiday: National Day, July 10

■ ECONOMY

Overview: tourism and offshore banking are features of this stable, middle-income developing nation
GDP: US$5.58 billion, per capita US$20,000; real growth rate 3% (1999 est.)
Inflation: 1.61% (year-end 2000)
Industries: accounts for 5% of GDP; banking, tourism, cement, oil refining and transshipment, salt production, rum, aragonite, pharmaceuticals, spiral welded steel pipe
Labour Force: approx. 150,000; 30% government, 40% hotels and restaurants, 10% business services, 5% agriculture
Unemployment: 9% (1998 est.)
Agriculture: accounts for 3% of GDP; dominated by small-scale producers; principal products—citrus fruit, vegetables, poultry; large net importer of food
Natural Resources: salt, aragonite, timber

■ FINANCE/TRADE

Currency: Bahamian dollar ($B) = 100 cents
International Reserves Excluding Gold: US$335 million (Jan. 2001)
Gold Reserves: none (Jan. 2001)
Budget: revenues US$766 million; expenditures US$845 million, including capital expenditures US$97 million (1997–98 est.)
Defence Expenditures: 4.58% of central government expenditure (1999)
Education Expenditures: 18.73% of central government expenditure (1999)
External Debt: US$349 million (1998)
Exports: US$305 million (2000); commodities: pharmaceuticals, cement, rum, crawfish; partners: US 90%, UK 10%
Imports: US$1.995 billion (2000); commodities: foodstuffs, manufactured goods, mineral fuels; partners: Nigeria 21%, US 35%, Japan 13%, Angola 11%

■ COMMUNICATIONS

Daily Newspapers: 3

Televisions: 227/1,000 inhabitants (1997 est.)
Radios: 729/1,000 inhabitants (1997 est.)
Telephones: 369 lines/1,000 inhabitants (1999)

■ TRANSPORTATION

Motor Vehicles: 59,000; 47,000 passenger cars (1996 est.)
Roads: 2,693 km; 1,546 km paved
Railway: none
Air Traffic: 704,000 passengers carried (1997)
Airports: 62; 33 have paved runways (1999 est.)

Canadian Embassy: Consulate of Canada, Shirley Street Plaza, Nassau; mailing address: Consulate of Canada, P.O. Box SS-6371, Nassau, Bahamas. Tel: (1-242) 393-2123. Fax: (1-242) 393-1305. Email: broks@bahamas.net.bs
Embassy in Canada: High Commission for the Commonwealth of the Bahamas, 50 O'Connor St, Ste 1313, Ottawa ON K1P 6L2. Tel: (613) 232-1724. Fax: (613) 232-0097. Email: ottawa-mission@bahighco.com

Bahrain

Long-Form Name: State of Bahrain
Capital: Manama

■ GEOGRAPHY

Area: 620 sq. km
Coastline: 161 km
Climate: arid; mild, pleasant winters; very hot, humid summers
Environment: there are no natural fresh water resources; ground water and sea water are the sole sources for all water needs; dust storms; desertification; drought; coastal degradation resulting from oil industry
Terrain: mostly low desert plain rising gently to low central escarpment
Land Use: 1% arable land; 1% permanent crops; 6% meadows and pastures; 0% forest and woodland; 92% other; includes 10 sq. km irrigated
Location: Persian Gulf, E of Saudi Arabia

■ PEOPLE

Population: 634,137 (July 1999 est.)
Nationality: Bahraini
Age Structure: 0-14 yrs: 30%; 15-64: 67%; 65+: 3% (2000 est.)
Population Growth Rate: 1.78% (2000 est.)
Net Migration: 1.12 migrants/1,000 population (2000 est.)
Ethnic Groups: 63% Bahraini, 19% Asian, 10% other Arab, 8% Iranian
Languages: Arabic (official); English also widely spoken; Farsi, Urdu

Religions: Muslim (70% Shi'a, 30% Sunni)
Birth Rate: 20.61/1,000 population (2000 est.)
Death Rate: 3.89/1,000 population (2000 est.)
Infant Mortality: 20.48 deaths/1,000 live births (2000 est.)
Life Expectancy at Birth: 70.58 years male, 75.45 years female (2000 est.)
Total Fertility Rate: 2.82 children born/woman (2000 est.)
Literacy: 86.2% (1997)

■ GOVERNMENT

Leader(s): Prime Min. Khalifa bin Salman Al Khalifa, Amir Hamad bin Isa Al Khalifa
Government Type: traditional monarchy
Administrative Divisions: 12 municipalities (manatiq, sing. —mintaqah)
Nationhood: Aug. 15, 1971 (from UK)
National Holiday: National Day, Dec. 16

■ ECONOMY

Overview: petroleum production and processing are the backbone of the economy and any change in the world oil market affects the economy
GDP: US$8.6 billion, per capita US$13,700; real growth rate 4% (1999 est.)
Inflation: 1.10% (June 1999)
Industries: accounts for 46% of GDP; petroleum processing and refining, aluminum smelting, offshore banking, ship repairing
Labour Force: 295,000 (1998 est.); 42% of labour force is Bahraini; 78% industry, commerce and services, 21% government, 1% agriculture
Unemployment: 15% (1998 est.)
Agriculture: including fishing, accounts for 1% of GDP; not self-sufficient in food production; heavily subsidized sector produces fruit, vegetables, poultry, dairy products, shrimp and fish
Natural Resources: oil, associated and nonassociated natural gas, fish

■ FINANCE/TRADE

Currency: Bahraini dinar (BD) = 1,000 fils
International Reserves Excluding Gold: US$1.460 billion (Jan. 2001)
Gold Reserves: US$0.15 million fine troy ounces (Jan. 2001)
Budget: revenues US$1.5 billion; expenditures US$1.9 billion, capital expenditures US$n.a.(1999 budget)
Defence Expenditures: 17.56% of total govt. expenditures (1999)
Education Expenditures: 12.46% of central govt. expenditure (1999)
External Debt: US$2 billion (1997)

Exports: US$5.199 billion (2000); commodities: petroleum 80%, aluminum 7%, other 13%; partners: US, United Arab Emirates, Japan, Singapore, Saudi Arabia
Imports: US$4.273 billion (2000); commodities: non-oil 59%, crude oil 41%; partners: UK, Saudi Arabia, US, Japan

■ COMMUNICATIONS

Daily Newspapers: 4
Televisions: 433/1,000 inhabitants (1997 est.)
Radios: 533/1,000 inhabitants (1997 est.)
Telephones: 249 lines/1,000 inhabitants (1999)

■ TRANSPORTATION

Motor Vehicles: 178,000; 143,000 passenger cars (1997 est.)
Roads: 3,164 km; 2,433 km paved
Railway: none
Air Traffic: 1,165,000 passengers carried (1997)
Airports: 3; 2 have paved runways (1999 est.)

Canadian Embassy: The Canadian Embassy to Bahrain, c/o The Canadian Embassy, P.O. Box 94321, Riyadh 11693, Saudi Arabia. Tel: (011-966-1) 488-2288. Fax: (011-966-1) 488-1997. Email: ryadh@dfait-maeci.gc.ca
Embassy in Canada: The Embassy of the State of Bahrain, 3502 International Dr NW, Washington DC 20008, USA. Tel: (202) 342-0741. Fax: (202) 362-2192. Email: n.a.

Bangladesh

Long-Form Name: People's Republic of Bangladesh
Capital: Dhaka

■ GEOGRAPHY

Area: 144,000 sq. km
Coastline: 580 km
Climate: tropical; cool, dry winter (Oct. to Mar.); hot, humid summer (Mar. to June)
Environment: vulnerable to droughts; much of country routinely flooded during summer monsoon season (June to Oct.); overpopulation; deforestation; cyclones
Terrain: mostly flat alluvial plain; hilly in southeast
Land Use: 73% arable land; 2% permanent crops; 5% meadows and pastures; 15% forest and woodland; 5% other, includes 31,000 sq. km irrigated
Location: S Asia, bordering on Bay of Bengal

■ PEOPLE

Population: 129,194,224 (July 2000 est.)
Nationality: Bangladeshi

Age Structure: 0-14 yrs: 36%; 15-64: 60%; 65+: 4% (2000 est.)
Population Growth Rate: 1.59% (2000 est.)
Net Migration: -0.77migrants/1,000 population (2000 est.)
Ethnic Groups: 98% Bengali, 250,000 Biharis, less than 1 million tribals
Languages: Bangla (official), English widely used, 5% tribal dialects
Religions: 83% Muslim, 16% Hindu, less than 1% Buddhist, Christian and other
Birth Rate: 25.44/1,000 population (2000 est.)
Death Rate: 8.73/1,000 population (2000 est.)
Infant Mortality: 71.66 deaths/1,000 live births (2000 est.)
Life Expectancy at Birth: 60.40 years male, 59.91 years female (2000 est.)
Total Fertility Rate: 2.85 children born/woman (2000 est.)
Literacy: 40% (1998)

■ GOVERNMENT

Leader(s): Pres. Shahabuddin Ahmed, Prime Min. Sheikh Hasina Wazed. A presidential election is scheduled for October 1, 2001.
Government Type: republic
Administrative Divisions: 5 divisions
Nationhood: Dec. 16, 1971 (from Pakistan; Bangladesh formerly known as East Pakistan)
National Holiday: Independence Day, Mar. 26

■ ECONOMY

Overview: one of the poorest nations in the world; the economy is based on a small number of agricultural exports, which are vulnerable to natural disasters; few natural resources; frequent cyclones and floods, a rapidly growing labour force that cannot be absorbed by agriculture, a low level of industrialization, government interference with the economy, failure to exploit energy reserves, and inadequate power supplies all contribute to stifling economic growth
GDP: US$187 billion, per capita US$1,470; real growth rate 5.2% (1999 est.)
Inflation: 2.30% (year-end 2000)
Industries: accounts for 17% of GDP, jute manufacturing, food processing, cotton textiles, petroleum, urea fertilizer
Labour Force: 66 million (1999); 56.5% agriculture, 33.7% services, 9.8% industry; extensive export of labour to Saudi Arabia, United Arab Emirates, Oman and Kuwait
Unemployment: n.a.
Agriculture: accounts for about 30% of GDP, 65% of employment and 20% of exports; imports 10% of food grain requirements; world's largest exporter of jute; commercial products—jute, rice, wheat, tea, sugar cane, potatoes, beef, milk, poultry
Natural Resources: natural gas, arable land, timber

■ FINANCE/TRADE

Currency: taka (Tk) = 100 poisha
International Reserves Excluding Gold: US$1.433 billion (Jan. 2001)
Gold Reserves: US$0.109 million fine troy ounces (Jan. 2001)
Budget: revenues US$3.8 billion; expenditures US$5.5 billion, including capital expenditures of US$n.a. (1997)
Defence Expenditures: n.a.
Education Expenditures: 2.2% of central government expenditure (1997)
External Debt: US$17.534 billion (1999)
Exports: US$4.056 billion (2000); commodities: jute, tea, leather, shrimp, manufacturing; partners: US 25%, Western Europe 22%, Middle East 9%, Japan 8%, Eastern Europe 7%
Imports: US$7.304 billion (2000); commodities: food, petroleum and other energy, nonfood consumer goods, semiprocessed goods and capital equipment; partners: Western Europe 18%, Japan 14%, Middle East 9%, US 8%

■ COMMUNICATIONS

Daily Newspapers: 37
Televisions: 6/1,000 inhabitants (1998)
Radios: 50/1,000 inhabitants (1997)
Telephones: 3.0 lines/1,000 inhabitants (1999)

■ TRANSPORTATION

Motor Vehicles: 225,000; 152,000 passenger cars (1997 est.)
Roads: 201,182 km; 19,112 km paved
Railway: 2,745 km
Air Traffic: 1,315,000 passengers carried (1997)
Airports: 16; all have paved runways (1999 est.)

Canadian Embassy: The Canadian High Commission, House CWN 16/A, Rd. 48, Gulshan; mailing address: G.P.O. Box 569, Dhaka, Bangladesh. Tel: (011-880-2) 988-7091. Fax: (011-880-2) 88-30-43. Email: dhaka@dfait-maeci.gc.ca
Embassy in Canada: High Commission for the People's Republic of Bangladesh, 275 Bank St, Ste 302, Ottawa ON K2P 2L6. Tel: (613) 236-0138. Fax: (613) 567-3213. Email: bdootcanda@iosphere.net

Barbados

Long-Form Name: Barbados
Capital: Bridgetown

■ GEOGRAPHY

Area: 430 sq. km
Coastline: 97 km
Climate: tropical; rainy season (June to Oct.)
Environment: subject to hurricanes, especially June to Oct.; water pollution and soil erosion; landslides
Terrain: relatively flat; rises gently to a central highland region
Land Use: 37% arable land; 0% permanent crops; 5% meadows and pastures; 12% forest and woodland; 46% other, includes n.a. km irrigated
Location: Caribbean islands, N of Venezuela

■ PEOPLE

Population: 274,540 (July 2000 est.)
Nationality: Barbadian, or Bajan (colloquial)
Age Structure: 0-14 yrs: 22%; 15-64: 69%; 65+: 9% (2000 est.)
Population Growth Rate: 0.55% (2000 est.)
Net Migration: -0.32migrants/1,000 population (2000 est.)
Ethnic Groups: 80% African, 16% mixed, 4% European
Languages: English
Religions: 67% Protestant, 9% Methodist, 4% Roman Catholic, 9% other, including Moravian
Birth Rate: 14.45/1,000 population (2000 est.)
Death Rate: 8.68/1,000 population (2000 est.)
Infant Mortality: 12.37 deaths/1,000 live births (2000 est.)
Life Expectancy at Birth: 70.43 years male, 75.60 years female (2000 est.)
Total Fertility Rate: 1.70 children born/woman (2000 est.)
Literacy: 97.6% (1997)

■ GOVERNMENT

Leader(s): Head of State: Queen Elizabeth II/Gov. Gen. Sir Clifford Husbands. Prime Min. Owen Seymour Arthur
Government Type: parliamentary democracy
Administrative Divisions: 11 parishes
Nationhood: Nov. 30, 1966 (from UK)
National Holiday: Independence Day, Nov. 30

■ ECONOMY

Overview: has one of the highest standards of living of islands in the region; the tourist industry and traditional sugar cane cultivation are main parts of the economy; manufacturing and tourism have become increasingly important in recent years
GDP: US$2.9 billion, per capita US$11,200; real growth rate 4.4% (1998 est.)
Inflation: 2.44% (year-end 2000)
Industries: accounts for 15.6% of GDP; tourism, sugar, light manufacturing, component assembly for export
Labour Force: 136,000 (1998 est.); 39.9% community, social and business services, 15.2% trade and tourism, 10.5% manufacturing-
Unemployment: 12.3% (year-end 1998)
Agriculture: accounts for 4.9% of GDP; major cash crop is sugar cane; other crops—vegetables and cotton; not self-sufficient in food
Natural Resources: crude oil, fishing, natural gas

■ FINANCE/TRADE

Currency: Barbadian dollar ($BDS) = 100 cents
International Reserves Excluding Gold: US$446 million (Nov. 2000)
Gold Reserves: none (Nov. 2000)
Budget: revenues US$725.5 million; expenditures US$750.6 million, including capital expenditures of US$126.3 million (1997–98 est.)
Defence Expenditures: n.a.
Education Expenditures: n.a.
External Debt: US$589 million (1999)
Exports: US$214 million (2000); commodities: sugar and molasses, electrical components, clothing, rum, machinery and transport equipment; partners: US 30%, CARICOM, UK, Puerto Rico, Canada
Imports: US$1.009 billion (2000); commodities: foodstuffs, consumer durables, raw materials, crude oil; partners: US 34%, CARICOM, Japan, UK, Canada

■ COMMUNICATIONS

Daily Newspapers: 2
Televisions: 277/1,000 inhabitants (1997 est.)
Radios: 863/1,000 inhabitants (1997 est.)
Telephones: 427 lines/1,000 inhabitants (1999)

■ TRANSPORTATION

Motor Vehicles: 48,500; 45,000 passenger cars (1997 est.)
Roads: 1,600 km; 1,582 km paved
Railway: none
Air Traffic: n.a.
Airports: 1, with a paved runway (1999 est.)

Canadian Embassy: The Canadian High Commission, Bishop's Court Hill, St. Michael, Barbados; mailing address: P.O. Box 404, Bridgetown, Barbados. Tel: (246) 429-3550. Fax: (246) 429-3780. Email: bdgtn@dfait-maeci.gc.ca
Embassy in Canada: High Commission for Barbados, 130 Albert St, Ste 1204, Ottawa ON K1P 5G4. Tel: (613) 236-9517. Fax: (613) 230-4362. Email: ottawa@foreign.gov.bb

Belarus

Long-Form Name: Republic of Belarus
Capital: Minsk

■ GEOGRAPHY

Area: 207,600 sq. km
Coastline: none; landlocked
Climate: mild and moist, transitional between continental and maritime
Environment: southern region is badly contaminated with nuclear fallout from 1986 Chernobyl reactor accident; pesticide use results in extensive soil pollution
Terrain: land of forests, lakes, rivers, and marshes; soil poor, sandy, marshy
Land Use: 29% arable, 1% permanent crops and forest, 34% forests and woodland, 15% meadows and pastures, 21% other; includes 1,000 sq. km irrigated
Location: W Asia, bordering on Poland

■ PEOPLE

Population: 10,366,719 (July 2000 est.)
Nationality: Belarusian
Age Structure: 0-14 yrs: 19%; 15-64: 68%; 65+: 13% (2000 est.)
Population Growth Rate: -0.17% (2000est.)
Net Migration: 3.01 migrants/1,000 population (2000 est.)
Ethnic Groups: 77.9% Byelorussian, 13.2% Russian, 4.1% Polish, 2.9% Ukrainian, 1.9% other
Languages: Byelorussian, Russian
Religions: predominantly Roman Catholic and Eastern Orthodox
Birth Rate: 9.27/1,000 population (2000 est.)
Death Rate: 13.96/1,000 population (2000 est.)
Infant Mortality: 14.63deaths/1,000 live births (2000 est.)
Life Expectancy at Birth: 61.83 years male, 74.48 years female (2000 est.)
Total Fertility Rate: 1.25 children born/woman (2000 est.)
Literacy: 99.5% (1998)

■ GOVERNMENT

Leader(s): Pres. Aleksandr Lukashenko, Prime Min. Vladimir Yermoshin
Government Type: republic
Administrative Divisions: 6 regions (voblastsi, sing. — voblasts), 1 municipality (harady, sing. — horad)
Nationhood: Aug. 25, 1991 (from former Soviet Union)
National Holiday: Independence Day, July 3

■ ECONOMY

Overview: strong emphasis on mining and agriculture, with growing manufacturing (heavy machinery, chemicals, fertilizer) and services sector; Belarus is an important transport link for the former Soviet states
GDP: US$55.2 billion, per capita US$5,300; real growth rate 1.5% (1999 est.)
Inflation: 168.62% (year-end 2000)
Industries: accounts for 28% of GDP; machinery, tools, refineries, fertilizer production; about 50% of labour force is employed in industry
Labour Force: 5 million (1999); 27.4% manufacturing, 22.4% community, social and business services, 21.9% agriculture
Unemployment: 2.3%, but large numbers of underemployed (Dec. 1998)
Agriculture: accounts for almost 23% of GDP; potatoes, flax, rye, oats, barley, wheat, cattle breeding, milk, vegetables, pigs, potatoes, peat, forest resources
Natural Resources: oil and natural gas, potassium, forest land, peat deposits

■ FINANCE/TRADE

Currency: Belarusian ruble
International Reserves Excluding Gold: US$350 million Dec. 2000)
Gold Reserves: n.a.
Budget: revenues US$4 billion; expenditures US$4.1 billion, including capital expenditures US$180 million (1997 est.)
Defence Expenditures: 4.07% of total govt. expenditures (1999)
Education Expenditures: 3.44% of total govt. expenditures (1999)
External Debt: US$1.136 billion (1999)
Exports: US$6.713 billion (2000); agricultural and transport machinery, computers, refrigerators, foodstuffs; partners: Russia, Ukraine, Poland, Germany
Imports: US$7.807 billion (2000); commodities: fuels, raw materials, textiles, sugar; partners: Russia, Ukraine, Poland, Germany

■ COMMUNICATIONS

Daily Newspapers: 8
Televisions: 314/1,000 inhabitants (1998)
Radios: 296/1,000 inhabitants (1997)
Telephones: 251 lines/1,000 inhabitants (1999)

■ TRANSPORTATION

Motor Vehicles: n.a.
Roads: 63,355 km; 60,567 km hard-surfaced
Railway: 5,563 km (does not include industrial lines)
Air Traffic: 231,000 passengers carried (1997)

Airports: 118; 36 have paved runways (1998 est.)

Canadian Embassy: The Canadian Embassy to Belarus, c/o The Canadian Embassy, Reform Plaza, 10th Floor, Aleje Jerozolimskie 123, 02-017 Warsaw, Poland. Tel: (011-48-22) 584-3100. Fax: (011-48-22) 584-3190

Embassy in Canada: Embassy of the Republic of Belarus, 130 Albert St, Ste 600, Ottawa ON K1P 5G4. Tel: (613) 233-9994. Fax: (613) 233-8500. Email: belamb@igs.net

Belgium

Long-Form Name: Kingdom of Belgium
Capital: Brussels

■ GEOGRAPHY

Area: 30,510 sq. km
Coastline: 66 km
Climate: temperate; mild winters, cool summers; rainy, humid, cloudy
Environment: air and water pollution; acid rain
Terrain: flat coastal plains in northwest central rolling hills, rugged mountains of Ardennes Forest in southeast
Land Use: 24% arable land; 1% permanent crops; 20% meadows and pastures; 21% forest and woodland; 34% other; includes negligible irrigated
Location: NW Europe, bordering on North Sea

■ PEOPLE

Population: 10,241,506 (July 2000 est.)
Nationality: Belgian
Age Structure: 0-14 yrs: 18%; 15-64: 66%; 65+: 16% (2000 est.)
Population Growth Rate: 0.18% (2000 est.)
Net Migration: 0.98 migrants/1,000 population (2000 est.)
Ethnic Groups: 58% Flemish, 31% Walloon, 11% mixed or other
Languages: Dutch or Flemish spoken in north (Flanders), French in south (Wallonia), both languages official; small English-speaking minority in east, German 1%
Religions: 75% Roman Catholic, remainder Protestant or other
Birth Rate: 10.91/1,000 population (2000 est.)
Death Rate: 10.13/1,000 population (2000 est.)
Infant Mortality: 4.76 deaths/1,000 live births (2000 est.)
Life Expectancy at Birth: 74.47 years male, 81.30 years female (2000 est.)
Total Fertility Rate: 1.61 children born/woman (2000 est.)
Literacy: 99% (1998)

■ GOVERNMENT

Leader(s): Head of State: King Albert II. Prime Min. Guy Verhofstadt
Government Type: federal parliamentary democracy under a constitutional monarch
Administrative Divisions: 10 provinces
Nationhood: Oct. 4, 1830 (from the Netherlands)
National Holiday: National Day, July 21

■ ECONOMY

Overview: a small, private enterprise—based economy possessing few natural resources, it is therefore highly vulnerable to the state of world markets; burgeoning public debt offsets economic growth
GDP: US$243.4 billion, per capita US$23,900; real growth rate 1.8% (1999 est.)
Inflation: 2.55% (year-end 2000)
Industries: accounts for 27% of GDP; engineering and metal products, processed food and beverages, chemicals, basic metals, textiles, glass, petroleum, coal
Labour Force: 4 million (1999); 32.9% community, social and business services, 23.1% manufacturing, 17.5% trade and tourism
Unemployment: 10.7% (Jan. 2001)
Agriculture: accounts for 1.4% of GDP; emphasis on livestock production—beef, veal, pork, milk; major crops are sugar beets, fresh vegetables, fruit, grain and tobacco; net importer of farm products
Natural Resources: coal, natural gas

■ FINANCE/TRADE

Currency: Belgian franc (BF) = 100 centimes; Euro (EUR) as of March 1, 2002
International Reserves Excluding Gold: US$7.972 billion (Jan. 2001)
Gold Reserves: US$8.298 million fine troy ounces (Jan. 2001)
Budget: revenues US$116.5 billion, expenditures US$119 billion, including capital expenditures of US$10.7 billion (1998 est.)
Defence Expenditures: 3.2% of central government expenditure (1997)
Education Expenditures: 3.1% of central government expenditure (1997)
External Debt: US$28.3 billion (1999 est.)
Exports: US$180.102 billion (2000) Belgium-Luxembourg Economic Union; commodities: iron and steel, transportation equipment, tractors, diamonds, petroleum products; partners: European Community 74%, US 5%, Communist countries 2%
Imports: US$166.452 billion (2000) Belgium-Luxembourg Economic Union; commodities: fuels, grains, chemicals, foodstuffs; partners: European Community 72%, US 5%, oil-

exporting, less-developed countries 4%, Communist countries 3%

■ COMMUNICATIONS

Daily Newspapers: 30
Televisions: 510/1,000 inhabitants (1998)
Radios: 793/1,000 inhabitants (1997)
Telephones: 502 lines/1,000 inhabitants (1999)

■ TRANSPORTATION

Motor Vehicles: 5,000,000; 4,450,000 passenger cars (1997 est.)
Roads: 145,850 km, 117,701 km paved
Railway: 3,437 km
Air Traffic: 6,872,000 passengers carried (1997)
Airports: 42; 24 have paved runways (1999 est.)
Canadian Embassy: The Canadian Embassy, 2, Avenue de Tervuren, 1040 Brussels, Belgium. Tel: (011-32-2) 741-0611. Fax: (011-32-2) 741-0643. Email: bru@dfait-maeci.gc.ca
Embassy in Canada: Embassy of the Kingdom of Belgium, 80 Elgin St, 4th Fl, Ottawa ON K1P 1B7. Tel: (613) 236-7267. Fax: (613) 236-7882. Email: ambabel.ottawa@diplobel.org

Belize

Long-Form Name: Belize
Capital: Belmopan

■ GEOGRAPHY

Area: 22,960 sq. km
Coastline: 386 km
Climate: tropical; very hot and humid; rainy season (May to Feb.)
Environment: frequent devastating hurricanes (Sept. to Dec.) and coastal flooding, especially in south; deforestation; industrial and agricultural water pollution
Terrain: flat, swampy coastal plain; low mountains in south
Land Use: 2% arable land; 1% permanent crops; 2% meadows and pastures; 92% forest and woodland; 3% other, includes 20 sq. km irrigated
Location: Central (Latin) America, just S of Mexico bordering on Caribbean Sea

■ PEOPLE

Population: 249,183 (July 2000 est.)
Nationality: Belizean
Age Structure: 0-14 yrs: 43%; 15-64: 54%; 65+: 3% (2000 est.)
Population Growth Rate: 2.75% (2000 est.)
Net Migration: -0.0 migrants/1,000 population (2000 est.)
Ethnic Groups: 31% Creole, 44.1% Mestizo, 9.2% Maya, 6.2% Garifuna, 9.5% other

Languages: English (official), Spanish, Maya, Garifuna (Carib)
Religions: 62% Roman Catholic, 30% Protestant sects, 2% none, 6% other
Birth Rate: 32.29/1,000 population (2000 est.)
Death Rate: 4.81/1,000 population (2000 est.)
Infant Mortality: 25.97 deaths/1,000 live births (2000 est.)
Life Expectancy at Birth: 68.66 years male, 73.28 years female (2000 est.)
Total Fertility Rate: 4.14 children born/woman (2000 est.)
Literacy: 75% (1997)

■ GOVERNMENT

Leader(s): Head of State: Queen Elizabeth II/Gov. Gen. Colville Young. Prime Min. Said Musa
Government Type: parliamentary democracy
Administrative Divisions: 6 districts
Nationhood: Sept. 21, 1981 (from UK; Belize formerly known as British Honduras)
National Holiday: Independence Day, Sept. 21

■ ECONOMY

Overview: economy primarily based on agriculture and merchandising; sugar is the main crop; tourism and construction are becoming increasingly important
GDP: US$740 million, per capita US$3,100; real growth rate 4% (1999 est.)
Inflation: 0.61% (year-end 2000)
Industries: accounts for 22% of GDP; sugar refining, clothing, timber and forest products, furniture, rum, soap, beverages, cigarettes, tourism, garment production, citrus concentrates
Labour Force: 71,000 (1997 est.); 30% agriculture, 16% services, 15.4% government, 11.2% commerce, 27.4% other
Unemployment: 14.3% (1998 est.)
Agriculture: accounts for 22% of GDP (including fish and forestry) and 75% of export earnings; commercial crops include sugar cane, bananas, cocoa, citrus fruit; expanding output of lumber and cultured shrimp; net importer of basic foods
Natural Resources: arable land potential, timber, fish, hydroelectric power

■ FINANCE/TRADE

Currency: Belizean dollar ($BZ) = 100 cents
International Reserves Excluding Gold: US$116 million (Dec. 2000)
Gold Reserves: n.a.
Budget: revenues US$140 million; expenditures US$142 million, including capital expenditures of US$n.a. (1997-98 est.)
Defence Expenditures: 2% of GDP (1997-98)
Education Expenditures: n.a.

External Debt: US$351 million (1999)
Exports: US$251 million (2000); commodities: sugar, clothing, seafood, molasses, citrus, wood and wood products; partners: US 47%, UK, Trinidad and Tobago, Canada
Imports: US$404 million (2000); commodities: machinery and transportation equipment, food, manufactured goods, fuels, chemicals, pharmaceuticals; partners: US 55%, UK, Netherlands Antilles, Mexico

■ COMMUNICATIONS

Daily Newspapers: 0
Televisions: 165/1,000 inhabitants (1997 est.)
Radios: 533/1,000 inhabitants (1997 est.)
Telephones: 156 lines/1,000 inhabitants (1999)

■ TRANSPORTATION

Motor Vehicles: 5,600; 2,400 passenger cars (1997 est.)
Roads: 2,872 km; 488 km paved
Railway: none
Air Traffic: n.a.
Airports: 44; 3 have paved runways (1999 est.)
Canadian Embassy: Consulate of Canada, 85 North Front St, P.O. Box 610, Belize City, Belize. Tel: (011-501-2) 31-060. Fax: (011-501-2) 30-060. Email: cdcon.bze@btl.net
Embassy in Canada: c/o High Commission for Belize, 2535 Massachusetts Ave NW, Washington DC 20008, USA. Tel: (202) 332-9636. Fax: (202) 332-6888. Email: belize@oas.org

Benin

Long-Form Name: Republic of Benin
Capital: Porto Novo (official); Cotonou (de facto)

■ GEOGRAPHY

Area: 112,620 sq. km
Coastline: 121 km
Climate: tropical; hot, humid in south; semi-arid in north
Environment: hot, dry, dusty harmattan wind may affect north in winter; deforestation; desertification; recent droughts have severely affected marginal agriculture in north; insufficient safe drinking water
Terrain: mostly flat to undulating plain; some hills and low mountains
Land Use: 13% arable land; 4% permanent crops; 4% meadows and pastures; 31% forest and woodland; 48% other, includes 100 sq. km irrigated
Location: WC Africa, bordering on South Atlantic Ocean

■ PEOPLE

Population: 6,395,919 (July 2000 est.)
Nationality: Beninese (sing. & pl.)
Age Structure: 0-14 yrs: 47%; 15-64: 50%; 65+: 3% (2000 est.)
Population Growth Rate: 3.03% (2000 est.)
Net Migration: 0 migrants/1,000 population (2000 est.)
Ethnic Groups: 99% African (42 ethnic groups, most important being Fon, Adja, Yoruba, Bariba); 5,500 Europeans
Languages: French (official); also Fon, Yoruba, Fulami, Bariba
Religions: majority Animist, 15% Islam, 15% Christian
Birth Rate: 44.81/1,000 population (2000 est.)
Death Rate: 14.51/1,000 population (2000 est.)
Infant Mortality: 90.84 deaths/1,000 live births (2000 est.)
Life Expectancy at Birth: 49.24 years male, 51.16 years female (2000 est.)
Total Fertility Rate: 6.32 children born/woman (2000 est.)
Literacy: 38.5% (1999)

■ GOVERNMENT

Leader(s): Pres. Mathieu Kerekou
Government Type: republic under multi-party democratic rule
Administrative Divisions: 6 provinces
Nationhood: Aug. 1, 1960 (from France; Benin formerly known as Dahomey)
National Holiday: National Day, Aug. 1

■ ECONOMY

Overview: one of the least developed countries in the world; limited natural resources and an underdeveloped infrastructure characterize the economy; agricultural products are a major export
GDP: US$8.1 billion, per capita US$1,300; real growth rate 5% (1999 est.)
Inflation: 4.17% (year-end 2000)
Industries: accounts for 14% of GDP; palm oil and palm kernel oil processing, textiles, beverages, petroleum, cigarettes, construction materials, foodstuffs
Labour Force: 3.1 million (1999); 70.2% agriculture, 23.1% services, 6.6% industry
Unemployment: n.a.
Agriculture: accounts for 34% of GDP; small farms produce 90% of agricultural output; production is dominated by food crops—corn, sorghum, cassava, beans and rice; cash crops include cotton, palm oil and peanuts; poultry and livestock output has not kept up with consumption
Natural Resources: small offshore oil deposits, limestone, marble, timber

■ FINANCE/TRADE

Currency: Communauté financière africaine franc (CFAF) = 100 centimes
International Reserves Excluding Gold: US$431 million (Nov. 2000)
Gold Reserves: US$0.011 million fine troy ounces (Aug. 2000)
Budget: n.a.
Defence Expenditures: 6.8% of central government expenditure (1997)
Education Expenditures: 3.2% of central government expenditure (1997)
External Debt: US$1.686 billion (1999)
Exports: US$203 million (2000); partners: Brazil 18%, Portugal 11%, Morocco 10%, Libya 6%, also France
Imports: US$682 million (2000); partners: France 21%, UK 9%, Thailand 9%, Hong Kong 8%, also China

■ COMMUNICATIONS

Daily Newspapers: 1
Televisions: 10/1,000 inhabitants (1998)
Radios: 108/1,000 inhabitants (1997)
Telephones: 7.0 lines/1,000 inhabitants (1999)

■ TRANSPORTATION

Motor Vehicles: 56,000; 36,400 passenger cars (1997 est.)
Roads: 6,787 km; 1,357 km paved
Railway: 578 km
Air Traffic: 86,000 passengers carried (1997)
Airports: 5; 2 have paved runways (1999 est.)

Canadian Embassy: c/o The Canadian Embassy, P.O. Box 4104, Abidjan 01, CÔte d'Ivoire. Tel: (011-225) 20-30-07-00. Fax: (011-225) 20-30-07-20. Email: abdjn@dfait-maeci.gc.ca
Embassy in Canada: Embassy of the Republic of Benin, 58 Glebe Ave, Ottawa ON K1S 2C3. Tel: (613) 233-4429. Fax: (613) 233-8952. Email: ambaben2@on.aira.com

Bermuda

Long-Form Name: Commonwealth of Bermuda
Capital: Hamilton

■ GEOGRAPHY

Area: 58.8 sq. km
Climate: subtropical; mild, humid; gales, strong winds common in winter
Land Use: 6% arable land; 0% permanent crops; 0% meadows and pastures; 0% forest and woodland; 94% other
Location: North Atlantic Ocean, E of United States

■ PEOPLE

Population: 62,997 (July 2000 est.)
Nationality: Bermudian
Ethnic Groups: 58% black, 36% white and 6% other
Languages: English

■ GOVERNMENT

Colony Territory of: Dependent Territory of the United Kingdom
Leader(s): Head of State: Queen Elizabeth II/ Gov. Thorold Masefield. Prem. Jennifer Smith
Government Type: dependent territory of the UK, with internal self-government
National Holiday: Bermuda Day, May 24

■ ECONOMY

Overview: a successful tourist industry accounts for its high per capita income; the industrial sector is small, and agriculture is limited by the lack of suitable land; 80% of food must be imported

■ FINANCE/TRADE

Currency: Bermudian dollar ($Ber) = 100 cents

Canadian Embassy: The Canadian Commission to Bermuda, c/o The Canadian Consulate General, 1251 Avenue of the Americas, New York NY, 10020-1175, USA. Tel: (212) 596-1628. Fax: (212) 596-1790. Email: cngny@dfait-maeci.gc.ca
Representative to Canada: c/o British High Commission, 80 Elgin St, Ottawa ON K1P 5K7. Tel: (613) 237-1530. Fax: (613) 237-7980. Email should be sent using the appropriate format at the British High Commission's website at http://www.britain-in-canada.org

Bhutan

Long-Form Name: Kingdom of Bhutan
Capital: Thimphu

■ GEOGRAPHY

Area: 47,000 sq. km
Coastline: none: landlocked
Climate: varies; tropical in southern plains; cool winters and hot summers in central valleys; severe winters and cool summers in Himalayas
Environment: violent storms coming from the Himalayas were the source of the country's name, which means Land of the Thunder Dragon; soil erosion and limited access to water are ongoing problems
Terrain: mostly mountainous with some fertile valleys and savanna

Land Use: 2% arable land; negligible permanent crops; 6% meadows and pastures; 66% forest and woodland; 26% other; includes 340 sq. km irrigated
Location: S Asia

■ PEOPLE

Population: 2,005,222 (July 2000 est.)
Nationality: Bhutanese (sing. & pl.)
Age Structure: 0-14 yrs: 40%; 15-64: 56%; 65+: 4% (2000 est.)
Population Growth Rate: 2.19% (2000 est.)
Net Migration: 0 migrants/1,000 population (2000 est.)
Ethnic Groups: 50% Bhote, 35% ethnic Nepalese, 15% indigenous or migrant tribes
Languages: Bhotes speak various Tibetan dialects—the most widely spoken dialect is Dzongkha (official); Nepalese speak various Nepalese dialects
Religions: 75% Mahayana Buddhism (state religion), Hinduism (25%, mainly ethnic Nepalese)
Birth Rate: 36.22/1,000 population (2000 est.)
Death Rate: 14.32/1,000 population (2000 est.)
Infant Mortality: 110.99 deaths/1,000 live births (2000 est.)
Life Expectancy at Birth: 52.79 years male, 51.99 years female (2000 est.)
Total Fertility Rate: 5.13 children born/woman (2000 est.)
Literacy: 44.2% (1997 est.)

■ GOVERNMENT

Leader(s): King Jigme Singye Wangchuk
Government Type: monarchy; special treaty relationship with India
Administrative Divisions: 18 districts (dzongkhag, sing. & pl.)
Nationhood: Aug. 8, 1949 (from India)
National Holiday: National Day, Dec. 17

■ ECONOMY

Overview: agriculture and forestry are the bedrock of the economy; it is poorly developed due to omnipresent rugged topography
GDP: US$2.1 billion, per capita US$1,060; real growth rate 7% (1999 est.)
Inflation: 8.50% (Dec. 1998)
Industries: accounts for 37% of GDP; cement, chemical products, mining, distilling, food processing, handicrafts, wood products, calcium carbide. Industries are small and technologically underdeveloped
Labour Force: exact figures not available; there is a massive lack of skilled labour
Unemployment: n.a.
Agriculture: accounts for 38% of GDP and provides a living for 90% of the population; based on subsistence farming and animal husbandry; self-sufficient in food except for foodgrains; other production—rice, corn, root crops, citrus fruit, dairy and eggs
Natural Resources: timber, hydroelectricity, gypsum, calcium carbide, tourism potential

■ FINANCE/TRADE

Currency: ngultrum (Nu) = 100 chetrum; Indian currency is also legal tender
International Reserves Excluding Gold: US$282 million (Sept. 2000)
Gold Reserves: n.a.
Budget: exact figures n.a.; the government of India finances almost 60% of Bhutan's expenditures
Defence Expenditures: negligible
Education Expenditures: 16.01% of central govt. expenditure (2000)
External Debt: US$184 million (1999)
Exports: US$118 million (1997) commodities: cardamom, gypsum, timber, handicrafts, cement, fruit, electricity, precious stones, spices; partners: India, Bangladesh
Imports: US$137 million (1997) commodities: fuel and lubricants, grain, machinery and parts, vehicles, fabrics, rice; partners: India, Japan, UK, Germany, US

■ COMMUNICATIONS

Daily Newspapers: 0
Televisions: 5.5/1,000 inhabitants (1997)
Radios: 19/1,000 inhabitants (1997)
Telephones: 18 lines/1,000 inhabitants (1999)

■ TRANSPORTATION

Motor Vehicles: n.a.
Roads: 3,285 km; 1,994 surfaced
Railway: none
Air Traffic: 36,000 passengers carried (1996)
Airports: 2; 1 has paved runway (1999 est.)
Canadian Embassy: The Canadian High Commission, 7/8 Shantipath, Chanakyapuri, New Delhi 110021; mailing address: P.O. Box 5207, Chanakyapur, New Delhi, India. Tel: (011-91-11) 687-6500. Fax: (011-91-11) 687-6579. Email: delhi@dfait-maeci.gc.ca
Embassy in Canada: Consular Representation of Bhutan, 255 Consumers Road, Ste 401, Toronto ON M2J 5B6. Tel: (416) 498-3150. Fax: (416) 498-7296. Email: ecsondra@web.ca

Bolivia

Long-Form Name: Republic of Bolivia
Capital: La Paz (seat of government); Sucre (legal capital and seat of judiciary)

■ GEOGRAPHY

Area: 1,098,580 sq. km
Coastline: none: landlocked
Climate: varies with altitude; humid and tropical to cold and semi-arid
Environment: cold, thin air of high plateau is obstacle to efficient fuel combustion; over-grazing, soil erosion, desertification; deforest-ation, pollution of drinking water
Terrain: Andes Mountains, high plateau, hills, lowland plains in Amazon basin
Land Use: 2% arable land; negligible permanent crops; 24% meadows and pastures; 53% forest and woodland; 21% other; includes 1,750 sq. km irrigated
Location: C South America

■ PEOPLE

Population: 8,152,620 (July 2000 est.)
Nationality: Bolivian
Age Structure: 0-14 yrs: 39.11%; 15-64: 56.42%; 65+: 4.47% (2000 est.)
Population Growth Rate: 1.83% (2000 est.)
Net Migration: -1.47 migrants/1,000 population (2000 est.)
Ethnic Groups: 30% Quechua, 25% Aymara, 30% mixed,15% European
Languages: Spanish, Quechua and Aymara (all official)
Religions: 95% Roman Catholic; 5% Protestant, especially Methodist
Birth Rate: 28.15/1,000 population (2000 est.)
Death Rate: 8.36/1,000 population (2000 est.)
Infant Mortality: 60.44 deaths/1,000 live births (2000 est.)
Life Expectancy at Birth: 61.19 years male, 66.34 years female (2000 est.)
Total Fertility Rate: 3.66 children born/woman (2000 est.)
Literacy: 84.5% (1998)

■ GOVERNMENT

Leader(s): Pres. Jorge Fernando Quiroga Parliamentary and presidential elections scheduled for June 2002
Government Type: republic
Administrative Divisions: 9 departments (departmentos, sing. —departmento)
Nationhood: Aug. 6, 1825 (from Spain)
National Holiday: Independence Day, Aug. 6

■ ECONOMY

Overview: a poor economy vulnerable to price fluctuations for its small number of exports; market-oriented economic reforms and tighter fiscal discipline are leading to generally improving economic conditions
GDP: US$24.2 billion, per capita US$3,000; real growth rate 2% (1999 est.)

Inflation: 4.60% (year-end 2000)
Industries: accounts for 35.5% of GDP; mining, smelting, petroleum, food and beverage, tobacco, handicrafts, clothing; illicit drug industry reportedly produces the largest revenues
Labour Force: 3 million (1999); 29.1% trade and tourism, 26.2% community, social and business services, 19.4% manufacturing
Unemployment: 11.4% (1997); with extensive underemployment
Agriculture: accounts for about 16.6% of GDP (including forestry and fisheries); principal commodities—coffee, coca, cotton, corn, sugar cane, rice, potatoes, timber; self-sufficient in food
Natural Resources: tin, natural gas, crude oil, zinc, tungsten, antimony, silver, iron ore, lead, gold, timber, hydroelectric power

■ FINANCE/TRADE

Currency: Boliviano ($b) = 100 centavos
International Reserves Excluding Gold: US$617 million (Jan. 2001)
Gold Reserves: US$0.939 million fine troy ounces (Jan. 2001)
Budget: revenues US$2.7 billion; expenditures US$2.7 billion (1998)
Defence Expenditures: 7.68% of total govt. expenditure (1999)
Education Expenditures: 20.42% of govt. expenditure (1999)
External Debt: US$6.157 billion (1999)
Exports: US$1.158 billion (2000); commodities: metals 45%, natural gas 32%, coffee, soyabeans, sugar, cotton, timber; partners: Argentina, UK, US
Imports: US$1.849 billion (2000); commodities: food, petroleum, consumer goods, capital goods; partners: US, Brazil, Japan, Argentina

■ COMMUNICATIONS

Daily Newspapers: 18
Televisions: 116/1,000 inhabitants (1998)
Radios: 675/1,000 inhabitants (1997)
Telephones: 62 lines/1,000 inhabitants (1999)

■ TRANSPORTATION

Motor Vehicles: 433,000; 200,000 passenger cars (1997 est.)
Roads: 52,216 km; 2,872 km paved
Railway: 3,691 km
Air Traffic: 2,251,000 passengers carried (1997)
Airports: 1,109 airfields; 13 have paved runways (1999 est.)

Canadian Embassy: The Office of Canadian Cooperation, Avenida 20 de Octubre, 2475

Plaza Avaroa Sopacachi, La Paz; mailing address: Casilla Postal 13032, La Paz, Bolivia. Tel: (011-591-2) 432-838. Fax: (011-591-2) 430-250. Email: lapaz@dfait-maeci.gc.ca
Embassy in Canada: Embassy of the Republic of Bolivia, 130 Albert St, Ste 416, Ottawa ON K1P 5G4. Tel: (613) 236-5730. Fax: (613) 236-8237. Email: n.a.

Bosnia and Herzegovina

Long-Form Name: Republic of Bosnia and Herzegovina
Capital: Sarajevo

■ GEOGRAPHY

Area: 51,129 sq. km
Coastline: 20 km
Climate: hot summers and cold winters; regions with high elevation have short, cool summers and long, severe winters; mild, rainy winters along the coast
Environment: air pollution; scarce water; waste disposal sites limited; subject to frequent destructive earthquakes
Terrain: mountains and valleys
Land Use: 14% arable, 5% permanent crops, 20% meadows and pastures, 39% forests, 22% other; includes 20 sq. km irrigated
Location: SE Europe

■ PEOPLE

Population: 3,835,777 (July 2000 est.)
Nationality: Bosnian, Herzegovinian
Age Structure: 0-14 yrs: 20%; 15-64: 71%; 65+: 9% (2000 est.)
Population Growth Rate: 3.1% (2000 est.)
Net Migration: 25.92 migrants/1,000 population (2000 est.)
Ethnic Groups: 31% Serb, Bosniak 44%, Croat 17%, Yugoslav 5.5%, other 2.5%; Note: Bosniak has replaced Muslim as an ethnic term, partly to avoid confusion with the religious term Muslim, an adherent of Islam.
Languages: Croatian, Serbian, Bosnian
Religions: 40% Muslim, 31% Orthodox, 15% Catholic, 4% Protestant, 10% other
Birth Rate: 12.92/1,000 population (2000 est.)
Death Rate: 7.87/1,000 population (2000 est.)
Infant Mortality: 25.17 deaths/1,000 live births (2000 est.)
Life Expectancy at Birth: 68.78 years male, 74.38 years female (2000 est.)
Total Fertility Rate: 1.71 children born/woman (2000 est.)
Literacy: n.a.

■ GOVERNMENT

Leader(s): Presidential Chairman (Serb) Jozo Krizanovic. Head of Gov't.: Prime Min. Zlatko Lagumdzija. Note: the central govt. is headed by a tripartite presidency with one representative of each of the three major ethnic constituencies
Government Type: in transition to democracy
Administrative Divisions: 2 first-order administrative divisions
Nationhood: Apr. 1992 (from Yugoslavia)
National Holiday: Bilt National Day, Nov. 25

■ ECONOMY

Overview: though farms are almost entirely privately owned, they are small and inefficient, and food must be imported; inter-ethnic warfare has caused sharp decreases in industrial output and soaring unemployment
GDP: US$6.2 billion, per capita US$1,770; real growth rate 5% (1999 est.)
Inflation: n.a.
Industries: accounts for 23% of GDP; steel production, mining (esp. coal, iron ore, lead, zinc), manufacturing (esp. vehicle assembly, textiles, tobacco products, wood furniture), oil refining
Labour Force: 1.026 million (1999); 2% agriculture, 45% industry and mining
Unemployment: 35-40% (1999 est.)
Agriculture: accounts for 19% of GDP; regularly produces less than half the region's food needs; foothills of northern Bosnia support orchards, vineyards, livestock and some wheat and corn; long winters and heavy precipitation reduce agricultural output in mountains; farms are generally not very productive
Natural Resources: coal, iron, bauxite, manganese, timber, copper, lead, zinc, chromium, hydroelectric power

■ FINANCE/TRADE

Currency: convertible marka = 100 convertible pfenniga
International Reserves Excluding Gold: n.a.
Gold Reserves: n.a.
Budget: expenditures US$1.6 billion; revenues and capital expenditures unknown (2000 est.)
Defence Expenditures: 14.1% of central government expenditure (1997)
Education Expenditures: n.a.
External Debt: US$1.962 billion (1999)
Exports: n.a.
Imports: n.a.

■ COMMUNICATIONS

Daily Newspapers: 3
Televisions: 41/1,000 inhabitants (1998)

Radios: 248/1,000 inhabitants (1997)
Telephones: 96 lines/1,000 inhabitants (1999)

■ TRANSPORTATION

Motor Vehicles: n.a.
Roads: 21,846 km; 11,425 km paved
Railway: 1,021 km
Air Traffic: n.a.
Airports: 27; 9 have paved runways (1999 est.)

Canadian Embassy: The Canadian Embassy, Logavina 7, 71000 Sarajevo, Bosnia and Herzegovina. Tel: (011-387-33) 447-900. Fax: (011-387-33) 447-901. Email: sjevo@dfait-maeci.gc.ca
Embassy in Canada: Embassy of Bosnia and Herzogovina, 130 Albert St., Ste 805, Ottawa ON K1P 5G4. Tel: (613) 236-0028. Fax: (613) 236-1139. Email: n.a.

Botswana

Long-Form Name: Republic of Botswana
Capital: Gaborone

■ GEOGRAPHY

Area: 600,370 sq. km
Coastline: none: landlocked
Climate: subtropical to semi-arid; warm winters and hot summers
Environment: overgrazing; desertification; limited resources of fresh water, periodic droughts, sand and dust storms
Terrain: predominantly flat to gently rolling tableland; Kalahari Desert in southwest
Land Use: 1% arable land; 0% permanent crops; 46% meadows and pastures; 47% forest and woodland; 6% other; includes 20 sq. km irrigated
Location: S Africa

■ PEOPLE

Population: 1,576,470 (July 2000 est.)
Nationality: Motswana (sing.), Batswana (pl.)
Age Structure: 0-14 yrs: 41%; 15-64: 55%; 65+: 4% (2000 est.)
Population Growth Rate: 0.76% (2000 est.)
Net Migration: 0 migrants/1,000 population (2000 est.)
Ethnic Groups: 95% Batswana; about 4% Kalanga, Basarwa and Kgalagadi; about 1% white
Languages: English (official), Setswana
Religions: 50% indigenous beliefs, 50% Christian
Birth Rate: 29.63/1,000 population (2000 est.)
Death Rate: 22.08/1,000 population (2000 est.)

Infant Mortality: 61.68 deaths/1,000 live births (2000 est.)
Life Expectancy at Birth: 38.63 years male, 39.93 years female (2000 est.)
Total Fertility Rate: 3.80 children born/woman (2000 est.)
Literacy: 75.5% (1998)

■ GOVERNMENT

Leader(s): Pres. Festus Gontebanye Mogae; V. Pres. Seretse Ian Khama
Government Type: parliamentary republic
Administrative Divisions: 10 districts and 4 town councils
Nationhood: Sept. 30, 1966 (from UK; Botswana formerly known as Bechuanaland)
National Holiday: Independence Day, Sept. 30

■ ECONOMY

Overview: economy based on mining (diamonds) and traditionally, cattle raising and crops; exhibits high unemployment
GDP: US$5.7 billion, per capita US$3,900; real growth rate 6.5% (1999 est.)
Inflation: 8.71% (year-end 2000)
Industries: accounts for 46% of GDP; livestock processing; mining of diamonds, copper, nickel, coal, salt, soda ash, potash; tourism
Labour Force: 1 million (1999); 36.6% community, social and business services; 18% trade and tourism, 11.2% manufacturing; 19,000 are employed in various mines in South Africa
Unemployment: 20-40% (1999 est.)
Agriculture: plagued by erratic rainfall and poor soil; accounts for only 4% of GDP; subsistence farming predominates; cattle raising supports 50% of the population; must import large share of food needs
Natural Resources: diamonds, copper, nickel, salt, soda ash, potash, coal, iron ore, silver, natural gas

■ FINANCE/TRADE

Currency: pula (P) = 100 thebe
International Reserves Excluding Gold: US$6.073 billion (Nov. 2000)
Gold Reserves: n.a.
Budget: n.a.
Defence Expenditures: 1.2% of GDP (1999 - 00)
Education Expenditures: 8.6% of GNP (1997)
External Debt: US$462 million (1999)
Exports: US$2.36 billion (1999 est.); commodities: diamonds 88%, copper and nickel 5%, meat 4%, cattle, animal products; partners: Switzerland, US, UK, other European Community-associated members of Southern African Customs Union

Imports: US$2.05 billion (1999 est.); commodities: foodstuffs, vehicles, textiles, petroleum products; partners: Switzerland

■ COMMUNICATIONS

Daily Newspapers: 1
Televisions: 20/1,000 inhabitants (1998)
Radios: 156/1,000 inhabitants (1997)
Telephones: 77 lines/1,000 inhabitants (1999)

■ TRANSPORTATION

Motor Vehicles: 100,000; 83,000 passenger cars (1997 est.)
Roads: 18,482 km; 4,343 km paved
Railway: 971 km
Air Traffic: 116,000 passengers carried (1997)
Airports: 92; 10 have paved runways (1999 est.)
Canadian Embassy: The Consulate fo Canada, Vision Hire Building, Plot 182, Queen's Road, Gaborone, Botswana; mailing address: P.O. Box 882, Gaborone, Botswana. Tel: (011-267) 30-44-11. Fax: (011-267) 30-44-11. Email: n.a.
Embassy in Canada: c/o High Commission for the Republic of Botswana, 1531-1533 New Hampshire Ave. NW, Washington DC 20036, USA. Tel: (202) 244-4990. Fax: (202) 244-4164. Email: n.a.

Brazil

Long-Form Name: Federative Republic of Brazil
Capital: Brasilia

■ GEOGRAPHY

Area: 8,511,965 sq. km; includes Arquipélago de Fernando de Noronha, Atol das Rocas, Ilha da Trindade, Ilhas Martin Vaz and Penedos de São Pedro e São Paulo
Coastline: 7,491 km
Climate: mostly tropical, but temperate in south
Environment: recurrent droughts in northeast; floods and frost in south; deforestation in Amazon basin; air and water pollution in Rio de Janeiro and São Paulo and several other large cities
Terrain: mostly flat to rolling lowlands in north; some plains, hills, mountains and narrow coastal belt
Land Use: 5% arable land; 1% permanent crops; 22% meadows and pastures; 58% forest and woodland; 14% other; includes 28,000 sq. km irrigated
Location: E South America

■ PEOPLE

Population: 172,860,370 (July 2000 est.)
Nationality: Brazilian
Age Structure: 0-14 yrs: 29%; 15-64: 66%; 65+: 5% (2000 est.)

Population Growth Rate: 0.94% (2000 est.)
Net Migration: -0.03 migrants/1,000 population (2000 est.)
Ethnic Groups: Portuguese, Italian, German, Japanese, black, Amerindian; 55% white, 38% mixed, 6% black, 1% other
Languages: Portuguese (official), Spanish, English, French
Religions: 70% Roman Catholic (nominal)
Birth Rate: 18.84/1,000 population (2000 est.)
Death Rate: 9.37/1,000 population (2000 est.)
Infant Mortality: 38.04 deaths/1,000 live births (2000 est.)
Life Expectancy at Birth: 58.54 years male, 67.56 years female (2000 est.)
Total Fertility Rate: 2.13 children born/woman (2000 est.)
Literacy: 84% (1998)

■ GOVERNMENT

Leader(s): Pres. Fernando Henrique Cardoso, V. Pres. Marco Maciel
Government Type: federative republic
Administrative Divisions: 26 states (estados, sing. — estado) and 1 federal district (distrito federal)
Nationhood: Sept. 7, 1822 (from Portugal)
National Holiday: Independence Day, Sept. 7

■ ECONOMY

Overview: inflation has dropped sharply and sweeping reforms have boosted the economy, but the domestic debt remains burdensome. Brazil's natural resources remain a major, long-term economic strength
GDP: US$1.057 trillion, per capita US$6,150; real growth rate 0.8% (1999 est.)
Inflation: 7.04% (year-end 2000)
Industries: accounts for 36% of GDP; textiles and other consumer goods, shoes, chemicals, cement, lumber, iron ore, steel, motor vehicles and auto parts, metalworking, capital goods, tin
Labour Force: 79 million (1999); 34.9% community, social and business services, 22.8% agriculture, 15.2% industry
Unemployment: 7.5% (1999 est.)
Agriculture: accounts for 14% of GDP; world's largest producer and exporter of coffee and orange juice concentrate and second-largest exporter of soybeans; self-sufficient in food, except for wheat
Natural Resources: iron ore, manganese, bauxite, nickel, uranium, phosphates, tin, hydroelectricity, gold, platinum, crude oil, timber

■ FINANCE/TRADE

Currency: real (CR$) = 100 centavos
International Reserves Excluding Gold: US$35.119 billion (Jan. 2001)

Gold Reserves: US$1.663 million fine troy ounces (Jan. 2001)
Budget: revenues US$151 billion; expenditures US$149 billion, including capital expenditures of US$36 billion (1998)
Defence Expenditures: 1.9% of GDP (1999)
Education Expenditures: 5.1% of GDP (1997)
External Debt: US$244.673 billion (1999)
Exports: US$52.703 billion (2000); commodities: coffee, metallurgical products, foodstuffs, iron ore, automobiles and parts; partners: US 28%, European Community 26%, Latin America 11%, Japan 6%
Imports: US$57.300 billion (2000); commodities: crude oil, capital goods, chemical products, foodstuffs, coal; partners: Middle East and Africa 24%, European Community 22%, US 21%, Latin America 12%, Japan 6%

■ COMMUNICATIONS

Daily Newspapers: 380
Televisions: 316/1,000 inhabitants (1998)
Radios: 444/1,000 inhabitants (1997)
Telephones: 149 lines/1,000 inhabitants (1999)

■ TRANSPORTATION

Motor Vehicles: 16,700,000; 13,100,000 passenger cars (1997 est.)
Roads: 1.98 million km; 184,140 km paved
Railway: 27,882 km
Air Traffic: 24,307,000 passengers carried (1997)
Airports: 3,277 airfields; 541 have paved runways (1999 est.)
Canadian Embassy: Setor de Embaixadas Sul, Avenida das Nacoes, Quadra 803, Lote 16, Brasilia DF, 70410-900; mailing address: Caixa Postal 341, 70359-900 Brasilia DF, Brazil.. Tel: (011-55-61) 321-2171. Fax: (011-55-61) 321-4529. Email: brsla@dfait-maeci.gc.ca
Embassy in Canada: Embassy of the Federative Republic of Brazil, 450 Wilbrod St, Ottawa ON K1N 6M8. Tel: (613) 237-1090. Fax: (613) 237-6144. Email: mailbox@brasembottawa.org

British Indian Ocean Territory

Long-Form Name: British Indian Ocean Territory
Capital: None; Victoria (Seychelles) is administrative headquarters

■ GEOGRAPHY

Area: 60 sq. km
Climate: tropical maritime, hot and humid, moderated by trade winds
Land Use: no arable land; 0% permanent crops, meadows or pastures, 100% other
Location: Indian Ocean, the Chagos Archipelago island group E of Madagascar, S of India

■ PEOPLE

Population: no indigenous inhabitants; US and UK military personnel
Nationality: n.a.
Ethnic Groups: n.a. - no indigenous population
Languages: n.a. - no indigenous population

■ GOVERNMENT

Colony Territory of: Dependent Territory of the United Kingdom
Leader(s): Head of State: Queen Elizabeth II
Government Type: dependency of Great Britain
National Holiday: n.a.

■ ECONOMY

Overview: fishing, coconuts, guano fertilizer; all economic activity takes place on the largest island, Diego Garcia, where joint US–UK defence facilities are located; there are no industrial or agricultural activities on the islands

■ FINANCE/TRADE

Currency: pound sterling (£ or £ stg)

Canadian Embassy: c/o of the Canadian High Commission, Macdonald House, 1 Grosvenor Square, London W1K 4AB, England, UK. Tel: (011-44-20) 7258-6600. Fax: (011-44-20) 7258-6333. Email: Ldn@dfait-maeci.gc.ca
Representative to Canada: c/o British High Commission, 80 Elgin St, Ottawa ON K1P 5K7. Tel: (613) 237-1530. Fax: (613) 237-7980. Email should be sent using the appropriate form at the British High Commission's website at http://www.britain-in-canada.org

British Virgin Islands

Long-Form Name: British Virgin Islands
Capital: Road Town

■ GEOGRAPHY

Area: 150 sq. km; includes the island of Anegada
Climate: subtropical and humid; moderated by trade winds; hurricanes, and tropical storms occur from July to Oct.
Land Use: 20% arable; 7% permanent crops; 33% permanent pastures; 7% forests; 33% other
Location: Caribbean islands, E of Puerto Rico

■ PEOPLE

Population: 19,615 (July 2000 est.)
Nationality: British Virgin Islander

Ethnic Groups: 90% black, 10% white, Asian, and other
Languages: English (official)

■ GOVERNMENT

Colony Territory of: Dependent territory of the UK
Leader(s): Head of State: Queen Elizabeth II
Government Type: dependency of Great Britain
National Holiday: Territory Day, July 1

■ ECONOMY

Overview: one of the most prosperous economies in the Caribbean; highly dependent on tourism

■ FINANCE/TRADE

Currency: US dollar ($) = 100 cents

Canadian Embassy: c/o The Canadian High Commission, Macdonald House, 1 Grosvenor Square, London, W1K 4AB, England, UK. Tel: (011-44-20) 7258-6600. Fax: (011-44-20) 7258-6333. Email: Ldn@dfait-maeci.gc.ca
Representative to Canada: c/o British High Commission, 80 Elgin St, Ottawa ON K1P 5K7. Tel: (613) 237-1530. Fax: (613) 237-7980. Email should be sent using the appropriate form at the British High Commission's website at http://www.britain-in-canada.org

---

Brunei Darussalam

Long-Form Name: Negara Brunei Darussalam
Capital: Bandar Seri Begawan

■ GEOGRAPHY

Area: 5,770 sq. km
Coastline: 161 km
Climate: tropical; hot, humid, rainy
Environment: typhoons, earthquakes and severe floods occasionally occur
Terrain: flat coastal plain rises to mountainous east; hilly lowland in west
Land Use: 1% arable land; 1% permanent crops; 1% meadows and pastures; 85% forest and woodland; 12% other, includes 10 sq. km irrigated
Location: Indonesia (island of Borneo), bordering on South China Sea and Malaysia

■ PEOPLE

Population: 336,376 (July 2000 est.)
Nationality: Bruneian
Age Structure: 0-14 yrs: 31%; 15-64: 66%; 65+: 3% (2000 est.)
Population Growth Rate: 2.17% (2000 est.)
Net Migration: 4.25 migrants/1,000 population (2000 est.)

Ethnic Groups: 62% Malay, 15% Chinese, 6% indigenous, 17% other
Languages: Malay (official), English and Chinese
Religions: Islam (official, mainly Sunni Muslims); majority of Chinese are Buddhist, Confucian or Taoist
Birth Rate: 20.81/1,000 population (2000 est.)
Death Rate: 3.39/1,000 population (2000 est.)
Infant Mortality: 14.84 deaths/1,000 live births (2000 est.)
Life Expectancy at Birth: 71.23 years male, 76.06 years female (2000 est.)
Total Fertility Rate: 2.47 children born/woman (2000 est.)
Literacy: 90.1% (1997)

■ GOVERNMENT

Leader(s): Sultan, Prime Min. and Min. of Defence Sir Hassanal Bolkiah
Government Type: constitutional sultanate
Administrative Divisions: 4 districts (daerah-daerah, sing. —daerah)
Nationhood: Jan. 1, 1984 (from UK)
National Holiday: National Day, Feb. 23

■ ECONOMY

Overview: economy is based on crude oil and natural gas exports and the per capita GDP is one of the highest for underdeveloped nations; almost totally supported by exports of crude oil and natural gas
GDP: US$5.6 billion, per capita US$17,400; real growth rate 2.5% (1999 est.)
Inflation: n.a.
Industries: accounts for 46% of GDP; petroleum, liquefied natural gas, construction
Labour Force: approx. 150,000; 42% production of oil, natural gas and construction; 48% trade, services and other; 4% agriculture, forestry and fishing; 6% other
Unemployment: n.a.
Agriculture: accounts for 5% of GDP; imports about 80% of its food needs; principal crops and livestock include rice, cassava, bananas, buffalo and pigs
Natural Resources: crude oil, natural gas, timber

■ FINANCE/TRADE

Currency: Bruneian dollar ($B) = 100 cents
International Reserves Excluding Gold: n.a.
Gold Reserves: n.a.
Budget: n.a.
Defence Expenditures: 5.1% of GDP (1998)
Education Expenditures: n.a.
External Debt: none
Exports: US$2.04 billion (1998 est.); commodities: crude oil, liquefied natural gas, petroleum products; partners: Japan 55%

Imports: US$1.38 billion (1998 est.); commodities: machinery and transport equipment, manufactured goods, food, beverages, tobacco, consumer goods; partners: Singapore 31%, US 20%, Japan 6%

■ COMMUNICATIONS

Daily Newspapers: 1
Televisions: n.a.
Radios: n.a.
Telephones: 246 lines/1,000 inhabitants (1999)

■ TRANSPORTATION

Motor Vehicles: 166,000; 148,000 passenger cars (1997 est.)
Roads: 1,150 km; 399 km paved
Railway: 13 km private line
Air Traffic: 877,000 passengers carried (1997)
Airports: 2; 1 has paved runway (1999 est.)

Canadian Embassy: The High Commission of Canada, 5th Floor, Jalan McArthur Bldg., Bandar Seri Begawan; mailing address: P.O. Box 2808, Bandar Seri, Begawan B58675, Brunei Darussalam. Tel: (011-673-2) 22-00-43. Fax (011-673-2) 22-00-40. Email: bsbgn@dfait-maeci.gc.ca
Embassy in Canada: High Commission for Brunei, 395 Laurier Ave E, Ottawa ON K1N 6R4. Tel: (613) 234-5656. Fax: (613) 234-4397. Email: n.a.

Bulgaria

Long-Form Name: Republic of Bulgaria
Capital: Sofia

■ GEOGRAPHY

Area: 110,910 sq. km
Coastline: 354 km
Climate: temperate; cold, damp winters; hot, dry summers
Environment: subject to earthquakes, landslides, deforestation, air and water pollution
Terrain: mostly mountains with lowlands in north and south
Land Use: 43% arable land; 2% permanent crops; 14% meadows and pastures; 38% forest and woodland; 3% other, includes 12,370 sq. km irrigated
Location: SE Europe, bordering on Black Sea

■ PEOPLE

Population: 7,796,694 (July 2000 est.)
Nationality: Bulgarian
Age Structure: 0-14 yrs: 16%; 15-64: 68%; 65+: 16% (2000 est.)
Population Growth Rate: -1.16% (2000 est.)

Net Migration: -5.06 migrants/1,000 population (2000 est.)
Ethnic Groups: 83% Bulgarian, 8.5% Turk, 2.6% Gypsy, 2.5% Macedonian, 3.4% Armenian, Russian, Tatar and other
Languages: Bulgarian (official), Turkish; secondary languages closely correspond to ethnic breakdown
Religions: 85% Bulgarian Orthodox, 13% Muslim (practised by Turkish and Pomak minorities), 0.8% Jewish, 0.7% Roman Catholic, 0.5% Protestant, Gregorian-Armenian and other
Birth Rate: 8.06/1,000 population (2000 est.)
Death Rate: 14.63/1,000 population (2000 est.)
Infant Mortality: 15.13 deaths/1,000 live births (2000 est.)
Life Expectancy at Birth: 67.45 years male, 74.56 years female (2000 est.)
Total Fertility Rate: 1.13 children born/woman (2000 est.)
Literacy: 98% (1999)

■ GOVERNMENT

Leader(s): Pres. Petar Stoyanov, Prime Min. Simeon Saxe-Coburg-Gotha
Presidential elections held Nov. 18, 2001
Government Type: emerging parliamentary democracy
Administrative Divisions: 9 provinces (oblasti, sing. —oblast)
Nationhood: Sept. 22, 1908 (from Turkey)
National Holiday: Independence Day, Mar. 3

■ ECONOMY

Overview: heavily in debt with low growth, the economy is also hindered by antiquated industrial plants; continues to adjust to a market economy; the government's structural reform program includes privatization and, where appropriate, liquidation of state-owned enterprises; agricultural policies have been liberalized
GDP: US$34.9 billion, per capita US$4,300; real growth rate 2.5% (1999 est.)
Inflation: 10.39% (year-end 2000)
Industries: accounts for 29% of GDP; food processing, machine building and metal working, electronics, chemicals
Labour Force: 4 million (1999); 33.9% industry, 18% agriculture, 21.9% community, social and business services
Unemployment: 15% (1999 est.)
Agriculture: accounts for 21% of GNP; climate and soil conditions support livestock raising and the growing of various grain crops, oilseeds, vegetables, fruit and tobacco; more than one-third of the arable land devoted to grain; world's

fourth largest tobacco exporter; surplus food producer
Natural Resources: bauxite, copper, lead, zinc, coal, timber, arable land

■ FINANCE/TRADE

Currency: lev (pl. leva) (Lv) = 100 stotinki
International Reserves Excluding Gold: US$3.029 billion (Jan. 2001)
Gold Reserves: US$1.031 million fine troy ounces (Jan. 2001)
Budget: revenues US$4.69 billion; expenditures US$5.06 billion, capital expenditures US$n.a. (1999 est.)
Defence Expenditures: 8.38% of total govt. expenditure (1999)
Education Expenditures: 5.15% of central govt. expenditure (1999)
External Debt: US$9.872 billion (1999)
Exports: US$4.791 billion (2000); commodities: machinery and equipment 60.5%, agricultural products 14.7%, manufactured consumer goods 10.6%, fuels, minerals, raw materials and metals 8.5%, other 5.7%; partners: socialist countries 82.5%, developed countries 6.8%, less developed countries 10.7%
Imports: US$6.481 billion (2000); commodities: fuels, minerals, raw materials 45.2%, machinery and equipment 39.8%, manufactured consumer goods 4.6%, agricultural products 3.8%, other 6.6%; partners: socialist countries 80.5%, developed countries 15.1%, less developed countries 4.4%

■ COMMUNICATIONS

Daily Newspapers: 17
Televisions: 398/1,000 inhabitants (1998)
Radios: 543/1,000 inhabitants (1997)
Telephones: 354 lines/1,000 inhabitants (1999)

■ TRANSPORTATION

Motor Vehicles: 1,990,000; 1,680,000 passenger cars (1997 est.)
Roads: 36,759 km; 33,818 km hard-surfaced
Railway: 4,294 km
Air Traffic: 722,000 passengers carried (1997)
Airports: 216; 129 have paved runways (1999 est.)

Canadian Embassy: c/o The Canadian Embassy, 36 Nicolae Iorga, 71118 Bucharest, Romania; Postal Address: The Canadian Embassy, P.O. Box 117, Post Office No. 22, Bucharest, Romania. Tel (011-40-1) 307-5000. Fax (011-40-1) 307-5010. Email: bucst@dfait-maeci.gc.ca
Embassy in Canada: Embassy of the Republic of Bulgaria, 325 Stewart St, Ottawa ON K1N 6K5.

Tel: (613) 789-3215. Fax: (613) 789-3524. Email: mailmn@storm.ca

---

Burkina Faso

Long-Form Name: Burkina Faso
Capital: Ouagadougou

■ GEOGRAPHY

Area: 274,200 sq. km
Coastline: none: landlocked
Climate: tropical; warm, dry winters; hot, wet summers
Environment: recent droughts and desertification severely affecting marginal agricultural activities, population distribution, economy; overgrazing;
Terrain: mostly flat to dissected, undulating plains; hills in west and southeast
Land Use: 13% arable land; 0% permanent crops; 22% meadows and pastures; 50% forest and woodland; 15% other, includes 200 sq. km irrigated
Location: WC Africa

■ PEOPLE

Population: 11,946,065 (July 2000 est.)
Nationality: Burkinabe (sing. & pl.)
Age Structure: 0-14 yrs: 48%; 15-64: 49%; 65+: 3% (2000 est.)
Population Growth Rate: 2.71% (2000 est.)
Net Migration: -1.1 migrants/1,000 population (2000 est.)
Ethnic Groups: more than 50 tribes; principal tribe is Mossi (over 40% of pop.); other important groups are Gurunsi, Senufo, Lobi, Bobo, Mande and Fulani
Languages: French (official); tribal languages belong to Sudanic family, spoken by 90% of population
Religions: 40% indigenous beliefs, about 50% Muslim, 10% Christian (mainly Roman Catholic)
Birth Rate: 45.26/1,000 population (2000 est.)
Death Rate: 17.04/1,000 population (2000 est.)
Infant Mortality: 108.53 deaths/1,000 live births (2000 est.)
Life Expectancy at Birth: 46.29 years male, 47.18 years female (2000 est.)
Total Fertility Rate: 6.44 children born/woman (2000 est.)
Literacy: 22.5% (1998)

■ GOVERNMENT

Leader(s): Head of State, Head of Government & Chairman: Capt. Blaise Compaoré, Prime Min. Paramango Ernest Yonli
Government Type: parliamentary democracy

Administrative Divisions: 30 provinces
Nationhood: Aug. 5, 1960 (from France; Burkina Faso formerly known as Upper Volta)
National Holiday: Anniversary of the Revolution, Aug. 4

■ ECONOMY

Overview: a poor economy with high population density and few natural resources, it relies heavily on subsistence agriculture; economic development is hindered by a poor communications network; agriculture provides approximately one-third of national income
GDP: US$12.4 billion, per capita US$1,100; real growth rate 5.5% (1999 est.)
Inflation: -0.30% (year-end 2000)
Industries: accounts for 20% of GDP; agricultural processing plants; brewery, cement and brick plants; soap, cigarettes, textiles, gold mining and extraction; a few other small consumer goods enterprises
Labour Force: 5 million (1999); 86.6% agriculture, 4.3% industry, 9.1% services; 20% of male labour force migrates annually to neighbouring countries for seasonal employment
Unemployment: n.a.
Agriculture: accounts for 36% of GDP; cash crops—peanuts, shea nuts, sesame, cotton; food crops—sorghum, millet, corn, rice; livestock; not self-sufficient in food grains
Natural Resources: manganese, limestone, marble; small deposits of gold, antimony, copper, nickel, bauxite, lead, phosphates, zinc, silver

■ FINANCE/TRADE

Currency: Communauté financière africaine franc (CFAF) = 100 centimes
International Reserves Excluding Gold: US$199 million (Nov. 2000)
Gold Reserves: US$0.011 million fine troy ounces (Aug. 2000)
Budget: n.a.
Defence Expenditures: 12.3% of central government expenditure (1997)
Education Expenditures: 1.5% of GNP (1997)
External Debt: US$1.518 billion (1999)
Exports: US$354 million (2000); commodities: oilseeds, cotton, live animals, gold; partners: European Community 42%, Taiwan 17%, Ivory Coast 15%
Imports: US$668 million (2000); commodities: grain, dairy products, petroleum, machinery; partners: European Community 37%, Africa 31%, US 15%

■ COMMUNICATIONS

Daily Newspapers: 4
Televisions: 9/1,000 inhabitants (1998)

Radios: 33/1,000 inhabitants (1997)
Telephones: 4.0 lines/1,000 inhabitants (1999)

■ TRANSPORTATION

Motor Vehicles: 55,000; 35,600 passenger cars (1997 est.)
Roads: 12,506 km; 2,001 km paved
Railway: 622 km
Air Traffic: 97,000 passengers carried (1997)
Airports: 33; 2 have paved runways (1999 est.)
Canadian Embassy: The Canadian Embassy, rue Agostino Neto, Ouagadougou; mailing address: Office of the Canadian Embassy, P.O. Box 548, Ouagadougou 01, Province du Kadiogo, Burkina Faso. Tel: (011-226) 31-18-95. Fax (011-226) 31-19-00. Email: ouaga@dfait-maeci.gc.ca
Embassy in Canada: Embassy of Burkina Faso, 48 Range Rd, Ottawa ON K1N 8J4. Tel: (613) 238-4796. Fax: (613) 238-3812. Email: burkina.faso@sympatico.ca

Burundi

Long-Form Name: Republic of Burundi
Capital: Bujumbura

■ GEOGRAPHY

Area: 27,830 sq. km
Coastline: none: landlocked
Climate: temperate; warm; occasional frost in uplands
Environment: soil exhaustion; soil erosion; deforestation; flooding and landslides are natural hazards
Terrain: mostly rolling to hilly highland; some plains
Land Use: 44% arable land; 9% permanent crops; 36% meadows and pastures; 3% forest and woodland; 8% other, includes 140 sq. km irrigated
Location: EC Africa

■ PEOPLE

Population: 6,054,714 (July 2000 est.)
Nationality: Burundian
Age Structure: 0-14 yrs: 47%; 15-64: 50%; 65+: 3% (2000 est.)
Population Growth Rate: 3.15% (2000 est.)
Net Migration: 7.43 migrants/1,000 population (2000 est.)
Ethnic Groups: Africans: 85% Hutu (Bantu), 14% Tutsi (Hamitic), 1% Twa (Pygmy); non-Africans: 3,000 Europeans, 2,000 South Asians
Languages: Kirundi and French (official); Swahili used commercially
Religions: about 67% Christian (62% Roman Catholic, 5% Protestant), 32% indigenous beliefs, 1% Muslim

Birth Rate: 40.46/1,000 population (2000 est.)
Death Rate: 16.44/1,000 population (2000 est.)
Infant Mortality: 71.50 deaths/1,000 live births (2000 est.)
Life Expectancy at Birth: 45.23 years male, 47.16 years female (2000 est.)
Total Fertility Rate: 6.25 children born/woman (2000 est.)
Literacy: 46%(1998)

■ GOVERNMENT

Leader(s): Pres. Maj. Pierre Buyoya; First V. Pres. Ferderic Bamvuginyumvira; Second V. Pres. Mathias Sinamenye
Government Type: republic
Administrative Divisions: 15 provinces
Nationhood: July 1, 1962 (from UN trusteeship under Belgian administration)
National Holiday: Independence Day, July 1

■ ECONOMY

Overview: economy is heavily dependent on the coffee crop and therefore vulnerable to market conditions; there are only a few basic industries; massive ethnic-based violence has also interfered with economic activity
GDP: US$4.2 billion, per capita US$730; real growth rate -1% (1999 est.)
Inflation: 24.32% (year-end 2000)
Industries: accounts for 17% of GDP; light consumer goods such as blankets, shoes, soap; assembly of imports; public works construction; food processing
Labour Force: 4 million (1999); 39.6% community, social and business services, 14.8% manufacturing
Unemployment: n.a.
Agriculture: accounts for 46% of GDP; 90% of population dependent on subsistence farming; marginally self-sufficient in food production; cash crops—coffee, cotton, tea; food crops—corn, sorghum, sweet potatoes, bananas, manioc; livestock—meat, milk, hides and skins
Natural Resources: nickel, uranium, rare earth oxide, peat, cobalt, copper, platinum (not yet exploited), vanadium, hydroelectric power

■ FINANCE/TRADE

Currency: Burundi franc (FBu) = 100 centimes
International Reserves Excluding Gold: US$25 million (Jan. 2001)
Gold Reserves: US$0.172 million fine troy ounces (Jan. 2001)
Budget: revenues US$125 million, expenditures US$176 million, including capital expenditures of US$n.a. (2000 est.)
Defence Expenditures: 23.35% of central government expenditure (1999 est.)

Education Expenditures: 15.20% of central govt. expenditure (1999)
External Debt: US$1.131 billion (1999)
Exports: US$48 million (2000); commodities: coffee 88%, tea, hides and skins; partners: European Community 83%, US 5%, Asia 2%
Imports: US$135 million (2000); commodities: capital goods 31%, petroleum products 15%, foodstuffs, consumer goods; partners: European Community 57%, Asia 23%, US 3%

■ COMMUNICATIONS

Daily Newspapers: 1
Televisions: 4/1,000 inhabitants (1998)
Radios: 71/1,000 inhabitants (1997)
Telephones: 3 lines/1,000 inhabitants (1999)

■ TRANSPORTATION

Motor Vehicles: 20,000; 8,200 passenger cars (1997 est.)
Roads: 14,480 km; 1,028 km paved
Railway: none
Air Traffic: 9,000 passengers carried (1996)
Airports: 4; 1 has paved runways (1999 est.)

Canadian Embassy: c/o The Canadian High Commission, P.O. Box 30481, Nairobi, Kenya. Tel: (011-254-2) 21-48-04. Fax: (011-254-2) 22-69-87. Email: nrobi@dfait-maeci.gc.ca
Embassy in Canada: Embassy of the Republic of Burundi, 325 Dalhousie St., Suite 815, Ottawa ON K1N 7G2. Tel (613) 789-0414. Fax (613) 789-9537. Email: ambabucanada@infonet.ca

---

Cambodia

Long-Form Name: Kingdom of Cambodia
Capital: Phnom Penh

■ GEOGRAPHY

Area: 181,040 sq. km
Coastline: 443 km
Climate: tropical; rainy, monsoon season (May to Oct.); dry season (Dec. to Mar.); little seasonal temperature variation
Environment: a land of paddies and forests dominated by Mekong River and Tonle Sap; deforestation, monsoons; logging and strip mining are resulting in environmental degradation
Terrain: mostly low, flat plains; mountains in southwest and north
Land Use: 13% arable land; 0% permanent crops; 11% meadows and pastures; 66% forest and woodland; 10% other; includes 920 sq. km irrigated
Location: SE Asia, bordering on the Gulf of Siam

■ PEOPLE

Population: 12,212,306 (July 2000 est.)
Nationality: Cambodian
Age Structure: 0-14 yrs: 42%; 15-64: 55%; 65+: 3% (2000 est.)
Population Growth Rate: 2.27% (2000 est.)
Net Migration: 0 migrants/1,000 population (2000 est.)
Ethnic Groups: 90% Khmer (Cambodian), 5% Vietnamese, 1% Chinese, 4% other minorities
Languages: Khmer (official), French
Religions: 95% Theravada Buddhism, 5% Christianity
Birth Rate: 33.48/1,000 population (2000 est.)
Death Rate: 10.79/1,000 population (2000 est.)
Infant Mortality: 66.82 deaths/1,000 live births (2000 est.)
Life Expectancy at Birth: 54.44 years male, 58.74 years female (2000 est.)
Total Fertility Rate: 4.82 children born/woman (2000 est.)
Literacy: 38.5% (1998)

■ GOVERNMENT

Leader(s): King Norodom Sihanouk, Prime Min. Hun Sen
Government Type: liberal democracy under constitutional monarchy
Administrative Divisions: 20 provinces (khett, sing. & pl.) and 3 municipalities (krong, sing. & pl.)
Nationhood: Nov. 9, 1953 (from France)
National Holiday: Independence Day, Nov. 9

■ ECONOMY

Overview: a desperately poor country; the economy has suffered badly due to internal war; the country has not been able to feed its people; economy remains essentially rural, with 90% of the population dependent mainly on subsistence agriculture
GDP: US$8.2 billion, per capita US$710; real growth rate 4% (1999 est.)
Inflation: -0.79% (year-end 2000)
Industries: accounts for 20% of GDP; rice milling, fishing, wood and wood products, rubber, cement, gem mining
Labour Force: 6 million (1999); 74.4% agriculture, 6.7% industry, 18.9% services
Unemployment: 2.8% (1999 est.)
Agriculture: accounts for 43% of GDP, mainly subsistence farming except for rubber plantations; main crops—rice, rubber, corn; food shortages—rice, meat, vegetables, dairy products, sugar, flour
Natural Resources: timber, gemstones, some iron ore, manganese, phosphates, hydroelectricity potential

■ FINANCE/TRADE

Currency: new riel (KR) = 100 sen
International Reserves Excluding Gold: US$500 million (Jan. 2001)
Gold Reserves: n.a.
Budget: revenues US$327 million, expenditures US$393 million, including capital expenditures of US$n.a. (1999 est.)
Defence Expenditures: 2.4% of GDP (1998)
Education Expenditures: 2.9% of GNP (1997)
External Debt: US$2.262 billion total (1999)
Exports: US$821 million (1999 est.); commodities: timber, garments, rubber, soybeans, sesame; partners: Singapore, Japan, Thailand, Hong Kong, Indonesia, Malaysia, US
Imports: US$1.2 billion (1999 est.); commodities: cigarettes, construction materials, petroleum products, machinery, motor vehicles; partners: Singapore, Vietnam, Japan, Australia, Hong Kong, Indonesia

■ COMMUNICATIONS

Daily Newspapers: 0
Televisions: 123/1,000 inhabitants (1998)
Radios: 127/1,000 inhabitants (1997)
Telephones: 3 lines/1,000 inhabitants (1999)

■ TRANSPORTATION

Motor Vehicles: n.a.
Roads: 35,769 km, but some roads are in serious disrepair; 4,165 km paved
Railway: 603 km, much inoperational since 1973
Air Traffic: n.a.
Airports: 19; 6 have paved runways (1999 est.)
Canadian Embassy: The Canadian Embassy, Villa 9, RV Senei Vinnavaut Oum, Chaktamouk, Daun Penh District, Phnom Penh.. Tel: (011-855-23) 213-470. Fax: (011-855-23) 211-389. Email: pnmpn@dfait-maeci.gc.ca
Embassy in Canada: c/o Embassy of the Kingdom of Cambodia, 866 UN Plaza, Ste. 420, New York, NY 10017, USA. Tel (212) 223-0676. Fax (212) 223-0425. Email: cambodia@un.int

Cameroon

Long-Form Name: Republic of Cameroon
Capital: Yaoundé

■ GEOGRAPHY

Area: 475,440 sq. km
Coastline: 402 km
Climate: varies with terrain from tropical along coast to semi-arid and hot in north
Environment: recent volcanic activity with release of poisonous gases; deforestation;

overgrazing; desertification; diseases transmitted through the water supply are common

Terrain: coastal plain in southwest, dissected plateau in centre, mountains in west, plains in north

Land Use: 13% arable land; 2% permanent crops; 4% meadows and pastures; 78% forest and woodland; 3% other, includes 210 sq. km irrigated

Location: WC Africa, bordering on South Atlantic Ocean

■ PEOPLE

Population: 15,421,937 (July 2000 est.)
Nationality: Cameroonian
Age Structure: 0-14 yrs: 43%; 15-64: 54%; 65+: 3% (2000 est.)
Population Growth Rate: 2.47% (2000 est.)
Net Migration: n.a. migrants/1,000 population (2000 est.)
Ethnic Groups: over 200 tribes of widely differing background; 31% Cameroon Highlanders, 19% Equatorial Bantu, 11% Kirdi, 10% Fulani, 8% Northwestern Bantu, 7% Eastern Nigritic, 13% other African, less than 1% non-African
Languages: English and French (official), 24 major African language groups, including Fang, Bamileke, Duala
Religions: 51% indigenous beliefs, 33% Christian, 16% Muslim
Birth Rate: 36.60/1,000 population (2000 est.)
Death Rate: 11.89/1,000 population (2000 est.)
Infant Mortality: 70.87 deaths/1,000 live births (2000 est.)
Life Expectancy at Birth: 54.01 years male, 55.64 years female (2000 est.)
Total Fertility Rate: 4.88 children born/woman (2000 est.)
Literacy: 73.5% (1998)

■ GOVERNMENT

Leader(s): Pres. Paul Biya, Prime Min. Peter Mafany Musonge
Government Type: unitary republic; multi-party presidential regime
Administrative Divisions: 10 provinces
Nationhood: Jan. 1, 1960 (from UN trusteeship under French administration; Cameroon formerly known as French Cameroon)
National Holiday: National Day, May 20

■ ECONOMY

Overview: an offshore oil industry has boosted the economy but the government is now emphasizing diversification, particularly in agriculture

GDP: US$31.5 billion, per capita US$2,000; real growth rate 5.2% (1999 est.)
Inflation: 5.30% (year-end 1999)
Industries: accounts for 22% of GDP; crude oil products, small aluminum plant, food processing, light consumer goods industries, textiles, sawmills
Labour Force: 6.0 million (1999); 74% agriculture, 4.5% industry, 21.5% services
Unemployment: 30% (1998 est.)
Agriculture: the agriculture and forestry sectors provide employment for the majority of the population, contributing 42% to GDP and providing a high degree of self-sufficiency in staple foods
Natural Resources: crude oil, bauxite, iron ore, timber, hydroelectricity potential

■ FINANCE/TRADE

Currency: Communauté financière africaine franc (CFAF) = 100 centimes
International Reserves Excluding Gold: US$172 million (Nov. 2000)
Gold Reserves: US$0.03 million fine troy ounces (June 1998)
Budget: revenues US$2.23 billion; expenditures US$2.23 billion, including capital expenditures of US$n.a. (1997 est.)
Defence Expenditures: 9.52% of total govt. expenditure (1999)
Education Expenditures: 12.00% of central govt. expenditure (1999)
External Debt: US$9.443 billion (1999)
Exports: US$1.489 billion (2000); commodities: petroleum products 56%, coffee, cocoa, timber, manufacturing; partners: European Community 50%, US 3%
Imports: US$1.361 million (2000); commodities: machines and electrical equipment, transport equipment, chemical products, consumer goods; partners: France 42%, Japan 7%, US 4%

■ COMMUNICATIONS

Daily Newspapers: 2
Televisions: 32/1,000 inhabitants (1998)
Radios: 163/1,000 inhabitants (1997)
Telephones: 6 lines/1,000 inhabitants (1999)

■ TRANSPORTATION

Motor Vehicles: 153,000; 92,000 passenger cars (1997 est.)
Roads: 34,300 km; 4,288 km paved
Railway: 1,104 km
Air Traffic: 279,000 passengers carried (1997)
Airports: 50; 11 have paved runways (1999 est.)

Canadian Embassy: The Canadian High Commission, Immeuble Stamiatades, Place de

l'Hotel de Ville, Yaoundé, Cameroon; mailing address: P.O. Box 572, Douala, Cameroon. Tel: (011-237) 23-23-11. Fax: (011-237) 22-10-90: Email: yunde@dfait-maeci.gc.ca
Embassy in Canada: High Commission for the Republic of Cameroon, 170 Clemow Ave, Ottawa ON K1S 2B4. Tel: (613) 236-1522. Fax: (613) 236-3385. Email: cameroon@comnet.ca

Canada

Long-Form Name: Canada
Capital: Ottawa

■ GEOGRAPHY

Area: 9,976,140 sq. km
Coastline: 243,791 km
Climate: varies from temperate in south to subarctic and arctic in north
Environment: 80% of population concentrated within 160 km of US border; permafrost in north a serious obstacle to development; acid rain and ocean-water pollution resulting from industrial and agricultural activities are an increasing problem
Terrain: mostly plains with mountains in west and lowlands in southeast
Land Use: 5% arable land; negligible permanent crops; 3% meadows and pastures; 54% forest and woodland; 38% other, includes 7,100 sq. km irrigated
Location: N North America, bordering on North Atlantic Ocean, Arctic Ocean, North Pacific Ocean and United States

■ PEOPLE

Population: 31,281,092 (July 2000 est.)
Nationality: Canadian
Age Structure: 0-14 yrs: 19%; 15-64: 68%; 65+: 13% (2000 est.)
Population Growth Rate: 1.02% (2000 est.)
Net Migration: 6.2 migrants/1,000 population (2000 est.)
Ethnic Groups: 28% British, 23% French, 15% other European, 2% Amerindian, 6% Arab, 26% mixed background
Languages: English and French (both official)
Religions: 45% Roman Catholic, 12% United Church, 8% Anglican, 35% other
Birth Rate: 11.41/1,000 population (2000 est.)
Death Rate: 7.39/1,000 population (2000 est.)
Infant Mortality: 5.08 deaths/1,000 live births (2000 est.)
Life Expectancy at Birth: 76.02 years male, 83.00 years female (2000 est.)
Total Fertility Rate: 1.64 children born/woman (2000 est.)
Literacy: 99% (1998)

■ GOVERNMENT

Leader(s): Head of State: Queen Elizabeth II/Gov. Gen. Adrienne Clarkson. Prime Min. Jean Chrétien
Government Type: confederation with parliamentary democracy
Administrative Divisions: 10 provinces, 3 territories
Nationhood: July 1, 1867 (from UK)
National Holiday: Canada Day, July 1

■ ECONOMY

Overview: abundant natural resources, skilled labour force, and high-tech industrialization characterize a market-oriented economy; Canada can anticipate solid economic prospects in the future
GDP: US$722.3 billion, per capita US$23,300; real growth rate 3.6% (1999 est.)
Inflation: 2.75% (year-end 2000)
Industries: accounts for 31% of GDP; processsed and unprocessed minerals, food products, wood and paper products, transportation equipment, chemicals, fish products, petroleum, natural gas
Labour Force: 17 million (1999); 31.8% community, social and business services, 23.5% trade and tourism, 14.5% manufacturing
Unemployment: 7.4% (Feb. 2001)
Agriculture: accounts for 3% of GDP; one of the world's major producers and exporters of grain (wheat and barley); key source of US agricultural imports; large forest resources cover 35% of total land area
Natural Resources: nickel, zinc, copper, gold, lead, molybdenum, potash, silver, fish, timber, wildlife, coal, crude oil, natural gas

■ FINANCE/TRADE

Currency: dollar ($ or $Can) = 100 cents
International Reserves Excluding Gold: US$29.087 billion (Jan. 2001)
Gold Reserves: US$1.184 million fine troy ounces (Jan. 2001)
Budget: revenues US$121.3 billion; expenditures US$112.6 billion, capital expenditures US$1.7 billion (1998)
Defence Expenditures: 1.2% of GDP (1997-98)
Education Expenditures: 6.9% of GNP (1997)
External Debt: n.a.
Exports: US$271.881 billion (2000); commodities: newsprint, wood pulp, timber, grain, crude petroleum, natural gas, ferrous and nonferrous ores, motor vehicles; partners: US, Japan, UK, Germany, other European Community, former USSR countries
Imports: US$242.439 billion (2000); commodities: processed foods, beverages, crude petroleum, chemicals, industrial machinery,

motor vehicles, durable consumer goods, electronic computers; partners: US, Japan, UK, Germany, other European Community, Taiwan, S Korea, Mexico

■ COMMUNICATIONS

Daily Newspapers: 107
Televisions: 715/1,000 inhabitants (1998)
Radios: 1,077/1,000 inhabitants (1997)
Telephones: 655 lines/1,000 inhabitants (1999)

■ TRANSPORTATION

Motor Vehicles: 17,200,000; 13,600,000 passenger cars (1997 est.)
Roads: 901,902 km; 318,371 km paved
Railway: 36,114 km operational
Air Traffic: 23,981,000 passengers carried (1997)
Airports: 1,411; 515 have paved runways (1999 est.)

Canadian Embassy: n.a.
Embassy in Canada: n.a.

Cape Verde

Long-Form Name: Republic of Cape Verde
Capital: Praia

■ GEOGRAPHY

Area: 4,030 sq. km
Coastline: 965 km
Climate: temperate; warm, dry, very erratic summer precipitation
Environment: subject to prolonged droughts; harmattan wind can obscure visibility; volcanically and seismically active; deforestation; desertification; overgrazing and overfishing
Terrain: steep, rugged, rocky, volcanic
Land Use: 11% arable land; negligible permanent crops; 6% meadows and pastures; negligible forest and woodland; 83% other, includes 30 sq. km irrigated
Location: Atlantic Ocean W of Africa

■ PEOPLE

Population: 401,343 (July 2000 est.)
Nationality: Cape Verdean
Age Structure: 0-14 yrs: 44%; 15-64: 50%; 65+: 6% (2000 est.)
Population Growth Rate: 0.98% (2000 est.)
Net Migration: -12.49 migrants/1,000 population (2000 est.)
Ethnic Groups: approx. 71% Creole (mulatto), 28% African, 1% European
Languages: Portuguese and Crioulo, a blend of Portuguese and West African tongues
Religions: Roman Catholicism fused with indigenous beliefs

Birth Rate: 29.67/1,000 population (2000 est.)
Death Rate: 7.38/1,000 population (2000 est.)
Infant Mortality: 54.58 deaths/1,000 live births (2000 est.)
Life Expectancy at Birth: 65.63 years male, 72.29 years female (2000 est.)
Total Fertility Rate: 4.19 children born/woman (2000 est.)
Literacy: 71.0% (1997)

■ GOVERNMENT

Leader(s): Pres. Pedro Pires, Prime Min. Jose Maria Pereira Neves
Government Type: republic
Administrative Divisions: 14 districts (concelhos, sing. —concelho)
Nationhood: July 5, 1975 (from Portugal)
National Holiday: Independence Day, July 5

■ ECONOMY

Overview: a service-oriented economy, which suffers from a poor natural resource base, a high birth rate and a long-term drought
GDP: US$618 million, per capita US$1,500; real growth rate 5% (1999 est.)
Inflation: 7.60% (March 1999)
Industries: accounts for 19% of GDP, fish processing, salt mining, clothing factories, ship repair, construction materials, food and beverage production
Labour Force: n.a.; 52% agriculture (mostly subsistence), 25% services, 23% industry
Unemployment: n.a.
Agriculture: accounts for 13% of GDP; largely subsistence farming; bananas are the only export crop; annual food imports required; growth potential limited by poor soils and limited rainfall. Approximately 90% of food needs must be imported
Natural Resources: salt, basalt rock, pozzolana, limestone, kaolin, fish

■ FINANCE/TRADE

Currency: Cape Verdean escudo (C.V. Esc.) = 100 centavos
International Reserves Excluding Gold: US$29 million (Nov. 2000)
Gold Reserves: n.a.
Budget: revenues US$253.7 million; expenditures US$276 million, including capital expenditures of US$n.a. (1997 est.)
Defence Expenditures: 2.2% of GDP (1997 est.)
Education Expenditures: n.a.
External Debt: US$284 million (1999)
Exports: US$17 million (2000); commodities: fish, bananas, salt; partners: Portugal, Angola, Algeria, Belgium/Luxembourg, Italy
Imports: US$286 million (2000.); commodities:

petroleum, foodstuffs, consumer goods, industrial products; partners: Portugal, Netherlands, Spain, France, US, Germany

■ COMMUNICATIONS

Daily Newspapers: 0
Televisions: 4.9/1,000 inhabitants (1997 est.)
Radios: 181/1,000 inhabitants (1997 est.)
Telephones: 112 lines/1,000 inhabitants (1999)

■ TRANSPORTATION

Motor Vehicles: 18,000; 11,000 passenger cars (1997 est.)
Roads: 1,100 km; 858 km paved
Railway: none
Air Traffic: 237,000 passengers carried (1997)
Airports: 6; all have paved runways (1999 est.)

Canadian Embassy: c/o The Canadian Embassy, P.O. Box 3373, Dakar, Senegal. Tel: (011-221) 823-92-90. Fax: (011-221) 823-87-49. Email: dakar@dfait-maeci.gc.ca
Embassy in Canada: c/o Embassy of the Republic of Cape Verde, 3415 Massachusetts Ave NW, Washington DC 20007, USA. Tel: (202) 965-6820. Fax: (202) 965-1207. Email: n.a.

Cayman Islands

Long-Form Name: Cayman Islands
Capital: George Town (on Grand Cayman Island)

■ GEOGRAPHY

Area: 259 sq. km (three islands: Grand Cayman, Little Cayman, Cayman Brac)
Climate: tropical maritime; warm, rainy summers (May to Oct.); cool season: Nov. to March, hurricane-prone July to Nov.
Land Use: 0% arable, 0% permanent crops; 8% meadows and pastures; 23% forest and woodland; 69% other
Location: Caribbean Sea, S of Cuba

■ PEOPLE

Population: 34,763 (July 2000 est.)
Nationality: Caymanian
Ethnic Groups: 40% mixed, 20% white, 20% black, 20% expatriates of various ethnic groups, various Hispanic strains, descendants of European settlers
Languages: English (official)

■ GOVERNMENT

Colony Territory of: United Kingdom Crown Colony
Leader(s): Head of State: Queen Elizabeth II
Government Type: United Kingdom Crown Colony

National Holiday: Constitution Day (first Monday in July)

■ ECONOMY

Overview: chiefly tourism (70% of GDP and 75% of export earnings) and financial services; main export turtle products; imports: foodstuffs (about 90% of food and consumer goods must be imported), manufactured items, textiles, building materials, cars, petroleum products

■ FINANCE/TRADE

Currency: Caymanian dollar (CI$) = 100 cents
Canadian Embassy: c/o The Canadian High Commission, Macdonald House, 1 Grosvenor Square, London W1K 4AB, England, UK. Tel: (011-44-20) 7258-6600. Fax: (011-44-20) 7258-6333. Email: Ldn@dfait-maeci.gc.ca
Representative to Canada: British High Commission, 80 Elgin St, Ottawa ON K1P 5K7. Tel: (613) 237-1530. Fax: (613) 237-7980. Email should be sent using the appropriate form at the British High Commission's website at http://www.britain-in-canada.org

---

Central African Republic

Long-Form Name: Central African Republic
Capital: Bangui

■ GEOGRAPHY

Area: 622,984 sq. km
Coastline: none: landlocked
Climate: tropical; hot, dry winters; mild to hot, wet summers
Environment: hot, dry, dusty harmattan winds affect northern areas; poaching has diminished reputation as one of last great wildlife refuges; desertification and flooding; tap water is not safe to drink
Terrain: vast, flat to rolling, monotonous plateau; scattered hills in northeast and southwest
Land Use: 3% arable land; negligible permanent crops; 5% meadows and pastures; 75% forest and woodland; 17% other
Location: C Africa

■ PEOPLE

Population: 3,512,751 (July 2000 est.)
Nationality: Central African
Age Structure: 0-14 yrs: 43%; 15-64: 53%; 65+: 4% (2000 est.)
Population Growth Rate: 1.77% (2000 est.)
Net Migration: -1.42 migrants/1,000 population (2000 est.)
Ethnic Groups: about 80 ethnic groups, the majority of which have related ethnic and linguistic characteristics; 34% Baya, 27%

Banda, 10% Sara, 21% Mandjia, 4% Mboum, 4% m'Baka; 6,500 Europeans, of whom 3,600 are French
Languages: French (official); Sangho (lingua franca and national language); Arabic, Hunsa, Swahili
Religions: 25% indigenous beliefs, 25% Protestant, 25% Roman Catholic, 15% Muslim, 10% other; animistic beliefs and practices strongly influence the Christian majority
Birth Rate: 37.52/1,000 population (2000 est.)
Death Rate: 18.44/1,000 population (2000 est.)
Infant Mortality: 106.69 deaths/1,000 live births (2000 est.)
Life Expectancy at Birth: 42.26 years male, 45.84 years female (2000 est.)
Total Fertility Rate: 4.95 children born/woman (2000 est.)
Literacy: 44.5% (1998)

■ GOVERNMENT

Leader(s): Pres. Ange-Felix Patassé, Prime Min. Martin Ziguele
Government Type: republic
Administrative Divisions: 14 prefectures, 2 economic prefectures, 1 capital commune
Nationhood: Aug. 13, 1960 (from France; formerly known as Central African Empire)
National Holiday: National Day (proclamation of the republic), Dec. 1

■ ECONOMY

Overview: subsistence agriculture and forestry are the backbone of the economy. It suffers from a poor transportation infrastructure and a weak human resource base; diamond industry accounts for 54% of export earnings
GDP: US$5.8 billion, per capita US$1,700; real growth rate 5% (1999 est.)
Inflation: -1.49% (year-end 1999)
Industries: accounts for 21% of GDP; sawmills, breweries, diamond mining, textiles, footwear, assembly of bicycles and motorcycles
Labour Force: 2 million (1997 est.); 32.6% construction industries, 30.5% manufacturing, 17.6% agriculture
Unemployment: n.a.
Agriculture: accounts for 53% of GDP; self-sufficient in food production except for grain; commercial crops—cotton, coffee, tobacco, timber; food crops—manioc, yams, millet, corn, bananas
Natural Resources: diamonds, uranium, timber, gold, oil, hydroelectric potential

■ FINANCE/TRADE

Currency: Communauté financière africaine franc (CFAF) = 100 centimes

International Reserves Excluding Gold: US$124 million (Nov. 2000)
Gold Reserves: US$0.011 million fine troy ounces (June 1998)
Budget: n.a.
Defence Expenditures: n.a.
Education Expenditures: n.a.
External Debt: US$913 million (1999)
Exports: US$167 million (2000); commodities: diamonds, cotton, coffee, timber, tobacco; partners: France, Belgium, Italy, Japan, US
Imports: US$196 million (2000); commodities: food, textiles, petroleum products, machinery, electrical equipment, motor vehicles, chemicals, pharmaceuticals, consumer goods, industrial products; partners: France, other European Community, Japan, Algeria, former Yugoslavia

■ COMMUNICATIONS

Daily Newspapers: 3
Televisions: 5/1,000 inhabitants (1998)
Radios: 83/1,000 inhabitants (1997)
Telephones: 3 lines/1,000 inhabitants (1999)

■ TRANSPORTATION

Motor Vehicles: 20,000; 11,000 passenger cars (1997 est.)
Roads: 23,810 km; 429 km paved
Railway: none
Air Traffic: 86,000 passengers carried (1997)
Airports: 52; 3 have paved runways (1999 est.)

Canadian Embassy: The Canadian High Commission, P.O. Box 572, Yaounde, Cameroon. Tel: (011-236) 61-09-73. Fax: (011-236) 61-40-74. Email: oxfarmca@internet.cf
Embassy in Canada: c/o Embassy of the Central African Republic, 1618-22nd St NW, Washington DC 20008, USA. Tel: (202) 483-7800. Fax: (202) 332-9893. Email: n.a.

Chad

Long-Form Name: Republic of Chad
Capital: N'Djamena

■ GEOGRAPHY

Area: 1,284,000 sq. km
Coastline: none: landlocked
Climate: tropical in south, desert in north
Environment: hot, dry, dusty harmattan winds occur in north; drought and desertification adversely affecting south; subject to plagues of locusts; unsafe water supply
Terrain: broad, arid plains in centre, desert in north, mountains in northwest, lowlands in south
Land Use: 3% arable land; negligible permanent crops; 36% meadows and pastures; 26% forest

and woodland; 35% others, includes 140 sq. km irrigated
Location: NC Africa

■ PEOPLE

Population: 8,424,504 (July 2000 est.)
Nationality: Chadian
Age Structure: 0-14 yrs: 48%; 15-64: 49%; 65+: 3% (2000 est.)
Population Growth Rate: 3.31% (2000 est.)
Net Migration: 0 migrants/1,000 population (2000 est.)
Ethnic Groups: some 200 distinct ethnic groups, most of whom are Muslims in the north and centre, and non-Muslims in the south; some 150,000 non-indigenous, of whom 1,000 are French
Languages: French and Arabic (official); Sara and Sango in south; more than 100 different languages and dialects are spoken
Religions: 50% Muslim, 25% Christian, 25% animism
Birth Rate: 48.81/1,000 population (2000 est.)
Death Rate: 15.71/1,000 population (2000 est.)
Infant Mortality: 96.66 deaths/1,000 live births (2000 est.)
Life Expectancy at Birth: 48.50 years male, 52.56 years female (2000 est.)
Total Fertility Rate: 6.63 children born/woman (2000 est.)
Literacy: 45% (1998)

■ GOVERNMENT

Leader(s): Pres. Lt.-Gen. Idriss Deby, Prime Min. Nagoum Yamassoum
Government Type: republic
Administrative Divisions: 14 prefectures
Nationhood: Aug. 11, 1960 (from France)
National Holiday: Independence Day, Aug. 11

■ ECONOMY

Overview: one of the world's most underdeveloped countries; civil war, drought and food shortages have adversely affected the economy, which is based on subsistence farming and fishing
GDP: US$7.6 billion, per capita US$1,000; real growth rate 0.6% (1999 est.)
Inflation: 3.80% (year-end 2000)
Industries: accounts for 14% of GDP, cotton textile mills, slaughterhouses, soap, cigarettes, brewery, natron (sodium carbonate), construction materials
Labour Force: 4 million (1999); 42.3% manufacturing, 19.1% community, social and business services, 8.0% transportation and communication
Unemployment: n.a.

Agriculture: accounts for 38% of GDP; largely subsistence farming; cotton most important cash crop; food crops include sorghum, millet, peanuts, rice, potatoes, manioc; livestock—cattle, sheep, goats, camels; self-sufficient in food in years of adequate rainfall
Natural Resources: small quantities of crude oil (unexploited but exploration beginning), uranium, natron, kaolin, fish (Lake Chad)

■ FINANCE/TRADE

Currency: Communauté financière africaine franc (CFAF) = 100 centimes
International Reserves Excluding Gold: US$178 million (Dec. 2000)
Gold Reserves: US$0.011 million fine troy ounces (June 1998)
Budget: revenues US$198 million; expenditures US$218 million, including capital expenditures of US$146 million (1998 est.)
Defence Expenditures: 12.6% of central government expenditure (1997)
Education Expenditures: 1.7% of GNP (1997)
External Debt: US$1.142 billion (1999)
Exports: US$227 million (2000); commodities: cotton 43%, cattle 35%, textiles 5%, fish; partners: France, Nigeria, Cameroon
Imports: US$227 million (2000); commodities: machinery and transportation equipment 39%, industrial goods 20%, petroleum products 13%, foodstuffs 9%; partners: US, France

■ COMMUNICATIONS

Daily Newspapers: 1
Televisions: 1/1,000 inhabitants (1998)
Radios: 242/1,000 inhabitants (1997)
Telephones: 1 line/1,000 inhabitants (1999)

■ TRANSPORTATION

Motor Vehicles: 24,600; 10,000 passenger cars (1997 est.)
Roads: 33,400 km; 267 km paved
Railway: none
Air Traffic: 93,000 passengers carried (1997)
Airports: 49; 7 have paved runways (1999 est.)
Canadian Embassy: c/o The Canadian Embassy, Édifice Stamatiades, Place de l'Hôtel de Ville, Yaoundé; mailing address: CP 572, Yaoundé, Cameroon. Tel: (011-237) 23-23-11. Fax: (011-237) 22-10-90. Email: yunde@dfait-maeci.gc.ca
Embassy in Canada: c/o Embassy of the Republic of Chad, 2002 R St NW, Washington DC 20009, USA. Tel: (202) 462-4009. Fax: (202) 265-1937. Email: info@chadembassy.org

Channel Islands

Long-Form Name: Channel Islands; Guernsey:

Bailiwick of Guernsey; Jersey: Bailiwick of Jersey
Capital: St. Helier (Jersey), St. Peter Port (Guernsey)

■ GEOGRAPHY

Area: Jersey: 116 sq. km; Guernsey: 194 sq. km
Climate: temperate, with mild winters and cool summers
Land Use: Jersey: 66% arable, remainder n.a.; Guernsey: n.a.
Location: English Channel, off the coast of France

■ PEOPLE

Population: Jersey: 88,915; Guernsey: 64,080 (July 2000 est.)
Nationality: Channel Islander
Ethnic Groups: English, French
Languages: English (official), French (official only on Jersey), Norman-French dialect

■ GOVERNMENT

Colony Territory of: Dependent Territory of the United Kingdom
Leader(s): Head of State: Queen Elizabeth II. Jersey: Lt. Gov. and Commander-in-Chief Air Marshal Sir John Cheshire. Guernsey: Lt. Gov. and Commander-in-Chief Sir John Foley
Government Type: largely self-governing British Crown dependency
National Holiday: Liberation Day, May 9

■ ECONOMY

Overview: Jersey: economy is based chiefly on financial services, agriculture and tourism, vegetable and flower exports, Jersey cattle; Guernsey: tourism, financial services, Guernsey cattle, and tomato and flower exports make up backbone of the economy

■ FINANCE/TRADE

Currency: Jersey pound, Guernsey pound, both = 100 pence; both are at par with the British pound
Canadian Embassy: c/o The Canadian High Commission, Macdonald House, 1 Grosvenor Square, London W1K 4AB, England, UK. Tel: (011-44-20) 7258-6600. Fax: (011-44-20) 7258-6333. Email: Ldn@dfait-maeci.gc.ca
Representative to Canada: c/o British High Commission, 80 Elgin St, Ottawa ON K1P 5K7. Tel: (613) 237-1530. Fax: (613) 237-7980. Email should be sent using the appropriate form at the British High Commission's website at http://www.britain-in-canada.org

Chile

Long-Form Name: Republic of Chile
Capital: Santiago

■ GEOGRAPHY

Area: 756,950 sq. km
Coastline: 6,435 km
Climate: temperate; desert in north; cool and damp in south
Environment: subject to severe earthquakes, active volcanism, tsunami; Atacama Desert one of world's driest regions; desertification; deforestation; air and water pollution
Terrain: low coastal mountains; fertile central valley; rugged Andes in east
Land Use: 5% arable land; negligible permanent crops; 18% meadows and pastures; 22% forest and woodland; 55% other, includes 12,650 sq. km irrigated
Location: SW South America

■ PEOPLE

Population: 15,153,797 (July 2000 est.)
Nationality: Chilean
Age Structure: 0-14 yrs: 28%; 15-64: 65%; 65+: 7% (2000 est.)
Population Growth Rate: 1.17% (2000 est.)
Net Migration: 0 migrants/1,000 population (2000 est.)
Ethnic Groups: 95% European and European-Amerindian, 3% Amerindian, 2% other
Languages: Spanish
Religions: 89% Roman Catholic, 11% Protestant and small Jewish population
Birth Rate: 17.19/1,000 population (2000 est.)
Death Rate: 5.52/1,000 population (2000 est.)
Infant Mortality: 9.60 deaths/1,000 live births (2000 est.)
Life Expectancy at Birth: 72.43 years male, 79.22 years female (2000 est.)
Total Fertility Rate: 2.20 children born/woman (2000 est.)
Literacy: 95.5% (1998)

■ GOVERNMENT

Leader(s): Pres. Ricardo Lagos Escobar
Government Type: republic
Administrative Divisions: 13 regions (regiones, sing. —region)
Nationhood: Sept. 18, 1810 (from Spain)
National Holiday: Independence Day, Sept. 18

■ ECONOMY

Overview: economy remains largely dependent on a few sectors, particularly copper mining (copper is the single largest export product), fishing and forestry

GDP: US$185.1 billion, per capita US$12,400; real growth rate -1% (1999 est.)
Inflation: 3.84% (year-end 2000)
Industries: accounts for 33% of GDP; copper (Chile is the world's largest producer and exporter of copper), other minerals, foodstuffs, fish processing, iron and steel, wood and wood products, transport equipment, textiles, cement
Labour Force: 6.0 million (1999); 24.79 community, social and business services, 18.6% trade and tourism, 16.6% agriculture
Unemployment: 8.3% (Nov. 2000)
Agriculture: accounts for about 6% of GDP (including fishing and forestry); major exporter of fruit, fish and timber products; major crops—wheat, corn, grapes, beans, sugar beets, potatoes, fruit; net agricultural importer
Natural Resources: copper, timber, iron ore, nitrates, precious metals, molybdenum

■ **FINANCE/TRADE**

Currency: peso ($CH) = 100 centavos
International Reserves Excluding Gold: US$14.169 billion (Jan. 2001)
Gold Reserves: US$0.074 million fine troy ounces (Jan. 2001)
Budget: revenues US$17 billion; expenditures US$17 billion, including capital expenditures US$n.a. (1998 est.)
Defence Expenditures: 8.25% of total govt. expenditure (1999)
Education Expenditures: 16.80% of central govt. expenditure (1999)
External Debt: US$37.762 billion (1999)
Exports: US$18.158 billion (2000); commodities: copper 48%, industrial products 33%, molybdenum, iron ore, wood pulp, fishmeal, fruit; partners: European Community 34%, US 22%, Japan 10%, Brazil 7%
Imports: US$18.070 billion (2000); commodities: petroleum, wheat, capital goods, spare parts, raw materials; partners: European Community 23%, US 20%, Japan 10%, Brazil 9%

■ **COMMUNICATIONS**

Daily Newspapers: 52
Televisions: 232/1,000 inhabitants (1998)
Radios: 354/1,000 inhabitants (1997)
Telephones: 207 lines/1,000 inhabitants (1999)

■ **TRANSPORTATION**

Motor Vehicles: 1,375,000; 900,000 passenger cars (1997 est.)
Roads: 79,800 km; 11,012 km paved
Railway: 6,782 km
Air Traffic: 4,610,000 passengers carried (1997)
Airports: 370; 62 have paved runways (1999 est.)

Canadian Embassy: The Canadian Embassy, Edificio World Trade Centre, 12th Fl., Nueva Tajamar 481, Santiago, Chile; mailing address: Casilla 139-10, Santiago, Chile. Tel: (011-56-2) 362-9660. Fax: (011-56-2) 362-9663. Email: stago@dfait-maeci.gc.ca
Embassy in Canada: Embassy of the Republic of Chile, 50 O'Connor St, Ste 1413, Ottawa ON K1P 6L2. Tel: (613) 235-9940. Fax: (613) 235-1176. Email: echileca@embachile-canada.com

China

Long-Form Name: People's Republic of China
Capital: Beijing

■ **GEOGRAPHY**

Area: 9,596,960 sq. km
Coastline: 14,500 km
Climate: extremely diverse; tropical in south to subarctic in north
Environment: frequent typhoons (about five times per year along southern and eastern coasts), damaging floods, tsunamis, earthquakes; deforestation; soil erosion; industrial pollution; water and air pollution; desertification; lack of safe drinking water
Terrain: mostly mountains, high plateaus, deserts in west; plains, deltas and hills in east
Land Use: 10% arable land; negligible permanent crops; 43% meadows and pastures; 14% forest and woodland; 33% other; includes 498,720 sq. km irrigated
Location: SE Asia, bordering on South China Sea, Yellow Sea

■ **PEOPLE**

Population: 1,261,832,482 (July 2000 est.)
Nationality: Chinese
Age Structure: 0-14 yrs: 25%; 15-64: 68%; 65+: 7% (2000 est.)
Population Growth Rate: 0.9% (2000 est.)
Net Migration: -0.4 migrants/1,000 population (2000 est.)
Ethnic Groups: 91.9% Han Chinese; 8.1% Zhuang, Uigur, Hui, Yi, Tibetan, Miao, Manchu, Mongol, Buyi, Korean and other nationalities
Languages: Standard Chinese (Putonghua) or Mandarin (based on the Beijing dialect), Yue (Cantonese), Wu (Shanghainese), Minbei (Fuzhou), Minnan. The Tibetans, Uigurs, Mongols and others have their own languages
Religions: officially atheist, but traditionally pragmatic and eclectic; Confucianism, Taoism and Buddhism; approx. 2–3% Muslim, 1% Christian

Birth Rate: 16.12/1,000 population (2000 est.)
Death Rate: 6.73/1,000 population (2000 est.)
Infant Mortality: 28.92 deaths/1,000 live births (2000 est.)
Life Expectancy at Birth: 69.60 years male, 73.33 years female (2000 est.)
Total Fertility Rate: 1.82 children born/woman (2000 est.)
Literacy: 83% (1998)

■ GOVERNMENT

Leader(s): Pres. Jiang Zemin, Prem. Zhu Rongji
Government Type: Communist Party-led state
Administrative Divisions: 23 provinces (sheng, sing. & pl.), 5 autonomous regions (zizhigu, sing. & pl.), 4 government-controlled municipalities (shi, sing. & pl.)
Nationhood: People's Republic established Oct. 1, 1949
National Holiday: National Day, Oct. 1

■ ECONOMY

Overview: the Soviet-style, centrally planned economy has been recently altered to include increased local authority, which has led to greater production; population control is vital, but has been weakened by popular resistance and loss of authority by rural cadres. Decentralization of the economic system is slowly progressing
GDP: US$4.8 trillion, per capita US$3,800; real growth rate 7% (1999 est.)
Inflation: 0.26% (year-end 2000)
Industries: accounts for 35% of GDP; iron, steel, coal, machine building, armaments, textiles, petroleum, chemical fertilizer, cement, consumer durables, food processing
Labour Force: 750 million (1999); 60% agriculture, 17.1% industry, 6.9% community, social and business services
Unemployment: urban unemployment approx. 10% with substantially higher unemployment and underemployment in rural areas (1999 est.)
Agriculture: accounts for 15% of GDP; among the world's largest producers of rice, potatoes, sorghum, peanuts, tea, millet, barley and pork; commercial crops include cotton, other fibres and oilseeds; produces variety of livestock products; self-sufficient in food
Natural Resources: coal, iron ore, crude oil, mercury, tin, tungsten, antimony, manganese, molybdenum, vanadium, magnetite, aluminum, lead, zinc, uranium, world's greatest hydroelectricity potential

■ FINANCE/TRADE

Currency: yuan (¥), pl. yen; = 10 jiao

International Reserves Excluding Gold: US$168.623 billion (Jan. 2001)
Gold Reserves: US$12.7 million fine troy ounces (Jan. 2001)
Budget: n.a.
Defence Expenditures: 12.71% of total govt. expenditure (1998)
Education Expenditures: 1.86% of central govt. expenditure (1998)
External Debt: US$154.223 billion (1999)
Exports: US$249.297 billion (2000); commodities: manufactured goods, agricultural products, oilseeds, grain (rice and corn), oil, minerals; partners: US, Japan, former USSR countries, Singapore, Germany
Imports: US$206.132 billion (2000); commodities: grain (mostly wheat), chemical fertilizer, steel, industrial raw materials, machinery, equipment; partners: Japan, US, Germany, former USSR countries

■ COMMUNICATIONS

Daily Newspapers: 39
Televisions: 272/1,000 inhabitants (1998)
Radios: 333/1,000 inhabitants (1997)
Telephones: 86 lines/1,000 inhabitants (1999)

■ TRANSPORTATION

Motor Vehicles: 11,450,000; 4,700,000 passenger cars (1997 est.)
Roads: 1,210,000 km; 271,300 km paved
Railway: 65,650 km
Air Traffic: 52,277,000 passengers carried (1997)
Airports: 206; 192 have paved runways
Canadian Embassy: The Canadian Embassy, 19 Dong Zhi Men Wai St, Chao Yang District, Beijing 100600, People's Republic of China. Tel: (011-86-10) 6532-3536. Fax (011-86-10) 6532-4311. Email: beijing@dfait-maeci.gc.ca
Embassy in Canada: Embassy of the People's Republic of China, 515 St. Patrick St, Ottawa ON K1N 5H3. Tel: (613) 789-3434. Fax: (613) 789-1911. Email: cooffice@buildlink.com

Christmas Island

Long-Form Name: Territory of Christmas Island
Capital: The Settlement

■ GEOGRAPHY

Area: 135 sq. km (land area); includes one of the largest coral islands in the Pacific
Climate: tropical, with little seasonal variation; heat and humidity moderated by trade winds
Land Use: dry sandy soil does not permit much cultivation
Location: SE Asia, between Australia and Indonesia

■ PEOPLE

Population: 2,564 (July 2000 est.)
Nationality: Christmas Islander
Ethnic Groups: 61% Chinese, 25% Malay, 11% European, 3% other. There is no indigenous population
Languages: English, Chinese, Oriental and European-speaking minorities

■ GOVERNMENT

Colony Territory of: Dependent Territory of Australia
Leader(s): Head of State: Queen Elizabeth II. Administrator Bill Taylor appointed by Australian Commonwealth govt.
Government Type: dependency of Australia
National Holiday: n.a.

■ ECONOMY

Overview: extraction and export of rock phosphate dust was the only significant economic activity until 1987, when the mine was closed; it was reopened in 1990

■ FINANCE/TRADE

Currency: Australian dollar = 100 cents
Canadian Embassy: c/o The Canadian High Commission, Commonwealth Ave, Canberra A.C.T. 2600, Australia. Tel: (011-61-2) 6270-4000. Fax: (011-61-2) 6273-3285. Email: cnbra@dfait-maeci.gc.ca
Representative to Canada: c/o Australian High Commission, 50 O'Connor St, Ste 710, Ottawa ON K1P 6L2. Tel: (613) 236-0841. Fax: (613) 236-4376. Email: n.a.

Cocos (Keeling) Islands

Long-Form Name: Territory of Cocos (Keeling) Islands
Capital: West Island

■ GEOGRAPHY

Area: 14 sq. km
Climate: tropical maritime modified by southeast trade wind for 9 months of the year; moderate rainfall
Land Use: primarily subsistence agriculture
Location: Indian Ocean, SW of Sumatra

■ PEOPLE

Population: 635 (July 2000 est.)
Nationality: Cocos Islander
Ethnic Groups: West Island: Europeans; Home Island: Cocos Malays
Languages: English, Malay

■ GOVERNMENT

Colony Territory of: Dependent Territory of Australia
Leader(s): Head of State: Queen Elizabeth II. Administrator Bill Taylor (appointed by Gov. Gen. of Australia)
Government Type: territory of Australia; dependency placed under Australian govt. authority by Cocos (Keeling) Islands Act of 1955
National Holiday: n.a.

■ ECONOMY

Overview: little industrial activity; agriculture limited to copra and coconut cultivation

■ FINANCE/TRADE

Currency: Australian dollar = 100 cents

Canadian Embassy: c/o The Canadian High Commission, Commonwealth Ave, Canberra A.C.T. 2600, Australia. Tel: (011-61-2) 6270-4000. Fax: (011-61-2) 6273-3285. Email: cnbra@dfait-maeci.gc.ca
Representative to Canada: c/o Australian High Commission, 50 O'Connor St, Ste 710, Ottawa ON K1P 6L2. Tel: (613) 236-0841. Fax: (613) 236-4376. Email: n.a.

Colombia

Long-Form Name: Republic of Colombia
Capital: Bogotá

■ GEOGRAPHY

Area: 1,138,910 sq. km; includes Isla de Malpelo, Roncador Cay, Serrana Bank, and Serranilla Bank
Coastline: 3,208 km
Climate: tropical along coast and eastern plains; cooler in highlands
Environment: highlands subject to volcanic eruptions; deforestation; soil damage from overuse of pesticides; periodic droughts; air pollution
Terrain: mixture of flat coastal lowlands, plains in east, central highlands, some high mountains (Andes)
Land Use: 4% arable land; 1% permanent crops; 39% meadows and pastures; 48% forest and woodland; 8% other, includes 5,300 sq. km irrigated
Location: NW South America, bordering on Caribbean Sea, Pacific Ocean

■ PEOPLE

Population: 39,685,655 (July 2000 est.)
Nationality: Colombian

Age Structure: 0-14 yrs: 32%; 15-64: 63%; 65+: 5% (2000 est.)
Population Growth Rate: 1.68% (2000 est.)
Net Migration: -0.33migrants/1,000 population (2000 est.)
Ethnic Groups: 58% mestizo, 20% white, 14% mulatto, 4% black, 3% mixed black-Amerindian, 1% Amerindian
Languages: Spanish
Religions: 95% Roman Catholic
Birth Rate: 22.85/1,000 population (2000 est.)
Death Rate: 5.73/1,000 population (2000 est.)
Infant Mortality: 24.70 deaths/1,000 live births (2000 est.)
Life Expectancy at Birth: 66.43 years male, 74.27 years female (2000 est.)
Total Fertility Rate: 2.69 children born/woman (2000 est.)
Literacy: 91% (1998)

■ GOVERNMENT

Leader(s): Pres. Andrés Pastrana; V. Pres. Gustavo Bell
Presidential elections scheduled for May 2002
Government Type: republic; executive branch dominates government structure
Administrative Divisions: 32 departments (departmentos, sing. —departmento), 1 capital district (distrito capital)
Nationhood: July 20, 1810 (from Spain)
National Holiday: Independence Day, July 20

■ ECONOMY

Overview: traditionally coffee has been the main export, though other industries such as oil and coal are developing; drug-related violence is an increasing threat to economic growth
GDP: US$245.1 billion, per capita US$6,200; real growth rate -5% (1999 est.)
Inflation: 9.49% (year-end 2000)
Industries: accounts for 26% of GDP; textiles, food processing, oil, clothing and footwear, beverages, chemicals, metal products, cement; mining—gold, coal, emeralds, iron, nickel, silver, salt
Labour Force: 18 million (1999); 28.6% community, social and business services, 23.5% industry, 7.1% finance
Unemployment: 18.1% (Dec. 1999)
Agriculture: accounts for 19% of GDP; crops make up two-thirds and livestock one-third of agricultural output; climate and soils permit a wide variety of crops, such as coffee, rice, tobacco, corn, sugar cane, cocoa beans, oilseeds, vegetables; forest products and shrimp farming are increasing in importance
Natural Resources: crude oil, natural gas, coal, iron ore, nickel, gold, copper, emeralds

■ FINANCE/TRADE

Currency: peso ($Col) = 100 centavos
International Reserves Excluding Gold: US$8.998 billion (Jan. 2001)
Gold Reserves: US$0.328 million fine troy ounces (Jan. 2001)
Budget: revenues US$22 billion; expenditures US$24 billion, including capital expenditures US$n.a. (2000 est.)
Defence Expenditures: 13.29% of total govt. expenditure (1999)
Education Expenditures: 20.29% of central govt. expenditure (1999)
External Debt: US$34.538 billion (1999)
Exports: US$13.040 billion (2000); commodities: coffee 30%, petroleum 24%, coal, bananas, fresh cut flowers; partners: US 36%, European Community 21%, Japan 5%, Netherlands 4%, Sweden 3%
Imports: US$11.539 billion (2000); commodities: industrial equipment, transportation equipment, foodstuffs, chemicals, paper products; partners: US 34%, European Community 16%, Brazil 4%, Venezuela 3%, Japan 3%

■ COMMUNICATIONS

Daily Newspapers: 37
Televisions: 217/1,000 inhabitants (1998)
Radios: 581/1,000 inhabitants (1997)
Telephones: 160 lines/1,000 inhabitants (1999)

■ TRANSPORTATION

Motor Vehicles: 1,700,000; 1,150,000 passenger cars (1997 est.)
Roads: 115,564 km; 13,868 km paved
Railway: 3,380 km
Air Traffic: 9,189,000 passengers carried (1997)
Airports: 1,101; 90 have paved runways (1999 est.)

Canadian Embassy: The Canadian Embassy, Carrera 7, No. 115-33, Piso 14, Bogotá, Colombia; mailing address: Apartado Aereo 110067, Bogotá 2, Colombia. Tel: (011-57-1) 657-9800. Fax (011-57-1) 657-9912. Email: bgota@dfait-maeci.gc.ca
Embassy in Canada: Embassy of the Republic of Colombia, 360 Albert St, Ste 1002, Ottawa ON K1R 7X7. Tel: (613) 230-3760. Fax: (613) 230-4416. Email: n.a.

Comoros

Long-Form Name: Federal Islamic Republic of the Comoros
Capital: Moroni

■ GEOGRAPHY

Area: 2,170 sq. km
Coastline: 340 km
Climate: tropical marine; rainy season (Nov. to May)
Environment: soil degradation and erosion, resulting from crop cultivation on slopes without proper terracing; deforestation; cyclones possible during rainy season
Terrain: volcanic islands, interiors vary from steep mountains to low hills
Land Use: 35% arable; 10% permanent; 7% meadows; 18% forest; 30% other
Location: E of Africa, Indian Ocean/Mozambique Channel

■ PEOPLE

Population: 578,400 (July 2000 est.)
Nationality: Comoran
Age Structure: 0-14 yrs: 43%; 15-64: 54%; 65+: 3% (2000 est.)
Population Growth Rate: 3.05% (2000 est.)
Net Migration: 0 migrants/1,000 population (2000 est.)
Ethnic Groups: Antalote, Cafre, Makoa, Oimatsaha, Sakalava
Languages: French and Arabic (both official), Shaafi Islam (a Swahili dialect), Malagasy; majority speaks Comoran
Religions: 86% Sunni Muslim, 14% Roman Catholic
Birth Rate: 40.05/1,000 population (2000 est.)
Death Rate: 9.59/1,000 population (2000 est.)
Infant Mortality: 86.33 deaths/1,000 live births (2000 est.)
Life Expectancy at Birth: 57.85 years male, 62.28 years female (2000 est.)
Total Fertility Rate: 5.38 children born/woman (2000 est.)
Literacy: 55.4% (1997)

■ GOVERNMENT

Leader(s): Head of State: Col. Assoumani Azzali. Prime Min. Hamada Madi
Government Type: independent republic
Administrative Divisions: 3 islands
Nationhood: July 6, 1975 (from France)
National Holiday: Independence Day, July 6

■ ECONOMY

Overview: agriculture is the main sector of the economy though it does not feed citizens adequately; lack of natural resources makes Comoros one of the world's poorest countries
GDP: US$410 million, per capita US$725; real growth rate 0% (1998 est.)
Inflation: n.a.
Industries: accounts for 5% of GDP; perfume distillation, textiles, furniture, jewelry, soft drinks, construction materials
Labour Force: approx. 150,000; 80% agriculture, 6% industry, 14% services
Unemployment: n.a.
Agriculture: accounts for 40% of GDP; most of population works in subsistence agriculture and fishing; plantations produce cash crops for export—vanilla, cloves, perfume essences and copra; principal food crops—coconuts, bananas, cassava; large net food importer
Natural Resources: negligible

■ FINANCE/TRADE

Currency: Comoran franc (CFAF) = 100 centimes
International Reserves Excluding Gold: US$42 million (Dec. 2000)
Gold Reserves: US$0.001 million fine troy ounces (June 1998)
Budget: revenues US$48 million; expenditures US$53 million, including capital expenditures of US$n.a. (1997)
Defence Expenditures: n.a.
Education Expenditures: n.a.
External Debt: $201 million (1999)
Exports: US$20 million (2000); commodities: vanilla, cloves, perfume oil, copra; partners: US 53%, France 41%, Africa 4%, Germany 2%
Imports: US$114 million (2000.); commodities: rice and other foodstuffs, cement, petroleum products, consumer goods; partners: Europe 62% (France 22%, other 40%), Africa 5%, Pakistan, China and others 31%

■ COMMUNICATIONS

Daily Newspapers: 0
Televisions: 1.7/1,000 inhabitants (1997 est.)
Radios: 155/1,000 inhabitants (1997 est.)
Telephones: 10 lines/1,000 inhabitants (1999)

■ TRANSPORTATION

Motor Vehicles: n.a.
Roads: 880 km; 673 km paved
Railway: none
Air Traffic: 27,000 passengers carried (1996)
Airports: 4; all have paved runways (1999 est.)
Canadian Embassy: Canadian Embassy to the Comoros, c/o The Canadian High Commission, P.O. Box 1022, Dar-es-Salaam, Tanzania. Tel: (011-255-22) 211-2831. Fax: (011-255-22) 211-6897. Email: dslam@dfait-maeci.gc.ca
Embassy in Canada: Embassy of the Islamic Federal Republic of Comoros, c/o Permanent Mission of the Comoros to the UN, 420 East 50th Street, New York, NY 10022, USA. Tel: (212) 972-8010. Fax: (212) 983-4712. Email: comun@undp.org

Congo

Long-Form Name: Republic of the Congo
Capital: Brazzaville

■ GEOGRAPHY

Area: 342,000 sq. km
Coastline: 169 km
Climate: tropical; rainy season (Mar. to June); dry season (June to Oct.); constant high temperatures and humidity; particularly enervating climate astride the equator
Environment: deforestation; air and water pollution; unsafe water supply; about 70% of the population lives in Brazzaville, Pointe Noire or along the railroad between them
Terrain: coastal plain, southern basin, central plateau, northern basin
Land Use: 0% arable land; negligible permanent crops; 29% meadows; 62% forest; 9% other; includes 10 sq km irrigated
Location: WC Africa, bordering on South Atlantic Ocean

■ PEOPLE

Population: 2,830,961 (July 2000 est.)
Nationality: Congolese (sing. & pl.)
Age Structure: 0-14 yrs: 42%; 15-64: 54%; 65+: 4% (2000 est.)
Population Growth Rate: 2.23% (2000 est.)
Net Migration: 0 migrants/1,000 population (2000 est.)
Ethnic Groups: about 15 ethnic groups divided into some 75 tribes, almost all Bantu; most important ethnic groups are Kongo (48%) in south, Sangha (20%) and M'Bochi (12%) in the north, Teke (17%) in the centre; about 8,500 Europeans, mostly French
Languages: French (official); many African languages with Lingala and Kikongo most widely used
Religions: 50% Christian, 48% animist, 2% Muslim
Birth Rate: 38.61/1,000 population (2000 est.)
Death Rate: 16.35/1,000 population (2000 est.)
Infant Mortality: 101.55 deaths/1,000 live births (2000 est.)
Life Expectancy at Birth: 44.49 years male, 50.47 years female (2000 est.)
Total Fertility Rate: 5.06 children born/woman (2000 est.)
Literacy: 78.5% (1998)

■ GOVERNMENT

Leader(s): Pres. Denis Sassou-Nguesso
Government Type: republic
Administrative Divisions: 9 regions, 1 commune
Nationhood: Aug. 15, 1960 (from France; formerly known as Belgian Congo, then Congo/Leopoldvilles then Congo /Kinshasa)
National Holiday: Congolese National Day, Aug. 15

■ ECONOMY

Overview: oil revenues are responsible for one of the highest growth rates in Africa, though the country faces increasing foreign debt and is vulnerable to the oil market. Recent efforts at economic reform are beginning to show results
GDP: US$4.15 billion, per capita US$1,530; real growth rate 5% (1999 est.)
Inflation: -0.88% (year-end 2000)
Industries: accounts for 59% of GDP; petroleum, lumbering, cement, sawmills, brewery, sugar mills, palm oil, soap, cigarettes
Labour Force: 1 million (1999); 62.4% agriculture, 25.6% services, 11.9% industry
Unemployment: n.a.
Agriculture: accounts for 10% of GDP (including fishing and forestry); cassava accounts for 90% of food output; other crops—rice, corn, peanuts, vegetables; cash crops include coffee and cocoa; forest products important export earner; imports over 90% of food needs
Natural Resources: petroleum, timber, potash, lead, zinc, uranium, copper, phosphate, natural gas, hydroelectric potential

■ FINANCE/TRADE

Currency: Communauté financière africaine franc (CFAF) = 100 centimes
International Reserves Excluding Gold: US$89 million (Nov. 2000)
Gold Reserves: US$0.011 million fine troy ounces (June 1998)
Budget: revenues US$870 million; expenditures US$970 million including capital expenditures of US$n.a. (1997 est.)
Defence Expenditures: 17.62% of total govt. expenditure (1997)
Education Expenditures: 6.1% of GNP (1997)
External Debt: US$5.031 billion (1999)
Exports: US$1.511 billion (2000); commodities: crude petroleum 72%, lumber, plywood, coffee, cocoa, sugar, diamonds; partners: US, France, other European Community
Imports: US$796 billion (2000); commodities: foodstuffs, consumer goods, intermediate manufactures, capital equipment; partners: France, Italy, other European Community members, U.S., Germany, Spain, Japan, Brazil

■ COMMUNICATIONS

Daily Newspapers: 6
Televisions: 12/1,000 inhabitants (1998)
Radios: 124/1,000 inhabitants (1997)
Telephones: 8 lines/1,000 inhabitants (1999)

■ TRANSPORTATION

Motor Vehicles: 47,000; 30,000 passenger cars (1997 est.)
Roads: 12,800 km; 1,242 km paved
Railway: 795 km
Air Traffic: 245,000 passengers carried (1997)
Airports: 36; 4 have paved runways (1999 est.)
Canadian Embassy: The Canadian Embassy to the Republic of the Congo, P.O. Box 4037, Libreville, Gabon. Tel: (011-241) 73-73-54. Fax: (011-241) 73-73-88. Email: lbrve@dfait-maeci.gc.ca
Embassy in Canada: c/o Embassy of the Republic of the Congo, 4891 Colorado Ave NW, Washington DC 20011, USA. Tel: (202) 726-5500. Fax: (202) 726-1860. Email: n.a.

Congo (Democratic Republic)

Long-Form Name: Democratic Republic of the Congo
Capital: Kinshasa

■ GEOGRAPHY

Area: 2,345,410 sq. km
Coastline: 37 km
Climate: tropical; hot and humid in equatorial river basin; cooler and drier in southern highlands; cooler and wetter in eastern highlands
Environment: dense tropical rainforest in central river basin and eastern highlands; periodic droughts in south; water pollution, deforestation; poaching negatively affects wildlife populations
Terrain: vast central basin is a low-lying plateau; mountains in east
Land Use: 3% arable; negligible permanent crops; 7% meadows; 77% forest; 13% other; includes 100 sq. km irrigated
Location: C Africa, just barely bordering on South Atlantic Ocean

■ PEOPLE

Population: 51,964,999 (July 2000 est.)
Nationality: Congolese (sing. & pl.)
Age Structure: 0-14 yrs: 48%; 15-64: 49%; 65+: 3% (2000 est.)
Population Growth Rate: 3.19% (2000 est.)
Net Migration: 0.82 migrants/1,000 population (2000 est.)
Ethnic Groups: over 200 African ethnic groups, the majority are Bantu; four largest tribes—Mongo, Luba, Kongo (all Bantu) and the Mangbetu-Azande (Hamitic)—make up 45% of the population
Languages: French (official), Lingala, Swahili, Kinggwana, Kikongo, Tshiluba
Religions: 50% Roman Catholic, 20% Protestant, 10% Kimbanguist, 10% Muslim, 10% other syncretic sects and traditional beliefs
Birth Rate: 46.44/1,000 population (2000 est.)
Death Rate: 15.38/1,000 population (2000 est.)
Infant Mortality: 101.71 deaths/1,000 live births (2000 est.)
Life Expectancy at Birth: 46.72 years male, 50.83 years female (2000 est.)
Total Fertility Rate: 6.92 children born/woman (2000 est.)
Literacy: 77.0% (1997)

■ GOVERNMENT

Leader(s): Pres. Joseph Kabila
Government Type: dictatorship; presumably undergoing a transition to representative government
Administrative Divisions: 10 provinces and 1 city
Nationhood: June 30, 1960 (from Belgium; formerly known as Belgian Congo, then Congo/Leopoldville, then Congo/Kinshasa)
National Holiday: Anniversary of independence from Belgium, June 30, 1960

■ ECONOMY

Overview: despite its vast potential wealth, the Democratic Republic of the Congo continues to suffer from a decline in the national economy; tight fiscal policies have curbed inflation and currency depreciation; a barter economy flourishes in all but the largest cities
GDP: US$35.7 billion, per capita US$710; real growth rate 1% (1999 est.)
Inflation: -10% (Feb. 1998)
Industries: accounts for 17% of GDP; mining, mineral processing, consumer products (including textiles, footwear and cigarettes), processed foods and beverages, cement, diamonds
Labour Force: 20 million (1999); 71.5% agriculture, 12.9% industry, 15.6% services
Unemployment: n.a.
Agriculture: accounts for 58% of GDP; cash crops: coffee, sugar, palm oil, rubber, quinine; food crops: cassava, bananas, root crops, corn
Natural Resources: cobalt, copper, cadmium, crude oil, industrial and gem diamonds, gold, silver, zinc, manganese, tin, germanium, uranium, radium, bauxite, iron ore, coal, hydroelectric potential

■ FINANCE/TRADE

Currency: Congolese franc
International Reserves Excluding Gold: US$83 million (Dec. 1996)
Gold Reserves: US$0.05 million fine troy ounces (Dec. 1997)

Budget: n.a.
Defence Expenditures: 4.6% of GDP (1997)
Education Expenditures: 0.18% of total govt. expenditure (1997)
External Debt: US$11.906 billion (1999)
Exports: US$495 million (2000); commodities: copper 37%, coffee 24%, diamonds 12%, cobalt, crude oil; partners: US, Belgium, France, Germany, Italy, UK, Japan
Imports: US$396 million (2000); commodities: consumer goods, foodstuffs, mining and other machinery, transport equipment, fuels; partners: US, Belgium, France, Germany, Italy, Japan, UK

■ COMMUNICATIONS

Daily Newspapers: 9
Televisions: 135/1,000 inhabitants (1998)
Radios: 375/1,000 inhabitants (1997)
Telephones: less than 1 line/1,000 inhabitants (1999)

■ TRANSPORTATION

Motor Vehicles: 530,000; 330,000 passenger cars (1997 est.)
Roads: 157,000 km; n.a. km paved
Railway: 5,138 km
Air Traffic: n.a.
Airports: 233; 23 have paved runways (1999 est.)

Canadian Embassy: The Canadian Embassy to the Democratic Republic of Congo, 17 avenue Pumbu, Commune de Gombe, Democratic Republic of Congo; mailing address: P.O. Box 8431, Kinshasa 1, Democratic Republic of Congo. Tel: (011-243) 884-1276. Fax: (011-243) 884-1277. Email: knsha@dfait-maeci.gc.ca
Embassy in Canada: Embassy of the Democratic Republic of Congo, 18 Range Rd, Ottawa ON K1N 8J3. Tel: (613) 230-6391. Fax: (613) 230-1945. Email: n.a.

Cook Islands

Long-Form Name: Cook Islands
Capital: Avarua (on Rarotonga Island)

■ GEOGRAPHY

Area: 240 sq. km
Climate: mild year-round, moderated by trade winds
Land Use: 9% arable, 13% permanent crops, negligible meadows and pastures, negligible forest and woodland, 78% other
Location: S Pacific Ocean, NE of New Zealand

■ PEOPLE

Population: 20,407 (July 2000 est.)

Nationality: Cook Islander
Ethnic Groups: Polynesian 81.3%, Polynesian-European mixture 7.7%, Polynesian-other mixture 7.7%, European 2.4%, other 0.9%
Languages: English (official), Cook Islands Maori

■ GOVERNMENT

Colony Territory of: Territory in free association with New Zealand
Leader(s): Head of State: Queen Elizabeth II. Prime Min. Terepai Maoate
Government Type: self-governing territory in free association with New Zealand; Cook Island is fully responsible for internal affairs; New Zealand retains responsibility for external affairs, in consultation with the Cook Islands
National Holiday: Constitution Day, Aug. 4

■ ECONOMY

Overview: agriculture provides the backbone of the economy: copra, fruits, tomatoes; livestock: pigs, goats; fishing; manufacturing is limited

■ FINANCE/TRADE

Currency: New Zealand dollar (NZ$) = 100 cents

Canadian Embassy: c/o The Canadian High Commission, 3rd Fl, 61 Molesworth St, Thorndon, Wellington, New Zealand; postal address: c/o Box 12-049, Thorndon, Wellington, New Zealand. Tel: (011-64-4) 473-9577. Fax: (011-64-4)471-2082. Email: wlgtn@dfait-maeci.gc.ca
Representative to Canada: c/o New Zealand High Commission, Clarica Centre, 99 Bank St, Ste 727, Ottawa ON K1P 6G3. Tel: (613) 238-5991. Fax: (613) 238-5707. Email: nzhcott@istar.ca

Costa Rica

Long-Form Name: Republic of Costa Rica
Capital: San José

■ GEOGRAPHY

Area: 51,100 sq. km; includes Isla del Coco
Coastline: 1,290 km
Climate: tropical; dry season (Dec. to Apr.); rainy season (May to Nov.)
Environment: subject to occasional earthquakes, hurricanes along Atlantic coast; frequent flooding of lowlands at onset of rainy season; active volcanoes; deforestation; soil erosion
Terrain: coastal plains separated by rugged mountains
Land Use: 6% arable; 5% permanent; 46% meadows; 31% forest; 12% other, includes 1,200 sq. km irrigated

Location: Central (Latin) America, bordering on Caribbean Sea, Pacific Ocean

■ PEOPLE

Population: 3,710,558 (July 2000 est.)
Nationality: Costa Rican
Age Structure: 0-14 yrs: 32%; 15-64: 63%; 65+: 5% (2000 est.)
Population Growth Rate: 1.69% (2000 est.)
Net Migration: 0.54 migrants/1,000 population (2000 est.)
Ethnic Groups: 94% white (including mestizo), 3% black, 1% Indian, 1% Chinese, 1% other
Languages: Spanish (official), English is spoken around Puerto Limon
Religions: 95% Roman Catholic
Birth Rate: 20.69/1,000 population (2000 est.)
Death Rate: 4.31/1,000 population (2000 est.)
Infant Mortality: 11.49 deaths/1,000 live births (2000 est.)
Life Expectancy at Birth: 73.30 years male, 78.47 years female (2000 est.)
Total Fertility Rate: 2.52 children born/woman (2000 est.)
Literacy: 95% (1998)

■ GOVERNMENT

Leader(s): Pres. Miguel Angel Rodríguez Parliamentary and presidential elections scheduled for Feb. 2, 2002
Government Type: democratic republic
Administrative Divisions: 7 provinces (provincias, sing. —provincia
Nationhood: Sept. 15, 1821 (from Spain)
National Holiday: Independence Day, Sept. 15

■ ECONOMY

Overview: inflation and external debt are high, many people are underemployed; coffee and banana crops are vital
GDP: US$26 billion, per capita US$7,100; real growth rate 7% (1999 est.)
Inflation: 10.99% (year-end 2000)
Industries: accounts for 22% of GDP; food processing, textiles and clothing, plastics products, construction materials, fertilizer, tourism
Labour Force: 1 million (1999); 24.1% community, social and business services, 24.1% agriculture, 18.9% industry
Unemployment: 5.6% (1998 est.), but there is much underemployment
Agriculture: accounts for 14% of GDP and 70% of exports; cash commodities—coffee, beef, bananas, sugar; normally self-sufficient in food except for grain; depletion of forest resources resulting in lower timber output
Natural Resources: hydroelectricity potential

■ FINANCE/TRADE

Currency: colón (pl. colones) (C/) = 100 centimes
International Reserves Excluding Gold: US$830 million (Jan. 2001)
Gold Reserves: US$0.002 million fine troy ounces (Jan. 2001)
Budget: revenues US$1.93 billion, expenditures US$2.27 billion, including capital expenditures of US$n.a. (1999 est.)
Defence Expenditures: 3.1% of central government expenditure (1997)
Education Expenditures: 19.02% of central govt. expenditure (1999)
External Debt: US$4.182 billion (1999)
Exports: US$5.865 billion (2000); commodities: coffee, bananas, textiles, sugar; partners: US 75%, Germany, Guatemala, Netherlands, UK, Japan
Imports: US$6.372 billion (2000); commodities: petroleum, machinery, consumer durables, chemicals, fertilizer, foodstuffs; partners: US 35%, Japan, Guatemala, Germany

■ COMMUNICATIONS

Daily Newspapers: 6
Televisions: 387/1,000 inhabitants (1998)
Radios: 271/1,000 inhabitants (1997)
Telephones: 204 lines/1,000 inhabitants (1999)

■ TRANSPORTATION

Motor Vehicles: 121,000; 49,600 passenger cars (1997 est.)
Roads: 37,273 km; 7,827 km paved
Railway: 950 km
Air Traffic: 992,000 passengers carried (1997)
Airports: 155; 28 have paved runways (1999 est.)

Canadian Embassy: The Canadian Embassy, Oficentro Ejecutivo La Sabana-detrás de la Contraloría, Sabana Sur, San José; mailing address: Canadian Embassy, P.O. Box 351-1007, Centro Colon, San José, Costa Rica. Tel: (011-506) 296-4149. Fax: (011-506) 296-4270. Email: sjose@dfait-maeci.gc.ca
Embassy in Canada: Embassy of the Republic of Costa Rica, 325 Dalhousie St., Suite 407, Ottawa ON K1N 7G2. Tel: (613) 562-2855. Fax: (613) 562-2582. Email: n.a.

Côte d'Ivoire (Ivory Coast)

Long-Form Name: Republic of Côte d'Ivoire
Capital: Yamoussoukro

■ GEOGRAPHY

Area: 322,460 sq. km

Coastline: 515 km
Climate: tropical along coast, semi-arid in far north; three seasons: warm and dry (Nov. to Mar.), hot and dry (Mar. to May), hot and wet (June to Oct.)
Environment: coast has heavy surf and no natural harbours; severe deforestation; water pollution; heavy flooding is possible during rainy season
Terrain: mostly flat to undulating plains; mountains in northwest
Land Use: 8% arable; 4% permanent; 41% permanent pastures; 22% forest; 25% other; includes 680 sq. km irrigated
Location: WC Africa, bordering on South Atlantic Ocean

■ PEOPLE

Population: 15,980,950 (July 2000 est.)
Nationality: Ivorian
Age Structure: 0-14 yrs: 46.45%; 15-64: 51.36%; 65+: 2.19% (2000 est.)
Population Growth Rate: 2.58% (2000 est.)
Net Migration: 1.6 migrants/1,000 population (2000 est.)
Ethnic Groups: over 60 ethnic groups; most important are the Baoule 23%, Bete 18%, Senoufou 15%, Malinke 11% and Agni; about 2 million foreign Africans mostly Burkinabe; about 130,000 to 330,000 non-Africans (30,000 French and 100,000-300,000 Lebanese)
Languages: French (official), 60 native dialects, of which Dioula is the most widely spoken
Religions: 28% indigenous, 60% Muslim, 12% Christian
Birth Rate: 40.78/1,000 population (2000 est.)
Death Rate: 16.57/1,000 population (2000 est.)
Infant Mortality: 95.06 deaths/1,000 live births (2000 est.)
Life Expectancy at Birth: 43.72 years male, 46.63 years female (2000 est.)
Total Fertility Rate: 5.80 children born/woman (2000 est.)
Literacy: 44.5% (1998)

■ GOVERNMENT

Leader(s): President Laurent Gbagbo, Prime Min. Affi N'Guessan
Government Type: republic; multi-party presidential regime
Administrative Divisions: 50 departments (departements, sing. —departement)
Nationhood: Aug. 7, 1960 (from France)
National Holiday: National Day, Aug. 7

■ ECONOMY

Overview: despite attempts to diversify, the economy is largely dependent on agriculture and related industries; highly sensitive to fluctuations in world prices for coffee and cocoa and to weather conditions
GDP: US$25.7 billion, per capita US$1,600; real growth rate 5% (1999 est.)
Inflation: 2.46% (year-end 2000)
Industries: accounts for 18% of GDP; foodstuffs, wood processing, oil refinery, automobile assembly, textiles, fertilizer, beverages
Labour Force: 6 million (1999); 45.4% community, social and business services, 15.6% industry, 13.8% agriculture
Unemployment: n.a.
Agriculture: most important sector, contributing 32% to GDP and 80% to exports; cash crops include coffee, cocoa beans, timber, bananas, palm kernels, rubber; food crops; not self-sufficient in bread grain and dairy products
Natural Resources: crude oil, diamonds, manganese, iron ore, cobalt, bauxite, copper

■ FINANCE/TRADE

Currency: Communauté financière africaine franc (CFAF) = 100 centimes
International Reserves Excluding Gold: US$515 million (Nov. 2000)
Gold Reserves: US$0.045 million fine troy ounces (Aug. 2000)
Budget: revenues US$2.3 billion; expenditures US$2.6 billion, including capital expenditures of US$640 million (1997 est.)
Defence Expenditures: 4.0% of central government expenditure (1997)
Education Expenditures: 5.0% of GNP (1997)
External Debt: US$13.170 billion (1999)
Exports: US$4.343 million (2000) commodities: cocoa 30%, coffee 20%, tropical woods 11%, cotton, bananas, pineapples, palm oil; partners: France, Germany, Netherlands, US, Belgium, Spain
Imports: US$2.997 million (2000) commodities: manufactured goods and semifinished products 50%, consumer goods 40%, raw materials and fuels 10%; partners: France, other European Community, Nigeria, US, Japan

■ COMMUNICATIONS

Daily Newspapers: 12
Televisions: 70/1,000 inhabitants (1998)
Radios: 164/1,000 inhabitants (1997)
Telephones: 15 lines/1,000 inhabitants (1999)

■ TRANSPORTATION

Motor Vehicles: 255,000; 160,000 passenger cars (1997 est.)
Roads: 50,400 km; 4,889 km paved
Railway: 660 km

Air Traffic: 158,000 passengers carried (1997)
Airports: 36; 7 have paved runways (1999 est.)
Canadian Embassy: The Canadian Embassy, Immeuble Trade-Center, 23 rue Nogues, Le Plateau, Abidjan; mailing address: BP 4104, Abidjan 01, Côte d'Ivoire;. Tel: (011-225) 20-30-07-00. Fax: (011-225) 20-30-07-20. Email: abdjn@dfait-maeci.gc.ca
Embassy in Canada: Embassy of the Republic of Côte d'Ivoire, 9 Marlborough Ave, Ottawa ON K1N 8E6. Tel: (613) 236-9919. Fax: (613) 563-8287. Email: embaci@ican.net

---

Croatia

Long-Form Name: Republic of Croatia
Capital: Zagreb

■ GEOGRAPHY

Area: 56,538 sq. km
Coastline: 5,790 km
Climate: hot summers and cold winters; along coast, mild winters and dry summers
Environment: air pollution (including acid rain), damaged forests, coastal pollution; subject to frequent and destructive earthquakes
Terrain: flat plains along Hungarian border, low mountains and highlands along Adriatic coast, coastline and islands
Land Use: 21% arable, 2% permanent crops, 20% meadows and pastures, 38% forest and woodland, 19% other; includes 30 sq. km irrigated
Location: S Europe, bordering on Adriatic Sea

■ PEOPLE

Population: 4,282,216 (July 2000 est.)
Nationality: Croat
Age Structure: 0-14 yrs: 18%; 15-64: 67%; 65+: 15% (2000 est.)
Population Growth Rate: 0.93% (2000 est.)
Net Migration: 7.98 migrants/1,000 population (2000 est.)
Ethnic Groups: 78.1% Croat, 12.2% Serb, 0.9% Muslim, 0.5% Hungarian, 0.5% Slovenian, 0.4% Czech, 0.3% Albanian, 0.3% Montenegrin, 0.2% Roma, 6.6% other
Languages: Croatian 96%, other 4% (including Italian, Hungarian, Czech, Slovak and German)
Religions: 76.5% Catholic, 11.1% Orthodox, 1.2% Slavic Muslim, 0.4% Protestant, 10.8% others and unknown
Birth Rate: 12.82/1,000 population (2000 est.)
Death Rate: 11.51/1,000 population (2000 est.)
Infant Mortality: 7.35 deaths/1,000 live births (2000 est.)

Life Expectancy at Birth: 70.04 years male, 77.51 years female (2000 est.)
Total Fertility Rate: 1.94 children born/woman (2000 est.)
Literacy: 98% (1998)

■ GOVERNMENT

Leader(s): Pres. Stjepan Mesic, Prime Min. Ivica Racan
Government Type: parliamentary democracy
Administrative Divisions: 20 counties (zvpanije, sing. —zvpanija), 1 city
Nationhood: June 25, 1991, secession from federal Yugoslavia
National Holiday: Statehood Day, May 30

■ ECONOMY

Overview: tourism, manufacturing including chemicals, food products, petroleum, ships and textiles. War and internal strife have severely disrupted economy
GDP: US$23.9 billion, per capita US$5,100; real growth rate 0% (1999 est.)
Inflation: 5.42% (year-end 2000)
Industries: accounts for 24% of GDP; mining, fertilizers, plastics, chemicals, fabricated metal, pig iron and rolled steel products, paper, wood products, shipbuilding, food processing, beverages, sugar, cotton fabrics, machinery
Labour Force: 2 million (1999); 33.6% industry, 22.7% community, social and business services, 15.8% trade and tourism
Unemployment: 20% (1999 est.)
Agriculture: accounts for 10% of GDP; Croatia normally produces a food surplus, but much land has been put out of production by fighting; products include wheat, maize, potatoes, plums, fish, livestock, esp. cattle, sheep, pigs, poultry, cereal grains, citrus fruit, vegetables
Natural Resources: oil, salt, coal, bauxite, brown coal and lignite, iron ore, china clay, silver, hydroelectric power, calcium, natural asphalt

■ FINANCE/TRADE

Currency: Croatian kuna = 100 lipas
International Reserves Excluding Gold: US$3.247 billion (Jan. 2001)
Gold Reserves: none (Jan. 2001)
Budget: revenues US$6 billion, expenditures US$4.7 billion, including capital expenditures of US$n.a. (1998)
Defence Expenditures: 5.76% of total govt. expenditure (2000)
Education Expenditures: 7.77% of central govt. expenditure (2000)
External Debt: US$9.443 billion (1999)

Exports: US$4.390 billion (2000); machinery and transportation equipment and other manufactured goods; partners: mostly Italy, Germany, United States, successor states of the former USSR

Imports: US$7.911 billion (2000); machinery and transportation equipment, chemicals, raw materials

■ COMMUNICATIONS

Daily Newspapers: 10
Televisions: 272/1,000 inhabitants (1998)
Radios: 336/1,000 inhabitants (1997)
Telephones: 365 lines/1,000 inhabitants (1999)

■ TRANSPORTATION

Motor Vehicles: n.a.
Roads: 27,840 km; 23,497 km paved
Railway: 2,296 km
Air Traffic: 767,000 passengers carried (1997)
Airports: 67; 22 have paved runways (1999 est.)

Canadian Embassy: The Canadian Embassy, Prilaz Gjure Dezelica #4, 10000 Zagreb. Tel: (011-385-1) 488-1200. Fax: (011-385-1) 488-1230. Email: zagrb@dfait-maeci.gc.ca
Embassy in Canada: Embassy of the Republic of Croatia, 229 Chapel St., Ottawa ON K1N 7Y6. Tel: (613) 562-7820. Fax: (613) 562-7821. Email: embcrott@sprint.ca

Cuba

Long-Form Name: Republic of Cuba
Capital: Havana

■ GEOGRAPHY

Area: 110,860 sq. km
Coastline: 3,735 km
Climate: tropical; moderated by trade winds; dry season (Nov. to Apr.); rainy season (May to Oct.)
Environment: averages one hurricane every two years; water pollution and deforestation
Terrain: mostly flat to rolling plains with rugged hills and mountains in the southeast
Land Use: 24% arable; 7% permanent; 27% pasture; 24% forest; 18% other, including 9,100 sq. km irrigated
Location: West Indies, bordering on Caribbean Sea, Atlantic Ocean

■ PEOPLE

Population: 11,141,997 (July 2000 est.)
Nationality: Cuban
Age Structure: 0-14 yrs: 21%; 15-64: 69%; 65+: 10% (2000 est.)
Population Growth Rate: 0.39% (2000 est.)

Net Migration: -1.52 migrants/1,000 population (2000 est.)
Ethnic Groups: 51% mulatto, 37% white, 11% black, 1% Chinese
Languages: Spanish
Religions: Christianity (majority Roman Catholic)
Birth Rate: 12.68/1,000 population (2000 est.)
Death Rate: 7.31/1,000 population (2000 est.)
Infant Mortality: 7.51 deaths/1,000 live births (2000 est.)
Life Expectancy at Birth: 73.84 years male, 78.73 years female (2000 est.)
Total Fertility Rate: 1.60 children born/woman (2000 est.)
Literacy: 95.9% (1997)

■ GOVERNMENT

Leader(s): Pres. of the Council of State: Fidel Castro
Government Type: communist state
Administrative Divisions: 14 provinces (provincias, sing. —provincia) and 1 special municipality (municipio especial)
Nationhood: May 20, 1902 (from Spain Dec. 10, 1898; administered by the US from 1898 to 1902)
National Holiday: Rebellion Day, July 26; Liberation Day, Jan. 1

■ ECONOMY

Overview: state plays the primary role in the economy and controls practically all foreign trade; recent government reforms aim at alleviating serious shortages of food, consumer goods and services; tourism plays a key role in foreign currency earnings
GDP: US$18.6 billion, per capita US$1,700; real growth rate 6.2% (1999 est.)
Inflation: n.a.
Industries: accounts for 36.5% of GDP; sugar milling, petroleum refining, food and tobacco processing, textiles, chemicals, paper and wood products, metals (particularly nickel), cement, fertilizers, consumer goods, agricultural machinery
Labour Force: 5.0 million (1998); 47.7% services, 28.5% industry, 23.8% agriculture
Unemployment: 6% (1999 est.)
Agriculture: accounts for 7.4% of GDP (including fishing and forestry); key commercial crops—sugar cane, tobacco and citrus fruit; other products—coffee, rice, potatoes, meat, beans; world's largest sugar exporter; not self-sufficient in food
Natural Resources: cobalt, nickel, iron ore, copper, manganese, salt, timber, silica, petroleum

■ FINANCE/TRADE

Currency: peso ($) = 100 centavos
International Reserves Excluding Gold: n.a.
Gold Reserves: n.a.
Budget: revenues US$13.5 billion, expenditures US$14.3 billion, inc. capital expenditures of n.a. (2000 est.)
Defence Expenditures: n.a.
Education Expenditures: 6.7% of GNP (1997)
External Debt: US$11.2 billion (1998)
Exports: US$2.420 billion (2000); commodities: sugar, nickel, shellfish, citrus, tobacco, coffee; partners: Russia 30%, China 9%, Canada 10%, Japan 6%, Spain 4%
Imports: US$4.210 billion (2000); commodities: capital goods, industrial raw materials, food, petroleum; partners: Russia 10%, China 9%, Spain 9%, Mexico 5%, Italy 5%, Canada 4%, France 4%

■ COMMUNICATIONS

Daily Newspapers: 17
Televisions: 239/1,000 inhabitants (1998)
Radios: 353/1,000 inhabitants (1997)
Telephones: 39 lines/1,000 inhabitants (1999)

■ TRANSPORTATION

Motor Vehicles: n.a.
Roads: 60,858 km; 29,820 km paved
Railway: 4,807 km
Air Traffic: 1,117,000 passengers carried (1997)
Airports: 170; 77 have paved runways (1999 est.)
Canadian Embassy: The Canadian Embassy, Calle 30, No. 518 Esquina 7a, Avenida Miramar, Havana, Cuba. Tel: (011-53-7) 24-25-16. Fax: (011-53-7) 24-97-72. Email: havan@dfait-maeci.gc.ca
Embassy in Canada: Embassy of the Republic of Cuba, 388 Main St, Ottawa ON K1S 1E3. Tel: (613) 563-0141. Fax: (613) 563-0068. Email: cuba@iosphere.net

---

Cyprus

Long-Form Name: Republic of Cyprus
Capital: Nicosia

■ GEOGRAPHY

Area: 9,250 sq. km
Coastline: 648 km
Climate: temperate, Mediterranean with hot, dry summers and cool, wet winters
Environment: moderate earthquake activity; water resource problems (no natural reservoir catchments, seasonal disparity in rainfall and most potable resources concentrated in the Turkish-Cypriot area)

Terrain: central plain with mountains to north and south, plain along south coast
Land Use: 12% arable; 5% permanent; negligible permanent pastures; 13% forest; 70% other, including 390 sq. km irrigated
Location: Middle East, in the Mediterranean Sea

■ PEOPLE

Population: 758,363 (July 2000 est.)
Nationality: Cypriot
Age Structure: 0-14 yrs: 23%; 15-64: 66%; 65+: 11% (2000 est.)
Population Growth Rate: 0.6% (2000 est.)
Net Migration: 0.44 migrants/1,000 population (2000 est.)
Ethnic Groups: 78% Greek; 18% Turkish; 4% other
Languages: 80% Greek, Turkish, English
Religions: 78% Greek Orthodox; 18% Muslim; 4% Maronite, Armenian, Apostolic and other
Birth Rate: 13.27/1,000 population (2000 est.)
Death Rate: 7.68/1,000 population (2000 est.)
Infant Mortality: 8.07 deaths/1,000 live births (2000 est.)
Life Expectancy at Birth: 74.43 years male, 79.10 years female (2000 est.)
Total Fertility Rate: 1.95 children born/woman (2000 est.)
Literacy: 95.9% (1997)

■ GOVERNMENT

Leader(s): Pres. Glafkos Clerides
Government Type: republic; Greek Cypriots control the only internationally recognized government, however the country is divided by a UN-patrolled buffer zone. The northern portion of the island (approx. 40%) is a Turkish-Cypriot administered area. (In 1983 this area was declared the Turkish Republic of Northern Cyprus, but Turkey is the only nation to recognize this jurisdiction.)
Administrative Divisions: 6 districts
Nationhood: Aug. 16, 1960 (from UK)
National Holiday: Independence Day, Oct. 1 (Nov. 15 is celebrated as Independence Day in the Turkish area)

■ ECONOMY

Overview: remains heavily dependent on agriculture and government service, which together empty about 50% of the workforce
GDP: Greek Cypriot area: revenues US$9 billion, per capita US$15,400; real growth rate 3.0%; Turkish Cypriot area: revenues US$820 million, per capita US$5,000; real growth rate 5.3% (1998 est.)
Inflation: 4.14% (year-end 2000)
Industries: accounts for 20-22% of GDP; mining (iron pyrites, gypsum, asbestos); manufactured

products—beverages, footwear, clothing and cement—are principally for local consumption, tourism

Labour Force: 369,600 (1998); 67.4% services, 18.9% industry, 13.7% agriculture

Unemployment: Greek Cypriot area, 3.3% (1998 est.); Turkish Cypriot area, 6.4% (1997)

Agriculture: accounts for 6-12% of GDP; employs 25% of labour force; major crops—potatoes, vegetables, barley, grapes, olives and citrus fruit; vegetables and fruit provide 25% of export revenues

Natural Resources: copper, pyrites, asbestos, gypsum, timber, salt, marble, clay earth pigment

■ FINANCE/TRADE

Currency: Cypriot pound (£ or £C) = 100 cents and Turkish lira (TL) = 100 kurus

International Reserves Excluding Gold: US$1.766 billion (Nov. 2000)

Gold Reserves: US$0.464 million fine troy ounces (Oct. 2000)

Budget: Greek area: revenues US$2.9 billion; expenditures US$3.4 billion, including capital expenditures of US$345 million; Turkish area: revenues US$171 million; expenditures US$306 million, including capital expenditures of US$56.8 million (1997 est.)

Defence Expenditures: 3.94% of total govt. expenditure (1998)

Education Expenditures: 11.84% of central govt. expenditures (1998)

External Debt: Greek Cypriot area: US$1.27 billion; Turkish Cypriot: US$n.a. (1998)

Exports: US$1.013 billion (2000); commodities: citrus, potatoes, grapes, wine, cement, clothing and shoes; partners: Middle East and North Africa 37%, UK 27%, other European Community 11%, US 2%

Imports: US$3.661 billion (2000); commodities: consumer goods 23%, petroleum and lubricants 12%, food and feed grains, machinery; partners: European Community 60%, Middle East and North Africa 7%, US 4%

■ COMMUNICATIONS

Daily Newspapers: 9
Televisions: n.a.
Radios: n.a.
Telephones: 545 lines/1,000 inhabitants (1999)

■ TRANSPORTATION

Motor Vehicles: 340,000; 230,000 passenger cars (1997 est.)
Roads: 13,013 km; 7,619 km paved
Railway: none
Air Traffic: 1,278,000 passengers carried (1997)

Airports: 15; 12 have paved runways (1999 est.)

Canadian Embassy: The High Commission for Canada to Cyprus, c/o the Canadian Embassy, P.O. Box 3394, Damascus, Syria. Tel: (011-963-11) 611-6692. Fax: (011-963-11) 611-4000. Email: dmcus@dfait-maeci.gc.ca

Embassy in Canada: c/o Embassy of the Republic of Cyprus, 2211 R St NW, Washington DC 20008, USA. Tel: (202) 462-5772. Fax: (202) 483-6710. Email: cypembwash@earthlink.net OR Consulate General of Cyprus, 365 Bloor St E, Toronto, ON M4W 3L4 Tel: (416) 944 0998.

Czech Republic

Long-Form Name: Czech Republic
Capital: Prague

■ GEOGRAPHY

Area: 78,866 sq. km
Coastline: none: landlocked
Climate: temperate; cool summers; cold, cloudy, humid winters
Environment: air and water pollution and acid rain, which also damages the forests; recently there has been severe flooding
Terrain: Bohemia in the west consists of rolling plains, hills and plateaus surrounded by low mountains; Moravia in east consists of very hilly country
Land Use: 41% arable; 2% permanent crops; 11% permanent pastures; 34% forests and woodland; 12% other; includes 240 sq. km irrigated
Location: C Europe

■ PEOPLE

Population: 10,272,179 (July 2000 est.)
Nationality: Czech
Age Structure: 0-14 yrs: 16%; 15-64: 70%; 65+: 14% (2000 est.)
Population Growth Rate: -0.08% (2000 est.)
Net Migration: 0.95 migrants/1,000 population (2000 est.)
Ethnic Groups: 81.2% Czech, 3.1% Slovak, 0.2% Hungarian, 0.5% German, 0.6% Polish, 13.2% Moravian, 0.4% Silesian, 0.3% Gypsy, 0.5% other
Languages: Czech and Slovak
Religions: 39.8% atheist, 39.2% Roman Catholic, 4.6% Protestant, 3% Orthodox, 13.4% other
Birth Rate: 9.10/1,000 population (2000 est.)
Death Rate: 10.87/1,000 population (2000 est.)
Infant Mortality: 5.63 deaths/1,000 live births (2000 est.)

Life Expectancy at Birth: 71.01 years male, 78.22 years female (2000 est.)
Total Fertility Rate: 1.18 children born/woman (2000 est.)
Literacy: 99.9% (1999 est.)

■ GOVERNMENT

Leader(s): Pres. Vaclav Havel, Prem. Milos Zeman
Government Type: parliamentary democracy
Administrative Divisions: 73 districts (okresi, sing. —okres) and 4 municipalities (mesta, sing. —mesto)
Nationhood: Jan. 1, 1993 (from Czechoslovakia)
National Holiday: National Liberation Day, May 8; Founding of the Republic, Oct. 28

■ ECONOMY

Overview: economy is beginning the transition from a command to a market economy; economic growth is less important at this point than economic restructuring
GDP: US$120.8 billion, per capita US$11,700; real growth rate -0.5% (1999 est.)
Inflation: 3.90% (year-end 2000)
Industries: accounts for 42% of GDP; fuels, ferrous metallurgy, machinery and equipment, coal, motor vehicles, glass, armaments
Labour Force: 6 million (1999); 37.9% industry, 8.1% agriculture, 8.8% construction, 45.2% communications and other
Unemployment: 8.5% (Nov. 2000)
Agriculture: accounts for 5% of GDP; largely self-sufficient in food production; diversified crop and livestock production, including grains, sugar beets, potatoes, hops, fruit, hogs, cattle and poultry
Natural Resources: hard and soft coal, kaolin, clay, graphite

■ FINANCE/TRADE

Currency: koruna (pl. koruny) (Kcs) = 100 haleru
International Reserves Excluding Gold: US$12.956 billion (Jan. 2001)
Gold Reserves: US$0.446 million fine troy ounces (Jan. 2001)
Budget: revenues US$16.4 billion; expenditures US$17.3 billion, including capital expenditures US$n.a. (1999)
Defence Expenditures: 5.02% of total govt. expenditure (1999)
Education Expenditures: 10.13% of central govt. expenditure (1999)
External Debt: US$22.583 billion (1999)
Exports: US$28.113 billion (2000); commodities: machinery and equipment 58.5%, industrial consumer goods 15.2%, fuels, minerals and metals 10.6%, agricultural and forestry products 6.1%, other products 15.2%; partners: former USSR countries, Germany, Poland, Hungary, former Yugoslavia, Austria, Bulgaria, Romania, US
Imports: US$30.727 billion (2000); commodities: machinery and equipment 41.6%, fuels, minerals, metals 32.2%, agricultural and forestry products 11.5%, industrial consumer goods 6.7%, other products 8%; partners: former USSR countries, Germany, Poland, Hungary, former Yugoslavia, Austria, Bulgaria, Romania, US

■ COMMUNICATIONS

Daily Newspapers: 21
Televisions: 447/1,000 inhabitants (1998)
Radios: 803/1,000 inhabitants (1997)
Telephones: 371 lines/1,000 inhabitants (1999)

■ TRANSPORTATION

Motor Vehicles: 5,000,000; 4,600,000 passenger cars (1997 est.) (includes data for Slovakia)
Roads: 127,693 km; all paved
Railway: 9,435 km
Air Traffic: 1,448,000 passengers carried (1997)
Airports: 114; 43 have paved runways (1999 est.)
Canadian Embassy: The Canadian Embassy, Mickiewiczova 6, 125 33 Prague 6, Czech Republic. Tel: (011-420-2) 7210-1800. Fax: (011-420-2) 7210-1890. Email: prgue@dfait-maeci.gc.ca
Embassy in Canada: Embassy of the Czech Republic, 251 Cooper St. Ottawa ON, K2P 0G2. Tel: (613) 562-3875. Fax: (613) 562-3878. Email: ottawa@embassy.mzv.cz

Denmark

Long-Form Name: Kingdom of Denmark
Capital: Copenhagen

■ GEOGRAPHY

Area: 43,094 sq. km; includes the island of Bornholm in the Baltic Sea and the rest of metropolitan Denmark, but excludes the Faroe Islands and Greenland
Coastline: 7,314 km (inc. fjords, etc.)
Climate: temperate; humid and overcast; mild, windy winters and cool summers
Environment: air and water pollution; pollution of drinking water
Terrain: low and flat to gently rolling plains
Land Use: 60% arable land; negligible permanent crops; 5% meadows; 10% forest; 25% other, includes 4,350 sq. km irrigated

Location: N Europe, bordering on North Sea, Baltic Sea

■ PEOPLE

Population: 5,336,394 (July 2000 est.)
Nationality: Dane
Age Structure: 0-14 yrs: 18%; 15-64: 67%; 65+: 15% (2000 est.)
Population Growth Rate: 0.31% (2000 est.)
Net Migration: 1.95 migrants/1,000 population (2000 est.)
Ethnic Groups: Scandinavian, Inuit, Faroese, German
Languages: Danish, Faroese, Greenlandic (an Inuit dialect); small German-speaking minority
Religions: 91% Evangelical Lutheran, 2% other Protestant and Roman Catholic, 7% other
Birth Rate: 12.16/1,000 population (2000 est.)
Death Rate: 11.00/1,000 population (2000 est.)
Infant Mortality: 5.11 deaths/1,000 live births (2000 est.)
Life Expectancy at Birth: 73.95 years male, 79.27 years female (2000 est.)
Total Fertility Rate: 1.73 children born/woman (2000 est.)
Literacy: 99% (1998)

■ GOVERNMENT

Leader(s): Head of State: Margrethe II. Prime Min. Poul Nyrup Rasmussen
Government Type: constitutional monarchy
Administrative Divisions: 14 counties (amter, sing. —amt) and 2 kommunes; dependent areas inc.: Faroe Islands, Greenland (see Greenland entry for details)
Nationhood: became a constitutional monarchy in 1849
National Holiday: Birthday of the Queen, Apr. 16

■ ECONOMY

Overview: advanced agriculture and industry; extensive government welfare measures; highly dependent on foreign trade
GDP: US$127.7 billion, per capita US$23,800; real growth rate 1.3% (1999 est.)
Inflation: 2.92% (year-end 2000)
Industries: accounts for 27% of GDP; food processing, machinery and equipment, textiles and clothing, chemical products, electronics, construction, furniture and other wood products
Labour Force: 3 million (1999); 36% community, social and business services, 20.2% industry, 14.4% trade and tourism
Unemployment: 6.1% (Jan. 2001)
Agriculture: accounts for 4% of GNP and employs 5.6% of labour force (includes fishing); farm products account for nearly 15% of export revenues; principal products—meat, dairy, grain, potatoes, rape, sugar beets, fish; self-sufficient in food production
Natural Resources: crude oil, natural gas, fish, salt, limestone, sand and gravel

■ FINANCE/TRADE

Currency: krone (pl. kroner) (DKr) = 100 oere
International Reserves Excluding Gold: US$13.216 billion (Jan. 2001)
Gold Reserves: US$2.141 million fine troy ounces (Jan. 2001)
Budget: revenues US$59.7 billion; expenditures US$57.6 billion, including capital expenditures US$n.a. (1997 est.)
Defence Expenditures: 4.07% of total govt. expenditure (2000)
Education Expenditures: 12.69% of central govt. expenditure (2000)
External Debt: n.a.
Exports: US$46.237 billion (2000); commodities: meat and meat products, dairy products, transport equipment, fish, chemicals, industrial machinery; partners: US 6%, Germany, Norway, Sweden, UK, other European Community, Japan
Imports: US$41.911 billion (2000); commodities: petroleum, machinery and equipment, chemicals, grain and foodstuffs, textiles, paper; partners: US 7%, Germany, Netherlands, Sweden, UK, other European Community

■ COMMUNICATIONS

Daily Newspapers: 37
Televisions: 585/1,000 inhabitants (1998)
Radios: 1,141/1,000 inhabitants (1997)
Telephones: 685 lines/1,000 inhabitants (1999)

■ TRANSPORTATION

Motor Vehicles: 2,200,000; 1,830,000 passenger cars (1997 est.)
Roads: 71,437 km; all paved
Railway: 2,859 km operational
Air Traffic: 6,236,000 passengers carried (1997)
Airports: 118; 28 have paved runways (1999 est.)

Canadian Embassy: The Canadian Embassy, Kr. Bernikowsgade 1, 1105 Copenhagen K, Denmark. Tel: (011-45) 33-48-32-00. Fax: (011-45) 33-48-32-20. Email: copen@dfait-maeci.gc.ca
Embassy in Canada: Embassy of the Kingdom of Denmark, 47 Clarence St, Ste 450, Ottawa ON K1N 9K1. Tel: (613) 562-1811. Fax: (613) 562-1812. Email: danemb@cyberus.ca

Djibouti

Long-Form Name: Republic of Djibouti
Capital: Djibouti

■ GEOGRAPHY

Area: 22,000 sq. km
Coastline: 314 km
Climate: desert; torrid, dry
Environment: vast wasteland; desertification; droughts and earthquakes; occasional cyclones; inadequate safe drinking water
Terrain: coastal plain and plateau separated by central mountains
Land Use: 0% arable; 0% permanent; 9% permanent pastures; negligible forest; 91% other
Location: E Africa, bordering on Gulf of Aden

■ PEOPLE

Population: 451,442 (July 2000 est.)
Nationality: Djiboutian
Age Structure: 0-14 yrs: 43%; 15-64: 55%; 65+: 2% (2000 est.)
Population Growth Rate: 1.45% (2000 est.)
Net Migration: -11.63 migrants/1,000 population (2000 est.)
Ethnic Groups: 60% Somali (Issa), 35% Afar, 5% French, Arab, Ethiopian and Italian
Languages: French and Arabic (both official); Somali and Afar widely used
Religions: 94% Muslim, 6% Christian
Birth Rate: 40.98/1,000 population (2000 est.)
Death Rate: 14.87/1,000 population (2000 est.)
Infant Mortality: 103.32 deaths/1,000 live births (2000 est.)
Life Expectancy at Birth: 49.01 years male, 52.68 years female (2000 est.)
Total Fertility Rate: 5.80 children born/woman (2000 est.)
Literacy: 48.3% (1997)

■ GOVERNMENT

Leader(s): Pres. Ismail Omar Guelleh, Prime Min. Mohamed Dilleita
Government Type: republic
Administrative Divisions: 5 districts (cercles, sing. -cercle)
Nationhood: June 27, 1977 (from France; formerly known as French Territory of the Afars and Issao)
National Holiday: Independence Day, June 27

■ ECONOMY

Overview: based on service activities related to country's strategic location and status as a free trade zone; Djibouti is heavily dependent on foreign aid

GDP: US$550 million, per capita US$1,200; real growth rate 2% (1999 est.)
Inflation: 6.7% (Feb. 1997)
Industries: accounts for 20% of GDP; limited to a few small-scale enterprises, such as dairy products and mineral-water bottling
Labour Force: 282,000; 75% agriculture, 11% industry, 14% services
Unemployment: n.a.
Agriculture: accounts for only 3% of GDP; scanty rainfall limits crop production to mostly fruit and vegetables; half of population pastoral nomads herding goats, sheep and camels; imports bulk of food needs
Natural Resources: geothermal areas

■ FINANCE/TRADE

Currency: Djiboutian franc (DF) = 100 centimes
International Reserves Excluding Gold: US$62 million (Jan. 2001)
Gold Reserves: n.a.
Budget: revenues US$156 million; expenditures US$175 million, including capital expenditures of US%n.a. (1997 est.)
Defence Expenditures: 4.5% of GDP (1997)
Education Expenditures: n.a.
External Debt: US$280 million (1999)
Exports: US$19 million (2000); commodities: hides and skins, coffee (in transit); partners: Middle East 50%, Africa 43%, Western Europe 7%
Imports: US$271 million (2000); commodities: foods, beverages, transport equipment, chemicals, petroleum products; partners: European Community 36%, Africa 21%, Bahrain 14%, Asia 12%, US 2%

■ COMMUNICATIONS

Daily Newspapers: 0
Televisions: 62/1,000 inhabitants (1997 est.)
Radios: 115/1,000 inhabitants (1997 est.)
Telephones: 14 lines/1,000 inhabitants (1999)

■ TRANSPORTATION

Motor Vehicles: 16,500; 13,500 passenger cars (1997 est.)
Roads: 2,890 km; 364 km paved
Railway: 100 km
Air Traffic: n.a.
Airports: 12; 2 have paved runways (1999 est.)
Canadian Embassy: The Canadian Embassy to Djibouti, c/o The Canadian Embassy, P.O. Box 1130, Addis Ababa, Ethiopia. Tel: (011-251-1) 71-30-22. Fax: (011-251-1) 71-30-33. Email: addis@dfait-maeci.gc.ca
Embassy in Canada: Embassy of the Republic of Djibouti, 1156 15th St. NW, Ste 515,

Washington DC 20005, USA. Tel: (202) 331-0270. Fax: (202) 331-0302. Email: n.a.

Dominica

Long-Form Name: Commonwealth of Dominica
Capital: Roseau

■ GEOGRAPHY

Area: 754 sq. km
Coastline: 148 km
Climate: tropical; moderated by northeast trade winds; heavy rainfall
Environment: flash floods a constant hazard; occasional hurricanes
Terrain: rugged mountains of volcanic origin
Land Use: 9% arable; 13% permanent; 3% meadows; 67% forest and woodland; 8% other
Location: Caribbean islands, northern end of the Windward Islands

■ PEOPLE

Population: 71,540 (July 2000 est.)
Nationality: Dominican
Age Structure: 0-14 yrs: 29%; 15-64: 63%; 65+: 8% (2000 est.)
Population Growth Rate: -1.14% (2000 est.)
Net Migration: -22.39 migrants/1,000 population (2000 est.)
Ethnic Groups: mostly black; some Carib Indians
Languages: English (official); French patois widely spoken
Religions: 77% Roman Catholic; 15% Protestant, 2% none, 1% unknown, 5% other
Birth Rate: 18.27/1,000 population (2000 est.)
Death Rate: 7.30/1,000 population (2000 est.)
Infant Mortality: 17.13 deaths/1,000 live births (2000 est.)
Life Expectancy at Birth: 70.50 years male, 76.36 years female (2000 est.)
Total Fertility Rate: 2.05 children born/woman (2000 est.)
Literacy: 94% (1997)

■ GOVERNMENT

Leader(s): Pres. Crispin Anselm Sorhaindo, Prime Min. Pierre Charles
Government Type: parliamentary democracy
Administrative Divisions: 10 parishes
Nationhood: Nov. 3, 1978 (from UK)
National Holiday: Independence Day, Nov. 3

■ ECONOMY

Overview: dependent on agriculture and vulnerable to climatic conditions; tourist potential (undeveloped)

GDP: US$225 million, per capita US$3,400; real growth rate 2% (1998 est.)
Inflation: 0.85% (year-end 2000)
Industries: agricultural processing, tourism, soap and other coconut-based products, cigars, pumice mining, cement blocks, shoes. Industries account for 16% of GDP.
Labour Force: 25,000; agriculture 40%, industry and commerce 32%, services 28%
Unemployment: 20% (1999 est.)
Agriculture: accounts for 21% of GDP; principal crops—bananas, citrus fruit, coconuts, root crops; bananas provide the bulk of export earnings; forestry and fisheries potential not exploited
Natural Resources: timber, hydroelectric power, arable land

■ FINANCE/TRADE

Currency: East Caribbean dollar ($EC) = 100 cents
International Reserves Excluding Gold: US$29 million (Dec. 2000)
Gold Reserves: n.a.
Budget: revenues US$72 million; expenditures US$79.9 million, including capital expenditures of US$11.5 million (1997–98)
Defence Expenditures: n.a.
Education Expenditures: n.a.
External Debt: US$108 million (1999)
Exports: US$52 million (2000); commodities: bananas, coconuts, grapefruit, soap, galvanized sheets; partners: UK 72%, Jamaica 10%, Organization of Eastern Caribbean States 6%, US 3%, other 9%
Imports: US$150 million (2000); commodities: food, oils and fats, chemicals, fuels and lubricants, manufactured goods, machinery and equipment; partners: US 23%, UK 18%, CARICOM 15%, Organization of Eastern Carribean States 15%, Japan 5%, Canada 3%, other 21%

■ COMMUNICATIONS

Daily Newspapers: 0
Televisions: 83/1,000 inhabitants (1997 est.)
Radios: 643/1,000 inhabitants (1997 est.)
Telephones: 279 lines/1,000 inhabitants (1999)

■ TRANSPORTATION

Motor Vehicles: 5,700; 2,800 passenger cars (1997 est.)
Roads: 780 km; 393 km paved
Railway: none
Air Traffic: n.a.
Airports: 2; both have paved runways (1999 est.)
Canadian Embassy: c/o The Canadian High

Commission, Bishop's Court Hill, St. Michael, Barbados; mailing address: P.O. Box 404, Bridgetown, Barbados. Tel: (246) 429-3550. Fax: (246) 429-3780. Email: bdgtn@dfait-maeci.gc.ca
Embassy in Canada: c/o High Commission for the Countries of the Organization of Eastern Caribbean States, 130 Albert St, Ste 700, Ottawa ON K1P 5G4. Tel: (613) 236-8952. Fax: (613) 236-3042. Email: echcc@travel-net.com

Dominican Republic

Long-Form Name: Dominican Republic
Capital: Santo Domingo

■ GEOGRAPHY

Area: 48,730 sq. km
Coastline: 1,288 km
Climate: tropical maritime; little seasonal temperature variation
Environment: subject to occasional hurricanes (July to Oct.); deforestation; erosion and water shortage
Terrain: rugged highlands and mountains interspersed with fertile valleys
Land Use: 21% arable; 9% permanent; 43% meadows; 12% forest; 15% other, includes 2,300 sq. km irrigated
Location: West Indies, bordering on Haiti, Caribbean Sea, Atlantic Ocean

■ PEOPLE

Population: 8,442,533 (July 2000 est.)
Nationality: Dominican
Age Structure: 0-14 yrs: 34%; 15-64: 61%; 65+: 5% (2000 est.)
Population Growth Rate: 1.64% (2000 est.)
Net Migration: -4.04 migrants/1,000 population (2000 est.)
Ethnic Groups: 73% mixed, 16% white, 11% black
Languages: Spanish
Religions: 95% Roman Catholic
Birth Rate: 25.15/1,000 population (2000 est.)
Death Rate: 4.72/1,000 population (2000 est.)
Infant Mortality: 35.93 deaths/1,000 live births (2000 est.)
Life Expectancy at Birth: 71.12 years male, 75.38 years female (2000 est.)
Total Fertility Rate: 3.00 children born/woman (2000 est.)
Literacy: 83% (1998)

■ GOVERNMENT

Leader(s): Pres. Rafael Hipolito Mejia, V. Pres. Milagros Ortiz Bosch

Government Type: representative democracy
Administrative Divisions: 29 provinces (provincias, sing. —provincia) and 1 district (distrito)
Nationhood: Feb. 27, 1844 (from Haiti)
National Holiday: Independence Day, Feb. 27

■ ECONOMY

Overview: agriculture is the backbone of the economy (sugar cane); tourism and a free trade zone help; hurricane damage has adversely affected agriculture and infrastructure; the government is attempting to increase electric generating capacity, but there have been numerous delays
GDP: US$43.7 billion, per capita US$5,400; real growth rate 8.3% (1999 est.)
Inflation: 5.7% (Mar. 2000)
Industries: accounts for 30.8% of GDP; tourism, sugar processing, ferronickel and gold mining, textiles, cement, tobacco
Labour Force: 4 million (1999); 45.7% agriculture, 38.8% services, 15.5% industry
Unemployment: 13.8% (1999 est.)
Agriculture: accounts for 13.6% of GDP and employs almost half of labour force; sugar cane most important commercial crop, followed by coffee, cotton and cocoa; food crops; animal output; not self-sufficient in food
Natural Resources: nickel, bauxite, gold, silver

■ FINANCE/TRADE

Currency: Dominican peso ($RD) = 100 centavos
International Reserves Excluding Gold: US$517 million (Jan. 2001)
Gold Reserves: US$0.018 million fine troy ounces (Jan. 2001)
Budget: revenues US$2.3 billion; expenditures US$2.9 billion, including capital expenditures of US$867million (1999 est.)
Defence Expenditures: 4.61% of total govt. expenditure (1998)
Education Expenditures: 15.83% of central govt. expenditure (1998)
External Debt: US$4.771 billion (1999)
Exports: US$906 million (2000); commodities: sugar, coffee, cocoa, gold, ferronickel; partners: US (including Puerto Rico) 74%
Imports: US$6.350 billion (2000); commodities: foodstuffs, petroleum, cotton and fabrics, chemicals and pharmaceuticals; partners: US (including Puerto Rico) 36%

■ COMMUNICATIONS

Daily Newspapers: 12
Televisions: 95/1,000 inhabitants (1998)

Radios: 178/1,000 inhabitants (1997)
Telephones: 98 lines/1,000 inhabitants (1999)

■ TRANSPORTATION

Motor Vehicles: 209,000; 114,200 passenger cars (1997 est.)
Roads: 12,600 km; 6,224 km paved
Railway: 757 km
Air Traffic: 34,000 passengers carried (1997)
Airports: 28; 13 have paved runways (1999 est.)

Canadian Embassy: The Canadian Embassy, Capitan Eugenio de Marchena, No. 39, La Esperilla, Santo Domingo; mailing address: Apartado 2054, Santo Domingo 1, Dominican Republic. Tel: (809) 685-1136. Fax: (809) 682-2691. Email: sdmgo@dfait-maeci.gc.ca
Embassy in Canada: Embassy of the Dominican Republic, 130 Albert St., Suite 418, Ottawa ON, K1P 5G4. Tel: (613) 569-9893. Fax: (613) 569-8673. Email: n.a.

East Timor

Long-Form Name: Timor Leste or Timor Loro Sa'e
Capital: Dili

■ GEOGRAPHY

Area: 14,874 sq. km
Coastline: n.a.
Climate: tropical with little seasonal temperature variation
Environment: lack of safe drinking water; water is mainly underground and often far from villages
Terrain: extremely mountainous
Land Use: n.a.
Location: eastern half of the island of Timor, which lies between Indonesia and Australia

■ PEOPLE

Population: est. 800,000 (2000)
Nationality: East Timorese
Age Structure: n.a.
Population Growth Rate: n.a.
Net Migration: n.a.
Ethnic Groups: 12 ethnic groups including 78% Timorese, Indonesian, Chinese, other
Languages: 9 Austronesian language groups: Tetum (spoken by about 60% of the population), Mambai, Tokodede, Kemak, Galoli, Idate, Waima'a, Naueti and 3 Papuan langauge groups (Bunak, Makasae, Fatuluku)
Religions: Catholic 91%; Other (Muslim, Protestant, Hindu, Buddhist) 9%
Birth Rate: 36.5/1,000 population

Death Rate: 17.4/1,000 population
Infant Mortality: 135 deaths/1,000 live births
Life Expectancy at Birth: 46.7 years male; 48.2 years female
Total Fertility Rate: n.a.
Literacy: n.a.

■ GOVERNMENT

Leader(s): Transitional Administrator: Sergio Vieira de Mello (Brazil). Mari Alkatiri, leader of Fretelin, sworn in as leader of new council elected Sept. 2001.
Government Type: United National Transitional Administration in East Timor (UNTAET) empowered with all legislative and executive authority. After August 30, 1999, pro-independence referendum and October 1999 support from Indonesia's legislature, Indonesian militias mounted a violent reprisal against vote which sparked international intervention.
Administrative Divisions: 13 districts
Nationhood: October 25, 1999 (declared from Indonesia)
National Holiday: Independence Day, August 30

■ ECONOMY

Overview: fierce fighting in struggle for independence has damaged or destroyed most of East Timor's infrastructure; East Timor hopes to revive its economy by export profits from its high quality, organically grown coffee crop
GDP: n.a.; estimated per capita income is $225, half of what it was before independence
Inflation: n.a.
Industries: n.a.
Labour Force: 341,887 (est.)
Unemployment: 5,397 (est.)
Agriculture: cornerstone of East Timorese economy. It employs over 80% of the population and is the major source of foreign exchange revenue. While paddy and rainfed rice is the leading cash crop, other principal crops include food crops 51%, plantations 25.8%, livestock 20.5%, forestry 1% and fisheries 1%. High quality arabica coffee is also being produced.
Natural Resources: extremely rich in oil, natural gas and manganese

■ FINANCE/TRADE

Currency: US dollar (US$) = 100 cents
International Reserves Excluding Gold: n.a.
Gold Reserves: n.a.
Budget: $584.1 million (proposed for 2000-2001)
Defence Expenditures: n.a.

Education Expenditures: n.a.
External Debt: n.a.
Exports: n.a.
Imports: n.a.

■ COMMUNICATIONS

Daily Newspapers: n.a.
Televisions: n.a.
Radios: n.a.
Telephones: n.a.

■ TRANSPORTATION

Motor Vehicles: n.a.
Roads: n.a.
Railway: n.a.
Air Traffic: n.a.
Airports: n.a.

Canadian Embassy: c/o The Canadian Embassy, 5th Floor, Wisma Metropolitan, Jalan Jendral Sudirman, Jakarta 12920; mailing address: P.O.Box 8324/JKS.MP, Jakarta 12084, Indonesia. Tel: (011-62-21) 525-0709. Fax: (011-62-21) 571-2251. Email: jkrta@dfait-maeci.gc.ca
Embassy in Canada: c/o Embassy of the Republic of Indonesia, 55 Parkdale Ave, Ottawa On K1Y 1E5. Tel: (613) 724-1100. Fax: (613) 724-1105. Email: n.a.

Ecuador

Long-Form Name: Republic of Ecuador
Capital: Quito

■ GEOGRAPHY

Area: 283,560 sq. km
Coastline: 2,237 km
Climate: tropical along coast becoming cooler inland
Environment: subject to frequent earthquakes, landslides, volcanic activity; deforestation; desertification; soil erosion; periodic droughts
Terrain: coastal plain, inter-Andean central highlands and flat to rolling eastern jungle
Land Use: 6% arable; 5% permanent; 18% meadows; 56% forest; 15% other, includes 5,560 sq. km irrigated
Location: NW South America, bordering on Pacific Ocean

■ PEOPLE

Population: 12,920,092 (July 2000 est.)
Nationality: Ecuadorian
Age Structure: 0-14 yrs: 36.23%; 15-64: 59.40%; 65+: 4.37% (2000 est.)

Population Growth Rate: 2.04% (2000 est.)
Net Migration: -0.56 migrants/1,000 population (2000 est.)
Ethnic Groups: 65% mestizo (mixed Indian and Spanish), 25% Indian, 7% Spanish, 3% black
Languages: Spanish (official), Indian languages, especially Quechua
Religions: 95% Roman Catholic
Birth Rate: 26.51/1,000 population (2000 est.)
Death Rate: 5.52/1,000 population (2000 est.)
Infant Mortality: 35.13 deaths/1,000 live births (2000 est.)
Life Expectancy at Birth: 68.26 years male, 73.99 years female (2000 est.)
Total Fertility Rate: 3.18 children born/woman (2000 est.)
Literacy: 90.5% (1998)

■ GOVERNMENT

Leader(s): Pres. Gustavo Noboa, V. Pres. Pedro Pinto
Government Type: republic
Administrative Divisions: 22 provinces (provincias, sing. —provincia)
Nationhood: May 24, 1822 (from Spain; Battle of Pichincha)
National Holiday: Independence Day, Aug. 10

■ ECONOMY

Overview: vulnerable to international oil prices; the banana crop, second in importance only to oil, has been hurt by EC import quotas and banana blight; strict austerity program has resulted in economic stabilization
GDP: US$54.5 billion, per capita US$4,300; real growth rate -8% (1999 est.)
Inflation: 96.09% (year-end 2000)
Industries: accounts for 36% of GDP; food processing, textiles, metal works, paper products, chemicals, fishing, timber, petroleum
Labour Force: 5 million (1999); 29.7% trade and tourism, 27.7% community, social and business services, 17.5% industry
Unemployment: 12%, with widespread underemployment (Nov. 1998 est.)
Agriculture: accounts for 14% of GDP and 35% of labour force (including fishing and forestry); leading producer and exporter of bananas and balsawood; crop and livestock sector; net importer of food-grain, dairy products and sugar
Natural Resources: petroleum, fish, timber, hydroelectric power

■ FINANCE/TRADE

Currency: sucre (S/) = 100 centavos; in Mar. 2000 the government announced a plan to phase out the sucre and use the US dollar

International Reserves Excluding Gold: US$721 million (Jan. 2001)
Gold Reserves: US$0.414 million fine troy ounces (Jan. 2001)
Budget: revenues US$5.1 billion; expenditures US$5.1 billion, including capital expenditures (1999)
Defence Expenditures: 3.4% of GDP (1998)
Education Expenditures: 3.5% of GNP (1997)
External Debt: US$14.506 billion (1999)
Exports: US$4.822 billion (2000); commodities: petroleum 47%, coffee, bananas, cocoa products, shrimp, fish products; partners: US 58%, Latin America, Caribbean, European Community countries
Imports: US$3.446 billion (2000); commodities: transport equipment, vehicles, machinery, chemicals, petroleum; partners: US 28%, Latin America, Caribbean, European Community, Japan

■ **COMMUNICATIONS**

Daily Newspapers: 29
Televisions: 293/1,000 inhabitants (1998)
Radios: 419/1,000 inhabitants (1997)
Telephones: 91 lines/1,000 inhabitants (1999)

■ **TRANSPORTATION**

Motor Vehicles: 684,000; 258,000 passenger cars (1997 est.)
Roads: 43,197 km; 8,165 km paved
Railway: 812 km
Air Traffic: 1,791,000 passengers carried (1997)
Airports: 182; 57 have paved runways (1999 est.)
Canadian Embassy: The Canadian Embassy, Avenida 6 de Diciembre, 2816 y Paul Rivet, Edificio Josueth Gonzalez, 4th Fl., Quito, Ecuador; mailing address: P.O. Box 17-11-6512, Quito, Ecuador. Tel: (011-593-2) 564-795. Fax: (011-593-2) 503-108. Email: quito@dfait-maeci.gc.ca
Embassy in Canada: Embassy of the Republic of Ecuador, 50 O'Connor St, Ste 316, Ottawa ON K1P 6L2. Tel: (613) 563-8206. Fax: (613) 235-5776. Email: mecuacan@sprint.ca

---

Egypt

Long-Form Name: Arab Republic of Egypt
Capital: Cairo

■ **GEOGRAPHY**

Area: 1,001,450 sq. km
Coastline: 2,450 km
Climate: desert; hot, dry summers with moderate winters
Environment: Nile is only perennial water source; increasing soil salinization below Aswan High Dam; hot, driving windstorm called khamsin occurs in spring; water pollution; desertification; urbanization and erosion are decreasing the arable land available
Terrain: vast desert plateau interrupted by Nile valley and delta
Land Use: 2% arable; 0% permanent; 0% meadows; negligible forest; 98% other, includes 32,460 sq. km irrigated
Location: NE Africa, bordering on Mediterranean Sea, Red Sea

■ **PEOPLE**

Population: 68,359,979 (July 2000 est.)
Nationality: Egyptian
Age Structure: 0-14 yrs: 35%; 15-64: 61%; 65+: 4% (2000 est.)
Population Growth Rate: 1.72% (2000 est.)
Net Migration: -0.35 migrants/1,000 population (2000 est.)
Ethnic Groups: 99% Eastern Hamitic stock; 1% Greek, Italian, Syro-Lebanese, Armenian
Languages: Arabic (official); English and French
Religions: 94% Muslim (mostly Sunni), 6% Coptic Christian and other
Birth Rate: 25.38/1,000 population (2000 est.)
Death Rate: 7.83/1,000 population (2000 est.)
Infant Mortality: 62.32 deaths/1,000 live births (2000 est.)
Life Expectancy at Birth: 61.29 years male, 65.47 years female (2000 est.)
Total Fertility Rate: 3.15 children born/woman (2000 est.)
Literacy: 53.5% (1998)

■ **GOVERNMENT**

Leader(s): Pres. Mohammed Hosni Mubarak, Prime Min. Atef Mohamed Ebeid
Government Type: republic
Administrative Divisions: 26 governorates (muhafazat, sing. —muhafazah)
Nationhood: Feb. 28, 1922 (from UK; formerly known as United Arab Republic)
National Holiday: Anniversary of the Revolution, July 23

■ **ECONOMY**

Overview: urban population growth puts pressure on the agricultural sector; having difficulty with its debt servicing; vulnerable to oil prices; unemployment has become a growing problem
GDP: US$200 billion, per capita US$3,000; real growth rate 5% (1999 est.)
Inflation: 2.68% (year-end 2000)

Industries: accounts for 32% of GDP, textiles, food processing, tourism, chemicals, petroleum, construction, cement, metals
Labour Force: 24 million (1999); 31.3% agriculture, 22.2% community, social and business services, 15.4% industry
Unemployment: 11.8% (1999 est.)
Agriculture: accounts for 17% of GDP and employs more than one-third of labour force; dependent on irrigation water from the Nile; world's fifth largest cotton exporter; other crops include rice, corn, wheat, beans, fruit, vegetables; not self-sufficient in food
Natural Resources: crude oil, natural gas, iron ore, phosphates, manganese, limestone, gypsum, talc, asbestos, lead, zinc

■ **FINANCE/TRADE**

Currency: Egyptian pound (LE) = 100 piasters
International Reserves Excluding Gold: US$12.913 billion (Dec. 2000)
Gold Reserves: US$2.432 million fine troy ounces (Dec. 2000)
Budget: revenues US$20.7 billion; expenditures US$22.3 billion, including capital expenditures of US$n.a. (1998-99 est.)
Defence Expenditures: 9.43% of central government expenditure (1997)
Education Expenditures: 14.76% of central government expenditure (1997)
External Debt: US$30.404 billion (1999)
Exports: US$4.276 billion (2000); commodities: raw cotton, crude and refined petroleum, cotton yarn, textiles; partners: US, European Community, Japan, Eastern Europe
Imports: US$14.671 billion (2000); commodities: foods, machinery and equipment, fertilizers, wood products, durable consumer goods, capital goods; partners: US, European Community, Japan, Eastern Europe

■ **COMMUNICATIONS**

Daily Newspapers: 17
Televisions: 122/1,000 inhabitants (1998)
Radios: 324/1,000 inhabitants (1997)
Telephones: 75 lines/1,000 inhabitants (1999)

■ **TRANSPORTATION**

Motor Vehicles: 1,711,000; 1,300,000 passenger cars (1997 est.)
Roads: 64,000 km; 49,984 km paved
Railway: 4,955 km
Air Traffic: 4,416,000 passengers carried (1997)
Airports: 90; 71 have paved runways (1999 est.)

Canadian Embassy: The Canadian Embassy, Arab International Bank Building, 5 Midan El Saraya el Kobra, Garden City, Cairo, Egypt; mailing address: P.O. Box 1667, Cairo, Egypt. Tel: (011-20-2) 794-3110. Fax: (011-20-2) 796-3548. Email: cairo@dfait-maeci.gc.ca

Embassy in Canada: Embassy of the Arab Republic of Egypt, 454 Laurier Ave E, Ottawa ON K1N 6R3. Tel: (613) 234-4931. Fax: (613) 234-9347. Email: n.a.

El Salvador

Long-Form Name: Republic of El Salvador
Capital: San Salvador

■ **GEOGRAPHY**

Area: 21,040 sq. km
Coastline: 307 km
Climate: tropical; rainy season (May to Oct.), dry season (Nov. to Apr.)
Environment: the Land of Volcanoes; subject to frequent and sometimes very destructive earthquakes; deforestation; soil erosion and pollution; water pollution
Terrain: mostly mountains with narrow coastal belt and central plateau
Land Use: 27% arable; 8% permanent; 29% meadows; 5% forest; 31% other, includes 1,200 sq. km irrigated
Location: Central (Latin) America, bordering on Pacific Ocean

■ **PEOPLE**

Population: 6,122,515 (July 2000 est.)
Nationality: Salvadoran
Age Structure: 0-14 yrs: 38%; 15-64: 57%; 65+: 5% (2000 est.)
Population Growth Rate: 1.87% (2000 est.)
Net Migration: -4.02 migrants/1,000 population (2000 est.)
Ethnic Groups: 90% mestizo, 1% Amerindian, 9% white
Languages: Spanish, Nahua spoken among some Indians
Religions: approx. 75% Roman Catholic, with activity by Protestant groups throughout the country
Birth Rate: 29.02/1,000 population (2000 est.)
Death Rate: 6.27/1,000 population (2000 est.)
Infant Mortality: 29.22 deaths/1,000 live births (2000 est.)
Life Expectancy at Birth: 66.14 years male, 73.52 years female (2000 est.)
Total Fertility Rate: 3.38 children born/woman (2000 est.)
Literacy: 78% (1998)

■ GOVERNMENT

Leader(s): Pres. Francisco Flores Perez, V. Pres. Carlos Quintanilla
Government Type: republic
Administrative Divisions: 14 departments (departmentos, sing. —departmento)
Nationhood: Sept. 15, 1821 (from Spain)
National Holiday: Independence Day, Sept. 15

■ ECONOMY

Overview: in recent years inflation has fallen to unprecedented levels and exports have grown considerably; even so, sizeable fiscal deficits persist; the trade deficit has been offset by remittances from the many Salvadorans living abroad
GDP: US$18.1 billion, per capita US$3,100; real growth rate 2.2% (1999 est.)
Inflation: 2.27% (year-end 2000)
Industries: accounts for 22% of GDP; food processing, textiles, non-metallic products, tobacco, beverages, clothing, petroleum products, cement
Labour Force: 3 million (1999); 35.8% agriculture, 19.6% community, social and business services, 17.4% trade and tourism
Unemployment: 7.7% (1997 est.)
Agriculture: accounts for 12% of GDP and 40% of labour force (including fishing and forestry); coffee most important commercial crop; other products—sugar cane, corn, rice, beans, oilseeds, beef, dairy products, shrimp; not self-sufficient in food
Natural Resources: hydroelectricity and geothermal power, crude oil

■ FINANCE/TRADE

Currency: colón (pl. colones) (C/) = 100 centavos
International Reserves Excluding Gold: US$1.840 billion (Jan. 2001)
Gold Reserves: US$0.469 million fine troy ounces (Jan. 2001)
Budget: revenues US$1.5 billion, expenditures US$1.73 billion, including capital expenditures of US$n.a. (1999)
Defence Expenditures: 7.95% of total govt. expenditure (1999)
Education Expenditures: 21.68% of central govt. expenditure (1999)
External Debt: US$4.014 billion (1999)
Exports: US$1.342 billion (2000); commodities: coffee 60%, sugar, cotton, shrimp; partners: US 49%, Germany 24%, Guatemala 7%, Costa Rica 4%, Japan 4%
Imports: US$3.796 billion (2000); commodities: petroleum products, consumer goods, foodstuffs, machinery, construction materials, fertilizer; partners: US 40%, Guatemala 12%, Venezuela 7%, Mexico 7%, Germany 5%, Japan 4%

■ COMMUNICATIONS

Daily Newspapers: 5
Televisions: 675/1,000 inhabitants (1998)
Radios: 464/1,000 inhabitants (1997)
Telephones: 76 lines/1,000 inhabitants (1999)

■ TRANSPORTATION

Motor Vehicles: 80,100; 35,300 passenger cars (1997 est.)
Roads: 10,029 km; 1,986 km paved
Railway: 602 km
Air Traffic: 1,701,000 passengers carried (1997)
Airports: 85; 4 have paved runways (1999 est.)

Canadian Embassy: Office of the Canadian Embassy, Centro Financiero Gigante, Alameda Roosevelt y 63 Avenida Sur, Torre A, Lobby 2, Colonia Escalon, San Salvador, El Salvador. Tel: (011-503) 279-4655. Fax: (011-503) 279-0765. Email: ssal@dfait-maeci.gc.ca
Embassy in Canada: Embassy of the Republic of El Salvador, 209 Kent St, Ottawa ON K2P 1Z8. Tel: (613) 238-2939. Fax: (613) 238-6940. Email: embajada@elsalvador.ca.org

Equatorial Guinea

Long-Form Name: Republic of Equatorial Guinea
Capital: Malabo

■ GEOGRAPHY

Area: 28,051 sq. km
Coastline: 296 km
Climate: tropical; always hot, humid
Environment: subject to violent windstorms; desertification; unsafe drinking water
Terrain: coastal plains rise to interior hills; islands are volcanic
Land Use: 5% arable; 4% permanent; 4% meadows; 46% forest; 41% other
Location: WC Africa, bordering on South Atlantic Ocean

■ PEOPLE

Population: 474,214 (July 2000 est.)
Nationality: Equatorial Guinean or Equatoguinean
Age Structure: 0-14 yrs: 43%; 15-64: 54%; 65+: 3% (2000 est.)
Population Growth Rate: 2.47 (2000 est.)
Net Migration: 0 migrants/1,000 population (2000 est.)
Ethnic Groups: indigenous population of Bioko, primarily Bubi, some Fernandinos; Rio Muni,

primarily Fang; less than 1,000 Europeans, mostly Spanish
Languages: Spanish (official), pidgin English, Fang,·Bubi, Ndowe, Bujeba, Anobones and Corisqueño
Religions: natives all nominally Christian and predominantly Roman Catholic; some pagan practices retained (5%)
Birth Rate: 38.13/1,000 population (2000 est.)
Death Rate: 13.40/1,000 population (2000 est.)
Infant Mortality: 94.83 deaths/1,000 live births (2000 est.)
Life Expectancy at Birth: 51.53 years male, 55.65 years female (2000 est.)
Total Fertility Rate: 4.94 children born/woman (2000 est.)'
Literacy: 79.9% (1997)

■ GOVERNMENT

Leader(s): Pres. Teodoro Obiang Nguema Mbasogo, Prime Min. Candido Muatetema Rivas
Government Type: republic in transition to multi-party democracy
Administrative Divisions: 7 provinces (provincias, sing. —provincia)
Nationhood: Oct. 12, 1968 (from Spain; formerly Spanish Guinea)
National Holiday: Independence Day, Oct. 12

■ ECONOMY

Overview: the economy is recovering from destruction by a past regime; subsistence agriculture, forestry and fishing predominate; little industry; many undeveloped natural resources, but increased exploitation of recently discovered natural gas resources is boosting the economy
GDP: US$960 million, per capita US$2,000; real growth rate 15% (1999 est.)
Inflation: n.a.
Industries: accounts for 60% of GDP; petroleum, fishing, sawmilling
Labour Force: n.a.; 66% agriculture, 23% services, 11% industry
Unemployment: 30% (1998)
Agriculture: accounts for 20% of GDP; cash crops—timber and coffee from Rio Muni, cocoa from Bioko; food crops—rice, yams, cassava, bananas, tobacco, oil, palm nuts, manioc, livestock
Natural Resources: timber, crude oil, small unexploited deposits of gold, manganese, uranium

■ FINANCE/TRADE

Currency: Communauté financière africaine franc (CFAF) = 100 centimes

International Reserves Excluding Gold: US$17 million (Nov. 2000)
Gold Reserves: n.a.
Budget: n.a.
Defence Expenditures: n.a.
Education Expenditures: n.a.
External Debt: US$271 million (1999)
Exports: US$396 million (2000); commodities: coffee, timber, cocoa beans; partners: Spain 44%, Germany 19%, Italy 12%, Netherlands 11%
Imports: US$30 million (2000); commodities: petroleum, food, beverages, clothing, machinery; partners: Spain 34%, Italy 16%, France 14%, Netherlands 8%

■ COMMUNICATIONS

Daily Newspapers: 1
Televisions: 8.4/1,000 inhabitants (1997 est.)
Radios: 380/1,000 inhabitants (1997 est.)
Telephones: 13 lines/1,000 persons (1999)

■ TRANSPORTATION

Motor Vehicles: 10,500; 6,500 passenger cars (1997 est.)
Roads: 2,880 km, none paved
Railway: none
Air Traffic: 21,000 passengers carried (1997)
Airports: 3; 2 have paved runways (1999 est.)
Canadian Embassy: The Canadian Embassy to Equatorial Guinea, c/o P.O. Box 4037, Libreville, Gabon. Tel: (011-241) 73-73-54. Fax (011-241) 73-73-88. Email: lbrve@dfait-maeci.gc.ca
Embassy in Canada: Embassy of Equatorial Guinea, 2020 16th St, NW, Washington DC 20009, USA. Tel: (202) 518-5700. Fax: (202) 518-5252. Email: n.a.

Eritrea

Long-Form Name: State of Eritrea
Capital: Asmara (formerly Asmera)

■ GEOGRAPHY

Area: 121,320 sq. km
Coastline: 1,151 km mainland coast; 2,234 km including island coastlines
Climate: hot, dry desert along Red Sea coast, cooler and wetter in central highlands, semi-arid in west
Environment: frequent droughts, famine, deforestation, soil erosion, overgrazing
Terrain: highlands descending to coastal desert in east, hilly in northwest, flat to rolling plains in southwest
Land Use: 12% arable, 1% permanent crops, 49% meadows and pastures, 6% forests and

woodland, 32% other; includes 280 sq. km irrigated
Location: E Africa

■ **PEOPLE**

Population: 4,135,933 (July 2000 est.)
Nationality: Eritrean
Age Structure: 0-14 yrs: 43%; 15-64: 54%; 65+: 3% (2000 est.)
Population Growth Rate: 3.86% (2000 est.)
Net Migration: 8.22 migrants/1,000 population (2000 est.)
Ethnic Groups: 50% ethnic Tigrinya, 40% Tigre and Kunama, 4% Afar, 3% Saho (Red Sea coast-dwellers), 3% other
Languages: Afar, Amharic, Tigre and Kunama, Cushitic dialects, Tigrinya, Nora Bana, Arabic
Religions: Muslim, Coptic Christian, Roman Catholic, Protestant
Birth Rate: 42.71/1,000 population (2000 est.)
Death Rate: 12.30/1,000 population (2000 est.)
Infant Mortality: 76.66 deaths/1,000 live births (2000 est.)
Life Expectancy at Birth: 53.36 years male, 58.29 years female (2000 est.)
Total Fertility Rate: 5.93 children born/woman (2000 est.)
Literacy: 25% (1997)

■ **GOVERNMENT**

Leader(s): Pres. Isaias Afworki, V. Pres. Ahmed Sherifo Mahmud
Government Type: transitional govt.
Administrative Divisions: 8 provinces (awraja)
Nationhood: May 24, 1993 (from Ethiopia)
National Holiday: National Day (independence from Ethiopia), May 24

■ **ECONOMY**

Overview: with independence from Ethiopia, Eritrea faces the bitter economic problems of a small and desperately poor nation; subsistence farming will continue to be the people's economic mainstay; production is augmented by remittances from abroad, and there are long-term prospects for revenue from offshore oil development, offshore fishing, and tourism; Ethiopia is largely dependent on Eritrean ports for foreign trade
GDP: US$2.9 billion, per capita US$750; real growth rate 3% (1999 est.)
Inflation: n.a.
Industries: accounts for 20% of GDP; food processing, beverages, textiles, clothing manufacture
Labour Force: 2.0 million (1998); 80% agriculture, 20% industry and commerce

Unemployment: n.a.
Agriculture: accounts for 18% of GDP; livestock, fish, vegetables, sorghum, cotton, coffee and tobacco
Natural Resources: gold, potash, copper, zinc, salt, fish

■ **FINANCE/TRADE**

Currency: nafka = 100 cents
International Reserves Excluding Gold: n.a.
Gold Reserves: n.a.
Budget: revenues US$283.9 million; expenditures US$351.6 million, including capital expenditures of US$n.a. (1997 est.)
Defence Expenditures: 28.6% of GDP (1997)
Education Expenditures: 1.8% of GNP (1997)
External Debt: US$254 million (1999)
Exports: US$52.9 million (1997); commodities: livestock, sorghum, textiles, food, small manufactures; partners: Ethiopia, Sudan, Saudi Arabia, US, Italy, Yemen
Imports: US$489.4 million (1997); commodities: processed goods, machinery, petroleum products; partners: Ethiopia, Saudi Arabia, Italy, United Arab Emirates

■ **COMMUNICATIONS**

Daily Newspapers: 0
Televisions: 14/1,000 inhabitants (1998)
Radios: 91/1,000 inhabitants (1997)
Telephones: 7 lines/1,000 inhabitants (1999)

■ **TRANSPORTATION**

Motor Vehicles: n.a.
Roads: 4,010 km, 874 km paved
Railway: 317 km; not operational
Air Traffic: n.a.
Airports: 21; 3 have paved runways (1999 est.)

Canadian Embassy: The Canadian Embassy to Eritrea, c/o P.O. Box 1130, Addis Ababa, Ethiopia. Tel: (011-251-1) 71-30-22. Fax: (011-251-1) 71-30-33. Email: addis@dfait-maeci.gc.ca
Embassy in Canada: Embassy of the State of Eritrea, 75 Albert St., Suite 610, Ottawa, ON K1P 5E7. Tel: (613) 234-3989. Fax: (613) 234-6213. Email: n.a.

Estonia

Long-Form Name: Republic of Estonia
Capital: Tallinn

■ **GEOGRAPHY**

Area: 45,226 sq. km

Coastline: 3,794 km
Climate: wet, moderate winter; long windy autumn; warm sunny summer; late and short spring
Environment: severe air pollution, soil and ground water contamination (chemicals and petroleum products), radioactive waste; frequent spring floods are a natural hazard
Terrain: marshy lowlands, sloping coastal plain; islands account for 10% of the region
Land Use: 25% arable, negligible permanent crops; 11% meadows and pastures; 44% forest and woodland; 20% other; includes 110 sq. km irrigated
Location: NE Europe, bordering on Baltic Sea

■ PEOPLE

Population: 1,431,471 (July 2000 est.)
Nationality: Estonian
Age Structure: 0-14 yrs: 18%; 15-64: 68%; 65+: 14% (2000 est.)
Population Growth Rate: -0.59% (2000 est.)
Net Migration: -0.79 migrants/1,000 population (2000 est.)
Ethnic Groups: 65.1% Estonian, 28.1% Russian, 2.5% Ukrainian, 1.5% Byelorussian, 1% Finn, 1.8% other
Languages: Estonian (official), Russian, Latvian, Lithuanian, English and German also spoken
Religions: Lutheran, Orthodox Christian
Birth Rate: 8.45/1,000 population (2000 est.)
Death Rate: 13.55/1,000 population (2000 est.)
Infant Mortality: 12.92 deaths/1,000 live births (2000 est.)
Life Expectancy at Birth: 63.40 years male, 75.79 years female (2000 est.)
Total Fertility Rate: 1.19 children born/woman (2000 est.)
Literacy: 100% (1998 est.)

■ GOVERNMENT

Leader(s): Pres. Lennart Meri, Prime Min. Mart Laar
Parliamentary and presidential elections scheduled for fall 2001.
Government Type: parliamentary democracy
Administrative Divisions: 15 counties (maakonnad, sing. —maakond)
Nationhood: Sept. 6, 1991 (from Soviet Union)
National Holiday: Independence Day, Feb. 24

■ ECONOMY

Overview: market reforms and stabilizing measures are rapidly transforming the economy; living standards and incomes are rising, but so are unemployment and inflation
GDP: US$7.9 billion, per capita US$5,600; real growth rate -0.5% (1999 est.)

Inflation: 4.02% (year-end 2000)
Industries: accounts for 30.7% of GDP; electronics, electrical engineering, textiles, clothing, footwear, shipbuilding
Labour Force: 1 million (1999); 24.6% industry, 25.1% community, social and business services, 12.9% trade and tourism
Unemployment: 11.7% (1999 est.); large numbers of underemployed
Agriculture: contributes 3.6% to GDP, and employs 20% of labour force; dairy products, pork, poultry, eggs, fruit, vegetables; net exports of meat, fish, dairy products, potatoes
Natural Resources: fish, shale, phosphorites, amber, limestone, peat, dolomite, arable land

■ FINANCE/TRADE

Currency: kroon (pl. kroons) = 100 sents
International Reserves Excluding Gold: US$855 million (Jan. 2001)
Gold Reserves: US$0.008 million fine troy ounces (Jan. 2001)
Budget: revenues US$1.37 billion; expenditures US$1.37 billion, including capital expenditures of US$n.a. (1997 est.)
Defence Expenditures: 4.04% of govt. expenditure (1999)
Education Expenditures: 9.40% of central govt. expenditure (1999)
External Debt: US$2.879 billion (1999)
Exports: US$3.133 billion (2000); dairy products, fish, furniture, electrical power, meat; partners: Russia and other former Soviet republics 50%, West 50%
Imports: US$4.241 billion (2000); machinery 45%, oil 13%, chemicals 12%; partners: Finland, Russia

■ COMMUNICATIONS

Daily Newspapers: 15
Televisions: 480/1,000 inhabitants (1998)
Radios: 693/1,000 inhabitants (1997)
Telephones: 357 lines/1,000 inhabitants (1999)

■ TRANSPORTATION

Motor Vehicles: n.a.
Roads: 49,480 km; 10,935 km paved
Railway: 1,018 km (does not include industrial lines)
Air Traffic: 231,000 passengers carried (1997)
Airports: 5; all have paved runways (1997 est.)
Canadian Embassy: Office of the Canadian Embassy, Toom Kooli 13, 2nd Fl, 10130 Tallinn, Estonia. Tel: (011-372) 627-3311. Fax: (011-372) 627-3312. Email: n.a.
Embassy in Canada: c/o Embassy of the Republic of Estonia, 260 Dalhousie St, Ste 210, Ottawa

ON K1N 7E4. Tel: (613) 789-4222. Fax: (613) 789-9555. Email: n.a.

Ethiopia

Long-Form Name: Federal Democratic Republic of Ethiopia
Capital: Addis Ababa

■ GEOGRAPHY

Area: 1,127,127 sq. km
Coastline: none; landlocked
Climate: tropical with wide topographic-induced variation; prone to extended droughts
Environment: geologically active Great Rift Valley susceptible to earthquakes, volcanic eruptions; deforestation; overgrazing; soil erosion; desertification; frequent droughts; famine
Terrain: high plateau with central mountain range divided by Great Rift Valley
Land Use: 12% arable; 1% permanent; 40% meadows; 25% forest; 22% other; includes 1,900 sq. km irrigated
Location: E Africa, between Somalia and Sudan

■ PEOPLE

Population: 64,117,452 (July 2000 est.)
Nationality: Ethiopian
Age Structure: 0-14 yrs: 47%; 15-64: 50%; 65+: 3% (2000 est.)
Population Growth Rate: 2.76% (2000 est.)
Net Migration: 0.14 migrants/1,000 population (2000 est.)
Ethnic Groups: 40% Oromo, 32% Amhara and Tigrean, 9% Sidamo, 6% Shankella, 6% Somali, 4% Afar, 2% Gurage, 1% other
Languages: Amharic (official), Tigrinya, Orominga, Guaraginga, Somali, Arabic, English (major foreign language taught in schools)
Religions: 45–50% Muslim, 35–40% Ethiopian Orthodox, 12% animist, 5% other
Birth Rate: 45.13/1,000 population (2000 est.)
Death Rate: 17.63/1,000 population (2000 est.)
Infant Mortality: 101.29 deaths/1,000 live births (2000 est.)
Life Expectancy at Birth: 44.41 years male, 45.94 years female (2000 est.)
Total Fertility Rate: 7.07 children born/woman (2000 est.)
Literacy: 36% (1998)

■ GOVERNMENT

Leader(s): Pres. Ghidada Negasso, Prem. Zenawi Meles
Government Type: federal republic

Administrative Divisions: 9 states and 2 chartered cities
Nationhood: oldest (at least 2,000 years) independent country in Africa and one of the oldest in the world
National Holiday: National Day, May 28

■ ECONOMY

Overview: remains one of the poorest and least developed countries in the world; its economy is based on agriculture and suffers from recent periods of drought, poor cultivation practices and the deterioration of internal security conditions
GDP: US$33.3 billion, per capita US$560; real growth rate 0% (1999 est.)
Inflation: -0.04% (year-end 2000)
Industries: accounts for 12% of GDP, cement, textiles, food processing, beverages, chemicals, metals processing, oil refinery
Labour Force: 27 million (1999); 80% agriculture, 12% services, 8% industry
Unemployment: n.a.
Agriculture: accounts for 46% of GDP even though frequent droughts, poor cultivation practices and state economic policies keep farm output low; famines not uncommon; estimated 50% of agricultural production at subsistence level
Natural Resources: small reserves of gold, platinum, copper, potash, natural gas

■ FINANCE/TRADE

Currency: birr (Br) = 100 cents
International Reserves Excluding Gold: US$375 million (March 2000)
Gold Reserves: US$0.020 million fine troy ounces (March 2000)
Budget: revenues US$1 billion; expenditures US$1.48 billion, including capital expenditures of US$415 million (1997 est.)
Defence Expenditures: 2.5% of GDP (1998-99)
Education Expenditures: 4.0% of GNP (1997)
External Debt: US$5.551 billion (1999)
Exports: US$508 million (2000); commodities: coffee 60%, hides; partners: US, Germany, Djibouti, Japan, Yemen, France, Italy
Imports: US$1.366 billion (2000); commodities: food, fuels, capital goods; partners: former USSR countries, Italy, Germany, Japan, UK, US, France

■ COMMUNICATIONS

Daily Newspapers: 4
Televisions: 5/1,000 inhabitants (1998)
Radios: 195/1,000 inhabitants (1997)
Telephones: 3 lines/1,000 inhabitants (1999)

■ TRANSPORTATION

Motor Vehicles: 69,000; 46,400 passenger cars (1997 est.)
Roads: 28,500 km; 4,275 km paved
Railway: 681 km
Air Traffic: 772,000 passengers carried (1996)
Airports: 85; 11 have paved runways (1999 est.)
Canadian Embassy: The Canadian Embassy, Old Airport Area, Higher 23, Kebele 12, House Number 122, Addis Ababa; mailing address: P.O. Box 1130, Addis Ababa, Ethiopia. Tel: (011-251-1) 71-30-22. Fax: (011-251-1) 71-30-33. Email: addis@dfait-maeci.gc.ca
Embassy in Canada: Embassy of the Federal Democratic Republic of Ethiopia, 151 Slater St, Ste 210, Ottawa ON K1P 5H3. Tel: (613) 235-6637. Fax: (613) 235-4638. Email: infoethi@magi.com

Falkland Islands

Long-Form Name: Colony of the Falkland Islands
Capital: Stanley (on East Falkland)

■ GEOGRAPHY

Area: numerous islands covering 12,173 sq. km
Climate: damp, cool, temperate; strong winds, esp. in spring; occasional snow all year
Land Use: 99% pastureland
Location: S South America, in the South Atlantic Ocean

■ PEOPLE

Population: 2,826 (July 2000 est.)
Nationality: Falkland Islander
Ethnic Groups: almost 100% British descent
Languages: English

■ GOVERNMENT

Colony Territory of: Dependent Territory of the United Kingdom
Leader(s): Head of State: Queen Elizabeth II. Governor Donald Lamont
Government Type: dependent territory of the UK, although in 1990 Argentina declared the Falklands and other British-held South Atlantic Islands part of new Argentine province Tierra del Fuego
National Holiday: Liberation Day, June 14

■ ECONOMY

Overview: heavily agricultural, esp. sheep farming, with wool main product; fishing: illex squid; exports tend to outweigh imports in value; chief trading partner: United Kingdom

■ FINANCE/TRADE

Currency: Falkland Islands pound (FKP) = 100 pence, at parity with the British pound sterling

Canadian Embassy: c/o The Canadian High Commission, Macdonald House, 1 Grosvenor Square, London W1K 4AB, England, UK. Tel: (011-44-20) 7258-6600. Fax: (011-44-20) 7445-3302. Email: Ldn@dfait-maeci.gc.ca
Representative to Canada: c/o British High Commission, 80 Elgin St, Ottawa ON K1P 5K7l. Tel: (613) 237-1530. Fax: (613) 237-7980. Email should be sent using the appropriate form at the British High Commission's website at http://www.britain-in-canada.org

Faroe Islands

Long-Form Name: Faroe Islands
Capital: Tórshavn (island of Stremoy)

■ GEOGRAPHY

Area: 1,399 sq. km (total of 18 islands and some reefs)
Climate: cold and windy; mild winters, cool summers; foggy
Land Use: 6% arable; 94% other
Location: Norwegian Sea (N Atlantic Ocean), N of Scotland

■ PEOPLE

Population: 45,296 (July 2000 est.)
Nationality: Faroese (sing. & pl.)
Ethnic Groups: Scandinavian
Languages: Faroese (derived from Old Norse), Danish

■ GOVERNMENT

Colony Territory of: Dependent Territory of Denmark
Leader(s): Queen Margrethe II of Denmark, represented by High Comm. Vibeke Larsen; Prime Min. Anfinn Kallsberg
Government Type: dependency with some degree of self-rule
National Holiday: Birthday of the Queen, Apr. 16

■ ECONOMY

Overview: fishing main industry, now in decline, which poses great danger to the economy; steep coastline and treacherous currents make trading by sea difficult; exports: fish and fish products; partners: Denmark, Norway, Sweden, Germany, United States

■ FINANCE/TRADE

Currency: Danish krone (kr) = 100 oere

Canadian Embassy: c/o The Canadian Embassy, Kr. Bernikowsgade 1, 1105 Copenhagen K, Denmark. Tel: (011-45) 33-48-32-00. Fax: (011-45) 33-48-32-20. Email: copen@dfait-maeci.gc.ca
Representative to Canada: c/o Embassy of the Kingdom of Denmark, 47 Clarence St, Ste 450, Ottawa ON K1N 9K1. Tel: (613) 562-1811. Fax: (613) 562-1812. Email: danemb@cyberus.ca

Fiji

Long-Form Name: Republic of the Fiji Islands
Capital: Suva

■ GEOGRAPHY

Area: 18,270 sq. km; includes 332 islands of which approx. 110 are inhabited
Coastline: 1,129 km
Climate: tropical marine; only slight seasonal temperature variation
Environment: subject to hurricanes from Nov. to Jan.; deforestation and soil erosion
Terrain: mostly mountains of volcanic origin
Land Use: 10% arable; 4% permanent; 10% meadows; 65% forest; 11% other; includes 10 sq. km irrigated
Location: Pacific Ocean, N of New Zealand

■ PEOPLE

Population: 832,494 (July 2000 est.)
Nationality: Fijian
Age Structure: 0-14 yrs: 33%; 15-64: 63%; 65+: 4% (2000 est.)
Population Growth Rate: 1.41% (2000 est.)
Net Migration: -3.6 migrants/1,000 population (2000 est.)
Ethnic Groups: 44% Indian, 51% Fijian, 5% European, other Pacific Islanders, overseas Chinese and others
Languages: English (official); Fijian; Hindi
Religions: Christianity 52%, Hinduism 38%, Muslim 8%, other 2%
Birth Rate: 23.48/1,000 population (2000 est.)
Death Rate: 5.78/1,000 population (2000 est.)
Infant Mortality: 14.45 deaths/1,000 live births (2000 est.)
Life Expectancy at Birth: 65.54 years male, 70.45 years female (2000 est.)
Total Fertility Rate: 2.89 children born/woman (2000 est.)
Literacy: 91.8% (1997)

■ GOVERNMENT

Leader(s): Pres. Ratu Josefa Iloilo, Prime Min. Laisenia Qarase
Government Type: republic. The government was destabilized by a coup and hostage taking that began May 19, 2000; it ended with the release of final hostages of deposed elected government on July 13, 2000. A new president was elected by the Great Council of Chiefs on July 13.
Administrative Divisions: 4 divisions and 1 dependency
Nationhood: Oct. 10, 1970 (from UK)
National Holiday: Independence Day, Oct. 10

■ ECONOMY

Overview: the economy, based on agriculture, has recovered from military coups, droughts and a drop in tourism; sugar exports are a major source of income
GDP: US$5.9 billion, per capita US$7,300; real growth rate 7.8% (1999 est.)
Inflation: 1.09% (year-end 2000)
Industries: accounts for 25.5% of GDP; sugar, copra, tourism, gold, silver, fishing, clothing, lumber, small cottage industries
Labour Force: 235,000; 29.3% community, social and business services, 24.9% industry, 14.5% trade and tourism
Unemployment: 6% (1997 est.)
Agriculture: accounts for 16.5% of GDP; principal cash crop is sugar cane; coconuts, cassava, rice, sweet potatoes and bananas; small livestock sector includes cattle, pigs, horses and goats; annual fish catch is significant
Natural Resources: timber, fish, gold, copper, offshore oil potential

■ FINANCE/TRADE

Currency: Fijian dollar ($F) = 100 cents
International Reserves Excluding Gold: US$367 million (Jan. 2001)
Gold Reserves: US$0.001 million fine troy ounces (Jan. 2001)
Budget: revenues US$540.65 million; expenditures US$742.65 million, including capital expenditures US$n.a. (1997 est.)
Defence Expenditures: 1.1% of GDP (1998)
Education Expenditures: n.a.
External Debt: US$163 million (1999)
Exports: US$447 million (2000); commodities: sugar 49%, copra, processed fish, lumber; partners: UK 45%, Australia 21%, US 4.7%
Imports: US$737 million (2000); commodities: food 15%, petroleum products, machinery, consumer goods; partners: US 48%, New Zealand, Australia, Japan

■ COMMUNICATIONS

Daily Newspapers: 1
Televisions: 25/1,000 inhabitants (1997 est.)
Radios: 600/1,000 inhabitants (1997 est.)
Telephones: 101 lines/1,000 inhabitants (1999)

■ TRANSPORTATION

Motor Vehicles: 59,000; 30,000 passenger cars (1997 est.)
Roads: 3,440 km; 1,692 km paved
Railway: 597 km
Air Traffic: 517,000 passengers carried (1997)
Airports: 25; 3 have paved runways (1999 est.)
Canadian Embassy: The Canadian Embassy to Fiji, c/o The Canadian High Commission, P.O. Box 12-049, Thorndon, Wellington, New Zealand. Tel: (011-679) 721-936. Fax: (011-679) 750-666. Email: wlgtn@dfait-maeci.gc.ca
Embassy in Canada: Embassy of the Republic of Fiji, 630 Third Ave, 7th Fl, New York NY 10017, USA. Tel: (212) 687-4130. Fax: (212) 687-3963. Email: n.a.

Finland

Long-Form Name: Republic of Finland
Capital: Helsinki

■ GEOGRAPHY

Area: 337,030 sq. km
Coastline: 1,126 km excluding islands and coastal indentations
Climate: cold temperate; potentially subarctic, but comparatively mild because of moderating influence of the North Atlantic Current, Baltic Sea and more than 60,000 lakes
Environment: permanently wet ground covers approx. 30% of land; air and water pollution
Terrain: mostly low, flat to rolling plains interspersed with lakes and low hills
Land Use: 8% arable; 0% permanent; 0% meadows; 76% forest; 16% other; includes 640 sq. km irrigated
Location: N Europe, bordering on Baltic Sea

■ PEOPLE

Population: 5,167,486 (July 2000 est.)
Nationality: Finn
Age Structure: 0-14 yrs: 18%; 15-64: 67%; 65+: 15% (2000 est.)
Population Growth Rate: 0.17% (2000 est.)
Net Migration: 0.58 migrants/1,000 population (2000 est.)
Ethnic Groups: 93% Finn, 6% Swede, 0.11% Lapp, 0.12% Gypsy, 0.02% Tatar
Languages: 93.5% Finnish, 6.3% Swedish (both official); small Lapp-and Russian-speaking minorities; business language is English
Religions: 89% Evangelical Lutheran, 9% atheist, 1% Eastern Orthodox, 1% other
Birth Rate: 10.80/1,000 population (2000 est.)
Death Rate: 9.73/1,000 population (2000 est.)
Infant Mortality: 3.82 deaths/1,000 live births (2000 est.)
Life Expectancy at Birth: 73.74 years male, 81.20 years female (2000 est.)
Total Fertility Rate: 1.70 children born/woman (2000 est.)
Literacy: 99% (1998)

■ GOVERNMENT

Leader(s): Pres. Tarja Halonen, Prime Min. Paavo Lipponen
Government Type: republic
Administrative Divisions: 6 provinces (laanit, sing. -laani)
Nationhood: Dec. 6, 1917 (from Soviet Union)
National Holiday: Independence Day, Dec. 6

■ ECONOMY

Overview: the manufacturing sector and trade are vital to this highly industrialized, largely free market economy; because of the climate, agricultural development is limited to maintaining self-sufficiency in basic products. Unemployment is a continuing problem
GDP: US$108.6 billion, per capita US$21,000; real growth rate 3.5% (1999 est.)
Inflation: 3.37% (year-end 2000)
Industries: accounts for 32% of GDP; metal manufacturing and shipbuilding, forestry and wood processing (pulp, paper), copper refining, foodstuffs, textiles, clothing
Labour Force: 3 million (1999); 33.9% community, social and business services, 19.2% industry, 14.6% trade and tourism
Unemployment: 8.3% (Jan. 2001)
Agriculture: accounts for 5% of GDP (including forestry); livestock production, especially dairy cattle, predominates; forestry is an important export earner; main crops—cereals, sugar beets, potatoes; 85% self-sufficient, but short of food and fodder grains
Natural Resources: timber, copper, zinc, iron ore, silver

■ FINANCE/TRADE

Currency: markkaa, or Finmark = 100 pennia; Euro (EUR) as of March 1, 2002
International Reserves Excluding Gold: US$7.446 billion (Jan. 2001)
Gold Reserves: US$1.577 million fine troy ounces (Jan. 2001)

Budget: revenues US$41· billion; expenditures US$41 billion, including capital expenditures of US$n.a. (1997 est.)
Defence Expenditures: 2.0% of GDP (1999)
Education Expenditures: 10.38% of central govt. expenditure (1998)
External Debt: n.a.
Exports: US$43.375 billion (2000); commodities: timber, paper and pulp, ships, machinery, clothing and footwear; partners: European Community 44.2% (UK 13%, Germany 10.8%), former USSR countries 14.9%, Sweden 14.1%, US 5.8%
Imports: US$31.556 billion (2000); commodities: foodstuffs, petroleum and petroleum products, chemicals, transport equipment, iron and steel, machinery, textile yarn and fabrics, fodder grains; partners: European Community 43.5% (Germany 16.9%, UK 6.8%), Sweden 13.3%, former USSR countries 12.1%, US 6.3%

■ COMMUNICATIONS

Daily Newspapers: 56
Televisions: 640/1,000 inhabitants (1998)
Radios: 1,496/1,000 inhabitants (1997)
Telephones: 557 lines/1,000 inhabitants (1999)

■ TRANSPORTATION

Motor Vehicles: 2,270,000; 2,000,000 passenger cars (1997 est.)
Roads: 77,895 km; 49,853 km paved
Railway: 5,865 km
Air Traffic: 6,002,000 passengers carried (1997)
Airports: 157; 69 have paved runways (1999 est.)

Canadian Embassy: The Canadian Embassy, Pohjois Esplanadi 25B, 00100 Helsinki; mailing address: Box 779, 00101 Helsinki, Finland. Tel: (011-358-9) 17-11-41. Fax (011-358-9) 60-10-60. Email: hsnki@dfait-maeci.gc.ca
Embassy in Canada: Embassy of Finland, 55 Metcalfe St, Ste 850, Ottawa ON K1P 6L5. Tel: (613) 236-2389. Fax: (613) 238-1474. Email: finembott@synapse.net

France

Long-Form Name: French Republic
Capital: Paris

■ GEOGRAPHY

Area: 547,030 sq. km; includes Corsica and the rest of metropolitan France, but excludes the overseas administrative divisions
Coastline: 3,427 km (includes Corsica, 644 km)
Climate: generally cool winters and mild summers, but mild winters and hot summers along the Mediterranean
Environment: most of large urban areas and industrial centres in Rhône, Garonne, Seine or Loire River basins; occasional warm, tropical winds known as mistrals are in central south; air and water pollution; acid rain
Terrain: mostly flat plains or gently rolling hills in north and west; remainder is mountainous, especially Pyrenees in south and Alps in east
Land Use: 33% arable; 2% permanent; 20% meadows; 27% forest; 18% other, includes 16,300 sq. km irrigated
Location: W Europe, bordering on Atlantic Ocean, Mediterranean Sea

■ PEOPLE

Population: 59,329,691 (July 2000 est.)
Nationality: Frenchman, Frenchwoman
Age Structure: 0-14 yrs: 19%; 15-64: 65%; 65+: 16% (2000 est.)
Population Growth Rate: 0.38% (2000 est.)
Net Migration: 0.66 migrants/1,000 population (2000 est.)
Ethnic Groups: Celtic and Latin with Teutonic, Slavic, North African, Indochinese and Basque minorities
Languages: French (100% of population); rapidly declining regional dialects (Provençal, Breton, Alsatian, Corsican, Catalan, Basque, Flemish)
Religions: 90% Roman Catholic, 2% Protestant, 1% Jewish, 1% Muslim (North African workers), 6% unaffiliated
Birth Rate: 12.27/1,000 population (2000 est.)
Death Rate: 9.14/1,000 population (2000 est.)
Infant Mortality: 4.51 deaths/1,000 live births (2000 est.)
Life Expectancy at Birth: 74.85 years male, 82.89 years female (2000 est.)
Total Fertility Rate: 1.75 children born/woman (2000 est.)
Literacy: 99% (1998)

■ GOVERNMENT

Leader(s): Pres. Jacques Chirac, Prime Min. Lionel Jospin
Presidential elections scheduled for April 2002
Government Type: republic
Administrative Divisions: 22 regions; dependent areas inc.: French Polynesia, Guadeloupe, Guiana (French Guiana), Martinique, Mayotte, New Caledonia, Réunion, St. Pierre and Miquelon, Southern and Antarctic Territories, Wallis and Futuna Islands
Nationhood: unified by Clovis in 486, First Republic proclaimed in 1792
National Holiday: Taking of the Bastille, July 14

■ ECONOMY

Overview: one of the world's most developed economies; largely self-sufficient in agricultural products; the leading agricultural producer in Western Europe; highly diversified industrial sector; economic integration into the European Community has unknown consequences; unemployment is rising rapidly
GDP: US$1.373 trillion, per capita US$23,300 real growth rate 2.7% (1999 est.)
Inflation: 1.70% (year-end 2000)
Industries: accounts for 26.1% of GDP; steel, machinery, chemicals, automobiles, metallurgy, aircraft, electronics, mining, textiles, food processing, tourism
Labour Force: 27 million (1999); 34.3% community, social and business services, 16.6% trade and tourism, 10.1% finance
Unemployment: 11% (1999 est.)
Agriculture: accounts for 3.3% of GNP (including fishing and forestry); one of the world's top five wheat producers; self-sufficient for most temperate-zone foods; shortages include fats and oils and tropical produce, but overall net exporter of farm products
Natural Resources: coal, iron ore, bauxite, fish, timber, zinc, potash

■ FINANCE/TRADE

Currency: franc (F or FF) = 100 centimes; Euro (EUR) as of Feb. 18, 2002
International Reserves Excluding Gold: US$32.800 billion (Jan. 2001)
Gold Reserves: US$97.245 million fine troy ounces (Jan. 2001)
Budget: revenues US$325 billion; expenditures US$360 billion, including capital expenditures of US$n.a. (1999 est.)
Defence Expenditures: 6.4% of central government expenditure (1997)
Education Expenditures: 6.0% of GNP (1997)
External Debt: n.a.
Exports: US$292.890 billion (2000); commodities: machinery and transportation equipment, chemicals, foodstuffs, agricultural products, iron and steel products, textiles and clothing; partners: Germany 15.8%, Italy 12.2%, UK 9.8%, Belgium/Luxembourg 8.9%, Netherlands 8.7%, US 6.7%, Spain 5.6%, Japan 1.8%, former USSR countries 1.3%
Imports: US$297.550 billion (2000); commodities: crude oil, machinery and equipment, agricultural products, chemicals, iron and steel products; partners: Germany 19.4%, Italy 11.5%, Belgium/Luxembourg 9.2%, US 7.7%, UK 7.2%, Netherlands 5.2%, Spain 4.4%, Japan 4.1%, former USSR countries 2.1%

■ COMMUNICATIONS

Daily Newspapers: 117
Televisions: 601/1,000 inhabitants (1998)
Radios: 937/1,000 inhabitants (1997)
Telephones: 582/1,000 inhabitants (1999)

■ TRANSPORTATION

Motor Vehicles: 30,755,000; 25,500,000 passenger cars (1997 est.)
Roads: 893,300 km; all paved
Railway: 31,939 km
Air Traffic: 43,401,000 passengers carried (1997)
Airports: 474; 267 have paved runways (1999 est.)
Canadian Embassy: The Canadian Embassy, 35-37 avenue Montaigne, 75008, Paris, France. Tel: (011-33-1) 44-43-29-00. Fax: (011-33-1) 44-43-29-99. Email: paris@dfait-maeci.gc.ca
Embassy in Canada: Embassy of France, 42 Sussex Dr, Ottawa ON K1M 2C9. Tel: (613) 789-1795. Fax: (613) 562-3735. Email: politique@ambafrance-ca.org

French Guiana

Long-Form Name: Department of Guiana
Capital: Cayenne

■ GEOGRAPHY

Area: 91,000 sq. km
Climate: tropical, warm and humid, little seasonal temperature variation
Land Use: 90% forest and woodland; interior is uncultivated wilderness, with mineral and forest resources that have not been tapped; 10% of land is under cultivation; 20 sq. km are irrigated
Location: N South America, bordering on Atlantic Ocean

■ PEOPLE

Population: 172,605 (July 2000 est.)
Nationality: French Guianese
Ethnic Groups: 66% black or mulatto, 12% Caucasian, 12% East Indian, Chinese, Amerindian, 10% other
Languages: French (official), Creole patois

■ GOVERNMENT

Colony Territory of: Overseas Department of France
Leader(s): Head of State: Pres. Jacques Chirac (France), Prefect Henri Masse, Pres. of General Council Andre Lecante
Government Type: overseas department of France
National Holiday: Taking of the Bastille, July 14

■ ECONOMY

Overview: economy is closely tied to that of France through subsidies and imports;

agriculture: rice, manioc, sugar cane, livestock; forestry, fisheries, food processing industry; chief trading partners: France, EC countries, Japan, US; unemployment is particularly serious among younger workers

■ **FINANCE/TRADE**

Currency: French franc = 100 centimes

Canadian Embassy: c/o The Canadian Embassy, 35-57 avenue Montaigne, Paris 75008, France. Tel: (011-33-1) 44-43-29-00. Fax: (011-3-1) 44-43-29-99. Email: paris@dfait-maeci.gc.ca
Representative to Canada: c/o Embassy of France, 42 Sussex Dr, Ottawa ON K1M 2C9. Tel: (613) 789-1795. Fax: (613) 562-3735. Email: politique@ambafrance-ca.org

French Polynesia

Long-Form Name: Territory of French Polynesia
Capital: Papeete (Windward Islands)

■ **GEOGRAPHY**

Area: 4,167 sq. km, consisting of five island archipelagoes scattered widely over Eastern Pacific; uninhabited Clipperton Territory is a dependency of French Polynesia but does not form part of the territory
Climate: warm and humid; tropical but moderate
Land Use: 1% arable, 6% permanent crops, 5% meadows and pastures, 31% forest and woodland, 57% other
Location: south Pacific Ocean, NE of New Zealand

■ **PEOPLE**

Population: 249,110 (July 2000 est.)
Nationality: French Polynesian
Ethnic Groups: 78% Polynesian, 12% Chinese, 6% local French, 4% metropolitan French
Languages: French and Tahitian (both official)

■ **GOVERNMENT**

Colony Territory of: Overseas Territory of France
Leader(s): Pres. Jacques Chirac (France), represented by High Commissioner to French Polynesia Jean Aribaud
Government Type: French overseas territory
National Holiday: Taking of the Bastille, July 14

■ **ECONOMY**

Overview: agriculture: copra, tropical fruits grown for local consumption; tourism accounts for approximately 20% of GDP and is primary source of revenue; trading partners: France, UK, US

■ **FINANCE/TRADE**

Currency: CFP franc = 100 centimes
Canadian Embassy: c/o The Canadian Embassy, 35-37 avenue Montaigne, Paris 75008, France. Tel: (011-33-1) 44-43-29-00. Fax: (011-33-1) 44-43-29-99. Email: paris@dfait-maeci.gc.ca
Representative to Canada: c/o Embassy of France, 42 Sussex Dr, Ottawa ON K1M 2C9. Tel: (613) 789-1795. Fax: (613) 562-3735. Email: politique@ambafrance-ca.org

Gabon

Long-Form Name: Gabonese Republic
Capital: Libreville

■ **GEOGRAPHY**

Area: 267,667 sq. km
Coastline: 885 km
Climate: tropical; always hot, humid
Environment: deforestation and poaching
Terrain: narrow coastal plain; hilly interior; savanna in east and south
Land Use: 1% arable; 1% permanent; 18% meadows; 77% forest; 3% other; includes 40 sq. km irrigated
Location: WC Africa, bordering on South Atlantic Ocean

■ **PEOPLE**

Population: 1,208,436 (July 2000 est.)
Nationality: Gabonese (sing. & pl.)
Age Structure: 0-14 yrs: 33%; 15-64: 61%; 65+: 6% (2000 est.)
Population Growth Rate: 1.08% (2000 est.)
Net Migration: 0 migrants/1,000 population (2000 est.)
Ethnic Groups: about 40 Bantu tribes, including four major tribal groupings (Fang, Eshira, Bapounou, Bateke); approx. 154,000 other Africans and Europeans, including 6,000 French and 11,000 persons of mixed background
Languages: French (official), Fang, Myene, Bateke, Bapounou/Eschira, Bandjabi
Religions: 55–75% Roman Catholic, 1% Muslim, remainder animist
Birth Rate: 27.60/1,000 population (2000 est.)
Death Rate: 16.83/1,000 population (2000 est.)
Infant Mortality: 96.30 deaths/1,000 live births (2000 est.)
Life Expectancy at Birth: 48.94 years male, 51.26 years female (2000 est.)
Total Fertility Rate: 3.73 children born/woman (2000 est.)
Literacy: 66.2% (1997)

■ GOVERNMENT

Leader(s): Pres. El Hadj Omar Bongo, Prem. Jean-François Ntoutoume-Emane
Government Type: republic; multi-party presidential regime
Administrative Divisions: 9 provinces
Nationhood: Aug. 17, 1960 (from France)
National Holiday: Independence Day, Aug. 17

■ ECONOMY

Overview: economy is dependent on oil, which has contributed to an increase in per capita income; agricultural and industrial sectors are relatively underdeveloped
GDP: US$7.9 billion, per capita US$6,500; real growth rate 1.7% (1999 est.)
Inflation: 3.97% (year-end 1997)
Industries: accounts for 60% of GDP; sawmills, cement, petroleum, food and beverages; mining of increasing importance (especially manganese and uranium)
Labour Force: 1 million (1998); 75.5% agriculture, 10.8% industry, 13.7% services
Unemployment: 21% (1997 est.)
Agriculture: accounts for 10% of GDP (including fishing and forestry); cash crops—cocoa, coffee, palm oil; livestock not developed; importer of food; okoume (a tropical softwood) is the most important timber product
Natural Resources: crude oil, manganese, uranium, gold, timber, iron ore

■ FINANCE/TRADE

Currency: Communauté financière africaine franc (CFAF) = 100 centimes
International Reserves Excluding Gold: US$150 million (Nov. 2000)
Gold Reserves: US$0.013 million fine troy ounces (June 1998)
Budget: n.a.
Defence Expenditures: 7.0% of central government expenditure (1997)
Education Expenditures: 2.9% of GNP (1997)
External Debt: US$3.978 billion (1999)
Exports: US$2.643 billion (2000); commodities: crude oil 70%, manganese 11%, wood 12%, uranium 6%; partners: France 53%, US 22%, Germany, Japan
Imports: US$973 million (2000); commodities: foodstuffs, chemical products, petroleum products, construction materials, manufacturers, machinery; partners: France 48%, US 2.6%, Germany, Japan, UK

■ COMMUNICATIONS

Daily Newspapers: 2
Televisions: 55/1,000 inhabitants (1998)
Radios: 183/1,000 inhabitants (1997)
Telephones: 32 lines/1,000 inhabitants (1999)

■ TRANSPORTATION

Motor Vehicles: 39,500; 23,800 passenger cars (1997 est.)
Roads: 7,670 km; 629 km paved
Railway: 649 km
Air Traffic: 469,000 passengers carried (1997)
Airports: 61; 11 have paved runways (1999 est.)

Canadian Embassy: The Canadian Embassy, P.O. Box 4037 Libreville, Gabon. Tel: (011-241) 73-73-54. Fax: (011-241) 73-73-88. Email: lbrve@dfait-maeci.gc.ca
Embassy in Canada: Embassy of the Gabonese Republic, 4 Range Rd, Ottawa ON K1N 8J5. Tel: (613) 232-5301. Fax: (613) 232-6916. Email: ambgabon@sprint.ca

Gambia

Long-Form Name: Republic of the Gambia
Capital: Banjul

■ GEOGRAPHY

Area: 11,300 sq. km
Coastline: 80 km
Climate: tropical; hot, rainy season (June to Nov.); cooler, dry season (Nov. to May)
Environment: deforestation and desertification; diseases spread through the water supply are common
Terrain: flood plain of the Gambia River flanked by some low hills
Land Use: 18% arable; 0% permanent; 9% meadows; 28% forest; 45% other; includes 150 sq. km irrigated
Location: W Africa, bordering on Atlantic Ocean

■ PEOPLE

Population: 1,367,124 (July 2000 est.)
Nationality: Gambian
Age Structure: 0-14 yrs: 45%; 15-64: 52%; 65+: 3% (2000 est.)
Population Growth Rate: 3.2% (2000 est.)
Net Migration: 2.97 migrants/1,000 population (2000 est.)
Ethnic Groups: 99% African (42% Mandinka, 18% Fula, 16% Wolof, 10% Jola, 9% Serahuli, 4% other); 1% non-Gambian
Languages: English (official); Mandinka, Wolof, Fula, other indigenous vernaculars
Religions: 90% Muslim, 9% Christian, 1% indigenous beliefs

Birth Rate: 42.28/1,000 population (2000 est.)
Death Rate: 13.21/1,000 population (2000 est.)
Infant Mortality: 79.29 deaths/1,000 live births (2000 est.)
Life Expectancy at Birth: 51.29 years male, 55.16 years female (2000 est.)
Total Fertility Rate: 5.76 children born/woman (2000 est.)
Literacy: 33.1% (1997)

■ GOVERNMENT

Leader(s): Pres. Yahya Jammeh; V. Pres. Isatou Njie Saidy. Presidential election scheduled for October 18, 2001.
Government Type: republic
Administrative Divisions: 5 divisions and 1 city (Banjul)
Nationhood: Feb. 18, 1965 (from UK)
National Holiday: Independence Day, Feb. 18

■ ECONOMY

Overview: a poor country, lacking in natural resources and possessing a limited agricultural base of peanut products; the recent rebound in tourism has helped the economy
GDP: US$1.4 billion, per capita US$1,030; real growth rate 4.2% (1999 est.)
Inflation: 2.2% (Jan. 2000)
Industries: accounts for 13% of GDP; peanut processing, tourism, beverages, agricultural machinery assembly, woodworking, metalworking, clothing
Labour Force: approx. 450,000 economically active; 35.4% community, social and business services, 17% trade and tourism, 11.7% transportation and communication
Unemployment: n.a.
Agriculture: accounts for 23% of GDP and employs about 75% of the population; imports one-third of food requirements; major export crop is peanuts; forestry and fishing resources not fully exploited
Natural Resources: fish

■ FINANCE/TRADE

Currency: dalasi (D) = 100 butut
International Reserves Excluding Gold: US$107 million (Oct. 2000)
Gold Reserves: n.a.
Budget: revenues US$88.6 million; expenditures US$98.2 million, including capital expenditures US$n.a. (1997 est.)
Defence Expenditures: 2.0% of GDP (1996-97)
Education Expenditures: 4.9% of GNP (1997)
External Debt: US$459 million (1999)
Exports: US$9 million (2000); commodities: peanuts and peanut products, fish, cotton lint, palm kernels; partners: Ghana 49%, Europe 27%, Japan 12%, US 1%
Imports: US$210 million (2000); commodities: foodstuffs, manufacturers, raw materials, fuel, machinery and transport equipment; partners: Europe 55%, (European Community 39%, other 16%), Asia 20%, US 11%, Senegal 4%

■ COMMUNICATIONS

Daily Newspapers: 1
Televisions: 3/1,000 inhabitants (1998)
Radios: 168/1,000 inhabitants (1997)
Telephones: 23 lines/1,000 inhabitants (1999)

■ TRANSPORTATION

Motor Vehicles: 9,000; 8,000 passenger cars (1997 est.)
Roads: 2,700 km; 956 km paved
Railway: none
Air Traffic: n.a.
Airports: 1, with paved runway (1999 est.)

Canadian Embassy: The Canadian High Commission to the Gambia, c/o The Canadian Embassy, P.O. Box 3373, Dakar, Senegal. Tel: (011-221) 823-92-90. Fax: (011-221) 823-87-49. Email: dakar@dfait-maeci.gc.ca
Embassy in Canada: c/o High Commission for the Republic of the Gambia, 1155 15th St NW, Ste 1000, Washington DC 20005-2 USA. Tel: (202) 785-1399. Fax: (202) 785-1430. Email: n.a.

Gaza Strip

Long-Form Name: none
Capital: none

■ GEOGRAPHY

Area: 360 sq. km
Climate: temperate, mild winters, dry and warm to hot summers
Land Use: 24% arable; 39% permanent crops; 0% permanent pastures; 11% forests and woodland; 26% other; includes 120 sq. km irrigated
Location: Middle East, bordering on Mediterranean Sea, Egypt and Israel.

■ PEOPLE

Population: 1,132,063 (July 2000 est.)
Nationality: n.a.
Ethnic Groups: Palestinian Arab and other 99.4%, Jewish 0.6%
Languages: Arabic, Hebrew (spoken by Israeli settlers and many Palestinians), English (widely understood)

■ GOVERNMENT

Colony Territory of: claimed and occupied by Israel

Leader(s): local Palestinian authority is headed by Yasser Arafat, subject to Israeli authority

Government Type: Palestinian Legislative Council (Jan. 1996) has limited powers under interim self-governing agreements with Israel. Originally designated as a five-year interim arrangement in 1993, permanent status still under negotiation.

National Holiday: n.a.

■ ECONOMY

Overview: economic conditions in the Gaza Strip, under the responsibility of the Palestinian Authority since the Cairo Agreement of May 1994, have deteriorated since the early 1990s; the most serious negative social effect has been the emergence of chronic unemployment, which has risen to over 20%

■ FINANCE/TRADE

Currency: 1 new Israeli shekel = 100 new agorot

Canadian Embassy: n.a.
Representative to Canada: n.a.

Georgia

Long-Form Name: Republic of Georgia
Capital: T'bilisi

■ GEOGRAPHY

Area: 69,700 sq. km
Coastline: 310 km
Climate: Alpine to subtropical with warm, humid coastlands
Environment: soil, air and water pollution from toxic chemicals
Terrain: largely mountainous in north and south; lowlands open to Black Sea in west; Kura River Basin in east; good soils in river valley, flood plains and lowlands
Land Use: 34% forests and woodlands; 9% arable; 4% permanent crops; 25% meadows and pastures; 28% other, includes 4,000 sq. km irrigated
Location: SW Asia, bordering on Black Sea

■ PEOPLE

Population: 5,019,538 (July 2000 est.)
Nationality: Georgian
Age Structure: 0-14 yrs: 20%; 15-64: 67%; 65+: 13% (2000 est.)
Population Growth Rate: -0.62% (2000 est.)

Net Migration: -2.57 migrants/1,000 population (2000 est.)
Ethnic Groups: 70.1% Georgian, 8.1% Armenian, 6.3% Russian, 5.7% Azerbaijani, 3% Ossetian, 1.9% Greek, 1.8% Abkhazian, 1% Ukrainian, 2.1% other
Languages: Armenian 7%, Azeri 6%, Georgian 71% (official), Russian 9%, other 7%
Religions: Christian Orthodox 75%, Muslim 11%, Armenian Apostolic 8%, unknown 6%
Birth Rate: 10.87/1,000 population (2000 est.)
Death Rate: 14.52/1,000 population (2000 est.)
Infant Mortality: 52.94 deaths/1,000 live births (2000 est.)
Life Expectancy at Birth: 60.90 years male, 68.23 years female (2000 est.)
Total Fertility Rate: 1.41 children born/woman (2000 est.)
Literacy: 99% (1998)

■ GOVERNMENT

Leader(s): Pres. Eduard A. Shevardnadze
Government Type: republic
Administrative Divisions: 53 rayons (raionebi, sing. —raioni), 9 cities (k'alak'ebi, sing. — k'alak'i) and 2 autonomous regions (avtomnoy respubliki, sing. —avtom respublika)
Nationhood: April 9, 1991 (from Soviet Union)
National Holiday: Independence Day, May 26

■ ECONOMY

Overview: steel processing and light industry predominate; agriculture hindered by extensive wooded areas; international transportation services through key ports are Georgia's main hope for the future
GDP: US$11.7 billion, per capita US$2,300; real growth rate 3.5% (1999 est.)
Inflation: 19.12% (year-end 1999)
Industries: accounts for 23% of GDP; coal and non-ferrous metals refining, machinery and instruments, electrical engineering, chemical production, food processing, cloth, hosiery, shoes, vehicles, mining, esp. manganese, coal, baryta
Labour Force: 3 million (1998); 31% industry and construction, 25% agriculture and forestry, 44% other
Unemployment: 14.5% (1998 est.)
Agriculture: accounts for 32% of GDP; grapes, tobacco, bay leaves, tea, citrus fruit, sugar, vegetables, grains, tobacco, tung, silk, orchard fruit
Natural Resources: manganese deposits; sulphur and other medicinal springs, forest resources, hydropower, coal and oil

■ FINANCE/TRADE

Currency: lari (GEL) = 100 tetri
International Reserves Excluding Gold: n.a.
Gold Reserves: US$0.002 million fine troy ounces (Dec. 2000)
Budget: revenues US$364 million; expenditures US$568 million, including capital expenditures of US$n.a. (1998)
Defence Expenditures: 4.65% of total govt. expenditure (1999)
Education Expenditures: 5.48% of central govt. expenditure (1999)
External Debt: US$1.652 billion (1999)
Exports: US$176 million (2000); grain, fruit, vegetables, tea, electric mine cars, seamless pipes
Imports: US$961 million (2000); fuel, foodstuffs, machinery, equipment

■ COMMUNICATIONS

Daily Newspapers: n.a.
Televisions: 473/1,000 inhabitants (1998)
Radios: 555/1,000 inhabitants (1997)
Telephones: 123 lines/1,000 inhabitants (1999)

■ TRANSPORTATION

Motor Vehicles: n.a.
Roads: 20,700 km; 19,354 km hard-surfaced
Railway: 1,583 km
Air Traffic: 110,000 passengers carried (1997)
Airports: 28; 14 have paved runways

Canadian Embassy: The Canadian Embassy to Georgia, c/o The Canadian Embassy, Nenehatun Caddesi No. 75, Gaziosmanpasa 06700, Ankara, Turkey. Tel: (011-90-312) 459-9200. Fax: (011-90-312) 459-9362. Email: ankra@dfait-maeci.gc.ca
Embassy in Canada: Embassy of the Republic of Georgia, 1615 New Hampshire Ave. NW, Suite 300, Washington DC 20009, USA. Tel: (202) 387-2390. Fax: (202) 393-4537. Email: Georgiaemb@hotmail.com

Germany

Long-Form Name: Federal Republic of Germany
Capital: Berlin

■ GEOGRAPHY

Area: 357,021 sq. km
Coastline: 2,389 km
Climate: temperate; cool, wet summers; cool to cold, cloudy winters with frequent rain and snow; occasional warm, tropical föhn wind; high relative humidity

Environment: air and water pollution; significant deforestation in mountain regions due to environmental pollution
Terrain: flat plains; lowlands in north; central uplands; Bavarian Alps in southwest
Land Use: 33% arable land; 1% permanent crops; 15% meadows and pastures; 31% forest and woodland; 20% other, includes 4,750 sq. km irrigated
Location: NC Europe, bordering on North Sea, Baltic Sea

■ PEOPLE

Population: 82,797,408 (July 2000 est.)
Nationality: German
Age Structure: 0-14 yrs: 16%; 15-64: 68%; 65+: 16% (2000 est.)
Population Growth Rate: 0.29% (2000 est.)
Net Migration: 4.01 migrants/1,000 population (2000 est.)
Ethnic Groups: German 91.5%, Turkish 2.4%, Italian 0.7%, Greek 0.4%. Polish 0.4%, other 4.6%
Languages: German (official)
Religions: 45% Protestant, 37% Roman Catholic, 18% unaffiliated
Birth Rate: 9.35/1,000 population (2000 est.)
Death Rate: 10.49/1,000 population (2000 est.)
Infant Mortality: 4.77 deaths/1,000 live births (2000 est.)
Life Expectancy at Birth: 74.30 years male, 80.75 years female (2000 est.)
Total Fertility Rate: 1.38 children born/woman (2000 est.)
Literacy: 99% (1998)

■ GOVERNMENT

Leader(s): Chanc. Gerhard Schroeder, Pres. Johannes Rau
Government Type: federal republic
Administrative Divisions: 16 states (Laender, sing. —Land)
Nationhood: January 18, 1871 (unification of German Empire); West Germany and East Germany were unified on Oct. 3, 1990
National Holiday: German Unity Day, Oct. 3

■ ECONOMY

Overview: possesses the world's third most technologically powerful economy, after the US and Japan, but its capitalistic economy has begun to struggle under the burden of generous social benefits; unemployment is a long-term, not just cyclical, problem; the integration and upgrading of the Eastern German economy remains a costly long-term problem

GDP: US$1.864 trillion, per capita US$22,700; real growth rate 1.5% (1999 est.)
Inflation: 1.95% (year-end 2000)
Industries: accounts for 30.4% of GDP; iron, steel, coal, chemicals, vehicles, ships, machinery, food and beverages, electronics, brown coal, shipbuilding, textiles, petroleum refining
Labour Force: 41 million (1999); 30.8% industry, 28.2% community, social and business services, 14.9% trade and tourism
Unemployment: 11.1% (Jan. 2001)
Agriculture: agriculture, including fishing and forestry, accounts for about 1.2% of GDP; diversified crop and livestock farming, including wheat, potatoes, barley, sugar beets, fruit, livestock products; net importer of food
Natural Resources: iron ore, coal, potash, natural gas, copper, salt, nickel, timber

■ FINANCE/TRADE

Currency: Deutsche Mark (DM) = 100 Pfennige; Euro (EUR) as of Dec. 31, 2001; DM coins and notes allowed until March 1, 2002
International Reserves Excluding Gold: US$48.526 billion (Jan. 2001)
Gold Reserves: US$111.519 million fine troy ounces (Jan. 2001)
Budget: revenues US$996 billion; expenditures US$1.036 trillion, including capital expenditures US$n.a. (1999 est.)
Defence Expenditures: 1.5% of GDP (1998)
Education Expenditures: 4.8% of GNP (1997)
External Debt: n.a.
Exports: US$549.744 billion (2000); manufactured goods 88%, agricultural products 5%, raw materials 2.3%, other 4.7%; partners: EU 58%, Eastern Europe 8%, other West European countries 7.5%, US 7%, Japan 2.5%, other 17%
Imports: US$498.086 billion (2000); manufactured goods 74%, agricultural products 10%, fuels 6.4%, raw materials 6%, other 3.6%; partners: EU 56%, Eastern Europe 9%, other West European countries 7%, US 7%, Japan 5%, China 2.5%, other 13.5%

■ COMMUNICATIONS

Daily Newspapers: 375
Televisions: 580/1,000 inhabitants (1998)
Radios: 948/1,000 inhabitants (1997)
Telephones: 590 lines/1,000 inhabitants (1999)

■ TRANSPORTATION

Motor Vehicles: 47,000,000; 42,800,000 passenger cars (1997 est.)
Roads: 656,140 km; 650,891 km paved

Railway: 40,826 km
Air Traffic: 45,805,000 passengers carried (1997)
Airports: 615; 320 have paved runways (1999 est.)

Canadian Embassy: The Canadian Embassy, Friedrichstrasse 95, 10117, Berlin, Germany. Tel: (011-49-30) 20-312-0. Fax: (011-49-30) 20-312-590. Email: brlin@dfait-maeci.gc.ca
Embassy in Canada: Embassy of the Federal Republic of Germany, 1 Waverley St, Ottawa ON K2P 0T8. Tel: (613) 232-1101. Fax: (613) 594-9330. Email: GermanEmbassyOttawa@on.aibn.com

Ghana

Long-Form Name: Republic of Ghana
Capital: Accra

■ GEOGRAPHY

Area: 238,540 sq. km
Coastline: 539 km
Climate: tropical; warm and comparatively dry along southeast coast; hot and humid in southwest; hot and dry in north
Environment: recent drought in north severely affecting marginal agricultural activities; deforestation; overgrazing; soil erosion; dry, northeasterly harmattan wind (Jan. to Mar.); water pollution and insufficient safe drinking water
Terrain: mostly low plains with dissected plateau in south-central area
Land Use: 12% arable; 7% permanent crops; 22% meadows; 35% forest; 24% other; includes 60 sq. km irrigated
Location: WC Africa, bordering on South Atlantic Ocean

■ PEOPLE

Population: 19,533,560 (July 2000 est.)
Nationality: Ghanaian
Age Structure: 0-14 yrs: 42%; 15-64: 55%; 65+: 3% (2000 est.)
Population Growth Rate: 1.87% (2000 est.)
Net Migration: -0.89% migrants/1,000 population (2000 est.)
Ethnic Groups: 99.8% black African (major tribes—44% Akan, 16% Moshi-Dagomba, 13% Ewe, 8% Ga, 18.8% other), 0.2% European and other
Languages: English (official); African languages include Akan, Moshi-Dagomba, Ewe and Ga
Religions: 38% indigenous beliefs, 30% Muslim, 24% Christian, 8% other

Birth Rate: 29.81/1,000 population (2000 est.)
Death Rate: 10.22/1,000 population (2000 est.)
Infant Mortality: 57.43 deaths/1,000 live births (2000 est.)
Life Expectancy at Birth: 56.07 years male, 58.82 years female (2000 est.)
Total Fertility Rate: 3.95 children born/woman (2000 est.)
Literacy: 69% (1998)

■ GOVERNMENT

Leader(s): Pres. John Agyekum Kufuor, V. Pres. Aliu Mahama
Government Type: constitutional democracy
Administrative Divisions: 10 regions
Nationhood: Mar. 6, 1957 (from UK, formerly known as Gold Coast)
National Holiday: Independence Day, Mar. 6

■ ECONOMY

Overview: heavily dependent on cocoa, gold and timber exports; international assistance boosts this economy, which depends on good harvests; population growth is a burden
GDP: US$35.5 billion, per capita US$1,900; real growth rate 4.3% (1999 est.)
Inflation: 25.19% (year-end 2000)
Industries: accounts for 30% of GDP; mining, lumbering, light manufacturing, fishing, aluminum, food processing
Labour Force: 9 million (1999); 59.3% agriculture, 11.1% industry, 29.6% services
Unemployment: 20% (1997 est.)
Agriculture: accounts for 40% of GDP; major cash crop is cocoa; other crops: rice, coffee, cassava, peanuts, corn; normally self-sufficient in food
Natural Resources: gold, timber, industrial diamonds, bauxite, manganese, fish, rubber

■ FINANCE/TRADE

Currency: cedi (C/) = 100 pesewas
International Reserves Excluding Gold: US$196 million (Oct. 2000)
Gold Reserves: US$0.280 million fine troy ounces (Jan. 2001)
Budget: n.a.
Defence Expenditures: 0.7% of GDP (1999)
Education Expenditures: 4.2% of GNP (1997)
External Debt: US$6.928 billion (1999)
Exports: US$1.413 billion (2000); commodities: cocoa 60%, timber, gold, tuna, bauxite, and aluminum; partners: US 23%, UK, other European Community countries
Imports: US$1.897 billion (2000); commodities: petroleum 16%, consumer goods, foods, intermediate goods, capital equipment; partners: US 10%, UK, Germany, France, Japan, S Korea

■ COMMUNICATIONS

Daily Newspapers: 4
Televisions: 99/1,000 inhabitants (1998)
Radios: 238/1,000 inhabitants (1997)
Telephones: 8 lines/1,000 inhabitants (1999)

■ TRANSPORTATION

Motor Vehicles: 135,000; 90,000 passenger cars (1997 est.)
Roads: 39,409 km; 11,653 km hard-surfaced
Railway: 953 km
Air Traffic: 211,000 passengers carried (1997)
Airports: 12; 6 have paved runways (1999 est.)

Canadian Embassy: Canadian High Commission, 42 Independence Ave, Accra, Ghana; P.O. Box 1639, Accra, Ghana. Tel: (011-233-21) 77-37-91. Fax: (011-233-21) 77-37-92. Email: accra@dfait-maeci.gc.ca
Embassy in Canada: High Commission for the Republic of Ghana, 1 Clemow Ave, Ottawa ON K1S 2A9. Tel: (613) 236-0871. Fax: (613) 236-0874. Email: n.a.

Gibraltar

Long-Form Name: Gibraltar
Capital: Gibraltar

■ GEOGRAPHY

Area: 6.5 sq. km
Climate: warm, temperate, low precipitation, mild winters, warm summers
Land Use: almost 100% bare limestone (Rock of Gibraltar) and/or built up; no farmland
Location: Iberian Peninsula of S Spain, bordering on Mediterranean Sea

■ PEOPLE

Population: 29,481 (July 2000 est.)
Nationality: Gibraltarian
Ethnic Groups: Portuguese, Maltese, Spanish, Italian, English
Languages: English (used in schools and for official purposes), Spanish, Italian, Portuguese, Russian

■ GOVERNMENT

Colony Territory of: Dependent Territory of United Kingdom
Leader(s): Head of State: Queen Elizabeth II. Gov. David Durie; Chief Min. Peter Caruana
Government Type: dependent territory of the UK
National Holiday: Commonwealth Day (second Monday in March)

■ ECONOMY

Overview: tourism most important; industries: construction materials, beverage bottling; re-exports: tobacco, petroleum, wine; exports of local products negligible; must import all food; more than 70% of the economy is in the public sector

■ FINANCE/TRADE

Currency: Gibraltar pound = 100 pence

Canadian Embassy: c/o The Canadian High Commission, Macdonald House, 1 Grosvenor Square, London W1K 4AB, England, UK. Tel: (011-44-20) 7258-6600. Fax: (011-44-20) 7258-6333. Email: Ldn@dfait-maeci.gc.ca
Representative to Canada: c/o British High Commission, 80 Elgin St, Ottawa ON K1P 5K7. Tel: (613) 237-1530. Fax: (613) 237-7980. Email should be sent using the appropriate form at the British High Commission's website at http://www.britain-in-canada.org

---

Greece

Long-Form Name: Hellenic Republic
Capital: Athens

■ GEOGRAPHY

Area: 131,940 sq. km
Coastline: 13,676 km
Climate: temperate; mild, wet winter; hot, dry summer
Environment: subject to severe earthquakes; air pollution; archipelago of 2,000 islands; water pollution
Terrain: mostly mountainous with ranges extending into sea as peninsulas or chains of islands
Land Use: 19% arable; 8% permanent crops; 41% meadows; 20% forest; 12% other, includes 13,140 sq. km irrigated
Location: S Europe, bordering on Adriatic Sea

■ PEOPLE

Population: 10,601,527 (July 2000 est.)
Nationality: Greek
Age Structure: 0-14 yrs: 15%; 15-64: 67%; 65+: 18% (2000 est.)
Population Growth Rate: 0.21% (2000 est.)
Net Migration: 1.97 migrants/1,000 population (2000 est.)
Ethnic Groups: 98% Greek, 2% others
Languages: Greek (official); English, German and French widely understood
Religions: 98% Greek Orthodox, 1.3% Muslim, 0.7% other

Birth Rate: 9.82/1,000 population (2000 est.)
Death Rate: 9.64/1,000 population (2000 est.)
Infant Mortality: 6.51 deaths/1,000 live births (2000 est.)
Life Expectancy at Birth: 75.89 years male, 81.16 years female (2000 est.)
Total Fertility Rate: 1.33 children born/woman (2000 est.)
Literacy: 96.5% (1998)

■ GOVERNMENT

Leader(s): Pres. Konstandinos Stefanopoulos, Prime Min. Konstandinos Simitis
Government Type: presidential parliamentary government
Administrative Divisions: 51 prefectures (nomoi, sing. —omós) and 1 autonomous region
Nationhood: 1829 (from the Ottoman Empire)
National Holiday: Independence Day (proclamation of the war of independence), Mar. 25

■ ECONOMY

Overview: a large commodity trade deficit is offset by the successful tourism industry; economy is characterized by low GDP growth and high national debt
GDP: US$149.2 billion, per capita US$13,900; real growth rate 3% (1999 est.)
Inflation: 3.15% (year-end 2000)
Industries: accounts for 27.3% of GDP; food and tobacco processing, textiles, chemicals, metal products, tourism, mining, petroleum
Labour Force: 5 million (1999); 21.9% agriculture, 20.1% community, social and business services, 19% industry
Unemployment: 9.9% (1999 est.)
Agriculture: accounts for 8.3% of GDP (including fishing and forestry); self-sufficient in food; principal products—wheat, corn, barley, sugar beets, olives, tomatoes, wine, tobacco, potatoes, beef, mutton, pork, dairy products
Natural Resources: bauxite, lignite, magnesite, crude oil, marble, hydropower

■ FINANCE/TRADE

Currency: drachma (Dr) = 100 lepta; euro as of March 1, 2002
International Reserves Excluding Gold: US$6.410 billion (Jan. 2001)
Gold Reserves: US$4.000 million fine troy ounces (Jan. 2001)
Budget: revenues US$37 billion; expenditures US$45 billion, capital expenditures US$n.a. (1998 est.)
Defence Expenditures: 8.40% of total govt. expenditure (1998)

Education Expenditures: 10.82% of central govt. expenditure (1998)
External Debt: US$41.9 billion (1998)
Exports: US$10.501 billion (2000); commodities: manufactured goods, food and live animals, fuels and lubricants, raw materials; partners: Germany 24%, Italy 14%, non-oil-developing countries 11.8%, France 9.5%, US 7.1%, UK 6.8%
Imports: US$26.557 billion (2000); commodities: machinery and transport equipment, light manufactures, fuels and lubricants, foodstuffs, chemicals; partners: Germany 22%, non-oil-developing countries 14%, oil-exporting countries 13%, Italy 12%, France 8%, US 3.2%

■ COMMUNICATIONS

Daily Newspapers: 156
Televisions: 466/1,000 inhabitants (1998)
Radios: 477/1,000 inhabitants (1997)
Telephones: 528 lines/1,000 inhabitants (1999)

■ TRANSPORTATION

Motor Vehicles: 3,500,000; 2,440,000 passenger cars (1997 est.)
Roads: 117,000 km; 107,406 km paved
Railway: 2,548 km
Air Traffic: 7,061,000 passengers carried (1997)
Airports: 80; 64 have paved runways (1999 est.)

Canadian Embassy: The Canadian Embassy, 4 Ioannou Gennadiou St, Athens 115 21, Greece. Tel: (011-30-1) 727-3400. Fax: (011-30-1) 727-3460. Email: athns@dfait-maeci.gc.ca
Embassy in Canada: Embassy of the Hellenic Republic, 80 MacLaren St, Ottawa ON K2P 0K6. Tel: (613) 238-6271. Fax: (613) 238-5676. Email: greekembott@travel-net.com

Greenland

Long-Form Name: Grønland
Capital: Nuuk (Godthab)

■ GEOGRAPHY

Area: 2,175,600 sq. km
Climate: arctic to subarctic; cool summers, cold winters
Land Use: 1% meadow and pastures; negligible forest and woodland; 99% bare rock, snow and ice
Location: N North America, bordering on Atlantic Ocean, Greenland Sea, Arctic Ocean, Baffin Bay

■ PEOPLE

Population: 56,309 (July 2000 est.)

Nationality: Greenlander
Ethnic Groups: 87% Greenlander (Inuit and Greenland-born Caucasians), 13% Danish and others
Languages: Inuit dialects, Danish

■ GOVERNMENT

Colony Territory of: Dependent Territory of Denmark
Leader(s): Queen Margrethe II of Denmark, represented by High Comm. Gunnar Martens (to fall 2001); Prem. Jonathan Motzfeldt
Government Type: part of the Danish realm; self-governing overseas administrative division
National Holiday: Birthday of the Queen, Apr. 16

■ ECONOMY

Overview: dependent on annual subsidy from the Danish government; unemployment is on the increase; fishing is the most important industry; mineral resource exploitation is limited to lead and zinc

■ FINANCE/TRADE

Currency: Danish krone (DKr) = 100 oere

Canadian Embassy: c/o The Canadian Embassy, Kr. Bernikowsgade 1, 1105 Copenhagen K, Denmark. Tel: (011-45) 33-48-32-00. Fax: (011-45) 33-48-32-20. Email: copen@dfait-maeci.gc.ca
Representative to Canada: c/o Royal Danish Embassy, 47 Clarence St Ste 450, Ottawa ON K1N 9K1. Tel: (613) 562-1811. Fax: (613) 562-1812. Email: danemb@cyberus.ca

Grenada

Long-Form Name: Grenada
Capital: Saint George's

■ GEOGRAPHY

Area: 340 sq. km
Coastline: 121 km
Climate: tropical; tempered by northeast trade winds
Environment: lies on edge of hurricane belt; hurricane season lasts from June to Nov.
Terrain: volcanic in origin with central mountains
Land Use: 15% arable; 18% permanent crops; 3% meadows; 9% forest; 55% other
Location: Caribbean islands, just north of Venezuela

■ PEOPLE

Population: 89,018 (July 2000 est.)
Nationality: Grenadian

Age Structure: 0-14 yrs: 38%; 15-64: 58%; 65+: 4% (2000 est.)
Population Growth Rate: -0.36% (2000 est.)
Net Migration: -16.54 migrants/1,000 population (2000 est.)
Ethnic Groups: 82% black, some East Indians, Europeans, a few Arawak
Languages: English (official); some French patois
Religions: largely Roman Catholic; Anglican; other Protestant sects
Birth Rate: 20.96/1,000 population (2000 est.)
Death Rate: 8.02/1,000 population (2000 est.)
Infant Mortality: 14.63 deaths/1,000 live births (2000 est.)
Life Expectancy at Birth: 62.74 years male, 66.31 years female (2000 est.)
Total Fertility Rate: 2.42 children born/woman (2000 est.)
Literacy: 96% (1997)

■ GOVERNMENT

Leader(s): Head of State: Queen Elizabeth II/Gov. Gen. Daniel Williams. Prime Min. Keith Mitchell
Government Type: constitutional democracy
Administrative Divisions: 6 parishes and 1 dependency
Nationhood: Feb. 7, 1974 (from UK)
National Holiday: Independence Day, Feb. 7

■ ECONOMY

Overview: economy is based on agriculture (spices, tropical plants) and tourism; unemployment is high
GDP: US$360 million, per capita US$3,700; real growth rate 5% (1999 est.)
Inflation: 0.24% (year-end 1999)
Industries: accounts for 15% of GDP; food and beverage, textiles, light assembly operations, tourism, construction
Labour Force: approx. 45,000; services 31%, agriculture 24%, construction 8%, manufacturing 5%, other 32%
Unemployment: 15% (1997)
Agriculture: accounts for 9.7% of GDP, 80% of exports and employs 24% of the labour force; bananas, cocoa, nutmeg and mace are major crops; small-scale farms predominate
Natural Resources: timber, tropical fruit, deepwater harbours

■ FINANCE/TRADE

Currency: East Caribbean dollar ($EC) = 100 cents
International Reserves Excluding Gold: US$58 million (Dec. 2000)
Gold Reserves: US$n.a.

Budget: revenues US$85.8 million; expenditures US$102.1 million, including capital expenditures of US$28 million (1997)
Defence Expenditures: n.a.
Education Expenditures: n.a.
External Debt: US$152 million (1999)
Exports: US$23 million (2000); commodities: nutmeg 35%, cocoa beans 15%, bananas 13%, mace 7%, textiles; partners: US 4%, UK, Germany, Netherlands, Trinidad and Tobago
Imports: US$175 million (2000); commodities: machinery 24%, food 22%, manufactured goods 19%, petroleum 8%; partners: US 32%, UK, Trinidad and Tobago, Japan, Canada

■ COMMUNICATIONS

Daily Newspapers: n.a.
Televisions: 370/1,000 inhabitants (1997 est.)
Radios: 640/1,000 inhabitants (1997 est.)
Telephones: 315 lines/1,000 inhabitants (1999)

■ TRANSPORTATION

Motor Vehicles: n.a.
Roads: 1,040 km; 638 km paved
Railway: none
Air Traffic: n.a.
Airports: 3; all have paved runways (1999 est.)

Canadian Embassy: The Canadian High Commission to Grenada, c/o The Canadian High Commission, P.O. Box 404, Bridgetown, Barbados. Tel: (246) 429-3550. Fax: (246) 429-3780. Email: bdgtn@dfait-maeci.gc.ca
Embassy in Canada: c/o High Commission for the Countries of the Organization of Eastern Caribbean States, 130 Albert St, Ste 700, Ottawa ON K1P 5G4. Tel: (613) 236-8952. Fax: (613) 236-3042. Email: echcc@travel-net.com

---

Guadeloupe

Long-Form Name: Department of Guadeloupe
Capital: Basse-Terre (seat of govt.); each of the 7 inhabited islands has its own chief town

■ GEOGRAPHY

Area: 1,780 sq. km (2 main islands, 5 small islands, one small island group called Iles des Saintes)
Climate: subtropical tempered by trade winds; hot and humid May–Dec., cool and dry Dec.–April
Land Use: 14% arable, 4% permanent crops, 14% meadows and pastures, 39% forest and woodland, 29% other; includes 30 sq. km irrigated
Location: Caribbean, halfway along the Lesser Antilles arch between Puerto Rico and S America

■ PEOPLE

Population: 426,493 (July 2000 est.)
Nationality: Guadeloupian
Ethnic Groups: 90% black or mulatto, 5% white, less than 5% East Indian, Lebanese, Chinese
Languages: French, Creole dialect

■ GOVERNMENT

Colony Territory of: Dependency of France
Leader(s): Head of State: Pres. Jacques Chirac (France). Prefect Jean-François Carenco, Pres. General Council Jacques Gillot
Government Type: overseas department of France
National Holiday: Taking of the Bastille, July 14

■ ECONOMY

Overview: economy depends on agriculture, tourism, light industry and services; unemployment is especially high among youth; agriculture: includes bananas, sugar cane, rum, flowers, livestock; vegetables and tobacco grown for local consumption; forestry, fisheries, tourism, food processing; partners: France, Martinique

■ FINANCE/TRADE

Currency: French franc = 100 centimes

Canadian Embassy: c/o The Canadian Embassy, 35-37 avenue Montaigne, Paris, 75008, France. Tel: (011-331) 44-43-29-00. Fax: (011-331) 44-43-29-99. Email: paris@dfait-maeci.gc.ca
Representative to Canada: c/o Embassy of France, 42 Sussex Dr, Ottawa ON K1M 2C9. Tel: (613) 789-1795. Fax: (613) 562-3735. Email: politique@ambafrance-ca.org

Guam

Long-Form Name: Territory of Guam
Capital: Hagatna (Agana)

■ GEOGRAPHY

Area: 541.3 sq. km
Climate: tropical maritime, with little seasonal variation, but typhoon-prone and suffers from earthquakes; wet all year
Land Use: 11% arable, 11% permanent crops, 15% meadows and pastures, 18% forest and woodland, 45% other; interior is mountainous and volcanic hills dominate the south, but many forests in northern Guam have been cleared for farming and the construction of airfields; coconut trees grow throughout the island
Location: N Pacific Ocean, E of the Philippines

■ PEOPLE

Population: 154,623 (July 2000 est.)
Nationality: Guamanian
Ethnic Groups: 47% Chamorro, 25% Filipino, 10% Caucasian, 18% Chinese, Japanese, Korean and other
Languages: English (official), Chamorro, Japanese

■ GOVERNMENT

Colony Territory of: Unincorporated Outlying Territory of the United States
Leader(s): Head of State: Pres. George W. Bush (US); Gov. Carl T.C. Gutierrez
Government Type: unincorporated outlying territory of the US; executive powers of the legislature similar to those of an American state legislature
National Holiday: Guam Discovery Day (first Monday in March); also Liberation Day, July 21

■ ECONOMY

Overview: economy depends mainly on US military spending and on tourism; agriculture: corn, coconuts, sweet potatoes, cucumbers, watermelons, beans, livestock, esp. cattle and pigs, fruit, vegetables, fish; industry: textile manufacture, cement, petroleum, printing, plastics, ship repair; tourism of growing importance

■ FINANCE/TRADE

Currency: American dollar = 100 cents
Canadian Embassy: c/o The Canadian Embassy, 501 Pennsylvania Avenue NW, Washington DC 20001, USA. Tel: (202) 682-1740. Fax: (202) 682-7726. Email: wshdc-outpack@dfait-maeci.gc.ca
Representative to Canada: c/o Embassy of the United States of America, 490 Sussex Drive, Ottawa ON, K1N 1G8. Tel: (613) 238-5335. Fax: (613) 688-3097. Email inquiries are not accepted

Guatemala

Long-Form Name: Republic of Guatemala
Capital: Guatemala

■ GEOGRAPHY

Area: 108,890 sq. km
Coastline: 400 km
Climate: tropical; hot, humid in lowlands; cooler in highlands
Environment: numerous volcanoes in mountains, with frequent violent earthquakes; Caribbean

coast subject to hurricanes and other tropical storms; deforestation; soil erosion; water pollution
Terrain: mostly mountainous with narrow coastal plains and rolling limestone plateau (Petén)
Land Use: 12% arable; 5% permanent; 24% permanent pastures; 54% forest; 5% other; includes 1,250 sq, km irrigated
Location: northernmost Central (Latin) America, bordering on Caribbean Sea, Pacific Ocean

■ PEOPLE

Population: 12,639,939 (July 2000 est.)
Nationality: Guatemalan
Age Structure: 0-14 yrs: 42%; 15-64: 54%; 65+: 4% (2000 est.)
Population Growth Rate: 2.63% (2000 est.)
Net Migration: -1.89 migrants/1,000 population (2000 est.)
Ethnic Groups: 56% Ladino (mestizo-mixed Indian and European ancestry), 44% Indian
Languages: 60% Spanish, but 40% of the population speaks an Indian language as a primary tongue (23 Indian dialects, including Quiche, Cakchiquel, Kekchi)
Religions: predominantly Roman Catholic; also Protestant, traditional Mayan
Birth Rate: 35.05/1,000 population (2000 est.)
Death Rate: 6.92/1,000 population (2000 est.)
Infant Mortality: 47.03 deaths/1,000 live births (2000 est.)
Life Expectancy at Birth: 63.53 years male, 68.96 years female (2000 est.)
Total Fertility Rate: 4.66 children born/woman (2000 est.)
Literacy: 67.5% (1998)

■ GOVERNMENT

Leader(s): Pres. Alfonso Antonio Portillo; V. Pres. Juan Francisco Reyes
Government Type: republic
Administrative Divisions: 22 departments (departamento, pl. departamentos)
Nationhood: Sept. 15, 1821 (from Spain)
National Holiday: Independence Day, Sept. 15

■ ECONOMY

Overview: the inflation rate has dropped significantly as a result of government economic reforms, but political uncertainty casts a shadow over the agriculturally based economy
GDP: US$47.9 billion, per capita US$3,900; real growth rate 3.5% (1999 est.)
Inflation: 5.98% (year-end 2000)
Industries: accounts for 20% of GDP; sugar, textiles and clothing, furniture, chemicals, petroleum, metals, rubber, tourism

Labour Force: 4.0 million (1999); 36.9% community, social and business services, 26.1% agriculture, 16.6% industry
Unemployment: 7.5% (1999 est.)
Agriculture: accounts for 23% of GDP and employs 60% of the labour force; principal crops—sugar cane, corn, bananas, coffee, beans, cardamom; livestock—cattle, sheep, pigs, chickens; food importer
Natural Resources: crude oil, nickel, rare woods, fish, chicle, hydropower

■ FINANCE/TRADE

Currency: quetzal (pl. quetzalas) (Q) = 100 centavos
International Reserves Excluding Gold: US$1.713 billion (Jan. 2001)
Gold Reserves: US$0.208 million fine troy ounces (Jan. 2001)
Budget: n.a.
Defence Expenditures: 0.7% of GDP (1998)
Education Expenditures: 1.7% of GNP (1997)
External Debt: US$4.660 billion (1999)
Exports: US$2.574 billion (2000); commodities: coffee 38%, bananas 7%, sugar 7%, cardamom 4%; partners: US 29%, El Salvador, Germany, Costa Rica, Italy
Imports: US$4.641 billion (2000); commodities: fuel and petroleum products, machinery, grain, fertilizers, motor vehicles; partners: US 38%, Mexico, Germany, Japan, El Salvador

■ COMMUNICATIONS

Daily Newspapers: 7
Televisions: 126/1,000 inhabitants (1998)
Radios: 79/1,000 inhabitants (1997)
Telephones: 55 lines/1,000 inhabitants (1999)

■ TRANSPORTATION

Motor Vehicles: 199,000; 102,000 passenger cars (1997 est.)
Roads: 13,100 km; 3,616 km paved
Railway: 884 km
Air Traffic: 508,000 passengers carried (1997)
Airports: 477; 11 have paved runways (1999 est.)

Canadian Embassy: The Canadian Embassy, 13 Calle 8-44, Zone 10, Guatemala City; mailing address: P.O. Box 400, Guatemala City, Guatemala, C.A. Tel: (011-502) 333-61-02. Fax: (011-502) 333-61-61. Email: gtmla@dfait-maeci.gc.ca
Embassy in Canada: Embassy of the Republic of Guatemala, 130 Albert St, Ste 1010, Ottawa ON K1P 5G4. Tel: (613) 233-7237. Fax: (613) 233-0135. Email: embguate@webruler.com

Guinea

Long-Form Name: Republic of Guinea
Capital: Conakry

■ GEOGRAPHY

Area: 245,857 sq. km
Coastline: 320 km
Climate: generally hot and humid; monsoonal-type rainy season (June to Nov.) with southwesterly winds; dry season (Dec. to May) with northeasterly harmattan winds
Environment: hot, dry, dusty harmattan haze may reduce visibility during dry season; deforestation; insufficient safe drinking water
Terrain: generally flat coastal plain, hilly to mountainous interior
Land Use: 2% arable; negligible permanent crops; 22% permanent pastures; 59% forest; 17% other; includes 930 sq. km irrigated
Location: W Africa, bordering on Atlantic Ocean

■ PEOPLE

Population: 7,466,200 (July 2000 est.)
Nationality: Guinean
Age Structure: 0-14 yrs: 43.38%; 15-64: 53.95%; 65+: 2.68% (2000 est.)
Population Growth Rate: 1.95% (2000 est.)
Net Migration: -2.68 migrants/1,000 population (2000 est.)
Ethnic Groups: 40% Peuhl, 30% Malinke, 20% Sousou, 10% smaller tribes
Languages: French (official); each tribe has its own language; 8 official languages are taught in schools, including Fulani, Malinke, Soussou
Religions: 85% Muslim, 7% indigenous beliefs, 8% Christian
Birth Rate: 40.08/1,000 population (2000 est.)
Death Rate: 17.86/1,000 population (2000 est.)
Infant Mortality: 130.98 deaths/1,000 live births (2000 est.)
Life Expectancy at Birth: 43.16 years male, 48.02 years female (2000 est.)
Total Fertility Rate: 5.46 children born/woman (2000 est.)
Literacy: 37.9% (1997)

■ GOVERNMENT

Leader(s): Pres. Gen. Lansana Conté, Premier Lamine Sidime
Government Type: republic
Administrative Divisions: 4 administrative regions (regions administrative, sing. —region administrative) and 1 special zone (zone speciale)
Nationhood: Oct. 2, 1958 (from France; formerly known as French Guinea)

National Holiday: Anniversary of the Second Republic, Apr. 3

■ ECONOMY

Overview: although possessing numerous natural resources and potential for agricultural development, it is one of the poorest countries in the world; mining accounts for the bulk of Guinea's exports, and apart from the bauxite industry, foreign investment remains low
GDP: US$9.2 billion, per capita US$1,200; real growth rate 3.7% (1999 est.)
Inflation: n.a.
Industries: accounts for 31% of GDP; bauxite mining, alumina, diamond mining, light manufacturing and agricultural processing industries
Labour Force: 3.0 million (1999); 78.1% agriculture, 1.3% industry, 20.6% services
Unemployment: n.a.
Agriculture: accounts for 24% of GDP and employs 80% of the workforce (including fishing and forestry); mostly subsistence farming; principal products—rice, coffee, pineapples, palm kernels, cassava, sweet potatoes, timber; livestock—cattle, sheep and goats
Natural Resources: bauxite, iron ore, diamonds, gold, uranium, hydroelectricity, fish

■ FINANCE/TRADE

Currency: Guinean franc = 100 centimes
International Reserves Excluding Gold: US$168 million (June 2000)
Gold Reserves: n.a.
Budget: n.a.
Defence Expenditures: 8.0% of central government expenditure (1997)
Education Expenditures: 1.9% of GNP (1997)
External Debt: US$3.518 billion (1999)
Exports: US$695 million (1998 est.); commodities: alumina, bauxite, diamonds, coffee, pineapples, bananas, palm kernels; partners: US 33%, European Community 33%, Eastern Europe 20%, Canada
Imports: US$560 million (1998 est.); commodities: petroleum products, metals, machinery, transport equipment, foodstuffs, textiles and grain; partners: US 16%, France, Brazil

■ COMMUNICATIONS

Daily Newspapers: 0
Televisions: 41/1,000 inhabitants (1998)
Radios: 47/1,000 inhabitants (1997)
Telephones: 6 lines/1,000 inhabitants (1999)

■ TRANSPORTATION

Motor Vehicles: 33,000; 13,700 passenger cars (1997 est.)
Roads: 30,500 km; 5,033 km paved
Railway: 1,086 km
Air Traffic: 36,000 passengers carried (1997)
Airports: 15; 5 have paved runways (1999 est.)

Canadian Embassy: The Canadian Embassy, P.O. Box 99, Conakry, Guinea. Tel: (011-224) 46-23-95. Fax: (011-224) 46-42-35. Email: cnaky@dfait-maeci.gc.ca
Embassy in Canada: Embassy of the Republic of Guinea, 483 Wilbrod St, Ottawa ON K1N 6N1. Tel: (613) 789-8444. Fax: (613) 789-7560. Email: ambaguineaott@sympatico.ca

Guinea-Bissau

Long-Form Name: Republic of Guinea-Bissau
Capital: Bissau

■ GEOGRAPHY

Area: 36,120 sq. km
Coastline: 350 km
Climate: tropical; generally hot and humid; monsoon-type rainy season (June to Nov.) with southwesterly winds; dry season (Dec. to May) with northeasterly harmattan winds
Environment: hot, dry, dusty harmattan haze may reduce visibility during dry season; deforestation, soil erosion
Terrain: mostly low coastal plain rising to savanna in east
Land Use: 11% arable; 1% permanent crops; 38% meadows; 38% forest; 12% other; includes 17 sq. km irrigated
Location: W Africa, bordering on Atlantic Ocean

■ PEOPLE

Population: 1,285,715 (July 2000 est.)
Nationality: Guinean
Age Structure: 0-14 yrs: 42%; 15-64: 55%; 65+: 3% (2000 est.)
Population Growth Rate: 2.4% (2000 est.)
Net Migration: 0 migrants/1,000 population (2000 est.)
Ethnic Groups: approx. 99% African (including 30% Balanta, 20% Fula, 14% Manjaca, 13% Mandinga, 7% Papel); less than 1% European and mulatto
Languages: Portuguese (official); Crioulo (a Portuguese-based Creole), Balante and numerous African languages
Religions: 65% indigenous beliefs, 30% Muslim, 5% Christian
Birth Rate: 39.63/1,000 population (2000 est.)

Death Rate: 15.62/1,000 population (2000 est.)
Infant Mortality: 112.25 deaths/1,000 live births (2000 est.)
Life Expectancy at Birth: 46.77 years male, 51.37 years female (2000 est.)
Total Fertility Rate: 5.27 children born/woman (2000 est.)
Literacy: 33.6% (1997)

■ GOVERNMENT

Leader(s): Pres. Yala Koumba, Prime Min. Faustino Imbali
Government Type: republic
Administrative Divisions: 9 regions (regiões, singular–região)
Nationhood: Sept. 10, 1974 (from Portugal; formerly known as Portuguese Guinea)
National Holiday: Independence Day, Sept. 24

■ ECONOMY

Overview: this poor country is focusing on agricultural development; exploitation of mineral deposits is hampered by a weak infrastructure and high costs. The heavy foreign debt is a burden
GDP: US$1.1 billion, per capita US$900; real growth rate 9.5% (1999 est.)
Inflation: 8.64% (year-end 2000)
Industries: accounts for 11% of GDP, agricultural processing, beer, soft drinks
Labour Force: approx. 500,000 economically active; 82% agriculture, 4% industry, 14% services
Unemployment: n.a.
Agriculture: accounts for 54% of GDP; nearly 100% of exports and 90% of employment; rice is the staple; not self-sufficient in food; fishing and forestry not fully exploited; crops include corn, beans, cassava, cashew nuts, peanuts, palm kernels and cotton
Natural Resources: unexploited deposits of petroleum, bauxite, phosphates; fish, timber

■ FINANCE/TRADE

Currency: Communauté financière africaine (CFAF) franc = 100 centimes
International Reserves Excluding Gold: US$54 million (Nov. 2000)
Gold Reserves: n.a.
Budget: n.a.
Defence Expenditures: 13.0% of central government expenditure (1997)
Education Expenditures: n.a.
External Debt: US$931 million (1999)
Exports: US$30 million (2000); commodities: cashews, fish, peanuts, palm kernels; partners: Portugal, Spain, Switzerland, Cape Verde, China

Imports: US$75 million (2000); commodities: capital equipment, consumer goods, semiprocessed goods, foods, petroleum; partners: Portugal, former USSR countries, European Community, other European, Senegal, US

■ COMMUNICATIONS

Daily Newspapers: 1
Televisions: n.a.
Radios: 44/1,000 inhabitants (1997)
Telephones: 7 lines/1,000 inhabitants (1999)

■ TRANSPORTATION

Motor Vehicles: 6,900; 4,000 passenger cars (1997 est.)
Roads: 4,400 km; 453 km paved
Railway: none
Air Traffic: 21,000 passengers carried (1997)
Airports: 30; 3 have paved runways (1999 est.)

Canadian Embassy: The Canadian Embassy to Guinea-Bissau, c/o The Canadian Embassy, P.O. Box 3373, Dakar, Senegal. Tel: (011-221) 823-92-90. Fax: (011-221) 823-87-49. Email: dakar@dfait-maeci.gc.ca
Embassy in Canada: Embassy of the Republic of Guinea-Bissau, 15929 Yukon Lane (Rockville, Maryland), Washington DC 20855, USA. Tel: (301) 947-3958. Fax: (301) 947-3958. Email: n.a.

Guyana

Long-Form Name: Co-operative Republic of Guyana
Capital: Georgetown

■ GEOGRAPHY

Area: 214,970 sq. km
Coastline: 459 km
Climate: tropical; hot, humid, moderated by northeast trade winds; two rainy seasons (May to mid-Aug., mid-Nov. to mid-Jan.)
Environment: flash floods a constant threat during rainy seasons; water pollution; deforestation
Terrain: mostly rolling highlands; low coastal plain; savanna in south
Land Use: 2% arable; negligible permanent; 6% meadows; 84% forest; 8% other; includes 1,300 sq. km irrigated
Location: N South America, bordering on Atlantic Ocean

■ PEOPLE

Population: 697,286 (July 2000 est.)
Nationality: Guyanese

Age Structure: 0-14 yrs: 29%; 15-64: 66%; 65+: 5% (2000 est.)
Population Growth Rate: -0.1% (2000 est.)
Net Migration: -10.48 migrants/1,000 population (2000 est.)
Ethnic Groups: 51% East Indian, 44% black and mixed, 4% Amerindian, 1% European and Chinese
Languages: English, Hindi, Urdu, Amerindian dialects
Religions: 60% Christian, 30% Hindu, 9% Muslim, 1% other
Birth Rate: 17.94/1,000 population (2000 est.)
Death Rate: 8.42/1,000 population (2000 est.)
Infant Mortality: 39.07deaths/1,000 live births (2000 est.)
Life Expectancy at Birth: 61.08 years male, 67.15 years female (2000 est.)
Total Fertility Rate: 2.11 children born/woman (2000 est.)
Literacy: 98.1% (1997)

■ GOVERNMENT

Leader(s): Pres. Bharrat Jagdeo, Prime Min. Samuel Hinds
Government Type: republic
Administrative Divisions: 10 regions
Nationhood: May 26, 1966 (from UK; formerly known as British Guyana)
National Holiday: Republic Day, Feb. 23

■ ECONOMY

Overview: one of the world's poorest countries, with a per capita income less than one-fifth the South American average; electricity has been in short supply and constitutes a major barrier to production
GDP: US$1.86 billion, per capita US$2,500; real growth rate -1.8% (1999 est.)
Inflation: 6.15% (year-end 2000)
Industries: accounts for 32.5% of GDP; bauxite mining, sugar, rice milling, timber, fishing (shrimp), textiles, gold mining
Labour Force: n.a.; 26% industry, 27% agriculture, 47% services
Unemployment: n.a.
Agriculture: most important sector, accounting for 34.7% of GDP; sugar and rice are main crops; livestock include beef, pork, poultry; not self-sufficient in food; development potential exists for fishing and forestry
Natural Resources: bauxite, gold, diamonds, hardwood timber, shrimp, fish

■ FINANCE/TRADE

Currency: Guyanese dollar ($G) = 100 cents
International Reserves Excluding Gold: US$275 million (Nov. 2000)

Gold Reserves: n.a.
Budget: revenues US$220.1 million; expenditures US$286.4 million, including capital expenditures of US$86.6 million (1998)
Defence Expenditures: n.a.
Education Expenditures: n.a.
External Debt: US$1.527 billion (1999)
Exports: US$522 million (2000); commodities: bauxite, sugar, rice, shrimp, gold, molasses, timber, rum; partners: UK 37%, US 12%, Canada 10.6%, CARICOM 4.8%
Imports: US$654 million (2000); commodities: manufactures, machinery, food, petroleum; partners: CARICOM 41%, US 18%, UK 9%, Canada 3%

■ COMMUNICATIONS

Daily Newspapers: 2
Televisions: 65/1,000 inhabitants (1997 est.)
Radios: 602/1,000 inhabitants (1997 est.)
Telephones: 75 lines/1,000 inhabitants (1999)

■ TRANSPORTATION

Motor Vehicles: 33,000; 24,000 passenger cars (1997 est.)
Roads: 7,970 km; 590 km paved
Railway: 187 km; no public railroads
Air Traffic: 126,000 passengers carried (1997)
Airports: 51; 5 paved runways (1999 est.)
Canadian Embassy: Canadian High Commission, High and Young Streets, Georgetown; mailing address: P.O. Box 10880, Georgetown, Guyana. Tel: (011-592-2) 72081. Fax: (011-592-2) 58380. Email: grgtn@dfait-maeci.gc.ca
Embassy in Canada: High Commission for the Co-operative Republic of Guyana, Burnside Bldg, 151 Slater St, Ste 309, Ottawa ON K1P 5H3. Tel: (613) 235-7249. Fax: (613) 235-1447. Email: n.a.

Haiti

Long-Form Name: Republic of Haiti
Capital: Port-au-Prince

■ GEOGRAPHY

Area: 27,750 sq. km
Coastline: 1,771 km
Climate: tropical; semi-arid where mountains in east cut off trade winds
Environment: lies in the middle of the hurricane belt and subject to severe storms from June to Oct.; occasional flooding and earthquakes; deforestation; soil erosion, insufficient safe drinking water
Terrain: mostly rough and mountainous
Land Use: 20% arable; 13% permanent crops; 18% meadows; 5% forest; 44% other; includes 750 sq. km irrigated

Location: West Indies, bordering on Caribbean Sea, Atlantic Ocean

■ PEOPLE

Population: 6,867,995 (July 2000 est.)
Nationality: Haitian
Age Structure: 0-14 yrs: 41%; 15-64: 55%; 65+: 4% (2000 est.)
Population Growth Rate: 1.39% (2000 est.)
Net Migration: -2.97 migrants/1,000 population (2000 est.)
Ethnic Groups: 95% black, 5% mulatto and European
Languages: French (official) spoken by only 10% of population; all speak Creole
Religions: 80% Roman Catholic (of which an overwhelming majority also practice Voodoo), 16% Protestant, 4% other
Birth Rate: 31.97/1,000 population (2000 est.)
Death Rate: 15.13/1,000 population (2000 est.)
Infant Mortality: 97.10 deaths/1,000 live births (2000 est.)
Life Expectancy at Birth: 47.46 years male, 51.06 years female (2000 est.)
Total Fertility Rate: 4.50 children born/woman (2000 est.)
Literacy: 48% (1998)

■ GOVERNMENT

Leader(s): Pres. Jean-Bertrand Aristide, Prem. Jean-Marie Antoine Polynice Cherestal
Government Type: elected government
Administrative Divisions: 9 départments (départements, sing. —département)
Nationhood: Jan. 1, 1804 (from France)
National Holiday: Independence Day, Jan. 1

■ ECONOMY

Overview: about 75% of the population live in absolute poverty, and do not have access to safe drinking water, medical care or sufficient food; agriculture based on small-scale subsistence farming; trade sanctions have further damaged the economy
GDP: US$9.2 billion, per capita US$1,340; real growth rate 2.4% (1999 est.)
Inflation: 13.7% (year-end 2000)
Industries: accounts for 20% of GDP; sugar refining, textiles, flour milling, cement manufacturing, bauxite mining, tourism, light assembly industries based on imported parts
Labour Force: 3 million (1999); 50.4% agriculture, 43.9% services, 5.7% industry
Unemployment: 70%; widespread under-employment (1999)
Agriculture: accounts for 32% of GDP and employs 70% of workforce; mostly small-size subsistence farms; commercial crops include

coffee and sugar cane; staple crops include rice, corn, sorghum and mangoes

Natural Resources: bauxite, copper, gold, calcium carbonate

■ FINANCE/TRADE

Currency: gourde (G) = 100 centimes

International Reserves Excluding Gold: US$81 million (Aug. 1998)

Gold Reserves: US$0.001 million fine troy ounces (Jan. 2001)

Budget: revenues US$323million; expenditures US$363 million, including capital expenditures US$n.a. (1997-98 est.)

Defence Expenditures: n.a.

Education Expenditures: n.a.

External Debt: US$1.191 billion (1999)

Exports: US$165 million (2000); commodities: light manufactures 65%, coffee 17%, other agriculture 8%, other products 10%; partners: US 77%, France 5%, Italy 4%, Germany 3%, other industrial 9%, less developed countries 2%

Imports: US$982 million (2000); commodities: machines and manufactures 36%, food and beverages 21%, petroleum products 11%, fats and oils 12%, chemicals 12%; partners: US 65%, Netherlands Antilles 6%, Japan 5%, France 4%, Canada 2%, Asia 2%

■ COMMUNICATIONS

Daily Newspapers: 4

Televisions: 5.0/1,000 inhabitants (1998)

Radios: 55/1,000 inhabitants (1997)

Telephones: 9 lines/1,000 inhabitants (1999)

■ TRANSPORTATION

Motor Vehicles: 53,000; 32,000 passenger cars (1997 est.)

Roads: 4,160 km; 1,011 km paved

Railway: 40 km

Air Traffic: n.a.

Airports: 13; 3 have paved runways (1999 est.)

Canadian Embassy: The Canadian Embassy, Édifice Banque de Nova Scotia, route de Delmas, Port-au-Prince, Haiti; mailing address: C.P. 826, Port-au-Prince, Haiti. Tel: (011-509) 298-3050. Fax: (011-509) 298-3801. Email: prnce@dfait-maeci.gc.ca

Embassy in Canada: Embassy of the Republic of Haiti, 130 Albert St, Ste 1409, Ottawa ON K1P 5G4. Tel: (613) 238-1628. Fax (613) 238-2986. Email: bohio@sympatico.ca

---

Honduras

Long-Form Name: Republic of Honduras

Capital: Tegucigalpa

■ GEOGRAPHY

Area: 112,090 sq. km

Coastline: 820 km

Climate: subtropical in lowlands, temperate in mountains

Environment: subject to frequent, but generally mild, earthquakes; damaging hurricanes along Caribbean coast; deforestation; soil erosion; mining pollution of freshwater resources

Terrain: mostly mountainous in interior, narrow coastal plains

Land Use: 15% arable; 3% permanent; 14% permanent pastures; 54% forest and woodlands; 14% other; includes 740 sq. km irrigated

Location: Central (Latin) America, bordering on Caribbean Sea, Pacific Ocean

■ PEOPLE

Population: 6,249,598 (July 2000 est.)

Nationality: Honduran

Age Structure: 0-14 yrs: 43%; 15-64: 54%; 65+: 3% (2000 est.)

Population Growth Rate: 2.52% (2000 est.)

Net Migration: -2.17 migrants/1,000 population (2000 est.)

Ethnic Groups: 90% mestizo (mixed Indian and European), 7% Indian, 2% black, 1% white

Languages: Spanish, Indian dialects

Religions: about 97% Roman Catholic; small Protestant minority

Birth Rate: 32.65/1,000 population (2000 est.)

Death Rate: 5.31/1,000 population (2000 est.)

Infant Mortality: 31.29 deaths/1,000 live births (2000 est.)

Life Expectancy at Birth: 67.91 years male, 72.06 years female (2000 est.)

Total Fertility Rate: 4.26 children born/woman (2000 est.)

Literacy: 73% (1998)

■ GOVERNMENT

Leader(s): Pres. Carlos Roberto Flores. Presidential election scheduled for November 25, 2001.

Government Type: republic

Administrative Divisions: 18 departments (departamentos, sing. —departamento, plus 1 probable central district)

Nationhood: Sept. 15, 1821 (from Spain)

National Holiday: Independence Day, Sept. 15

■ ECONOMY

Overview: one of the poorest countries in the western hemisphere, with a high population growth rate, a high unemployment rate, a lack of basic services and an export sector vulnerable to world prices (coffee, bananas)

GDP: US$14.1 billion, per capita US$2,050; real growth rate -3% (1999 est.)
Inflation: 11.06% (year-end 2000)
Industries: accounts for 25% of GDP; agricultural processing (sugar and coffee), textiles, clothing, wood products
Labour Force: 2.0 million (1999); 38.2% agriculture, 19.9% community, social and business services, 37.4% undefined
Unemployment: 12%, with 30% under-employment (1999 est.)
Agriculture: accounts for 20% of GDP, over 60% of the labour force and 20% of exports; main products include bananas, coffee, timber, beef, citrus fruit, shrimp; importer of wheat
Natural Resources: timber, gold, silver, copper, lead, zinc, iron ore, antimony, coal, fish

■ FINANCE/TRADE

Currency: lempira (L) = 100 centavos
International Reserves Excluding Gold: US$1.279 billion (Jan. 2001)
Gold Reserves: US$0.021 million fine troy ounces (Jan. 2001)
Budget: revenues US$980 million; expenditures US$1.15 billion, including capital expenditures of US$n.a. (1998 est.)
Defence Expenditures: 0.6% of GDP (1998)
Education Expenditures: 3.6% of GNP (1997)
External Debt: US$5.333 billion (1999)
Exports: US$1.419 billion (2000); commodities: bananas, coffee, shrimp, lobster, minerals, lumber; partners: US 52%, Germany 11%, Japan, Italy, Belgium
Imports: US$2.870 billion (2000); commodities: machinery and transport equipment, chemical products, manufactured goods, fuel and oil, foodstuffs; partners: US 39%, Japan 9%, CACM, Venezuela, Mexico

■ COMMUNICATIONS

Daily Newspapers: 7
Televisions: 90/1,000 inhabitants (1998)
Radios: 386/1,000 inhabitants (1997)
Telephones: 44 lines/1,000 inhabitants (1999)

■ TRANSPORTATION

Motor Vehicles: 185,000; 80,000 passenger cars (1997 est.)
Roads: 15,400 km; 3,126 km paved
Railway: 595 km
Air Traffic: 474,000 passengers carried (1996 est.)
Airports: 119; 12 have paved runways (1999 est.)

Canadian Embassy: The Office of the Canadian Embassy, Centro Financiero BANEXPO, 3rd Floor, Bulevar San Juan Bosco, Colonia Payaqui, Tegucigalpa, Honduras, Postal Address: The Office of the Canadian Embassy, P.O. Box 3552, Tegucigalpa, Honduras. Tel: (011 504) 232-4551. Fax: (011 504) 232-8767. Email: tglpa@dfait-maeci.gc.ca
Embassy in Canada: Embassy of the Republic of Honduras, 151 Slater St, Ste 805, Ottawa ON K1P 5H3. Tel: (613) 233-8900. Fax: (613) 232-0193. Email: scastell@magma.ca

---

Hong Kong

Long-Form Name: Hong Kong Special Administrative Region
Capital: none

■ GEOGRAPHY

Area: 1,092 sq. km
Climate: tropical monsoon; cool and humid in winter, hot and rainy from spring through summer, warm and sunny in fall
Land Use: 6% arable land; 1% permanent crops; 1% meadows; 20% forest; 72% other, includes 20 sq. km irrigated
Location: SE Asia, bordering on South China Sea

■ PEOPLE

Population: 7,116,302 (July 2000 est.)
Nationality: Chinese
Ethnic Groups: 95% Chinese, 5% other
Languages: Chinese (Cantonese), English

■ GOVERNMENT

Colony Territory of: Special Administrative Region (SAR) of the People's Republic of China
Leader(s): Pres. of China, Jiang Zemin; Chief Exec. Tung Chee-hwa
Government Type: reverted to China July 1, 1997
National Holiday: National Day, Oct. 1-2; July 1 is celebrated as Hong Kong Special Administrative Region Establishment Day

■ ECONOMY

Overview: manufacturing and services (finance, business and professional) are the basis of the economy; natural resources are limited and food and raw materials must be imported

■ FINANCE/TRADE

Currency: Hong Kong dollar (HK$) = 100 cents
Canadian Embassy: c/o The Canadian Embassy, 19 Dong Zhi Men Wai, Chao Yang District 100600, Beijing, PDR China. Tel: (011-86-10) 6532-3536. Fax: (011-86-10) 6532-4311. Email: bejing@dfait-maeci.gc.ca

Representative to Canada: c/o Embassy of the People's Republic of China, 515 St. Patrick St, Ottawa ON K1N 5H3. Tel: (613) 789-3434. Fax: (613) 789-1911. Email: cooffice@buildlink.com

Hungary

Long-Form Name: Republic of Hungary
Capital: Budapest

■ GEOGRAPHY

Area: 93,030 sq. km
Coastline: none: landlocked
Climate: temperate; cold, cloudy, humid winter; warm summer
Environment: levees are common along many streams, but flooding occurs almost every year; pollution of air, soil and underground water resources
Terrain: mostly flat to rolling plains
Land Use: 51% arable; 3.6% permanent crops; 12.4% permanent pastures; 19% forest; 14% other, includes 2,060 sq. km irrigated
Location: C Europe

■ PEOPLE

Population: 10,138,844 (July 2000 est.)
Nationality: Hungarian
Age Structure: 0-14 yrs: 17%; 15-64: 68%; 65+: 15% (2000 est.)
Population Growth Rate: -0.33% (2000 est.)
Net Migration: 0.73 migrants/1,000 population (2000 est.)
Ethnic Groups: 89.9% Hungarian, 4% Gypsy, 2% Serb, 2.6% German, 0.8% Slovak, 0.7% Romanian
Languages: Hungarian (Magyar, official), 1.8% other
Religions: 67.5% Roman Catholic, 20% Calvinist, 5% Lutheran, 7.5% atheist and other
Birth Rate: 9.26/1,000 population (2000 est.)
Death Rate: 13.34/1,000 population (2000 est.)
Infant Mortality: 9.15 deaths/1,000 live births (2000 est.)
Life Expectancy at Birth: 67.00 years male, 76.05 years female (2000 est.)
Total Fertility Rate: 1.25 children born/woman (2000 est.)
Literacy: 99% (1998)

■ GOVERNMENT

Leader(s): Pres. Ferenc Madl; Prime Min. Victor Orban
Government Type: parliamentary democracy
Administrative Divisions: 19 counties (megyek, sing. —megye), 20 urban counties and 1 capital city (fovaros)

Nationhood: 1001 (unification by King Stephen I)
National Holiday: St. Stephen's Day, Aug. 20 (National Day)

■ ECONOMY

Overview: consolidated its stabilization program and undergone enough restructuring to become an established market economy; it appears to have entered a period of sustainable growth, gradually falling inflation, and stable external balances; the government's main economic priorities are to complete structural reforms, particularly in pension, taxation, and healthcare reforms
GDP: US$79.4 billion, per capita US$7,800; real growth rate 4% (1999 est.)
Inflation: 9.72% (year-end 2000)
Industries: accounts for 30% of GDP; mining, metallurgy, engineering industries, processed foods, textiles, chemicals (especially pharmaceuticals)
Labour Force: 5 million (1999); 29.1% industry, 28.4% community, social and business services, 13.2% agriculture
Unemployment: 10% (1999 est.)
Agriculture: accounts for 5% of GDP (including forestry) and 16% of employment; highly diversified crop-livestock farming; main crops—wheat, corn, sunflowers, potatoes, sugar beets; livestock—hogs, cattle, poultry and dairy products; self-sufficient in food
Natural Resources: bauxite, coal, natural gas, fertile soils, arable land

■ FINANCE/TRADE

Currency: forint (Ft) = 100 filler
International Reserves Excluding Gold: US$10.483 billion (Jan. 2001)
Gold Reserves: US$0.101 million fine troy ounces (Jan. 2001)
Budget: revenues US$13.5 billion; expenditures US$15.1 billion, including capital expenditures of US$n.a. (1999 est.)
Defence Expenditures: 2.29% of total govt. expenditure (1998)
Education Expenditures: 8.57% of total govt. expenditure (1998)
External Debt: US$29.042 billion (1999)
Exports: US$24.336 billion (2000); commodities: capital goods 36%, foods 24%, consumer goods 18%, fuels and minerals 11%, other 11%; partners: EU nations 65%, former USSR and Eastern Europe 35%
Imports: US$29.193 billion (2000); commodities: machinery and transport 28%, fuels 20%, chemical products 14%, manufactured consumer goods 16%, agriculture

6%, other 16%; partners: former USSR countries 43%, Eastern Europe 28%, less developed countries 23%, US 3%

■ COMMUNICATIONS

Daily Newspapers: 40
Televisions: 437/1,000 inhabitants (1998)
Radios: 689/1,000 inhabitants (1997)
Telephones: 371 lines/1,000 inhabitants (1999)

■ TRANSPORTATION

Motor Vehicles: 2,810,000; 2,310,000 passenger cars (1997 est.)
Roads: 188,203 km; 81,680 km paved
Railway: 7,606 km
Air Traffic: 1,635,000 passengers carried (1997)
Airports: 43; 16 have paved runways (1999 est.)

Canadian Embassy: The Canadian Embassy, Budakeszi ut 32, 1121 Budapest, Hungary. Tel.: (011-36-1) 392-3360. Fax: (011-36-1) 392-3390. Email: bpest@dfait-maeci.gc.ca
Embassy in Canada: Embassy of the Republic of Hungary, 299 Waverley St, Ottawa ON K2P 0V9. Tel: (613) 230-2717. Fax: (613) 230-7560. Email: sysadmin@huembott.org

Iceland

Long-Form Name: Republic of Iceland
Capital: Reykjavik

■ GEOGRAPHY

Area: 103,000 sq. km
Coastline: 4,988 km
Climate: temperate; moderated by North Atlantic Current; mild, windy winters; damp, cool summers
Environment: subject to earthquakes and volcanic activity; water pollution
Terrain: mostly plateau interspersed with mountain peaks, ice fields; coast deeply indented by bays and fjords
Land Use: 0% arable; 0% permanent; 23% meadows; 1% forest; 76% other
Location: NW Europe, island in Norwegian Sea, Atlantic Ocean

■ PEOPLE

Population: 276,365 (July 2000 est.)
Nationality: Icelander
Age Structure: 0-14 yrs: 23%; 15-64: 65%; 65+: 12% (2000 est.)
Population Growth Rate: 0.57% (2000 est.)
Net Migration: -2.3 migrants/1,000 population (2000 est.)

Ethnic Groups: homogeneous mixture of descendants of Norwegians and Celts
Languages: Icelandic
Religions: Christianity (predominantly Protestant)
Birth Rate: 14.86/1,000 population (2000 est.)
Death Rate: 6.87/1,000 population (2000 est.)
Infant Mortality: 3.58 deaths/1,000 live births (2000 est.)
Life Expectancy at Birth: 77.19 years male, 81.77 years female (2000 est.)
Total Fertility Rate: 2.03 children born/woman (2000 est.)
Literacy: 99% (1997)

■ GOVERNMENT

Leader(s): Pres. Olafur Ragnar Grimsson, Prime Min. David Oddsson
Government Type: constitutional republic
Administrative Divisions: 23 counties (syslar, sing. —sysla) and 14 independent towns (kaupstadhir, sing. —kaupstadhur)
Nationhood: June 17, 1944 (from Denmark)
National Holiday: Anniversary of the Establishment of the Republic, June 17

■ ECONOMY

Overview: basically capitalistic, but it has an extensive welfare system, low unemployment, and an unusually even distribution of income; depends heavily on the fishing industry and is vulnerable to changing world fish prices
GDP: US$6.42 billion, per capita US$23,500; real growth rate 4.5% (1999 est.)
Inflation: 5.16% (year-end 2000)
Industries: accounts for 21% of GDP; fish processing, aluminum smelting, ferro-silicon production, hydroelectricity
Labour Force: 131,000 (1999); 55% commerce, finance and services, 14% other manufacturing, 6% agriculture, 8% fish processing, 5% fishing
Unemployment: 2.4% (year-end 1999 est.)
Agriculture: accounts for about 15% of GDP (including fishing); fishing is the most important economic activity, contributing nearly 75% to export earnings; principal crops include potatoes and turnips; livestock—cattle, sheep; self-sufficient in crops
Natural Resources: fish, hydroelectric and geothermal power, diatomite

■ FINANCE/TRADE

Currency: króna (pl. krónur) (ISK) = 100 aurar
International Reserves Excluding Gold: US$365 million (Dec. 2000)
Gold Reserves: US$0.059 million fine troy ounces (Jan. 2001)

Budget: revenues US$n.a.; expenditures US$3 billion, including capital expenditures of US$146 million (1999 est.)
Defence Expenditures: none
Education Expenditures: 10.06% of central govt. expenditure (1998)
External Debt: US$2.6 billion (1999)
Exports: US$1.924 billion (2000); commodities: fish and fish products, animal products, aluminum, diatomite; partners: European Community 58.9% (UK 23.3%, Germany 10.3%), US 13.6%, former USSR countries 3.6%
Imports: US$2.521 billion (2000); commodities: machinery and transportation equipment, petroleum, foodstuffs, textiles; partners: European Community 58% (Germany 16%, Denmark 10.4%, UK 9.2%), US 8.5%, former USSR countries 3.9%

■ COMMUNICATIONS

Daily Newspapers: 5
Televisions: 355/1,000 inhabitants (1997 est.)
Radios: 940/1,000 inhabitants (1997 est.)
Telephones: 677 lines/1,000 inhabitants (1999)

■ TRANSPORTATION

Motor Vehicles: 144,000; 125,300 passenger cars (1997 est.)
Roads: 12,689 km; 3,439 km paved
Railway: none
Air Traffic: 1,334,000 passengers carried (1997)
Airports: 86; 12 have paved runways (1999 est.)

Canadian Embassy: The Consulate General of Canada, Suörlandsbraut 10, 108 Reykjavik, Iceland, Postal Address: The Consulate General of Canada, P.O. Box 8094, 128 Reykjavik, Iceland. Tel: (011 354) 5 68-08-20. Fax: (011 354) 5 68-08-99. Email: cantrade.canada@mmedia.is
Embassy in Canada: Embassy of the Republic of Iceland, 360 Albert St, 7th Fl Ste 710, Ottawa ON K1R 7X7. Tel: (613) 482-1944. Fax: (613) 482-1945. Email: n.a.

India

Long-Form Name: Republic of India
Capital: New Delhi

■ GEOGRAPHY

Area: 3,287,590 sq. km
Coastline: 7,000 km
Climate: varies from tropical monsoon in south to temperate in north
Environment: deforestation; soil erosion; overgrazing; air and water pollution; desertification, droughts, flash floods, severe thunderstorms common; earthquakes are a hazard
Terrain: upland plain (Deccan Plateau) in south, flat to rolling plain along the Ganges, deserts in west, Himalayas in north
Land Use: 56% arable; 1% permanent; 4% meadows; 23% forest; 16% other, includes 480,000 sq. km irrigated
Location: S Asia, bordering on Arabian Sea, Indian Ocean, Bay of Bengal

■ PEOPLE

Population: 1,014,003,817 (July 2000 est.)
Nationality: Indian
Age Structure: 0-14 yrs: 34%; 15-64: 62%; 65+: 4% (2000 est.)
Population Growth Rate: 1.58% (2000 est.)
Net Migration: -0.08 migrants/1,000 population (2000 est.)
Ethnic Groups: 72% Indo-Aryan, 25% Dravidian, 3% Mongoloid and other
Languages: Hindi (official, spoken by 30%); English; 19 regional languages, including Bengali, Tlegu, Marathi, Tamil, Urdu, Gujarati, Malayalam, Kannada, Oriya, Punjabi, Assamese, Kashmiri, Sindhi and Sanskrit; 24 languages spoken by a million or more persons each; numerous other languages
Religions: 80% Hindu, 14% Muslim, 2.4% Christian, 2% Sikh, 0.7% Buddhist, 0.5% Jains, 0.4% other
Birth Rate: 24.79/1,000 population (2000 est.)
Death Rate: 8.88/1,000 population (2000 est.)
Infant Mortality: 64.90 deaths/1,000 live births (2000 est.)
Life Expectancy at Birth: 61.89 years male, 63.13 years female (2000 est.)
Total Fertility Rate: 3.11 children born/woman (2000 est.)
Literacy: 53.5% (1997)

■ GOVERNMENT

Leader(s): Pres. Kocheril Raman Narayanan, Prime Min. Atal Behari Vajpayee
Government Type: federal republic
Administrative Divisions: 25 states and 7 union territories
Nationhood: Aug. 15, 1947 (from UK)
National Holiday: Anniversary of the Proclamation of the Republic, Jan. 26

■ ECONOMY

Overview: a mixture of traditional village farming and handicrafts, modern agriculture, old and new branches of industry and a multitude of support services; millions still live in poverty, hoping to benefit from modern farming techniques

GDP: US$1.805 trillion, per capita US$1,800; real growth rate 5.5% (1999 est.)
Inflation: 4.01% (year-end 2000)
Industries: accounts for 30% of GDP, textiles, food processing, steel, machinery, transportation equipment, cement, jute manufactures, mining, petroleum, power, chemicals, pharmaceuticals, electronics
Labour Force: 439 million (1999); 62.6% agriculture, 10.8% industry, 26.6% services
Unemployment: n.a.
Agriculture: accounts for 25% of GDP and employs 65% of labour force; self-sufficient in food grains; main crops—rice, wheat, oilseeds, cotton, jute, tea, sugar cane, potatoes; livestock— cattle, buffalo, sheep, goats and poultry; in top 10 of fishing nations
Natural Resources: coal, iron ore, manganese, mica, bauxite, titanium ore, chromite, petroleum, natural gas, diamonds, crude oil, limestone

■ FINANCE/TRADE

Currency: rupee (Rs) = 100 paise
International Reserves Excluding Gold: US$38.361 billion (Jan. 2001)
Gold Reserves: US$11.502 million fine troy ounces (Jan. 2001)
Budget: revenues US$42.12 billion; expenditures US$63.79 billion, including capital expenditures of US$13.8 billion (1998-99 est.)
Defence Expenditures: 15.41% of govt. expenditure (1999)
Education Expenditures: 2.99% of central govt. expenditure (1999)
External Debt: US$94.393 billion (1999)
Exports: US$40.966 billion (2000); commodities: tea, coffee, iron ore, fish products, manufactures; partners: European Community 25%, former USSR countries and Eastern Europe 17%, US 19%, Japan 10%
Imports: US$48.666 billion (2000); commodities: petroleum, edible oils, textiles, clothing, capital goods; partners: European Community 33%, Middle East 19%, Japan 10%, US 9%, former USSR countries and Eastern Europe 8%

■ COMMUNICATIONS

Daily Newspapers: n.a.
Televisions: 69/1,000 inhabitants (1998)
Radios: 121/1,000 inhabitants (1997)
Telephones: 27 lines/1,000 inhabitants (1999)

■ TRANSPORTATION

Motor Vehicles: 6,990,000; 4,300,000 passenger cars (1997 est.)
Roads: 3,319,644 km; 1,517,077 km hard-surfaced

Railway: 62,915 km
Air Traffic: 16,040,000 passengers carried (1997 est.)
Airports: 346; 238 have paved runways (1999 est.)

Canadian Embassy: The Canadian High Commission, 7/8 Shantipath, Chanakyapuri, New Delhi 110021; mailing address: The Canadian High Commission, P.O. Box 5207, Chanakyapuri, New Delhi 110021, India. Tel: (011-91-11) 687-6500. Fax: (011-91-11) 687-6579. Email: delhi@dfait-maeci.gc.ca
Embassy in Canada: High Commission for the Republic of India, 10 Springfield Rd, Ottawa ON K1M 1C9. Tel: (613) 744-3751. Fax: (613) 744-0913. Email: hicomind@sprint.ca

Indonesia

Long-Form Name: Republic of Indonesia
Capital: Jakarta

■ GEOGRAPHY

Area: 1,919,440 sq. km (13,677 islands)
Coastline: 54,716 km
Climate: tropical; hot, humid; more moderate in highlands
Environment: archipelago of more than 13,500 islands (6,000 inhabited); occasional floods, severe droughts and tsunamis; deforestation; environmental pollution
Terrain: mostly coastal lowlands; larger islands have interior mountains
Land Use: 10% arable; 7% permanent crops; 7% meadows; 62% forest; 14% other, includes 45,970 sq. km irrigated
Location: SE Asia, bordering on Indian Ocean

■ PEOPLE

Population: 224,784,210 (July 2000 est.)
Nationality: Indonesian
Age Structure: 0-14 yrs: 31%; 15-64: 65%; 65+: 4% (2000 est.)
Population Growth Rate: 1.63% (2000 est.)
Net Migration: 0 migrants/1,000 population (2000 est.)
Ethnic Groups: majority of Malay stock comprising 45% Javanese, 14% Sundanese, 7.5% Madurese, 7.5% coastal Malays, 26% other
Languages: Bahasa Indonesia (modified form of Malay; official); English and Dutch leading foreign languages; 25 local dialects, the most widely spoken of which is Javanese
Religions: 87% Muslim, 6% Protestant, 3% Roman Catholic, 2% Hindu, 1% Buddhist, 1% other

Birth Rate: 22.60/1,000 population (2000 est.)
Death Rate: 6.31/1,000 population (2000 est.)
Infant Mortality: 42.21 deaths/1,000 live births (2000 est.)
Life Expectancy at Birth: 65.61 years male, 70.42 years female (2000 est.)
Total Fertility Rate: 2.61 children born/woman (2000 est.)
Literacy: 85.5 (1998)

■ GOVERNMENT

Leader(s): Pres. Megawati Sukarnoputri, V. Pres. Hamzah Haz
Government Type: republic
Administrative Divisions: 23 provinces (propinsi-propinsi, sing. —propinsi), 2 special regions (daerah—daerah istimewa, sing. —daerah istimewa) and 1 special capital city district (daerah khusus ibukota)
Nationhood: Aug. 17, 1945 (Indonesia became legally independent from the Netherlands on Dec. 27, 1949; formerly known as Netherlands or Dutch East Indies)
National Holiday: Independence Day, Aug. 17

■ ECONOMY

Overview: a mixed economy with many socialist institutions and central planning but with a recent emphasis on deregulation and private enterprise; hampered by large population growth; possesses abundant natural wealth
GDP: US$610 billion, per capita US$2,800; real growth rate 0% (1999 est.)
Inflation: 3.72% (year-end 2000)
Industries: accounts for 35% of GDP; petroleum, textiles, mining, cement, chemical fertilizer production, timber, food, rubber
Labour Force: 99 million (1999); 54.1% agriculture, 10.3% industry, 37.6% services
Unemployment: 15-20%; 50% underemployment (1998 est.)
Agriculture: accounts for 21% of GDP; subsistence food production; small-holder and plantation production for export; rice, cassava, peanuts, rubber, cocoa, coffee, copra, other tropical products; the staple crop is rice; once the world's largest rice importer, Indonesia is now nearly self-sufficient
Natural Resources: crude oil, tin, natural gas, nickel, timber, bauxite, copper, fertile soils, coal, gold, silver

■ FINANCE/TRADE

Currency: rupiah (Rp) = 100 sen
International Reserves Excluding Gold: US$22.326 billion (Dec. 2000)
Gold Reserves: US$3.101 million fine troy ounces (Jan. 2001)

Budget: revenues US$25.4 billion; expenditures US$25.4 billion, including capital expenditures of US$n.a. (1999-00 est.)
Defence Expenditures: 3.48% of central government expenditure (1999)
Education Expenditures: 6.66% of central gov't expenditure (1999)
External Debt: US$150.096 billion (1999)
Exports: US$38.303 billion (2000); commodities: petroleum and liquefied natural gas 40%, timber 15%, textiles 7%, rubber 5%, coffee 3%; partners: Japan 42%, US 16%, Singapore 9%, European Community 11%
Imports: US$26.482 billion (2000); commodities: machinery 39%, chemical products 19%, manufactured goods 16%; partners: Japan 26%, European Community 19%, US 13%, Singapore 7%,

■ COMMUNICATIONS

Daily Newspapers: 69
Televisions: 136/1,000 inhabitants (1998)
Radios: 156/1,000 inhabitants (1997)
Telephones: 29 lines/1,000 inhabitants (1999)

■ TRANSPORTATION

Motor Vehicles: 4,600,000; 2,500,000 passenger cars (1997 est.)
Roads: 342,700 km; 158,670 km paved
Railway: 6,458 km
Air Traffic: 12,650,000 passengers carried (1997)
Airports: 446; 127 have paved runways (1999 est.)

Canadian Embassy: The Canadian Embassy, Flr 5 Wisma Metropolitan, Jalan Jendral Sudirman, Jakarta 12920; mailing address: P.O. Box 8324/JKS.MP, Jakarta 12084, Indonesia. Tel: (011-62-21) 525-0709. Fax: (011-62-21) 571-2251. Email: jkrta@dfait-maeci.gc.ca
Embassy in Canada: Embassy of the Republic of Indonesia, 55 Parkdale Ave, Ottawa ON K1Y 1E5. Tel: (613) 724-1100. Fax: (613) 724-1105. Email: info@prica.org

---

Iran

Long-Form Name: Islamic Republic of Iran
Capital: Tehran

■ GEOGRAPHY

Area: 1,648,000 sq. km
Coastline: 2,440 km
Climate: mostly arid or semi-arid, subtropical along Caspian coast
Environment: deforestation; overgrazing; desertification; air and water pollution; periodic droughts and floods

Terrain: rugged mountainous rim; high, central basin with deserts, mountains; small, discontinuous plains along both coasts
Land Use: 10% arable; 1% permanent crops; 27% meadows; 7% forest; 55% other, includes 94,000 sq. km irrigated
Location: SW Asia (Middle East), bordering on Persian Gulf

■ PEOPLE

Population: 65,619,636 (July 2000 est.)
Nationality: Iranian
Age Structure: 0-14 yrs: 34%; 15-64: 61%; 65+: 5% (2000est.)
Population Growth Rate: 0.83% (2000 est.)
Net Migration: -4.55 migrants/1,000 population (2000 est.)
Ethnic Groups: 51% Persian, 24% Azerbaijani, 7% Kurd, 8% Gilaki and Mazandarani, 2% Lur, 2% Baloch, 3% Arab, 2% Turkmen, 1% other
Languages: Farsi (Persian) (official) 58%, Turkic and Turkic dialects 26%, Kurdish 9%, Luri 2%, Balochi 1%, Turkish 1%, Arabic 1%, 2% other
Religions: 99% Muslim (89% Shia, 10% Sunni); Christianity, Judaism, Zoroastrianism 1%
Birth Rate: 18.29/1,000 population (2000 est.)
Death Rate: 5.45/1,000 population (2000 est.)
Infant Mortality: 30.02 deaths/1,000 live births (2000 est.)
Life Expectancy at Birth: 68.34 years male, 71.05 years female (2000 est.)
Total Fertility Rate: 2.20 children born/woman (2000 est.)
Literacy: 74.5% (1998)

■ GOVERNMENT

Leader(s): Pres. Mohammed Khatami, Supreme Religious Leader Ayatollah Mohammed Ali Hoseini Khamenei
Government Type: theocratic republic
Administrative Divisions: 28 provinces (ostanha, sing. —ostan)
Nationhood: Apr. 1, 1979, Islamic Republic of Iran proclaimed
National Holiday: Islamic Republic Day, Apr. 1

■ ECONOMY

Overview: economy is a mixture of central planning, state ownership of oil and other large enterprises, village agriculture, and small-scale private trading and service ventures; soaring external debt and high unemployment impede progress towards recovery from the economic devastation of the war with Iraq
GDP: US$347.6 billion, per capita US$5,300; real growth rate 1% (1999 est.)
Inflation: 14.48% (year-end 2000)

Industries: accounts for 34% of GDP; petroleum, petrochemicals, textiles, cement and other building materials, food processing (particularly sugar refining and vegetable oil production), metal fabricating (steel and copper)
Labour Force: 20 million (1999); 36.4% agriculture, 32.8% industry, 30.8% services
Unemployment: 25% (1999 est.)
Agriculture: accounts for 21% of GDP; principal products—rice, other grains, sugar beets, fruits, nuts, cotton, dairy products, wool, caviar; not self-sufficient in food
Natural Resources: petroleum, natural gas, coal, chromium, copper, iron ore, lead, manganese, zinc, sulphur

■ FINANCE/TRADE

Currency: 10 rials (RIs) = 1 toman
International Reserves Excluding Gold: n.a.
Gold Reserves: n.a.
Budget: revenues US$34.6 billion; expenditures US$34.9 billion, including capital expenditures of US$11.8 billion (1996-97)
Defence Expenditures: 8.05% of govt. expenditure (1999)
Education Expenditures: 15.64% of central govt. expenditure (1999)
External Debt: US$10.357 billion (1999)
Exports: US$17.500 billion (2000); commodities: petroleum 90%, carpets, fruit, nuts, hides; partners: Japan, Turkey, Italy, Netherlands, Spain, France, Germany
Imports: US$15.100 billion (2000); commodities: machinery, military supplies, metal works, foodstuffs, pharmaceuticals, technical services, refined oil products; partners: Germany, Japan, Turkey, UK, Italy

■ COMMUNICATIONS

Daily Newspapers: 32
Televisions: 157/1,000 inhabitants (1998)
Radios: 265/1,000 inhabitants (1997)
Telephones: 125 lines/1,000 inhabitants (1999)

■ TRANSPORTATION

Motor Vehicles: 2,239,000; 1,630,000 passenger cars (1997 est.)
Roads: 140,200 km; 49,440 km paved
Railway: 5,600 km
Air Traffic: 9,804,000 passengers carried (1997)
Airports: 288; 112 have paved runways (1999 est.)

Canadian Embassy: The Canadian Embassy to the Islamic Republic of Iran, 57 Shahid Javad-e-Sarafraz, Ostad-Motahari Ave, 15868 Tehran; mailing address: P.O. Box 11365-4647, Tehran, Iran. Tel: (011-98-21) 873-2623. Fax: (011-98-21) 873-3202. Email: teran@dfait-maeci.gc.ca

Embassy in Canada: Embassy of the Islamic Republic of Iran, 245 Metcalfe St, Ottawa ON K2P 2K2. Tel: (613) 235-5105. Fax: (613) 238-0379. Email: n.a.

Iraq

Long-Form Name: Republic of Iraq
Capital: Baghdad

■ GEOGRAPHY

Area: 437,072 sq. km
Coastline: 58 km
Climate: desert; mild to cool winters with dry, hot, cloudless summers
Environment: development of Tigris-Euphrates river systems contingent upon agreements with upstream riparians (Syria and Turkey); air and water pollution; soil degradation (salinization) and erosion; desertification
Terrain: mostly broad plains; reedy marshes in southeast; mountains along borders with Iran and Turkey
Land Use: 12% arable; 0% permanent crops; 9% meadows; 0% forest; 79% other, includes 25,500 sq. km irrigated
Location: SW Asia (Middle East), bordering on Persian Gulf

■ PEOPLE

Population: 22,675,617 (July 2000 est.)
Nationality: Iraqi
Age Structure: 0-14 yrs: 42%; 15-64: 55%; 65+: 3% (2000 est.)
Population Growth Rate: 2.86% (2000 est.)
Net Migration: 0 migrants/1,000 population (2000 est.)
Ethnic Groups: 75–80% Arab, 15–20% Kurdish, 5% Turkoman and other
Languages: Arabic (official), Kurdish (official in Kurdish region), Assyrian, Armenian
Religions: 97% Muslim (60–65% Shi'a, 32–37% Sunni), 3% Christian or other
Birth Rate: 35.04/1,000 population (2000 est.)
Death Rate: 6.40/1,000 population (2000 est.)
Infant Mortality: 62.49 deaths/1,000 live births (2000 est.)
Life Expectancy at Birth: 65.54 years male, 67.56 years female (2000 est.)
Total Fertility Rate: 4.87 children born/woman (2000 est.)
Literacy: 58% (1997)

■ GOVERNMENT

Leader(s): Pres. and Prem. Saddam Hussein at-Takriti; Deputy Premiers: Tariq Aziz, Hikmat Mizban Ibrahim al-Azzawi
Government Type: republic
Administrative Divisions: 18 provinces (muhafazat, sing. —muhafazah)
Nationhood: Oct. 3, 1932 (from League of Nations mandate under British administration)
National Holiday: Anniversary of the Revolution, July 17

■ ECONOMY

Overview: industrial production and foreign trade is centrally planned and managed while some small-scale industry and services and most agriculture is left to private enterprise; oil exports are at about 3/4 of their pre-war level; per capita food imports have increased significantly
GDP: US$59.9 billion, per capita US$2,700; real growth rate 13% (1999 est.)
Inflation: n.a.
Industries: accounts for 13% of GDP; petroleum, chemicals, textiles, construction materials, food processing
Labour Force: 6.0 million (1998); 79.7% services, 12.5% agriculture, 7.8% industry
Unemployment: n.a.
Agriculture: accounted for 6% of GNP and 30% of labour force before the Gulf War; principal products—wheat, barley, rice, vegetables, dates, other fruit, cotton, wool; livestock—cattle, sheep; not self-sufficient in food output
Natural Resources: crude oil, natural gas, phosphates, sulphur

■ FINANCE/TRADE

Currency: dinar = 1,000 fils
International Reserves Excluding Gold: n.a.
Gold Reserves: n.a.
Budget: n.a.
Defence Expenditures: n.a.
Education Expenditures: n.a.
External Debt: US$130 billion (1999 est.)
Exports: US$664 million (2000.); commodities: crude oil and refined products, machinery, chemicals, dates; partners: US, Brazil, former USSR countries, Italy, Turkey, France, Japan, former Yugoslavia
Imports: US$610 million (2000.); commodities: manufactures, food; partners: Turkey, US, Germany, UK, France, Japan, Romania, former Yugoslavia, Brazil

■ COMMUNICATIONS

Daily Newspapers: 4
Televisions: 83/1,000 inhabitants (1998)
Radios: 229/1,000 inhabitants (1997)
Telephones: 30 lines/1,000 inhabitants (1999)

■ TRANSPORTATION

Motor Vehicles: 1,040,000; 672,000 passenger cars (1997 est.)
Roads: 45,550 km; 38,400 km paved
Railway: 2,032 km
Air Traffic: n.a.
Airports: 113; 80 have paved runways (1999 est.)

Canadian Embassy: The Canadian Embassy to Iraq, c/o The Canadian Embassy, P.O. Box 815403, Amman, Jordan. 11180. Tel: (011-962-6) 566-61-24. Fax: (011-962-6) 568-92-27. Email: amman@dfait-maeci.gc.ca
Embassy in Canada: Embassy of the Republic of Iraq, 215 McLeod St, Ottawa ON K2P 0Z8. Tel: (613) 236-9177. Fax: (613) 567-1101. Email: n.a.

Ireland

Long-Form Name: Ireland
Capital: Dublin

■ GEOGRAPHY

Area: 70,280 sq. km
Coastline: 1,448 km
Climate: temperate maritime; modified by North Atlantic Current; mild winters, cool summers; consistently humid; overcast about half the time
Environment: deforestation and water pollution, especially of lakes, from agricultural runoff
Terrain: mostly level to rolling interior plains surrounded by rugged hills and low mountains; sea cliffs on west coast
Land Use: 13% arable; negligible permanent crops; 68% meadows; 5% forest; 14% other;
Location: NW Europe, (British Isles), bordering on Atlantic Ocean and Irish Sea

■ PEOPLE

Population: 3,797,257 (July 2000 est.)
Nationality: Irish
Age Structure: 0-14 yrs: 22%; 15-64: 67%; 65+: 11% (2000 est.)
Population Growth Rate: 1.16% (2000 est.)
Net Migration: 5.27 migrants/1,000 population (2000 est.)
Ethnic Groups: Celtic, with English minority
Languages: Irish (official first language, but use is limited) and English; English is the language generally used, with Gaelic spoken in a few areas, mostly along the western seaboard
Religions: 93% Roman Catholic, 3% Anglican, 1% atheist, 3% other
Birth Rate: 14.51/1,000 population (2000 est.)
Death Rate: 8.14/1,000 population (2000 est.)

Infant Mortality: 5.62 deaths/1,000 live births (2000 est.)
Life Expectancy at Birth: 74.06 years male, 79.74 years female (2000 est.)
Total Fertility Rate: 1.91 children born/woman (2000 est.)
Literacy: 99% (1998)

■ GOVERNMENT

Leader(s): Pres. Mary McAleese, Prime Min. Bertie Ahern
Government Type: republic
Administrative Divisions: 26 counties
Nationhood: Dec. 6, 1921 (from UK)
National Holiday: St. Patrick's Day, Mar. 17

■ ECONOMY

Overview: a small, open economy that is trade dependent; unemployment is high but inflation has been considerably lowered and the deficit burden relieved
GDP: US$73.7 billion, per capita US$20,300; real growth rate 8.4% (1999 est.)
Inflation: 5.56% (year-end 2000)
Industries: account for 39% of GDP, 80% of exports and employs almost 30% of the workforce; food products, brewing, textiles, clothing, chemicals, pharmaceuticals, machinery, transportation equipment, glass and crystal
Labour Force: 2 million (1999); 25.4% community, social and business services, 19.7% industry, 17.7% trade and tourism
Unemployment: 5.5% (1999)
Agriculture: accounts for 5% of GDP and 13% of the labour force; principal crops include turnips, barley, potatoes, sugar, beets, wheat; livestock—meat and dairy products; 85% self-sufficient in food; food shortages include bread grain, fruits, vegetables
Natural Resources: zinc, lead, natural gas, barite, copper, gypsum, limestone, dolomite, peat, silver

■ FINANCE/TRADE

Currency: Irish pound (£ or £Ir) = 100 pence; Euro (EUR) as of Feb. 10, 2002
International Reserves Excluding Gold: US$4.940 billion (Jan. 2001)
Gold Reserves: US$0.176 million fine troy ounces (Jan. 2001)
Budget: revenues US$25.3 billion; expenditures US$20.9 billion, including capital expenditures of US$2 billion (1999)
Defence Expenditures: 3.3% of total govt. expenditure (1997)
Education Expenditures: 13.58% of central govt. expenditure (1997)

External Debt: US$11 billion (1998)
Exports: US$72.246 billion (2000); commodities: live animals, animal products, chemicals, data processing equipment, industrial machinery; partners: European Community 74% (U.K. 35%, Germany 11%, France 9%), US 8%
Imports: US$47.298 billion (2000); commodities: food, animal feed, chemicals, petroleum and petroleum products, machinery, textiles, clothing; partners: European Community 66% (U.K. 42%, Germany 9%, France 4%), US 16%

■ COMMUNICATIONS

Daily Newspapers: 6
Televisions: 403/1,000 inhabitants (1998)
Radios: 699/1,000 inhabitants (1997)
Telephones: 478 lines/1,000 inhabitants (1999)

■ TRANSPORTATION

Motor Vehicles: 1,320,000; 1,100,00 passenger cars (1997 est.)
Roads: 92,500 km; 87,042 km paved
Railway: 1,947 km
Air Traffic: 8,964,000 passengers carried (1997)
Airports: 44; 17 have paved runways (1999 est.)
Canadian Embassy: The Canadian Embassy, 65 St Stephen's Green, Dublin 2, Ireland. Tel: (011-353-1) 478-1988. Fax: (011-353-1) 478-1285. Email: dubln@dfait-maeci.gc.ca
Embassy in Canada: Embassy of Ireland, 130 Albert St, Ste 1105, Ottawa ON K1P 5G4. Tel: (613) 233-6281. Fax: (613) 233-5835. Email: emb.ireland@sympatico.ca

Isle of Man

Long-Form Name: Isle of Man
Capital: Douglas

■ GEOGRAPHY

Area: 572 sq. km
Climate: temperate maritime, cool summers and mild winters, humid, overcast about half the time
Land Use: 9% arable; 0% permanent crops; 46% permanent pastures; 6% forests and woodland; 39% other;
Location: Irish Sea, between Great Britain and Northern Ireland

■ PEOPLE

Population: 73,117 (July 2000 est.)
Nationality: Manxman, Manxwoman
Ethnic Groups: Manx (Norse-Celtic descent), Briton
Languages: English, Manx, Gaelic

■ GOVERNMENT

Colony Territory of: Dependency of United Kingdom
Leader(s): Head of State: Queen Elizabeth II. Lt.-Gov. Ian David Macfadyen, Chief Min. Donald James Gelling
Government Type: Crown dependency administered in accordance with its own laws
National Holiday: Tynwald Day, July 5

■ ECONOMY

Overview: offshore banking, manufacturing, and tourism are key sectors of the economy; the government's policy of offering incentives to high-technology companies and financial institutions to locate on the island has paid off in expanding employment opportunities in high-income industries

■ FINANCE/TRADE

Currency: Manx pound = 100 pence; on a par with British pound sterling

Canadian Embassy: c/o The Canadian High Commission, Macdonald House, 1 Grosvenor Square, London W1K 4AB, England, UK. Tel: (011-44-20) 7258-6600. Fax: (011-44-20) 7258-6333. Email: Ldn@dfait-maeci.gc.ca
Representative to Canada: c/o British High Commission, 80 Elgin St, Ottawa ON K1P 5K7. Tel: (613) 237-1530. Fax: (613) 237-7980. Email should be sent using the appropriate form at the British High Commission's website at http://www.britain-in-canada.org

Israel

Long-Form Name: State of Israel
Capital: Jerusalem

■ GEOGRAPHY

Area: 20,770 sq. km
Coastline: 273 km
Climate: temperate; hot and dry in desert areas
Environment: sandstorms may occur during spring and summer; limited arable land and natural water resources pose serious constraints; deforestation
Terrain: Negev Desert in the south; low coastal plain; central mountains; Jordan Rift Valley
Land Use: 17% arable; 4% permanent crops; 7% permanent pastures; 6% forest; 66% other, includes 1,800 sq. km irrigated
Location: SW Asia (Middle East), bordering on Mediterranean Sea

■ PEOPLE

Population: 5,842,454 (July 2000 est.)
Nationality: Israeli
Age Structure: 0-14 yrs: 28%; 15-64: 63%; 65+: 9% (2000 est.)
Population Growth Rate: 1.67% (2000 est.)
Net Migration: 3.63 migrants/1,000 population (2000 est.)
Ethnic Groups: 80.1% Jewish, 19.9% non-Jewish (mostly Arab)
Languages: Hebrew (official); Arabic used officially for Arab minority; European languages (mostly English)
Religions: 82% Judaism, 14% Islam (mostly Sunni Muslim), 2% Christian and Druze, 2% other
Birth Rate: 19.32/1,000 population (2000 est.)
Death Rate: 6.22/1,000 population (2000 est.)
Infant Mortality: 7.90 deaths/1,000 live births (2000 est.)
Life Expectancy at Birth: 76.57 years male, 80.67 years female (2000 est.)
Total Fertility Rate: 2.60 children born/woman (2000 est.)
Literacy: 96% (1998)

■ GOVERNMENT

Leader(s): Prime Min. Ariel Sharon, Pres. Moshe Katzav
Government Type: parliamentary democracy
Administrative Divisions: 6 districts (mehozot, sing. —mehoz)
Nationhood: May 14, 1948 (from League of Nations mandate under British administration)
National Holiday: Independence Day, May 14; the Jewish calendar is lunar and the holiday may occur in Apr. or May

■ ECONOMY

Overview: a market economy with government participation; despite limited natural resources, this country has strong agriculture and industry sectors; transfer payments and foreign loans offset the deficit; the Palestinian uprising and Russian immigration stifle growth; high Jewish immigration from the former Soviet states has created massive housing problems
GDP: US$105.4 billion, per capita US$18,300; real growth rate 2.1% (1999 est.)
Inflation: 1.12% (year-end 2000)
Industries: accounts for 17% of GDP; food processing, diamond cutting and polishing, textiles, clothing, chemicals, metal products, military equipment, transport equipment, electrical equipment, miscellaneous machinery, potash mining, high-technology electronics, tourism

Labour Force: 3 million (1999); 36.1% community, social and business services, 14.3% trade and tourism, 20.9% industry
Unemployment: 8.9% (Nov. 2000)
Agriculture: accounts for 2% of GDP; largely self-sufficient in food production, except for bread grains; principal products—citrus and other fruit, vegetables, cotton; livestock products—beef, dairy and poultry
Natural Resources: copper, phosphates, bromide, potash, clay, sand, sulphur, asphalt, manganese, small amounts of natural gas and crude oil

■ FINANCE/TRADE

Currency: new Israeli shekel (NIS) = 100 new agorot
International Reserves Excluding Gold: US$23.728 billion (Jan. 2001)
Gold Reserves: none (Jan. 2001)
Budget: revenues US$40 billion; expenditures US$42.4 billion, capital expenditures US$n.a. (2000 est.)
Defence Expenditures: 9.5% of GDP (1999)
Education Expenditures: 14.06% of central govt. expenditure (1999)
External Debt: US$18.7 billion (1997)
Exports: US$30.520 billion (2000); commodities: polished diamonds, citrus and other fruit, textiles and clothing, processed foods, fertilizer and chemical products, military hardware, electronics; partners: US, UK, Germany, France, Belgium, Luxembourg, Italy
Imports: US$34.808 billion (2000); commodities: military equipment, rough diamonds, oil, chemicals, machinery, iron and steel, cereals, textiles, vehicles, ships, aircraft; partners: US, Germany, UK, Switzerland, Italy, Belgium, Luxembourg

■ COMMUNICATIONS

Daily Newspapers: 34
Televisions: 318/1,000 inhabitants (1998)
Radios: 520/1,000 inhabitants (1997)
Telephones: 471 lines/1,000 inhabitants (1999)

■ TRANSPORTATION

Motor Vehicles: 1,600,000; 1,220,000 passenger cars (1997 est.)
Roads: 15,965 km, all paved
Railway: 610 km
Air Traffic: 3,754,000 passengers carried (1997)
Airports: 58; 33 have paved runways (1999 est.)
Canadian Embassy: The Canadian Embassy, 3 Nirim St., 4th Fl, Tel Aviv, 67060; mailing address: P.O. Box 9442, Tel Aviv, Israel. Tel: (011-972-3) 636-3300. Fax: (011-972-3) 636-3380. Email: taviv@dfait-maeci.gc.ca

Embassy in Canada: Embassy of Israel, 50 O'Connor St, Ste 1005, Ottawa ON K1P 6L2. Tel: (613) 567-6450. Fax: (613) 237-8865. Email: ottawa@israel.org

Italy

Long-Form Name: Italian Republic
Capital: Rome

■ GEOGRAPHY

Area: 301,230 sq. km; includes Sardinia and Sicily
Coastline: 7,600 km
Climate: predominantly Mediterranean; Alpine in far north; hot, dry in south
Environment: regional risks include landslides, mudflows, snowslides, earthquakes, volcanic eruptions, flooding; land sinkage in Venice; serious air and water pollution
Terrain: mostly rugged and mountainous; some plains, coastal lowlands
Land Use: 31% arable; 10% permanent crops; 15% meadows; 23% forest; 21% other, includes 27,100 sq. km irrigated
Location: S Europe, bordering on Adriatic Sea, Mediterranean Sea

■ PEOPLE

Population: 57,634,327 (July 2000 est.)
Nationality: Italian
Age Structure: 0-14 yrs: 14%; 15-64: 68%; 65+: 18% (2000 est.)
Population Growth Rate: 0.09% (2000 est.)
Net Migration: 1.74 migrants/1,000 population (2000 est.)
Ethnic Groups: primarily Italian but population includes small clusters of German-, French- and Slovene-Italians in the north and Albanian-Italians in the south; Sicilians; Sardinians
Languages: Italian; parts of Trentino-Alto Adige region are predominantly German-speaking; significant French-speaking minority in Valle d'Aosta region; Slovene-speaking minority in the Trieste-Gorizia area
Religions: almost 100% nominally Roman Catholic
Birth Rate: 9.13/1,000 population (2000 est.)
Death Rate: 9.99/1,000 population (2000 est.)
Infant Mortality: 5.92 deaths/1,000 live births (2000 est.)
Life Expectancy at Birth: 75.85 years male, 82.41 years female (2000 est.)
Total Fertility Rate: 1.18 children born/woman (2000 est.)
Literacy: 98.5% (1998)

■ GOVERNMENT

Leader(s): Pres. Carlo Azeglio Ciampi, Prime Min. Silvio Berlusconi
Government Type: republic
Administrative Divisions: 20 regions (regioni, sing. —regione)
Nationhood: Mar. 17, 1861, Kingdom of Italy proclaimed
National Holiday: Anniversary of the Republic, June 2

■ ECONOMY

Overview: country is divided into a developed industrial north and an undeveloped agricultural south; an inadequate communications system, high pollution and economic integration into the European Union pose continuing challenges
GDP: US$1.212 trillion, per capita US$21,400; real growth rate 1.3% (1999 est.)
Inflation: 2.54% (year-end 2000)
Industries: accounts for 31.6% of GDP; machinery and transportation equipment, iron and steel, chemicals, food processing, textiles, motor vehicles
Labour Force: 26 million (1999); 21.7% industry, 21.4% trade and tourism, 28.5% community, social and business services
Unemployment: 11.5% (1999 est.)
Agriculture: accounts for 2.6% of GDP and 10% of the workforce; self-sufficient in foods other than meat and dairy products; principal crops— fruit, vegetables, grapes, potatoes, sugar beets, soybeans, grain, olives
Natural Resources: mercury, potash, marble, sulphur, dwindling natural gas and crude oil reserves, fish, coal

■ FINANCE/TRADE

Currency: lira (Lit) = 100 centesimi; Euro (EUR) as of March 1, 2002
International Reserves Excluding Gold: US$24.966 billion (Jan. 2001)
Gold Reserves: US$78.829 million fine troy ounces (Jan. 2001)
Budget: revenues US$530 billion; expenditures US$522 billion, including capital expenditures US$n.a. (1999 est.)
Defence Expenditures: 4.1% of central government expenditure (1997)
Education Expenditures: 4.9% of GNP (1997)
External Debt: n.a.
Exports: US$239.927 billion (2000); commodities: textiles, wearing apparel, metals, transportation equipment, chemicals; partners: European Community 57%, US 9%, OPEC 4%
Imports: US$231.998 billion (2000);

commodities: petroleum, industrial machinery, chemicals, metals, foods, agricultural products; partners: European Community 57%, OPEC 6%, US 6%

■ COMMUNICATIONS

Daily Newspapers: 78
Televisions: 486/1,000 inhabitants (1998)
Radios: 878/1,000 inhabitants (1997)
Telephones: 462 lines/1,000 inhabitants (1999)

■ TRANSPORTATION

Motor Vehicles: 34,000,000; 31,000,000 passenger cars (1997 est.)
Roads: 654,676 km; all paved
Railway: 19,394 km
Air Traffic: 28,184,000 passengers carried (1997)
Airports: 136; 97 have paved runways (1999 est.)
Canadian Embassy: The Canadian Embassy, Via G.B. de Rossi 27, 00161 Rome, Italy. Tel: (011-39-06) 445981. Fax: (011-39-06) 445 98750. Email: rome@dfait-maeci.gc.ca
Embassy in Canada: Embassy of the Italian Republic, 275 Slater St, 21st Fl, Ottawa ON K1P 5H9. Tel: (613) 232-2401. Fax: (613) 233-1484. Email: ambital@italyincanada.org

---

Jamaica

Long-Form Name: Jamaica
Capital: Kingston

■ GEOGRAPHY

Area: 10,990 sq. km
Coastline: 1,022 km
Climate: tropical; hot, humid; temperate interior
Environment: subject to hurricanes (especially July to Nov.); deforestation; water pollution
Terrain: mostly mountainous with narrow, discontinuous coastal plain
Land Use: 14% arable; 6% permanent; 24% meadows; 17% forest; 39% other, includes 350 sq. km irrigated
Location: West Indies, island in Caribbean Sea, just south of Cuba

■ PEOPLE

Population: 2,652,689 (July 2000 est.)
Nationality: Jamaican
Age Structure: 0-14 yrs: 30%; 15-64: 63%; 65+: 7% (2000 est.)
Population Growth Rate: 0.46% (2000 est.)
Net Migration: -8.39 migrants/1,000 population (2000 est.)
Ethnic Groups: 90.9% African, 7.3% mixed,

1.3% East Indian and Afro-East Indian, 0.2% white, 0.2% Chinese and Afro-Chinese, 0.1% other
Languages: English (official), Creole
Religions: 60% Protestant, 5% Roman Catholic, 35% other
Birth Rate: 18.51/1,000 population (2000 est.)
Death Rate: 5.51/1,000 population (2000 est.)
Infant Mortality: 14.61 deaths/1,000 live births (2000 est.)
Life Expectancy at Birth: 73.26 years male, 77.26 years female (2000 est.)
Total Fertility Rate: 2.11 children born/woman (2000 est.)
Literacy: 86% (1998)

■ GOVERNMENT

Leader(s): Head of State: Queen Elizabeth II/Gov. Gen. Howard Cooke. Prime Min. Percival J. Patterson
Government Type: parliamentary democracy
Administrative Divisions: 14 parishes
Nationhood: Aug. 6, 1962 (from UK)
National Holiday: Independence Day, first Monday in Aug.

■ ECONOMY

Overview: key sectors in this island economy are bauxite and tourism; continued tight fiscal policies have helped slow inflation and stabilize the exchange rate, but have resulted in the slowdown of economic growth
GDP: US$8.8 billion, per capita US$3,350; real growth rate -0.5% (1999 est.)
Inflation: 8.17% (year-end 2000)
Industries: accounts for 42.1% of GDP; tourism, bauxite mining, textiles, food processing, light manufactures
Labour Force: 1 million (1999); 26.1% agriculture, 29.9% community, social and business services, 16.2% finance
Unemployment: 15.5% (1998)
Agriculture: accounts for about 7.4% of GDP, 22% of workforce and 17% of exports; principal crops—sugar cane, bananas, coffee, citrus, potatoes and vegetables; not self-sufficient in grain, meat and dairy products
Natural Resources: bauxite, gypsum, limestone

■ FINANCE/TRADE

Currency: Jamaican dollar ($J) = 100 cents
International Reserves Excluding Gold: US$1.053 billion (Dec. 2000)
Gold Reserves: n.a.
Budget: revenues US$2.27 billion; expenditures US$3.66 billion, including capital expenditures of US$1.265 billion (1998-99 est.)

Defence Expenditures: 2.4% of central government expenditure (1997)
Education Expenditures: 7.4% of GNP (1997)
External Debt: US$3.913 billion (1999)
Exports: US$1.268 billion (2000); commodities: bauxite, alumina, sugar, bananas; partners: US 40%, UK, Canada, Trinidad and Tobago, Norway
Imports: US$3.016 billion (2000); commodities: petroleum, machinery, food, consumer goods, construction goods; partners: US 46%, UK, Venezuela, Canada, Japan, Trinidad and Tobago

■ COMMUNICATIONS

Daily Newspapers: 3
Televisions: 182/1,000 inhabitants (1998)
Radios: 480/1,000 inhabitants (1997)
Telephones: 199 lines/1,000 inhabitants (1999)

■ TRANSPORTATION

Motor Vehicles: 58,900; 43,500 passenger cars (1997 est.)
Roads: 18,700 km; 13,100 km paved
Railway: 370 km
Air Traffic: 1,400,000 passengers carried (1997)
Airports: 36; 11 have paved runways (1999 est.)
Canadian Embassy: The Canadian High Commission, 3 West Kings House Road, Kingston 10, Jamaica; mailing address: The Canadian High Commission, P.O. Box 1500, Kingston 10, Jamaica. Tel: (876) 926-1500. Fax: (876) 511-3494. Email: kngtn@dfait-maeci.gc.ca
Embassy in Canada: Jamaican High Commission, 275 Slater St, Ste 800, Ottawa ON K1P 5H9. Tel: (613) 233-9311. Fax: (613) 233-0611. Email: jhcott@comnet.ca

Japan

Long-Form Name: Japan
Capital: Tokyo

■ GEOGRAPHY

Area: 377,835 sq. km; includes Bonin Islands (Ogasawara-gunto), Daito-shoto, Minamijima, Okinotori-shima, Ryukyu Islands (Nansei-shoto) and Volcano Islands (Kazan-retto)
Coastline: 29,751 km
Climate: varies from tropical in south to cool temperate in north
Environment: many dormant and some active volcanoes; about 1,500 seismic occurrences (mostly tremors) every year; subject to tsunamis; acid rain caused by industrial emissions

Terrain: mostly rugged and mountainous
Land Use: 11% arable; 1% permanent crops; 2% permanent pastures; 67% forest and woodland; 19% other, includes 27,820 sq. km irrigated
Location: E Asia, bordering on Sea of Japan, North Pacific Ocean

■ PEOPLE

Population: 126,549,976 (July 2000 est.)
Nationality: Japanese
Age Structure: 0-14 yrs: 15%; 15-64: 68%; 65+: 17% (2000 est.)
Population Growth Rate: 0.18% (2000 est.)
Net Migration: 0 migrants/1,000 population (2000 est.)
Ethnic Groups: 99.4% Japanese, 0.6% other (mostly Korean)
Languages: Japanese
Religions: most Japanese observe both Shinto and Buddhist rites; about 16% belong to other faiths, including 0.8% Christian
Birth Rate: 9.96/1,000 population (2000 est.)
Death Rate: 8.15/1,000 population (2000 est.)
Infant Mortality: 3.91 deaths/1,000 live births (2000 est.)
Life Expectancy at Birth: 77.51 years male, 84.05 years female (2000 est.)
Total Fertility Rate: 1.41 children born/woman (2000 est.)
Literacy: 99% (1998)

■ GOVERNMENT

Leader(s): Emperor Tsegu no Miya Akihito; Prime Min. Junichiro Koizumi
Government Type: constitutional monarchy
Administrative Divisions: 47 prefectures
Nationhood: 660 BC, traditional founding by Emperor Jimmu; May 3, 1947 constitutional monarchy established
National Holiday: Birthday of the Emperor, Dec. 23

■ ECONOMY

Overview: impressive economic growth and status as the second largest industrial economy in the world is due to government-industry cooperation and a strong work ethic; known for high-tech industry; the crowding of habitable land and the aging population are two major long-term problems
GDP: US$2.95 trillion, per capita US$23,400; real growth rate 0.3% (1999 est.)
Inflation: -0.64% (year-end 2000)
Industries: accounts for 35% of GDP, metallurgy, engineering, electrical and electronics, textiles, chemicals, automobiles, fishing

Labour Force: 68 million (1999); 22.3% community, social and business services, 23.7% industry; 7.1% agriculture
Unemployment: 4.7% (Jan. 2001)
Agriculture: accounts for 2% of GDP; highly subsidized and protected sector, with crop yields among highest in the world; main crops—rice, sugar beets, vegetables, fruit; animal products include pork, poultry, dairy and eggs; about 50% self-sufficient in food
Natural Resources: negligible mineral resources, fish

■ FINANCE/TRADE

Currency: yen (pl. yen) (¥)
International Reserves Excluding Gold: US$349.896 billion (Jan. 2001)
Gold Reserves: US$24.547 million fine troy ounces (Jan. 2001)
Budget: revenues US$463 billion; expenditures US$809 billion, including capital expenditures of US$94 billion (2000-2001 est.)
Defence Expenditures: 0.9% of GDP (1998–99)
Education Expenditures: 3.6% of GNP (1997)
External Debt: n.a.
Exports: US$479.174 billion (2000); commodities: manufactures 97% (including machinery 38%, motor vehicles 17%, consumer electronics 10%); partners: US 34%, Southeast Asia 22%, Western Europe 21%, Communist countries 5%, Middle East 5%
Imports: US$379.450 billion (2000); commodities: manufactures 42%, fossil fuels 30%, foodstuffs 15%, nonfuel raw materials 13%; partners: Southeast Asia 23%, US 23%, Middle East 15%, Western Europe 16%, Communist countries 7%

■ COMMUNICATIONS

Daily Newspapers: 122
Televisions: 707/1,000 inhabitants (1998)
Radios: 955/1,000 inhabitants (1997)
Telephones: 558 lines/1,000 inhabitants (1999)

■ TRANSPORTATION

Motor Vehicles: 69,700,000; 47,000,000 passenger cars (1997 est.)
Roads: 1,152,207 km; 863,003 km paved
Railway: 23,671 km
Air Traffic: 94,998,000 passengers carried (1997)
Airports: 171; 140 have paved runways (1999 est.)
Canadian Embassy: The Canadian Embassy, 3-38 Akasaka 7-chome, Minato-ku, Tokyo 107-8503, Japan. Tel: (011-81-3) 5412-6200. Fax: (011-81-3) 5412-6303. Email: tokyo@dfait-maeci.gc.ca

Embassy in Canada: Embassy of Japan, 255 Sussex Dr, Ottawa ON K1N 9E6. Tel: (613) 241-8541. Fax: (613) 241-2232. Email: n.a.

Jordan

Long-Form Name: Hashemite Kingdom of Jordan
Capital: Amman

■ GEOGRAPHY

Area: 89,213 sq. km
Coastline: 26 km
Climate: mostly arid desert; rainy season in west (Nov. to Apr.)
Environment: lack of natural water resources; deforestation; overgrazing; soil erosion; desertification
Terrain: mostly desert plateau in east, highland area in west; Great Rift Valley separates East and West Banks of the Jordan River
Land Use: 4% arable land; 1% permanent crops; 9% permanent pastures; 1% forest; 85% other; includes 630 sq. km irrigated
Location: SW Asia (Middle East), on Arabian Peninsula

■ PEOPLE

Population: 4,998,564 (July 2000 est.)
Nationality: Jordanian
Age Structure: 0-14 yrs: 38%; 15-64: 59%; 65+: 3% (2000 est.)
Population Growth Rate: 3.1% (2000 est.)
Net Migration: 7.4 migrants/1,000 population (2000 est.)
Ethnic Groups: 98% Arab, 1% Circassian, 1% Armenian
Languages: Arabic (official); English widely understood among upper and middle classes
Religions: Islam (92% Sunni Muslim, Shia minority), 8% Christianity
Birth Rate: 26.24/1,000 population (2000 est.)
Death Rate: 2.63/1,000 population (2000 est.)
Infant Mortality: 21.11 deaths/1,000 live births (2000 est.)
Life Expectancy at Birth: 74.94 years male, 79.93 years female (2000 est.)
Total Fertility Rate: 3.44 children born/woman (2000 est.)
Literacy: 88.5% (1998)

■ GOVERNMENT

Leader(s): King Abdullah II, Prem. Ali Abu al-Ragheb
Government Type: constitutional monarchy
Administrative Divisions: 12 governorates (muhafazat, sing. —muhafazah)

Nationhood: May 25, 1946 (from League of Nations mandate under British administration; formerly known as Trans-Jordan)
National Holiday: Independence Day, May 25

■ ECONOMY

Overview: imports are outweighing exports and foreign aid makes up the difference; droughts are a potential threat; debt, poverty and unemployment remain problems; economic recovery is unlikely without substantial foreign aid, debt relief and economic reform
GDP: US$16 billion, per capita US$3,500; real growth rate 2.0% (1999 est.)
Inflation: 0.59% (year-end 1999)
Industries: accounts for 25% of GDP; phosphate mining, petroleum refining, cement, potash, light manufacturing
Labour Force: 1.1 million (1999); 9.1% transportation and communication industries, 57.7% services, 16.1% industry
Unemployment: official rate 15%, but actually 25-30% (1999 est.)
Agriculture: accounts for 3% of GDP; principal products are wheat, barley, citrus fruit, tomatoes, melons, olives; livestock—sheep, goats, poultry; large net importer of food
Natural Resources: phosphates, potash, shale oil

■ FINANCE/TRADE

Currency: Jordanian dinar (JD) = 1,000 fils
International Reserves Excluding Gold: US$3.322 billion (Jan. 2001)
Gold Reserves: US$0.401 million fine troy ounces (Dec. 2000)
Budget: revenues US$2.8 billion; expenditures US$3.1 billion, including capital expenditures of US$n.a. (2000 est.)
Defence Expenditures: 19.23% of total govt. expenditure (1999)
Education Expenditures: 16.23% of central govt. expenditure (1999)
External Debt: US$8.947 billion (1999)
Exports: US$1.895 billion (2000); commodities: fruit and vegetables, phosphates, fertilizers; partners: Iraq, Saudi Arabia, India, Kuwait, Japan, China, former Yugoslavia, Indonesia
Imports: US$4.376 billion (2000); commodities: crude oil, textiles, capital goods, motor vehicles, foodstuffs; partners: European Community, US, Saudi Arabia, Japan, Turkey, Romania, China, Taiwan

■ COMMUNICATIONS

Daily Newspapers: 4
Televisions: 86/1,000 inhabitants (1998)
Radios: 287/1,000 inhabitants (1997)

Telephones: 87 lines/1,000 inhabitants (1999)

■ TRANSPORTATION

Motor Vehicles: 265,000; 175,000 passenger cars (1997 est.)
Roads: 8,000 km, all paved
Railway: 677 km
Air Traffic: 1,353,000 passengers carried (1997)
Airports: 20; 16 have paved runways (1999 est.)
Canadian Embassy: The Canadian Embassy, Pearl of Shmeisani Bldg, Shmeisani, Amman, Jordan; mailing address: P.O. Box 815403, Amman, Jordan 11180. Tel: (011-962-6) 566-61-24. Fax: (011-962-6) 568-92-27. Email: amman@dfait-maeci.gc.ca
Embassy in Canada: Embassy of the Hashemite Kingdom of Jordan, 100 Bronson Ave, Ste 701, Ottawa ON K1R 6G8. Tel: (613) 238-8090. Fax: (613) 232-3341. Email: n.a.

Kazakhstan

Long-Form Name: Republic of Kazakhstan
Capital: Astana; in December 1998 the government was moved from Almaty to Astana

■ GEOGRAPHY

Area: 2,717,300 sq. km
Coastline: none; landlocked; Kazakhstan borders the Aral Sea (1,015 km) and the Caspian Sea (1,894 km)
Climate: dry desert climate; arid and semi-arid; hot summers and cold winters
Environment: drought and desertification; lack of fresh water; drying up of Aral Sea is causing increased concentrations of chemical pesticides and natural salts; industrial pollution, including radioactive or toxic chemical sites
Terrain: desert and steppe; plains in western Siberia to oasis and desert in Central Asia
Land Use: 12% arable; 11% permanent crops; 57% meadows and pastures; 4% forests; 16% other; includes 22,000 sq. km irrigated
Location: C Asia, bordering on Caspian Sea

■ PEOPLE

Population: 16,733,227 (July 2000 est.)
Nationality: Kazakhstani
Age Structure: 0-14 yrs: 27%; 15-64: 65%; 65+: 8% (2000 est.)
Population Growth Rate: -0.05% (2000 est.)
Net Migration: -6.7 migrants/1,000 population (2000 est.)
Ethnic Groups: 46% Kazakh, 34.7% Russian, 4.9% Ukrainian, 3.1% German, 2.3% Uzbek, 1.9% Tatar, 7.1% other

Languages: Kazakh (official, spoken by over 40% of population), Russian (official, spoken by two-thirds of population), German, Ukrainian
Religions: primarily Sunni Muslim (47%) and Eastern Orthodox (44%), Protestant (2%), other 7%
Birth Rate: 16.78/1,000 population (2000 est.)
Death Rate: 10.56/1,000 population (2000 est.)
Infant Mortality: 59.39 deaths/1,000 live births (2000 est.)
Life Expectancy at Birth: 57.73 years male, 68.93 years female (2000 est.)
Total Fertility Rate: 2.03 children born/woman (2000 est.)
Literacy: 99% (1998)

■ GOVERNMENT

Leader(s): Pres. Nursultan A. Nazarbayev, Prem. Kasymzhomart Tokayev
Government Type: republic
Administrative Divisions: 14 oblasts (oblystar, sing. —oblysy) and 3 cities (gala, sing. — galasy)
Nationhood: Dec. 16, 1991 (from Soviet Union)
National Holiday: Day of the Republic, Oct. 25

■ ECONOMY

Overview: predominantly mining and manufacturing; agriculture possible only with irrigation; serious pollution problems, lack of modern technology and little experience in foreign markets hamper economic progress
GDP: US$54.5 billion, per capita US$3,200; real growth rate 1.7% (1999 est.)
Inflation: 13.17% (year-end 2000)
Industries: accounts for 30% of GDP; coal refining, oil and natural gas extraction, mining, agricultural machinery, electric motors, construction materials
Labour Force: 8 million (1999) 25.9% community, social and business services, 23.9% agriculture, 15.8% industry
Unemployment: 13.7%; large numbers of underemployed (1998 est.)
Agriculture: accounts for 10% of GDP, and employs one quarter of labour force; wheat, cotton, rice, vineyard and orchard crops, sheep, cattle
Natural Resources: fish, oil, natural gas, zinc, coal, lead, iron ore, rare metals, tungsten, copper, zinc, manganese, bauxite, gold

■ FINANCE/TRADE

Currency: tenge = 100 tiyn
International Reserves Excluding Gold: US$1.826 billion (Jan. 2001)
Gold Reserves: US$1.845 million fine troy ounces (Jan. 2001)

Budget: revenues US$3.1 billion; expenditures US$3.6 billion, including capital expenditures of US$n.a. (1999 est.)
Defence Expenditures: 4.70% of central government expenditure (1999)
Education Expenditures: 4.33% of central government expenditure (1999)
External Debt: US$6.182 billion (1999)
Exports: US$8.380 billion (2000): fuels, karakul fleece, wool, industrial products
Imports: US$4.533 billion (2000): fuel, industrial products; partners: mostly Asian countries

■ COMMUNICATIONS

Daily Newspapers: 3
Televisions: 231/1,000 inhabitants (1998)
Radios: 384/1,000 inhabitants (1997)
Telephones: 108 lines/1,000 inhabitants (1999)

■ TRANSPORTATION

Motor Vehicles: n.a.
Roads: 119,390 km; 103,272 km hard-surfaced
Railway: 14,400 km
Air Traffic: 568,000 passengers carried (1997)
Airports: 10; 9 have paved runways

Canadian Embassy: The Canadian Embassy, 34 Karasai Batir St, Almaty 480100, Kazakhstan. Tel: (011-7-3272) 50-11-51. Fax: (011-7-3272) 582-493. Email: almat@dfait-maeci.gc.ca
Embassy in Canada: c/o The Embassy of the Republic of Kazakhstan, 1401 16th Street NW, Washington, DC 20036, USA. Tel: (202) 232-5488. Fax: (202) 232-5845. Email: kazak@intr.net

Kenya

Long-Form Name: Republic of Kenya
Capital: Nairobi

■ GEOGRAPHY

Area: 582,650 sq. km
Coastline: 536 km
Climate: varies from tropical along coast to arid in interior
Environment: unique physiography supports abundant and varied wildlife of scientific and economic value, but poaching is a continuing problem; deforestation; soil erosion; desertification; glaciers on Mt. Kenya; deteriorating water quality
Terrain: low plains rise to central highlands bisected by Great Rift Valley; fertile plateau in west

Land Use: 7% arable; 1% permanent crops; 37% permanent pastures; 30% forest; 25% other; includes 660 sq. km irrigated
Location: E Africa, bordering on Indian Ocean

■ PEOPLE

Population: 30,339,770 (July 2000 est.)
Nationality: Kenyan
Age Structure: 0-14 yrs: 43%; 15-64: 54%; 65+: 3% (2000 est.)
Population Growth Rate: 1.53% (2000 est.)
Net Migration: 0 migrants/1,000 population (2000 est.)
Ethnic Groups: 22% Kikuyu, 14% Luhya, 13% Luo, 12% Kalenjin, 11% Kamba, 6% Kisii, 6% Meru, 1% Asian, European and Arab, 15% other
Languages: English and Swahili (official); Kikuyu and Luo are widely spoken; numerous indigenous languages
Religions: 28% Roman Catholic, 26% indigenous beliefs, 38% Protestant, 8% other
Birth Rate: 29.35/1,000 population (2000 est.)
Death Rate: 14.08/1,000 population (2000 est.)
Infant Mortality: 68.74 deaths/1,000 live births (2000 est.)
Life Expectancy at Birth: 46.95 years male, 49.04 years female (2000 est.)
Total Fertility Rate: 3.66 children born/woman (2000 est.)
Literacy: 80.5% (1998)

■ GOVERNMENT

Leader(s): Pres. Daniel T. arap Moi, V. Pres. George Saitoti
Government Type: republic
Administrative Divisions: 7 provinces and 1 area
Nationhood: Dec. 12, 1963 (from UK; formerly known as British East Africa)
National Holiday: Independence Day, Dec. 12

■ ECONOMY

Overview: a large annual population growth, a deteriorating infrastructure and a shortage of arable land threaten economic growth; vulnerable to weather conditions
GDP: US$45.1 billion, per capita US$1,600; real growth rate 1.5% (1999 est.)
Inflation: 5.86% (year-end 2000)
Industries: accounts for 18% of GDP; small-scale consumer goods (plastic, furniture, batteries, textiles, soap, cigarettes, flour), agricultural processing, oil refining, cement, tourism
Labour Force: 15 million (1999); 43.2% community, social and business services, 18.9% agriculture, 13.1% industry
Unemployment: 50% in urban areas (1998 est.)

Agriculture: accounts for 26% of GDP and 65% of exports; cash crops include coffee, tea, sisal, pineapple; food products—corn, wheat, sugar cane, fruit, vegetables, dairy products; food output not sufficient for existing population
Natural Resources: gold, limestone, diatomite, salt barytes, magnesite, feldspar, sapphires, fluorspar, garnets, wildlife, hydropower

■ FINANCE/TRADE

Currency: Kenyan shilling (KSh) = 100 cents
International Reserves Excluding Gold: US$881 million (Dec. 2000)
Gold Reserves: none (Dec. 2000)
Budget: revenues US$2.91 billion; expenditures US$2.97 billion, including capital expenditures of US$n.a. (2000 est.)
Defence Expenditures: 1.9% of GDP (1998-99)
Education Expenditures: 6.5% of GNP (1997)
External Debt: US$6.562 billion (1999)
Exports: US$1.795 billion (2000); commodities: coffee 20%, tea 18%, manufactures 15%, petroleum products 10%; partners: Western Europe 45%, Africa 22%, Far East 10%, US 4%, Middle East 3%
Imports: US$3.096 billion (2000); commodities: machinery and transportation equipment 36%, raw materials 33%, fuels and lubricants 20%, food and consumer goods 11%; partners: Western Europe 49%, Far East 20%, Middle East 19%, US 7%

■ COMMUNICATIONS

Daily Newspapers: 4
Televisions: 21/1,000 inhabitants (1998)
Radios: 104/1,000 inhabitants (1997)
Telephones: 10 lines/1,000 inhabitants (1999)

■ TRANSPORTATION

Motor Vehicles: 364,900; 271,000 passenger cars (1997 est.)
Roads: 63,800 km; 8,868 km paved
Railway: 2,778 km
Air Traffic: 836,000 passengers carried (1997)
Airports: 230; 21 have paved runways (1999 est.)

Canadian Embassy: The Canadian High Commission, Comcraft House, Hailé Sélassie Ave, Nairobi; mailing address: The Canadian High Commission, P.O. Box 30481, Nairobi, Kenya. Tel: (011-254-2) 21-48-04. Fax: (011-254-2) 22-69-87. Email: nrobi@dfait-maeci.gc.ca
Embassy in Canada: High Commission for the Republic of Kenya, 415 Laurier Ave E, Ottawa ON K1N 6R4. Tel: (613) 563-1773. Fax: (613) 233-6599. Email: kenrep@on.aibn.com

Kiribati

Long-Form Name: Republic of Kiribati
Capital: Tarawa

■ GEOGRAPHY

Area: 717 sq. km
Coastline: 1,143 km
Climate: tropical; marine, hot and humid, moderated by trade winds
Environment: typhoons can occur anytime, but usually Nov. to Mar.
Terrain: mostly low-lying coral atolls surrounded by extensive reefs
Land Use: negligible arable; 51% permanent crops; 0% meadows; 3% forest; 46% other; includes n.a. sq. km irrigated
Location: SW Pacific Ocean, NE of Australia

■ PEOPLE

Population: 91,985 (July 2000 est.); 20 of Kiribati's 33 islands are inhabited
Nationality: I-Kiribati (sing. & pl.)
Age Structure: 0-14 yrs: 41%; 15-64: 56%; 65+: 3% (2000 est.)
Population Growth Rate: 2.34% (2000 est.)
Net Migration: 0 migrants/1,000 population (2000 est.)
Ethnic Groups: Micronesian
Languages: English (official), Gilbertese
Religions: 52.6% Roman Catholic, 40.9% Protestant (Congregational), some Seventh-Day Adventist and Baha'i
Birth Rate: 32.43/1,000 population (2000 est.)
Death Rate: 9.01/1,000 population (2000 est.)
Infant Mortality: 55.36 deaths/1,000 live births (2000 est.)
Life Expectancy at Birth: 56.89 years male, 62.82 years female (2000 est.)
Total Fertility Rate: 4.40 children born/woman (2000 est.)
Literacy: 90.6% (1997 est.)

■ GOVERNMENT

Leader(s): Pres. Teburoro Tito, V. Pres. Tewareka Tentoa
Government Type: republic
Administrative Divisions: 3 units
Nationhood: July 12, 1979 (from UK; formerly known as Gilbert Islands)
National Holiday: Independence Day, July 12

■ ECONOMY

Overview: economy has fluctuated widely in recent years and copra production and a good fish catch have provided a boost; at present there is a moderate but steady growth trend
GDP: US$74 million, per capita US$860; real growth rate 2.5% (1999 est.). Kinibati's revenues are supplemented by a nearly equal amount from external sources
Inflation: n.a.
Industries: accounts for 7% of GDP; fishing, handicrafts
Labour Force: n.a.
Unemployment: n.a., but massive under-employment
Agriculture: accounts for 14% of GDP (including fishing); copra and fish contribute 65% to exports; subsistence farming predominates; food crops—taro, breadfruit, sweet potatoes, vegetables; not self-sufficient in food
Natural Resources: tuna fishing

■ FINANCE/TRADE

Currency: Australian dollar ($A) = 100 cents
International Reserves Excluding Gold: n.a.
Gold Reserves: n.a.
Budget: n.a.
Defence Expenditures: n.a.
Education Expenditures: n.a.
External Debt: n.a.
Exports: US$6 million (2000); commodities: fish 55%, copra 42%; partners: European Community 20%, Marshall Islands 12%, US 8%, American Samoa 4%
Imports: US$29 million (2000); commodities: foodstuffs, fuel, transportation equipment; partners: Australia 39%, Japan 21%, New Zealand 6%, UK 6%, US 3%

■ COMMUNICATIONS

Daily Newspapers: 0
Televisions: 11/1,000 inhabitants (1997 est.)
Radios: 184/1,000 inhabitants (1997 est.)
Telephones: 43 lines/1,000 inhabitants (1999)

■ TRANSPORTATION

Motor Vehicles: n.a.
Roads: 670 km; n.a. km paved
Railway: none
Air Traffic: 28,000 passengers carried (1997)
Airports: 21; 4 have paved runways (1999 est.)

Canadian Embassy: The Canadian High Commission to Kiribati, c/o The Canadian High Commission, P.O. Box 12-049, Thorndon, Wellington, New Zealand. Tel: (011-64-4) 473-9577. Fax: (011-64-4) 471-2082. Email: wlgtn@dfait-maeci.gc.ca
Embassy in Canada: c/o New Zealand High Commission, Clarica Centre, 99 Bank St, Ste 727, Ottawa, ON K1P 6G3. Tel: (613)

238-5991. Fax: (613) 238-5707. Email: nzhcott@istar.ca

Korea (North)

Long-Form Name: Democratic People's Republic of Korea
Capital: Pyongyang

■ GEOGRAPHY

Area: 120,540 sq. km
Coastline: 2,495 km
Climate: temperate with rainfall concentrated in summer
Environment: isolated mountainous interior, nearly inaccessible and sparsely populated; late-spring droughts often followed by severe flooding
Terrain: mostly hills and mountains separated by deep, narrow valleys; coastal plains wide in west, discontinuous in east
Land Use: 14% arable; 2% permanent; negligible meadows; 61% forest; 23% other, includes 14,600 sq. km irrigated
Location: E Asia, bordering on Yellow Sea, Sea of Japan

■ PEOPLE

Population: 21,687,550 (July 2000 est.)
Nationality: Korean
Age Structure: 0-14 yrs: 26%; 15-64: 68%; 65+: 6% (2000 est.)
Population Growth Rate: 1.35% (2000 est.)
Net Migration: 0 migrants/1,000 population (2000 est.)
Ethnic Groups: Korean (racially homogeneous)
Languages: Korean
Religions: Buddhism and Confucianism; Taoism, Shamanism, Chonodogyu; autonomous religious activities are now almost nonexistent; government-sponsored religious groups exist to provide an illusion of religious freedom
Birth Rate: 20.43/1,000 population (2000 est.)
Death Rate: 6.88/1,000 population (2000 est.)
Infant Mortality: 24.29 deaths/1,000 live births (2000 est.)
Life Expectancy at Birth: 67.76 years male, 73.86 years female (2000 est.)
Total Fertility Rate: 2.30 children born/woman (2000 est.)
Literacy: 99% (1998)

■ GOVERNMENT

Leader(s): Chairman National Defense Commission Kim Jong-Il, Chairman of Supreme People's Assembly Kim Yong-nam, Prime Min. Hong Song-nam
Government Type: authoritarian socialist state; one-person dictatorship

Administrative Divisions: 9 provinces (do, sing. & pl.) and 3 special cities si, sing. & pl.)
Nationhood: Sept. 9, 1948
National Holiday: Independence Day (DPRK Foundation Day), Sept. 9

■ ECONOMY

Overview: a command economy that is almost completely socialized, with state-owned industry and collectivization of agriculture; state control over economic affairs is unusually tight even for a socialist country
GDP: US$22.6 billion, per capita US$1,000; real growth rate 1% (1999 est.)
Inflation: n.a.
Industries: accounts for 42% of GDP; machine building, military products, electric power, chemicals, mining, metallurgy, textiles, food processing
Labour Force: 9.6 million economically active; 42.8% agricultural, 26.9% services, 30.3% industry
Unemployment: n.a.
Agriculture: accounts for about 30% of GNP and 36% of workforce; principal crops—rice, corn, potatoes, soybeans, pulses; fish; livestock and livestock products—cattle, hogs, pork, eggs; not self-sufficient in grain
Natural Resources: coal, lead, tungsten, zinc, graphite, magnesite, iron ore, copper, gold, pyrites, salt, fluorspar, hydroelectricity

■ FINANCE/TRADE

Currency: North Korean won (Wn) = 100 chon
International Reserves Excluding Gold: n.a.
Gold Reserves: n.a.
Budget: n.a.
Defence Expenditures: 25% to 33% of GDP (1998 est.)
Education Expenditures: n.a.
External Debt: n.a.
Exports: US$680 million (1998 est.); commodities: minerals, metallurgical products, agricultural products, manufactures; partners: former USSR countries, China, Japan, Germany, Hong Kong, Singapore
Imports: US$954 million (1998 est.); commodities: petroleum, machinery and equipment, coking coal, grain; partners: former USSR countries, Japan, China, Germany, Hong Kong, Singapore

■ COMMUNICATIONS

Daily Newspapers: 3
Televisions: 53/1,000 inhabitants (1998)
Radios: 147/1,000 inhabitants (1997)
Telephones: 46 lines/1,000 inhabitants (1999)

■ TRANSPORTATION

Motor Vehicles: n.a.
Roads: 31,200 km; 1,997 km paved
Railway: 5,000 km
Air Traffic: 280,000 passengers carried (1997)
Airports: 49; 22 have paved runways

Canadian Embassy: The Canadian Embassy to the Democratic People's Republic of Korea, c/o The Canadian Embassy, 19 Dong Zhi Men Wai St., Chao Yang District, Beijing 100600, People's Republic of China. Tel: (011-86-10) 6532-3536. Fax: (011-86-10) 6532-4311. Email: bejing@dfait-maeci.gc.ca
Embassy in Canada: none

Korea (South)

Long-Form Name: Republic of Korea
Capital: Seoul

■ GEOGRAPHY

Area: 98,480 sq. km
Coastline: 2,413 km
Climate: temperate, with rainfall heavier in summer than winter
Environment: occasional typhoons bring high winds and floods; earthquakes in southwest; air and water pollution in large cities
Terrain: mostly hilly and mountainous; wide coastal plains in west and south
Land Use: 19% arable; 2% permanent crops; 1% meadows; 65% forest; 13% other, includes 13,350 sq. km irrigated
Location: E Asia, bordering on Yellow Sea, Sea of Japan

■ PEOPLE

Population: 47,470,969 (July 2000 est.)
Nationality: Korean
Age Structure: 0-14 yrs: 22%; 15-64: 71%; 65+: 7% (2000 est.)
Population Growth Rate: 0.93% (2000 est.)
Net Migration: 0 migrants/1,000 population (2000 est.)
Ethnic Groups: homogeneous; small Chinese minority (about 20,000)
Languages: Korean; English widely taught in high school
Religions: 48.6% Christianity, 47.4% Buddhism, 3% Confucianism, 1% other
Birth Rate: 15.12/1,000 population (2000 est.)
Death Rate: 5.85/1,000 population (2000 est.)
Infant Mortality: 7.85 deaths/1,000 live births (2000 est.)
Life Expectancy at Birth: 70.75 years male, 78.54 years female (2000 est.)

Total Fertility Rate: 1.72 children born/woman (2000 est.)
Literacy: 97.2% (1997)

■ GOVERNMENT

Leader(s): Pres. Kim Dae-jung, Prime Min. Yi Han-tong
Government Type: republic
Administrative Divisions: 9 provinces (do, sing. & pl.) and 6 special cities (gwangyoksi, sing. & pl.)
Nationhood: Aug. 15, 1948
National Holiday: Independence Day, Aug. 15

■ ECONOMY

Overview: dynamic growth is attributed to the planned development of an export-oriented economy in a strongly entrepreneurial society; labour unrest has hurt its record of noninflationary growth; economic growth has recovered in recent years
GDP: US$625.7 billion, per capita US$13,300; real growth rate 10% (1999 est.)
Inflation: 2.26% (year-end 2000)
Industries: accounts for 45% of GDP; textiles, clothing, footwear, food processing, chemicals, steel, electronics, automobile production, shipbuilding
Labour Force: 24 million (1999); 25.1% trade and tourism, 23.9% industry, 14.8% agriculture
Unemployment: 4.6% (Jan. 2001)
Agriculture: accounts for 5% of GDP and 21% of workforce (including fishing and forestry); main crops—rice, root crops, barley, vegetables, fruit; livestock and livestock products—cattle, hogs, chickens, milk, eggs; self-sufficient in food, except for wheat; fish catch is seventh largest in the world
Natural Resources: coal, tungsten, graphite, molybdenum, lead, hydroelectricity

■ FINANCE/TRADE

Currency: South Korean won (W) = 100 chun
International Reserves Excluding Gold: US$95.077 billion (Jan. 2001)
Gold Reserves: US$0.440 million fine troy ounces (Jan. 2001)
Budget: revenues US$68.9 billion; expenditures US$82.3 billion, including capital expenditures of US$14.5 billion (1998 est.)
Defence Expenditures: 16.29% of govt. expenditure (1997)
Education Expenditures: 19.56% of central govt. expenditure (1997)
External Debt: US$129.784 billion (1999)
Exports: US$171.832 billion (2000); commodities: textiles, clothing, electronic and electrical equipment, footwear, machinery, steel,

automobiles, ships, fish; partners: US 33%, Japan 21%
Imports: US$155.458 billion (2000); commodities: machinery, electronics and electronic equipment, oil, steel, transport equipment, textiles, organic chemicals, grains; partners: Japan 28%, US 25%

■ COMMUNICATIONS

Daily Newspapers: 60
Televisions: 346/1,000 inhabitants (1998)
Radios: 1,033/1,000 inhabitants (1997)
Telephones: 438/1,000 inhabitants (1999)

■ TRANSPORTATION

Motor Vehicles: 10,000,000; 7,000,000 passenger cars (1997 est.)
Roads: 86,990 km; 64,808 km paved
Railway: 6,240 km
Air Traffic: 35,506,000 passengers carried (1997)
Airports: 103; 67 have paved runways (1999 est.)

Canadian Embassy: The Canadian Embassy, Fl. 10 & 11, Kolon Building, 45 Mugyo-Dong, Jung-Ku, Seoul 100-170, Korea; mailing address: P.O. Box 6299, Seoul 100-662 Korea. Tel: (011-82-2) 3455-6000. Fax: (011-82-2) 755-0686. Email: seoul@dfait-maeci.gc.ca
Embassy in Canada: Embassy of the Republic of Korea, 150 Boteler St, Ottawa ON K1A 5A6. Tel: (613) 244-5010. Fax: (613) 244-5043. Email: cultural@emb-korea.ottawa.on.ca

Kuwait

Long-Form Name: State of Kuwait
Capital: Kuwait

■ GEOGRAPHY

Area: 17,820 sq. km
Coastline: 499 km
Climate: dry desert; intensely hot summers; short, cool winters
Environment: large and sophisticated desalination plants are required for adequate drinking water supply; air and water pollution; desertification
Terrain: flat to slightly undulating desert plain
Land Use: negligible arable; 0% permanent crops; 8% meadows; negligible forest; 92% other; includes 20 sq. km irrigated
Location: SW Asia (Middle East), on Arabian Peninsula, bordering on Persian Gulf

■ PEOPLE

Population: 1,973,572 (July 2000 est.)
Nationality: Kuwaiti

Age Structure: 0-14 yrs: 29.36%; 15-64: 68.32%; 65+: 2.32% (2000 est.)
Population Growth Rate: 3.44% (2000 est.)
Net Migration: 14.77 migrants/1,000 population (2000 est.)
Ethnic Groups: 45% Kuwaiti, 35% other Arab, 9% South Asian, 4% Iranian, 7% other
Languages: Arabic (official); Kurdish, Farsi, English (commercial) widely spoken
Religions: 85% Muslim (30% Shi'a, 45% Sunni, 10% other), 15% Christian, Hindu, Parsi and other
Birth Rate: 22.04/1,000 population (2000 est.)
Death Rate: 2.45/1,000 population (2000 est.)
Infant Mortality: 11.55 deaths/1,000 live births (2000 est.)
Life Expectancy at Birth: 75.27 years male, 76.92 years female (2000 est.)
Total Fertility Rate: 3.26 children born/woman (2000 est.)
Literacy: 80.5% (1998)

■ GOVERNMENT

Leader(s): Prime Min. Shaikh Saad al-Abdullah al-Salim al-Sabah; Emir: Shaikh Jabir al-Ahmad al-Jabir al-Sabah
Government Type: nominal constitutional monarchy
Administrative Divisions: 5 governorates (muhafazat, sing. -muhafazah)
Nationhood: June 19, 1961 (from UK)
National Holiday: National Day, Feb. 25

■ ECONOMY

Overview: a small and relatively open economy with crude oil reserves of about 10% of world reserves; lacks water and has practically no arable land, thus preventing development of agriculture; with the exception of fish, it depends almost wholly on food imports
GDP: US$44.8 billion, per capita US$22,500; real growth rate 1.1% (1999 est.)
Inflation: 3.01% (year-end 1999)
Industries: petroleum (accounts for 55% of GDP and 90% of export revenues), petrochemicals, desalination, food processing, salt, construction
Labour Force: 1 million (1999); 45% services, 20% construction, 12% trade, 9% manufacturing, 3% finance and real estate, 2% agriculture, 2% power and water, 1% mining and quarrying
Unemployment: n.a.
Agriculture: virtually none; dependent on imports for food; about 75% of potable water (adversely affected by the Gulf War) must be distilled or imported
Natural Resources: petroleum, fish, shrimp, natural gas

■ FINANCE/TRADE

Currency: dinar (KD) = 1,000 fils
International Reserves Excluding Gold: US$7.727 billion (Jan. 2001)
Gold Reserves: US$2.539 million fine troy ounces (Jan. 2001)
Budget: revenues US$10 billion; expenditures US$13 billion, including capital expenditures US$n.a. (1999 est.)
Defence Expenditures: 22.70% of govt. expenditure (1999)
Education Expenditures: 13.91% of central govt. expenditure (1999)
External Debt: US$9.27 billion (1998 est.)
Exports: US$11.514 billion (2000); commodities: oil 90%; partners: Japan, Italy, Germany, US
Imports: US$7.464 billion (2000); commodities: food, construction material, vehicles and parts, clothing; partners: Japan, US, Germany, UK

■ COMMUNICATIONS

Daily Newspapers: 8
Televisions: 491/1,000 inhabitants (1998)
Radios: 660/1,000 inhabitants (1997)
Telephones: 240 lines/1,000 inhabitants (1999)

■ TRANSPORTATION

Motor Vehicles: 693,000; 538,000 passenger cars (1997 est.)
Roads: 4,450 km; 3,590 km paved
Railway: none
Air Traffic: 2,114,000 passengers carried (1997)
Airports: 7; 4 have paved runways (1999 est.)

Canadian Embassy: The Canadian Embassy, Villa 24, Area 4, 24 Mutawakel St, Da Aiyah, Kuwait; mailing address: P.O. Box 25281, 13113, Safat, Kuwait City, Kuwait. Tel: (011-965) 256-3025. Fax: (011-965) 256-0173. Email: kwait@dfait-maeci.gc.ca
Embassy in Canada: Embassy of the State of Kuwait, 80 Elgin St, Ottawa, ON K1P 1C6. Tel: (613) 780-9999. Fax: (613) 780-9905. Email: info@embassyofkuwait.com

---

Kyrgyzstan

Long-Form Name: Kyrgyz Republic
Capital: Bishkek

■ GEOGRAPHY

Area: 198,500 sq. km
Coastline: none: landlocked
Climate: dry continental to polar in high Tien Shan; subtropical in south; glacial Alpine; moderate in valley regions

Environment: frequent severe earthquakes; water pollution and water-borne diseases are widespread
Terrain: mountainous; 75% of land covered by snow and glaciers; peaks of Tien Shan rise to 7,000 meters, and associated valleys and basins encompass the entire nation
Land Use: land is cultivated mainly in valleys; 7% arable; negligible permanent crops, 44% meadows and pastures; 4% forest and woodland; 45% other; includes 9,000 sq. km irrigated
Location: C Asia, bordering on China

■ PEOPLE

Population: 4,685,230 (July 2000 est.)
Nationality: Kyrgyzstani
Age Structure: 0-14 yrs: 36%; 15-64: 58%; 65+: 6% (2000 est.)
Population Growth Rate: 1.43% (2000 est.)
Net Migration: -2.81 migrants/1,000 population (2000 est.)
Ethnic Groups: 52.4% Kirghiz, 18% Russian, 12.9% Uzbeks, 2.5% Ukrainian, 2.4% German, 1.6% Tatars, 10.2% other
Languages: Kirghiz and Russian (both official) and Dungan
Religions: 75% Muslim, 20% Eastern Orthodox, 5% other
Birth Rate: 26.29/1,000 population (2000 est.)
Death Rate: 9.15/1,000 population (2000 est.)
Infant Mortality: 77.08 deaths/1,000 live births (2000 est.)
Life Expectancy at Birth: 59.06 years male, 67.90 years female (2000 est.)
Total Fertility Rate: 3.22 children born/woman (2000 est.)
Literacy: 97% (1997)

■ GOVERNMENT

Leader(s): Pres. Askar Akayev; Prime Min. Kurmanbek Bakiyev
Government Type: republic
Administrative Divisions: 6 oblasttar (sing. — oblast) and 1 city (sing. —shaar)
Nationhood: August 31, 1991 (from Soviet Union)
National Holiday: National Day, Dec. 2; also Independence Day, Aug. 31

■ ECONOMY

Overview: a small, poor, mountainous country with a predominantly agricultural economy; has been one of the most progressive countries of the former Soviet Union in carrying out market reforms; foreign assistance played a substantial role in the country's recent economic turnaround

GDP: US$10.3 billion, per capita US$2,300; real growth rate 3.4% (1999 est.)
Inflation: 18.69% (year-end 2000)
Industries: accounts for 20% of GDP; small machinery, cement, shoes, furniture and appliances, electronics, electrical engineering, silk making, rare earth metals
Labour Force: 2 million (1999); 33% agriculture and forestry, 28% industry and construction, 39% other
Unemployment: 6%; large numbers of underemployed (1998 est.)
Agriculture: accounts for 45% of GDP; wheat, barley, beets, cotton, fruit, vegetables, yaks, potatoes, cotton, grain, tobacco, livestock (mainly sheep); irrigation required
Natural Resources: mercury, antimony, zinc, tungsten deposits, coal, natural gas, oil, nepheline, bismuth, mercury, lead, zinc

■ FINANCE/TRADE

Currency: Kyrgyzstani som = 100 tyiyn
International Reserves Excluding Gold: US$234 million (Jan. 2001)
Gold Reserves: US$0.083 million fine troy ounces (Jan. 2001)
Budget: n.a.
Defence Expenditures: 10.12% of central government expenditure (1999)
Education Expenditures: 22.33% of central government expenditure (1998)
External Debt: US$1.699 billion (1999)
Exports: US$786 million (2000); agricultural products, antimony, silk, carpets, nonferrous metals, electrical equipment, cotton, wool, meat, tobacco, gold, mercury, hydropower, machinery, consumer goods; partners: China, UK
Imports: US$513 million (2000); grain, lumber, industrial products, metals, fuel, machinery, consumer goods; partners: Turkey, Cuba, US, Germany

■ COMMUNICATIONS

Daily Newspapers: 3
Televisions: 45/1,000 inhabitants (1998)
Radios: 112/1,000 inhabitants (1997)
Telephones: 76 lines/1,000 inhabitants (1999)

■ TRANSPORTATION

Motor Vehicles: n.a.
Roads: 18,500 km; 16,854 km paved or graveled
Railway: 370 km, plus industrial lines
Air Traffic: 423,000 passengers carried (1997)
Airports: 54; 14 have paved runways

Canadian Embassy: c/o The Canadian Embassy, 34 Karasai Batir St, Almaty 480100, Kazakhstan. Tel: (011-7-3272) 50-11-51. Fax: (011-7-3272) 582-493. Email: almat@dfait-maeci.gc.ca
Embassy in Canada: c/o Embassy of the Kyrgyz Republic, 1732 Wisconsin Ave NW, Washington DC 20007, USA. Tel: (202) 338-5141. Fax: (202) 338-5139. Email: n.a.

Laos

Long-Form Name: Lao People's Democratic Republic
Capital: Vientiane

■ GEOGRAPHY

Area: 236,800 sq. km
Coastline: none: landlocked
Climate: tropical monsoon; rainy season (May to Nov.); dry season (Dec. to Apr.)
Environment: deforestation; soil erosion; subject to floods; limited safe drinking water
Terrain: mostly rugged mountains; some plains and plateaus
Land Use: 3% arable land; negligible permanent crops; 3% meadows; 54% forest; 40% other; includes between 750 and 2,169 sq. km irrigated
Location: SE Asia

■ PEOPLE

Population: 5,497,459 (July 2000 est.)
Nationality: Laotian or Lao
Age Structure: 0-14 yrs: 43%; 15-64: 54%; 65+: 3% (2000 est.)
Population Growth Rate: 2.5% (2000 est.)
Net Migration: 0 migrants/1,000 population (2000 est.)
Ethnic Groups: mostly Laotian; Vietnamese, Kha, Thai, Meo, Hmong, Yao, Chinese, European, Indian and Pakistani minorities
Languages: Lao (official), French, English, tribal languages
Religions: 60% Buddhist, 40% animist and other
Birth Rate: 38.29/1,000 population (2000 est.)
Death Rate: 13.35/1,000 population (2000 est.)
Infant Mortality: 94.80 deaths/1,000 live births (2000 est.)
Life Expectancy at Birth: 51.22 years male, 55.02 years female (2000 est.)
Total Fertility Rate: 5.21 children born/woman (2000 est.)
Literacy: 58.6% (1997)

■ GOVERNMENT

Leader(s): Pres. Khamtai Siphandon, Prime Min. Boungnang Volachit
Government Type: communist state
Administrative Divisions: 16 provinces (khoueng, sing. & pl.) and 1 municipality (kampheng

nakhon, sing. & pl.) and 1 special zone
(khethiset, sing. & pl.)
Nationhood: July 19, 1949 (from France)
National Holiday: National Day (proclamation of
the Lao People's Democratic Republic), Dec. 2

■ ECONOMY

Overview: one of the world's poorest nations,
landlocked with a primitive infrastructure; while
traditionally a communist centrally planned
economy with government ownership and
control of productive enterprises, the
government is now decentralizing control and
encouraging some private enterprise; heavily
dependent on foreign aid
GDP: US$7 billion, per capita US$1,300; real
growth rate 5.2% (1999 est.)
Inflation: 25.09% (year-end 2000)
Industries: accounts for 22% of GDP; tin
mining, timber, electric power, agricultural
processing
Labour Force: 1-1.5 million (1999 est.); 75.7%
agriculture, 7.1% industry, 17.2% services
Unemployment: 5.7% (1997 est.)
Agriculture: accounts for 51% of GDP and
employs most of the labour force; subsistence
farming predominates; normally self-sufficient;
principal crops—rice (80% of cultivated land),
potatoes, vegetables, coffee, sugar cane, cotton
Natural Resources: timber, hydroelectricity,
gypsum, tin, gold, gemstones

■ FINANCE/TRADE

Currency: new kip (NK) = 100 at
International Reserves Excluding Gold: US$139
million (Dec. 2000)
Gold Reserves: US$0.017 million fine troy
ounces (Jan. 2001)
Budget: revenues US$202.7 million;
expenditures US$385.1 million, capital
expenditures US$n.a. (1997-98 est.)
Defence Expenditures: 17.5% of central
government expenditure (1997)
Education Expenditures: 2.1% of GNP (1997)
External Debt: US$2.527 billion (1999)
Exports: US$341 million (2000); wood products,
electricity, tin, consumer goods; partners:
Vietnam, Thailand, Germany, France
Imports: US$521 million (2000); machinery and
equipment, fuel, vehicles; partners: Thailand,
Japan, Vietnam, China, Singapore

■ COMMUNICATIONS

Daily Newspapers: 3
Televisions: 4/1,000 inhabitants (1998)
Radios: 143,1,000 inhabitants (1997)
Telephones: 6 lines/1,000 inhabitants (1999)

■ TRANSPORTATION

Motor Vehicles: 21,000; 10,000 passenger cars
(1997 est.)
Roads: 21,716 km; 9,673.5 km paved
Railway: none
Air Traffic: 125,000 passengers carried (1997)
Airports: 52; 9 have paved runways (1999 est.)

Canadian Embassy: The Canadian Embassy to
Laos, c/o P.O. Box 2090, Bangkok 10501
Thailand. Tel: (011-66-2) 636-0540. Fax: (011-
66-2) 636-0565. Email: bngkk@dfait-
maeci.gc.ca
Embassy in Canada: Embassy of the Lao
People's Democratic Republic, 2222 S St NW,
Washington DC 20001, USA. Tel: (202) 332-
6416. Fax: (202) 332-4923. Email: n.a.

Latvia

Long-Form Name: Republic of Latvia
Capital: Riga

■ GEOGRAPHY

Area: 64,589 sq. km
Coastline: 531 km
Climate: maritime, wet, moderate winters
Environment: air and water pollution, soil and
groundwater contaminated with chemicals and
petroleum products at military bases
Terrain: hilly, forested land with many lakes and
shallow valleys
Land Use: 27% arable, negligible permanent
crops, 13% meadows and pastures, 46% forest,
14% other; includes 160 sq. km irrigated
Location: NE Europe, bordering on Baltic Sea

■ PEOPLE

Population: 2,404,926 (July 2000 est.)
Nationality: Latvian
Age Structure: 0-14 yrs: 17%; 15-64: 68%; 65+:
15% (2000 est.)
Population Growth Rate: -0.84% (2000 est.)
Net Migration: -1.32 migrants/1,000 population
(2000 est.)
Ethnic Groups: 56.5% Latvian, 30.4% Russian,
4.3% Belorussian, 2.8% Ukrainian, 2.6% Polish,
3.4% other
Languages: Lettish (official), Lithuanian,
Russian, some others
Religions: Lutheran, Catholic, Russian Orthodox
Birth Rate: 7.80/1,000 population (2000 est.)
Death Rate: 14.88/1,000 population (2000 est.)
Infant Mortality: 15.71 deaths/1,000 live births
(2000 est.)
Life Expectancy at Birth: 62.48 years male, 74.62
years female (2000 est.)

Total Fertility Rate: 1.13 children born/woman (2000 est.)
Literacy: 100% (1998)

■ GOVERNMENT

Leader(s): Pres. Vaira Vike-Freiberga, Prime Min. Andris Berzins
Government Type: parliamentary democracy
Administrative Divisions: 26 counties (sing. — rajons) and 7 municipalities
Nationhood: Sept. 6, 1991 (from Soviet Union)
National Holiday: Independence Day, Nov. 18

■ ECONOMY

Overview: lacks natural resources, aside from its arable land and small forests; its most valuable economic asset is its workforce, which is better educated and disciplined than in most of the former Soviet republics; rapidly moving towards a dynamic market economy, but the transition has seen dramatic declines in both GDP and industrial production
GDP: US$9.8 billion, per capita US$4,200; real growth rate 0% (1999 est.)
Inflation: 2.65% (year-end 2000)
Industries: accounts for 29% of GDP and 31% of labour force; manufacturing of railroad cars, paper, woolen goods, electronics and engineering, food processing
Labour Force: 1.0 million (1999); 41% industry, 16% forestry and agriculture, 43% services
Unemployment: 9.6% (1999 est.), but large numbers of underemployed
Agriculture: accounts for 8% of GDP, employs 9% of labour force and has become largely privatized; poor soil hinders agriculture products including grain, beets, potatoes, cattle and dairy farming, poultry, fishing
Natural Resources: forests, peat deposits, amber, dolomite, hydroelectric power, arable land

■ FINANCE/TRADE

Currency: lat = 100 santims
International Reserves Excluding Gold: US$812 million (Jan. 2001)
Gold Reserves: US$0.249 milllion fine troy ounces (Jan. 2001)
Budget: revenues US$1.33 billion, expenditures US$1.27 billion, including capital expenditures of US$n.a. (1998 est.)
Defence Expenditures: 2.50% of total govt. expenditure (1999)
Education Expenditures: 4.85% of central govt. expenditure (1999)
External Debt: US$2.657 billion (1999)
Exports: US$1.867 billion (2000); vehicles, household appliances, electric power; partners: Russia 21%, Germany 14%, UK 14%, Sweden 8%

Imports: US$3.187 billion (2000): fuels, cars, chemicals and metal products; partners: Russia 16%, Germany 16%, Finland 10%, Sweden 8%

■ COMMUNICATIONS

Daily Newspapers: 24
Televisions: 492/1,000 inhabitants (1998)
Radios: 710/1,000 inhabitants (1997)
Telephones: 300 lines/1,000 inhabitants (1999)

■ TRANSPORTATION

Motor Vehicles: n.a.
Roads: 59,178 km; 22,843 km paved
Railway: 2,412 km
Air Traffic: 229,000 passengers carried (1997)
Airports: 50; 36 have paved runways

Canadian Embassy: The Canadian Embassy, Doma Laukums 4, 4th Fl, Riga LV-1977, Latvia. Tel. (011-371) 783-0141. Fax: (011-371) 783-1040. Email: riga@dfait-maeci.gc.ca
Embassy in Canada: Embassy of the Republic of Latvia, 280 Albert St Ste 300, Ottawa, ON, K1P 5G8. Tel: (613) 238-6014. Fax: (613) 238-7044. Email: n.a.

Lebanon

Long-Form Name: Lebanese Republic
Capital: Beirut

■ GEOGRAPHY

Area: 10,400 sq. km
Coastline: 225 km
Climate: Mediterranean; mild to cool, wet winters with hot, dry summers; heavy snowfall in winter in Lebanon Mountains
Environment: deforestation; soil erosion; air and water pollution; desertification
Terrain: narrow coastal plain; al Biqa' separates Lebanon and Anti-Lebanon Mountains; rugged terrain historically helped isolate, protect and develop numerous factional groups based on religion, clan and ethnicity.
Land Use: 21% arable; 9% permanent crops; 1% meadow; 8% forest; 61% other, includes 860 sq. km irrigated
Location: SW Asia (Middle East), bordering on Mediterranean Sea

■ PEOPLE

Population: 3,578,036 (July 2000 est.)
Nationality: Lebanese (sing. & pl.)
Age Structure: 0-14 yrs: 28%; 15-64: 65%; 65+: 7% (2000 est.)
Population Growth Rate: 1.38% (2000 est.)
Net Migration: 0 migrants/1,000 population (2000 est.)

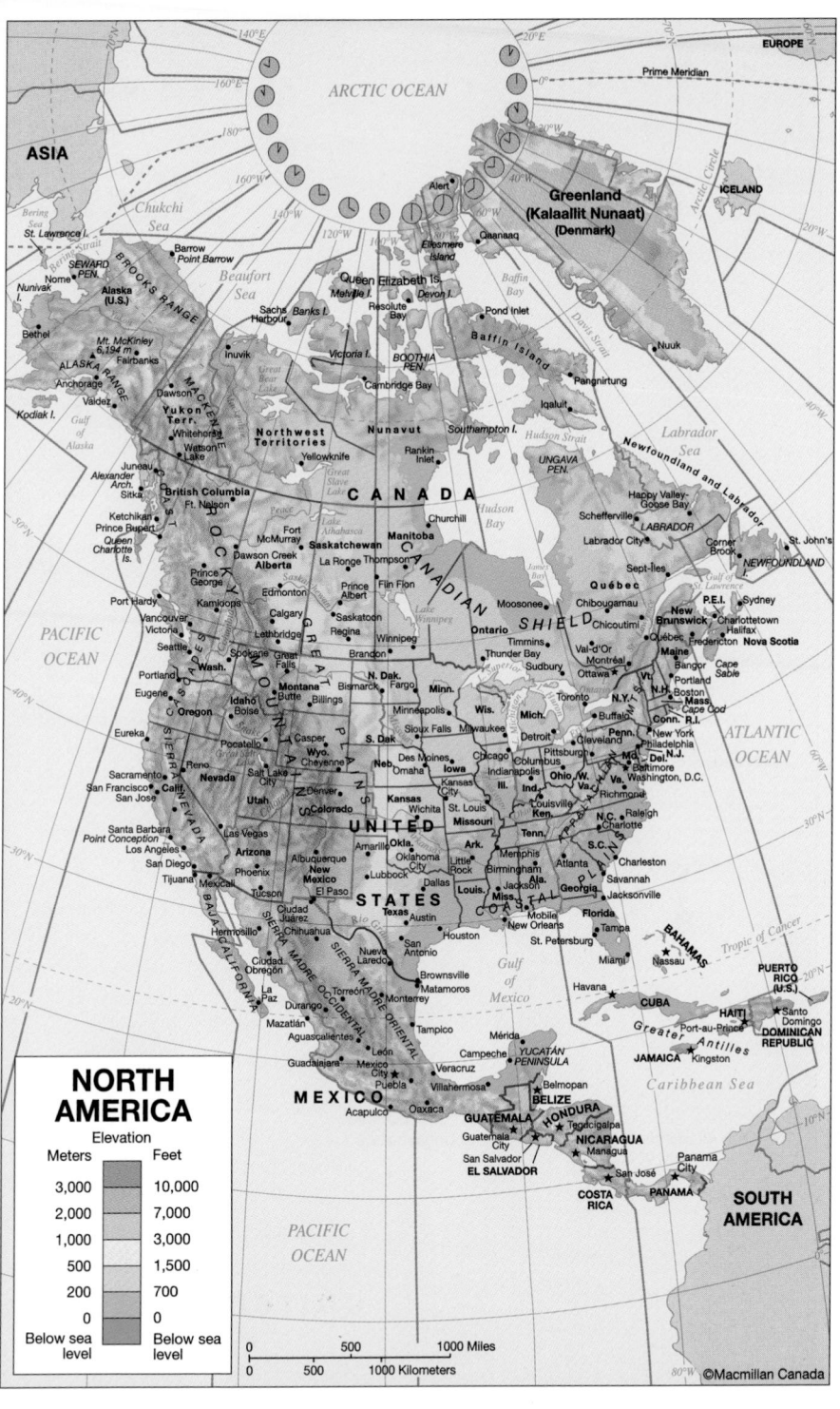

NORTH AMERICA

Elevation

Meters	Feet
3,000	10,000
2,000	7,000
1,000	3,000
500	1,500
200	700
0	0
Below sea level	Below sea level

©Macmillan Canada

All islands in Hudson, James, and Ungava Bays are part of Nunavut.

©Macmillan Canada

CANADA

Elevation

Meters	Feet
3,000	10,000
2,000	7,000
1,000	3,000
500	1,500
200	700
0	0
Below sea level	Below sea level

Kalaallit Nunaat (Greenland) (Den.)

Baffin Bay

Davis Strait

Arctic Circle

Baffin Island

esmere sland

on I.

n a v u t

• Iqaluit

Labrador Sea

Southampton I.

ATLANTIC OCEAN

Ungava Bay

LABRADOR

Hudson Bay

Happy Valley–Goose Bay

Newfoundland and Labrador

Island of Newfoundland

Churchill

Belcher Islands

Labrador City

• St. John's

Corner Brook

James Bay

Québec

Sept-Îles •

Anticosti Island

St-Pierre and Miquelon (Fr.)

Moosonee •

Baie Comeau •

Gulf of Saint Lawrence

Prince Edward Island

Rimouski

Sydney •

Cape Breton Island

Ontario

Rouyn-Noranda •

Chicoutimi •

New Brunswick

Moncton •

Charlottetown

Lake Nipigon

Québec •

Nova Scotia

Fredericton •

Dartmouth

er

Timmins •

Sherbrooke •

Saint John

Halifax

Lake Superior

Sault Ste. Marie •

Montréal

Hull

Sudbury •

North Bay •

Ottawa

ATLANTIC OCEAN

Owen Sound •

Kingston •

Lake Huron

Oshawa •

Toronto •

Lake Ontario

Hamilton •

Sarnia •

• London

Windsor •

Lake Erie

Lake Michigan

	100	200	300 Miles
0	200	400 Kilometers	

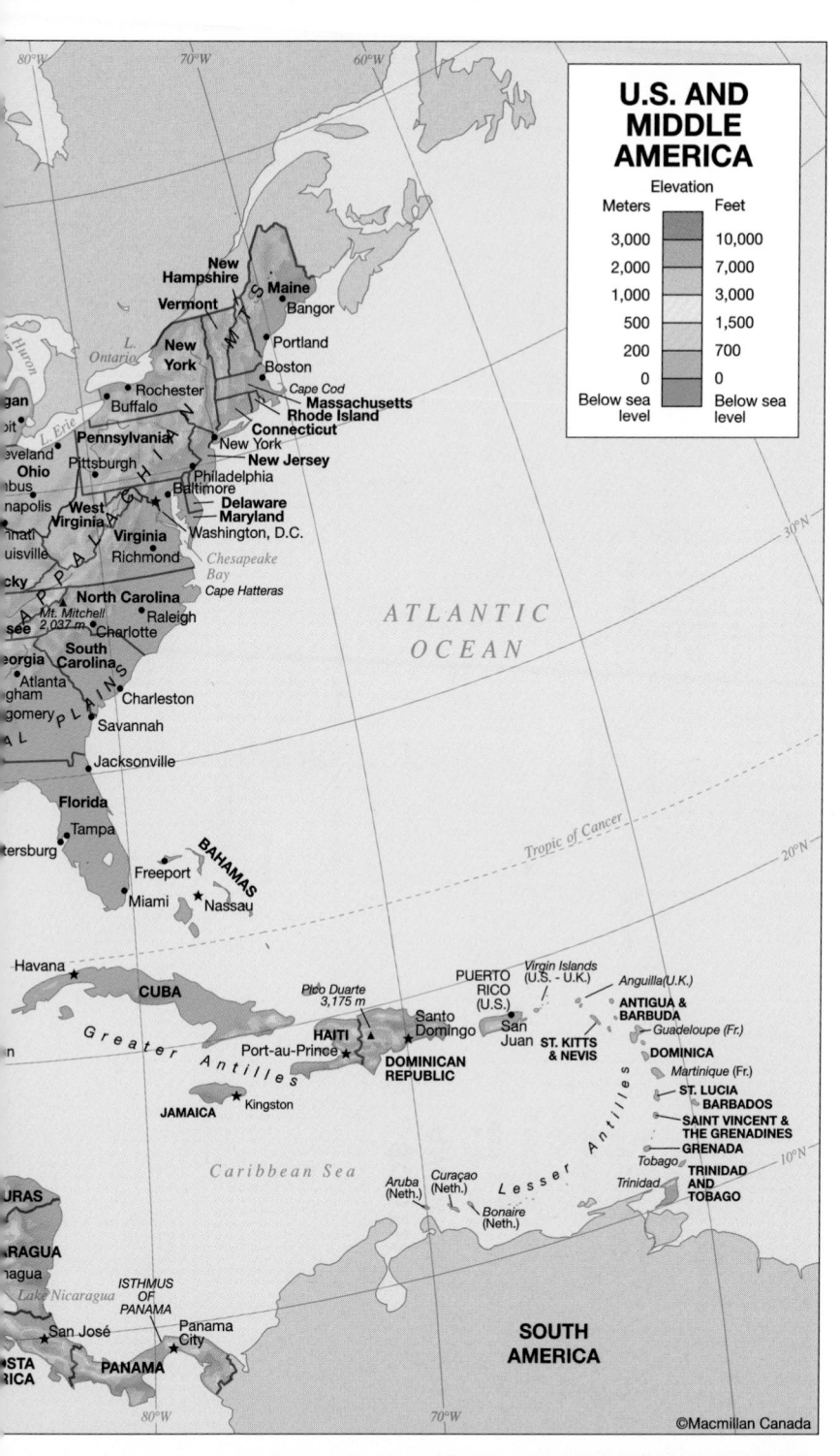

U.S. AND MIDDLE AMERICA

Elevation

Meters		Feet
3,000		10,000
2,000		7,000
1,000		3,000
500		1,500
200		700
0		0
Below sea level		Below sea level

80°W
70°W
60°W

New Hampshire
Vermont
Maine
Bangor
Portland
New York
Boston
L. Ontario
Rochester
Buffalo
Cape Cod
Massachusetts
Rhode Island
Connecticut
New York
New Jersey
L. Erie
Pennsylvania
Philadelphia
Ohio
Pittsburgh
Baltimore
Delaware
eveland
West Virginia
Maryland
Washington, D.C.
Virginia
Richmond
Chesapeake Bay
Cape Hatteras
uisville
cky
North Carolina
Mt. Mitchell 2,037 m
Raleigh
see
Charlotte
South Carolina
eorgia
Atlanta
gham
Charleston
gomery
Savannah
AL
Jacksonville

L. Huron
gan
bit
ibus
napolis
inati
Cleveland

APPALACHIAN MTS.
COASTAL PLAIN

ATLANTIC OCEAN

30°N

Florida
Tampa
tersburg
BAHAMAS
Freeport
Miami
Nassau

Tropic of Cancer

20°N

Havana
CUBA

PUERTO RICO (U.S.)
Virgin Islands (U.S. - U.K.)
Anguilla (U.K.)
ANTIGUA & BARBUDA
Guadeloupe (Fr.)
Pico Duarte 3,175 m
Santo Domingo
San Juan
ST. KITTS & NEVIS
DOMINICA
HAITI
Martinique (Fr.)
Port-au-Prince
DOMINICAN REPUBLIC
ST. LUCIA
BARBADOS
SAINT VINCENT & THE GRENADINES
GRENADA
Tobago
TRINIDAD AND TOBAGO
Trinidad

Greater Antilles

JAMAICA
Kingston

Lesser Antilles

Caribbean Sea

Aruba (Neth.)
Curaçao (Neth.)
Bonaire (Neth.)

10°N

URAS
RAGUA
nagua
Lake Nicaragua
ISTHMUS OF PANAMA
San José
Panama City
STA RICA
PANAMA

SOUTH AMERICA

80°W
70°W

©Macmillan Canada

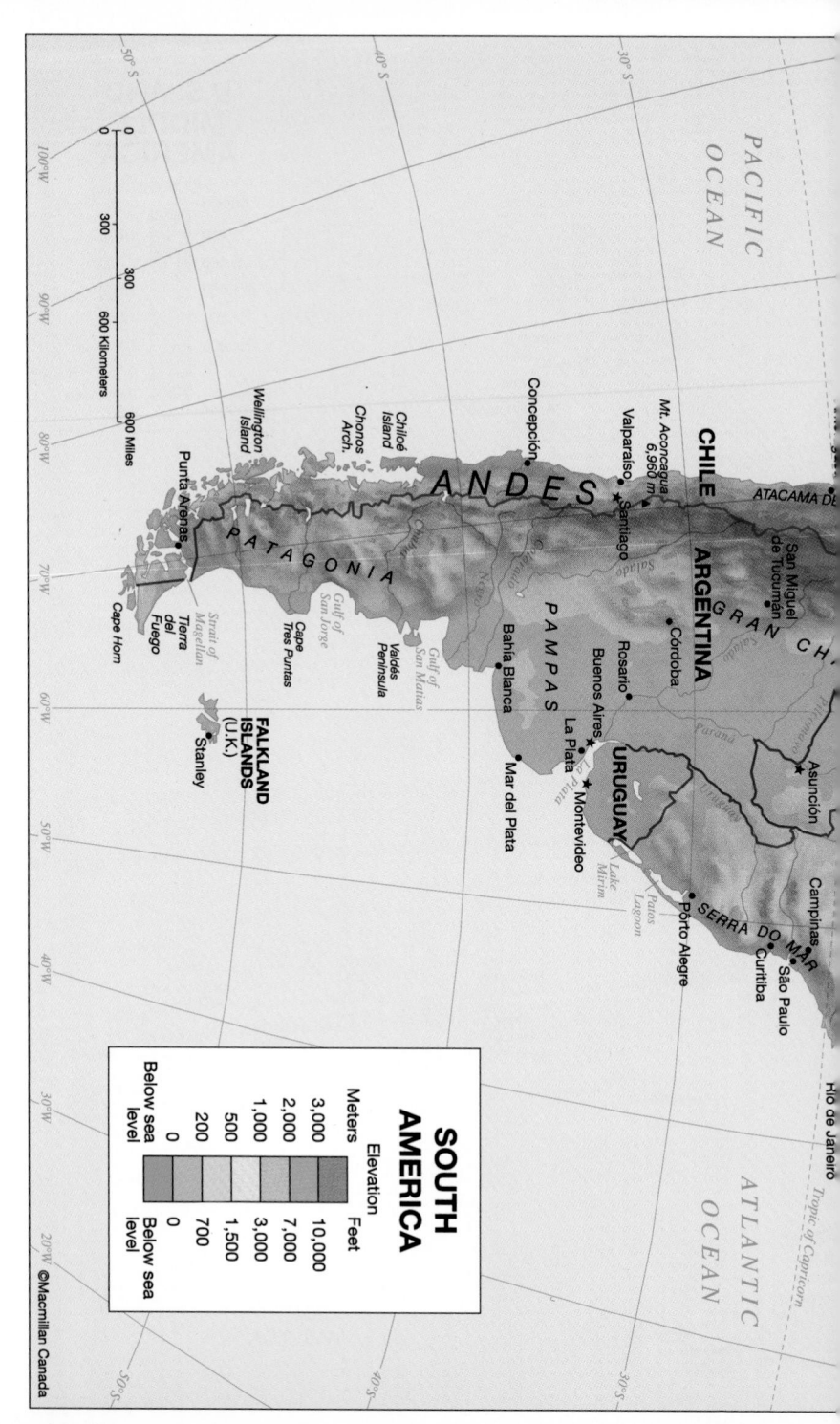

SOUTH AMERICA

Elevation

Meters	Feet
3,000	10,000
2,000	7,000
1,000	3,000
500	1,500
200	700
0	0
Below sea level	Below sea level

©Macmillan Canada

PACIFIC OCEAN

ATLANTIC OCEAN

CHILE

ARGENTINA

URUGUAY

ANDES

PATAGONIA

PAMPAS

GRAN CH

ATACAMA DE

Mt. Aconcagua 6,960 m

Valparaíso
Santiago
Concepción
Chiloé Island
Chonos Arch.
Wellington Island
Punta Arenas
Cape Horn
Tierra del Fuego
Strait of Magellan
Gulf of San Jorge
Valdés Peninsula
Cape Tres Puntas
Gulf of San Matías
Bahía Blanca
Mar del Plata
La Plata
Buenos Aires
Rosario
Córdoba
San Miguel de Tucumán
Asunción
Porto Alegre
Curitiba
São Paulo
Campinas
Rio de Janeiro
Montevideo
Stanley

FALKLAND ISLANDS (U.K.)

SERRA DO MAR

Lake Mirim
Patos Lagoon
Paraná
Uruguay
Salado

Tropic of Capricorn

0 300 600 Kilometers
0 300 600 Miles

50°S 40°S 30°S
100°W 90°W 80°W 70°W 60°W 50°W 40°W 30°W 20°W

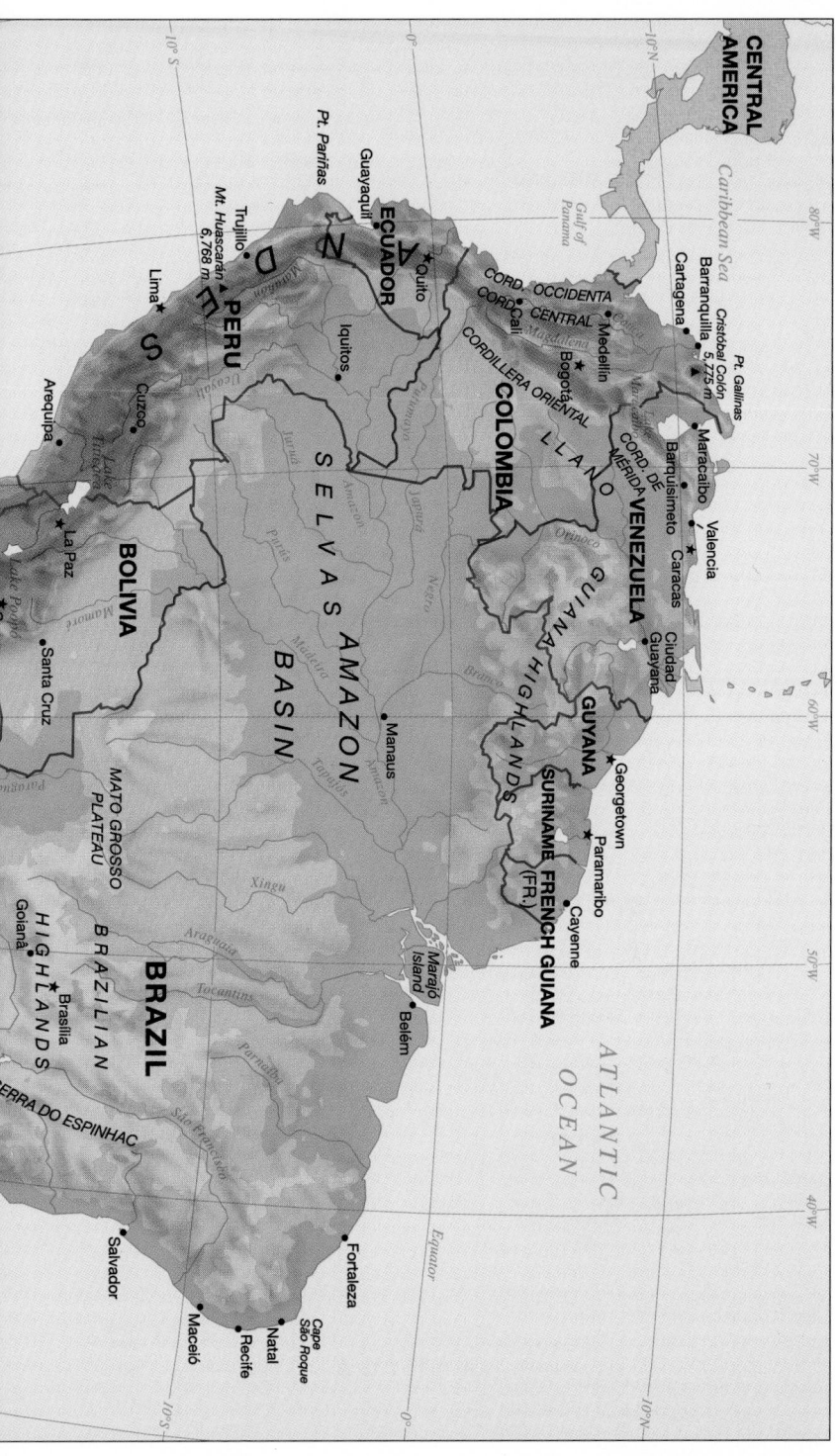

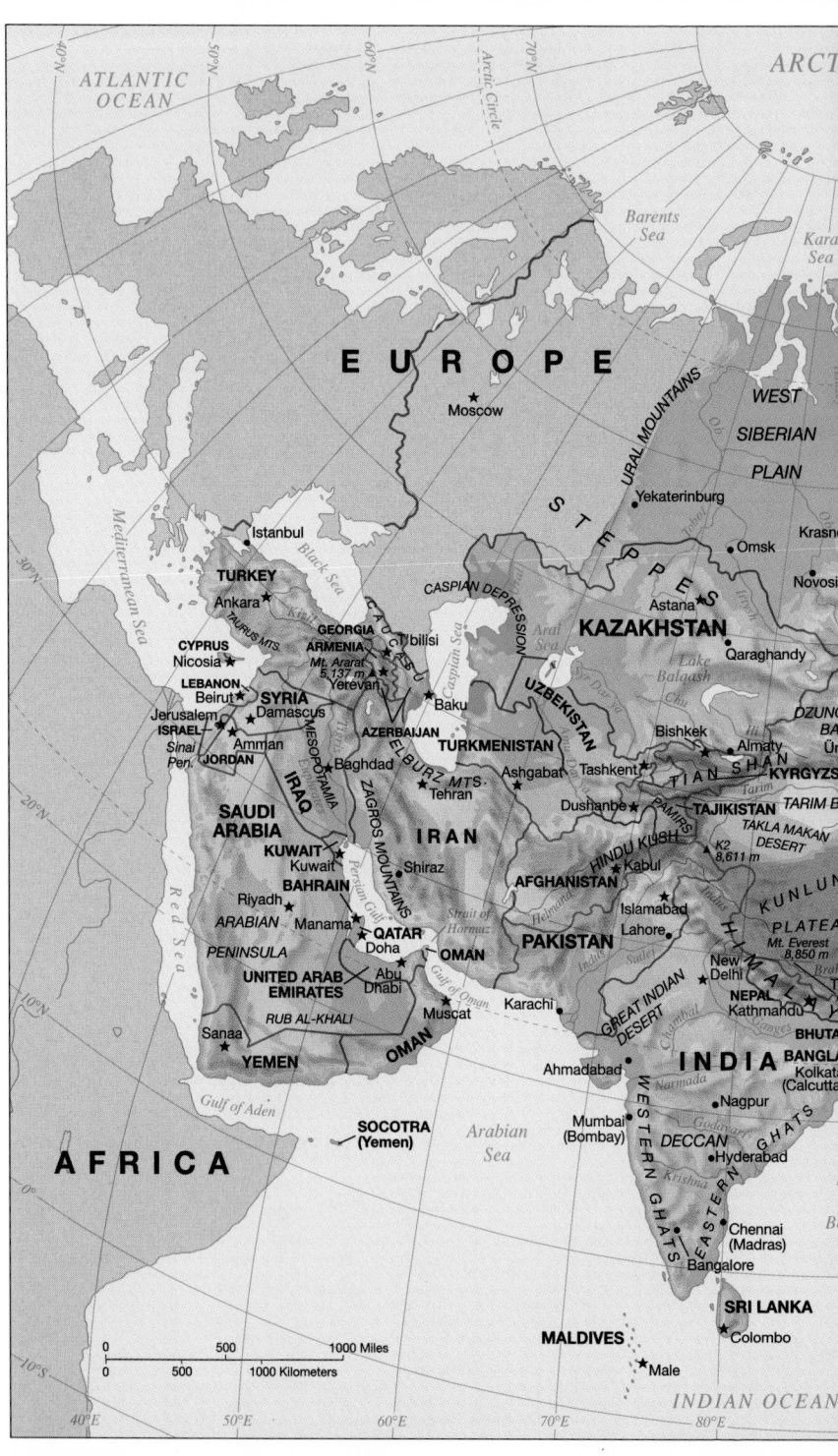

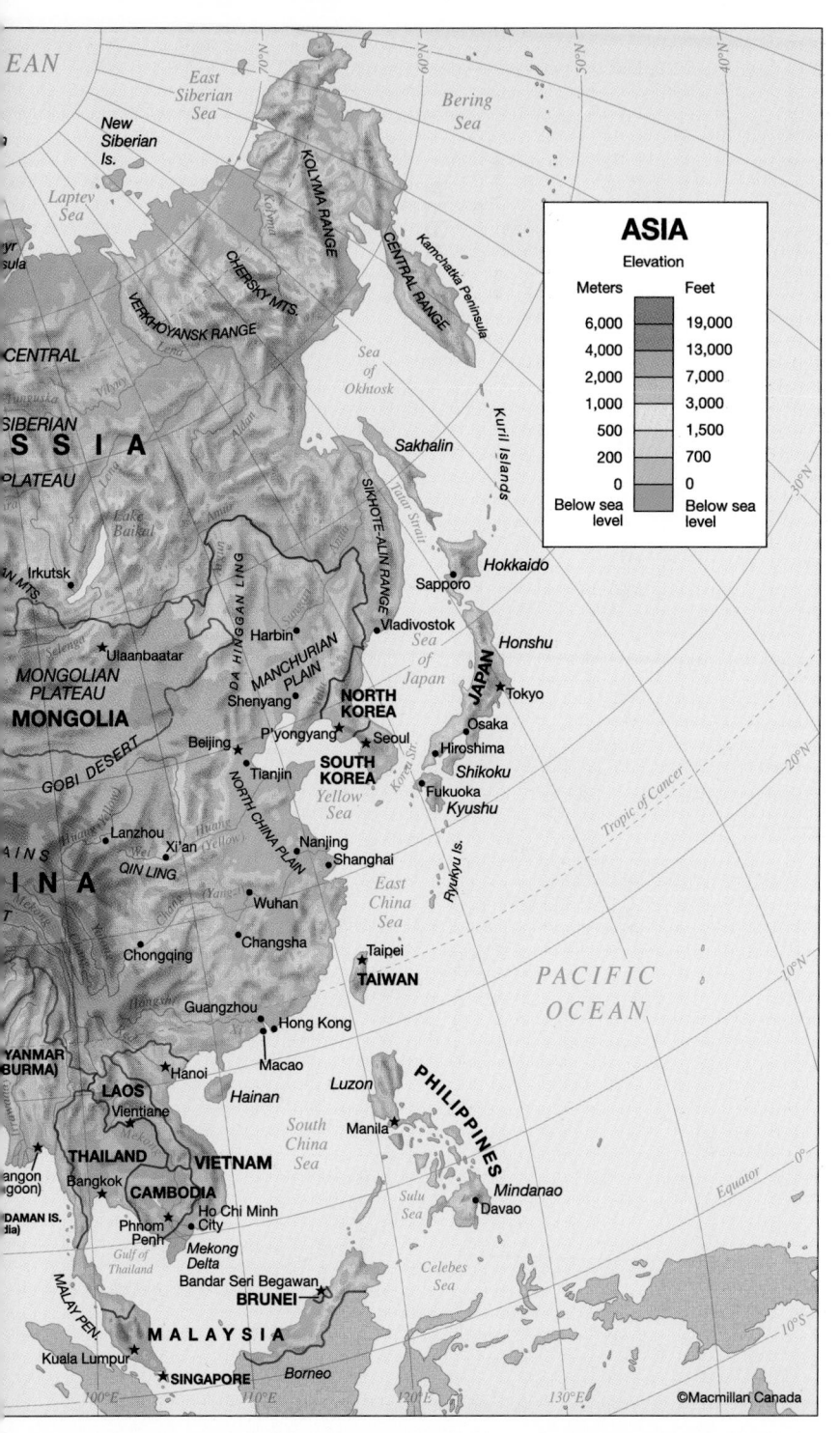

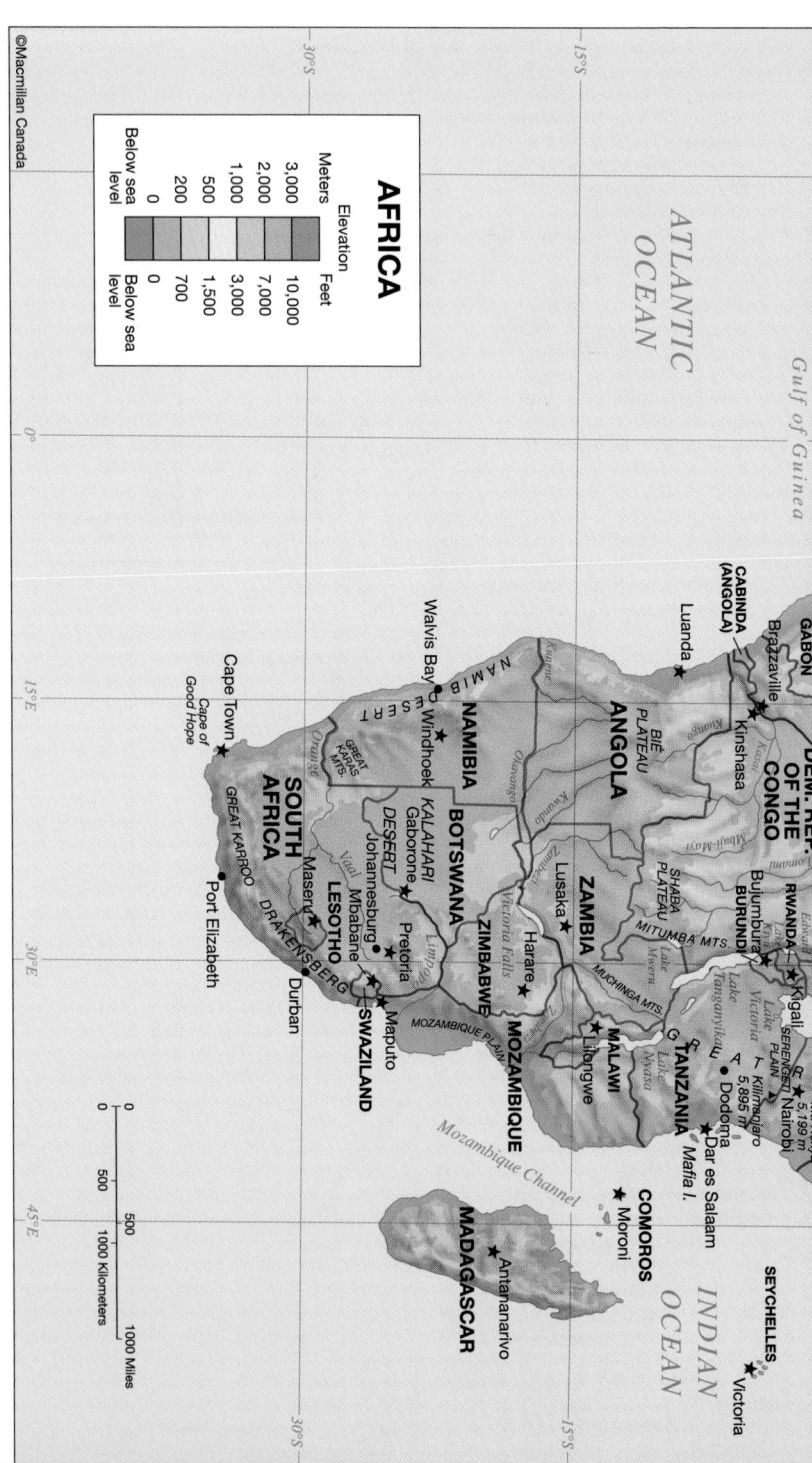

AFRICA

Elevation

Meters	Feet
3,000	10,000
2,000	7,000
1,000	3,000
500	1,500
200	700
0	0
Below sea level	Below sea level

ATLANTIC OCEAN

Gulf of Guinea

São Tomé
Libreville
GABON
CONGO
Brazzaville
CABINDA (ANGOLA)
Kinshasa
DEM. REP. OF THE CONGO
Luanda
BIÉ PLATEAU
ANGOLA
SHABA PLATEAU
MITUMBA MTS.
RWANDA
Kigali
BURUNDI
Bujumbura
Lake Victoria
Lake Tanganyika
SERENGETI PLAIN
Mt. Kenya 5,199 m
Nairobi
Kilimanjaro 5,895 m
TANZANIA
Dodona
Dar es Salaam
Mafia I.

Walvis Bay
Windhoek
NAMIB DESERT
NAMIBIA
GREAT KARAS MTS.
Orange
KALAHARI DESERT
Gaborone
BOTSWANA
Lusaka
ZAMBIA
MUCHINGA MTS.
Victoria Falls
Harare
ZIMBABWE
Lake Malawi
MALAWI
Lilongwe
MOZAMBIQUE

Cape Town
Cape of Good Hope
GREAT KARROO
SOUTH AFRICA
Vaal
Johannesburg
Pretoria
Mbabane
SWAZILAND
Maseru
LESOTHO
DRAKENSBERG
Durban
Port Elizabeth
Maputo
MOZAMBIQUE PLAIN
Limpopo
Mozambique Channel

COMOROS
Moroni

SEYCHELLES
Victoria

MADAGASCAR
Antananarivo

INDIAN OCEAN

0° Equator

15°S

30°S

0°

15°E

30°E

45°E

0 500 1000 Miles
0 500 1000 Kilometers

©Macmillan Canada

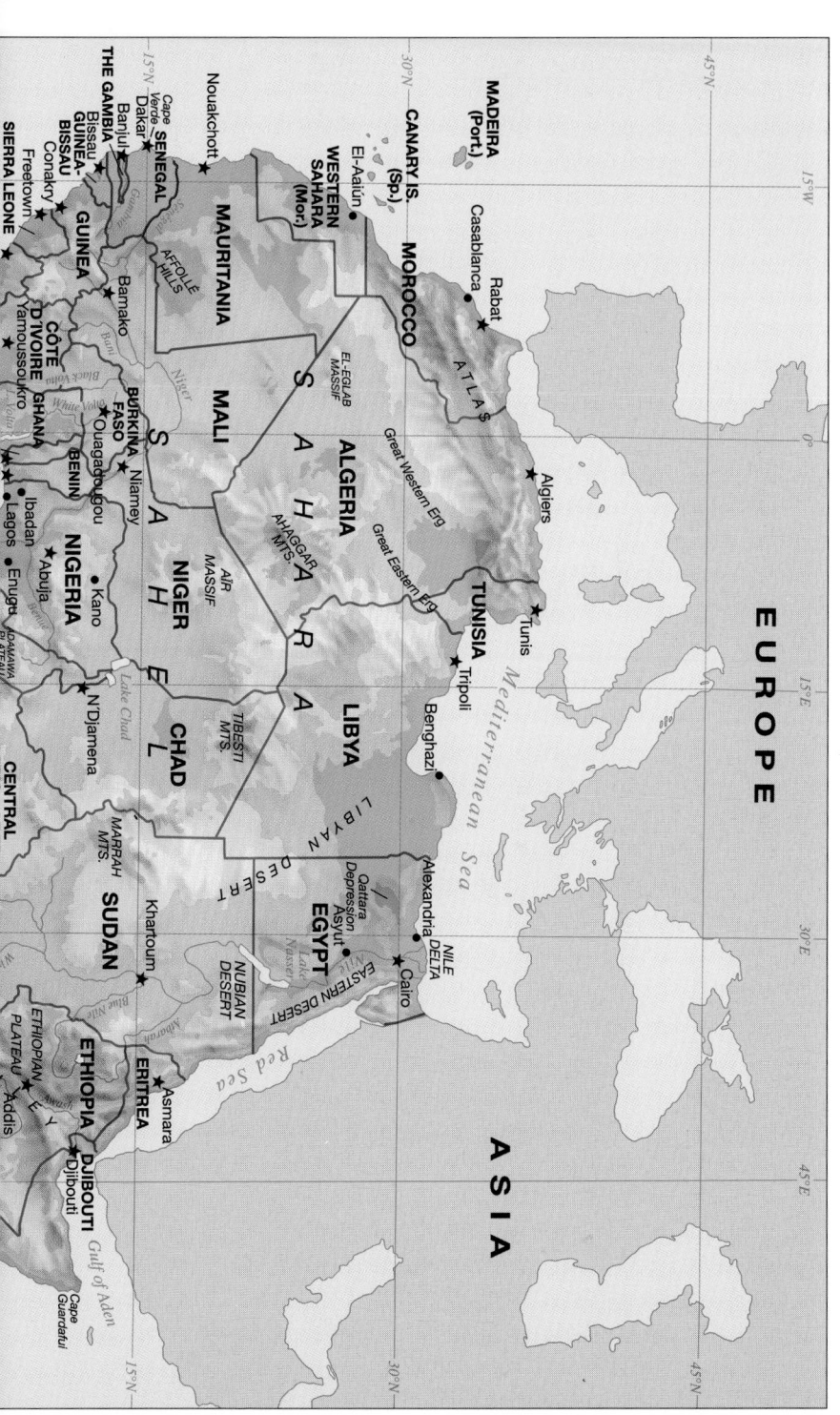

ASIA

Tropic of Cancer

Taiwan

NORTHERN MARIANA ISLANDS (U.S.)

Hainan

South China Sea

Philippine Islands

Philippine Sea

Guam (U.S.)

FEDERATED STATES OF MICRONESIA

Koror *Yap*
Palau Chuuk ★ Palikir

Celebes Sea

Caroline Islands

Leuser 3,466 m
▲ ●Medan

Manado

Sumatra

Pontianak *Borneo*

Molucca Is.

0°

Padang

Bangka Celebes Ceram
Kerinci 3,800 m Jambi Buru Ambon
Palembang Banjarmasin Ujung Pandang *Banda Sea*

Jayapura

Bismarck Arch.

Bismarck Sea

WEST IRIAN *MAOKE MTS.*
Jaya Peak 5,029 m New Guinea

New Britain

Jakarta ★

Java Sea

I N D O N E S I A

Aru

PAPUA NEW GUINEA

Solomon Sea

Bandung *Java* Surabaya *Bali* Sumbawa Flores
Yogyakarta Malang *Lombok* *Sumba* **EAST TIMOR**

Arafura Sea

Torres Strait

Pt. Moresby

Timor *Timor Sea* Cape York

Darwin **ARNHEM LAND**

Gulf of Carpentaria

CAPE YORK PENINSULA

Great Barrier Reef

15°S

KIMBERLEY PLATEAU

Northern Territory

Townsville

Cor Sea

North West Cape

GREAT SANDY DESERT

AUSTRALIA

HAMERSLEY RA.

MACDONNELL RANGES

Alice Springs

GREAT DIVIDING RANGE

Tropic of Capricorn

GIBSON DESERT

Ayers Rock ▲ 868 m
MUSGRAVE

SIMPSON DESERT

Queensland

GREAT ARTESIAN BASIN

Brisban

GREAT VICTORIA DESERT

Western Australia

South Australia

Lake Eyre

30°S

●Perth

NULLARBOR PLAIN

New South Wales

Newcastle

Cape Leeuwin

Great Australian Bight

Adelaide

Victoria

AUSTRALIAN ALPS

●Sydney
Canberra, A.C.T.
▲ Mt. Kosciusko 2,228 m
Cape Howe

Melbourne

Bass Strait

Tas

I N D I A N   O C E A N

45°S

Tasmania
●Hobart

South East Cape

©Macmillan Canada

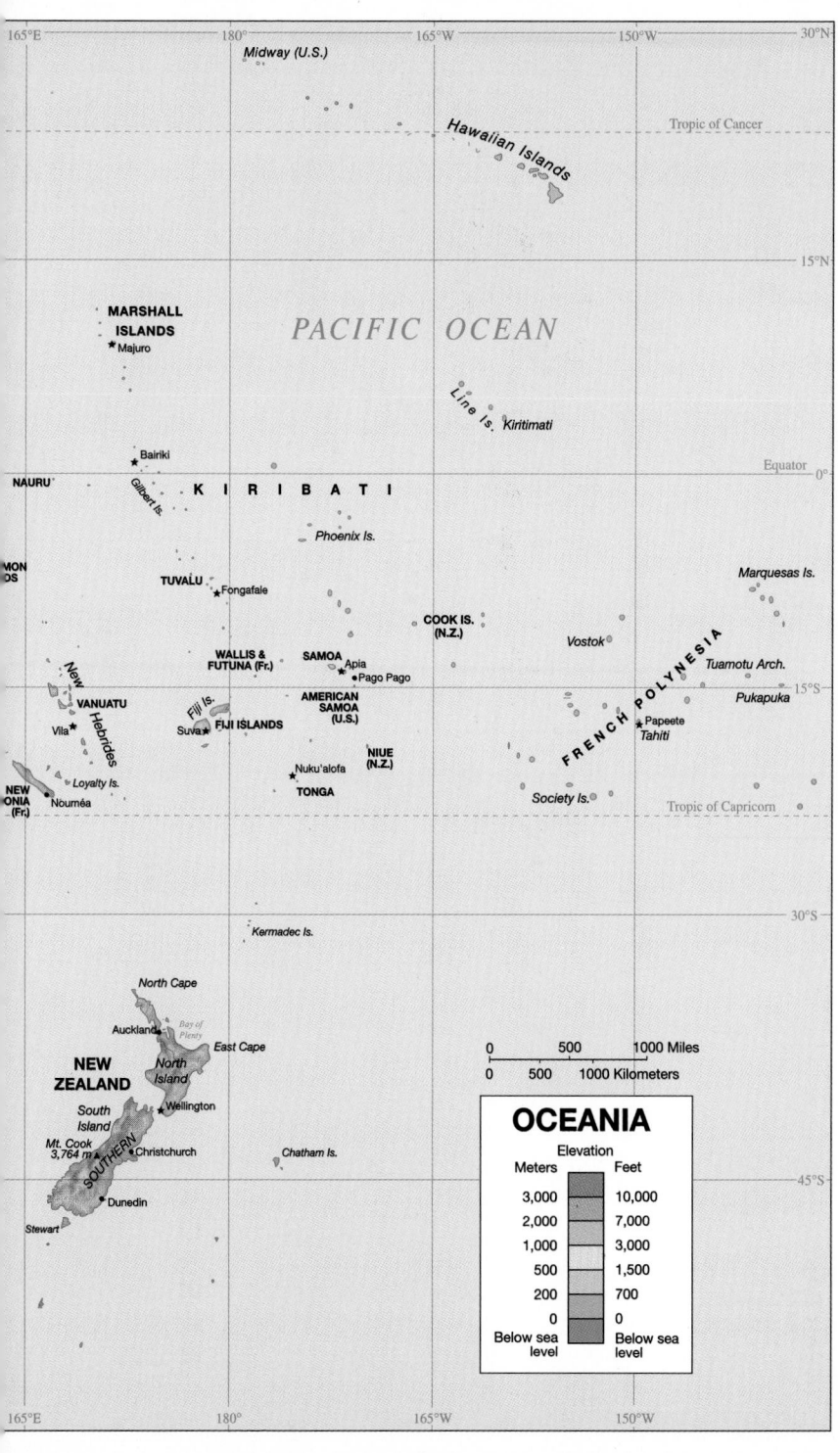

165°E — 180° — 165°W — 150°W — 30°N

Midway (U.S.)

Tropic of Cancer

Hawaiian Islands

— 15°N

MARSHALL
ISLANDS
★ Majuro

PACIFIC OCEAN

Line Is.

Kiritimati

Equator 0°

Bairiki ★

NAURU

Gilbert Is.

K I R I B A T I

MON
OS

Phoenix Is.

Marquesas Is.

TUVALU   Fongafale

COOK IS.
(N.Z.)

Vostok

FRENCH POLYNESIA

Tuamotu Arch.

New

WALLIS &
FUTUNA (Fr.)

SAMOA
Apia
Pago Pago

15°S

VANUATU

Fiji Is.

AMERICAN
SAMOA
(U.S.)

Pukapuka

Hebrides

Vila ★   Suva ★ FIJI ISLANDS

Papeete
Tahiti

NEW
ONIA
(Fr.)

Loyalty Is.

Nouméa

Nuku'alofa

NIUE
(N.Z.)

TONGA

Society Is.

Tropic of Capricorn

30°S

Kermadec Is.

North Cape

Auckland

Bay of
Plenty

East Cape

0   500   1000 Miles

0   500   1000 Kilometers

NEW
ZEALAND

North
Island

South
Island

Wellington

SOUTHERN

Mt. Cook
3,764 m Christchurch

Chatham Is.

45°S

Dunedin

Stewart

OCEANIA

Elevation

Meters		Feet
3,000		10,000
2,000		7,000
1,000		3,000
500		1,500
200		700
0		0
Below sea level		Below sea level

165°E — 180° — 165°W — 150°W

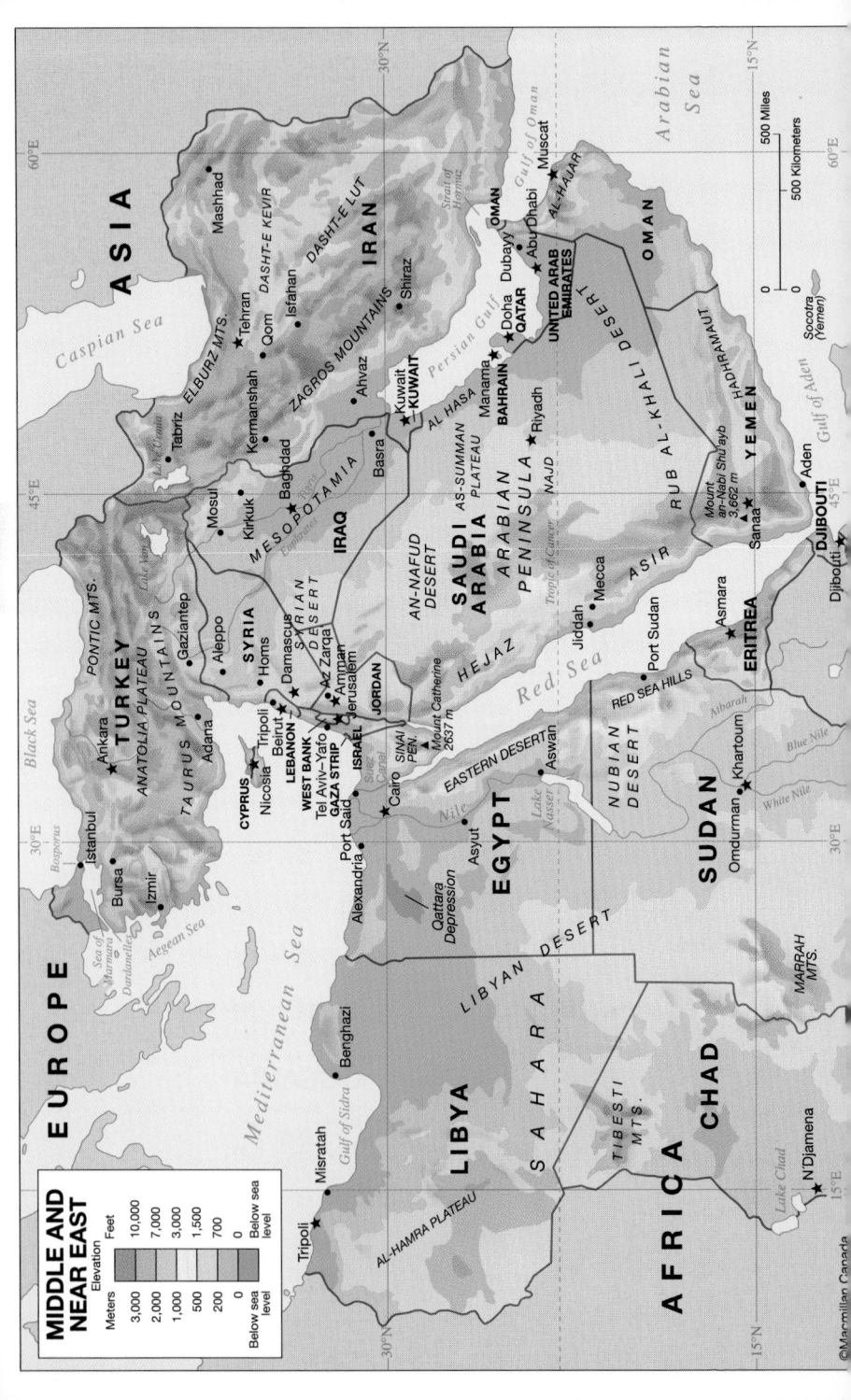

MIDDLE AND NEAR EAST

Elevation

Meters	Feet
3,000	10,000
2,000	7,000
1,000	3,000
500	1,500
200	700
0	0
Below sea level	Below sea level

EUROPE

ASIA

AFRICA

Black Sea

Caspian Sea

Sea of Marmara

Bosporus

Dardanelles

Aegean Sea

Mediterranean Sea

Gulf of Sidra

Arabian Sea

Gulf of Oman

Strait of Hormuz

Persian Gulf

Gulf of Aden

Red Sea

Socotra (Yemen)

TURKEY

Istanbul
Bursa
Izmir
Ankara ★
Adana
Gaziantep

PONTIC MTS.
ANATOLIA PLATEAU
TAURUS MOUNTAINS

Lake Van
Lake Urmia

IRAN

Tabriz
Mashhad
Tehran ★
Qom
Isfahan
Kermanshah
Shiraz
Ahvaz

ELBURZ MTS.
DASHT-E KEVIR
DASHT-E LUT
ZAGROS MOUNTAINS

SYRIA

Aleppo
Homs
Damascus ★
Az Zarqa
Amman

SYRIAN DESERT

IRAQ

Mosul
Kirkuk
Baghdad ★
Basra

MESOPOTAMIA

Tigris
Euphrates

CYPRUS
Nicosia ★

LEBANON
Beirut ★
Tripoli

ISRAEL
Tel Aviv–Yafo
Jerusalem ★
WEST BANK
GAZA STRIP

JORDAN
Amman ★

KUWAIT
Kuwait ★

BAHRAIN
Manama ★

QATAR
Doha ★

UNITED ARAB EMIRATES
Abu Dhabi ★
Dubayy

OMAN
Muscat ★
AL-HAJAR

SAUDI ARABIA
Riyadh ★
Mecca
Jiddah

AL HASA
AS-SUMMAN PLATEAU
ARABIAN PENINSULA
NAJD
AN-NAFUD DESERT
HEJAZ
ASIR
RUB AL-KHALI DESERT
HADHRAMAUT

YEMEN
Sana ★
Aden
Mount an-Nabi Shu'ayb 3,662 m

DJIBOUTI
Djibouti ★

ERITREA
Asmara ★

EGYPT
Cairo ★
Alexandria
Port Said
Asyut
Aswan

Suez Canel
SINAI PEN.
Mount Catherine 2637 m
EASTERN DESERT
Qattara Depression
LIBYAN DESERT
Nile
Lake Nasser
Tropic of Cancer

LIBYA
Tripoli ★
Benghazi
Misratah

AL-HAMRA PLATEAU
SAHARA

SUDAN
Khartoum ★
Omdurman
Port Sudan
Aswan

NUBIAN DESERT
RED SEA HILLS
Atbarah
Blue Nile
White Nile

CHAD
N'Djamena ★

MARRAH MTS.
TIBESTI MTS.
Lake Chad

500 Miles
500 Kilometers
0

© Macmillan Canada

15°N
30°E
45°E
60°E
15°N
30°N

Ethnic Groups: 95% Arab, 4% Armenian, 1% other
Languages: Arabic and French (both official); Armenian, English, Kurdish
Religions: Muslim 70% (Sunni, Shia and Druse), Christian 30% (mainly Maronite; also, Armenian, Greek and Syrian sects and Protestants)
Birth Rate: 20.26/1,000 population (2000 est.)
Death Rate: 6.42/1,000 population (2000 est.)
Infant Mortality: 29.30 deaths/1,000 live births (2000 est.)
Life Expectancy at Birth: 68.87 years male, 73.74 years female (2000 est.)
Total Fertility Rate: 2.08 children born/woman (2000 est.)
Literacy: 85% (1998)

■ GOVERNMENT

Leader(s): Pres. Emile Jamil Lahud; Prime Min. Rafiq Hariri
Government Type: republic
Administrative Divisions: 5 governorates (muhafazat, sing. —muhafazah)
Nationhood: Nov. 22, 1943 (from League of Nations mandate under French administration)
National Holiday: Independence Day, Nov. 22

■ ECONOMY

Overview: factional infighting has led to deterioration of the infrastructure and disrupted normal economic activity in what used to be the centre for Middle Eastern banking; high unemployment; growing shortages; international aid is vital
GDP: US$16.2 billion, per capita US$4,500; real growth rate 1% (1999 est.)
Inflation: 13.8% (Feb. 1997)
Industries: accounts for 27% of GDP; banking, food processing, textiles, cement, oil refining, chemicals, jewelry, some metal fabricating
Labour Force: 1 million (1999); 27.4% industry, 58.4% services, 14.3% agriculture
Unemployment: 18% (1997 est.)
Agriculture: accounts for about 12% of GDP; principal products—citrus fruit, vegetables, potatoes, olives, tobacco, hemp (hashish), sheep and goats; not self-sufficient in grain
Natural Resources: limestone, iron ore, salt; water-surplus state in a water-deficit region

■ FINANCE/TRADE

Currency: Lebanese pound (£L) = 100 piasters
International Reserves Excluding Gold: US$5.932 billion (Jan. 2001)
Gold Reserves: US$9.222 milllion fine troy ounces (Jan. 2001)
Budget: revenues US$4.9 billion; expenditures US$8.36 billion, including capital expenditures of US$n.a. (1999 est.)
Defence Expenditures: 10.64% of total govt. expenditure (1999)
Education Expenditures: 7.23% of central govt. expenditure (1999)
External Debt: US$8.441 billion (1999)
Exports: US$717 million (2000); commodities: agricultural products, chemicals, textiles, metals and jewelry; partners: 21% Saudi Arabia, 9.5% Switzerland, 6% Jordan, 12% Kuwait, 5% US
Imports: US$6.253 billion (2000); commodities: consumer goods, machinery and transport equipment, petroleum products; partners: 14% Italy, 12% France, 6% US, 5% Turkey, 3% Saudi Arabia

■ COMMUNICATIONS

Daily Newspapers: 15
Televisions: 352/1,000 inhabitants (1998)
Radios: 906/1,000 inhabitants (1997)
Telephones: 201 lines/1,000 inhabitants (1999)

■ TRANSPORTATION

Motor Vehicles: n.a.
Roads: 7,300 km; 6,200 km paved
Railway: 399 km; railroad system in disrepair, considered inoperable
Air Traffic: 857,000 passengers carried (1997)
Airports: 9; 7 have paved runways (1999 est.)

Canadian Embassy: The Canadian Embassy, Coolrite Building, 434 Autostrade, Jal-ed-Dib, Lebanon; mailing address: P.O. Box 60163, Jal-el-Dib, Beirut, Lebanon. Tel: (011-961-4) 713-900. Fax: (011-961-4) 710-595. Email: berut@dfait-maeci.gc.ca
Embassy in Canada: Embassy of the Lebanese Republic, 640 Lyon St, Ottawa ON K1S 3Z5. Tel: (613) 236-5825. Fax: (613) 232-1609. Email: emblebanon@synapse.net

Lesotho

Long-Form Name: Kingdom of Lesotho
Capital: Maseru

■ GEOGRAPHY

Area: 30,355 sq. km
Coastline: none: landlocked
Climate: temperate; cool to cold, dry winters; hot, wet summers
Environment: population pressure forcing settlement in marginal agricultural areas results in overgrazing, severe soil erosion, soil exhaustion; desertification
Terrain: mostly highland with some plateaus, hills and mountains

Land Use: 11% arable; 0% permanent crops; 66% meadows; 0% forest; 23% other; includes 30 sq. km irrigated
Location: S Africa

■ PEOPLE

Population: 2,143,141 (July 2000 est.)
Nationality: Mosotho (sing.), Basotho (pl.)
Age Structure: 0-14 yrs: 40%; 15-64: 56%; 65+: 4% (2000 est.)
Population Growth Rate: 1.65% (2000 est.)
Net Migration: -0.64 migrants/1,000 population (2000 est.)
Ethnic Groups: 99.7% Sotho; 0.3% Europeans, Asians and other
Languages: Sesotho (southern Sotho) and English (official); also Zulu and Xhosa
Religions: 80% Christian, indigenous beliefs
Birth Rate: 31.74/1,000 population (2000 est.)
Death Rate: 14.59/1,000 population (2000 est.)
Infant Mortality: 82.97 deaths/1,000 live births (2000 est.)
Life Expectancy at Birth: 49.78 years male, 51.84 years female (2000 est.)
Total Fertility Rate: 4.15 children born/woman (2000 est.)
Literacy: 71.3% (1997)

■ GOVERNMENT

Leader(s): King Letsie III, Prime Min. Pakalitha Mosisili
Government Type: parliamentary constitutional monarchy
Administrative Divisions: 10 districts
Nationhood: Oct. 4, 1966 (from UK: formerly known as Basutoland)
National Holiday: Independence Day, Oct. 4

■ ECONOMY

Overview: the economy is hampered by the geography of the country (small, landlocked and mountainous) and the lack of natural resources other than water; subsistence farming is the main occupation; labourers in South Africa make remittances; industry is growing in importance
GDP: US$4.7 billion, per capita US$2,240; real growth rate -10% (1998 est.)
Inflation: 6.13% (year-end 2000)
Industries: accounts for 42% of GDP; light manufacturing, milling, canning, leather, jute production, textiles, clothing, light engineering, food, beverages, handicrafts, tourism
Labour Force: 1 million (1999); 23.3% agriculture, 33.1% industry, 43.6% services
Unemployment: substantial unemployment and underemployment (1999)
Agriculture: accounts for 14% of GDP; very

primitive, mostly subsistence farming and livestock; principal crops are corn, wheat, pulses, sorghum and barley
Natural Resources: some diamonds and other minerals, water, agricultural and grazing land

■ FINANCE/TRADE

Currency: loti, maloti (pl.) = 100 lisente
International Reserves Excluding Gold: US$413 million (Jan. 2001)
Gold Reserves: n.a.
Budget: n.a.
Defence Expenditures: 6.54% of central government expenditure (1998)
Education Expenditures: 26.71% of central government expenditure (1998)
External Debt: US$686 million (1999)
Exports: US$194 million (1998); commodities: wool, mohair, wheat, cattle, peas, beans, corn, hides, skins, baskets; partners: South Africa 53%, European Community 30%, North and South America 13%
Imports: US$863 million (1998).; commodities: corn, building materials, clothing, vehicles, machinery, medicines, petroleum, oil and lubricants; partners: South Africa 95%, European Community 2%

■ COMMUNICATIONS

Daily Newspapers: 2
Televisions: 25/1,000 inhabitants (1998)
Radios: 49/1,000 inhabitants (1997)
Telephones: 10 lines/1,000 inhabitants (1999)

■ TRANSPORTATION

Motor Vehicles: n.a.
Roads: 4,955 km; 887 km paved
Railway: 2.6 km, owned, operated by and included in the statistics for South Africa
Air Traffic: 10,000 passengers carried (1997)
Airports: 29; 4 have paved runways (1999 est.)

Canadian Embassy: The Canadian High Commission to Lesotho, c/o Canadian Embassy, Private Bag X13, Hatfield 0028, Pretoria, South Africa. Canadian Consulate, P.O. Box 1191, Maseru 100, Lesotho. Tel: (011-266) 314-187. Fax: (011-266) 314-187. Email: bwhite@lesoff.co.za
Embassy in Canada: c/o High Commission for the Kingdom of Lesotho, 2511 Massachusetts Ave NW, Washington DC 20008, USA. Tel: (202) 797-5533. Fax: (202) 234-6815. Email: n.a.

Liberia

Long-Form Name: Republic of Liberia
Capital: Monrovia

■ GEOGRAPHY

Area: 111,370 sq. km
Coastline: 579 km
Climate: tropical; hot, humid; dry winters with hot days and cool to cold nights; wet, cloudy summers with frequent heavy showers
Environment: West Africa's largest tropical rain forest, subject to deforestation; soil erosion is increasingly a problem; river pollution
Terrain: mostly flat to rolling coastal plains rising to rolling plateau and low mountains in northeast
Land Use: 1% arable; 3% permanent crops; 59% permanent pastures; 18% forest; 19% other; includes 20 sq. km irrigated
Location: W Africa, bordering on South Atlantic Ocean

■ PEOPLE

Population: 3,164,156 (July 2000 est.)
Nationality: Liberian
Age Structure: 0-14 yrs: 43%; 15-64: 54%; 65+: 3% (2000 est.)
Population Growth Rate: 1.94% (2000 est.)
Net Migration: -11.22 migrants/1,000 population (2000 est.)
Ethnic Groups: 95% indigenous African tribes, including Kpelle, Bassa, Gio, Kru, Grego, Mano, Krahn, Gola, Gbandi, Lom, Kissi, Vai and Bella; 2.5% descendants of repatriated slaves known as Americo-Liberians, and 2.5% Congo People (descendants of immigrants from the Caribbean who had been slaves)
Languages: English (official); 20 local languages of the Niger-Congo language group; English used by approx. 20%
Religions: 70% traditional, 20% Muslim, 10% Christian
Birth Rate: 47.22/1,000 population (2000 est.)
Death Rate: 16.58/1,000 population (2000 est.)
Infant Mortality: 134.63 deaths/1,000 live births (2000 est.)
Life Expectancy at Birth: 49.60 years male, 52.49 years female (2000 est.)
Total Fertility Rate: 6.43 children born/woman (2000 est.)
Literacy: 48.4% (1997)

■ GOVERNMENT

Leader(s): Pres. Charles Taylor, V. Pres. Moses Zeh Blah
Government Type: republic
Administrative Divisions: 13 counties
Nationhood: July 26, 1847
National Holiday: Independence Day, July 26

■ ECONOMY

Overview: civil war since 1990 has destroyed much of Liberia's economy, especially the infrastructure in and around Monrovia; many businesspeople have fled the country, taking capital and expertise with them; the government must encourage foreign investment to restore the infrastructure and to raise incomes
GDP: US$2.85 billion, per capita US$1,000; real growth rate 0.5% (1999 est.)
Inflation: n.a.
Industries: accounts for 15% of GDP; rubber processing, food processing, construction materials, furniture, palm oil processing, mining (iron ore, diamonds)
Labour Force: n.a; 74.2% agriculture, 16.4% services, 9.4% industry
Unemployment: 70%
Agriculture: accounts for 50% of GDP (including fishing and forestry); principal products—rubber, timber, coffee, cocoa, rice, cassava, palm oil, sugar cane, bananas, sheep and goats; not self-sufficient in food, imports 25% of rice consumption
Natural Resources: iron ore, timber, diamonds, gold, hydropower

■ FINANCE/TRADE

Currency: Liberian dollar ($L) = 100 cents
International Reserves Excluding Gold: none (Oct. 2000)
Gold Reserves: n.a.
Budget: n.a.
Defence Expenditures: 2.9% of GDP (1998)
Education Expenditures: n.a.
External Debt: US$2.077 billion (1999)
Exports: US$1.328 billion (2000); commodities: diamonds, iron ore, rubber, timber, coffee; partners: US, EU, Netherlands, Singapore
Imports: US$1.036 billion (2000); commodities: mineral fuels, chemicals, machinery, foodstuffs; partners: EU, US, Japan, China, Netherlands

■ COMMUNICATIONS

Daily Newspapers: 6
Televisions: 29/1,000 inhabitants (1997)
Radios: 329/1,000 inhabitants (1997)
Telephones: 2 lines/1,000 inhabitants (1999)

■ TRANSPORTATION

Motor Vehicles: 28,700; 17,800 passenger cars (1997 est.)
Roads: 10,600 km; 657 km paved
Railway: 490 km
Air Traffic: n.a.
Airports: 45; 2 have paved runways (1999 est.)

Canadian Embassy: The Canadian Embassy to Liberia, c/o Canadian Embassy, P O Box 4104, Abidjan 01, Cote d'Ivoire. Tel: (011-225) 20-

30-07-00. Fax: (011-225) 20-30-07-20. Email: abdjn@dfait-maeci.gc.ca
Embassy in Canada: consular address: Consulate of Liberia, 519 Spadina Rd, Toronto ON M5P 2W6. Email: Liberia@iname.com

Libya

Long-Form Name: Socialist People's Libyan Arab Jamahiriya
Capital: Tripoli

■ GEOGRAPHY

Area: 1,759,540 sq. km
Coastline: 1,770 km
Climate: Mediterranean along coast; dry, extreme desert interior
Environment: hot, dry, dust-laden ghibli (a southern wind lasting one to four days in spring and fall); desertification; dust storms; sparse natural surface-water resources
Terrain: mostly barren, flat to undulating plains, plateaus, depressions
Land Use: 1% arable; 0% permanent; 8% meadows; 0% forest; 91% other; includes 4,700 sq. km irrigated
Location: N Africa, bordering on Mediterranean Sea

■ PEOPLE

Population: 5,115,450 (July 2000 est.)
Nationality: Libyan
Age Structure: 0-14 yrs: 36%; 15-64: 60%; 65+: 4% (2000 est.)
Population Growth Rate: 2.42% (2000 est.)
Net Migration: 0 migrants/1,000 population (2000 est.)
Ethnic Groups: 97% Berber and Arab; some Greeks, Maltese, Italians, Egyptians, Pakistanis, Turks, Indians and Tunisians
Languages: Arabic (official); Italian and English widely understood in major cities, Berber
Religions: 97% Sunni Muslim, 3% Christian and other
Birth Rate: 27.68/1,000 population (2000 est.)
Death Rate: 3.51/1,000 population (2000 est.)
Infant Mortality: 30.08 deaths/1,000 live births (2000 est.)
Life Expectancy at Birth: 73.34 years male, 77.66 years female (2000 est.)
Total Fertility Rate: 3.71 children born/woman (2000 est.)
Literacy: 76.5% (1997)

■ GOVERNMENT

Leader(s): Leader Col. Mu'ammar Abu Minyar al-Qadhafi. Sec. of Gen. People's Congress Muhammad al-Zanati

Government Type: Jamahiriya (a state of the masses); in theory, governed by the populace through local councils; in fact, a military dictatorship
Administrative Divisions: 25 municipalities (baladiyat, sing. —baladiyah)
Nationhood: Dec. 24, 1951 (from Italy)
National Holiday: Revolution Day, Sept. 1

■ ECONOMY

Overview: a socialist-oriented economy that depends largely on revenues from the oil sector; cutbacks on imports due to declining oil revenues have led to shortages of foodstuffs and basic goods; must import 75% of its food needs, as poor soil and climate limit agricultural production
GDP: US$39.3 billion, per capita US$7,900; real growth rate 2% (1999 est.)
Inflation: n.a.
Industries: accounts for 47% of GDP; petroleum, food processing, textiles, handicrafts, cement
Labour Force: 2 million (1998); 28.9% industry, 53% services, 18.1% agriculture
Unemployment: 30% (1998 est.)
Agriculture: accounts for 7% of GDP; cash crops—wheat, barley, olives, dates, citrus fruit, peanuts; 75% of food is imported
Natural Resources: crude oil, natural gas, gypsum

■ FINANCE/TRADE

Currency: Libyan dinar (LD) = 1,000 dirhams
International Reserves Excluding Gold: US$9.839 billion (Nov. 2000)
Gold Reserves: n.a.
Budget: revenues US$3.6 billion; expenditures US$5.1 billion, including capital expenditures of US$n.a. (1998 est.)
Defence Expenditures: 19.7% of central government expenditure (1997)
Education Expenditures: n.a.
External Debt: US$4 billion (1998 est.)
Exports: US$5.894 billion (2000); commodities: petroleum, peanuts, hides; partners: Italy, former USSR countries, Germany, Spain, France, Belgium/Luxembourg, Turkey
Imports: US$4.613 billion (2000); commodities: machinery, transport equipment, food, manufactured goods; partners: Italy, former USSR countries, Germany, UK, Japan

■ COMMUNICATIONS

Daily Newspapers: 4
Televisions: 126/1,000 inhabitants (1998)
Radios: 233/1,000 inhabitants (1997)
Telephones: 101 lines/1,000 inhabitants (1999)

■ TRANSPORTATION

Motor Vehicles: 904,000; 592,000 passenger cars (1997 est.)
Roads: 83,200 km; 47,590 km paved
Railway: none
Air Traffic: 571,000 passengers carried (1997)
Airports: 142; 59 have paved runways (1999 est.)

Canadian Embassy: The Canadian Embassy, Al-Fateh Tower, 7th Fl, P.O. Box 93392, Al-Fateh Tower Post Office, Tripoli, Libya. Tel: (011-218-21) 335-1633. Fax: (011-218-21) 335-1630. Email: n.a.
Embassy in Canada: Embassy of the Socialist People's Libyan Arab Jamahiriya, 81 Metcalfe St Ste 1000, Ottawa ON K1P 6K7. Tel: (613) 230-0919. Fax: (613) 230-0683. Email: n.a.

Liechtenstein

Long-Form Name: Principality of Liechtenstein
Capital: Vaduz

■ GEOGRAPHY

Area: 160 sq. km
Coastline: none: landlocked
Climate: continental; cold, cloudy winters with frequent snow or rain; cool to moderately warm, cloudy, humid summers
Environment: variety of microclimatic variations based on elevation
Terrain: mostly mountainous (Alps) with Rhine Valley in western third
Land Use: 24% arable; 0% permanent crops; 16% meadows; 35% forest; 25% other; includes n.a. sq. km irrigated
Location: C Europe, bordering on Switzerland and Austria

■ PEOPLE

Population: 32,207 (July 2000 est.)
Nationality: Liechtensteiner
Age Structure: 0-14 yrs: 18%; 15-64: 71%; 65+: 11% (2000 est.)
Population Growth Rate: 1.02% (2000 est.)
Net Migration: 5.03 migrants/1,000 population (2000 est.)
Ethnic Groups: 87.5% Alemannic, 12.5% Italian, Turkish and other
Languages: German (official), also Alemannic dialect
Religions: 87.3% Roman Catholic, 8.3% Protestant, 2.8% other, 1.6% unknown
Birth Rate: 11.83/1,000 population (2000 est.)
Death Rate: 6.64/1,000 population (2000 est.)
Infant Mortality: 5.07 deaths/1,000 live births (2000 est.)

Life Expectancy at Birth: 75.16 years male, 82.47 years female (2000 est.)
Total Fertility Rate: 1.49 children born/woman (2000 est.)
Literacy: 100% (1997)

■ GOVERNMENT

Leader(s): Head of State: Prince Hans Adam II von und zu Liechtenstein. Prime Min. Otmar Hasler
Government Type: hereditary constitutional monarchy
Administrative Divisions: 11 communes (gemeinden, sing. —gemeinde)
Nationhood: Jan. 23, 1719, Imperial Principality of Liechtenstein established
National Holiday: Assumption Day, Aug. 15

■ ECONOMY

Overview: a prosperous economy based mainly on small-scale light industry and some farming; economy closely tied to that of Switzerland in a customs union; known for low business taxes and easy incorporation rules
GDP: US$730 million, per capita US$23,000; real growth rate n.a. (1998 est.)
Inflation: n.a.
Industries: electronics, metal manufacturing, textiles, ceramics, pharmaceuticals, food products, precision instruments, tourism
Labour Force: approx. 23,500; of which 13,847 are foreigners; 46% industry, trade and building, 52% services, 2% agriculture, fishing, forestry and horticulture
Unemployment: 1.8% (Feb. 1999)
Agriculture: livestock, vegetables, corn, barley, wheat, potatoes, grapes
Natural Resources: hydroelectric potential, arable land

■ FINANCE/TRADE

Currency: Swiss franc, franken, or franco (SwF) = 100 centimes, rappen, or centesimi
International Reserves Excluding Gold: n.a.
Gold Reserves: n.a.
Budget: revenues US$424.2 million; expenditures US$414.1 million, including capital expenditures US$n.a. (1998 est.)
Defence Expenditures: defence is the responsibility of Switzerland
Education Expenditures: n.a.
External Debt: none
Exports: exact figures not available; small speciality machinery, dental products, stamps, hardware, pottery; partners: EU and EFTA countries, especially Switzerland
Imports: exact figures not available; commodities: machinery, metal goods, textiles,

foodstuffs, motor vehicles; partners: EU countries, Switzerland

■ COMMUNICATIONS

Daily Newspapers: 2
Televisions: 372/1,000 inhabitants (1997 est.)
Radios: 652/1,000 inhabitants (1997 est.)
Telephones: 609 lines/1,000 inhabitants (1999)

■ TRANSPORTATION

Motor Vehicles: n.a.
Roads: 250 km; all paved
Railway: 18.5 km, owned, operated and included in statistics for Austria
Air Traffic: n.a.
Airports: none
Canadian Embassy: The Canadian Embassy to Liechtenstein, c/o the Canadian Embassy, P.O. Box 3000, Berne 6, Switzerland. Tel: (011-41-31) 357-32-00. Fax: (011-41-31) 357-32-10. Email: bern@dfait-maeci.gc.ca
Embassy in Canada: Embassy of Liechtenstein, c/o Embassy of Switzerland, 5 Marlborough Ave, Ottawa ON K1N 8E6. Tel: (613) 235-1837. Fax: (613) 563-1394. Email: vertretung@ott.rep.admin.ch

Lithuania

Long-Form Name: Republic of Lithuania
Capital: Vilnius

■ GEOGRAPHY

Area: 65,200 sq. km
Coastline: 99 km
Climate: transitional, between maritime and continental; mild, with moderate precipitation
Environment: risk of accidents from the two Chernobyl-type reactors; at military bases, contamination of soil and groundwater with chemicals and petroleum products
Terrain: undulating glacial terrain; rivers, lakes and swamps predominate
Land Use: 35% arable; 12% permanent crops; 7% permanent pastures; 31% forest; 15% other; includes 430 sq. km irrigated
Location: NE Europe, bordering on Baltic Sea

■ PEOPLE

Population: 3,620,756 (July 2000 est.)
Nationality: Lithuanian
Age Structure: 0-14 yrs: 19%; 15-64: 67%; 65+: 14% (2000 est.)
Population Growth Rate: -0.29% (2000 est.)
Net Migration: 0.16 migrants/1,000 population (2000 est.)

Ethnic Groups: 80.6% Lithuanian, 8.7% Russian, 7% Polish, 1.6% Byelorussian, 2.1% other
Languages: Lithuanian (official), Russian, Polish
Religions: predominantly Protestant, Roman Catholic, Russian Orthodox
Birth Rate: 9.77/1,000 population (2000 est.)
Death Rate: 12.87/1,000 population (2000 est.)
Infant Mortality: 14.67 deaths/1,000 live births (2000 est.)
Life Expectancy at Birth: 63.07 years male, 75.41 years female (2000 est.)
Total Fertility Rate: 1.34 children born/woman (2000 est.)
Literacy: 99.5% (1998)

■ GOVERNMENT

Leader(s): Pres. Valdas Adamkus, Prime Min. Algirdas Mikolas Brazauskas
Government Type: parliamentary democracy
Administrative Divisions: 44 regions (rajonai, sing. —rajonas) and 11 municipalities
Nationhood: Sept. 6, 1991 (from Soviet Union)
National Holiday: Statehood Day, Feb. 16

■ ECONOMY

Overview: arable land and strategic location are Lithuania's only important natural resources; Lithuania remains highly dependent on Russia for energy, raw materials, grains and markets for its products
GDP: US$17.3 billion, per capita US$4,800; real growth rate -3% (1999 est.)
Inflation: 1.01% (year-end 2000)
Industries: accounts for 32% of GDP and employs 42% of labour force; heavy engineering, shipbuilding, production of building materials, nuclear and electric power production; electric motors, television sets, appliances, refining, fertilizer
Labour Force: 2 million (1999); 26.9% industry, 22% community, social and business services, 19% agriculture
Unemployment: 10% (1999); large numbers of underemployed
Agriculture: accounts for 10% of GDP and employs approximately 18% of labour force; beef and dairy cattle and related products, pigs, poultry, grains, flax, potatoes and other vegetables, eggs, fish, dairy products; net exporter of meat, milk and eggs
Natural Resources: amber, peat

■ FINANCE/TRADE

Currency: litas (pl. litai) = 100 centas
International Reserves Excluding Gold: US$1.283 billion (Jan. 2001)

Gold Reserves: US$0.186 million fine troy ounces (Jan. 2001)
Budget: revenues US$1.5 billion; expenditures US$1.7 billion, including capital expenditures of US$n.a. (1997 est.)
Defence Expenditures: 3.32% of govt. expenditure (1999)
Education Expenditures: 5.65% of central govt. expenditure (1999)
External Debt: US$3.584 billion (1999)
Exports: US$3.723 billion (2000); 18% electronics, 5% petroleum products, 10% food, 6% chemicals; partners: 40% Russia, 16% Ukraine, 32% other former Soviet republics, 12% West
Imports: US$5.380 billion (2000); 24% oil, 14% machinery, 8% chemicals, grain; partners: 62% Russia, 18% Belarus, 10% other former Soviet republics, 10% West (1989)

■ COMMUNICATIONS

Daily Newspapers: 19
Televisions: 459/1,000 inhabitants (1998)
Radios: 513/1,000 inhabitants (1997)
Telephones: 312 lines/1,000 inhabitants (1999)

■ TRANSPORTATION

Motor Vehicles: n.a.
Roads: 71,375 km; 64,951 km paved
Railway: 2,002 km
Air Traffic: 237,200 passengers carried (1997)
Airports: 96; 25 have paved runways

Canadian Embassy: Office of the Canadian Embassy, Gedimino pr. 64, 2001 Vilnius, Lithuania. Tel: (011-370) 222-0865. Fax: (011-370) 222-0884. Email: n.a.
Embassy in Canada: Embassy of the Republic of Lithuania, 130 Albert St, Ste 204, Ottawa, ON K1P 5G4. Tel: (613) 567-5458. Fax: (613) 567-5315. Email: litemb@storm.ca

---

Luxembourg

Long-Form Name: Grand Duchy of Luxembourg
Capital: Luxembourg

■ GEOGRAPHY

Area: 2,586 sq. km
Coastline: none: landlocked
Climate: modified continental with mild winters, cool summers
Environment: deforestation; air and water pollution in urban areas
Terrain: mostly gently rolling uplands with broad, shallow valleys; uplands to slightly mountainous in the north; steep slope down to Moselle floodplain in the southeast
Land Use: 24% arable; 1% permanent crops; 20% meadows; 21% forest; 34% other; including 10 sq. km irrigated shared with Belgium
Location: NC Europe, bordering on Belgium, France and Germany

■ PEOPLE

Population: 437,389 (July 2000 est.)
Nationality: Luxembourger
Age Structure: 0-14 yrs: 19%; 15-64: 67%; 65+: 14% (2000 est.)
Population Growth Rate: 1.27% (2000 est.)
Net Migration: 9.21 migrants/1,000 population (2000 est.)
Ethnic Groups: Celtic base, with French and German blend; also guest and worker residents
Languages: Luxembourgisch (official), German (written language of commerce and press), French (administrative), English
Religions: 97% Roman Catholic, 3% Protestant and Jewish
Birth Rate: 12.45/1,000 population (2000 est.)
Death Rate: 8.91/1,000 population (2000 est.)
Infant Mortality: 4.83 deaths/1,000 live births (2000 est.)
Life Expectancy at Birth: 73.84 years male, 80.63 years female (2000 est.)
Total Fertility Rate: 1.70 children born/woman (2000 est.)
Literacy: 99% (1997)

■ GOVERNMENT

Leader(s): Head of State: Henri, Grand Duke of Luxembourg. Prime Min. Jean-Claude Juncker
Government Type: constitutional monarchy
Administrative Divisions: 3 districts
Nationhood: 1839 (Grand Duchy)
National Holiday: National Day (public celebration of the Grand Duke's birthday), June 23

■ ECONOMY

Overview: a stable economy featuring moderate growth, low inflation and negligible unemployment; is in an economic union with Belgium for trade and most financial matters, and is also closely connected economically with the Netherlands; financial sector is strong; industrial sector is becoming increasingly diversified
GDP: US$14.7 billion, per capita US$34,200; real growth rate 4.2% (1999 est.)
Inflation: 3.15% (year-end 2000)
Industries: accounts for 23% of GDP; banking, iron and steel, food processing, chemicals, metal

products, engineering, tires, glass, aluminum
Labour Force: 236,400 (1998 est.); 14% community, social and business services, 20% trade and tourism, mining and manufacturing 16%, construction 11%, transportation and communication 8%, other 42%
Unemployment: 2.6% (Nov. 2000)
Agriculture: accounts for only 1% of GDP (including forestry); principal products—barley, oats, potatoes, wheat, fruits, wine grapes; cattle-raising widespread
Natural Resources: iron ore (no longer exploited), arable land

■ FINANCE/TRADE

Currency: Luxembourg franc (LuxF) = 100 centimes; Euro (EUR) as of March 1, 2002
International Reserves Excluding Gold: US$76 million (Jan. 2001)
Gold Reserves: US$0.076 million fine troy ounces (Jan. 2001)
Budget: revenues US$4.73 billion; expenditures US$4.71 billion, including capital expenditures US$n.a. (2000 est.)
Defence Expenditures: n.a.
Education Expenditures: n.a
External Debt: n.a.
Exports: US$7.545 billion (2000); commodities: finished steel products, chemicals, rubber products, glass, aluminum, other industrial products; partners: European Community 75%, US 6%
Imports: US$10.203 billion (2000); commodities: minerals, metals, foodstuffs, quality consumer goods; partners: Germany 40%, Belgium 35%, France 15%, US 3%

■ COMMUNICATIONS

Daily Newspapers: 5
Televisions: 451/1,000 inhabitants (1997 est.)
Radios: 651/1,000 inhabitants (1997 est.)
Telephones: 724 lines/1,000 inhabitants (1999)

■ TRANSPORTATION

Motor Vehicles: 251,000; 233,000 passenger cars (1997 est.)
Roads: 5,166 km; all paved
Railway: 274 km
Air Traffic: 560,000 passengers carried (1997)
Airports: 2; 1 has paved runways (1999 est.)
Canadian Embassy: The Canadian Embassy to Luxembourg, c/o 2, Avenue de Tervuren, 1040 Brussels, Belgium. Tel: (011-32-2) 741-0611. Fax: (011-32-2) 741-0643. Email: bru@dfait-maeci.gc.ca
Embassy in Canada: Embassy of the Grand Duchy of Luxembourg, 2200 Massachusetts Ave NW, Washington DC 20008, USA. Tel: (202) 265-4171. Fax: (202) 328-8270. Email: info@luxembourg-usa.org

Macau

Long-Form Name: Macau Special Administrative Region
Capital: none

■ GEOGRAPHY

Area: 21 sq. km (a peninsula and three small islands)
Climate: subtropical maritime; marine with cool winters, warm summers
Land Use: 98% built-up; almost no agricultural lands or fresh water resources
Location: SE coast of China, bordering on South China Sea

■ PEOPLE

Population: 445,594 (July 2000 est.)
Nationality: Chinese
Ethnic Groups: Chinese 95%, Portuguese 3%, other 2%
Languages: Portuguese (official), Cantonese, English widely spoken

■ GOVERNMENT

Colony Territory of: Special Administrative Region of China
Leader(s): Pres. Jiang Zemin (China), Chief Executive Edmund Ho Hau Wah
Government Type: reverted to China Dec. 20, 1999
National Holiday: National Day, Oct. 1-2; Dec. 20 is celebrated as Macau Special Administrative Region Establishment Day

■ ECONOMY

Overview: gambling and tourism; industry confined to textiles, fireworks, toy-making, plastics; imports almost all energy, food and water from China

■ FINANCE/TRADE

Currency: pataca (pl. patacas) = 100 avos

Canadian Embassy: n.a.
Representative to Canada: none

Macedonia

Long-Form Name: The Former Yugoslav Republic of Macedonia
Capital: Skopje

■ GEOGRAPHY

Area: 25,333 sq. km
Coastline: none: landlocked
Climate: hot, dry summers and autumns; winters relatively cold with heavy snowfall
Environment: high earthquake hazard; air pollution from metallurgical plants
Terrain: mountainous, with deep valleys and basins; three large lakes
Land Use: 24% arable land, 2% permanent crops, 25% permanent pastures, 39% forests, 10% other; includes 830 sq. km irrigated
Location: SE Europe

■ PEOPLE

Population: 2,041,467 (July 2000 est.)
Nationality: Macedonian
Age Structure: 0-14 yrs: 23%; 15-64: 67%; 65+: 10% (2000 est.)
Population Growth Rate: 0.04% (2000 est.)
Net Migration: -5.66 migrants/1,000 population (2000 est.)
Ethnic Groups: 66.6% Macedonian, 22.7% Albanian, 4% Turkish, 2.1% Serb, 2.2% Gypsies, 2.4% other
Languages: 70% Macedonian, 21% Albanian, 3% Turkish, 3% Serbo-Croatian, 3% other
Religions: 67% Eastern Orthodox, 30% Muslim, 3% other
Birth Rate: 13.73/1,000 population (2000 est.)
Death Rate: 7.69/1,000 population (2000 est.)
Infant Mortality: 13.35 deaths/1,000 live births (2000 est.)
Life Expectancy at Birth: 71.58 years male, 76.19 years female (2000 est.)
Total Fertility Rate: 1.82 children born/woman (2000 est.)
Literacy: 94% (1997)

■ GOVERNMENT

Leader(s): Pres. Boris Trajkovski, Prime Min. Ljubco Georgievski
Government Type: emerging democracy
Administrative Divisions: 34 counties (opstinas, sing. —opstina)
Nationhood: Sept. 17, 1991 (from Yugoslavia)
National Holiday: Independence Day, Sept. 8

■ ECONOMY

Overview: although it is the poorest of the six republics of the dissolved Yugoslav federation, Macedonia can meet its basic food requirements; new economic ties are necessary, however, to keep living standards from falling to a bare subsistence level; all oil, gas, modern machinery and parts must be imported; continued political upheaval prevents return to settled economic conditions; an important supplement to GDP is the remittances from thousands of Macedonians working in Germany and other West European countries; continued recovery depends on Macedonia's ability to attract investment, to redevelop trade ties with Greece and Serbia and Montenegro, and to maintain its commitment to economic liberalization
GDP: adjusted for purchasing power parity: US$7.6 billion, per capita US$3,800; real growth rate 2.5% (1999 est.)
Inflation: -1.26% (year-end 1999)
Industries: accounts for 32% of GDP; level of technology is generally low; basic liquid fuels, coal, metallic chromium, lead, zinc; Macedonia is one of the seven legal cultivators of the opium poppy for the world pharmaceutical industry
Labour Force: 1 million (1999); 35.2% industry, 20.2% community, social and business services, 11.6% trade and tourism
Unemployment: 35% (1999 est.)
Agriculture: highly labour-intensive; accounts for 13% of GDP. Rice, tobacco, corn, millet and wheat are the chief crops; livestock production includes beef, pork and poultry
Natural Resources: chromium, lead, zinc, manganese, tungsten, nickel, iron ore, asbestos, timber

■ FINANCE/TRADE

Currency: denar = 100 deni
International Reserves Excluding Gold: US$972 million (Jan. 2001)
Gold Reserves: US$0.112 million fine troy ounces (Jan. 2001)
Budget: n.a.
Defence Expenditures: 2.5% of GDP (1999)
Education Expenditures: 5.1% of GNP (1997)
External Debt: US$1.433 billion (1999)
Exports: US$1.292 billion (2000); manufactured goods, machinery and transportation equipment, raw materials, food and livestock, tobacco and beverages, chemicals; partners: mostly the former Yugoslav republics, Germany, Albania, Greece
Imports: US$2.156 billion (2000); fuel and lubricants, machinery and transport equipment, food and livestock, chemicals, raw materials, manufactures; partners: other former Yugoslav republics, Germany, Albania, Greece, Bulgaria

■ COMMUNICATIONS

Daily Newspapers: 3
Televisions: 250/1,000 inhabitants (1998)
Radios: 200/1,000 inhabitants (1997)
Telephones: 234 lines/1,000 inhabitants (1999)

■ TRANSPORTATION

Motor Vehicles: n.a.
Roads: 8,684 km; 5,540 km paved
Railway: 699 km operational
Air Traffic: 229,000 passengers carried (1997)
Airports: 16; 10 have paved runways (1999 est.)
Canadian Embassy: Office of the Canadian Embassy, 44 Mitropolit Teodosij Gologanov, 1000 Skopje, Former Yugoslav Republic of Macedonia, Tel: (011-389-91) 125-228. Fax: (011-389-91) 122-681. Email: skpje@dfait-maeci.gc.ca
Embassy in Canada: Embassy of the Former Yugoslav Republic of Macedonia, 130 Albert St Ste 1006, Ottawa, ON, K1P 5G4. Tel: (613) 234-3882. Fax: (613) 233-1852. Email: emb.macedonia.ottawa@sympatico.ca

---

Madagascar

Long-Form Name: Republic of Madagascar
Capital: Antananarivo

■ GEOGRAPHY

Area: 587,040 sq. km
Coastline: 4,828 km
Climate: tropical along coast, temperate inland, arid in south
Environment: subject to periodic cyclones; deforestation; overgrazing; soil erosion; desertification; water pollution
Terrain: narrow coastal plain; high plateau and mountains in centre
Land Use: 4% arable; 1% permanent crops; 41% permanent pastures; 40% forest; 14% other, includes 10,870 sq. km irrigated
Location: island in the Indian Ocean, E of Africa

■ PEOPLE

Population: 15,506,472 (July 2000 est.)
Nationality: Malagasy
Age Structure: 0-14 yrs: 45%; 15-64: 52%; 65+: 3% (2000 est.)
Population Growth Rate: 3.02% (2000 est.)
Net Migration: 0 migrants/1,000 population (2000 est.)
Ethnic Groups: basic split between highlanders of predominantly Malayo-Indonesian origin (Merina and Betsileo) and coastal tribes, collectively termed the Côtiers, with mixed African, Malayo-Indonesian and Arab ancestry (Betsimisaraka, Tsimihety, Antaiska, Sakalava)
Languages: French and Malagasy (both official)
Religions: 52% indigenous beliefs; approx. 41% Christian, 7% Muslim
Birth Rate: 42.92/1,000 population (2000 est.)
Death Rate: 12.69/1,000 population (2000 est.)

Infant Mortality: 85.26 deaths/1,000 live births (2000 est.)
Life Expectancy at Birth: 52.71 years male, 57.26 years female (2000 est.)
Total Fertility Rate: 5.84 children born/woman (2000 est.)
Literacy: 47% (1997)

■ GOVERNMENT

Leader(s): Pres. Didier Ratsiraka, Prime Min. Tantely Andrianarivo
Government Type: republic
Administrative Divisions: 6 provinces (faritany)
Nationhood: June 26, 1960 (from France; formerly known as Malagasy Republic)
National Holiday: Independence Day, June 26

■ ECONOMY

Overview: a poor country, hampered by high population growth and a GDP growth rate that is not keeping pace; agriculture is the basis of the economy; industrial development is hurt by government policies restricting imports of equipment and spare parts
GDP: US$11.5 billion, per capita US$780; real growth rate 4.5% (1999 est.)
Inflation: 12.03% (year-end 2000)
Industries: accounts for 12% of GDP; agricultural processing (meat canneries, soap factories, breweries, tanneries, sugar refining), light consumer goods industries (textiles, glassware), cement, automobile assembly plant, paper, petroleum
Labour Force: 7.0 million (1999); 59.2% community, social and business services, 26.7% agriculture
Unemployment: n.a.
Agriculture: accounts for 34% of GDP; cash crops—coffee, vanilla, sugar cane, cloves, cocoa; food crops—rice, cassava, beans, bananas, peanuts; almost self-sufficient in rice
Natural Resources: graphite, chromite, coal, bauxite, salt, quartz, tar sands, semi-precious stones, mica, fish

■ FINANCE/TRADE

Currency: Malagasy franc (FMG) = 100 centimes
International Reserves Excluding Gold: US$283 million (Jan. 2001)
Gold Reserves: n.a.
Budget: revenues US$553 million; expenditures US$735 million, including capital expenditures of US$n.a. (1998 est.)
Defence Expenditures: 8.5% of govt. expenditure (1997)
Education Expenditures: 1.9% GNP (1997)
External Debt: US$4.409 billion (1999)

Exports: US$238 million (2000); commodities: coffee 45%, vanilla 15%, cloves 11%, sugar, petroleum products; partners: France, Japan, Italy, Germany, US

Imports: US$501 million (2000); commodities: intermediate manufactures 30%, capital goods 28%, petroleum 15%, consumer goods 14%, food 13%; partners: France, Germany, UK, other European Community, US

■ COMMUNICATIONS

Daily Newspapers: 5
Televisions: 21/1,000 inhabitants (1998)
Radios: 192/1,000 inhabitants (1997)
Telephones: 3 lines/1,000 inhabitants (1999)

■ TRANSPORTATION

Motor Vehicles: 74,700; 58,900 passenger cars (1997 est.)
Roads: 49,837 km; 5,781 km paved
Railway: 883 km
Air Traffic: 575,000 passengers carried (1997)
Airports: 133; 29 have paved runways (1999 est.)

Canadian Embassy: The Canadian Embassy to Madagascar, P.O. Box 1022, Dar-es-Salaam, Tanzania. Tel: (011-255-22) 211-2831. Fax: (011-255-22) 211-6897. Email: ambamadott@on.aibn.com
Embassy in Canada: Embassy of the Republic of Madagascar, 649 Blair Rd, Gloucester, ON KIJ 7M4. Tel: (613) 744-7995. Fax: (613) 744-2530. Email: ambamadott@on.aibn.com

Malawi

Long-Form Name: Republic of Malawi
Capital: Lilongwe

■ GEOGRAPHY

Area: 118,480 sq. km
Coastline: none: landlocked
Climate: tropical; rainy season (Nov. to May); dry season (May to Nov.)
Environment: deforestation; water pollution; soil degradation
Terrain: narrow elongated plateau with rolling plains, rounded hills, some mountains
Land Use: 34% arable; 0% permanent crops; 20% meadows; 39% forest; 7% other; includes 280 sq. km irrigated
Location: SE Africa

■ PEOPLE

Population: 10,385,849 (July 2000 est.)
Nationality: Malawian
Age Structure: 0-14 yrs: 45%; 15-64: 52%; 65+: 3% (2000 est.)

Population Growth Rate: 1.61% (2000 est.)
Net Migration: 0 migrants/1,000 population (2000 est.)
Ethnic Groups: Chewa, Nyanja, Tumbuko, Yao, Lomwe, Sena, Tonga, Ngoni, Ngonde, Asian, European
Languages: English and Chichewa (both official); other languages important regionally
Religions: 55% Protestant, 20% Roman Catholic, 25% Muslim, traditional indigenous beliefs
Birth Rate: 38.49/1,000 population (2000 est.)
Death Rate: 22.44/1,000 population (2000 est.)
Infant Mortality: 122.28 deaths/1,000 live births (2000 est.)
Life Expectancy at Birth: 37.20 years male, 37.98 years female (2000 est.)
Total Fertility Rate: 5.33 children born/woman (2000 est.)
Literacy: 58.5% (1998)

■ GOVERNMENT

Leader(s): Pres. Bakili Muluzi; Pres. Justin Malewezi
Government Type: multi-party democracy
Administrative Divisions: 24 districts
Nationhood: July 6, 1964 (from UK; formerly known as Nyasaland)
National Holiday: Independence Day, July 6; Republic Day, July 6

■ ECONOMY

Overview: one of the world's least developed countries; the economy is predominantly agricultural, with about 90% of the population living in rural areas; economy depends heavily on foreign aid
GDP: US$9.4 billion, per capita US$940; real growth rate 4.2% (1999 est.)
Inflation: 29.49% (year-end 2000)
Industries: accounts for 29% of GDP; agricultural processing (tea, tobacco, sugar), sawmilling, cement, consumer goods
Labour Force: 5.0 million (1999); 54% agriculture, 12.9% industry, 12.7% services
Unemployment: n.a.
Agriculture: accounts for 37% of GDP; crops: tobacco, sugar cane, cotton, tea, corn; subsistence crops: cattle and goats
Natural Resources: limestone; unexploited deposits of uranium, coal and bauxite

■ FINANCE/TRADE

Currency: kwacha (K) = 100 tambala
International Reserves Excluding Gold: US$312 million (Jan. 2001)
Gold Reserves: US$0.010 million fine troy ounces (Jan. 2001)

Budget: revenues US$490 million, expenditures US$523 million, including capital expenditures of US$n.a. (1999-2000 est.)
Defence Expenditures: n.a.
Education Expenditures: 5.4% of GNP (1997)
External Debt: US$2.751 billion (1999)
Exports: US$341 million (2000); commodities: tobacco, tea, sugar, coffee, peanuts; partners: US, UK, Zambia, South Africa, Germany
Imports: US$524 million (2000); commodities: food, petroleum, semimanufactures, consumer goods, transportation equipment; partners: South Africa, Japan, US, UK, Zimbabwe

■ COMMUNICATIONS

Daily Newspapers: 5
Televisions: 2/1,000 inhabitants (1998)
Radios: 249/1,000 inhabitants (1997)
Telephones: 4 lines/1,000 inhabitants (1999)

■ TRANSPORTATION

Motor Vehicles: 54,300; 25,400 passenger cars (1997 est.)
Roads: 28,400 km; 5,254 km paved
Railway: 789 km
Air Traffic: 158,000 passengers carried (1997)
Airports: 44; 5 have paved runways (1999 est.)
Canadian Embassy: The Canadian High Commission to Malawi, c/o The Canadian High Commission, 5199 United Nations Ave, Lusaka; mailing address: P.O. Box 31313 Lusaka, Zambia. Tel: (011-260-1) 25-08-33. Fax: (011-260-1) 25-41-76. Email: lsaka@dfait-maeci.gc.ca
Embassy in Canada: High Commission for the Republic of Malawi, 7 Clemow Ave, Ottawa ON K1S 2A9. Tel: (613) 236-8931. Fax: (613) 236-1054.   Email: malawi.highcommission@sympatico.ca

Malaysia

Long-Form Name: Malaysia
Capital: Kuala Lumpur

■ GEOGRAPHY

Area: 329,750 sq. km; includes Sabah and Sarawak
Coastline: 4,675 km total (2,068 km Peninsular Malaysia, 2,607 km East Malaysia)
Climate: tropical; annual southwest (Apr. to Oct.) and northeast (Oct. to Feb.) monsoons
Environment: subject to flooding; air and water pollution; deforestation
Terrain: coastal plains rising to hills and mountains
Land Use: 3% arable; 12% permanent crops; negligible meadows; 68% forest; 17% other, includes 2,941 sq. km irrigated
Location: SE Asia, bordering on South China Sea

■ PEOPLE

Population: 21,793,293 (July 2000 est.)
Nationality: Malaysian
Age Structure: 0-14 yrs: 35%; 15-64: 61%; 65+: 4% (2000 est.)
Population Growth Rate: 2.01% (2000 est.)
Net Migration: 0 migrants/1,000 population (2000 est.)
Ethnic Groups: 58% Malay and other indigenous, 26% Chinese, 7% Indian, 9% other
Languages: Peninsular Malaysia: Malay (official), English, Chinese dialects, Tamil; State of Sabah: English, Malay, numerous tribal dialects; Chinese State of Sarawak: English, Malay, Mandarin, numerous tribal languages
Religions: Peninsular Malaysia: Muslim (Malays), Buddhist (Chinese), Hindu (Indians); State of Sabah: 38% Muslim, 17% Christian, 45% other; Chinese State of Sarawak: 35% tribal religions, 24% Buddhist and Confucianist, 20% Muslim, 16% Christian, 5% other
Birth Rate: 25.30/1,000 population (2000 est.)
Death Rate: 5.25/1,000 population (2000 est.)
Infant Mortality: 20.96 deaths/1,000 live births (2000 est.)
Life Expectancy at Birth: 68.22 years male, 73.63 years female (2000 est.)
Total Fertility Rate: 3.29 children born/woman (2000 est.)
Literacy: 86% (1998)

■ GOVERNMENT

Leader(s): Paramount Ruler: (Sultan) Tunku Salahuddin, Prime Min. Mahathir bin Mohamad
Government Type: constitutional monarchy nominally headed by the paramount ruler (king) and a bicameral parliament
Administrative Divisions: 13 states (negeri—negeri, sing. —negeri) and 2 federal territories (wilaya-wilaya persekutuan, sing. —wilayah persekutuan)
Nationhood: Aug. 31, 1957 (from UK)
National Holiday: National Day, Aug. 31

■ ECONOMY

Overview: vulnerable to recession or a fall in world commodity prices because of its high export dependence; the world's largest producer of semiconductor devices; the majority of the rural population subsists at the poverty level but recent increases in economic output have improved living standards and real income;

foreign investment has increased significantly in recent years

GDP: US$229.1 billion, per capita US$10,700; real growth rate 5% (1999 est.)

Inflation: 1.53% (year-end 2000)

Industries: accounts for 46% of GDP; rubber and oil palm processing and manufacturing, light manufacturing industries, electronics, tin mining and smelting, logging and processing timber, logging, petroleum production, agriculture processing, petroleum production and refining, logging`

Labour Force: 9 million (1999); 26% agriculture, 19.9% industry, 19.9% services

Unemployment: 3% (1999 est.)

Agriculture: accounts for 12% of GDP; Peninsular Malaysia—natural rubber, palm oil, rice; Sabah—mainly subsistence; main crops—rubber, timber, coconut, rice; Sarawak—main crops—rubber, timber, pepper; there is a deficit of rice in all areas

Natural Resources: tin, crude oil, timber, copper, iron ore, natural gas, bauxite

■ FINANCE/TRADE

Currency: ringgit ($M) = 100 sen

International Reserves Excluding Gold: US$29.048 billion (Jan. 2001)

Gold Reserves: US$1.170 million fine troy ounces (Jan. 2001)

Budget: revenues US$23.2 billion; expenditures US$27.6 billion, including capital expenditures of US$n.a. (1999)

Defence Expenditures: 2.1% of GDP (1998)

Education Expenditures: 4.9% of GNP (1997-98)

External Debt: US$45.939 billion (1999)

Exports: US$75.563 billion (2000); commodities: natural rubber, palm oil, tin, timber, petroleum, electronics, light manufactures; partners: Singapore, Japan, former USSR countries, European Community, Australia, US

Imports: US$80.875 billion (2000); commodities: food, crude oil, consumer goods, intermediate goods, capital equipment, chemicals; partners: Japan, Singapore, Germany, UK, Thailand, China, Australia, US

■ COMMUNICATIONS

Daily Newspapers: 42

Televisions: 166/1,000 inhabitants (1998)

Radios: 420/1,000 inhabitants (1997)

Telephones: 203 lines/1,000 inhabitants (1999)

■ TRANSPORTATION

Motor Vehicles: 3,100,000; 3,050,000 passenger cars (1997 est.)

Roads: 94,500 km; 70,970 km paved

Railway: Peninsular Malaysia: 1,672 km; Sabah: 134 km; Sarawak: none

Air Traffic: 15,592,000 passengers carried (1997)

Airports: 115; 32 have paved runways (1999 est.)

Canadian Embassy: The Canadian High Commission, Flr 7 and 15, Plaza OSK, 172 Jalan Ampang, 50450 Kuala Lumpur, Malaysia; mailing address: P.O. Box 10990, 50732 Kuala Lumpur, Malaysia. Tel: (011-60-3) 2718-3333. Fax: (011-60-3) 2718-3399. Email: klmpr@dfait-maeci.gc.ca

Embassy in Canada: High Commission for Malaysia, 60 Boteler St, Ottawa ON K1N 8Y7. Tel: (613) 241-5182. Fax: (613) 241-5214. Email: mwottawa@istar.ca

Maldives

Long-Form Name: Republic of Maldives

Capital: Malé

■ GEOGRAPHY

Area: 300 sq. km; 1,190 coral islands grouped in 26 atolls

Coastline: 644 km

Climate: tropical; hot, humid; dry, northeast monsoon (Nov. to Mar.); rainy, southwest monsoon (June to Aug.)

Environment: future rise in ocean level could obliterate large parts of the country; freshwater supplies are limited

Terrain: flat with elevations of only 2.5 metres

Land Use: 10% arable; 0% permanent crops; 3% meadows; 3% forest; 84% other; includes n.a. sq. km irrigated

Location: islands in the Indian Ocean, S of India

■ PEOPLE

Population: 301,475 (July 2000 est.)

Nationality: Maldivian

Age Structure: 0-14 yrs: 46%; 15-64: 51%; 65+: 3% (2000 est.)

Population Growth Rate: 3.06% (2000 est.)

Net Migration: 0 migrants/1,000 population (2000 est.)

Ethnic Groups: mixtures of Sinhalese, Dravidian, Arab and African

Languages: Dhivehi (Maldivian dialect of Sinhara; script derived from Arabic); English spoken by most government officials

Religions: Sunni Muslim

Birth Rate: 38.96/1,000 population (2000 est.)

Death Rate: 8.32/1,000 population (2000 est.)

Infant Mortality: 65.52 deaths/1,000 live births (2000 est.)

Life Expectancy at Birth: 61.05 years male, 63.40 years female (2000 est.)
Total Fertility Rate: 5.62 children born/woman (2000 est.)
Literacy: 95.7% (1997)

■ GOVERNMENT

Leader(s): Pres. Maumoun Abdul Gayoom
Government Type: republic
Administrative Divisions: 19 atolls (atolhu, sing. & pl.) and 1 other first-order administrative division
Nationhood: July 26, 1965 (from UK)
National Holiday: Independence Day, July 26

■ ECONOMY

Overview: based on fishing, tourism and shipping; fishing is the largest industry; tourism has become one of the largest and most important sources of revenue
GDP: US$540 million, per capita US$1,800; real growth rate 7% (1999 est.)
Inflation: -1.10% (year-end 2000)
Industries: accounts for 18% of GDP; fishing and fish processing, tourism, shipping, boat building, some coconut processing, garments, woven mats, coir (rope), handicrafts
Labour Force: approx. 70,000; 25% agriculture, 21% industry, 21% services, transportation and communication 10%, other 23%
Unemployment: negligible
Agriculture: accounts for almost 20% of GDP (including fishing); fishing more important than farming; limited production of coconuts, corn, sweet potatoes; most staple foods must be imported
Natural Resources: fish

■ FINANCE/TRADE

Currency: rufiyaa (Rf) = 100 laari
International Reserves Excluding Gold: US$124 million (Jan. 2001)
Gold Reserves: US$0.002 million fine troy ounces (Jan. 2001)
Budget: revenues US$166 million, expenditures US$192 million, including capital expenditures US$80 million (1999 est.)
Defence Expenditures: 18.25% of govt. expenditure (1998 est.)
Education Expenditures: 17.97% of central govt. expenditure (1999)
External Debt: US$217 million (1999)
Exports: US$76 million (2000); commodities: fish 57%, clothing 39%; partners: Thailand, Western Europe, Sri Lanka
Imports: US$389 million (2000); commodities: intermediate and capital goods 47%, consumer goods 42%, petroleum products 11%; partners: Japan, Western Europe, Thailand

■ COMMUNICATIONS

Daily Newspapers: 2
Televisions: 33/1,000 inhabitants (1997 est.)
Radios: 116/1,000 inhabitants (1997 est.)
Telephones: 80 lines/1,000 inhabitants (1999)

■ TRANSPORTATION

Motor Vehicles: n.a.
Roads: Malé has 9.6 km of coral highways within the city
Railway: none
Air Traffic: 189,000 passengers carried (1997)
Airports: 5; 2 have paved runways (1999 est.)

Canadian Embassy: The Canadian High Commission to Maldives, c/o The Canadian High Commission, P.O. Box 1006, Colombo 7, Sri Lanka. Tel: (011-94-75) 69-58-41. Fax: (011-94-75) 35-38-29. Email: clmbo@dfait-maeci.gc.ca
Embassy in Canada: Embassy of the Maldives, c/o High Commission for the Democratic Socialist Republic of Sri Lanka, 333 Laurier Ave W, Ste 1204, Ottawa ON K1P 1C1. Tel: (613) 233-8449. Fax: (613) 238-8448. Email: lankacom@magi.com

Mali

Long-Form Name: Republic of Mali
Capital: Bamako

■ GEOGRAPHY

Area: 1,240,000 sq. km
Coastline: none: landlocked
Climate: subtropical to arid; hot and dry Feb. to June; rainy, humid and mild June to Nov.; cool and dry Nov. to Feb.
Environment: hot, dust-laden harmattan haze common during dry seasons; soil erosion; desertification; deforestation
Terrain: mostly flat to rolling northern plains covered by sand; savanna in south, rugged hills in northeast
Land Use: 2% arable; 0% permanent crops; 25% meadows; 6% forest; 67% other; includes 780 sq. km irrigated
Location: NW Africa

■ PEOPLE

Population: 10,685,948 (July 2000 est.)
Nationality: Malian
Age Structure: 0-14 yrs: 47%; 15-64: 50%; 65+: 3% (2000 est.)

Population Growth Rate: 2.98% (2000 est.)
Net Migration: -0.37 migrants/1,000 population (2000 est.)
Ethnic Groups: 50% Mande (Bambara, Malinke, Sarakole), 17% Peul, 12% Voltaic, 6% Songhai, 10% Tuareg and Moor, 5% other
Languages: French (official); Bambara spoken by about 80% of the population; numerous African languages
Religions: 90% Muslim, 9% indigenous beliefs, 1% Christian
Birth Rate: 49.23/1,000 population (2000 est.)
Death Rate: 19.10/1,000 population (2000 est.)
Infant Mortality: 123.25 deaths/1,000 live births (2000 est.)
Life Expectancy at Birth: 45.50 years male, 47.85 years female (2000 est.)
Total Fertility Rate: 6.89 children born/woman (2000 est.)
Literacy: 38% (1998)

■ GOVERNMENT

Leader(s): Pres. Alpha Oumar Konare, Prime Min. Mande Sidibe
Presidential elections scheduled for May 2002
Government Type: republic
Administrative Divisions: 8 regions
Nationhood: Sept. 22, 1960 (from France; formerly French Sudan)
National Holiday: Anniversary of the Proclamation of the Republic, Sept. 22

■ ECONOMY

Overview: among the poorest countries in the world, with 65% of its land area desert or semidesert; economic activity is largely confined to the area irrigated by the Niger; industrial activity is concentrated on processing farm commodities
GDP: US$8.5 billion, per capita US$820; real growth rate 5% (1999 est.)
Inflation: -0.68% (year-end 2000)
Industries: accounts for 21% of GDP; small local consumer goods and processing, construction, phosphate, gold, fishing
Labour Force: 5.0 million (1999); 85.5% agriculture, 12.5% services, 2% industry
Unemployment: n.a.
Agriculture: accounts for 46% of GDP; most production based on small subsistence farms; cotton and livestock products account for over 70% of exports; other crops—millet, rice, corn, vegetables, peanuts; livestock—cattle, sheep and goats
Natural Resources: gold, phosphates, kaolin, salt, limestone, uranium; bauxite, iron ore, manganese, tin and copper deposits are known but not exploited

■ FINANCE/TRADE

Currency: Communauté financière africaine franc (CFAF) = 100 centimes
International Reserves Excluding Gold: US$291 million (Nov. 2000)
Gold Reserves: US$0.19 million fine troy ounces (Aug. 2000)
Budget: revenues $730 million; expenditures $770 million, including capital expenditures of n.a. (1997 est.)
Defence Expenditures: 7.2% of central government expenditure (1997)
Education Expenditures: 2.2% of GNP (1997)
External Debt: US$3.183 billion (1999)
Exports: US$512 million (2000); commodities: livestock, peanuts, dried fish, cotton, skins; partners: mostly franc zone (monetary area including France's former colonies in Africa) and Western Europe
Imports: US$731 million (2000); commodities: textiles, vehicles, petroleum products, machinery, sugar, cereals; partners: mostly franc zone (monetary area including France's former colonies in Africa) and Western Europe

■ COMMUNICATIONS

Daily Newspapers: 3
Televisions: 12/1,000 inhabitants (1998)
Radios: 54/1,000 inhabitants (1997)
Telephones: 3 lines/1,000 inhabitants (1999)

■ TRANSPORTATION

Motor Vehicles: 41,800; 24,700 passenger cars (1997 est.)
Roads: 15,100 km; 1,827 km paved
Railway: 729 km
Air Traffic: 86,000 passengers carried (1997)
Airports: 28; 6 have paved runways (1999 est.)

Canadian Embassy: The Canadian Embassy, P.O. Box 198, Bamako, Mali. Tel: (011-223) 21-22-36. Fax: (011-223) 21-43-62. Email: bmako@dfait-maeci.gc.ca
Embassy in Canada: Embassy of the Republic of Mali, 50 Goulburn Ave, Ottawa ON K1N 8C8. Tel: (613) 232-1501. Fax: (613) 232-7429. Email: n.a.

Malta

Long-Form Name: Republic of Malta
Capital: Valletta

■ GEOGRAPHY

Area: 316 sq. km
Coastline: 140 km

Climate: Mediterranean with mild, rainy winters and hot, dry summers
Environment: numerous bays provide good harbours; fresh water very scarce, increasing reliance on desalination
Terrain: mostly low, rocky, flat to dissected plains; many coastal cliffs
Land Use: 38% arable; 3% permanent crops; 0% meadows; 0% forest; 59% other, includes 10 sq. km irrigated
Location: Mediterranean Sea, S of Sicily

■ PEOPLE

Population: 391,670 (July 2000 est.)
Nationality: Maltese (sing. & pl.)
Age Structure: 0-14 yrs: 20%; 15-64: 67%; 65+: 13% (2000 est.)
Population Growth Rate: 0.74% (2000 est.)
Net Migration: 2.39 migrants/1,000 population (2000 est.)
Ethnic Groups: mixture of Arab, Sicilian, Norman, Spanish, Italian, English
Languages: Maltese and English (both official), Italian widely spoken
Religions: 98% Roman Catholic
Birth Rate: 12.75/1,000 population (2000 est.)
Death Rate: 7.70/1,000 population (2000 est.)
Infant Mortality: 5.94 deaths/1,000 live births (2000 est.)
Life Expectancy at Birth: 75.49 years male, 80.62 years female (2000 est.)
Total Fertility Rate: 1.92 children born/woman (2000 est.)
Literacy: 91.1% (1997)

■ GOVERNMENT

Leader(s): Pres. Guido De Marco, Prime Min. Eddie Fenech Adami
Government Type: parliamentary democracy
Administrative Divisions: none
Nationhood: Sept. 21, 1964 (from UK)
National Holiday: Independence Day, Sept. 21

■ ECONOMY

Overview: manufacturing and tourism are important; economy is dependent on foreign trade and services (food, water and energy); Malta produces only 20% of its food needs, has a limited supply of fresh water and lacks domestic energy sources
GDP: US$5.3 billion, per capita US$13,800; real growth rate 4% (1999 est.)
Inflation: 2.37% (year-end 2000)
Industries: accounts for 26% of GDP; tourism, ship repair yard, clothing, construction, food manufacturing, textiles, footwear, clothing, beverages, tobacco

Labour Force: approx. 144,000; 22% industry, 66% services, other 12%
Unemployment: 5.5% (1999)
Agriculture: accounts for 3% of GDP; 20% self-sufficient overall; main products—potatoes, cauliflower, grapes, wheat, barley, tomatoes, citrus, cut flowers, green peppers, hogs, poultry, eggs; adequate supplies of vegetables, poultry, milk, pork products; seasonal or periodic shortages
Natural Resources: limestone, salt

■ FINANCE/TRADE

Currency: Maltese lira (LM) = 100 cents
International Reserves Excluding Gold: US$1.557 million (July 2000)
Gold Reserves: US$0.006 million fine troy ounces (July 2000)
Budget: revenues US$1.32 billion; expenditures US$1.76 billion, including capital expenditures of US$n.a. (1998 est.)
Defence Expenditures: 2.09% of central govt. expenditure (1997)
Education Expenditures: 12.18% of govt. expenditure (1997)
External Debt: US$10.600 billion (1999)
Exports: US$2.295 million (2000); commodities: clothing, textiles, footwear, ships; partners: Germany 31%, UK 14%, Italy 14%
Imports: US$3.182 billion (2000); commodities: food, petroleum, nonfood raw materials; partners: Germany 19%, UK 17%, Italy 17%, US 11%

■ COMMUNICATIONS

Daily Newspapers: 2
Televisions: 714/1,000 inhabitants (1997 est.)
Radios: 651/1,000 inhabitants (1997 est.)
Telephones: 512 lines/1,000 inhabitants (1999)

■ TRANSPORTATION

Motor Vehicles: 141,200; 122,100 passenger cars (1997 est.)
Roads: 1,742 km; 1,677 km paved
Railway: none
Air Traffic: 1,054,000 passengers carried (1997)
Airports: 1, with a paved runway (1999 est.)

Canadian Embassy: The Canadian High Commission to Malta, c/o The Canadian Embassy, Via G.B. de Rossi 27, 00161 Rome, Italy. Tel: (011-39-06) 445981. Fax: (011-39-06) 445 98750. Email: rome@dfait-maeci.gc.ca
Embassy in Canada: High Commission for Malta, 2017 Connecticut Ave NW, Washington DC 20008, USA. Tel: (202) 462-3611. Fax: (202) 387-5470. Email: n.a.

Marshall Islands

Long-Form Name: Republic of the Marshall Islands
Capital: Majuro

■ GEOGRAPHY

Area: 181.3 sq. km; 2 island chains of 30 atolls and 1,152 islands
Coastline: 370.4 km
Climate: islands border typhoon belt; wet season, May to Nov.; hot and humid
Environment: occasional typhoons; insufficient fresh water
Terrain: low coral limestone and sand islands
Land Use: 0% arable, 60% permanent crops, 0% meadows or forests, 40% other; includes n.a. sq. km irrigated
Location: Oceania, in North Pacific Ocean, SW of Hawaii

■ PEOPLE

Population: 68,126 (July 2000 est.)
Nationality: Marshallese (sing. & pl.)
Age Structure: 0-14 yrs: 50%; 15-64: 48%; 65+: 2% (2000 est.)
Population Growth Rate: 3.88% (2000 est.)
Net Migration: 0 migrants/1,000 population (2000 est.)
Ethnic Groups: Micronesian
Languages: English (official), two major Marshallese dialects, Japanese
Religions: Christian (predominantly Protestant)
Birth Rate: 45.17/1,000 population (2000 est.)
Death Rate: 6.40/1,000 population (2000 est.)
Infant Mortality: 40.95 deaths/1,000 live births (2000 est.)
Life Expectancy at Birth: 63.72 years male, 67.36 years female (2000 est.)
Total Fertility Rate: 6.61 children born/woman (2000 est.)
Literacy: 93% (1997)

■ GOVERNMENT

Leader(s): Pres. Kessai Note
Government Type: constitutional government in free association with the US
Administrative Divisions: 33 municipalities
Nationhood: Oct. 21, 1986 (from US-administered UN trusteeship)
National Holiday: Proclamation of the Republic of the Marshall Islands, May 1

■ ECONOMY

Overview: agriculture and tourism are the backbone of the economy; industry is on a small scale, limited to handicrafts, copra and fish processing; imports far exceed exports; foreign aid is vital
GDP: US$105 million, per capita US$1,670; real growth rate -5% (1998)
Inflation: n.a.
Industries: accounts for 13% of GDP; copra, fish, tourism, crafts; offshore banking is in its infancy
Labour Force: n.a.
Unemployment: n.a.
Agriculture: accounts for 15% of GDP; coconuts, taro, cacao, breadfruit, fruits, poultry, tomatoes, melons, cattle
Natural Resources: phosphate, marine products, minerals

■ FINANCE/TRADE

Currency: United States dollar = 100 cents
International Reserves Excluding Gold: n.a.
Gold Reserves: n.a.
Budget: n.a.
Defence Expenditures: defence is the responsibility of the US
Education Expenditures: n.a.
External Debt: n.a.
Exports: US$28 million (1997est.); fish, coconut oil, trochus shells; partners: US, Japan, Australia
Imports: US$58 million (1997 est.); foodstuffs, machinery, equipment, fuels, beverages, tobacco; partners: US, Japan, Australia, New Zealand

■ COMMUNICATIONS

Daily Newspapers: n.a.
Televisions: n.a.
Radios: n.a.
Telephones: 62 lines/ 1,000 inhabitants (1999)

■ TRANSPORTATION

Motor Vehicles: n.a.
Roads: paved roads on major islands only
Railway: none
Air Traffic: 33,000 passengers carried (1997)
Airports: 16; 4 have paved runways (1999 est.)

Canadian Embassy: The Canadian Embassy to the Marshall Islands, c/o The Canadian High Commission, Commonwealth Ave., Canberra A.C.T., Australia. Tel: (011-61-2) 6270-4000. Fax: (011-61-2) 6273-3285. Email: cnbra@dfait-maeci.gc.ca
Embassy in Canada: c/o Embassy of the Republic of the Marshall Islands, 2433 Massachusetts Ave NW, Washington DC 20008, USA. Tel: (202) 234-5414. Fax: (202) 232-3236. Email: n.a.

Martinique

Long-Form Name: Department of Martinique
Capital: Fort-de-France

■ GEOGRAPHY

Area: 1,100 sq. km
Climate: tropical, moderated by trade winds; rainy season (June to Oct.)
Land Use: 8% arable; 8% permanent crops; 17% permanent pastures; 44% forest; 23% other, includes 40 sq. km irrigated
Location: Caribbean Islands, halfway along the Lesser Antilles arch between Puerto Rico and Venezuela

■ PEOPLE

Population: 414,516 (July 2000 est.)
Nationality: Martiniquais
Ethnic Groups: 90% black, remainder a mix of black African and Latin ancestry, Caucasian 5%
Languages: French (official), majority speak Creole

■ GOVERNMENT

Colony Territory of: Overseas Department of France
Leader(s): Pres. Jacques Chirac (France), Prefect Michel Cadot
Government Type: overseas department of France
National Holiday: Taking of the Bastille, National Day, July 14

■ ECONOMY

Overview: most of the meat, vegetable and grain requirements must be imported; industry: food processing, oil refining, chemical engineering; agriculture: pineapples, tobacco, cotton, bananas, sugar, rum, livestock; forest products; fishing; chief trading partners: France, UK, Guadeloupe

■ FINANCE/TRADE

Currency: French franc (F) = 100 centimes

Canadian Embassy: c/o The Canadian Embassy 35-37 avenue Montaigne, 75008 Paris, France. Tel: (011-33-1) 44-43-29-00. Fax: (011-33-1) 44-43-29-99. Email: paris@dfait-maeci.gc.ca
Representative to Canada: c/o Embassy of France, 42 Sussex Dr, Ottawa ON K1M 2C9. Tel: (613) 789-1795. Fax: (613) 562-3735. Email: politique@ambafrance-ca.org

Mauritania

Long-Form Name: Islamic Republic of Mauritania
Capital: Nouakchott

■ GEOGRAPHY

Area: 1,030,700 sq. km
Coastline: 754 km
Climate: desert; constantly hot, dry, dusty
Environment: hot, dry, dust/sand-laden sirocco wind blows primarily in Mar. and Apr.; desertification; only perennial river is the Senegal; overgrazing and insufficient fresh water
Terrain: mostly barren, flat plains of the Sahara; some central hills
Land Use: 0% arable; 0% permanent crops; 38% meadows; 4% forest; 58% other; includes 490 sq. km irrigated
Location: NW Africa, bordering on Atlantic Ocean

■ PEOPLE

Population: 2,667,859 (July 2000 est.)
Nationality: Mauritanian
Age Structure: 0-14 yrs: 46%; 15-64: 52%; 65+: 2% (1999 est.)
Population Growth Rate: 2.94% (2000 est.)
Net Migration: 0 migrants/1,000 population (2000 est.)
Ethnic Groups: 30% Maur, 40% mixed Maur-black, 30% black
Languages: Hasaniya Arabic and Wolof (both official), Pular, Soninke
Religions: nearly 100% Muslim
Birth Rate: 43.36/1,000 population (2000 est.)
Death Rate: 13.97/1,000 population (2000 est.)
Infant Mortality: 78.15 deaths/1,000 live births (2000 est.)
Life Expectancy at Birth: 48.70 years male, 52.87 years female (2000 est.)
Total Fertility Rate: 6.29 children born/woman (2000 est.)
Literacy: 41% (1998)

■ GOVERNMENT

Leader(s): Pres. Maaouya Ould Sid Ahmed Taya; Prime Min. Cheikh Ould Mohamed El Avia
Government Type: republic
Administrative Divisions: 12 regions and 1 capital district
Nationhood: Nov. 28, 1960 (from France)
National Holiday: Independence Day, Nov. 28

■ ECONOMY

Overview: most of the population is engaged in agricultural and livestock production; substantial iron ores; threatened by foreign overexploitation of fishing areas; in recent years, droughts, conflicts with Senegal, rising energy costs and economic mismanagement have resulted in a substantial build-up of foreign debt; short-term growth prospects are dismal
GDP: US$4.9 billion, per capita US$1,910; real growth rate 3.7% (1999 est.)
Inflation: 3.25% (year-end 2000)
Industries: accounts for 31% of GDP; fishing, fish processing, mining of iron ore and gypsum
Labour Force: 1 million (1999); 69.4% agriculture, 21.7% services, 8.9% industry
Unemployment: n.a.
Agriculture: accounts for 25% of GDP (including fishing); largely subsistence farming, nomadic cattle and sheep herding except in Senegal river valley; crops—dates, millet, sorghum, root crops; fish products number-one export; large food deficit in years of drought
Natural Resources: iron ore, gypsum, fish, copper, phosphate

■ FINANCE/TRADE

Currency: ouguiya (UM) = 5 Khoums
International Reserves Excluding Gold: US$284 million (Sept. 2000)
Gold Reserves: US$0.012 million fine troy ounces (Sept. 2000)
Budget: n.a.
Defence Expenditures: n.a.
Education Expenditures: 5.1% of GNP (1997)
External Debt: US$2.528 billion (1999)
Exports: US%592 million (2000); commodities: iron ore, processed fish, small amounts of gum arabic and gypsum, unrecorded but numerically significant cattle exports to Senegal; partners: European Community 57%, Japan 39%, Ivory Coast 2%
Imports: US$294 million (2000); commodities: foodstuffs, consumer goods, petroleum products, capital goods; partners: European Community 79%, Africa 5%, US 4%, Japan 2%

■ COMMUNICATIONS

Daily Newspapers: 2
Televisions: 91/1,000 inhabitants (1998)
Radios: 151/1,000 inhabitants (1997)
Telephones: 6 lines/1,000 inhabitants (1999)

■ TRANSPORTATION

Motor Vehicles: 27,000; 17,800 passenger cars (1997 est.)

Roads: 7,660 km; 866 km paved
Railway: 704 km
Air Traffic: 245,000 passengers carried (1997)
Airports: 26; 8 have paved runways (1999 est.)

Canadian Embassy: The Canadian Embassy to Mauritania, c/o The Canadian Embassy, P.O. Box 3373, Dakar, Senegal. Tel: (011-221) 823-9290. Fax: (011-221) 823-8749. email: dakar@dfait-maeci.gc.ca
Embassy in Canada: Embassy of the Islamic Republic of Mauritania, 121 Sherwood Dr, Ottawa ON K1V 3V1. Tel: (613) 237-3283. Fax: (613) 237-3287. Email: info@ambarimca.org

---

Mauritius

Long-Form Name: Republic of Mauritius
Capital: Port Louis

■ GEOGRAPHY

Area: 1,860 sq. km; includes Agalega Islands, Cargados Carajos Shoals (St. Brandon) and Rodriques
Coastline: 177 km
Climate: tropical modified by southeast trade winds; warm, dry winter (May to Nov.); hot, wet, humid summer (Nov. to May)
Environment: subject to cyclones (Nov. to Apr.); almost completely surrounded by reefs; water pollution is a growing problem
Terrain: small coastal plain rising to discontinuous mountains encircling central plateau
Land Use: 49% arable; 3% permanent crops; 3% meadows; 22% forest; 23% other, includes 170 sq. km irrigated
Location: Indian Ocean, E of Africa (E of Madagascar)

■ PEOPLE

Population: 1,179,368 (July 2000 est.)
Nationality: Mauritian
Age Structure: 0-14 yrs: 26%; 15-64: 68%; 65+: 6% (2000 est.)
Population Growth Rate: 0.89% (2000 est.)
Net Migration: -0.93 migrants/1,000 population (2000 est.)
Ethnic Groups: 68% Indo-Mauritian, 27% Creole, 3% Sino-Mauritian, 2% Franco-Mauritian
Languages: English (official), Creole, French, Hindi, Urdu, Hakka, Bojpoori
Religions: 52% Hindu, 28% Christian (mostly Roman Catholic with a few Anglicans), 17% Muslim, 3% other

Birth Rate: 16.66/1,000 population (2000 est.)
Death Rate: 6.83/1,000 population (2000 est.)
Infant Mortality: 17.73 deaths/1,000 live births (2000 est.)
Life Expectancy at Birth: 66.98 years male, 75.04 years female (2000 est.)
Total Fertility Rate: 2.02 children born/woman (2000 est.)
Literacy: 83.0% (1997)

■ **GOVERNMENT**

Leader(s): Pres. Cassam Uteem, Prime Min. Anerood Jugnauth
Government Type: parliamentary democracy
Administrative Divisions: 9 administrative districts and 3 dependencies
Nationhood: Mar. 12, 1968 (from UK)
National Holiday: Independence Day, Mar. 12

■ **ECONOMY**

Overview: based on sugar, manufacturing (textiles) and tourism; industrialization programs stress increasing exports
GDP: US$12.3 billion, per capita US$10,400; real growth rate 4% (1999 est.)
Inflation: 4.20% (year-end 2000)
Industries: accounts for 29% of GDP; food processing (largely sugar milling), textiles, wearing apparel, chemical and chemical products, metal products, transport equipment, nonelectrical machinery, tourism
Labour Force: approx. 525,000; 14% agriculture, 36% industry, 24% community, social and business services, 26% other
Unemployment: 9.8% (1997 est.)
Agriculture: accounts for 10% of GDP; about 90% of cultivated land in sugar cane (which accounts for 40% of export earnings); other products—tea, corn, potatoes, bananas, pulses, cattle, goats, fish; net food importer, especially rice and fish
Natural Resources: arable land, fish

■ **FINANCE/TRADE**

Currency: rupee (Mau Rs) = 100 cents
International Reserves Excluding Gold: US$781 million (Jan. 2001)
Gold Reserves: US$0.062 million fine troy ounces (Jan. 2001)
Budget: revenues US$1.1 billion, expenditures US$1.2 billion, including capital expenditures US$n.a. (1999 est.)
Defence Expenditures: 0.85% of total govt. expenditure (1999)
Education Expenditures: 15.81% of central govt. expenditure (1999)
External Debt: US$2.464 billion (1999)
Exports: US$1.588 billion (2000); commodities:

textiles 44%, sugar 40%, light manufactures 10%; partners: European Community 77%, US 15%
Imports: US$2.119 billion (2000); commodities: manufactured goods 50%, capital equipment 17%, foodstuffs 13%, petroleum products 8%, chemicals 7%; partners: European Community, US, South Africa, Japan

■ **COMMUNICATIONS**

Daily Newspapers: 6
Televisions: 226/1,000 inhabitants (1998)
Radios: 368/1,000 inhabitants (1997)
Telephones: 224 lines/1,000 inhabitants (1999)

■ **TRANSPORTATION**

Motor Vehicles: 83,050; 70,000 passenger cars (1997 est.)
Roads: 1,910 km; 1,834 km paved
Railway: none
Air Traffic: 804,000 passengers carried (1997)
Airports: 5; 2 have paved runways (1999 est.)

Canadian Embassy: The Canadian High Commission to Mauritius, c/o The Canadian High Commission, Private Bag X13, Hatfield 0028, Pretoria, South Africa. Tel: (011-27-12) 422-3000. Fax: (011-27-12) 422-3052. Email: pret@dfait-maeci.gc.ca
Embassy in Canada: c/o Embassy of Mauritius, 4301 Connecticut Avenue NW, Ste 441, Washington DC 20008, USA. Tel: (202) 244-1491. Fax: (202) 966-0983. Email: mauritius.embassy@prodigy.net

Mayotte

Long-Form Name: Territorial Collectivity of Mayotte
Capital: Mamoutzou

■ **GEOGRAPHY**

Area: 374 sq. km
Climate: tropical maritime; hot, humid rainy season during northeastern monsoon (Nov. to May), dry season is cooler (May to Nov.)
Land Use: 20,000 acres under agricultural cultivation
Location: Mozambique Channel, off E coast of Africa

■ **PEOPLE**

Population: 155,911 (July 2000 est.)
Nationality: Mahorais (sing. & pl.)
Ethnic Groups: Antalote, Cafre, Makoa, Oimatsaha, Sakalava
Languages: French (official), Mahorian (a Swahili dialect)

■ GOVERNMENT

Colony Territory of: Territorial Collectivity of France
Leader(s): Pres. Jacques Chirac (France), Prefect Pierre Bayle
Government Type: French territorial collectivity
National Holiday: Taking of the Bastille, July 14

■ ECONOMY

Overview: industry: lobster, shrimp; agriculture: pineapples, bananas, mangoes, breadfruit, cassava, ylang-ylang, vanilla, coffee, spices; must import a large portion of its food requirements, mainly from France; chief trading partners: France, UK, South Africa, Bahrain, Thailand, Réunion

■ FINANCE/TRADE

Currency: French franc (F) = 100 centimes

Canadian Embassy: c/o The Canadian Embassy, 35-37 avenue Montaigne, 75008 Paris, France. Tel: (011-33-1) 44-43-29-00. Fax: (011-33-1) 44-43-29-99. Email: paris@dfait-maeci.gc.ca
Representative to Canada: c/o Embassy of France, 42 Sussex Dr., Ottawa ON K1M 2C9. Tel: (613) 789-1795. Fax: (613)562-3735. Email: politique@ambafrance-ca.org

Mexico

Long-Form Name: United Mexican States
Capital: Mexico

■ GEOGRAPHY

Area: 1,972,550 sq. km
Coastline: 9,330 km
Climate: varies from tropical to desert
Environment: subject to tsunamis along the Pacific coast and destructive earthquakes in the centre and south; natural water resources scarce and polluted; deforestation; erosion widespread; desertification; serious air pollution
Terrain: high, rugged mountains, low coastal plains, high plateaus and desert
Land Use: 12% arable, 1% permanent crops; 39% meadows; 26% forest; 22% other, includes 61,000 sq. km irrigated
Location: Central (Latin) America, bordering on United States, Gulf of Mexico, Pacific Ocean

■ PEOPLE

Population: 100,349,766 (July 2000 est.)
Nationality: Mexican
Age Structure: 0-14 yrs: 34%; 15-64: 62%; 65+: 4% (2000 est.)
Population Growth Rate: 1.53% (2000 est.)

Net Migration: -2.84 migrants/1,000 population (2000 est.)
Ethnic Groups: 60% mestizo (Indian-Spanish), 30% Amerindian or predominantly Amerindian, 9% white or predominantly white, 1% other
Languages: Spanish, also indigenous (Mayan) languages
Religions: 89% Roman Catholic, 6% Protestant, 5% other
Birth Rate: 23.15/1,000 population (2000 est.)
Death Rate: 5.05/1,000 population (2000 est.)
Infant Mortality: 26.19 deaths/1,000 live births (2000 est.)
Life Expectancy at Birth: 68.47 years male, 74.66 years female (2000 est.)
Total Fertility Rate: 2.67 children born/woman (2000 est.)
Literacy: 91% (1998)

■ GOVERNMENT

Leader(s): Pres. Vicente Fox
Government Type: federal republic operating under a centralized government
Administrative Divisions: 31 states (estados, sing. —estado) and 1 federal district (distrito federal)
Nationhood: Sept. 16, 1810 (from Spain)
National Holiday: Independence Day, Sept. 16

■ ECONOMY

Overview: outlook remains positive, but this country still needs to overcome many structural problems as it strives to modernize its economy and raise living standards; income distribution is very unequal, with the top 20% of income earners accounting for 55% of income; trade with the US and Canada has nearly doubled since NAFTA was implemented in 1994
GDP: US$865.5 billion, per capita US$8,500; real growth rate 3.7% (1999 est.)
Inflation: 9.50% (year-end 2000)
Industries: accounts for 29% of GDP; food and beverages, tobacco, chemicals, iron and steel, petroleum, mining, textiles, clothing, transportation equipment, tourism
Labour Force: 40 million (1999); 57% services, 22.9% agriculture, 20.1% industry
Unemployment: 2.5% (1998); plus considerable underemployment
Agriculture: accounts for 5% of GDP and over 25% of labour force; large number of small farms at subsistence level; major food crops—corn, wheat, rice, beans; cash crops—cotton, coffee, fruit, tomatoes
Natural Resources: crude oil, silver, copper, gold, lead, zinc, natural gas, timber

■ FINANCE/TRADE

Currency: peso ($Mex) = 100 centavos

International Reserves Excluding Gold: US$39.421 billion (Jan. 2001)
Gold Reserves: US$0.240 million fine troy ounces (Jan. 2001)
Budget: revenues US$117 billion; expenditures US$123 billion, capital expenditures US$n.a. (1998 est.)
Defence Expenditures: 1.0% of GDP (1999)
Education Expenditures: 4.9% of GNP (1997)
External Debt: US$166.960 billion (1999)
Exports: US$148.447 billion (2000); commodities: crude oil, oil products, coffee, shrimp, engines, cotton; partners: US 66%, European Community 16%, Japan 11%
Imports: US$158.429 billion (2000); commodities: grain, metal manufactures, agricultural machinery, electrical equipment; partners: US 62%, European Community 18%, Japan 10%

■ COMMUNICATIONS

Daily Newspapers: 295
Televisions: 261/1,000 inhabitants (1998)
Radios: 325/1,000 inhabitants (1997)
Telephones: 112 lines/1,000 inhabitants (1999)

■ TRANSPORTATION

Motor Vehicles: 12,330,000; 8,200,000 passenger cars (1997 est.)
Roads: 323,977 km; 96,221 km paved
Railway: 31,048 km
Air Traffic: 17,266,000 passengers carried (1997)
Airports: 1,806; 233 have paved runways (1999 est.)

Canadian Embassy: The Canadian Embassy, Calle Schiller no. 529, Rincon del Bosque, Colonia Polanco, 11580 Mexico; mailing address: Apartado Postal 105-05, 11580 Mexico, Mexico. Tel: (011-52-5) 724-7900. Fax: (011-52-5) 724-7980. Email: mxico@dfait-maeci.gc.ca
Embassy in Canada: Embassy of the United Mexican States, 45 O'Connor St, Ste 1500, Ottawa ON K1P 1A4. Tel: (613) 233-8988. Fax: (613) 235-9123. Email: info@embamexcan.com

Micronesia

Long-Form Name: Federated States of Micronesia
Capital: Palikir

■ GEOGRAPHY

Area: 702 sq. km.; 4 major island groups totalling 607 islands
Coastline: 6,112 km

Climate: tropical; heavy rainfall all year long, particularly in the eastern islands
Environment: occasional severe typhoons mostly from June to Dec.
Terrain: varies from high, mountainous islands to low coral atolls; volcanic outcroppings
Land Use: n.a.
Location: Oceania, in the N Pacific Ocean, NE of Australia

■ PEOPLE

Population: 133,144 (July 2000 est.)
Nationality: Micronesian
Age Structure: n.a.
Population Growth Rate: 3.28% (2000 est.)
Net Migration: 11.65 migrants/1,000 population (2000 est.)
Ethnic Groups: 9 Micronesian and Polynesian groups
Languages: English (offical and common), local languages including Pohnpeian, Yapese, Trukese and Kosrean
Religions: Roman Catholic 50%, Protestant 47%, other or none 3%
Birth Rate: 27.09/1,000 population (2000 est.)
Death Rate: 5.95/1,000 population (2000 est.)
Infant Mortality: 33.48 deaths/1,000 live births (2000 est.)
Life Expectancy at Birth: 66.67 years male, 70.62 years female (2000 est.)
Total Fertility Rate: 3.83 children born/woman (2000 est.)
Literacy: 89% (1998 est.)

■ GOVERNMENT

Leader(s): Pres. Leo Falcam; V. Pres. Redley Killion
Government Type: constitutional government in free association with the United States
Administrative Divisions: 4 states
Nationhood: Nov. 3, 1986 (from US-administered UN Trusteeship)
National Holiday: Proclamation of the Federated States of Micronesia, May 10

■ ECONOMY

Overview: mostly subsistence farming and fishing; few economically viable mineral deposits; region's remote location and lack of adequate facilities hinders development of tourism potential; considerably dependant on financial assistance from the US
GDP: US$240 million, per capita US$2,000; real growth rate 3% (1997)
Inflation: n.a.
Industries: accounts for 4% of GDP; fish processing, crafts, tourism, construction

Labour Force: n.a.; two-thirds are government employees
Unemployment: n.a.
Agriculture: accounts for 19% of GDP; pepper, tropical fruits and vegetables, coconuts, pigs, chickens
Natural Resources: forests, marine products, deep-sea minerals

■ FINANCE/TRADE

Currency: US dollar ($) = 100 cents
International Reserves Excluding Gold: US$106 million (Jan. 2001)
Gold Reserves: n.a.
Budget: n.a.
Defence Expenditures: n.a.
Education Expenditures: n.a.
External Debt: US$111 million (1997 est.)
Exports: exact figures not available; commodities: fish, garments, bananas, pepper; partners: Japan, US, Guam
Imports: exact figures not available; commodities: food, manufactures, machinery and equipment, beverages; partners: US, Japan, Australia

■ COMMUNICATIONS

Daily Newspapers: n.a.
Televisions: n.a.
Radios: n.a.
Telephones: 80 lines/1,000 inhabitants (1999)

■ TRANSPORTATION

Motor Vehicles: n.a.
Roads: 240 km; 42 km paved
Railway: none
Air Traffic: n.a.
Airports: 6; 5 have paved runways (1999 est.)

Canadian Embassy: Canadian Embassy to the Federated States of Micronesia, c/o The Canadian High Commission, Commonwealth Avenue, Canberra ACT 2600, Australia, Tel: (011 61 2) 6270-4000. Fax: (011 61 2) 6273-3285. Email: cnbra@dfait-maeci.gc.ca
Embassy in Canada: c/o The Embassy of the Republic of the Philippines, 130 Albert St Ste 606, Ottawa, ON K1P 5G4. Tel: (613) 233-1121. Fax: (613) 233-4165. Email: ottawape@istar.ca

Moldova

Long-Form Name: Republic of Moldova
Capital: Chisinau

■ GEOGRAPHY

Area: 33,843 sq. km
Coastline: none: landlocked
Climate: mild sunny winters; warm rainy summers; long dry autumns
Environment: heavy use of agricultural chemicals, including banned pesticides such as DDT, has contaminated groundwater and soil; erosion severe due to poor farming methods
Terrain: hilly plains in north; southern steppe
Land Use: 53% arable, 14% permanent crops, 13% permanent pastures, 13% forest, 7% other, includes 3,110 sq. km irrigated
Location: E Europe, bordering on Ukraine and Romania

■ PEOPLE

Population: 4,430,654 (July 2000 est.)
Nationality: Moldovan
Age Structure: 0-14 yrs: 23%; 15-64: 67%; 65+: 10% (2000 est.)
Population Growth Rate: 0.0% (2000 est.)
Net Migration: -0.31 migrants/1,000 population (2000 est.)
Ethnic Groups: 64.5% Moldavian, 13.8% Ukrainian, 13% Russian, 3.5% Gagauz, 1.5% Jews, 3.7% other
Languages: Moldavan (official), Russian, Ukrainian, Gagauz (a Turkish dialect)
Religions: 98.5% Eastern Orthodox, 1.5% Jewish, minority Baptists (note that almost all churchgoers are ethnic Moldovan; the Slavic population are not churchgoers)
Birth Rate: 12.86/1,000 population (2000 est.)
Death Rate: 12.58/1,000 population (2000 est.)
Infant Mortality: 43.32 deaths/1,000 live births (2000 est.)
Life Expectancy at Birth: 59.92 years male, 69.22 years female (2000 est.)
Total Fertility Rate: 1.63 children born/woman (2000 est.)
Literacy: 98.5% (1998)

■ GOVERNMENT

Leader(s): Pres. Vladimir Voronin, Prime Min. Vasile Tarlev
Government Type: republic
Administrative Divisions: 10 juletule (sing. juletul), 1 autonomous territorial unit and 1 municipality
Nationhood: Aug. 27, 1991 (from Soviet Union)
National Holiday: Independence Day, Aug. 27

■ ECONOMY

Overview: predominantly agricultural, with important manufacturing sector; Moldova has a

climate favourable to agriculture, and this is where the bulk of economic development has taken place
GDP: US$9.7 billion, per capita US$2,200; real growth rate -4.4% (1999 est.)
Inflation: 31.29% (year-end 2000)
Industries: accounts for 35% of GDP; machinery and appliances, hosiery, refined sugar, vegetable oil, canned food, shoes, textiles
Labour Force: 2 million (1999); 40.5% agriculture, 20.6% services, 19.2% industry
Unemployment: 2%; also large numbers of underemployed (Sept. 1998)
Agriculture: accounts for 31% of GDP; grapes and other fruits, vegetables, sugar, wheat and cereal grains, tobacco, oil, essential oil crops
Natural Resources: lignite, phosphorites, gypsum, arable land

■ FINANCE/TRADE

Currency: leu (pl. lei)
International Reserves Excluding Gold: US$227 million (Jan. 2001)
Gold Reserves: n.a.
Budget: revenues US$536 million; expenditures US$594 million, including capital expenditures of US$n.a. (1998 est.)
Defence Expenditures: 1% of GDP (1999)
Education Expenditures: 4.79% of central govt. expenditure (1999)
External Debt: US$943 million (1999)
Exports: US$449 million (2000); wine, grapes, other agricultural products, machinery, pumps
Imports: US$617 million (2000); fuels, metals and metal products, consumer products, foodstuffs

■ COMMUNICATIONS

Daily Newspapers: 4
Televisions: 297/1,000 inhabitants (1998)
Radios: 740/1,000 inhabitants (1997)
Telephones: 127 lines/1,000 inhabitants (1999)

■ TRANSPORTATION

Motor Vehicles: n.a.
Roads: 12,300 km; 10,738 km hard-surfaced
Railway: 1,328 km, which does not include industrial lines
Air Traffic: 46,000 passengers carried (1997)
Airports: 26; 8 have paved runways

Canadian Embassy: The Canadian Embassy to Moldova, c/o The Canadian Embassy, P.O. Box 117, Post Office No. 22, 71118 Bucharest, Romania. Tel: (011-40-1) 307-5000. Fax: (011-40-1) 307-5010. Email: bucst@dfait-maeci.gc.ca
Embassy in Canada: Embassy of the Republic of Moldova, 2101 S. St NW, Washington DC

20008, USA. Tel: (202) 667-1130. Fax: (202) 667-1204. Email: ciobanu@dgsys.com

---

Monaco

Long-Form Name: Principality of Monaco
Capital: Monaco

■ GEOGRAPHY

Area: 1.95 sq. km
Coastline: 4.1 km
Climate: Mediterranean with mild, wet winters and hot, dry summers
Environment: almost entirely urban
Terrain: hilly, rugged, rocky
Land Use: almost 100% urban
Location: W Europe, bordering on France and Mediterranean Sea

■ PEOPLE

Population: 31,693 (July 2000 est.)
Nationality: Monegasque or Monacan
Age Structure: 0-14 yrs: 15%; 15-64: 62%; 65+: 23% (2000 est.)
Population Growth Rate: 0.48% (2000 est.)
Net Migration: 7.89 migrants/1,000 population (2000 est.)
Ethnic Groups: 47% French, 16% Monegasque, 16% Italian, 21% other
Languages: French (official), English, Italian, Monegasque
Religions: 95% Roman Catholic
Birth Rate: 9.94/1,000 population (2000 est.)
Death Rate: 13.06/1,000 population (2000 est.)
Infant Mortality: 5.92 deaths/1,000 live births (2000 est.)
Life Expectancy at Birth: 74.88 years male, 83.00 years female (2000 est.)
Total Fertility Rate: 1.76 children born/woman (2000 est.)
Literacy: 99% (1997 est.)

■ GOVERNMENT

Leader(s): Prince Rainier III, Min. of State Patrick Leclercq
Government Type: constitutional monarchy
Administrative Divisions: 4 districts (quartiers, sing. —quartier)
Nationhood: 1419, rule by the House of Grimaldi
National Holiday: National Day, Nov. 19

■ ECONOMY

Overview: a popular resort, attracting tourists to its casinos and pleasant climate; no income tax and low business taxes make it a tax haven; no data is published on the economy
GDP: US$870 million, per capita US$27,000; real growth rate n.a. (1999 est.)

Inflation: n.a.
Industries: pharmaceuticals, food processing, precision instruments, glassmaking, printing, tourism
Labour Force: n.a.
Unemployment: 3.1% (1998)
Agriculture: none
Natural Resources: none

■ **FINANCE/TRADE**

Currency: French franc (F) = 100 centimes
International Reserves Excluding Gold: n.a.
Gold Reserves: n.a.
Budget: n.a.
Defence Expenditures: defence is the responsibility of France
Education Expenditures: n.a.
External Debt: n.a.
Exports: n.a.; full customs integration with France, which collects and rebates Monegasque trade duties
Imports: n.a.; full customs integration with France, which collects and rebates Monegasque trade duties

■ **COMMUNICATIONS**

Daily Newspapers: 1
Televisions: 788/1,000 inhabitants (1997 est.)
Radios: 1,072/1,000 inhabitants (1997 est.)
Telephones: n.a.

■ **TRANSPORTATION**

Motor Vehicles: 21,000; 17,000 passenger cars (1997 est.)
Roads: 50 km paved city streets only
Railway: 1.7 km
Air Traffic: 44,000 passengers carried (1997)
Airports: Monaco is linked to the airport in Nice, France, by helicopter service

Canadian Embassy: The Canadian Consulate General, c/o The Canadian Embassy, 35 av Montaigne, 75008 Paris, France. Tel: (011-33-1) 44-43-22-51. Fax: (011-33-1) 44-43-29-99. email: paris@dfait-maeci.gc.ca
Embassy in Canada: Consulate of Monaco, 1500 Sherbrooke St W, Ste 1500, Montreal PQ H3A 2W1. Tel: (514) 849-0589. Fax: (514) 631-2771. Email: n.a.

Mongolia

Long-Form Name: Mongolia
Capital: Ulan Bator

■ **GEOGRAPHY**

Area: 1,565,000 sq. km
Coastline: none: landlocked

Climate: desert; continental (large daily and seasonal temperature ranges)
Environment: harsh and rugged; water resources are severely limited; deforestation is a problem; spring dust storms are a natural hazard
Terrain: vast semidesert and desert plains; mountains in west and southwest; Gobi desert in southeast
Land Use: 1% arable; 0% permanent crops; 80% meadows; 9% forest; 10% other; includes 800 sq. km irrigated
Location: EC Asia, bordering China and Russia

■ **PEOPLE**

Population: 2,650,952 (July 2000 est.)
Nationality: Mongolian
Age Structure: 0-14 yrs: 34%; 15-64: 62%; 65+: 4% (2000 est.)
Population Growth Rate: 1.54% (2000 est.)
Net Migration: 0 migrants/1,000 population (2000 est.)
Ethnic Groups: 90% Mongol, 4% Kazakh, 2% Chinese, 2% Russian, 2% other
Languages: Kazakh and Khalkha Mongol is spoken by over 90% of population; minor languages include Turkic, Russian, Chinese and English
Religions: no state religion; predominantly Buddhist Lamaism and Shamanism, Islam 4%
Birth Rate: 21.53/1,000 population (2000 est.)
Death Rate: 6.14/1,000 population (2000 est.)
Infant Mortality: 41.22 deaths/1,000 live births (2000 est.)
Life Expectancy at Birth: 64.98 years male, 69.64 years female (2000 est.)
Total Fertility Rate: 2.40 children born/woman (2000 est.)
Literacy: 84.0% (1997)

■ **GOVERNMENT**

Leader(s): Pres. Natsagiin Bagabandi, Prime Min. Nambaryn Enkhbayar
Government Type: republic
Administrative Divisions: 18 provinces (aymguud, sing. —aymag) and 3 municipalities (hotuud, sing. —hot)
Nationhood: Mar. 13, 1921 (from China; formerly known as Outer Mongolia)
National Holiday: National Day, July 11

■ **ECONOMY**

Overview: severe climate, widely dispersed population and largely unproductive land have hindered economic development; one-quarter of the population lives below the poverty line; traditionally based on agriculture and the breeding of livestock (has highest number of livestock per person in the world); recently

extensive mineral resources have been developed
GDP: US$6.1 billion, per capita US$2,320; average real growth rate 3.5% (1999 est.)
Inflation: 7.57% (year-end 1999)
Industries: accounts for 24% of GDP; processing of animal products, building materials, food and beverage, mining (particularly coal), copper
Labour Force: 1 million (1999); 39.9% agriculture, 21% industry, 39.2% services
Unemployment: 4.5% (1998)
Agriculture: accounts for 33% of GDP; 90% of exports, and provides livelihood for about 50% of the population; livestock raising predominates (sheep, goats, horses); crops— wheat, barley, potatoes, forage
Natural Resources: oil, coal, copper, molybdenum, tungsten, phosphates, tin, nickel, zinc, wolfram, fluorspar, gold

■ **FINANCE/TRADE**

Currency: tughrik (Tug) = 100 mongos
International Reserves Excluding Gold: US$170 million (Jan. 2001)
Gold Reserves: US$0.085 million fine troy ounces (Jan. 2001)
Budget: revenues US$260 million, expenditures US$366 million, including capital expenditures US$n.a. (1999)
Defence Expenditures: 8.32% of central government expenditure (1998)
Education Expenditures: 8.03% of central government expenditure (1998)
External Debt: US$891 million (1999)
Exports: US$435 million (2000); commodities: livestock, animal products, wool, hides, fluorspar, nonferrous metals, minerals; partners: former USSR countries 80%
Imports: US$455 million (2000); commodities: machinery and equipment, fuels, food products, industrial consumer goods, chemicals, building materials, sugar, tea; partners: former USSR countries 80%

■ **COMMUNICATIONS**

Daily Newspapers: 4
Televisions: 63/1,000 inhabitants (1998)
Radios: 151/1,000 inhabitants (1997)
Telephones: 39 lines/1,000 inhabitants (1999)

■ **TRANSPORTATION**

Motor Vehicles: n.a.
Roads: 49,250 km; 1,674 km paved
Railway: 1,928 km
Air Traffic: 240,000 passengers carried (1997)
Airports: 34; 8 have paved runways
Canadian Embassy: The Canadian Embassy to Mongolia, c/o The Canadian Embassy, 19 Dong

Zhi Men Wai St, Chao Yang District, Beijing 100600, China. Tel: (011-86-10) 6532-3536. Fax: (011-86-10) 6532-4311. Email: bejing@dfait-maeci.gc.ca

Embassy in Canada: Embassy of Mongolia, 2833 M St NW, Washington DC 20007, USA. Tel: (202) 333-7117. Fax: (202) 298-9227. Email: n.a.

Montserrat

Long-Form Name: Montserrat
Capital: Plymouth (abandoned in 1997 due to volcanic activity) Interim government buildings are located in Brades

■ **GEOGRAPHY**

Area: 100 sq. km
Climate: tropical, no well-defined rainy season; June to Nov. hottest; prone to hurricanes
Land Use: 20% arable, 0% permanent crops, 10% meadows and pastures, 40% forests, 30% other; includes n.a. sq. km irrigated
Location: Carribbean island, SE of Puerto Rico

■ **PEOPLE**

Population: 6,409 (July 2000 est.)
Nationality: Montserratian
Ethnic Groups: descendants of British, French, Irish settlers; also black
Languages: English (official)

■ **GOVERNMENT**

Colony Territory of: Crown Colony of the United Kingdom
Leader(s): Head of State: Queen Elizabeth II. Gov. Anthony Longrigg, Chief Min. John Osborne
Government Type: dependent territory of the UK
National Holiday: Celebration of the Birthday of the Queen, second Saturday in June

■ **ECONOMY**

Overview: manufacturing accounts for 85% of exports: leather goods, cotton clothing, electronics, plastic bags, herbal teas, ornamental plants, tropical fruit; the economy is heavily dependent on imports, making it vulnerable to fluctuations in world prices; ongoing major volcanic activity is hindering economic activity

■ **FINANCE/TRADE**

Currency: Eastern Caribbean dollar = 100 cents

Canadian Embassy: c/o Macdonald House, 1 Grosvenor Square, London WIK 4AB, England, UK. Tel: (011-44-20) 7258-6600. Fax: (011-44-20) 7258-6333. Email: Ldn@dfait-maeci.gc.ca

Representative to Canada: c/o High Commission for the Countries of the Organization of Eastern Caribbean States, 130 Albert St, Ste 700, Ottawa ON K1P 5G4. Tel: (613) 236-8952. Fax: (613) 236-3042. Email: echcc@travel-net.com

Morocco

Long-Form Name: Kingdom of Morocco
Capital: Rabat

■ GEOGRAPHY

Area: 446,550 sq. km
Coastline: 1,835 km
Climate: Mediterranean, becoming more extreme in the interior
Environment: northern mountains geologically unstable and subject to earthquakes; desertification; unsafe water supply; land degradation
Terrain: mostly mountains with rich coastal plains
Land Use: 21% arable; 1% permanent crops; 47% permanent pastures; 20% forest; 11% other, includes 12,580 sq. km irrigated
Location: NW Africa, bordering on Atlantic Ocean

■ PEOPLE

Population: 30,122,350 (July 2000 est.)
Nationality: Moroccan
Age Structure: 0-14 yrs: 35%; 15-64: 60%; 65+: 5% (2000 est.)
Population Growth Rate: 1.74% (2000 est.)
Net Migration: -1.21 migrants/1,000 population (2000 est.)
Ethnic Groups: 99.1% Arab-Berber, 0.7% non-Morrocan, 0.2% Jewish
Languages: Arabic (official); several Berber dialects; French is language of business, government, diplomacy and post-primary education
Religions: 98.7% Sunni Muslim, 1.1% Christian, 0.2% Jewish
Birth Rate: 24.60/1,000 population (2000 est.)
Death Rate: 6.02/1,000 population (2000 est.)
Infant Mortality: 49.72 deaths/1,000 live births (2000 est.)
Life Expectancy at Birth: 66.92 years male, 71.44 years female (2000 est.)
Total Fertility Rate: 3.13 children born/woman (2000 est.)
Literacy: 47% (1998)

■ GOVERNMENT

Leader(s): King Sidi Mohammed VI, Prime Min. Abderrahmane Youssoufi
Government Type: constitutional monarchy

Administrative Divisions: 37 provinces and 2 municipalities (wilayas)
Nationhood: Mar. 2, 1956 (from France)
National Holiday: Throne Day or Sete de Throne, July 30 (anniversary of King Mohammed VI's accession to the throne)

■ ECONOMY

Overview: faces the problems typical of developing countries: restraining government spending, reducing constraints on private activity and foreign trade, and keeping inflation manageable
GDP: US$108 billion, per capita US$3,600; real growth rate 0% (1999 est.)
Inflation: 1.89% (year-end 2000)
Industries: accounts for 30% of GDP, phosphate rock mining and processing, food processing, leather goods, textiles, construction, tourism
Labour Force: 11 million (1999); 45.6% agriculture, 29.4% services, 25% industry
Unemployment: 19% (1998 est.)
Agriculture: accounts for 16% of GDP; 50% of employment and 30% of export value; not self-sufficient in food; cereal farming and livestock raising predominate; barley, wheat, citrus fruit, wine, vegetables, olives
Natural Resources: phosphates, iron ore, manganese, lead, zinc, fish, salt

■ FINANCE/TRADE

Currency: dirham (DH) = 100 centimes
International Reserves Excluding Gold: US$4.699 billion (Jan. 2001)
Gold Reserves: US$0.706 million fine troy ounces (Jan. 2001)
Budget: revenues US$9.1 billion; expenditures US$10 billion, including capital expenditures US$1.7 billion (1998-99 est.)
Defence Expenditures: 3.8% of GDP (1997-98)
Education Expenditures: 5.0% of GNP (1997)
External Debt: US$19.060 billion (1999)
Exports: US$7.450 billion (2000); commodities: food and beverages 30%, semiprocessed goods 23%, consumer goods 21%, phosphates 17%; partners: European Community 58%, India 7%, Japan 5%, former USSR countries 3%, US 2%
Imports: US$11.439 billion (2000); commodities: capital goods 24%, semi-processed goods 22%, raw materials 16%, fuel and lubricants 16%, food and beverages 13%, consumer goods 10%; partners: European Community 53%, US 11%, Canada 4%, Iraq 3%, former USSR countries 3%, Japan 2%

■ COMMUNICATIONS

Daily Newspapers: 22
Televisions: 160/1,000 inhabitants (1998)

Radios: 241/1,000 inhabitants (1997)
Telephones: 53 lines/1,000 inhabitants (1999)

■ TRANSPORTATION

Motor Vehicles: 1,380,000; 1,040,000 passenger cars (1997 est.)
Roads: 57,847 km; 30,254 km paved
Railway: 1,907 km
Air Traffic: 2,638,000 passengers carried (1997)
Airports: 70; 26 have paved runways (1999 est.)

Canadian Embassy: The Canadian Embassy, 13 bis, rue Jaafar As-Sadik; Rabat-Agdal; mailing address: CP 709, Rabat-Agdal, Morocco. Tel: (011-212-37) 68-74-00. Fax: (011-212-37) 68-74-30. Email: rabat@dfait-maeci.gc.ca.
Embassy in Canada: Embassy of the Kingdom of Morocco, 38 Range Rd, Ottawa ON K1N 8J4. Tel: (613) 236-7391. Fax: (613) 236-6164. Email: sifamaot@videotron.net

---

Mozambique

Long-Form Name: Republic of Mozambique
Capital: Maputo

■ GEOGRAPHY

Area: 801,590 sq. km
Coastline: 2,470 km
Climate: tropical to subtropical
Environment: severe drought and floods occur in south; desertification; water pollution; danger of cyclones
Terrain: mostly coastal lowlands, uplands in centre, high plateaus in northwest, mountains in west
Land Use: 4% arable; negligible permanent crops; 56% meadows; 18% forest; 22% other; includes 1,180 sq. km irrigated
Location: SE Africa, bordering on Mozambique Channel

■ PEOPLE

Population: 19,104,696 (July 2000 est.)
Nationality: Mozambican
Age Structure: 0-14 yrs: 43%; 15-64: 54%; 65+: 3% (2000 est.)
Population Growth Rate: 1.47% (2000 est.)
Net Migration: 0 migrants/1,000 population (2000 est.)
Ethnic Groups: 99.66% indigenous tribal groups; about 0.06% Europeans, 0.2% Euro-Africans, 0.08% Indians
Languages: Portuguese (official); English; many indigenous dialects
Religions: 50% indigenous beliefs, 30% Christian, 20% Muslim
Birth Rate: 37.99/1,000 population (2000 est.)

Death Rate: 23.29/1,000 population (2000 est.)
Infant Mortality: 139.86 deaths/1,000 live births (2000 est.)
Life Expectancy at Birth: 38.34 years male, 36.68 years female (2000 est.)
Total Fertility Rate: 4.93 children born/woman (2000 est.)
Literacy: 42% (1998)

■ GOVERNMENT

Leader(s): Pres. Joaquím Alberto Chissano, Prime Min. Pascoal Manuel Mocumbi
Government Type: republic
Administrative Divisions: 10 provinces (provincias, sing. —provincia)
Nationhood: June 25, 1975 (from Portugal)
National Holiday: Independence Day, June 25

■ ECONOMY

Overview: internal disorder, lack of government administrative control and a growing foreign debt have contributed to the country's failure to exploit the economic potential of its agricultural, hydropower and transportation resources; depends on much foreign aid; industry operates at only 20–40% of capacity
GDP: US$18.7 billion, per capita US$1,000; real growth rate 10% (1999 est.)
Inflation: 2.03% (year-end 1999)
Industries: accounts for 18% of GDP; food, beverages, chemicals (fertilizer, soap, paints), petroleum products, textiles, nonmetallic mineral products (cement, glass, asbestos), tobacco
Labour Force: 9.0 million (1999); 84.5% agriculture, 7.4% industry, 8.1% services
Unemployment: n.a.
Agriculture: accounts for 34% of GDP, over 90% of labour force and about 90% of exports; cash crops—cotton, cashew nuts, sugar cane, tea, shrimp; other crops—cassava, corn, rice, tropical fruit; not self-sufficient in food
Natural Resources: coal, titanium, natural gas, hydropower

■ FINANCE/TRADE

Currency: metical (pl. meticais) (Mt) = 100 centavos
International Reserves Excluding Gold: US$725 million (Dec. 2000)
Gold Reserves: n.a.
Budget: revenues US$402 million; expenditures US$799 million, including capital expenditures US$n.a. (1997 est.)
Defence Expenditures: 4.7% of GDP (1997)
Education Expenditures: n.a.
External Debt: US$6.959 billion (1999)
Exports: US$190 million (2000); commodities:

shrimp 48%, cashews 21%, sugar 10%, copra 3%, citrus 3%; partners: US, Western Europe, Germany, Japan
Imports: US$939 million (2000); commodities: food, clothing, farm equipment, petroleum; partners: US, Western Europe, former USSR countries

■ COMMUNICATIONS

Daily Newspapers: 2
Televisions: 5/1,000 inhabitants (1998)
Radios: 40/1,000 inhabitants (1997)
Telephones: 4 lines/1,000 inhabitants (1999)

■ TRANSPORTATION

Motor Vehicles: 88,800; 67,600 passenger cars (1997 est.)
Roads: 30,400 km; 5,685 km paved
Railway: 3,131 km
Air Traffic: 188,000 passengers carried (1997)
Airports: 170; 22 have paved runways (1999 est.)

Canadian Embassy: The Canadian Embassy, avenida Julius Nyerere, No. 1128, Maputo; mailing address: P.O. Box 1578, Maputo, Mozambique. Tel: (011-258-1) 492-623. Fax: (011-258-1) 492-667. Email: mputo@dfait-maeci.gc.ca
Embassy in Canada: High Commission for the Republic of Mozambique, 1990 M St NW, Ste 570, Washington DC 20036, USA. Tel: (202) 293-7146. Fax: (202) 835-0245. Email: n.a.

Myanmar

Long-Form Name: Union of Myanmar (formerly Burma)
Capital: Rangoon

■ GEOGRAPHY

Area: 678,500 sq. km
Coastline: 1,930 km
Climate: tropical monsoon; cloudy, rainy, hot, humid summers (southwest monsoon, June to Sept.); less cloudy, scant rainfall, mild temperatures, lower humidity during winter (northeast monsoon, Dec. to Apr.)
Environment: subject to destructive earthquakes and cyclones; flooding and landslides common during rainy season (June to Sept.); deforestation
Terrain: central lowlands ringed by steep, rugged highlands
Land Use: 15% arable land; 1% permanent crops; 1% meadows and pastures; 49% forest and woodland; 34% other, includes 10,680 sq. km irrigated
Location: SE Asia, bordering on Bay of Bengal

■ PEOPLE

Population: 41,734,853 (July 2000 est.)
Nationality: Burmese
Age Structure: 0-14 yrs: 30%; 15-64: 65%; 65+: 5% (1999 est.)
Population Growth Rate: 0.64% (2000 est.)
Net Migration: -1.85 migrants/1,000 population (2000 est.)
Ethnic Groups: 68% Burmese, 9% Shan, 7% Karen, 4% Rakhine, 3% Chinese, 2% Mon, 2% Indian, 5% other
Languages: Myanmar (Burmese); minority ethnic groups have their own languages
Religions: 89% Buddhist, 11% animist beliefs, Muslim, Christian or other
Birth Rate: 20.61/1,000 population (2000 est.)
Death Rate: 12.35/1,000 population (2000 est.)
Infant Mortality: 75.30 deaths/1,000 live births (2000 est.)
Life Expectancy at Birth: 53.60 years male, 56.29 years female (2000 est.)
Total Fertility Rate: 2.37 children born/woman (2000 est.)
Literacy: 84% (1998)

■ GOVERNMENT

Leader(s): Chairman and Prime Min. General Than Shwe
Government Type: military regime
Administrative Divisions: 7 divisions (yin-mya, sing. —yin), 7 states (pyine-mya, sing. —pyine)
Nationhood: Jan. 4, 1948 (from UK)
National Holiday: Independence Day, Jan. 4

■ ECONOMY

Overview: dependent on agriculture and vulnerable to world market conditions (especially for rice); has been unable to achieve much improvement in export earnings due to falling prices for many of its export commodities
GDP: US$59.4 billion, per capita US$1,200; real growth rate 4.6% (1999 est.)
Inflation: -0.11% (year-end 2000)
Industries: accounts for 11% of GDP; agricultural processing; textiles and footwear; wood and wood products; petroleum refining; mining of copper, tin, tungsten, iron; construction materials; pharmaceuticals; fertilizer
Labour Force: 24 million (1999); 69.1% agriculture, 8.9% trade and tourism, 7.2% industry
Unemployment: 7.1% (official 1997-98 estimate)
Agriculture: accounts for 59% of GDP; self-sufficient in food; principal crops: rice, corn, oilseed, sugar cane, pulses; world's largest stand of hardwood trees; rice and teak account for

55% of exports; world's largest producer of opium poppies

Natural Resources: crude oil, timber, tin, antimony, zinc, copper, tungsten, lead, coal, some marble, limestone, precious stones, natural gas

■ FINANCE/TRADE

Currency: kyat (K) = 100 pyas
International Reserves Excluding Gold: US$255 million (Nov. 2000)
Gold Reserves: US$0.231 million fine troy ounces (Nov. 2000)
Budget: n.a.
Defence Expenditures: 31.94% of govt. expenditure (1998)
Education Expenditures: 7.72% of central govt. expenditure (1998)
External Debt: US$5.999 billion (1999)
Exports: US$1.283 billion (2000); commodities: teak, rice, oilseed, metals, rubber, gems; partners: Southeast Asia, India, China, European Community, Africa
Imports: US$2.386 billion (2000); commodities: machinery, transport equipment, chemicals, food products; partners: Japan, European Community, former socialist nations, China, Southeast Asia

■ COMMUNICATIONS

Daily Newspapers: 5
Televisions: 7/1,000 inhabitants (1998)
Radios: 95/1,000 inhabitants (1997)
Telephones: 6 lines/1,000 inhabitants (1999)

■ TRANSPORTATION

Motor Vehicles: 69,000; 35,000 passenger cars (1997 est.)
Roads: 28,200 km; 3,440 km paved
Railway: 3,991 km
Air Traffic: 334,000 passengers carried (1997)
Airports: 80; 10 have paved runways (1999 est.)

Canadian Embassy: The Canadian Embassy to Myanmar, c/o The Canadian Embassy, 990 Rama IV, Abdulrahim Place, 15th Fl, Bangrak, Bangkok 10500, Thailand; mailing address: P.O. Box 2090, Bangkok 10501, Thailand. Tel: (011-66-2) 636-0540. Fax: (011-66-2) 636-0566. Email: bngkk@dfait-maeci.gc.ca
Embassy in Canada: Embassy of the Union of Myanmar, 85 Range Rd, Ste 902/903, Ottawa ON K1N 8J6. Tel: (613) 232-6434. Fax: (613) 232-6435. Email: meott@magma.ca

---

Namibia

Long-Form Name: Republic of Namibia
Capital: Windhoek

■ GEOGRAPHY

Area: 825,418 sq. km
Coastline: 1,572 km
Climate: desert; hot, dry; rainfall sparse and erratic
Environment: inhospitable with very limited natural water resources; drought and desertification
Terrain: mostly high plateau; Namib Desert along coast; Kalahari Desert in east
Land Use: 1% arable; 0% permanent crops; 46% permanent pastures; 22% forest; 31% other; includes 60 sq. km irrigated
Location: SW Africa, bordering on South Atlantic Ocean

■ PEOPLE

Population: 1,771,327 (July 2000 est.)
Nationality: Namibian
Age Structure: 0-14 yrs: 43%; 15-64: 53%; 65+: 4% (2000 est.)
Population Growth Rate: 1.57% (2000 est.)
Net Migration: 0 migrants/1,000 population (2000 est.)
Ethnic Groups: 87.5% black, 6% white, 6.5% mixed; about 50% of the population belong to the Ovambo tribe and 9% to the Kavangos tribe
Languages: white population: 60% Afrikaans, 33% German, 7% English (all official); several indigenous languages
Religions: 90% Christian, 10% traditional religions
Birth Rate: 35.23/1,000 population (2000 est.)
Death Rate: 19.49/1,000 population (2000 est.)
Infant Mortality: 70.88 deaths/1,000 live births (2000 est.)
Life Expectancy at Birth: 44.33 years male, 40.53 years female (2000 est.)
Total Fertility Rate: 4.89 children born/woman (2000 est.)
Literacy: n.a.

■ GOVERNMENT

Leader(s): Pres. Sam Nujoma, Prime Min. Hage Geingob
Government Type: republic
Administrative Divisions: 13 regions
Nationhood: Mar. 21, 1990 (from South Africa)
National Holiday: Independence Day, Mar. 21

■ ECONOMY

Overview: very dependent on the mining industry to extract and process minerals for export; world's fifth largest producer of uranium; rich diamond deposits; more than 50% of the population depends on subsistence agriculture
GDP: US$7.1 billion, per capita US$4,300; real growth rate 3% (1999 est.)

Inflation: 8.60% (year-end 1999)
Industries: meat packing, fish processing, dairy products; mining accounts for 30% of GDP (copper, lead, zinc, diamonds, uranium)
Labour Force: 1 million (1999); 43.5% agriculture, 21.9% industry, 34.8% services
Unemployment: 30-40%, including underemployment (1997 est.)
Agriculture: accounts for 12% of GDP (including fishing); mostly subsistence farming; livestock raising major source of cash income; crops: millet, sorghum, peanuts; large unfulfilled fish catch potential; needs to import food
Natural Resources: diamonds, copper, uranium, gold, lead, tin, zinc, salt, vanadium, natural gas, fish, hydroelectric potential; suspected deposits of coal and iron ore

■ FINANCE/TRADE

Currency: Namibian dollar = 100 cents
International Reserves Excluding Gold: US$303 million (Jan. 2001)
Gold Reserves: none (Jan. 2001)
Budget: revenues US$883 million; expenditures US$950 million, including capital expenditures of US$n.a. (1998)
Defence Expenditures: 2.6% of GDP (1997-98)
Education Expenditures: 9.1% of GNP (1997)
External Debt: US$159 million (1999 est.)
Exports: US$1.40 billion (1999 est.); commodities: diamonds, uranium, zinc, copper, meat, processed fish, karakul skins; partners: South Africa, UK, Spain, Japan
Imports: US$1.50 billion (1999 est.); commodities: foodstuffs, manufactured consumer goods, machinery and equipment; partners: South Africa, Germany, US, Japan

■ COMMUNICATIONS

Daily Newspapers: 4
Televisions: 37/1,000 inhabitants (1998)
Radios: 144/1,000 inhabitants (1997)
Telephones: 64 lines/1,000 inhabitants (1999)

■ TRANSPORTATION

Motor Vehicles: 129,000; 62,500 passenger cars (1997 est.)
Roads: 63,258 km; 5,250 km paved
Railway: 2,382 km
Air Traffic: 214,000 passengers carried (1997)
Airports: 135; 22 have paved runways (1999 est.)
Canadian Embassy: The Canadian High Commission to Namibia, c/o The Canadian High Commission, 1103 Arcadia St, Hatfield 0083, Pretoria; mailing address: Private Bag X13, Hatfield 0028, Pretoria, South Africa. Tel.: (011-27-12) 422-3000. Fax: (011-27-12) 422-3052. Email: pret@dfait-maeci.gc.ca

Embassy in Canada: High Commission for the Republic of Namibia, 1605 New Hampshire Ave NW, Washington DC 20009, USA. Tel: (202) 986-0540. Fax: (202) 986-0443. Email: n.a.

Nauru

Long-Form Name: Republic of Nauru
Capital: no capital city as such; government offices in Yaren

■ GEOGRAPHY

Area: 21 sq. km
Coastline: 30 km
Climate: tropical; monsoonal; rainy season (Nov. to Feb.)
Environment: only 53 km south of equator; periodic droughts; water supply limited and unreliable
Terrain: sandy beach rises to fertile ring around raised coral reefs with phosphate plateau in centre
Land Use: 0% arable; 0% permanent; 0% meadows; 0% forest; 100% other
Location: island in the Pacific Ocean, NE of Australia

■ PEOPLE

Population: 11,845 (July 2000 est.)
Nationality: Nauruan
Age Structure: 0-14 yrs: 41%; 15-64: 57%; 65+: 2% (2000 est.)
Population Growth Rate: 2.05% (2000 est.)
Net Migration: 0 migrants/1,000 population (2000 est.)
Ethnic Groups: 58% Nauruan, 26% other Pacific Islander, 8% Chinese, 8% European
Languages: Nauruan, a distinct Pacific Island language (official); English widely understood, spoken and used for most government and commercial purposes
Religions: Christian (two-thirds Nauruan Protestant, one-third Roman Catholic)
Birth Rate: 27.86/1,000 population (2000 est.)
Death Rate: 7.34/1,000 population (2000 est.)
Infant Mortality: 10.90 deaths/1,000 live births (2000 est.)
Life Expectancy at Birth: 57.35 years male, 64.50 years female (2000 est.)
Total Fertility Rate: 3.71 children born/woman (2000 est.)
Literacy: n.a.

■ GOVERNMENT

Leader(s): Pres. Bernard Dowiyogo
Government Type: republic
Administrative Divisions: 14 districts

Nationhood: Jan. 31, 1968 (from UN trusteeship under Australia, New Zealand and UK; formerly known as Pleasant Island)
National Holiday: Independence Day, Jan. 31

■ ECONOMY

Overview: most other resources are imported; has one of the highest per capita incomes in the Third World; the rehabilitation of mined land and the replacement of income from phosphates are serious long-term considerations
GDP: n.a.
Inflation: n.a.
Industries: phosphate mining, financial services, coconuts
Labour Force: n.a.
Unemployment: 0%
Agriculture: coconuts; other agricultural activities are negligible; almost completely dependent on imports for food and water
Natural Resources: phosphates

■ FINANCE/TRADE

Currency: Australian dollar ($A) = 100 cents
International Reserves Excluding Gold: n.a.
Gold Reserves: n.a.
Budget: n.a.
Defence Expenditures: no formal defence structure
Education Expenditures: n.a.
External Debt: US$33.3 million
Exports: n.a.; commodities: phosphates; partners: Australia, New Zealand
Imports: n.a.; commodities: food, fuel, manufacturers, building materials, machinery; partners: Australia, UK, New Zealand, Japan

■ COMMUNICATIONS

Daily Newspapers: 0
Televisions: 42/1,000 inhabitants (1997 est.)
Radios: 590/1,000 inhabitants (1997 est.)
Telephones: n.a.

■ TRANSPORTATION

Motor Vehicles: n.a.
Roads: 30 km; 24 km paved
Railway: 3.9 km
Air Traffic: 137,000 passengers carried (1997)
Airports: 1, with a paved runway (1999 est.)
Canadian Embassy: c/o The Canadian High Commission, Commonwealth Ave, Canberra A.C.T. 2600, Australia. Tel: (011-61-2) 6270-4000. Fax: (011-61-2) 6273-3285. Email: cnbra@dfait-maeci.gc.ca
Embassy in Canada: c/o Australian High Commission, 50 O'Connor St, Ste 710, Ottawa ON K1P 6L2. Tel: (613) 236-0841. Fax: (613) 236-4376. Email: n.a.

Nepal

Long-Form Name: Kingdom of Nepal
Capital: Kathmandu

■ GEOGRAPHY

Area: 140,800 sq. km
Coastline: none: landlocked
Climate: varies from cool summers and severe winters in north to subtropical summers and mild winters in south
Environment: contains eight of the world's 10 highest peaks; flooding, drought, landslides; deforestation; soil erosion; water pollution
Terrain: flat river plain of the Ganges in south, central hilly region, rugged Himalayas in north
Land Use: 17% arable; negligible permanent crops; 15% meadows; 42% forest; 26% other, includes 8,500 sq. km irrigated
Location: SC Asia, bordering on India and Tibet

■ PEOPLE

Population: 24,702,119 (July 2000 est.)
Nationality: Nepalese
Age Structure: 0-14 yrs: 41%; 15-64: 56%; 65+: 3% (2000 est.)
Population Growth Rate: 2.34% (2000 est.)
Net Migration: 0 migrants/1,000 population (2000 est.)
Ethnic Groups: Newars, Indians, Tibetans, Gurungs, Magars, Tamangs, Bhotias, Rais, Limbus, Sherpas, as well as many smaller groups
Languages: Nepali (official); 20 languages divided into numerous dialects
Religions: 90% Hindu, 5% Buddhist, 3% Muslim, 2% other; only official Hindu state in the world, although no sharp distinction between many Hindu and Buddhist groups; small groups of Muslims and Christians
Birth Rate: 33.83/1,000 population (2000 est.)
Death Rate: 10.41/1,000 population (2000 est.)
Infant Mortality: 75.93 deaths/1,000 live births (2000 est.)
Life Expectancy at Birth: 58.30 years male, 57.35 years female (2000 est.)
Total Fertility Rate: 4.68 children born/woman (2000 est.)
Literacy: 39% (1998)

■ GOVERNMENT

Leader(s): King Gyanendra Bir Bikram Shah, Prime Min. Sher Bahadur Deuba
Government Type: parliamentary democracy
Administrative Divisions: 14 zones (anchal, sing. & pl.)
Nationhood: 1768, unified by Prithvi Narayan Shah

National Holiday: Birthday of His Majesty the King, Dec. 28

■ ECONOMY

Overview: one of the poorest and most underdeveloped countries in the world; agriculture provides the backbone of the economy, employing more than 80% of the population; there have been attempts to expand into other economic sectors

GDP: US$27.4 billion, per capita US$1,100; real growth rate 3.4% (1999 est.)

Inflation: 1.54% (year-end 2000)

Industries: accounts for 22% of GDP; small rice, jute, sugar and oilseed mills, cigarettes, textiles, cement, brick; tourism, carpet production

Labour Force: 11 million (1999); 93% agriculture, 6.5% services, 0.6% industry

Unemployment: n.a., but substantial rate of underemployment

Agriculture: accounts for 41% of GDP and 80% of workforce; farm products—rice, corn, wheat, sugar cane, root crops, milk, buffalo meat; not self-sufficient in food, particularly in drought years

Natural Resources: quartz, water, timber, hydroelectric potential, scenic beauty; small deposits of lignite, copper, cobalt, iron ore

■ FINANCE/TRADE

Currency: rupee (NRs) = 100 paisa

International Reserves Excluding Gold: US$933 million (July 2000)

Gold Reserves: US$0.153 million fine troy ounces (July 2000)

Budget: n.a.

Defence Expenditures: 5.63% of total govt. expenditure (2000)

Education Expenditures: 14.41% of central govt. expenditure (2000)

External Debt: US$2.970 billion (1999)

Exports: US$$474 million (1998); commodities: clothing, carpets, leather goods, grain; partners: India 38%, US 23%, UK 6%, other Europe 9%

Imports: US$1.246 billion (1998); commodities: petroleum products 20%, fertilizer 11%, machinery 10%; partners: India 36%, Japan 13%, Europe 4%, US 1%

■ COMMUNICATIONS

Daily Newspapers: 29

Televisions: 6/1,000 inhabitants (1998)

Radios: 38/1,000 inhabitants (1997)

Telephones: 11 lines/1,000 inhabitants (1999)

■ TRANSPORTATION

Motor Vehicles: n.a.

Roads: 13,223 km; 4,073 km paved

Railway: 101 km

Air Traffic: 755,000 passengers carried (1997)

Airports: 45; 5 have paved runways (1999 est.)

Canadian Embassy: The Canadian Embassy to Nepal, c/o The Canadian Cooperation Office, Lazimpat, Kathmandu, Nepal; mailing address: P.O. Box 4574, Kathmandu, Nepal. Tel: (011-9771) 415-193. Fax: (011-9771) 410-422. Email: cco@cco.org.np

Embassy in Canada: Embassy of the Kingdom of Nepal, 2131 Leroy Place NW, Washington DC 20008, USA. Tel: (202) 667-4550. Fax: (202) 667-5534. Email: nepali@erols.com

Netherlands

Long-Form Name: Kingdom of the Netherlands

Capital: Amsterdam; seat of government: The Hague

■ GEOGRAPHY

Area: 41,532 sq. km

Coastline: 451 km

Climate: temperate; marine; cool summers and mild winters

Environment: nearly half of the land area is below sea level and protected from the North Sea by dikes; water and air pollution

Terrain: mostly coastal lowland and reclaimed land (polders); some hills in southeast

Land Use: 25% arable; 3% permanent crops; 25% permanent pastures; 8% forest; 39% other, includes 6,000 sq. km irrigated

Location: NW Europe, bordering on North Sea

■ PEOPLE

Population: 15,892,237 (July 2000 est.)

Nationality: Dutchman, Dutchwoman

Age Structure: 0-14 yrs: 18%; 15-64: 68%; 65+: 14% (2000 est.)

Population Growth Rate: 0.57% (2000 est.)

Net Migration: 2.3 migrants/1,000 population (2000 est.)

Ethnic Groups: 91% Dutch, 9% Moroccans, Turks and others

Languages: Dutch, Frisian

Religions: 62% Christianity, of which 34% is Roman Catholic and 25% is Protestant; most of the rest do not profess a religion

Birth Rate: 12.12/1,000 population (2000 est.)

Death Rate: 8.72/1,000 population (2000 est.)

Infant Mortality: 4.42 deaths/1,000 live births (2000 est.)

Life Expectancy at Birth: 75.40 years male, 81.28years female (2000 est.)

Total Fertility Rate: 1.64 children born/woman (2000 est.)

Literacy: 99% (1998)

■ GOVERNMENT

Leader(s): Head of State: Queen Beatrix. Prem. Willem (Wim) Kok
Government Type: constitutional monarchy
Administrative Divisions: 12 provinces (provincien, sing. provincie); dependent areas: Aruba, Netherland Antilles
Nationhood: 1579 (from Spain)
National Holiday: Queen's Day, Apr. 30

■ ECONOMY

Overview: a highly developed and affluent economy based on private enterprise; numerous government-backed welfare programs; trade and financial sectors are the strongest part of the economy
GDP: US$365.1 billion, per capita US$23,100; real growth rate 3.4% (1999 est.)
Inflation: 2.52% (year-end 2000)
Industries: contributes 26.8% to the GDP; agro-industries, metal and engineering products, electrical machinery and equipment, chemicals, petroleum, fishing, construction, micro-electronics
Labour Force: 7 million (1999); 35.4% community, social and business services, 19.2% trade and tourism, 18% industry
Unemployment: 2.7% (Oct. 2000)
Agriculture: accounts for 3.5% of GDP and 4% of labour force; animal production predominates; crops—grains, potatoes, sugar beets, fruits, vegetables; shortages of grain, fats and oils
Natural Resources: natural gas, crude oil, fertile soil

■ FINANCE/TRADE

Currency: guilder, gulden or florin (f.) = 100 cents; Euro (EUR) as of Jan. 28, 2002
International Reserves Excluding Gold: US$8.484 billion (Jan. 2001)
Gold Reserves: US$29.315 million fine troy ounces (Jan. 2001)
Budget: revenues US$163 billion; expenditures US$170 billion, including capital expenditures of US$n.a. (1999 est.)
Defence Expenditures: 3.86% of govt. expend-itures (1997)
Education Expenditures: 9.97% total govt. expenditures (1997)
External Debt: none
Exports: US$199.621 billion (2000); commodities; agricultural products, processed foods and tobacco, natural gas, chemicals, metal products, textiles, clothing; partners: European Community 74.9% (Germany 28.3%, Belgium-

Luxembourg 14.2%, France 10.7, UK 10.2%), US 4.7%
Imports: US$198.468 billion (2000); com-modities: raw materials and semifinished products, consumer goods, transportation equipment, crude oil, food products; partners: European Community 63.8% (Germany 26.5%, Belgium-Luxembourg 23.1%, UK 8.1%), US 7.9%

■ COMMUNICATIONS

Daily Newspapers: 38
Televisions: 543/1,000 inhabitants (1998)
Radios: 978/1,000 inhabitants (1997)
Telephones: 607 lines/1,000 inhabitants (1999)

■ TRANSPORTATION

Motor Vehicles: 6,490,000; 5,750,000 passenger cars (1997 est.)
Roads: 125,575 km; 113,018 km paved
Railway: 2,739 km
Air Traffic: 17,890,000 passengers carried (1997)
Airports: 28; 19 have paved runways (1999 est.)

Canadian Embassy: The Canadian Embassy, Sophiaalaan 7, 2514JP, The Hague, Netherlands. Tel: (011-31-70) 311-1600. Fax: (011-31-70) 311-1620. Email: hague@dfait-maeci.gc.ca
Embassy in Canada: Embassy of the Kingdom of the Netherlands, 350 Albert St, Ste 2020, Ottawa ON K1R 1A4. Tel: (613) 237-5030. Fax: (613) 237-6471. Email: nlgovott@net com.ca

---

Netherlands Antilles

Long-Form Name: Netherlands Antilles
Capital: Willemstad

■ GEOGRAPHY

Area: 960 sq. km, 2 island groups
Climate: tropical maritime, moderated by northeasterly trade winds, short rainy season
Land Use: islands mostly too rocky for agriculture; only 10% is arable land; 0% permanent crops, 0% meadows and pastures, 0% forest, 90% other; includes n.a. sq. km irrigated
Location: West Indies, just north of Venezuela

■ PEOPLE

Population: 210,134 (July 2000 est.)
Nationality: Netherlands Antillean
Ethnic Groups: mixed African 85%, Carib Indian, European, Latin, Oriental
Languages: Dutch (official), Papiamento

(derived from Dutch, Spanish, Portuguese), English

■ GOVERNMENT

Colony Territory of: Dependent Territory of the Netherlands
Leader(s): Chief of State: Queen Beatrix/Gov. Jaime M. Saleh. Prime Min. Miguel Pourier
Government Type: dependency with internal self-government
National Holiday: Queen's Day, Apr. 30

■ ECONOMY

Overview: unlike many Latin American countries, the Netherlands Antilles has avoided crushing external debt; Curaçao has one of the largest ship-repair dry docks in the western hemisphere; almost all consumer goods must be imported; chief trading partner: UK

■ FINANCE/TRADE

Currency: Netherlands Antilles guilder, gulden or florin = 100 cents

Canadian Embassy: c/o The Canadian Embassy, 7, 2514JP The Hague, Netherlands. Tel: (011-31-70) 311-1600. Fax: (011-31-70) 311-1620. Email: hague@dfait-maeci.gc.ca
Representative to Canada: c/o Embassy of the Kingdom of the Netherlands, 350 Albert St, Ste 2020, Ottawa ON K1R 1A4. Tel: (613) 237-5030. Fax: (613) 237-6471. Email: nlgovott@netcom.ca

New Caledonia

Long-Form Name: Territory of New Caledonia and Dependencies
Capital: Nouméa

■ GEOGRAPHY

Area: 19,060 sq. km (a peninsula and three small islands)
Climate: humid, subtropical maritime, modified by southeast trade winds
Land Use: 0% arable, 0% permanent crops, 12% meadow and pasture, 39% forest and woodland, 49% other; includes 160 sq. km irrigated
Location: SW Pacific Ocean (Melanesia), E of Australia

■ PEOPLE

Population: 201,816 (July 2000 est.)
Nationality: New Caledonian
Ethnic Groups: 42.5% Melanesian, 37.1% European, 8.4% Wallisian, 3.8% Polynesian, 3.6% Indonesian, 1.6% Vietnamese, 3% other

Languages: French (official), 28 Melanesian and Polynesian languages

■ GOVERNMENT

Colony Territory of: Overseas Territory of France
Leader(s): Pres. Jacques Chirac (France), High Commissioner and Prefect Thierry Lataste
Government Type: overseas territory of France since 1956
National Holiday: Taking of the Bastille, July 14

■ ECONOMY

Overview: only a negligible portion of the land is arable, and most food must be imported; the backbone of the economy is nickel export

■ FINANCE/TRADE

Currency: CFP franc = 100 centimes

Canadian Embassy: c/o The Canadian Embassy, 35-37 avenue Montaigne 75008 Paris, France. Tel: (011-33-1) 44-43-29-00. Fax: (011-33-1) 44-43-29-99. Email: paris@dfait-maeci.gc.ca
Representative to Canada: c/o Embassy of France, 42 Sussex Dr, Ottawa ON K1M 2C9. Tel: (613) 789-1795. Fax: (613) 562-3735. Email: politique@ambafrance-ca.org

New Zealand

Long-Form Name: New Zealand
Capital: Wellington

■ GEOGRAPHY

Area: 268,680 sq. km
Coastline: 15,134 km
Climate: temperate with sharp regional contrasts
Environment: earthquakes are common though usually not severe; deforestation and soil degradation are increasing; occasional volcanic activity
Terrain: predominantly mountainous with some large coastal plains
Land Use: 9% arable; 5% permanent crops; 50% meadows and pastures; 28% forest and woodland; 8% other, includes 2,850 sq. km irrigated
Location: SE of Australia, bordering on Tasman Sea, Pacific Ocean

■ PEOPLE

Population: 3,819,762 (July 2000 est.)
Nationality: New Zealander
Age Structure: 0-14 yrs: 23%; 15-64: 66%; 65+: 11% (2000 est.)
Population Growth Rate: 1.17% (2000 est.)

Net Migration: 4.95 migrants/1,000 population (2000 est.)
Ethnic Groups: 79.1% European, 9.7% Maori, 3.8% Pacific Islander, 7.4% other
Languages: English (official), Maori
Religions: 75% Christian, 18% unspecified, 7% Hindu, Confucian, other
Birth Rate: 14.28/1,000 population (2000 est.)
Death Rate: 7.57/1,000 population (2000 est.)
Infant Mortality: 6.39 deaths/1,000 live births (2000 est.)
Life Expectancy at Birth: 74.85 years male, 80.93 years female (2000 est.)
Total Fertility Rate: 1.80 children born/woman (2000 est.)
Literacy: 99% (1998)

■ GOVERNMENT

Leader(s): Head of State: Queen Elizabeth II/Gov. Gen. Silvia Cartwright. Prime Min. Helen Clark
Government Type: parliamentary democracy
Administrative Divisions: 93 counties, 9 districts, 3 town districts; dependent areas inc.: the Cook Islands, the Kermadec Islands, Niue, the Ross Dependency (uninhabited except for scientific personnel), Tokelau
Nationhood: Sept. 26, 1907 (from UK)
National Holiday: Waitangi Day, Feb. 6

■ ECONOMY

Overview: government has been reorienting from an agrarian to an open, free-market economy that can compete in the global community; inflation has been reduced; growth has been sluggish, unemployment has been at an all-time high
GDP: US$63.8 billion, per capita US$17,400; real growth rate 3.1% (1999 est.)
Inflation: 2.62% (year-end 2000)
Industries: accounts for 23% of GDP; food processing, wool production, wood and paper products, textiles, machinery, transportation equipment, banking and insurance, tourism, mining
Labour Force: 2 million (1999); 28.7% community, social and business services, 21.1% trade and tourism, 17% industry
Unemployment: 7% (year-end 1999 est.)
Agriculture: accounts for 8% of GDP and 11% of workforce; livestock predominates: wool, meat, dairy products; crops: wheat, barley, potatoes, pulses, fruit and vegetables; fish; surplus producer of farm products
Natural Resources: natural gas, iron ore, sand, coal, timber, hydroelectricity, gold, limestone

■ FINANCE/TRADE

Currency: New Zealand dollar (NZ$) = 100 cents
International Reserves Excluding Gold: US$2.952 billion (Jan. 2001)
Gold Reserves: none (Jan. 2001)
Budget: revenues US$24.9 billion; expenditures US$23.7 billion, including capital expenditures US$n.a. (1997–98 est.)
Defence Expenditures: 3.07% of total govt. expenditure (1999)
Education Expenditures: 15.83% of central govt. expenditure (1999)
External Debt: US$53 billion (1998)
Exports: US$12.381 billion (2000); commodities: wool, lamb, mutton, beef, fruit, fish, cheese, manufactures, chemicals, forestry products; partners: European Community 18.3%, Japan 17.9%, Australia 17.5%, US 13.5%
Imports: US$13.199 billion (2000); commodities: petroleum, consumer goods, motor vehicles, industrial equipment; partners: Australia 19.7%, Japan 16.9%, European Community 16.9%, US 15.3%, Taiwan 3%

■ COMMUNICATIONS

Daily Newspapers: 23
Televisions: 508/1,000 inhabitants (1998)
Radios: 990/1,000 inhabitants (1997)
Telephones: 496 lines/1,000 inhabitants (1999)

■ TRANSPORTATION

Motor Vehicles: 2,110,000; 1,770,000 passenger cars (1997 est.)
Roads: 92,200 km; 53,568 km paved
Railway: 3,913 km
Air Traffic: 9,435,000 passengers carried (1997)
Airports: 111; 44 have paved runways (1999 est.)

Canadian Embassy: The Canadian High Commission, 61 Molesworth St, 3rd Floor, Thorndon, Wellington; mailing address: P.O. Box 12049, Thorndon, Wellington, New Zealand. Tel: (011-64-4) 473-9577. Fax: (011-64-4) 471-2082. Email: wlgtn@dfait-maeci.gc.ca
Embassy in Canada: New Zealand High Commission, Clarica Centre, 99 Bank St, Ste 727, Ottawa ON K1P 6G3. Tel: (613) 238-5991. Fax: (613) 238-5707. Email: nzhcott@istar.ca

Nicaragua

Long-Form Name: Republic of Nicaragua
Capital: Managua

■ GEOGRAPHY

Area: 129,494 sq. km
Coastline: 910 km
Climate: tropical in lowlands, cooler in highlands
Environment: subject to destructive earthquakes, volcanoes, landslides and occasional severe hurricanes; deforestation; soil erosion; water pollution
Terrain: extensive Atlantic coastal plains rising to central interior mountains; narrow Pacific coastal plain interrupted by volcanoes
Land Use: 9% arable; 1% permanent crops; 46% meadows; 27% forest; 17% other; includes 880 sq. km irrigated
Location: Central (Latin) America, bordering on Caribbean Sea, Pacific Ocean

■ PEOPLE

Population: 4,812,569 (July 2000 est.)
Nationality: Nicaraguan
Age Structure: 0-14 yrs: 40%; 15-64: 57%; 65+: 3% (2000 est.)
Population Growth Rate: 2.2% (2000 est.)
Net Migration: -1.35 migrants/1,000 population (2000 est.)
Ethnic Groups: 69% mestizo, 17% white, 9% black, 5% Indian
Languages: Spanish (official); English- and Indian-speaking minorities on Atlantic coast
Religions: 95% Roman Catholic, 5% Protestant
Birth Rate: 28.26/1,000 population (2000 est.)
Death Rate: 4.90/1,000 population (2000 est.)
Infant Mortality: 34.79 deaths/1,000 live births (2000 est.)
Life Expectancy at Birth: 66.81 years male, 70.77 years female (2000 est.)
Total Fertility Rate: 3.27 children born/woman (2000 est.)
Literacy: 67% (1998)

■ GOVERNMENT

Leader(s): Pres. José Arnoldo Aleman, V. Pres. Leopoldo Navarro
Parliamentary and presidential elections held Nov. 4, 2001
Government Type: republic
Administrative Divisions: 15 departments (departamentos, sing. —departamento) and 2 autonomous regions (regiones autonomistas, sing. —region autonomista)
Nationhood: Sept. 15, 1821 (from Spain)
National Holiday: Independence Day, Sept. 15

■ ECONOMY

Overview: based on the export of coffee and cotton; government control is extensive, including the financial system, wholesale purchasing, production, sales, foreign trade and distribution of goods; many shortages; high inflation
GDP: US$12.5 billion, per capita US$2,650; real growth rate 6.3% (1999 est.)
Inflation: 11.21% (year-end 1999)
Industries: accounts for 22% of GDP; food processing, chemicals, metal products, textiles, clothing, petroleum refining and distribution, beverages, footwear
Labour Force: 2 million (1999); 37.7% services, 46.5% agriculture, 15.8% industry
Unemployment: 10.5%; underemployment approximately 36% (1999 est.)
Agriculture: accounts for 34% of GDP; cash crops—coffee, bananas, sugar cane, cotton; food crops—rice, corn, cassava, citrus fruit, beans; variety of animal products—beef, veal, pork, poultry, dairy; war has lowered self-sufficiency in food
Natural Resources: gold, silver, copper, tungsten, lead, zinc, timber, fish

■ FINANCE/TRADE

Currency: gold córdoba ($C) = 100 centavos
International Reserves Excluding Gold: US$423 million (Jan. 2000)
Gold Reserves: n.a.
Budget: revenues US$527 million; expenditures US$617 million, including capital expenditures US$n.a. (1998 est.)
Defence Expenditures: 1.2% of GDP (1998)
Education Expenditures: 3.9% of GNP (1997)
External Debt: US$6.986 billion (1999)
Exports: US$631 million (2000); commodities: coffee, cotton, sugar, bananas, seafood, meat, chemicals; partners: CEMA 15%, OECD 75%, others 10%
Imports: US$1.845 billion (2000); commodities: petroleum, food, chemicals, machinery, clothing; partners: CEMA 55%, European Community 20%, Latin America 10%, others 10%

■ COMMUNICATIONS

Daily Newspapers: 4
Televisions: 190/1,000 inhabitants (1998)
Radios: 285/1,000 inhabitants (1997)
Telephones: 30 lines/1,000 inhabitants (1999)

■ TRANSPORTATION

Motor Vehicles: 148,000; 73,000 passenger cars (1997 est.)
Roads: 16,382 km; 1,818 km paved
Railway: none

Air Traffic: 51,000 passengers carried (1997)
Airports: 182; 11 have paved runways (1999 est.)
Canadian Embassy: The Office of the Canadian Embassy, Costado Oriental de la Casa Nazareth, Una Quadra Arriba, Calle Noval, Managua. Mailing address: The Office of the Canadian Embassy, Apartado Postal 25, Managua, Nicaragua. Tel: (011-505) 268-0433. Fax: (011-505) 268-0437. Email: mngua@dfait-maeci.gc.ca
Embassy in Canada: Embassy of the Republic of Nicaragua, 1627 New Hampshire Ave NW, Washington DC 20009, USA. Tel: (202) 939-6537. Fax: (202) 939-6545. Email: n.a.

Niger

Long-Form Name: Republic of Niger
Capital: Niamey

■ GEOGRAPHY

Area: 1,267,000 sq. km
Coastline: none: landlocked
Climate: mostly hot, dry, dusty; tropical in extreme south
Environment: recurrent drought and desertification severely affecting marginal agricultural activities; overgrazing; soil erosion
Terrain: desert and sand dunes; hills in north
Land Use: 3% arable land; 0% permanent crops; 7% meadows; 2% forest; 88% other; includes 660 sq. km irrigated
Location: WC Africa

■ PEOPLE

Population: 10,075,511 (July 2000 est.)
Nationality: Nigerian
Age Structure: 0-14 yrs: 48%; 15-64: 50%; 65+: 2% (2000 est.)
Population Growth Rate: 2.75% (2000 est.)
Net Migration: -0.75 migrants/1,000 population (2000 est.)
Ethnic Groups: 56% Hausa; 22% Djerma; 8.5% Fula; 8% Tuareg; 4.3% Beri Beri (Kanouri); 1.2% Arab, Toubou and Gourmantche; about 1,200 French expatriates
Languages: French (official); Hausa (50%), Djerma, also Tuareg, Fulani
Religions: 80% Muslim, remainder indigenous beliefs and Christians
Birth Rate: 51.45/1,000 population (2000 est.)
Death Rate: 23.17/1,000 population (2000 est.)
Infant Mortality: 124.90 deaths/1,000 live births (2000 est.)
Life Expectancy at Birth: 41.43 years male, 41.11 years female (2000 est.)
Total Fertility Rate: 7.16 children born/woman (2000 est.)

Literacy: 14.5% (1998)

■ GOVERNMENT

Leader(s): Pres. Mamadou Tandja, Prime Min. Hama Amadou
Government Type: republic
Administrative Divisions: 7 departments (departements, sing. —departement); 1 capital district (capitale district)
Nationhood: Aug. 3, 1960 (from France)
National Holiday: Republic Day, Dec. 18

■ ECONOMY

Overview: about 90% of the population is engaged in livestock rearing and farming; depends heavily on exploitation of uranium deposits, thus vulnerable to demand for uranium; increasing external debt is a problem; GDP growth cannot keep pace with the rapid population growth
GDP: US$9.6 billion, per capita US$1,000; real growth rate 2% (1999 est.)
Inflation: 2.90% (year-end 2000)
Industries: accounts for 18% of GDP; cement, brick, rice mills, small cotton gins, textiles, chemicals, oilseed presses, slaughterhouses and a few other small light industries; uranium production began in 1971
Labour Force: 5 million (1999); 85% agriculture, 2.7% industry, 12.3% services
Unemployment: n.a.
Agriculture: accounts for 40% of GDP and 90% of labour force; cash crops—cowpeas, cotton, peanuts; food crops—millet, sorghum, cassava, rice; livestock—cattle, sheep, goats; self-sufficient in food except in drought years
Natural Resources: uranium, coal, iron ore, tin, phosphates, gold, petroleum

■ FINANCE/TRADE

Currency: Communauté financière africaine franc (CFAF) = 100 centimes
International Reserves Excluding Gold: US$51 million (Nov. 2000)
Gold Reserves: US$0.011 million fine troy ounces (Aug. 2000)
Budget: revenues US$377 million; expenditures US$377 million, including capital expenditures of US$105 million (1999 est.)
Defence Expenditures: 6.9% of central government expenditures (1997)
Education Expenditures: 2.3% of GNP (1997)
External Debt: US$1.621 billion (1999)
Exports: US$291 million (2000); commodities: uranium 76%, livestock, cowpeas, onions, hides, skins; partners: n.a.
Imports: US$385 million (2000); commodities: petroleum products, primary materials,

machinery, vehicles and parts, electronic equipment, pharmaceuticals, chemical products, cereals, foodstuffs; partners: n.a.

■ COMMUNICATIONS

Daily Newspapers: 1
Televisions: 27/1,000 inhabitants (1998)
Radios: 69/1,000 inhabitants (1997)
Telephones: 2 lines/1,000 inhabitants (1999)

■ TRANSPORTATION

Motor Vehicles: 51,600; 37,500 passenger cars (1997 est.)
Roads: 10,100 km; 798 km paved
Railway: none
Air Traffic: 86,000 passengers carried (1997)
Airports: 27; 9 have paved runways (1999 est.)
Canadian Embassy: Office of the Canadian Embassy, Boulevard Mali Béro, Niamey, Niger; mailing address: Box 362, Niamey, Niger. Tel: (011-227) 75-36-86. Fax: (011-227) 75-31-07. Email: niamy@dfait-maeci.gc.ca
Embassy in Canada: Embassy of the Republic of Niger, 38 Blackburn Ave, Ottawa ON K1N 8A3. Tel: (613) 232-4291. Fax: (613) 230-9808. Email: n.a.

Nigeria

Long-Form Name: Federal Republic of Nigeria
Capital: Abuja

■ GEOGRAPHY

Area: 923,768 sq. km
Coastline: 853 km
Climate: varies; equatorial in south, tropical in centre, arid in north
Environment: recent droughts in north severely affecting marginal agricultural activities; desertification; soil degradation, rapid deforestation
Terrain: southern lowlands merge into central hills and plateaus; mountains in southeast, plains in north
Land Use: 33% arable; 3% permanent crops; 44% permanent pastures; 12% forest; 8% other, includes 9,570 sq. km irrigated
Location: WC Africa, bordering on South Atlantic Ocean

■ PEOPLE

Population: 123,337,822 (July 2000 est.)
Nationality: Nigerian
Age Structure: 0-14 yrs: 44%; 15-64: 53%; 65+: 3% (2000 est.)
Population Growth Rate: 2.67% (2000 est.)
Net Migration: 0.28 migrants/1,000 population (2000 est.)

Ethnic Groups: more than 250 tribal groups; Hausa and Fulani of the north, Yoruba of the southwest and Ibos of the southeast make up 65% of the population; about 27,000 non-Africans
Languages: English (official); Hausa, Yoruba, Ibo, Fulani and several other languages also widely used
Religions: 50% Muslim, 40% Christian, 10% indigenous beliefs
Birth Rate: 40.16/1,000 population (2000 est.)
Death Rate: 13.72/1,000 population (2000 est.)
Infant Mortality: 74.18 deaths/1,000 live births (2000 est.)
Life Expectancy at Birth: 51.58 years male, 51.55 years female (2000 est.)
Total Fertility Rate: 5.66 children born/woman (2000 est.)
Literacy: 61% (1998)

■ GOVERNMENT

Leader(s): Pres. Olusegun Obasanjo; V. Pres. Atiku Abubakar
Government Type: military government since Dec. 1983; the present regime has announced democratization beginning Oct. 1998
Administrative Divisions: 36 states and 1 territory
Nationhood: Oct. 1, 1960 (from UK)
National Holiday: Independence Day, Oct. 1

■ ECONOMY

Overview: dependent on oil and vulnerable to oil prices; agricultural production cannot keep pace with rapid population growth and Nigeria, once a large exporter of food, must now import foodstuffs; high inflationary pressures are a concern; government efforts to reduce Nigeria's dependence on oil exports and to sustain noninflationary economic growth have been hampered by inadequate new investment and endemic corruption
GDP: US$110.5 billion, per capita US$970; real growth rate 2.7% (1999 est.)
Inflation: 6.94% (year-end 2000)
Industries: accounts for 42% of GDP; crude oil, natural gas, coal, tin, columbite; palm oil, peanut, cotton, rubber, petroleum, wood, hides and skins; textiles, cement, building materials, food products, footwear, chemicals, printing, ceramics, steel
Labour Force: 50 million (1999); 44.6% agriculture, 51.2% services, 4.2% industry
Unemployment: n.a.
Agriculture: accounts for 33% of GDP and half of labour force; inefficient small-scale farming dominates; once a large net exporter of food and now an importer; cash crops—cocoa, peanuts, palm oil, rubber; food crops—corn, rice,

sorghum, millet, cassava, yams, fishing and forestry
Natural Resources: crude oil, tin, columbite, iron ore, coal, limestone, lead, zinc, natural gas

■ FINANCE/TRADE

Currency: naira (N) = 100 kobo
International Reserves Excluding Gold: n.a.
Gold Reserves: US$0.69 million fine troy ounces (Jan. 1997)
Budget: adjusted for purchasing power parity: revenues US$13.9 billion; expenditures US$13.9 billion, including capital expenditures of US$n.a. (1998 est.)
Defence Expenditures: 0.7% of GDP (1999)
Education Expenditures: 0.7% of GNP (1997)
External Debt: US$29.358 billion (1999)
Exports: US$12.187 billion (2000); commodities: oil 95%, cocoa, palm kernels, rubber; partners: European Community 51%, US 32%
Imports: US$14.282 billion (2000); commodities: consumer goods, capital equipment, chemicals, raw materials; partners: European Community, US

■ COMMUNICATIONS

Daily Newspapers: 25
Televisions: 66/1,000 inhabitants (1998)
Radios: 223/1,000 inhabitants (1997)
Telephones: 4 lines/1,000 inhabitants (1999)

■ TRANSPORTATION

Motor Vehicles: 970,000; 590,200 passenger cars (1997 est.)
Roads: 194,394 km; 60,068 km paved
Railway: 3,557 km
Air Traffic: 318,000 passengers carried (1997)
Airports: 71; 37 have paved runways (1999 est.)
Canadian Embassy: The Canadian High Commission, 3A Bobo St, Maitama, Abuja FCT, Nigeria. Tel: (011-234-9) 413-9910. Fax: (011-234-9) 413-9911. Email: abuja@dfait-maeci.gc.ca
Embassy in Canada: High Commission for the Federal Republic of Nigeria, 295 Metcalfe St, Ottawa, ON K2P 1R9. Tel: (613) 236-0522. Fax: (613) 236-0529. Email: hc@nigeriahighcommottawa.com

---

Niue

Long-Form Name: Niue
Capital: Alofi

■ GEOGRAPHY

Area: 260 sq. km, world's largest uplifted coral island

Climate: tropical maritime, modified by southeasterly trade winds
Land Use: 19% arable, 8% permanent crops, 4% meadows and pastures, 19% forest, 50% other; includes n.a. sq. km irrigated
Location: Pacific Ocean, NE of New Zealand

■ PEOPLE

Population: 2,113 (July 2000 est.)
Nationality: Niuean
Ethnic Groups: Polynesian
Languages: English, Polynesian closely related to Tongan and Samoan

■ GOVERNMENT

Colony Territory of: Territory of New Zealand
Leader(s): Head of State: Queen Elizabeth II. Prem. Sani Lakatani
Government Type: self-governing parliamentary democracy in free association with New Zealand
National Holiday: Waitangi Day, Feb. 6

■ ECONOMY

Overview: heavily dependent on aid from New Zealand; govt. expenditures regularly exceed revenues; agriculture includes coconuts, honey, limes, root crops, livestock; chief trading partner: New Zealand

■ FINANCE/TRADE

Currency: New Zealand dollar = 100 cents
Canadian Embassy: c/o The Canadian High Commission, 3rd Fl, 61 Molesworth St, Thorndon, Wellington, New Zealand; Mailing address: c/o P.O. Box 12-049, Thorndon, Wellington, New Zealand. Tel: (011-64-4) 473-9577. Fax: (011-64-4) 471-2082. Email: wlgtn@dfait-maeci.gc.ca
Representative to Canada: c/o New Zealand High Commission, Clarica Centre, 99 Bank St, Ste 727, Ottawa ON K1P 6G3. Tel: (613) 238-5991. Fax: (613) 238-5707. Email: nzhcott@istar.ca

---

Norfolk Island

Long-Form Name: Territory of Norfolk Island
Capital: Kingston (administrative centre), Burnt Pine (commercial centre)

■ GEOGRAPHY

Area: 34.6 sq. km
Climate: subtropical, mild, little seasonal variation
Land Use: 0% arable, 0% permanent crops, 25% meadows and pastures, 0% forests, 75% other; includes no irrigated land

Location: S Pacific Ocean, E of Australia

■ PEOPLE

Population: 1,892 (July 2000 est.)
Nationality: Norfolk Islander
Ethnic Groups: majority descendants of Polynesians and British (the latter crew members of the British naval ship Bounty)
Languages: English (official), Norfolk (a mixture of 18th-century English and ancient Tahitian)

■ GOVERNMENT

Colony Territory of: Dependent Territory of Australia
Leader(s): Queen Elizabeth II, represented by Admin. Anthony J. Messner
Government Type: a largely self-governing dependency, territory of Australia
National Holiday: Pitcairners' Arrival Day Anniversary, June 8

■ ECONOMY

Overview: tourism is backbone of economy; revenues from tourism have helped the agricultural sector become self-sufficient in beef, poultry and eggs; export of indigenous fruit and vegetables

■ FINANCE/TRADE

Currency: Australian dollar = 100 cents
Canadian Embassy: c/o The Canadian High Commission, Commonwealth Ave, Canberra, A.C.T. 2600, Australia. Tel: (011-61-2) 6270-4000. Fax: (011-61-2) 6273-3285. Email: cnbra@dfait-maeci.gc.ca
Representative to Canada: c/o Australian High Commission, 50 O'Connor St, Ste 710, Ottawa ON K1P 6L2. Tel: (613) 236-0841. Fax: (613) 236-4376. Email: n.a.

Northern Marianas

Long-Form Name: The Commonwealth of the Northern Mariana Islands
Capital: Saipan

■ GEOGRAPHY

Area: 477 sq. km (combined land area of 16 islands)
Climate: tropical maritime, moderated by northeasterly trade winds; little seasonal temperature variation
Land Use: 21% arable on Saipan Island; volcanic islands too mountainous for cultivation; chief agricultural use is grazing; 19% meadows and pastures; no irrigated land

Location: Pacific Ocean, E of the Philippines

■ PEOPLE

Population: 71,912 (July 2000 est.)
Nationality: no descriptive term; American citizenship
Ethnic Groups: Chamorro, Carolinians and other Micronesians, Caucasian, Japanese, Chinese, Korea
Languages: English (official), Chamorro, Carolinian, Japanese; 86% of the population speaks a language other than English at home

■ GOVERNMENT

Colony Territory of: Outlying Territory of the United States
Leader(s): Head of State: Pres. George W. Bush (US); Head of Government: Pedro P. Tenorio
Government Type: commonwealth in political union with the US; self-governing with locally elected governing body
National Holiday: Commonwealth Day, Jan. 8

■ ECONOMY

Overview: economy benefits from US financial assistance, but the rate of funding has declined as local revenues have increased; tourism is growing in importance and now employs approximately 50% of the workforce; agriculture: cattle, coconuts, breadfruit, vegetables

■ FINANCE/TRADE

Currency: American dollar = 100 cents
Canadian Embassy: c/o The Canadian Embassy, 501 Pennsylvania Ave. NW, Washington DC 20001, USA. Tel: (202) 682-1740. Fax: (202) 456-7726. Email: wshdc-outpack@dfait-maeci.gc.ca
Representative to Canada: c/o Embassy of the United States of America, 490 Sussex Dr., Ottawa, ON, K1N 1G8. Tel: (613) 238-5335. Fax: (613) 688-3097. Email inquiries are not accepted

Norway

Long-Form Name: Kingdom of Norway
Capital: Oslo

■ GEOGRAPHY

Area: 324,220 sq. km
Coastline: 21,925 km (3,491 km mainland; 2,413 km large islands; 16,093 km long fjords; numerous small islands and minor indentations); one of the longest and most rugged coastlines in the world

Climate: temperate along coast, modified by North Atlantic Current; colder interior; rainy year-round on west coast

Environment: air and water pollution; acid rain damages forests and adversely affects lakes and threatens fish stocks

Terrain: glaciated; mostly high plateaus and rugged mountains broken by fertile valleys; small, scattered plains; coastline deeply indented by fjords; arctic tundra in north

Land Use: 3% arable; 0% permanent crops; negligible meadows, 27% forest; 70% other; includes 970 sq. km irrigated

Location: N Europe, bordering on Norwegian Sea, North Sea

■ PEOPLE

Population: 4,481,162 (July 2000 est.)

Nationality: Norwegian

Age Structure: 0-14 yrs: 20%; 15-64: 65%; 65+: 15% (2000 est.)

Population Growth Rate: 0.50% (2000 est.)

Net Migration: 2.13 migrants/1,000 population (2000 est.)

Ethnic Groups: Germanic (Nordic, Alpine, Baltic) and racial-cultural minority of 20,000 Lapps

Languages: Norwegian (official); small Lapp- and Finnish-speaking minorities

Religions: Lutheran (88%, state church), other Protestant and Roman Catholic 4%, none 3.2%, other 4.8%

Birth Rate: 12.79/1,000 population (2000 est.)

Death Rate: 9.89/1,000 population (2000 est.)

Infant Mortality: 3.98 deaths/1,000 live births (2000 est.)

Life Expectancy at Birth: 75.73 years male, 81.77 years female (2000 est.)

Total Fertility Rate: 1.81 children born/woman (2000 est.)

Literacy: 99% (1998)

■ GOVERNMENT

Leader(s): King Harald V, Prime Min. Jens Stoltenberg

Government Type: constitutional monarchy

Administrative Divisions: 19 provinces (fylker, sing. —fylke); dependent areas inc.: Bouvet Island (uninhabited), Jan Mayen (uninhabited), Peter I Island (uninhabited), Queen Maud Land (uninhabited), Svalbard

Nationhood: Oct. 26, 1905 (from Sweden)

National Holiday: Constitution Day, May 17

■ ECONOMY

Overview: a small country with high dependence on international trade; a prosperous capitalist nation that has extensive welfare measures; concerns are the aging population, increased economic integration with Europe and the balance between private and public influence in economic decisions

GDP: US$111.3 billion, per capita US$25,100; real growth rate 0.8% (1999 est.)

Inflation: 3.09% (year-end 2000)

Industries: accounts for 26.3% of GDP; petroleum and gas, food processing, shipbuilding, pulp and paper products, metal, chemicals, timber, mining, textiles, fishing

Labour Force: 2 million (1999); 38.7% community, social and business services, 17.4% trade and tourism, 14.6% industry

Unemployment: 3.0% (Jan. 2001)

Agriculture: accounts for 2.2% of GDP and 6% of labour force; among world's top 10 fishing nations; livestock output exceeds value of crops; over half of food needs imported

Natural Resources: rich in natural resources: crude oil, copper, natural gas, pyrites, nickel, iron ore, zinc, lead, fish, timber, hydropower

■ FINANCE/TRADE

Currency: krone (pl. kroner) (NKr) = 100 oere

International Reserves Excluding Gold: US$23.174 billion (Jan. 2001)

Gold Reserves: US$1.184 million fine troy ounces (Jan. 2001)

Budget: revenues US$69.7 billion, expenditures US$60.1 billion, including capital expenditures US$n.a. (2000 est.)

Defence Expenditures: 6.39% of total govt. expenditure (1998)

Education Expenditures: 6.79% of central govt. expenditure (1998)

External Debt: none

Exports: US$51.827 billion (2000); commodities: petroleum and petroleum products 25%, natural gas 11%, fish 7%, aluminum 6%, ships 3.5%, pulp and paper; partners: UK 26%, European Free Trade Association 16.3%, less developed countries 14%, Sweden 12%, Germany 12%, US 6%, Denmark 5%

Imports: US$32.527 billion (2000); commodities: machinery, fuels and lubricants, transportation equipment, chemicals, foodstuffs, clothing, ships; partners: Sweden 18%, less developed countries 18%, Germany 14%, Denmark 8%, UK 7%, Japan 5%

■ COMMUNICATIONS

Daily Newspapers: 83

Televisions: 579/1,000 inhabitants (1998)

Radios: 915/1,000 inhabitants (1997)

Telephones: 709 lines/1,000 inhabitants (1999)

■ TRANSPORTATION

Motor Vehicles: 2,210,000; 1,700,000 passenger cars (1997 est.)
Roads: 90,741 km; 67,602 km paved
Railway: 4,012 km
Air Traffic: 13,759,000 passengers carried (1997)
Airports: 103; 67 have paved runways (1999 est.)
Canadian Embassy: The Canadian Embassy, Wergelandsveien #7, 0244 Oslo, Norway. Tel: (011-47) 22-99-53-00. Fax: (011-47) 22-99-53-01. Email: oslo@dfait-maeci.gc.ca
Embassy in Canada: Embassy of the Kingdom of Norway, Royal Bank Centre, 90 Sparks St, Ste 532, Ottawa ON K1P 5B4. Tel: (613) 238-6571. Fax: (613) 238-2765. email: emb.ottawa @mfa.no

Oman

Long-Form Name: Sultanate of Oman
Capital: Masqat or Muscat

■ GEOGRAPHY

Area: 212,460 sq. km
Coastline: 2,092 km
Climate: dry desert; hot, humid along coast; hot, dry interior; strong southwest summer monsoon (May to Sept.) in far south
Environment: summer winds often raise large sandstorms and dust storms in interior; sparse natural freshwater resources are threatened by increasing soil salinity
Terrain: vast central desert plain, rugged mountains in north and south
Land Use: 0% arable; negligible permanent crops; 5% meadows; 0% forest; 95% other; includes 580 sq. km irrigated
Location: SW Asia (Middle East), bordering on Arabian Sea

■ PEOPLE

Population: 2,533,389 (July 2000 est.)
Nationality: Omani
Age Structure: 0-14 yrs: 41%; 15-64: 57%; 65+: 2% (2000 est.)
Population Growth Rate: 3.46% (2000 est.)
Net Migration: 0.65 migrants/1,000 population (2000 est.)
Ethnic Groups: almost entirely Arab, with small Balochi, Zanzibari, Pakistani and Indian groups
Languages: Arabic (official); English, Balochi, Urdu, Indian dialects
Religions: 75% Ibadhi Muslim; remainder Sunni Muslim, Shi'a Muslim, Hindu minority
Birth Rate: 38.08/1,000 population (2000 est.)
Death Rate: 4.16/1,000 population (2000 est.)

Infant Mortality: 23.28 deaths/1,000 live births (2000 est.)
Life Expectancy at Birth: 69.66 years male, 74.00 years female (2000 est.)
Total Fertility Rate: 6.08 children born/woman (2000 est.)
Literacy: 67.1 (1997)

■ GOVERNMENT

Leader(s): Sultan and Prime Min. Qaboos bin Sa'id Al Said
Government Type: absolute monarchy; independent, with residual UK influence
Administrative Divisions: 6 regions (mintaqat, sing. —mintaqah) and 2 governorates (muhafazat, sing. —muhafazah)
Nationhood: 1650, expulsion of the Portuguese
National Holiday: National Day, Nov. 18

■ ECONOMY

Overview: depends on the success of its oil industry, which has 15 years' supply at the current rate of extraction; subsistence agriculture is the major employment, and the general populace relies on imported food
GDP: US$19.6 billion, per capita US$8,000; real growth rate 4% (1999 est.)
Inflation: -1.11% (year-end 2000)
Industries: accounts for 40% of GDP; crude oil production and refining, natural gas production, construction, cement, copper
Labour Force: 1 million (1999); 50% agriculture, 21.8% industry, 28.6% services; 58% of labour force are non-Omani
Unemployment: n.a.
Agriculture: accounts for 3% of GDP and 40% of labour force (including fishing); less than 2% of land cultivated; largely subsistence farming (dates, limes, bananas, alfalfa, vegetables, camels, cattle); not self-sufficient in food
Natural Resources: crude oil, copper, asbestos, some marble, limestone, chromium, gypsum, natural gas

■ FINANCE/TRADE

Currency: Omani rial (RO) = 1,000 baiza
International Reserves Excluding Gold: US$2.175 billion (Jan. 2001)
Gold Reserves: US$0.291 million fine troy ounces (Jan. 2001)
Budget: revenues US$4 billion; expenditures US$5.6 billion, including capital expenditures of US$n.a. (1999 est.)
Defence Expenditures: 32.20% of govt. expenditure (1999)
Education Expenditures: 15.71% of central govt. expenditure (1999)

External Debt: US$3.603 billion (1999)
Exports: US$7.750 billion (2000); commodities: petroleum, re-exports, processed copper, dates, nuts, fish; partners: Japan, S Korea, Thailand
Imports: US$5,215 billion (2000); commodities: machinery, transportation equipment, manufactured goods, food, livestock, lubricants; partners: Japan, United Arab Emirates, UK, Germany, US

■ COMMUNICATIONS

Daily Newspapers: 4
Televisions: 595/1,000 inhabitants (1998)
Radios: 598/1,000 inhabitants (1997)
Telephones: 90 lines/1,000 inhabitants (1999)

■ TRANSPORTATION

Motor Vehicles: 300,000; 209,000 passenger cars (1997 est.)
Roads: 32,800 km; 9,840 km paved
Railway: none
Air Traffic: 1,678,000 passengers carried (1997)
Airports: 142; 6 have paved runways (1999 est.)

Canadian Embassy: The Canadian Embassy to Oman, c/o The Canadian Embassy, P.O. Box 94321, Riyadh 11693, Saudi Arabia. Tel: (011-966-1) 488-2288. Fax: (011-966-1) 488-1997. Email: ryadh@dfait-maeci.gc.ca
Embassy in Canada: c/o Embassy of the Sultanate of Oman, 2535 Belmont Rd. NW, Washington DC 20008, USA. Tel: (202) 387-1980. Fax: (202) 745-4933. Email: n.a.

Pakistan

Long-Form Name: Islamic Republic of Pakistan
Capital: Islamabad

■ GEOGRAPHY

Area: 803,940 sq. km
Coastline: 1,046 km along Gulf of Oman and Arabian Sea
Climate: mostly hot, dry desert; temperate in northwest; arctic in north
Environment: frequent earthquakes, occasionally severe especially in north and west; flooding along the Indus after heavy rains (July and Aug.); deforestation; soil erosion; desertification; water pollution from raw sewage
Terrain: flat Indus plain in east; mountains in north and northwest; Balochistan plateau in west
Land Use: 27% arable; 1% permanent crops; 6% meadows; 5% forest; 61% other, includes 171,100 sq. km irrigated
Location: SW Asia (Middle East), bordering on Arabian Sea

■ PEOPLE

Population: 141,553,775 (July 2000 est.)
Nationality: Pakistani
Age Structure: 0-14 yrs: 41%; 15-64: 55%; 65+: 4% (2000 est.)
Population Growth Rate: 2.17% (2000 est.)
Net Migration: -0.9 migrants/1,000 population (2000 est.)
Ethnic Groups: Punjabi, Sindhi, Pashtun (Pathan), Baloch, Muhajir (immigrants from India and their descendants)
Languages: Urdu (official), Punjab (spoken by majority), Sindhi, Pushto, English
Religions: 97% Muslim (77% Sunni, 20% Shi'a), 3% Christian, Hindu and other
Birth Rate: 32.11/1,000 population (2000 est.)
Death Rate: 9.51/1,000 population (2000 est.)
Infant Mortality: 82.49 deaths/1,000 live births (2000 est.)
Life Expectancy at Birth: 60.27 years male, 61.91 years female (2000 est.)
Total Fertility Rate: 4.56 children born/woman (2000 est.)
Literacy: 43% (1998)

■ GOVERNMENT

Leader(s): Pres. and Chief Exec. Lt.-Gen Pervez Musharraf
Government Type: federal republic
Administrative Divisions: 4 provinces, 1 territory and 1 capital territory
Nationhood: Aug. 14, 1947 (from UK; formerly West Pakistan)
National Holiday: Pakistan Day (proclamation of the republic), Mar. 23

■ ECONOMY

Overview: long-standing economic weaknesses such as indebtedness, a small tax base, large population and dependence on cotton exports hamper the economy
GDP: US$282 billion, per capita US$2,000; real growth rate 3.1% (1999 est.)
Inflation: 4.37% (year-end 2000)
Industries: accounts for 26.6% of GDP; textiles, food processing, beverages, petroleum products, construction materials, clothing, paper products, international finance, shrimp
Labour Force: 50 million (1999); 47.4% agriculture, 12.4% industry, 13.3% community, social and business services
Unemployment: 7% (1999 est.)
Agriculture: 25.2% of GDP, over 50% of labour force; world's largest continuous irrigation system; cotton, wheat, rice, sugar cane, fruits, vegetables, livestock (milk, beef, mutton, eggs); self-sufficient in food grain

Natural Resources: land, extensive natural gas reserves, limited crude oil, poor quality coal, iron ore, copper, salt, limestone

■ FINANCE/TRADE

Currency: Pakistani rupee (PRs) = 100 paisa
International Reserves Excluding Gold: US$1.143 billion (Jan. 2001)
Gold Reserves: US$2.091 million fine troy ounces (Jan. 2001)
Budget: revenues US$10 billion; expenditures US$11.7 billion, including capital expenditures US$n.a. (1998-99)
Defence Expenditures: 3.9% of GDP (1999-00)
Education Expenditures: 2.7% of GNP (1997)
External Debt: US$34.423 billion (1999)
Exports: US$8.696 billion (2000); commodities: rice, cotton, textiles, clothing; partners: European Community 31%, US 11%, Japan 11%
Imports: US$10.522 billion (2000); commodities: petroleum, petroleum products, machinery, transportation, equipment, vegetable oils, animal fats, chemicals; partners: European Community 26%, Japan 15%, US 11%

■ COMMUNICATIONS

Daily Newspapers: 264
Televisions: 88/1,000 inhabitants (1998)
Radios: 98/1,000 inhabitants (1997)
Telephones: 22 lines/1,000 inhabitants (1999)

■ TRANSPORTATION

Motor Vehicles: 1,100,000; 800,000 passenger cars (1997 est.)
Roads: 247,811 km; 141,252 km paved
Railway: 8,163 km
Air Traffic: 5,883,000 passengers carried (1997 est.)
Airports: 118; 82 have paved runways (1999 est.)

Canadian Embassy: The Canadian High Commission, Diplomatic Enclave, Sector G-5, Islamabad; mailing address: The Canadian High Commission, G.P.O. Box 1042, Islamabad, Pakistan. Tel: (011-92-51) 227-91-00. Fax: (011-92-51) 227-91-88. Email: isbad@dfait-maeci.gc.ca
Embassy in Canada: High Commission for the Islamic Republic of Pakistan, Burnside Bldg, 151 Slater St, Ste 608, Ottawa ON K1P 5H3. Tel: (613) 238-7881. Fax: (613) 238-7296. Email: parepottawa@sprint.ca

---

Palau

Long-Form Name: Republic of Palau

Capital: Koror (on Koror Island); a new capital is being built 20 km northeast

■ GEOGRAPHY

Area: 458 sq. km (26 islands and 300+ islets)
Coastline: 1,519 km
Climate: tropical, warm year-round; wet season, May to Dec.; dry season, Jan. to April; typhoon-prone with violent winds and heavy rain, esp. in July
Environment: inadequate facilities for waste management; typhoons
Terrain: about 200 islands; topography varies from high and mountainous to low coral reef islands; northern islands of volcanic origin, fertile and extensively cultivated; southern islands too rugged for habitation
Land Use: n.a.
Location: W Pacific Ocean (Micronesia), E of the Philippines

■ PEOPLE

Population: 18,766 (July 2000 est.)
Nationality: Palauan
Age Structure: 0-14 yrs: 27%; 15-64: 68%; 65+: 5% (2000 est.)
Population Growth Rate: 1.75% (2000 est.)
Net Migration: 5.01 migrants/1,000 population (2000 est.)
Ethnic Groups: Polynesian, Malayan, Melanesian, mixtures
Languages: English (official in all states), Sonsorolese, Angaur, Japanese, Tobi, Palauan
Religions: Christian, Modekngei, a religion indigenous to Palau
Birth Rate: 19.88/1,000 population (2000 est.)
Death Rate: 7.35/1,000 population (2000 est.)
Infant Mortality: 17.12 deaths/1,000 live births (2000 est.)
Life Expectancy at Birth: 65.47 years male, 71.88 years female (2000 est.)
Total Fertility Rate: 2.47 children born/woman (2000 est.)
Literacy: 92% (1997)

■ GOVERNMENT

Leader(s): Pres. Tommy Remengesau, V. Pres. Sandra Pierantozzi
Government Type: constitutional government in free association with the US
Administrative Divisions: 18 states
Nationhood: Oct. 1, 1994 (from US-administered UN trusteeship)
National Holiday: Constitution Day, July 9

■ ECONOMY

Overview: subsistence agriculture and fishing;

some tourism; government is main employer; phosphate deposits on northern islands; largely dependent on imports from the US
GDP: US$160 million, per capita US$8,800; real growth rate 10% (1997 est.)
Inflation: n.a.
Industries: some fishing and agriculture, tourism, crafts, garment making
Labour Force: n.a.
Unemployment: 7%
Agriculture: subsistence-level cultivation of coconuts, copra, yams, cassava
Natural Resources: marine resources, minerals (especially gold), forests

■ FINANCE/TRADE

Currency: American dollar (US$) = 100 cents
International Reserves Excluding Gold: n.a.
Gold Reserves: n.a.
Budget: revenues US$52.9 million; expenditures US$59.9 million, including capital expenditures of USn.a. (1997 est.)
Defence Expenditures: defence is the responsibility of the US
Education Expenditures: n.a.
External Debt: n.a.
Exports: exact figures not available; fish, copra, handicrafts; partners: US, Japan
Imports: exact figures not available; machinery, equipment, fuels; partners: US

■ COMMUNICATIONS

Daily Newspapers: n.a.
Televisions: 586/1,000 inhabitants (1997 est.)
Radios: 639/1,000 inhabitants (1997 est.)
Telephones: n.a.

■ TRANSPORTATION

Motor Vehicles: n.a.
Roads: 61 km; 36 km paved
Railway: none
Air Traffic: n.a.
Airports: 3; 1 has a paved runway (1999 est.)

Canadian Embassy: c/o The Canadian Embassy, 501 Pennsylvania Ave NW, Washington DC 20001, USA. Tel: (202) 682-1740. Fax: (202) 456-7726. email: washdc-outpack@dfait-maeci.gc.ca
Embassy in Canada: c/o Embassy of the United States of America, 490 Sussex Drive, Ottawa, ON, K1N 1G8, Tel: (613) 238-5335. Fax: (613) 688-3097. Email inquiries are not accepted

Panama

Long-Form Name: Republic of Panama
Capital: Panama

■ GEOGRAPHY

Area: 78,200 sq. km
Coastline: 2,490 km
Climate: tropical; hot, humid, cloudy; prolonged rainy season (May to Jan.), short dry season (Jan. to May)
Environment: dense tropical forest in east and northwest is threatened by deforestation; water pollution and soil degradation
Terrain: interior mostly steep, rugged mountains and dissected, upland plains; coastal areas largely plains and rolling hills
Land Use: 7% arable; 2% permanent crops; 20% meadows; 44% forest; 27% other; includes 320 sq. km irrigated
Location: Central (Latin) America, bordering on S America, Caribbean Sea, Pacific Ocean

■ PEOPLE

Population: 2,808,268 (July 2000 est.)
Nationality: Panamanian
Age Structure: 0-14 yrs: 31%; 15-64: 63%; 65+: 6% (2000 est.)
Population Growth Rate: 1.34% (2000 est.)
Net Migration: -1.16 migrants/1,000 population (2000 est.)
Ethnic Groups: 70% mestizo (mixed Indian and European ancestry), 14% West Indian, 10% white, 6% Indian
Languages: Spanish (official), 14% English; many Panamanians are bilingual
Religions: 85% Roman Catholic, 15% Protestant
Birth Rate: 19.53/1,000 population (2000 est.)
Death Rate: 4.98/1,000 population (2000 est.)
Infant Mortality: 20.80 deaths/1,000 live births (2000 est.)
Life Expectancy at Birth: 72.74 years male, 78.31 years female (2000 est.)
Total Fertility Rate: 2.32 children born/woman (2000 est.)
Literacy: 91.5% (1998)

■ GOVERNMENT

Leader(s): Pres. Mireya Elisa Moscoso, First V. Pres. Arturo Ulises Vallarino
Government Type: constitutional republic
Administrative Divisions: 9 provinces (provincias, sing. provincia) and 2 territories (comarca)
Nationhood: Nov. 3, 1903 (from Colombia; became independent from Spain Nov. 28, 1821)
National Holiday: Independence Day, Nov. 3

■ ECONOMY

Overview: political instability, lack of credit and the erosion of business confidence have drastically hurt the economy; exports are stagnant; unemployment and economic reform are two of the greatest challenges the government must face

GDP: US$21billion, per capita US$7,600; real growth rate 4.4% (1999 est.)
Inflation: 1.45% (year-end 2000)
Industries: accounts for 25% of GDP; manufacturing and construction activities, petroleum refining, brewing, cement and other construction materials, sugar mills
Labour Force: 1 million (1999); 26.9% community, social and business services; 26.3% agriculture, 9.5% industry
Unemployment: 13.1% (1997 est.)
Agriculture: accounts for 8% of GDP and 27% of labour force; bananas, rice, corn, coffee, sugar cane, livestock, fishing, importer of food grain, vegetables, milk products
Natural Resources: copper, mahogany forests, shrimp. hydroelectric potential

■ FINANCE/TRADE

Currency: balboa (B) = 100 centesimos
International Reserves Excluding Gold: US$873 million (Jan. 2001)
Gold Reserves: n.a.
Budget: revenues US$2.4 billion; expenditures US$2.4 billion, including capital expenditures of US$341 million (1997 est.)
Defence Expenditures: 3.99% of total govt. expenditure (1998)
Education Expenditures: 17.63% of central govt. expenditure (1998)
External Debt: US$7.313 billion (1999)
Exports: US$833 million (2000); commodities: bananas 40%, shrimp 27%, coffee 4%, sugar, petroleum products; partners: US 90%, Central America and Caribbean, European Community
Imports: US$3.503 billion (2000); commodities: foodstuffs 16%, capital goods 9%, crude oil 16%, consumer goods, chemicals; partners: US 35%, Central America and Caribbean, European Community, Mexico, Venezuela

■ COMMUNICATIONS

Daily Newspapers: 7
Televisions: 187/1,000 inhabitants (1998)
Radios: 299/1,000 inhabitants (1997)
Telephones: 164 lines/1,000 inhabitants (1999)

■ TRANSPORTATION

Motor Vehicles: 226,800; 144,000 passenger cars (1997 est.)
Roads: 11,258 km; 3,783 km paved
Railway: 335 km
Air Traffic: 772,000 passengers carried (1997)
Airports: 115; 41 have paved runways (1999 est.)

Canadian Embassy: The Canadian Embassy, World Trade Center, 1st Floor, Calle 53 Este y Calle 5 B Sur, Urbanización Marbella City, Panama; Postal Address: The Canadian Embassy, Apartado Postal 0832-2446, Estafeta World Trade Center, Panama City, Panama. Tel: (011-507) 264-9731. Fax: (011-507) 263-8083. Email: panama@dfait-maeci.gc.ca
Embassy in Canada: Embassy of the Republic of Panama, 130 Albert St, Ste 300, Ottawa ON K1P 5G4. Tel: (613) 236-7177. Fax: (613) 236-5775. Email: pancanem@travel-net.com

---

Papua New Guinea

Long-Form Name: Independent State of Papua New Guinea
Capital: Port Moresby

■ GEOGRAPHY

Area: 462,840 sq. km
Coastline: 5,152 km
Climate: tropical; northwest monsoon (Dec. to Mar.), southeast monsoon (May to Oct.); slight seasonal temperature variation
Environment: one of the world's largest swamps along southwest coast; some active volcanoes; frequent earthquakes and mudslides; pollution and deforestation
Terrain: mostly mountains with coastal lowlands and rolling foothills
Land Use: 0.1% arable; 1% permanent crops; negligible meadows; 92.9% forest; 6% other; includes n.a. sq. km irrigated
Location: Pacific Ocean, Coral Sea N of Australia

■ PEOPLE

Population: 4,926,984 (July 2000 est.)
Nationality: Papua New Guinean
Age Structure: 0-14 yrs: 39%; 15-64: 58%; 65+: 3% (2000 est.)
Population Growth Rate: 2.47% (2000 est.)
Net Migration: 0 migrants/1,000 population (2000 est.)
Ethnic Groups: predominantly Melanesian and Papuan; some Negrito, Micronesian and Polynesian
Languages: pidgin, English, Motu (all official); also 715 local languages
Religions: 22% Roman Catholic, 16% Lutheran, 8% Presbyterian/Methodist/London Missionary Society, 5% Anglican, 4% Evangelical Alliance, 1% Seventh-Day Adventists, 10% other Protestant sects, 34% indigenous beliefs
Birth Rate: 32.68/1,000 population (2000 est.)
Death Rate: 8.00/1,000 population (2000 est.)
Infant Mortality: 59.89 deaths/1,000 live births (2000 est.)
Life Expectancy at Birth: 61.05 years male, 65.26 years female (2000 est.)

Total Fertility Rate: 4.38 children born/woman (2000 est.)
Literacy: 70% (1998)

■ GOVERNMENT

Leader(s): Head of State: Queen Elizabeth II/Gov. Gen. Silas Atopare. Prime Min. Mekere Morauta
Government Type: parliamentary democracy
Administrative Divisions: 20 provinces
Nationhood: Sept. 16, 1975 (from UN trusteeship under Australian administration)
National Holiday: Independence Day, Sept. 16

■ ECONOMY

Overview: country has abundant natural resources but exploitation has been hampered by the rugged terrain and the high cost of developing an infrastructure; subsistence agriculture is the livelihood for 85% of the population; mining accounts for about 60% of export earnings
GDP: US$11.6 billion, per capita US$2,500; real growth rate 3.6% (1999 est.)
Inflation: 14.93% (year-end 1999)
Industries: accounts for 34.5% of GDP; copra crushing, oil palm processing, plywood processing, wood chip production, gold, silver, copper, construction, tourism
Labour Force: 2 million (1999); 85% agriculture, 10.2% industry,
Unemployment: n.a.
Agriculture: 28.2% of GDP; fertile soils and favourable climate permits cultivating a wide variety of crops; cash crops: coffee, cocoa, coconuts, palm kernels; other products: tea, rubber, sweet potatoes, fruit, vegetables, poultry, pork; net importer of food for urban centres
Natural Resources: gold, copper, silver, natural gas, timber, oil potential, fisheries

■ FINANCE/TRADE

Currency: kina (K) = 100 toea
International Reserves Excluding Gold: US$240 million (May 2000)
Gold Reserves: US$0.063 million fine troy ounces (May 2000)
Budget: revenues US$1.6 billion; expenditures US$1.9 billion, including capital expenditures (1998 est.)
Defence Expenditures: 1.0% of GDP (1998)
Education Expenditures: 22.06% of central govt. expenditure (1999)
External Debt: US$2.847 billion (1999)
Exports: US$2.095 billion (2000); commodities: gold, copper ore, coffee, copra, palm oil, timber, lobster; partners: Germany, Japan, Australia, UK, Spain, US
Imports: US$1.643 billion (2000); commodities: machinery and transport equipment, fuels, food, chemicals, consumer goods; partners: Australia, Singapore, Japan, US, New Zealand, UK

■ COMMUNICATIONS

Daily Newspapers: 2
Televisions: 24/1,000 inhabitants (1998)
Radios: 97/1,000 inhabitants (1997)
Telephones: 13 lines/1,000 inhabitants (1999)

■ TRANSPORTATION

Motor Vehicles: 99,300; 21,600 passenger cars (1997 est.)
Roads: 19,600 km; 686 km paved
Railway: none
Air Traffic: 1,114,000 passengers carried (1997)
Airports: 492; 19 have paved runways (1999 est.)

Canadian Embassy: The Canadian High Commission to Papua New Guinea, c/o The Canadian High Commission, Commonwealth Ave, Canberra A.C.T. 2600, Australia. Tel: (011-61-2) 6270-4000. Fax: (011-61-2) 6273-3285. Email: cnbra@dfait-maeci.gc.ca
Embassy in Canada: c/o High Commission for Papua New Guinea, 1779 Massachusetts Ave NW, Ste 805, Washington DC 20036, USA. Tel: (202) 745-3680. Fax: (202) 745-3679. Email: KunduWash@aol.com

---

Paraguay

Long-Form Name: Republic of Paraguay
Capital: Asunción

■ GEOGRAPHY

Area: 406,750 sq. km
Coastline: none: landlocked
Climate: subtropical; varies from temperate in east to semi-arid in far west
Environment: local flooding in southeast (early Sept. to June); poorly drained plains may become boggy (early Oct. to June); deforestation and water pollution are increasing
Terrain: grassy plains and wooded hills east of Río Paraguay; Gran Chaco region west of Río Paraguay mostly low, marshy plain near the river and dry forest and thorny scrub elsewhere
Land Use: 6% arable; 0% permanent crops; 55% permanent pastures; 32% forest; 7% other; includes 670 sq. km irrigated
Location: C South America

■ PEOPLE

Population: 5,585,828 (July 2000 est.)
Nationality: Paraguayan
Age Structure: 0-14 yrs: 39%; 15-64: 56%; 65+: 5% (2000 est.)
Population Growth Rate: 2.64% (2000 est.)
Net Migration: -0.09 migrants/1,000 population (2000 est.)
Ethnic Groups: 95% mestizo (Spanish and Indian), 5% white and Indian
Languages: Spanish (official), Guarani
Religions: 90% Roman Catholic; 10% Mennonite and other Protestant denominations
Birth Rate: 31.27/1,000 population (2000 est.)
Death Rate: 4.81/1,000 population (2000 est.)
Infant Mortality: 30.81 deaths/1,000 live births (2000 est.)
Life Expectancy at Birth: 71.22 years male, 76.27 years female (2000 est.)
Total Fertility Rate: 4.16 children born/woman (2000 est.)
Literacy: 92.5% (1998)

■ GOVERNMENT

Leader(s): Pres. Luis Angel Gonzalez Macchi, V. Pres. Julio Cesar Franco
Government Type: constitutional republic
Administrative Divisions: 17 departments (departamentos, sing. —departamento) and 1 capital city
Nationhood: May 14, 1811 (from Spain)
National Holiday: Independence Days, May 14–15

■ ECONOMY

Overview: in the absence of significant mineral or petroleum resources, the economy is based on agriculture; has a large hydroelectric power potential; is vulnerable to climatic conditions and international commodity prices for agricultural exports; nontraditional exports are growing rapidly
GDP: US$19.9 billion, per capita US$3,650; real growth rate -1% (1999 est.)
Inflation: 8.98% (year-end 2000)
Industries: accounts for 21% of GDP; meat packing, oilseed crushing, milling, brewing, textiles, other light consumer goods, cement, construction
Labour Force: 2 million (1999); 26.8% trade and tourism, 17.7% industry, 33.1% services
Unemployment: 12% (1998 est.)
Agriculture: accounts for 28% GDP and 45% of labour force; cash crops: cotton, sugar cane; other crops: corn, wheat, tobacco, soybeans, cassava, fruit and vegetables; animal products:

beef, pork, eggs, milk; surplus producer of timber; self-sufficient in most foods
Natural Resources: iron ore, manganese, limestone, hydropower, timber

■ FINANCE/TRADE

Currency: guaraní (pl. guaraníes) (G/) = 100 centimos
International Reserves Excluding Gold: US$661 million (Jan. 2001)
Gold Reserves: US$0.035 million fine troy ounces (Jan. 2001)
Budget: n.a.
Defence Expenditures: 1.4% of GDP (1998)
Education Expenditures: 4.0% of GNP (1997)
External Debt: US$2.514 billion (1999)
Exports: US$1.237 billion (2000); commodities: cotton, soybeans, timber, vegetable oils, coffee, tung oil, meat products; partners: European Community 37%, Brazil 25%, Argentina 10%, Chile 6%, US 6%
Imports: US$3.697 billion (2000); commodities: capital goods 35%, consumer goods 20%, fuels and lubricants 19%, raw materials 16%, foodstuffs, beverages and tobacco 10%; partners: Brazil 30%, European Community 20%, US 18%, Argentina 8%, Japan 7%

■ COMMUNICATIONS

Daily Newspapers: 5
Televisions: 101/1,000 inhabitants (1998)
Radios: 182/1,000 inhabitants (1997)
Telephones: 55 lines/1,000 inhabitants (1999)

■ TRANSPORTATION

Motor Vehicles: 121,000; 71,000 passenger cars (1997 est.)
Roads: 29,500 km; 15,000 km paved
Railway: 971 km
Air Traffic: 196,000 passengers carried (1997)
Airports: 937; 10 have paved runways (1999 est.)

Canadian Embassy: The Canadian Embassy to Paraguay, 1598 Casilla de Correo, 1425 Buenos Aires, Argentina. Tel: (011-54-11) 4805-3032. Fax: (011-54-11) 4806-1209. Email: bairs@dfait-maeci.gc.ca
Embassy in Canada: Embassy of the Republic of Paraguay, 151 Slater St, Ste 501, Ottawa, ON K1P 5H3. Tel: (613) 567-1283. Fax: (613) 567-1679. Email: embapar@magmacom.com

---

Peru

Long-Form Name: Republic of Peru
Capital: Lima

■ GEOGRAPHY

Area: 1,285,220 sq. km
Coastline: 2,414 km
Climate: varies from tropical in east to dry desert in west
Environment: subject to earthquakes, tsunamis, landslides, mild volcanic activity; deforestation; overgrazing; soil erosion; desertification; air pollution in Lima; shares control of Lago Titicaca, world's highest navigable lake, with Bolivia
Terrain: western coastal plain (costa), high and rugged Andes in centre (sierra), eastern lowland jungle of Amazon Basin (selva)
Land Use: 3% arable: negligible permanent crops; 21% meadows; 66% forest; 10% other, includes 12,800 sq. km irrigated
Location: W South America, bordering on Pacific Ocean

■ PEOPLE

Population: 27,012,899 (July 2000 est.)
Nationality: Peruvian
Age Structure: 0-14 yrs: 35%; 15-64: 61%; 65+: 4% (2000 est.)
Population Growth Rate: 1.75% (2000 est.)
Net Migration: -1.1 migrants/1,000 population (2000 est.)
Ethnic Groups: 45% Indian; 37% mestizo (mixed Indian and European ancestry); 15% white; 3% black, Japanese, Chinese and other
Languages: Spanish and Quechua (official), Aymara
Religions: predominantly Roman Catholic
Birth Rate: 24.48/1,000 population (2000 est.)
Death Rate: 5.84/1,000 population (2000 est.)
Infant Mortality: 40.60 deaths/1,000 live births (2000 est.)
Life Expectancy at Birth: 67.63 years male, 72.50 years female (2000 est.)
Total Fertility Rate: 3.04 children born/woman (2000 est.)
Literacy: 89% (1998)

■ GOVERNMENT

Leader(s): Pres. Alejandro Toledo, Prime Min. Roberto Dañino
Government Type: constitutional republic
Administrative Divisions: 24 departments (departamentos, sing. —departamento) and 1 constitutional province (provincia constitucional)
Nationhood: July 28, 1821 (from Spain)
National Holiday: Independence Day, July 28

■ ECONOMY

Overview: revival of growth in GDP continues to be restricted by the large amount of public and private resources being devoted to strengthening internal security; deficit spending and poor relations with international lenders are problems; labour unrest has cut production; food shortages; world's largest producer of coca (for cocaine)
GDP: US$116 billion, per capita US$4,400; real growth rate 2.4% (1999 est.)
Inflation: 3.76% (year-end 2000)
Industries: accounts for 42% of GDP, mining of metals, petroleum, fishing, textiles, clothing, food processing, cement, auto assembly, steel, shipbuilding, metal fabrication
Labour Force: 9 million (1999); 34.1% trade and tourism, 28.6% community, social and business services, 6% finance
Unemployment: 7.7%, plus extensive underemployment (1997)
Agriculture: accounts for 13% of GDP and 35% of labour force; commercial crops: coffee, cotton, sugar cane; other crops: rice, wheat, potatoes, plantains, coca; animal products: poultry, meats, dairy, wool; not self-sufficient in grain or vegetable oil; fish catch of 6.9 million metric tons
Natural Resources: copper, silver, gold, petroleum, timber, fish, iron ore, coal, phosphate, potash

■ FINANCE/TRADE

Currency: nuevo sol (pl. soles) (S/.) = 100 centimos
International Reserves Excluding Gold: US$8.363 billion (Jan. 2001)
Gold Reserves: US$1.100 million fine troy ounces (Jan. 2001)
Budget: n.a.
Defence Expenditures: 1.4% of GDP (1998)
Education Expenditures: 2.9% of GNP (1997)
External Debt: US$32.284 billion (1999)
Exports: US$7.002 billion (2000); commodities: fishmeal, cotton, sugar, coffee, copper, iron ore, refined silver, lead, zinc, crude petroleum and by-products; partners: European Community 22%, US 20%, Japan 11%, Latin America 8%, former USSR countries 4%
Imports: US$8.797 billion (2000); commodities: foodstuffs, machinery, transport equipment, iron and steel semimanufactures, chemicals, pharmaceuticals; partners: US 23%, Latin America 16%, European Community 12%, Japan 7%, Switzerland 3%

■ COMMUNICATIONS

Daily Newspapers: 74
Televisions: 144/1,000 inhabitants (1998)
Radios: 273/1,000 inhabitants (1997)
Telephones: 67 lines/1,000 inhabitants (1999)

■ TRANSPORTATION

Motor Vehicles: 775,000; 500,000 passenger cars (1997 est.)
Roads: 72,900 km; 8,700 km paved
Railway: 1,988 km
Air Traffic: 2,725,000 passengers carried (1997)
Airports: 234; 44 have paved runways (1999 est.)

Canadian Embassy: The Canadian Embassy, Calle Libertad 130, Miraflores, Lima, Peru; mailing address: Casilla 18-1126, Correo Miraflores, Lima, Peru. Tel: (011-51-1) 444-4015. Fax: (011-51-1)242-4050. Email: lima@dfait-maeci.gc.ca
Embassy in Canada: Embassy of the Republic of Peru, 130 Albert St, Ste 1901, Ottawa ON K1P 5G4. Tel: (613) 238-1777. Fax: (613) 232-3062. Email: embperuca@sprint.ca

Philippines

Long-Form Name: Republic of the Philippines
Capital: Manila

■ GEOGRAPHY

Area: 300,000 sq. km
Coastline: 36,289 km
Climate: tropical marine; northeast monsoon (Nov. to Apr.); southwest monsoon (May to Oct.)
Environment: astride typhoon belt, usually affected by 15 and struck by five to six cyclonic storms per year; subject to landslides, active volcanoes, destructive earthquakes, tsunami; deforestation; soil erosion; water pollution
Terrain: mostly mountains with narrow to extensive coastal lowlands
Land Use: 19% arable; 12% permanent crops; 4% meadows; 46% forest; 19% other, includes 15,800 sq. km irrigated
Location: SE of China, bordering on South China Sea, Pacific Ocean

■ PEOPLE

Population: 81,159,644 (July 2000 est.)
Nationality: Filipino
Age Structure: 0-14 yrs: 37%; 15-64: 59%; 65+: 4% (2000 est.)
Population Growth Rate: 2.07% (2000 est.)
Net Migration: -1.02 migrants/1,000 population (2000 est.)
Ethnic Groups: 91.5% Christian Malay, 4% Muslim Malay, 1.5% Chinese, 3% other
Languages: Pilipino (native national language based on Tagalog) and English (both official); Spanish also spoken, also 76 indigenous languages including Cebuano, Tagalog, Iloco, Ifugao

Religions: 83% Roman Catholic, 9% Protestant, 5% Muslim, 3% Buddhist and other
Birth Rate: 27.85/1,000 population (2000 est.)
Death Rate: 6.13/1,000 population (2000 est.)
Infant Mortality: 29.52 deaths/1,000 live births (2000 est.)
Life Expectancy at Birth: 64.65 years male, 70.46 years female (2000 est.)
Total Fertility Rate: 3.48 children born/woman (2000 est.)
Literacy: 95% (1998)

■ GOVERNMENT

Leader(s): Pres. Gloria Macapagal-Arroyo, V. Pres. Teofisto Guingona
Government Type: republic
Administrative Divisions: 14 regions, divided into 73 provinces and 61 chartered cities
Nationhood: July 4, 1946 (from US)
National Holiday: Independence Day (from Spain), June 12

■ ECONOMY

Overview: drought and power supply problems have hampered production; world's largest exporter of coconuts and coconut products
GDP: US$282 billion, per capita US$3,600; real growth rate 2.9% (1999 est.)
Inflation: 4.36% (year-end 2000)
Industries: accounts for 32% of GDP; textiles, pharmaceuticals, chemicals, wood products, food processing, electronics assembly, petroleum refining, fishing
Labour Force: 32 million (1999); 45.8% agriculture, 17.1% community, social and business services, 9.5% industry
Unemployment: 9.6% (Oct. 1998)
Agriculture: accounts for about 20% of GDP and 45% of labour force; major crops: rice, coconuts, corn, sugarcane, bananas, pineapples, mangoes; animal products: pork, eggs, beef: net exporter of farm products: fish catch of 2 million metric tons annually
Natural Resources: timber, crude oil, nickel, cobalt, silver, gold, salt, copper

■ FINANCE/TRADE

Currency: peso (P) = 100 centavos
International Reserves Excluding Gold: US$12.460 billion (Jan. 2001)
Gold Reserves: US$7.268 million fine troy ounces (Jan. 2001)
Budget: revenues US$14.5 billion; expenditures US$12.6 billion, including capital expenditures US$n.a. (1998 est.)
Defence Expenditures: 5.10% of total govt. expenditure (1999)
Education Expenditures: 19.42% of central govt. expenditure (1999)

External Debt: US$52.022 billion (1999)
Exports: US$29.464 billion (2000); commodities: electrical equipment 19%, textiles 16%, minerals and ores 11%, farm products 10%, coconut 10%, chemicals 5%, fish 5%, forest products 4%; partners: US 36%, European Community 19%, Japan 18%, ESCAP 9%, ASEAN 7%
Imports: US$25.468 billion (2000); commodities: raw materials 53%, capital goods 17%, petroleum products 17%; partners: US 25%, Japan 17%, Economic and Social Commission for Asia and Pacific 13%, European Community 11%, Association of Southeast Asian Nations 10%, Middle East 10%

■ COMMUNICATIONS

Daily Newspapers: 47
Televisions: 108/1,000 inhabitants (1998)
Radios: 159/1,000 inhabitants (1997)
Telephones: 39 lines/1,000 inhabitants (1999)

■ TRANSPORTATION

Motor Vehicles: n.a.
Roads: 199,950 km; 39,590 km paved
Railway: 897 km; 492 km operational
Air Traffic: 7,475,000 passengers carried (1997)
Airports: 266; 76 have paved runways (1999 est.)

Canadian Embassy: The Canadian Embassy, 9th and 11th Fl, Allied Bank Centre, 6754 Ayala Ave, Makati, Manila, Philippines; mailing address: P.O. Box 2168, Makati CPO 1261, Manila, Philippines. Tel: (011-63-2) 867-0001. Fax: (011-63-2) 810-4299. Email: manil@dfait-maeci.gc.ca
Embassy in Canada: Embassy of the Republic of the Philippines, 130 Albert St, Ste 606, Ottawa ON K1P 5G4. Tel: (613) 233-1121. Fax: (613) 233-4165. Email: ottawape@istar.ca

---

Pitcairn Islands

Long-Form Name: Pitcairn, Henderson, Ducie and Oeno Islands
Capital: Adamstown

■ GEOGRAPHY

Area: 47 sq. km (Pitcairn and 3 small uninhabited islands)
Climate: tropical, hot, humid, modified by southeasterly trade winds; rainy season from Nov. to March
Land Use: rugged but fertile interior
Location: S Pacific Ocean, E of French Polynesia

■ PEOPLE

Population: 54 (July 2000 est.)

Nationality: Pitcairn Islander
Ethnic Groups: descendants of Polynesians and British (the latter crew members of the British naval ship Bounty)
Languages: English (official), Tahitian-English dialect

■ GOVERNMENT

Colony Territory of: Dependent Territory of the United Kingdom
Leader(s): Head of State: Queen Elizabeth II (UK)
Government Type: dependency of the UK
National Holiday: Celebration of the Birthday of the Queen, second Saturday in June

■ ECONOMY

Overview: inhabitants subsist on fishing and farming; fertile soil of the valleys produces wide variety of fruit and vegetables; bartering is an important part of the economy; imports: fuel oil, machinery, building materials; no exports other than small tourist trade with passing ships

■ FINANCE/TRADE

Currency: New Zealand dollar = 100 cents

Canadian Embassy: c/o The Canadian High Commission, Macdonald House, 1 Grosvenor Square, London, W1K 4AB. Tel: (011-44-20) 7258-6600. Fax: (011-44-20) 7258-6333. Email: Ldn@dfait-maeci.gc.ca
Representative to Canada: c/o British High Commission, 80 Elgin St, Ottawa ON K1P 5K7. Tel: (613) 237-1530. Fax: (613) 237-7980. Email should be sent using the appropriate form at the British High Commission's website at http://www.britain-in-canada.org

---

Poland

Long-Form Name: Republic of Poland
Capital: Warsaw

■ GEOGRAPHY

Area: 312,683 sq. km
Coastline: 491 km along Baltic Sea
Climate: temperate with cold, cloudy, moderately severe winters with frequent precipitation; mild summers with frequent showers and thundershowers
Environment: plain crossed by a few meandering streams; severe air and water pollution in south; flat terrain; lack of natural barriers; recently there has been severe flooding
Terrain: mostly flat plain, mountains along southern border
Land Use: 47% arable; 1% permanent crops;

13% meadows; 29% forest; 10% other; includes 1,000 sq. km irrigated
Location: NE Europe, bordering on Baltic Sea

■ PEOPLE

Population: 38,646,023 (July 2000 est.)
Nationality: Polish, Pole
Age Structure: 0-14 yrs: 19%; 15-64: 69%; 65+: 12% (2000 est.)
Population Growth Rate: -0.04 (2000 est.)
Net Migration: -0.49 migrants/1,000 population (2000 est.)
Ethnic Groups: 97.6% Polish, 1.3% German, 0.6% Ukrainian, 0.5% Byelorussian
Languages: Polish
Religions: 95% Roman Catholic (about 75% practising), 5% Russian Orthodox, Protestant and other
Birth Rate: 10.13/1,000 population (2000 est.)
Death Rate: 9.99/1,000 population (2000 est.)
Infant Mortality: 9.61 deaths/1,000 live births (2000 est.)
Life Expectancy at Birth: 69.01 years male, 77.60 years female (2000 est.)
Total Fertility Rate: 1.38 children born/woman (2000 est.)
Literacy: 99% (1998)

■ GOVERNMENT

Leader(s): Pres. Aleksander Kwasniewski, Prime Minister Leszek Miller
Government Type: republic
Administrative Divisions: 16 provinces (wojewodztwa, sing. -wojewodztwo)
Nationhood: Nov. 11, 1918, independent republic proclaimed
National Holiday: Constitution Day, May 3; Independence Day, Nov. 11

■ ECONOMY

Overview: continues to make good progress in the difficult transition to a free-market economy; in contrast to the vibrant expansion of private non-farm activity, the large agricultural component remains handicapped by structural problems, surplus labour, inefficient small farms, and lack of investment
GDP: US$276.5 billion, per capita US$7,200; real growth rate 3.8% (1999 est.)
Inflation: 10.13% (year-end 2000)
Industries: accounts for 31% of GDP, machine building, iron and steel, extractive industries, chemicals, shipbuilding, food processing, glass, beverages, textiles
Labour Force: 20 million (1999); 26.7% agriculture, 24.3% industry, 18.7% community, social and business services
Unemployment: 15.6% (Jan. 2001)

Agriculture: accounts for 5% GDP and 27% of labour force; 75% of output from private farms, 25% from state farms; low productivity; leading European producer of rye, rapeseed and potatoes; wide variety of other crops and livestock; major exporter of pork products
Natural Resources: coal, sulphur, copper, natural gas, silver, lead, salt

■ FINANCE/TRADE

Currency: zloty (pl. zlotych) (Zl) = 100 groszy
International Reserves Excluding Gold: US$26.562 billion (Dec. 2000)
Gold Reserves: US$3.306 million fine troy ounces (Dec. 2000)
Budget: revenues US$31.6 billion; expenditures US$34.8 billion, including capital expenditures US$n.a. (1999 est.)
Defence Expenditures: 4.15% of total govt. expenditure (1999)
Education Expenditures: 4.67% of total govt. expenditure (1999)
External Debt: US$54.268 billion (1999)
Exports: US$30.615 billion (2000); commodities: machinery and equipment 63%, fuels, minerals and metals 14%, manufactured consumer goods 14%, agricultural and forestry products 5%; partners: former USSR countries 25%, Germany 12%, Czech and Slovak Republics 6%
Imports: US$48.346 billion (2000); commodities: machinery and equipment 36%, fuels, minerals and metals 35%, manufactured consumer goods 9%, agricultural and forestry products 12%; partners: former USSR countries 23%, Germany 13%, Czech and Slovak Republics 6%

■ COMMUNICATIONS

Daily Newspapers: 55
Televisions: 413/1,000 inhabitants (1998)
Radios: 523/1,000 inhabitants (1997)
Telephones: 263 lines/1,000 inhabitants (1999)

■ TRANSPORTATION

Motor Vehicles: 9,120,000; 7,580,000 passenger cars (1997 est.)
Roads: 381,046 km; 249,966 km paved
Railway: 23,420 km
Air Traffic: 1,998,000 passengers carried (1997)
Airports: 123; 85 have paved runways (1999 est.)
Canadian Embassy: The Canadian Embassy, Reform Plaza, 10th Fl, Aleje Jerozolimski 123, 02-017 Warsaw, Poland. Tel: (011-48-22) 584-3100. Fax: (011-48-22) 584-3190. Email: wsaw@dfait-maeci.gc.ca
Embassy in Canada: Embassy of the Republic of Poland, 443 Daly Ave, Ottawa ON K1N 6H3.

Tel: (613) 789-0468. Fax: (613) 789-1218.
Email: n.a.

Portugal

Long-Form Name: Portuguese Republic
Capital: Lisbon

■ GEOGRAPHY

Area: 92,391 sq. km; includes Azores and
Madeira Islands
Coastline: 1,793 km
Climate: maritime temperature; cool and rainy in
north, warmer and drier in south
Environment: air pollution and soil degradation
are accelerating; coastal water pollution; Azores
subject to severe earthquakes
Terrain: mountainous north, rolling plains in
south
Land Use: 26% arable; 9% permanent crops; 9%
meadows; 36% forest; 20% other, includes
6,300 sq, km irrigated
Location: SW Europe, bordering on North
Atlantic Ocean

■ PEOPLE

Population: 10,048,232 (July 2000 est.)
Nationality: Portuguese
Age Structure: 0-14 yrs: 17%; 15-64: 68%; 65+:
15% (2000 est.)
Population Growth Rate: 0.18% (2000 est.)
Net Migration: 0.50 migrants/1,000 population
(2000 est.)
Ethnic Groups: homogeneous Mediterranean
stock in mainland, Azores and Madeira Islands;
citizens of black African descent who
immigrated to mainland during decolonization
number less than 100,000
Languages: Portuguese (official), English,
French
Religions: 97% Roman Catholic, 1% Protestant,
2% other
Birth Rate: 11.49/1,000 population (2000 est.)
Death Rate: 10.20/1,000 population (2000 est.)
Infant Mortality: 6.05 deaths/1,000 live births
(2000 est.)
Life Expectancy at Birth: 72.24 years male, 79.49
years female (2000 est.)
Total Fertility Rate: 1.47 children born/woman
(2000 est.)
Literacy: 91.5% (1998)

■ GOVERNMENT

Leader(s): Pres. Jorge Sampaio, Prem. Antonio
Guterres
Government Type: parliamentary democracy
Administrative Divisions: 18 districts (distritos,
sing. -distrito) and 2 autonomous regions
(regioes autonomas, sing. -regiao autonoma)
Nationhood: 1140; independent republic
proclaimed Oct. 5, 1910
National Holiday: Day of Portugal, June 10

■ ECONOMY

Overview: the economy has grown recently due
to strong domestic consumption and investment
spending; government is promoting
privatization measures; the global slowdown
and tight financial policies to combat inflation
have caused economic growth to slow
GDP: US$151.4 billion, per capita US$15,300;
real growth rate 3.2% (1999 est.)
Inflation: 2.87% (year-end 2000)
Industries: accounts for 36% of GDP; textiles
and footwear; wood pulp, paper and cork;
metalworking; oil refining; chemicals; fish
canning; wine; tourism
Labour Force: 5 million (1999); 24.8%
community, social and business services, 23.4%
industry, 19.5% trade and tourism
Unemployment: 4.6% (1999 est.)
Agriculture: accounts for 4% of GDP and 20% of
labour force; small inefficient farms; imports
more than half of food needs; major crops:
grain, potatoes, olives, grapes; livestock sector:
sheep, cattle, goats, poultry, meat, dairy
products
Natural Resources: fish, forests (cork), tungsten,
iron ore, uranium ore, marble

■ FINANCE/TRADE

Currency: escudo (Esc) = 100 centavos; Euro
(EUR) as of March 1, 2002
International Reserves Excluding Gold: US$9.049
billion (Jan. 2001)
Gold Reserves: US$19.506 million fine troy
ounces (Jan. 2001)
Budget: n.a.
Defence Expenditures: 2.6% of GDP (1997)
Education Expenditures: 5.8% of GNP (1997)
External Debt: US$13.1 billion (1997 est.)
Exports: US$23.035 billion (2000); com-
modities: cotton textiles, cork and cork
products, canned fish, wine, timber and timber
products, resin, machinery, appliances; partners:
European Community 72%, other developed
countries 13%, US 6%
Imports: US$37.981 billion (2000); com-
modities: petroleum, cotton, foodgrains,
industrial machinery, iron and steel, chemicals;
partners: European Community 67%, other
developed countries 13%, less developed
countries 15%, US 4%

■ COMMUNICATIONS

Daily Newspapers: 27
Televisions: 542/1,000 inhabitants (1998)
Radios: 304/1,000 inhabitants (1997)
Telephones: 423 lines/1,000 inhabitants (1999)

■ TRANSPORTATION

Motor Vehicles: 3,680,700; 2,750,000 passenger cars (1997 est.)
Roads: 68,732 km; 59,110 km surfaced
Railway: 2,850 km
Air Traffic: 6,281,000 passengers carried (1997)
Airports: 66; 40 have paved runways (1999 est.)

Canadian Embassy: The Canadian Embassy, Avenida da Liberdade, 196-200, 3rd Floor, 1269-121 Lisbon, Portugal. Tel: (011-351) 21-316-46-00. Fax: (011-351) 21-316-46-91. Email: lsbon@dfait-maeci.gc.ca
Embassy in Canada: Embassy of Portugal, 645 Island Park Dr, Ottawa ON K1Y 0B8. Tel: (613) 729-0883. Fax: (613) 729-4236. Email: embportugal@embportugal-ottawa.org

---

Puerto Rico

Long-Form Name: Commonwealth of Puerto Rico
Capital: San Juan

■ GEOGRAPHY

Area: 9,104 sq. km
Climate: tropical marine, mild, little seasonal temperature variation
Land Use: 4% arable; 5% permanent crops; 26% permanent pastures; 16% forest; 49% other, includes 390 sq. km irrigated
Location: West Indies, bordering on Caribbean Sea, Atlantic Ocean

■ PEOPLE

Population: 3,915,798 (July 2000 est.)
Nationality: Puerto Rican (US citizens)
Ethnic Groups: almost entirely Hispanic
Languages: Spanish (official); English is widely understood

■ GOVERNMENT

Colony Territory of: Commonwealth associated with the US
Leader(s): Pres. George W. Bush, Gov. Sila Maria Calderon
Government Type: commonwealth associated with the US
National Holiday: US Independence Day, July 4

■ ECONOMY

Overview: economy (one of the most dynamic in the Caribbean region) has benefited from heavy US investment; new industries include pharmaceuticals and electronics; tourism is important; sugar production has lost out to dairy production and other livestock products as the main facet of the agricultural sector

■ FINANCE/TRADE

Currency: American dollar ($US) = 100 cents

Canadian Embassy: c/o The Canadian Embassy, 501 Pennsylvania Ave NW, Washington DC 20001, USA. Tel: (202) 682-1740. Fax: (202) 456-7726. Email: wshdc-outpack@dfait-maeci.gc.ca
Representative to Canada: c/o Embassy of the United States of America, 490 Sussex Drive, Ottawa, ON, K1N 1G8. Tel: (613) 238-5335. Fax: (613) 688-3097. Email inquiries are not accepted

---

Qatar

Long-Form Name: State of Qatar
Capital: Doha

■ GEOGRAPHY

Area: 11,437 sq. km
Coastline: 563 km
Climate: desert; hot, dry; humid and sultry in summer
Environment: haze, dust storms, sandstorms common; limited freshwater resources mean increasing dependence on large-scale desalination facilities
Terrain: mostly flat and barren desert covered with loose sand and gravel
Land Use: 1% arable; 0% permanent crops; 5% meadows; 0% forest; 94% other; includes 80 sq. km irrigated
Location: SW Asia (Middle East, Arabian Peninsula), bordering on Persian Gulf

■ PEOPLE

Population: 744,483 (July 2000 est.)
Nationality: Qatari
Age Structure: 0-14 yrs: 26%; 15-64: 71%; 65+: 3% (2000 est.)
Population Growth Rate: 3.35% (2000 est.)
Net Migration: 21.58 migrants/1,000 population (2000 est.)
Ethnic Groups: 40% Arab, 18% Pakistani, 18% Indian, 10% Iranian, 14% other
Languages: Arabic (official); English is commonly used as second language

Religions: Islam (native Qataris—less than one-third of the population—principally adhere to orthodox Wahhabi sect of Sunni Muslims)
Birth Rate: 16.07/1,000 population (2000 est.)
Death Rate: 4.19/1,000 population (2000 est.)
Infant Mortality: 22.14 deaths/1,000 live births (2000 est.)
Life Expectancy at Birth: 69.92 years male, 74.94 years female (2000 est.)
Total Fertility Rate: 3.25 children born/woman (2000 est.)
Literacy: 80.0% (1997)

■ GOVERNMENT

Leader(s): Amir Shaykh Hamad bin Khalifa Al Thani. Prime Min. Shaykh 'Abd Allah ibn Khalifa Al Thani
Government Type: traditional monarchy
Administrative Divisions: 9 municipalities (baladiyah, sing. —baladiyah)
Nationhood: Sept. 3, 1971 (from UK)
National Holiday: Independence Day, Sept. 3

■ ECONOMY

Overview: has one of the highest per capita GDPs in the world, due to oil revenues; reserves should not be completely depleted for about 20 years; production and export of natural gas is becoming increasingly important; oil has given Qatar a per capita GDP comparable to the leading West European industrial countries
GDP: US$12.3 billion, per capita US$17,100; real growth rate 1.5% (1999 est.)
Inflation: -1.02% (year-end 2000)
Industries: accounts for 49% of GDP; crude oil production and refining, fertilizers, petrochemicals, steel, cement
Labour Force: n.a.; 3% agriculture, 28% industry, 69% services; 83% of labour force in private sector is non-Qatari
Unemployment: n.a.
Agriculture: farming and grazing on small scale, less than 1% of GDP; commercial fishing increasing in importance; most food imported
Natural Resources: crude oil, natural gas, fish

■ FINANCE/TRADE

Currency: Qatari riyal (QR) = 100 dirhams
International Reserves Excluding Gold: n.a.
Gold Reserves: US$0.019 million fine troy ounces (Nov. 2000)
Budget: revenues US$5 billion; expenditures US$4 billion, including capital expenditures of US$n.a. (1999-00 est.)
Defence Expenditures: 8.1% of GDP (1999-00)
Education Expenditures: n.a.
External Debt: US$10 billion (1998 est.)
Exports: US$4.125 billion (2000) commodities:

petroleum products 90%, steel, fertilizers; partners: France, Germany, Italy, Japan, Spain
Imports: US$3.575 billion (2000) commodities: foodstuffs, beverages, animal and vegetable oils, chemicals, machinery and equipment; partners: European Community, Japan, Arab countries, US, Australia

■ COMMUNICATIONS

Daily Newspapers: 5
Televisions: 308/1,000 inhabitants (1997 est.)
Radios: 343/1,000 inhabitants (1997 est.)
Telephones: 263 lines/1,000 inhabitants (1999)

■ TRANSPORTATION

Motor Vehicles: 184,000; 97,000 passenger cars (1997 est.)
Roads: 1,230 km; 1,107 km paved
Railway: none
Air Traffic: 1,165,000 passengers carried (1997)
Airports: 4; 2 have paved runways (1999 est.)

Canadian Embassy: The Canadian Embassy to Qatar, c/o The Canadian Embassy, Villa 24, Area 4, Plot 121, 24 Al-Mutawakel St, Da Aiyah, Kuwait City, Kuwait; mailing address: P.O. Box 25281, 13113, Safat, Kuwait City, Kuwait. Tel: (011-965) 256-3025. Fax: (011-965) 256-0173. Email: kwait@dfait-maeci.gc.ca
Embassy in Canada: Embassy of the State of Qatar, c/o Permanent Mission of the State of Qatar to the United Nations, 809 UN Plaza, First Ave 4th Fl, New York NY 10017, USA. Tel: (212) 486-9335. Fax: (212) 758-4952. Email: n.a.

Réunion

Long-Form Name: Department of Réunion
Capital: Saint-Denis

■ GEOGRAPHY

Area: 2,512 sq. km; uninhabited islands of Juan de Nova, Europa, Bassas da India, Iles Glorieuses, Tromelin administered by Réunion but do not form part of the territory; Mauritius and the Seychelles claim Tromelin, Madagascar claims all 5 islands
Climate: tropical, but more moderate at higher elevations; May to Nov.; cool and dry; Nov. to April: hot and rainy
Land Use: volcanic island; some cultivation of indigenous plants and cash crops such as corn; 17% arable, 2% permanent crops, 5% meadows and pastures, 35% forest, 41% other; includes 60 sq. km irrigated
Location: Indian Ocean, E of Africa (E of Madagascar)

■ PEOPLE

Population: 720,934 (July 2000 est.)
Nationality: Réunionese
Ethnic Groups: French Creoles, African, Malagasy, Pakistani, Indian and Chinese minorities
Languages: French (official), Creole vernacular

■ GOVERNMENT

Colony Territory of: Overseas Department of France
Leader(s): Pres. Jacques Chirac (France); Prefect Gonthier Friederici
Government Type: overseas department of France
National Holiday: Taking of the Bastille, July 14

■ ECONOMY

Overview: agriculture-based economy, of which sugar cane is the backbone; government is promoting the development of the tourist industry; socioeconomic tensions between classes with widely disparate living standards; economy heavily depends on financial assistance from France

■ FINANCE/TRADE

Currency: French franc = 100 centimes
Canadian Embassy: c/o The Canadian Embassy, 35-37 avenue Montaigne, 75008, Paris, France. Tel: (011-33-1) 44-43-29-00. Fax: (011-33-1) 44043-29-99. Email: paris@dfait-maeci.gc.ca
Representative to Canada: c/o Embassy of France, 42 Sussex Dr, Ottawa ON K1M 2C9. Tel: (613) 789-1795. Fax: (613) 562-3735. Email: politique@ambafrance-ca.org

---

Romania

Long-Form Name: Romania
Capital: Bucharest

■ GEOGRAPHY

Area: 237,500 sq. km
Coastline: 225 km
Climate: temperate; cold, cloudy winters with frequent snow and fog; sunny summers with frequent showers and thunderstorms
Environment: frequent earthquakes most severe in south and southwest; geologic structure and climate promotes landslides; water pollution; air pollution in south; soil degradation
Terrain: central Transylvanian Basin is separated from the plain of Moldavia on the east by the Carpathian Mountains and separated from the Walachian Plain on the south by the Transylvanian Alps
Land Use: 41% arable; 3% permanent crops; 21% meadows; 29% forest; 6% other, includes 31,020 sq. km irrigated
Location: SE Europe, bordering on Black Sea

■ PEOPLE

Population: 22,411,121 (July 2000 est.)
Nationality: Romanian
Age Structure: 0-14 yrs: 18%; 15-64: 68%; 65+: 14% (2000 est.)
Population Growth Rate: -0.21% (2000 est.)
Net Migration: -0.6 migrants/1,000 population (2000 est.)
Ethnic Groups: 89.5% Romanian; 7.1% Hungarian; 0.5% German; 2.9% Ukrainian, Serb, Croat, Russian, Turk and Gypsy
Languages: Romanian (official), Hungarian, German; French and English also spoken
Religions: 70% Romanian Orthodox; 6% Roman Catholic; 24% Calvinist, Lutheran, Jewish, Baptist, unaffiliated
Birth Rate: 10.76/1,000 population (2000 est.)
Death Rate: 12.29/1,000 population (2000 est.)
Infant Mortality: 19.84 deaths/1,000 live births (2000 est.)
Life Expectancy at Birth: 66.10 years male, 73.99 years female (2000 est.)
Total Fertility Rate: 1.35 children born/woman (2000 est.)
Literacy: 98% (1998)

■ GOVERNMENT

Leader(s): Pres. Ion Iliescu, Prime Min. Adrian Nastase
Government Type: republic
Administrative Divisions: 40 counties (judete, sing. -judet) and 1 municipality (municipiu)
Nationhood: 1881 (from Turkey); republic proclaimed Dec. 30, 1947
National Holiday: National Day of Romania, Dec. 1

■ ECONOMY

Overview: industry suffers from an aging capital plant and shortages of energy; agriculture sector has suffered from drought and mismanagement; private enterprise is increasing in importance; growing budget deficit, inflation, unemployment and a deteriorating infrastructure hamper economic progress
GDP: US$87.4 billion, per capita US$3,900; real growth rate -4.8% (1999 est.)
Inflation: 45.67% (year-end 2000)
Industries: accounts for 51% of GDP; mining, timber, construction materials, metallurgy, chemicals, machine building, food processing, petroleum
Labour Force: 11 million (1999); 27.4% industry, 33% agriculture, 10.1% community, social and business services

Unemployment: 10.5% (Dec. 2000)
Agriculture: 23% of GDP and 28% of labour force; major wheat and corn producer, sugar beets, sunflower seeds, potatoes, milk, eggs, meat
Natural Resources: crude oil (reserves being exhausted), timber, natural gas, coal, iron ore, salt, arable land, hydropower

■ FINANCE/TRADE

Currency: leu (pl. lei) = 100 bani
International Reserves Excluding Gold: US$3.998 billion (Jan. 2001)
Gold Reserves: US$3.375 million fine troy ounces (Jan. 2001)
Budget: revenues US$11.2 billion; expenditures US$12.7 billion, including capital expenditures of US$n.a. (1999 est.)
Defence Expenditures: 7.25% of total govt. expenditure (1997)
Education Expenditures: 9.42% of total govt. expenditure (1997)
External Debt: US$9.367 billion (1999)
Exports: US$6.894 billion (2000); commodities: machinery and equipment 34.7%, fuels, minerals and metals 24.7%, manufactured consumer goods 16.9%, agricultural materials and forestry products 11.9%, other 11.6%; partners: former USSR countries 27%, Eastern Europe 23%, European Community 15%, US 5%, China 4%
Imports: US$8.420 billion (2000); commodities: fuels, minerals and metals 51%, machinery and equipment 26.7%, agricultural and forestry products 11%, manufactured consumer goods 4.2%; partners: Communist countries 60%, non-communist countries 40%

■ COMMUNICATIONS

Daily Newspapers: 106
Televisions: 233/1,000 inhabitants (1998)
Radios: 319/1,000 inhabitants (1997)
Telephones: 167 lines/1,000 inhabitants (1999)

■ TRANSPORTATION

Motor Vehicles: 3,000,000; 2,460,000 passenger cars (1997 est.)
Roads: 153,359 km; 103,671 km paved
Railway: 11,385 km
Air Traffic: 995,000 passengers carried (1997)
Airports: 62; 25 have paved runways (1999 est.)

Canadian Embassy: The Canadian Embassy, 36, Nicolae Iorga, Bucharest 71118; mailing address: P.O. Box 117, Post Office No. 22, Bucharest, Romania. Tel: (011-40-1) 307-5000. Fax: (011-40-1) 307-5010. Email: bucst@dfait-maeci.gc.ca
Embassy in Canada: Embassy of Romania, 655 Rideau St, Ottawa ON K1N 6A3. Tel: (613) 789-3709. Fax: (613) 789-4365. Email: romania@cyberus.ca

Russia

Long-Form Name: Russian Federation
Capital: Moscow

■ GEOGRAPHY

Area: 17,075,200 sq. km
Coastline: 37,653 km
Climate: ranges from steppes in south through humid continental, subarctic in Siberia to tundra in polar north; winters vary—cool along Black Sea, frigid in Siberia; summers—warm in the steppes to cool along Arctic coast
Environment: cold desert in north; volcanic activity; only small percentage of land is arable—much is too far north; permafrost over much of Siberia; severe land, air and water pollution; deforestation and soil erosion
Terrain: rolling western plains, north-south ridge of Ural Mountains, central plateau, rugged eastern uplands
Land Use: 8% arable; 46% forests and woodland; 4% meadows and pastures; 42% steppe and cold desert; includes 40,000 sq. km irrigated
Location: E Europe and N Asia, bordering on Barents Sea, Baltic Sea, Black Sea, Caspian Sea

■ PEOPLE

Population: 146,001,176 (July 2000 est.)
Nationality: Russian
Age Structure: 0-14 yrs: 18%; 15-64: 69%; 65+: 13% (2000 est.)
Population Growth Rate: -0.38% (2000 est.)
Net Migration: 1.02 migrants/1,000 population (2000 est.)
Ethnic Groups: 81.5% Russians; 3.8% Tatars, 1.2% Chuvash, 0.9% Bashkir, 0.8% Belorussian, 3% Ukrainian, remainder inc. Chechens, Germans, Udmurts, Mari, Kazakhs, Avars, Jews, Moldavians and Armenians
Languages: Russian (official), Tartar, Ukrainian
Religions: Christianity (Russian Orthodox) with substantial Muslim populations and other religious minorities
Birth Rate: 9.02/1,000 population (2000 est.)
Death Rate: 13.80/1,000 population (2000 est.)
Infant Mortality: 20.33 deaths/1,000 live births (2000 est.)
Life Expectancy at Birth: 61.95 years male, 72.69 years female (2000 est.)
Total Fertility Rate: 1.25 children born/woman (2000 est.)
Literacy: 99.5% (1998)

■ GOVERNMENT

Leader(s): Pres. Vladimir V. Putin; Prem. Mikhail Kasyanov
Government Type: federation
Administrative Divisions: 49 oblasts (oblastey, sing. —oblast), 21 autonomous republics (avtonomnyk respublik, sing. —avtonomnaya respublika), 10 autonomous okrugs (avtonomnykh okrugov, sing. —avtonomnyy okrug), 6 krays (krayer, sing. —kray), 2 federal cities (gorod) and 1 autonomous oblast (avtonomnaya oblast)
Nationhood: Aug. 24, 1991 (from Soviet Union)
National Holiday: Independence Day, June 12

■ ECONOMY

Overview: a vast country with a great many natural resources, a well-educated population, and a diverse but declining industrial base; 25% of the population lives below the poverty line and the country continues to experience formidable difficulties in moving from its old centrally planned economy to a modern market economy; the severity of Russia's economic problems is dramatized by the large annual decline in population, caused by environmental hazards, poor health care, and other factors
GDP: US$620.3 billion, per capita US$4,200; real growth rate 3.2% (1999 est.)
Inflation: 20.75% (year-end 2000)
Industries: accounts for 38.5% of GDP; natural gas refining, steel and coal production and processing, all forms of machine building, shipbuilding, transportation equipment, consumer durables, communications and agricultural equipment, medical and scientific instruments
Labour Force: 78 million (1999); 25.9% industry, 25.9% community, social and business services, 15.4% agriculture
Unemployment: 12.4% (1999); substantial underemployment
Agriculture: accounts for 8.4% of GDP; grain, sugar beets, sunflower seeds, meat, milk, vegetables, fruit
Natural Resources: iron ore, coal, oil, gold, platinum, copper, zinc, lead, tin, rare metals; climate, terrain and distance hinder exploitation

■ FINANCE/TRADE

Currency: ruble (rbl.) = 100 kopeks
International Reserves Excluding Gold: US$25.889 billion (Jan. 2001)
Gold Reserves: US$12.498 million fine troy ounces (Jan. 2001)
Budget: revenues US$24.08 billion; expenditures US$26.82 billion, including capital expenditures US$n.a. (1999 est.)

Defence Expenditures: 12.34% of total govt. expenditure (1999)
Education Expenditures: 1.74% of total govt. expenditure (1999)
External Debt: US$173.940 billion (1999)
Exports: US$98.342 billion (2000); commodities: fuels, wood products, metals, chemicals, wide range of manufactured products
Imports: US$45.453 billion (2000); commodities: machinery, medicine, foodstuffs, consumer products

■ COMMUNICATIONS

Daily Newspapers: 285
Televisions: 420/1,000 inhabitants (1998)
Radios: 418/1,000 inhabitants (1997)
Telephones: 210 lines/1,000 inhabitants (1999)

■ TRANSPORTATION

Motor Vehicles: 24,000,000; 14,100,000 passenger cars (1997 est.)
Roads: 948,000 km; 336,000 km paved
Railway: 150,000 km
Air Traffic: 20,419,000 passengers carried (1997)
Airports: 2,517; 630 have paved runways

Canadian Embassy: The Canadian Embassy, 23 Starokonyushenny Per, Moscow, 121002 Russia. Tel: (011-7-095) 956-6666. Fax: (011-7-095) 232-9948. Email: mosco@dfait-maeci.gc.ca
Embassy in Canada: Embassy of the Russian Federation, 285 Charlotte St, Ottawa ON K1N 8L5. Tel: (613) 235-4341. Fax: (613) 236-6342. Email: rusemb@intranet.ca

---

Rwanda

Long-Form Name: Rwandese Republic
Capital: Kigali

■ GEOGRAPHY

Area: 26,338 sq. km
Coastline: none: landlocked
Climate: temperate; two rainy seasons (Feb. to Apr., Nov. to Jan.); mild in mountains with frost and snow possible
Environment: deforestation; overgrazing; soil exhaustion; soil erosion; periodic droughts
Terrain: mostly grassy uplands and hills; mountains in west
Land Use: 35% arable; 13% permanent crops; 18% meadows; 22% forest; 12% other; includes 40 sq. km irrigated
Location: EC Africa

■ PEOPLE

Population: 7,229,129 (July 2000 est.)

Nationality: Rwandan
Age Structure: 0-14 yrs: 43%; 15-64: 54%; 65+: 3% (2000 est.)
Population Growth Rate: 1.14% (2000 est.)
Net Migration: -2.46 migrants/1,000 population (2000 est.)
Ethnic Groups: 84% Hutu, 15% Tutsi, 1% Twa (Pygmoid)
Languages: Kinyarwanda, French, English (all official); Kiswahili used in commercial centres
Religions: 65% Christian (mostly Roman Catholic), 9% Protestant, 1% Muslim, 25% indigenous beliefs and other
Birth Rate: 34.78/1,000 population (2000 est.)
Death Rate: 20.95/1,000 population (2000 est.)
Infant Mortality: 120.06 deaths/1,000 live births (2000 est.)
Life Expectancy at Birth: 38.58 years male, 40.13 years female (2000 est.)
Total Fertility Rate: 5.07 children born/woman (2000 est.)
Literacy: 64% (1998)

■ GOVERNMENT

Leader(s): Pres. Paul Kagame, Prime Min. Bernard Makuza
Government Type: republic; presidential system in which military leaders hold key offices
Administrative Divisions: 12 prefectures
Nationhood: July 1, 1962 (from UN trusteeship under Belgian administration)
National Holiday: Independence Day, July 1

■ ECONOMY

Overview: a poor nation whose economy is severely hampered by civil war, which has damaged infrastructure and economic prospects; agricultural sector dominates, with coffee and tea making up 80–90% of total exports; manufacturing is largely restricted to the processing of agricultural products
GDP: US$5.9 billion, per capita US$720; real growth rate 5.3% (1996 est.)
Inflation: 4.30% (year-end 2000)
Industries: accounts for 20% of GDP mining of cassiterite (tin ore) and wolframite (tungsten ore), tin, cement, agricultural processing, small-scale beverage production, soap, furniture, shoes, plastic goods, textiles, cigarettes
Labour Force: 4 million (1999); 92.8% agriculture, 4.3% services, 3% industry and commerce
Unemployment: n.a.
Agriculture: accounts for 44% of GDP and about 90% of labour force; cash crops: coffee, tea, pyrethrum (insecticide made from chrysanthemums); main food crops: bananas, beans, sorghum, potatoes; stock raising; self-

sufficiency declining; country imports foodstuffs as farm production fails to keep up with population growth; coffee and tea constitute 80–90% of total exports
Natural Resources: gold, cassiterite (tin ore), wolframite (tungsten ore), natural gas, hydropower

■ FINANCE/TRADE

Currency: Rwandan franc (RF) = 100 centimes
International Reserves Excluding Gold: US$186 million (Jan. 2001)
Gold Reserves: none (Jan. 2001)
Budget: revenues US$202 million; expenditures US$361 million, including capital expenditures of US$n.a. (1998 est.)
Defence Expenditures: 3.8% of GDP (1999)
Education Expenditures: n.a.
External Debt: US$1.292 billion (1999)
Exports: US$59 million (2000); commodities: coffee 85%, tea, tin, cassiterite, wolframite, pyrethrum; partners: Germany, Belgium, Italy, Uganda, UK, France, US
Imports: US$213 million (2000); commodities: textiles, foodstuffs, machines and equipment, capital goods, steel, petroleum products, cement and construction material; partners: US, Belgium, Germany, Kenya, Japan

■ COMMUNICATIONS

Daily Newspapers: 1
Televisions: 0/1,000 inhabitants (1998)
Radios: 102/1,000 inhabitants (1997)
Telephones: 2 lines/1,000 inhabitants (1999)

■ TRANSPORTATION

Motor Vehicles: 27,800; 11,900 passenger cars (1997 est.)
Roads: 12,000 km; 1,000 km paved
Railway: none
Air Traffic: n.a.
Airports: 8; 4 have paved runways (1999 est.)

Canadian Embassy: Office of the Canadian Embassy, rue Akagera, P.O. Box 1177, Kigali, Rwanda. Tel: (011-250) 73210. Fax: (011-250) 72719. Email: kgali@dfait-maeci.gc.ca
Embassy in Canada: Embassy of the Republic of Rwanda, c/o 1714 New Hampshire NW, Washington DC 20009, USA. Tel: (202) 232-2882. Fax: (202) 232-4544. Email: n.a.

Saint Helena

Long-Form Name: Saint Helena
Capital: Jamestown

■ GEOGRAPHY

Area: 410 sq. km
Climate: tropical marine; little seasonal variation
Land Use: 6% arable, 0% permanent crops, 6% meadows and pastures, 6% forests, 82% other; includes n.a. sq. km irrigated
Location: S Atlantic Ocean, SW of Africa

■ PEOPLE

Population: 7,212 (July 2000 est.)
Nationality: Saint Helenian
Ethnic Groups: Europeans, East Indians, Africans
Languages: English (official)

■ GOVERNMENT

Colony Territory of: Dependent Territory of the United Kingdom
Leader(s): Head of State: Queen Elizabeth II; Gov. and Commander-in-Chief David James Hollamby
Government Type: dependent territory of the UK
National Holiday: Celebration of the Birthday of the Queen, second Saturday in June

■ ECONOMY

Overview: depends primarily on financial assistance from UK; fishing, livestock raising and sale of handicrafts provide income for local population; due to the lack of jobs, many inhabitants have emigrated

■ FINANCE/TRADE

Currency: Saint Helenian pound = 100 pence (at par with British pound)

Canadian Embassy: c/o The Canadian High Commission, Macdonald House, 1 Grosvenor Square, London W1K 4AB, England, UK. Tel: (011-44-20) 7258-6600. Fax: (011-44-20) 7258-6333. email: Ldn@dfait-maeci.gc.ca
Representative to Canada: c/o British High Commission, 80 Elgin St, Ottawa ON K1P 5K7. Tel: (613) 237-1530. Fax: (613) 237-7980. Email should be sent using the appropriate form at the British High Commission's website at http://www.britain-in-canada.org

---

Saint Kitts and Nevis

Long-Form Name: Federation of Saint Kitts and Nevis
Capital: Basseterre

■ GEOGRAPHY

Area: 261 sq. km
Coastline: 135 km

Climate: subtropical tempered by constant sea breezes; little seasonal temperature variation; rainy season (May to Nov.)
Environment: subject to hurricanes (July to Oct.)
Terrain: volcanic with mountainous interiors
Land Use: 22% arable; 17% permanent crops; 3% meadows; 17% forest; 41% other; includes n.a. sq. km irrigated
Location: Caribbean islands E of Puerto Rico

■ PEOPLE

Population: 38,819 (July 2000 est.)
Nationality: Kittian or Kittitian, Nevisian
Age Structure: 0-14 yrs: 30%; 15-64: 61%; 65+: 9% (2000 est.)
Population Growth Rate: -0.22% (2000 est.)
Net Migration: -11.85 migrants/1,000 population (2000 est.)
Ethnic Groups: mainly of black African descent
Languages: English
Religions: Anglican, other Protestant sects, Roman Catholic
Birth Rate: 19.06/1,000 population (2000 est.)
Death Rate: 9.38/1,000 population (2000 est.)
Infant Mortality: 16.72 deaths/1,000 live births (2000 est.)
Life Expectancy at Birth: 67.95 years male, 73.68 years female (2000 est.)
Total Fertility Rate: 2.43 children born/woman (2000 est.)
Literacy: 90.0% (1997)

■ GOVERNMENT

Leader(s): Head of State: Queen Elizabeth II/Gov. Gen. Cuthbert Montraville Sebastian. Prime Min. Vance Amory
Government Type: constitutional monarchy
Administrative Divisions: 14 parishes
Nationhood: Sept. 19, 1983 (from UK)
National Holiday: Independence Day, Sept. 19

■ ECONOMY

Overview: traditionally dependent on the growing and processing of sugar cane and on remittances from overseas workers; tourism and export-oriented manufacturing are increasing
GDP: US$244 million, per capita US$6,000; real growth rate 1.6% (1998 est.)
Inflation: 3.91% (year-end 1999)
Industries: accounts for 22.5% of GDP; sugar processing, tourism, cotton, salt, copra, clothing, footwear, beverages
Labour Force: approx. 20,000 (1999)
Unemployment: 4.5% (1997)
Agriculture: accounts for 5.5% of GDP; cash crop: sugar cane; subsistence crops: rice, yams, vegetables, bananas; fishing potential but not fully exploited; most food imported

Natural Resources: negligible

■ FINANCE/TRADE

Currency: East Caribbean dollar ($EC) = 100 cents

International Reserves Excluding Gold: US$45 million (Dec. 2000)

Gold Reserves: n.a.

Budget: revenues US$64.1 million; expenditures US$73.3 million, including capital expenditures of US$10.4 million (1997 est.)

Defence Expenditures: n.a.

Education Expenditures: n.a.

External Debt: US$136 million (1999)

Exports: US$39 million (2000); commodities: sugar, manufactures, postage stamps; partners: US 53%, UK 22%, Trinidad and Tobago 5%, OECS 5%

Imports: US$151 million (2000); commodities: foodstuffs, intermediate manufactures, machinery, fuels; partners: US 36%, UK 12%, Trinidad and Tobago 6%, Canada 3%, Japan 3%, OECS 4%

■ COMMUNICATIONS

Daily Newspapers: 0

Televisions: 257/1,000 inhabitants (1997 est.)

Radios: 721/1,000 inhabitants (1997 est.)

Telephones: 518 lines/1,000 inhabitants (1999)

■ TRANSPORTATION

Motor Vehicles: n.a.

Roads: 320 km; 136 km paved

Railway: 58 km

Air Traffic: n.a.

Airports: 2, both with paved runways (1999 est.)

Canadian Embassy: The Canadian High Commission to Saint Kitts and Nevis, c/o The Canadian High Commission, Bishop's Court Hill, St. Michael, Barbados; mailing address: P.O. Box 404, Bridgetown, Barbados. Tel: (246) 429-3550. Fax: (246) 429-3780. Email: bdgtn@dfait-maeci.gc.ca

Embassy in Canada: c/o High Commission for the Countries of the Organization of Eastern Caribbean States, 130 Albert St Ste 700, Ottawa ON K1P 5G4. Tel: (613) 236-8952. Fax: (613) 236-3042. Email: echcc@travel-net.com

Saint Lucia

Long-Form Name: Saint Lucia

Capital: Castries

■ GEOGRAPHY

Area: 620 sq. km

Coastline: 158 km

Climate: tropical, moderated by northeast trade winds; dry season from Jan. to Apr., rainy season from May to Aug.

Environment: subject to hurricanes and volcanic activity; deforestation; soil erosion

Terrain: volcanic and mountainous with some broad, fertile valleys

Land Use: 8% arable; 21% permanent crops; 5% meadow; 13% forest; 53% other; includes 10 sq. km irrigated

Location: Caribbean islands, N of Venezuela

■ PEOPLE

Population: 156,260 (July 2000 est.)

Nationality: Saint Lucian

Age Structure: 0-14 yrs: 33%; 15-64: 62%; 65+: 5% (2000 est.)

Population Growth Rate: 1.21% (2000 est.)

Net Migration: -4.67 migrants/1,000 population (2000 est.)

Ethnic Groups: 90% African descent, 6% mixed, 3% East Indian, 1% Caucasian

Languages: English (official), French patois

Religions: 90% Roman Catholic, 7% Protestant, 3% Anglican

Birth Rate: 22.19/1,000 population (2000 est.)

Death Rate: 5.43/1,000 population (2000 est.)

Infant Mortality: 15.64 deaths/1,000 live births (2000 est.)

Life Expectancy at Birth: 68.74 years male, 76.14 years female (2000 est.)

Total Fertility Rate: 2.42 children born/woman (2000 est.)

Literacy: 82.0% (1997)

■ GOVERNMENT

Leader(s): Head of State: Queen Elizabeth II/Gov. Gen. Calliopa Pearlette Louisy. Prime Min. Kenny Anthony

Government Type: parliamentary democracy

Administrative Divisions: 11 quarters

Nationhood: Feb. 22, 1979 (from UK)

National Holiday: Independence Day, Feb. 22

■ ECONOMY

Overview: depends on strong agricultural (bananas) and tourist industry sectors; expanding industrial base supported by foreign investment in manufacturing and activities such as data processing; vulnerable to droughts and tropical storms

GDP: US$656 million, per capita US$4,300; real growth rate 2.9% (1998 est.)

Inflation: 5.35% (year-end 1999)

Industries: accounts for 32.3% of GDP; clothing,

electronic component assembly, beverages, tourism, lime and coconut processing
Labour Force: 43,800.
Unemployment: n.a.
Agriculture: accounts for 10.7% GDP and 43% of labour force; crops: bananas, coconuts, vegetables, citrus fruit, root crops, cocoa; imports food for the tourist industry
Natural Resources: forests, sandy beaches, minerals (pumice), mineral springs, geothermal potential

■ FINANCE/TRADE

Currency: EC dollar (EC$) = 100 cents
International Reserves Excluding Gold: US$79 million (Dec. 2000)
Gold Reserves: n.a.
Budget: revenues US$141.2 million; expenditures US$146.7 million, including capital expenditures of US$25.1 million (1997-98 est.)
Defence Expenditures: n.a.
Education Expenditures: n.a.
External Debt: US$181 million (1999)
Exports: US$63 million (2000); commodities: bananas 67%, cocoa, vegetables, fruit, coconut oil, clothing; partners: UK 55%, CARICOM 21%, US 18%, other 6%
Imports: US$365 million (2000); commodities: manufactured goods 22%, machinery and transportation equipment 21%, food and live animals 20%, mineral fuels, foodstuffs, machinery and equipment, fertilizers, petroleum products; partners: US 33%, UK 16%, CARICOM 14.8%, Japan 6.5%, other 29.7%

■ COMMUNICATIONS

Daily Newspapers: 0
Televisions: 205/1,000 inhabitants (1997 est.)
Radios: 710/1,000 inhabitants (1997 est.)
Telephones: 266 lines/1,000 inhabitants (1999)

■ TRANSPORTATION

Motor Vehicles: 12,300; 11,400 passenger cars (1997 est.)
Roads: 1,210 km; 63 km paved
Railway: none
Air Traffic: n.a.
Airports: 2, both with paved runways (1999 est.)

Canadian Embassy: The Canadian High Commission to Saint Lucia, c/o The Canadian High Commission, Bishop's Court Hill, St. Michael, Barbados; mailing address: P.O. Box 404, Bridgetown, Barbados. Tel: (246) 429-3550. Fax: (246) 429-3780. Email: bdgtn@dfait-maeci.gc.ca

Embassy in Canada: c/o High Commission for the Countries of the Organization of Eastern Caribbean States, 130 Albert St Ste 700, Ottawa ON K1P 5G4. Tel: (613) 236-8952. Fax: (613) 236-3042. email: echcc@travel-net.com

Saint Pierre and Miquelon

Long-Form Name: Territorial Collectivity of Saint Pierre and Miquelon
Capital: Saint-Pierre

■ GEOGRAPHY

Area: 242 sq. km, 8 small islands
Climate: cold and wet, misty and foggy, windy spring and autumn, moist, temperate summers, cold and snowy winters
Land Use: 13% arable, 0% permanent crops, 0% meadows and pastures, 4% forest, 83% other; includes n.a. km irrigated
Location: N Atlantic Ocean, S of Newfoundland

■ PEOPLE

Population: 6,896 (July 2000 est.)
Nationality: Frenchman, Frenchwoman
Ethnic Groups: descendants of French settlers, Basques and Bretons (French fishermen)
Languages: French, English

■ GOVERNMENT

Colony Territory of: Territorial Collectivity of France
Leader(s): Pres. Jacques Chirac (France); Prefect Jean-François Tallec
Government Type: territorial collectivity with internal self-government
National Holiday: Taking of the Bastille, July 14

■ ECONOMY

Overview: fishing, and the servicing of fishing fleets operating off the coast of Newfoundland, have long been an important part of the economy; agriculture: some vegetables and livestock for local consumption; partners: UK, Canada, EEC

■ FINANCE/TRADE

Currency: French franc = 100 centimes
Canadian Embassy: c/o The Canadian Embassy, 35-37 avenue Montaigne, 75008 Paris, France. Tel: (011-33-1) 44-43-29-00. Fax: (011-33-1) 44-43-29-99. Email: paris@dfait-maeci.gc.ca
Representative to Canada: c/o Embassy of France, 42 Sussex Dr, Ottawa ON K1M 2C9. Tel: (613) 789-1795. Fax: (613) 562-3735. Email: politique@ambafrance-ca.org

Saint Vincent and the Grenadines

Long-Form Name: Saint Vincent and the Grenadines
Capital: Kingstown

■ GEOGRAPHY

Area: 389 sq. km
Coastline: 84 km
Climate: tropical; little seasonal temperature variation; rainy season (May to Nov.)
Environment: subject to hurricanes; Soufrière volcano is a constant threat; water pollution along coasts
Terrain: volcanic, mountainous; Soufrière volcano on the island of Saint Vincent
Land Use: 10% arable; 18% permanent crops; 5% meadows; 36% forest; 31% other; includes 10 sq. km irrigated
Location: Caribbean islands, N of Venezuela

■ PEOPLE

Population: 115,461 (July 2000 est.)
Nationality: Saint Vincentian or Vincentian
Age Structure: 0-14 yrs: 30%; 15-64: 63%; 65+: 7% (2000 est.)
Population Growth Rate: 0.43% (2000 est.)
Net Migration: -7.75 migrants/1,000 population (2000 est.)
Ethnic Groups: 66% black African descent; remainder mixed, with some white, East Indian, Carib Indian
Languages: English (official), some French patois
Religions: Anglican, Methodist, Roman Catholic, Seventh-Day Adventist
Birth Rate: 18.25/1,000 population (2000 est.)
Death Rate: 6.21/1,000 population (2000 est.)
Infant Mortality: 17.06 deaths/1,000 live births (2000 est.)
Life Expectancy at Birth: 70.60 years male, 74.06 years female (2000 est.)
Total Fertility Rate: 2.11 children born/woman (2000 est.)
Literacy: 82.0% (1997)

■ GOVERNMENT

Leader(s): Head of State: Queen Elizabeth II/Gov. Gen. Sir Charles James Antrobus, Prime Min. Ralph Gonsalves
Government Type: parliamentary democracy
Administrative Divisions: 6 parishes
Nationhood: Oct. 27, 1979 (from UK)
National Holiday: Independence Day, Oct. 27

■ ECONOMY

Overview: overdependence on the weather-plagued banana crop as a major export earner has caused high unemployment; has been unsuccessful in diversifying into new industries
GDP: US$309 million, per capita US$2,600; real growth rate 4% (1999 est.)
Inflation: 0.20% (year-end 2000)
Industries: accounts for 17.5% of GDP; food processing (sugar, flour), cement, furniture, rum, starch, sheet metal, beverage
Labour Force: n.a.
Unemployment: n.a.
Agriculture: accounts for 10.6% of GDP and 60% of labour force; provides bulk of exports; products: bananas, arrowroot (world's largest producer), coconuts, sweet potatoes, spices; small numbers of cattle, sheep, hogs, goats; small fish catch used locally
Natural Resources: negligible

■ FINANCE/TRADE

Currency: EC dollar ($EC) = 100 cents
International Reserves Excluding Gold: US$55 million (Dec. 2000)
Gold Reserves: n.a.
Budget: revenues US$85.7 million; expenditures US$98.6 million, including capital expenditures of US$25.7 million (1997 est.)
Defence Expenditures: negligible
Education Expenditures: 15.32% of total govt. expenditure (1999)
External Debt: US$192 million (1999)
Exports: US$48 million (2000); commodities: bananas, eddoes and dasheen (taro), arrowroot starch, copra; partners: CARICOM 37%, UK 43%, US 15%
Imports: US$174 million (2000); commodities: foodstuffs, machinery and equipment, chemicals and fertilizers, minerals and fuels; partners: US 42%, CARICOM 19%, UK 15%

■ COMMUNICATIONS

Daily Newspapers: 0
Televisions: 156/1,000 inhabitants (1997 est.)
Radios: 667/1,000 inhabitants (1997 est.)
Telephones: 209 lines/1,000 inhabitants (1999)

■ TRANSPORTATION

Motor Vehicles: 8,200; 5,000 passenger cars (1997 est.)
Roads: 1,040 km; 320 km paved
Railway: none
Air Traffic: n.a.
Airports: 6, 5 with paved runways (1999 est.)

Canadian Embassy: The Canadian High Commission to Saint Vincent and the Grenadines, c/o The Canadian High Commission, Bishop's Court Hill, St. Michael, Barbados; mailing address: P.O. Box 404,

Bridgetown, Barbados. Tel: (246) 429-3550. Fax: (246) 429-3780. Email: bdgtn@dfait-maeci.gc.ca

Embassy in Canada: c/o High Commission for the Countries of the Organization of Eastern Caribbean States, 130 Albert St Ste 700, Ottawa ON K1P 5G4. Tel: (613) 236-8952. Fax: (613) 236-3042. email: echcc@travel-net.com

Samoa

Long-Form Name: Independent State of Samoa
Capital: Apia

■ GEOGRAPHY

Area: 2,860 sq. km
Coastline: 403 km
Climate: tropical; rainy season lasts from Oct. to March, dry season from May to Oct.
Environment: volcanism and typhoons are natural hazards; soil erosion
Terrain: interior is rocky, with volcanic mountains; narrow coastal plain
Land Use: 19% arable, 24% permanent crops, 0% meadows and pastures, 47% forest and woodland, 10% other; includes n.a. sq. km irrigated
Location: South Pacific Ocean, E of Australia and NE of New Zealand

■ PEOPLE

Population: 179,466 (July 2000 est.)
Nationality: Samoan
Age Structure: 0-14 yrs: 33%; 15-64: 61%; 65+: 6% (2000 est.)
Population Growth Rate: -0.22% (2000 est.)
Net Migration: -11.59 migrants/1,000 population (2000 est.)
Ethnic Groups: 92.6% Samoan, 7% European-Polynesian; 0.4% Europeans
Languages: Samoan (Polynesian), also English
Religions: almost 100% Christianity
Birth Rate: 15.59/1,000 population (2000 est.)
Death Rate: 6.24/1,000 population (2000 est.)
Infant Mortality: 32.75 deaths/1,000 live births (2000 est.)
Life Expectancy at Birth: 66.48 years male, 72.06 years female (2000 est.)
Total Fertility Rate: 3.50 children born/women (2000 est.)
Literacy: 98% (1997)

■ GOVERNMENT

Leader(s): Head of State Tanumafili II Malietoa, Prime Min. Tuialepa Sailele Malielegaoi
Government Type: constitutional monarchy under a native chief
Administrative Divisions: 11 districts

Nationhood: Jan. 1, 1962
National Holiday: National Day, June 1

■ ECONOMY

Overview: heavily agriculture-oriented, and disease and pests have done much damage in recent years; tourism has become the most important growth industry; the flexibility of the labor market is a basic strength for future economic gains
GDP: US$485 million; per capita US$2,100, real growth rate 1.8% (1998 est.)
Inflation: 0.97% (year-end 2000)
Industries: accounts for 25% of GDP; fishing, timber, food processing, tourism
Labour Force: n.a.; 65% agriculture, 30% services, 5% industry
Unemployment: n.a.
Agriculture: makes up 40% of GDP; mostly coconuts and fruit
Natural Resources: fish, forest resources, hydroelectric potential

■ FINANCE/TRADE

Currency: tala ($WS) = 100 sene
International Reserves Excluding Gold: US$66 million (Jan. 2001)
Gold Reserves: n.a.
Budget: revenues US$118 million; expenditures US$128 million, including capital expenditures US$n.a. (1997 est.)
Defence Expenditures: n.a.
Education Expenditures: n.a.
External Debt: US$192 million (1999)
Exports: US$15 million (2000); commodities: coconut oil and cream, copra, fish, beer; partners: New Zealand, American Samoa, Australia, Germany, US
Imports: US$106 million (2000); commodities: intermediate goods, food, capital goods; partners: New Zealand, Australia, Fiji, US

■ COMMUNICATIONS

Daily Newspapers: 0
Televisions: 61/1,000 inhabitants (1997 est.)
Radios: 992/1,000 inhabitants (1997 est.)
Telephones: 49 lines/1,000 inhabitants (1999)

■ TRANSPORTATION

Motor Vehicles: 2,600; 1,200 passenger cars (1997 est.)
Roads: 790 km; 332 km paved
Railway: none
Air Traffic: 75,000 passengers carried (1997)
Airports: 3; 1 has paved runways (1999 est.)
Canadian Embassy: The Canadian High Commission to Western Samoa, c/o The Canadian High Commission, P.O. Box 12049,

Thorndon, Wellington, New Zealand. Tel: (011-64-4) 473-9577. Fax: (011-64-4) 471-2082. Email: wlgtn@dfait-maeci.gc.ca
Embassy in Canada: c/o Samoa High Commission, 800 Second Ave, Ste 400D, New York NY 10017, USA. Tel: (212) 599-6196. Fax: (212) 599-0797. Email: samoa@un.int

San Marino

Long-Form Name: Republic of San Marino
Capital: San Marino

■ GEOGRAPHY

Area: 60.5 sq. km
Coastline: none: landlocked
Climate: Mediterranean; mild to cool winters; warm, sunny summers
Environment: dominated by the Appenines
Terrain: rugged mountains
Land Use: 17% arable; 0% permanent crops; 0% meadows; 0% forest; 83% other; includes n.a. sq. km irrigated
Location: S Europe (E Italy)

■ PEOPLE

Population: 26,937 (July 2000 est.)
Nationality: Sammarinese
Age Structure: 0-14 yrs: 16%; 15-64: 68%; 65+: 16% (2000 est.)
Population Growth Rate: 1.49% (2000 est.)
Net Migration: 11.62 migrants/1,000 population (2000 est.)
Ethnic Groups: Sammarinese, Italian
Languages: Italian
Religions: Roman Catholic
Birth Rate: 10.88/1,000 population (2000 est.)
Death Rate: 7.65/1,000 population (2000 est.)
Infant Mortality: 6.33 deaths/1,000 live births (2000 est.)
Life Expectancy at Birth: 77.57 years male, 85.02 years female (2000 est.)
Total Fertility Rate: 1.29 children born/woman (2000 est.)
Literacy: 96% (1997)

■ GOVERNMENT

Leader(s): Captains-Regent: Loris Francini and Alberto Cecchetti
Government Type: republic
Administrative Divisions: 9 municipalities (castelli, sing. —castello)
Nationhood: 301 (by tradition)
National Holiday: Anniversary of the Foundation of the Republic, Sept. 3

■ ECONOMY

Overview: tourism and the sale of postage stamps are vital to the economy; tourism itself contributes more than 50% to the GDP; key industries are clothing, electronics, ceramics, agricultural products, wine and cheese
GDP: US$500 million, per capita $20,000; real growth rate 4.8% (1997 est.)
Inflation: n.a.
Industries: wine, olive oil, cement, leather, textiles, tourism
Labour Force: n.a.
Unemployment: 3.7% (May. 1999)
Agriculture: employs 3% of labour force; products: wheat, grapes, corn, olives, meat, cheese, hides; small numbers of cattle, pigs, horses; depends on Italy for food imports
Natural Resources: building stone

■ FINANCE/TRADE

Currency: Italian lire (Lit) = 100 centesimi; San Marino also mints its own coins
International Reserves Excluding Gold: n.a.
Gold Reserves: n.a.
Budget: n.a.
Defence Expenditures: n.a.
Education Expenditures: n.a.
External Debt: n.a.
Exports: n.a.; trade data are included in the statistics for Italy
Imports: n.a.; see exports

■ COMMUNICATIONS

Daily Newspapers: 3
Televisions: 334/1,000 inhabitants (1997 est.)
Radios: 593/1,000 inhabitants (1997 est.)
Telephones: 689 lines/1,000 inhabitants (1999)

■ TRANSPORTATION

Motor Vehicles: 30,000; 25,000 passenger cars (1997 est.)
Roads: 220 km; n.a. km paved
Railway: none
Air Traffic: n.a.
Airports: none
Canadian Embassy: The Canadian Consulate to San Marino, c/o The Canadian Embassy, Via G.B. de Rossi, 27, 00161 Rome, Italy. Tel: (011-39-06) 445981. Fax: (011-39-06) 445 98750. Email: rome@dfait-maeci.gc.ca
Embassy in Canada: c/o Consulate of San Marino, 20 Queen St W Ste 3300, P.O. Box 33, Toronto ON M5H 3R3. Tel: (416) 971-4848. Fax: (416) 971-4849. Email: blette@lette.com

São Tomé and Príncipe

Long-Form Name: Democratic Republic of São Tomé and Príncipe
Capital: São Tomé

■ GEOGRAPHY

Area: 1,001 sq. km
Coastline: 209 km
Climate: tropical; hot, humid; one rainy season (Oct. to May)
Environment: deforestation; soil degradation
Terrain: volcanic, mountainous
Land Use: 2% arable; 36% permanent crops; 1% meadows; 0% forest; 61% other; includes 100 sq. km irrigated
Location: S Atlantic Ocean, off W African Coast

■ PEOPLE

Population: 159,883 (July 2000 est.)
Nationality: São Toméan
Age Structure: 0-14 yrs: 48%; 15-64: 48%; 65+: 4% (2000 est.)
Population Growth Rate: 3.16 (2000 est.)
Net Migration: -3.62 migrants/1,000 population (2000 est.)
Ethnic Groups: mestiço, angolares (descendants of Angolan slaves), forros (descendants of freed slaves), servicais (contract labourers from Angola, Mozambique and Cape Verde), tongas (children of servicais born on the islands) and European (primarily Portuguese)
Languages: Portuguese (official), Crioulo
Religions: Roman Catholic, Evangelical Protestant, Seventh-Day Adventist
Birth Rate: 42.98/1,000 population (2000 est.)
Death Rate: 7.76/1,000 population (2000 est.)
Infant Mortality: 50.41 deaths/1,000 live births (2000 est.)
Life Expectancy at Birth: 63.84 years male, 66.70 years female (2000 est.)
Total Fertility Rate: 6.08 children born/woman (2000 est.)
Literacy: 75% (1997)

■ GOVERNMENT

Leader(s): Pres. Fradique de Menezes
Government Type: republic
Administrative Divisions: 2 provinces
Nationhood: July 12, 1975 (from Portugal)
National Holiday: Independence Day, July 12

■ ECONOMY

Overview: the economy is hampered by overdependence on cocoa production, which has substantially declined in recent years because of drought and mismanagement; imports 90% of food needs as well as all fuels and most manufactured goods; government is attempting to restructure economy and reduce debt burden
GDP: US$169 million, per capita US$1,100; real growth rate 1.5% (1999 est.)
Inflation: n.a.

Industries: accounts for 19% of GDP; light construction, shirts, soap, beer, fisheries, shrimp processing
Labour Force: n.a.; most of population engaged in subsistence agriculture and fishing. There are shortages of skilled workers.
Unemployment: 50% (1998 est.)
Agriculture: 23% of GDP; primary source of exports; cash crops: cocoa (85%), coconuts, palm kernels, coffee; food products: bananas, papayas, beans, poultry, fish; not self-sufficient in food grain and meat
Natural Resources: fish, hydropower

■ FINANCE/TRADE

Currency: dobra (Db) = 100 centimos
International Reserves Excluding Gold: US$6 million (June 1998)
Gold Reserves: n.a.
Budget: n.a.
Defence Expenditures: n.a.
Education Expenditures: n.a.
External Debt: US$254 million (1999)
Exports: US$4.90 million (1999 est.); commodities: cocoa 85%, copra, coffee, palm oil; partners: Germany, Netherlands, China
Imports: US$19.50 million (1999 est.); commodities: machinery and electrical equipment 54%, food products 23%, other 23%; partners: Portugal, Germany, Angola, China

■ COMMUNICATIONS

Daily Newspapers: 0
Televisions: 144/1,000 inhabitants (1997 est.)
Radios: 238/1,000 inhabitants (1997 est.)
Telephones: 31 lines/1,000 inhabitants (1999)

■ TRANSPORTATION

Motor Vehicles: n.a.
Roads: 320 km; 218 km paved
Railway: none
Air Traffic: 25,000 passengers carried (1997)
Airports: 2, both with paved runways (1999 est.)
Canadian Embassy: The Canadian Embassy to São Tomé and Príncipe, c/o The Canadian Embassy, P.O. Box 4037 Libreville, Gabon. Tel: (011-241) 73-73-54. Fax: (011-241) 73-73-88. Email: lbrve@dfait-maeci.gc.ca
Embassy in Canada: Embassy of São Tomé and Príncipe, 400 Park Ave, 7th Fl, New York, NY 10022. Tel: (212) 317-0533. Fax: (212) 317-0580. Email: n.a.

Saudi Arabia

Long-Form Name: Kingdom of Saudi Arabia
Capital: Riyadh (royal); Jeddah (administrative)

■ GEOGRAPHY

Area: 1,960,582 sq. km
Coastline: 2,640 km
Climate: harsh, dry desert with great extremes of temperature
Environment: no perennial rivers or permanent water bodies; developing extensive coastal seawater desalination facilities; desertification; coastal pollution; frequent dust and sand storms
Terrain: mostly uninhabited, sandy desert
Land Use: 2% arable; 0% permanent crops; 56% permanent pastures; 1% forest; 41% other; includes 4,350 sq. km irrigated
Location: SW Asia (Middle East), bordering on Persian Gulf, Arabian Sea, Red Sea

■ PEOPLE

Population: 22,023,506 (July 2000 est.)
Nationality: Saudi
Age Structure: 0-14 yrs: 43%; 15-64: 55%; 65+: 2% (2000 est.)
Population Growth Rate: 3.28% (2000 est.)
Net Migration: 1.36 migrants/1,000 population (2000 est.)
Ethnic Groups: 90% Arab, 10% Afro-Asian
Languages: Arabic (official); English (business language)
Religions: Muslim (85% Sunni, 15% Shia)
Birth Rate: 37.47/1,000 population (2000 est.)
Death Rate: 6.02/1,000 population (2000 est.)
Infant Mortality: 52.90 deaths/1,000 live births (2000 est.)
Life Expectancy at Birth: 66.11 years male, 69.51 years female (2000 est.)
Total Fertility Rate: 6.30 children born/woman (2000 est.)
Literacy: 73.5% (1998)

■ GOVERNMENT

Leader(s): King and Prime Min. Fahd bin 'Abd al-'Aziz Al Sa'ud
Government Type: monarchy
Administrative Divisions: 13 provinces (mintaqat, sing. —mintaqah)
Nationhood: Sept. 23, 1932 (unification)
National Holiday: Unification of the Kingdom, Sept. 23

■ ECONOMY

Overview: has the largest reserves of petroleum in the world and is the largest exporter of petroleum; the government is working toward the privatization of the economy;
GDP: US$191 billion, per capita US$9,000; real growth rate 1.6% (1999 est.)
Inflation: -0.81% (year-end 2000)

Industries: accounts for 47% of GDP; crude oil production, petroleum refining, basic petrochemicals, cement, small steel-rolling mill, construction, fertilizer, plastic
Labour Force: 7 million (4 million foreign workers) (1999); 34% government, 28% industry, 22% services, 16% agriculture
Unemployment: n.a.
Agriculture: accounts for 6% of GDP; fastest growing economic sector; subsidized by government; products: wheat, barley, tomatoes, melons, dates, citrus fruit, mutton, chickens, eggs, milk; approaching self-sufficiency in food
Natural Resources: crude oil, natural gas, iron ore, gold, copper

■ FINANCE/TRADE

Currency: riyal (SR) = 100 halalah
International Reserves Excluding Gold: US$17.137 billion (Jan. 2001)
Gold Reserves: US$4.596 million fine troy ounces (Jan. 2001)
Budget: revenues US$41.9 billion; expenditures US$49.4 billion, including capital expenditures US$n.a. (2000 est.)
Defence Expenditures: 12% of GDP (1997 est.)
Education Expenditures: 7.5% of GNP (1997)
External Debt: US$28 billion (1998 est.)
Exports: US$62.250 billion (2000); commodities: petroleum and petroleum products 89%; partners: Japan 26%, US 26%, France 6%, Bahrain 6%
Imports: US$29.754 billion (2000); commodities: manufactured goods, transportation equipment, construction materials, processed food products; partners: US 20%, Japan 18%, UK 16%, Italy 11%

■ COMMUNICATIONS

Daily Newspapers: 13
Televisions: 262/1,000 inhabitants (1998)
Radios: 321/1,000 inhabitants (1997)
Telephones: 129 lines/1,000 inhabitants (1999)

■ TRANSPORTATION

Motor Vehicles: 3,000,000; 1,710,000 passenger cars (1997 est.)
Roads: 146,524 km; 44,104 km paved
Railway: 1,390 km
Air Traffic: 11,738,000 passengers carried (1997)
Airports: 205; 72 have paved runways (1999 est.)

Canadian Embassy: The Canadian Embassy, Diplomatic Quarter, Riyadh; mailing address: P.O. Box 94321, Riyadh 11693, Saudi Arabia. Tel: (011-966-1) 488-2288. Fax: (011-966-1) 488-1997. Email: ryadh@dfait-maeci.gc.ca

Embassy in Canada: Royal Embassy of Saudi Arabia, 99 Bank St, Ste 901, Ottawa ON K1P 6B9. Tel: (613) 237-4100. Fax: (613) 237-0567. Email: n.a.

Senegal

Long-Form Name: Republic of Senegal
Capital: Dakar

■ GEOGRAPHY

Area: 196,190 sq. km
Coastline: 531 km
Climate: tropical; hot, humid; rainy season (Dec. to Apr.) has strong southeast winds; dry season (May to Nov.) dominated by hot, dry harmattan wind
Environment: lowlands seasonally flooded; deforestation; overgrazing; soil degradation; wildlife populations are endangered by poaching
Terrain: generally low, rolling, plains rising to foothills in southeast
Land Use: 12% arable; 0% permanent crops; 16% permanent pastures; 54% forest; 18% other, includes 710 sq. km irrigated
Location: W Africa, bordering on Atlantic Ocean

■ PEOPLE

Population: 9,987,494 (July 2000 est.)
Nationality: Senegalese (sing. & pl.)
Age Structure: 0-14 yrs: 45%; 15-64: 52%; 65+: 3% (2000 est.)
Population Growth Rate: 2.94% (2000 est.)
Net Migration: 0 migrants/1,000 population (2000 est.)
Ethnic Groups: 43.3% Wolof, 23.8% Fulani, 14.7% Serer, 3.7% Diola, 3% Mandingo, 1% European and Lebanese, 10.5% other
Languages: French (official); Wolof, Pulaar, Diola, Mandingo
Religions: 92% Muslim, 6% indigenous beliefs, 2% Christian (mostly Roman Catholic)
Birth Rate: 37.94/1,000 population (2000 est.)
Death Rate: 8.57/1,000 population (2000 est.)
Infant Mortality: 58.08 deaths/1,000 live births (2000 est.)
Life Expectancy at Birth: 60.60 years male, 63.82 years female (2000 est.)
Total Fertility Rate: 5.21 children born/woman (2000 est.)
Literacy: 34.6% (1997)

■ GOVERNMENT

Leader(s): Pres. Abdoulaye Wade, Prime Min. Madior Boye

Government Type: republic under multi-party democratic rule
Administrative Divisions: 10 regions
Nationhood: April 4, 1960 (from France)
National Holiday: Independence Day, Apr. 4

■ ECONOMY

Overview: tourism has emerged as a great boon to the economy; fishing is the main economic resource; mining (phosphate) has been hurt by reduced worldwide demand for fertilizers in recent years; limited resource base, environmental degradation and very high population growth continue to delay improvements
GDP: US$16.6 billion, per capita US$1,650; real growth rate 5% (1999 est.)
Inflation: 0.73% (year-end 2000)
Industries: accounts for 20% of GDP; fishing, agricultural processing, phosphate mining, petroleum refining, building materials
Labour Force: 4 million (1999); 80.6% agriculture, 6.2% industry, 13.1% services
Unemployment: n.a.; urban youth 40%
Agriculture: including fishing, accounts for 19% of GDP; major products: peanuts (cash crop), millet, corn, sorghum, rice, cotton, tomatoes, green vegetables; estimated two-thirds self-sufficient in food; fish catch of 354,000 metric tons
Natural Resources: fish, phosphates, iron ore

■ FINANCE/TRADE

Currency: Communauté financière africaine franc (CFAF) = 100 centimes
International Reserves Excluding Gold: US$347 million (Nov. 2000)
Gold Reserves: US$0.029 million fine troy ounces (Aug. 2000)
Budget: n.a.
Defence Expenditures: 1.4% of GDP (1997)
Education Expenditures: 3.7% of GNP (1997)
External Debt: US$3.705 billion (1999)
Exports: US$927 million (2000); commodities: manufactures 30%, fish products 27%, peanuts 11%, petroleum products 11%, phosphates 10%; partners: US, France, other European Community, Ivory Coast, India
Imports: US$1.391 billion (2000); commodities: semimanufactures 30%, food 27%, durable consumer goods 17%, petroleum 12%, capital goods 14%; partners: US, France, other European Community, Nigeria, Algeria, China, Japan

■ COMMUNICATIONS

Daily Newspapers: 1

Televisions: 41/1,000 inhabitants (1998)
Radios: 142/1,000 inhabitants (1997)
Telephones: 18 lines/1,000 inhabitants (1999)

■ TRANSPORTATION

Motor Vehicles: 160,000; 110,000 passenger cars (1997 est.)
Roads: 14,576 km; 4,271 km paved
Railway: 906 km
Air Traffic: 166,000 passengers carried (1997)
Airports: 20; 10 have paved runways (1999 est.)

Canadian Embassy: The Canadian Embassy, 45 av. de la République, P.O. Box 3373, Dakar, Senegal. Tel: (011-221) 823-92-90. Fax: (011-221) 823-87-49. Email: dakar@dfait-maeci.gc.ca
Embassy in Canada: Embassy of the Republic of Senegal, 57 Marlborough Ave, Ottawa ON K1N 8E8. Tel: (613) 238-6392. Fax: (613) 238-2695. Email: ambassn@sympatico.ca

---

Serbia and Montenegro

Long-Form Name: Federal Republic of Yugoslavia (self-proclaimed)
Capital: Belgrade (Serbia), Podgorica (Montenegro)

■ GEOGRAPHY

Area: 102,350 sq. km (Serbia 88,412 sq. km, Montenegro 13,938 sq. km)
Coastline: 199 km (Montenegro 199 km, Serbia 0 km)
Climate: continental in north; continental and Mediterranean in central region; south— Adriatic climate along coast, hot and dry summers, relatively cold winters, with heavy snowfall inland
Environment: coastal water pollution from sewage outlets, esp. in tourist-related areas; air and water pollution; subject to earthquakes
Terrain: varied: rich fertile plain in north, limestone ranges and basins in east, mountains and hills in southeast, high shoreline with no islands in southwest
Land Use: 30% arable, 5% permanent crops, 20% meadows and pastures, 25% forests, 20% other
Location: S Europe, bordering Adriatic Sea

■ PEOPLE

Population: 10,662,087 (July 2000 est.)
Nationality: Serb, Montenegrin
Age Structure: Serbia: 0-14 yrs: 20%; 15-64: 65%; 65+: 15% (2000 est.) Montenegro 0-14 yrs: 22%; 15-64: 66%; 65+: 12% (2000 est.)
Population Growth Rate: Serbia: 0.73% Montenegro: -12.22% (2000 est.)

Net Migration: Serbia: 6.26 migrants/1,000 population (2000 est.) Montenegro: 29.18 migrants/1,000 population (2000 est.)
Ethnic Groups: 62.6% Serb, 16.5% Albanian, 5% Montenegrin, 3.4% Yugoslav, 3.3% Hungarian, 9.2% other
Languages: 95% Serbian, 5% Albanian
Religions: 65% Orthodox, 19% Muslim, 4% Roman Catholic, 1% Protestant, 11% other
Birth Rate: 12.20/1,000 population (Serbia); 14.90/1,000 population (Montenegro) (2000 est.)
Death Rate: 11.08/1,000 population (Serbia); 7.90/1,000 population (Montenegro) (2000 est.)
Infant Mortality: 20.13 deaths/1,000 live births (Serbia); 10.97 deaths/1,000 live births (Montenegro) (2000 est.)
Life Expectancy at Birth: 69.31 years male, 75.72 years female (Serbia); 71.45 years male, 79.82 years female (Montenegro) (2000 est.)
Total Fertility Rate: 1.70 children born/woman (Serbia); 1.96 children born/woman (Montenegro) (2000 est.)
Literacy: n.a.

■ GOVERNMENT

Leader(s): President: Vojislav Kostunica, Prime Min. Dragisa Pesic
Government Type: republic
Administrative Divisions: 2 republics (republike, sing. —republika) and 2 nominally autonomous provinces (autonomna pokrajine, sing. — autonomna pokrajina)
Nationhood: April 11, 1992 (from Yugoslavia)
National Holiday: St. Vitus Day, June 28

■ ECONOMY

Overview: bloody ethnic warfare has caused destabilization of republic boundaries and the break-up of important inter-republic trade connections; the economic boom anticipated by the government after the suspension of UN sanctions has failed to take place, largely due to government mismanagement of the economy
GDP: US$20.6 billion, per capita US$1,800; real growth rate -20% (1999 est.)
Inflation: n.a.
Industries: accounts for 50% of GDP; machine building, metallurgy, mining, consumer goods, electronics, petroleum products, chemicals, pharmaceuticals
Labour Force: 1.6 million economically active (1999 est.); 41% industry, 35% services, 12% trade and tourism, 7% transportation and communication, 5% agriculture
Unemployment: 30% (1999 est.)
Agriculture: accounts for 20% of GDP; cereals, cotton, oilseed plants, chicory, fodder crops,

fruit, vegetables, tobacco, olives, citrus, rice, livestock (sheep, goats)
Natural Resources: oil, gas, coal, antimony, copper, lead, gold, chrome, pyrite, hydropower

■ FINANCE/TRADE

Currency: Yugoslav New Dinar (YD) = 100 paras
International Reserves Excluding Gold: US$2.549 billion (Jan. 1998)
Gold Reserves: n.a.
Budget: n.a.
Defence Expenditures: 6.5% of GDP (1999)
Education Expenditures: n.a.
External Debt: US$12.949 billion (1999)
Exports: US$2.450 million (2000); manufactured goods, food, live animals, raw materials; partners: Russia, Italy, Germany
Imports: US$2.950 million (2000); machinery, transport equipment, fuels and lubricants, manufactured goods, chemicals, food, live animals, raw materials; partners: Germany, Italy, Russia

■ COMMUNICATIONS

Daily Newspapers: 18
Televisions: 259/1,000 inhabitants (1998)
Radios: 297/1,000 inhabitants (1997)
Telephones: 214 lines/1,000 inhabitants (1999)

■ TRANSPORTATION

Motor Vehicles: 1,333,000; 1,002,000 passenger cars (1997 est.)
Roads: 48,603 km; 28,822 km paved
Railway: 4,095 km
Air Traffic: n.a.
Airports: 48; 19 have paved runways (1999 est.)

Canadian Embassy: The Canadian Embassy, 75 Kneza Milosa, 11000 Belgrade, Yugoslavia. Tel: (011-381-11) 64-46-66. Fax: (011-381-11) 64-14-80. Email: bgrad@dfait-maeci.gc.ca
Embassy in Canada: Embassy of the Federal Republic of Yugoslavia, 17 Blackburn Ave, Ottawa ON K1N 8A2. Tel: (613) 233-6289. Fax: (613) 233-7850. Email: ottambyu@capitalnet.com

Seychelles

Long-Form Name: Republic of Seychelles
Capital: Victoria

■ GEOGRAPHY

Area: 455 sq. km
Coastline: 491 km
Climate: tropical marine; humid; cooler season

during southeast monsoon (late May to Sept.); warmer season during northwest monsoon (Mar. to May)
Environment: lies outside the cyclone belt, so severe storms are rare; short droughts possible; no fresh water, catchments collect rain
Terrain: 40 granitic and about 50 coralline islands; Mahé Group is granitic, narrow coastal strip, rocky, hilly; others are coral, flat, elevated reefs
Land Use: 2% arable; 13% permanent crops; 0% meadows; 11% forest; 74% other; includes n.a. sq. km irrigated
Location: Indian Ocean, NE of Madagascar

■ PEOPLE

Population: 79,326 (July 2000 est.)
Nationality: Seychellois sing. & pl.)
Age Structure: 0-14 yrs: 29%; 15-64: 65%; 65+: 6% (2000 est.)
Population Growth Rate: 0.49% (2000 est.)
Net Migration: -6.3 migrants/1,000 population (2000 est.)
Ethnic Groups: Seychellois (mixture of Asians, Africans, Europeans)
Languages: English, French (both official), Creole
Religions: 90% Roman Catholic, 8% Anglican, 2% other
Birth Rate: 17.99/1,000 population (2000 est.)
Death Rate: 6.74/1,000 population (2000 est.)
Infant Mortality: 17.74 deaths/1,000 live births (2000 est.)
Life Expectancy at Birth: 64.87 years male, 76.12 years female (2000 est.)
Total Fertility Rate: 1.85 children born/woman (2000 est.)
Literacy: 58% (1997)

■ GOVERNMENT

Leader(s): Pres. France Albert René, V. Pres. James Michel
Government Type: republic
Administrative Divisions: 23 administrative districts
Nationhood: June 29, 1976 (from UK)
National Holiday: National Day, June 18 (1993 adoption of a new constitution)

■ ECONOMY

Overview: the government is moving to reduce the high dependence on tourism by promoting the development of farming, fishing and small-scale manufacturing, yet it is also encouraging foreign investment in order to upgrade hotels and other services
GDP: US$590 million, per capita US$7,500; real growth rate 1.8% (1999 est.)

Inflation: 6.29% (year-end 2000)
Industries: accounts for 21% of GDP; tourism employs 30% of labour force; mostly subsistence farming; cash crops: coconuts, cinnamon, vanilla; other products: sweet potatoes, cassava, bananas; broiler chickens; large share of food needs imported; expansion of tuna fishing under way
Labour Force: n.a.; 19% industry, 57% services, 14% government, 10% agriculture
Unemployment: n.a.
Agriculture: accounts for 4% of GDP, mostly subsistence farming; cash crops: coconuts, cinnamon, vanilla; large share of food needs to be imported; tuna fishing is increasing in importance
Natural Resources: fish, copra, cinnamon trees

■ FINANCE/TRADE

Currency: Seychelles rupee (SRe) = 100 cents
International Reserves Excluding Gold: US$41 million (Nov. 2000)
Gold Reserves: n.a.
Budget: n.a.
Defence Expenditures: 2.88% of total govt. expenditure (1998)
Education Expenditures: 8.57% of govt. expenditure (1998)
External Debt: US$172 million (1999)
Exports: US$167 million (2000); commodities: fish, copra, cinnamon bark, petroleum products (re-exports); partners: France 63%, Pakistan 12%, Réunion 10%, UK 7%
Imports: US$361 million (2000); commodities: manufactured goods, food, tobacco, beverages, machinery and transportation equipment, petroleum products; partners: UK 20%, France 14%, South Africa 13%, PDRY 13%, Singapore 8%, Japan 6%

■ COMMUNICATIONS

Daily Newspapers: 1
Televisions: 139/1,000 inhabitants (1997 est.)
Radios: 529/1,000 inhabitants (1997 est.)
Telephones: 248 lines/1,000 inhabitants (1999)

■ TRANSPORTATION

Motor Vehicles: 8,500; 6,800 passenger cars (1997 est.)
Roads: 280 km; 176 km paved
Railway: none
Air Traffic: 384,000 passengers carried (1997)
Airports: 14; 6 have paved runways (1999 est.)

Canadian Embassy: The Canadian High Commission to Seychelles, c/o The Canadian High Commission, 38 Mirambo St, Dar-es-Salaam; mailing address: P.O. Box 1022, Dar-es-Salaam, Tanzania. Tel: (011-255-22) 211-2831. Fax: (011-255-22) 211-6897. Email: dslam@dfait-maeci.gc.ca
Embassy in Canada: High Commission for the Republic of Seychelles, 800 Second Ave, Ste 400C, New York NY 10017, USA. Tel: (212) 972-1785. Fax: (212) 972-1786. Email: seychelles@un.int

Sierra Leone

Long-Form Name: Republic of Sierra Leone
Capital: Freetown

■ GEOGRAPHY

Area: 71,740 sq. km
Coastline: 402 km
Climate: tropical; hot, humid; summer rainy season (May to Dec.); winter dry season (Dec. to Apr.)
Environment: extensive mangrove swamps hinder access to sea; sand and dust storms; deforestation; soil degradation; population pressure negatively affects land
Terrain: coastal belt of mangrove swamps, wooded hill country, upland plateau, mountains in east
Land Use: 7% arable; 1% permanent crops; 31% meadows; 28% forest; 33% other; includes 290 sq. km irrigated
Location: W Africa, bordering on North Atlantic Ocean

■ PEOPLE

Population: 5,232,624 (July 2000 est.)
Nationality: Sierra Leonean
Age Structure: 0-14 yrs: 45%; 15-64: 52%; 65+: 3% (2000 est.)
Population Growth Rate: 3.67% (2000 est.)
Net Migration: 10.61 migrants/1,000 population (2000 est.)
Ethnic Groups: 90% native African (30% Temne, 39% Mende, other 30%); 10% Creole, European, Lebanese and Asian
Languages: English (official); regular use limited to literate minority; principal vernaculars are Mende in south and Temne in north; Krio is the language of the resettled ex-slave population of the Freetown area and is lingua franca
Religions: 60% Muslim, 10% Christian, 30% traditional beliefs
Birth Rate: 45.63/1,000 population (2000 est.)
Death Rate: 19.58/1,000 population (2000 est.)
Infant Mortality: 148.66 deaths/1,000 live births (2000 est.)

Life Expectancy at Birth: 42.37 years male, 48.21 years female (2000 est.)
Total Fertility Rate: 6.08 children born/woman (2000 est.)
Literacy: 37.2% (1997)

■ GOVERNMENT

Leader(s): Pres. Ahmad Tejan Kabbah, V. Pres. Albert Joe Demby
Government Type: constitutional democracy
Administrative Divisions: 3 provinces and 1 area
Nationhood: Apr. 27, 1961 (from UK)
National Holiday: Republic Day, Apr. 27

■ ECONOMY

Overview: the economic and social infrastructure is underdeveloped; subsistence agriculture is the backbone of the economy; problems include unemployment, large trade deficits; diamond mining is an important source of national income
GDP: US$2.5 billion, per capita US$500; real growth rate -10% (1999 est.)
Inflation: -0.84% (year-end 2000)
Industries: accounts for 16% of GDP; mining (diamonds, bauxite, rutile), small-scale manufacturing (beverages, textiles, cigarettes, footwear), petroleum refinery
Labour Force: 2 million (1998); 69.6% agriculture, 14.1% industry, 16.4% services
Unemployment: n.a.
Agriculture: accounts for 52% of GDP and two-thirds of the labour force, largely subsistence farming; cash crops: coffee, cocoa, palm kernels; harvest of food staple rice meets 80% of domestic needs; annual fish catch averages 53,000 metric tons
Natural Resources: diamonds, titanium ore, bauxite, iron ore, gold, chromite

■ FINANCE/TRADE

Currency: leone (Le) = 100 cents
International Reserves Excluding Gold: US$61 million (Jan. 2001)
Gold Reserves: n.a.
Budget: n.a.
Defence Expenditures: 33.0% of central government expenditure (1997)
Education Expenditures: n.a.
External Debt: US$1.249 billion (1999)
Exports: US$9 million (2000); commodities: rutile 50%, bauxite 17%, cocoa 11%, diamonds 3%, coffee 3%; partners: US, UK, Belgium, Germany, (Western Europe)
Imports: US$154 million (2000); commodities: capital goods 40%, food 32%, petroleum 12%, consumer goods 7%, light industrial goods;

partners: US, European Community, Japan, China, Nigeria

■ COMMUNICATIONS

Daily Newspapers: 1
Televisions: 13/1,000 inhabitants (1998)
Radios: 253/1,000 inhabitants (1997)
Telephones: 4 lines/1,000 inhabitants (1999)

■ TRANSPORTATION

Motor Vehicles: 42,500; 21,000 passenger cars (1997 est.)
Roads: 11,300 km; 904 km paved
Railway: 84 km
Air Traffic: 15,000 passengers carried (1996)
Airports: 10; 1 has paved runway (1999 est.)
Canadian Embassy: The Canadian High Commission to Sierra Leone, c/o The Canadian Embassy, PO Box 99, Conakry, Guinea. Tel: (011-224) 46-23-95. Fax: (011-224) 46-42-35. Email: cnaky@dfait-maeci.gc.ca
Embassy in Canada: c/o High Commission for the Republic of Sierra Leone, 1701-19th St NW, Washington DC 20009, USA. Tel: (202) 939-9261. Fax: (202) 483-1793. Email: n.a.

Singapore

Long-Form Name: Republic of Singapore
Capital: Singapore

■ GEOGRAPHY

Area: 647.5 sq. km
Coastline: 193 km
Climate: tropical; hot, humid, rainy; no pronounced rainy or dry seasons; thunderstorms occur on 40% of all days (67% of days in Apr.)
Environment: mostly urban and industrialized; water supply is limited
Terrain: lowland; gently undulating central plateau contains water catchment area and nature preserve
Land Use: 2% arable; 6% permanent crops; 0% meadows; 5% forest; 87% other; includes n.a. sq. km irrigated
Location: SE Asia (southern tip of Malaysia), bordering on South China Sea

■ PEOPLE

Population: 4,151,264 (July 2000 est.)
Nationality: Singaporean
Age Structure: 0-14 yrs: 18%; 15-64: 75%; 65+: 7% (2000 est.)
Population Growth Rate: 3.54% (2000 est.)
Net Migration: 26.8 migrants/1,000 population (2000 est.)

Ethnic Groups: 77% Chinese, 14% Malay, 7.6% Indian, 1.4% other
Languages: Chinese (Mandarin), Malay, Tamil and English (all official); Malay (national)
Religions: majority of Chinese are Buddhists or atheists; Malays nearly all Muslim (minorities are Christians, Hindus, Sikhs, Taoists, Confucianists)
Birth Rate: 12.79/1,000 population (2000 est.)
Death Rate: 4.21/1,000 population (2000 est.)
Infant Mortality: 3.65 deaths/1,000 live births (2000 est.)
Life Expectancy at Birth: 77.10 years male, 83.23 years female (2000 est.)
Total Fertility Rate: 1.16 children born/woman (2000 est.)
Literacy: 92% (1998)

■ GOVERNMENT

Leader(s): Pres. Sellapan Rama Nathan, Prime Min. Goh Chok Tong
Government Type: parliamentary republic within Commonwealth
Administrative Divisions: none
Nationhood: Aug. 9, 1965 (from Malaysia)
National Holiday: National Day, Aug. 9

■ ECONOMY

Overview: has an open entrepreneurial economy with strong service and manufacturing sectors and good international trading links; growth has traditionally run at high rates; per capita GDP is among the highest in Asia; rising labour costs continue to adversely affect Singapore's competitiveness
GDP: US$98 billion, per capita US$27,800; real growth rate 5.5% (1999 est.)
Inflation: 1.36% (year-end 2000)
Industries: accounts for 28% of GDP; petroleum refining, electronics, oil drilling equipment, rubber processing and rubber products, processed food and beverages, ship repair, entrepôt trade, financial services, biotechnology
Labour Force: 2 million (1998); 27% industry, 22.8% trade and tourism, 21.6% community, social and business services
Unemployment: 5.4% (Jan. 2000)
Agriculture: minor importance in the economy; self-sufficient in poultry and eggs; must import most other food; major crops: rubber, copra, fruit, vegetables
Natural Resources: fish, deepwater ports

■ FINANCE/TRADE

Currency: Singapore dollar ($S) = 100 cents
International Reserves Excluding Gold: US$80.022 billion (Jan. 2001)
Gold Reserves: n.a.

Budget: revenues US$13.9 billion; expenditures US$16.9 billion, including capital expenditures US$8.1 billion (1998-99 est.)
Defence Expenditures: 27.94% of central government expenditure (1998)
Education Expenditures: 18.20% of central government expenditure (1998)
External Debt: n.a.
Exports: US$127.986 billion (2000); commodities (includes transshipments to Malaysia): petroleum products, rubber electronics, manufactured goods; partners: US 24%, Malaysia 14%, Japan 9%, Thailand 6%, Hong Kong 5%, Australia 3%, Germany 3%
Imports: US$123.187 billion (2000); commodities (includes transshipments from Malaysia): capital equipment, petroleum, chemicals, manufactured goods, foodstuffs; partners: Japan 22%, US 16%, Malaysia 15%, European Community 12%, Kuwait 1%

■ COMMUNICATIONS

Daily Newspapers: 8
Televisions: 348/1,000 inhabitants (1998)
Radios: 822/1,000 inhabitants (1997)
Telephones: 482 lines/1,000 inhabitants (1999)

■ TRANSPORTATION

Motor Vehicles: 545,000; 390,000 passenger cars (1997 est.)
Roads: 3,122 km; 3,038 km paved
Railway: 38.6 km
Air Traffic: 12,981,000 passengers carried (1997)
Airports: 9; all have paved runways (1999 est.)
Canadian Embassy: Canadian High Commission, IBM Towers, 14th & 15th Fls, 80 Anson Rd, Singapore 079907; mailing address: Robinson Rd, P.O. Box 845, Singapore 901645. Tel: (011-65) 325-3200. Fax: (011-65) 325-3297. Email: spore@dfait-maeci.gc.ca
Embassy in Canada: c/o High Commission for the Republic of Singapore, 231 East 51st St, New York NY 10022, USA. Tel: (212) 826-0840. Fax: (212) 826-2964. Email: n.a.

Slovakia

Long-Form Name: Slovak Republic
Capital: Bratislava

■ GEOGRAPHY

Area: 48,845 sq. km
Coastline: none: landlocked
Climate: temperate: cool summers, cold, cloudy, humid winters
Environment: severe damage to forests from acid rain; industrial air pollution from metallurgical plants poses risks to human health

Terrain: rugged mountains in central region and north, lowlands in south
Land Use: 31% arable; 3% permanent crops; 17% permanent pastures; 41% forests; 8% other; includes 800 sq. km irrigated
Location: C Europe

■ PEOPLE

Population: 5,407,956 (July 2000 est.)
Nationality: Slovak
Age Structure: 0-14 yrs: 19%; 15-64: 69%; 65+: 12% (2000 est.)
Population Growth Rate: 0.12% (2000 est.)
Net Migration: 0.53 migrants/1,000 population (2000 est.)
Ethnic Groups: 85.7% Slovak, 10.6% Hungarian, 1.6% Gypsy, 1.0% Czech, 0.3% Ruthenian, 0.3% Ukrainian, 0.1% German, 0.1% Polish, 0.3% other
Languages: Slovak (official), Hungarian
Religions: 60.3% Roman Catholic, 9.7% atheist, 8.4% Protestant, 4.1% Orthodox, 17.5% other
Birth Rate: 10.00/1,000 population (2000 est.)
Death Rate: 9.29/1,000 population (2000 est.)
Infant Mortality: 9.18 deaths/1,000 live births (2000 est.)
Life Expectancy at Birth: 69.71 years male, 77.98 years female (2000 est.)
Total Fertility Rate: 1.25 children born/woman (2000 est.)
Literacy: 99.0% (1998)

■ GOVERNMENT

Leader(s): Pres. Rudolf Schuster, Prime Min. Mikulas Dzurinda
Government Type: parliamentary democracy
Administrative Divisions: 8 departments (kraje, sing. —kraj)
Nationhood: Jan. 1, 1993 (from Czechoslovakia)
National Holiday: Slovak Constitution Day, Sept. 1; Anniversary of Slovak National Uprising, Aug. 29

■ ECONOMY

Overview: continues the difficult transition from a centrally controlled economy to a modern market-oriented economy; private activity now makes up more than two-thirds of GDP. Slovakia continues to experience difficulty in attracting foreign investment
GDP: US$45.9 billion, per capita US$8,500; real growth rate 1.9% (1999 est.)
Inflation: 12.04% (year-end 2000)
Industries: accounts for 33% of GDP; mining, chemicals, metalworking, consumer appliances, plastics, armaments
Labour Force: 3 million (1999); 29.3% industry, 26.4% community, social and business services, 12.4% agriculture

Unemployment: 20% (1999 est.)
Agriculture: accounts for 5% of GDP; very diversified crop and livestock production including grains, livestock, poultry; mostly self-sufficient in food
Natural Resources: brown coal and lignite, iron ore, copper, manganese, salt, gas

■ FINANCE/TRADE

Currency: koruna (pl. koruny) (Kc) = 100 halierov
International Reserves Excluding Gold: US$4.007 billion (Nov. 2000)
Gold Reserves: US$1.290 million fine troy ounces (Nov. 2000)
Budget: revenues US$5.4 billion; expenditures US$5.8 billion, including capital expenditures US$n.a. (1999 est.)
Defence Expenditures: 4.76% of central government expenditure (1999)
Education Expenditures: 10.74% of central government expenditure (1999)
External Debt: US$9.150 billion (1999)
Exports: US$11.803 billion (2000); machinery and transport equipment, chemicals, fuels, minerals, agricultural products; partners: Czech Republic, successor states of the former USSR, Germany, Poland, Austria, France, US, UK
Imports: US$12.682 billion (2000); machinery and transport equipment, fuels, lubricants, manufactured goods, chemicals, agricultural products

■ COMMUNICATIONS

Daily Newspapers: 19
Televisions: 402/1,000 inhabitants (1998)
Radios: 580/1,000 inhabitants (1997)
Telephones: 307 lines/1,000 inhabitants (1999)

■ TRANSPORTATION

Motor Vehicles: included in the data for the Czech Republic
Roads: 17,710 km; 17,533 km paved
Railway: 3,660 km
Air Traffic: 81,000 passengers carried (1997)
Airports: 36; 18 have paved runways (1999 est.)

Canadian Embassy: The Canadian Embassy to Slovakia, Miskkova 28D, 81100 Bratislava, Slovak Republic. Tel: (011-421-7) 5244-2175. Fax: (011-421-7) 5249-9995. Email: masson yensen@canemb.sk
Embassy in Canada: Embassy of the Slovak Republic, 50 Rideau Terrace, Ottawa ON K1M 2A1. Tel: (613) 749-4442. Fax: (613) 749-4989. Email: slovakemb@sprint.ca

Slovenia

Long-Form Name: Republic of Slovenia
Capital: Ljubljana

■ GEOGRAPHY

Area: 20,253 sq. km
Coastline: 46.6 km
Climate: Mediterranean climate on the coast, continental climate with mild to hot summers and cold winters in the plateaus and eastern valleys
Environment: pollution of Sava River; heavy metals and toxic chemicals along coast; forest damage from air pollution; subject to flooding and earthquakes
Terrain: short coastal strip, alpine mountain region, mixed mountains and valleys and numerous rivers in east
Land Use: 12% arable; 3% permanent crops; 24% meadows and pastures; 54% forests and woodland; 7% other includes 20 sq. km irrigated
Location: southern Europe, bordering on Adriatic Sea

■ PEOPLE

Population: 1,927,593 (July 2000 est.)
Nationality: Slovene
Age Structure: 0-14 yrs: 16%; 15-64: 69%; 65+: 15% (2000 est.)
Population Growth Rate: 0.12% (2000 est.)
Net Migration: 1.75 migrants/1,000 population (2000 est.)
Ethnic Groups: 88% Slovene, 3% Croat, 2% Serb, 1% Bosniak, 0.6% Yugoslav, 0.4% Hungarian, 5% other
Languages: 91% Slovenian, 6% Serbo-Croatian, 3% other
Religions: 71% Roman Catholic, 1% Lutheran, 1% Muslim, 4.3% athiest, 23% other
Birth Rate: 9.35/1,000 population (2000 est.)
Death Rate: 9.90/1,000 population (2000 est.)
Infant Mortality: 4.56 deaths/1,000 live births (2000 est.)
Life Expectancy at Birth: 70.97 years male, 78.97 years female (2000 est.)
Total Fertility Rate: 1.28 children born/woman (2000 est.)
Literacy: 99% (1998)

■ GOVERNMENT

Leader(s): Pres. Milan Kucan, Prime Min. Janez Drnovsek
Government Type: parliamentary democratic republic
Administrative Divisions: 136 municipalities (obcine, sing. —obcina) and 11 urban municipalities (obcine mestne, sing. —obcina mestna)
Nationhood: June 25, 1991 (from Yugoslavia)
National Holiday: National Statehood Day, June 25

■ ECONOMY

Overview: tourism has suffered due to internal strife; destruction of trade channels and the influx of tens of thousands of refugees have interfered with economic recovery after secession from Yugoslavia; there are efforts toward the privatization of major industrial firms; inflation and unemployment rates are gradually beginning to drop; chief trading partners: Germany, Italy, former Soviet countries, France, Austria, US
GDP: US$21.4 billion, per capita US$10,900; real growth rate 3.5% (1999 est.)
Inflation: 10.85% (year-end 2000)
Industries: accounts for 35% of GDP; metallurgy, furniture, sports equipment, steel, cars, sugar, cement, textiles, machine tools
Labour Force: 1 million (1999); 39.3% industry, 23.1% community, social and business services, 11.1% trade and tourism
Unemployment: 7.9% (1998)
Agriculture: accounts for 4% of GDP; products include wheat, maize, sugar beets, potatoes, cabbages, livestock (esp. cattle, sheep, pigs, poultry); fishing, forestry; many other agricultural products must be imported
Natural Resources: brown coal and lignite deposits, lead, zinc, mercury, uranium, silver, hydropower

■ FINANCE/TRADE

Currency: Slovenian tolar = 100 stotins (at parity with Yugoslav dinar)
International Reserves Excluding Gold: US$3.113 billion (Jan. 2001)
Gold Reserves: none (Jan. 2001)
Budget: revenues US$8.11 billion; expenditures US$8.32 billion, including capital expenditures (1997 est.)
Defence Expenditures: 12.5% of central government expenditure (1997)
Education Expenditures: 5.7% of GNP (1997)
External Debt: US$4.4 billion (1998 est.)
Exports: US$8.652 billion (2000); machinery, semifinished goods, raw materials, electric motors, transportation equipment, clothing, foodstuffs
Imports: US$10.145 billion (2000); raw materials, semifinished goods, machinery, foodstuffs

■ COMMUNICATIONS

Daily Newspapers: 7
Televisions: 356/1,000 inhabitants (1998)
Radios: 406/1,000 inhabitants (1997)
Telephones: 378 lines/1,000 inhabitants (1999)

■ TRANSPORTATION

Motor Vehicles: n.a.
Roads: 19,586 km; 17,745 km paved
Railway: 1,201 km
Air Traffic: 404,000 passengers carried (1997)
Airports: 14; 6 have paved runways (1999 est.)

Canadian Embassy: The Canadian Embassy to Slovenia, c/o The Canadian Embassy Budakeszi ut 32, 1121 Budapest, Hungary. Tel.: (011-36-1) 392-3360. Fax: (011-36-1) 392-3390. Email: bpest@dfait-maeci.gc.ca
Embassy in Canada: Embassy of the Republic of Slovenia, 150 Metcalfe St, Ste 2101, Ottawa, ON K2P 1P1. Tel: (613) 565-5781. Fax: (613) 565-5783. Email: n.a.

Solomon Islands

Long-Form Name: Solomon Islands
Capital: Honiara (on island of Guadalcanal)

■ GEOGRAPHY

Area: 28,450 sq km
Coastline: 5,313 km
Climate: tropical monsoon; few extremes of temperature and weather
Environment: subject to typhoons, which are rarely destructive; geologically active region with frequent earth tremors; soil degradation and deforestation; deterioration of coral reefs
Terrain: mostly rugged mountains with some low coral atolls
Land Use: 1% arable; 1% permanent crops; 1% meadows; 88% pastures; 9% other; includes n.a. sq. km irrigated
Location: Melanesia, Pacific Ocean, E of New Guinea

■ PEOPLE

Population: 466,194 (July 2000 est.)
Nationality: Solomon Islander
Age Structure: 0-14 yrs: 44%; 15-64: 53%; 65+: 3% (2000 est.)
Population Growth Rate: 3.04% (2000 est.)
Net Migration: 0 migrants/1,000 population (2000 est.)
Ethnic Groups: 93% Melanesian, 4% Polynesian, 1.5% Micronesian, 0.8% European, 0.3% Chinese, 0.4% other

Languages: English (official), Pidgin, 120 local languages
Religions: 34% Anglican, 19% Roman Catholic, 17% South Seas Evangelical, 25% other Protestant, 5% other
Birth Rate: 34.79/1,000 population (2000 est.)
Death Rate: 4.35/1,000 population (2000 est.)
Infant Mortality: 25.26 deaths/1,000 live births (2000 est.)
Life Expectancy at Birth: 68.86 years male; 73.81 years female (2000 est.)
Total Fertility Rate: 4.80 children born/woman (2000 est.)
Literacy: 62.0% (1997)

■ GOVERNMENT

Leader(s): Head of State: Queen Elizabeth II/Gov. Gen. John Lapli. Prime Min. Manasseh Sogavare
Government Type: parliamentary democracy
Administrative Divisions: 7 provinces and 1 town
Nationhood: July 7, 1978 (from UK; formerly known as British Solomon Islands)
National Holiday: Independence Day, July 7

■ ECONOMY

Overview: about 90% of the population depend on subsistence agriculture, fishing and forestry for at least part of their livelihood; possesses an abundance of undeveloped mineral resources; little manufacturing activity—most manufactured goods must be imported uncontrolled government spending is leading to national financial ruin despite a rich natural resource base
GDP: US$1.21 billion, per capita US$2,650; real growth rate 3.5% (1999 est.)
Inflation: 8.26% (year-end 1999)
Industries: account for 3.5% of GDP; copra, fish (tuna)
Labour Force: approx. 27,000; 41.5% community, social and business services, 23.7% agriculture, 11.9% trade and tourism
Unemployment: n.a.
Agriculture: including fishing and forestry, accounts for approx. 50% of GDP; mostly subsistence farming; cash crops: cocoa, beans, coconuts, palm kernels, timber; other products: rice, potatoes, vegetables, fruit, cattle, pigs; not self-sufficient in food grains; 90% of fish catch is exported
Natural Resources: fish, forests, gold, bauxite, phosphates, lead, zinc, nickel

■ FINANCE/TRADE

Currency: Solomon Islands dollar ($SI) = 100 cents

International Reserves Excluding Gold: US$35 million (Nov. 2000)
Gold Reserves: n.a.
Budget: revenues US$147 million; expenditures US$168 million, including capital expenditures US$n.a. (1997 est.)
Defence Expenditures: negligible
Education Expenditures: n.a.
External Debt: US$160 million (1999)
Exports: US$130 million (2000); commodities: fish 46%, timber 31%, copra 5%, palm oil 5%; partners: Japan 51%, UK 12%, Thailand 9%, Netherlands 8%, Australia 2%, US 2%
Imports: US$145 million (2000); commodities: plant and machinery 30%, fuel 19%, food 16%; partners: Japan 36%, US 23%, Singapore 9%, UK 9%, New Zealand 9%, Australia 4%, Hong Kong 4%, China 3%

■ COMMUNICATIONS

Daily Newspapers: 0
Televisions: 6.4/1,000 inhabitants (1997 est.)
Radios: 122/1,000 inhabitants (1997 est.)
Telephones: 19 lines/1,000 inhabitants (1999)

■ TRANSPORTATION

Motor Vehicles: n.a.
Roads: 1,360 km; 34 km paved
Railway: none
Air Traffic: 94,000 passengers carried (1997)
Airports: 33; 2 have paved runways (1999 est.)

Canadian Embassy: The Canadian High Commission to Solomon Islands, c/o The Canadian High Commission, Commonwealth Ave, Canberra A.C.T. 2600, Australia. Tel: (011-61-2) 6270-4000. Fax: (011-61-2) 6273-3285. Email: cnbra@dfait-maeci.gc.ca
Embassy in Canada: c/o High Commission for the Solomon Islands, 800-2nd Ave, Ste 400L, New York NY 10017, USA. Tel: (212) 599-6192. Fax: (212) 661-8925. Email: simny@solomons.com

Somalia

Long-Form Name: Somalia
Capital: Mogadishu

■ GEOGRAPHY

Area: 637,657 sq. km
Coastline: 3,025 km
Climate: desert; northeast monsoon (Dec. to Feb.), cooler southwest monsoon (May to Oct.); irregular rainfall; hot, humid periods (tangambili) between monsoons
Environment: recurring droughts; frequent dust storms over eastern plains in summer; deforestation; overgrazing; soil erosion; desertification
Terrain: mostly flat to undulating plateau rising to hills in north
Land Use: 2% arable; negligible permanent crops; 69% permanent pastures; 26% forest; 3% other; includes 1,800 sq. km irrigated
Location: E Africa, bordering on Gulf of Aden, Indian Ocean

■ PEOPLE

Population: 7,253,137 (July 2000 est.)
Nationality: Somali
Age Structure: 0-14 yrs: 44%; 15-64: 53%; 65+: 3% (2000 est.)
Population Growth Rate: 2.9% (2000 est.)
Net Migration: 0 migrants/1,000 population (2000 est.)
Ethnic Groups: 85% Somali, rest mainly Bantu; 30,000 Arabs, 3,000 Europeans, 800 Asians
Languages: Somali (official); Arabic, Italian, English
Religions: almost entirely Sunni Muslim, small Christian community
Birth Rate: 47.70/1,000 population (2000 est.)
Death Rate: 18.69/1,000 population (2000 est.)
Infant Mortality: 125.77 deaths/1,000 live births (2000 est.)
Life Expectancy at Birth: 44.66 years male, 47.85 years female (2000 est.)
Total Fertility Rate: 7.18 children born/woman (2000 est.)
Literacy: 24% (1997)

■ GOVERNMENT

Leader(s): Pres. Abidiqasim Salad Hassan appointed by interim-parliament of 245 clan chiefs in 2000. Prime Min. Ali Khalif Galayr. Not supported by Somaliland or Puntland. State of anarchy continues; government structures absent
Government Type: n.a.
Administrative Divisions: 18 regions (plural n.a., sing. —gobolka)
Nationhood: July 1, 1960 (from a merger of British Somaliland, which became independent from the UK on June 26, 1960, and Italian Somaliland, which became independent from the Italian-administered UN trusteeship on July 1, 1960, to form the Somali Republic)
National Holiday: Anniversary of the Revolution, Oct. 21

■ ECONOMY

Overview: nomads or semi-nomads who are dependent upon livestock for their livelihoods make up about 50% of the population; one of the world's least developed countries, possessing few resources; problems include high external debt, double-digit inflation and bitter civil war which has devastated much of the economy

GDP: US$4.3 billion, per capita US$600; real growth rate n.a.% (1999 est.)

Inflation: n.a.

Industries: accounts for 10% of GDP; based on processing of agricultural products; sugar refining, textiles, petroleum refining

Labour Force: n.a.; 75.6% agriculture, 8.4% industry, 16% services

Unemployment: n.a.

Agriculture: livestock accounts for 59% of GDP and 65% of export revenue: cattle, sheep, goats; fishing potential largely unexploited; crops: bananas, sorghum, corn, mangoes, sugar cane; not self-sufficient in food

Natural Resources: uranium and largely unexploited reserves of iron ore, tin, gypsum, bauxite, copper, salt

■ FINANCE/TRADE

Currency: Somali shilling (So.Sh.) = 100 cents

International Reserves Excluding Gold: n.a.

Gold Reserves: n.a.

Budget: n.a.

Defence Expenditures: n.a.

Education Expenditures: n.a.

External Debt: US$2.606 billion (1999)

Exports: US$41 million (2000); commodities: livestock, hides, skins, bananas, fish; partners: US 0.5%, Saudi Arabia, Italy, Germany

Imports: US$45 million (2000); commodities: textiles, petroleum products, foodstuffs, construction materials; partners: US 13%, Italy, Germany, Kenya, UK, Saudi Arabia

■ COMMUNICATIONS

Daily Newspapers: 2

Televisions: 15/1,000 inhabitants (1997)

Radios: 53/1,000 inhabitants (1997)

Telephones: 2 lines/1,000 inhabitants (1999)

■ TRANSPORTATION

Motor Vehicles: 20,000; 10,000 passenger cars (1997 est.)

Roads: 22,100 km; 2,608 km paved

Railway: none

Air Traffic: n.a.

Airports: 61; 7 have paved runways (1999 est.)

Canadian Embassy: The Canadian Embassy to Somalia, c/o The Canadian High Commission, Comcraft House, 6th Fl, Hailé Sélassie Ave, Nairobi, Kenya; mailing address: The Canadian High Commission, P.O. Box 30481, Nairobi, Kenya. Tel: (011-254-2) 21-48-04. Fax: (011-254-2) 22-69-87. Email: nrobi@dfait-maeci.gc.ca

Embassy in Canada: c/o The High Commission for the Republic of Kenya, 415 Laurier Ave E, Ottawa ON K1N 6R4. Tel: (613) 563-1773. Fax: (613) 233-6599. Email: kenrep@on.aibn.com

South Africa

Long-Form Name: Republic of South Africa

Capital: Pretoria (administrative), Cape Town (legislative), Bloemfontein (judicial)

■ GEOGRAPHY

Area: 1,219,912 sq. km; includes Walvis Bay, Marion Island, and Prince Edward Island

Coastline: 2,798 km

Climate: mostly semi-arid; subtropical along coast; sunny days, cool nights

Environment: lack of important arterial rivers or lakes requires extensive water conservation and control measures; prolonged droughts and increasing water pollution exacerbate the problem

Terrain: vast interior plateau rimmed by rugged hills and narrow coastal plain

Land Use: 10% arable; 1% permanent crops; 67% meadows; 7% forest; 15% other, includes 12,700 sq. km irrigated

Location: S Africa, bordering on Indian Ocean, South Atlantic Ocean

■ PEOPLE

Population: 43,421,021 (July 2000 est.)

Nationality: South African

Age Structure: 0-14 yrs: 32%; 15-64: 63%; 65+: 5% (2000 est.)

Population Growth Rate: 0.5% (2000 est.)

Net Migration: -1.9 migrants/1,000 population (2000 est.)

Ethnic Groups: 75.2% black, 13.6% white, 8.6% coloured, 2.6% Indian

Languages: 11 official languages: Afrikaans, English, Ndebele, Pedi, Sotho, Swazi, Tsonga, Tswana, Venda, Xhosa, Zulu

Religions: most of whites, coloureds and approx. 60% of blacks are Christian; approx. 60% of Indians are Hindu, 20% Muslim

Birth Rate: 24.56/1,000 population (2000 est.)

Death Rate: 14.69/1,000 population (2000 est.)

Infant Mortality: 58.88 deaths/1,000 live births (2000 est.)

Life Expectancy at Birth: 50.41 years male, 51.81 years female (2000 est.)

Total Fertility Rate: 2.47 children born/woman (2000 est.)

Literacy: 84.5% (1998)

■ GOVERNMENT

Leader(s): Pres. Thabo Mvuyelwa Mbeki
Government Type: republic
Administrative Divisions: 9 provinces; after the election bringing Mandela to power, all 10 black homelands and 4 provinces existing earlier were dissolved
Nationhood: May 31, 1910 (from UK)
National Holiday: Freedom Day, April 27

■ ECONOMY

Overview: there is great disparity in living standards between the white minority (favoured) and the black majority; international embargoes against the country (because of its policy of apartheid) hurt the economy; burgeoning unemployment; has rich mineral resources (diamonds)
GDP: US$296.1 billion, per capita US$6,900; real growth rate 3% (1999 est.)
Inflation: 5.20% (year-end 1999)
Industries: accounts for 35% of GDP; mining (world's largest producer of platinum, gold, chrome), automobile assembly, metalworking, machinery, textile, iron and steel, chemical, fertilizer, foodstuffs
Labour Force: 17 million (1999); 28.3% industry, 26.5% community, social and business services, 15.4% trade and tourism
Unemployment: 30.0%, with high underemployment (1999 est.)
Agriculture: accounts for 5% of GDP and 30% of labour force; diversified agriculture, with emphasis on livestock; products: cattle, poultry, sheep, wool, milk, beef, corn, wheat; sugar cane, fruit, vegetables; self-sufficient in food
Natural Resources: gold, chromium, antimony, coal, iron ore, manganese, nickel, phosphates, tin, uranium, gem diamonds, platinum, copper, vanadium, salt, natural gas

■ FINANCE/TRADE

Currency: rand (R) = 100 cents
International Reserves Excluding Gold: US$6.053 billion (Jan. 2001)
Gold Reserves: US$5.900 million fine troy ounces (Jan. 2001)
Budget: n.a.
Defence Expenditures: 5.6% of central government expenditure (1997)
Education Expenditures: 7.9% of GNP (1997)
External Debt: US$24.158 billion (1999)
Exports: US$26.042 billion (2000); commodities: gold 40%, minerals and metals 23%, food 6%, chemicals 3%; partners: Germany, Japan, UK, US, other European Community, Hong Kong
Imports: US$26.811 billion (2000); commodities: machinery 27%, chemicals 11%, vehicles and aircraft 11%, textiles, scientific instruments, base metals; partners: US, Germany, Japan, UK, France, Italy, Switzerland

■ COMMUNICATIONS

Daily Newspapers: 17
Televisions: 125/1,000 inhabitants (1998)
Radios: 317/1,000 inhabitants (1997)
Telephones: 125 lines/1,000 inhabitants (1999)

■ TRANSPORTATION

Motor Vehicles: 6,280,000; 4,120,000 passenger cars (1997 est.)
Roads: 534,131 km; 63,027 km paved
Railway: 21,431 km
Air Traffic: 7,274,000 passengers carried (1997)
Airports: 744; 143 have paved runways (1999 est.)

Canadian Embassy: The Canadian High Commission, 1103 Arcadia, Hatfield 0083, Pretoria; mailing address: Private Bag X13, Hatfield 0028, South Africa. Tel: (011-27-12) 422-3000. Fax: (011-27-12) 422-3052. Email: pret@dfait-maeci.gc.ca
Embassy in Canada: Embassy of the Republic of South Africa, 15 Sussex Dr, Ottawa ON K1M 1M8. Tel: (613) 744-0330. Fax: (613) 741-1639. Email: safrica@ottawa.net

Spain

Long-Form Name: Kingdom of Spain
Capital: Madrid

■ GEOGRAPHY

Area: 504,782 sq. km; includes Balaeric Islands, Canary Islands, Ceuta, Melilla, Islas Chafarinas, Peñón de Vélez de la Gomera
Coastline: 4,964 km
Climate: temperate; clear, hot summers in interior, more moderate and cloudy along coast; cloudy, cold winters in interior, partly cloudy and cool along coast
Environment: deforestation; air and water pollution; soil degradation; desertification; periodic droughts
Terrain: large, flat to dissected, rugged hills; Pyrenees in north
Land Use: 30% arable; 9% permanent crops; 21% meadows; 32% forest; 8% other, includes 34,530 sq. km irrigated
Location: SW Europe, bordering on Mediterranean Sea and N Atlantic Ocean

■ PEOPLE

Population: 39,996,671(July 2000 est.)

Nationality: Spanish or Spaniard
Age Structure: 0-14 yrs: 15%; 15-64: 68%; 65+: 17% (2000 est.)
Population Growth Rate: 0.11% (2000 est.)
Net Migration: 0.88 migrants/1,000 population (2000 est.)
Ethnic Groups: composite of Mediterranean and Nordic types
Languages: Castilian Spanish; second languages include 17% Catalan (northeast), 7% Galician (northwest), 2% Basque (north)
Religions: 99% Roman Catholic, 1% other sects
Birth Rate: 9.22/1,000 population (2000 est.)
Death Rate: 9.03/1,000 population (2000 est.)
Infant Mortality: 4.99 deaths/1,000 live births (2000 est.)
Life Expectancy at Birth: 75.32 years male, 82.49 years female (2000 est.)
Total Fertility Rate: 1.15 children born/woman (2000 est.)
Literacy: 97% (1998)

■ GOVERNMENT

Leader(s): King Juan Carlos I, Pres. Jose Maria Aznar
Government Type: parliamentary monarchy
Administrative Divisions: 17 autonomous communities (comunidades autonomas, sing. — comunidad autonoma)
Nationhood: 1492 (expulsion of the Moors and unification)
National Holiday: National Day, Oct. 12

■ ECONOMY

Overview: advocates liberalization, privatization, and deregulation of the economy, and has introduced some tax reforms to that end; adjustment to the monetary and other economic policies of an integrated Europe will pose difficult challenges in the next few years
GDP: US$677.5 billion, per capita US$17,300; real growth rate 3.6% (1999 est.)
Inflation: 3.43% (year-end 2000)
Industries: accounts for 33.6% of GDP; textiles and apparel (including footwear), food and beverages, metals and metal manufacturing, chemicals, shipbuilding, automobiles, machine tools
Labour Force: 17 million (1999); 64% services, 28% manufacturing and mining, 8% agriculture
Unemployment: 16% (1999 est.)
Agriculture: accounts for 3.2% of GDP and 14% of labour force; major products: grain, vegetables, olives, wine grapes, sugar beets, citrus fruit, beef, pork, poultry, dairy; largely self-sufficient in food; fish catch of 1.4 million metric tons
Natural Resources: coal, lignite, iron ore, uranium, mercury, pyrites, fluorspar, gypsum, zinc, lead, tungsten, copper, kaolin, potash, hydropower

■ FINANCE/TRADE

Currency: peseta (Pta) = 100 centimos; Euro (EUR) as of March 1, 2002
International Reserves Excluding Gold: US$31.807 billion (Jan. 2001)
Gold Reserves: US$16.829 million fine troy ounces (Jan. 2001)
Budget: revenues US$115 billion, expenditures US$125 billion, including capital expenditures US$n.a. (1998 est.)
Defence Expenditures: 6.0% of central government expenditure (1997)
Education Expenditures: 5.0% of GNP (1997)
External Debt: n.a.
Exports: US$110.044 billion (2000); commodities: foodstuffs, live animals, wood, footwear, machinery, chemicals; partners: European Community 66%, US 8%, other developed countries 9%
Imports: US$152.768 billion (2000); commodities: petroleum, footwear, machinery, chemicals, grain, soybeans, coffee, tobacco, iron and steel, timber, cotton, transport equipment; partners: European Community 57%, US 9%, other developed countries 13%, Middle East 3%

■ COMMUNICATIONS

Daily Newspapers: 87
Televisions: 506/1,000 inhabitants (1998)
Radios: 333/1,000 inhabitants (1997)
Telephones: 410 lines/1,000 inhabitants (1999)

■ TRANSPORTATION

Motor Vehicles: 18,300,000; 14,900,000 passenger cars (1997 est.)
Roads: 346,858 km; 343,389 km paved
Railway: 13,950 km
Air Traffic: 30,316,000 passengers carried (1997)
Airports: 105; 70 have paved runways (1999 est.)
Canadian Embassy: The Canadian Embassy, Calle Nunez de Balboa, 35, 28001 Madrid; mailing address: Apartado 587, 28080 Madrid, Spain. Tel: (011-34) 91-423-3252. Fax: (011-34) 91-423-3251. Email: mdrid@dfait-maeci.gc.ca
Embassy in Canada: Embassy of the Kingdom of Spain, 74 Stanley Ave, Ottawa ON, K1M IP4. Tel: (613) 747-2252. Fax: (613) 744-1224. Email: embespca@mail.mae.es

---

Sri Lanka

Long-Form Name: Democratic Socialist Republic of Sri Lanka
Capital: Colombo

■ GEOGRAPHY

Area: 65,610 sq. km
Coastline: 1,340 km
Climate: tropical; monsoonal; northeast monsoon (Dec. to Mar.); southwest monsoon (June to Oct.)
Environment: occasional cyclones, tornados; deforestation; soil erosion; pollution of fresh water resources
Terrain: mostly low, flat to rolling plain; mountains in south-central interior
Land Use: 14% arable; 15% permanent crops; 7% meadows; 32% forest; 32% other, includes 5,500 sq. km irrigated
Location: Indian Ocean, S of India

■ PEOPLE

Population: 19,238,575 (July 2000 est.)
Nationality: Sri Lankan
Age Structure: 0-14 yrs: 26%; 15-64: 67%; 65+: 7% (2000 est.)
Population Growth Rate: 0.89% (2000 est.)
Net Migration: -1.47 migrants/1,000 population (2000 est.)
Ethnic Groups: 74% Sinhalese; 18% Tamil; 7% Moor; 1% Burgher, Malay and Veddha
Languages: Sinhala (official); Sinhala and Tamil are the national languages; Sinhala spoken by about 74% of population, Tamil spoken by about 18%; English commonly used in government and spoken by about 10% of the population
Religions: 69% Buddhist, 15% Hindu (Tamil speakers), 8% Christian, 8% Muslim
Birth Rate: 16.78/1,000 population (2000 est.)
Death Rate: 6.43/1,000 population (2000 est.)
Infant Mortality: 16.51 deaths/1,000 live births (2000 est.)
Life Expectancy at Birth: 69.33 years male, 74.45 years female (2000 est.)
Total Fertility Rate: 1.98 children born/woman (2000 est.)
Literacy: 91% (1998)

■ GOVERNMENT

Leader(s): Pres. Chandrika Bandaranaike Kumaratunga, Prime Min. Ratnasiri Wickramanayake
Government Type: republic
Administrative Divisions: 8 provinces
Nationhood: Feb. 4, 1948 (from UK; formerly known as Ceylon)
National Holiday: Independence and National Day, Feb. 4

■ ECONOMY

Overview: sustained economic growth, coupled with low population growth, has pushed Sri Lanka from the ranks of the poorest countries however civil war between Sinhalese and Tamils continues to disrupt
GDP: US$50.5 billion, per capita US$2,600; real growth rate 3.7% (1999 est.)
Inflation: 6.18% (year-end 2000)
Industries: accounts for 19% of GDP; processing of rubber, tea, coconuts and other agricultural commodities; cement, petroleum refining, textiles, tobacco. The apparel industry has surpassed all other kinds of manufacturing
Labour Force: 8 million (1999); 38.7% agriculture, 18.3% community, social and business services, 12.7% industry
Unemployment: 9.5% (1998 est.)
Agriculture: accounts for 21% of GDP and almost 45% of labour force; most important staple crop is paddy rice; other field crops: sugar cane, grains, pulses, oilseeds, roots; spices; cash crops: tea, rubber, coconuts; animal products: milk, eggs, hides, meat; not self-sufficient in rice production
Natural Resources: limestone, graphite, mineral sands, gems, phosphates, clay, hydropower

■ FINANCE/TRADE

Currency: rupee (SL Re) = 100 cents
International Reserves Excluding Gold: US$1.039 billion (Dec. 2000)
Gold Reserves: US$0.626 million fine troy ounces (Jan. 2001)
Budget: revenues US$2.7 billion; expenditures US$4.2 billion, including capital expenditures of US$1.1 billion (1998 est.)
Defence Expenditures: 14.99% of total govt. expenditure (1999)
Education Expenditures: 10.96% of govt. expenditure (1999)
External Debt: US$9.473 billion (1999)
Exports: US$4.846 billion (2000); commodities: tea, textiles and garments, petroleum products, coconut, rubber, agricultural products, gems and jewelry, marine products; partners: US 26%, Egypt, Iraq, UK, Germany, Singapore, Japan
Imports: US$6.373 billion (2000); commodities: petroleum, machinery and equipment, textiles and textile materials, wheat, transportation equipment, electrical machinery, sugar, rice; partners: Japan, Saudi Arabia, US 5.6%, India, Singapore, Germany, UK, Iran

■ COMMUNICATIONS

Daily Newspapers: 9
Televisions: 92/1,000 inhabitants (1998)
Radios: 209/1,000 inhabitants (1997)
Telephones: 36 lines/1,000 inhabitants (1999)

■ TRANSPORTATION

Motor Vehicles: 468,900; 220,000 passenger cars (1997 est.)

Roads: 11,285 km; 10,721 km paved
Railway: 1,463 km
Air Traffic: 1,232,000 passengers carried (1997)
Airports: 14, 12 have paved runways (1999 est.)
Canadian Embassy: The Canadian High Commission, 6 Gregory's Rd, Cinnamon Gardens, Colombo 7, Sri Lanka; mailing address: P.O. Box 1006, Colombo 7, Sri Lanka. Tel: (011-94-75) 69-58-41. Fax: (011-94-75) 35-38-29. Email: clmbo@dfait-maeci.gc.ca
Embassy in Canada: High Commission for the Democratic Socialist Republic of Sri Lanka, 333 Laurier Ave W, Ste 1204, Ottawa ON K1P 1C1. Tel: (613) 233-8449. Fax: (613) 238-8448. Email: lankacom@magi.com

Sudan

Long-Form Name: Republic of the Sudan
Capital: Khartoum

■ GEOGRAPHY

Area: 2,505,810 sq. km
Coastline: 853 km
Climate: tropical in south; arid desert in north; rainy season (Apr. to Oct.)
Environment: dominated by the Nile and its tributaries; dust storms; desertification; unsafe drinking water resources; overhunting threatens wildlife population
Terrain: generally flat, featureless plain; mountains in east and west
Land Use: 5% arable; negligible permanent crops; 46% permanent pastures; 19% forest; 30% other; includes 19,460 sq. km irrigated
Location: NE Africa, bordering on Red Sea

■ PEOPLE

Population: 35,079,814 (July 2000 est.)
Nationality: Sudanese
Age Structure: 0-14 yrs: 45%; 15-64: 53%; 65+: 2% (2000 est.)
Population Growth Rate: 2.84% (2000 est.)
Net Migration: 0.05 migrants/1,000 population (2000 est.)
Ethnic Groups: 52% black, 39% Arab, 6% Beja, 2% foreigners, 1% other
Languages: Arabic (official), Nubian, Ta Bedawie, diverse dialects of Nilotic, Nilo-Hamatic and Sudanic languages, English; program of Arabization in process
Religions: 70% Sunni Muslim (in north), 25% indigenous beliefs, 5% Christian (mostly in south and Khartoum)
Birth Rate: 38.58/1,000 population (2000 est.)
Death Rate: 10.28/1,000 population (2000 est.)
Infant Mortality: 70.21 deaths/1,000 live births (2000 est.)

Life Expectancy at Birth: 55.49 years male, 57.66 years female (2000 est.)
Total Fertility Rate: 5.47 children born/woman (2000 est.)
Literacy: 53.3% (1997)

■ GOVERNMENT

Leader(s): Pres. Omar Hassan Ahmed al-Bashir
Government Type: transitional; government was civilianized after the ruling military junta was dissolved on Oct. 16, 1993
Administrative Divisions: 26 states (wilayat, sing. —wilayah)
Nationhood: Jan. 1, 1956 (from Egypt and UK; formerly known as Anglo-Egyptian Sudan)
National Holiday: Independence Day, Jan. 1

■ ECONOMY

Overview: a very poor country, hurt by civil war, chronic political instability, adverse weather and counterproductive governmental economic policies; agriculture is the economic base. It employs 80% of the labour force and focuses chiefly on processing agricultural produce; international aid is helping the country manage a high foreign debt, but creditors want economic reform
GDP: US$32.6 billion, per capita US$940; real growth rate 3% (1999 est.)
Inflation: 15.99% (year-end 1999)
Industries: accounts for 17% of GDP; cotton ginning, textiles, cement, edible oils, sugar, soap distilling, shoes, petroleum refining
Labour Force: 11 million (1998); 63.4% agriculture, 4.3% industry, 32.3% services
Unemployment: n.a.
Agriculture: accounts for 41% of GDP and 80% of labour force; untapped potential for higher farm production; water shortages; two-thirds of land area suitable for crops and livestock; major products: cotton, oilseeds, sorghum, millet, wheat, gum arabic, sheep; marginally self-sufficient in most foods
Natural Resources: modest reserves of crude oil, iron ore, copper, chromium ore, zinc, tungsten, mica, silver, crude oil

■ FINANCE/TRADE

Currency: Sudanese dinar (LSd) = 100 piastres; Sudanese pound was discontinued in July 1999
International Reserves Excluding Gold: US$238 million (April 2000)
Gold Reserves: n.a.
Budget: revenues US$1.2 billion; expenditures US$1.3 billion, including capital expenditures of US$n.a. (2000 est.)
Defence Expenditures: 53.8% of central government expenditure (1997)

Education Expenditures: 0.9% of GNP (1997)
External Debt: US$16.132 billion (1999)
Exports: US$650 million (2000); commodities: cotton 43%, sesame, gum arabic, peanuts; partners: Western Europe 46%, Saudi Arabia 14%, Eastern Europe 9%, Japan 9%, US 3%
Imports: US$1.975 billion (2000); commodities: petroleum products, manufactured goods, machinery and equipment, medicines and chemicals; partners: Western Europe 32%, Africa and Asia 15%, US 13%, Eastern Europe 3%

■ COMMUNICATIONS

Daily Newspapers: 5
Televisions: 87/1,000 inhabitants (1998)
Radios: 271/1,000 inhabitants (1997)
Telephones: 6 lines/1,000 inhabitants (1999)

■ TRANSPORTATION

Motor Vehicles: 75,000 registered vehicles, including 35,000 passenger cars (1996)
Roads: 11,900 km; 4,320 km paved
Railway: 5,311 km
Air Traffic: 333,000 passengers carried (1997)
Airports: 61; 12 have paved runways (1999 est.)

Canadian Embassy: The Canadian Embassy to the Sudan, 10th St, Off Sharia al Baladia, Khartoum East, Sudan. Tel: (011-249-11) 79-03-20. Fax: (011-249-11) 79-03-21. Email: Khrtm@dfait-maeci.gc.ca
Embassy in Canada: Embassy of the Republic of the Sudan, 354 Stewart St, Ottawa ON K1N 6K8. Tel: (613) 235-4000. Fax: (613) 235-6880. Email: sudanembassy-canada@home.com

Suriname

Long-Form Name: Republic of Suriname
Capital: Paramaribo

■ GEOGRAPHY

Area: 163,270 sq. km
Coastline: 386 km
Climate: tropical; moderated by trade winds
Environment: mostly tropical rain forest; deforestation resulting from logging for export; mining causes pollution of inland waterways
Terrain: mostly rolling hills; narrow coastal plain with swamps
Land Use: 0% arable; 0% permanent crops; 0% meadows; 96% forest; 4% other; includes 600 sq. km irrigated
Location: N South America, bordering on Atlantic Ocean

■ PEOPLE

Population: 431,303 (July 2000 est.)
Nationality: Surinamer
Age Structure: 0-14 yrs: 32%; 15-64: 62%; 65+: 6% (2000 est.)
Population Growth Rate: 0.65% (2000 est.)
Net Migration: -8.92 migrants/1,000 population (2000 est.)
Ethnic Groups: 37% Hindustani (East Indian), 31% Creole (black and mixed), 15% Javanese, 10% Maroons, 2% Amerindian, 2% Chinese, 1% European, 2% other
Languages: Dutch (official), Hindustani 32%, Javanese 15%; the majority can speak the native language Sranang Tongo (Taki-Taki); English is also widely spoken
Religions: 27.4% Hindu, 19.6% Muslim, 22.8% Roman Catholic, 25.2% Protestant (predominantly Moravian), about 5% indigenous beliefs
Birth Rate: 21.08/1,000 population (2000 est.)
Death Rate: 5.69/1,000 population (2000 est.)
Infant Mortality: 25.06 deaths/1,000 live births (2000 est.)
Life Expectancy at Birth: 68.71 years male, 74.14 years female (2000 est.)
Total Fertility Rate: 2.50 children born/woman (2000 est.)
Literacy: 93.5% (1997)

■ GOVERNMENT

Leader(s): Pres. Ronald Venetiaan, V. Pres and Prime Min. Jules Ajodhia
Government Type: constitutional democracy
Administrative Divisions: 10 districts (distrikten, sing. distrikt)
Nationhood: Nov. 25, 1975 (from Netherlands; formerly known as Netherlands Guiana or Dutch Guiana)
National Holiday: Independence Day, Nov. 25

■ ECONOMY

Overview: the economy is vulnerable to world prices for its bauxite, which provides more than 15% of the GDP and 65+% of export earnings. Guerrilla activity has targeted the economic infrastructure; high inflation, high unemployment, widespread black-market activity and hard currency shortfalls continue to characterize the economy
GDP: US$1.48 billion, per capita US$3,400; real growth rate -1% (1999 est.)
Inflation: 64.30% (year-end 2000)
Industries: accounts for 22% of GDP; bauxite mining, alumina and aluminum production, lumbering, food processing, fishing

Labour Force: approx. 100,000; 20% agriculture, 8.9% industry, 49.4% services, 15.2% trade and tourism
Unemployment: 20% (1997)
Agriculture: accounts for 13% of GDP and 25% of export earnings; paddy rice planted on 85% of arable land and represents 60% of total farm output; other products: bananas, palm kernels, coconuts, plantains, peanuts, beef, chicken; shrimp and forestry products of increasing importance
Natural Resources: timber, hydropower potential, fish, shrimp, bauxite, iron ore and modest amounts of nickel, copper, platinum, gold

■ **FINANCE/TRADE**

Currency: Surinamese guilder, gulden or florin (Sf) = 100 cents
International Reserves Excluding Gold: US$70 million (May 1999)
Gold Reserves: US$0.373 million fine troy ounces (May 1999)
Budget: adjusted for purchasing power parity: revenues US$317 million; expenditures US$333 million, including capital expenditures of US$52 million (1997 est.)
Defence Expenditures: 1.6% of GDP (1997 est.)
Education Expenditures: n.a.
External Debt: US$175.6 million (19968 est.)
Exports: US$414 million (2000); commodities: alumina, bauxite, aluminum, rice, wood and wood products, shrimp and fish, bananas; partners: Netherlands 28%, US 22%, Norway 18%, Japan 11%, Brazil 10%, UK 4%
Imports: US$439 million (2000); commodities: capital equipment, petroleum, foodstuffs, cotton, consumer goods; partners: US 34%, Netherlands 20%, Trinidad and Tobago 8%, Brazil 5%, UK 3%

■ **COMMUNICATIONS**

Daily Newspapers: 2
Televisions: 146/1,000 inhabitants (1997 est.)
Radios: 695/1,000 inhabitants (1997 est.)
Telephones: 171 lines/1,000 inhabitants (1999)

■ **TRANSPORTATION**

Motor Vehicles: 66,000; 46,900 passenger cars (1997 est.)
Roads: 4,530 km; 1,178 km paved
Railway: 166 km
Air Traffic: 279,000 passengers carried (1997)
Airports: 46; 5 have paved runways (1999 est.)

Canadian Embassy: The Canadian Embassy to Suriname, c/o Canadian High Commission, High and Young Streets, Georgetown; mailing address: P.O. Box 10880, Georgetown, Guyana. Tel. (011-592-2) 72-081. Fax: (011-592-2) 58-380. Email: grgtn@dfait-maeci.gc.ca
Embassy in Canada: c/o Embassy of the Republic of Suriname, Van Ness Center, 4301 Connecticut Ave NW, Ste 460, Washington DC 20008, USA. Tel: (202) 244-7488. Fax: (202) 244-5878. Email: embsur@erols.com

---

Svalbard

Long-Form Name: Svalbard
Capital: Longyearbyen

■ **GEOGRAPHY**

Area: 62,049 sq. km, 5 large islands, many smaller ones
Climate: arctic, tempered by mild Atlantic winds, cool suumers, cold winters
Land Use: undeveloped except for mining establishments; no trees—the only bushes are crowberry and cloudberry
Location: Arctic Ocean, midway between Norway and the North Pole

■ **PEOPLE**

Population: 2,416 (July 2000 est.)
Nationality: Norwegian
Ethnic Groups: 62% Russian and Ukrainian; 38% Norwegian
Languages: Norwegian, Russian

■ **GOVERNMENT**

Colony Territory of: Dependent Territory of Norway
Leader(s): Head of State: King Harald V (Norway)
Government Type: Territory of Norway
National Holiday: n.a.

■ **ECONOMY**

Overview: tourism most important; coal mining only industry (the Norwegian state-owned company employs almost 60% of the population); some trapping of seal, polar bear, fox and walrus

■ **FINANCE/TRADE**

Currency: Norwegian krone = 100 oere

Canadian Embassy: c/o The Canadian Embassy, Wergelandsveien 7, 0244 Oslo, Norway. Tel: (011-47) 22-99-53-00. Fax: (011-47) 22-99-53-01. Email: oslo@dfait-maeci.gc.ca
Representative to Canada: c/o Embassy of the Kingdom of Norway, Royal Bank Centre, 90

Sparks St, Ste 532, Ottawa ON K1P 5B4. Tel: (613) 238-6571. Fax: (613) 238-2765. Email: emb.ottawa@mfa.no

Swaziland

Long-Form Name: Kingdom of Swaziland
Capital: Mbabane (administrative); Lobamba (legislative)

■ GEOGRAPHY

Area: 17,363 sq. km
Coastline: none: landlocked
Climate: varies from tropical to near temperate
Environment: overhunting and overgrazing; soil degradation; soil erosion; limited safe drinking water
Terrain: mostly mountains and hills; some moderately sloping plains
Land Use: 11% arable; 0% permanent crops; 62% meadows; 7% forest; 20% other; includes 670 sq. km irrigated
Location: S Africa

■ PEOPLE

Population: 1,083,289 (July 2000 est.)
Nationality: Swazi
Age Structure: 0-14 yrs: 46%; 15-64: 52%; 65+: 2% (2000 est.)
Population Growth Rate: 2.02% (2000 est.)
Net Migration: 0 migrants/1,000 population (2000 est.)
Ethnic Groups: 97% African, 3% European
Languages: English and siSwati (official); government business conducted in English
Religions: 60% Christian, 40% indigenous beliefs
Birth Rate: 40.64/1,000 population (2000 est.)
Death Rate: 20.40/1,000 population (2000 est.)
Infant Mortality: 108.95 deaths/1,000 live births (2000 est.)
Life Expectancy at Birth: 39.54 years male, 41.37 years female (2000 est.)
Total Fertility Rate: 5.87 children born/woman (2000 est.)
Literacy: 77.5% (1997)

■ GOVERNMENT

Leader(s): King Mswati III; Premier Barnabas Sibusiso Dlamini
Government Type: monarchy; independent member of Commonwealth
Administrative Divisions: 4 districts
Nationhood: Sept. 6, 1968 (from UK)
National Holiday: Somhlolo (Independence) Day, Sept. 6

■ ECONOMY

Overview: is based on subsistence agriculture and is closely tied to that of its neighbour, South Africa, from which it receives 90% of its imports and to which it sends about half of its exports; manufacturing focuses on the processing of agricultural products; mining is becoming less important; overgrazing, soil deterioration and recurrent droughts are persistent problems
GDP: US$4.2 billion, per capita US$4,200; real growth rate 3.1% (1999 est.)
Inflation: 16.70% (year-end 2000)
Industries: accounts for 48% of GDP; mining (coal and asbestos), wood pulp, sugar; asbestos is declining in importance
Labour Force: n.a.; 74% agriculture, 17% services, 9% industry; 24,000–29,000 employed in South Africa
Unemployment: n.a.
Agriculture: accounts for 10% of GDP and over 60% of labour force; mostly subsistence agriculture; cash crops: sugar cane, citrus fruit, cotton, pineapple; other crops and livestock: corn, sorghum, peanuts, cattle, goats, sheep; not self-sufficient in grain
Natural Resources: asbestos, coal, clay, tin, hydroelectric power, quarry stone, talc, forests and small gold and diamond deposits

■ FINANCE/TRADE

Currency: lilangeni (pl. emalangeni) (E) = 100 cents
International Reserves Excluding Gold: US$376 million (Jan. 2001)
Gold Reserves: n.a.
Budget: n.a.
Defence Expenditures: n.a.
Education Expenditures: n.a.
External Debt: US$258 million (1999)
Exports: US$825 million (1999); commodities: sugar, asbestos, wood pulp, citrus, canned fruit, soft drink concentrates; partners: South Africa, UK, US
Imports: US$1.05 billion (1999); commodities: motor vehicles, machinery, transport equipment, chemicals, petroleum products, foodstuffs; partners: South Africa, US, UK

■ COMMUNICATIONS

Daily Newspapers: 3
Televisions: 19/1,000 inhabitants (1997 est.)
Radios: 143/1,000 inhabitants (1997 est.)
Telephones: 31 lines/1,000 inhabitants (1999)

■ TRANSPORTATION

Motor Vehicles: 36,755; 28,523 passenger cars (1997 est.)

Roads: 2,896 km; n.a. km paved
Railway: 297 km
Air Traffic: 41,000 passengers carried (1997)
Airports: 18; 1 has paved runway (1999 est.)

Canadian Embassy: The Canadian High Commission to Swaziland, c/o The Canadian Embassy, 1103 Arcadia St, Hatfield 0083, Pretoria; mailing address: Private Bag X13, Hatfield 0028, Pretoria, South Africa. Tel: (011-27-12) 422-3000. Fax (011-27-12) 422-3052. Email: pret@dfait-maeci.gc.ca
Embassy in Canada: High Commission for the Kingdom of Swaziland, 3400 International Dr NW, Ste 3M, Washington DC, 20008, Tel: (202) 234-5002, Fax: (202) 234-8254. Email: swaziland@compuserve.com

Sweden

Long-Form Name: Kingdom of Sweden
Capital: Stockholm

■ GEOGRAPHY

Area: 449,964 sq. km
Coastline: 3,218 km
Climate: temperate in south with cold, cloudy winters and cool, partly cloudy summers, subarctic in north
Environment: water pollution; acid rain; ice floes in coastal waters hinder navigation
Terrain: mostly flat or gently rolling lowlands; mountains in west
Land Use: 7% arable; 0% permanent crops; 1% meadows; 68% forest; 24% other; includes 1,250 sq. km irrigated
Location: N Europe, bordering on Baltic Sea

■ PEOPLE

Population: 8,873,052 (July 2000 est.)
Nationality: Swedish, Swede
Age Structure: 0-14 yrs: 18%; 15-64: 64%; 65+: 18% (2000 est.)
Population Growth Rate: 0.02% (2000 est.)
Net Migration: 0.86 migrants/1,000 population (2000 est.)
Ethnic Groups: homogeneous white population; small Lappish minority; about 12% foreign born or first-generation immigrants (Finns, Yugoslavs, Danes, Norwegians, Greeks, Turks)
Languages: Swedish (official), small Lapp- and Finnish-speaking minorities; immigrants speak native languages
Religions: 94% Evangelical Lutheran, 1.5% Roman Catholic, 4.5% other
Birth Rate: 10.01/1,000 population (2000 est.)

Death Rate: 10.62/1,000 population (2000 est.)
Infant Mortality: 3.49 deaths/1,000 live births (2000 est.)
Life Expectancy at Birth: 76.95 years male, 82.37 years female (2000 est.)
Total Fertility Rate: 1.53 children born/woman (2000 est.)
Literacy: 99% (1998)

■ GOVERNMENT

Leader(s): King Carl XVI Gustaf, Prime Min. Goran Persson
Government Type: constitutional monarchy
Administrative Divisions: 21 counties (lan, sing. & pl.)
Nationhood: June 6, 1523, constitutional monarchy established
National Holiday: Day of the Swedish Flag, June 6

■ ECONOMY

Overview: a mixed system of high-tech capitalism and extensive welfare benefits; has benefited from neutrality in world wars; economy is heavily oriented toward foreign trade; has excellent communications systems but faces loss of competitive edge as inflation and unemployment rates rise
GDP: US$184 billion, per capita US$20,700; real growth rate 3.8% (1999 est.)
Inflation: 1.00% (year-end 2000)
Industries: accounts for 30.5% of GDP; iron and steel, precision equipment (bearings, radio and telephone parts, armaments), wood pulp and paper products, processed foods, motor vehicles
Labour Force: 5 million (1999); 40.4% community, social and business services, 18.3 industry, 14.3 % trade and tourism
Unemployment: 4.4% (Jan. 2001)
Agriculture: accounts for 2.2% of GDP; animal husbandry predominates, with milk and dairy products accounting for 37% of farm income; main crops: grains, sugar beets, potatoes; 100% self-sufficient in grains and potatoes, 85% self-sufficient in sugar beets
Natural Resources: zinc, iron ore, lead, copper, silver, timber, uranium, hydropower potential

■ FINANCE/TRADE

Currency: krona (pl. kronor) (Skr) = 100 oere
International Reserves Excluding Gold: US$14.033 billion (Jan. 2001)
Gold Reserves: US$5.961 million fine troy ounces (Jan. 2001)
Budget: n.a.
Defence Expenditures: 5.59% of govt. expenditure (1999)

Education Expenditures: 6.58% of total govt. expenditure (1999)
External Debt: n.a.
Exports: US$82.289 billion (2000); commodities: machinery, motor vehicles, paper products, pulp and wood, iron and steel products, chemicals, petroleum and petroleum products; partners: European Community 52.1%, (Germany 12.1%, UK 11.2%, Denmark 6.8%), US 9.8%, Norway 9.3%
Imports: US$68.610 billion (2000); commodities: machinery, petroleum and petroleum products, chemicals, motor vehicles, foodstuffs, iron and steel, clothing; partners: European Community 55.8%, (Germany 21.2%, UK 8.6%, Denmark 6.6%), US 7.5%, Norway 6%

■ COMMUNICATIONS

Daily Newspapers: 94
Televisions: 531/1,000 inhabitants (1998)
Radios: 932/1,000 inhabitants (1997)
Telephones: 665 lines/1,000 inhabitants (1999)

■ TRANSPORTATION

Motor Vehicles: 4,00,000; 3,800,000 passenger cars (1997 est.)
Roads: 210,907 km; 163,453 km paved
Railway: 12,821 km
Air Traffic: 11,327,000 passengers carried (1997)
Airports: 256; 147 have paved runways (1999 est.)
Canadian Embassy: The Canadian Embassy, Tegelbacken 4 (Flr 7), Stockholm, Sweden; mailing address: P.O. Box 16129; S-10323 Stockholm, Sweden. Tel: (011-46-8) 453-3000. Fax: (011-46-8) 24-24-91. email: stkhm@dfait-maeci.gc.ca
Embassy in Canada: Embassy of Sweden, Mercury Court, 377 Dalhousie St, Ottawa ON K1N 9N8. Tel: (613) 241-8553. Fax: (613) 241-2277. Email: sweden@cyberus.ca

---

Switzerland

Long-Form Name: Swiss Confederation
Capital: Bern

■ GEOGRAPHY

Area: 41,290 sq. km
Coastline: none: landlocked
Climate: temperate, but varies with altitude; cold, cloudy, rainy/snowy winters; cool to warm, cloudy, humid summers with occasional showers
Environment: dominated by Alps; air and water pollution; avalanches, flash floods and landslides are natural hazards

Terrain: mostly mountains (Alps in south, Jura in northwest) with a central plateau of rolling hills, plains and large lakes
Land Use: 10% arable; 2% permanent crops; 28% permanent pastures; 32% forest; 28% other; includes 250 sq. km irrigated
Location: C Europe

■ PEOPLE

Population: 7,262,372 (July 2000 est.)
Nationality: Swiss (sing. & pl.)
Age Structure: 0-14 yrs: 17%; 15-64: 68%; 65+: 15% (2000 est.)
Population Growth Rate: 0.30% (2000 est.)
Net Migration: 1.38 migrants/1,000 population (2000 est.)
Ethnic Groups: total population: 65% German, 18% French, 10% Italian, 1% Romansch, 6% other
Languages: 65% German, 18% French, 12% Italian, 1% Raeto-Romansch (all official), 4% other
Religions: 47.6% Roman Catholic, 44.3% Protestant, 8.1% other
Birth Rate: 10.40/1,000 population (2000 est.)
Death Rate: 8.75/1,000 population (2000 est.)
Infant Mortality: 4.53 deaths/1,000 live births (2000 est.)
Life Expectancy at Birth: 76.73 years male, 82.63 years female (2000 est.)
Total Fertility Rate: 1.47 children born/woman (2000 est.)
Literacy: 99% (1998)

■ GOVERNMENT

Leader(s): Pres. Moritz Leuenberger, V. Pres. Kasper Villiger
Government Type: federal republic
Administrative Divisions: 26 cantons
Nationhood: Aug. 1, 1291
National Holiday: Anniversary of the Founding of the Swiss Confederation, Aug. 1

■ ECONOMY

Overview: country has the highest per capita output, general living standards, education and science, healthcare and diet standards in Europe; important banking and tourist sectors; low inflation and negligible unemployment is due partly to government policies; has rejected membership in the European Economic Community
GDP: US$197 billion, per capita US$27,100; real growth rate 1.4% (1999 est.)
Inflation: 1.58% (year-end 2000)
Industries: accounts for 31.1% of GDP; machinery, chemicals, watches, textiles, precision instruments

Labour Force: 4 million (1999); 24.3% industry, 23.6% community, social and business services, 20.3% trade and tourism
Unemployment: 1.9% (Feb. 2001)
Agriculture: accounts for 2.8% of GDP; dairy farming predominates; less than 50% self-sufficient; food shortages: fish, refined sugar, fats and oils (other than butter), grains, eggs, fruit, vegetables, meat
Natural Resources: hydropower potential, timber, salt; scenic beauty

■ **FINANCE/TRADE**

Currency: Swiss franc, franken, or franco (SwF) = 100 centimes, rappen, or centesimi
International Reserves Excluding Gold: US$30.278 billion (Jan. 2001)
Gold Reserves: US$77.265 million fine troy ounces (Jan. 2001)
Budget: revenues US$32.66 billion; expenditures US$34.89 billion, including capital expenditures of US$2.3 billion (1998 est.)
Defence Expenditures: 4.98% of total govt. expenditure (1998)
Education Expenditures: 2.30% of total govt. expenditure (1998)
External Debt: n.a.
Exports: US$74.897 billion (2000); commodities: machinery and equipment, precision instruments, metal products, foodstuffs, textiles and clothing; partners: Europe 64% (European Community 56%, other 8%), US 9%, Japan 4%
Imports: US$76.135 billion (2000); commodities: agricultural products, machinery and transportation equipment, chemicals, textiles, construction materials; partners: Europe 79% (European Community 72%, other 7%), US 5%

■ **COMMUNICATIONS**

Daily Newspapers: 88
Televisions: 535/1,000 inhabitants (1998)
Radios: 1,000/1,000 inhabitants (1997)
Telephones: 699 lines/1,000 inhabitants (1999)

■ **TRANSPORTATION**

Motor Vehicles: 3,700,000; 3,300,000 passenger cars (1997 est.)
Roads: 71,059 km; all paved
Railway: 4,492 km
Air Traffic: 12,482,000 passengers carried (1997)
Airports: 67; 42 have paved runways (1999 est.)

Canadian Embassy: Canadian Embassy, Kirchenfeldstrasse 88, 3005 Berne, Switzerland; mailing address: Box 3000, Berne 6, Switzerland. Tel: (011-41-31) 357-32-00. Fax:

(011-41-31) 357-32-10. Email: bern@dfait-maeci.gc.ca
Embassy in Canada: Embassy of Switzerland, 5 Marlborough Ave, Ottawa ON K1N 8E6. Tel: (613) 235-1837. Fax: (613) 563-1394. Email: vertretung@ott.rep.admin.ch

Syria

Long-Form Name: Syrian Arab Republic
Capital: Damascus

■ **GEOGRAPHY**

Area: 185,180 sq. km; including 1,295 sq. km of Israeli-occupied territory
Coastline: 193 km
Climate: mostly desert; hot, dry, sunny summers (June to Aug.) and mild, rainy winters (Dec. to Feb.) along coast
Environment: deforestation; overgrazing; soil erosion; desertification; unsafe drinking water
Terrain: primarily semi-arid and desert plateau; narrow coastal plain; mountains in west
Land Use: 28% arable; 4% permanent crops; 43% meadows; 3% forest; 22% other; includes 9,060 sq. km irrigated
Location: SW Asia (Middle East), bordering on Mediterranean Sea

■ **PEOPLE**

Population: 16,305,659 (July 2000 est.)
Nationality: Syrian
Age Structure: 0-14 yrs: 41%; 15-64: 56%; 65+: 3% (2000 est.)
Population Growth Rate: 2.58% (2000 est.)
Net Migration: 0 migrants/1,000 population (2000 est.)
Ethnic Groups: 90.3% Arab; 9.7% Kurds, Armenians and other
Languages: Arabic (official), Kurdish, Armenian, Aramaic, Circassian; English and French widely understood
Religions: 74% Sunni, 16% Alawite, Druze and other Muslim sects, 10% Christian
Birth Rate: 31.11/1,000 population (2000 est.)
Death Rate: 5.29/1,000 population (2000 est.)
Infant Mortality: 34.86 deaths/1,000 live births (2000 est.)
Life Expectancy at Birth: 67.35 years male, 69.64 years female (2000 est.)
Total Fertility Rate: 4.06 children born/woman (2000 est.)
Literacy: 72% (1998)

■ **GOVERNMENT**

Leader(s): Pres. Bashar al-Asad, V. Pres. Abd al-Halim ibn Said Khaddam. Prime Min. Muhammad Mustafa Miru

Government Type: republic under leftwing military regime
Administrative Divisions: 14 provinces (muhafazat, sing. —muhafazah)
Nationhood: Apr. 17, 1946 (from League of Nations mandate under French administration; formerly known as United Arab Republic)
National Holiday: National Day, Apr. 17

■ ECONOMY

Overview: economic difficulties are due, in part, to severe drought in several recent years, costly but unsuccessful attempts to match Israel's military strength, a fall-off in Arab aid and insufficient foreign exchange earnings to buy needed imports; agricultural output is poor; a major long-term concern is the additional drain of upstream Euphrates water by Turkey once its vast dam and irrigation projects are completed
GDP: US$42.2 billion, per capita US$2,500; real growth rate 0% (1999 est.)
Inflation: -0.41% (year-end 2000)
Industries: accounts for 22% of GDP, textiles, food processing, beverages, tobacco, phosphate rock mining, petroleum
Labour Force: 5 million (1999); 62.9% services, 22% agriculture, 15.1% industry
Unemployment: 12-15% (1998 est.)
Agriculture: accounts for 29% of GDP; all major crops (wheat, barley, cotton, lentils, chickpeas) grown on rain-fed land causing wide swings in yields; animal products: beef, lamb, eggs, poultry, milk; not self-sufficient in grain or livestock products
Natural Resources: crude oil, phosphates, chrome and manganese ores, asphalt, iron ore, rock salt, marble, gypsum

■ FINANCE/TRADE

Currency: Syrian pound (£S) = 100 piastres
International Reserves Excluding Gold: n.a.
Gold Reserves: US$0.833 million fine troy ounces (Dec. 2000)
Budget: revenues US$3.5 billion; expenditures US$4.2 billion, including capital expenditures of US$n.a. (1997 est.)
Defence Expenditures: 24.77% of total govt. expenditure (1998)
Education Expenditures: 10.20% of total govt. expenditure (1998)
External Debt: US$22.369 billion (1999)
Exports: US$14.777 billion (2000); commodities: petroleum, textiles, fruit and vegetables, phosphates; partners: Italy, Romania, former USSR countries, US, Iran, France
Imports: US$13.202 billion (2000); commodities: petroleum, machinery, base

metals, foodstuffs and beverages; partners: Iran, Germany, former USSR countries, France, Libya, US

■ COMMUNICATIONS

Daily Newspapers: 8
Televisions: 70/1,000 inhabitants (1998)
Radios: 278/1,000 inhabitants (1997)
Telephones: 95 lines/1,000 inhabitants (1999)

■ TRANSPORTATION

Motor Vehicles: 352,900; 134,000 passenger cars (1997 est.)
Roads: 36,377 km; 26,299 km paved
Railway: 2,750 km
Air Traffic: 694,000 passengers carried (1997)
Airports: 104; 24 have paved runways (1999 est.)

Canadian Embassy: The Canadian Embassy, Lot 12, Mezzeh Autostrade, Damascus, Syria; mailing address: P.O. Box 3394, Damascus, Syria. Tel: (011-963-11) 611-6692. Fax: (011-963-11) 611-4000. Email: dmcus@dfait-maeci.gc.ca
Embassy in Canada: Embassy of the Syrian Arab Republic, 151 Slater St., Suite 1000, Ottawa, ON, K1P 5H3, Tel: (613) 569-5556, Fax: (613) 569-3800. Email: n.a.

Taiwan

Long-Form Name: Taiwan
Capital: Taipei

■ GEOGRAPHY

Area: 35,980 sq. km; includes the Pescadores, Matsu and Quemoy
Coastline: 1,566.3 km
Climate: tropical; marine; rainy season during southwest monsoon (June to Aug.)
Environment: subject to earthquakes and typhoons; water and air pollution
Terrain: eastern two-thirds mostly rugged mountains; flat to gently rolling plains in west
Land Use: 24% arable; 1% permanent crops; 5% meadows; 55% forest; 15% other; includes n.a. sq. km irrigated
Location: island, SE of China, bordering on South and East China Seas, Pacific Ocean

■ PEOPLE

Population: 22,191,087 (July 2000 est.)
Nationality: Chinese
Age Structure: 0-14 yrs: 22%; 15-64: 70%; 65+: 8% (2000 est.)
Population Growth Rate: 0.81% (2000 est.)
Net Migration: -0.38 migrants/1,000 population (2000 est.)

Ethnic Groups: 84% Taiwanese, 14% mainland Chinese, 2% aborigine
Languages: Mandarin Chinese (official); Taiwanese and Hakka dialects also used
Religions: 93% mixture of Buddhist, Islam, Confucian and Taoist, 5% Christian, 3% other
Birth Rate: 14.42/1,000 population (2000 est.)
Death Rate: 5.91/1,000 population (2000 est.)
Infant Mortality: 7.06 deaths/1,000 live births (2000 est.)
Life Expectancy at Birth: 73.62 years male, 79.32 years female (2000 est.)
Total Fertility Rate: 1.76 children born/woman (2000 est.)
Literacy: 94% (1998)

■ GOVERNMENT

Leader(s): Pres. Chen Shui-bian, V. Pres. Annette Lu. Prime Min. Chang Chun-hsiung
Government Type: multi-party democratic regime
Administrative Divisions: 16 counties (hsien, sing. & pl.), 5 municipalities (shih, sing. & pl.), 2 special municipalities (chuan-shih, sing. & pl.)
Nationhood: n.a.
National Holiday: National Day (Anniversary of the Revolution), Oct. 10

■ ECONOMY

Overview: dynamic capitalist economy with gradually decreasing guidance of investment and foreign trade by government authorities and partial government ownership of some large banks and industrial firms
GDP: US$357 billion, per capita US$16,100; real growth rate 5.5% (1999 est.)
Inflation: n.a.
Industries: accounts for 33% of GDP, textiles, clothing, chemicals, electronics, food processing, plywood, sugar milling, cement, shipbuilding, petroleum
Labour Force: 9.4 million (1997 est.); 52% services, 38% industry, 10% agriculture
Unemployment: 2.9% (1999 est.)
Agriculture: accounts for 3% of GDP; heavily subsidized sector; major crops: rice sugar cane, sweet potatoes, fruit, vegetables; livestock: hogs, poultry, beef, milk, cattle; not self-sufficient in wheat, soybeans, corn; fish catch expanding, 1.4 million metric tons
Natural Resources: small deposits of coal, natural gas, limestone, marble and asbestos

■ FINANCE/TRADE

Currency: New Taiwan dollar (NT$) = 100 cents
International Reserves Excluding Gold: US$61.888 billion (Dec. 1997)
Gold Reserves: n.a.
Budget: revenues US$36.82 billion; expenditures US$40.53 billion, including capital expenditures of US$n.a. (1999 est.)
Defence Expenditures: 2.8% of GDP (1998–99)
Education Expenditures: n.a.
External Debt: US$35 billion (Sept. 1999)
Exports: US$121.528 billion (1999); commodities: textiles 16%, electrical machinery 19%, general machinery and equipment 14%, telecommunications equipment 9%, basic metals and metal products 5%, foodstuffs 0.9%, plywood and wood products 1.3%; partners: US 36.2%, Japan 13.7%
Imports: US$110.961 billion (1999); commodities: machinery and equipment 15.9%, crude oil 5%, chemical and chemical products 11.1%, basic metals 7.4%, foodstuffs 2%; partners: Japan 31%, US 23%, Saudi Arabia 8.6%

■ COMMUNICATIONS

Daily Newspapers: n.a.
Televisions: n.a.
Radios: n.a.
Telephones: n.a.

■ TRANSPORTATION

Motor Vehicles: 5,225,000; 4,300,000 passenger cars (1997 est.)
Roads: 34,901 km; 31,271 km paved
Railway: 2,481 km
Air Traffic: n.a.
Airports: 38; 35 have paved runways (1999 est.)

Canadian Embassy: none
Embassy in Canada: none

Tajikistan

Long-Form Name: Republic of Tajikistan
Capital: Dushanbe

■ GEOGRAPHY

Area: 143,100 sq. km
Coastline: none; landlocked
Climate: continental; severe winters in east; extremely hot summers; wet spring; semi-arid to polar in Pamir mountains
Environment: lack of fresh water; little land suitable for cultivation; industrial pollution
Terrain: mountains and glaciers constitute 93% of land area, predominantly herding and nonagricultural
Land Use: 6% arable, negligible permanent crops, 25% meadows and pastures, 4% forest and woodland, 65% other, includes 6,390 sq. km irrigated
Location: C Asia, bordering on China and Afghanistan

■ PEOPLE

Population: 6,440,732 (July 2000 est.)
Nationality: Tajik, Tajikistani
Age Structure: 0-14 yrs: 42%; 15-64: 54%; 65+: 4% (2000 est.)
Population Growth Rate: 2.12% (2000 est.)
Net Migration: -3.71 migrants/1,000 population (2000 est.)
Ethnic Groups: 64.9% Tajik, 25% Uzbek, 3.5% Russian (declining due to emigration), 6.6% other
Languages: Tajik (official), Uzbek, Russian
Religions: 80% Sunni Muslim, 5% Shia Muslim, 15% other
Birth Rate: 33.56/1,000 population (2000 est.)
Death Rate: 8.64/1,000 population (2000 est.)
Infant Mortality: 117.42 deaths/1,000 live births (2000 est.)
Life Expectancy at Birth: 60.95 years male, 67.38 years female (2000 est.)
Total Fertility Rate: 4.35 children born/woman (2000 est.)
Literacy: 99% (1998)

■ GOVERNMENT

Leader(s): Pres. Emomali Rahmonov, Prime Min. Oqil Oqilov
Government Type: republic
Administrative Divisions: 2 oblasts (viloyatho, sing. —viloyat) and 1 autonomous oblast (viloyati mukhtori)
Nationhood: Sept. 9, 1991 (from Soviet Union)
National Holiday: National Day, Sept. 9

■ ECONOMY

Overview: mostly mining and manufacturing with strong agricultural sector; industry and agriculture have been producing at reduced capacity due to civil unrest; currency incompatibility with neighbouring countries is straining trade relations; depends on aid from Russia and Uzbekistan and on international aid for much of its basic subsistence needs
GDP: US$6.2 billion, per capita US$1,020; real growth rate 2% (1999 est.)
Inflation: n.a.
Industries: accounts for 24% of GDP; aluminum and electrochemical plants, textile machinery, silk and carpet mills; zinc, lead, chemicals and fertilizers, cement, vegetable oil, refrigerators and freezers
Labour Force: 2 million (1999); 43% agriculture and forestry, 22% industry and construction, 35% other
Unemployment: 5.7% (Dec. 1998); also large numbers of underemployed
Agriculture: accounts for 34% of GDP; cotton, grapes, fruit, grains, silkworm farming, cattle breeding, sheep, goats, pigs

Natural Resources: coal, oil, rare metals, rock crystal, mica, gold, hydropower potential, uranium, mercury, zinc, lead

■ FINANCE/TRADE

Currency: Tajik ruble (R) = 100 tanga
International Reserves Excluding Gold: n.a.
Gold Reserves: n.a.
Budget: n.a.
Defence Expenditures: 15.70% of central govt. expenditure (1998)
Education Expenditures: 3.00% of total govt. expenditure (1998)
External Debt: US$889 million (1999)
Exports: US$727 million (2000); commodities: fruit, plant products, aluminum; partners: other Central Asian countries
Imports: US$696 million (2000); commodities: fuel, machinery, foodstuffs; partners: other Central Asian countries

■ COMMUNICATIONS

Daily Newspapers: 2
Televisions: 285/1,000 inhabitants (1998)
Radios: 142/1,000 inhabitants (1997)
Telephones: 35 lines/1,000 inhabitants (1999)

■ TRANSPORTATION

Motor Vehicles: n.a.
Roads: 13,700 km; 11,330 km hard-surfaced
Railway: 480 km, not including industrial lines
Air Traffic: 594,000 passengers carried (1997)
Airports: 59; 14 have paved runways (1999 est.)

Canadian Embassy: The Canadian Embassy to Tajikistan, c/o The Canadian Embassy, 34 Kasarai Batir St, Almaty 480100, Kazakhstan. Tel: (011-7-3272) 50-11-51. Fax: (011-7-3272) 582-493. Email: almat@dfait-maeci.gc.ca
Embassy in Canada: n.a.

Tanzania

Long-Form Name: United Republic of Tanzania
Capital: Dar es Salaam

■ GEOGRAPHY

Area: 945,087 sq. km
Coastline: 1,424 km
Climate: varies from tropical along coast to temperate in highlands
Environment: deforestation; lack of water limits agriculture; recent droughts affected marginal agriculture
Terrain: plains along coast; central plateau; highlands in north, south; Kilimanjaro is highest point in Africa
Land Use: 3% arable; 1% permanent crops; 40%

meadows; 38% forest; 18% other; includes 1,500 sq. km irrigated
Location: E Africa, bordering on Indian Ocean

■ PEOPLE

Population: 35,306,126 (July 2000 est.)
Nationality: Tanzanian
Age Structure: 0-14 yrs: 45%; 15-64: 52%; 65+: 3% (2000 est.)
Population Growth Rate: 2.57% (2000 est.)
Net Migration: -1.59 migrants/1,000 population (2000 est.)
Ethnic Groups: 99% native African consisting of well over 100 tribes; 1% Asian, European and Arab
Languages: Swahili and English (official); English primarily language of commerce, administration and higher education; Swahili widely understood and generally used for communication between ethnic groups
Religions: mainland: 45% Christian, 35% Muslim, 20% indigenous beliefs; Zanzibar: almost all Muslim
Birth Rate: 40.17/1,000 population (2000 est.)
Death Rate: 12.88/1,000 population (2000 est.)
Infant Mortality: 80.97 deaths/1,000 live births (2000 est.)
Life Expectancy at Birth: 51.32 years male, 53.23 years female (2000 est.)
Total Fertility Rate: 5.51 children born/woman (2000 est.)
Literacy: 73% (1998)

■ GOVERNMENT

Leader(s): Pres. Benjamin William Mkapa, Prem. Frederick Sumaye
Government Type: republic
Administrative Divisions: 25 regions
Nationhood: April 26, 1964; Tanganyika became independent on Dec. 9, 1961 (from UN trusteeship under British administration); Zanzibar became independent Dec. 19, 1963 (from UK); Tanganyika united with Zanzibar Apr. 26, 1964 to form the political unit that was renamed Tanzania on Oct. 29, 1964
National Holiday: Union Day, Apr. 26

■ ECONOMY

Overview: world aid is increasing the availability of imports and providing funds to rehabilitate this country's deteriorated economic infrastructure; this poor economy is heavily dependent on agriculture; industry is largely confined to processing agricultural products; mining is increasing in importance; recent banking reforms have helped increase private sector growth and investment
GDP: US$23.3 billion, per capita US$550; real growth rate 4% (1999 est.)

Inflation: 5.92% (year-end 2000)
Industries: accounts for 17% of GDP; primarily agricultural processing (sugar, beer, cigarettes, sisal twine), diamond mines, oil refineries, shoes, cement, textiles, wood products, fertilizer
Labour Force: 17 million (1999); 90% agriculture, 10% industry and commerce
Unemployment: n.a.
Agriculture: accounts for 49% of GDP, 85% of exports and employs 90% of workforce; topography and climatic conditions limit cultivated crops to only 5% of land area; cash crops: coffee, sisal, tea, cotton, pyrethrum (insecticide made from chrysanthemums), cashews, tobacco, cloves (Zanzibar); corn, wheat, beans, fruit and vegetables grown for local consumption
Natural Resources: hydropower potential, tin, phosphates, iron ore, coal, diamonds, gemstones, gold, natural gas, nickel

■ FINANCE/TRADE

Currency: Tanzania shilling (TSh) = 100 cents
International Reserves Excluding Gold: US$983 million (Jan. 2001)
Gold Reserves: n.a.
Budget: revenues US$1 billion; expenditures US$1.3 billion, including capital expenditures of US$n.a. (1999 est.)
Defence Expenditures: 10.7% of central government expenditure (1997)
Education Expenditures: n.a.
External Debt: US$7.968 billion (1999)
Exports: US$667 million (2000); commodities: coffee, cotton, sisal, cashew nuts, meat, tobacco, tea, diamonds, coconut products, pyrethrum, cloves; partners: Germany, UK, US, Netherlands, Japan
Imports: US$1.559 billion (2000); commodities: manufactured goods, machinery and transportation equipment, cotton piece goods, crude oil, foodstuffs; partners: Germany, UK, US, Iran, Japan, Italy

■ COMMUNICATIONS

Daily Newspapers: 3
Televisions: 21/1,000 inhabitants (1998)
Radios: 279/1,000 inhabitants (1997)
Telephones: 5 lines/1,000 inhabitants (1999)

■ TRANSPORTATION

Motor Vehicles: 133,800; 55,000 passenger cars (1997 est.)
Roads: 88,200 km; 3,704 paved
Railway: 3,569 km
Air Traffic: 218,000 passengers carried (1997)
Airports: 129; 11 have paved runways (1999 est.)

Canadian Embassy: The Canadian High Commission, 38 Mirambo St, Dar-es-Salaam; mailing address: P.O. Box 1022, Dar-es-Salaam, Tanzania. Tel: (011-255-22) 211-2831. Fax: (011-255-22) 211-6897. Email: dslam@dfait-maeci.gc.ca

Embassy in Canada: High Commission for the United Republic of Tanzania, 50 Range Rd, Ottawa ON, K1N 8J4. Tel: (613) 232-1500. Fax: (613) 232-5184. Email: tzottawa@synapse.net

Thailand

Long-Form Name: Kingdom of Thailand
Capital: Bangkok

■ GEOGRAPHY

Area: 514,000 sq. km
Coastline: 3,219 km
Climate: tropical; rainy, warm, cloudy southwest monsoon (mid-May to Sept.); dry, cool, northeast monsoon (Nov. to mid-Mar.); southern isthmus always hot and humid
Environment: air and water pollution; land subsidence in Bangkok area; deforestation; soil erosion; illegal hunting threatens wildlife populations
Terrain: central plain; eastern plateau (Khorat); mountains elsewhere
Land Use: 34% arable; 6% permanent crops; 2% permanent pastures; 26% forest; 32% other, includes 44,000 sq. km irrigated
Location: SE Asia, bordering on Gulf of Siam and Andaman Sea

■ PEOPLE

Population: 61,230,874 (July 2000 est.)
Nationality: Thai (sing. & pl.)
Age Structure: 0-14 yrs: 24%; 15-64: 70%; 65+: 6% (2000 est.)
Population Growth Rate: 0.93% (2000 est.)
Net Migration: 0 migrants/1,000 population (2000 est.)
Ethnic Groups: 75% Thai, 14% Chinese, 11% other
Languages: Thai; English is the secondary language of the elite; small minorities speak Chinese, Malay, indigenous languages
Religions: 95% Buddhist (Theravada), 3.8% Muslim, 0.5% Christianity, 0.1% Hinduism, 0.6% other
Birth Rate: 16.86/1,000 population (2000 est.)
Death Rate: 7.53/1,000 population (2000 est.)
Infant Mortality: 31.48 deaths/1,000 live births (2000 est.)
Life Expectancy at Birth: 65.29 years male, 71.97 years female (2000 est.)

Total Fertility Rate: 1.88 children born/woman (2000 est.)
Literacy: 95% (1998)

■ GOVERNMENT

Leader(s): King Phumiphon Adunyadet (Rama IX), Prem. Thaksin Chinnawat
Government Type: constitutional monarchy
Administrative Divisions: 76 provinces (changwat, sing. & pl.)
Nationhood: 1238 (traditional founding date); never colonized
National Holiday: Birthday of His Majesty the King, Dec. 5

■ ECONOMY

Overview: with the currency depreciation and the collapse of domestic demands; imports have fallen by more than a third recently; foreign investment for new projects, the long-time catalyst of Thailand's economic growth, has also slowed
GDP: US$388.7 billion, per capita US$6,400; real growth rate 4% (1998 est.)
Inflation: 1.55% (year-end 2000)
Industries: accounts for 39% of GDP, tourism is the largest source of foreign exchange; textiles and garments, agricultural processing, beverages, tobacco, cement, other light manufacturing, such as jewelry; electric appliances and components, integrated circuits, furniture, plastics
Labour Force: 37 million (1999); 60.3% agriculture, 11.2% trade and tourism, 11.1% industry
Unemployment: 3.3% (Nov. 1999)
Agriculture: accounts for 12% of GDP and 57% of labour force; leading producer and exporter of rice and cassava; other crops: rubber, corn, sugar cane, coconuts, soybeans; self-sufficient in food except for wheat
Natural Resources: tin, rubber, natural gas, tungsten, tantalum, timber, lead, fish, gypsum, lignite, fluorite

■ FINANCE/TRADE

Currency: baht (pl. baht) (B) = 100 satang
International Reserves Excluding Gold: US$32.169 billion (Jan. 2001)
Gold Reserves: US$2.367 million fine troy ounces (Jan. 2001)
Budget: revenues US$20 billion; expenditures US$23 billion, including capital expenditures of US$n.a. (1999 est.)
Defence Expenditures: 6.64% of govt. expenditure (1999)
Education Expenditures: 17.30% of govt. expenditure (1999)

External Debt: US$96.335 billion (1999)
Exports: US$72.696 billion (2000); commodities: textiles 12%, fishery products 12%, rice 8%, tapioca 8%, jewelry 6%, manufactured gas, corn, tin; partners: US 18%, Japan 14%, Singapore 9%, Netherlands, Malaysia, Hong Kong, China
Imports: US$54.140 billion (2000); commodities: machinery and parts 23%, petroleum products 13%, chemicals 11%, iron and steel, electrical appliances; partners: Japan 26%, US 14%, Singapore 7%, Germany, Malaysia, UK

■ COMMUNICATIONS

Daily Newspapers: 30
Televisions: 236/1,000 inhabitants (1998)
Radios: 232/1,000 inhabitants (1997)
Telephones: 86 lines/1,000 inhabitants (1999)

■ TRANSPORTATION

Motor Vehicles: 5,700,000; 1,550,000 passenger cars (1997 est.)
Roads: 64,600 km; 62,985 km paved
Railway: 3,940 km
Air Traffic: 14,236,000 passengers carried (1997)
Airports: 106; 56 have paved runways (1999 est.)
Canadian Embassy: The Canadian Embassy, 990 Rama IV, Abdulrahim Place, 15th Fl, Bangkok 10500, Thailand; mailing address: P.O. Box 2090, Bangkok 10501, Thailand. Tel: (011-66-2) 636-0540. Fax: (011-66-2) 636-0566. Email: bngkk@dfait-maeci.gc.ca
Embassy in Canada: The Royal Thai Embassy, 180 Island Park Dr, Ottawa ON K1Y 0A2. Tel: (613) 722-4444. Fax: (613) 722-6624. Email: thaicommott@sympatico.ca

---

Togo

Long-Form Name: Togolese Republic
Capital: Lomé

■ GEOGRAPHY

Area: 56,785 sq. km
Coastline: 56 km
Climate: tropical; hot, humid in south; semi-arid in north
Environment: hot, dry harmattan wind; recent droughts affecting agriculture; deforestation
Terrain: gently rolling savanna in north; low coastal plain with extensive lagoons and marshes
Land Use: 38% arable; 7% permanent crops; 4% meadows; 17% forest; 34% other; includes 70 sq. km irrigated
Location: WC Africa, bordering on South Atlantic Ocean

■ PEOPLE

Population: 5,018,502 (July 2000 est.)
Nationality: Togolese (sing. & pl.)
Age Structure: 0-14 yrs: 46%; 15-64: 51%; 65+: 3% (2000 est.)
Population Growth Rate: 2.7% (2000 est.)
Net Migration: 0.16 migrants/1,000 population (2000 est.)
Ethnic Groups: 37 tribes; largest and most important are Ewe, Mina and Kabyè; under 1% European and Syrian-Lebanese
Languages: French, both official and language of commerce; major African languages are Ewe and Mina in the south and Dagomba and Kabyè in the north
Religions: about 70% indigenous beliefs, 20% Christian, 10% Muslim
Birth Rate: 38.02/1,000 population (2000 est.)
Death Rate: 11.18/1,000 population (2000 est.)
Infant Mortality: 71.55 deaths/1,000 live births (2000 est.)
Life Expectancy at Birth: 52.75 years male, 56.70 years female (2000 est.)
Total Fertility Rate: 5.50 children born/woman (2000 est.)
Literacy: 55% (1998)

■ GOVERNMENT

Leader(s): Pres. Gen. Gnassingbé Eyadéma, Prime Min. Agbeyome Kodjo
Government Type: republic; one-party presidential regime under transition to multiparty democratic rule
Administrative Divisions: 5 regions
Nationhood: Apr. 27, 1960 (from UN trusteeship under French administration; formerly known as French Togo)
National Holiday: Independence Day, Apr. 27

■ ECONOMY

Overview: an underdeveloped country that is heavily dependent on subsistence agriculture and phosphate mining; self-sufficient in basic foodstuffs when harvests are normal; political unrest and widespread strikes have interfered with economic activity
GDP: US$8.6 billion, per capita US$1,700; real growth rate 4% (1999 est.)
Inflation: 1.89% (year-end 2000)
Industries: accounts for 21% of GDP; phosphate mining, agricultural processing, cement, handicrafts, textiles, beverages
Labour Force: 2 million (1999); 64.3% agriculture, 6.3% industry, 29.4% services
Unemployment: n.a.
Agriculture: accounts for 42% of GDP and 64% of labour force; cash crops: coffee, cocoa, cotton; food crops: yams, cassava, corn, beans,

rice, millet, sorghum, fish, livestock
Natural Resources: phosphates, limestone, marble, arable land

■ FINANCE/TRADE

Currency: Communauté financière africaine franc (CFAF) = 100 centimes
International Reserves Excluding Gold: US$112 million (Nov. 2000)
Gold Reserves: US$0.013 million fine troy ounces (Aug. 2000)
Budget: revenues US$242 million; expenditures US$262 million, including capital expenditures US$n.a. (1997 est.)
Defence Expenditures: 11.6% of central government expenditure (1997)
Education Expenditures: 4.5% of GNP (1997)
External Debt: US$1.500 billion (1999)
Exports: US$227 million (2000); commodities: phosphates, cocoa, coffee, cotton, manufactures, palm kernels; partners: European Community 70%, Africa 9%, US 2%, other 19%
Imports: US$425 million (2000); commodities: food, fuels, durable consumer goods, other intermediate goods, capital goods; partners: European Community 69%, Africa 10%, Japan 7%, US 4%, other 10%

■ COMMUNICATIONS

Daily Newspapers: 1
Televisions: 18/1,000 inhabitants (1998)
Radios: 218/1,000 inhabitants (1997)
Telephones: 8 lines/1,000 inhabitants (1999)

■ TRANSPORTATION

Motor Vehicles: 110,000; 75,000 passenger cars (1997 est.)
Roads: 7,520 km; 2,376 km paved
Railway: 525 km
Air Traffic: 86,000 passengers carried (1997)
Airports: 9; 2 have paved runways (1999 est.)

Canadian Embassy: The Canadian Embassy to Togo, c/o Canadian High Commission, 42 Independence Ave, Accra, Ghana; P.O. Box 1639, Accra, Ghana. Tel: (011-233-21) 77-37-91. Fax: (011-233-21) 77-37-92. Email: accra@dfait-maeci.gc.ca
Embassy in Canada: Embassy of the Republic of Togo, 12 Range Rd, Ottawa ON K1N 8J3. Tel: (613) 238-5916. Fax: (613) 235-6425. Email: n.a.

Tokelau

Long-Form Name: Tokelau
Capital: none; each atoll has its own administrative centre

■ GEOGRAPHY

Area: 10 sq. km, 3 atolls
Climate: tropical maritime, moderated by trade winds (April–Nov.)
Land Use: 0% arable, permanent crops, meadows/pastures or forests; 100% other; includes no irrigated land
Location: S Pacific Ocean, NE of Australia

■ PEOPLE

Population: 1,458 (July 2000 est.)
Nationality: Tokelauan
Ethnic Groups: Polynesian
Languages: Tokelauan, English

■ GOVERNMENT

Colony Territory of: Overseas Territory of New Zealand
Leader(s): Head of State: Queen Elizabeth II
Government Type: territory of New Zealand
National Holiday: Waitangi Day, Feb. 6

■ ECONOMY

Overview: Tokelau's small size, great distance from markets and lack of resources greatly hinder economic development; copra is only agricultural product of significance; the people rely on aid from New Zealand, supplemented by revenue from postage stamps, souvenir coins, and handicrafts

■ FINANCE/TRADE

Currency: New Zealand dollar = 100 cents

Canadian Embassy: c/o The Canadian High Commission, 3rd Fl, 61 Molesworth St. Thorndon, Wellington, New Zealand; mailing address: P.O. Box 12049, Thorndon, Wellington, New Zealand. Tel: (011-64-4) 6270-4000. Fax: (011-64-4) 471-2082. Email: wlgtn@dfait-maeci.gc.ca
Representative to Canada: c/o New Zealand High Commission, Clarica Centre, 99 Bank St, Ste 727, Ottawa ON K1P 6G3. Tel: (613) 238-5991. Fax: (613) 238-5707. Email: nzhcott@istar.ca

Tonga

Long-Form Name: Kingdom of Tonga
Capital: Nuku'alofa

■ GEOGRAPHY

Area: 748 sq. km; archipelago of 170 islands, of which 36 are inhabited
Coastline: 419 km
Climate: tropical; modified by trade winds; warm season (Dec. to May), cool season (May to Dec.)

Environment: subject to cyclones (Oct. to Apr.); deforestation and overhunting of native animals
Terrain: most islands have limestone base formed from uplifted coral formation; others have limestone overlying volcanic base
Land Use: 24% arable; 43% permanent crops; 6% meadows; 11% forest; 16% other; includes n.a. sq. km irrigated
Location: Pacific Ocean, NW of New Zealand

■ PEOPLE

Population: 102,321 (July 2000 est.)
Nationality: Tongan
Age Structure: 0-14 yrs: 42%; 15-64: 54%; 65+: 4% (2000 est.)
Population Growth Rate: 1.91% (2000 est.)
Net Migration: 0 migrants/1,000 population (2000 est.)
Ethnic Groups: Polynesian; about 300 Europeans
Languages: Tongan, English
Religions: Christian; Free Wesleyan Church claims over 30,000 adherents
Birth Rate: 24.92/1,000 population (2000 est.)
Death Rate: 5.86/1,000 population (2000 est.)
Infant Mortality: 14.45 deaths/1,000 live births (2000 est.)
Life Expectancy at Birth: 65.54 years male, 70.45 years female (2000 est.)
Total Fertility Rate: 3.20 children born/woman (2000 est.)
Literacy: n.a.

■ GOVERNMENT

Leader(s): King Taufa'ahau Tupou IV, Prince and Prime Min. Prince Lavaka ata Ulukalala
Government Type: hereditary constitutional monarchy
Administrative Divisions: three island groups
Nationhood: June 4, 1970 (from UK; formerly known as Friendly Islands)
National Holiday: Emancipation Day, June 4

■ ECONOMY

Overview: the economy's base is agriculture though the country must import a high proportion of its food, for the most part from New Zealand; tourism is the main source of hard currency; the country also remains dependent on sizeable external aid and remittances to offset its trade deficit.
GDP: US$232 million, per capita US$2,100; real growth rate -1.5% (1998 est.)
Inflation: 5.91% (year-end 2000)
Industries: accounts for 10% of GDP; tourism, fishing
Labour Force: n.a.; 70% agriculture, 30% mining
Unemployment: n.a.
Agriculture: accounts for 30% of GDP and 70% of labour force; dominated by coconut, copra and banana production; squash, vanilla beans, cocoa, coffee, ginger, black pepper
Natural Resources: fish, fertile soil

■ FINANCE/TRADE

Currency: pa'anga ($T) = 100 seniti
International Reserves Excluding Gold: US$27 million (Jan. 2001)
Gold Reserves: n.a.
Budget: n.a.
Defence Expenditures: n.a.
Education Expenditures: n.a.
External Debt: US$64 million (1999)
Exports: US$12 million (2000); commodities: coconut oil, desiccated coconut, copra, bananas, taro, vanilla beans, fruit, vegetables, fish; partners: New Zealand 54%, Australia 30%, US 8%, Fiji 5%
Imports: US$74 million (2000); commodities: food products, beverages, tobacco, fuels, machinery, transport equipment, chemicals, building materials; partners: New Zealand 39%, Australia 25%, Japan 9%, US 6%, European Community 5%

■ COMMUNICATIONS

Daily Newspapers: 1
Televisions: 19/1,000 inhabitants (1997 est.)
Radios: 596/1,000 inhabitants (1997 est.)
Telephones: 93 lines/1,000 inhabitants (1999)

■ TRANSPORTATION

Motor Vehicles: n.a.
Roads: 680 km; 184 km paved
Railway: none
Air Traffic: 49,000 passengers carried (1997)
Airports: 6; 1 have paved runways (1999 est.)

Canadian Embassy: The Canadian High Commission to Tonga, c/o The Canadian High Commission, 61 Molesworth St, 3rd Floor, Thorndon, Wellington; mailing address: P.O. Box 12-049, Thorndon, Wellington, New Zealand. Tel: (011-64-4) 473-9577. Fax: (011-64-4) 471-2082. Email: wlgtn@dfait-maeci.gc.ca
Embassy in Canada: Embassy of the Kingdom of Tonga, 250 East 51st St, New York NY 10022, USA. Tel: (917) 369-1025. Fax: (917) 369-1024. Email: n.a.

Trinidad and Tobago

Long-Form Name: Republic of Trinidad and Tobago
Capital: Port of Spain

■ GEOGRAPHY

Area: 5,128 sq. km
Coastline: 362 km
Climate: tropical; rainy season (June to Dec.)
Environment: outside usual path of hurricanes and other tropical storms; water pollution and soil deterioration; oil pollution of beaches
Terrain: mostly plains with some hills and low mountains
Land Use: 15% arable; 9% permanent crops; 2% meadows; 46% forest; 28% other, includes 220 sq. km irrigated
Location: West Indies, off N coast of South America

■ PEOPLE

Population: 1,175,523 (July 2000 est.)
Nationality: Trinidadian, Tobagonian
Age Structure: 0-14 yrs: 25%; 15-64: 68%; 65+: 7% (2000 est.)
Population Growth Rate: -0.49% (2000 est.)
Net Migration: -9.92 migrants/1,000 population (2000 est.)
Ethnic Groups: 40% black, 40% East Indian, 14% mixed, 1% white, 1% Chinese, 4% other
Languages: English (official), Hindi, French, Spanish, Chinese
Religions: Christianity 61%, Hinduism 24%, Islam 6%, 9% other
Birth Rate: 13.84/1,000 population (2000 est.)
Death Rate: 8.84/1,000 population (2000 est.)
Infant Mortality: 25.76 deaths/1,000 live births (2000 est.)
Life Expectancy at Birth: 65.45 years male, 70.59 years female (2000 est.)
Total Fertility Rate: 1.83 children born/woman (2000 est.)
Literacy: 97.8% (1997)

■ GOVERNMENT

Leader(s): Pres. Arthur Napoleon Raymond Robinson, Prime Min. Basdeo Panday.
Government Type: parliamentary democracy
Administrative Divisions: 8 counties, 3 municipalities and 1 ward
Nationhood: Aug. 31, 1962 (from UK)
National Holiday: Independence Day, Aug. 31

■ ECONOMY

Overview: the economy has suffered in recent years because of the sharp decline in the price of oil; the unemployment rate has risen due to the government's austerity programs; the government is seeking to diversify the country's export base
GDP: US$9.41 billion, per capita US$8,500; real growth rate 5% (1999 est.)
Inflation: 3.56% (year-end 2000)

Industries: accounts for 44% of GDP; petroleum, chemicals, tourism, food processing, cement, beverage, cotton textiles
Labour Force: approx. 560,000 economically active (1999); 30.4% community, social and business services, 11.3% agriculture, 10.9% construction
Unemployment: 14.2% (1998)
Agriculture: accounts for approx. 2% of GDP; highly subsidized sector; major crops: cocoa and sugar cane; sugar cane acreage is being shifted into rice, citrus, coffee, vegetables; must import large share of food needs
Natural Resources: crude oil, natural gas, asphalt

■ FINANCE/TRADE

Currency: Trinidad and Tobago dollar ($TT) = 100 cents
International Reserves Excluding Gold: US$1.295 billion (June 2000)
Gold Reserves: US$0.060 million fine troy ounces (Dec. 2000)
Budget: revenues US$1.54 billion; expenditures US$1.6 billion, including capital expenditures of US$117.3 million (1998)
Defence Expenditures: 5.4% of central government expenditure (1997)
Education Expenditures: 3.6% of GNP (1997)
External Debt: US$2.462 billion (1999)
Exports: US$2.448 billion (2000); commodities (including re-exports): petroleum and petroleum products 70%, fertilizer, chemicals 15%, steel products, sugar, cocoa, coffee, citrus; partners: US 61%, European Community 15%, CARICOM 9%, Latin America 7%, Canada 3%
Imports: US$3.127 billion (2000); commodities: raw materials 41%, capital goods 30%, consumer goods 29%; partners: US 42%, European Community 21%, Japan 10%, Canada 6%, Latin America 6%, CARICOM 4%

■ COMMUNICATIONS

Daily Newspapers: 4
Televisions: 334/1,000 inhabitants (1998)
Radios: 534/1,000 inhabitants (1997)
Telephones: 216 lines/1,000 inhabitants (1999)

■ TRANSPORTATION

Motor Vehicles: 155,000; 128,000 passenger cars (1997 est.)
Roads: 8,320 km; 4,252 km paved
Railway: minimal agricultural railway system near San Fernando
Air Traffic: 807,000 passengers carried (1997)
Airports: 6; 3 have paved runways (1999 est.)

Canadian Embassy: The Canadian High Commission, Maple House, 3-3A Sweet Briar

Road, St. Clair, Port of Spain, Trinidad and Tobago; mailing address: P.O. Box 1246, Port-of-Spain, Trinidad and Tobago. Tel: (868) 622-6232. Fax: (868) 628-1830. Email: pspan-ag@dfait-maeci.gc.ca
Embassy in Canada: High Commission for the Republic of Trinidad and Tobago, 200 First Ave, 3rd Level, Ottawa ON K1S 2G6. Tel: (613) 232-2418. Fax: (613) 232-4349. Email: ottawa@ttmissions.com

Tunisia

Long-Form Name: Republic of Tunisia
Capital: Tunis

■ GEOGRAPHY

Area: 163,610 sq. km
Coastline: 1,148 km
Climate: temperate in north with mild, rainy winters and hot, dry summers; desert in south
Environment: deforestation; overgrazing; soil erosion; desertification; ineffective disposal of toxic and hazardous wastes
Terrain: mountains in north; hot, dry central plain; semi-arid south merges into the Sahara
Land Use: 19% arable; 13% permanent crops; 20% meadows; 4% forest; 44% other, includes 3,850 sq. km irrigated
Location: N Africa, bordering on Mediterranean Sea

■ PEOPLE

Population: 9,593,402 (July 2000 est.)
Nationality: Tunisian
Age Structure: 0-14 yrs: 30%; 15-64: 64%; 65+: 6% (2000 est.)
Population Growth Rate: 1.17% (2000 est.)
Net Migration: -0.7 migrants/1,000 population (2000 est.)
Ethnic Groups: 98% Arab-Berber, 1% European, less than 1% Jewish
Languages: Arabic (official); Arabic and French (commerce)
Religions: 98% Muslim, 1% Christian, less than 1% Jewish
Birth Rate: 17.38/1,000 population (2000 est.)
Death Rate: 4.98/1,000 population (2000 est.)
Infant Mortality: 30.09 deaths/1,000 live births (2000 est.)
Life Expectancy at Birth: 72.14 years male, 75.36 years female (2000 est.)
Total Fertility Rate: 2.04 children born/woman (2000 est.)
Literacy: 68% (1998)

■ GOVERNMENT

Leader(s): Pres. Gen. Zine El Abidine Ben Ali,
Prime Min. Mohamed Ghannouchi
Government Type: republic
Administrative Divisions: 23 governorates
Nationhood: Mar. 20, 1956 (from France)
National Holiday: National Day, Mar. 20

■ ECONOMY

Overview: diverse economy, with important agriculture, mining, energy, tourism, and manufacturing sectors; governmental control of economic affairs has gradually lessened over the past decade with increasing privatization of trade and commerce, simplification of the tax structure, and a prudent approach to debt
GDP: US$52.6 billion, per capita US$5,500; real growth rate 6% (1999 est.)
Inflation: 2.93% (year-end 2000)
Industries: accounts for 28% of GDP; petroleum, mining (particularly phosphate and iron ore), textiles, footwear, food, beverages, tourism
Labour Force: 4 million (1999); 21.6% agriculture, 16.3% industry, 62.1% services
Unemployment: 16.5% (1999 est.)
Agriculture: accounts for 12% of GDP; output subject to severe fluctuations because of frequent droughts; export crops: olives, dates, oranges, almonds; other products: grain, sugar beets, wine grapes, poultry, beef, dairy; not self-sufficient in food
Natural Resources: crude oil, phosphates, iron ore, lead, zinc, salt, arable land

■ FINANCE/TRADE

Currency: Tunisian dinar (D) = 1,000 millimes
International Reserves Excluding Gold: US$1.353 billion (July 2000)
Gold Reserves: US$0.218 million fine troy ounces (July 2000)
Budget: revenues US$5.1 billion; expenditures US$5.8 billion, including capital expenditures of US$1.6 billion (1999 est.)
Defence Expenditures: 5.3% of govt. expenditure (1997)
Education Expenditures: 18.01% of total govt. expenditure (2000)
External Debt: US$11.872 billion (1999)
Exports: US$5,846 billion (2000); commodities: hydrocarbons, agricultural products, phosphates and chemicals; partners: European Community 73%, Middle East 9%, US 1%, Turkey, former USSR countries
Imports: US$8.809 billion (2000); commodities: industrial goods and equipment 57%, hydrocarbons 13%, food 12%, consumer goods; partners: European Community 68%, US 7%, Canada, Japan, former USSR countries, China, Saudi Arabia, Algeria

■ COMMUNICATIONS

Daily Newspapers: 8
Televisions: 198/1,000 inhabitants (1998)
Radios: 223/1,000 inhabitants (1997)
Telephones: 90 lines/1,000 inhabitants (1999)

■ TRANSPORTATION

Motor Vehicles: 531,000; 248,000 passenger cars (1997 est.)
Roads: 23,100 km; 18,226 km paved
Railway: 2,168 km
Air Traffic: 1,779,000 passengers carried (1997)
Airports: 32; 15 have paved runways (1999 est.)

Canadian Embassy: Canadian Embassy, 3, rue du Sénégal, Place d'Afrique, 1002 Tunis-Belvedere, Tunisia; mailing address: CP 31, Le Belvédère, 1002, Tunis-Belvedere, Tunisia. Tel: (011-216-1) 796-577. Fax: (011-216-1) 792-371. Email: tunis@dfait-maeci.gc.ca
Embassy in Canada: Embassy of the Republic of Tunisia, 515 O'Connor St, Ottawa ON, K1S 3P8. Tel: (613) 237-0330. Fax: (613) 237-7939. Email: n.a.

Turkey

Long-Form Name: Republic of Turkey
Capital: Ankara

■ GEOGRAPHY

Area: 780,580 sq. km
Coastline: 7,200 km
Climate: temperate; hot, dry summers with mild, wet winters; harsher in interior
Environment: subject to severe earthquakes, especially along major river valleys in west; water and air pollution; desertification
Terrain: mostly mountains; narrow coastal plain; high central plateau (Anatolia)
Land Use: 32% arable; 4% permanent crops; 16% meadows; 26% forest; 22% other, includes 36,740 sq. km irrigated
Location: SW Asia (Near East), bordering on Mediterranean Sea, Black Sea, Aegean Sea

■ PEOPLE

Population: 65,666,677 (July 2000 est.)
Nationality: Turk
Age Structure: 0-14 yrs: 29%; 15-64: 65%; 65+: 6% (2000 est.)
Population Growth Rate: 1.27% (2000 est.)
Net Migration: 0 migrants/1,000 population (2000 est.)
Ethnic Groups: 80% Turkish, 20% Kurd
Languages: Turkish (official), Kurdish 7%, Arabic; English (business language)

Religions: 99.8% Muslim (mostly Sunni), 0.2% other (mostly Christian and Jewish)
Birth Rate: 18.65/1,000 population (2000 est.)
Death Rate: 5.96/1,000 population (2000 est.)
Infant Mortality: 48.90 deaths/1,000 live births (2000 est.)
Life Expectancy at Birth: 68.63 years male, 73.41 years female (2000 est.)
Total Fertility Rate: 2.16 children born/woman (2000 est.)
Literacy: 84% (1998)

■ GOVERNMENT

Leader(s): Pres. Ahmet Necdet Sezer, Prime Min. Bulent Ecevit
Government Type: republican parliamentary democracy
Administrative Divisions: 80 provinces (iller, sing. —il)
Nationhood: Oct. 29, 1923 (successor state to the Ottoman Empire)
National Holiday: Anniversary of the Declaration of the Republic, Oct. 29

■ ECONOMY

Overview: has a strong and rapidly growing private sector, yet the state still plays a major role in basic industry, banking, transport, and communications; its most important industry and largest exporter is textiles and clothing, which is almost entirely in private hands Note: Major economic disruption in August 1999 due to a massive earthquake
GDP: US$409.4 billion, per capita US$6,200; real growth rate -5% (1999 est.)
Inflation: 54.92% (year-end 2000)
Industries: accounts for 29% of GDP; textiles, food processing, mining (coal, chromite, copper, boron minerals), steel, petroleum, construction, lumber, paper
Labour Force: 31 million (1999); 43.6% agriculture, 15% industry, 14% community, social and business services; about 1,000,000 Turks work abroad
Unemployment: 7.3%, plus 6.9% under-employment (April 1999 est.)
Agriculture: accounts for 18% of GDP and 46% the labour force; products: tobacco, cotton, grain, olives, sugar beets, pulses, citrus fruit, variety of animal products; self-sufficient in food most years
Natural Resources: antimony, coal, chromium, mercury, copper, borate, sulphur, iron ore

■ FINANCE/TRADE

Currency: Turkish lira (TL) = 100 kurus
International Reserves Excluding Gold: US$25.119 billion (Jan. 2001)

Gold Reserves: US$3.739 million fine troy ounces (Jan. 2001)
Budget: revenues US$45.2 billion; expenditures US$66.7 billion, including capital expenditures of US$3.4 billion (1999)
Defence Expenditures: 8.15% of total govt. expenditure (1999)
Education Expenditures: 11.28% of total govt. expenditure (1999)
External Debt: US$101.796 billion (1999)
Exports: US$27.594 billion (2000); commodities: industrial products 70%, crops and livestock products 25%; partners: Germany 18.4%, Iraq 8.5%, Italy 8.2%, US 6.5%, UK 4.9%, Iran 4.7%
Imports: US$53.707 billion (2000); commodities: crude oil, machinery, transport equipment, metals, pharmaceuticals, dyes, plastics, rubber, mineral fuels, fertilizers, chemicals; partners: Germany 14.3%, US 10.6%, Iraq 10.0%, Italy 7.0%, France 5.8%, UK 5.2%

■ COMMUNICATIONS

Daily Newspapers: 57
Televisions: 286/1,000 inhabitants (1998)
Radios: 180/1,000 inhabitants (1997)
Telephones: 278 lines/1,000 inhabitants (1999)

■ TRANSPORTATION

Motor Vehicles: 4,400,000; 3,300,000 passenger cars (1997 est.)
Roads: 382,397; 95,599 km paved
Railway: 8,607 km operational
Air Traffic: 9,380,000 passengers carried (1997)
Airports: 118; 82 have paved runways (1999 est.)
Canadian Embassy: The Canadian Embassy, Nenehatun Caddesi 75, Gaziosmanpasa, 06700 Ankara, Turkey. Tel: (011-90-312) 459-9200. Fax: (011-90-312) 459-9361. Email: ankra@dfait-maeci.gc.ca
Embassy in Canada: Embassy of the Republic of Turkey, 197 Wurtemburg St, Ottawa ON K1N 8L9. Tel: (613) 789-4044. Fax: (613) 789-3442. Email: turkish@magna.ca

---

Turkmenistan

Long-Form Name: Turkmenistan
Capital: Ashkhabad

■ GEOGRAPHY

Area: 488,100 sq. km
Coastline: landlocked; 1,768 km coastline along Caspian Sea
Climate: subtropical desert; long, extremely hot summers; short and cold winters; rainfall occurs only in the mountains

Environment: soil and groundwater contaminated with chemicals and pesticides; salinization and waterlogging of soil due to poor irrigation methods; desertification in some areas; prone to earthquakes
Terrain: flat to rolling sandy desert; Caspian Sea in west
Land Use: 3% arable, 0% permanent crops, 63% pastures and meadows, 8% forests, 26% other, includes 13,000 sq. km irrigated
Location: WC Asia, bordering on Caspian Sea

■ PEOPLE

Population: 4,518,268 (July 2000 est.)
Nationality: Turkmen
Age Structure: 0-14 yrs: 38%; 15-64: 58%; 65+: 4% (2000 est.)
Population Growth Rate: 1.87% (2000 est.)
Net Migration: -1.11 migrants/1,000 population (2000 est.)
Ethnic Groups: 77% Turkmen, 6.7% Russian, 9.2% Uzbek, 2% Kazakh, 5.1% other
Languages: 72% Turkmen (official), 12% Russian, 9% Uzbek, 7% other
Religions: 89% Muslim, 9% Eastern Orthodox, 2% unknown
Birth Rate: 28.88/1,000 population (2000 est.)
Death Rate: 9.04/1,000 population (2000 est.)
Infant Mortality: 73.30 deaths/1,000 live births (2000 est.)
Life Expectancy at Birth: 57.29 years male, 64.71 years female (2000 est.)
Total Fertility Rate: 3.63 children born/woman (2000 est.)
Literacy: 98% (1997)

■ GOVERNMENT

Leader(s): Pres. Saparmurad Niyazov
Government Type: republic
Administrative Divisions: 5 regions (welayatlar, sing. —welayat)
Nationhood: Oct. 27, 1991 (from Soviet Union)
National Holiday: Independence Day, Oct. 27

■ ECONOMY

Overview: mining produces the greatest part of Turkmenistan's economic production value, but agriculture is the chief occupation; industry leans heavily toward the energy sector (gas, oil), but the lack of pipeline access to hard currency markets limits expansion; efforts at gas and oil export expansion will take many more years to pay off
GDP: US$7.7 billion, per capita US$1,800; real growth rate 9% (1999 est.)
Inflation: n.a.
Industries: accounts for 62% of GDP; oil production and refining, natural gas extraction,

chemicals, electrical engineering, fertilizer, carpets, textiles and clothing, food processing
Labour Force: 2 million (1999); 42% agriculture and forestry, 21% industry and construction, 37% other
Unemployment: n.a.
Agriculture: accounts for 10% of GDP; irrigation is mandatory for agriculture; products include cotton, grains, livestock, fish
Natural Resources: extensive mineral deposits, including the world's largest sulfur deposits; oil, natural gas, coal, potassium, salts, sulphur

■ FINANCE/TRADE

Currency: manat = 100 tenesi
International Reserves Excluding Gold: n.a.
Gold Reserves: n.a.
Budget: n.a.
Defence Expenditures: 15.6% of central government expenditure (1997)
Education Expenditures: n.a.
External Debt: US$2.015 billion (1999)
Exports: US$2.333 billion (2000); oil, natural gas, electric power, clothing and textiles, petroleum products, carpets; partners: Hong Kong, Switzerland, US, former Soviet Union, Germany, Turkey
Imports: US$1.014 billion (2000); machinery, foodstuffs, consumer products, plastics and rubber, textiles; partners: US, former Soviet Union, Turkey, Germany, Cyprus

■ COMMUNICATIONS

Daily Newspapers: n.a.
Televisions: 201/1,000 inhabitants (1998)
Radios: 276/1,000 inhabitants (1997)
Telephones: 82 lines/1,000 inhabitants (1999)

■ TRANSPORTATION

Motor Vehicles: n.a.
Roads: 24,000 km; 19,488 km paved
Railway: 2,187 km
Air Traffic: 523,000 passengers carried (1997)
Airports: 64; 22 have paved runways (1998 est.)
Canadian Embassy: c/o The Canadian Embassy, Nenehatun Caddesi 75, Gaziosmanpasa 06700, Ankara, Turkey. Tel: (011-90-312) 459-9200. Fax: (011-90-312) 459-9361. Email: ankra@dfait-maeci.gc.ca
Embassy in Canada: c/o Embassy of the Republic of Turkmenistan, 2207 Massachusetts Ave NW, Washington DC 20008, USA. Tel: (202) 588-1500. Fax: (202) 588-0697. Email: n.a.

Turks and Caicos

Long-Form Name: The Turks and Caicos Islands
Capital: Grand Turk (Cockburn Town)

■ GEOGRAPHY

Area: 430 sq. km; 30+ small cays, of which only 8 are inhabited
Climate: sunny, relatively dry, equable climate with moderating winds; occasional hurricanes
Land Use: 2% arable, 0% permanent crops, meadows, forests, 98% other; includes n.a. sq. km irrigated
Location: West Indies (S Atlantic Ocean), N of Dominican Republic

■ PEOPLE

Population: 17,502 (July 2000 est.)
Nationality: none (British citizens)
Ethnic Groups: black majority
Languages: English (official)

■ GOVERNMENT

Colony Territory of: Colony of the United Kingdom
Leader(s): Head of State: Queen Elizabeth II/Gov. Mervyn Jones. Head of government: Chief Min. Derek H. Taylor
Government Type: dependent territory of the United Kingdom
National Holiday: Constitution Day, Aug. 30

■ ECONOMY

Overview: fishing is the most important activity; exports include lobster, conch, other fish products; imports include food and drink, tobacco, maufactured goods; tourism; offshore banking; chief trading partner: US

■ FINANCE/TRADE

Currency: US dollar (US$) = 100 cents

Canadian Embassy: c/o The Canadian High Commission, Macdonald House, 1 Grosvenor Square, London W1K 4AB, England, UK. Tel: (011-44-20) 7258-6600. Fax: (011-44-20) 7258-6333. Email: Ldn@dfait-maeci.gc.ca
Representative to Canada: c/o British High Commission, 80 Elgin St, Ottawa ON K1P 5K7. Tel: (613) 237-1530. Fax: (613) 237-7980. Email should be sent using the appropriate form at the British High Commission's website at http://www.britain-in-canada.org

Tuvalu

Long-Form Name: Tuvalu
Capital: Funafuti

■ GEOGRAPHY

Area: 26 sq. km

Coastline: 24 km
Climate: tropical; moderated by easterly trade winds (Mar. to Nov.); westerly gales and heavy rain (Nov. to Mar.)
Environment: severe tropical storms are rare; no natural safe drinking water resources
Terrain: very low-lying and narrow coral atolls
Land Use: the 9 coral atolls have just enough soil to allow for subsistence agriculture; there are also coconut groves
Location: S Pacific Ocean, NE of Australia

■ PEOPLE

Population: 10,838 (July 2000 est.)
Nationality: Tuvaluan
Age Structure: 0-14 yrs: 34%; 15-64: 61%; 65+: 5% (2000 est.)
Population Growth Rate: 1.41% (2000 est.)
Net Migration: 0 migrants/1,000 population (2000 est.)
Ethnic Groups: 96% Polynesian
Languages: Tuvaluan, English
Religions: 97% Congregationalist (Church of Tuvalu), 1.4% Seventh Day Adventists, 1% Baha'i, 0.6% other
Birth Rate: 21.78/1,000 population (2000 est.)
Death Rate: 7.66/1,000 population (2000 est.)
Infant Mortality: 23.30 deaths/1,000 live births (2000 est.)
Life Expectancy at Birth: 64.21 years male, 68.53 years female (2000 est.)
Total Fertility Rate: 3.11 children born/woman (2000 est.)
Literacy: n.a.

■ GOVERNMENT

Leader(s): Head of State: Queen Elizabeth II/Gov. Gen. Sir Tomasi Puapua. Acting Prime Min. Lagitupu Tuilimu
Government Type: constitutional monarchy with a parliamentary democracy
Administrative Divisions: none
Nationhood: Oct. 1, 1978 from UK (formerly known as Ellice Islands)
National Holiday: Independence Day, Oct. 1

■ ECONOMY

Overview: scattered group of 9 coral atolls with poor soil; a small economy, no known mineral resources and few exports; receives money from the sale of stamps and coins and worker remittances as well as an international trust fund; subsistence farming and fishing are the primary economic activities
GDP: n.a.
Inflation: n.a.
Industries: fishing, tourism, copra, fish
Labour Force: n.a.

Unemployment: n.a.
Agriculture: coconuts, copra, fish
Natural Resources: fish

■ FINANCE/TRADE

Currency: Australian dollar ($A) or Tuvaluan dollar ($T) = 100 cents
International Reserves Excluding Gold: n.a.
Gold Reserves: n.a.
Budget: n.a.
Defence Expenditures: n.a.
Education Expenditures: n.a.
External Debt: n.a.
Exports: n.a.; commodities: copra; partners: Fiji, Australia, New Zealand
Imports: n.a.; commodities: food, animals, fuels, machinery, manufactures; partners: Fiji, Australia, New Zealand

■ COMMUNICATIONS

Daily Newspapers: 0
Televisions: 13.0/1,000 inhabitants (1997 est.)
Radios: 369/1,000 inhabitants (1997 est.)
Telephones: n.a.

■ TRANSPORTATION

Motor Vehicles: n.a.
Roads: 8 km gravel roads
Railway: none
Air Traffic: n.a.
Airports: 1; no paved runway (1999 est.)

Canadian Embassy: The Canadian High Commission to Tuvalu, c/o The Canadian High Commission, 61 Molesworth St, 3rd Fl, Thorndon, Wellington; mailing address: P.O. Box 12-049, Thorndon, Wellington, New Zealand. Tel: (011-64-4) 473-9577. Fax: (011-64-4) 471-2082. Email: wlgtn@dfait-maeci.gc.ca
Embassy in Canada: c/o New Zealand High Commission, Clarica Centre, 99 Bank St, Ste 727, Ottawa, ON K1P 6G3. Tel: (613) 238-5991. Fax: (613) 238-5707. Email: nzhcott@istar.ca

U.S. Virgin Islands

Long-Form Name: Virgin Islands of the United States
Capital: Charlotte Amalie

■ GEOGRAPHY

Area: 352 sq. km
Climate: subtropical, tempered by easterly trade winds, relatively low humidity, little seasonal temperature variation; rainy season May to Nov.
Land Use: 15% arable; 6% permanent crops;

26% meadows; 6% forest; 47% other; includes n.a. sq. km irrigated
Location: Caribbean islands, just E of Puerto Rico

■ PEOPLE

Population: 120,917 (July 2000 est.)
Nationality: Virgin Islander
Ethnic Groups: 74% West Indian (45% born in the Virgin Islands and 29% born elsewhere in the West Indies), 13% US mainland, 5% Puerto Rican, 8% other (80% black, 15% white, 5% other); 14% of Hispanic origin
Languages: English (official), but Spanish and Creole are widely spoken

■ GOVERNMENT

Colony Territory of: Dependent Territory of the United States
Leader(s): Head of State: George W. Bush, Gov. Dr. Charles Wesley Turnbull
Government Type: organized, unincorporated territory of the US
National Holiday: Transfer Day, Mar. 31 (1917, from Denmark to the US)

■ ECONOMY

Overview: tourism is the primary economic activity accounting for more than 70% of GDP and 70% of employment; some manufacturing; small agricultural sector (most food is imported); international business and financial services are a small but growing sector

■ FINANCE/TRADE

Currency: US dollar ($) = 100 cents

Canadian Embassy: c/o The Canadian Embassy, 501 Pennsylvania Ave NW, Washington DC 20001, USA. Tel: (202) 682-1740. Fax: (202) 456-7726. Email: wshdc-outpack@dfait-maeci.gc.ca
Representative to Canada: c/o Embassy of the United States of America, 490 Sussex Dr, Ottawa, ON, K1N 1G8. Tel: (613) 238-5335. Fax: (613) 688-3097. Email inquiries are not accepted

Uganda

Long-Form Name: Republic of Uganda
Capital: Kampala

■ GEOGRAPHY

Area: 236,040 sq. km
Coastline: none; landlocked
Climate: tropical; generally rainy with two dry seasons (Dec. to Feb., June to Aug.); semi-arid in northeast
Environment: straddles equator; deforestation; overgrazing; soil erosion; widespread poaching
Terrain: mostly plateau with rim of mountains
Land Use: 25% arable; 9% permanent crops; 9% permanent pastures; 28% forest; 29% other; includes 90 sq. km irrigated
Location: EC Africa

■ PEOPLE

Population: 23,317,560 (July 2000 est.)
Nationality: Ugandan
Age Structure: 0-14 yrs: 51%; 15-64: 47%; 65+: 2% (2000 est.)
Population Growth Rate: 2.72% (2000 est.)
Net Migration: -2.4 migrants/1,000 population (2000 est.)
Ethnic Groups: 17% Baganda, 12% Karamojong, 8% Basogo, 8% Iteso, 6% Langi, 6% Rwanda, 5% Bagisu, 4% Acholi, 4% Lugbara, 3% Bunyro, 27% other
Languages: English (official); Luganda and Swahili widely used; other Bantu and Nilotic languages
Religions: 33% Roman Catholic, 33% Protestant, 16% Muslim, rest indigenous beliefs
Birth Rate: 48.04/1,000 population (2000 est.)
Death Rate: 18.44/1,000 population (2000 est.)
Infant Mortality: 93.25 deaths/1,000 live births (2000 est.)
Life Expectancy at Birth: 42.22 years male, 43.67 years female (2000 est.)
Total Fertility Rate: 6.96 children born/woman (2000 est.)
Literacy: 65% (1998)

■ GOVERNMENT

Leader(s): Pres. Yoweri Kaguta Museveni, Prime Min. Apollo Nsibambi
Parliamentary elections held June 26, 2001
Government Type: republic
Administrative Divisions: 39 districts
Nationhood: Oct. 9, 1962 (from UK)
National Holiday: Independence Day, Oct. 9

■ ECONOMY

Overview: despite substantial natural resources, the economy has been ruined by years of political instability, mismanagement and civil war; the government has started a reform program which is partly aimed at lowering high inflation and increasing export earnings; agriculture is the most important economic sector
GDP: US$24.2 billion, per capita US$1,060; real growth rate 5.5% (1999 est.)
Inflation: 2.83% (year-end 2000)

Industries: accounts for 17% of GDP; sugar, brewing, tobacco, cotton textile, cement
Labour Force: 11 million (1999); 85.9% agriculture, 4.4% industry, 9.7% services
Unemployment: n.a.
Agriculture: accounts for 44% of GDP and 86% of labour force; coffee, tea and tobacco are the main export crops
Natural Resources: copper, cobalt, limestone, salt, hydropower, arable land

■ FINANCE/TRADE

Currency: Ugandan shilling (USh) = 100 cents
International Reserves Excluding Gold: US$808 million (Dec. 2000)
Gold Reserves: n.a.
Budget: revenues US$959 million; expenditures US$1.04 billion, including capital expenditures of US$n.a. (1998-99)
Defence Expenditures: 23.9% of central government expenditure (1997)
Education Expenditures: 2.6% of GNP (1997)
External Debt: US$4.077 billion (1999)
Exports: US$494 million (2000); commodities: coffee 97%, cotton, tea; partners: US 25%, UK 18%, France 11%, Spain 10%
Imports: US$1.436 billion (2000); commodities: petroleum products, machinery, cotton piece goods, metals, transportation equipment, food; partners: Kenya 25%, UK 14%, Italy 13%

■ COMMUNICATIONS

Daily Newspapers: 2
Televisions: 27/1,000 inhabitants (1998)
Radios: 128/1,000 inhabitants (1997)
Telephones: 3 lines/1,000 inhabitants (1999)

■ TRANSPORTATION

Motor Vehicles: 51,000; 24,400 passenger cars (1997 est.)
Roads: 27,000 km; 1,800 km paved
Railway: 1,241 km
Air Traffic: 100,000 passengers carried (1997)
Airports: 26; 4 have paved runways (1999 est.)

Canadian Embassy: The Canadian High Commission to Uganda, c/o The Canadian High Commission, Comcraft House, Hailé Sélassie Ave, Nairobi, Kenya; mailing address: The Canadian High Commission, P.O. Box 30481, Nairobi, Kenya. Tel: (011-254-2) 21-48-04. Fax: (011-254-2) 22-69-87. Email: nrobi@dfait-maeci.gc.ca
Embassy in Canada: High Commission for the Republic of Uganda, 231 Cobourg St, Ottawa ON K1N 8J2. Tel: (613) 789-7797. Fax: (613) 789-8909. Email: ugacom@comnet.ca

Ukraine

Long-Form Name: Ukraine
Capital: Kiev

■ GEOGRAPHY

Area: 603,700 sq. km
Coastline: 2,782 km
Climate: temperate continental; subtropical on southern Crimean coast; moderate rainfall in north; drier in southern regions
Environment: air and water pollution, unsafe drinking water, deforestation, radiation contamination around Chernobyl nuclear power plant
Terrain: Carpathian mountains in west, marshy in north, remainder flat fertile plains (steppes) and plateaux
Land Use: 58% arable, 2% permanent crops, 13% meadows and pastures, 18% forest, 9% other, includes 26,050 sq. km irrigated
Location: E Europe, bordering on Black Sea

■ PEOPLE

Population: 49,153,027 (July 2000 est.)
Nationality: Ukrainian
Age Structure: 0-14 yrs: 18%; 15-64: 68%; 65+: 14% (2000 est.)
Population Growth Rate: -0.83% (2000 est.)
Net Migration: -0.84 migrants/1,000 population (2000 est.)
Ethnic Groups: 73% Ukrainian, 22% Russian, 1% Jewish, 4% other
Languages: Ukrainian, Russian, Romanian, Polish
Religions: predominantly Eastern Orthodox and Roman Catholic; Uniate Church re-legalized in 1991; also, Autocephalous Orthodox Church, Greek rite Catholic
Birth Rate: 9.03/1,000 population (2000 est.)
Death Rate: 16.48/1,000 population (2000 est.)
Infant Mortality: 21.67 deaths/1,000 live births (2000 est.)
Life Expectancy at Birth: 60.39 years male, 71.85 years female (2000 est.)
Total Fertility Rate: 1.26 children born/woman (2000 est.)
Literacy: 99.5% (1998)

■ GOVERNMENT

Leader(s): Pres. Leonid Kuchma, Prime Min. Anatoliy Kinakh
Government Type: republic
Administrative Divisions: 24 oblasts (oblasti, sing. —oblast), 1 autonomous republic (avtomnaya respublika), 2 municipalities (mista, sing. —misto) with oblast status
Nationhood: Dec. 1, 1991 (from Soviet Union)
National Holiday: Independence Day, Aug. 24

■ ECONOMY

Overview: mining and heavy industry, with very strong agricultural sector; food surplus area of former USSR; internal political disputes are hobbling economic progress

GDP: US$109.5 billion, per capita US$2,200; real growth rate -0.4% (1999 est.)

Inflation: 22.68% (year-end 1999)

Industries: accounts for 26% of GDP and 33% of labour force; industries include: mining, manufacturing of machinery, food processing, chemicals, electric and electronic equipment, coal, electric power, food processing (esp. sugar)

Labour Force: 25 million (1999); 32% industry and construction, 24% agriculture and forestry, 17% health and cultural services, 27% other

Unemployment: 4.3% (Dec. 1999) officially registered, but there is extensive unregistered unemployment or underemployment

Agriculture: accounts for about 12%; corn, wheat, sugar beets, sunflower seeds, barley, tobacco; livestock includes cattle, pigs, goats, sheep, vegetables, milk, sugar beets

Natural Resources: coal, manganese, oil, gypsum, iron, lead, zinc, titanium, natural gas, oil, salt, sulphur, graphite, mercury, timber, arable land

■ FINANCE/TRADE

Currency: hryvnia (pl. hryvni) = 100 kopiykas

International Reserves Excluding Gold: US$1.456 billion (Jan. 2001)

Gold Reserves: US$0.454 million fine troy ounces (Jan. 2001)

Budget: revenues US$8.3 billion; expenditures US$8.8 billion, including capital expenditures US$n.a. (1999 est.)

Defence Expenditures: 8.4% of central government expenditure (1997)

Education Expenditures: 7.3% of GNP (1997)

External Debt: US$14.136 billion (1999)

Exports: US$14.767 billion (2000): minerals, agricultural products, heavy machinery, vehicles, airplanes

Imports: US$18.465 billion (2000): machinery and equipment, chemicals, textiles, energy

■ COMMUNICATIONS

Daily Newspapers: 44

Televisions: 490/1,000 inhabitants (1998)

Radios: 884/1,000 inhabitants (1997)

Telephones: 199 lines/1,000 inhabitants (1999)

■ TRANSPORTATION

Motor Vehicles: n.a.

Roads: 176,310 km; 170,139 km paved

Railway: 23,350 km

Air Traffic: 1,190,000 passengers carried (1997)

Airports: 706; 163 have paved runways

Canadian Embassy: The Canadian Embassy, 31 Yaroslaviv Val St, Kiev 01901, Ukraine. Tel: (011-380-44) 464-1144. Fax: (011-380-44) 464-0598. Email: kiev@dfait-maeci.gc.ca

Embassy in Canada: Embassy of Ukraine, 310 Somerset St W, Ottawa ON K2P 0J9. Tel: (613) 230-2961. Fax: (613) 230-2400. Email: ukrembassy@on.aibn.com

United Arab Emirates

Long-Form Name: United Arab Emirates

Capital: Abu Dhabi

■ GEOGRAPHY

Area: 82,880 sq. km

Coastline: 1,318 km

Climate: desert; cooler in eastern mountains

Environment: frequent dust and sand storms; lack of natural freshwater resources being overcome by desalination plants; desertification

Terrain: flat, barren coastal plain; desert wasteland; mountains in east

Land Use: 2% permanent pastures; 98% other; includes 50 sq. km irrigated

Location: SW Asia (Middle East), Arabian Peninsula bordering on Persian Gulf

■ PEOPLE

Population: 2,369,153 (July 2000 est.)

Nationality: Emiri or Emirian

Age Structure: 0-14 yrs: 30%; 15-64: 68%; 65+: 2% (2000 est.)

Population Growth Rate: 1.61% (2000 est.)

Net Migration: 1.82 migrants/1,000 population (2000 est.)

Ethnic Groups: 19% Emiri, 23% other Arab, 50% South Asian (fluctuating), 8% other expatriates (includes Westerners and East Asians); less than 20% of the population are United Arab Emirates citizens

Languages: Arabic (official); Farsi and English widely spoken in major cities; Hindi, Urdu

Religions: 96% Muslim (16% Shi'a); 4% Christian, Hindu and other

Birth Rate: 18.00/1,000 population (2000 est.)

Death Rate: 3.68/1,000 population (2000 est.)

Infant Mortality: 17.17 deaths/1,000 live births (2000 est.)

Life Expectancy at Birth: 71.64 years male, 76.61 years female (2000 est.)

Total Fertility Rate: 3.29 children born/woman (2000 est.)

Literacy: 74.8% (1997)

■ GOVERNMENT

Leader(s): Pres. Zayid bin Sultan Al Nuhayyan, V. Pres. and Prime Min. Maktum bin Rashid al-Maktum

Government Type: federation with specified powers delegated to the United Arab Emirates central government and other powers reserved to member emirates

Administrative Divisions: 7 emirates (imarat, sing. -imarah)

Nationhood: Dec. 2, 1971 (from UK; formerly known as Trucial States)

National Holiday: National Day, Dec. 2

■ ECONOMY

Overview: an open economy tied to the world prices for oil and gas; currently has a high standard of living; crude oil reserves should last for over 100 years at present levels of production; the government is encouraging privatization measures

GDP: US$41.5 billion, per capita US$17,700; real growth rate 2.5% (1999 est.)

Inflation: n.a.

Industries: accounts for 52% of GDP; petroleum, fishing, petrochemicals, construction materials, some boat building, handicrafts, pearling

Labour Force: 1.38 million (1999 est.): 38% industry, 4.5% agriculture, 57.3% services

Unemployment: n.a.

Agriculture: accounts for 3% of GDP and 6% of labour force; cash crop: dates; food products: vegetables, watermelons, poultry, eggs, dairy, fish; only 25% self-sufficient in food

Natural Resources: crude oil and natural gas

■ FINANCE/TRADE

Currency: Emirian dirham (Dh) = 100 fils

International Reserves Excluding Gold: US$13.523 billion (Dec. 2000)

Gold Reserves: US$0.397 million fine troy ounces (Dec. 2000)

Budget: revenues US$5.5 billion; expenditures US$6.2 billion, including capital expenditures US$n.a. (1999 est.)

Defence Expenditures: 30.06% of central government expenditure (1999)

Education Expenditures: 17.33% of central government expenditure (1999)

External Debt: US$15.5 billion (1998 est.)

Exports: US$43.506 billion (2000); commodities: crude oil 75%, natural gas, re-exports, dried fish, dates; partners: US, European Community, Japan, Singapore, Korea

Imports: US$35.575 billion (2000); commodities: food, consumer and capital goods; partners: European Community, Japan, US

■ COMMUNICATIONS

Daily Newspapers: 7

Televisions: 130/1,000 inhabitants (1997 est.)

Radios: 345/1,000 inhabitants (1997)

Telephones: 332 lines/1,000 inhabitants (1999)

■ TRANSPORTATION

Motor Vehicles: 400,000; 320,000 passenger cars (1997 est.)

Roads: 1,088 km, all paved

Railway: none

Air Traffic: 4,720,000 passengers carried (1997)

Airports: 40; 22 have paved runways (1999 est.)

Canadian Embassy: The Canadian Embassy, Villa No. 440, 26th St, Rowdah District, Abu Dhabi, UAE; mailing address: P.O. Box 6970, Abu Dhabi, UAE. Tel: (011-971-2) 446-969. Fax: (011-971-2) 458-787. Email: abdbi@dfait-maeci.gc.ca

Embassy in Canada: c/o Embassy of the United Arab Emirates, 45 O'Connor St, Ste 1800 World Exchange Plaza, Ottawa, ON, K1P 1A4, Tel: (613) 565-7272, Fax: (613) 565-8007. Email: safara@uae-embassy.com

United Kingdom

Long-Form Name: United Kingdom of Great Britain and Northern Ireland

Capital: London

■ GEOGRAPHY

Area: 244,820 sq. km

Coastline: 12,429 km

Climate: temperate; moderated by prevailing southwest winds over the North Atlantic Current; more than half of the days are overcast

Environment: pollution control measures improving air, water quality; because of heavily indented coastline, no location is more than 125 km from tidal waters

Terrain: mostly rugged hills and low mountains; level to rolling plains in east and southeast

Land Use: 25% arable; negligible permanent crops; 46% meadows; 10% forest; 19% other; includes 1,080 sq. km irrigated

Location: NW Europe, bordering on North Sea, Atlantic Ocean

■ PEOPLE

Population: 59,511,464(July 2000 est.)

Nationality: British or Briton

Age Structure: 0-14 yrs: 19%; 15-64: 65%; 65+: 16% (2000 est.)

Population Growth Rate: 0.25% (2000 est.)

Net Migration: 1.07 migrants/1,000 population (2000 est.)

Ethnic Groups: 81.5% English, 9.6% Scottish, 2.4% Irish, 1.9% Welsh, 1.8% Ulster, 2.8% West Indian, Indian, Pakistani and other
Languages: English, Welsh (about 26% of population of Wales), Scottish form of Gaelic (about 60,000 in Scotland)
Religions: 73% Anglican, 23% Roman Catholic, 3% Muslim, 0.1% Sikh, 0.2% Presbyterian, 0.5% Methodist, 0.2% Jewish
Birth Rate: 11.76/1,000 population (2000 est.)
Death Rate: 10.38/1,000 population (2000 est.)
Infant Mortality: 5.63 deaths/1,000 live births (2000 est.)
Life Expectancy at Birth: 74.97 years male, 80.49 years female (2000 est.)
Total Fertility Rate: 1.74 children born/woman (2000 est.)
Literacy: 99% (1998)

■ GOVERNMENT

Leader(s): Head of State: Queen Elizabeth II. Prime Min. Tony Blair
Government Type: constitutional monarchy
Administrative Divisions: 47 counties, 7 metropolitan counties, 26 districts, 9 regions and 3 island areas; dependent areas include: Anguilla, Bermuda, British Antarctic Territory (uninhabited except for variable population of research stations – about 300 persons), British Indian Ocean Territory, British Virgin Islands, Cayman Islands, Channel Islands, Falkland Islands, Gibraltar, Guernsey, Isle of Man, Jersey, Montserrat, Pitcairn, Saint Helena, South Georgia (uninhabited except for scientific station and 500 persons in a whaling/sealing settlement), South Sandwich Islands (uninhabited), Turks and Caicos Islands
Nationhood: Jan. 1, 1801, United Kingdom established
National Holiday: Celebration of the Birthday of the Queen, second Saturday in June

■ ECONOMY

Overview: essentially capitalist economy; intensive agricultural practices produce 60% of domestic food needs with only 1% of the labour force; strong service sector; industry is declining in importance
GDP: US$1.29 trillion, per capita US$21,800; real growth rate 1.9% (1999 est.)
Inflation: 2.93% (year-end 2000)
Industries: accounts for 25.3% of GDP and 25% of labour force; machinery and transportation equipment, metals, food processing, paper and paper products, textiles, chemicals, clothing, other consumer goods, motor vehicles, aircraft, shipbuilding, petroleum, coal
Labour Force: 30 million (1999); 62.8% services, 1.2% agriculture, 1.9% energy, 25% manufacturing and construction, 9.1% government
Unemployment: 3.5% (Dec. 2000)
Agriculture: accounts for only 1.7% of GDP; highly mechanized and efficient farms; wide variety of crops and livestock products produced; about 60% self-sufficient in food and feed needs
Natural Resources: coal, crude oil, natural gas, tin, limestone, iron ore, salt, clay, chalk, gypsum, lead, silica

■ FINANCE/TRADE

Currency: pound sterling (£ or £ stg) = 100 pence
International Reserves Excluding Gold: US$41.772 billion (Jan. 2001)
Gold Reserves: US$14.860 million fine troy ounces (Jan. 2001)
Budget: revenues US$541 billion; expenditures US$507.5 billion, including capital expenditures US$35.1 billion (1998 est.)
Defence Expenditures: 7.10% of central government expenditure (1999)
Education Expenditures: 3.73% of total govt. expenditure (1999)
External Debt: n.a.
Exports: US$232.482 billion (2000); commodities: manufactured goods, machinery, fuels, chemicals, semifinished goods, transport equipment; partners: European Community 50.4% (Germany 11.7%, France 10.2%, Netherlands 6.8%), US 13%, Communist countries 2.3%
Imports: US$279.706 billion (2000); commodities: manufactured goods, machinery, semifinished goods, foodstuffs, consumer goods; partners: European Community 52.5% (Germany 16.6%, France 8.8%, Netherlands 7.8%), US 10.2%, Communist countries 2.1%

■ COMMUNICATIONS

Daily Newspapers: 99
Televisions: 645/1,000 inhabitants (1998)
Radios: 1,436/1,000 inhabitants (1997)
Telephones: 567 lines/1,000 inhabitants (1999)

■ TRANSPORTATION

Motor Vehicles: 28,800,000; 25,000,000 passenger cars (1997 est.)
Roads: 371,603 km, all paved
Railway: 16,878 km
Air Traffic: 62,763,000 passengers carried (1997)
Airports: 498; 357 have paved runways (1999 est.)
Canadian Embassy: The Canadian High Commission, Macdonald House, 1 Grosvenor Square, London W1K 4AB, England, UK. Tel: (011-44-20) 7258-6600. Fax: (011-44-20) 7258-6333. Email: Ldn@dfait-maeci.gc.ca

Embassy in Canada: British High Commission, 80 Elgin St, Ottawa ON K1P 5K7. Tel: (613) 237-1530. Fax: (613) 237-7980. Email should be sent using the appropriate form at the British High Commission's website at http://www.britain-in-canada.org

United States

Long-Form Name: United States of America
Capital: Washington, D.C.

■ GEOGRAPHY

Area: 9,629,091 sq. km; includes only the 50 states and District of Columbia
Coastline: 19,924 km
Climate: mostly temperate, but varies from tropical (Hawaii) to arctic (Alaska); arid to semi-arid in west with occasional warm, dry chinook wind
Environment: pollution control measures improving air and water quality; acid rain; agricultural fertilizer and pesticide pollution; management of sparse natural water resources in west; desertification; tsunamis, volcanoes and earthquake activity around Pacific; permafrost in Alaska
Terrain: vast central plain, mountains in west, hills and low mountains in east; rugged mountains and broad river valleys in Alaska; rugged, volcanic topography in Hawaii
Land Use: 19% arable; negligible permanent crops; 25% meadows; 30% forest; 26% other, includes 207,000 sq. km irrigated
Location: North America, bordering on Canada, Mexico, Pacific Ocean, Atlantic Ocean

■ PEOPLE

Population: 275,562,673 (July 2000 est.)
Nationality: American
Age Structure: 0-14 yrs: 21%; 15-64: 66%; 65+: 13% (2000 est.)
Population Growth Rate: 0.91% (2000 est.)
Net Migration: 3.5 migrants/1,000 population (2000 est.)
Ethnic Groups: 83.5% white, 12.4% black, 3.3% Asian, 0.8% other
Languages: predominantly English; sizable Spanish-speaking minority
Religions: 56% Protestant (including 21% Baptist, 12% Methodist, 8% Lutheran, 4% Presbyterian, 3% Episcopalian), 28% Roman Catholic, 2% Jewish, 4% other, 10% none
Birth Rate: 14.20/1,000 population (2000 est.)
Death Rate: 8.70/1,000 population (2000 est.)
Infant Mortality: 6.82 deaths/1,000 live births (2000 est.)

Life Expectancy at Birth: 74.24 years male, 79.90 years female (2000 est.)
Total Fertility Rate: 2.06 children born/woman (2000 est.)
Literacy: 99.0% (1998)

■ GOVERNMENT

Leader(s): Pres. George W. Bush, V. Pres. Richard B. Cheney
Government Type: federal republic
Administrative Divisions: 50 states and 1 district; dependent areas include: American Samoa, Baker Island, Federated States of Micronesia, Guam, Howland Island, Jarvis Island, Johnston Atoll, Kingman Reef, Marshall Islands, Midway Islands (inhabited by U.S. military personnel), Northern Marianas, Palau, Palymyra Atoll, Puerto Rico (for details see Puerto Rico entry), Virgin Islands (for details see Virgin Islands entry), Wake Island (military base)
Nationhood: July 4, 1776 (from England)
National Holiday: Independence Day, July 4

■ ECONOMY

Overview: market-oriented economy with a very large private sector; a powerful and diversified economy, with high per capita GNP; problems include the significant budget and trade deficits, large medical costs for the aging population and inadequate investment in industry and infrastructure
GDP: US$9.255 trillion, per capita US$33,900; real growth rate 4.1% (1999 est.)
Inflation: 3.38% (year-end 2000)
Industries: accounts for 18% of GDP and 25.3% of labour force; highly diversified industry; petroleum, steel, motor vehicles, aerospace, telecommunications, chemicals, electronics, food processing, consumer goods, fishing, lumber, mining
Labour Force: 139 million (1999); 35.5% community, social and business services, 20.8% trade and tourism, 16.4% industry
Unemployment: 4.6% (March 2001)
Agriculture: accounts for 2% of GDP and 2.8% of labour force; favourable climate and soils support a wide variety of crops and livestock production; world's second largest producer and top exporter of grain; surplus food producer; fish catch of 4.4 million metric tons
Natural Resources: coal, copper, lead, molybdenum, phosphates, uranium, bauxite, gold, iron, mercury, nickel, potash, silver, tungsten, zinc, crude oil, natural gas, timber

■ FINANCE/TRADE

Currency: US dollar ($ or $US) = 100 cents

International Reserves Excluding Gold: US$54.477 billion (Nov. 2000)
Gold Reserves: US$261.610 million fine troy ounces (Jan. 2001)
Budget: revenues US$1.828 trillion; expenditures US$1.703 trillion, including capital expenditures US$n.a. (1999)
Defence Expenditures: 15.22% of govt. expenditure (1999)
Education Expenditures: 1.80% of govt. expenditure (1999)
External Debt: n.a.
Exports: US$767.019 billion (2000); commodities: capital goods, automobiles, industrial supplies and raw materials, consumer goods, agricultural products; partners: Canada 22.9%, Japan 11.8%
Imports: US$1.2 trillion (2000); commodities: crude and partly refined petroleum, machinery, automobiles, consumer goods, industrial raw materials, food and beverages; partners: Japan 19.6%, Canada 19.1%

■ COMMUNICATIONS

Daily Newspapers: 1,520
Televisions: 847/1,000 inhabitants (1998)
Radios: 2,146/1,000 inhabitants (1997)
Telephones: 664 lines/1,000 inhabitants (1999)

■ TRANSPORTATION

Motor Vehicles: 212,000,000; 137,000,000 passenger cars (1997 est.)
Roads: 6,348,227 km; 3,732,757 km paved
Railway: 240,000 km
Air Traffic: 590,571,000 passengers carried (1997)
Airports: 14,572; 5,174 have paved runways (1999 est.)

Canadian Embassy: The Canadian Embassy, 501 Pennsylvania Ave, NW, Washington DC 20001, USA. Tel: (202) 682-1740. Fax: (202) 682-7726. Email: wshdc-outpack@dfait-maeci.gc.ca
Embassy in Canada: Embassy of the United States of America, 490 Sussex Dr, Ottawa, ON, K1N 1G8. Tel: (613) 238-5335. Fax: (613) 688-3097. Email inquiries are not accepted

Uruguay

Long-Form Name: Oriental Republic of Uruguay
Capital: Montevideo

■ GEOGRAPHY

Area: 176,220 sq. km
Coastline: 660 km
Climate: warm temperate; freezing temperatures almost unknown

Environment: subject to seasonally high winds, droughts, floods; industrial pollution from Brazil
Terrain: mostly rolling plains and low hills; fertile coastal lowland
Land Use: 7% arable; negligible permanent crops; 77% meadows; 6% forest; 10% other; includes 7,700 sq. km irrigated
Location: SE South America, bordering on Atlantic Ocean

■ PEOPLE

Population: 3,334,074 (July 2000 est.)
Nationality: Uruguayan
Age Structure: 0-14 yrs: 24%; 15-64: 63%; 65+: 13% (2000 est.)
Population Growth Rate: 0.77% (2000 est.)
Net Migration: -0.63 migrants/1,000 population (2000 est.)
Ethnic Groups: 88% white, 8% mestizo, 4% black
Languages: Spanish, Brazilero
Religions: 66% nominally Roman Catholic, 2% Protestant, 2% Jewish, 30% other
Birth Rate: 17.42/1,000 population (2000 est.)
Death Rate: 9.06/1,000 population (2000 est.)
Infant Mortality: 15.14 deaths/1,000 live births (2000 est.)
Life Expectancy at Birth: 71.90 years male, 78.75 years female (2000 est.)
Total Fertility Rate: 2.37 children born/woman (2000 est.)
Literacy: 97.5% (1998)

■ GOVERNMENT

Leader(s): Pres. Jorge Batlle, V. Pres Luis Hierro
Government Type: republic
Administrative Divisions: 19 departments (departamentos, sing. —departamento)
Nationhood: Aug. 25, 1828 (from Brazil)
National Holiday: Independence Day, Aug. 25

■ ECONOMY

Overview: a small economy with favourable climate, good soils and considerable hydropower potential; problems include high inflation rates, a large domestic debt and frequent strikes; growth in the agriculture and fishing sectors has spurred recovery; unemployment is on the rise and hobbles economic progress
GDP: US$28 billion, per capita US$8,500; real growth rate -2.5% (1999 est.)
Inflation: 4.76% (year-end 2000)
Industries: accounts for 28% of GDP and 19% of labour force; meat packing, oil refining, manufacturing, foodstuffs, engineering, transport equipment, sugar, textiles, leather apparel, tires

Labour Force: 2 million (1999); 36.6% community, social and business services, 21.1% industry, 17.9% trade and tourism, 15.3% agriculture

Unemployment: 12% (1999)

Agriculture: accounts for 10% of GDP and 11% of labour force; meat processing, wool and hides, sugar, textiles, footwear, leather apparel, tires, cement, fishing, petroleum refining, wine, wheat, rice, corn, sorghum; self-sufficient in most basic foods

Natural Resources: arable land, hydropower potential, minor minerals

■ FINANCE/TRADE

Currency: new peso (N$Ur) = 100 centesimos

International Reserves Excluding Gold: US$2.556 billion (Jan. 2001)

Gold Reserves: US$0.833 million fine troy ounces (Jan. 2001)

Budget: revenues US$4.4 billion; expenditures US$4.6 billion, including capital expenditures of US$500 million (1998 est.)

Defence Expenditures: 4.09% of total govt. expenditure (1999)

Education Expenditures: 7.76% of total govt. expenditure (1999)

External Debt: US$7.447 billion (1999)

Exports: US$2.375 billion (2000); commodities: hides and leather goods 17%, beef 10%, wool 9%, fish 7%, rice 4%; partners: Brazil 17%, US 15%, Germany 10%, Argentina 10%

Imports: US$3.466 billion (2000); commodities: fuels and lubricants 15%, metals, machinery, transportation equipment, industrial chemicals; partners: Brazil 24%, Argentina 14%, US 8%, Germany 8%

■ COMMUNICATIONS

Daily Newspapers: 36

Televisions: 241/1,000 inhabitants (1998)

Radios: 607/1,000 inhabitants (1997)

Telephones: 250 lines/1,000 inhabitants (1999)

■ TRANSPORTATION

Motor Vehicles: 525,000; 475,000 passenger cars (1997 est.)

Roads: 8,983 km; 8,085 km paved

Railway: 2,073 km

Air Traffic: 544,000 passengers carried (1997)

Airports: 65; 15 have paved runways (1999 est.)

Canadian Embassy: The Canadian Embassy, Plaza Independencia 749, off. 102, 11100 Montevideo, Uruguay. Tel: (011-598-2) 902-20-30. Fax: (011-598-2) 902-20-29. Email: mvdeo@dfait-maeci.gc.ca

Embassy in Canada: Embassy of the Eastern Republic of Uruguay, 130 Albert St, Ste 1905, Ottawa ON K1P 5G4. Tel: (613) 234-2727. Fax: (613) 233-4670. Email: uruott@iosphere.net

Uzbekistan

Long-Form Name: Republic of Uzbekistan

Capital: Tashkent

■ GEOGRAPHY

Area: 447,400 sq. km

Coastline: landlocked; 420 km coastline along Aral Sea

Climate: dry continental; warm to hot summers; cool to cold winters; semi-arid grassland in east

Environment: drying up of the Aral Sea is resulting in increasing concentrations of chemical pesticides and natural salts; water and soil pollution

Terrain: flat to rolling deserts and semideserts, mountains, shrinking Aral Sea in west

Land Use: 9% arable, 1% permanent crops, 46% meadows and pastures, 3% forest, 41% other, includes 40,000 sq. km irrigated

Location: C Asia

■ PEOPLE

Population: 24,755,519 (July 2000 est.)

Nationality: Uzbekistani

Age Structure: 0-14 yrs: 37%; 15-64: 58%; 65+: 5% (2000 est.)

Population Growth Rate: 1.6% (2000 est.)

Net Migration: -2.18 migrants/1,000 population (2000 est.)

Ethnic Groups: 80% Uzbek, 5.5% Russian, 1.5% Tartars, 5% Tajiks, 3% Kazakhs, 2.5% Kara-Kalpaks, 2.5% other

Languages: 74.3% Uzbek (official), 14.2% Russian, 4.4% Tajik, 7.1% other

Religions: predominantly Sunni Muslim and Eastern Orthodox

Birth Rate: 26.18/1,000 population (2000 est.)

Death Rate: 8.02/1,000 population (2000 est.)

Infant Mortality: 72.13 deaths/1,000 live births (2000 est.)

Life Expectancy at Birth: 60.09 years male, 67.52 years female (2000 est.)

Total Fertility Rate: 3.09 children born/woman (2000 est.)

Literacy: 99.0% (1997)

■ GOVERNMENT

Leader(s): Pres. Islam A. Karimov, Prem. Otkir Sultonov

Government Type: republic

Administrative Divisions: 12 (wiloyatlar, sing. — wiloyat), 1 autonomous republic (respublikasi), 1 city (shahri)

Nationhood: Aug. 31, 1991 (from Soviet Union)
National Holiday: Independence Day, Sept. 1

■ ECONOMY

Overview: despite the need for irrigation, agriculture is the predominant economic sector; small industrial sector, mining; inflation is skyrocketing and economic problems are numerous; more than 60% of the population is living in overcrowded rural villages
GDP: US$59.3 billion, per capita US$2,500; real growth rate -1% (1999 est.)
Inflation: n.a.
Industries: accounts for 27% of GDP; chemicals and gas, machine building, metalmaking, textile manufacture, clothing, butter, preserves, vegetable oil, textiles
Labour Force: 10 million (1999); 39% agriculture and forestry, 24% industry and construction, 37% other
Unemployment: 0.4% (1997); also large numbers of underemployed
Agriculture: accounts for 27% of GDP, vegetables, cotton, grains, almonds, fruit, livestock; 97% of all crops are grown on irrigated land
Natural Resources: gold, nonferrous metals, coal, natural gas, petroleum, uranium, silver, copper

■ FINANCE/TRADE

Currency: som
International Reserves Excluding Gold: n.a.
Gold Reserves: n.a.
Budget: revenues US$4.4 billion, expenditures US$4.7 billion, including capital expenditures of US$1.1 billion (1997 est.)
Defence Expenditures: 6.1% of central government expenditure (1997)
Education Expenditures: 7.7% of GNP (1997)
External Debt: US$4.163 billion (1999)
Exports: US$3.217 billion (2000): cotton, agricultural products, machinery; partners: Russia, Ukraine, Eastern and Western Europe
Imports: US$3.247 billion (2000): foodstuffs, machinery, consumer products; partners: principally other former Soviet states, Czech Republic, Western Europe

■ COMMUNICATIONS

Daily Newspapers: 3
Televisions: 275/1,000 inhabitants (1998)
Radios: 465/1,000 inhabitants (1997)
Telephones: 66 lines/1,000 inhabitants (1999)

■ TRANSPORTATION

Motor Vehicles: n.a.
Roads: 81,600 km; 71,237 km hard-surfaced
Railway: 3,380 km, plus industrial lines

Air Traffic: 1,566,000 passengers carried (1997)
Airports: 3; all have paved runways (1997 est.)

Canadian Embassy: c/o The Canadian Embassy, 23 Starokonyushenny Pereulok, Moscow 121002, Russia. Tel: (011-7-095) 956-6666. Fax: (011-7-095) 232-9948. Email: mosco@dfait-maeci.gc.ca
Embassy in Canada: c/o The Embassy of the Republic of Uzbekistan, 1746 Massachusetts Ave. NW, Washington, DC 20036. Tel: (202) 887-5300. Fax: (202) 293-6804. Email: n.a.

Vanuatu

Long-Form Name: Republic of Vanuatu
Capital: Port Vila

■ GEOGRAPHY

Area: 14,760 sq. km
Coastline: 2,528 km
Climate: tropical; moderated by southeast trade winds
Environment: subject to tropical cyclones or typhoons (Jan. to Apr.); volcanism causes minor earthquakes; lack of safe drinking water
Terrain: mostly mountains of volcanic origin; narrow coastal plains
Land Use: 2% arable; 10% permanent crops; 2% meadows; 75% forests and woodlands; 11% other; includes n.a. sq. km irrigated
Location: South Pacific Ocean, NE of Australia

■ PEOPLE

Population: 189,618 (July 2000 est.)
Nationality: Ni-Vanuatu (sing. & pl.)
Age Structure: 0-14 yrs: 37%; 15-64: 60%; 65+: 3% (2000 est.)
Population Growth Rate: 1.74% (2000 est.)
Net Migration: 0 migrants/1,000 population (2000 est.)
Ethnic Groups: 94% indigenous Melanesian, 4% French, remainder Vietnamese, Chinese and various Pacific Islanders
Languages: English and French (both official); pidgin (known as Bislama or Bichelama)
Religions: 36.7% Presbyterian, 15% Anglican, 15% Catholic, 7.6% indigenous beliefs, 6.2% Seventh-Day Adventist, 3.8% Church of Christ, 15.7% other
Birth Rate: 25.93/1,000 population (2000 est.)
Death Rate: 8.52/1,000 population (2000 est.)
Infant Mortality: 62.52 deaths/1,000 live births (2000 est.)
Life Expectancy at Birth: 59.23 years male, 61.98 years female (2000 est.)
Total Fertility Rate: 3.29 children born/woman (2000 est.)

Literacy: 64.0% (1997)

■ GOVERNMENT

Leader(s): Pres. John Bani, Prime Min. Edward Natapei
Government Type: republic
Administrative Divisions: 6 provinces
Nationhood: July 30, 1980 (from France and UK; formerly known as New Hebrides)
National Holiday: Independence Day, July 30

■ ECONOMY

Overview: economy is based on subsistence farming, fishing and tourism; few mineral deposits; a small light industry sector sees to local needs; tax revenues come largely from import duties
GDP: US$245 million, per capita US$1,300; real growth rate n.a.% (1999 est.)
Inflation: 1.96% (year-end 1999)
Industries: accounts for 13% of GDP; food and fish freezing, meat canning, wood processing
Labour Force: n.a.; 65% agriculture, 32% services, 3% industry
Unemployment: n.a.
Agriculture: accounts for 24% of GDP and 65% of labour force; export crops: cocoa, coffee and fish; subsistence crops: copra, taro, yams, coconuts, fruit and vegetables
Natural Resources: manganese, hardwood forests, fish

■ FINANCE/TRADE

Currency: vatu (VT) = 100 centimes
International Reserves Excluding Gold: US$37 million (Jan. 2001)
Gold Reserves: n.a.
Budget: n.a.
Defence Expenditures: negligible
Education Expenditures: n.a.
External Debt: US$65 million (1999)
Exports: US$35 million (2000); commodities: copra 37%, cocoa 11%, meat 9%, fish 8%, timber 4%; partners: Netherlands 34%, France 27%, Japan 17%, Belgium 4%, New Caledonia 3%, Singapore 2%
Imports: US$92 million (2000); commodities: machines and vehicles 25%, food and beverages 23%, basic manufactures 18%, raw materials and fuels 11%, chemicals 6%; partners: Australia 36%, Japan 13%, New Zealand 10%, France 8%, Fiji 5%

■ COMMUNICATIONS

Daily Newspapers: 0
Televisions: 10.5/1,000 inhabitants (1997 est.)
Radios: 327/1,000 inhabitants (1997 est.)
Telephones: 28 lines/1,000 inhabitants (1999)

■ TRANSPORTATION

Motor Vehicles: 6,300; 4,000 passenger cars (1997 est.)
Roads: 1,070 km; 256 km paved
Railway: none
Air Traffic: 75,000 passengers carried (1997)
Airports: 32; 3 have paved runways (1999 est.)

Canadian Embassy: The Canadian High Commission to Vanuatu, c/o The Canadian High Commission, Commonwealth Ave, Canberra A.C.T. 2600, Australia. Tel: (011-61-2) 6270-4000. Fax: (011-61-2) 6273-3285. Email: cnbra@dfait-maeci.gc.ca

Vatican City

Long-Form Name: State of the Vatican City, or the Holy See
Capital: Vatican City

■ GEOGRAPHY

Area: 0.44 sq. km
Coastline: none: landlocked
Climate: temperate; mild, rainy winters (Sept. to mid-May) with hot, dry summers (May to Sept.)
Environment: urban
Terrain: low hill
Land Use: 100% built-up
Location: S Europe (W Italy)

■ PEOPLE

Population: 880 (July 2000 est.)
Nationality: n.a.
Age Structure: n.a.
Population Growth Rate: 1.15% (2000 est.)
Net Migration: n.a.

Ethnic Groups: primarily Italians and Swiss but also many other nationalities
Languages: Italian, Latin and various other languages
Religions: Roman Catholic
Birth Rate: n.a.
Death Rate: n.a.
Infant Mortality: n.a.
Life Expectancy at Birth: n.a.
Total Fertility Rate: n.a.
Literacy: 100%

■ GOVERNMENT

Leader(s): Head, Roman Catholic Church, Pope John Paul II (Karol Wojtyla)
Government Type: monarchical-sacerdotal state
Administrative Divisions: none
Nationhood: Feb. 11, 1929 (from Italy)

National Holiday: Installation Day of the Pope (John Paul II), Oct. 22; also Christmas, Easter, Feast of Saints Peter and Paul (June 29), and other holy days of obligation

■ ECONOMY

Overview: economy is supported financially by contributions (known as Peter's Pence) from Roman Catholics throughout the world, the sale of postage stamps, tourist mementos, fees for admission to museums and the sale of publications
GDP: n.a.
Inflation: n.a.
Industries: printing and production of a small amount of mosaics and staff uniforms; worldwide banking and financial activities
Labour Force: approximately 1,500 Vatican City employees divided into three categories: executives, office workers, salaried employees
Unemployment: n.a.
Agriculture: none
Natural Resources: none

■ FINANCE/TRADE

Currency: Vatican Lira (Lit) = 100 centesimi (at par with Italian lira)
International Reserves Excluding Gold: n.a.
Gold Reserves: n.a.
Budget: revenues US$209.6 million, expenditures US$198.5 million, including capital expenditures US$n.a. (1997)
Defence Expenditures: defence is the responsibility of Italy
Education Expenditures: n.a.
External Debt: n.a.
Exports: n.a.
Imports: n.a.

■ COMMUNICATIONS

Daily Newspapers: 1
Televisions: n.a.
Radios: n.a.
Telephones: n.a.

■ TRANSPORTATION

Motor Vehicles: n.a.
Roads: no highways, all city streets
Railway: 862 m
Air Traffic: none
Airports: none

Canadian Embassy: The Canadian Embassy, Via della Conciliazione 4/D, 00193 Rome, Italy. Tel. (011-39-06) 6830-7316. Fax: (011-39-06) 6880-6283. Email: vatcn@dfait-maeci.gc.ca
Embassy in Canada: Apostolic Nunciature, 724 Manor Ave, Rockcliffe Park, Ottawa ON K1M 0E3. Tel: (613) 746-4914. Fax: (613) 746-4786. Email: nuncioap@istar.ca

Venezuela

Long-Form Name: The Bolivarian Republic of Venezuela
Capital: Caracas

■ GEOGRAPHY

Area: 912,050 sq. km
Coastline: 2,800 km
Climate: tropical; hot, humid; more moderate in highlands
Environment: subject to floods, rockslides, mud slides; periodic droughts; increasing industrial pollution in Caracas and Maracaibo
Terrain: Andes Mountains and Maracaibo lowlands in northwest; central plains (llanos); Guyana highlands in southwest
Land Use: 4% arable; 1% permanent crops; 20% meadows; 34% forest; 41% other; includes 1,900 sq. km irrigated
Location: N South America, bordering on Caribbean Sea

■ PEOPLE

Population: 23,542,649 (July 2000 est.)
Nationality: Venezuelan
Age Structure: 0-14 yrs: 33%; 15-64: 63%; 65+: 4% (2000 est.)
Population Growth Rate: 1.6% (2000 est.)
Net Migration: -0.19 migrants/1,000 population (2000 est.)
Ethnic Groups: 67% mestizo, 21% white, 10% black, 2% Indian
Languages: Spanish (official); Indian dialects spoken by approximately 200,000 Amerindians in the remote interior
Religions: 96% nominally Roman Catholic, 2% Protestant, 2% other
Birth Rate: 21.09/1,000 population (2000 est.)
Death Rate: 4.94/1,000 population (2000 est.)
Infant Mortality: 26.17 deaths/1,000 live births (2000 est.)
Life Expectancy at Birth: 70.05 years male, 76.31 years female (2000 est.)
Total Fertility Rate: 2.51 children born/woman (2000 est.)
Literacy: 92.0% (1998)

■ GOVERNMENT

Leader(s): Pres. Hugo Chavez, V. Pres. Adina Bastidas
Government Type: republic
Administrative Divisions: 23 states (estados, sing. —estado), 1 federal district (distrito federal) and 1 federal dependency (dependencia federal)

Nationhood: July 5, 1811 (from Spain)
National Holiday: Independence Day, July 5

■ ECONOMY

Overview: petroleum is the backbone of the economy, accounting for 27% of GDP, 78% of total exports and more than half of government revenue; it is likely to become even more important as the state petroleum company plans to double its production over the next 10 years
GDP: US$182.8 billion, per capita US$8,000; real growth rate -7.2% (1999 est.)
Inflation: 16.20% (year-end 2000)
Industries: accounts for 63% of GDP; petroleum, iron-ore mining, construction materials, food processing, textiles, steel, aluminum, motor vehicle assembly
Labour Force: 9 million (1999); 27.5% community, social and business services, 22.2% trade and tourism, 15.5% industry (1993)
Unemployment: 18% (1999 est.)
Agriculture: accounts for 4% GDP; products: corn, sorghum, sugar cane, rice, bananas, vegetables, coffee, beef, pork, milk, eggs, fish; not self-sufficient in food other than meat
Natural Resources: crude oil, natural gas, iron ore, gold, bauxite, other minerals, hydropower, diamonds

■ FINANCE/TRADE

Currency: bolívar (Bs) = 100 centimos
International Reserves Excluding Gold: US$13.910 billion (Jan. 2001)
Gold Reserves: US$11.290 million fine troy ounces (Jan. 2001)
Budget: revenues US$26.4 billion; expenditures US$27 billion, including capital expenditures of US$n.a. (2000 est.)
Defence Expenditures: 9.8% of central government expenditure (1997)
Education Expenditures: 5.2% of GNP (1997)
External Debt: US$35.852 billion (1999)
Exports: US$29.502 billion (2000); commodities: petroleum 81%, bauxite and aluminum, iron ore, agricultural products, basic manufactures; partners: US 50.3%, Germany 5.3%, Japan 4.1%
Imports: US$16.298 billion (2000); commodities: foodstuffs, chemicals, manufactures, machinery and transport equipment; partners: US 44%, Germany 8.5%, Japan 6%, Italy 5%, Brazil 4.4%

■ COMMUNICATIONS

Daily Newspapers: 86
Televisions: 185/1,000 inhabitants (1998)
Radios: 468/1,000 inhabitants (1997)
Telephones: 109 lines/1,000 inhabitants (1999)

■ TRANSPORTATION

Motor Vehicles: 2,025,000; 1,500,000 passenger cars (1997 est.)
Roads: 96,155 km; 32,308 km paved
Railway: 584 km
Air Traffic: 4,020,000 passengers carried (1997)
Airports: 366; 122 have paved runways (1999 est.)

Canadian Embassy: The Canadian Embassy, 6a Av. Entre 3a y 5a, Transv. de Altamira, Altamira, Edificio Omni, Caracas, Venezuela. mailing address: Apartado 62302, Caracas 1060A, Venezuela. Tel: (011-58-2) 264-0833. Fax: (011-58-2) 261-8741. Email: crcas@dfait-maeci.gc.ca
Embassy in Canada: Embassy of the Republic of Venezuela, 32 Range Rd, Ottawa ON K1N 8J4. Tel: (613) 235-5151. Fax: (613) 235-3205. Email: embavene@travel-net.com

---

Vietnam

Long-Form Name: Socialist Republic of Vietnam
Capital: Hanoi

■ GEOGRAPHY

Area: 329,560 sq. km
Coastline: 3,444 km (excluding islands)
Climate: tropical in south; monsoonal in north with hot, rainy season (mid-May to mid-Sept.) and warm, dry season (mid-Oct. to mid-Mar.)
Environment: occasional typhoons (May to Jan.) with extensive flooding; soil deterioration; inadequate supply of safe drinking water
Terrain: low, flat delta in south and north; central highlands; hilly, mountainous far north and northwest
Land Use: 17% arable; 4% permanent crops; 1% meadows; 30% forest; 48% other, includes 18,600 sq. km irrigated
Location: SE Asia, bordering on South China Sea

■ PEOPLE

Population: 78,773,873 (July 2000 est.)
Nationality: Vietnamese (sing. & pl.)
Age Structure: 0-14 yrs: 33%; 15-64: 62%; 65+: 5% (2000 est.)
Population Growth Rate: 1.49% (2000 est.)
Net Migration: -0.51 migrants/1,000 population (2000 est.)
Ethnic Groups: 85–90% predominantly Vietnamese; 3% Chinese; more than 60 ethnic minorities including Muong, Thai, Meo, Khmer, Man, Cham; other mountain tribes
Languages: Vietnamese (official), French,

Chinese, English, Khmer, tribal languages (Mon-Khmer and Malayo-Polynesian)
Religions: Buddhist, Confucian, Taoist, Roman Catholic, indigenous beliefs, Islamic, Protestant
Birth Rate: 21.62/1,000 population (2000 est.)
Death Rate: 6.26/1,000 population (2000 est.)
Infant Mortality: 31.13 deaths/1,000 live births (2000 est.)
Life Expectancy at Birth: 66.84 years male, 71.87 years female (2000 est.)
Total Fertility Rate: 2.53 children born/woman (2000 est.)
Literacy: 92.5% (1998)

■ GOVERNMENT

Leader(s): Pres. Tran Duc Luong, Prime Min. Phan Van Khai
Government Type: communist state
Administrative Divisions: 58 provinces (tinh, sing. & pl.), 3 municipalities (thu do, sing. & pl.)
Nationhood: Sept. 2, 1945 (from France)
National Holiday: Independence Day, Sept. 2

■ ECONOMY

Overview: centrally planned, developing economy with extensive government ownership and control of production facilities; dependent on foreign aid; high rate of population growth and high unemployment combine to form the economy's most serious problem
GDP: US$143.1 billion, per capita US$1,850; real growth rate 4.8% (1999 est.)
Inflation: n.a.
Industries: accounts for 33% of GDP; food processing, textiles, machine building, mining, cement, chemical fertilizer, glass, tires, oil, fishing
Labour Force: 40 million (1999); 65% agriculture, 11.8% industry, 20.7% services
Unemployment: n.a.
Agriculture: accounts for 26% of GDP; rice, corn, potatoes make up 50% of farm output; commercial crops (rubber, soybeans, coffee, tea, bananas) and animal products other 50%; not self-sufficient in rice
Natural Resources: phosphates, coal, manganese, bauxite, chromate, offshore oil deposits, forests

■ FINANCE/TRADE

Currency: dong (pl. dong) (D) = 100 xu
International Reserves Excluding Gold: US$2.728 billion (Sept. 2000)
Gold Reserves: n.a.
Budget: n.a.
Defence Expenditures: 11.1% of central govt. expenditure (1997)

Education Expenditures: 13.90% of total govt. expenditure (1999)
External Debt: US$23.260 billion (1999)
Exports: US$7.029 billion (2000); commodities: agricultural and handicraft products, coal, minerals, ores; partners: former USSR countries, Eastern Europe, Japan, Singapore
Imports: US$10.980 billion (2000); commodities: petroleum, steel products, railroad equipment, chemicals, medicines, raw cotton, fertilizer, grain; partners: former USSR countries, Eastern Europe, Japan, Singapore

■ COMMUNICATIONS

Daily Newspapers: 10
Televisions: 47/1,000 inhabitants (1998)
Radios: 107/1,000 inhabitants (1997)
Telephones: 27 lines/1,000 inhabitants (1999)

■ TRANSPORTATION

Motor Vehicles: 178,000; 80,000 passenger cars (1997 est.)
Roads: 93,300 km; 23,418 km paved
Railway: 2,652 km
Air Traffic: 2,527,000 passengers carried (1997)
Airports: 48; 36 have paved runways
Canadian Embassy: The Canadian Embassy, 31 Hung Vuong Street, Hanoi, Vietnam, Tel: (011 84 4) 823-5500, Fax: (011 84 4) 823-5333. Email: hanoi@dfait-maeci.gc.ca
Embassy in Canada: Embassy of the Socialist Republic of Vietnam, 470 Wilbrod St, Ottawa, ON KIN 6M8. Tel: (613) 236-0772. Fax: (613) 236-2704. Email: vietem@istar.ca

Wallis and Futuna

Long-Form Name: Territory of the Wallis and Futuna Islands
Capital: Mata-Utu

■ GEOGRAPHY

Area: 274 sq. km
Climate: tropical maritime, rainy season (Nov. to April); cool, dry season (May to Oct.)
Land Use: 5% arable, 20% permanent crops, 0% meadows and pasture, 0% forests, 75% other; includes n.a. sq. km irrigated
Location: SW Pacific Ocean, E of Australia

■ PEOPLE

Population: 15,283 (July 2000 est.)
Nationality: Wallisian, Futunan, or Wallis and Futuna Islanders
Ethnic Groups: Polynesians, and descendants of French settlers

Languages: Wallisian, Futunian (Polynesian languages), French

■ **GOVERNMENT**

Colony Territory of: Overseas Territory of France
Leader(s): Head of State: Pres. Jacques Chirac (France)
Government Type: overseas territory of France
National Holiday: n.a.

■ **ECONOMY**

Overview: agriculture includes copra, cassava, yams, taro roots, bananas; livestock includes pigs and goats; considerable imports, negligible exports

■ **FINANCE/TRADE**

Currency: CFP franc = 100 centimes
Canadian Embassy: c/o The Canadian Embassy, 35-37 avenue Montaigne, 75008, Paris, France. Tel: (011-33-1) 44-43-29-00. Fax: (011-33-1) 44-43-29-99. Email: paris@dfait-maeci.gc.ca
Representative to Canada: c/o Embassy of France, 42 Sussex Dr, Ottawa ON K1M 2C9. Tel: (613) 789-1795. Fax: (613) 562-3735. Email: politique@ambafrance-ca.org

West Bank

Long-Form Name: none
Capital: none

■ **GEOGRAPHY**

Area: 5,860 sq. km
Climate: temperate, temperature and precipitation vary with altitude, warm to hot summers, cool to mild winters
Land Use: 27% arable; 0% permanent crops; 32% permanent pastures; 1% forests and woodland; 40% other; includes n.a. sq. km irrigated
Location: Middle East, between Israel and Jordan

■ **PEOPLE**

Population: 2,020,298 (July 2000 est.)
Nationality: n.a.
Ethnic Groups: Palestinian Arab and other 83%, Jewish 17%
Languages: Arabic, Hebrew (spoken by Israeli settlers and many Palestinians), English (widely understood)

■ **GOVERNMENT**

Colony Territory of: claimed and occupied by Israel

Leader(s): local Palestinian authority is headed by Yasser Arafat, subject to Israeli authority
Government Type: Palestinian Legislative Council (Jan. 1996) has limited powers under interim self-governing agreements with Israel. Originally designated as a five-year interim arrangement in 1993, permanent status still under negotiation.
National Holiday: n.a.

■ **ECONOMY**

Overview: as for Gaza Strip

■ **FINANCE/TRADE**

Currency: 1 new Israeli shekel= 100 new agorot; 1 Jordanian dinar = 1,000 fils.

Canadian Embassy: n.a.
Representative to Canada: n.a.

Western Sahara

Long-Form Name: Western Sahara
Capital: none

■ **GEOGRAPHY**

Area: 266,000 sq. km
Coastline: 1,110 km
Climate: Mediterranean to arid; hot, dry desert; rain is rare; cold offshore air currents produce fog and heavy dew
Environment: desertification, sparse water and arable land; hot and dry and dust/sand-laden sirocco wind; harmattan haze
Terrain: mostly barren rocky desert; small mountains in south and northeast
Land Use: 0% arable; 0% permanent crops, 19% permanent pastures, 0% forests, 81% other; includes n.a. sq. km irrigated
Location: NW Africa, bordering on Atlantic Ocean

■ **PEOPLE**

Population: 244,943 (July 2000 est.)
Nationality: Sahrawi, Sahraoui
Age Structure: n.a.
Population Growth Rate: 2.29% (2000 est.)
Net Migration: -6.05 migrants/1,000 population (2000 est.)
Ethnic Groups: Arabs, Berbers
Languages: Hassaniya Arabic, Moroccan Arabic
Religions: Islam (almost 100% Sunni Muslim)
Birth Rate: 45.07/1,000 population (2000 est.)
Death Rate: 16.11/1,000 population (2000 est.)
Infant Mortality: 133.59 deaths/1,000 live births (2000 est.)

Life Expectancy at Birth: 48.65 years male, 51.33 years female (2000 est.)
Total Fertility Rate: 6.64 children born/woman (2000 est.)
Literacy: n.a.

■ GOVERNMENT

Leader(s): under de facto control of Morocco
Government Type: under Moroccan occupation; legal status and matters of sovereignty remain unresolved
Administrative Divisions: none (under de facto control of Morocco)
Nationhood: n.a.
National Holiday: n.a.

■ ECONOMY

Overview: economy severely disrupted by Moroccan occupation and ongoing guerrilla warfare; poor in natural resources and with inadequate rainfall, most food must be imported; all aspects of the economy are controlled by the Moroccan government
GDP: n.a.
Inflation: n.a.
Industries: phosphate mining, fishing, handicrafts
Labour Force: approx. 12,000 (1999 est.); 50% of the people are engaged in subsistence farming and animal husbandry
Unemployment: n.a.
Agriculture: limited to subsistence agriculture; some grain production, livestock (esp. sheep, goats, camels); cash economy exists largely for the garrison forces
Natural Resources: rich phosphate deposits, iron ore

■ FINANCE/TRADE

Currency: Moroccan dirham (DH) = 100 centimes
International Reserves Excluding Gold: n.a.
Gold Reserves: n.a.
Budget: n.a.
Defence Expenditures: n.a.
Education Expenditures: n.a.
External Debt: n.a.
Exports: phosphates main export product; Morocco claims and administers Western Sahara, so trade partners are included in overall Moroccan accounts
Imports: fuel for fishing fleet; most of the country's food supply must be imported; partners, see exports

■ COMMUNICATIONS

Daily Newspapers: n.a.

Televisions: 24.5/1,000 inhabitants (1997 est.)
Radios: 229/1,000 inhabitants (1997 est.)
Telephones: n.a.

■ TRANSPORTATION

Motor Vehicles: n.a.
Roads: 6,200 km; 1,350 km surfaced
Railway: none
Air Traffic: n.a.
Airports: 12; 3 have paved runways (1999 est.)

Canadian Embassy: none
Embassy in Canada: none

Yemen

Long-Form Name: Republic of Yemen
Capital: Sana'a (political capital); Aden (commercial capital)

■ GEOGRAPHY

Area: 527,970 sq. km
Coastline: 1,906 km
Climate: hot, dry desert in the south to temperate in central region and north; harsh desert in the east
Environment: desertification, overgrazing, lack of natural fresh water, soil erosion, summer dust and sand storms
Terrain: narrow coastal plain; western mountains, northern desert interior
Land Use: 3% arable land; 0% permanent crops; 30% meadows and pasture; 4% forest and woodland; 63% other; includes 3,600 sq. km irrigated
Location: SW Asia (Middle East), bordering on Red Sea

■ PEOPLE

Population: 17,479,206 (July 2000 est.)
Nationality: Yemeni
Age Structure: 0-14 yrs: 47%; 15-64: 49%; 65+: 4% (2000 est.)
Population Growth Rate: 3.36% (2000 est.)
Net Migration: 0 migrants/1,000 population (2000 est.)
Ethnic Groups: predominantly Arab; Afro-Arab, Indian, Somali and European minorities
Languages: Arabic
Religions: predominantly Muslim; Christian and Hindu minorities in the south
Birth Rate: 43.44/1,000 population (2000 est.)
Death Rate: 9.86/1,000 population (2000 est.)
Infant Mortality: 70.28 deaths/1,000 live births (2000 est.)
Life Expectancy at Birth: 58.10 years male, 61.64 years female (2000 est.)

Total Fertility Rate: 7.05 children born/woman (2000 est.)
Literacy: 44% (1998)

■ GOVERNMENT

Leader(s): Pres. Ali Abdallah Salih, Prime Min. Abd al-Qadir Ba Jamal
Government Type: republic
Administrative Divisions: 17 governorates (muhafazat, sing. —muhafazah)
Nationhood: May 22, 1990
National Holiday: Proclamation of the Republic, May 22

■ ECONOMY

Overview: future economic level depends heavily on Western assistance; North: low level of domestic industry once self-sufficient in food but now dependent on imports; South: economic growth among the slowest of all Arab countries
GDP: US$12.7 billion, per capita US$750; real growth rate 4% (1999 est.)
Inflation: 7.91% (year-end 1998)
Industries: accounts for 42% of GDP; petroleum, cotton, textiles, leather goods, food processing, handicrafts, cement, small aluminum products factory
Labour Force: 5 million (1999); most people are employed in agriculture
Unemployment: n.a.
Agriculture: in the north, agriculture accounts for 20% GDP; main crops include fruit (grapes) and cotton; in the south, agriculture accounts for 17% GDP and 45% of the labour force; the main agricultural product is livestock (cattle, camels, sheep, goats, poultry)
Natural Resources: salt deposits, petroleum, fish, marble, coal, gold, lead, nickel, copper

■ FINANCE/TRADE

Currency: Yemeni rial (YR) = 100 fils
International Reserves Excluding Gold: US$2.605 billion (Oct. 2000)
Gold Reserves: US$0.005 million fine troy ounces (Oct. 2000)
Budget: revenues US$1.8 billion; expenditures US$1.95 billion, including capital expenditures of US$n.a. (1999 est.)
Defence Expenditures: 18.77% of total govt. expenditure (1999)
Education Expenditures: 21.81% of govt. expenditure (1999)
External Debt: US$4.610 billion (1999)
Exports: US$1.867 billion (2000); crude oil, cotton, coffee, vegetables, cotton, animal hides, fish; partners: US, Japan, Singapore
Imports: US$2.167 billion (2000); textiles and other manufactured consumer goods, petroleum products, sugar, grain, flour, other foodstuffs, cement, grain, consumer goods, crude oil, machinery, chemicals; partners: nations of the former Soviet Union, UK, Ethiopia

■ COMMUNICATIONS

Daily Newspapers: 3
Televisions: 29/1,000 inhabitants (1998)
Radios: 64/1,000 inhabitants (1997)
Telephones: 17 lines/1,000 inhabitants (1999)

■ TRANSPORTATION

Motor Vehicles: 516,000; 230,000 passenger cars (1997 est.)
Roads: 67,000 km; 7,700 km paved
Railway: none
Air Traffic: 707,000 passengers carried (1997)
Airports: 50; 13 have paved runways (1999 est.)

Canadian Embassy: The Canadian Embassy to Yemen, c/o Canadian Embassy, Diplomatic Quarter, P.O. Box 94321, Riyadh 11693, Saudi Arabia. Tel: (011-966-1) 488-2288. Fax: (011-966-1) 488-1997. Email: ryadh@dfait-maeci.gc.ca
Embassy in Canada: Embassy of the Republic of Yemen, 788 Island Park Drive, Ottawa ON K1Y OC2. Tel: (613) 729-6627. Fax: (613) 729-8915. Email: ghamdan@sprint.ca

Yugoslavia

see Serbia and Montenegro

Zambia

Long-Form Name: Republic of Zambia
Capital: Lusaka

■ GEOGRAPHY

Area: 752,614 sq. km
Coastline: none: landlocked
Climate: tropical; modified by altitude; rainy season (Oct. to Apr.)
Environment: deforestation; soil erosion; desertification; air pollution and resultant acid rain; tropical storms are a natural hazard from Nov. to Apr.
Terrain: mostly high plateau with some hills and mountains
Land Use: 7% arable; 0% permanent crops; 40% meadows; 39% forest; 14% other; includes 460 sq. km irrigated
Location: SC Africa

■ PEOPLE

Population: 9,582,418 (July 2000 est.)
Nationality: Zambian
Age Structure: 0-14 yrs: 48%; 15-64: 50%; 65+: 2% (2000 est.)
Population Growth Rate: 1.95% (2000 est.)
Net Migration: -0.33 migrants/1,000 population (2000 est.)
Ethnic Groups: 98.7% African, 1.1% European, 0.2% other
Languages: English (official); about 70 indigenous languages
Religions: 50–75% Christian, 24–49% Muslim and Hindu, remainder indigenous beliefs
Birth Rate: 41.90/1,000 population (2000 est.)
Death Rate: 22.08/1,000 population (2000 est.)
Infant Mortality: 92.38 deaths/1,000 live births (2000 est.)
Life Expectancy at Birth: 37.08 years male, 37.41 years female (2000 est.)
Total Fertility Rate: 5.62 children born/woman (2000 est.)
Literacy: 76% (1998)

■ GOVERNMENT

Leader(s): Pres. Frederick Chiluba, V. Pres. Enoch Kavindele
Parliamentary and presidential elections scheduled for Nov. 2001
Government Type: republic
Administrative Divisions: 9 provinces
Nationhood: Oct. 24, 1964 (from UK; formerly known as Northern Rhodesia)
National Holiday: Independence Day, Oct. 24

■ ECONOMY

Overview: economy continues to decline due to a sustained drop in copper production and ineffective economic policies; problems include a high inflation rate, high population growth and severe drought
GDP: US$8.5 billion, per capita US$880; real growth rate 1.5% (1999 est.)
Inflation: 19.1% (Jan. 1998)
Industries: accounts for 30.6% of GDP; copper mining and processing, transport, construction, foodstuffs, beverages, chemicals, textiles and fertilizer
Labour Force: 4 million (1999); 37.9% agriculture, 7.8% industry, 54.9% services
Unemployment: 25% (1998)
Agriculture: accounts for 20.6% of GDP and 85% of labour force; food production is insufficient for country's needs; crops: corn (food staple), sorghum, rice, peanuts, sunflower, tobacco, cotton, sugar cane, cassava; cattle, goats, beef, eggs produced; marginally self-sufficient in corn

Natural Resources: copper, cobalt, zinc, lead, coal, emeralds, gold, silver, uranium, hydropower potential

■ FINANCE/TRADE

Currency: kwacha (K) = 100 ngwee
International Reserves Excluding Gold: US$245 million (Dec. 2000)
Gold Reserves: n.a.
Budget: revenues US$606 million; expenditures US$547 million, including capital expenditures of US$61 million (1998 est.)
Defence Expenditures: 3.93% of govt. expenditure (1999)
Education Expenditures: 14.45% of govt. expenditure (1999)
External Debt: US$5.853 billion (1999)
Exports: US$698 million (2000); commodities: copper, zinc, cobalt, lead, tobacco; partners: European Community, Japan, South Africa, US
Imports: US$682 million (2000); commodities: machinery, transportation equipment, foodstuffs, fuels, manufactures; partners: European Community, Japan, South Africa, US

■ COMMUNICATIONS

Daily Newspapers: 3
Televisions: 137/1,000 inhabitants (1998)
Radios: 121/1,000 inhabitants (1997)
Telephones: 9 lines/1,000 inhabitants (1999)

■ TRANSPORTATION

Motor Vehicles: 215,500; 142,000 passenger cars (1997 est.)
Roads: 66,781 km; n.a. km paved
Railway: 2,164 km
Air Traffic: 50,000 passengers carried (1997)
Airports: 112; 12 have paved runways (1999 est.)
Canadian Embassy: The Canadian High Commission, 5199 United Nations Ave, Lusaka; mailing address: P.O. Box 31313, 10101 Lusaka, Zambia. Tel: (011-260-1) 25-08-33. Fax: (011-260-1) 25-41-76. Email: lsaka@dfait-maeci.gc.ca
Embassy in Canada: High Commision for the Republic of Zambia, c/o Embassy of Zambia, 2419 Massachusetts Ave NW, Washington DC 20008, USA. Tel: (202) 265-9717. Fax: (202) 332-0826. Email: zambia@tmn.com

---

Zimbabwe

Long-Form Name: Republic of Zimbabwe
Capital: Harare

■ GEOGRAPHY

Area: 390,580 sq. km
Coastline: none: landlocked

Climate: tropical; moderated by altitude; rainy season (Nov. to Mar.)

Environment: recurring droughts; floods and severe storms are rare; deforestation; soil erosion; air and water pollution; desertification; poaching has significantly reduced the black rhinoceros population, which was once the largest concentration of the species anywhere in the world

Terrain: mostly high plateau with higher central plateau (high veld); mountains in east

Land Use: 7% arable; less than 1% permanent crops (coffee plantations); 13% meadows; 23% forest and woodland; 57% other; includes 1,930 sq. km irrigated

Location: S Africa

■ PEOPLE

Population: 11,342,521 (July 2000 est.)
Nationality: Zimbabwean
Age Structure: 0-14 yrs: 40%; 15-64: 57%; 65+: 3% (2000 est.)
Population Growth Rate: 0.26% (2000 est.)
Net Migration: 0 migrants/1,000 population (2000 est.)
Ethnic Groups: 98% African (71% Shona, 16% Ndebele, 11% other), 1% white, 1% mixed and Asian
Languages: English (official); Shona and Sindebele, numerous minor tribal dialects
Religions: 50% syncretic (part Christian, part indigenous beliefs), 25% Christian, 24% indigenous beliefs, a few Muslim
Birth Rate: 25.00/1,000 population (2000 est.)
Death Rate: 22.43/1,000 population (2000 est.)
Infant Mortality: 62.25 deaths/1,000 live births (2000 est.)
Life Expectancy at Birth: 39.18 years male, 36.34 years female (2000 est.)
Total Fertility Rate: 3.34 children born/woman (2000 est.)
Literacy: 88% (1998)

■ GOVERNMENT

Leader(s): Pres. Robert Mugabe
Presidential elections scheduled for March 2002
Government Type: parliamentary democracy
Administrative Divisions: 8 provinces and 2 cities with provincial status
Nationhood: Apr. 18, 1980 (from UK; formerly known as Southern Rhodesia)
National Holiday: Independence Day, Apr. 18

■ ECONOMY

Overview: severe droughts have adversely affected this agriculture-based economy in recent years; the government is working to consolidate earlier progress in developing a market-oriented economy

GDP: US$26.5 billion, per capita US$2,400; real growth rate 0% (1999 est.)
Inflation: 58.52% (year-end 1999)
Industries: accounts for 32% of GDP; mining (minerals and metals account for 40% of exports), steel, clothing and footwear, chemicals, foodstuffs, fertilizer, beverages, transportation equipment, wood products
Labour Force: 5 million (1999); 29.9% community, social and business services, 25.9% agriculture, 15.1% industry (1992)
Unemployment: 50% (1999 est.)
Agriculture: accounts for 28% of GDP; 40% of land area divided into 4,500 large commercial farms and 42% in communal lands; crops: corn (food staple), cotton, tobacco, wheat, coffee, sugar cane, peanuts; livestock: cattle, sheep, goats, pigs; self-sufficient in food
Natural Resources: coal, chromium ore, asbestos, gold, nickel, copper, iron ore, vanadium, lithium, tin

■ FINANCE/TRADE

Currency: Zimbabwean dollar ($Z) = 100 cents
International Reserves Excluding Gold: US$184 million (Jan. 2001)
Gold Reserves: US$0.486 million fine troy ounces (Jan. 2001)
Budget: revenues US$2.5 billion; expenditures US$2.9 billion, including capital expenditures of US$29 million (1997 est.)
Defence Expenditures: 7.09% of central government expenditure (1997)
Education Expenditures: 24.20% of central government expenditure (1997)
External Debt: US$4.566 billion (1999)
Exports: US$1.927 billion (2000); commodities: agriculture 34% (tobacco 21%, other 13%), manufactures 19%, gold 11%, ferrochrome 11%, cotton 6%; partners: Europe 55% (European Community 41%, Netherlands 6%, other 8%), Africa 22% (South Africa 12%, other 10%), US 8%, Japan 4%
Imports: US$2.564 billion (2000); commodities: machinery and transportation equipment 37%, other manufactures 22%, chemicals 16%, fuels 15%; partners: European Community 31%, Africa 29% (South Africa 21%, other 8%), US 8%, Japan 4%

■ COMMUNICATIONS

Daily Newspapers: 2
Televisions: 30/1,000 inhabitants (1998)
Radios: 93/1,000 inhabitants (1997)
Telephones: 21 lines/1,000 inhabitants (1999)

■ TRANSPORTATION

Motor Vehicles: 358,000; 250,000 passenger cars (1997 est.)
Roads: 18,338 km; 8,692 km paved
Railway: 2,759 km
Air Traffic: 790,000 passengers carried (1997)
Airports: 459; 18 have paved runways (1999 est.)

Canadian Embassy: The Canadian High Commission, 45 Baines Ave, Harare, Zimbabwe; mailing address: P.O. Box 1430, Harare, Zimbabwe. Tel: (011-263-4) 252-181. Fax: (011-263-4) 252-186. Email: hrare@dfaitmaeci.gc.ca

Embassy in Canada: High Commission for the Republic of Zimbabwe, 332 Somerset St W, Ottawa ON K2P 0J9. Tel: (613) 237-4388. Fax: (613) 563-8269. Email: zim.highcomm@sympatico.ca

The Next WTO Ministerial Conference

*T*he World Trade Organization will be holding its fourth Ministerial Conference—from November 9 to 13, 2001, in Doha, the capital city of Qatar. Previous Ministerial Conferences were held in Singapore (1996), Geneva (1998) and Seattle (1999).

This uppermost decision-making body of the WTO is mandated to meet a minimum of every two years. The group has the authority to make decisions on any matter under any WTO Agreement. Preparatory meetings began in earnest after February 8, 2001, when the decision to meet in Qatar was taken. The negotiations concerning the agenda reflect issues that were raised in Seattle and the agenda that failed at the 1999 meeting. The goal of the 2001 Ministerial Conference is to agree to begin another round of negotiations that will bring multi-lateral trade in agriculture and services under the same type of existing arrangements concerning manufactured goods.

Preparations for the Qatar meetings included 35 plenary meetings of the Council in an effort to create a process of consultation from the "bottom up" and counter criticisms that the WTO was heavily influenced by major industrial nations and multi-national corporations. Goals of those meetings included progress toward improving technical assistance and market access for least-developed countries. Further meetings were held for smaller, resource-poor delegations that cannot afford residence in Geneva, to ensure that their positions were represented.

In addition to the attendance of member delegates in Qatar, 647 NGOs (non-governmental organizations) have been confirmed as eligible to attend the Ministerial Conference. Organizers have restricted the NGOs to one representative each, citing limitations on available accommodations. Member delegations were also asked to restrict their representation. (WTO protesters, who successfully disrupted the Ministerial meeting in Seattle, were also busy, organizing an international day of protest against the WTO for November 9th.)

One of the items on the agenda in Doha will be the formal adoption of agreements to admit both China and Chinese Taipei (a separate customs territory that includes Taiwan) to the WTO. On Sept. 17, 2001, the WTO Director-General announced that the Working Party on China's Accession had successfully concluded negotiations on the terms of China's membership. Chinese Taipei reached agreement on its membership application on September 18th. Once the agreements are formally adopted by the WTO, each new member must ratify its deal; 30 days after ratification, full membership is conferred.

While China was one of the original signatories to the GATT (the WTO's predecessor) in 1948, after the revolution in 1949, the country abandoned international trade negotiation activity—until 1986. The impact of adding China to the WTO framework will be significant. In 2000, China was the 7th largest exporter and 8th leading importer of manufactured goods (exports US$249.2 billion; imports US$225.1 billion). China also ranked high in the area of commercial services: 12th leading exporter with US$297.7 billion; 10th largest importer $34.8 billion. That said, China's share of merchandise exports represented 3.9 percent of the world's total, while imports were 3.4 percent.

For a general description of the WTO see page 274 or visit www.wto.org

Astronomy has taught us that the universe is more complex than the ancients thought. Though less dependent on the "patterns" in the sky, we continue the exploration. The skies act not simply as a guide, but also as a frontier to be explored.

Our Solar System

Our solar system consists of our sun, at least nine planets and smaller bodies such as asteroids, comets and moons. The dominant member of this family is the sun, our nearest star. The sun is an enormous ball of hot, glowing gas, mostly hydrogen and helium. Its powerful pull of gravity holds the planets, asteroids and comets in orbit around it.

The planets have been known since people first turned their gaze skyward. The ancient Greeks called them "wanderers" because they moved through the sky relative to the fixed stars. Five planets can be seen without a telescope: Mercury, Venus, Mars, Jupiter and Saturn. They are visible because they reflect the light of the sun.

In order of distance from the sun, the planets are Mercury, Venus, Earth, Mars, Jupiter, Saturn, Uranus, Neptune and Pluto.

All the planets revolve (orbit) around the sun in the same counter-clockwise direction. The closer to the sun, the greater their speed. Except for Pluto, all the orbits lie in nearly the same plane in space, like marbles rolling on a table top.

Our Place in the Universe Although the solar system seems enormous, it is quite small compared to the whole universe. Our sun is only one star among the hundreds of billions that make up our spiral-shaped galaxy, the **Milky Way**. It takes our sun, with planets in tow, about 250 million years to orbit around the Milky Way just once. All the stars that we see at night are in a small, nearby portion of our galaxy. There may be billions of galaxies in the universe, each containing billions of stars of its own.

The Birth of our Solar System Approximately 4.6 billion years ago (billions of years after the galaxies were formed)

astronomers believe that a vast cloud of gas and dust collapsed and formed a spinning disk. Gravitation compacted so much material in the centre that extremely high pressures and temperatures lit a nuclear fire—our sun began to shine. Meanwhile, any remaining lumps of hot solids and gases slowly collected to become the planets, moons, asteroids and comets.

Our Solar System The planets of the solar system can be divided into two groups. The inner planets, Mercury, Venus, Earth and Mars, are the **terrestrial**, or Earth-like, planets. These are small rocky worlds with metal cores and thin atmospheres, except for airless Mercury. Jupiter, Saturn, Uranus and Neptune make up the realm of the **gas giants**. These planets do not have a solid surface, but are made up of layers of gases and clouds, possibly with rocky cores the size of Earth. The gas giants are huge: a thousand Earths could easily fit inside Jupiter. Saturn's rings may be the most famous feature of the solar system but rings are also found around Jupiter, Uranus and Neptune.

Pluto is unique and does not fit into either of these two groups. It is a tiny world of rock and ice, smaller than the Earth's moon, and with an extremely thin atmosphere.

Separating the terrestrial planets from the gas giants is the **asteroid belt**, a region of space between Mars and Jupiter where as many as 50,000 rocky objects may orbit the sun. Asteroids, often called minor planets, range from gravel-size, or smaller, to the 1,000-km-wide Ceres. They may be the remains of a small, shattered planet.

Over 60 moons, or satellites, are found in the solar system. All the planets, except for Mercury and Venus, have at least one moon orbiting them. Some of these moons are fascinating worlds in their own right: **Phobos** and **Deimos**, the moons of Mars, may be captured asteroids; **Io**, one of Jupiter's moons, has many active volcanoes; **Europa**, another one of Jupiter's moons, may have a subterranean ocean; **Titan**, a moon of Saturn, has an atmosphere thicker than

Earth's. Jupiter with its 16 known moons, Saturn with its 18 and Uranus with its 17 are like miniature solar systems.

Exploring the Solar System Most of the planets have been visited by space probes from Earth: Mercury was visited in 1974 by *Mariner 10*, Soviet *Venera* spacecraft landed on Venus several times in the 1970s while *Viking 1* and *2* landed on Mars in 1976. The best spacecraft views of Jupiter and Saturn were obtained by *Voyager 1* and *2* in 1979 and 1980–81 respectively. *Voyager 2* went on to Uranus in 1986 and Neptune in August 1989. These spacecraft made discoveries not possible from the Earth: craters on Mercury, volcanoes and great valleys on Mars, Jupiter's ring and 10 new moons of Uranus were only a few.

Recent missions include the *Ulysses* mission, launched in 1990, which finished its second orbit of the sun in 1997-98. The spacecraft will do a south polar pass of the sun from September 2000 to January 2001. The combined NASA/ESA (European Space Agency) *Cassini* mission to Saturn was launched in October 1997. *Cassini* will enter orbit around Saturn July 2004.

On July 4, 1997, the Pathfinder mission to Mars made a successful landing, sending back data and pictures. In November 1996 the Mars Global Surveyor (MGS) was launched on a mapping and photography mission. Mapping began in March 1999 and pictures taken in June 2000 showed features resembling water erosion in over 200 places. Scientists had previously thought that the red planet was too cold and the atmosphere too thin to allow water to exist. For the latest releases from the MGS, visit http://mars.jpl.nasa.gov/mgs. The Mars Odyssey spacecraft lifted off April 7, 2001 and was expected to reach the Red Planet in late October for a mission intended to look for signs of past life.

Our Solar System at a Glance

	Distance from Sun (million km)	Equatorial Diameter (km)	Gravity (Earth=1)	Mass (Earth=1)	Period of Orbit about the Sun	Period of Rotation on Axis (days)	Number of known Moons
Sun	—	1 392 000	27.90	332 830	—	25.38	—
Mercury	57.9	4 878	0.38	0.06	88.0 days	58.60	0
Venus	108.2	12 104	0.91	0.8	224.7 days	243.00	0
Earth	149.6	12 756	1.00	1.0	365.3 days	0.99	1
Mars	227.9	6 787	0.38	0.1	1.88 years	1.02	2
Jupiter	778.4	142 800	2.54	317.8	11.86 years	0.41	28
Saturn	1 426.7	120 000	1.08	95.2	29.63 years	0.42	30
Uranus	2 868.7	51 200	0.91	14.5	83.97 years	0.71	21
Neptune	4 498.2	48 680	1.19	17.2	164.80 years	0.67	8
Pluto	5 906.3	2 390	0.06	0.002	248.63 years	6.38	1

Source: *NASA 2001; http://solarsystem.nasa.gov/features/planets/planetsfeat.html*

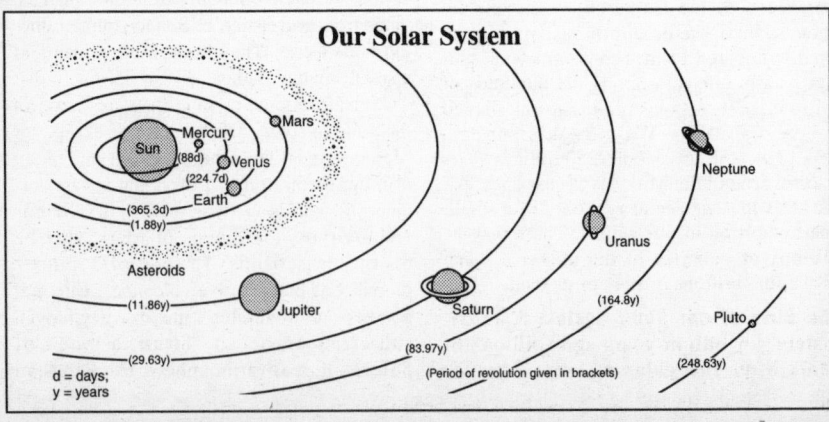

Our Solar System

Sun (88d)
Mercury
Venus (224.7d)
Earth (365.3d) (1.88y)
Mars
Asteroids
Jupiter (11.86y)
Saturn (29.63y)
Uranus (83.97y)
Neptune (164.8y)
Pluto (248.63y)

d = days; y = years

(Period of revolution given in brackets)

International Space Station (ISS)

Sixteen countries have been contributing to the International Space Station (ISS), a project that first got serious attention (and funding) in 1993. That project is now a reality that orbits 400 km above the Earth, at an inclination of 51.6° to the equator.

The actual assembly of the ISS began in December 1998, when the first stage—the Functional Cargo Block—was launched from Kazakstan. That first launch put the propulsion, command and control systems in place with the Zarya module. A six-man crew went up in December 1998 to do some assembly of the space station in orbit—they added the Unity module. In June 1999, tools and a crane were added to assist in construction. On May 19, 2000 a seven-member crew began to ready the space station for residents. On July 25, 2000 the third big component of the station, Zvezda, docked with the ISS. A NASA mission in mid-September took supplies up after a Russian supply ship with oxygen generators, toilet components and other gear had made Zvezda habitable. The September NASA mission installed equipment such as power and data cables as well as bringing supplies. Crew members also tested air filters and heaters aboard the unit. The first permanent crew (two Russians and an American) were scheduled to begin a five-month residence in early November 2000.

Canada's Marc Garneau visited the station as part of a mission (Nov. 30-Dec. 11, 2000) to install the station's first solar panels, which will eventually generate 110 kilowatts of power. Col. Chris Hadfield became the first Canadian to walk in space (April 19-May 1, 2001), when he installed CANADARM2, part of Canada's contribution to the station. The station is expected to be finished in 2006.

Other contributions to the project include a pressurized lab and logistics transport vehicles (European Space Agency); a lab with "attached exposed facility" and logistics transport vehicles (Japan); and research modules, a service module with its own life support and habitation system, a science power platform to supply electrical power, more logistics transport vehicles and a Soyuz spacecraft for emergency crew return and transfer (Russia).

The completed station would weigh almost 450 metric tons, were it on Earth. It will be 108m by 88m, with about the same volume as the fuselage of Boeing 747 or three ordinary houses. It will accommodate up to seven people at once. Its orbit was chosen because it can be reached by launch vehicles from each of the international partners; the orbit also allows observation of 85 percent of the globe and 95 percent of the world's population.

The ISS was originally planned to establish a permanent laboratory where gravity, temperature and air pressure could be manipulated to create conditions that would be impossible to achieve in Earth-bound labs. The site will be used for testing scientific and engineering hypotheses, and for conducting research in biology, chemistry, physics, ecology and medicine. The space station will also serve as a test site for new technologies for advanced industrial materials, medical research and new communications technology.

The participants in the ISS program are the United States; Canada; European Space Agency partners Belgium, Denmark, France, Germany, Italy, the Netherlands, Norway, Spain, Sweden, Switzerland, and the United Kingdom; plus Japan, Russia and Brazil. Each partner will contribute astronauts to crew the finished station, and have access to its labs for research and experiments.

The International Space Station is the largest scientific cooperative program in history. For more news and information, visit NASA at http://www.nasa.gov/station/.

Some Astronomical Terms

Asteroid Any of the thousands of small, rocky objects that orbit the Sun. Some pass closer to the Sun than Earth does and others have orbits that take them well beyond Jupiter. The largest asteroid is one called Ceres.

Big Bang The primeval explosion that most astronomers think gave rise to the universe as we see it today, in which clusters of galaxies are moving apart from one another. Astronomers calculate the Big Bang happened about 15 to 20 billion years ago.

Black Hole An object whose gravitational pull is so strong that—within a certain distance of it—nothing can escape, not even light. Black holes are thought to result from the collapse of certain very massive stars, but other kinds have been postulated as well: **mini black holes**, for example, which might have been formed in the turbulence shortly after the Big Bang. **Supermassive black holes**—with masses millions of times the Sun's—may exist in the cores of large galaxies.

Comet A small chunk of ice, dust and rocky material (a few kilometres across) which, when it comes close enough to the Sun, can develop a tenuous "tail." The tail of a comet is made of gas and dust that have been driven off the comet's surface by the Sun's energy. The tail always points away from the Sun (no matter in what direction the comet is moving).

Eclipse The blocking of all or part of the light from one object by another.

Galaxy A large assemblage of stars (and sometimes interstellar gas and dust), typically containing millions to hundreds of billions of member stars. A galaxy is held together by the gravitational attraction of its member stars (and other material) to one another.

Light-Year The distance light travels in one year in a vacuum. Since light travels at a speed of about 300,000 km per second, a light-year is roughly 9.5 trillion km long.

Magnitude A way of expressing the brightness of astronomical objects, inherited from the Greeks. In the magnitude system, a lower number indicates a brighter object (for example, a 1st-magnitude star is brighter than a 3rd-magnitude star). Each step in magnitude corresponds to a brightness difference of about 2.5. Stars of the 6th magnitude are the faintest the unaided human eye can see.

Meteor A bit of solid debris from space, burning up in the Earth's atmosphere because of friction with the air. Before entering Earth's atmosphere, the body is called a meteoroid. If any of the object survives its fiery passage through the air, the parts that hit the ground are called **meteorites.**

Milky Way Galaxy A spiral galaxy, with a disk approximately 100,000 light-years across, containing roughly 400 billion stars. Our Sun is in the disk about two-thirds of the way from the centre. It takes about 200 million years to orbit the centre of the Milky Way once.

Neutron Star A crushed remnant left over when a very massive star explodes. Some neutron stars are known to spin very rapidly, at least at the beginning, and can be detected as **pulsars**: rapidly flashing sources of radio radiation or visible light. The pulses are produced by the spinning of a neutron star, much as a lighthouse beacon appears to flash off, on and off.

Nova A star that abruptly and temporarily increases its brightness by a factor of hundreds of thousands.

Orbit The path of one body around another (such as the Moon around the Earth) or around the centre of gravity of a number of objects (such as the Sun's 200-million-year path around the centre of our galaxy).

Planet A major object that orbits around a star.

Quasar One of a class of very distant (typically billions of light years away), extremely bright, and very small objects. Quasar means "quasistar"—that is, something that looks like a star but can't actually be a star.

Red Giant A very large distended, and relatively cool star in the final stages of its life.

Solar System The Sun and all things orbiting it, including the nine major planets, their satellites, and all the asteroids and comets.

Supernova An explosion that marks the end of a very massive star's life. When it occurs, the star can outshine all the other stars in a galaxy in total for several days, and may leave behind a crushed core (perhaps a neutron star or a black hole).

White Dwarf The collapsed remnant of a relatively low-mass star (roughly one and a half times the Sun's mass and less), which has exhausted the fuel for its nuclear reactions and shines only by radiating its stored up heat.

Source: *The Astronomical Society of the Pacific, San Francisco, CA*

Phases of the Moon, 2002

(Eastern Standard Time)

New Moon	First Quarter	Full Moon	Last Quarter
			Jan 05, 10:55 PM
Jan 13, 08:29 AM	Jan 21, 12:46 PM	Jan 28, 05:50 PM	Feb 04, 08:33 AM
Feb 12, 02:41 AM	Feb 20, 07:02 AM	Feb 27, 04:17 AM	Mar 05, 08:24 PM
Mar 13, 09:02 PM	Mar 21, 09:28 PM	Mar 28, 01:25 PM	Apr 04, 10:29 AM
Apr 12, 02:27 PM	Apr 20, 07:48 AM	Apr 26, 10:00 PM	May 04, 02:16 AM
May 12, 05:45 AM	May 19, 02:42 PM	May 26, 06:51 AM	Jun 02, 07:05 PM
Jun 10, 06:46 PM	Jun 17, 07:29 PM	Jun 24, 04:42 PM	Jul 02, 12:19 PM
Jul 10, 05:26 AM	Jul 16, 11:47 PM	Jul 24, 04:07 AM	Aug 01, 05:22 AM
Aug 08, 02:15 PM	Aug 15, 05:12 AM	Aug 22, 05:29 PM	Aug 30, 09:31 PM
Sep 06, 10:10 PM	Sep 13, 01:08 PM	Sep 21, 01:59 PM	Sep 29, 12:03 PM
Oct 06, 06:17 AM	Oct 13, 12:33 AM	Oct 21, 02:20 AM	Oct 29, 12:28 AM
Nov 04, 03:30 PM	Nov 11, 03:52 PM	Nov 19, 08:34 PM	Nov 27, 10:46 AM
Dec 04, 02:34 AM	Dec 11, 10:48 AM	Dec 19, 02:10 PM	Dec 26, 07:31 PM

Daylight Saving Time (Summer Time) is kept in most places across Canada. It starts at 2 a.m. on Sunday, April 7, 2002 when clocks go forward one hour. Clocks return to Standard Time at 2 a.m. on Sunday, October 27 when clocks go back one hour. To get wristwatch time in the Eastern Time Zone between April 7 and October 27 *add* one hour to the times listed.

Across Canada, there are six Standard Time Zones. To adjust to wristwatch time in another time zone, add or subtract the following to the times listed in the table: Newfoundland (+1hr 30m), Atlantic (+1hr), Central (-1hr), Mountain (-2hr), Pacific (-3hr).

Organizations

Canadian Astronomical Society:
An organization of professional astronomers. Contact: Serge Demers, CASCA Secretary, Département de Physique, Université de Montréal, Montreal, Quebec H3C 3J7.
Business office: R. Hayes
Dept. of Physics, Queen's University, Kingston, ON K7L 3N6
Tel: (613) 533-6000 x74431; Fax: (613) 533-6463
Web site: http://www.casca.ca.

Royal Astronomical Society of Canada (RASC):
The Society is an organization of amateur and professional astronomers open to anyone interested in astronomy. The Society publishes the annual *Observer's Handbook* as well as other publications. It has more than 4,500 members in 23 clubs across Canada. National Headquarters is located at 136 Dupont Street, Toronto, Ontario M5R 1V2 Tel: (416) 924-7973.
Web site: http://www.rasc.ca.

Fireball From The Beginning

T he dawn twilight of Jan. 18, 2000 saw a remarkable sight in the skies over the Yukon and northern British Columbia: a fireball, with a trail of illuminated dust behind it. The cause of that fireball was a 200,000-kilogram lump of dirt, left over from the birth of the solar system, and still carrying within it some of the primitive organic materials from that time. The fireball, moving at about 16 kilometres a second, roared across the Yukon, passing within 20 kilometres of Whitehorse before exploding in the air and coming to Earth on frozen Tagish Lake, B.C.

Had the meteorite not landed on ice, it would have probably been lost—most such objects disintegrate in the atmosphere and pieces that make it to the ground crumble within a few days. What's more, the pieces—still chilled from 4 billion years in deep space—landed on ice and stayed frozen, so that they didn't lose the volatile organic compounds they contain. The fragments have been picked up for study. "No meteorite has ever been collected like that before," one researcher said.

Events in the 2002 Sky

January

1   Jupiter at Opposition. The giant planet will be at its closest approach to Earth. This is the best time to view and photograph Jupiter and its moons.

3-5   Quadrantids Meteor Shower. This will be an average show for the Quadrantids due to the near quarter moon. Best viewing will be to the East after midnight.

February

Sky will be mostly uneventful in February. The new moon is Feb. 12 and the full moon is Feb. 28

March

20   The Vernal Equinox occurs at 2:16 p.m. EST. There will be equal amounts of day and night. This is also the first day of Spring.

April

21-23   Lyrid Meteor Shower. This year's show for the Lyrids will be average due to the near full moon. Look for meteors radiating from the constellation of Lyra after midnight.

May

5-6   Eta Aquarids Meteor Shower. This should be an average show due to the near quarter moon. The radiant point for this shower will be in the constellation of Aquarius. Best viewing is usually to the east after midnight.

June

10   An annular solar eclipse will occur, with a path across the Pacific Ocean. Partial phases will be visible from most of North America except for the northeast. (See Eclipses, page 571.)

21   The Summer Solstice occurs at 9:24 a.m. EDT. The Sun is at its highest point in the sky and it will be the longest day of the year. This is the first day of summer in the northern hemisphere.

July

28-29   Southern Delta Aquarids Meteor Shower. Don't expect too much from this shower due to the near full moon. The radiant point for this shower will be in the constellation of Aquarius. Best viewing is usually to the east after midnight.

August

11-13   Perseids Meteor Shower. This should be a great year for the Perseids. The thin crescent moon will set early allowing even the faint meteors to be seen. Best viewing is usually to the east after midnight. The shower will peak on August 12.

20   Uranus at Opposition. The giant blue planet will be at its closest approach to Earth. Those with good telescopes should be able to make out the planet's tiny blue disk.

September

23   The Autumnal Equinox begins at 12:56 a.m. EDT. There will be equal amounts of day and night. This is also the first day of autumn.

October

21-22   Orionids Meteor Shower. This will be a disappointing year for the Orionids due to the glare of the full moon. The radiant point for this shower is in the constellation of Orion. Best viewing, if any, will be to the east after midnight.

November

17-18   Leonid Meteor Shower. The near full moon will be a big problem this year for the Leonids. Find a good site far from city lights and expect to see only the brightest meteors. Look for the shower radiating from the constellation Leo after midnight.

December

13-15   Geminids Meteor Shower. The moon could be a problem this year. Best viewing will be far from city lights. The radiant point for this shower will be in the constellation of Gemini. Best viewing will be after the moon sets, well after midnight.

17   Saturn at Opposition. The ringed planet will be at its closest approach to Earth. This is the best time to view and photograph Saturn and its moons.

21   The Winter Solstice occurs at 8:15 p.m. EST. The Sun is at its lowest point in the sky and it will be the shortest day of the year. This is the first day of winter in the northern hemisphere.

Eclipses in 2002

The year 2002 features two eclipses of the Sun and three of the moon. The lunar eclipses are all penumbral, meaning the moon is not in the darkest part of the Earth's shadow and the effect may be subtle and hard to see.

May 26

Penumbral Lunar Eclipse: The first eclipse of the year is a deep penumbral lunar eclipse, only visible in parts of western Canada at moonset.

June 10

Annular Solar Eclipse: The first solar eclipse of 2002 is annular, or ring-shaped, with a path that stretches across the Pacific Ocean. Partial phases will be visible from eastern Asia and most of North America except for the northeast. The greatest eclipse will occur at 23:48:15 GMT about 2 600 kilometres northwest of the Hawaiian Islands and lasts about 23 seconds.

June 24

Penumbral Lunar Eclipse: The year's second lunar eclipse follows two weeks after the annular solar eclipse and is nominally visible in the Eastern hemisphere. Unfortunately, it will be so shallow as to be all but invisible, even for the sharpest-eyed observers.

November 19-20

Penumbral Lunar Eclipse: The last penumbral lunar eclipse of 2002 is also the deepest lunar eclipse of the year. It will be visible from the Americas, Europe, Africa and central Asia. Eastern Canada will see a full eclipse, while the west will see a partial eclipse. In Canada, the eclipse will start about 23:32 GMT and end at 04:01 GMT (Nov 20).

December 4

Total Solar Eclipse: Not visible in Canada. The eclipse track starts in the Atlantic off the west coast of Angola, crosses southern Africa and the Indian Ocean and ends at sunset in southern Australia. A partial eclipse will be seen in most of Africa, western Australia and Antarctica.

> **WARNING: SPECIAL PRECAUTIONS MUST BE TAKEN TO OBSERVE THE SUN AT ALL TIMES. AT NO TIME DURING A PARTIAL SOLAR ECLIPSE CAN THE SUN BE OBSERVED SAFELY WITH THE UNPROTECTED HUMAN EYE.**

Space Information on the World Wide Web

NASA Home Page http://www.nasa.gov
NASA provides links to the massive amount of information the agency has placed on the Web, as well as links to other space-related sites in the United States and other countries.
Space Telescope Science Institute http://www.stsci.edu
This is the site for the Hubble Telescope.

Cassini Mission to Saturn: http://www.jpl.nasa.gov/cassini/
Images, mission status, student activities.

Getting down on Mars: *A one-stop shopping site for people interested in all aspects of the Red Planet is http://mars.jpl.nasa.gov/. Learn about the evidence for water, the search for traces of former life, and the spacecraft that are studying Mars's surface. If you dream of walking on the ochre dunes of Mars, try http://spaceflight.nasa.gov/mars/, where you'll learn about plans for human exploration of the solar system.*

Canadian Space Agency *(see page 572) has a home page dedicated to our Space Science Program, including an overview that goes back to our first observatory in 1839, and details of current work being done in Space Life Sciences, Atmospheric Sciences, Space Astronomy, Microgravity Sciences and Solar Terrestrial Relations. http://www.science.sp-agency.ca is the home of the Space Science Program.*

The Canadian Space Agency (CSA)

The CSA was created by an act of Parliament on December 14, 1990; its mission is to "promote the peaceful use and development of space for the social and economic benefit of Canadians." Its more immediate job is to co-ordinate Canada's space programs and manage our space-related activities.

Canadian experience in space predates the creation of the CSA: Canadians designed and built the first Canadian satellite in time for a launch on Sept. 9, 1962. *Alouette I* made us the third country in space (after Russia and the US), and was the first satellite to return useful information on the ionosphere, (the layer of the upper atmosphere that affects long-distance radio transmissions).

In 1972, Canada launched *Anik A1* and became the first country to have a commercial communications satellite network. It made nation-wide, real-time television possible. It also brought reliable telephone service to the North for the first time. *Anik E-2* still provides services to television networks and telephone systems, and facilitates activities such as the transmission of newspaper copy to printing plants across the country.

In 1976, Canada and the United States launched a joint venture communications satellite, *Hermes*, which became the prototype for direct broadcast satellites. In 1981, the Canadian-designed and built Remote Manipulator System or CANADARM, was used on the Space Shuttle *Columbia*. Operated by two hand controls from the comfort of the space shuttle's cabin, the Canadarm allows astronauts to take satellites from the cargo bay and position them in space; it is also designed to snare satellites already in orbit and place them into the cargo bay for a return to Earth.

The Canadian Astronaut Program has been in operation since 1983; see page 567 for details.

Canada and the International Space Station: Canada's contribution is the Mobile Servicing System (MSS), consisting of equipment and facilities on the ISS and on the ground. The sophisticated CANADARM2 is part of this system, as is a robotic hand (known formally as a Special Purpose Dexterous Manipulator or SPDM). These pieces and the CANADARM2 will be used for assembly and maintenance tasks on the space station. The arm, together with the hand, can manipulate delicate objects; the CANADARM2 can work with large objects. The CSA is working on a Canadian Space Vision System to assist those using the equipment. Ground support for the devices will be at CSA headquarters in St. Hubert, Quebec. Training, logistics support and other resources will be used to monitor the condition of the equipment and train personnel to use it.

RadarSat, launched in 1995, is the country's first Earth Observation satellite. This remote sensing satellite is in a near-polar orbit 800 km above the Earth. RadarSat produces images of the Earth's surface using a microwave Synthetic Aperture Radar (SAR) system. (Similar devices use optical sensors; unlike them, Radarsat can function night or day, and through clouds, fog or smoke.)

RadarSat II, to be launched in 2003, will be an advanced SAR satellite. Personnel in fields as diverse as ice navigation, cartography, geological exploration, maritime surveillance, disaster relief operations, and agriculture and forestry surveillance will be able to use the data images as the markets served by RadarSat I expand. Visit http://www.space.gc.ca/about/csagla/earthenvir/ for updates on Canada's Earth Observation technology.

Canadian Space Agency

Canadian Space Agency (CSA) http://www.space.gc.ca
Information on Canada's contribution to space research and Canada's astronauts, including regular updates on the International Space Station.

Canadian Astronaut Office http://www.space.gc.ca/csa_sectors/human_presence

Canada's Astronauts

The Canadian Astronaut Program began in 1983 when Canada was invited to send an astronaut on the U.S. space shuttle. A permanent corps of Canadian astronauts who could co-ordinate and conduct Canadian experiments in space was created as a result.

The first recruiting drive for the astronaut program resulted in 4,300 applications. Six were successful. In 1992, a second invitation for recruits went out and another 5,000 applications poured in. Four more candidates were selected, based on a combination of academic background, professional experience, health and communication skills.

The first Canadian astronaut to fly in space was **Dr. Marc Garneau**. He conducted a set of experiments in space science, space technology, and life sciences during Mission 41-G, from October 5-13, 1984, aboard the Space Shuttle *Challenger*. **Dr. Steve MacLean** flew on the Space Shuttle mission STS-52, aboard *Columbia*, from October 22 to November 1, 1992, and conducted a second set of these experiments.

January 22-30, 1992, **Dr. Roberta Bondar** flew aboard *Discovery* during Mission STS-42. She served as the prime Canadian Payload Specialist for the first International Microgravity Laboratory mission; she conducted more than 43 experiments on behalf of 13 countries.

In November 1995, **Col. Chris Hadfield** was the first Canadian Mission Specialist to participate in a Space Shuttle mission as a crew member and the first Canadian on board the Russian Space Station *Mir* when he flew aboard *Atlantis* during Mission STS-74, from November 12-20, 1995.

In May 1996, **Dr. Marc Garneau** made his second space flight, as a Mission Specialist aboard Space Shuttle *Endeavor*. This Mission, STS-77, was a rendezvous and proximity mission using the SPARTAN-207 satellite. Once again, the CANADARM played a large role in this run-up to the assembly of the International Space Station (ISS). This mission also carried the commercial SPACEHAB module and two Canadian experiments, one in material processing and one in biology.

Dr. Robert Thirsk flew as a Payload Specialist on Mission STS-78, also known as the Life and Microgravity Spacelab flight, launched on June 20, 1996. During the 17-day mission, Dr. Thirsk conducted a series of 43 life and microgravity experiments aboard the Spacelab—a fully-equipped international space laboratory carried in the Shuttle's cargo bay.

On August 7, 1997, **Bjarni Tryggvason** was Payload Specialist for flight on STS-85. He tested the Microgravity Vibration Isolation Mount (MIM) and performing material science and fluid physics experiments designed to examine sensitivity to spacecraft vibrations. This work was directed at developing better understanding of the need for systems such as the MIM on the International Space Station (ISS) and on the effect of vibrations on the many experiments to be performed on the ISS.

The CSA's **Dr. Dave Williams** was one of seven astronauts to participate in the STS-90 mission on board the Space Shuttle *Columbia* from April 17 to May 3, 1998. Dr. Williams and his fellow crew members conducted a total of 26 life science experiments designed to study the effects of microgravity on the brain and parts of the central nervous system.

During this mission Williams served as official crew medical officer. On July 21, 1998, Dr. Williams was appointed Director of the Space and Life Sciences Directorate at NASA's Johnson Space Centre in Houston.

In August 1996, **Julie Payette** began mission specialist training at the Johnson Space Centre, working for the Astronaut Office's Robotics branch. Initial astronaut training was completed in April 1999; Payette visited the ISS in May 1999 as part of STS-96, a 10-day logistics and resupply mission.

Dr. Marc Garneau flew his third space mission Nov. 30, 2000, when he installed the first of four sets of solar panels on the ISS. **Col. Chris Hadfield** became the first Canadian to walk in space in April 2001, when he uncrated, installed, and tested CANADARM2 (part of Canada's contribution to the multi-billion-dollar-project) on the ISS.

Source: *Canadian Space Agency* http://www.space.gc.ca

Constellations

Astronomers have divided the sky into 88 well-defined areas called constellations. They are named after people, animals or objects. The pattern of bright stars in some constellations (such as Orion or Scorpius) resembles the person, animal, or object they are named after but in most constellations it is difficult to see a pattern among the stars. The largest constellation is Hydrus, followed by Virgo and Ursa Major. The smallest is Crux.

Constellation	Meaning
Andromeda	Daughter of Cassiopeia
Antlia	The Air Pump
Apus	Bird of Paradise
Aquarius	The Water-bearer
Aquila	The Eagle
Ara	The Altar
Aries	The Ram
Auriga	The Charioteer
Bootes	The Herdsman
Caelum	The Chisel
Camelopardalis	The Giraffe
Cancer	The Crab
Canes Venatici	The Hunting Dogs
Canis Major	The Big Dog
Canis Minor	The Little Dog
Capricornus	The Horned Goat
Carina	The Keel
Cassiopeia	The Queen
Centaurus	The Centaur
Cepheus	The King
Cetus	The Whale
Chamaeleon	The Chameleon
Circinus	The Compasses
Columba	The Dove
Coma Berenices	Berenice's Hair
Corona Australis	The Southern Crown
Corona Borealis	The Northern Crown
Corvus	The Crow
Crater	The Cup
Crux	The Cross
Cygnus	The Swan
Delphinus	The Dolphin
Dorado	The Goldfish
Draco	The Dragon
Equuleus	The Little Horse
Eridanus	A River
Fornax	The Furnace
Gemini	The Twins
Grus	The Crane (bird)
Hercules	The Son of Zeus
Horologium	The Clock
Hydra	The Water Snake (f)
Hydrus	The Water Snake (m)
Indus	The Indian
Lacerta	The Lizard
Leo	The Lion
Leo Minor	The Little Lion
Lepus	The Hare
Libra	The Balance
Lupus	The Wolf
Lynx	The Lynx
Lyra	The Lyre
Mensa	Table Mountain
Microscopium	The Microscope
Monoceros	The Unicorn
Musca	The Fly
Norma	The Square
Octans	The Octant
Ophiuchus	The Serpent-bearer
Orion	The Hunter
Pavo	The Peacock
Pegasus	The Winged Horse
Perseus	Rescuer of Andromeda
Phoenix	The Phoenix
Pictor	The Painter
Pisces	The Fishes
Piscis Austrinus	The Southern Fish
Puppis	The Stern
Pyxis	The Compass
Reticulum	The Reticle
Sagitta	The Arrow
Sagittarius	The Archer
Scorpius	The Scorpion
Sculptor	The Sculptor
Scutum	The Shield
Serpens	The Serpent
Sextans	The Sextant
Taurus	The Bull
Telescopium	The Telescope
Triangulum	The Triangle
Triangulum Australe	The Southern Triangle
Tucana	The Toucan
Ursa Major	The Great Bear[1]
Ursa Minor	The Little Bear[2]
Vela	The Sails
Virgo	The Maiden
Volans	The Flying Fish
Vulpecula	The Fox

(1) Commonly known as the Big Dipper. (2) Commonly known as The Little Dipper

Observatories in Canada

Maritime Region:

☐ Burke-Gaffney Observatory
Department of Astronomy and Physics, Saint Mary's University, Halifax, NS B3H 3C3. Open: Nov. to Mar. at 7 p.m. and April to June at 9 p.m., every 1st and 3rd Sat. From June to Sept. open every Sat. Tel: (902) 496-8257. Web site: http://mnbsun.stmarys.ca/bgo/bgo.html

☐ University of New Brunswick
Brydon Jack Observatory Museum, P.O. Box 4400, Fredericton, NB E3A 5A3. Oldest observatory in Canada, 1851. No charge. Summer (by appointment).

Central Canada:

☐ David Dunlap Observatory
University of Toronto, P.O. Box 360, Richmond Hill, Ont. L4C 4Y6. Open Wednesday mornings from 10 to 11:30 a.m. From April to Sept. Open also on Saturday evenings. Reservations required. Tel: (905) 884-2112.

☐ **Helen B. Hogg Observatory**
Canada Science and Technology Museum. 1867 St. Laurent Blvd. Ottawa, Ont. K1G 5A3. Tel: (613) 991-3044.

☐ **Hume Cronyn Memorial Observatory**
University of Western Ontario, London, Ont. N6A 3K7. Late Oct. to early April by reservation. From June to Aug. on Saturday evenings at 8:30 p.m. Tel: (519) 661-3183. Web site: phobos.astro.uwo.ca/~dfgray/pub-nit.html.

☐ **Science North Solar Observatory** 100 Ramsey Lake Rd., Sudbury, Ont. P3A 2K3. Viewing of the solar spectrum and the Sun in hydrogen-alpha and white light in a darkened theatre. Open most days. Tel: (705) 522-3701.

Western Canada:

☐ **Climenhaga Observatory**
Dept. of Physics and Astronomy, University of Victoria, P.O. Box 3055 Stn Csc, Victoria, BC V8W 3P6. Tel: (250) 721-7700. Open daily. Web site: http://astrowww.phys.uvic.ca/climenhaga/obs/telescope.html

☐ **Rothney Astrophysical Observatory**
Physics and Astronomy Dept., University of Calgary, Calgary, Alta. T2N 1N4. Tel: (403) 220-5385. Web site: http://www.ucalgary.ca/~milone/rao.html.

☐ **Dominion Astrophysical Observatory** RR #5, 5071 West Saanich Rd., Victoria, BC V8X 4M6. Open throughout the year Mon. to Fri. 9:15 a.m. to 4:30 p.m. In summer, May to Aug., open from 9:00 a.m. until 8 p.m. Sun. to Fri., as well as on Sat from 9:30 a.m. to 11:00 p.m.

☐ **Dominion Radio Astrophysical Observatory**
P.O. Box 248, Penticton, BC V2A 6K3. Conducted tours. Sun., July–Aug. only, 2–5 p.m. Visitors' centre open year-round during daytime. Tel: (250) 493-2277.

☐ **H.R. Macmillan Planetarium and Gordon Southam Observatory**
1100 Chestnut St., Vancouver, B.C. V6J 3J9. Open Fri.-Sun., and statutory holidays 12 p.m.-5 p.m. and 7 p.m.-11 p.m., weather and volunteer staff permitting. Tel: (604) 763-4431.

☐ **Devon Observatory** Dept. of Physics, University of Alberta, Edmonton, Alta T6G 2J1.

☐ **University of Saskatchewan Observatory**
108 Wiggins Road, Saskatoon, Sask. S7N 5E6. Tel: (306) 966-6434.

☐ **University of British Columbia Observatory**
2219 Main Mall, Vancouver, BC V6T 1W5. Free public observing on clear Sat. eve. Tel: (604) 224-6186 (observing) or (604) 228-2802 (tours).

Planetariums

Maritime Region:

☐ **Burke-Gaffney Planetarium**
Saint Mary's University, Department of Astronomy, Halifax, NS B3H 3C3.

☐ **The Halifax Planetarium**
The education section of the Nova Scotia Museum of Natural History. 1747 Summer St., Halifax, NS B3H 3A6. Tel: (902) 424-7370. Located in the Sir James Dunn Building, Dalhousie Univeristy. The education section of the Nova Scotia Museum of Natural History. Open on Tuesday evenings at 7 p.m. Free. Tel: (902) 424-7353.

Central Canada:

☐ **Doran Planetarium**
Laurentian University, Ramsey Lake Rd., Sudbury, Ont. P3E 2C6. Tel: (705) 675-1151, ext. 2222. Web site: http://www.laurentian.ca/.

☐ **Planetarium de Montréal** 1000 St. Jacques St. W., Montreal, Que. H3C 1G7. Tel: (514) 872-4530. Live shows in French and English. Open daily. Web site: http://www.planetarium.montreal.qc.ca/.

☐ **McLaughlin Planetarium**
Royal Ontario Museum: 100 Queen's Park, Toronto, Ont. M5S 2C6. Tel: (416) 586-5549 (switchboard). On-going astronomy program using STARLAB planetariums for school and public programming only. Phone (416) 586-5801 for information. Recorded astronomy information line (416) 586-5736.

☐ **William J. McCallion Planetarium**
Department of Physics and Astronomy, McMaster University, 1280 Main Street, Hamilton, ON L8S 4M1. Tel: (905) 525-9140.

Western Canada:

☐ **Calgary Centennial Planetarium**
Alberta Science Centre, 701-11 St. S.W., P.O. Box 2100, Stn. M. Calgary, Alta. T2P 2M5. Tel: (403) 221-3700.

☐ **Edmonton Space Sciences Centre**
Coronation Park, 1121-142 St., Edmonton. Alta T5M 4A1. Tel: (780) 452-9100 or (780) 451-3344. Features planetarium Star Theatre, IMAX film theatre, exhibit galleries, telescope shop and bookstore. Open daily.

☐ **H.R. MacMillan Planetarium**
1100 Chestnut St., Vancouver, B.C. V6J 3J9. Tel: (604) 738-7827.Web site: http://pacific-space-centre.bc.ca/.

☐ **Manitoba Planetarium**
Museum of Man and Nature. 190 Rupert Ave., Winnipeg, Man. R3B 0N2. Tel: (204) 956-2830 (switchboard). Shows daily except some Mondays. Museum gift shop has scientific books and equipment. Web site: http://portal.mbnet.mb.ca/Manitoba Museum. Also worth a visit is the section on the Manitoba Centre for UFO Studies.

EARTH SCIENCES

The earth sciences include **geology** (the study of earth's origin and composition), **ocean-ography** (the study of ocean water, currents, life-forms and the ocean floor), **paleontology** (the study of fossils and ancient life-forms), and **meteorology** (the study of earth's atmosphere, including weather and climate). This section includes material on geology and paleontology. Meteorology can be found in the section on Climate (see pages 9–23).

The Geological Survey of Canada

The Geological Survey of Canada (GSC) is Canada's first scientific agency, and one of the first of its kind in the world. The agency was created to survey and map mineral deposits in Canada's nearly 1 million square kilometres of land and freshwater lakes, and more than 6 million square kilometres of coastal boundaries.

The Survey began life in Montreal in 1842. Under the first director William Edmond Logan, a Canadian businessman turned geologist, its initial task was a search for coal, the main industrial fuel at the time. The search, throughout Upper and Lower Canada, was unsuccessful, but Logan did find mineable deposits of copper and other metallic minerals.

Soon Survey geologists were undertaking expeditions westward. In the 1880s another director, George Mercer Dawson, became a noted ethnologist in Western Canada, as well as pioneer geologist. His reports included observations of the Haida people of British Columbia. During his expeditions he took many photographs of settlements and totem poles, capturing a glimpse of a vanishing landscape.

In 1992 the Geological Survey marked its 150th anniversary. While the task of mapping Canada's geology remains its central focus, the computerized Survey of the 1990s is very different from the one started by Sir William Logan. The Survey now undertakes an ever-expanding range of research—from exploring questions related to global change to those concerning natural hazards such as earthquakes, landslides, volcanoes, floods and ground instability.

For more information on the Geological Survey and its programs, contact: Com-munications Office, Geological Survey of Canada, 601 Booth Street, Ottawa, Ontario K1A OE8.

Geological Cyberspace Connections

*W*ant to get a different look at the map of Canada? How about a map that shows the ages of rock from coast to coast? Or where people live? Or how the various aboriginal languages are distributed? Just click on http://www.atlas.gc.ca, for the National Atlas of Canada, online version. The system offers a variety of ready-made maps on a host of fascinating topics. If you want to massage geographical data on your own, try the GeoGratis web site of Canada's Centre for Remote Sensing (http://geogratis.cgdi.gc.ca), where digital geographical data is available free of charge. And for more detailed information about individual cities, or maps of small regions of the country, try Statistics Canada (http://statcan.ca/).

Common Geological Terms

Continental shelf: Submerged edge of continent, extending to depths of less than 200 metres, and largely made up of sedimentary rock.

Earthquake: A sudden motion or trembling in the earth caused by the release of slowly accumulated strain along a fault line or through volcanic activity.

Echo Sounding: A determination of water depth by measuring the time required for a sonic or ultrasonic signal to travel to the bottom of a body of water and back to the ship emitting the signal.

Epicentre: Point on the earth's surface directly above the focus of an earthquake, usually the location of the most severe damage.

Erosion: Breakdown and wearing away of rocks on the earth's surface by the action of water, waves, glaciers, wind and underground water. ▶

► **Fault:** a fracture in the earth's crust along which there has been displacement of the rock on either side, relative to one another.

Geothermal energy: energy that can be extracted from the earth's internal heat, usually in the form of emissions of hot water, steam, and gas.

Glacier: a large ice mass formed on land by recrystallisation of compacted snow.

Ice Field: An extensive area of interconnected glaciers. An ice field is known as pack ice when floating on the sea.

Igneous Rock: Rock formed when a mass of molten magma cools and solidifies on or below earth's surface. One of three main classes of rock.

Magma: Molten rocky material (mostly silica) beneath the earth's surface. Reaching the surface red hot through volcanic activity, it cools and becomes lava.

Metamorphic rock: Rock formed when preexisting rocks are altered by marked changes in temperature, pressure, or shearing stress. One of three major rock groups.

Sedimentary rock: Rock formed from the accumulation of loose material deposited by water, wind and ice, and solidified by compaction.

Seismograph: a device that records the seismic vibrations of an earthquake. The wave disturbances caused by earthquakes have different speeds and require different lengths of time to reach the surface.

Tectonic plates: Rigid outer layer of the earth's crust consists of about ten large plates, which "float" horizontally across the denser inner crust. The boundaries of these plates are zones of intense activity, and give rise to mountain building, volcanoes, changes in the ocean floor, and earthquakes.

Tsunami: Particular form of ocean wave produced by an earthquake in the ocean floor, noted for its destructive force.

Volcano: A vent in the earth's crust through which magma, rock fragments, dust, gases, and ash are ejected from below earth's surface.

Composition of the Earth

Core: The earth's core lies about 2,900 km below the surface, and consists of two layers: a solid inner core and an outer liquid layer. The inner core is a solid mass, 3,200 km in diameter, probably composed of compressed iron with small amounts of other metals such as nickel. The outer core (the only liquid layer) is about 3,470 km in radius and gives rise to earth's magnetic fields.

Mantle: Accounting for about 82 percent of earth's volume, the mantle is denser than the crust, and probably increases in density close to the core. The mantle extends from the core to about 90 km below the higher mountains, and to about 5 km beneath parts of the ocean crust.

Crust: The outside crust of planet earth ranges in thickness from 5 to 50 km. The relatively light, granite-like rock forming the continents overlies a thinner magnesium-iron layer that makes up the ocean floor. The continental blocks "float" on the denser layer forming the ocean bed.

Hydrosphere: A layer of water covering over 70% of the earth's crust, including all water on or near the surface of the planet.

Atmosphere: The lightest part of earth is the atmosphere, a gaseous envelope surrounding the planet. The atmosphere consists of nitrogen, oxygen, water vapour and argon. Less than 0.1% is composed of other gases. Gases have weight, so the atmosphere is densest near earth's surface, and thins towards the vacuum of space.

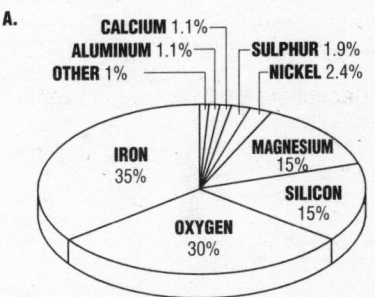

A.
- CALCIUM 1.1%
- ALUMINUM 1.1%
- OTHER 1%
- SULPHUR 1.9%
- NICKEL 2.4%
- IRON 35%
- MAGNESIUM 15%
- SILICON 15%
- OXYGEN 30%

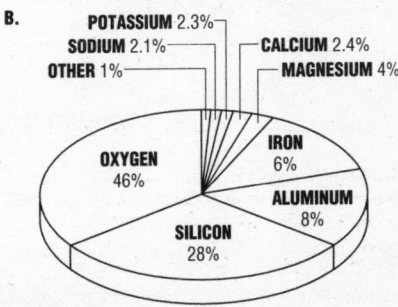

B.
- POTASSIUM 2.3%
- SODIUM 2.1%
- OTHER 1%
- CALCIUM 2.4%
- MAGNESIUM 4%
- OXYGEN 46%
- IRON 6%
- ALUMINUM 8%
- SILICON 28%

▲

Relative abundance of elements by weight of elements in the whole earth (A) and in the earth's crust (B).

Earthquakes

Although the earth's surface seems completely stable, it is constantly moving and changing. Layers of rock in the earth's crust, called plates, push and pull each other until they bend or stretch.

Vibrations or "seismic waves" emanate from the source of the breakage out through the earth, causing the planet to quiver or ring like a tuning fork. The waves can be so minor that the quake will not be felt by humans, or so severe it will change the physical landscape of the area.

Earthquakes can happen all over the world, but they tend to reoccur along weaknesses in the crust, called faults. By studying the patterns of earthquakes, scientists determine the areas at greatest risk and compile the information in seismic zoning maps. In this way, building regulations can be applied to earthquake zones to minimize possible damage.

The most common method of measuring an earthquake's magnitude is the Richter Scale. It estimates the force from recordings of seismic waves taken by an instrument called a seismometer. the scale is logarithmic, so that each numeric reading is ten times greater in recorded amplitude.

The intensity of an earthquake can also be measured through the Modified Mercalli Scale. In addition to mechanical recordings, it uses witness accounts to describe the effects of an earthquake.

Measuring Earthquakes

Richter		Modified Mercali	
2.5	Generally felt, but not recorded.	I	Not felt except by a very few
		II	Felt only by a few persons at rest, especially on upper floors of buildings
3.5	Felt by many people.	III	Felt noticeably indoors. Standing cars may rock slightly. Most people do not recognize.
		IV	During daytime felt by many indoors, outdoors by a few. Dishes, windows and doors disturbed; walls creak. At night, some awaken. Sensation like a heavy truck passing.
		V	Felt by nearly everyone; many awakened. Some dishes and windows broken; some objects over-turned. Trees, poles and other tall objects disturbed.
4.5	Some local damage may occur.	VI	Felt by all, many run outdoors. Heavy furniture moves; occasionally plaster falls and chimneys damaged. Overall damage slight.
		VII	Everyone runs outdoors. Well-built structures suffer negligible damage; slight to moderate damage in well-built homes; poorly constructed buildings suffer considerable damage. Noticed by people in moving cars.
6.0	A destructive earthquake	VIII	Damage slight in specially designed structures; considerable in ordinary substantial buildings, with partial collapse; great in poorly-built structures. Chimneys fall. Heavy furniture overturned. Disturbs people driving cars. Sand and mud ejected in small amounts.
		IX	Damage to specially designed structures considerable. Buildings shifted off foundations. Conspicuous ground cracks. Underground pipes broken.

▶

Richter			Modified Mercali
7.0	A major earthquake, about 10 occur each year	X	Some well-built wooden structures destroyed; most masonry and frame structures destroyed. Ground badly cracked. Rails bent. Landslides considerable.
8.0	Great earthquake, occurs once every five to 10 years	XI	Few masonry structures remain standing. Bridges destroyed. Broad fissures in ground. Underground pipelines out of service. Earth slumps, and land slips in soft ground.
		XII	Damage total. Waves seen on ground surface. Lines of sight and levels distorted. Objects thrown upward into air.

World's Major Earthquakes

Date		Location	Deaths	Magnitude
1902	Dec. 16	Turkestan	4 500	—
1905	Apr. 4	India, Kangra	19 000	8.6
1905	Sep. 8	Italy, Calabria	2 500	7.9
1906	Aug. 17	Chile, Santiago	20 000	8.6
1907	Oct. 21	Central Asia	12 000	8.1
1908	Dec. 28	Italy, Messina	83 000	7.5
1915	Jan. 13	Italy, Avezzano	29 980	7.5
1920	Dec. 16	China, Gansu	200 000	8.6
1923	Sep. 1	Japan, Kwanto-Tokyo-Yokohama	143 000	8.3
1925	Mar. 16	China, Yunnan	5 000	7.1
1927	Mar. 7	Japan, Tango	3 020	7.9
1927	May 22	China, near Xining	200 000	8.3
1929	May 1	Iran	3 300	7.4
1932	Dec. 25	China, Gansu	70 000	7.6
1933	Mar. 2	Japan, Sanriku	2 990	8.9
1934	Jan. 15	India, Behar-Nepal	10 700	8.4
1935	Apr. 20	Formosa	3 280	7.1
1935	May 30	Pakistan, Quetta	30 000	7.6
1939	Jan. 25	Chile, Chillan	28 000	8.3
1939	Dec. 26	Turkey, Erzincan	30 000	7.6
1948	June 28	Japan, Fukui	5 390	7.3
1949	Aug. 5	Ecuador, Ambato	6 000	6.8
1960	Feb. 29	Morocco, Agadir	15 000	5.9
1960	May 22	Chile	5 000	7.3
1966	Aug. 19	Turkey, Varto	2 520	7.1
1968	Aug. 31	Iran	20 000	7.3
1970	May 31	Peru	66 000	7.8
1972	Apr. 10	Southern Iran	5 054	7.1
1972	Dec. 23	Nicaragua, Managua	5 000	6.2
1974	Dec. 28	Pakistan	5 300	6.2
1976	Feb. 4	Guatemala	23 000	7.5
1976	June 30	Westirian, Indonesia	5 000	7.1
1976	July 27	China, Tangshan	255 000	8.0
1976	Aug. 16	Philippines, Mindanao	8 000	7.9
1976	Nov. 24	Turkey	4 000	7.3
1978	Sep. 16	Iran	25 000	7.8
1980	Oct. 10	Algeria	4 500	7.7
1980	Nov. 23	Southern Italy	4 800	7.2
1981	June 11	Southern Iran	3 000	6.9
1985	Sep. 19	Mexico, Michoacan	15 000	8.1
1988	Dec. 7	Turkey-USSR	25 000	7.0
1990	June 20	Western Iran	50 000	7.7
1993	Sept. 30	India	9 500	6.4
1995	Jan. 17	Kobe, Japan	6 000	7.2
1998	Feb. 1	Afghanistan	5 000	6.9
1999	Aug. 17	Turkey	12 000	7.4
2001	Jan. 26	India, Gujarat	20 085	7.7

Source: *U.S. Geological Survey*

Earthquakes in Canada

Scientists estimate that more than 1,000 earthquakes are recorded in Canada each year. Most measure less than 3 on the Richter scale. The southwest corner of British Columbia is the most active earthquake region (more than 200 every year). Other active regions include coastal BC, the southern Yukon, the Mackenzie Valley in the Northwest Territories, the Arctic Islands, and parts of Ontario and Québec (especially the Ottawa and St Lawrence valleys).

Date		Location	Magnitude
1918	Dec. 6	Vancouver Island	7.0
1925	March 1	Charlevoix-Kamouraska region,Québec	6.7
1929	May 6	Off Queen Charlotte Islands	7.0
1929	Nov. 18	Atlantic Ocean. South of Newfoundland	7.2
1933	Nov. 20	Baffin Bay	7.3
1935	Nov. 1	Québec-Ontario border	6.2
1946	June 23	Vancouver Island	7.3
1949	Aug. 22	Off Queen Charlotte Islands	8.1
1958	July 10	Alaska-BC border	7.9
1970	June 24	South of Queen Charlotte Islands	7.4
1976	Dec. 20	West of Vancouver Island	6.8
1979	Feb. 28	Yukon-Alaska border	7.5
1980	Dec. 17	West of Vancouver Island	6.8
1985	Dec. 23	Mackenzie region, NWT	6.9
1988	Nov. 25	Saguenay region, Quebec	6.0
1989	Dec. 25	Northern Quebec	6.1
1992	April 6	West of Vancouver Island	6.8

Source: *Geological Survey of Canada*

For more information on earthquakes, contact the following divisions of the Geological Survey of Canada:

Geophysics Division
1 Observatory Crescent
Ottawa, Ont.
K1A 0Y3
Tel (24 hrs): (613) 995-5558

Pacific Geoscience Centre
P.O. Box 6000
9860 West Saanich
Sidney, BC V8L 4B2
Tel (24 hrs): (604) 363-6500

Geological Time Periods

The story of planet earth is one of continuous change. Fossils, rock records and radioactive dating show three marked changes in the patterns of plant and animal life. These times of change in the most recent 570 million years of the earth's history are divided by geologists into three eras: Paleozoic (ancient life); Mesozoic (age of reptiles); and Cenozoic (age of mammals). The more than 4 billion years before the start of the Paleozoic era are referred to as Precambrian time. Each geological unit is divided further: the eras into periods, the periods into epochs.

The names of the time periods are taken either from the geographic locality where the fossil information was best displayed or first studied, or from some characteristic of the geological formations. For example, the Jurassic period is named from the Jura Mountains of France and Switzerland, and the Carboniferous is named from the coal-bearing sedimentary rocks. ▶

Era	Period	Epoch	Years Ago	Changes and Characteristics
➤ Precambrian Time			4.5 bil.?	Cooling and melting of the earth's crust. Evidence of bacteria, the first known living things, about 3.5 billion years ago.
Paleozoic	Cambrian		575 mil.	Seas spread across North America. First fishes appear. Greatest development of invertebrates.
	Ordovician		480 mil.	Floods sometimes cover two-thirds of North America. Jawless fish appear. Algae become plentiful.
	Silurian		435 mil.	Coral reefs are formed. First amphibians and forests of fernlike trees appear.
	Devonian		405 mil.	Gas and oil are formed. Many kinds of fish in seas and fresh water. First insects appear.
	Carboniferous —Mississippian		350 mil.	Warm, moist climate produces great forests that later become coal beds. Fish and amphibians plentiful.
	—Pennsylvanian		310 mil.	Appalachian Mountains are formed. Large amounts of coal are formed. First reptiles appear.
	Permian		270 mil.	Ural Mountains are formed. Glaciers in southern hemisphere melt. Gas, oil and salt are formed. Reptiles developing.
Mezozoic	Triassic		225 mil.	Reptiles dominate the earth. First mammals appear.
	Jurassic		180 mil.	Shallow seas invade continents. Dinosaurs reach their largest size. First birds appear.
	Cretaceous		130 mil.	Seas spread over the land. Flowering plants appear. Dinosaurs die out. Most chalk deposits are made.
Cenozoic	Tertiary	Paleocene	65 mil.	Mountains become higher. Climates less uniform. Mammals, flowering plants become common.
		Eocene	50 mil.	Climate mild. Seas flood shores of continents. Primitive apes, early horses and elephants appear.
		Oligocene	38 mil.	Climate mild. Alps and Himalayas begin to rise. Many volcanoes. Oil and natural gas are formed.
		Miocene	27 mil.	Climate mild. Rocky Mountains and Sierra Nevadas forming. Flowering plants and trees resemble modern kinds.
		Pliocene	10 mil.	Climate cooling. Mountains rising in western Canada. Many volcanoes. Birds and mammals spread around the world. Humans appear near end of epoch.
	Quaternary	Pleistocene	1.5 mil.	Great ice sheets cover northern hemisphere. Climate cool. Mountains continue to rise in North America. Early humans reach Europe and North America.
		Recent, or Holocene	10 000	Glaciers melt and Great Lakes are formed. Climate warm. Humans live in most parts of the earth, develop agriculture, use metals, domesticate animals.

Source: *Gage Canadian Dictionary by Walter S. Avis, et al. Copyright © 1983 Gage Publishing Limited. Reproduced by permission.*

Lithoprobe

(by Horst Heise, Communications Adviser)

When European explorers called North America the "New World" they reversed geological time. In reality, our ancestral continent, Laurentia, formed long before the forces of plate tectonics shaped their building blocks into Eurasia, South America and Africa.

Tracing our continent's dramatic assembly is the purpose of Canada's national Lithoprobe project (a probe or study of the lithosphere—the Earth's crust), our biggest earth-science undertaking ever and the first of its kind. More than 750 specialists (including over 400 post-graduate and post-doctoral students) from the various branches of the earth sciences have joined the project. Since 1984, Lithoprobe scientists have been constructing a "moving" image of what North America has gone through during the last four billion years, and published about 1,000 technical papers on the subject.

From its beginning, Lithoprobe has included experts from all earth science specialties, including geologists, geophysicists and geochemists, as well as the whole geoscience community. The project has been funded by the Natural Sciences and Engineering Research Council of Canada and the Geological Survey of Canada, and supported by provincial agencies, and mining and oil companies when operating in their spheres of interest.

In hard-rock mining areas Lithoprobe showed that seismic reflection surveys could provide good lithological and structural leads. Given Canada's reliance on mineral resources, this technique is of fundamental importance to existing as well as future mining communities.

The project intends to trace the growth of our continent from its beginning until today. Canada's four-billion-year-old rocks belong to a piece of old continental crust which then became part of the Slave Province.

The Slave Province (a geological designation) is one of six "original" microcontinents or **cratons** of the Archean age which eventually drifted into each other to form the heart of the Canadian Shield. The other cratons have been named Rae, Hearne, Wyoming, Superior and Nain. Whatever land had been in the oceans between the craton, even the ocean floor itself, was squeezed into a series of mountain belts (**orogens**) in the biggest, most widely spread round of continental collision the world has ever known, accompanied by an enormous outpouring of magma, which formed a brand new crust.

This giant welding process occurred in the **Early Proterozoic** period and the new mountain belts created included ranges that exist today as only eroded remains that look like welds uniting the Archean pieces.

Rifting turned into continent splitting in the west where a wide continental slope received the sediments on which the prairies now produce grain, and oil and gas reserves are found. The same happened in the east a while later, when a massive supercontinent resulted from an earlier orogen split (roughly where the St. Lawrence River is today) and a wide ocean developed. It in turn was pushed out of existence in a series of tectonic squeezes which ended with the creation of the Appalachians. Comparatively recently, the Atlantic opened, and is still widening today. Out west, the Rockies formed during the Early Tertiary, while tectonic processes have kept BC growing westward since Jurassic times.

■ Tracking the Canadian Mosaic

Many bits and pieces have become part of the "Canadian mosaic" during the continent's long geologic past, including portions of old and new continents, islands or ocean floor which have drifted in from many parts of the world. Depending on where in Canada we live, its underground once may be been in tropical seas (parts of Saskatchewan, for instance) or shivered at Himalayan heights (large portions of Ontario and Quebec) or, in geological terms, not existed until fairly recently. Piecing the geological story of our continent together is like having to choose from a pile of not one but several jigsaw puzzles of various ages in which individual pieces likely were reshaped before they occupied their present positions. They may have come from various depths in the crust, or been newly formed during tectonic activity; developed long ago or more recently, either here or far away.

Earth's geologic history began with our planet's cooling 4.6 billion years ago, leading to the formation of the planet's outer crust, which became a patchwork of individual, moving pieces or "plates." Our own continent, North America, currently is moving westward at a fairly good pace, about 4 or 5 cm per year, about as fast as one's fingernails grow. That translates into 4,000 to 5,000 km in 100 million years—a small portion of Earth's lifetime (comparable to just 31 minutes of a 24-hour day).

The North American continent grew through a progressive sticking together, or **accretion**, of smaller into bigger pieces of land. But there were also continental breakups that involved huge supercontinents. As well, the flowing magma created new lithosphere that was added to the continents and the ocean floors.

As crustal plates meet, one may slip below the other, for instance the heavier oceanic plates slide under lighter continental crust. This tectonic action is called **subduction**. Portions of a subducted plate may become attached to the underside of the overlying crustal pate, but most of the subduction plate will be recycled into the mantle, where it melts, perhaps to enter into another cycle of melting, outpouring and cooling.

Such a subduction zone was discovered under Vancouver Island in 1984, when a first geophysical test section proved the feasibility of the Lithoprobe project. This survey across Vancouver Island sounded the underground with seismic reflection signals. It showed conclusively how a portion of the Pacific Ocean seafloor was vanishing under Vancouver Island and on into the depths of Earth, causing a trail of earthquakes and tremors and, farther inland, volcanoes to line up parallel to the west coast. This investigation, and Lithoprobe's subsequent work there, was the first major earth-science investigation to cross an ocean-continent-subduction zone.

■ A Growing Continent

All of the Canadian Cordillera (with the exception of the volcanoes along the west coast), from the foothills in the east to the offshore in the west, is not where it used to be. All of it has been pushed, crunched or extended. The eastern portions are thrusted packages of sediments which previously had been laid down on the continental slope of the older North American continent. Part of this package still lies mostly undisturbed east of the Rockies in Alberta and in northeastern BC, and in the Western Canada Sedimentary Basin, which harbours western Canada's huge reserves of oil and gas.

Lithoprobe's west coast experiment was followed by an 1100-km long transect study and cross section all the way from the Juan de Fuca Ridge west of Vancouver Island to southwestern Alberta. This Southern Cordillera transect provided earth scientists with a rich record of how plate tectonics have worked in the recent past, and what the results of these processes look like.

Farther east, Lithoprobe looked at the Superior Province, in the heart of the Canadian Shield. Its age is Archean, the eon which comprises almost half of Earth's history, and the major period of its crustal formation. Archean rocks of the world, although a relatively small fraction of the exposed continental crust, contain a disproportionate amount of the world's mineral wealth, including more than half of the world's gold and significant base metal reserves. Also, the vast majority of useful diamond deposits come from deep lithospheric roots beneath Archean cratons and in some parts beneath the Superior craton.

The oldest rocks known on Earth, just over 4 billion years old, are in the Slave geological province, in the western Northwest Territories. The Slave contains rocks formed between 4 and 2.5 billion years ago; it is a relatively small member of the Archean family of microcontinents.

The Slave craton is significantly different from the much larger Superior Province. It has different rock compositions; the type, setting and timing of gold and base metal mineralization is different. More of the Slave's volcanic rocks are somewhat lighter, and a greater precentage of sedimentary rocks is present. Oldest rocks in the Slave craton are much older than in the Superior Province; still, the Slave Province appears to be a fragment of a yet earlier and bigger craton. Structures also differ, intensifying the quest for tectonic evidence from our oldest geological past.

Other revelations from Lithoprobe include evidence that the area from South Dakota, through the exposed shield in Saskatchewan-Manitoba and across Hudson Bay to northern Quebec was once part of a vast ocean—more than 5,000 kms wide—and scattered tropical islands and archipelagoes like those in the southwest Pacific. (Try to picture yourself on Bali while digging out from the next Saskatchewan blizzard.) The clues are geological markers such as the origin of the rocks and the time markers imprinted by various, mostly tectonic, processes. Saskatchewan's and Manitoba's South Sea remnants began to form after a previous continent split, which created an initial rift, comparable to the present Red Sea-Gulf of Aden area. This water body, comparable to the Pacific Ocean, was in the area where wheat fields now sway in the breeze.

Lithoprobe is scheduled to continue until 2003. Visit the project's Web site at http://www.geop.ubc.ca/Lithoprobe/public.html for an overview, an explanation of Lithoprobe techniques, and details of current research and educational resources. The program has a set of slides and other materials available for educational use; for more information you can also contact the Lithoprobe Secretariat at the University of British Columbia, Vancouver, BC V6T 1Z4.

Minerals

Minerals are all around us—everything from ice on the sidewalk in winter to the salt you sprinkle on French fries. Each mineral species has a definite chemical composition and a crystal structure.Therefore, ice is mineral because it is solid, but water is not because it is liquid. Sea shells are not minerals because, although they are solid, they are organic—formed by living creatures.

The physical properties of minerals—their form and hardness—are easy to recognize. Specimens may be composed of large showy crystals or millions of tiny crystals fused together. The external shape (or habit) is determined by the internal arrangement of atoms. The atoms are joined together in a framework to form minute building blocks. Called the crystal structure, the arrangement of atoms is unique for each mineral. The habit is also partly the result of the environment in which a mineral grows. If there is enough space during growth, the mineral develops smooth external crystals. However, conditions are seldom ideal and more often than not, minerals grow together as masses of fibres, grains, plates or spheres. The hardness of a mineral—its resistance to scratching—is measured by the Mohs scale.

The optical properties of minerals—lustre, colour and transparency—are easily observed by the unaided eye; other optical properties are determined with microscopes. Lustre is the quality of light reflected from the surface of a mineral. For instance, the highly reflective surfaces of pyrite produce the metallic lustre characteristics of most sulphide minerals. Many silicates, carbonates and otherminerals have a softer, but still bright, glassy or vitreous lustre. Minerals with surfaces that reflect light more diffusely, such as serpentine asbestos or cyanotrichite, are said to have silky or earthly lustres. Lustre is reliable means of distinguishing minerals.

Colour can also be very distinctive, but is not always reliable in identifying most minerals because even minerals of the same species can occur in many colours. Quartz, which is quite common, can be as clear as water or the deepest purple because of flaws in the mineral's crystal structure. Colour can also be affected by the presence of major elements in the mineral: copper in azurite produces an intense azure blue; arsenic makes realgar appear red; and curite is coloured orange by uranium. Colour can also be produced by physical structure. When light strikes very thin layers within the structure of labradorite, the mineral glows with iridescent colours, an effect much like that of sunlight striking a film of gasoline on a puddle, causing a rainbow of colour.

Determining the chemical composition and crystal structure of minerals requires laboratory techniques and tools such as the electron microbe, a reliable tool for analysing chemical composition. Crystal structure is determined using an X-ray diffractometer. Other mineral properties such as magnetism, fluorescence and radioactivity are more easily detected: magnetite and pyrrhotite are noticeably magnetic; some minerals, such as scheelite, fluoresce strongly in ultra-violet light; and all uranium and thorium-bearing minerals are radioactive. The radiation can easily be detected with a Geiger counter or scintillometer.

Mohs Scale of Hardness

Mohs scale indicates the relative hardness of minerals. Each mineral listed is hard enough to scratch a smooth surface of those below it. On this scale, a polymer-like polyethylene would have a hardness of about 1, a finger nail 2.5, a penny 5, window glass 5.5, and the blade of a pocket knife 6.5. Tool steel has a hardness of about 7, and easily cuts glass.

10	Diamond
9	Corundum
8	Topaz
7	Quartz
6	Orthoclase
5	Apatite
4	Fluorite
3	Calcite
2	Gypsum
1	Talc

Source: *Geological Survey of Canada*

Earth Sciences Museums

Maritime Region:

☐ St. Lawrence Miner's Museum
P.O. Box 1992, St. Lawrence, Nfld A0E 2V0.
Tel: (709) 873-2222. No charge. Open in summer.

☐ Fundy Geological Museum
4028 Eastern Avenue, Parrsboro, NS B0M 1S0.
Tel: (902) 254-3814. Entrance fee. Open June to Oct.
from 9:30 am to 5:30 pm, Nov. to May from Tues. to
Sat. to 5:00 pm. Web site:
http://www.ednet.ns.ca/educ/museum/ fundy.html.

☐ Inverness Miner's Museum
Lower Railway Street, Inverness, NS B0E 1N0. Tel:
(902) 258-2097. Entrance fee. Open all year.

☐ Springhill Miner's Museum
P.O. Box 610, Black River Road, Springhill, NS
B0M 1X0. Tel: (902) 597-3449.
Entrance fee. Open spring, summer and fall.

Central Canada:

☐ Alcan Museum and Archives
1188 Sherbrooke Street West, Montreal, Que.
H3A 3G2. Tel: (514) 848-8187. No charge. Open all year.

☐ Canadian Museum of Nature, Viola Macmillan Mineral Gallery
240 McLeod St. at Metcalfe, Ottawa, Ont. K1P 6P4.
Tel: (613) 566-4730. Entrance fee. Closed Monday
(Oct.–Apr.), Christmas Day and New Year's Day.

☐ Logan Hall
Geological Survey of Canada, 601 Booth Street,
Ottawa, Ont. K1A 0E8. Tel: (613)995-4261. No charge.
Open all year. Closed on weekends and holidays.

☐ Musée de Géologie
Laval University, Pavillon Pouliot, 4th floor,
Sainte Foy, Que. G1K 7P4. Tel: (418) 656-2131.
No charge. Open all year.

☐ Musée mineralogique et minier de Thetford Mines
711 Smith Blvd. South, Thetford Mines, Que.
G6G 5T3. Entrance fee. Open all year.
Tel: (418) 335-2123.

☐ Musée régional mines de Malartic
650 rue da la Paix, Abitibi East, Malartic, Que. J0Y
1Z0. Tel: (819) 757-4677. Entrance fee. Open all year.

☐ Earth Sciences Museum
University of Waterloo, Waterloo, Ont. N2L 3G1.
Tel: (519) 885-1211, ext. 2469. No charge.
Open weekdays from 8:30 am to 4:30 pm.
Web site: http://www.science.uwaterloo.ca/earth/
museum/museum.html.

☐ Miller Museum of Geology
Queen's University, Miller Hall, Kingston, Ont. K7L 3N6.
Tel: (613) 545-2597. No charge. Open all year.

☐ Oil Museum of Canada
2423 Kelly Road, Oil Springs, (35 km southeast of
Sarnia), Ont. N0N 1P0. Tel: (519) 834-2840. Entrance
fee. Open in summer and fall. Tours all year.

☐ The Petrolia Discovery Foundation
4381 Discovery Line, Petrolia, Ont. N0N 1R0.
Tel: (519) 882-0897. Entrance fee. Open in summer
and fall.

☐ Royal Ontario Museum, INCO Gallery of Earth Sciences
100 Queen's Park, Toronto, Ont. M5S 2C6.
Tel: (416) 586-5549. Entrance fee. Closed Christmas,
New Year's Day.

☐ Timmins Museum
70 Legion Drive, South Porcupine, Ont. P4N 1B3. Tel:
(705) 235-5066. No charge. Open all year.

Western Canada:

☐ Stonewall Quarry Park
200 North Main Street, Stonewall, Man. R0C 2Z0.
Tel: (204) 467-5354. Entrance fee. Open all year.

☐ Geological Museum
University of Saskatchewan, Geological Sciences
Building, Saskatoon, Sask. S7N 0W0.
Tel: (306) 966-5683. No charge. Open all year.

☐ Frank Slide Interpretive Centre
1 km north of Frank, Alta T0K 0E0.
Tel: (403) 562-7388. No charge. Open all year.

☐ Museum of Geology
University of Alberta, basement of Earth Sciences
Building, Edmonton, Alta T6G 2E3.
Tel: (403) 492-3265. No charge. Open all year.

☐ Royal Tyrrell Museum of Palaeontology
Hwy. 838, Midland Provincial Park, Drumheller, Alta
T0J 0Y0. Tel: (403) 823-7707. Entrance fee.
Open all year. Web site: http://www.tyrrell.com/.

☐ Dinosaur Provincial Park
Patricia, Alta T0J 2K0. Tel: (403) 378-4342.
No charge. Open all year.

☐ British Columbia Museum of Mining
PO Box 188, Britannia Beach, BC V0N 1J0.
Tel: (604) 896-2233. Entrance fee. Open in summer
and fall. All year for groups.

☐ M.Y. Williams Geological Museum
University of British Columbia, 6339 Stores Road,
Vancouver, BC V6T 2B4. Tel: (604) 228-5586.
No charge. Open all year.

☐ Princeton and District Museums
167 Vermilion Street, Princeton, BC V0X 1W0.
Tel: (250) 295-7588. No charge. Summer (June 30–
August 31.)

☐ Keno City Mining Museum
Centre Street, Keno City, Yukon Y0B 1M0.
Tel: (867) 995-2792. No charge. Open in summer.

PHYSICAL SCIENCES

Physics and chemistry constitute the physical sciences. **Chemistry** concerns itself with the composition, properties, and reactions of substances. Organic chemistry, one of the two main branches of chemistry, specializes in the composition, properties, and reactions of hydrocarbon compounds. The other branch, inorganic chemistry, deals primarily with the elements and compounds that do not include hydrocarbons. **Physics** concerns itself with universal aspects of nature—forces, energy, structure of matter, and their interactions. Some of its particular fields are: plasma physics, optics and quantum optics, particle physics, geophysics, biophysics, and acoustics. As basic sciences, physics and chemistry permeate all sciences and technologies.

Common Chemistry Terms

Acid: a substance that in liquid form will turn blue litmus paper red, react with alkalis (bases) to form salts, and dissolve metals to form salts.

Alkali: Any compound that has chemical qualities of a base, such as reacting with acid to form salts.

Atomic Weight (Mass): The relative mass of an atom, based on a scale in which a specific carbon atom is assigned a mass value of 12.

Base: an alkaline substance, either molecular or ionic in form, that will accept or receive a proton from another chemical unit.

Catalyst: a substance that accelerates a chemical reaction without becoming a part of the end product of the reaction.

Compound: A substance formed by the combination of two or more chemical elements that cannot be separated from the combination by physical means. The constituent atoms, however, can usually be separated by means of chemical reactions.

Electron: A negatively-charged particle that moves in orbit about the nucleus of an atom.

Element: A substance composed of atoms with the same atomic number or the same number of protons in their nuclei.

Isotope: One of two or more atoms having the same atomic number, but a different mass number.

Mass Number: the atomic weight of an isotope, calculated from the number of protons and neutrons in the nucleus.

Matter: Anything that has weight or fills space, such as a solid, liquid, or gas.

Polymer: a huge molecule composed of repeating units of the same molecule.

Valence: a number that represents the combining power of an element, ion, or radical.

Common Physics Terms

Acceleration: the rate of change of velocity with respect to time.

Anode: The positive terminal of an electric current flow. In a vacuum tube, electrons flow from the cathode to the anode.

Cathode: The negative terminal of an electric current system. In vacuum tube, the filament serves as the source electrons.

Conduction: the transfer of heat by molecular motion from a source of high temperature to a region of lower temperature, tending towards a result of equalized temperatures.

Convection: The mechanical transfer of heated molecules of a gas or liquid from a source to another area, as when a room is warmed by the movement of air molecules heated by a radiator.

Electromotive Force: The force that causes the movement of electrons through an electrical circuit.

Energy: the ability to perform work. Energy may be changed from one form to another, as from heat to light, but normally it cannot be created or destroyed.

Force: the influence on a body that causes it to accelerate.

Heat: A form of energy that results from the disordered motion of molecules. As the motion becomes more rapid and disordered, the amount of heat is increased.

Mass: a measure of the amount of matter. Near the surface of earth, it is roughly equivalent to weight.

Momentum: the mathematical product of the mass of a moving object and its velocity.

Velocity: The speed with which an object travels over a specified distance during a measured amount of time.

Weight: The force on a body produced by the downward pull of gravity on it.

Basic Laws of Physics

■ Newton's Laws of Motion

Newton's laws apply to objects in a vacuum, and are difficult to observe in the "real" world where forces such as friction affect all objects.

First Law: Any object at rest tends to stay at rest, and a body in motion will continue that motion with a constant velocity unless acted upon by some external unbalanced force.

Second Law: The acceleration of an object is directly proportional to the force acting upon it, and is inversely proportional to the mass of the object.

Third Law: Every action generates an equal and opposite reaction.

■ Gravity

When an object is dropped near the surface of the earth, it increases in speed as it falls. By rolling balls down inclined planes Galileo discovered that acceleration due to gravity is the same for all objects, independent of their weight (mass). For example, if you drop this book and a brick simultaneously, they will reach to floor at the same time. You can try the same experiment with a heavy book and a single sheet of paper. The paper is affected by the resistance of the air. Then crumple the paper, and try again.

Gravity is the force that tends to attract objects to the centre of a celestial body, such as the earth, the moon or Mars. The weight of an object at the earth's surface is mainly due to the force of gravity between the earth and the object. The force exerted by the earth varies with the object's distance from the centre of the earth. Therefore the weight of an object is not the same at the earth's surface as it is on the moon or in space.

■ Laws of Thermodynamics

Sadi Carnot (1796-1832) stated in his work *Reflections on the Motive Power of Fire* that mechanical energy could be produced by the simple transfer of heat.

First Law: In a closed system, energy appears to be conserved in all but nuclear reactions and other extreme conditions.

Second Law: In a closed system, heat never travels from a low to a higher temperature in a self sustaining process. In a closed system, entropy (disorder) always increases.

■ Two Basic Laws of Quantum Physics

Heisenberg's Uncertainty Principle: It is impossible to specify completely the position and momentum of a particle, such as an electron.

Pauli's Exclusion Principle: No two electrons of the same atom can have identical values for all four quantum numbers: at least one quantum number must be different.

Loudness of Sounds

Sound is measured in decibels. A decibel is a unit for measuring the relative intensity of a sound, equal to one-tenth of a bel. A bel indicates the amount of energy in the form of sound transmitted to one sq cm of the ear. The bel was named after Alexander Graham Bell.

The decibel scale advances geometrically instead of arithmetically. Twenty decibels represents not twice as much noise as ten, but 10 times as much. The 80-decibel level of a pneumatic drill is 100 times as noisy as the 60-decibel level of a quiet motor.

Source: *Dictionary of Science, Barnhardt, American Heritage Series*

Intensity (decibels)	Loudness	Intensity (decibels)	Loudness
0	Threshold of hearing	70	Loud conversation
10 (1 bel)	Virtual silence	80	Door slamming
20	Quiet room	90	Busy typing room
30	Watch ticking at 1 m	100	Near loud motor horn
40	Quiet street	110	Pneumatic drill
50	Quiet conversation	120	Near airplane engine
60	Quiet motor at 1 m	130	Threshold of pain

The Elements

(name, symbol and atomic number)

An element is a substance composed of atoms that are chemically alike—each atom has an identical number of protons in its nucleus. Furthermore, there is no known process to break these elements down into more fundamental substances.

Name	Symbol	Number	Name	Symbol	Number	Name	Symbol	Number
actinium	Ac	89	gold	Au	79	potassium	K	19
aluminum	Al	13	hafnium	Hf	72	praseodymium	Pr	59
americium	Am	95	hassium	Hs	108	promethium	Pm	61
antimony	Sb	51	helium	He	2	protactinium	Pa	91
argon	Ar	18	holmium	Ho	67	radium	Ra	88
arsenic	As	33	hydrogen	H	1	radon	Rn	86
astatine	At	85	indium	In	49	rhenium	Re	75
barium	Ba	56	iodine	I	53	rhodium	Rh	45
berkelium	Bk	97	iridium	Ir	77	rubidium	Rb	37
beryllium	Be	4	iron	Fe	26	ruthenium	Ru	44
bismuth	Bi	83	krypton	Kr	36	rutherfordium	Rf	104
bohrium	Bh	107	lanthanum	La	57	samarium	Sm	62
boron	B	5	lawrencium	Lr	103	scandium	Sc	21
bromine	Br	35	lead	Pb	82	seaborgium	Sg	106
cadmium	Cd	48	lithium	Li	3	selenium	Se	34
calcium	Ca	20	lutetium	Lu	71	silicon	Si	14
californium	Cf	98	magnesium	Mg	12	silver	Ag	47
carbon	C	6	manganese	Mn	25	sodium	Na	11
cerium	Ce	58	meitnerium	Mt	109	strontium	Sr	38
cesium	Cs	55	mendelevium	Md	101	sulfur	S	16
chlorine	Cl	17	mercury	Hg	80	tantalum	Ta	73
chromium	Cr	24	molybdenum	Mo	42	technetium	Tc	43
cobalt	Co	27	neodymium	Nd	60	tellurium	Te	52
copper	Cu	29	neon	Ne	10	terbium	Tb	65
curium	Cm	96	neptunium	Np	93	thallium	Tl	81
dubnium	Db	105	nickel	Ni	28	thorium	Th	90
dysprosium	Dy	66	niobium	Nb	41	thulium	Tm	69
einsteinium	Es	99	nitrogen	N	7	tin	Sn	50
erbium	Er	68	nobelium	No	102	titanium	Ti	22
europium	Eu	63	osmium	Os	76	tungsten	W	74
fermium	Fm	100	oxygen	O	8	ununnilium*	Uun	110
fluorine	F	9	palladium	Pd	46	unununium*	Uuu	111
francium	Fr	87	phosphorus	P	15	ununbium*	Uub	112
gadolinium	Gd	64	platinum	Pt	78	ununquadium*	Uuq	114
gallium	Ga	31	plutonium	Pu	94	ununhexium*	Uuh	116
germanium	Ge	32	polonium	Po	84	ununoctium*	Uuo	118
						uranium	U	92
						vanadium	V	23
						xenon	Xe	54
						ytterbium	Yb	70
						yttrium	Y	39
						zinc	Zn	30
						zirconium	Zr	40

*temporary name

What is the Periodic Table?

*T*he *Periodic Table of Elements (shown opposite) has its roots in the 19th century when chemists calculated how much one atom of an element weighed in comparison to another. The resulting weight was known as the atomic mass and measured in atomic mass units (amu). (An amu is a mass equal to 1/12 of the mass of the most common form of carbon atom.) As the list of elements was compiled and ranked in order of mass, chemists noted that every seven or eight elements had similar properties.*

By 1869 Dimitri Mendeleyev was confident enough to rearrange the list of elements to group those with similar properties and leave blanks for the missing ones. Mendeleyev only had 63 elements; the table now has 109 named elements (some artificially created) and at least six others have been found but not named.

Early in the 20th century, the table was further refined when atoms were found to be made up of protons and electrons. The number of protons and electrons is equal in one atom and this number was designated the element's atomic number. The table now shows the elements in order according to their atomic number and their atomic mass.

Periodic Table of Elements

gases

non-metals

other metals

transition metals

rare earth elements

Z	Symbol	Weight
1	H	1.00
2	He	4.00
3	Li	6.94
4	Be	9.01
5	B	10.81
6	C	12.01
7	N	14.01
8	O	15.99
9	F	18.99
10	Ne	20.18
11	Na	22.98
12	Mg	24.30
13	Al	26.98
14	Si	28.08
15	P	30.97
16	S	32.06
17	Cl	35.45
18	Ar	39.95
19	K	39.09
20	Ca	40.08
21	Sc	44.95
22	Ti	47.88
23	V	50.94
24	Cr	51.99
25	Mn	54.94
26	Fe	55.84
27	Co	58.93
28	Ni	58.69
29	Cu	63.54
30	Zn	65.39
31	Ga	69.72
32	Ge	72.61
33	As	74.92
34	Se	78.96
35	Br	79.90
36	Kr	83.80
37	Rb	85.46
38	Sr	87.62
39	Y	88.90
40	Zr	91.22
41	Nb	92.91
42	Mo	95.94
43	Tc	(98)
44	Ru	101.07
45	Rh	102.91
46	Pd	106.42
47	Ag	107.87
48	Cd	112.41
49	In	114.82
50	Sn	118.71
51	Sb	121.76
52	Te	127.60
53	I	126.90
54	Xe	131.29
55	Cs	132.90
56	Ba	137.33
71	Lu	174.97
72	Hf	178.49
73	Ta	180.95
74	W	183.84
75	Re	186.21
76	Os	190.2
77	Ir	192.22
78	Pt	195.08
79	Au	196.97
80	Hg	200.59
81	Tl	204.38
82	Pb	207.2
83	Bi	208.98
84	Po	(209)
85	At	(210)
86	Rn	(222)
87	Fr	(223)
88	Ra	226.02
103	Lr	(262)
104	Rf	(263)
105	Db	(262)
106	Sg	(266)
107	Bh	(264)
108	Hs	(269)
109	Mt	(268)
110	Uun	(272)
111	Uuu	(272)
112	Uub	(277)
114	Uuq	(289)
116	Uuh	(289)
118	Uuo	(293)

lanthanoids

Z	Symbol	Weight
57	La	138.91
58	Ce	140.12
59	Pr	140.91
60	Nd	144.24
61	Pm	(145)
62	Sm	150.36
63	Eu	151.96
64	Gd	157.25
65	Tb	158.93
66	Dy	162.50
67	Ho	164.93
68	Er	167.26
69	Tm	168.93
70	Yb	173.04

actinoids

Z	Symbol	Weight
89	Ac	227.03
90	Th	232.04
91	Pa	231.04
92	U	238.03
93	Np	237.05
94	Pu	(244)
95	Am	(243)
96	Cm	(247)
97	Bk	(247)
98	Cf	(251)
99	Es	(252)
100	Fm	(257)
101	Md	(258)
102	No	(259)

This is a table which shows the properties of the elements, in the order of their atomic mass or number, and arranged in horizontal rows (periods) and vertical columns (groups) to illustrate the occurrence of similarities in the structure of their atoms. When the elements are arranged in this order, their chemical and physical properties show repeatable trends. This pattern in properties occurs periodically; that is, the pattern is repeated in an orderly manner over time.

The order of the elements is that of their atomic numbers, the integers which are equal to the positive electrical charges of the atomic nuclei expressed in electronic units.

Elements that are listed with their atomic weights in brackets are radioactive and have variable weights. Since the various isotopes weigh differently at different times due to decay (that is, an isotope will be heavier at its creation than later on), the atomic mass of the most stable isotope is listed.

FOCUS ON...

Neutrino News

On June 18, 2001, physicists from Canada, the U.S. and the U.K. announced they had solved a 30-year-old puzzle—the mystery of the missing solar neutrinos. Canada's Sudbury Neutrino Observatory (SNO) showed that neutrinos change as they travel from the core of the Sun to the Earth.

The discovery means that the current understanding of what goes on in the interior of the Sun is more or less correct, but it also implies that neutrinos actually have a small amount of mass—something not predicted by the so-called Standard Model of sub-atomic physics. Neutrinos are tiny, neutral elementary particles that only interact with other matter via the weak nuclear force. The very weakness of the weak force means matter is almost transparent to neutrinos. The Sun produces enormous numbers of neutrinos—more than two hundred trillion trillion trillion neutrinos every second. But, since they rarely interact, these neutrinos pass through the Sun and the earth (and you) unhindered.

The existence of the neutrino was suggested by Wolfgang Pauli in 1930 as a solution to a nagging problem in a nuclear process called beta decay. In this process, it seemed that energy always went missing; Pauli suggested it was carried away by this hypothetical particle, which was dubbed the neutrino, or "little neutral one," by Enrico Fermi. It would be another 26 years before the first neutrino was detected.

In time, it was shown there were actually three types (called flavours) of neutrinos— the electron-neutrino (ne), the muon-neutrino (nu) and the tau-neutrino (nt). The Sun produces only electron-neutrinos.

About 30 years ago, Princeton physicist John Bahcall calculated how many electron-neutrinos should be produced by the Sun (a number called the neutrino flux) and experimenters set about trying to confirm his calculations. Indeed, experiments showed that neutrinos from the Sun were reaching the Earth—but not as many as predicted by the models. In fact, about two-thirds of the expected neutrinos were missing.

Two things could be wrong. Either the models of how the Sun behaves were incorrect, which would be a severe blow for theories that are otherwise very successful. Or the electron-neutrinos were somehow changing into one of the other flavours between here and the Sun—a phenomenon called "oscillation." This is not as weird as it sounds; something similar is known to happen with some other particles. But in order for oscillation to occur, the neutrinos must have at least some mass.

This was called the Solar Neutrino Problem—and the Sudbury Neutrino Observatory was built to solve it. Earlier observatories were unable to detect all three flavours of neutrinos, leaving open the possibility that some were being missed.

The construction of the Observatory began in 1990 and was completed in 1998 at a cost of $73 million. The detector was built 6,800 feet under ground, in INCO Limited's Creighton mine near Sudbury, Ont., where the rock screens out almost all particles except the neutrinos.

SNO is a heavy-water Cherenkov detector, which means that it relies on light flashes produced by the extremely rare collisions of neutrinos with other particles—only about 10 a day. The particles in question are in 1,000 tonnes of heavy water—a rare, natural variant of water whose hydrogen atoms have an extra neutron. The heavy water is contained in a 12-metre diameter acrylic vessel.

Neutrinos react with the heavy water to produce flashes of light called Cherenkov radiation. This light is then detected by an array of 9,600 photomultiplier tubes mounted on a geodesic support structure surrounding the heavy water vessel. The detector is immersed in light (normal) water within a 10-storey-high barrel-shaped cavity excavated from Norite rock. The detector laboratory is extremely clean to reduce background signals from radioactive elements present in the mine dust, which would otherwise hide the very weak signal from neutrinos.

The Observatory began taking data in April, 1999. A little more than two years later, researchers presented their initial results at the Canadian Association of

Physicists Annual Conference at Victoria, B.C. The findings were the first direct evidence for neutrino oscillation.

The result is important because there are so many neutrinos that even a small mass for each one would enable them to have an effect on the evolution of the Universe through their gravitational effects. Indeed, the SNO team was able to say that the sum of the masses of all three was more than 0.05 electron-volts (eV) and less than 8.4 eV. (For such tiny masses, scientists usually use energy values, relying on the well-known link between energy and matter defined by Albert Einstein. An electron-volt is so little energy it would take more than 600 million trillion eV per second to light a 100-watt light bulb.)

"Even though there is an enormous number of neutrinos in the universe, the mass limits show that neutrinos make up only a small fraction of the total mass and energy content," says Hamish Robertson, a U.S. member of the SNO team and professor of physics at the University of Washington in Seattle.

Detecting neutrinos from the sun is also a way to see the sun's interior. The neutrinos produced in the core of the sun escape unhindered; this is why SNO is often referred to as the "window on the sun," since the neutrinos act as a probe on the mechanisms in the solar core.

"We now have high confidence that the discrepancy (in neutrinos) is not caused by problems with the models of the Sun but by changes in the neutrinos themselves as they travel from the core of the Sun to the Earth," said Art McDonald, SNO Project Director and professor of physics at Queen's University in Kingston, Ont. "Earlier measurements had been unable to provide definitive results showing that this transformation from solar electron neutrinos to other types occurs. The new results from SNO, combined with previous work, now reveal this transformation clearly, and show that the total number of electron neutrinos produced in the Sun are just as predicted by detailed solar models."

The finding that electron-neutrinos from the Sun transform into neutrinos of another type is very important for a full understanding of the Universe at the most microscopic level. This oscillation of neutrino types is not allowed in the Standard Model of elementary particles—so theoreticians will now be spending sleepless nights trying to find the best way to incorporate this new data into more comprehensive theories.

As their first results were being announced, the SNO scientists began the next phase of their measurements, by adding salt to the heavy water. This will allow them to study another neutrino reaction with deuterium that provides a large sensitivity to all neutrino types. Their further measurements can address the transformation of neutrino type with even greater sensitivity, as well as studying other properties of neutrinos, of the Sun and supernovae.

How does the sun shine?

*I*n the 19th century, eminent scientists, such as Lord Kelvin and Hermann von Helmholtz, thought that the energy produced by gravitational contraction caused the sun to shine. But that energy could only account for about 30 million years of existence—and geological evidence was pointing to a much greater age for the earth and therefore the sun.

The first hint of the correct answer came with the discovery of radioactivity, followed early in the 20th century by the theory of relativity and quantum mechanics. Key was the finding that four hydrogen atoms weigh more than one helium atom; if hydrogen atoms fused together to form helium, the excess mass (in the form of energy) would be enough to power the sun for billions of years.

But it would take enormous energy to cause hydrogen atoms to fuse. Where could that energy have come from? According to the modern theory of stellar evolution, the sun is heated to the enormous temperatures at which nuclear fusion can occur by gravitational energy released as the solar mass contracts from a large gas cloud. So the 19th-century physicists were partly right; gravitational energy ignited nuclear fusion in the sun.

Source: *www.nobel.se/physics/articles*

The International System of Units (SI)

The Systeme Internationale (SI) or metric system was developed in France in 1799. By 1880 many European countries and much of South America had adopted the system as a common language of measurements.

The pressures of global trade have persuaded many of the English-speaking countries to adopt a uniform international standard of measure. Canada adopted the metric system in 1970.

Name	Symbol	Quantity
■ SI Base Units		
metre	m	length
kilogram	kg	mass
second	s	time
ampere	A	electric current
kelvin	K	thermodynamic temperature
mole	mol	amount of substance
candela	cd	luminous intensity
■ SI Supplementary Units		
radian	rad	plane angle
steradian	sr	solid angle
■ Common SI Derived Units With Special Names		
hertz	Hz	frequency
pascal	Pa	pressure, stress
watt	W	power, radiant flux
volt	V	electric potential, electromotive force
newton	N	force
joule	J	energy, work
coulomb	C	electric charge
ohm	Ω	electric resistance
farad	F	electric capacitance
■ Common Units Used With the SI		
litre	L	volume or capacity $(= 1\ dm^3)$
degree Celsius	°C	temperature $(= 1\ K;\ 0°C = 273.2\ K)$

hectare	ha	area $(= 10\ 000\ m^2)$
tonne	t	mass $(= 1000\ kg)$
electronvolt	eV	energy $(= 0.160\ aJ)$
nautical mile	M	distance (navigation) $(= 1852\ m)$
knot	kn	speed (navigation) $(= 1\ M/h)$
standard atmosphere	atm	atmospheric pressure $(= 101.3\ kPa)$

■ SI Prefixes

Name	Symbol	Multiplying Factor*
exa-	E	10^{18}
peta-	P	10^{15}
tera-	T	10^{12}
giga-	G	10^9
mega-	M	10^6
kilo-	k	10^3
hecto-	h	10^2
deca-	da	10
deci-	d	10^{-1}
centi-	c	10^{-2}
milli-	m	10^{-3}
micro-	μ	10^{-6}
nano-	n	10^{-9}
pico-	p	10^{-12}
femto-	f	10^{-15}
atto-	a	10^{-18}

*$10^2 = 100$; $10^3 = 1\ 000$; $10^{-1} = 0.1$; $10^{-2} = 0.01$; Thus, 2 km = 2 x 1 000 = 2 000 m ; 3 cm = 3 x 0.01 = 0.03 m

Source: *Gage Canadian Dictionary*

Large Numbers

1 thousand	1 000
1 million	1 000 000 or 10^6
1 milliard: used in Europe, USSR, former French possessions	1 000 000 000 or 10^9
1 billion:	1 000 000 000 000 or 10^{12}
—Canada, the United States and France	1 000 000 000 or 10^9
1 trillion:	1 000 000 000 000 000 000 or 10^{18}
—Canada and the United States	1 000 000 000 000 or 10^{12}

Source: *World Weights and Measures*

Science Centres and Museums

Maritime Region:

☐ **Discovery Centre**
1593 Barrington Street, Halifax, NS. Entrance fee.
Open daily. Tel: (902) 492-4422, Fax: (902) 492-3170
Web site: http://www.discoverycentre.ns.ca.

☐ **Electrical Engineering Museum**
University of New Brunswick, Dept. of Electrical
Engineering, Head Hall, Fredericton, NB No charge.
Open winter, spring and fall.

☐ **Nova Scotia Museum of Industry**
147 Foord Street, Stellarton, NS B0K 1S0.
Entrance fee. Open daily. Tel: (902) 755-5425.
Web site: http://www.museum.gov.ns.ca/moi/index.htm.

Central Canada:

☐ **Museum of Visual Science and Optometry**
University of Waterloo, Optometry Building,
Columbia Street, Waterloo, Ont. N2L 3G1.
Tel: (519) 885-1211, ext. 3405. No charge.
Open all year.Web site:
http://www.optometry.uwaterloo.ca/~museum.

☐ **Hamilton Museum of Steam and Technology**
900 Woodward Avenue, Hamilton, Ont. L8H 7N2.
Tel: (416) 549-5225. Entrance fee. Open all year.

☐ **National Museum of Science and Technology**
1867 St. Laurent Blvd., Ottawa, Ont. K1G 5A3.
Tel: (613) 991-3044. Entrance fee. Open all year.
Web site: http://science-tech.nmstc.ca/.

☐ **Ontario Science Centre**
770 Don Mills Road, Toronto, Ont. M3C 1T3.
Tel : (416) 696-1000. Open daily (except Christmas Day).
Web site: http://www.osc.on.ca/.

☐ **Science North**
100 Ramsay Lake Road, Sudbury, Ont. P3E 5S9.
Tel: (705) 522-3700 Entrance fee. Open all year.
Web site: http://www.sciencenorth.on.ca.

Western Canada:

☐ **Calgary Science Centre**
701-11 Street SW, Calgary, Alta T2P 2M5.
Tel: (403) 221-3700, Fax: (403) 237-0186
No charge. Open all year, closed Mondays.
Web site: http://www.calgaryscience.ca.

☐ **Edmonton Space and Science Centre**
11211-142 Street, Edmonton, Alta T5M 4A1.
Tel: (403) 452-9100, Fax: (403) 455-5882.
Entrance fee. Open all year.
Web site: http://www.planet.con.net/~essc/start.html.

☐ **Energeum**
640-5th Avenue S.W., Main Floor, Energy Resources
Building, Calgary, Alta T2P 3G4. Tel: (403) 297-4293,
Fax: (403) 297-3757. No charge. Open all year.

☐ **The Interior Space and Science Centre**
2704 Highway 6, Vernon, BC V1T 5G5. Tel: & Fax:
(250) 545-3644. No charge. Open all year, Monday
to Friday.

☐ **Saskatchewan Science Centre**
Winnipeg Street and Wascana Drive, Regina, Sask.
S4P 3M3. Entrance fee. Open all year.
Tel: 1 800 667-6300 or (306) 791-7900.
Web site: http://www.sciencecentre.sk.ca.

☐ **Science World**
1455 Quebec Street, Vancouver, BC V6A 3Z7.
Tel: (604) 443-7440, Fax: (604) 443-7430.
Entrance fee. Open daily, except Christmas Day.
Web site: www.scienceworld.bc.ca.

A Concrete Solution?

*E*very year, human beings use 5 billion tonnes of concrete worldwide. This makes for strong
buildings, but it has a significant downside: making Portland cement, the key ingredient of
concrete, releases vast quantities of carbon dioxide into the atmosphere.

That's why Professor Moncef Nehdi of the University of Western Ontario, under a grant
from the Natural Sciences and Engineering Research Council, is trying to alter the make-up of
concrete to minimize the need for Portland cement.

Portland cement is mainly limestone, together with other materials containing aluminum and
silica. The raw materials are ground, heated until they fuse, and then cooled into a "clinker"
that is crushed to a fine powder. But during the heating, carbon dioxide is given off: estimates
are that production of Portland cement will reach 2 billion tonnes by 2010, and making that
much cement will release about 2 billion tonnes of carbon dioxide.

Nehdi is trying to use large volumes of recycled mineral waste to produce an economic and
environmentally efficient self-compacting concrete that will also have a low cement content,
meaning less carbon dioxide released into the atmosphere.
Source: *NSERC*

SCIENCE AT WORK

Individual Canadians have been awarded recognition in the ranks of the world's preeminent scientists and researchers, as our lists of Nobel Prize winners and the Canadian Engineering and Science Hall of Fame both show.

Canadian Nobel Laureates in Science and Medicine

1923	Drs. Banting, Macleod and Collip	Medicine and Physiology	For the discovery of insulin
1971	Dr. Gerhard Herzberg	Chemistry	For his contributions to the knowledge of electronic structure, particularly free radicals
1986	Dr. John Polanyi	Chemistry	For contributions concerning the dynamics of elementary chemical reactions
1993	Dr. Michael Smith	Chemistry	Co-winner for work on genetic codes
1994	Bertram Brockhouse	Physics	Co-winner for study on atoms

Canadian Science and Engineering Hall of Fame

The inductees into the Canadian Science and Engineering Hall of Fame are outstanding researchers, inventors, and innovators who have won worldwide recognition for their accomplishments. The Hall of Fame portrait gallery is located at the NRC laboratories on Sussex Drive in Ottawa. Inductees are announced each October. The Hall of Fame web site can be accessed at http://www.nrc.ca.

The Inductees

Maude Abbott (1869–1940) . . . . Pathologist and specialist in congenital heart disease
Sir Frederick Banting (1891–1941) . . . . Co-discoverer of insulin; Nobel laureate
Alexander Graham Bell (1847–1922) . . . . . . Inventor of the telephone
J. Armand Bombardier (1907–1964) . . . . Inventor of the snowmobile
Bertram Brockhouse (1918–) . . . . Physicist who pioneered use of neutron scattering in study of atoms
Douglas Harold Copp (1915–1998) . . . . Discoverer of calcitonin, a hormone used in the treatment of osteoporosis
Reginald Fessenden (1866–1932) . . . . Pioneer in the development of the radio
Sir Sanford Fleming (1827–1915) . . . . Architect of the transcontinental railway; inventor of time zones
Gerald Heffernan (1919–) . . . . Innovation in steel production, developer of the environment-friendly "mini-mill"
Gerhard Herzberg (1904–99) . . . . Astrophysicist and Nobel laureate
Harold Elford Johns (1915–1998) . . . . Developer of the cobalt-60 cancer therapy unit in 1951.
George J. Klein (1904–92) . . . . Design engineer, the most productive inventor in 20th century Canada
Hugh Le Caine (1914–77) . . . . Physicist; designed the first musical synthesizer
Sir William Logan (1798–1875) . . . . First director of the Geological Survey of Canada
Elizabeth "Elsie" MacGill (1905–80) . . . . . . Aeronautical engineer, oversaw WWII production of Hawker Hurricane fighter aircraft
Frances G. McGill (1877–1959) . . . . Pioneer in forensic pathology
Frère Marie-Victorin (1885–1944) . . . . Botanist, author and teacher
Andrew G.L. MacNaughton (1887–1966) . . . Inventor of cathode-ray detection finder and military leader
Margaret Newton (1887–1971) . . . . Plant pathologist, who developed techniques to combat wheat rust
Joseph-Alphonse Ouimet (1908–88) . . . . . . Inventor, engineer and CBC president
Wilder Penfield (1891–1976) . . . . Neurosurgeon who developed surgical treatments for epilepsy
John Polanyi (1929–) . . . . Nobel laureate; contributed to the development of laser chemistry
Charles E. Saunders (1867–1937) . . . . Developed fast-ripening Marquis wheat
Michael Smith (1932–2000) . . . . Chemistry researcher, genetic codes and DNA
Edgar William Richard Steacie (1900–62) . . Researcher (free radical chemistry), and educator
Wallace Turnbull (1870–1954) . . . . Inventor of the variable pitch propellor

Source: *National Research Council*

The National Research Council

Canada's National Research Council was established in 1916, with the country at war and millions of men and women serving overseas. The NRC's goal was to develop Canadian science—a goal that is still its focus. Some highlights from the NRC's history:

1916-1927: Magnesite, a mineral used in the coating of high-temperature industrial furnaces, was imported for years because domestic ores weren't pure enough. NRC-financed researchers found a simple way of eliminating the impurities, so Canada could cut its dependence on imports.

1928-1932: From 1924 to 1938, Canadian medical researchers worked with the NRC to find a vaccine against tuberculosis. Their work helped make the BCG vaccine the main weapon against the disease.

George Klein (1904-1992), a Canadian inventor and a longtime NRC employee, produced an almost endless list of inventions: aircraft skis, an electric wheelchair for quadriplegics, a microsurgery staple gun and a retractable antenna that is still standard equipment on satellites

1933-1945: The NRC helped develop radar (for "radio distance and ranging") during World War II. Today, radar is essential to make travel safer by air, land and sea.

Before World War II began, the NRC enlisted **Sir Frederick Banting**, the discoverer of insulin, to lead research on combat-related medicine. Banting's team worked on wound infections, shock, penicillin, a typhus vaccine, blood substitutes and plastic surgery.

1946-1952: The NRC's Harry Stevinson developed a reliable emergency locator beacon for downed aircraft. In 1957, the Crash Position Indicator was introduced for military use, and by 1960 was available for commercial aircraft.

If you or someone you know wears a **pacemaker**, the technology that made it possible was developed by the NRC in the late 1940s by Jack Hopps.

1953-1963: In 1958, the NRC built one of the world's earliest cesium beam atomic clocks—accurate to a few millionths of a second per year. By the 1970s, NRC time was being used to set official time scales and clocks around the world.

Canola oil, which can sometimes take the place of butter on popcorn, is used to make margarine, cooking oils, lubricants and inks. In the 1940s, the NRC worked helped to develop a hybrid canola plant, and today canola is one of Canada's leading cash crops.

1964-1971: In 1971, Dr. Gerhard Herzberg of the NRC won a Nobel Prize in chemistry for his work in identifying molecules in space.

If you've ever played a **synthesizer**, you owe the experience to an NRC scientist. Hugh Le Caine invented the first one in the world 1945.

1972-1980: In 1973, the NRC opened a centre to retrieve and analyse data from flight recorders (more commonly known as black boxes).

Also in 1973, the **Canada-France-Hawaii Telescope** opened, high on the frigid, barren top of the Hawaiian volcano Mauna Kea. It can produce images almost as sharp as those from the Hubble Space Telescope—and it's much easier to repair.

1981-1989: The NRC developed an optical security patch that changes colour in different lights. The patch is used on paper money and drivers' licences to prevent counterfeiting.

Saran Narang made a major medical breakthrough when he produced **synthetic insulin** for use by diabetics.

1990-2001: In May 1996, Canadian astronaut Marc Garneau retrieved a satellite in flight using the CANADARM—with the help of the Space Vision System, a technology developed by the NRC.

In the early 1990s, NRC experts introduced various fingerprint detection methods that are still used by the RCMP and other police forces.

A Whiff of the Future

*T*he National Research Council's specialists don't like to rest on their laurels. After developing a bomb sniffer in the 1970s, which received recognition worldwide as the best way to find hidden bombs, they started looking at new ideas. Researchers saw the sniffer was perfect to detect things such as drugs; the Trace Narcotics Detector is now used by law enforcement agencies in Canada, the U.S. and the Middle East. The next step? Sniffers that combine vapour-sampling techniques with a new technology called ion mobility spectroscopy, in order to detect the freshness of seafood or identify tree species for harvesting.

2000 Nobel Prize Winners

Each October the Swedish academies for physics, chemistry and medicine announce the winners of the Nobel Prizes in science. The awards are named after Alfred Nobel, the Swedish-born chemist and businessman who invented dynamite and smokeless gunpowder. The science prizes, as well as a prize for literature and one for peace, are financed by an endowment from Nobel's estate. The prize for economics is financed by the Swedish national bank. Korea's Kim Dae Jung won the peace prize for reconciliation with North Korea. Gao Xingjian of China won the literature prize. The economics prize went to James J. Heckman for contributions to the theory selective sample analysis and to Daniel L. McFadden for contributing to the theory of discrete choice.

The 2000 prize in **chemistry** went to Alan Heeger of the University of California, Alan MacDiarmid of the University of Pennsylvania, and Hideki Shirakawa of the University of Tsukuba for the discovery of conductive polymers.

The **physics** prize was awarded to Zhores Alferov of the Ioffe Physico-Technical Institute and Herbert Kroemer of the University of California for developing new semiconductors used in high-speed electronics and to Jack Kilby of Texas Instruments Inc. for his part in inventing integrated circuits.

The **medicine and physiology** prize went to Arvid Carlsson of the University of Goteborg, Paul Greengard of Rockefeller University, and Eric Kandel of Columbia University for discoveries about signal transduction in the nervous system.

> The offical Web site of the Nobel Foundation can be found at http://www.nobel.se. The site offers information on The Nobel Foundation, the various institutions that award the prizes and an Electronic Nobel Museum Project that allows browsers to look into a searchable database of all the prizes and winners; take a virtual tour of some Nobel facilities and access a library of related books and papers.
>
> There is also a Nobel Internet Archive (not affiliated with The Nobel Foundation) that can be searched by category, year or name. Winners biographies can also be accessed at this site. It can be found at http://www.nobelprizes.com.

2000 Manning Award Winners

The Manning Awards recognize and encourage innovation in Canada by honouring individuals who have created and promoted a new concept, process or product which is beneficial to society. Administered by the Calgary-based Ernest C. Manning Foundation, the awards are presented annually. For the 2001 winners, visit http://www.manningawards.ca.

PRINCIPAL AWARD: Pierre Côté of Oakville, Ont. for his development of ZeeWeed, a unique filtration membrane that represents a revolution in water treatment. ZeeWeed can be used to purify water, including the treatment of ground or surface water for drinking or the purification of municipal and industrial wastewater before discharge to the environment.

AWARD OF DISTINCTION: Abraham Friedman, of Montreal, PQ, for his development of the Grow Home, a narrow-front rowhouse that has enabled Canadians with annual incomes as low as $25,000 to become homeowners. To date, more than 10,000 units have been built in Canada.

INNOVATION AWARD: Quinn Holtby of Edmonton, Alta for developing a comprehensive oil well bore fluid containment system for drilling and service rigs known as the "Kelly Kan/Katch Kan." His system has allowed the petroleum industry to create a cleaner, dryer and safer work environment and prevents environmental damage at the wellsite.

Fred Marsh of Kamloops, B. C. for the Marsh Flexible Goal Peg System—a safer system to hold goal nets in place. Under normal conditions, the pegs bend and return to their original position. But with a strong impact, the net pops off the pegs, preventing serious injury to the player. This successful system was adopted by the NHL and has been in use since 1991.

YOUNG CANADIAN INNOVATION AWARDS:
Erin Stewart, Chatham, Ont. (knee pad to prevent patellofemoral syndrome); Avaleigh Milne and Travis Beamish,Kingston, Ont. (impacts of anesthetics on the human body); David Laflamme, Sherbrooke, PQ (testing effects of an extract of Ginkgo Biloba); Alex McKelvey, Toronto, Ont.(developing a wireless and comprehensive email system.)

Source: *The Manning Awards*

Patents

If you have an idea for a new gizmo, what is required to have it patented? The Patent Office judges the idea based the following criteria:

1) the gizmo must be the first of its kind in the world;
2) the gizmo must be useful, and most importantly, it must work;
3) the gizmo must be obviously ingenious to others familiar with the field.

A patent gives you the right to exclude others from making, using or selling an invention from the day the patent is granted until 20 years after filing. Patents also provide useful technical information to the public. Although individual inventors still apply for patents, the majority of applications now come from large corporations. Patents are granted by individual countries; so the protection of a Canadian patent extends throughout Canada alone. Patent rights in the United States or elsewhere must be applied for separately in the individual countries.

A Canadian patent application can be filed from any Canada Post outlet across the country. Detailed information on the application procedure for Patents, Trademarks, Copyrights and Industrial and Integrated Circuits Designs can be obtained from the Canadian Intellectual Property Office in Hull, Québec. (819) 953-7620.

There are now a number of World Wide Web sites that are of interest to inventors. These include:

The Canadian Intellectual Property Office (CIPO)
http://cipo.gc.ca
CIPO's web site has information on Canadian Patents, Trademarks, Copyrights, Industrial Designs and Integrated Circuit Topographies. Trademarks can now be filed on line.

The Canadian Innovation Centre
http://www.innovationcentre.ca
The Canadian Innovation Centre is a not-for-profit corporation dedicated to helping Canadians commercialize their technological innovations. (The Centre issues a publication, *Eureka!*, quarterly.)

Canadian Technology Network
http://www.nrc.ca/ctn
Part of the National Reseearch Council site, CTN gives small and medium-sized technology businesses access to a cross-country network of expert advisors.

US Patent and Trademark Office
http://www.uspto.gov/
General information about US Patents and Trademarks is available, and the site has direct links to other national patent offices.

The Centre for Networked Information Discovery and Retrieval (CNIDR-US Patent Project)
http://patents.cnidr.org
You can access the US Patent Classifications Database at this site. You can also access the patent database and do a search for existing patents.

Research Chairs Program

I *n the 2000 federal budget, the Government of Canada set aside $900 million to establish 2,000 Canada Research Chairs in universities across the country by 2005; about 400 researchers will be named to the new chairs each year. The goal is to help Canadian universities, together with their affiliated research institutes and hospitals, to become world-class research centres by providing funds so they can recruit top researchers. There are two types of appointments: seven-year renewable Chairs, to be filled by established research leaders, and five-year Chairs, to be filled by up-and-coming young researchers who have the potential to be leaders.*

FOCUS ON...

Synchrotrons

They're calling it the "field of beams"—the football field-sized, $173.5-million Canadian Light Source (CLS). The project, now under construction in Saskatoon, is the largest science project in Canada in 30 years. It is scheduled for completion in 2003 and will begin operating as a non-profit research facility in 2004.

At the heart of the CLS project is a state-of-the-art, third-generation **synchrotron**, a device that produces light—mainly X-rays—of such brightness and energy that they can be used for unprecedented scientific and technological research.

Like a giant microscope, this brilliant light source allows matter to be examined at the atomic scale—from cross-sectional images of a mosquito's knee to the nanosecond-by-nanosecond behaviour of protein molecules such as antibodies.

In the synchrotron, electrons are accelerated to nearly the speed of light and forced into a circular path by magnets. As they speed along this curved path, the electrons emit bright infrared, ultraviolet and X-ray light, which is directed down "beamlines" to work stations where researchers do their experiments. Ultimately, up to 50 different experiments could be carried out at one time.

This relatively new light source will be used to probe the structure of matter, investigate chemical reactions, develop new drugs, design new microchips for more powerful computers, manufacture tiny biomedical implants and create new materials such as stronger metal alloys for airplane wings.

Worldwide, about 70 percent of all beam time on synchrotrons is used for materials research. Synchrotron light has been used to explore the properties of materials as diverse as semi-conductors, glass, muscle fibres and plastics.

The ultrabright X-rays are being used to help industry develop solvent-free paints,

find new ways to manufacture biodegradable plastics that could be eaten by bugs, and study the surfaces and interfaces between materials (research which can help tackle corrosion problems in cars, planes and pipelines.

There are also medical and biotechnological uses, such as determining the three-dimensional structure of proteins, knowledge that might lead to new and better drugs or perhaps increase the winter hardiness of wheat. Recent preliminary research published in the peer-reviewed journal *Nature* suggests that synchrotron analysis of a single hair from a woman may reveal whether she has breast cancer.

The project was officially launched in the fall of 1999, but it was the culmination of years of planning, negotiation and hard work. Though the word synchrotron is still new to many Canadians, scientists have been calling for a Canadian synchrotron since the mid-1970s.

But Canada continued to be without such a facility, forcing those researchers who wished to use synchrotron light to travel elsewhere. Then, in early 1996, the Natural Sciences and Engineering Research Council began reviewing proposals for a homegrown synchrotron. The CLS project began as a collaborative venture between the University of Saskatchewan, the City of Saskatoon, the Province of Saskatchewan and the Government of Canada. In 1999, the Canada Foundation for Innovation (CFI) got the project off the ground with a grant of $56.4 million.

According to a 1996 study, the CLS will attract $35 million annually to Canada in commercial research and development spending, add almost $122 million to Canada's gross domestic product during construction and $12 million per year once the facility becomes operational. It will also create 200 permanent jobs.

To find out more, visit the CLS website: http://www.cls.usask.ca.

ATMOSPHERIC SCIENCE

A Glossary of Weather Terms

Air mass: an extensive body of air with a fairly uniform distribution of moisture and temperature throughout.

Alberta clipper: named after the clipper sailing ships, which at one time were the fastest vessels on the seas. These storms zip along at 64 km/h, preceded by about 5 cm of light, powdery snow and followed by violent winds capable of reaching 100 km/h. This often results in severe blowing and drifting with blizzard conditions that can leave many roads impassable.

Atmosphere: the envelope of air surrounding the earth. Most weather events are confined to the lower 10 km of the atmosphere.

Atmospheric pressure: the force exerted on the earth by the weight of the atmosphere.

Blizzard: severe winter weather condition characterized by low temperatures, strong winds above 40 km/h, and visibility of less than 1 km due to blowing snow; condition lasts three hours or more.

Blowing snow: snow lifted from the earth's surface by the wind to a height of two metres or more. Blowing snow is higher than drifting snow.

Bright sunshine: sunshine intense enough to burn a mark on recording paper mounted in the Campbell-Stokes sunshine recorder. The daily period of bright sunshine is less than that of visible sunshine because the sun's rays are not intense enough to burn the paper just after sunrise, near sunset and under cloudy conditions.

Chinook (also snow-eater): a dry, warm, strong wind that blows down the eastern slopes of the Rocky Mountains in North America. The warmth and dryness are due principally to heating by compression as the air descends the mountain slope.

Cold wave: an occurrence of dangerous cold conditions, when temperatures often dip below -18°C, that usually lasts longer than a few days.

Crepuscular rays: clouds to excite any sky photographer. Crepuscular rays are caused by streaks or beams of sunlight shining through openings in large cumulonimbus clouds on the horizon. The beams reach down and outward from behind the clouds. If they focus upward, toward a point in the sky opposite the sun, they are called anticrepuscular rays. Sometimes they are called sun beams crossing the sky or Jacob's ladder. Sailors refer to them as "the sun drawing water." The dark bands you see crossing the sky are the shadows from clouds.

Cyclone: a generic term that describes all classes of storms from local thunderstorms and tiny dust devils to monstrous hurricanes and typhoons. It comes from the Greek word, *kyklon*, meaning cycle, circle or coil of a snake and refers to all circular wind systems.

Deep low: used to describe the central barometric pressure of a low [usually when it is about 975 millibars (97.50 kPa or less)]. Often has winds of gale to storm force around the low.

Developing low: a low in which the central pressure is decreasing with time. Winds would normally increase as the low deepens.

Dew point temperature: the temperature at which air becomes saturated, allowing condensation of water vapour as frost, fog, dew, mist or precipitation.

Drizzle: precipitation consisting of numerous minute water droplets which appear to float; the droplets are much smaller than in rain.

El Niño: Near the end of most years, the normally cold Peru Current that sweeps northward along the South American coast from southern Chile to the equator is replaced by a warm southward flowing coastal current. Centuries ago the local fishermen named this the "Christ child current," because it appeared around the Christmas season. Every few years it was unusually intense and over time the term El Niño became more closely associated with occasional intense warmings.

Filling low: a low in which the central pressure is increasing with time., i.e. the low is gradually weakening.

Flash floods: a very rapid rise of water with little or no advance warning, most often when an intense thunderstorm drops a huge rainfall on a fairly small area in a very short space of time.

Fog: a cloud based at the earth's surface consisting of tiny water droplets or, under very cold conditions, ice crystals or ice fog; generally found in calm or low wind conditions. Under foggy conditions, visibility is reduced to less than one km. ▶

Frazil ice: [French Canadian] during the freeze-up period ice forms on the river surface and ice crystals or frazil develop within the river, especially in open turbulent water slightly below 0°C. Frazil ice is very common in rapids.

Freezing precipitation: supercooled water drops of drizzle, or rain which freeze on impact to form a coating of ice upon the ground or any objects they strike.

Front: the boundary between two different air masses which have originated from widely separated regions. A cold front is the leading edge of an advancing cold air mass, while a warm front is the trailing edge of a retreating cold air mass.

Frost: the deposit of ice crystals that occurs when the air temperature is at or below the freezing point of water. The term frost is also used to describe the icy deposits of water vapor that may form on the ground or on other surfaces like car windshields, which are colder than the surrounding air and which have a temperature below freezing.

Gale: a strong wind. A gale warning is issued for expected winds of 65 to 100 km/h (34 to 47 knots).

Gust: a sudden, brief increase in wind speed, for generally less than 20 seconds.

Heat wave: a period with more than three consecutive days of maximum temperatures at or above 32°C.

High pressure: a term for an area of high (maximum) pressure with a closed, clockwise (in the Northern Hemisphere) circulation of air.

Humidex: a measure of what hot weather "feels like." Air of a given temperature and moisture content is equated in comfort to air with a higher temperature and that of negligible moisture content. At a humidex of 30°C some people begin to experience discomfort. [*see* chart on p. 591.]

Hurricanes: tropical systems are classed into several categories depending on maximum strength, usually measured by maximum sustained wind speed. A *tropical disturbance* is simply a moving area of thunderstorms in the tropics that maintains its identity for 24 hours or more. A *tropical depression* is a cyclonic system originating over the tropics with a highest sustained wind speed of up to 61 km/h. A *tropical storm* has a highest sustained wind speed of between 62 and 117 km/h. A *hurricane* has wind speeds of 118 km/h or more.

Ice pellets: precipitation consisting of fragments of ice, 5 mm or less in diameter, that bounce when hitting a hard surface, making a sound upon impact.

Inversion: the term refers to a temperature increase with height, where the usual pattern is a decrease in temperature within increasing height.

Isobar: a line on a weather map or chart connecting points of equal pressure. The large concentric lines on television or newspaper weather maps are isobars.

Killing frost: a frost severe enough to end the growing season, usually when the air temperature falls below -2°C.

Land breeze: a small-scale wind set off when the air temperature over water is warmer than that over adjacent land. The land breeze develops at night and blows from the land out to the sea or onto the lake. Its counterpart is the sea or lake breeze.

Low pressure: an area of low (minimum) atmospheric pressure that has a closed counter-clockwise circulation in the Northern Hemisphere.

Peak wind (gust): the highest instantaneous wind speed recorded for a specific time period.

Plough winds: these belong to a family of strong, straight-line downburst winds found in thunderstorms. These winds rush to the ground with great force, maybe 100 to 150 km/h and occasionally even higher. Damage usually covers an area less than 3 km across. Plough winds are capable of toppling trees, lifting roofs, and ripping apart houses and other structures.

Precipitation: any and all forms of water, whether liquid or solid, that fall from the atmosphere and reach the earth's surface. A day with measurable precipitation is a day when the water equivalent of the precipitation is equal to or greater than 0.2 mm.

Probability of precipitation (POP): subjective numerical estimates of your chances of encountering measurable precipitation at some time during the forecast period. For example, a 40% probability of rain means there are four chances in 10 of getting wet. They cannot be used to predict when, where or how much precipitation will occur.

Relative humidity: the ratio of water vapour in the air at a given temperature to the maximum which could exist at that temperature. It is usually expressed as a percentage.

Ridge: an elongated area of high pressure extending from the centre of a high pressure region; the opposite of a trough. ▶

Sea breeze: a small-scale wind set off when the air temperature over land is greater than that over the adjacent sea. The sea breeze develops during the day and blows from the sea to the land. Its counterpart is the land breeze.

Sleet: is not what you think. In the United States, sleet is frozen raindrops that bounce when they hit the surface. It is not as treacherous to drive on as is freezing rain. What Americans call sleet a Canadian would call ice pellets or frozen raindrops. They are spherical or irregular shapes with a diameter of 5 mm or less. Pellets do not stick to trees or wires. On the other hand, sleet to a British weather watcher is a mix of rain and partly melted snowflakes.

Small craft warning: issued when winds over the coastal marine areas are expected to reach and maintain speeds of 20 to 33 knots.

Snow: precipitation consisting of white or translucent ice crystals and often agglomerated into snowflakes. A day with measurable snow is a day when the total snowfall is at least 0.2 cm.

Squall: a strong, sudden wind which generally lasts a few minutes then quickly decreases in speed. Squalls are generally associated with severe thunderstorms.

Storm track: the path taken by a low-pressure centre.

Storm warning: the wind warning that is issued to mariners when winds are expected to be 48 to 63 knots.

Thunderstorm: a local storm, usually produced by a cumulonimbus cloud, and always accompanied by thunder and lightning. A thunderstorm day is a day when thunder is heard or when lightning is seen (rain and snow need not have fallen).

Tornado (also twister): a violently rotating column of air that is usually visible as a funnel cloud hanging from dark thunderstorm clouds. It is one of the least extensive of all storms, but in violence, it is the most destructive.

Trough: an elongated area of low pressure extending from the centre of a low pressure region; the opposite of a ridge.

Tsunami: also known (incorrectly) as a tidal wave. "Tsunami" comes from Japanese and means "harbour wave." It is a wave set in motion by an undersea movement such as an earthquake or a landslide. These waves can travel up to 1,000 km/h over long distances, hitting the shore with tremendous force.

Typhoon: a severe tropical cyclone in the Western Pacific Ocean, counterpart of the Atlantic hurricane.

Virga: streaks of falling rain that evaporate before reaching the ground.

Watches and warnings: Environment Canada alerts Canadians to severe storms by issuing weather watches and warnings. Usually the first message is the severe thunderstorm watch. If a watch is issued in your area, maintain your routine, but keep an eye skyward for threatening weather, and listen to radio and television for further weather information. When severe local storms are building, or have actually been sighted or detected by radar, then warnings are issued and updated. These may be either severe thunderstorm warnings or tornado warnings. Warnings mean you should be on the alert.

Waterspout: A waterspout is not really a waterspout. Often called a tornado over water, the actual water spray involved does not extend from the surface to the cloud, but 3 to 10 metres above the water surface. Like the tornado, the waterspout is very brief. Sailors believed one way of breaking up a waterspout was to fire a cannon through it.

Weatheradio: this is the name of Environment Canada's weather information broadcast network. The network has transmitters in every region and listeners need a receiver, which can be purchased from electronic equipment dealers, to pick up the broadcasts. Weatheradio signals warnings of severe weather automatically to receivers equipped with special alarm devices for that purpose.

Westerlies (west-wind belt): the pronounced west-to-east motion of the atmosphere centred over middle latitudes from about 35 to 65° latitude.

Willy-willies: refers to small, circular winds such as dust devils or whirlwinds in Australia, not very hazardous. Before 1950, willy-willies referred to much larger, more destructive typhoons or hurricanes.

Wind chill: a measure of the effect we feel when strong winds are combined with freezing tempera-tures. The index is in temperature-like units, explaining the way skin feels in a comparable temperature on a calm day, i.e., if it's –10°C and the wind chill is –20, it means your skin feels as cold as it would on a calm day at –20°C.

Wind direction: the direction from which the wind is blowing.

Source: *Environment Canada*

Humidex

RELATIVE HUMIDITY (%)

DBT (°C)	100	95	90	85	80	75	70	65	60	55	50	45	40	35	30	25	20
43													56	54	51	49	47
42											56	56	54	52	50	48	46
41										57	54	54	52	50	48	46	44
40								56	56	54	53	52	51	49	47	44	43
39							57	53	54	52	51	51	49	47	45	43	41
38					58	57	55	51	51	50	49	49	47	46	43	42	40
37				57	56	54	53	49	50	48	47	47	45	43	42	40	
36			58	56	54	52	51	48	48	47	45	45	43	42	40	38	
35	58	58	57	53	52	51	49	46	47	45	43	43	42	41	38	37	
34	55	57	55	51	50	48	47	43	44	43	42	42	41	39	37	36	
33	52	54	52	49	47	46	45	41	42	41	39	40	38	37	36	34	
32	50	51	50	46	45	44	43	40	40	39	38	38	37	36	34	33	
31	48	49	48	44	43	42	41	38	38	37	36	36	35	34	33	31	
30	46	47	46	43	42	41	39	36	37	36	34	35	34	33	31	31	
29	43	45	44	41	39	38	37	34	35	34	33	33	32	31	30		
28	41	42	41	38	37	36	35	32	33	32	31	32	31	29	28		
27	39	40	39	36	35	34	33	31	31	31	29	30	29	28	28		
26	37	38	37	34	33	33	32	29	30	29	28	28	28	27			
25	35	36	35	33	32	31	30	27	28	28	27	27	27	26			
24	33	34	33	31	30	29	28	26	27	26	25	26	26	25			
23	33	32	32	28	28	27	26	24	24	24	23	24	23				
22	31	29	29	27	27	26	26		24	23	23	23					
21	29	29	28														

DRY BULB TEMPERATURE (DEGREES CELSIUS)

Humidex (°C)	Degree of Comfort
20 - 29	Comfortable
30 - 39	Varying degrees of discomfort
40 - 45	Almost everyone uncomfortable
46 and over	Many types of labour must be restricted

■ In hot weather, our bodies regulate core temperature by using our sweat glands to shed water. Sweating doesn't cool the body, but the evaporation of sweat on your skin removes heat because it takes energy (heat) to change the liquid on your skin to vapour in the air. However, when it's humid, the air itself is already full of moisture and it can't absorb the moisture we are trying to shed, making us sticky and uncomfortable.

Ultra-Violet Index

Ultra-violet radiation is short-wavelength radiation that is part of the spectrum, just beyond visible violet light. These waves can harm both plant and animal life—the shorter of the UV wavelengths, known as UV-B, can cause sunburn, skin cancer and cataracts in humans and animals, and can also reduce agricultural productivity.

These rays are usually blocked by the protective ozone layer in the stratosphere, found between 10 and 50 km above the Earth. Ozone is a form of oxygen that has thee atoms instead of two and is created when ordinary oxygen interacts with ultraviolet radiation from the sun. Ozone can be destroyed by chemicals released into the air—most notably by the breakdown of chlorofluorocarbons (CFCs). CFCs have been used in air-conditioning, refrigeration and in some plastics manufacturing and CFC molecules are stable enough to last 100 years in the atmosphere—long enough to drift into the stratosphere where UV-B rays can break them down to produce free chlorine atoms. It is the chlorine atoms that destroy ozone.

In the 1970s, scientists had a theory that the chemicals drifting in the atmosphere could destroy the ozone layer. In the winter of 1985 NASA discovered a hole in the ozone layer over Antarctica. In recent years the continuing depletion of the ozone layer has resulted its general thinning, and in holes of varying sizes at the poles from time to time. Various attempts have been made to phase out the use of ozone-depleting chemicals all over the world, particularly at the Earth Summit in Rio de Janeiro in June 1992. While progress has been made, it is important to realize that more UV-B rays are getting through the atmosphere and there is a higher risk of UV-B generated health problems.

In May 1992, Canada's weather service launched a daily ultraviolet index as part of the forecast, the first country in the world to do so. The purpose of the index is to warn people about the dangers of over-exposure to the sun. Several other countries, including Australia, New Zealand, the Netherlands, Germany, Great Britain and the United States, have now started their own programs closely modelled on the Canadian UV index.

The amount of UV-B is measured on a scale of 0 to 10, with 10 being a typical amount you would receive on a summer day in the tropics. The higher the number, the faster you'll sunburn. (Sunburn times are for light untanned skin; times would be somewhat longer for those with darker skin.)

UV Index	Category	Sunburn Time
over 9	extreme	less than 15 minutes
7 - 9	high	about 20 minutes
4 - 7	moderate	about 30 minutes
0 - 4	low	more than one hour

Source: *Environment Canada*

Why Wind Chill Matters

*O*n a calm winter day, our bodies insulate us from cold temperatures by warming a thin layer of air close to our skin (the boundary layer). When the wind blows, it takes away this protective layer, exposing our skin to cold, moving air. Our bodies expend more energy warming up a new layer, and if each one keeps getting blown away, our skin temperature will drop, and we will feel colder.

How much heat you keep or lose depends not just on the wind. Good quality clothing with high insulating properties traps air, for a thicker boundary layer around the body to keep in the heat. Wet clothing or footwear loses this property; the water creates body-heat loss that nearly equals the condition of exposed skin.

Your body type also determines how quickly you lose or increase heat—people with a tall, slim build become cold much faster than those who are shorter and heavier. Physical activity (walking or skiing) increases metabolism and generates body heat; those with less muscle mass (children or the elderly) find it harder to get warm. None of this matters until the temperature drops. Then, check not just the outside temperature but also the wind chill to make sure you're properly dressed.

Weather Records

	Canada	United States	World
Highest maximum air temperature	45.0° Midale and Yellowgrass, Sask. July 5, 1937	56.7° Death Valley, CA July 10, 1913	58.0° Al'aziziyah, Libya Sept. 13, 1922
Lowest minimum air temperature	-63.0° Snag, YT Feb. 3, 1947	-62.1° Prospect Creek Camp, AK Jan. 23, 1971	-89.6° Vostok, Antarctica July 21, 1983
Coldest month	-47.9° Eureka, NWT Feb. 1979		
Highest sea-level pressure	107.95 kPa Dawson, YT Feb. 2, 1989	107.86 kPa Northway, AK Jan. 31, 1989	108.38 kPa Agata, Siberia USSR Dec. 31, 1968
Lowest sea-level pressure	94.02 kPa St. Anthony, Nfld Jan. 20, 1977	89.23 kPa Matecumbe Key, FL Sept. 2, 1935	87 kPa in eye of Typhoon Tip (Pacific Ocean) Oct. 12, 1979
Greatest precipitation in 24hrs	489.2 mm Ucluelet Brynnor Mines, BC Oct. 6, 1967	1 090 mm Alvin, TX	1 869.9 mm Cilaos, La Réunion Is. March 15, 1952
Greatest precipitation in one month	2 235.5 mm Swanson Bay, BC Nov. 1917	2 717.8 mm Kukui, HI March 1942	9 300 mm Cherrapunji, India July 1861
Greatest precipitation in one year	9 341.1 mm Henderson Lake, BC 1998	17 902.7 mm Kukui, HI 1982	26 461.2 mm Cherrapunji, India Aug. 1860-July 1861
Greatest average annual precipitation	7 m Henderson Lake, BC	11 684 mm Mt. Waialeaie, Kauai, HI	11 684 mm Mt. Waialeaie, Kauai, HI
Least annual precipitation	13.6 mm Arctic Bay, NWT 1949	0.0 Bagdad, CA Oct. 3, 1912 to Nov. 8, 1914	0.0 Arica, Chile—no rain for 14 years
Greatest average annual snowfall	1 518 cm Glacier Mt. Fidelity, BC	1 461 cm Rainer Paradise Ranger Station, WA	
Greatest snowfall in one season	2 446.9 cm Revelstoke/Mt. Copeland, BC 1971–72	2 896 cm Mt. Baker, WA 1998–99	
Greatest snowfall in one month	535.8 cm Haines Apps. No 2, BC Dec. 1959	990.6 cm Tamarack, CA Jan. 1911	
Greatest snowfall in one day	145 cm Tahtsa Lake West, BC Feb. 11, 1999	193 cm Silver Lake, CO April 14–15, 1921	
Highest average annual number of thunderstorm days	36 days London, Ont.	96 days Fort Meyers, FL	322 days Bogor, Indonesia
Heaviest hailstone	290 g Cedoux, Sask. Aug. 27, 1973	758 g Coffeyville, KS Sept. 3, 1970	15 000 g Guangdong province of China April 19, 1995
Highest average annual wind speed	36 km/h Cape Warwick, Resolution Island, NWT	56.3 km/h Mt. Washington, NH	
Highest wind speed for 1 hr	201.1 km/h Cape Hopes Advance (Quaqtaq), Que. Nov. 18, 1931	362.0 km/h Mt. Washington, NH April 12, 1934	
Highest average hours of fog	1 890 hrs Argentia, Nfld	2 552 hrs Cape Disappointment, WA	

Source: *Environment Canada*

Wind Chill Hazards

Check the wind chill before you go outdoors in the winter, and make sure you are well prepared for the weather. Even moderate wind chills can be dangerous if you are outside for long periods.

In parts of the country with a milder climate (Southern Ontario, Southern British Columbia and the Atlantic provinces except Labrador), a wind chill warning is issued at -35°C. Further north, people have grown more accustomed to the cold, and have adapted to the more severe conditions. Because of this, Environment Canada issues warnings at progressively colder wind chill values as you move north. Most of Canada hears a warning at -45°C. The residents of the Arctic and Northern Manitoba, Northern Ontario and Northern Quebec are warned at -53°C, and -63°C in the high Arctic.

Wind Chill (°C)	Description	Health Concern	What to do
0 to –9	Low	• Slight increase in discomfort.	• Dress warmly, with the outside temperature in mind.
–9 to –24	Moderate	• Uncomfortable. • Exposed skin feels cold. • Risk of hypothermia if outside for long periods without adequate protection	• Dress in layers of warm clothing, with an outer layer that is wind resistant • Wear a hat, mittens and scarf • Keep active.
–25 to –44	Cold	• Risk of skin freezing (frostbite). Check extremities (fingers, toes, ears and face) for numbness or whiteness. Risk of hypothermia if outside for long periods without adequate protection	• Dress in layers of warm clothing, with an outer layer that is wind resistant. Cover all exposed skin, particularly your face and hands. Wear a hat, mittens and a scarf, neck tube or face mask. Keep active.
–45 to –62 WARNING LEVEL	Very cold	• Exposed skin may freeze in minutes. Check extremities frequently for numbness or whiteness (frostbite). Serious risk of hypothermia if outside for long periods.	• Be careful. Dress very warmly in layers of clothing, with an outer layer that is wind resistant. Cover all exposed skin, particularly your face and hands. Wear a hat, mittens and a scarf, neck tube or face mask. Limit outdoor activities to short periods. Be ready to cut short or cancel outdoor activities. Keep active.
–63 and colder DANGER!	Extreme	• Outdoor conditions are hazardous. Exposed skin may freeze in seconds.	• Stay indoors.

Source: *Environment Canada*

Jack Frost Nipping at your Window-Pane

Is Jack Frost partly responsible for our relative wealth and comfort here in Canada? U.S. researchers William Masters and Margaret McMillan think so. In a study in the Journal of Economic Growth in 2001, they argue that countries where there's a hard frost every year are healthier and more productive than those countries where the ground never freezes.

Masters and McMillan propose two reasons why frost is important-disease and agriculture. A country like Canada, where mosquitoes and other disease carriers die every winter, doesn't suffer much from endemic diseases, such as malaria and yellow fever. As well, the frost allows the accumulation of organic material that enriches the soil-material that is recycled back to its constituents much more quickly in the tropics. The frost also acts as a way of storing moisture until it's needed in the spring, so that farmers don't have to rely on unreliable seasonal rains.

So our climate has two advantages according to Masters: we have better soil and we're not too sick to work it; and frost helps people control disease and builds up topsoil.

Source: *Purdue University*

The Beaufort Wind Scale

Beaufort forces range from 0 in calm conditions, to 12 in a hurricane. Rear-Admiral Sir Francis Beaufort of the British Royal Navy devised the scale in 1805. It originally referred to the amount of sail a full-rigged ship could carry in specific wind conditions. In light air, just one sail would be taken in; in a moderate gale, seven would come down; and in a heavy storm the number would be eleven, therefore Beaufort force 11. The Beaufort scale has been modified and modernized several times. Basically though, the idea is to estimate wind speed by watching the effects of wind on such things as flags, trees, smoke, water surface and even people. The scale is still widely used today.

Beaufort Wind Force	Wind Speed (km/h)	Wind Type	Descriptive Effects
0	0–1	calm	smoke rises vertically
1	2–5	light air	smoke drifts slowly
2	6–11	light breeze	leaves rustle; wind vanes move
3	12–19	gentle breeze	leaves and twigs in constant motion
4	20–29	moderate breeze	small branches move; raises dust and loose paper moves along
5	30–38	fresh breeze	small trees sway
6	39–50	strong breeze	large branches in continuous motion; telephone wires whistle
7	51–61	near gale	whole trees in motion; wind affects walking
8	62–74	gale	twigs and small branches break off trees
9	75–87	strong gale	branches break; shingles blow from roofs
10	88–101	storm	trees snap and uproot; some damage to buildings
11	102–117	violent storm	property damage widespread
12	118–	hurricane	severe and extensive damage

Source: *Environment Canada*

Tornado Intensity Scale

Tornadoes are classified by the destruction they leave behind. They are rated from F0 to F5, F standing for Fujita, one of the world's leading experts on tornadoes.

F-Scale	Winds (km/h)	Length (km)	Width	Damage
0 (very weak)	under 116	< 1.5	under 15m	Light damage; minor roof, tree, chimney, antenna and sign damage
1 (weak)	117-180	1.6-5	50m	Moderate damage; barns torn apart; mobile homes pushed off foundations; trees snapped; cars pushed off roads; sheet metal buildings destroyed
2 (strong)	181-252	5.1-15.9	160m	Considerable damage; roofs torn off schools, homes and businesses; debris from barns scattered; trailers disintegrated; large trees uprooted; concrete block buildings destroyed
3 (severe)	253-332	16-50	161-500m	Severe damage; roofs and walls of schools, homes and buildings blown away; large trees uprooted; weaker homes completely disappear
4 (devastating)	333-419	51-159	0.5-1.4km	Interior and exterior walls of all homes blown apart; cars thrown more than 300m in the air
5 (incredible)	420-512	160-507	1.5-16km	Strongly built homes completely blown away; bizarre phenomena such as straw driven through fence posts

Source: *Environment Canada*

The Saffir-Simpson Hurricane Intensity Scale

Category	Maximum Sustained Wind Speed (km/h)	Minimum Surface Pressure (kPa)	Storm Surge (m)	Remarks
1 (minimal)	119-153	>=98.0	1.0-1.7	Damage to trees and signs. Low-lying flooding. Small craft torn from mooring.
2 (moderate)	154-177	97.9-96.5	1.8-2.6	Trees blown down; damage to mobile homes and roofs. Marinas flooded; evacuation of shores.
3 (extensive)	178-209	96.4-94.5	2.7-3.8	Some structural damage to small buildings; serious coastal flooding;mobile homes destroyed.
4 (extreme)	210-249	94.4-92.0	3.9-5.6	Extensive damage: doors, roofs, windows; major damage to lower floors of buildings near shore. Major beach erosion.Massive evacuation from shore possible.
5 (catastrophic)	>250	<92.0	>5.6	Small buildings blown away; complete destruction of mobile homes; massive evacuation within 10 to 20 km of shore possible.

Source: *H.S. Saffir, P.E. and Dr. R. Simpson*

Hurricane Names in 2002

*T*he names chosen for tropical storms in the Atlantic Ocean, Gulf of Mexico and the
Caribbean Sea for 2002 are: Arthur, Bertha, Cristobal, Dolly, Edouard, Fay, Gustav,
Hanna, Isidore, Josephine, Kyle, Lili, Marco, Nana, Omar, Paloma, Rene, Sally, Teddy, Vicky,
and Wilfred. The names for eastern Pacific tropical storms (those west of 140 W) are: Alma,
Boris, Cristina, Douglas, Elida, Fausto, Genevieve, Hernan, Iselle, Julio, Kenna, Lowell,
Marie, Norbert, Odile, Polo, Rachel, Simon, Trudy, Vance, Winnie, Xavier, Yolanda, Zeke.
Other regions of the world have their own naming system for violent storms.

Since 1953, Atlantic tropical storms have been named from lists originated by the National
Hurricane Centre and now maintained and updated by an international committee of the World
Meteorological Organization (WMO). The lists featured only women's names until 1979, when
men's and women's names were alternated. Six lists are used in rotation. Thus, the 2002 list
will be used again in 2008.

Hurricanes that have a severe impact on lives or the economy are remembered for
generations, and some go into weather history. If a hurricane has had a major impact, any
country affected by the storm can request that the name of the hurricane be "retired" by
agreement of the WMO. Retiring a name actually means that it cannot be reused for at least
10 years, to facilitate historic references, legal actions, and insurance claim activities, and
avoid public confusion with another storm of the same name.

Three hurricane names from the 1996 list have been retired, so that on the 2002 list,
Cristobal has replaced Cesar, Fay has replaced Fran, and Hanna has replaced Hortense.

FOCUS ON...

Air Quality

Air pollution affects the health of all of us, especially children, the elderly and those with respiratory and cardiac conditions.

According to federal government studies, 5,000 deaths a year can be attributed to air pollution; the Ontario Medical Association says air pollution costs Ontario citizens more than $1 billion a year in hospital admissions, emergency room visits and absenteeism. Figures from the Toronto Public Health Department alone show that air pollution causes 1,000 deaths a year and numerous health-related problems.

■ What do we mean by air pollution?

When we think of air pollution, we usually think of smog, which is indeed an important factor in air quality. Smog is composed mostly of ground-level ozone and fine particles. Ozone is created when nitrogen oxides and volatile organic compounds combine in the presence of sunlight, which is why smog is primarily a summer phenomenon.

Sulphur dioxide (SO_2), a colourless gas, smells like burnt matches. It can be oxidized to sulphur trioxide, which in the presence of water is easily transformed to sulphuric acid mist or rain. SO_2 can be oxidized to form acid aerosols. It is also a precursor to sulphates, one of the main components of respirable particles in the atmosphere.

SO_2 comes mainly from smelters and utilities, iron and steel mills, petroleum refineries and pulp and paper mills. Small sources include residential, commercial and industrial space heating

Exposure to high levels of SO_2 can cause breathing problems, respiratory illness, changes in the lung's defences and worsening respiratory and cardiovascular disease. People with asthma or chronic lung or heart disease are the most sensitive to SO_2. It also damages trees and crops.

Ozone (O_3), a colourless, odourless gas, is a major component of smog. Ozone results from reactions between nitrogen oxides and volatile organic carbons in the presence of sunlight. High levels typically occur from May to September, between noon and early evening.

Exposure to high levels of O_3 results in chest tightness, coughing and wheezing. People with respiratory and heart problems are at a higher risk for such problems. Ozone also causes noticeable damage in many crops, garden plants and trees.

Nitrogen Dioxide (NO_2), a reddish-brown gas with a pungent and irritating odour, transforms in the air to make gaseous nitric acid and toxic organic nitrates. NO_2 also plays a major role in producing ground-level ozone, and is a precursor to nitrates, which contribute to increased respirable particle levels.

All combustion in air produces oxides of nitrogen, of which NO_2 is the major one. Much of it comes from the transportation sector—cars and trucks. Much of the remainder comes from power generation, metal production and incineration. There are also small natural sources of NO_2.

NO_2 irritates the lungs and can lower resistance to respiratory infection. People with asthma and bronchitis are especially sensitive.

Total reduced sulphur compounds (TRS) produce offensive odours similar to rotten eggs or cabbage. Industrial sources of TRS include the steel industry, pulp and paper mills, refineries and sewage treatment facilities. Natural sources include swamps, bogs and marshes.

TRS compounds are not normally considered a health hazard. They are, however, a primary cause of odours.

Carbon monoxide (CO), a colourless, odourless and tasteless but poisonous gas, is produced primarily by incomplete burning of fossil fuels. Most of it comes from cars and trucks, but a significant amount comes from by metal production.

CO enters the bloodstream and reduces oxygen delivery to the organs and tissues. People with heart disease are particularly sensitive. Exposure to high levels is linked with impairment of: vision, work capacity, learning ability and performance of difficult tasks.

Suspended particles in the atmosphere consist of either solid particles or fine liquid droplets. They include aerosols, smoke, fumes, dust, fly ash and pollen.

Particles in the atmosphere have been characterized according to size, mainly because of the different health effects from particles of different diameters. Particles with diameters less than 100 microns (millionths of a metre) are classified as total suspended particles (TSP). Particles less than 10 microns and 2.5 microns in diameter are defined as inhalable particles (PM_{10}) and respirable particles ($PM_{2.5}$), respectively. The smaller the particle, the further it will penetrate into the lungs. Most particle emissions from human activity fall into the TSP size range.

Particles come from both natural and man-made sources. Natural sources include windblown soil and mineral particles, volcanic ash, sea salt spray and biological materials such as pollen, spores, bacteria and smoke from forest fires. Man-made sources include windblown dust from agricultural soil, roads and construction sites and particles from combustion of fossil fuels.

The greatest effect on health is from particles 10 microns or less in diameter, which can aggravate bronchitis, asthma and other respiratory diseases. People with asthma, cardiovascular or lung disease, as well as children and elderly people, are considered to be the most sensitive.

■ How is air quality measured?

The federal government, the provinces and many municipalities measure what is called an Air Quality Index (AQI). This uses real-time data from measuring stations to calculate the amount of several common pollutants in the air. The list of measured pollutants varies from place to place, but Ontario's Air Quality Index serves as an example.

In Ontario, a network of 33 monitoring stations continuously measures six common pollutants: sulphur dioxide, ozone, nitrogen dioxide, total reduced sulphur compounds, carbon monoxide and suspended particles. The quantity of each is measured on an appropriate scale and the AQI for a locality is based on whichever is highest on a particular day. (See Ontario's air quality web site: http://www.air qualityontario.com.)

If the AQI falls below 32, the air is considered good or very good. An AQI reading between 32 and 49 indicates moderate air quality, and an AQI reading from 50 to 99 indicates poor air quality. A reading over 100 indicates very poor air quality.

Canada maintains two air-monitoring networks. The National Air Pollution (NAPS) Network is a joint federal, provincial, territorial and municipal network established in 1969. It is primarily an urban network, with 239 air monitoring stations in 136 municipalities. The augmented Canadian Air and Precipitation Monitoring Network (CAPMoN) is a rural network with 23 air monitoring stations in Canada and one in the United States.

The NAPS Network gathers measurements on the components of smog—ozone, particulate matter, sulphur dioxide, carbon monoxide, nitrogen oxides and volatile organic compounds. The CAPMoN has been in operation for over 20 years. Its initial focus was on acid rain, but now smog pollutants are also measured at some sites.

Environment Canada is refurbishing and expanding the networks under a $29-million, five-year program. The new money will be used to establish up to ten new NAPS Network monitoring stations, refurbish approximately 50 critical monitoring stations as well as to replace aging instrumentation throughout the network. Some of the money will be used to add measurements of ozone and particulate matter at several stations of the augmented CAPMoN.

The federal government is also working on improving the science of clean air, giving $60 million to the Canadian Foundation for Climate and Atmospheric Sciences (CFCAS). The Foundation announced its first round of research projects on February 15, 2001.

On December 7, 2000, Canada signed an agreement to reduce transboundary smog with the United States through an Ozone Annex under the 1991 Canada-U.S. Air Quality Agreement. Measures to improve air pollution monitoring, air pollution reporting and to ensure cleaner vehicles and cleaner fuels have been announced as part of a $120 million investment to enable Canada to meet its commitments under the Annex.

Source: *Government of Ontario, Environment Canada*

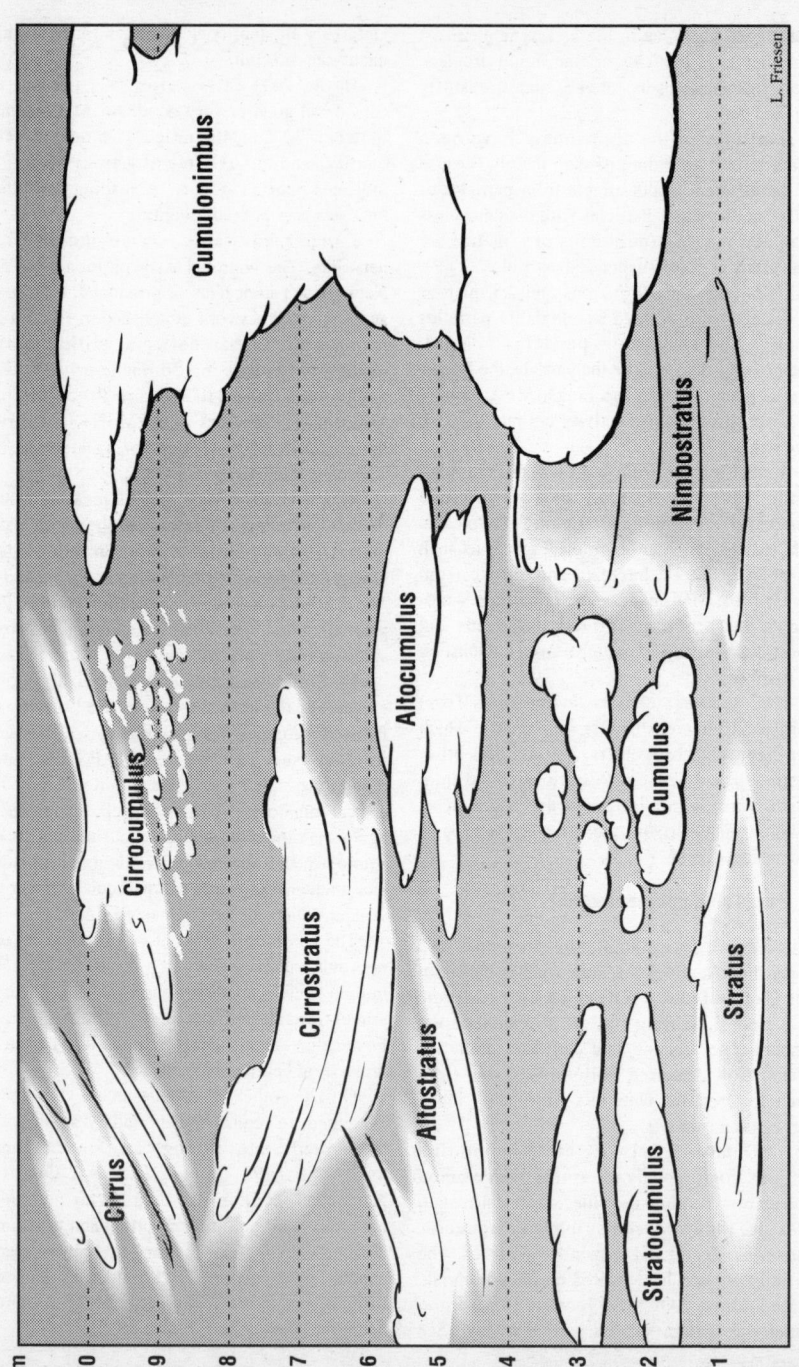

L. Friesen

km
10
9
8
7
6
5
4
3
2
1

Cirrus

Cirrocumulus

Cirrostratus

Cumulonimbus

Altocumulus

Altostratus

Nimbostratus

Cumulus

Stratocumulus

Stratus

Ten Basic Cloud Types

1. Cirrus
Thin wispy small white clouds that often occur as feathery filaments or long streamers stretching across the sky. Often their ends are swept by strong winds giving it the look of a mare's tail.

2. Cirrostratus
White uniform veil of thin transparent cloud. Sky still appears bright with a halo around the sun. Cloud sheets are small or extensive.

3. Cirrocumulus
Thin bands of either continuous or patchy small clouds, white or pale grey in colour. Cloud base occurs above 6,000 m.; ripple or rib pattern gives it a look of fish-scales, referred to as a "mackerel sky."

4. Altocumulus
Either patchy or continuous middle cumulus cloud with a dappled or rippled appearance. Thicker and lower version of cirrocumulus that is associated with changeable weather and perhaps rain.

5. Alto stratus
Grey pale uniform layer of cloud in which the sun may appear weakly. Too thick and low for halos to be seen, however, through the overcast, the sun can be seen weakly. A sign of precipitation within a few hours.

6. Stratocumulus
Low layers of grey or whitish clouds with occasional dark patches that have a well-defined rounded or undulating appearance. May have a few breaks, but usually total cloud cover extends for hundreds of kilometres.

7. Stratus
A grey uniform low blanket of cloud that may be continuous or patchy, often producing light drizzle. The base is between the surface and 300 m, often obscuring hill tops and tall buildings. Looks like high drifting fog or making for a dull, grey day.

8. Nimbostratus
A thick low level (600 m) deck of cloud providing continuous rain or snow. Usually covers the entire sky and completely hides the sun.

9. Cumulus
White puffy clouds that often form by day and disappear by night. Well-defined base begins at 600 to 1,200 m; upper parts are cauliflower-like. Associated with fair weather, blue sky and no precipitation.

10. Cumulonimbus
Giant impressive cumulus clouds with dark base and a smooth anvil-shaped top. Called the kings of the sky, they are the biggest of all clouds, often towering in excess of 10 km. Often associated with severe thunderstorms and sometimes hail or tornadoes. In heavy rain, cumulonimbus clouds have a dark ominous base and a curtain of rain.

Source: *Environment Canada*

Weather Symbols

Meteorologists in Canada, China and Croatia—in fact, all around the world—use a standard set of symbols in constructing detailed weather maps. Here are some samples of these universal weather symbols:

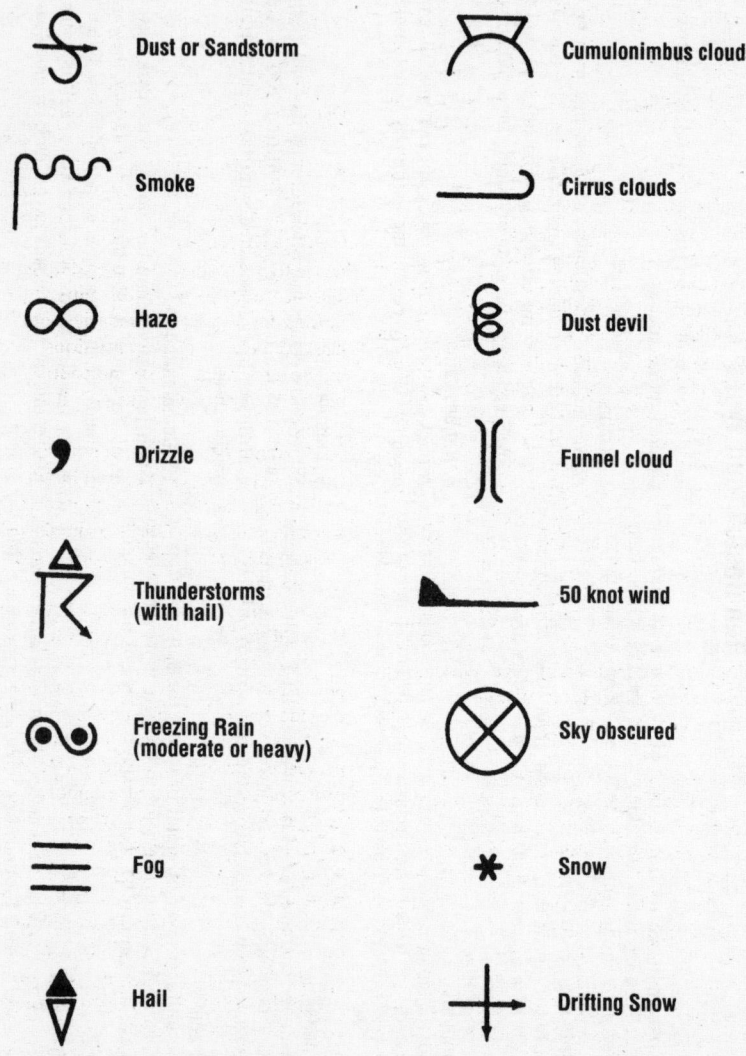

Dust or Sandstorm	Cumulonimbus clouds
Smoke	Cirrus clouds
Haze	Dust devil
Drizzle	Funnel cloud
Thunderstorms (with hail)	50 knot wind
Freezing Rain (moderate or heavy)	Sky obscured
Fog	Snow
Hail	Drifting Snow

Source: *Environment Canada*

Revisiting the Kyoto Protocol

International negotiators gathered in Bonn, Germany late in July, 2001 to save the Kyoto Protocol on climate change. Despite the high-profile withdrawal of the U.S., 180 countries—including Canada—reached a compromise on general principles. Another meeting, in Marrakesh, Morocco in October 2001, will iron out details so that individual countries can begin ratifying the agreement.

■ The Facts of Climate Change

Climate change is a global problem; a central cause of climate change is thought to be greenhouse gases (GHGs) such as methane and carbon dioxide. Many GHGs form naturally, but without human activity, it's unlikely there would be a crisis. Heating and cooling buildings, using energy at home and work, driving vehicles to move people and goods, powering industrial processes— all contribute extra GHGs. Greenhouse gases are so called because they act like the glass in a greenhouse—trapping the warmth of the sun. This is a good thing for hothouse tomatoes, but bad for the Earth: Scientists believe that the warming trend they see will damage the polar ice caps, cause sea levels to rise, increase the number of extremely violent weather events and cause agricultural patterns to change. In Canada, climate change will affect fishing, farming, forestry, lakes, rivers, coastal communities and the North.

Since 1948, Environment Canada has been keeping nationwide records; there has been a general warming over the past two decades. In fact, six of the warmest 10 springs occurred in the past 20 years. As of spring 2000, Canada had experienced three years of above-normal temperatures. For most of the country the difference was 1 or 2 degrees C; for southern Manitoba and northern Ontario, it was close to 3 degrees. Elsewhere, scientists are recording disquieting changes—the oceans are warming, ice caps *are* melting, there's open water at the North Pole. The Intergovernmental Panel on Climate Control (IPCC), set up by the World Meteorological Organization and United Nations Environ-

ment Program, estimates that world temperatures will rise on average between 1.4 and 5.8 degrees this century.

■ Consensus for Action

To deal with the issue, more than 160 countries gathered in Kyoto, Japan in December 1997, and agreed to reduce GHG emissions. The agreement that set out those targets, and the options available to countries to achieve them, became known as the Kyoto Protocol. Canada's target is to reduce its GHG emissions to 6 percent below 1990 levels by the period between 2008 and 2012. The protocol becomes binding when it is ratified by at least 55 countries, covering at least 55 percent of the emissions addressed by the agreement. So far, no country that has taken on a target has ratified the Kyoto Protocol.

A stumbling block has been the administrative framework within which countries will meet their Kyoto targets. Since the signing, nations have been meeting every year to define the rules, but until Bonn, without success.

One of the elements of the Kyoto Protocol that Canada favours is the inclusion of what are called "sinks"—forests and agricultural soils that can remove carbon dioxide from the atmosphere. Sinks can be enhanced through sustainable management practices in forestry and on farms. The protocol says a limited number of carbon sink activities can be part of a country's strategy to meet its obligations. At Bonn, Canada was seeking a broader definition of what activities would qualify; the Canadian position prevailed. If sinks were included in only a limited way, Canadian negotiators argued, important sectors and many countries would have no incentive to manage their forests and farms properly.

The protocol also includes three market-based instruments known as the Kyoto Mechanisms that allow countries to earn or buy credits outside their borders. The **Clean Development Mechanism (CDM)** is a way to earn credits by investing in emission reduction projects in developing countries. For example, a Canadian firm might invest in wind farms in Africa. The African country decreases its reliance on fossil fuel and its greenhouse gas emissions. Under the CDM, the Canadian firm receives what are called "certified emission reduction credits"; these credits can be used towards meeting Canada's Kyoto target.

Joint Implementation is a way to earn credits by investing in emission reduction projects in developed countries that have taken on a Kyoto target. In a manner similar to the CDM, a Canadian firm with expertise in oil and gas pipeline technologies might help to improve the efficiency of and reduce leakage from a pipeline in eastern Europe. Both countries benefit—Canada gets emission credits and the host nation gets a more efficient, less polluting pipeline.

Finally, **International Emissions Trading** allows developed countries that have taken on a Kyoto target to buy and sell credits among themselves. So, for example, Canada might be able to reduce its emissions more than its agreed target. Another country, finding it more difficult to achieve its target, can buy the excess Canadian credits. The net effect on the Earth's atmosphere is that GHG emissions have been reduced overall—and the more efficient country is rewarded financially.

Two other aspects are important: There must be a way to ensure that countries that take on a target actually try to meet it. And developing countries must be included, in a way that lets them continue to develop while reducing their GHG emissions. As well, some small countries—especially those on low-lying islands—will need international aid to deal with the consequences of global climate change. Canada has been seeking what the government calls a balanced package that deals with sinks, the three Kyoto Mechanisms and a compliance mechanism, and that also addresses the priorities of developing countries.

■ **Implementation Plans**

In a statement after the Bonn compromise, Prime Minister Jean Chrétien said Canada wants to meet most of its Kyoto obligations through domestic action rather than through buying and selling emission credits. Canada, he said, is already set to reduce emissions by 65 megatons—one third of the Kyoto target—and will be looking for ways to achieve the rest in the next few years. Canada has also committed $45 million to financial assistance for developing nations to fight climate change.

With the Bonn meeting over, negotiators returned home with the task of making the protocol into law. Canada will likely ratify the agreement in 2002, government spokesmen said. Exactly how Canada will move to meet the rest of its obligations remains to be seen. But there are options: Britain uses a stick, fining GHG polluters, while Germany prefers the carrot approach, offering price incentives for greener electricity.

Business is scrambling to link investment strategies with saving the world: The emissions credits are already starting to have a monetary value. In late July, 2001, energy giant Royal Dutch/Shell predicted a traded price of $5 a ton of carbon in 2005, rising to $20 a ton by 2012. Putting a cash value on reducing GHG emissions will create incentives to cut emissions and invest in non-polluting technologies.

The U.S. walked away from the Kyoto deal. U.S. spokesman said they wouldn't try to block progress on the accord, as long as it doesn't affect American interests. But whether the deal can succeed in the long term without U.S. participation remains to be seen.

Economists cannot agree on the costs of climate control. World Bank spokesmen said that the compromise likely means the cost will be lower than expected—about 1 per cent of GDP between now and 2010, for the 39 industrialized nations (including Canada) that the pact requires to cut emissions to 94.8 percent of 1990 levels by 2012.

There is also a cost for doing nothing. The World Health Organization estimates that the penalty for failing to reduce the levels of air pollution could be as high as 8 million premature deaths around the world between 2000 and 2020.

LIFE SCIENCES

The life sciences consist of diverse disciplines that share a knowledge base centered around the same fundamental question, "What is life?" Beginning with biology (the study of living organisms), the life sciences soon included: zoology (the study of animals), botany (the study of plants), and taxonomy (the study of the classification of living things).

Over the last century, an ever increasing variety of subdisciplines and approaches to studying life have arisen: microbiology (the study of microorganisms), genetics (the study of heredity), biochemistry (the study of chemical compounds and reactions in living organisms), ecology (the study of the relationships between living things and their environment), and ethology (the study of animal behaviour). Most recently these disciplines have been joined by biotechnology (the study and use of organisms or their components for the manufacture or production of commercial substances, aided by techniques of genetic manipulation).

Common Life Sciences Terms

Aerobic: Life processes that depend on the presence of oxygen.

Algae: Simple rootless plants that grow in bodies of water in relative proportion to the amount of nutrients available.

Allergen: Any of various sorts of material that, as a result of coming into contact with appropriate tissues, induce a state of sensitivity and/or resistance to infection or toxic substances.

Anaerobic: Life processes that occur in the absence of oxygen.

Animal: A vertebrate (having a bony skeleton or one made of cartilage) or invertebrate (lacking a spine or skeleton) species including, but not limited to, humans and other mammals, birds, fish, and shellfish.

Bacteria: Single cell microorganisms that possess cell walls. Some cause disease and some are beneficial.

Baleen: Horny plates with fringed inner edges attached to the upper jaw of Mysticeti type whales, such as right and blue whales. The baleen are used to filter plankton and other food from water.

Biodiversity: The total diversity within an ecosystem, including genetic variation among species, diversity of life forms, and ecosystem diversity.

Biomass: The amount of living matter in a given unit of the environment.

Biosphere: The portion of Earth (upwards at least to a height of 10,000 m and downward to the ocean floor and a 100 km below the planet's surface) and the atmosphere surrounding it that supports life.

Bloom: A seasonal, dense growth of small marine plants, i.e., phytoplankton.

Coniferous: Refers to a softwood, cone bearing tree.

Deciduous: Refers to a hardwood, leaf dropping tree.

Effluent Waste: Material discharged into the environment, treated or untreated.

Flood Tide: Interim period of tide between low and high water; a rising tide.

Lagoon: Shallow pond where sunlight, bacterial action and oxygen work to purify waste water.

Marsh: Wet, soft, low-lying land that provides a natural habitat for many plants and animals.

Molt: The periodic casting off or shedding of the outer body covering (feathers, hair, skin, or cuticle) by birds, mammals, and reptiles.

Nutrients: Elements or compounds essential to growth and development of living things: carbon, oxygen, nitrogen, potassium, and phosphorus.

Osmosis: Tendency of a fluid to pass through a permeable membrane, such as the wall of a living cell, into a less concentrated solution, so as to equalize concentrations on both sides of the membrane.

Photosynthesis: A process of biochemical change in which plant cells, using light as an energy source, manufacture simple sugars from oxygen and carbon dioxide.

Regeneration (forests): The renewal of a forest by natural processes (self-sown seed or root suckers), as well as by sowing or planting new tree stock.

Synthesis: Production of a substance by the union of elements or simpler chemical compounds.

Tailings: Residue of raw materials or waste separated out during the processing of wood or minerals products.

Tidal Marsh: Low, flat marshlands crossed by interlaced channels and tidal sloughs, and subject to tidal inundation from the ocean, normally, the only vegetation present is salt-tolerant rushes and grasses.

Tide: Alternate rising and falling of water levels twice each lunar day, due to gravitational attraction of the moon and the sun in conjunction with the Earth's rotational force.

Major Groups of Living Organisms

All life forms are classified in a hierarchical series of groups. Taxonomy, the science of such classification, was introduced by Swedish scientist, Carolus Linneaus (1707–78).

The purpose of classification is to provide each plant or animal on the planet with a unique name by which it is known; to describe it so it may be recognized by anyone; and to place it within a system that shows its relationship to other plants and animals.

The system is flexible, allowing updating as more is learned about individual species and their history.

Naming

The scientific naming of species involves two Latin names. The first word in the species name denotes the Genus the species belongs to. For example, the first word in the scientific name of the Monarch butterfly is *Danaus*. The Monarch belongs to the Genus Danaus.

The second word in the scientific name is particular to a species and can be quite arbitrary. Sometimes species names refer to a person, a country, a particular feature of the animal or plant, or a food source. The second word in the scientific name for the Monarch is plexippus. Thus, the scientific name of the Monarch is *Danaus plexippus*.

A species usually also has a common or more familiar name. For example, people seldom refer to the Monarch butterfly as Danaus plexippus.

Species

The basic level in the system is species. The interpretation of differences and similarities between species is often subjective; so the number and name of a species may change. Also new species are still being found and identified.

Genus

Species with a number of common features are grouped together in Genera. The number of different species in a genus can vary from one to several hundred. Again identification is subjective and the number of genera is not fixed.

Family

Genera are further grouped into Families. Butterfly genera are broadly divided into four major families: 1) Papilionidae (swallowtails); 2) Pierodae (whites and sulphurs); 3) Nymphalidae (brush-footed); and 4) Lycaenidae (hairstreaks, coppers, and blues).

Order

Families that share major characteristics are grouped into Orders. For example, butterflies, along with moths, belong to the Order Lepidoptera or insects with scales. The word comes from the Greek words *lepis* (scale) and *pteron* (wing). Classification at this level can be a very complex structure of orders, sub-orders, and sub-sub-orders.

Class

Further up the hierarchy, all Orders belong to a Class. Members of each class show charac-teristics indicating a common evolutionary descent.

Phylum

At the next level, butterflies, for example, are members of the Phylum Arthropoda, along with millipedes, spiders, and crustaceans, among others. The word Phylum comes from the Greek *phulon* or race.

Kingdom

At the highest level of the hierarchy, butterflies along with other living creatures, including humans, are members of the Animal Kingdom.

Extinct and Endangered Species in Canada, 2001

The following list has been prepared by the Committee on the Status of Endangered Wildlife in Canada.

The "Extinct" category refers to any species that was indigenous to Canada that no longer exists anywhere in the world. The "Extirpated" category refers to any species that no longer exists in the wild but does occur elsewhere. The "Endangered" category refers to any species threatened with imminent extinction or extirpation throughout all or most of its Canadian range.

For more information, visit the Web site http://www.speciesatrisk.gc.ca.

Species	Habitat	Year Documented
EXTINCT CATEGORY		
Mammals		
Caribou, Woodland	(Queen Charlotte Islands population) BC	1920s, 1984
Mink, Sea	Atlantic coastal waters	1894
Birds		
Auk, Great	QC, NB, NS, NF	1844
Duck, Labrador	QC, NB, NS, NF	1875
Pigeon, Passenger	SK, MB, ON, QC, NB, NS, PE	1914
Fish		
Cisco, Deepwater	ON	1952
Cisco, Longjaw	ON	1975
Dace, Banff Longnose	AB	1986
Stickleback, Benthic (Hadley Lake)	BC	1999
Stickleback, Limnetic (Hadley Lake)	BC	1999
Walleye, Blue	ON	1965
Molluscs		
Limpet, Eelgrass	QC, NS, NF	1929
EXTIRPATED CATEGORY		
Mammals		
Bear, Grizzly	(Prairie population) AB, SK,MB	1880s
Ferret, Black-footed	AB, SK, MB	1974
Walrus, Atlantic	Atlantic coastal waters	1850
Whale, Grey	Atlantic population	prior 1800
Birds		
Grouse, Sage	(British Columbia population) BC	not observed since 1960's
Prairie-Chicken, Greater	AB, SK, MB, ON	last reported 1987 (SK)
Reptiles		
Lizard, Pygmy Short-Horned	(British Columbia population) BC	last reported 1898, near Osoyoos, BC
Rattlesnake, Timber	ON	1941
Fish		
Chub, Gravel	ON	last reported 1958, Thames River drainage
Paddlefish	ON	1917
Molluscs		
Wedgemussel, Dwarf	NB	1968
Lepidopterans[1]		
Blue, Karner	ON	1991
Elfin, Frosted	ON	1988
Marble, Island	BC	prior 1910
Plants		
Blue-eyed Mary	ON	not observed since 1954
Tick-trefoil, Illinois	ON	not observed since 1888
ENDANGERED CATEGORY		
Mammals		
Badger, American	BC, ON	2000
Caribou, Peary	(Banks Island population) (High Arctic population) NT, NU	1991

▶

▶ Caribou, Woodland .... (Atlantic - Gaspésie population) QC 2000
Fox, Swift .... AB, SK 1998
Marmot, Vancouver Island .... BC 1997
Marten, American .... (Newfoundland population) NF.................. 1996
Whale, Beluga .... St. Lawrence River population 1997
　　　　　　　　　　　　　　　　　　　Ungava Bay population 1988
　　　　　　　　　　　　　　　　　　　Southeast Baffin Island–
　　　　　　　　　　　　　　　　　　　　Cumberland Sound population 1990
Whale, Bowhead .... Eastern Arctic population 1980
　　　　　　　　　　　　　　　　　　　Western Arctic population 1986
Whale, Right .... Atlantic and Pacific Oceans 1990
Wolverine .... (Eastern population) QC, NF 1989

Birds
Bobwhite, Northern .... ON 1994
Chat, Western Yellow-breasted .... BC 2000
Crane, Whooping .... NT, NU 1978
Curlew, Eskimo .... All provinces and territories except BC 2000
Flycatcher, Acadian .... ON 1994
Grouse, Sage .... (Prairie population) AB, SK 1998
Owl, Barn .... (Eastern population) ON, QC 1999
Owl, Burrowing .... BC, AB, MB, SK 1995
Owl, Northern Spotted .... BC 1999
Plover, Mountain .... AB, SK 1987
Plover, Piping .... AB, SK, MB, ON, QC, NB, NS, PE, NF 1985
Rail, King .... ON 1994
Shrike, Loggerhead .... (Eastern population) MB, ON, QC 1991
Sparrow, Henslow's .... ON 1993
Tern, Roseate .... QC, NB, NS 1999
Thrasher, Sage .... BC, AB, SK 1992
Warbler, Kirtland's........................... ON 1999
Warbler, Prothonotary...................... ON 1996
Woodpecker, White-headed................ BC 2000

Amphibians
Frog, Northern Cricket .... ON 1990
Frog, Northern Leopard .... (Southern Mountain population) BC 1998
Frog, Oregon Spotted .... BC 1999
Frog, Rocky Mountain Tailed .... BC 2000
Reptiles
Racer, Blue .... ON 1991
Snake, Lake Erie Water .... ON 1991
Snake, Night .... BC 2001
Snake, Sharp-tailed .... BC 1999
Turtle, Leatherback .... Atlantic & Pacific Oceans 1981

Fish
Dace, Nooksack.............................. BC 1996
Lamprey, Morrison Creek .... BC 1999
Salmon, Atlantic .... (Inner Bay of Fundy populations) NB, NS ... 2001
Stickleback, Benthic Paxton .... BC 1999
Lake (Texada Island)
Stickleback, Benthic Vananda Creek .... BC 1999
Stickleback, Limnetic Paxton .... BC 1999
Lake (Texada Island)
Stickleback, Limnetic Vananda Creek ... BC 1999
Sucker, Salish .... BC 1986
Trout, Aurora .... ON 2000
Whitefish, Atlantic (Acadian) .... NS 1984

Molluscs
Bean, Rayed .... ON 1999
Lampmussel, Wavy-rayed .... ON 1999
Mussel, Mudpuppy .... ON 2001
Physa, Hotwater .... BC 1998
Riffleshell, Northern .... ON 1999
Snail, Banff Springs .... AB 1997
Snuffbox .... ON 2001

Lepidopterans[1]
Blue, Island .... BC .... 2000 ▶

▶ Checkerspot, Taylor's .... BC 2000
Ringlet, Maritime .... QC, NB 1997

Plants
Agalinis, Gattinger's .... ON 1999
Agalinis, Skinner's .... ON 1999
Ammannia, Scarlet .... BC, ON 1999
Avens, Eastern Mountain .... NS 1999
Balsamroot, Deltoid .... BC 1996
Bluehearts .... ON 1998
Braya, Long's .... NF 1997
Bugbane, Tall .... BC 2001
Bulrush, Bashful (Few-flowered Club-rush) ...... ON 2000
Bush-clover, Slender .... ON 1999
Buttercup, Water-plantain .... BC 1996
Cactus, Eastern Prickly Pear .... ON 1998
Coreopsis, Pink .... NS 1999
Cryptanthe, Tiny .... AB, SK 1998
Fern, Southern Maidenhair .... BC 1998
Gentian, White Prairie .... ON 1991
Ginseng, American .... ON, QC 1999
Goat's-rue, Virginia .... ON 1996
Goldenrod, Showy .... ON 1999
Lady's-slipper, Small White .... MB, ON 1999
Lotus, Seaside Birds-foot .... BC 1996
Lousewort, Furbish's .... NB 1998
Lupine, Prairie .... BC 1996
Milkwort, Pink .... ON 1998
Mountain-mint, Hoary .... ON 1998
Mulberry, Red .... ON 1999
Orchid, Western Prairie Fringed .... MB 2000
Owl-clover, Bearded .... BC 1998
Paintbrush, Golden .... BC 1995
Plantain, Heart-leaved .... ON 1998
Pogonia, Large Whorled .... ON 1998
Pogonia, Nodding .... ON 1999
Pogonia, Small Whorled .... ON 1998
Quillwort, Engelmann's .... ON 1992
Sanicle, Bear's-foot .... BC 2001
Sedge, False Hop .... ON, QC 1997
Sedge, Juniper .... ON 1999
Sprike-rush, Horsetail .... ON 2000
Sundew, Thread-leaved .... NS 1991
Thistle, Pitcher's .... ON 1999
Toothcup .... BC, ON 1999
Tree, Cucumber .... ON 1999
Trillium, Drooping .... ON 1996
Twayblade, Purple .... ON 1999
Willow, Barrens .... NF 2001
Wintergreen, Spotted .... YT, NT, BC, AB 2000
Wood-poppy .... ON 1993
Woodsia, Blunt-lobed .... ON, QC 1994
Woolly-heads, Tall .... (Pacific population) BC 2001

Lichens
Seaside Centipede .... BC 1996

Mosses
Moss, Apple .... BC 1997

Source: *Committee on Status of Endangered Wildlife in Canada*
(1) Lepidopteran: Order of insects with four wings covered by fine scales; butterflies and moths.

Geographical Locations

AB Alberta	NF Newfoundland	ON Ontario
BC British Columbia	NS Nova Scotia	PE Prince Edward Island
MB Manitoba	NT Northwest Territories	QC Quebec
NB New Brunswick	NU Nunavut	SK Saskatchewan
		YT Yukon Territory

The Human Genome Project

On June 26, 2000, US scientists announced that they had finished "sequencing the genome." In some quarters the achievement was hailed as the greatest advance since Charles Darwin's *Origin of Species* was published. What's it all about? It's about the "mapping" or sequencing of all the DNA in an organism. In the case of the Human Genome Project, it's about mapping all the DNA in us. Why does it matter? (And what language are they speaking?)

■ It Starts with DNA

Deoxyribonucleic acid, better known as DNA, has four chemical components or bases. The bases are adenine, cytosine, guanine and thymine or A, C, G and T. It is the pattern of organization of A, C, G and T that determines how a particular gene (portion of DNA) directs the production of proteins and holds genetic information that gets passed (copied) to new cells.

What the participants in the Genome project did was take purified DNA and use computerized sequencing devices to read the order of the four chemicals in every chromosome and in each of the tens of thousands of genes that make up the human organism. While the sequencing is done, much work remains to find out what all of the information means. (Some have suggested that while we've got the "book of life" in our hands, it's written in a foreign language.)

■ What could it mean?

Figuring out the biochemical code for all our genes is likely the first (vital) step in figuring out what each protein does, how it works with the rest of the proteins and how the process all relates to making up and maintaining a healthy human being. (Or, conversely, what happens when things go wrong.) Some raise the spectre of designer babies or discrimination based on an analysis of an individual's genes (for instance, an insurance company could refuse coverage for those found to have a genetic predisposition to cancer—and these are genuine concerns. Others are hoping to go beyond the keys to hundreds of diseases—all the way to cures. Drugs could be designed to work with a particular person's genetic make-up, for maximum effectiveness with few side effects. Scientists can already see which of the thousands of genes are active in a particular tissue sample and are starting to probe the mysteries of diseases such as diabetes or Alzheimer's.

■ Who did the work?

Commercial enterprises raced an international consortium of scientists funded by the US and Great Britain to do the initial sequencing. A number of other countries have human genome research programs as well, including Australia, Brazil, Canada, China, Denmark, France, Germany, Israel, Italy, Japan, Korea, Mexico, the Netherlands, Russia and Sweden. A major issue has been "who owns the work"? The government-funded project has steadily posted its findings on a public database for all to use. In other quarters, the debate over the right to patent certain sequences has led to concerns that key information will be held for the benefit of only a few.

■ What's happening in Canada?

Genome Canada, a non-profit corporation set up to support research into genomics, committed $176 million in early 2001 to 17 research projects and 5 genome centres across Canada. In June, 2001, the corporation announced another competition, with up to $165 million more to be invested in worthwhile projects.

"What Genome Canada has allowed us to do is dream, and dream big," said Willie Davidson, dean of science at Simon Fraser University and head of a project to map the genome of the Atlantic salmon. "I've been dreaming about this for 20 years."

Other projects include examining the legal, ethical and social aspects of genomic research, building a database of protein structures, tracing the evolution of prokaryotes (single-celled creatures without nuclei), studying the environmental interactions of certain bacteria, tracking the genetic changes that take place when a cell becomes cancerous and a host of others.

All told, British Columbia got $46 million for studies relating to fisheries, health, the environment and forestry. The Prairie region got $19 million for studies relating to agriculture and to ethical and legal issues. Ontario researchers are studying health and legal and ethical issues, to the tune of $47 million. In Quebec, $52 million will finance research into health and ethical/legal issues. In the Maritimes, research into the environment, evolution, and health will consume $12 million.

For more information, visit http://www.Genome Canada.ca

FOCUS ON...

The Question of Life

Where did life on Earth begin? Conventional wisdom says it began on the planet about 3 billion years ago, perhaps underwater, or in tidal pools. But scientists have speculated for years about another possibilities—that life came to Earth from somewhere else.

Known as "panspermia," such theories have always been proposed by a minority of thinkers, including the Swedish chemist and Nobel laureate Svante Arrhenius and the British astronomers Fred Hoyle and Chandra Wickramasinghe. There are two main reasons they have not won widespread acceptance: It's hard to imagine how living materials could form in space and it is equally hard to imagine how living material could come to Earth without being destroyed in the process.

But early in 2001, NASA scientists, duplicating the harsh conditions of cold interstellar space in their laboratory, created primitive cells that mimic the membranes found in all living things. The work by scientists at NASA Ames Research Center is important because some scientists believe that the delivery—by comets, meteorites and interplanetary dust—of similar organic compounds born in interstellar space might have "kick-started" life on Earth.

The research leader, Dr. Louis Allamandola, said the discovery implies that life could be everywhere in the universe.

The researchers from Ames's Astrochemistry Laboratory and the Department of Chemistry and Biochemistry at the University of California, Santa Cruz, used simple, everyday chemicals to create "proto"-cells. It is a process that happens all the time in the dense molecular clouds of space, according to Dr. Allamandola.

The scientists re-created the conditions found in the cold vacuum of space, and then shone ultraviolet radiation—found everywhere—on a series of simple ices. (Interstellar ices are made of familiar everyday chemicals such as water, methanol (wood alcohol), ammonia and carbon monoxide that are frozen together.)

Irradiating the ices created solid materials which, when immersed in water, spontaneously created soap bubble-like membranous structures that contained both an "inside" and an "outside" layer.

This new work appears to show that the early chemical steps believed to be important for the origin of life do not require an already-formed planet. Instead, they seem to take place in deep space long before planet formation occurs. In other words, vastness of space could be filled with chemical compounds that, if they land in a hospitable environment like our Earth, can readily jump-start life.

Membranes are important in all modern life forms, and are thought to be a key element in the development of life, because they protect the chemistry involved in life processes from being disrupted. "Membranes are like a house," said team member Jason Dworkin of the SETI (Search for Extraterrestrial Intelligence) Institute. "Maybe these molecules were just the raw lumber lying around that allowed origin-of-life chemicals to move in and set up housekeeping or construct their own houses."

The research was part of NASA's astro-biology program, which is aimed at finding out how life originated, and how likely it is that life exists elsewhere than Earth.

The obvious place to look for extra-terrestrial life is the planet Mars; researchers are still debating whether mysterious structures found inside a meteorite that came from Mars are evidence of life long ago.

Early in 2001, an international team of researchers reported what they called compelling evidence that certain crystals in the Martian meteorite ALH84001 are of biological origin, created by "bacteria" native to the Red Planet. It remains to find the bacteria themselves, said Dr. Imre Friedmann, an NRC senior research fellow at NASA Ames.

Other researchers, however, were sceptical, arguing that non-biological processes could equally well have created the crystals. The debate seems likely to continue.

Zoos and Aquariums*

Maritime Region:

☐ **Aquarium and Marine Centre**
C.P. 1010, 2nd Avenue, Shippigan, NB E0B 2P0.
Tel: (506) 336-3013 Fax: (506) 336-3057.
Entrance fee. Open May to September.
http://inter.gov.nb.ca/dfa/aecm.htm

☐ **Cherry Brook Zoo**
901 Foster Thurston Drive, Saint John, NB E2K 5H9.
Tel: (506) 634-1440. Fax: (506) 634-0717.
Entrance fee. Open all year. E-mail: noah@nbnet.nb.ca

☐ **Magnetic Hill Zoo**
100 Worthington Avenue, Moncton, NB E1C 9Z3.
Tel: (506) 384-0303 Fax (506) 853-3569.
Open May to October, with limited openings on
winter weekends. Entrance fee.
www.greatermoncton.com/mhzoo/index.html

Central Canada:

☐ **Aquarium du Québec**
1675, avenue des Hotels, Sainte-Foy, Que. G1W 4S3.
Tel: (418) 659-5266. Fax: (418) 646-9238.
Entrance fee. Open all year.
www.aquarium.qc.ca/aquarium.html

☐ **The Biodøme de Montréal**
An environmental museum. 4777, avenue Pierre-de
Coubenin, Montréal, Que. H1V 1B3. Tel: (514) 868-
3000. Fax: (514) 868-3065. Entrance fee. Open all
year. www.ville.montreal.qc.ca/biodome/bdm.htm

☐ **Parc safari Africain**
850 Route 202, Hemmingford, Que. J0L 1H0.
Tel: (514) 247-2727 Fax: (514) 247-3563.
Entrance fee. Open mid-May to Labour Day.
www.parcsafari.com

☐ **Saint-Félicien Zoo**
2230 Boulevarde du Jardin, Saint-Félicien, Que.
G8K 2P8. Tel: (418) 679-0543 Fax: (418) 679-3647.
Entrance fee. Open mid-May to mid-October.
www.zoosauvage@destination.ca

☐ **Société Zoologique de Granby**
525, rue Saint-Hubert, Granby, Que. J2G 5P3.
Tel: (450) 372-9113. Fax: (450) 372-5531.
Entrance fee. Open May to September.
www.zoogranby.qc.ca

☐ **African Lion Safari and Game Farm**
R.R#1, Cambridge, Ont. N1R 5S2.
Tel: (519) 623-2620. Fax: (519) 623-9542.
Entrance fee. Open summer. www.lionsafari.com

☐ **Bowmanville Zoological Park**
340 King Street East, Bowmanville, Ont. L1C 3K5.
Tel: (905) 623-5655 Fax: (905) 623-9675.

☐ **Jungle Cat World**
3667 Concession 6, Orono, Ont. L0B 1M0.
Tel: (905) 983-5016. Fax: (905) 983 9858.
Entrance fee. Open March to November.
www.junglecatworld.com

☐ **Toronto Zoo**
361A Old Finch Avenue, Scarborough, Ont. M1B 5K7.

Tel: (416) 392-5900. Fax: (416) 392-5934. Entrance
fee. Open all year. www.torontozoo.com

Western Canada:

☐ **Assiniboine Park Zoo**
2355 Corydon Avenue, Winnipeg, Man. R3P 0R5.
Tel: (204) 986-6921 Fax: (204) 832-5420. Entrance
fee. Open all year.

☐ **Saskatoon Zoo**
1903 Forest Drive, Saskatoon, Sask. S7S 1G9.
Tel: (306) 975-3382 Fax: (306) 975-3326.
Entrance fee. Open all year.

☐ **Alberta Birds of Prey**
P.O. Box 1150, Coaldale, Alta T1M 1M9.
Tel: (403) 345-4262.

☐ **Calgary Zoo, Botanical Garden and Prehistoric
Park**
P.O. Box 3036, Station "B," 1300 Zoo Road NE,
Calgary, Alta T2M 4R8. Tel: (403) 232-9300
Fax: (403) 237-7582. Entrance fee. Open all year.
www.calgaryzoo.ab.ca

☐ **Marine Life Department/Dolphin Lagoon**
West Edmonton Mall, #2472, 8770-170 Street,
Edmonton, Alta T5T 4M2. Tel: (403) 444-5346
Fax: (403) 444-5266.
www.westedmall.com/parks/dolphin.htm

☐ **Valley Zoo and John Janzen Nature Centre**
P.O. Box 2359, 13315 Buena Vista Road, Edmonton,
Alta T5J 2R7. Tel: (403) 496-6911 Fax: (403) 944-
7529. Entrance fee. Open all year.
ww.ualberta.ca/EDMONTON/CONTRIB/jjanzen/

☐ **Barrett Aviaries**
3745 Melrose Road, Qualicum Beach, BC V9K 1V3.
Tel: (250) 752-2912 Fax: (250) 752-1600.

☐ **Crystal Garden**
713 Douglas Street, Victoria, BC V8W 1N8.
Tel: (250) 381-1277 Fax: (250) 383-1218.
Entrance fee. Open all year.
www.bcpcc.com/crystal

☐ **Greater Vancouver Zoological Centre**
5048-264 Street, Aldergrove, BC V4W 1N7.
Tel: (604) 856-6825 Fax: (604) 857-9008.
www.greatervancouverzoo.com

☐ **Kamloops Wildlife Park**
P.O. Box 698, East Trans Canada Highway, Kamloops,
BC V2C 5L7. Tel: (250) 573-3242 Fax: (250) 573-2406.
Entrance fee. Open all year.
www.kamloopswildlife.com

☐ **Mountain View Farms Breeding and
Conservation Centre** 8011-240th St., Langley, BC
V3A 4P9. Tel: (604) 688-0553 Fax: (604) 688-7330.
www.mtnviewfarms.com

☐ **Vancouver Aquarium Marine Science Centre**
P.O. Box 3232, Stanley Park, Vancouver, BC V6B 3X8.
Tel: (604) 659-3474 Fax: (604) 659-3515. Entrance
fee. Open all year. www.vanaqua.org

*Accredited by the Canadian Association of Zoos and
Aquariums.

Canada may well have been one of the best kept secrets on the world's arts and entertainment scene, but the secret is getting harder and harder to keep as artists like David Cronenberg, Alanis Morissette, Robert LePage, and Carol Shields make their mark. Historically, the small size and scattered nature of the Canadian market made dissemination of Canadian works of art and entertainment products difficult. But the years following World War II saw an explosion of activity in every sector, fuelled by public institutions such as the CBC, the Canada Council for the Arts, and the National Film Board and similar provincial and local agencies. Canadian content requirements for broadcasters and tax and investment measures favouring Canadian publishers have also helped foster successful, if fragile, publishing and recording industries. In 1996 all levels of government devoted $5.8 billion to culture (this includes federal support for the CBC and provincial and local support for public libraries). Restraints on public spending over the past two decades have caused emphasis to be placed on private investment and on production for foreign markets. During the 1990s, film and TV production saw a 200 percent increase in foreign investment and a 33 percent increase in private sector Canadian investment. At the same time Canadian authors, agents and publishers found the sale of foreign rights to be a lucrative stream of revenue in a world hungry to read the work of writers such as Shields, Michael Ondaatje, Anne Michaels and Anne-Marie MacDonald.

MAJOR ARTS COUNCILS

The Canada Council: 350 Albert St, Box 1047, Ottawa, Ont., K1P 5V8; tel: (613) 566-4414 (toll-free:1-800-263-5588); fax: (613) 566-4390; e-mail: [employee name]@canadacouncil.ca (see personnel directory at website);website: www.canadacouncil.ca.

Alberta Foundation for the Arts: Alberta Community Development, 901 Standard Life Centre, 10405 Jasper Ave, Edmonton, Alta, T5J 4R7; tel: (780) 427-9968; fax: (780)422-9132; e-mail: afa@mcd.gov.ab.ca; Website: http://www.affta.ab.ca

British Columbia Arts Council: Box 9819, Stn. Prov. Govt., Victoria, BC, V8W 9W3; tel: (250) 356-1718; fax: (250) 387-4099; e-mail: csbinfo@tbc.gov.bc.ca; Website: www.bcartscouncil.gov.bc.ca

Manitoba Arts Council: 525-93 Lombard Avenue, Winnipeg, Man., R3B 3B1; tel: (204) 945-2237; fax: 945-5925; website: www.gov.mb.ca/cgi-bin/print_hit_bold.pl/chc/archives/MAC/mac.html?Manitoba+Arts+Council#first_hit

New Brunswick Arts Board: P.O. Box 6000, Fredericton, NB, E3B-5H1; tel: (506) 453-4307; fax (506) 453-6043; e-mail: artsboard@gov.nb.ca

Newfoundland and Labrador Arts Council: Box 98, St. John's, Nfld, A1C 5H5; tel: (709) 726-2212; fax: (709)726-0619; e-mail: nlacmail@newcomm.net; website: www.nlac.nf.ca

Northwest Territories Arts Council: Department of Education, Culture and Employment, Government of the Northwest Territories, Box 1320, Yellowknife, NWT, X1A 2L9; phone: (867) 920-3103; fax: (867) 873-0205

Nova Scotia Arts Council: P.O. Box 1559, CRO, Halifax, NS, B3J-2Y3; phone: (902) 422-1123; fax (902) 422-1445; e-mail: nsartscouncil@ns.sympatico.ca

Ontario Arts Council: 151 Bloor St. W., Toronto, ON M5S 1T6; phone: (416) 961-1660; fax: (416) 961-7796 (Toll-free: 1-800-387-0058); e-mail: info@arts.on.ca; website: www.arts.on.ca

P.E.I. Council of the Arts: tel:(902) 368-4410

Conseil des arts et des lettres du Quebec: Quebec bureau: 79, boulevard René-Lévesque Est, bureau 320, Quebec, G1R 5N5; tel: (418) 643-1707, (Toll-free) 1-800-897-1707; fax: (418) 643-4558; Montreal bureau: 500, Place d'Armes, 15e étage, Montréal, QC, H2Y 2W2; tel: (514) 864-3350, (Toll-free)1-800-608-3350; fax: (514) 864-4160; e-mail. affaires.publiques@calq.gouv.qc.ca; website: www.calq.gouv.qc.ca/fr/index.htm

Saskatchewan Arts Board: 3rd Floor, 3475 Albert Street Regina, Saskatchewan S4S 6X6; tel: (306) 787-4056, (Toll-free, Saskatchewan only)1-800-667-7526; fax: (306) 787-4199; e-mail: sab@artsboard.sk.ca

Yukon Tourism, Arts Branch: Box 2703, Whitehorse, Yukon, Y1A 2C6; tel: (867) 667-8589, (Toll-free within Yukon) 1-800-661-0408; fax: (867) 393-6456. e-mail: arts@gov.yk.ca; website: www.artsykon.com

TELEVISION

Television first reached Canada in the 1940s from border stations in the United States. The Canadian Broadcasting Corporation's TV services were launched in 1952. The launch in English Canada was less than auspicious; the first image to appear on the screen was the CBC logo presented upside down. The CBC recovered its poise and the network grew rapidly, opening stations across the country and broadcasting its programs on affiliated private stations.

CBC TV was joined by the private Canadian Television Network in 1961. The CanWest/Global system began in the 1970s and has become Canada's third major television network. Through the 1980s and 1990s the CRTC has licensed dozens of specialty cable services to ensure that Canadian services offer viewers a full range of choices.

While the most-watched television programs in Canada continue to be American dramas and situation comedies, Canadian broadcasters have scored considerable success with programs such as *Wojek*, *The King of Kensington*, *Street Legal*, and *Due South*. Canadian producers have been particularly successful with children's programs such as *Mr. Dressup* and with sketch comedy programs including *The Wayne and Shuster Comedy Hour*, *This Hour Has 22 Minutes*, and *SCTV*.

Today the television market accounts for 70 percent of the 14,000 film projects undertaken in Canada each year. Much of that production is destined for air in the United States and other countries as international coproduction becomes an increasingly popular way of funding television programs around the world.

Canada's Television Classification System

In the fall of 1997, a television classification system was formally launched on Canadian airwaves to help Canadians identify programming suitable to various age groups. There are seven classification levels. Although violence is the most important content consideration, each classification also includes information on coarse language, nudity and sex. The classifications are designed for use with V-chip technology which enables parents to block reception of undesirable programs. A Canadian V-chip system using the following classifications is expected to be operational in 2001.

 Children: Might contain occasional comedic, unrealistic depictions of violence. No offensive language. No sex or nudity.

 Children Over 8 Years: Might include mild physical violence, comedic violence, comic horror, special effects; fantasy, supernatural, or animated violence. No profanity. No sex or nudity.

 General: Violence is minimal and infrequent. Contains no frightening special effects not required by the storyline. May contain inoffensive slang. No profanity. No sex or nudity.

 Parental Guidance: Moderate violence which must be justified within the context of the storyline. Might contain mild profanity, suggestive language, some nudity.

 Over 14 Years: Might contain intense scenes of violence. Could include frequent profanity. Mght include scenes of nudity and/or sexual activity.

 Adults: Depictions of violence are intended for adult viewing, and thus are not suitable for audiences under 18 years of age. Might contain graphic language and explicit portrayals of sex and/or nudity.

Exempt: News, sports, documentaries, and other information programming, talk shows, music videos, and variety programming.

Source: *Media Awareness Network, www.media-awareness.ca*

The DTV Revolution Begins

In 2001 Canadian broadcasting took a major step towards realizing the multi-channel universe that industry observers have been predicting for the past decade. In November 2000, the Canadian Radio-television and Telecommunications Commission (CRTC) approved 21 applications for new digital television services which cable, satellite and other television delivery systems will be required to carry. Approximately 200 more services were approved pending their ability to negotiate distribution deals with cable and satellite companies.

The services granted mandatory carriage were:

BookTelevision—The
    Channel

Connect

FashionTelevision—The
    Channel

Health Network Canada

Land and Sea

LCN Affaires

Men TV

Perfecto, La Chaîne

PrideVision

Réseau Info Sports

Télé Ha! Ha!

The Biography Channel

The Canadian Documentary
    Channel

The Independent Film
    Channel Canada

The Issues Channel

13th Street

Travel TV

13e rue

Wisdom: Canada's Body,
    Mind & Spirit Channel

Women's Sports Network

ZDTV Canada

A number of these channels had their premieres in September 2001.

While the new channels originate as analog signals, they are converted into digital signals for transmission via satellite and on cable. Because cable's analog capacity is pretty much full, any new services will have to be transmitted this way because digital signals take up so much less bandwidth. In order to receive the digital services, viewers require a set-top box that converts the signals back to analog for viewing on conventional TV sets.

Fully digitized television, which is produced as well as transmitted digitally and designed for viewing on a new generation of digital TV sets, is expected to appear in Canada after 2006, its scheduled roll-out in the United States. Digital's two principle formats—High Definition and Standard Definition—will bring major improvements in picture and sound quality, and give the broadcasting system virtually unlimited capacity for new services. Industry groups say that analog broadcasting is expected to continue well past 2010, and that many consumers will continue to use analog sets with the help of converters.

Sources: *CRTC, Canadian Digital Television*

Canada Mourns Mr. Dressup

It's not often that an American entertainer finds greener fields for their career in Canada. But that's exactly what happened to U.S.-born children's performer Ernie Coombs when he emigrated north in the early 1960s. Coombs, whose sudden death Canada mourned on September 18, 2001, was known to several generations of Canadians as Mr. Dressup. At CBC Television, Coombs found a sympathetic environment for the enlightened and nurturing children's programming that became his specialty. He developed the Mr. Dressup character at first for a weekday afternoon programme entitled Butternut Square. Mr. Dressup was given his own show in 1967 in which he performed with his fellow hosts, puppets Casey and Finnegan. It remained in production for an unprecedented 29 seasons until, in 1996, Coombs decided to retire from the grind of weekly television. After that the show continued to enjoy success in reruns, while Coombs continued to enthrall Canada's children in live productions.

The CRTC: Canada's Communications Watchdog

The Canadian Radio-television and Telecommunications Commission (CRTC) regulates all aspects of the Canadian broadcasting system. It grants licences to radio and television broadcasters, enforces the conditions of those licences and reviews broadcaster performance at regularly scheduled hearings. Created under the Broadcasting Act of 1968, the Commission inherited a long tradition of government supervision of broadcasting in Canada. Radio broadcasting was regulated in its early days under the Radiotelegraph Act. In the 1930s responsibility for radio was shifted to the newly-created Canadian Broadcasting Corporation. Private broadcasters were unhappy with a system that gave their public sector competitor the right to supervise their businesses and so an independent regulator, the Board of Broadcast Governors (BBG), was formed in 1958. The Broadcasting Act of 1968 replaced the BBG with the CRTC. The commission scored a success with the establishment of Canadian content regulations in 1971 for radio. Through the 1980s and 1990s it insisted on higher levels of quality Canadian programming from private television broadcasters and oversaw the introduction of dozens of new specialty services on cable and satellite television. While the CRTC also supervises telecommunications it announced in 1999 that it would not attempt to regulate the Internet.

Web site: *www.crtc.gc.ca*

The Gemini Awards, 2000

The Gemini Awards were established in 1986 to honor outstanding contributions to the Canadian television industry. Given out annually by the Academy of Canadian Cinema and Television, the Geminis grew out of the former ACTRA Awards, last presented in 1985. The 15th Geminis were given out Oct. 28–30, 2000.

Dramatic series . . . . *DaVinci's Inquest*
Comedy series . . . . *This Hour Has 22 Minutes*
TV movie . . . . *Dr. Lucille: The Lucille Teasdale Story*
Actor (dramatic series) . . . . Michael Riley, *Power Play*, "What It All Meant"
Actor (dramatic program) . . . . Jonathan Scarfe, The Sheldon Kennedy Story
Supporting actor (dramatic program or mini-series) . . . . Robert Wisden, *The Sheldon Kennedy Story*
Supporting actor (dramatic series) . . . . Pedro Salvin, *Peter Benchley's Amazon*, "The Chosen"
Actress (dramatic series) . . . . Torri Higginson, *The City*, "Properties of Light"
Actress (dramatic program) . . . . Colleen Rennison, *A Feeling Called Glory*
Supporting actress (dramatic program or mini-series) . . . . Shirley Douglas, *Shadow Lake*
Supporting actress (dramatic series) . . . . Shannon Lawson, *The City*, "Free Fall"
Performance (performing arts program or series) . . . . Juan Chioran, *Dracula*
Performance (comedy program or series) . . . . Cathy Jones, Rick Mercer, Greg Thomey, Mary Walsh,
This Hour Has 22 Minutes, Season 7, "Episode 21"
Performance (variety program or series) . . . . Brigitte Gall, *Brigitte Gall: Joan of Montreal*
Animated program or series . . . . *Angela Anaconda*, p. Steven DeNure, Neil Court,
Joanna Ferrone, John Mariella, Sue Rose, Beth Stevenson
Children's or Youth program or series . . . . *Incredible Story Studio*, p. Kevin DeWalt,
Robert de Lint, Rob King, Virginia Thompson
Documentary series . . . . *The View From Here*
Lifestyle information series . . . . *Foodessence*
Best Talk/General Information Series . . . . *Skylight*
Sports program . . . . *Legends of Hockey: The Second Season*
News Information series . . . . *the fifth estate*
Performing arts program . . . . *Tall Tales From The Long Corner*
Short dramatic program . . . . *A Feeling Called Glory*
Science, technology, nature, environment or adventure documentary program . . . . *After Darwin*

Source: *Academy of Canadian Cinema and Television*

The Most-Watched Television Programs in Canada[1]

Top 10 Programs

1. Academy Awards (CTV)
2. *Who Wants to be a Millionaire?* (Wednesday Special, CTV)
3. *Who Wants to be a Millionaire?* (Thursday Special, CTV)
4. *Who Wants to be a Millionaire?* (Wednesday Special 2, CTV)
5. *Academy Awards Pre-Show* (CTV)
6. *Who Wants to be a Millionaire?* (Thursday Special 2, CTV)
7. Grey Cup Game 2000 (CBC)
8. Emmy Awards (CTV)
9. Golden Globe Awards (CTV)
10. *Titanic (CTV)*

Top 10 Regularly Scheduled Programs[2]

1. *The Sopranos* (CTV)
2. *E.R.* (CTV)
3. Stanley Cup Finals (CBC)
4. NHL Playoffs, Round Two (CBC)
5. *Law and Order* (CTV)
6. NHL Playoffs, Round One (CBC)
7. *Who Wants to be a Millionaire?* (all episodes averaged, CTV)
8. World Skating Championships (CTV)
9. *Third Watch* (CTV)
10. *The West Wing* (CTV)

Source: *List based on data provided by Nielsen Media Research*
(1) Persons 2+ for the period Aug. 28, 2000-Sept. 2, 2001. (2) Five episodes minimum.

The Prime-Time Emmy Awards, 1999–2000

The 2000–01 Emmy Awards, presented on behalf of the US Academy of Television Arts and Sciences, were postponed twice: the September 16th telecast was called off after the terrorist attacks on New York and Washington; the rescheduled broadcast for October 7th was scrubbed as military action began against Afghanistan. In contention: *The Sopranos* led the nominees with 22, followed by 18 for *The West Wing*. For information concerning the winners of 2000–01 Emmy Awards, visit www.emmys.tv

OUTSTANDING DRAMA SERIES . . . . *The West Wing*, NBC
Actor (drama series) . . . . James Gandolfini, *The Sopranos*, HBO
Actress (drama series) . . . . Sela Ward, *Once And Again*, ABC
Supporting actor (drama series) . . . . Richard Schiff, *The West Wing*, NBC
Supporting actress (drama series) . . . . Allison Janney, *The West Wing*, NBC
Directing (drama series) . . . . Thomas Schlamme, *The West Wing*, Pilot, NBC
Writing (drama series) . . . . Aaron Sorkin, Rick Cleveland, *The West Wing*. "In Excelsis Deo," NBC

OUTSTANDING COMEDY SERIES . . . . *Will & Grace*, NBC
Actor (comedy series) . . . . Michael J. Fox, *Spin City*, ABC
Actress (comedy series) . . . . Patricia Heaton, *Everybody Loves Raymond*, CBS
Supporting actor (comedy series) . . . . Sean Hayes, *Will & Grace*, NBC
Supporting actress (comedy series) . . . . Megan Mullally, *Will & Grace*, NBC
Writing (comedy series) . . . . Linwood Boomer, *Malcolm In The Middle*, Pilot, FOX

OUTSTANDING MINISERIES . . . . *The Corner*, HBO
Actor (miniseries or movie) . . . . Jack Lemmon, *Tuesdays With Morrie*, ABC
Actress (miniseries or movie) . . . . Halle Berry, *Introducing Dorothy Dandridge*, HBO
Supporting actor (miniseries or movie) . . . . Hank Azaria, *Tuesdays With Morrie*, ABC
Supporting actress (miniseries or movie) . . . . Vanessa Redgrave, *If These Walls Could Talk 2*, HBO
Directing (miniseries or movie) . . . . Charles S. Dutton, *The Corner*, HBO
Writing (miniseries or movie) . . . . David Simon, David Mills, *The Corner*, HBO

OUTSTANDING VARIETY, MUSIC OR COMEDY SERIES . . . . *The Chris Rock Show*, HBO
OUTSTANDING VARIETY, MUSIC OR COMEDY SPECIAL . . . *Saturday Night Live: The 25th Anniversary Special*, NBC
Directing (variety or music) . . . . Paul Miller, *1998 Tony Awards*, CBS
Writing (variety or music) . . . . Eddie Izzard, *Eddie Izzard: Dress To Kill*, HBO
Performance (variety or music) . . . . Eddie Izzard, *Eddie Izzard: Dress To Kill*, HBO

OUTSTANDING TV MOVIE . . . . *Tuesdays With Morrie*, ABC

Television Networks and Cable Services

Arts & Entertainment Network (A&E): 235 E 45th St, New York, NY 10017. (212) 210-1328

Atlantic Television System & Atlantic Satellite Network: Box 1653, 2885 Robie St, Halifax, N.S. B3K 4P5. (902) 453-4000.

Bravo!: 299 Queen St W, Toronto, Ont. M5V 2Z5 (416) 591-5757

C-SPAN (Cable Satellite Public Affairs Network): 400 N. Capitol St. NW, Suite 650, Washington, DC 20001. (202) 737-3220

Cable News Network (CNN): 1 CNN Centre, Box 105366, Atlanta, GA 30348-5366. (404) 827-1700

Canadian Broadcasting Corporation (CBC): Box 500 Stn. A, Toronto, Ont. M5W 1E6. (416) 205-3311

Canal Famille: 2100 Sainte-Catherine ouest, Bureau 800, Montreal, Que. H3H 2T3. (514) 939-3150

CanWest/Global Communications Corp.: 201 Portage Ave, 31st Flr, TD Centre, Winnipeg, Man. R3B 3L7. (204) 956-2025

Capital Cities/ABC, Inc.: 77 W 66th St, New York, NY 10023-6298. (212) 456-7777

CHUM Limited: 1331 Yonge St, Toronto, Ont. M4T 1Y1. (416) 925-6666.

Columbia Broadcasting System (CBS): 51 W 52nd St, New York, NY 10019. (212) 975-4321

Country Music Television: 2806 Opreyland Dr., Nashville, TN 37214. (615) 871-5830

CTV Television Network Ltd.: Box Stn. O, 9 Channel Ct., Toronto, Ont. M4A 2M9. (416) 595-4100

Discovery Channel: 2225 Sheppard Ave E, Suite 100, Toronto, Ont. M2J 5C2

The Family Channel Inc.: BCE Place, 181 Bay St., Box 787, Toronto, Ont. M5J 2T3. (416) 956-2030

Fox Broadcasting Co.: P.O. Box 900, Beverly Hills, CA 90213-0900. (310) 369-1000

Global Television Network: 81 Barber Greene Rd, Don Mills, Ont. M3C 2A2 (416) 446-5311

Inuit Broadcasting Corporation: 217 Laurier Ave W, Ste 703, Ottawa, Ont. K1P 5J6. (613) 235-1892

Life Network: 1155 Leslie St, Toronto, Ont. M3C 2J6. (416) 444-9494

Maclean Hunter Limited: 777 Bay St, Toronto, Ont. M5W 1A7. (416) 596-5103

The Movie Network/First Choice: BCE Place, 181 Bay St., Box 787, Toronto, Ont. M5J 2T3. (416) 956-2010

MuchMusic Network: 299 Queen St W, Toronto, Ont. M5V 2Z5. (416) 591-5757

MusiquePlus: 1355 Sainte-Catherine est, Montreal, Que. H3B 1A5. (514) 284-7587

National Broadcasting Company (NBC): 30 Rockefeller Plaza, New York, NY 10112. (212) 664-4444

Premier Choix TVEC Inc.: 2100 Sainte-Catherine ouest, #800 Montreal, Que. H3H 2T3. (514) 939-3150

Public Broadcasting Service (PBS): 1320 Braddock Place, Alexandria, VA 22314-1698. (703) 739-5000

Le Reseau des Sports: 1755 Boul. René-Lévesque est, Bur. 300, Montreal, Que. H2K 4P6. (514) 599-2244

Rogers Broadcasting Ltd.: 36 Victoria St, Toronto, Ont. M5C 1H3. (416) 864-2000

Showcase Television Inc.: 121 Bloor St E, #200, Toronto, Ont. M4W 1B9 (416) 967-2473

Société de radio-télévision du Quebec (Radio-Quebec): 800, rue Fullum, Montreal, Que. H2K 3L7. (514) 521-2424

The Sports Network (TSN): 2225 Sheppard Ave E, Suite 100, Willowdale, Ont. M2J 5C2. (416) 494-1212

Telelatino Network Inc.: 5125 Steeles Ave W, Weston, Ont. M9L 1R5. (416) 744-8200

TVOntario (TVO): Box 200, Stn Q, Toronto, Ont. M4T 2T1. (416) 484-2600

Vision TV: 80 Bond St, Toronto, Ont. M5B 1X2. (416) 368-3194

The Weather Channel: 1 Robert Speck Parkway, Ste 1600, Mississauga, Ont. L4Z 4B3. (905) 566-9511

Women's Television Network: 300-1661Portage Ave, Winnipeg, Man. R3J 3T7. (204) 783-5116

YTV Canada Inc.: 64 Jefferson Ave, Unit 18, Toronto, Ont. M6K 3H3. (416) 534-1191

RADIO

Radio Broadcasting has played an integral part in Canada's cultural development. The first radio licence was issued in 1919 to an experimental station based in Montreal. Radio stations proliferated in the 1920s. Railway companies were among Canada's first radio broadcasters, presenting programs for the enjoyment of passengers aboard their trains. However, most stations devoted themselves almost entirely to music and other programming imported from the United States. In 1936 the Canadian Broadcasting Corporation was formed to help remedy the situation. By the end of WWII, the corporation was operating two networks in English-the Trans-Canada and Dominion networks-and one network in French. CBC's news service was born out of the need to keep Canadians informed of overseas action during the war. Andrew Allan's *Stage* and other dramatic programs were the backbone of the "Golden Age" of Canadian radio from 1945 to 1955. Private radio continued to rely heavily on American music programming, a situation that remained unchanged until 1971, when they were compelled to accept quotas by the federal regulator (see **Music** p. 630, **CRTC** p.626). CBC Radio languished after the introduction of television until a 1971 revamp of its programming lead to the creation of *Morningside*, *As It Happens* and *Sunday Morning* and added popular morning and "drive-home" local information shows to the schedule. Private radio continues to embrace the trend towards specialized program "niches" (country, classical, "oldies," and "all-news" etc.). That trend is expected to intensify in the next few years as digital radio provides virtually unlimited signal capacity.

Pre-Tax Profitability-Private Radio In Canada[1]

	1996	1997	1998	1999	2000
Total revenue	814 242 576	868 762 090	940 068 322	973 753 638	1 023 438 508
Total expenses	726 589 657	748 844 883	780 237 412	793 262 926	820 375 901
Depreciation	29 143 135	29 704 893	30 775 165	31 357 056	36 112 002
Interest	37 298 279	29 859 139	47 730 174	58 246 542	45 312 360
Adjustments	12 985 733	9 509 039	1 291 925	2 006 036	10 514 517
Pre-tax profits	8 225 779	50 844 145	80 033 656	88 881 080	111 123 723

Source: *CRTC*   (1) Reported in millions of dollars.

Radio Distribution Undertakings in Canada

	1997	1998	1999	2000	2001
AM[1]	559	546	540	498	476
FM[2]	1 269	1 321	1 324	1 258	1 357
Total	**1 828**	**1 867**	**1 864**	**1 756**	**1 833**

Source: *CRTC*

(1) AM includes low-power relay transmitters.

(2) FM includes community and campus stations, educational, native, ethnic stations and low power radio announcement systems.

MUSIC

The watershed year in the Canadian music industry was 1971, when the federal government imposed Canadian content regulations on the country's radio stations. These regulations helped build a domestic recording industry that has produced several generations of world-class pop stars including Bryan Adams, Céline Dion, Sarah MacLauchlan and Shania Twain.

Montreal, Toronto, and Vancouver have consistently served as centres for the Canadian popular music industry. But other cities have served as hotbeds at various periods. Winnipeg in the 1960s was dubbed the Liverpool of Canada for a scene that launched the careers of Neil Young and the

Guess Who. The Ottawa Valley has long been a place of musical ferment owing to the interaction of the its Irish, Scottish, and French settlers. Bruce Cockburn and Alanis Morrissette are two of the National Capital Region's best known alumni.

Nova Scotia and Newfoundland have historically been home to vibrant Celtic folk traditions and the 1990s saw the rise of Atlantic Canada as a major centre for music production in Canada. Those traditions have been parlayed into commercial success for artists such as The Rankins, singer Rita MacNeil, and folk/rock fiddlers Ashley MacIsaac and Natalie McMaster.

The Juno Awards, 1992–2001

The Juno Awards were established in 1975 to honor achievement in the Canadian recording industry. The name was chosen to honor Pierre Juneau, former head of the Canadian Radio-television and Telecommunications Commission (CRTC) which instituted "Canadian content" requirements in the nation's broadcast industry.

Nominations for most major Juno categories are determined by record sales, although the actual winners are selected by a vote of members of the

Canadian Academy of Recording Arts & Sciences.

Nominees must be Canadian citizens or landed immigrants and must have resided in Canada during the year prior to their nomination. Eligible recordings don't require national distribution, but must be available for retail sale in Canada.

The latest awards were announced March 4, 2001. The awards ceremony was broadcast live from the Copps Coliseum in Hamilton, Ont.

Canadian Entertainer of the Year

1992	Bryan Adams
1993	The Tragically Hip
1994	The Rankin Family
1995	The Tragically Hip
1996	Shania Twain

Best Selling Album (Foreign or Domestic)

2000	*Millennium*, Backstreet Boys
2001	*The Marshall Mathers LP*, Eminem

Best Album

1992	*Mad Mad World*, Tom Cochrane
1993	*Ingenue*, k.d. lang
1994	*Harvest Moon*, Neil Young
1995	*Colour of My Love*, Celine Dion
1996	*Jagged Little Pill*, Alanis Morissette
1997	*Trouble at the Henhouse*, The Tragically Hip
1998	*Clumsy*, Our Lady Peace
1999	*Let's Talk About Love*, Celine Dion
2000	*Supposed Former Infatuation Junkie*, Alanis Morissette
2001	*Maroon*, Barenaked Ladies

Best Single

1992	"Life Is a Highway," Tom Cochrane
1993	"Beauty and the Beast," Celine Dion/Peabo Bryson
1994	"Fare Thee Well Love," The Rankin Family
1995	"Could I Be Your Girl," Jann Arden
1996	"You Oughta Know," Alanis Morissette
1997	"Ironic," Alanis Morissette
1998	"Building a Mystery," Sarah McLachlan
1999	"One Week," Barenaked Ladies
2000	"Bobcaygeon," The Tragically Hip
2001	"I'm Like A Bird," Nelly Furtado

Best Female Artist

1992	Celine Dion
1993	Celine Dion
1994	Celine Dion
1995	Jann Arden
1996	Alanis Morissette
1997	Celine Dion
1998	Sarah McLachlan
1999	Celine Dion
2000	Chantal Kreviazuk
2001	Jann Arden

Best Male Artist

1992	Tom Cochrane
1993	Leonard Cohen
1994	Roch Voisine
1995	Neil Young
1996	Colin James
1997	Bryan Adams
1998	Paul Brandt
1999	Jim Cuddy
2000	Bryan Adams
2001	Neil Young

Best Group

1992	Crash Test Dummies
1993	Barenaked Ladies
1994	The Rankin Family
1995	The Tragically Hip

▶

▶ 1996 . . . . Blue Rodeo
1997 . . . . The Tragically Hip
1998 . . . . Our Lady Peace
1999 . . . . Barenaked Ladies
2000 . . . . Matthew Good Band
2001 . . . . Barenaked Ladies

Best Songwriter

1992 . . . . Tom Cochrane
1993 . . . . k.d. lang
1994 . . . . Leonard Cohen
1995 . . . . Jann Arden
1996 . . . . Alanis Morissette (with Glen Ballard)
1997 . . . . Alanis Morissette (with Glen Ballard)
1998 . . . . Sarah McLachlan/Pierre Marchand
1999 . . . . Bryan Adams,(w' co-songwriter)
Phil Thornalley "On A Day Like Today;"
(w' co-songwriter) Eliott Kennedy,"When You're Gone"
2000 . . . . . . Shania Twain, "Man! I Feel Like A Woman,"
(co-Songwriter Robert John "Mutt" Lange);
"You've Got A Way," (co-Songwriter Robert John "Mutt"
Lange); "That Don't Impress Me Much,"
(co-Songwriter Robert John "Mutt" Lange)
2001 . . . . . Nelly Furtado, "Turn Off The Light," "I'm Like
A Bird," "...on the radio (remember the days)"

Best New Solo Artist

1994 . . . . Jann Arden
1995 . . . . Susan Aglukark
1996 . . . . Ashley MacIsaac
1997 . . . . Terri Clark
1998 . . . . Holly McNarland
1999 . . . . Melanie Doane
2000 . . . . Tal Bachman
2001 . . . . Nelly Furtado

Best New Group

1994 . . . . The Waltons
1995 . . . . Moist
1996 . . . . The Philosopher Kings
1997 . . . . The Killjoys
1998 . . . . Leahy
1999 . . . . Johnny Favourite Swing Orchestra
2000 . . . . Sky
2001 . . . . Nickelback

Best Selling Francophone Album

1994 . . . . *Album de Peuple: Tome 2*
1995 . . . . *Coup de tête*
1996 . . . . *D'eux*
1997 . . . . *Live À Paris*
1998 . . . . *Marie Michèle Desrosiers*
Chante Les Classiques de Noël
1999 . . . . *S'il Suffisait D'Aimer*, Celine Dion
2000 . . . . *En Catimini*, La Chicane
2001 . . . . *Un grand noël d'amour*, Ginette Reno

Best Country Female Artist

1992 . . . . Cassandra Vasik
1993 . . . . Michelle Wright
1994 . . . . Cassandra Vasik
1995 . . . . Michelle Wright

1996 . . . . Shania Twain
1997 . . . . Shania Twain
1998 . . . . Shania Twain
1999 . . . . Shania Twain
2000 . . . . Shania Twain
2001 . . . . Terri Clark

Best Country Male Artist

1992 . . . . George Fox
1993 . . . . Gary Fjellgaard
1994 . . . . Charlie Major
1995 . . . . Charlie Major
1996 . . . . Charlie Major
1997 . . . . Paul Brandt
1998 . . . . Paul Brandt
1999 . . . . Paul Brandt
2000 . . . . Paul Brandt
2001 . . . . Paul Brandt

Best Country Group or Duo

1992 . . . . Prairie Oyster
1993 . . . . Tracey Prescott & Lonesome Daddy
1994 . . . . The Rankin Family
1995 . . . . Prairie Oyster
1996 . . . . Prairie Oyster
1997 . . . . The Rankin Family
1998 . . . . Farmer's Daughter
1999 . . . . Leahy
2000 . . . . The Rankins
2001 . . . . The Wilkinsons

Best Pop/Adult Album

2000 . . . . . . *Colour Moving And Still*, Chantal Kreviazuk
2001 . . . . *Maroon*, Barenaked Ladies

Best Rock Album

1992 . . . . *Roll the Bones*, Rush
1993 . . . . *Doin' the Nasty*, Slik Toxik
1994 . . . . *Dig*, I. Mother Earth
1995 . . . . *Suffersystem*, Monster Voodoo Machine
1996 . . . . *Jagged Little Pill*, Alanis Morissette
2000 . . . . *Beautiful Midnight*, Matthew Good Band
2001 . . . . *Music @ Work*, The Tragically Hip

Best Alternative Album

1998 . . . . *Glee*, Bran Van 3000
1999 . . . . *Rufus Wainwright*, Rufus Wainwright
2000 . . . . *Julie Doiron and the Wooden Stars*,
Julie Doiron and the Wooden Stars
2001 . . . . *Mass Romantic*, The New Pornographers

Best Rap Recording

1992 . . . . "My Definition of a Boombastic Jazz Style,"
Dream Warriors
1993 . . . . *Keep It Slammin'*, Devon
1994 . . . . *One Track Mind*, TBTBT
1995 . . . . *Certified*, Ghetto Concept
1996 . . . . *E-Z On Tha Motion*, Ghetto Concept
1997 . . . . *What It Takes*, Choclair
1998 . . . . *Cash Crop*, Rascalz
1999 . . . . *Northern Touch*, Rascalz featuring
Choclair, Kardinal Offishall, Thrust and Checkmate ▶

▶ 2000 . . . . *Ice Cold*, Choclair
2001 . . . . *Balance*, Swollen Members

Best Dance Recording

1992 . . . . "Everyone's a Winner (Chocolate Movement
Mix)," Bootsauce
1993 . "Love Can Move Mountains (Club Mix)," Celine Dion
1994 . . . . "Thankful (Raw Club Mix)," Red Light
1995 . . . . "Higher Love (Club Mix)," Capital Sound
1996 . . "A Deeper Shade of Love (Extended Mix)," Camille
1997 . . . . "Astroplane" (City of Love Mix), BKS
1998 . . . . "Euphoria" (Rabbit in the Moon Mix), Delerium
1999 . . . . *Broken Bones*, Love Inc.
2000 . . . . *Silence*, Delerium
2001 . . . . *Into The Night*, Love Inc

Best Contemporary Jazz Album

1992 . . . . *For the Moment*, Renee Rosnes;
In Transition, Brian Dickinson; *The Brass Is Back*,
Rob McConnell and The Boss Brass
1993 . . . . *My Ideal*, P.J. Perry
1994 . . . . *Don't Smoke in Bed*, Holly Cole Trio
1995 . . *The Merlin Factor*, Jim Hillman & The Merlin Factor
1996 . . . . *NOJO*, Neufeld-Occhipinti Jazz Orchestra
1997 . . . . *Africville Suite*, Joe Sealy
1998 . . . . *Metalwood*, Metalwood
1999 . . . . *Metalwood 2*, Metalwood
2000 . . . . *...so far*, D.D. Jackson
2001 . . . . *Compassion*, François Carrier Trio

Best Vocal Jazz Album

2000 . . . . *When I Look In Your Eyes*, Diana Krall
2001 . . . . *Both Sides Now*, Joni Mitchell

Best Mainstream/Traditional Jazz Album

1994 . *Fables and Dreams*, Dave Young/Phil Dwyer Quartet
1995 . . . . *Free Trade*, Free Trade
1996 . . . . *Vernal Fields*, Ingrid Jensen
1997 . . . . *Ancestors*, Renee Rosnes
1998 . . . . *In the Mean Time*, The Hugh Fraser Quintet
1999 . . . . *The Atlantic Sessions*, Kirk MacDonald
2000 . . . . *Deep In A Dream*, Pat LaBarbera
2001 . . . . *Rob McConnell Tentet*, Rob McConnell Tentet

Best R&B/Soul Recording

1992 . . . . "Call My Name," Love & Sas
1993 . . . . "Once in a Lifetime," Love & Sas
1994 . . . . "The Time is Right,"Rupert Gayle
1995 . . . . "First Impressions for the Bottom Jigglers,"
Bass is Base
1996 . . . . "Deborah Cox," Deborah Cox
1997 . . . . "Feelin' Alright," Carlos Morgan
1998 . . . . *Things Just Ain't the Same*, Deborah Cox
1999 . . . . *One Wish*, Deborah Cox
2000 . . . . *Thinkin' About You*, 2Rude
featuring Latoya & Miranda
2001 . . . . *Sleepless*, jacksoul

Best Blues/Gospel Album

1994 . . . . *South at Eight/North at Nine*, Colin Linden
1995 . . . . *Joy to the World Jubilation V*,
Montreal Jubilation Gospel Choir
1996 . . . . *That River*, Jim Byrnes
1997 . . . . *Right To Sing The Blues*, Long John Baldry

Best Blues Album

1998 . . . . *National Steel*, Colin James
1999 . . . . *Blues Weather*, Fathead
2000 . . . . *Gust Of Wind*, Ray Bonneville
2001 . . . . *Love Comin' Down*, Sue Foley

Best Gospel Album

1998 . . . . *Romantics and Mystics*, Steve Bell
1999 . . . . *Life Is*, Sharon Riley & Faith Chorale
2000 . . . . . . *Legacy Of Hope*, Deborah Klassen
2001 . . . . *Simple Songs*, Steve Bell

Best Reggae/Calypso Recording

1994 . . . . *Informer*, Snow
1995 . . . . . . *Class and Credential*, Carla Marshall
1996 . . . . *Now and Forever*, Sattalites
1997 . . . . *Nana Maclean*, Nana Maclean
1998 . . . . *Catch de Vibe*, Messenjah
1999 . . . . *Vision*, Frankie Wilmot
2000 . . . . *Heart & Soul*, Lazo
2001 . . . . . *Lenn Hammond*, Lenn Hammond

Best Global Album

1992 . . . . *The Gathering*, Various Artists
1993 . . . . *Spirits of Havana*, Jane Bunnett
1994 . . . . *El Camino Real*, Ancient Cultures
1995 . . . . *Africa+*, Eval Manigat
1996 . . . . *Music From Africa*, Takadja
1997 . . . . *Africa Do Brasil*, Paulo Ramos Group
1998 . . . . *La Llorona*, Lhasa
1999 . . . . *La Llorona*, Lhasa
2000 . . . . *Omnisource*, Madagascar Slim
2001 . . . . *Ritmo + Soul*, Jane Bunnett
And The Spirits Of Havana

Best Roots and Traditional Album

1992 . . . . . *Saturday Night Blues*, Various Artists; *The Visit*,
Loreena McKennitt
1993 . . . . . *Jusqu'aux P'tites Heures*, La Bouttine Souriante
1994 . . . . *My Skies*, James Keelaghan
1995 . . . . *The Mask and Mirror*, Loreena McKennitt
1996 . . . *Hi: How Are You Today?*, Ashley MacIsaac (solo);
Gypsies & Lovers, The Irish Descendants (group)
1997 . . . . *drive-in movie*, Fred Eaglesmith (solo);
Matapedia, Kate & Anna McGarrigle (group)
1998 . . . . *Other Songs*, Ron Sexsmith (solo)
Molinos, The Paperboys (group)
1999 . . . . *Heartstrings*, Willie P. Bennett (solo)
The McGarrigle Hour, Kate & Anna McGarrigle (group)
2000 . . . . *Breakfast In New Orleans Dinner In Timbuktu*, Bruce
Cockburn (solo) *Kings Of Love*, Blackie & The Rodeo Kings (group)
2001 . . . . *Jenny Whiteley*, Jenny Whiteley (solo)
Tri-Continental, Tri-Continental, Bill Bourne,
Lester Quitzau, Madagascar Slim (group)

Instrumental Artist(s) of the Year

1992 . . . . Shadowy Men on a Shadowy Planet
1993 . . . . Ofra Harnoy
1994 . . . . Ofra Harnoy
1995 . . . . André Gagnon
1996 . . . . Liona Boyd
1997 . . . . Ashley MacIsaac
1998 . . . . Leahy ▶

Best Instrumental Album

1999 ...... *My Roots Are Showing*, Natalie MacMaster
2000 .... *In My Hands*, Natalie MacMaster
2001........................ *Free Fall*, Jesse Cook

Best Classical Album (solo or chamber ensemble)

1992 ..... *Franz Liszt: Années de Pelerinage*, Louis Lortie
1993 .... *Beethoven: Piano Sonatas*, Louis Lortie
1994 .... *Beethoven: Piano Sonatas, Op. 10, No. 1-3*,
Louis Lortie
1995....... *Erica Goodman Plays Canadian Harp Music*,
Erica Goodman
1996. *Aikan: Grande Sonate/Sonatine*, Marc-André Hamelin
1997............ *Scriabin: The Complete Piano Sonatas*,
Marc-Andre Hamelin
1998............ *Marc-André Hamelin plays Franz Liszt*,
Marc-André Hamelin
1999 ...... *Bach: Well-Tempered Clavier – Book 1*,
Angela Hewitt
2000........ *Schumann: String Quartets*, St. Lawrence
String Quartet
2001.. *Bach: The Six Sonatas & Partitas For Solo Violin*,
James Ehnes

Best Classical Album (large ensemble)

1992.......... *Debussy: Pelleas et Melisande*, Orchestre
Symphonique de Montréal, Charles Dutoit
1993 ... *Handel: Excerpts from Floridante*, Tafelmusik
1994 .. *Handel: Concerti Grossi, Op. 3, No. 1-6*, Tafelmusik
1995 .. *Bach: Brandenburg Concertos Nos. 1-6*, Tafelmusik
1996 .... *Shostakovich: Symphonies 5 & 9*, Orchestra
Symphonique de Montréal
1997 .... *Ginastera/Villa-Lobos/Evangelista*,
I Musici de Montreal
1998 ...... *Mozart Horn Concertos*, James Sommerville,
CBC Vancouver Orchestra, Mario Bernardi
1999 .... *Handel: Music For The Royal Fireworks*,
Tafelmusik, Jeanne Lamon (Musical Director)
2000...... *Respighi: La Boutique Fantasque*, Orchestre
Symphonique de Montréal
2001 ..... *Sibelius: Lemminkäinen Suite — Night Ride
And Sunrise*, Toronto Symphony Orchestra

Best Classical Album (vocal or choral performance)

1995.............. *Berlioz: Les Troyens*, Vocal Soloists,
Choeur et Orchestre symphonique de Montréal
1995 .. *Ben Heppner Sings Richard Strauss*, Ben Heppner,
Toronto Symphony Orchestra, Andrew Davis, conductor
1997.. *Berlioz: La Damnation de Faust*, Choeur et Orcheste
symphonique de Montreal, Charles Dutoit, Conductor
1998..... *Soirée Francaise*, Michel Schade, Russel Braun,
Canadian Opera Company Orchestra, Richard Bradshaw
1999........ *Songs Of Travel*, Gerald Finley (baritone),
Stephen Ralls (piano)
2000......... *German Romantic Opera*, Ben Heppner
2001 ...... *G.F. Handel: Apollo e Dafne Silete Venti*,
Karina Gauvin; Russell Braun; Les violons du Roy

Best Classical Composition

1992......... *Concerto For Piano & Chamber Orchestra*,
Michael Conway Baker
1993 .... *Concerto for Flute and Orchestra*,
R. Murray Schafer
1994.................... *Among Friends*, Chan Ka Nin
1995........... *Sketches From Natal*, Malcolm Forsyth
1996 .... *Concerto For Violin and Orchestra*,
Andrew P. MacDonald
1997.................... *Picasso Suite*, Harry Somers
1998 .... *Electra Rising*, Malcolm Forsyth
1999 ..... *Concerto For Wind Orchestra*, Colin McPhee
2000 ..... *Shattered Night, Shivering Stars*, Alexina Louie
2001 . *From The Diary Of Anne Frank*, Oskar Morawetz

Best Children's Album

1992........ *Vivaldi's Ring of Mystery*, Susan Hammond/
Classical Kids
1993 .... *Waves of Wonder*, Jack Grunsky
1994................ *Tchaikovsky Discovers America*,
SusanHammond/Classical Kids
1995 .... *Bananaphone*, Raffi
1996 .... *Celery Stalks at Midnight*, Al Simmons
1997 ...... *Songs From the Treehouse*, Martha Johnson
1998................... *Livin' in a Shoe*, Judy & David
1999 . *Mozart's Magnificent Voyage*, Susan Hammond's
Classical Kids
2000........ *Skinnamarink TV*, Sharon, Lois and Bram
2001 .... *Sing & Dance*, Jack Grunsky

Producer of the Year

1992.................................. Bryan Adams
1993 ..... k.d. lang/Ben Mink (Greg Penny, co-producer)
1994 .... Steve MacKinnon/Marc Jordan
(Greg Penny, co-producer)
1995.......................... Robbie Robertson
1996.................. Michael-Phillip Wojewoda
1997 .... Garth Richardson
1998 .... Pierre Marchand
1999.......... Colin James (co-producer, Joe Hardy)
2000..................... Tal Bachman and Bob Rock
2001 ...... Gerald Eaton, Brian West and Nelly Furtado

Best Video

1992 .... *Into the Fire* (Sarah McLachlan), Phil Kates
1993...... *Closing Time* (Leonard Cohen), Curtis Wehrfritz
1994.... *I Would Die For You* (Jann Arden), Jeth Weinrich
1995 .... *Tunnel of Trees* (Gogh Van Go), Lyne Charlebois
1996 .... *Good Mother* (Jann Arden), Jeth Weinrich
1997........ *Burned Out Car* (Junkhouse), Jeth Weinrich
1998 .... *Gasoline* (Moist), Javier Aguilera
1999...... *Forestfire*, Javier Aguilera (David Usher)
2000................ *So Pure*, Alanis Morissette
2001................. Rob Heydon (for Edwin), *Alive*

Best Music of Aboriginal Canada Recording

1995.............................. Susan Aglukark
1996........ Jerry Alfred & The Medicine Beat
1997 .... Buffy Ste. Marie
2000........ *Falling Down*, Chester Knight & The Wind
2001.................... *Nipaiamianan*, Florent Vollant

Source: *Canadian Academy of Recording Arts & Sciences*

The East Coast Music Awards, 2001

The East Coast Music Awards were established in 1989 to honor outstanding contributions to the Canadian music industry by artists performing, recording, or rooted in Atlantic Canada, and to celebrate that region's distinct musical heritage in English and in French. The 13th annual ECMAs were presented Feb. 8–11, 2001 in Charlottetown, PEI.

Male Artist Of The Year . . . . Lenni Gallant
Female Artist Of The Year . . . . Damhnait Doyle
Group Of The Year . . . . The Barra MacNeils
Songwriter Of The Year . . Gordie Sampson, Fred Lavery
Single Of The Year . . . . . "Tattooed," Damhnait Doyle
Video Of The Year . . . . Damhnait Doyle
Album Of The Year . . . . *Lennie Gallant Live*
New Artist Of The Year . . . . . The Carson Downey Band
Entertainer Of The Year . . . . The Fables
Country Artist/Group Of The Year . . . . . . Julian Austin
Pop/Rock Artist/Group Of The Year . . . Damhnait Doyle
Instrumental Artist/Group Of The Year
. . . . Natalie MacMaster
Alternative Artist/Group Of The Year . . . . Arlibido
Jazz Artist/Group Of The Year . . . . Jive Kings

Blues Artist/Group Of The Year . The Carson Downey Band
Gospel Artist/Group Of The Year . . . . The LaPointes
Children's Artist/Group Of The Year . . . . . Teresa Doyle
Urban Recording Of The Year . . . . *Annick Gagnon*,
Annick Gagnon
Classical Recording Of The Year . . . . . *At the Rim of the
Carol-Singing Sea*,
Newfoundland Symphony Youth Choir
Roots/Traditional Solo Artist Of The Year
. . . . Lennie Gallant
Roots/Traditional Group Of The Year . . The Ennis Sisters
Francophone Recording Of The Year
. . . . Grand Dérangement
Aboriginial Artist/Group Of The Year
. . . . George Paul and the Red Ochre Band

The Grammy Awards, 1995–2000

Grammy winners are selected annually by the 6,000 voting members of The Recording Academy, based on artistic and/or technical excellence.

The titles for song of the year are followed by the names of the songwriters. The 2000 Grammy winners were announced Feb. 21, 2001.

Best Record
1995 "Kiss From A Rose," Seal
1996 "Change the World," Eric Clapton
1997 "Sunny Came Home," Shawn Colvin
1998 "My Heart Will Go On," Celine Dion
1999 "Smooth," Santana featuring Rob Thomas
2000 "Beautiful Day," U2

Best Album
1995 *Jagged Little Pill*, Alanis Morissette
1996 *Falling Into You*, Celine Dion
1997 *Time Out Of Mind*, Bob Dylan
1998 *The Miseducation of Lauryn Hill*, Lauryn Hill
1999 *Supernatural*, Santana
2000 *Two Against Nature*, Steely Dan

Best Song
1995 "Kiss From A Rose," Seal
1996 "Change the World," Eric Clapton, Wynonna
1997 "Sunny Came Home," Shawn Colvin
1998 "My Heart Will Go On," James Harper,
Will Jennings
1999 "Smooth," Itaal Shur & Rob Thomas, songwriters
2000 "Beautiful Day," U2

Best Male Pop Vocal
1995 "Kiss From A Rose," Seal
1996 "Change the World," Eric Clapton
1997 "Candle in the Wind 1997," Elton John
1998 "My Father's Eyes," Eric Clapton
1999 "Brand New Day," Sting
2000 "Again," Lenny Kravitz

Best Female Vocal
1995 "No More 'I Love You's'," Annie Lennox
1996 "Un-Break My Heart," Toni Braxton
1997 "Building A Mystery," Sarah McLachlan
1998 "My Heart Will Go On," Celine Dion
1999 "I Will Remember You," Sarah McLachlan
2000 "There Goes the Neighbourhood," Sheryl Crow

Best Female Country Vocal Performance
1995 "Baby, Now That I've Found You," Alison Krauss
1996 "Blue," LeAnn Rimes
1997 "How Do I Live," Trisha Yearwood
1998 "You're Still The One," Shania Twain
1999 "Man! I Feel Like A Woman!" Shania Twain
2000 "Breathe," Faith Hill

Best Jazz Vocal Performance
1995 "An Evening With Lena Horne," Lena Horne
1996 "New Moon Daughter," Cassandra Wilson
1997 "Dear Ella," DeeDee Bridgewater
1998 "I Remember Miles," Shirley Horn
1999 "When I Look In Your Eyes," Diana Krall
2000 "In The Moment — Live In Concert," Dianne Reeves

Best Instrumental Soloist(s) Performance
(with Orchestra)
1995 Itzhak Perlman, The American Album (Works Of
Bernstein, Barber, Foss)
1996 Yefim Bronfman, Bartok: The Three Piano
Concertos
1997 Yo-Yo Ma & David Zinman, Premieres – Cello
Concertos (Works Of Danielpour, Kirchner, Rouse) ▶

▶ 1998 Anne-Sophie Mutter & Krzysztof Penderecki,
Penderecki: Violin Con. No. 2 Metamorphosen
1999 Prokofiev: Piano Concertos. Nos. 1 & 3; Bartók:
Piano Con. No. 3, Martha Argerich & the
Montreal Symphony Orchestra
2000 "Maw: Violin Concerto," Joshua Bell & the London
Philharmonic Orchestra

Best New Artist
1995 Hootie & The Blowfish
1996 LeAnn Rimes
1997 Paula Cole
1998 Lauryn Hill
1999 Christina Aguilera
2000 Shelby Lynne

Source: *National Academy of Recording Arts & Sciences*   Note: Canadian artist set in bold type.

The ADISQ ("Félix") Awards, 2000

The Felix Awards have been presented annually since 1978 by ADISQ, the umbrella group representing the Québec music, video, and performance industry, to acknowledge achievement in Canada's French language music and performance scene. The 22nd awards were held at ADISQ's annual gala in Montreal, November 6, 2000.

Popular Song of the Year *Je n't'aime plus*, Mario Pelchat
Group of the Year . . . . .La Chicane
Best Female Vocalist . . . . .Isabelle Boulay
Best Male Vocalist . . . . .Bruno Pelletier
Album of the Year (pop-rock) . . . .*D'autres rives*,
Bruno Pelletier
Album of the Year (popular) . . . .*Scènes d'amour*,
Isabelle Boulay
Album of the Year (rock) . . . .*À l'ombre de l'ange*,
Éric Lapointe
Album of the Year (traditional) . . . .*100 ans de folklore*
de chez nous, various artists
Album of the Year (hip-hop) . .*Mentalité moune morne...*
(ils n'ont pas compris), Muzion
Album of the Year (jazz) . . . . . .*Little Zab*, Yannick Rieu
Bestselling Album . . .*À l'ombre de l'ange*, Éric Lapointe
Album of the Year (urban/techno) . .*The East Infection*,
Ramasutra
Best Quebec Artist In a Language Other Than French
. . . . .Lara Fabian
Best Artist from "la francophonie," . . . .Louise Attaque
(France)

Achievement by a Quebec Artist Outside Québec
. . . . .Lynda Lemay
Best World Music Artist (québecois) . .Lilison Di Kinara
Writer/Composer of the Year . . . . .Daniel Boucher
Album of the Year (country) . . .*Hommage à mes amis*,
Bobby Hachey
Album of the Year (classical, large ensemble)
. . . .*Boris Godounov de Moussorgsky*
Joseph Rouleau et l'Orchestre Métropolitain
Album of the Year (classical, soloist/small ensemble)
. . . .*Let's Dance*, Angèle Dubeau et La Pietà
Video of the Year . . . .*Mon ange*, Éric Lapointe
Album of the Year (children's) . . . .*2000 et un enfants*,
Dan Bigras
Album of the Year (instrumental) . .*François Cousineau*,
François Cousineau
Album of the Year (humour) . . . . . .*Roule-toi par terre!*
Crampe en masse,
Ghyslain Dufresne, Mathieu Gratton
Album of the Year (original soundtrack)
. . . .*Pin-Pon, le film*, Yves Soutière,
Thomas Gratton et Philippe Lambert

Celine Dion: A Mom At Last!

*P*op diva Celine Dion undertook a new career on Jan. 25, 2001 when she delivered a six-pound, eight-ounce son at a Florida hospital. The baby, Rene-Charles, had been generating as many headlines as his famous mum even before his birth. Dion gave her desire to have a child as one of the main reasons for her "retirement" after a 1999 farewell concert in Montreal. Efforts by Dion and her manager/husband Rene Angelil to conceive a child through in vitro fertilization were widely publicized in the tabloid press. Those efforts came about after Angelil was diagnosed with cancer and a tumour was removed from his neck. In 2000, Dion threatened a $20-million lawsuit against the **National Enquirer** after the paper published a false story claiming she was pregnant with twins. But, in interviews following Rene-Charles' birth, Dion said she could end up being the mother of twins after all. It seems a second egg was fertilized during the in vitro process and left frozen at the New York clinic that conducted the treatment. Dion told a Quebec magazine that she would definitely be going back to New York to retrieve it.

Canadian Music Hall of Fame

The Canadian Academy of Recording Arts and Sciences instituted a Hall of Fame Award in 1978 to honour Canadians who have contributed to the greater international recognition of Canadian artists and music.

■ Winners

1978	Guy Lombardo	1986	Gordon Lightfoot			Domenic Troiano
	Oscar Peterson	1987	The Guess Who			John Kay
1979	Hank Snow	1989	The Band			Zal Yanovsky
1980	Paul Anka	1990	Maureen Forrester	1997		Lenny Breau
1981	Joni Mitchell	1991	Leonard Cohen			Gil Evans
1982	Neil Young	1992	Ian & Sylvia			Maynard Ferguson
1983	Glenn Gould	1993	Anne Murray			Moe Kauffman
1984	The Crewcuts	1994	Rush			Rob McConnell
	The Diamonds	1995	Buffy Sainte-Marie	1998		David Foster
	The Four Lads	1996	David Clayton-Thomas	1999		Luc Plamondon
1985	Wilf Carter		Denny Doherty	2000		Bruce Fairbairn

2001 INDUCTEE

■ Bruce Cockburn

Singer/songwriter Bruce Cockburn was inducted into the Canadian Music Hall of Fame at the 30th Anniversary Juno Awards on March 4th, 2001. His induction honoured a 30-year career that includes 20 gold and platinum albums and 11 Juno Awards. In a stirring acceptance speech, Cockburn, known as much for his passionate political activism as for his extraordinary musicianship, said he felt honoured to have been part of a period that he believes will prove seminal in the development of Canadian culture.

"In the '60s," he said, "when I was just beginning to play for people and write songs, the world began to recognize its oneness. We had McLuhan and Vatican II; we had Swami Vishnu Devananda dropping chrysanthemums from the air over Belfast and Suez. We had a generation of people worldwide who began to appreciate their common burdens and strengths instead of fixating on what separated them.

"There is a dark side," he cautioned. "That is, promotion of uniformity by those whose interest is power, for profit. Their job is easier if we're all the same—if we all like whatever they tell us to like."

Source: *Canadian Academy of Recording Arts and Sciences   http://www.juno-awards.ca/caras/*

The Canadian Academy of Recording Arts and Sciences (CARAS)

T his organization was originally created to administer and promote the Juno Awards. It has since expanded its mandate to link members of the Canadian music community and members of the public interested in the Canadian music and recording industry. The Junos themselves remain the centrepiece, to recognize (and reward) outstanding achievement in recorded music. The broadcast of the Junos brings singers, musicians, songwriters, producers and other creative talent together and to the attention of both a national audience and foreign markets.

CARAS uses a website to achieve its goals beyond the awards: a home page for the Canadian Music Hall of Fame has biographies, photos and sound clips from the inductees. In addition, CARAS is building a database containing information about Canadian music, and all of its artists and creators. Known as JAMA (Juno Awards Music Archive), the site boasted almost 2,000 entries in March of 1998 and is still growing. Browsers can access biographies, images, discographies and audio clips of Canadian artists. Check it out at http://www.juno-awards.ca

Canadian Country Music Awards, 2001

Fans' Choice Award:	Terri Clark
Female Artist of the Year	Carolyn Dawn Johnson
Male Artist of the Year	Jason McCoy
Single of the Year	"Complicated," Carolyn Dawn Johnson
Album of the Year	*Room With A View*, Carolyn Dawn Johnson
Vocal Duo or Group of the Year	The Wilkinsons
Music Video of the Year	"No Fear," Terri Clark
Song of the Year	"Complicated," Carolyn Dawn Johnson
Roots Artist or Group of the Year	Natalie MacMaster
Rising Star	Carolyn Dawn Johnson

Source: *Canadian Country Music Awards*

Top 50 Albums in Canada, 2000

Artist, Title	Artist, Title
1. Eminem, *Marshall Mathers LP*	26. Various Artists, *Mission Impossible 2 Soundtrack*
2. Britney Spears, *Oops! I Did It Again*	27. Celine Dion, *All The Way—A Decade of Song*
3. 'N SYNC, *No Strings Attached*	28. Madonna, *Music*
4. Beatles, *1*	29. 3 Doors Down, *Better Life*
5. Sanatana, *Supernatural*	30. Various Artists, *2000 Grammy Nominees*
6. Backstreet Boys, *Black and Blue*	31. Various Artists, *Now! 5*
7. Various Artists, *Muchdance 2001*	**32. Shania Twain, *Come On Over***
8. Various Artists, *Big Shiny Tunes 5*	33. Kid Rock, *Devil Without A Cause*
9. Limp Bizkit, *Chocolate Starfish & the Hot Dog Flavored Water*	34. Aqua, *Aquarius*
10. Creed, *Human Clay*	35. Kid Rock, *History of Rock*
11. Dr. Dre, *Chronic 2001*	36. Blink-182, *Enema of the State*
12. Macy Gray, *On How Life Is*	37. S Club 7, *S Club*
13. Enrique Iglesias, *Enrique*	38. Sting, *Brand New Day*
14. Red Hot Chili Peppers, *Californication*	39. Pink, *Can't Take Me Home*
15. Destiny's Child, *Writing's on the Wall*	40. Various Artists, *Women & Song 4*
16. Moby, *Play*	41. Savage Garden, *Affirmation*
17. Christina Aguilera, *Christina Aguilera*	42. Backstreet Boys, *Millennium*
18. Various Artists, *Muchdance 2000*	43. Papa Roach, *Infest*
19. U2, *All That You Can't Leave Behind*	44. Bon Jovi, *Crush*
20. Lenny Kravitz, *Greatest Hits*	45. Various Artists, *Planet Pop 2001*
21. Faith Hill, *Breathe*	**46. The Tragically Hip, *Music @ Work***
22. Various Artists, *Big Shiny Tunes 4*	**47. Ginette Reno, *Un Grand Noel d'Amour***
23. Matchbox Twenty, *Mad Season*	48. ABBA, *Gold—Greatest Hits*
24. Dixie Chicks, *Fly*	49. Eiffel 65, *Europop*
25. Marc Anthony, *Marc Anthony*	50. Offspring, *Conspiracy of One*

Source: *Chart information supplied by SoundScan. Copyright © 2000 by SoundScan, Inc. All rights reserved.* SoundScan
Note: Canadian artists set in bold type.

Top 50 Hit Singles, 2000

Artist, Title	Artist, Title
1. Madonna, Music- Maxi Single	27. Mariah Carey, Thank God I Found You
2. Madonna, American Pie	28. Modjo, Lady/Hear Me Tonight-Remix
3. Hampton the Hampster, Hampsterdance Song	29. Sonique, Feels So Good Part 1 & 2
4. 'N SYNC, Bye, Bye, Bye	30. Whitney Houston, Could I Have This Kiss Forever
5. Backstreet Boys, Shape of My Heart	31. Love Inc., Here Comes the Sunshine
6. Souldecision, Faded	32. The Bratt Pack, Carousel
7. Sting, Desert Rose/Brand New Day	33. Shaft, Mucho Mambo
8. U2, Beautiful Day Single #1	34. Christina Aguilera, What A Girl Wants
9. The Moffatts, Bang Bang Bang	35. Snow, Everybody Wants To Be Like You
10. Alice Deejay, Better Off Alone	36. Bob Marley, Sun Is Shining (Remixes)
11. U2, Beautiful Day Single #2	37. Portishead, Glorytimes
12. Pearl Jam, Last Kiss	38. Destiny's Child, Say My Name
13. Aqua, Cartoon Heroes	39. Sonique, It Feels So Good
14. Pink, There You Go	40. Kim Lukas, All I Really Want
15. Pearl Jam, Nothing As It Seems	41. Eiffel 65, Blue
16. Toni Braxton, He Wasn't Man Enough	42. David Bowie/Bing Crosby, Peace On Earth/Little
17. Joee, I Don't Believe You	Drummer
18. Oasis, Let It Out	43. Britney Spears, Oops I Did It Again
19. Santana, Maria Maria	43. Backstreet Boys, Show Me the Meaning of Being
20. Darude, Sandstorm	Lonely
21. Delerium, Silence	45. Vengaboys, Megamix
22. O-Town, Liquid Dreams	46. Elissa, Mamboleo
23. Spice Girls, Holler/Let Love Lead the Way	47. Jacksoul, Can't Stop
24. Hanson, This Time Around	48. Filter, Take A Picture
25. Eiffel 65, Move Your Body	**49. Kardinal Offishal, Hustlin'**
26. Lara Fabian, I Will Love Again	50. Various Artists, Pokemon World

Source: *Chart information supplied by SoundScan. Copyright © 2000 by SoundScan, Inc. All rights reserved.*
Note: Canadian artists set in bold type.

MTV Video Music Awards, 2001

Best Video of the Year . . . "Lady Marmalade", Christina Aguilera, Lil' Kim, Mya, Pink f/ Missy "Misdemeanor" Elliott
Best Rock Video . . . . "Rollin", Limp Bizkit
Best R&B Video . . . . "Survivor", Destiny's Child
Best Hip Hop Video . . . . "Ms. Jackson", Outkast
Viewer's Choice . . . . "Pop", 'N SYNC
Best Rap Video . . . . "Ride Wit Me", Nelly
Best Direction . . . . Fatboy Slim, "Weapon of Choice"
Best Female Video . . . . "Let Me Blow Ya Mind", Eve f/ Gwen Stefani
Best Pop Video . . . . "Pop", 'N SYNC
Best Video from a Film . . . "Lady Marmalade", Christina Aguilera, Lil' Kim, Mya, Pink f/ Missy "Misdemeanor" Elliott
Best New Artist . . . . "Fallin", Alicia Keys
Best Group Video . . . . "Pop", 'N SYNC
Best Male Video . . . . "South Side", Moby f/ Gwen Stefani
Best Dance Video . . . . "Pop", 'N SYNC
Best Breakthrough Video . . . . "Weapon of Choice", Fatboy Slim
Best Art Direction . . . . "Weapon of Choice", Fatboy Slim
Special Effects . . . . "RockDJ", Robbie Williams
Best Editing . . . . "Weapon of Choice", Fatboy Slim
Best Choreography . . . . "Weapon of Choice", Fatboy Slim
Best Cinematography . . . . "Weapon of Choice", Fatboy Slim

Source: *MTV: Music Television*

The MuchMusic Video Awards, 2000*

Best Rock Video	"Load Me Up," Matthew Good Band
Best Pop Video	"Misery," The Moffatts
Best Post-Production	"Rubbin'," Choclair
Best Cinematography	"Breathe Or Die," Dream Warriors
Best Video	"Load Me Up," Matthew Good Band
Best Director	The Tragically Hip,"My Music At Work"
Best Rap Video	"Let's Ride," Choclair
Best Soul/R and B Video	"Dissin' Us," 2 Rude featuring Jully Black and Grimmi Grimmi
Best Independent Video	"Money or Love," Saukrates
Best Dance Video	"Here Comes The Sunshine," Love Inc.
Best International Video	"Californication," Red Hot Chili Peppers
MuchMoreMusic Award	"Man, I Feel Like A Woman," Shania Twain
Best French Video	"Je Combats Le Spleen," Stefie Shock
VideoFACT Award	"DEEP," Serial Joe
Lifetime achievement award	The Guess Who
People's choice, favourite Canadian artist	"Alive," Edwin
People's choice, favourite Canadian group	"Is Anybody Home?," Our Lady Peace
People's choice, favourite Canadian video	"Is Anybody Home?," Our Lady Peace
People's choice, favourite international artist	"The Real Slim Shady," Eminem
People's choice, favourite international group	"Bye Bye Bye," 'N SYNC

Source: *MuchMusic Network*   *2001 Awards were cancelled.

Recording Industry Sales, 2000–2001[1]

These two charts examine the amount—and dollar value—of music purchased in a variety of forms between June 30–May 31, for 2000 and 2001. Sales information is supplied by members of the Canadian Recording Industry Association. Units and dollar amounts are expressed in the thousands.

'000s Units Shipped	2001	2000	% change
Total Music Video	668	456	46%
Total Singles	172	175	-2%%
Cassette		436945	-54%
CD		15 89217 590	-10%
Total Albums		16 32818 535	-12%
Grand Total	**17 168**	**19 166**	**-10%**

Net Value of Sales ($000s)	2001	2000	% change
Total Music Videos	$8 414	$5 103	65%
Total Singles	794	814	-2%
Cassette		2 2195 819	-62%
CD		189 798211 678	-10%
Total Albums		192 017217 497	-12%
Grand Total	**$219 225**	**$223 414**	**-10%**

Note: The categories of DCC/Mini Disc and Cassette Single have been eliminated from the report due to negligible sales.

Source: *Canadian Recording Industry Association*   (1) For the period ending May 31st.

The Rock and Roll Hall of Fame

The Rock and Roll Hall of Fame was established in 1984. The Rock and Roll Hall of Fame and Museum opened in September 1995 in Cleveland, Ohio.

■ **ARTISTS (Year Elected)**

Aerosmith (2001)
The Allman Brothers Band (1995)
The Animals (1994)
LaVern Baker (1991)
Hank Ballard (1990)
The Band (1994)
The Beach Boys (1988)
The Beatles (1988)
The Bee Gees (1997)
Chuck Berry (1986)

Bobby "Blue" Bland (1992)
Booker T. & The MG's (1992)
David Bowie (1996)
James Brown (1986)
Ruth Brown (1993)
Buffalo Springfield (1997)
Solomon Burke (2001)
The Byrds (1991)
Johnny Cash (1992)
Ray Charles (1986)
Eric Clapton (2000)

The Coasters (1987)
Eddie Cochran (1987)
Sam Cooke (1986)
Cream (1993)
Creedence Clearwater Revival (1993)
Crosby, Stills and Nash (1997)
Bobby Darin (1990)
Bo Diddley (1987)
Dion (1989)
Fats Domino (1986)
The Doors (1993)

▶

▶ The Drifters (1988)
Bob Dylan (1988)
The Eagles (1998)
Earth, Wind and Fire (2000)
Duane Eddy (1994)
The Everly Brothers (1986)
The Flamingos (2001)
Fleetwood Mac (1998)
The Four Seasons (1990)
The Four Tops (1990)
Aretha Franklin (1987)
Marvin Gaye (1987)
Grateful Dead (1994)
Al Green (1995)
Bill Haley (1987)
Buddy Holly (1986)
The Jimi Hendrix Experience (1992)
John Lee Hooker (1991)
The Impressions (1991)
The Isley Brothers (1992)
Michael Jackson (2001)
Etta James (1993)
Jefferson Airplane (1996)
Billy Joel (1999)
Elton John (1994)
Janis Joplin (1995)
B.B. King (1987)
The Jackson Five (1997)
The Kinks (1990)
Gladys Knight and the Pips (1996)
Led Zeppelin (1995)
Lloyd Price (1998)
John Lennon (1994)
Jerry Lee Lewis (1986)
Little Richard (1986)
Little Willie John (1996)
The Lovin' Spoonful (2000)
Frankie Lyman and the Teenagers
  (1993)
The Mamas and the Papas (1998)
Bob Marley (1994)
Martha and the Vandellas (1995)
Curtis Mayfield (1999)
Paul McCartney (1999)
Joni Mitchell (1997)
Clyde McPhatter (1987)
The Moonglows (2000)
Van Morrison (1993)
Ricky Nelson (1987)
Roy Orbison (1987)
Parliament Funkadelic (1997)
Carl Perkins (1987)

Wilson Pickett (1991)
Pink Floyd (1996)
The Platters (1990)
Elvis Presley (1986)
Queen (2001)
Bonnie Raitt (2000)
Otis Redding (1989)
Jimmy Reed (1991)
Smokey Robinson (1987)
The Rolling Stones (1989)
Sam & Dave (1992)
Santana (1998)
Del Shannon (1999)
The Shirelles (1996)
Paul Simon (2001)
Simon and Garfunkel (1990)
Sly and the Family Stone (1993)
Dusty Springfield (1999)
Bruce Springsteen (1999)
Steely Dan (2001)
Rod Stewart (1994)
The Supremes (1988)
The Staple Singers (1999)
James Taylor (2000)
The Temptations (1989)
Ike and Tina Turner (1991)
Big Joe Turner (1987)
Ritchie Valens (2001)
Gene Vincent (1998)
The Velvet Underground (1996)
Muddy Waters (1987)
The Who (1990)
Jackie Wilson (1987)
Stevie Wonder (1989)
The Yardbirds (1992)
The Young Rascals (1997)
Neil Young (1995)
Frank Zappa (1995)

■ **NON-PERFORMERS**
Paul Ackerman (1995)
Dave Bartholomew (1991)
Ralph Bass (1991)
Chris Blackwell (2001)
Leonard Chess (1987)
Dick Clark (1993)
Clive Davis (2000)
Tom Donahue (1996)
Lamont Dozier, Brian Holland
  & Eddie Holland (1990)
Ahmet Ertegun (1987)
Leo Fender (1992)

Alan Freed (1986)
Milt Gabler (1993)
Gerry Goffin & Carole King (1990)
Berry Gordy, Jr. (1988)
Bill Graham (1992)
Jerry Leiber & Mike Stoller (1987)
George Martin (1999)
Syd Nathan (1997)
Johnny Otis (1994)
Sam Phillips (1986)
Doc Pomus (1992)
Phil Spector (1989)
Allen Toussaint (1998)
Jerry Wexler (1987)

■ **LIFETIME ACHIEVEMENT
  AWARDS**
Willie Dixon (1994)
Nesuhi Ertegun (1991)
John Hammond (1986)

■ **EARLY INFLUENCES**
Louis Armstrong (1990)
Charles Brown (1999)
Charlie Christian (1990)
Nat "King" Cole (2000)
Willie Dixon (1994)
Woody Guthrie (1988)
Billie Holiday (2000)
Howlin' Wolf (1991)
The Ink Spots (1989)
Mahalia Jackson (1997)
Elmore James (1992)
Robert Johnson (1986)
Louis Jordan (1987)
Lead Belly (1988)
Bill Monroe (1997)
Jelly Roll Morton (1998)
The Orioles (1995)
Les Paul (1988)
Professor Longhair (1992)
Ma Rainey (1990)
Jimmie Rodgers (1986)
Pete Seeger (1996)
Bessie Smith (1989)
The Soul Stirrers (1989)
T-Bone Walker (1987)
Dinah Washington (1993)
Hank Williams (1987)
Bob Wills & His Texas Playboys
  (1999)
Jimmy Yancey (1986)

Source: *Rock and Roll Hall of Fame Foundation*

Music Festivals in Canada

Classical music festivals and competitions across Canada have played an essential role in the development of the country's musical talent since the first local music festival was organized in Edmonton in 1908. By 1953, every province had at least one festival in operation. The Federation of Canadian Music Festivals was founded in 1949 to coordinate their activities and, in Canada's centennial year (1967), the first all-Canadian music competition was held in Saint John, N.B.

Today, the Federation reports a total of 230 festivals occurring in Canada each year. These festivals attract some 140,000 entries involving the participation of as many as half a million people. Attendance at local festivals averages 450,000, while provincial festivals average audiences of 6,000 people. The festivals are important to young musicians as much for the prestige they bestow on participants as for the prizes and scholarships offered to help with their studies. The Federation is made up of provincial associations that are responsible for supporting local festivals and organizing festivals to determine the provincial champions at various levels. These champions represent their home province at the National Music Festival. In 1973, the national competition was instituted on an annual basis. Since 1981, the national festival has been held in a different province each year.

Major Classical and New Music Festivals

In addition to the network of amateur music festivals sponsored by the Federation of Canadian Music Festivals, professional and a number of other amateur music festivals take place across Canada each year.

The Banff International String Quartet Competition, Banff, Alberta, August-September: This triennial competition was created in 1983 to mark the 50th anniversary of The Banff Centre for the Arts. The Banff International String Quartet Competition (BISQC) has since become recognized as one of the world's leading international music competitions. The next competition will be held in 2002. Tel. (403) 762-6100.

The Winnipeg Symphony Orchestra New Music Festival, Winnipeg, Manitoba, February 1-9: First presented in January 1992, the Festival has drawn international participation, earned critical acclaim, and enjoyed a growing audience. It is now considered one of Canada's most important forums for new work. Tel. (204) 949-3999.

The Ottawa Chamber Music Festival, Ottawa, Ont., July-August: The Ottawa Chamber Music Society produces a two-week summer programme of chamber music featuring the highest calibre of local, national and international artists. Concerts take place in downtown Ottawa, mostly in churches. Tel. (613) 234-8008.

Festival of the Sound, Parry Sound, Ont. July-August: Talks by renowned scholars, open rehearsals and concerts reflecting a wide variety of classical genres make this noted Ontario festival on the shores of Georgian Bay. Tel. (705) 746-2410.

The Saskatoon Symphonies Festival of New Music, Saskatoon, Saskatchewan, April: Events include small chamber groups, a jazz brunch, concerts by the Saskatchewan Chamber Orchestra, and an after hours club. Also includes world premieres of new works such as *Batoche* a chamber opera based on the life of Louis Riel, by composer Bill Pura. The Festival of New Music puts the prairies on the cutting edge of creative music making. Tel. (306) 665-6414.

Festival international de Lanaudière, Joliette, Québec, June-August: This six-week event is one of largest and longest classical music festivals in Canada. Some 30 concerts are presented by as many as 1,300 musicians for up to 48,000 visitors. Most concerts for soloists and smaller ensembles are held in the many churches of the Joliette area. Larger groups such as the Montréal Symphony Orchestra perform at the Lanaudière Amphitheatre. The festival is renowned for its emphasis on new work and young artists. The 2002 edition of the Festival international de Lanaudière is scheduled to begin June 28. Tel. 1-800-245-7636.

MusicFest Canada, location varies, May: This six day annual national event brings together more than 11,000 of Canada's finest young musicians who perform for recognition as the country's foremost musical ensembles. Participants range in age from 12-24 years and are drawn from the elementary, high school, college and university levels. Tel. (403) 717-1766.

MOVIES

Canada has been a world leader in documentary filmmaking, producing renowned artists such as Donald Brittain and Harry Rasky primarily through the National Film Board of Canada. The film board has also helped bring Canada to prominence as a producer of animation, and short subjects. Canadians have made an enormous contribution to the Hollywood feature film industry, from film mogul Louis B. Mayer to acclaimed director Norman Jewison to stars including Mary Pickford, Dan Ackroyd, Michael J. Fox, John Candy and Keanu Reeves. The Department of Canadian Heritage estimates that 20 percent of those employed in the Hollywood film industry are Canadian and that about 60 percent of the software used in U.S. film productions was developed by Canadians. Made-in-Canada features by filmmakers such as Denys Arcand, David Cronenburg, Atom Egoyan, and Patricia Rozema have enjoyed considerable critical and "art house" success around the world. In the 1990s, Canadian features twice won the Special Grand Jury Prize at the Cannes Film Festival. However, with U.S. distribution houses controlling 85 percent of the theatrical market, only one in twenty features gaining commercial release in Canada is produced in Canada.

Toronto International Film Festival, 2001

The 26th annual festival was held Sept. 6 to 15 in 2001, showing 326 films from over 56 countries. This is widely regarded as North America's major film festival.

People's Choice Award . . . . *Le Fabuleux Destin d'Amélie Poulain*, Jean-Pierre Jeunet, France
Discovery Award . . . . *Chicken Rice War*, CheeK, Singapore
Fipresci Award . . . . *Inch'Allah Dimanche*, Yamina Benguigui, France
Best Canadian First Feature . . . . **Inertia, Sean Garrity**
Best Canadian Feature Film. . . . . **Atanarjuat (The Fast Runner), Zacharias Kunuk**
Best Canadian Short Film . . . . **FILM(DZAMA), deco dawson**

Source: *Toronto International Film Festival*

Montreal World Film Festival, 2001

The 25th annual Festival des Films du Monde was held from Aug. 23rd to Sept 3rd, 2001.

Grand Prix of the Americas (tie) . . . . *Baran*, Majid Majidi (Iran), *Torzok (Abandoned)*, Arpad Sopsits (Hungary)
Special Grand Prix of the Jury . . . . *El Hijo de la Novia (The Son of the Bride)*,
Juan José Campanella (Argentina/Spain)
Best Director . . . . Oliver Hirschbiegel (Germany), *Das Experiment (The Experiment)*
Best Actress . . . . **Sandrine Kiberlain, Nicole Garcia, Mathilde Seigner,**
Betty Fisher et Autres Histoures, Claude Miller (France/Canada)
Best Actor . . . . Robert Stadlober, *Engel & Joe* (Germany)
Best Screenplay . . . . **Catherine Martin, *Mariage* (Canada)**
Best Short Film. . . . . *Still Life*, Sima Urale (New Zealand)
People's Choice Award . . . . *Der Tunnel (The Tunnel)*, Roland Suso Richter (Germany)

Source: *Montreal World Film Festival*

Genie Awards, 1990–2000

The Genie Awards have been presented since 1980 by the Academy of Canadian Cinema and Television to honor achievement in the Canadian film industry. Awards apply to films released in the previous year. Voting is conducted in a two-step process whereby the winners are chosen by all academy members from among the five nominees selected in each category by their respective craft branches. The 2000 awards were presented Jan. 29, 2001.

1990

Picture . . . . *Jesus de Montréal*
Actor . . . . Lothaire Bluteau, *Jesus de Montréal*
Actress . . . . Rebecca Jenkins, *Bye Bye Blues*
Sup. Actor . . . . Remy Girard, *Jesus de Montréal*
Sup. Actress . . . . Robyn Stevan, *Bye Bye Blues*
Director . . . . Denys Arcand, *Jesus de Montréal*

1991

Picture . . . . *Black Robe*
Actor . . . . Remy Girard, *Amoureux fou*
Actress . . . . Pascale Montpetit, *H*
Sup. Actor . . . . August Schellenberg, *Black Robe*
Sup. Actress . . . . Danielle Proulx, *Amoureux fou*
Director . . . . Bruce Beresford, *Black Robe*

1992

Picture . . . . *Naked Lunch*
Actor . . . . Tony Nardi, *La Sarrasine*
Actress . . . . Janet Wright, *Bordertown Café*
Sup. Actor . . . . Michael Hogan, *Solitaire*
Sup. Actress . . . . Monique Mercure, *Naked Lunch*
Director . . . . David Cronenberg, *Naked Lunch*

1993

Picture . . . . *Thirty-Two Short Films about Glenn Gould*
Actor . . . . Tom McCamus, *I Love A Man in Uniform*
Actress . . . . Sheila McCarthy, *The Lotus Eaters*
Sup. Actor . . . . Kevin Tighe, *I Love A Man in Uniform*
Sup. Actress . . . . Nicola Cavendish, *The Grocer's Wife*
Director . . . . François Girard, *Thirty-Two Short Films about Glenn Gould*

1994

Picture . . . . *Exotica*
Actor . . . . Maury Chaykin, *Whale Music*
Actress . . . . Sandra Oh, *Double Happiness*
Sup. Actor . . . . Don McKellar, *Exotica*
Sup. Actress . . . . Martha Henry, *Mustard Bath*
Director . . . . Atom Egoyan, *Exotica*

1995

Picture . . . . *Le Confessionnal*
Actor . . . . David La Haye, *L'Enfant D'Eau*
Actress . . . . Helena Bonham Carter, *Margaret's Museum*
Sup. Actor . . . . Kenneth Welsh, *Margaret's Museum*
Sup. Actress . . . . Kate Nelligan, *Margaret's Museum*
Director . . . . Robert Lepage, *Le Confessionnal*

1996

Picture . . . . *Lilies*
Actor . . . . . . William Hutt, *Long Day's Journey Into Night*
Actress . . . Martha Henry, *Long Day's Journey Into Night*

Sup. Actor . . . Peter Donaldson, *Long Day's Journey Into Night*
Sup. Actress . . . . Martha Burns, *Long Day's Journey Into Night*
Director . . . . David Cronenburg, *Crash*

1997

Picture . . . . *The Sweet Hereafter*
Actor . . . . Ian Holm, *The Sweet Hereafter*
Actress . . . . Molly Parker, *Kissed*
Sup. Actor . . . . Peter MacNeill, *The Hanging Garden*
Sup. Actress . . . . . Seana McKenna, *The Hanging Garden*
Director . . . . Atom Egoyan, *The Sweet Hereafter*

1998

Picture . . . . *The Red Violin*
Actor . . . . Roshan Seth, *Such a Long Journey*
Actress . . . . Sandra Oh, *Last Night*
Sup. Actor . . . . Callum Keith Rennie, *Last Night*
Sup. Actress . . . . Monique Mercure, *Conquest*
Director . . . . François Girard, *The Red Violin*

1999

Picture . . . . *Sunshine*
Actor . . . . Bob Hoskins, *Felicia's Journey*
Actress . . . . Sylvie Moreau, *Post Mortem*
Sup. Actor . . . . Mark McKinney, *Dog Park*
Sup. Actress . . . . . Catherine O'Hara, *The Life Before This*
Director . . . . Jeremy Podeswa, *The Five Senses*

2000

Picture . . . . *Maelström*
Actor . . . . Tony Nardi, *My Father's Angel*
Actress . . . . Marie-Josée Croze, *Maelström*
Sup. Actor . . . . Martin Cummins, *Love Come Down*
Sup. Actress . . . . Helen Shaver, *We All Fall Down*
Director . . . . Denis Villeneuve, *Maelström*
Original Screenplay . . . . Denis Villeneuve, *Maelström*
Cinematography . . . . André Turpin, *Maelström*
Film Editing . . . . Susan Shipton, *Possible Worlds*
Art Direction . . . . Danièle Rouleau, *Possible Worlds*
Costume Design . . . . Michel Robidas, *Stardom*
Overall Sound . . . . Daniel Pellerin, Paul Adlaf, Peter Kelly, Brad Thornton, Brad Zoern, *Love Come Down*
Sound Editing . . . . David McCallum, Fred Brennan, Susan Conley, Steven Hammond, Garrett Kerr, Jane Tattersall, Robert Warchol, *Love Come Down*
Music Score . . . . Patric Caird, *Here's to Life!*
Best Feature Length Documentary . . . . Ron Mann, *Grass*
Best Animated Short . . . . Michael Scott, Eugene Fedorenko, Rose Newlove, David Verrall, *Village of Idiots*
Best Live Action Short Drama . . . . André Théberge, Alain Jacques, *Le p'tit Varius*

Motion Picture Academy Awards (Oscars™)

1990

Picture . . . . *Dances With Wolves*, Orion
Actor . . . . Jeremy Irons, *Reversal of Fortune*
Actress . . . . Kathy Bates, *Misery*
Sup. Actor . . . . Joe Pesci, *Good Fellas*
Sup. Actress . . . . Whoopi Goldberg, *Ghost*
Director . . . . Kevin Costner, *Dances With Wolves*

1991

Picture . . . . *The Silence of the Lambs*, Orion
Actor . . . . Anthony Hopkins, *The Silence of the Lambs*
Actress . . . . Jodie Foster, *The Silence of the Lambs*
Sup. Actor . . . . Jack Palance, *City Slickers*
Sup. Actress . . . . Mercedes Ruehl, *The Fisher King*
Director . . . . . Jonathan Demme, *The Silence of the Lambs*

1992

Picture . . . . *Unforgiven*, Clint Eastwood, producer
Actor . . . . Al Pacino, *Scent of A Woman*
Actress . . . . Emma Thompson, *Howards End*
Sup. Actor . . . . Gene Hackman, *Unforgiven*
Sup. Actress . . . . Marisa Tomei, *My Cousin Vinny*
Director . . . . Clint Eastwood, *Unforgiven*

1993

Picture . . . . *Schindler's List*, Steven Spielberg,
Gerald R. Molen, Branko Lustig, producers
Actor . . . . Tom Hanks, *Philadelphia*
Actress . . . . Holly Hunter, *The Piano*
Sup. Actor . . . . Tommy Lee Jones, *The Fugitive*
Sup. Actress . . . . Anna Paquin, *The Piano*
Director . . . . Steven Spielberg, *Schindler's List*

1994

Picture . . . . *Forrest Gump*, SteveTisch,
Wendy Finerman, Steve Sharkey, producers
Actor . . . . Tom Hanks, *Forrest Gump*
Actress . . . . Jessica Lange, *Blue Sky*
Sup. Actor . . . . Martin Landau, *Ed Wood*
Sup. Actress . . . . Dianne Wiest, *Bullets Over Broadway*
Director . . . . Robert Zemeckis, *Forrest Gump*

1995

Picture . . . . *Braveheart*, Mel Gibson, Alan Ladd, Jr., and
Bruce Davey, producers
Actor . . . . Nicolas Cage, *Leaving Las Vegas*
Actress . . . . Susan Sarandon, *Dead Man Walking*
Sup. Actor . . . . Kevin Spacey, *The Usual Suspects*
Sup. Actress . . . . Mira Sorvino, *Mighty Aphrodite*
Director . . . . Mel Gibson, *Braveheart*

1996

Picture . . . . . *The English Patient*, Saul Zaentz, producer
Actor . . . . Geoffrey Rush, *Shine*
Actress . . . . Frances McDormand, *Fargo*
Sup. Actor . . . . Cuba Gooding, Jr., *Jerry Maguire*
Sup. Actress . . . . . Juliette Binoche, *The English Patient*
Director . . . . Anthony Minghella, *The English Patient*

1997

Picture . . . . *Titanic*, James Cameron,
Jon Landau, producers
Actor. . . . . Jack Nicholson, *As Good as It Gets*
Actress . . . . Helen Hunt, *As Good as It Gets*
Sup. Actor . . . . Robin Williams, *Good Will Hunting*
Sup. Actress . . . . Kim Basinger, *L.A. Confidential*
Director . . . . James Cameron, *Titanic*

1998

Picture . . . . *Shakespeare in Love*, Donna Gigliotti,
Marc Norman, David Parfitt, Harvey Weinstein,
Edward Zwick, producers
Actor . . . . Roberto Benigni, *Life is Beautiful*
Actress. . . . . Gwyneth Paltrow, *Shakespeare in Love*
Sup. Actor . . . . James Coburn, *Affliction*
Sup. Actress . . . . Judi Dench, *Shakespeare in Love*
Director. . . . . Steven Spielberg, *Saving Private Ryan*

1999

Picture . . . . *American Beauty*, Bruce Cohen
and Dan Jinks, producers
Actor . . . . Kevin Spacey, *American Beauty*
Actress . . . . Hilary Swank, *Boys Don't Cry*
Sup. Actor . . . . . . Michael Caine, *The Cider House Rules*
Sup. Actress . . . . Angelina Jolie, *Girl Interrupted*
Director . . . . Sam Mendes, *American Beauty*

2000

Picture . . . . . . *Gladiator*, Douglas Wick, David Franzoni,
Branko Lustig, producers
Actor . . . . Russell Crowe, *Gladiator*
Actress . . . . Julia Roberts, *Erin Brockovich*
Sup. Actor. . . . . Benicio Del Toro, *Traffic*
Sup. Actress . . . . Marcia Gay Harden, *Pollock*
Director . . . . Steven Soderbergh, *Traffic*
Foreign-Language Film . . . . *Crouching Tiger
Hidden Dragon*, Taiwan
Original Screenplay. . . Cameron Crowe, *Almost Famous*
Screenplay Adaptation . . . . Stephen Gaghan, *Traffic*
Cinematography . . . . . Conrad L. Hall, *American Beauty*
Editing . . . . Stephen Mirrione, *Traffic*
Original Score (Dramatic) . . . . Tan Dun,
Crouching Tiger, Hidden Dragon
Original Song . . . . . Bob Dylan, "Things Have Changed"
Art Direction . Tim Yip, *Crouching Tiger, Hidden Dragon*
Costume Design. . . . . Janty Yates, *Gladiator*
Sound Scott Millan, Bob Beemer, Ken Weston, *Gladiator*
Sound Editing . . . . Jon Johnson, *U-571*
Makeup . . . . Rick Baker, Gail Ryan, *Topsy-Turvy*
Visual Effects . . . . John Nelson, Neil Corbould,
Tim Burke, Rob Harvey, *Gladiator*
Documentary Feature . . . . Mark Jonathan Harris,
Deborah Oppenheimer, *Into the Arms of Strangers*
Documentary Short Subject . Tracy Seretean, *Big Mama*

Source: © Academy of Motion Picture Arts and Sciences

2000 Oscar™ Nominations

Picture: *Chocolat; Crouching Tiger, Hidden Dragon; Erin Brockovich; Gladiator; Traffic.*

Actor: Javier Bardem, *Before Night Falls*; Russell Crowe, *Gladiator*; Tom Hanks, *Castaway*; Ed Harris, *Pollock*; Geoffrey Rush, *Quills.*

Actress: Joan Allen, *The Contender*; Juliette Binoche, *Chocolat*; Ellen Burstyn, *Requiem for a Dream*; Laura Linney, *You Can Count On Me.*

Supporting Actor: Jeff Bridges, *The Contender*; Willem Dafoe, *Shadow of the Vampire*; Benicio Del Toro, *Traffic*; Albert Finney, *Erin Brockovich*; Joaquin Phoenix, *Gladiator.*

Supporting Actress: Judi Dench, *Chocolat*; Marcia Gay Harden, *Pollock*; Kate Hudson, *Almost Famous*; Frances McDormand, *Almost Famous*; Julie Walters, *Billy Elliot.*

Director: Stephen Daldry, *Billy Elliot*; Ang Lee, *Crouching Tiger, Hidden Dragon*; Steven Soderbergh, *Erin Brockovich*; Ridley Scott, *Gladiator*; Steven Soderbergh, *Traffic.*

Foreign-Language Film: *Amores Perros*, Mexico; *Crouching Tiger, Hidden Dragon*, Taiwan; *Divided We Fall*, Czech R.; *Everybody Famous!*, Belgium; *The Taste of Others*, France.

Original Screenplay: Cameron Crowe, *Almost Famous*; Lee Hall, *Billy Elliot*; Susannah Grant, *Erin Brockovich*; David Franzoni, John Logan, William Nicholson, *Gladiator*; Kenneth Lonergan, *You Can Count On Me.*

Screenplay Adaptation: Robert Nelson Jacobs, *Chocolat*; Wang Hui Ling, James Schamus, Tsai Kuo Jung, *Crouching Tiger, Hidden Dragon*; Ethan & Joel Cohen, *O Brother Where Art Thou?*; Stephen Gaghan, *Traffic*; Steve Kloves, *Wonder Boys.*

Cinematography: Peter Pau, *Crouching Tiger, Hidden Dragon*; John Mathieson, *Gladiator*; Lajos Koltai, *Malena*; Roger Deakins, *O Brother Where Art Thou?*; Caleb Deschanel, *The Patriot.*

Original Song: Randy Newman, "A Fool In Love"; Björk, "I've Seen It All"; Jorge Calandrelli, Tan Dun, James Schamus, "A Love Before Time"; Sting, David Hartley, "My Funny Friend and Me"; Bob Dylan, "Things Have Changed".

Source: © *Academy of Motion Picture Arts and Sciences*

The Sundance Film Festival Awards

The Sundance Film Festival was held January 18–28 in Park City, Utah, USA.

Documentary Grand Jury Prize . . . . . *Southern Comfort*, dir. Kate Davis

Dramatic Grand Jury Prize . . . . *The Believer*, dir. Henry Bean

Documentary Audience Award. (joint winners) *Dogtown and Z-Boys*, dir. Stacy Peralta and *Scout's Honor*, dir. Tom Shepard.

Dramatic Audience Award . *Hedwig and The Angry Inch*, dir. John Cameron Mitchell

World Cinema Audience Award . . . . . . *The Road Home*, dir. by Zhang Yimou

Documentary Directing Award . . . . Stacy Peralta, *Dogtown and Z-Boys*

Dramatic Directing Award . . . . John Cameron Mitchell, *Hedwig and The Angry Inch*

The Freedom of Expression Award . . . . . *Scout's Honor*, dir. Tom Shepard

Waldo Salt Screenwriting Award. . . . Christopher Nol *Memento*

Dramatic Special Jury Prize . . . . Tom Wilkinson and Sissy Spacek, *In The Bedroom*.

Documentary Special Jury Prize . *Children Underground*, dir. Edet Belzberg.

Jury Prize in Latin American Cinema. . . . (joint winners) *Possible Loves*, dir. Sandra Werneck, and *Without a Trace*, dir. Maria Navaro.

Jury Prize in Short Filmmaking . . . . . . *Gina, An Actress, Age 29*, dir. Paul Harrill

Source: *Sundance Film Festival*

The Berlin Film Festival Awards

The 51st annual Berlin Film Festival (also known as the "Berlinale") was held February 7–18, 2001.

Golden Berlin Bear . . . . . . *Intimacy*, dir. Patrice Chéreau

Silver Berlin Bear . . *Beijing Bicycle*, dir. Wang Xiaoshuai

Silver Berlin Bear . . . . *Italian for Beginners*, dir. Lone Scherfig

Best Actress . . . . Kerry Fox, *Intimacy*

Best Actor . . . . Benicio del Toro, *Traffic*

Best Director . . . . . . Lin Cheng-Sheng, *Betelnut Beauty*

Alfred Bauer Prize (film debut) . . . . *The Swamp*, Lucrecia Martel

Best European film . . . . . . *Intimacy*, dir. Patrice Chéreau

Source: *Berlin Film Festival*

The Cannes Film Festival Awards, 1991–2000

1991

Best Film................................*Barton Fink* (USA)
Special Grand Jury Prize.......*La belle noiseuse* (France)
Best Director........Joel Coen & Ethan Coen, *Barton Fink*
Best Actor...................John Turturro, *Barton Fink*
Best Actress.....Irène Jacob, *The Double Life of Veronica*

1992

Best Film..............*The Best Intentions* (Switzerland)
Special Grand Jury Prize........*Il Ladro di Bambini* (Italy)
Best Director.................Robert Altman, *The Player*
Best Actor....................Tim Robbins, *The Player*
Best Actress........Pernilla August, *The Best Intentions*

1993

Best Film .. (tie) *The Piano*, (New Zealand), *Farewell To My
Concubine* (China)
Special Grand Jury Prize ...*Faraway, So Close!* (Germany)
Best Director.......................Mike Leigh, *Naked*
Best Actor.......................David Thewlis, *Naked*
Best Actress....................Holly Hunter, *The Piano*

1994

Best Film...........................*Pulp Fiction*, (USA)
Special Grand Jury Prize ...*Burnt by the Sun* (Russia) and
To Live! (China)
Best Director..............Nanni Moretti, *Journal intime*
Best Actor......................Ge You, *To Live!*
Best Actress..............Virna Lisi, *la Reine Margot*

1995

Special Grand Jury Prize................*Crash* (Canada)
Best Director...................Joel Coen, *Fargo* (U.S.)
Best Actor.................(tie) Daniel Autueil & Pascal
Duquenne, *The Eighth Day* (France)
Best Actress.......Brenda Blethyn, *Secrets and Lies* (UK)
Palme d'Or.......................*Secrets and Lies* (UK)

1996

Special Grand Jury Prize ....*The Sweet Hereafter* (Canada)
Best Director....Wong Kar-Wai, *Happy Together* (Hong Kong)
Best Actor............Sean Penn, *She's So Lovely* (U.S)
Best Actress.............Kathy Burke, *Nilby Mouth* (U.K)
Palme d'Or.................(tie) *Unagi* (The Eel) (Japan)
The Taste of Cherry (Iran)

1997

Grand Jury Prize.................*La Vita e Bella* (Italy)
Special Jury Prize.........*La Classe de Neige* (France);
Festen (Denmark)
Best Director ...John Boorman, *The General* (Great Britain)
Best Actor..............Peter Mullan, *My Name is Joe*
(Great Britain)
Best Actress......Elodie Bouchez and Natacha Regnier,
La Vie Revee des Anges (France)
Palme d'Or......*Eternity and a Day*, Theo Angelopoulos
(Greece)

1998

Grand Jury Prize.................*L'humanité* (France)
Jury Prize.........................*A Carta* (Portugal)
Best Director...........Pedro Almodovar, *Todo Sobre
Mi Madre* (Spain)
Best Actor.....Emmanuel Schotté, *L'humanité* (France)
Best Actress.....Séverine Cancele, *L'humanité* (France)
and Emilie Dequenne, *Rosetta* (Belgium)
Palme d'Or...............*Rosetta*, Luc and Jean-Pierre
Dardenne (Belgium)

1999

Grand Prize............*Guizi Lai Le*, Jiang Wen (China)
Jury Prize......*Sånger Från Andra Våningen* (Sweden);
Takhté Siah (Iran)
Best Director.............Edward Yang, *Yi Yi* (Taiwan)
Best Actor....................Tony Leung Chiu-Wai,
In the Mood for Love (China)
Best Actress ......Björk, *Dancer in the Dark* (Denmark)
Palme d'Or *Dancer in the Dark*, Lars von Trier (Denmark)

2000

Grand Prize ....*The Piano Teacher*, Michael Haneke
(Austria/Germany)
Caméra d'Or.............***Atanarjuat The Fast Runner*,
Zacharias Kunuk (Canada)**
Best Director.......(joint winners) Joel Coen, *The Man
Who Wasn't There* (USA);
David Lynch, *Mulholland Drive* (USA).
Best Actor . Benoit Magimel, *The Piano Teacher* (France)
Best Actress.......................Isabelle Huppert,
The Piano Teacher (France)
Palme d'Or ......*The Son's Room*, Nanni Moretti (Italy)

Source: *The Cannes Film Festival*

Atanarjuat: The Fast Runner

*T*he first Innu film ever, by Canada's Zacharias Kunuk, claimed the Cannes Film Festival's
Caméra d'Or award for 2001.

Kunuk says he got the idea of transferring traditional storytelling techniques to film when he
first heard his elders tell stories of the hunt when they returned from the land. In 1981 he bought
his first video camera and was inspired by the way children would gather at his window whenever
he sat down to review his tapes.

"We want to show how our ancestors survived by the strength of their community and their
wits," he says of his company, Isuma Productions, "and how new ways of storytelling today can
help our community survive another thousand years."

GOVERNOR GENERAL'S PERFORMING ARTS AWARDS

The Governor General's Performing Arts Awards were inaugurated in 1992 to pay tribute to the lifetime achievements of outstanding artists in a variety of creative fields. The motto of the awards, "The Arts Engage and Inspire Us," reflects the cultural contribution made by recipients chosen from theatre, dance, classical music/opera, popular music, film and broadcasting. The awards are presented annually in November by the Governor General and are administered by the Governor General's Performing Arts Awards Foundation.

■ Winners 1995–2000

1995
Denys Arcand, writer/director
Maureen Forrester, opera singer
Peter Gzowski, writer/broadcaster
Paul Hébert, actor/director
Anne Murray, singer
Jeanne Renaud, dancer/choreographer

1996
Francois Barbeau, artist/designer/teacher
Michel Brault, cameraman/director
Martha Henry, actor/director
Joni Mitchell, singer/songwriter
Luc Plamondon, songwriter
Grant Strate, dancer/choreographer/teacher
Martha Lou Henley, arts volunteer/benefactor
Jon Kimura Parker, pianist

1998
Paul Buissoneau, theatre director/actor/writer
Bruce Cockburn, singer-songwriter
Rock Demers, film producer

The Royal Canadian Air Farce, comedians
Arnold Spohr, dancer/choreographer
Jon Vickers, opera singer
Joseph H. Shoctor, arts volunteer/benefactor
Denis Marleau, theatre director

1999
Mario Bernardi, conductor
David Cronenberg, film maker
Denise Filiatrault, actor/writer/director
Mavor Moore, actor/writer/director
Louis Quilico, opera singer
Ginette Reno, singer
Sam Sniderman, entrepreneur
Michel Tremblay, playwright

2000
Janette Bertrand
Walter Carsen
Tom C. ("Stompin' Tom") Connors
Fernand Nault
Christopher Newton
Teresa Stratas
Donald Sutherland

2001 Winners

■ Mario Bernardi, C.C.

The discipline of his work, the conscientiousness of his programming, and the outstanding results he has achieved as an orchestra builder have earned Maestro Mario Bernardi a reputation as the foremost Canadian conductor of his generation.

Maestro Bernardi was born in Kirkland Lake, Ontario, in 1930, and studied at the Venice Conservatory in Italy and at Toronto's Royal Conservatory of Music. He made his opera conducting debut in 1957 with the COC, and in 1963 was appointed Coach and Assistant Conductor at the Sadler's Wells Opera Company, London (now the English National Opera). From 1966 to 1968 he was

Photo Credit: Malak Photography

co-Music Director there, the first and only Canadian to be so honoured.

In 1969 he became the Founding Conductor of the National Arts Centre Orchestra (NACO) in Ottawa. He was appointed Conductor Laureate in 1997, a position he still holds. Maestro Bernardi is Principal Conductor of the CBC Vancouver Orchestra (since 1983) and Conductor Laureate of the Calgary Philharmonic (since 1992).

■ Diane Dufresne

Quebec singing superstar Diane Dufresne has been an icon on the francophone music scene for close to four decades. Her raw passion, boundless energy, flamboyant sense of spectacle, and consummate professionalism have transcended linguistic barriers, catapulted her to the summit of an extraordinary career. By emphasising her Quebec roots and the works of Quebec chansonniers, she has made *joual* rock around the globe.

Ms. Dufresne was born in Montreal in 1944. She made her public debut in 1965 and went to Paris where she perfected her *métier* as a *chanteuse*.

Photo Credit: Jean-François Bérubé

Returning to Montreal, she appeared in Clémence Desrochers' revue *Les Girls*, a huge hit across the province. During the summers of 1970-71 she performed with musician François Cousineau at the Théâtre d'été de la Marjolaine, where she discovered rock music—and never looked back.

Her best-known singles include *Oxygène*, *Rock pour un gars d'bicyc'*, *Le parc Belmont*, *Que*, and *Le 304*. She has released over 20 albums.

■ Max Ferguson, O.C.

A master satirist, philosopher and prankster, Max Ferguson has hosted several eclectic shows. He was born in 1924 in Durham, England and lived most of his early life in London, Ontario. After working at London radio station CFPL, he joined CBC Halifax in December 1946 as an announcer, newscaster and disc jockey. It was there that Mr. Ferguson created his most memorable character, "Rawhide," as well as several others (including the mellifluous announcer Marvin Mellobell and old Ma Perkins).

Photo Credit: Cindy Taylor

CBC transferred Ferguson to Toronto in 1949 and put his program on the national network, where it remained on air for 17 consecutive years. Every weekday morning, Canadians tuned in to the irascible Rawhide delivering a satirical analysis of Canadian cultural and political events. From 1954 to 1961 Ferguson hosted two television programs, the nightly *Gazette* on CBC Halifax and CBC Toronto's *Tabloid*. His long-running *The Max Ferguson Show*, a weekly radio program of variety and commentary, ran every Saturday from October 1, 1962 to September 5, 1998. He retired from CBC Radio in 1998.

■ Evelyn Hart, C.C.

Internationally-renowned prima ballerina Evelyn Hart has devoted her life to her art and to helping Canada become an internationally recognized centre of dance excellence. During her 25 years with Canada's

Royal Winnipeg Ballet (RWB), the oldest ballet company in North America, she has raised the company's artistic standards and become one of Winnipeg's most renowned cultural ambassadors.

Photo Credit: David Cooper

Evelyn Hart was born in Toronto in 1956 and began her dance training in London when she was 14. She attended the National Ballet School in Toronto before moving to Winnipeg to study at the Royal Winnipeg Ballet School, Professional Division. She joined the RWB *corps de ballet* in 1976, and was promoted to soloist in 1978 and to principal dancer in 1979.

■ Christopher Plummer, C.C.

On stage or on screen, in roles ranging from Shakespeare's Hamlet to journalist Mike Wallace in the Oscar-nominated *The Insider* to the complex and legendary John Barrymore, Christopher Plummer radiates versatility, discipline, and a confident grace and intensity.

He was born in Toronto in 1929 and grew up in Montreal. He began acting professionally immediately after graduating from high school, made his Broadway debut in 1954, and appeared as Jason opposite Dame Judith Anderson's Medea at the Théâtre Sarah Bernhardt in Paris. His association with the Stratford Festival of Canada goes back to its formative years. He made his debut there in 1956 as the young and fiery Henry V, and over the next decade played a succession of leading roles including Hamlet, Cyrano de Bergerac, and Macbeth.

Photo Credit: Ken Duncan

He was a leading actor at Great Britain's National Theatre and the Royal Shakespeare Company, and has enjoyed award-winning successes on Broadway. Film roles have included the Academy Award-winning *The Sound of Music*, *The Man Who Would Be King* and *The Insider*. His television appearances include the award-winning BBC *Hamlet at Elsinore*, *The Thorn Birds* and *On Golden Pond*.

■ Anne-Claire Poirier

In 1967, Anne-Claire Poirier finished *De mère en fille*, the first feature-length Quebec film by a woman, marking the debut of a major body of work: "political cinema from a woman's point of view, engaged in the most important liberation movement of our era," as she herself described it.

Photo Credit: Jean-Pierre Joly

Anne-Claire Poirier was born in St-Hyacinthe, Quebec, in 1932. After completing a degree in law, she became an actor and after a short stint at Radio-Canada began working at the National Film Board of Canada (NFB) in 1960 as an assistant director and editor. Her directorial debut soon followed, with *30 minutes, Mr. Plummer* (1963) and *La Fin des étés* (1964), her first fictional film, co-written with author Hubert Aquin.

In 1969 she and Jeanne Morazain developed a major series called *En tant que femmes*, designed to showcase Quebec woman directors. In 1975 Anne-Claire Poirier was named Executive Producer and Studio Chief of the NFB's French production unit.

■ Thea Borlase
(Ramon John Hnatyshyn Award for Voluntarism in the Performing Arts)

Thea Borlase is recognized in Moncton and around the region in both linguistic communities as a woman of incredible dedication and integrity, giving selflessly of her time and her person to the advancement of creativity through the performing arts. It is largely thanks to her vision and determination that Moncton's historic Capitol Theatre, a 1920s vaudeville house restored to its former glory and re-opened in 1993, enjoys the success it does today as a first-class performing arts facility.

Born Theodora May Mitchell in London in 1921, Thea Borlase was drawn to music and

drama from an early age. She served in the Women's Royal Naval Service (WRENS) during World War II, and emigrated to Canada in 1946.

There she joined *Stage Door '56*, a highly successful amateur theatre company and helped found the Moncton District Drama Council. She served as President of the New Brunswick Drama League, and from 1982 to 1992 she was the Atlantic Regional Officer of the Canada Council for the Arts.

■ Édouard Lock and La La La Human Steps
(National Arts Centre Award)

A leading figure in the world of contemporary dance, Édouard Lock has influenced, challenged, and shaped this art form beyond borders. One cannot speak or write about contemporary dance in Canada—or indeed internationally—without acknowledging the breadth of his capacity and genius. His influence over the past 20 years has been phenomenal: he has created a unique choreographic language, literally transforming the landscape of contemporary dance and building his company, La La La Human Steps, into one of the world's most exciting and innovative dance troupes.

Photo Credit: Jean-François Bérubé

Édouard Lock was born in Casablanca, Morocco, in 1954 and emigrated to Quebec when he was three. He became interested in dance at the age of nineteen, and worked with various Montreal dance companies including the Groupe Nouvelle Aire and Les Grands Ballets Canadiens.

Photo Credit: Shari Melanson

THEATRE

Toronto is now considered the third largest production centre of live theatre in the English speaking world (following New York, and London, England). The English Canadian theatre scene has undergone exponential growth since the birth of the Stratford Shakespearean Festival at Stratford, Ont. in 1954. The alternative theatre movement that swept English Canada in the 1970s established producers of Canadian drama in every large centre. Diminishing government support in the 1980s and 1990s led to more emphasis on commercial Canadian productions of British, French and American "megamusicals" while development of new and experimental work has passed increasingly to independent artists often appearing at a cross-Canada network of "fringe" festivals.

Theatrical activity in French Canada burgeoned in the 1950s and 1960s as playwrights such as Marcel Dubé (*Un Simple Soldat*) and Gratien Gélinas (`*Tit Coq*) explored the social and moral issues confronting Québecers in their own dialect. This movement reached its apex in the work of Michel Tremblay in the early 1970s. More recently, Quebec theatre has also excelled in less verbal forms of theatre such as the spectacles produced by Cirque du Soleil, while the "total theatre" productions of Quebec City writer/performer/director Robert LePage have garnered critical acclaim around the world.

Dora Awards, 2001

The Doras, honoring excellence in Toronto theatrical productions, were first handed out in 1981. Named for Dora Mavor Moore, a teacher and director who helped establish professional theatre in Canada in the 1930s and 1940s, the awards are chosen annually from over 200 productions. The 2001 Dora Mavor Moore Awards, honoring the best of the Toronto community's performing arts, were held January 25, 2001 at the Pantages Theatre.

Outstanding New Play . . . . *I, Claudia*, Kristen Thomson
Outstanding New Musical . . . . *Iron Road*, Chan Ka Nin & Mark Brownell
Outstanding Production of a Play . . . . *Platonov,* Soulpepper Theatre Company Outstanding Production of a Musical . . . . *Billy Budd*, Canadian Opera Company
Outstanding Direction of a Play . . . . Ian McElhinny, *Stones In His Pockets*
Outstanding Direction of a Musical . . . . Neil Armfield, *Billy Budd*
Outstanding Performance by a Male in a Principle Role-Play . . . . Conleth Hill, *Stones In His Pockets*
Outstanding Performance by a Female in a Principal Role-Play . . . . *I, Claudia*, Kristen Thomson
Performance by a Male in a Principal Role-Musical . . . . Russell Braun, *Billy Budd*
Outstanding Performance by a Female in a Principal Role-Musical . . . . Louise Pitre, *Mamma Mia!*
Outstanding Performance in a Featured Role-Play or Musical . . . . Diego Matamoros, *Platonov*
Outstanding Production for Young Audiences . . . . *The Beauty Machine*, Young Peoples Theatre
Outstanding Set Design . . . . Brian Thomson, *Billy Budd*
Outrastanding Costume Design . . . . Shadowland-Anne Barber, Brad Harley & Luisa Milan, *New France*

Independent Theatre
Outstanding New Play or Musical . . . . *Radio:30*, Chris Earle
Outstanding Production . . . . *The Doll House*, DV&T Theatre Company
Outstanding Direction . . . . Vikki Anderson, *The Doll House*
Outstanding Performance by a Female . . . . Fiona Byrne, *The Doll House*
Outstanding Performance by a Male . . . . Ben Carlson, *The Doll House*
Outstanding Set Design . . . . Vikki Anderson, *The Doll House*
Outstanding Costume Design . . . . Shawn Kerwin, *The Doll House*

Source: *Toronto Theatre Alliance*

Jessie Awards, 2001

Named for professional theatre pioneer Jessie Richardson, these awards honour excellence in and raise awareness of professional theatre in Vancouver. Winners of the 18th annual awards were announced June 10, 2001.

Small Theatre

Outstanding Original Play or Musical	*The Waterhead (Three by Three)*, Aaron Bushkowsky
Outstanding Production	Kicked, *Touchstone Theatre*
Larry Lillo Award for Outstanding Direction	Katrina Dunn, *Kicked*, Touchstone Theatre
Outstanding Performance by an Actress in a Lead Role	Kendra Fanconi, *Box2*, Radix Theatre
Outstanding Performance by an Actor in a Lead Role	Donald Adams, *Kicked*, Touchstone Theatre
Outstanding Performance by an Actress in a Supporting Role	Kathleen Duborg, *Be Still*, Gateway Theatre
Outstanding Performance by an Actor in a Supporting Role	Donald Adams, *Dona Flor and her Two Husbands*, Electric Company
Outstanding Costume Design	Christine Reimer, *Dona Flor and her Two Husbands*, Electric Company
Outstanding Set Design of a Play	David Roberts, *Be Still*, Gateway Theatre
Outstanding Lighting Design	Del Surjik, *Three in the Back, Two in the Head*, Pi Theatre & Rumble Productions
Outstanding Sound Design or Original Composition	Noah Drew, *Kicked*, Touchstone Theatre

Large Theatre

Outstanding Production	*She Loves Me*, Arts Club Theatre
Larry Lillo Award for Outstanding Direction	Morris Panych, *She Loves Me*, Arts Club Theatre
Outstanding Performance by an Actress in a Lead Role	Seana McKenna, *Wit*, Vancouver Playhouse
Outstanding Performance by an Actor in a Lead Role	Mark Hildreth, *Candida*, Vancouver Playhouse
Outstanding Performance by an Actress in a Supporting Role	Lois Anderson, *Candida*, Vancouver Playhouse
Outstanding Performance by an Actor in a Supporting Role	Steven E. Miller, *Guys and Dolls*, Vancouver Playhouse
Outstanding Set Design of a Play or Musical	Ken MacDonald *Art*, Arts Club Theatre
Outstanding Lighting Design of a Play or Musical	Alan Brodie, *Art*, Arts Club Theatre
Outstanding Sound Design or Original Composition	John McCulloch, *The Mystery of Irma Vepp*, Arts Club Theatre
Outstanding Costume Design of a Play or Musical	*She Loves Me*, Arts Club Theatre

Source: *Jessies Richardson Society*

Theatre Highlights for 2002

Arts Club Theatre, Vancouver

The Arts Club opens the new year with a production of U.S. playwright Arthur Miller's powerful postwar saga, *All My Sons*, which unmasks the passions, secrets and lies that bind together a hard-headed family and their neighbours in the aftermath of World War II. The production runs from January 25 to February 24. *Dames at Sea*, runs from February 1 to March 2. A sweet little girl from a faraway Hometown comes to make it big on Broadway in this "good old-fashioned musical" which spoofs 1930s Hollywood films. The 1999 Pulitzer-Prize-winning comedy *Dinner With Friends* by Donald Margulies runs from March 8 to April 7. The play looks at what happens to two couples when one of them splits up. Playwright Morris Panych presents *The Dishwashers*, an edgy new comedy that examines the lives of four highly educated young dishwashers with nothing in common but their lowly occupation. The production runs form March 29 to April 27.

Vancouver Playhouse, Vancouver

Molière's *The School for Wives* tells the story of a rich man who trains the perfect wife for himself, only to have her fall for another man. It runs January 7 to February 7. Michael Healey's award-winning drama *The Drawer Boy* (February 11 to March 9) explores the boundary between art and reality as a young actor lives with two farmers while researching a play. *The Rainmaker*, the play whose film version became a classic starring Katherine Hepburn and Burt Lancaster, runs March 18 to April 13.

Theatre Calgary, Calgary

From January 29 to February 16, 2002, Theatre Calgary presents Sam Shepard's *True West*, an adroitly constructed comedy with serious overtones. Arthur Miller's classic modern tragedy, *Death of a Salesman* follows from February 26 to March 23. Rod Beattie stars as stockbroker-turned-farmer Walt Wingfield in *Wingfield On Ice*, the latest in the highly acclaimed Wingfield series of plays by Dan Needles, opening April 9 and running to May 4.

Globe Theatre, Regina

A seamless sequence of scenes and sonnets make up *Shakespeare Unplugged*, devised and directed by Ed Thomason. The production is from Nova Scotia's Willpower Theatre and runs in Regina January 9 to 23. *Grace*, by Michael Lewis MacLennan is a gritty drama, exploring the lives of six strangers whose paths cross and recross over a 24-hour period.

Winner of the 1996 Canadian National Playwriting Competition, the show runs February 6 to 20. Dario Fo's classic satire, *Accidental Death of an Anarchist*, will be presented in a new Canadian adaption by Micheline Chevrier March 13 to 27. Timothy Findley's *Elizabeth Rex* follows April 24 to May 8. The Governor General's Award winning play documents a fictional encounter between Elizabeth I and one of Shakespeare's actors as recounted by Shakespeare himself.

Manitoba Theatre Centre, Winnipeg

Syncopation award-winning new romantic comedy by Allan Knee runs January 2 to 26. It's a funny, tender look at the American dream, set in New York's Lower East Side before the First World War. *Vinci*, a new play by Manitoba playwright Maureen Hunter follows February 7 to March 2. The play is about the enigmatic forces that helped shape Leonardo de Vinci's life. In Marie Jones's *Stones in His Pockets* (March 7 to 30) a myriad of characters take the stage in an insightful and hilarious account of a Hollywood film crew invading a remote town in western Ireland. *The Rainmaker* (see Vancouver Playhouse) runs April 25 to May 18.

The Stratford Festival, Stratford, Ont.

Highlights on the festival's main stage in 2002 include *King Lear*, which will feature renowned Canadian film and stage star Christopher Plummer in the title role. Plummer, who has starred in films including *The Sound of Music*, *The Battle of Britain*, and *The Insider*, will be directed by noted British director Jonathan Miller. *King Lear* will run from August to November at the Festival Theatre.

2002 is the Stratford Festival's 50th anniversary. To mark the occasion, the festival will open a new performance space, the Studio Theatre. Planned for productions in the new space are *The Mandrake*, by Niccolo Machiavelli, *The Two Noble Kinsmen* by William Shakespeare and John Fletcher and *The Swanne, Part One: The Death of Cupid* by Peter Hinton. Also planned for the Studio is a festival of one-act plays by Timothy Findley, Paul Dunn, Anton Piatigorsky, Celia McBride, Ian Ross, Jean Cocteau, Jean-Paul Sartre and Federico Fellini.

Mirvish Productions, Toronto

Allan Knee's *Syncopation* runs at the Winter Garden Theatre January 30 to March 18 (see Manitoba Theatre Centre). The Winter Garden will also host *Zadie's Shoes*, March 23 to May 11. The play, by Adam Pettle, tells the touching story of a well-meaning gambler who can't resist another test of his luck. It was a surprise hit in last year's Factory Theatre season. *Peggy Sue Got Married*, an exhilarating musical adaptation of the hit comedy motion picture, will run at the Elgin Theatre in May and June. The Mirvishes will present *Blast!*, at the Hummingbird Centre, June 4 to 29. This musical extravaganza won the 2001 Tony Award for Best Special Theatrical event.

Tarragon Theatre, Toronto

High-level meetings to negotiate the departure of Québec from Canada are charged by personal impulses toward seduction and betrayal in *Plan B*, by Michael Healey (January 8 to February 10). In Daniel Brooks's *The Good Life* secrets are revealed, hidden passions implied; some bonds are strengthened, and others destroyed at a dinner party for six people—two couples and two single men (March 5 to April 7). Joan Macleod's *The Shape of a Girl* follows March 26 to April 8. It tells of an adolescent girl who becomes obsessed by a killing among teenagers in Victoria, and questions a moral climate that could lead to such horror. *Well*, by Jonathan Wilson recounts a man's return to the site where, as a child, he fell down a well and became a media icon. The play runs April 30 to June 2.

Theatre Passe Muraille, Toronto

Dreams of Blonde & Blue M.J. Kang's compelling portrait of a family struggling to escape the past and embrace the future January 24 to February 10. Monologist Ted Johns performs an updated version of *The Great School Crisis*, his satirical critique of Ontario's educational system, a hit at the Blyth Festival in 1999 March 14 to 31. *Thunderstick*, a cliché-busting comedy of conflict and political intrigue from native journalist and playwright Ken Williams follows April 18 to May 5. *Boxhead* is a surreal comedy by Darren O'Donnell in which science and the nature of existence clash. It runs from May 30 to June 16.

The National Arts Centre, Ottawa

Vinci, by Maureen Hunter, runs January 10 to 26 (see Manitoba Theatre Centre). NAC adds a dash of Coward February 28 to March 16 with Noel Coward's *Present Laughter*. Tom Stoppard's Indian Ink follows May 9 to 25. The play opens in 1930, at the close of the British colonial era in India, where free-spirited English poet Flora Crewe has struck up a friendship with Nirad Das, a local artist. Some fifty years later in London, her biographer struggles to piece together the details of Flora's life. *When We Were Singing* runs February 12 to March 2 as part of NAC's Studio Stage Series. It's a hip, funny and bittersweet musical about illusion and disillusion in the 1990s by Dorothy Dittrich. The Studio series continues April 30, with *Belle*, Florence Gibson's chronicle for reconstruction-era America. Directed by Ken Gass who directed the play's acclaimed world premiere in Toronto in February 2000.

Centaur Theatre, Montreal

The storm of the century is the subject in *Freeze* by Stephen Orloy. Set during the catastrophic ice storm in 1999, the play chronicles a Montreal couple's hilarious journey through those incredible days and weeks. The play runs January 29 to March 10. Centaur presents *Moon for the Misbegotten*, part of Eugene O'Neill's cycle of plays about the ill-starred Tyrone family. *Dinner With Friends* by Donald Margulies runs April 2 to May 12 (see Arts Club Theatre). *The Cripple of Inishmaan*, by Martin McDonagh, tells the story of Cripple Billy a young Irish boy who seeks fame and fortune when he learns that Hollywood director Robert Flaherty is coming to a neighbouring island to film his documentary *Man of Aran*. Directed by Ben Barnes, artistic director of Ireland's Abbey Theatre, the production runs May 7 to June 2.

Summer Theatre in Canada

Blyth Festival
P.O. Box 10, Blyth, Ont.
N0M 1H0

Charlottetown Festival
Confederation Centre of Arts
145 Richmond St.
Charlottetown, PEI
C1A 1J1

Huron Country Playhouse
R.R. #1, Grand Bend, Ont.
N0M 1T0

Kawartha Summer Theatre
P.O. Box 161, 2 Lindsay St. S.
Lindsay, Ont. K9V 4S1

Lighthouse Festival Theatre
P.O. Box 1208, Port Dover, Ont.
N0A 1N0

Nanaimo Festival
P.O. Box 626, Nanaimo, B.C.
V9R 5L9 (Michael McLaughlin)

Port Credit Summer Theatre
161 Lakeshore Road W.
Mississauga, Ont. L5H 1G3

Red Barn Theatre
P.O. Box 291,
Jackson's Point, Ont. L0E 1L0

Shaw Festival Theatre
P.O. Box 774
Niagara-on-the-Lake, Ont.
L0S 1J0

Stephenville Festival
149 Montana Dr.
Stephenville, Nfld. A2N 2T4

Stratford Shakespearean Festival
P.O. Box 520, Stratford, Ont.
N5A 6V2

Theatre Orangeville
87 Broadway,
Orangeville Opera House
Orangeville, Ont.
L9W 1K1

Thousand Islands Playhouse
P.O. Box 241,
Gananoque, Ont. K7G 2T8

Upper Canada Playhouse
P.O. Box 852,
Morrisburg, Ont.
K0C 1X0

Sources Include: *The Professional Association of Canadian Theatres*

Major Theatre Companies in Canada

MARITIMES

Mermaid Theatre of Nova Scotia: Box 2697, Windsor, N.S. B0N 2T0

Mulgrave Road Co-op Theatre: Box 219, Guysborough, N.S. B0H 1N0

Neptune Theatre Foundation: #B24, 1903 Barrington St., Halifax, N.S. B3J 3L7

Ship's Company Theatre: P.O. Box 275, Parrsboro, N.S. B0M 1S0

Theatre New Brunswick: Box 566, Fredericton, N.B. E3B 5A6

CENTRAL CANADA

Buddies in Bad Times: 12 Alexander St, Toronto, Ont. M5R 1E8

Canadian Stage Company: 26 Berkeley St, Toronto, Ont. M5A 2W3

Centaur Theatre Company: 453, rue Saint-François-Xavier, Montreal, Que. H2Y 2T1

La Compagnie Jean Ducepe: 1400 rue Saint-Urbain, Montreal, Que. H2X 2M5

Company of Sirens: 736 Bathurst St, Toronto, Ont. M5S 2R4

Factory Theatre: 125 Bathurst St, Toronto, Ont. M5V 2R2

Grand Theatre Company (Theatre London): 471 Richmond St, London, Ont. N6A 3E4

Great Canadian Theatre Company: 910 Gladstone Ave, Ottawa, Ont. K1R 6Y4

Gryphon Theatre: Box 454, Barrie, Ont. L4M 4T7

Magnus Theatre Company: The Central School Bldg., 10 South Algoma St, Thunder Bay, Ont. P7B 3A7

National Arts Centre: Box 1534, Stn. B, Ottawa, Ont. K1P 5W1

Native Earth Performing Arts: 503-720 Bathurst St, Toronto, Ont. M5S 2R4

Nightwood Theatre: 6000-317 Adelaide St W, Toronto, Ont. M5V 1T2

The Piggery: Box 390, North Hatley, Que. J0B 2C0

Princess of Wales Theatre: 300 King St W, Toronto, Ont. M5V 1J2

Royal Alexandra Theatre: 260 King St W, Toronto, Ont. M5V 1H9

Saidye Bronfman Centre for the Arts: 5170 Chemin de la Côte, Ste.-Catherine, Montreal, Que. H3Y 1M7

Soulpepper Theatre Company: P.O Box 199, 260 Adelaide St. E., Toronto, Ont. M5A 1N1

Sudbury Theatre Centre: Box 641, Stn. B, Sudbury, Ont. P3E 4P8

Tarragon Theatre: 30 Bridgman Ave, Toronto, Ont. M5R 1X3

Theatre Aquarius: 190 King William St., Hamilton, Ont. L8R 1A8

Théâtre de la Bordée: 1105, rue Saint-Jean, #201, Quebec, Que. G1R 1S3

Théâtre du Nouveau Monde: 137, Saint-Ferdinand, #201, Montreal, Que. H4C 2S7

Théâtre du Rideau Vert: 269 Rene Levesque G, Que., Que. G1R 2B3

Le Théâtre du Trident: 580, ave Grande-Allée est, #20, Quebec, Que. G1R 2K2

Theatre Passe Muraille: 16 Ryerson Ave, Toronto, Ont. M5T 2P3

Young People's Theatre: 165 Front St E, Toronto, Ont. M5A 3Z4

WESTERN CANADA

Alberta Theatre Projects: 220-9th Ave SE, Calgary, Alta. T2G 5C4

Arts Club Theatre: 1585 Johnson St, Vancouver, B.C. V6H 3R9

Belfry Theatre: 1291 Gladstone Ave, Victoria, B.C. V8T 1G5

Citadel Theatre: 9828-101A Ave, Edmonton, Alta. T5J 3C6

Globe Theatre: 1801 Scarth St, Regina, Sask. S4P 2G9

Manitoba Theatre Centre: 174 Market Ave, Winnipeg, Man. R3B 0P8

Manitoba Theatre for Young People: 89 Princess St, Winnipeg, Man. R3B 2X5

New Bastion Theatre Company: 625 Superior Ave, Victoria, BC. V8V 1V1

Nightcap Productions: Box 1646, Saskatoon, Sask. S7K 3R8

Persephone Theatre: 2802 Rusholme Rd, Saskatoon, Sask. S7L 0H2

Popular Theatre Alliance of Manitoba: 2-413 Selkirk Ave, Winnipeg, Man. R2W 2M4

Prairie Theatre Exchange: 389 Portage Ave, Portage Place, Unit Y300, Winnipeg, Man. R3B 3H6

Tamahnous Theatre Workshop Society: 222-275 Woodland Dr, Vancouver, B.C. V5L 3S7

Theatre Calgary: 220-9th Ave. SE, Calgary, Alta. T2G 5C4

Theatre Network Society: 10708-124th St, Edmonton, Alta. T5M 0H1

25th Street Theatre: 420 Duchess St, Saskatoon, Sask. S7K 0R1

Vancouver Playhouse: 160 West 1st Ave, Vancouver, B.C. V5Y 1A4

Western Canada Theatre Company: Box 329, Kamloops, BC V2C 5K9

Sources Include: *The Professional Association of Canadian Theatres*

DANCE

Canada is home to strong traditions in both classical and contemporary dance. Founded in 1938, The Royal Winnipeg Ballet is the second oldest company in North America and was the first in the Commonwealth to receive a Royal charter. Since 1951, the Toronto-based National Ballet of Canada has provided a home to major talents including prima ballerinas Karen Kain and Veronica Tennant. It has also been a favoured stopping place for international greats such as the late Rudolph Nureyev. The National Ballet was instrumental in facilitating the 1979 defection of Russia's Mikhail Barishnykov in Toronto. Barishnykov danced his first performances as a free man with the National Ballet, an event whose anniversary was marked in 1999 with the presentation of an honorary doctorate to Baryshnikov at the University of Toronto.

Major Ballet Companies

Alberta Ballet: 141-18th Avenue SW, Calgary, AB, T2S 0B8

Ballet British Columbia: #102, 1101 West Broadway, Vancouver, B.C. V6H 1G2

Ballet Jorgen: 213B Glebeholme Blvd., Toronto, Ont., M4J 1S8

Ballet North: 12245-131 St., Edmonton, Alta. T5L 1M8

Les Grands Ballets Canadiens: 4816 rue Rivard, Montreal, Que. H2J 2N6

Royal Winnipeg Ballet: 380 Graham Ave., Winnipeg, Man. R3C 4K2

The National Ballet of Canada: The Walter Carson Centre, 470 Queen's Quay W, Toronto, Ont. M5V 3K4

Major Contemporary and Jazz Dance Companies

Les Ballets Jazz de Montréal: 3450 rue St-Urbain, Montreal, Que. H2X 2N5

Contemporary Dancers Canada: 109 Pulford St., Winnipeg, Man. R3L 1X8

Dancemakers: 927 Dupont St., Toronto, Ont. M6H 1Z1

Decidedly Jazz Danceworks: 1514 - 4 St. SW, Calgary, Alta. T2R 0Y4

Desrosiers Dance Theatre: 103-219 Broadview Ave., Toronto, Ont. M4M 2G3

Fortier Danse Création: Box 605, Stn. C., Montreal, Que. H2L 4L5

Margie Gillis Dance Foundation: 502-3575 boul. St. Laurent, #502, Montreal, Que. H2X 2T7

Danny Grossman Dance Company: 511 Bloor St. W., Toronto, Ont. M5S 1Y4

LaLaLa Human Steps: #206, 5655 av. du Parc, Montreal, Que. H2V 4H2

Le Groupe de la Place Royale: 2 Daly Ave., Ste. 2, Ottawa, Ont. K1N 6E2

Karen Jamieson Dance Company: 221 E. 16th Ave., Vancouver, B.C. V5T 2T5

Kompany!: #810, 10136-100th St., Edmonton, Alta. T5J 0P1

Mascall Dance: 1130 Jervis St., Vancouver, B.C. V6E 2C7

O Vertigo Danse: 4455 rue de Rouen, Montreal, Que. H1V 1H1

La Fondation Jean-Pierre Perreault: 2022 Rue Sherbrooke Est, Montreal, Que. H2K 1B9

Gina Lori Riley Dance Enterprises: 3277 Sandwich St., Windsor, Ont. N9C 1A9

Toronto Dance Theatre: 80 Winchester St., Toronto, Ont. M4X 1B2

Canadian Children's Dance Theatre: 509 Parliament St. Toronto, Ont. M4X 1P3

Compagnie Marie Chouinard: #615-3981 boul. St.-Laurent, Montreal, Wue. H2W 1Y5

Dance Arts Vancouver: #402-873 Beatty St. Vancouver, BC V6B 2M6

Source: *Dance Umbrella of Ontario*

BOOKS, MAGAZINES, NEWSPAPERS

According to the Association of Canadian Book Publishers, book publishing is a $1.7 billion enterprise in Canada. Eleven million English-speaking Canadians regularly read books, twice as many as in 1978, and Canadian-owned publishing firms publish over 80 percent of Canadian-authored titles. The association also reports that export of Canadian books has tripled since 1989. Canadian authors regularly win international acclaim and, in recent years Canadians have won the Pulitzer Prize, the Booker Prize, and the Orange Prize for Fiction.

Magazine publishing in Canada is an $866 million business in which domestic magazines take a 30 percent share of the market. The industry was dealt a serious blow in 2000 when the federal government was forced by the World Trade Organization to abandon tax measures aimed at protecting the advertising market from nominally Canadian "split run" editions of U.S. magazines. In 2001 the federal government responded with the creation of the $150,000,000 Canada Magazine Fund designed to offset revenue losses due to increased foreign competition.

Recent years have seen major shifts in newspaper ownership. Montreal-based Québecor Inc. took control of the Sun newspaper chain. Canada's oldest newspaper dynasty, that of the Thomson family, divested itself of most of its newspaper holdings, while, in 2000 the newspaper empire of Conrad Black's Hollinger Inc. sold its interests in Southam Newspapers to Winnipeg television magnate Izzy Asper's Canwest Global Corporation. The withdrawal followed a dramatic expansion in Hollinger's newspaper holdings during the late 1990s. In August 2001, Black sold his remaining shares in the *National Post* newspaper to the Asper family.

The Governor General's Literary Awards, 1991–2000

The Governor General's Literary Awards, Canada's foremost literary prizes, are presented annually to recognize and reward Canadian writers. The awards were initiated in 1937 by the Canadian Authors' Association with the agreement of Governor General Baron Tweedsmuir (novelist John Buchan), and were administered by the Association until 1958.

The Awards are now administered by the Canada Council which appoints juries composed of literary specialists who select the best English and French-language works in each of 6 best categories: drama, fiction, poetry, non-fiction, and beginning in 1987, children's literature (text and illustration) and translation. The juries review all books by Canadian authors, illustrators and translators published in Canada or abroad during the previous year (Oct. 1–Sept. 30). In the case of translation, the original work must also be a Canadian-authored title. Winners receive a medal from the Governor General, $10,000 and a specially-bound copy of their award-winning book. The 2000 winners were announced Nov. 14, 2000.

English

—1991—

Fiction . . . . *Such a Long Journey*, Rohinton Mistry
Non-fiction . . . . *Occupied Canada*, Robert Hunter and Robert Calihoo
Poetry . . . . *Night Field*, Don McKay
Drama . . . . *Amigo's Blue Guitar*, Joan MacLeod

—1992—

Fiction . . . . *The English Patient*, Michael Ondaatje
Non-fiction . . . . *Revenge of the Land: A century of greed, tragedy and murder on a Saskatchewan Farm*, Maggie Siggins
Poetry . . . . *Inventing the Hawk*, Lorna Crozier
Drama . . . . *Possible Worlds, A Short History of Night*, John Mighton

—1993—

Fiction	*The Stone Diaries*, Carol Shields
Non-fiction	*Touch the Dragon*, Karen Connelly
Poetry	*Forest of the Medieval World*, Don Coles
Drama	*Fronteras Americanas*, Guillermo Verdecchia

—1994—

Fiction	*A Discovery of Strangers*, Rudy Wiebe
Non-fiction	*Rogue Primate: An Exploration of Human Domestication*, John A. Livingston
Poetry	*Cantos from a Small Room*, Robert Hilles
Drama	*The Ends of the Earth*, Morris Panych

—1995—

Fiction	*The Roaring Girl*, Greg Hollingshead
Non-fiction	*Shadow Maker: The Life of Gwendolyn MacEwen*, Rosemary Sullivan
Poetry	*Voice*, Anne Szumigalski
Drama	*Three in the Back, Two in the Head*, Jason Sherman

—1996—

Fiction	*The Englishman's Boy*, Guy Vanderhaeghe
Non-fiction	*The Unconscious Civilization*, John Raulston Saul
Poetry	*Apostrophes: Woman at a Piano*, E.D. Blodgett
Drama	*The Monument*, Colleen Wagner

—1997—

Fiction	*The Underpainter*, Jane Urquhart
Non-fiction	*Drumblair-Memories of an American Childhood*, Rachel Manley
Poetry	*Land to Light On*, Dionne Brand
Drama	*fareWel*, Ian Ross

—1998—

Fiction	*Forms of Devotion*, Diane Schoemperlen
Non-fiction	*Lines on the Water—A Fisherman's Life on the Miramichi*, David Adams Richards
Poetry	*White Stone: The Alice Poems*, Stephanie Bolster
Drama	*Harlem Duet*, Djanet Sears

—1999—

Fiction	*Elizabeth and After*, Matt Cohen
Non-fiction	*Water*, Marq de Villiers
Poetry	*Songs for Relinquishing the Earth*, Jan Zwicky
Drama	*The Drawer Boy*, Michael Healey

—2000—

Fiction	*Anil's Ghost*, Michael Ondaatje
Non-fiction	*Notes from the Hyena's Belly*, Nega Mezlekia
Poetry	*Another Gravity*, Don McKay
Drama	*Elizabeth Rex*, Timothy Findley
Translation	*Just Fine*, Robert Majzels
Children's Literature (Illustration)	*Yuck, a Love Story*, Marie-Louise Gay
Children's Literature (Text)	*Looking for X*, Deborah Ellis

French

—1991—

Fiction	*La Croix du Nord*, André Brochu
Non-fiction	*Le Jaguar et le Tamanoir*, Bernard Arcand
Poetry	*Chant pour un Québec Iointain*, Madeleine Gagnon
Drama	*Mon oncle Marcel qui vague vague près du métro Berri*, Gilbert Dupuis

—1992—

Fiction	*L'enfant chargé de songes*, Anne Hébert
Non-fiction	*La Radissonie. Le pays de la baie James*, Pierre Turgeon
Poetry	*Andromède attendra*, Gilles Cyr
Translation	*La mémoire postmoderne. Essai sur l'artcanadien contemporain*, Jean Papineau
Children's Literature (Illustration)	*Simon et la ville de carton*, Gille Tibo
Children's Literature (Text)	*Victor*, Christiane Duchesne

—1993—

Fiction	*Cartique des Plaines*, Nancy Huston
Non-fiction	*Le littérature de l'exiguité*, François Paré
Poetry	*Le Saut de L'ange*, Denise Desautels
Drama	*Celle-la*, Daniel Danis

—1994—

Fiction	*Le Petit Aigle à tête blanche*, Robert Lalonde
Non-fiction	*Du sida*, Chantal Saint-Jarre
Poetry	*Aknos*, Fulvio Caccia
Drama	*French Town*, Michel Ouellette

—1995—

Fiction	*Les Oiseaux de Saint-John Perse*, Nicole Houde
Non-fiction	*Louis-Antoine Dessaulles*, Yvan Lamonde
Poetry	*Pour orchestre et poète seul*, Émile Martel
Drama	*Les Quatre Morts de Marie*, Carole Fréchette

—1996—

Fiction	*Soifs*, Marie-Claire Blais
Non-fiction	*Le Naufrage de l'universite-Et autres essais d'epistemologie politique*
Poetry	*Le Quator de l' errance, La traversee du desert*
Drama	*Le Passage de L'Indiana*, Normand Charette

—1997—

Fiction	*Cet imperceptible mouvement*, Aude
Non-fiction	*Enfants du néant et mangeurs d'âmes-Guerre, culture et société en Iroquoisie ancienne*, Roland Viau
Poetry	*Romans-fleuves*, Pierre Nepveu
Drama	*Dits et Inédits*, Yvan Bienvenue

—1998—

Fiction	*La Terre ferme*, Christiane Frenette
Non-fiction	*Intérieurs du nouveau monde: essais dur les littératures du Québec et des Amériques*, Pierre Nepveu
Poetry	*Le Part de feu/Le Deuil de la rancune*, Suzanne Jacob
Drama	*15 secondes*, François Archambault

—1999—

Fiction . . . . *La Danse juive*, Lise Tremblay
Non-fiction. . . . . *Le Mal du Nord*, Pierre Perrault
Poetry . . . . *Conversations*, Herménégilde Chiasson
Drama . . . . *Il n'y a que l'amour*, Jean Marc Dalpé

—2000—

Fiction. . . . . *Un vent se lève qui éparpille*, Jean Marc Dalpé
Non-fiction . . . . *Genèse des nations et cultures du Nouveau Monde*, Gérard Bouchard
Poetry . . . . *La Marche de l'aveugle sans son chien*, Normand de Bellefeuille
Drama . . . . *Littoral*, Wajdi Mouawad
Translation . . . . Lori Saint-Martin, Paul Gagné, *Un parfum de cèdre*
Children's Literature (Illustration) . . . . *L'Écharpe rouge*, Anne Villeneuve
Children's Literature (Text) . . . . *Un été de Jade*, Charlotte Gingras

Source: *The Canada Council*

The Stephen Leacock Award for Humour

Stephen Butler Leacock was born in England in 1869. He was educated at Upper Canada College, University of Toronto (B.A.), and the University of Chicago (Ph.D.). He taught at UCC, and later lectured in political science at McGill. His literary output included works in history, economics and political science, although by far the most popular were his humour books. By the time of his death in 1944, he was the best-known humourist in the English-speaking world.

Canada's highest award for humour is given annually at a ceremony in Leacock's hometown of Orillia, Ontario.

Year	Author	Title
1997	Arthur Black	*Black in the Saddle Again*
1998	Mordecai Richler	*Barney's Version*
1999	Stuart McLean	*Home from the Vinyl Café*
2000	Arthur Black	*Black Tie and Tales*
2001	Stuart McLean	*Vinyl Café Unplugged*

Source: *The Leacock Home*

Mordecai Richler 1931–2001

*T*he month of July 2001 was marked by an outpouring of grief for author Mordecai Richler, who died suddenly on July 3 just days after receiving chemotherapy treatment for kidney cancer. Television specials, multi-page spreads in Canada's national newspapers and commemorative events across the country marked his passing, an unprecedented display of mourning for a Canadian literary figure. Richler was one of the country's most prolific writers, penning 10 novels (including **The Apprenticeship of Duddy Kravitz**, **St. Urbain's Horseman**, **Barney's Version**, **Solomon Gursky Was Here**, and **Joshua Then and Now**), screenplays (for the film adaptations of **Duddy Kravitz** and **Joshua**), children's books (**Jacob Two-Two Meets the Hooded Fang** and **Jacob-Two-Two and the Dinosaur**), and countless articles and essays.

Raised in the rough-and-tumble Jewish neighbourhood around St. Urbain Street in depression- and wartime-era Montreal, Richler left Canada after the war for Europe, settling finally in Great Britain. There he established himself as the Canadian member of the group of writers known as the Angry Young Men who elucidated working class disillusionment with traditional British society. While Richler will be remembered for his vivid and penetrating depictions of Jewish Montreal, his most enduring gift to Canadian letters was his satirical work, both as a commentator and a novelist.

The Giller Prize, 1996–2000

The Giller Prize awards $25,000 annually to the author of the best Canadian novel or short story collection published in English. The award was founded in 1994 by Toronto businessman Jack Rabinovitch in honour of his late wife, literary journalist Doris Giller.

The 2000 Giller Prize was presented November 2, 2000.

Year	Author	Title
1996	Margaret Atwood	*Alias Grace*
1997	Mordecai Richler	*Barney's Version*
1998	Alice Munro	*The Love of a Good Woman*
1999	Bonnie Burnard	*A Good House*
2000	Michael Ondaatje	*Anil's Ghost*
	David Adams Richards	*Mercy Among the Children*

The Booker Prize, 1996–2000

The Booker Prize recognizes the best work of English fiction published in the Commonwealth, South Africa and Ireland. It is sponsored by Booker McConnell Ltd., an international food and agriculture business, and administered by the Booker Prize Book Trust, a British educational charity. Since 1984, the value of the Booker Prize has been £15,000.

Year	Author	Title
1996	Graham Swift	*Last Orders*
1997	Arundhati Roy	*God of Small Things*
1998	Ian McEwan	*Amsterdam*
1999	J.M. Coetzee	*Disgrace*
2000	**Margaret Atwood**	***The Blind Assassin***

Pulitzer Prizes, 2000

The winners of these annual American literary awards were announced on April 18, 2001.

Fiction	Michael Chabon, *The Amazing Adventures of Kavalier & Clay*
Non-fiction	Herbert P. Bix, *Hirohito and the Making of Modern Japan*
Poetry	Stephen Dunn, *Different Hours*
Drama	David Auburn, *Proof*
Biography	David Levering Lewis, *W.E.B. Du Bois: The Fight for Equality and the American Century, 1919-1963*
History	Joseph J. Ellis, *Founding Brothers: The Revolutionary Generation*
News Reporting	Staff, *Miami Herald* (Elián Gonzalez raid)
Investigative Reporting	David Willman, *Los Angeles Times* (Unsafe prescription drugs)

Atwood Takes the Booker Prize

*A*fter three attempts, Canadian author Margaret Atwood became the first Canadian to lay sole claim to Britain's Booker Prize on November 8, 2000. Atwood won for her tenth novel, **The Blind Assassin**. *(Set in the 1930s, the book tells the story of 82-year-old Iris Chase, and the events around her sister's mysterious, early death.)*

It was Atwood's fourth nomination for the prestigious $120,000 award. At the time of the award, Atwood admitted to not having prepared an acceptance speech, assuming it was a waste of time after her previous shortlistings.

Bestselling Books in Canada, 2000

Fiction

1. *Scarlet Feather*, by Maeve Binchy
2. **Anil's Ghost, by Michael Ondaatje**
3. **The Blind Assassin, by Margaret Atwood**
4. *The Brethren*, by John Grisham
5. *The Bear And The Dragon*, by Tom Clancy
6. *Winter's Heart*, by Robert Jordan
7. **Vinyl Cafe: Unplugged, by Stuart McLean**
8. *No Great Mischief*, by Alistair MacLeod
9. **A Good House, by Bonnie Burnard**
10. **Mercy Among The Children, by David Adams Richards**

Source: *The Globe and Mail*

Non-fiction

1. *Tuesdays With Morrie*, by Mitch Albom
2. *'Tis*, by Frank McCourt
3. *The Rock Says*, by The Rock
4. *Have A Nice Day*, by Mick (Mankind) Foley
5. *In A Sunburned Country*, by Bill Bryson
6. **Canada: A People's History, by Don Gillmor and Pierre Turgeon**
7. *The Beatles Anthology*, by The Beatles
8. *Ten Things I Wish I'd Known*, by Maria Shriver
9. *On Writing*, by Stephen King
10. **Trudeau Albums, by Peter Gzowski et al**

Canadian books set in bold type.

National Magazine Awards, 2001

These annual awards were given June 1, 2001 by the National Magazine Awards Foundation. In 2001 there were gold and silver awards in 33 categories, including writing, design and photography.

One-of-a-Kind Articles	Sarah Hampson, "Place of Worship," *Toronto Life*
Humour	Paul Quarrington, "A Little Place I Know," *Outdoor Canada*
Business	Trevor Cole, "Nickelled and Damned," *Report on Business Magazine*
Science & Technology	Timothy Taylor, "Time Warp," *Saturday Night*
Health and Medicine	Yanick Villedieu, "L'homme rapaillé," *L'actualité*
Still-Life Photography	Andrzej Pluta, "Balm and Beauty and Hosanna," *Border Crossings*
Fashion	Brad MacIver, Chris Chapman, Susie Sheffman, "Beauty in the Bungalow," *Fashion*
Politics	Guy Lawson, "The Whispering Campaign," *Saturday Night*
Investigative Reporting	Gordon Laird, "This Land is Whose Land?," *THIS Magazine*
Fiction	Cynthia Flood, "Religious Knowledge," *Prism International*
Arts and Entertainment	Urjo Kareda, "Sold Out," *Toronto Life*
Sports and Recreation	Charles Foran, "The Trials of Marty McSorley," *Saturday Night*
Photojournalism	Lynne Cohen, "A Conjugal Visit," *Saturday Night*
Personal journalism	Cynthia Brouse, "Gross Encounters," *Toronto Life*
Portrait Photography	Chris Buck, "Floored," *Shift*
Columns	Urjo Kareda, "Coming to a theatre near you.../Money well spent /Raising the barre," *Toronto Life*
Service	Ann Dowsett Johnston & Staff, "Measuring Excellence," *Maclean's*
Travel	Russell Monk, "The Other Side of Remote," *Outpost*
How-To	Linda Pim, "10 Ways to Save Your Local Woods," *Seasons*
Essays	Alberto Manguel, "The Toronto That Is," *Toronto Life*
Profiles	Norman Doidge, "Love, Friendship and the Art of Dying," *Saturday Night*
Poetry	Sarah Klassen, "In Retrospect," *Arc*
Editorial Package	Peeter Kopvillem & Staff, "Pierre Elliott Trudeau," *Maclean's*
Words and Pictures	Karen Connelly, Yuric Dojc, Matthew Rogers, Gary Salewicz, Gary Ross, Sandra Latini, "City of Nations," *Toronto Life*
Social Affairs	Pierre Cayouette, " L'eau qui tue," *L'actualité*
Magazine Covers	Leanne Shapton, "Saul Bellow," *Saturday Night*
President's Medal	Norman Doidge, *Saturday Night*
Magazine of the Year	*AZURE*
Best New Magazine	*Moneysense*
Alexander Ross Award for Best New Magazine Writer	Matthew McKinnon
Foundation Award for Outstanding Achievement	Ken Rodmell

Source: *National Magazine Awards Foundation*

Top Canadian Paid-Circulation Magazines, 2001

Magazine	Circulation[1]
Reader's Digest (Canadian English edition)	1 001 022
Chatelaine (English language edition)	735 059
TV Guide	561 107
Canadian Living	547 763
Maclean's	506 428
Time (Canadian edition)	317 325
Séléction du Reader's Digest (Canadian French edition)	221 187
Canadian Geographic	205 401
TV Hebdo	189 716
Châtelaine (French language edition)	187 913
Coupe de Pouce	172 413
Flare	160 221
7 Jours	130 229

Source: *CARD: Media Information Network*

(1) Average total paid circulation for most recently reported 6 month period as of August 2001.

Media Convergence In Canada

*M*edia convergence is both a technical and an economic phenomenon. Digital technology has made it possible for journalists working in print to become suppliers of information to broadcast media and vice versa. The same technology makes it possible for both of these traditional media to work in tandem with internet-based platforms. Given the trend in mergers and acquisitions that has continued unabated worldwide since the 1980s, corporations involved in the different areas of the communications field have made logical merger partners. The 2000 takeover of U.S. media giant Time Warner by internet service provider America Online created a media behemoth that included the internet, cable television, publishing and film and TV production among its holdings.

The latest round of media mergers hit Canada later that year when Bell Canada Enterprises acquired the CTV television network, and CanWest Global, owners of Global Television, took over Hollinger Inc.'s Canadian newspapers and internet assets. The Hollinger deal instantly made CanWest Canada's largest newspaper publisher, with 13 major dailies and 126 community newspapers in its stable, plus a 50 percent stake in the **National Post** newspaper. BCE added a print dimension to its holdings in January 2001 by forming Bell Globemedia, a joint venture with Thomson Corp which put CTV, the **Globe and Mail** newpaper, and Sympatico internet service under one roof.

The mergers paved the way for resource sharing between newspapers and television outlets, but concerns were raised as to the impact this would have on the variety of voices in the Canadian media. In response, the Canadian Radio-television and Telecommunications Commission (CRTC) ruled on August 2, 2001 that, while TV and newspapers could share newsgathering and other resources, they would be required to maintain separate management structures. In addition, the media organizations involved would have to set up monitoring committees to take complaints from employees and the public concerning their new relationships.

Top Canadian Daily Newspapers, 2001

Newspaper	Daily[2]		Circulation[1] Saturday	Sunday
Toronto Star	454 409		686 652	457 893
Globe and Mail	354 574		416 457	
National Post	332 188		396 413	
Journal de Montreal	262 233		321 616	268 279
Toronto Sun	230 618		170 440	389 108
La Presse	194 147		285 823	201 383
Vancouver Sun	185 632	(M-Th)	244 748	
	217 442	(F)		
Vancouver Province	161 689			198 437
Ottawa Citizen	140 535		181 637	137 139
Montreal Gazette	138 087		178 570	135 905
Edmonton Journal	414 237	(M-Th/Sat);	137 473	
	163 748	(F)		
Winnipeg Free Press	123 777		178 471	129 226
Calgary Herald	110 851	(M-Th)	128 559	111 086
	148 012	(F)		
Hamiltion Spectator	109 098		126 617	
Le Journal de Quebec	96 396		123 242	99 069
London Free Press	94 844		118 394	
Halifax Chronicle Herald	89 910		58 928	
Windsor Star	75 604		87 478	
Victoria-Times Columnist	74 810	(M-Sat)		74 944
Edmonton Sun	73 728	(M-Sat)		106 878

Source: *CARD: Media Information Network*

(1) Average total paid circulation for most recently reported 6-month period as of August 2001. Ranked by weekday circulation.

(2) Monday to Friday unless otherwise indicated.

National Newspaper Awards, 2001

These annual awards were announced in Montreal on May 3, 2001.

Editorial Writing	Henry Aubin, *Montreal Gazette*
Spot News Photography	Paul Chiasson, The Canadian Press
Feature Photography	Andrew Stawicki, *Toronto Star*
Spot News Reporting	Andrew McIntosh, *National Post*
International Reporting	Linda Diebel, *Toronto Star*
Sports Writing	Gary Mason, *Vancouver Sun*
Feature Writing	Jill Mahoney, Kim Lunman, Erin Anderssen, *Globe and Mail*
Columns	Margaret Wente, *Globe and Mail*
Sports Photography	Ryan Remiorz, The Canadian Press
Enterprise Reporting	Les Papp, *Toronto Star*
Critical Writing	Doug Saunders, *Globe and Mail*
Layout and Design	Roger Watanabe, *Vancouver Sun*
Editorial Cartooning	Serge Chapleau, *La Presse*
Business Reporting	David Baines, *Vancouver Sun*
Local Reporting	Rob Tripp, *Kingston Whig-Standard*

Source: *Canadian Newspaper Association*

GALLERIES AND MUSEUMS

Canadian art is a time-honoured tradition with the oldest surviving work of prehistoric First Nations carving dating back to 5,000 B.C. European traditions were slow to take hold in the colonial regime. Bishop Laval established the country's first school of art near Quebec in 1675 and religious art dominated the Canadian scene until the 19th century when Paul Kane and Cornelius Krieghoff became the country's first genre painters, rendering scenes of native and settler life respectively. After the establishment of major art institions such as the Royal Canadian Academy of Art (1880) and the Ontario College of Art (1875), landscape became the dominant form of Canadian painting, a trend that peaked with the formation of the Group of Seven in 1920 (see article below). Abstract art reached Canada in the 1940s and gained its first domestic expression in the work of Montreal's automatiste painters, lead by Jean Paul Riopelle and Paul-Emile Borduas, working under the influence of cubism and the French surreallists. Art in English Canada remained under the sway of the Group of Seven and that of British representational trends in portraiture and urban landscape until the formation in 1954 and subsequent international success of Painters Eleven in Toronto. This group which featured Jack Bush, Kazuo Nakamura, Jock MacDonald, William Ronald, and Harold Town drew heavily on the abstract expressionist movement in the United States for inspiration and its members scored success in New York critical circles of the period. Leadership reverted to Montreal in the 1960s with the emergence of painters devoted to the op art school focussing on experiments in visual effects and surface dynamics. While magic realist painters such as Nova Scotia's Alex Colville, and Newfoundland's Christopher Pratt and Manitoba-born naïve painter William Kurelek kept representational painting popular through the 1970s, a new generation of artists such as Michael Snow, Greg Curnoe, General Idea, and Iain Baxter followed the international trend away from painting into conceptual art exploring new media such as film, photography, performance and installation art. The 1980s saw a rebirth in interest in representational painting with the emergence of neo-expressionist influenced work from groups such as Vancouver's New Romantics and Toronto's ChromaZone Collective. Today the Canadian art scene features artists working in every conceivable medium and genre. Their work is shown in artist run collectives, commercial galleries and larger public galleries in every major centre.

Group of Seven

The Group of Seven held its first exhibition at the Art Gallery of Toronto in May 1920. The original members included J.E.H. MacDonald, Lawren Harris, A.Y. Jackson, Arthur Lismer, F.H. Varley, Frank Johnston and Franklin Carmichael.

In 1924, Johnston resigned from the Group and, in 1926, A.J. Casson was invited to join. In the later years of the Group, two new members, Edwin Holgate and Lionel Lemoine FitzGerald, were added. The Group held its final exhibition in Dec. 1931 and disbanded in 1932.

Tom Thomson, who drowned in 1917, was never a member of the Group of Seven, though his boldly-colored works depicting the rugged landscape of northern Ontario became associated with its style of painting.

By breaking with the traditional, European, painting style popular in Canada in the 1920s, The Group of Seven made a huge impact on Canadian art. Although originally reviled by critics, the Group had gained wide acceptance and popularity by the 1930s. Today, the Group's paintings are exhibited in every major gallery in Canada.

J.E.H. **MacDonald** (1873–1932)
Lawren **Harris** (1885–1970)
Alexander Young (A.Y.) **Jackson** (1882–1974)
Arthur **Lismer** (1885–1969)
Frederick Horsman **Varley** (1881–1969)
Frank Hans **Johnston** (1888–1949)
Frank **Carmichael** (1890–1945)
Alfred Joseph (A.J.) **Casson** (1898–1992)
Edwin **Holgate** (1892–1977)
Lionel Lemoine **FitzGerald** (1890–1956)
Tom **Thomson** (1877–1917)

Source: *Looking at Landscape,* Dwight Siegner, The McMichael Canadian Art Collection

Gallery and Museum Highlights, 2002

Glenbow Museum, Calgary

Glenbow's showing of *Pop Revolution* (February 16-May 26) is an exclusive Canadian engagement for the innovative exhibit from New York's Museum of Modern Art. It follows the emergence of Pop Art from post Second World War consumerism, explores its insights, criticism, and often light-hearted takes on life in our modern, material world. From Marilyn Monroe to Chairman Mao, from soup cans to fighter planes, visitors will examine the creative work of Andy Warhol, Roy Lichtenstein, Robert Indiana, Jasper Johns, and other prominent Pop artists of the 1960s and early 1970s. *The Group of Seven in Western Canada* (June 15-October) explores how the Toronto-based group played a significant role in the shaping the identity and history of western Canada. This show will include approximately 250 works by Group artists plus 30 to 50 by their western contemporaries.

Art Gallery of Ontario, Toronto

The AGO began a yearlong celebration of its 100th anniversary on September 15, 2001 with *House Guests: Contemporary Artists in The Grange* which continues until January 27, 2002. The juxtaposition of contemporary work with the historical setting of the Grange (the building that originally housed the gallery) is the first in a series of reinstallation of work from the galleries' collections in unusual settings. In 2000, the AGO received a major gift of 242 prints by the Canadian artist, David Blackwood. *Celebrating the Centennial: David Blackwood's Fire Down on the Labrador* will include working proofs, drawings and the original plate for Blackwood's best known plate, "Fire Down on the Labrador" (1980). The exhibition runs March 30-June 23. *Celebrating the Centennial: Recent Acquisitions of European Prints and Drawings* (to March 17) includes a selection of recent gifts and purchases of major European prints and drawings. *Video Primer*, running until March 24, includes work by 50 video artists from Canada, the United States and various other countries. It explores the medium's evolution and the themes that have engaged video artists from the outset.

Yes Yoko Ono (February 22-May 20) is the first large-scale multimedia retrospective of Yoko Ono's work to be mounted in North America since 1971. The 150 works in the exhibition are from the 1960s to the present with a focus on the her work from the 1960s, and aims to establish Ono as a pivotal figure in the development of the post-war international avant-garde.

As part of a cultural partnership with Russia's Hermitage Museum, AGO presents *Canadian Works to the State Hermitage Museum, Russia*, an assembly of Canadian works from its collection which will be sent to Russia (June-September). *Dreaming With Open Eyes: The Schwarz Collection of Dada and Surrealist Art* (June 7-September 1) comprises over 200 works from the collection donated to the Israel Museum in 1998. They include painting, sculpture, objects, drawing, prints, collages, photographs, artist's books, and other publications and ephemera representing the work of such artists as Marcel Duchamp, Man Ray and Max Ernst.

Royal Ontario Museum, Toronto

Papiers à la Mode: Illusions of Fashion by Isabelle de Borchgrave and Rita Brown, on view to January 20, is a collection of over 30 life-size costumes reproduced entirely in paper and inspired by key moments in international fashion design of the 18th to 20th centuries. *More Than Keeping Cool: Chinese Fans and Fan Paintings* (to April 28) showcases the beauty, as well the function, of an indispensable object in the daily life of the Chinese from the 16th to 20th centuries. Many of the artifacts, hidden away in the ROM vaults for over 80 years, will be on public display for the first time.

National Gallery of Canada, Ottawa

From February 1 to May 5, 2002, the National Gallery celebrates Vancouver artist Gathie Falk. Organized by the Vancouver Art Gallery, the exhibition, which comprises 78 pieces, will focus on significant bodies of the Vancouver artist's work, dating from the early ceramic sculptures of the 1970s to the complex mixed-media installations of the present.

No Man's Land: The Photographs of Lynne Cohen (February 1-May 12) will be the first full examination of this Canadian photographer's work, from pieces produced in the mid-1970s to her most recent photographs. Her photographs constitute a complex, multi-layered commentary about our culture, its illusions and contradictions, and the slightly insane hopes and dreams we share as a society.

The large body of innovative and completely original prints made by Betty Goodwin which brought the artist to national and international attention between 1969 and 1976, will be the subject of an exhibition running May 31-September 2. These prints are best known by the series that included vests and shirts as her subjects.

In partnership with the Art Gallery of Ontario, the National Gallery will present the first major retrospective of the work of Canadian painter Tom Thomson (1877-1917) in over 30 years (June 7-September 8). The exhibition will comprise approximately 125 paintings and will enable visitors to view the broad range of Thomson's artistic production throughout his brief career.

Printmaking in Italy, c.1550-c.1630 will reconsider the history of printmaking in Italy from the middle of the 16th century up to the 1620s, a period which saw a massive increase in the volume of print production. This exhibition runs October 1, 2002-January 1, 2003. Organized by the Musée d'art contemporain de Montréal in collaboration with the National Gallery, one of the first large-scale Canadian presentations of work by David Rabinowitch will be on view October 1, 2002-January 1, 2003.

Canadian Museum of Civilization, Hull

Lifelines: Canada's East Coast Fisheries runs to February 24. This major exhibition–developed by the Canadian Museum of Civilization in collaboration with four Atlantic museums–explores the fascinating history of the fisheries, the region's lively culture, and the stakes involved in protecting our marine resources. From May 16 to October 14, *Vikings: The North Atlantic Saga* will mark the first time that artifacts from all the regions visited during the Vikings' westward expansion have been exhibited together. Among the treasures are silver hoards, pagan grave finds dated 800 to 1050 A.D., looted jewellery, medieval church carvings and saga manuscripts from the 13th and 14th centuries. Themes of exploration, new frontiers, human independence and stewardship of the planet weave the displays together. The exhibit also looks at the mysteries of Viking shipbuilding and navigation, and theories about the disappearance of the Norse colonies in Greenland.

Montreal Museum of Fine Art

From January 23 to April 14 the museum spotlights the work of German photographer Herbert List (1903-1975). The exhibition of 170 prints is the first time that List's different genres have been presented together. *Francisco Goya and Jake and Dinos Chapman: "Disasters of War"* (to January 27) features two series: Francisco Goya's "Disasters of War" (1810-1820) and its contemporary counterpart, eighty prints from "Disasters of War II" by British artists Jake and Dinos Chapman. This parallel presentation highlights the perpetuity of war as a theme in art and illustrates significant changes in the image from Goya's era to our own. In *Piranesi-Goya: "Roma Fantastica" and "The Sleep of Reason"* (to January 27) 300 prints from the Gabriele Mazzotta Foundation in Milan by two of the greatest printmakers of the 18th and early 19th century combine to illustrate the apogee and final disillusionment of the Enlightenment in Europe.

Raphaël to Tiepolo: Master Italian Paintings from the Budapest Museum of Fine Arts runs April 24-August 4. This exhibition features 43 works from the major Italian schools of the 15th to the 18th century masters like Lorenzo Monaco, Sassetta, Filippo Lippi, Raphael, Titian, Sebastiano del Piombo, Tintoretto, Veronese, Bernardo Strozzi, Annibale Carracci, Bernardo Bellotto and Giovani Battista Tiepolo. The works present a variety of subjects, from religious and mythological themes to portraits.

Beaverbrook Museum, Fredericton

Canvas of War: Canada's War Art, runs January 27-April 17. This exhibition, organized by the Canadian War Museum, is the first major exhibition of Canadian war art of both world wars. A.Y. Jackson, Arthur Lismer, Alex Colville and Jack Shadbolt are among the artists represented. A retrospective on the work of Vancouver artist Gathie Falk runs September 15-November 17 (see the National Gallery of Canada). Other exhibitions for 2002 include *Sylvat Aziz and Leesa Streifler* (April 28-June 23), *Glenn Priestley: From Tabor Hill to Keswick Ridge* (April 28-June 23), *Traditions of Portraiture* (July 2-September 1), *Impressionist Paintings* (November 24-January 28, 2003) and *The Birth of the Modern* (November 24-January 28, 2003).

Art Gallery of Nova Scotia, Halifax

Allan Harding MacKay: Source/Derivations (to February 3) consists of new drawings and photo transparent "derivations" inspired by the 1923 painting The Red Cloak by Edith A. Smith, which the artist discovered in the AGNS Permanent Collection during his two month of his artist-in-residency at the gallery in 1999. *Art as Language*, is a project of AGNS's Education Gallery that includes an interactive component. This exhibition is designed to help visitors understand and appreciate the stories told by families who are new to Canada. Running until March 3, it highlights how the visual arts can serve as a place to communicate, to build relationships, and to build a new home for newcomers.

Manitoba's "National Treasure"

*T*he Hudson's Bay Company Gallery at the Manitoba Museum of Man and Nature houses Manitoba's National Treasure—the Hudson's Bay Company Museum Collection. The collection was donated to the museum in 1994. A new wing was completed in 1998 to accommodate a collection that spans three centuries of the Company's colourful history and contains more than 10,000 artifacts.

Half of the collection originated in First Nations, Métis and Inuit communities. The items illustrate traditional lifestyles and unique adaptations to the world of the commercial fur trade. These artifacts were acquired by the HBC through purchase, trade, ceremonial gift exchange and donations from fur traders and their families. The European-Canadian Collection includes furnishings from the head office in London, England; personal belongings; commemorative medals; trade goods; and objects related to navigation, exploration and retail. The Fine Art Collection features 17th century antique maps and watercolours by Peter Rindisbacher, painted at Red River in the 1820s.

The gallery is linked to the Nonsuch Gallery and its full-scale replica of the ship which, in 1688, carried fur traders into Hudson's Bay for the first time.

The Hudson's Bay Company Gallery tells the story of one of the oldest commercial enterprises still in existence and of its impact on the history of Canada. The artifacts reveal an amazing story that includes the quest for the fabled North West Passage and the establishment of a trading empire encompassing a vast area from Labrador to Vancouver Island to what is now the northwestern United States, even touching on Alaska, Kamchatka, Hawaii and China.

Major Public Art Galleries in Canada

Art Gallery of Greater Victoria: 1040 Moss St., Victoria, B.C. V8V 4P1 (604) 384-4101

Art Gallery of Nova Scotia: P.O. Box 2262, Halifax, N.S. B3J 3C8 (902) 424-7542

Art Gallery of Ontario: 317 Dundas St. W., Toronto, Ont. M5T 1G4 (416) 979-6648

Art Gallery of Windsor: 3100 Howard Ave., Windsor, Ont. N8X 3Y8 (519) 258-7111

Beaverbrook Art Gallery: P.O. Box 605, Fredericton, N.B. E3B 5A6 (506) 458-8545

Confederation Centre Art Gallery and Museum: 145 Richmond St., Charlottetown, P.E. C1A 1J1 (902) 628-6111

Dunlop Art Gallery: P.O. Box 2311, Regina, Sask. S4P 3Z5 (306) 777-6040

Edmonton Art Gallery: 2 Sir Winston Churchill Sq., Edmonton, Alta. T5J 2C1 (403) 422-6223

McMichael Canadian Art Collection: 10365 Islington Ave., Kleinburg, Ont. L0J 1C0 (905) 893-1121

Montreal Museum of Fine Arts: 1379-1380 Sherbrooke St. W., P.O. Box 3000, Stn. H, Montreal, Que. H3G 2T9 (514) 285-1600

Musee d'Art Contemporain de Montreal: 185 St. Catherine St. W, Montreal, Que. H2X 1Z8 (514) 847-6212

Musée du Québec: Parc des Champs de Bataille, 1, rue Wolfe/Montcalm, Quebec, Que. G1R 5H3 (418) 643-2150

National Gallery of Canada: 380 Sussex Dr., Ottawa, Ont. K1N 9N4 (613) 990-1985

Thunder Bay Art Gallery: P.O. Box 1193, Station F, Thunder Bay, Ont. P7C 4X9 (807) 577-6427

Vancouver Art Gallery: 750 Hornby St., Vancouver, B.C. V6Z 2H7 (604) 662-4700

Winnipeg Art Gallery: 300 Memorial Blvd., Winnipeg, Man. R3C 1V1 (204) 786-6641

Major Public Museums in Canada

Canadian Centre for Architecture: 1920 rue Baile, Montreal, Que. H3A 1E9 (514) 939-7000

Canadian Museum of Civilization: 100 Laurier St., Box 3100, Stn B, Hull, Que. J8X 4H2 (819) 776-7000

Canadian Museum of Contemporary Photography: 1 Rideau Canal, P.O. Box 465, Station A, Ottawa, Ont. K1N 9N6 (613) 990-8257

Canadian Museum of Nature: P.O. Box 3443, Station D, Ottawa, Ont. K1P 6P4 (613) 566-4700

Canadian War Museum: 330 Sussex Dr., Ottawa, Ont. K1A 0M8 (613) 996-1420

Glenbow-Alberta Institute: 130-9th Ave. SE, Calgary, Alta. T2G 0P3 (403) 268-4100

Manitoba Museum of Man and Nature: 190 Rupert Ave., Winnipeg, Man. R3B 0N2 (204) 956-2830

Maritime Museum of the Atlantic: 1675 Lower Water St., Halifax, N.S. B3J 1S3 (902) 429-7490

McCord Museum of Canadian History: 690, rue Sherbrooke ouest, Montreal, Que. H3A 1E9 (514) 398-7100

Musée de la Civilisation: 85, rue Dalhousie, C.P. 155, Succursale B, Quebec, Que. G1K 7A6 (418) 643-2158

New Brunswick Museum: 277 Douglas Ave., Saint John, N.B. E2K 1E5 (506) 643-2300

Newfoundland Museum: 285 Duckworth St., P.O. Box 8700, St. John's, Nfld. A1B 4J6 (709) 729-2329

Nova Scotia Museum: 1747 Summer St., Halifax, N.S. B3H 3A6 (902) 424-6471

Prince of Wales Northern Heritage Centre: P.O. Box 1320, Yellowknife, N.W.T. X1A 2L9 (867) 873-7551

Provincial Museum of Alberta: 12845-102nd Ave., Edmonton, Alta. T5N 0M6 (403) 453-9100

Royal British Columbia Museum: P.O. Box 9815, Stn. Prov. Govt., Victoria, B.C. V8W 9W2 (250) 387-3701

Royal Ontario Museum: 100 Queen's Park, Toronto, Ont. M5S 2C6 (416) 586-8000

Royal Saskatchewan Museum: Wascana Park, College and Albert, Regina, Sask. S4P 3V7 (306) 787-2815

Vancouver Museum: 1100 Chestnut St., Vancouver, B.C. V6J 3J9 (604) 736-4431

Prince Edward Island Museum and Heritage Foundation: 2 Kent St., Charlottetown, PEI C1A 1M6 (902) 368-6600

Governor General's Awards in Visual and Media Arts

These annual awards, funded and administered by the Canada Council for the Arts, were created in June 1999. Six prizes are awarded for distinguished career achievement in the visual and media arts, and one prize for distinguished contributions to the visual and media arts through voluntarism, philanthropy, board governance or community outreach activities. The second annual Governor General's awards were announced March 14, 2001.

2001 Winners

■ **Douglas Cardinal,** architect, Ottawa, Ontario
Douglas Cardinal's trademark curvilinear, organic buildings, sensitively placed into the landscape like sculptures, have been called an indigenous Canadian style of architecture. Over 36 years, the Calgary-born Cardinal has undertaken a wide variety of projects, ranging from homes to government and institutional buildings. His most notable projects include the spectacular Canadian Museum of Civilization in Hull, Quebec; the award-winning St. Mary's Church in Red Deer, Alberta; the Grande Prairie Regional College and the Ponoka Provincial Building.

■ **Tom Dean,** Visual Artist
Tom Dean's 30-year career is marked by a rare consistency that is evident in a fascination with the meaning of both ordinary and mythical objects. From the earliest pieces of the 1970s to his showing at the 1999 Venice Biennale, Tom Dean's powerful body of work has given a strong voice to contemporary Canadian art. His work is found in the permanent collections of the Montreal Museum of Fine Arts, the Musée d'art contemporain de Montréal and the National Gallery of Canada.

■ **Russell C. Goodman,** Stained Glass Artist
Russell C. Goodman is the modern master of a medieval medium. He has worked in stained glass for almost 50 years, cutting, painting, firing and glazing the best of antique glass. He has designed and installed over 1,000 stained glass windows, including those in St. Andrew's Presbyterian Church (Thunder Bay), Christ Church United (Mississauga), Donway United Church and St. Augustine's of Canterbury (both in Toronto). Goodman's sensitivity to space and coloured light can also be found in the windows of private and public buildings.

■ **Jamelie Hassan,** Visual Artist
Jamelie Hassan's multi-media installations, photo-based and video work have been important features in the Canadian visual art milieu since the early 1970s. Her work has focused on issues of cultural and personal identity, exclusion, displacement, language and communication. The complexity of her installation and multi-media work has attracted critical attention across Canada as well as internationally, including the United States, Europe, the Middle East and Japan. Her work can be found in various public collections, including those of the Art Gallery of Ontario, the National Gallery of Canada and the New Museum of Contemporary Art in New York.

■ **Liz Magor,** Visual Artist
Liz Magor's sculptures, installation pieces and photographic works examine the notion of Canadianness that is reflected more often in literature than in contemporary visual arts. Her work has been exhibited in major Canadian public art galleries and museums, including the National Gallery of Canada, the Art Gallery of Ontario, and the Vancouver Art Gallery, as well as abroad. She represented Canada at the prestigious Venice Biennale in 1987.

■ **Alanis Obomsawin,** Filmmaker
Alanis Obomsawin is an internationally renowned documentary filmmaker, whose work has led to a better understanding of the history and culture of Aboriginal peoples. Her independent spirit and vision are reflected in a significant body of film work for the National Film Board of Canada that includes *Kanehsatake: 270 Years of Resistance* (about the 1990 Oka crisis), *Rocks at Whiskey Trench*, *My Name is Kahentiiosta* and *Mother of Many Children*.

■ **Joan Chalmers,** Philanthropist
Joan Chalmers has distinguished herself not only for her financial support for the arts, but by the energy she has devoted to the development of the arts, especially fine crafts. She has brought wisdom and leadership to countless arts boards, including those of the Canadian Crafts Council, the World Crafts Council, Aid to Artisans, the Glenn Gould Foundation and the Stratford Festival.

Festivals And Events, 2002

As well as festivals in the various branches of the performing arts, communities across Canada celebrate local, national and international culture with a wide variety of events. Here is a sample of the fairs and festivals available to visitors across Canada. Note that dates are subject to change and interested visitors should contact the numbers given, or the tourist bureaus of the respective provinces and territories.

■ Newfoundland and Labrador
Twillingate's Fish, Fun and Folk Festival, Twillingate, July: This festival of Newfoundland heritage features music games and lots of seafood. Tel. (709) 884-5376.

Gander's 15th Annual Festival of Flight, Gander, July-August: Described as "Newfoundland's Biggest Kitchen Party," the festival includes live music, seafood, fireworks and demolition derbies. Tel. (709) 651-2930.

Trinity-Conception Fall Fair, Harbour Grace, September: The 44th annual fair will include the Miss Newfoundland & Labrador Pageant, a talent search contest, farm days, arts and crafts contest, agricultural contests, amusement park, parade, and nightly entertainment. Tel. (709) 596-6201.

Grand Falls-Windsor Red Maple Festival, Grand Falls-Windsor, October-November: This community fall festival features swimming, hockey, tournament, ball hockey tournament, teen dances, adult dances and community skating. It concludes with a huge bonfire and mini-fireworks at Centennial Field. Tel. (709) 489-0450.

■ Prince Edward Island
Lucy Maude Montgomery Festival, Cavendish and Area, August: Two days of wholesome family fun and an opportunity to learn more about Montgomery and her time. Experience old-fashioned community events. Hear readings from Montgomery's work. Improve your writing skills at writers' workshops. Learn about her biography and history at the memorial service. Enjoy traditional and children's entertainment. Tel. (902) 963-7874.

Old Home Week/PEI Exhibition, Charlottetown, August: Atlantic Canada's premiere exhibition and entertainment experience. Harness racing, equestrian and livestock shows, midway, parade, commercial exhibits, food fest, entertainment, agriculture, handicraft and garden displays. Tel. (902) 629-6623.

International Shellfish Festival, Charlottetown, September: A celebration of P.E.I. shellfish including oysters, mussels and clams. Featuring the Polar Foods International Eastern Canadian Oyster Shucking Championships, the Great Paderno Chowder Challenge and island entertainment. Tel. (902) 892-4455.

■ Nova Scotia
Nova Scotia International Tattoo, Halifax, June 29-July 7: The world's largest annual indoor show presents acts performed by over 2,000 military and civilian performers from Canada and around the world. The program offers a unique combination of music, dance, drama, gymnastics, comedy and military displays. Tel. (902) 420-1114.

Yarmouth Seafest, Yarmouth, July: This community event celebrates Yarmouth's connection to a seafaring heritage. Key elements include a giant street parade, antique car show, bagpiper's walk and tea with the Mayor. It also features the largest fireworks display in Southwest Nova Scotia and the fabulous Fish Feast. Tel. (902) 742-5355.

Festival Acadien de Clare, Clare, July: Canada's largest and oldest Acadian festival. Theatre, hikes, races, parades, a deep-sea fishing tournament and other competitions are all a part of the event. Tel. (902) 769-3655.

■ New Brunswick
Shediac Lobster Festival, Shediac, first week of July: The Shediac Lobster Festival is an annual event held in the first week of July. Visitors are invited to discover the region's lobster and Acadian culture. Parades, races, entertainment and fireworks are all part of the festivities. Tel. (506) 532-1122.

New Brunswick Highland Games and Scottish Festival, Fredericton, late July: This event features pipeband competitions, individual piping and drumming competitions, highland dancing competitions, heavy events contests, clan heritage genealogy workshop, celtic music, ceilidh and concerts under the stars. It also includes fiddling, whisky tasting, celtic guitar, step dancing, and genealogy workshops. Tel. 1-888-368-4444, (506) 452-9244.

La Foire Brayonne, Edmundston, August: Internationally renowned, this popular festival offers three main activities: concerts, cultural activities and sports events. It celebrates the heritage of local Francophones and it is one of the biggest Francophone festivals outside Québec. Tel. (506) 739-6608.

■ Quebec

The Quebec Winter Carnival, Quebec City, February 1-17: is a unique and exciting event that has enlivened the world's snow capital for 48 years. It draws nearly 1 million visitors every year. For 17 consecutive days, the Carnival offers sporting, artistic, and cultural activities that provide grown-ups and children alike an opportunity to rediscover the wonders of winter. The main Carnival attractions are located in the heart of Old Quebec. These include dogsled races, canoe races, parades, ice fishing, flapjack breakfasts and toboggan runs. Tel. 1-877-BONJOUR.

Montreal Wine and Spirits Show, Montreal, March 14-17: Grape growers from around the world gather for this international-calibre show which includes wine-tasting and conferences that put quality wines and spirits in the limelight. To prolong the experience of discovery, take some of these unique products home with you. This biennial event is for adults only and is held in years ending in an even number. Tel. 1-877-BONJOUR.

Quebec Summer Festival, Quebec City, July: This is the biggest French-language stage and street performance event in North America. Over 1,000 artists from up to 20 countries perform in as many as 500 shows. Tel. 1-877-BONJOUR.

■ Ontario

Winterlude, Ottawa, weekends February 1-17: The world's largest skating rink (the Rideau Canal) is the centrepiece of this annual winter carnival. But the bed races, polar bear golf, buskers on ice, hot air balloon fiesta, ice sculptures and figure skating that contribute to the festivities take place throughout the National Capital Region. Tel. 1-800-363-4465.

Caravan, Toronto, June: Caravan brings together a broad range of multicultural groups for a nine-day extravaganza of food, entertainment and fun. A full range of International Pavilions, as well as major Special Theme downtown Pavilions highlight the festival. From the colourful Alentejo Portuguese Pavilion to the exotic Waikiki Hawaiian Pavilion and the tiny, charming Novgorod Russian Pavilion, the festival features a world-wide array of music, dance and arts. For many visitors, it's the food that makes Caravan a year-after-year favourite, and many families visit several Pavilions a night, for appetizers at one, main courses at another and desserts at a third Caravan Passports provide unlimited admission to almost 750 shows in nine days. Tel. (416) 977-0466.

Great Rendezvous Festival, Thunder Bay, second week of July: This 10-day festival commemorates the historic arrival of the voyageur brigades and features rustic camps, authentic canoes, unique crafts, historic games, music and spirited fun. Tel. (807) 625-2149.

Caribana™, Toronto, August: Celebrating its 35th anniversary in 2002, Caribana™ is the largest Caribbean festival in North America. Presented by the Caribbean Cultural Committee, the two-week festival attracts over a million participants annually. Tel. (416) 465-4884.

■ Manitoba

Groundswell Presents Street Scenes, Winnipeg, April 19. Winnipeg welcomes spring by taking to the streets of the Exchange District with this festival of street entertainment that includes music and theatre on the sidewalk, buskers on the corners, and brass trios in doorways.

Red River Exhibition, Winnipeg, June: Family entertainment starts with a parade and continues with a giant midway, nightly entertainment and attractions, innovative displays and creative exhibits. Tel. (204) 888-6990.

Winnipeg International Children's Festival, Winnipeg, June: The Winnipeg International Children's Festival provides world-standard performing arts and participatory activities which are educational, entertaining and accessible to young people from all social, economic and ethnic backgrounds. Activities include Authors' Reading Tent, Circus and Magic Partnership Tent, hands-on activities, puppet making and more. Tel. (204) 958-4741.

Brandon Summer Fair, Brandon, June: A horse show, agricultural events, a midway and tribal village are among the events that draw 100,000 people to this event each year. Tel. (204) 726-3590.

Winnipeg Folklorama, Winnipeg, August: The provincial capital celebrates cultural diversity at this two-week annual festival. Pavilions throughout the city feature ethnic cuisine, entertainment and crafts. Tel. (204) 982-6210.

Winnipeg Oktoberfest, Winnipeg, September: This is one of the largest indoor Canadian festivals featuring the finest in Bavarian delicacies, domestic and imported beverages as well as traditional German-style entertainment daily. Tel. (204) 956-1720.

■ Saskatchewan

The Prince Albert Winter Festival, Prince Albert, February 9-24: The 24th annual Prince Albert Winter Festival includes children's carnival, talent shows, arts & crafts, international food and entertainment, guest artists, sled dog races and snow sculptures. Tel. (306) 764-7595.

Vesna Festival, Saskatoon, May: A celebration of Ukrainian culture including artisans, fine arts cultural displays and, of course, lots of dancing. (306) 934-1803.

Shorebirds and Friends, Wadena, June: Each year some 250,000 shorebirds return to Saskatchewan's Quill Lakes. This is an annual celebration of the event which includes bird-watching tours and guided tours of wildlife habitats. Tel. 1-888-338-2145.

Taste of Saskatchewan, Saskatoon, July: More than 24 Saskatoon restaurants serve three of their favourite house dishes in an outdoor setting in Friendship Park. Available for sampling are Chinese, Greek, Italian, Indian, Native and Cajun foods. Live entertainment includes some of Saskatchewan's finest performers. Tel. (306) 975-3175.

■ Alberta

Banff Festival of the Arts, Banff, June-August: The Banff Centre hosts this annual gathering of approximately 1,000 performing artists working and performing with its stellar international faculty in a picturesque Rocky Mountain setting. Dance, drama, opera, music, jazz, Aboriginal arts, journalism, media arts and visual arts events are included. Tel. 1-800-565-9989.

Stampede 2002, Calgary, July 5-14: The Calgary Stampede is Canada's premiere celebration of western heritage and culture and one of the top such events in all of North America. Organizers promise visitors more to see and do over 10 days than they will ever be able to manage-from rides to pancakes, horses to light shows, rodeos to stage shows, chuckwagons to displays of Alberta Agriculture, top name acts on the Coke Stage. Western duds are a must! Tel. 1-800-661-1767, (403) 269-9822.

Klondike Days, Edmonton, July 18–27: More than 750,000 fair visitors attend this exposition which starts with a colourful parade and continues with 10 days of midway rides and attractions, excellent live entertainment, chuckwagon racing, the Feature Country Showcase, great shopping and, of course, the little mini-donuts that have become the fair's trademark. Tel.1-888-800-PARK (7275), (780) 471-7210.

Edmonton International Street Performers Festival, Edmonton, July: The arts take to the streets for this nine-day festival. Clowns, jugglers, musicians, mimes, street artists and many other Canadian and international street acts perform their work in Edmonton's Churchill Square, in the heart of the city's arts district. Performances take place 10 a.m. to 10 p.m. daily. The presence of a festival tent in Churchill Square ensures that performances proceed daily, rain or shine. Tel. (780) 425-5162.

Buffalo Days Pow Wow at Head-Smashed-In Buffalo Jump, Head-Smashed-In Buffalo Jump, July: Native dancers from across North America compete at this annual event, held at a World Heritage site used by aboriginal peoples for almost 6,000 years. The weekend extravaganza features three days of Native dance competitions, a traditional tipi village and a natural outdoor setting. Tel. (403) 553-2731.

■ British Columbia

Kamloops Cowboy Festival, Kamloops, March 3-10: The BC Cowboy Heritage Society presents this festival which includes a western trade show, western art, western music and cowboy poetry. It supports the preservation of cowboy heritage in BC and institutions such as the BC Cowboy Hall of Fame which holds its induction ceremony at the Cowboy Festival. Tel. 1-888-763-2224.

Victoria Harbour Festival, Victoria, May: This ten-day celebration bridges two holiday long weekends, Canada's Victoria Day and U.S. Memorial Day. Featured under the festival umbrella are events, ranging from a literary festival to a rodeo, with many family-oriented entertainment, cultural and sporting events in between. The Victoria Day Parade and internationally renowned Swiftsure International Yacht Race are part of the festivities. Tel. (250) 592-9098.

Nanaimo International World Championship Bathtub Race, Nanaimo, July: The off-the-wall race of unusual home-made watercraft is the centrepiece for a weekend featuring a wide range of activities around Departure Bay. Tel. (250) 753-7223.

Okanagan Wine Festival, Okanagan Valley, Sept.-Oct.: 2002 marks the 22nd annual edition of this celebration of the grape harvest in one of the country's most prestigious winemaking regions. Events take place at wineries, restaurants and attractions all along the Okanagan valley. Tel. (250) 861-6654.

■ Yukon

Yukon Sourdough Rendezvous Festival, Whitehorse, February 22-25: This winter festival has sports, arts, as well as traditional games. The entertainment ranges from dog races, to Can Can Dancers, from Snow Shoe Shufflers to the International Winter Air Show. Tel. (867) 667-2148.

Dawson City's Yukon Gold Panning Championships, Dawson City, July 1: As part of its Canada Day celebrations, Dawson City celebrates the art that put Yukon on the map. The annual competition is open to amateurs and professionals from Yukon and around the world and includes time trials as well as the finals. Tel. (867) 993-5575.

Whitehorse to Dawson City Yukon River Bathtub Race, Yukon River, August: This bathtub race offers one of the longest and toughest courses in the world. Participants are expected to cover 780 kilometres in two days! Tel. (867) 777-3536.

■ Northwest Territories

Caribou Carnival, Yellowknife, March 26-28: The Caribou Carnival is Yellowknifers' favourite spring event. The Queen and Princess contests are featured, as well as snowmobile races. Also included in the carnival is the NMI Mobility Canadian Championship Dog Derby. The biggest purse in the Northwest Territories is offered for this 3-day, 240 km (142 miles) race on Great Slave Lake. The 42 annual race will feature mushers from across North America and around the world. Tel: (867) 873-4262.

Raven Mad Daze, Yellowknife, June: The longest day of the year is cause for celebration in Yellowknife. The town closes its streets to traffic as thousands of people party all night and stay up with the sun. The action includes live music, dancing, late-night sidewalk sales, food, children's games and more. Tel. (867) 873-3408.

NWT Mining Week, Yellowknife, June: Eight-day festival celebrating mining and exploration in the NWT. Mine-rescue competitions, mine tours, geology hikes, interactive street displays, demonstrations and seismic station tours. Contact: NWT Chamber of Mines. Tel: (867) 873-5281.

Great Northern Arts Festival, Inuvik, July: This is the territory's premier cultural festival. Each summer in mid July, the people of Inuvik welcome over 120 visual and performing artists from across the Northwest Territories, Nunavut and Yukon, and visitors from around the world. The festival features an extensive exhibit and sale of fine arts and crafts, as well as an exciting program filled with demonstrations, workshops, cultural presentations and entertainment. Tel. (867) 777-3536.

■ Nunavut

Nunavut Day, throughout Nunavut, July 9: Residents of Nunavut celebrate both the coming of summer and the founding of Nunavut on this day. Events take place across the new territory. Among the activities in Baker Lake are foot and bicycle races, a tea-boiling contest and traditional Inuit games. Tel. 1-800-491-7910.

CANADIAN HALL OF FAME

The following list is not meant to be exhaustive, but rather a listing of prominent Canadians, and those whose reputations and those whose reputation is inextricably linked to Canada, from all fields.

A

ABBOTT, John Joseph Caldwell (Sir), politics. St Andrews, Lower Canada, 1821–93. Canada's third prime minister.

ABBOTT, Maude Elizabeth Seymour, medicine. St Andrews, Que., 1869–1940. Specialist in congenital heart disease. *History of Medicine in the Province of Quebec.*

ABBOTT, Roger, performing arts. Eng., 1946. Actor and co-producer of CBC's *Royal Canadian Air Farce*; noted for impersonation of Jean Chrétien.

ABEL, Sidney Gerald (Sid), sports. Melville, Sask., 1918–2000. Hockey player; 1949–52 considered best offensive unit when centred with Gordie Howe and Ted Lindsay (Detroit Red Wings); four-time all-star.

ABERDEEN, Ishbel Maria Marjoribanks Gordon (Lady), reformer. Eng., 1857–1939. Helped create National Council of Women, Victorian Order of Nurses.

ABERHART, William "Bible Bill", politics. Hibbard Twp, Ont., 1878–1943. Founded Social Credit party; Alberta premier 1935–43.

ACORN, Milton, literary arts. Charlottetown, PEI, 1923–86. Radical poet. "The Island Means Minago."

ADAMS, Bryan, performing arts. Kingston, Ont., 1959. Singer/songwriter; rock star. *Reckless.*

ADAMS, Ian, literary arts. Tanzania, 1937. Novelist, nonfiction writer. *S, Portrait of a Spy; The Trudeau Papers.*

ADAMS, Thomas, city planner. Scot., 1871–1940. Father of the Canadian Planning Movement.

AFFLECK, Raymond Tait, visual arts. Penticton, BC, 1922–89. Architect; designed Place Ville Marie, Place Bonaventure.

AGLUKARK, Susan, performing arts. Arviat, NWT, 1966. Singer/songwriter; first Inuit recording artist.

AIRD, John Black, politics. Toronto, Ont., 1923–95. Liberal senator; Ontario lieutenant-governor 1980–85.

AISLIN (b. Christopher Terry Mosher), visual arts. Ottawa, Ont., 1942. *Montreal Gazette* cartoonist; sports caricaturist.

AITKEN, William Maxwell (Lord Beaverbrook), literary arts. Maple, Ont., 1879–1964. Publisher; newspaper magnate; British Conservative cabinet minister.

AKEEAKTASHUK, visual arts. Hudson Bay, Ont., 1898–1954. Sculptor; first important Inuit carver.

ALBANI, Emma (b. Louise Cecile Emma Lajeunesse), performing arts. Chambly, Que., 1847–1930. Opera singer; grand diva excelled in Wagnerian opera, popular in Britain and US.

ALCOCK, John Alfred, Expert in laser and plasma physics; winner of Herzberg medal in 1975. Scotland, 1938.

ALEXANDER, Lincoln MacCauley, politics. Toronto, Ont., 1922. First Black in Parliament; Ont. lieutenant-governor 1985–91.

ALLAN, Hugh (Sir), business. Scot., 1810–82. Railway promoter; suspected of electoral bribery for soliciting favours in Pacific Scandal (1873).

ALLAN, Ted (b. Allan Herman), performing arts. Montreal, Que., 1916–95. Author; screenwriter. *Lies My Father Told Me; Bethune: The Making of a Hero.*

ALLEMAGNE, John Cameron, literary arts. Toronto, Ont., 1951. Reporter, columnist, food writer. *The Importance of Lunch.*

ALLEN, Charlotte Vale, literary arts. Toronto, Ont., 1941. Writer, lecturer on child abuse. *Daddy's Girl.*

ALLEN, John F. (Jack), science. Winnipeg, Man., 1908. Co-discoverer of superfluidity in liquid helium.

ALLEN, Montagu (Sir), sports. Montreal, Que., 1860–1951. Financier and sportsman who donated Allen Cup in 1908 for senior amateur competition in Canada.

ALLEN, Ralph, literary arts. Winnipeg, Man., 1913–66. Influential *Maclean's* editor (1946–60).

ALMOND, Paul, performing arts. Montreal, Que., 1931. Film director. *Act of the Heart.*

ALTMAN, Sidney, science. Montreal, Que., 1939. Microbiologist; 1989 Nobel Prize in chemistry for role in research into chemical cell reactions.

AMIEL, Barbara, media. Eng., 1940s. Journalist; conservative political and social columnist.

AMOS, Beth (b. Bessie Rymer), performing arts. St Catharines, Ont., 1915–95. Actor. *Jake and the Kid; Miracle at Indian Creek; Canadian Bacon.*

ANDERSON, Doris Hilda, literary arts. Toronto, Ont., 1921. Writer; feminist; editor, *Chatelaine* 1958–77.

ANDERSON, Frank Ross, sports. Edmonton, Alta, 1938–1980. International chess master; won gold medals in Amsterdam (1954) and in Munich (1958).

ANDERSON, Pamela Denise, performing arts. Ladysmith, BC, 1967. Voluptuous actress who has starred in *Baywatch, Barb Wire.*

ANDERSON, Reid Bryce, performing arts. New Westminster, BC, 1949. Dancer; ballet director of National Ballet of British Columbia; later National Ballet of Canada.

ANDRE, Brother (b. Alfred Bissette), religion. St Gregoire d'Iberville, Lower Canada, 1845–1937. Mystic; built Montreal's St Joseph's Oratory.

ANGILIK, Paul Apak, performing arts. Hall Beach, NWT, 1954–98. Documentary filmmaker of Inuit life; adventurer; contributor to Inuit Broadcasting Corporation.

ANKA, Paul Albert, performing arts. Ottawa, Ont., 1941. Singer/songwriter; composed more than 400 songs. "My Way."

APPLEBAUM, Louis, performing arts. Toronto, Ont., 1918–2000. Composer; writer of opera, concerts, film scores.

APPLEYARD, Peter, performing arts. Eng., 1928. Jazz musician; vibraphonist; TV personality. "Swing Fever."

APPS, Charles Joseph Sylvanus (Syl), sports. Paris, Ont., 1915–98. Hockey player; Toronto Maple Leafs (1936–48); 3-time all-star; pole vault contender in 1936 Olympics; 1937 Canadian Athlete of the Year.

AQUIN, Hubert, literary arts. Montreal, Que., 1929–77. Novelist; modernist writer. *Neige Noire.*

ARBOUR, Louise, law. Montreal, Que., 1947. Judge for Supreme Court of Ontario; appointed to Supreme Court of Canada in 1999. From 1996–99 was chief prosecutor for UN's international war crimes tribunal.

ARCAND, Denys, performing arts. Deschambault, Que., 1941. Film director. *Decline of the American Empire.*

ARCHAMBAULT, Louis, visual arts. Montreal, Que., 1915. Sculptor; his work is in many museum collections.

ARCHER, Violet, performing arts. Montreal, Que., 1913–2000. Internationally recognized classical music composer, inspired by Canadian folk music. *Prairie Profiles.*

ARDEN, Elizabeth (b. Florence Nightingale Graham), business. Woodbridge, Ont., 1884–1966. Founder of the Elizabeth Arden cosmetics empire, Arden was a pioneer in mass advertising and built the business from a small shop in New York City in 1914 to today's vast chain of spas and beauty salons.

ARDEN, Jann (b. Jann Arden Richards), performing arts. Calgary, Alta, 1962. Juno-award winning pop singer, songwriter. *Happy?; Time for Mercy.*

ARTHUR, Eric Ross, visual arts. New Zealand, 1898–1982. Architectural conservancy advocate; writer. *Toronto: No Mean City; The Barn: A Vanishing Landmark in North America.*

ASPER, Israel Harold, business. Minnedosa, Man., 1932. Financier; founder Global-TV; columnist; author.

ATHANS, George S. Jr., sports. Kelowna, BC, 1952. Three-time world water ski champion.

ATKINSON, Joseph, media. Newcastle, Ont., 1865–1948. Journalist; built *Toronto Star* into nation's largest newspaper.

ATWOOD, Margaret Eleanor, literary arts. Ottawa, Ont., 1939. Prolific novelist with international following. *The Handmaid's Tale, Alias Grace.*

AUBERT de GASPE, Philippe-Ignace François, literary arts. Quebec City, Que., 1814–41. Novelist; wrote first French-Cdn novel. *L'influence d'un livre* (1837).

AUF DER MAUR, Nick, journalism. Montreal, Que., 1942–98. Long-time columnist for *Montreal Gazette*; co-wrote biography of Brian Mulroney: *The Boy from Baie Comeau.*

AUGUSTYN, Frank Joseph, performing arts. Hamilton, Ont., 1953. Former principal dancer, National Ballet of Canada; director, Ottawa Ballet.

AVERY, Oswald, science. Halifax, NS, 1877–1955. First person to show agent responsible for transferring genetic information was DNA, not a protein as previously thought.

AXWORTHY, Norman Lloyd, politics. North Battleford, Sask., 1939. Liberal minister of external affairs; defense.

AYKROYD, Daniel Edward (Dan), performing arts. Ottawa, Ont., 1952. Actor/comedian. *Saturday Night Live, Ghostbusters.*

BACHMAN, Randy, performing arts. Winnipeg, Man., 1946. Rock musician; guitarist for Guess Who, Bachman-Turner Overdrive. *American Woman.*

BAETZ, Reuben, politics. Chelsey, Ont., 1923–96. Executive director of Canadian Council on Social Development; proponent of national unemployment insurance program.

BAFFIN, William, exploration and discovery. Eng., 1584–1622. Made two Arctic voyages in search of the Northwest Passage; first to conclude Hudson Bay did not lead westward; explored Baffin Island.

BAGSHAW, Elizabeth Catherine, medicine. Victoria County, Ont., 1881–1982. Pioneering woman doctor who, from 1932–66, was medical director of Canada's first (illegal) birth control clinic in Hamilton, Ont., responding to women's financial needs during Depression years.

BAILEY, Brian, business. Galahad, Alta, 1958. Women's sportswear designer; launched label with own name in 1988; later under Iscariot Design; active fashion business promoter.

BAILEY, Donovan, sports. Jamaica, 1967. Track star who won 100 m race at world record time, 9.84, at 1996 Olympics in Atlanta.

BAIRD, Elizabeth Carol, literary arts. Stratford, Ont., 1939. Food writer with *Canadian Living Magazine* and the *Toronto Star;* author of several cookbooks. *Classic Canadian Cooking; Elizabeth Baird's Favourites.*

BAKER, Carroll, performing arts. Bridgewater, NS, 1949. Singer; country music star.

BALDWIN, Robert, politics. York, Ont., 1804–58. Proponent of responsible government; co-premier (with LaFontaine) of Upper Canada.

BALLARD, Harold Edwin, sports. Toronto, Ont., 1903–90. Sports capitalist; irascible owner of Toronto Maple Leafs, Hamilton Tiger Cats.

BANTING, Frederick Grant, (Sir) medicine. Alliston, Ont., 1891–1941. Medical researcher; co-discoverer of insulin; Nobel Prize for medicine, 1923.

BARBEAU, Charles Marius, ethnologist. St-Marie-de-Beauce, Que., 1883–1969. Eminent folklorist.

BARFOOT, Joan Louise, literary arts. Owen Sound, Ont., 1947. Novelist. *Dancing in the Dark; Family News; Charlotte and Claudia Keeping in Touch.*

BARKER, William George (Billy), military. Dauphin, Man., 1894–1930. Fighter pilot awarded Victoria Cross for 60 solo combat missions against German aircraft during WWI.

BARLOW, Maude Victoria, politics. Toronto, Ont., 1947. Political/human rights activist, author. Chair, Council of Canadians.

BARR, Murray Llewellyn, medicine. Belmont, Ont., 1908. Anatomist; developed chromosome analysis to diagnose genetic disorders.

BARRY, James (b. Miranda Stewart), medicine. Eng., 1795–1865. In 1857 appointed inspector general of military hospitals in Province of Canada; as a woman disguised as a man, was the first woman doctor to work in Canada.

BASINSKI, Zbigniew Stanislaw, science. Poland, 1928. Outstanding metal physics researcher.

BASSETT, John White Hughes, media. Ottawa, Ont., 1915–98. Media executive.

BASSETT-SEGUSO, Carling Kathrin, sports. Toronto, Ont., 1967. Top-ranked Canadian tennis player.

BATA, Sonja Ingrid, public service. Switzerland, 1926. Founder of the Bata Shoe Museum in Toronto; wife of shoe retailing entrepreneur Thomas Bata.

BATA, Thomas John, business. Czech., 1914. Industrialist; chairman, Bata Shoes; in over 70 countries.

BATEMAN, Robert McLellan, visual arts. Toronto, Ont., 1930. Painter; major international wildlife artist.

BAUER, David William (Father), sports. Kitchener, Ont., 1925–88. Hockey coach; father of Cdn Olympic hockey.

BAUMANN, Alexander (Sasha), sports. Czech., 1964. Swimmer; gold medals in 200 m, 400 m individual medley, 1984 Olympics; 1984 top male athlete.

BEARDY, Quentin Pickering Jackson, visual arts. Island Lake, Man., 1944–84. Graphic stylist using Cree legends.

BEATTY, Henry Perrin, politics. Toronto, Ont., 1950. President of CBC, 1995–98; former PC cabinet minister.

BECK, Adam (Sir), business. Baden, Canada W, 1857–1925. Hydro commissioner; built Ontario Hydro.

BECKER, Abigail, military. Frontenac Cty, UC, 1831–1905. Heroine; saved men shipwrecked on Lake Erie.

BECKWITH, John, literary arts/performing arts. Victoria, BC, 1927. Composer; writer; critic. *The Shivaree.*

BEDARD, Myriam, sports. Loretteville, Que., 1969. Biathlete; two gold medals, biathlon, '94 Olympics.

BEDDOES, Dick, media. Daysland, Alta, 1926–91. Colourful sportswriter, broadcaster, hockey commentator with the Vancouver *Sun, Globe & Mail,* Edmonton *Bulletin;* broadcaster on CFRB radio in Toronto. *Pal Hal,* a profile of Harold Ballard.

BEECROFT, Norma Marian, performing arts. Oshawa, Ont., 1934. Composer; avant-garde musician. "From Dreams of Brass."

BEERS, William George, medicine/sports. Montreal, Que., 1843–1900. Popularized lacrosse; Dean, Canada's first dental college.

BEGIN, Monique, politics. Italy, 1936. First Quebec woman in Commons; health minister.

BELANGER, Michel, business. Lévis, Que., 1929–97. President of Quebec's National Bank; 1991–92 was co-chairman of Belanger-Campeau Commission which examined constitutional concerns in Quebec.

BELIVEAU, Jean Arthur, sports. Trois-Rivières, Que., 1931. Hockey player; stylish Montreal Canadiens centre, 1953–71; 507 goals.

BELL, Alexander Graham, invention. Scot., 1847–1922. Invented telephone; worked on iron lung, phonograph, seawater desalination.

BELL, George Maxwell (Max), business. Regina, Sask., 1912–72. Industrialist; principal, FP Publications and sportsman.

BELL, Marilyn, sports. Toronto, Ont., 1937. First person to swim Lake Ontario (1954).

BELL, Robert Edward, science. Ladner, BC, 1918–92. Nuclear physicist; discovered proton radioactivity.

BELLOW, Saul, literary arts. Lachine, Que., 1915. Nobel Prize for Literature. *Herzog.*

BELZBERG, Samuel, business. Calgary, Alta, 1928. Financier; developed real estate financing in W Canada; founder, First City Trust.

BENMERGUI, Ralph, CBC radio and television personality; host of television programs *Friday Night!,* CBC's *Midday;* frequent host for CBC Radio's *This Morning.* Morocco, 1955.

BENNETT, Richard Bedford, first Viscount, politics. Hopewell Hill, NB, 1870–1947. Prime minister of Canada 1930–35.

BENNETT, William Andrew Cecil (W.A.C.), politics. Hastings, NB, 1900–79. Social Credit premier of BC, 1952–72.

BENNETT, William Richards, politics. Kelowna, BC, 1932. Social Credit premier of BC, 1975–86.

BENOIT, Jehane, media. Montreal, Que., 1904–87. Food expert; cookbook writer; featured on TV; authority on Cdn/Québécois cooking.

BENY, Roloff (b. Wilfred Roy), visual arts. Medicine Hat, Alta, 1924–84. Photographer; lavish travel books. *India.*

BERBICK, Trevor, sports. Jamaica, 1952. Boxer; Canadian heavyweight champion (1978–85); WBC world heavyweight champion (1986).

BERCZY, William (b. Johann Albrecht Ulrich Moll), visual arts. Germany, 1744–1813. Painter, architect; most famous for his portraits of the native leader Joseph Brant. Also designed church decorations for Christ Church Montreal, in 1903.

BERESFORD-HOWE, Constance Elizabeth, literary arts. Montreal, Que., 1922. Novelist. *Night Studies.*

BERGER, Thomas Rodney, politics. Victoria, BC, 1933. Jurist; proponent of aboriginal rights; commissioner, Mackenzie Valley Pipeline Inquiry.

BERLIN, Boris, Long associated with Toronto's Royal Conservatory of Music, taught many of Canada's leading pianists; author and co-author of major pedagogical works. *Basics of Ear Training.* Russia, 1907–2001.

BERNARDI, Mario, performing arts. Kirkland Lake, Ont., 1930. Conductor, Calgary Philharmonic.

BERNIER, Sylvie, sports. Quebec City, Que., 1964. Diver; gold medal, 3 m springboard,1984 Olympics.

BERTON, Pierre, literary arts. Whitehorse, YT, 1920. Popular historian; author and media personality. *The Last Spike.*

BESRE, Jean, performing arts. Sherbrooke, Que., 1936–2001. Beloved Quebec television and stage actor; for many years starred in popular TV series *Jamais deux sans toi* and *La P'tite Semaine;* also performed in children's programs and wrote musical comedy *Madeleine de Verchères.*

BESSETTE, Gerard, literary arts. Ste-Anne-de-Sabrevois, Que., 1920. Novelist, poet, literary critic. *Mes romans et moi.*

BEST, Charles Herbert, medicine. USA, 1899–1978. Physiologist; co-discoverer of insulin.

BETHUNE, Henry Norman, medicine. Gravenhurst, Ont., 1890–1939. Surgeon; hero in China, where he died helping revolutionary army.

BEY, Salome, performing arts. USA, 1938?. Singer, songwriter, actress. Noted for jazz, blues, spirituals. Wrote and starred in *Indigo,* a history of blues. *Shimmytime.*

BIG BEAR, politics. Ft. Carlton, Sask., 1825–88. Cree leader; opposed treaties on grounds they would destroy Cree way of life.

BIGELOW, Dr. Wilfred Gordon, medicine. Brandon, Man., 1913. Surgeon; developed first cardiac pacemaker.

BILLES, Alfred Jackson, business. Toronto, Ont., 1902–95. Co-founder in 1922 of Canada-wide chain Canadian Tire Corporation.

BILLES, John William, business. Toronto, Ont., 1896–1956. Original founder of Canadian Tire chain of hardware stores.

BINNS, Patrick George, politics. Weyburn, Sask., 1948. PC premier of PEI, 1996.

BIRDSELL, Sandra, literary arts. Hamiota, Man., 1942. Novelist who weaves domestic and feminist themes into her work. *The Missing Child; The Chrome Suite.*

BIRKS, Henry, business. Montreal, Que., 1840–1928. Silversmith who founded national jewelry chain Henry Birks and Sons, opening his first store in 1879 in Montreal.

BIRNEY, Alfred Earle, literary arts. Calgary, Alta, 1904–1995. Narrative poet and professor. *David and Other Poems.*

BISHOP, William Avery (Billy), military. Owen Sound, Ont., 1894–1956. WWI flying ace; downed 72 enemy planes.

BISSELL, Keith, performing arts. Meaford, Ont., 1912–92. Composer of choral, vocal, organ, orchestral and chamber music; folksong arrangements for piano and voice; commissioned by Lois Marshall, Charles Peaker and others.

BISSOONDATH, Neil Devindra, literary arts. Trinidad, 1955. Novelist, short story writer. *A Casual Brutality.*

BLACK, Arthur, media. Toronto, Ont., 1943. Syndicated journalist and broadcaster; host of CBC Radio's *Basic Black,* a program incorporating humour, interviews and music. *Wit and Wisdom of Arthur Black.*

BLACK, Conrad Moffat, business. Montreal, Que., 1944. Press baron; owner of Hollinger Inc. newspaper empire.

BLACK, Davidson, medicine. Toronto, Ont., 1884–1934. China-based anatomist, scholar and anthropologist; identified Peking Man, an ancient human species of *Homo erectus.*

BLAIS, Marie-Claire, literary arts. Quebec City, Que., 1939. Influential novelist. *Une Saison dans la vie d'Emmanuel.*

BLAISE, Clark Lee, literary arts. USA, 1940. Writer; explorer of the displaced person. *Resident Alien.*

BLAKE, Hector "Toe", sports. Victoria Mines, Ont., 1912–95. Hockey player; coached Montreal Canadiens to eight Stanley Cups, 1955–68.

BLAKENEY, Allan Emrys, politics. Bridgewater, NS, 1925. NDP premier of Saskatchewan 1971–82.

BLISS, John William Michael, politics. Leamington, Ont., 1941. Author, history commentator. *Right Honorable Men: The Descent of Canadian Politics from Macdonald to Mulroney.*

BLOHM, Hans Ludwig, visual arts. Germany, 1927. Photographer; author of many photography books. *The Beauty of the Maritimes.*

BLONDIN-ANDREWS, Ethel, politics. Fort Norman, NWT, 1951. In 1988, first native woman elected to Parliament, for Western Arctic (Lib).

BLUMENFELD, Hans, city planner. Germany, 1892–1988. Urban planner; author. *The Modern Metropolis.*

BLYTHE, Dominic, performing arts. Eng., 1947. Actor with Stratford Festival, Ont.

BOCHNER, Lloyd, performing arts. Toronto, Ont., 1924. Character actor who has appeared in TV series *Dynasty* and *Santa Barbara* and in movies. *Naked Gun 2½.*

BODOGH, Marilyn, sports. Toronto, Ont., 1955. Curling. Two-time world champion (skip) in women's curling; member of Team Canada.

BOGGS, Jean Sutherland, visual arts. Peru, 1922. Art curator; National Gallery curator, 1966–76.

BOLDT, Arnie, sports. Osler, Sask., 1957. One-legged high jumper holds disabled world record (2.08 m).

BOLT, Carol, literary arts. Winnipeg, Man., 1941. Playwright; socially conscious writer. *One Night Stand.*

BOMBARDIER, Joseph Armand, invention. Valcourt, Que., 1908–64. Inventor; developer of snowmobiles.

BONDAR, Roberta Lynn, science. Sault Ste Marie, Ont., 1945. Astronaut; first Canadian woman in space.

BONISTEEL, Roy, media. Ameliasburg, Ont., 1930. Host of CBC television's *Man Alive* series 1967–89; early career as a radio producer for church organizations. *In Search of Man Alive.*

BORDEN, Robert Laird (Sir), politics. Grand Pré, NS, 1854–1937. Canada's prime minister throughout WWI (1911–20).

BORDUAS, Paul-Emile, visual arts. St-Hilaire, Que., 1905–60. Painter; founded Automatistes. *L'etoile noire.*

BORSOS, Phillip, performing arts. Tasmania, 1954–95. Filmmaker. *The Grey Fox* (winner of Best Picture and Best Director, 1982 Genie Awards); *Bethune.*

BOSSY, Michael, sports. Montreal, Que., 1957. Hockey player; NY Islanders winger; nine 50-goal seasons.

BOTSFORD, Sara, performing arts. Dobie, Que., 1952. Stage, film and TV actress. *Bay Boy; E.N.G.*

BOTTERELL, Edmund Henry, science. Vancouver, BC, 1906–97. Neurosurgeon who initiated program into spinal chord injury research; during WWII devoted to rehabilitation of veterans.

BOUCHARD, Lucien, politics. St-Coeur-de-Marie, Que., 1938. Founder and leader of Bloc Québécois; leader of Parti Québécois; premier of Quebec, 1996–2001.

BOUCHER, Gaetan, sports. Charlesbourg, Que., 1958. Speedskater; two gold medals (1000 m,1500 m) and a bronze medal (500 m) 1984 Winter Olympics.

BOUEY, Gerald Keith, business. Axford, Sask., 1920. Banker; governor.

BOURASSA, Henri, politics. Montreal, Que., 1868–1952. Federalist; founded *Le Devoir* newspaper.

BOURASSA, Jocelyne, sports. Shawinigan-Sud, Que., 1947. Golf champion, winner of many awards, including La Canadienne 1973 LPGA event; Golf Personality of the Year, Golf Canada, 1972.

BOURASSA, Robert, politics. Montreal, Que., 1933–96. Quebec premier 1970–76, 1985–93.

BOURGEOYS, Marguerite, religion. France, 1620–1700. Religious educator; canonized, 1982.

BOURGET, Ignace, religion. Lauzon, Que., 1799–1885. Catholic bishop of Montreal; avid ultra-Montanist opposed secular Quebec.

BOURNE, Shae-Lynn, sports. Chatham, Ont., 1976. Ice dancing; with Victor Kraatz won Canadian title, 1993–96; third in World Championships, 1996.

BOURQUE, James, politics. Wandering River, Alta, 1935–96. Aboriginal activist appointed to Privy Council, 1992. Co-director of policy for Royal Commission on Aboriginal Peoples, 1994.

BOURQUE, Raymond, sports. Montreal, Que., 1960. Hockey player; Boston Bruins defenceman; four-time Norris Trophy winner.

BOWELL, Mackenzie (Sir), politics. Eng., 1823–1917. Canada's fifth prime minister (1894–96).

BOWER, John William (Johnny), sports. Prince Albert, Sask., 1924. Hockey player. Long-time goalkeeper for New York Rangers, Toronto Maple Leafs; led Leafs to four Stanley Cup wins.

BOWERING, George Harry, literary arts. Penticton, BC, 1935. Prolific poet and prose writer. "Burning Water."

BOWMAN, Scotty, sports. Montreal, Que., 1933. Hockey coach; won six Stanley Cups; five with Montreal.

BOYD, Liona, performing arts. Eng., 1950. Acclaimed classical guitarist. *The Guitar—Liona Boyd.*

BOYLE, Joseph Whiteside, exploration and discovery. Toronto, Ont., 1867–1923. Adventurer "Klondike Joe"; mining entrepreneur; national hero in Romania.

BOYLE, Willard S., invention. Amherst, NS, 1924. Physicist who co-invented the charge-coupled device for camcorders and telescopes.

BRACKEN, John, politics. Ellisville, Ont., 1883–1969. Cons. Manitoba premier 1922–42.

BRAITHWAITE, Max, literary arts. Nokomis, Sask., 1911–95. Prairie novelist noted for autobiographical novel *Why Shoot the Teacher?*

BRAND, Oscar, performing arts. Winnipeg, Man., 1920. Folksinger; recorded 80 albums; author folk song collections. *Squid Jiggin' Ground.*

BRANT, Joseph (b. Thayendanegea), politics/religion. USA, 1742–1807. Mohawk leader; British loyalist during American Revolution; translated Bible into Mohawk.

BRANT, Mary "Molly", c1736–96. Politics.

BRASSARD, Jean-Luc, sports. Valleyfield, Que., 1972. Skier; gold medal moguls 1994 Olympics.

BRASSEUR, Isabelle, sports. Kingsbury, Que., 1970. Skater; with Lloyd Eisler won 1993 pairs world title, two Olympic bronze medals (1992).

BRAULT, Jacques, literary arts. Montreal, Que., 1933. Poet; playwright; novelist. *Agonie.*

BRAUN, Eric, performing arts. Internationally renowned baritone opera singer; Braun's repertoire spanned classical and modern works, with a special emphasis on Schubert, Wagner and Schumann. Windsor, Ont., 1934–2001.

BREAU, Lenny, performing arts. USA, 1941–84. Guitarist; singer; composer of jazz, country, folk and pop; aired on CBC radio in 1940s and 1950s.

BREBEUF, Jean de, religion. France, 1593–1649. Jesuit martyr; missionary at Sainte Marie among the Hurons.

BRILL, Debbie, sports. Mission, BC, 1953. High jumper; originated "Brill bend" jumping style.

BRITTAIN, Donald, visual arts. Ottawa, Ont., 1928–89. Documentary filmmaker. *On Guard for Thee.*

BROADBENT, John Edward (Ed), politics. Oshawa, Ont., 1936. National leader, NDP 1975–89.

BROADFOOT, Dave, performing arts. Toronto, Ont., 1925. Comedian; Sergeant Renfrew character on *Royal Canadian Air Farce.*

BROCK, Isaac (Sir), military. Eng., 1769–1812. Soldier; War of 1812 hero; died at Queenston Heights.

BROCKHOUSE, Bertram Neville, science. Lethbridge, Alta, 1918. Pioneer of use of thermal neutrons to study aspects of behaviour of condensed matter systems at atomic level. Won 1994 Nobel Prize for physics.

BRONFMAN, Charles Rosner, business. Montreal, Que., 1931. Industrialist; chairman, Cemp Investments Ltd; former owner, Montreal Expos.

BRONFMAN, Edgar M., business. Montreal, Que., 1929. Industrialist; CEO, Seagram's Ltd; president, World Jewish Congress.

BRONFMAN, Samuel, business. Brandon, Man., 1891–1971. Capitalist; distiller (Seagram Co. Ltd) and philanthropist.

BROOKS, Marilyn, Fashion designer launched innovative Unicorn boutique in Toronto, Ont., in 1963; founder of Marilyn Brooks boutique chain. USA, 1932.

BROSSARD, Nicole, literary arts. Montreal, Que., 1943. Formalist poet. "Mecanique jongleuse suivi de masculin grammaticale."

BROWN, Arthur Royal "Roy", military. Carleton Place, Ont., 1893–1944. On April 21, 1918, shot down Germany's Red Baron, Manfred von Richthofen.

BROWN, George, media/politics. Scot., 1818–80. Journalist; founded *Toronto Globe* (1844); as reformer, played major role in Confederation.

BROWN, John George "Kootenai", exploration and discovery. Ire., 1839–1916. Adventurer; army official; prospector; whisky trader; established Waterton Lakes Natl Park.

BROWN, Rosemary, politics. Jamaica, 1930. Activist; head, Ontario Human Rights Assn; former NDP leadership candidate.

BROWNING, Kurt, sports. Rocky Mountain House, Alta, 1966. World figure skating champion, 1989–91, 1993.

BRUHN, Erik Belton Evers, performing arts. Denmark, 1928–86. Dancer; choreographer; guiding figure for National Ballet.

BRULE, Etienne, exploration and discovery. France, 1592–1633. Explorer; first known European to reach Lake Superior.

BRZOZOWICZ, Czelaw Peter, engineering. Poland, 1911–97. Structural engineer consulted on Toronto's original subway line, Niagara Falls Skylon Tower and CN Tower in Toronto.

BUCHAN, John, first Baron Tweedsmuir, literary arts. Scot., 1875–1940. Thriller novelist, wrote *The 39 Steps*; governor general, 1935–40.

BUCHANAN, John MacLennan, politics. Sydney, NS, 1931. Conservative premier of NS, 1978–90.

BUCK, Tim, politics. Eng., 1891–1973. Radical politician; led Canadian Commmunist Party, 1929–61.

BUCKE, Richard Maurice, medicine. Eng., 1837–1902. Physician; writer; advocate for the mentally ill; spiritual writer. *Cosmic Consciousness.*

BUCZYNSKI, Walter, performing arts. Toronto, Ont., 1933. Pianist and composer of orchestral, chamber, vocal and piano music; soloist internationally in 1960s and 1970s. *Songs of War; Ressurection II.*

BUJOLD, Geneviève, performing arts. Montreal, Que., 1942. Actress; international star. *Dead Ringers.*

BULL, Gerald Vincent, invention. North Bay, Ont., 1928–90. Inventor; weapons designer; murdered mysteriously.

BURKA, Petra, sports. Holland, 1946. Figure skater; women's world champion, 1965.

BURNARD, Bonnie, literary arts. Petrolia, Ont., 1945. Novelist; her *A Good House* won the 1999 Giller Prize. *Women of Influence,* short stories.

BURNS, Tommy (b. Noah Brusso), sports. Hanover, Ont., 1881–1955. Boxer; world heavyweight champion, 1906–08.

BURR, Raymond William Stacy, performing arts. New Westminster, BC, 1917–93. Actor; TV's Perry Mason, 1957–66, 1985–93.

BURROUGHS, Jackie, performing arts. Eng., 1942. Actress; versatile performer; Hetty in *Road to Avonlea.*

BUSH, John Hamilton (Jack), visual arts. Toronto, Ont., 1909–77. Abstract artist. "Bridge Passage."

BUTALA, Sharon Annette, literary arts. Nipawin, Sask., 1940. Novelist, short story writer, playwright. *Coming Attractions; The Fourth Archangel.*

BUTCHART, Robert Pim, business. Owen Sound, Ont., 1856–1943. In 1888 founded Owen Sound Portalnd Cement Co.; later turned quarries in Victoria, BC, into famed Butchart Gardens.

BY, John, military. Eng., 1779–1836. Engineer; built Rideau Canal, Quebec fortifications.

BYNG, Julian Hedworth George, first Viscount, military. Eng., 1862–1935. Soldier; governor general, 1921–26.

CABOT, John (b. Giovanni Caboto), exploration and discovery. Italy, c. 1450–99. First N American landing since the Vikings.

CABOT, Sebastian, performing arts. Eng., 1918–76. Portly, bearded character actor in film and television. *The Captain's Paradise, The Beachcombers, Family Affair.*

CAIN, Larry, sports. Toronto, Ont., 1963. Canoeist; gold (500 m) and silver (1000 m) medals, 1984 Olympics.

CALDER, Frank Arthur, politics. Nass Harbour, BC, 1915. Native politician; Nishga leader; BC MLA.

CALDWELL, Zoe, performing arts. Australia, 1933. Actor, director. *The Prime of Miss Jean Brodie.*

CALLAGHAN, Barry, literary arts. Toronto, Ont., 1937. Founder of *Exile: A Literary Quarterly;* novelist, journalist; son of Morley Callaghan.

CALLAGHAN, Morley Edward, literary arts. Toronto, Ont., 1903–90. Novelist; memoirist. *The Loved and the Lost.*

CALLBECK, Catherine, politics. Central Bedeque, PEI, 1939. First woman to be elected premier. Liberal premier of PEI 1993–96.

CALLUM, Keith Rennie, performing arts. England, 1960. Actor noted for role as Stanley Raymond Kowalski in CBC Mountie comedy/drama *Due South;* also appeared in movies *My Life as a Dog; Hard Core Logo;* and in TV series *The X-Files.*

CALLWOOD, June, public service. Chatham, Ont., 1924. Journalist; civil libertarian, AIDS activist.

CALVERT, Lorne Albert, politics. Moose Jaw, Sask., 1952. NDP premier of Saskatchewan 2001–; formerly minister of social services.

CAMERON, Elspeth MacGregor, literary arts. Toronto, Ont., 1943. Biographer. *Robertson Davies: An Appreciation; Hugh MacLennan: A Writer's Life; Irving Layton: A Portrait.*

CAMERON, James, literary arts. Eng., 1910. Philosopher; essayist; poet. "Images of Authority."

CAMERON, James, performing arts. Kapuskasing, Ont., 1954. Hollywood-based director of action movies including *Terminator* series, *Aliens, True Lies, Titanic.*

CAMERON, Michelle, sports. Calgary, Alta, 1962. Gold medalist in sychronized swimming with Carolyn Waldo, 1988 Olympics.

CAMERON, Silver Donald, literary arts. Toronto, Ont., 1937. Novelist, critic, editor, playwright. *Dragon Lady; Wind, Whales and Whisky: A Cape Breton Voyage.*

CAMERON, Thomas Wright Moir, medicine. Scot., 1894–1947. Parasitologist; pioneered study of parasitic worms.

CAMP, Dalton Kingsley, politics. Woodstock, NB, 1920. PC consultant; newspaper columnist.

CAMPBELL, Alexander (Sir), politics. Eng., 1822–92. Tory leader; Father of Confederation.

CAMPBELL, Avril Phaedra "Kim", politics. Port Alberni, BC, 1947. First woman prime minister of Canada, June 1993–December 1993.

CAMPBELL, Clarence, sports. Fleming, Sask., 1905–84. Sports administrator; headed NHL, 1946–77.

CAMPBELL, Douglas, performing arts. Scot., 1922. Actor at Stratford Festival, Ont. Co-founder of Canadian Players.

CAMPBELL, Gordon, politics. Vancouver, BC, 1948. Liberal party premier of British Columbia 2001–; formerly mayor of Vancouver.

CAMPBELL, Neve, performing arts. Guelph, Ont., 1973. Actress/dancer noted for role in Canadian TV series *Catwalk;* appeared in the US TV series *Party of 5;* also films *The Craft;* and the cult hit *Scream.*

CAMPBELL, Nicholas, performing arts. Toronto, Ont., 1952. Versatile actor, screenwriter, director; star of CBC's *DaVinci's Inquest;* also film *The Omen;* and TV production of *Come Back Little Sheba.*

CAMPBELL, Norman Kenneth, performing arts. USA, 1924. Music producer; innovative developer of ballet and musicals.

CAMPEAU, Robert, business. Sudbury, Ont., 1923. Financier; exemplar of 1980s expansionist business mania; developer; retail store magnate.

CANDY, John Franklin, performing arts. Toronto, Ont., 1950–94. Actor; comedian; bearish *SCTV* regular (Johnny LaRue, William B.); film star. *Uncle Buck.*

CAPLAN, Elinor, politics. Toronto, Ont., 1944. Liberal MP; former chairman of management board, has held various portfolios in provincial government, including minister of citizenship and immigration.

CARDINAL, Douglas Joseph, visual arts. Red Deer, Alta, 1934. Métis architect; Canadian Museum of Civilization.

CARDINAL, Tantoo, performing arts. Fort McMurray, Alta, 1951. Native actress who has appeared in films, *Big Bear, Smoke Signals, Black Robe* and CBC's *North of 60.*

CARELESS, James Maurice Stockford, literary arts. Historian; has written extensively on the effect of cities expanding into the hinterland. *Canada: A Story of Challenge; Brown of the Globe.* Toronto, Ont., 1919.

CARIOU, Len, performing arts. St Boniface Man., 1939. Theatre director and actor; associated with Manitoba Theatre Centre; Stratford Festival, Ont.; and in England and US. Tony Award for Stephen Sondheim's *Sweeney Todd* in New York, 1979.

CARLE, Gilles, visual arts. Maniwaki, Que., 1929. Film director. *La Vrai Nature de Bernadette.*

CARLETON, Guy (Sir), first Baron Dorchester, politics. Ire., 1724–1808. Quebec governor, 1768–78, 1785–95; supporter of French traditions.

CARMAN, William Bliss, literary arts. Fredericton, NB, 1861–1929. Poet; journalist. "The Pipes of Pan."

CARMICHAEL, Franklin, visual arts. Orillia, Ont., 1890–1945. Group of Seven founding member.

CARNEGIE, Herb, sports. Toronto, Ont., 1919. Outstanding hockey player, winner of four MVP awards with Black Aces, a semipro team with Quebec Senior Hockey League, during the 1940s and '50s; Carnegie, whose parents were Jamaican, was barred from NHL because of his race.

CARNEY, Patricia, PC minister of energy, mines and resources and international trade; entered Senate in 1990. China, 1935.

CARR, Emily, visual arts. Victoria, BC, 1871–1945. Painter of NW coastal Indians and nature.

CARR, Shirley, politics. Niagara Falls, Ont., First Woman to lead CUPE, Canada's largest union. President Emeritus, Canadian Labour Congress.

CARREY, James (Jim), performing arts. Jackson's Point, Ont., 1962. Comedic actor. *Ace Ventura; The Mask; Batman Forever.*

CARRIER, Roch, literary arts. Beauce, Que., 1937. Novelist; playwright. *La Guerre, Yes Sir!*

CARSON, John Elmer (Jack), performing arts. Carman, Man., 1910–63. Square-jawed film actor. *Mildred Pierce.*

CARTER, Emmett (Cardinal), religion. Montreal, Que., 1912. As Toronto Cardinal, helped get full funding for Catholic schools.

CARTER, Wilf, performing arts. Port Hilford, NS, 1904–96. Singer; father of Canadian country music.

CARTIER, Georges-Etienne (Sir), politics. St Antoine, UC, 1814–73. Father of Confederation; joint premier of United Canada, 1857–62.

CARTIER, Jacques, exploration and discovery. France, 1491–1557. Credited with European discovery of Canada; first explorer of St. Lawrence River.

CARVER, Brent, performing arts. Cranbrook, BC, 1951. Versatile actor active at Ontario's Stratford Festival (*Hamlet; Pirates of Penzance*); television (CBC's *Street Legal*); in musical comedy (*Jacques Brel Is Alive and Well and Living in Paris*); and on film (*The Wars*).

CARVER, Humphrey Stephen Mumford, politics. Eng., 1902–95. Key figure in Central Mortgage and Housing Corporation 1950s–60s; formed Co-operative Commonwealth Federation, forerunner of NDP.

CASGRAIN, Thérèse, politics. Montreal, Que., 1896–1981. Won Quebec women the right to vote (1940) and hold provincial office; leader of Quebec's CCF party in 1951.

CASSON, Alfred Joseph (A.J.), visual arts. Toronto, Ont., 1898–1992. Member, Group of Seven. *Country Store.*

CATHERWOOD, Ethel, sports. Haldimand Cty, Ont., 1909. High jumper; gold in high jump, 1928 Olympics.

CAVOUKIAN, Artin and Lucie, visual arts. Egypt, Armenia, 1915–95, 1923–95. Clientele of photographer Artin with wife Lucie included world leaders.

CHALMERS, Floyd Sherman, public service. USA, 1898–1993. Instituted Floyd S. Chalmers Foundation funding for arts in Canada.

CHAMBERLAIN, Douglas Thomas, performing arts. Toronto, Ont., 1933. Character actor; roles in classics, comedy and light opera, associated with Ontario's Stratford Festival; *Spring Thaw* revue; also at Charlottetown Festival and Vancouver Playhouse Theatre.

CHAMPLAIN, Samuel de, exploration and discovery. France, 1567–1635. Explorer; important cartographer/ geographer; "Father of New France."

CHANG, Simon, business. China, 1950. Fashion designer; also branched into fragrances, accessories, uniforms for restaurants and salon design.

CHANG, Thomas Ming Sui, medicine/science. China, 1933. Physiologist; expert on artificial cells and organs.

CHAPMAN, John Herbert, science. London, Ont., 1921–79. Physicist; lead role in Canada's satellite program.

CHAPUT-ROLLAND, Solange, media. Montreal, Que., 1919. Writer; broadcaster; Québécoise federalist.

CHAREST, Jean J., politics. Sherbrooke, Que., 1958. Led PC rump after '93 federal electoral debacle.

CHARLEBOIS, Robert, performing arts. Montreal, Que., 1945. Singer/songwriter. "Solidaritude."

CHARLEVOIX, Pierre François Xavier de, literary arts. France, 1682–1761. Historian; first complete history of New France.

CHAYKIN, Maury, performing arts. USA, 1949. Prolific actor has appeared in *Jacob Two-Two Meets the Hooded Fang; Dances With Wolves.*

CHEE CHEE, Benjamin (b. Kenneth Thomas Benjamin), visual arts. Temagami, Ont., 1944–77. Ojibwa artist; blockstamped abstract and animal, bird images; noted for use of movement and humour.

CHERRY, Don, sports. Kingston, Ont., 1934. Hockey coach; commentator; feisty nationalist.

CHERRY, Zena, media. Prince Albert, Sask., 1915–2000. Longtime social columnist for Toronto's *Globe and Mail*. "After a Fashion."

CHEVALIER, Leo, business. Montreal, Que., 1934–2000. Fashion designer of international lines.

CHIPMAN, Ward, law. St John, NB, 1787–1851. Jurist; chief justice of NB; noted abolitionist.

CHIRAEFF, Ludmilla, performing arts. Latvia, 1924. Choreographer; founder, Les Grands Ballets Canadiennes.

CHISHOLM, George Brock, medicine. Oakville, Ont., 1896–1971. Psychiatrist; early opponent of pollution, nuclear arms; first head of World Health Org.

CHONG, Rae Dawn, performing arts. Vancouver, BC, 1962. Film actress. *Quest for Fire.*

CHONG, Thomas (Tommy), performing arts. Edmonton, Alta, 1938. Actor; half of Cheech and Chong comedy team. *Cheech and Chong's Nice Dreams.*

CHOUART DES GROSEILLIERS, Medard, exploration and discovery. France, 1618–90. Explorer; fur trader; with Radisson opened western fur trade.

CHOUINARD, Josée, sports. Rosemont, Que., 1969. Three-time Canadian figure skating champion.

CHRETIEN, Joseph Jacques Jean, politics. Shawinigan, Que., 1934. Became prime minister of Canada, general election 1993.

CHRETIEN, Raymond, politics. Shawinigan, Que., 1942. Canadian ambassador to the United States 1994–.

CHRISTENSEN, Hayden, performing arts. Vancouver, BC, 1981. Actor; has gained new role in *Star Wars* series as the young Anakin Skywalker. *Higher Ground.*

CHRISTIE, Robert Wallace, performing arts. Toronto, Ont., 1920–96. Played at Ontario's Stratford Festival; Old Vic in London, Eng.; famous for portrayal of John A. MacDonald.

CHRISTIE, William Mellis, business. Scot., 1829–1900. Biscuit manufacturer; Christie Biscuits founder.

CHUVALO, George, sports. Toronto, Ont., 1937. Boxer; fought three world champions; never knocked down. Anti-drug crusader.

CLAIR, Frank, sports. USA, 1917. Football coach; 174 wins (Ottawa Rough Riders) tops CFL coaches.

CLANCY, Francis Michael "King", sports. Ottawa, Ont., 1903–86. Hockey player; defenceman, Ottawa Senators, Toronto Maple Leafs; lively raconteur.

CLARK, Charles Joseph (Joe), politics. High River, Alta, 1939. Prime minister of Canada 1979–80. Leader of federal Progressive Conservative Party, 1998–.

CLARK, Greg, literary arts. Toronto, Ont., 1892–1977. Journalist and humorist, winner of Leacock Award for Humour.

CLARK, Karl Adolf, Georgetown, Ont., invention.

CLARK, Susan, performing arts. Sarnia, Ont., 1940. Actress who has appeared in Hollywood movies, television. *Murder by Decree; Coogan's Bluff; Webster.*

CLARK, Wayne, business. Drumheller, Alta, 1949. Canadian fashion designer noted for his dramataic evening wear and high-quality sportswear.

CLARKE, Austin Chesterfield, literary arts. Barbados, 1934. Novelist, short story writer. *Proud Empires; Nine Men Who Laughed.*

CLARKSON, Adrienne Louise, media/politics. Hong Kong, 1939. Broadcaster; long-time CBC host. *Take Thirty.* Appointed governor-general of Canada, 1999.

CLAYTON-THOMAS, David, performing arts. Eng., 1941. Singer; member, Blood, Sweat and Tears. *Spinning Wheel.*

COCHRANE, Tom, performing arts. Lynn Lake, Man., 1953. Singer, songwriter, guitarist. Led Toronto-based quintet, Tom Cochrane and Red Rider, formed in 1976. *Breaking Curfew.* Went solo in 1991 with *Mad, Mad World.* "Life is a Highway."

COCKBURN, Bruce, performing arts. Ottawa, Ont., 1945. Singer/songwriter; politically conscious performer. *Dancing in the Dragon's Jaws.*

COE-JONES, Dawn, sports. Lake Cowichan, BC, 1961. Golfer; leading pro; 1993 LPGA title.

COHEN, Leonard, literary arts/performing arts. Montreal, Que., 1934. Poet; singer. *Flowers for Hitler, I'm Your Man.*

COHEN, Matt, literary arts. Kingston, Ont., 1942–2000. Short story writer, novelist, translator. *The Colour of War; Living on Water; Freud: The Paris Notebooks.*

COHEN, Morris (Moishe) Abraham "Two-Gun", military. Eng., 1889–1970. China hand; confidant of Sun Yat-sen; general in Chinese army.

COHEN, Samuel Nathan, literary arts. Sydney, NS, 1923–71. Critic; Canada's first serious drama critic.

COHON, George, business. USA, 1937. CEO, Cdn McDonald's restaurants; philanthropist.

COLDWELL, James William (Major), politics. Eng., 1888–1974. CCF founder; leader, 1942–60.

COLE, Holly, performing arts. Halifax, NS, 1963. Jazz/pop singer with distinctive contralto voice; founder of the Holly Cole Trio. *Don't Smoke in Bed; Christmas Blues; Dear Dark Heart.*

COLE, Jack, business. Toronto, Ont., 1920–97. With brother Carl started Coles chain of bookstores in Toronto, which later became national; created Coles Notes, study booklets for students, in 1947.

COLEMAN, Kathleen Blake (Kit), media. Toronto, Ont., 1864–1915. First woman war correspondent.

COLICOS, John, performing arts. Toronto, Ont., 1928–2000. Stage actor; Stratford Festival regular.

COLLENETTE, David M., Liberal MP; has been minister of transportation, national defense and veteran affairs. England, 1946.

COLLIP, James Bertram, medicine. Belleville, Ont., 1892–1965. Biochemist; co-discoverer of insulin.

COLOMBO, John Robert, literary arts. Kitchener, Ont., 1936. Anthologist; prolific compiler of reference books. *Colombo's Canadian Quotations.*

COLVILLE, Alexander, visual arts. Toronto, Ont., 1920. Realistic painter; designed centennial coins.

COMFORT, Charles Fraser, visual arts. Scot., 1900–94. Artist, graphic designer, created murals for Toronto Stock Exchange; director of National Gallery of Canada 1960–65.

CONACHER, Lionel Pretoria, sports. Toronto, Ont., 1901–54. Canada's Athlete of the Half-Century (1900–1950).

CONNOR, Ralph (b. Charles William Gordon), literary arts. West Indian Lands, Glengarry County, Canada West 1860–1937. Popular novelist, preacher of "red-blooded" Christianity. *The Sky Pilot.*

CONNORS, Charles Thomas "Stompin' Tom", performing arts. Saint John, NB, 1936. Country singer; nationalist performer. *Across This Land with Stompin' Tom.*

COOK, George Ramsay, literary arts. Alameda, Sask., 1931. Prolific historian. *Canada: A Modern Study; The Maple Leaf Forever.*

COOK, James, exploration and discovery. Eng., 1728–79. Navigator; explored Newfoundland and Northwest coasts.

COOK, Myrtle, sports. Toronto, Ont., 1902–85. Member of the women's track and field team in the 1928 Amsterdam Olympics, setting world record in 100 m race during Olympic trials; sports journalist for the *Montreal Star;* active on Olympic committees throughout career.

COOKE, Jack Kent, business. Hamilton, Ont., 1912–97. Capitalist; flamboyant owner of newspapers, radio stations, sports teams (Washington Redskins).

COOMBS, Ernest Arthur (Ernie), performing arts. USA, 1927–2001. Children's entertainer; CBC's "Mr. Dressup."

COON COME, Matthew, politics. Mistassini, Que., 1956. Grand Chief of the Assembly of First Nations 2000–.

COOP, Jane Austin, performing arts. Saint John, NB, 1950. Classical pianist; has appeared with both national and international orchestras; Beethoven specialist.

COPP, Harold, science. Toronto, Ont., 1915. Physiologist; discovered calcitonon, hormone that regulates calcium in blood.

COPPS, Sheila Maureen, politics. Hamilton, Ont., 1952. Liberal deputy prime minister.

CORBEIL, Carole, literary arts. Montreal, Que., 1952–2000. Award-winning journalist and novelist wrote *Voice-Over*, which won City of Toronto Book Award in 1993, and *In the Wings*.

CORMIER, Ernest, visual arts. Montreal, Que., 1885–1980. Architect; designed University of Montreal.

CORNISH, Judith, business. Toronto, Ont., 1958. With partner Joyce Gunhouse designs Comrags fashion design label.

CORRIGAL, Jim, sports. Barrie, Ont., 1946. Football player. Lineman with Toronto Argonauts 1970–81; four-time CFL all-star.

COSENTINO, Frank, sports. Hamilton, Ont., 1937. Football player; CFL quarterback, 1960–69; sports history writer; prof., physical education.

COSTAIN, Thomas Bertram, literary arts. Brantford, Ont., 1885–1965. Historical novelist. *High Towers.*

COUGHTRY, Graham, visual arts. St Lambert, Que., 1931–99. Abstract figurative painter; exhibited in New York's Guggenheim Museum, Museum of Modern Art, as well as across Canada.

COULTHARD, Jean, performing arts. Vancouver, BC, 1908. Composer. "The Pines of Emily Carr."

COUPLAND, Douglas Campbell, literary arts. Germany. 1961. Novelist; humorist. *Generation X.*

COURNOYEA, Nellie J., politics. Aklavik, NWT, 1940. First woman aboriginal leader of Northwest Territories.

COWAN, Garry, sports. Kitchener, Ont., 1938. Golfer; twice US amateur champion (1966, 1971).

CRANSTON, Toller, sports. Hamilton, Ont., 1949. Skater; brought innovation and artistry to men's figure skating.

CRAWLEY, Frank Radford "Budge", visual arts. Ottawa, Ont., 1911–87. Film producer. *The Rowdyman.*

CREIGHTON, Donald Grant, literary arts. Toronto, Ont., 1902–79. Historian; developed literary side of history.

CREIGHTON, Mary Helen, performing arts. Dartmouth, NS, 1899–1989. Folk music expert specializing in English, French, Gaelic, Mi'kmaq and Nova Scotian music; associated with National Museum of Canada.

CREMAZIE, Claude Joseph Olivier "Octave", literary arts. Quebec City, Que., 1827–79. Father of French Canadian poetry. "Le Drapeau de Carillon."

CREMO, Lee, performing arts. Cape Breton, NS, 1939–99. Six-time winner of Maritime Old-Time Fiddling Contest; mix of Irish, Scottish, Mi'kmaq Indian music; winner of Canadian title at Alberta Tar Sands Competition.

CROLL, David Arnold, politics. Russia, 1900–91. Liberal MLA in 1934; first Jewish cabinet minister (1955).

CROMBIE, David Edward, politics. Toronto, Ont., 1936. Civic reformer; Toronto mayor 1973–78.

CRONENBERG, David, visual arts. Toronto, Ont., 1943. Film director; inventive horror; science fiction filmmaker. *Videodrome, Crash.*

CRONYN, Hume (b. Hume Blake), performing arts. London, Ont., 1911. Stage actor; film character player. *Cocoon.*

CROSBIE, John Carnell, politics. St John's, Nfld, 1931. PC minister of fisheries and oceans; international trade; justice.

CROTHERS, William, sports. Markham, Ont., 1940. Runner; silver medal (800 m), 1964 Olympics.

CROW, John William, business. Eng., 1937. Economist; governor of Bank of Canada, 1987–94.

CROWFOOT, military. Belly R, Alta, 1830–90. Blackfoot chief, diplomat.

CUDDY, James Gordon (Jim), performing arts. Toronto, Ont., 1955. Lead singer for rock group Blue Rodeo.

CUMMINGS, Burton, performing arts. Winnipeg, Man., 1947. Rock singer; lead singer, The Guess Who; later solo artist. *My Own Way to Rock.*

CUNARD, Samuel (Sir), business. Halifax, NS, 1787–1865. Shipowner; founded Cunard Line forerunner.

CURNOE, Gregory Richard, visual arts. London, Ont., 1936–92. Fine artist whose paintings often incorporated written words; also created collages, drawings, prints.

CURRIE, Arthur William (Sir), military. Strathroy, Ont., 1875–1933. Commander, Canadian corps, WWI.

CURRIE, Philip, science. Toronto, Ont., 1948. Curator of dinosaurs for Alberta's Royal Tyrrel Museum in Drumheller and world leader in paleontology; recently discovered a feathered dinosaur that proved birds were dinosaurs.

CURTOLA, Robert Allen (Bobby), performing arts. Thunder Bay, Ont., 1944. Singer; early teen idol. "Fortune Teller."

CYR, Louis, sports. Napierville, Que., 1863–1912. World's strongest man, 1880–1990.

DAFOE, Allan Roy, medicine. Madoc, Ont., 1883–1943. Small-town physician who delivered the Dionne quintuplets, 28 May 1934; later faced accusations of exploiting the sisters.

DAFOE, John Wesley, media. Combermere, Ont., 1866–1944. Journalist; influential editor, *Winnipeg Free Press.*

DAIGLE, Sylvie, sports. Sherbrooke, Que., 1962. Won gold in 1988 Calgary Olympics in short track speed skating, as well as silver and bronze medals; five-time world champion.

DAIR, Carl, visual arts. Welland, Ont., 1912–67. Internationally recognized designer, topographer; created Cartier, first modern Canadian typeface. *Design with Type.*

DALE, Cynthia, performing arts. Toronto, Ont., 1961. Actress known for roles in TV series *Street Legal; Taking the Falls.* Also movie *Moonstruck.*

DANBY, Kenneth Edison (Ken), visual arts. Sault Ste Marie, Ont., 1940. Painter of realistic sports figures.

DANCE, Helen Oakley, performing arts. Toronto, Ont., 1913–2001. Record producer, jazz and blues historian and journalist, Dance was a contemporary of jazz greats such as Duke Wellington; also civil-rights supporter.

DANKO, Rick, performing arts. Simcoe, Ont., 1943–99. Founder and vocal/bass member of folk, blues, rock group The Band, subject of director Martin Scorcese's film *The Last Waltz.*

DAUDELIN, Charles, visual arts. Granby, Que., 1920–2001. Abstract artist, sculptor whose spiritually themed works are displayed in Canada and France. Designed awards for France-Canada and Jutra prizes.

DAUDELIN, Robert, performing arts. West Shefford, Que., 1939. Film administrator; writer; producer; director. Founder of movie critic magazine *Objectif;* International Film Festival in Montreal; director of Cinémathèque québécoise.

DAVEY, Keith, politics. Toronto, Ont., 1926. Long-time Liberal Party strategist.

DAVIES, Robertson William, literary arts. Thamesville, Ont., 1913–95. Novelist; playwright. *Fifth Business.*

DAVIS, Andrew, performing arts. Eng., 1944. Conductor of Toronto Symphony Orchestra 1975–88; participated in 1978 TSO visit to People's Republic of China.

DAVIS, Donald, performing arts. Newmarket, Ont., 1928–98. Distinguished Shakespearean actor, played Ontario's Stratford Festival; also appeared in TV roles: *Mission Impossible.* Co-founder of Toronto's Crest Theatre.

DAVIS, Fred, media. Toronto, Ont., 1921–96. Broadcaster and host of long-running CBC panel show "Front Page Challenge" (1957–95).

DAVIS, Victor, sports. Guelph, Ont., 1964–89. Swimmer; three medals 1984 Olympics; gold in 200 m breaststroke.

DAVIS, Warren, performing arts. Peterborough, Ont., 1926–95. CBC newsman. *The National; This Hour Has Seven Days.*

DAVIS, William Grenville, politics. Brampton, Ont., 1929. PC premier of Ontario, 1971–85.

DAWSON, George Mercer, science. Pictou, NS, 1849–1901. Geologist; surveyed much of northern and western Canada.

DAWSON, John William (Sir), science. Pictou, NS, 1820–99. Geologist; made McGill a leading university; founded Royal Society of Canada.

DAY, James, sports. Thornhill, Ont., 1946. Equestrian; team gold medal, 1968 Olympics.

DAY, Stockwell, politics. Barrie, Ont., 1950. Former provincial treasurer for Alberta; Canadian Reform Alliance Conservative Party leader, 2000–.

DE CARLO, Yvonne (b. Peggy Yvonne Middleton), performing arts. Vancouver, BC, 1924. Actress; film/TV star. *The Munsters.*

DE LA ROCHE, Mazo (b. Maisie Roche), literary arts. Newmarket, Ont., 1879–1961. Prolific popular novelist. *Jalna.*

de VILLIERS, Priscilla, politics. Pretoria, S. Africa, 1942. Activist and founder of CAVEAT, Canadians Against Violence Everywhere Advocating Its Termination.

DEL GRANDE, Louis, performing arts. USA, 1942. Actor, producer, writer. Starred in CBC TV series *Seeing Things.*

DENNYS, Louise, literary arts. Egypt, 1948. Vice-president and publisher at Knopf Canada.

DEPOE, Norman Reade, media. USA, 1917–80. CBC's Ottawa correspondent in the 1960s, Depoe was respected for his high standards in both national and international reporting during his career; also helped build CBC network in the 1950s.

DESCHENES, Jules, law. Montreal, Que., 1923–2000. Jurist; Que. chief justice; chairman, Inquiry of War Criminals in Canada.

DESJARDINS, Alphonse, business. Lévis, Que., 1854–1920. Banker; established first Caisse populaire (credit union) in 1900.

DESMARAIS, Paul, business. Sudbury, Ont., 1927. Industrialist; chairman of Power Corp., controlling trust, insurance and paper companies.

DESMOND, Trudy, performing arts. USA, 1946–99. Ballad and jazz singer, appeared in 1970 revue Spring Thaw. *My One and Only Love,* a tribute to Gershwin.

DEWAR, Marion, politics. Montreal, Que., 1928. Mayor, Ottawa, 1978–85; NDP MP.

DEWDNEY, Christopher, literary arts. London, Ont., 1951. Eclectic poet. *The Immaculate Perception: The Recent Artifacts from the Institute of Applied Fiction.*

DEWHURST, Colleen, performing arts. Montreal, Que., 1926–91. Actress who cultivated an earth-mother persona; noted for TV and film roles and performances in Albee and O'Neill plays. *Annie Hall; Murphy Brown.*

DeWOLF, Harry George, military. Bedford, NS, 1903–2000. Most decorated officer in Canadian Armed Forces; at helm of HMS *Haida* during Allied invasion of Normandy.

DHALIWAL, Herb, Liberal MP, minister of fisheries and oceans. India, 1952.

DIAMOND, Abel Joseph (Jack), visual arts. South Africa, 1932. Leading architect; designed Toronto's central YMCA; York University (Toronto) Student Centre; Jerusalem City Hall; Burns Building, Calgary.

DIAMOND, Billy, politics/business. Waskaganish, Que., 1949. Cree chief who successfully negotiated for native rights during James Bay hydroelectric project in Quebec; founder of Cree-owned airline Air Creebec.

DICKENS, Francis Jeffrey, military. Eng., 1844–86. Policeman; novelist's son; inspector in NWMP.

DICKINS, Clennell Haggerston "Punch", exploration and discovery. Portage la Prairie, Man., 1899–1995. Adventurer. First to fly length of MAcKenzie River and above Arctic Circle.

DICKINSON, Peter Allgood Rastall, visual arts. England, 1925–61. International style architect responsible for postwar development: Benvenuto Apartments, Prudential Building (Toronto); CIBC, Windsor Plaza (Montreal).

DICKSON, Robert George Brian, law. Yorkton, Sask., 1916–98 Chief justice of Canada, 1984–90.

DIEFENBAKER, John George, politics. Neustadt, Ont., 1895–1979. Prime minister of Canada 1957–63. (PC)

DION, Celine, performing arts. Montreal, Que., 1968. Popular Quebec chanteuse. "Unison."

DION, Stéphane, politics. Quebec City, Que., 1955. Political scientist; Liberal Minister of Intergovernmental Affairs 1996–.

DIONNE, Marcel, sports. Drummondville, Que., 1951. Hockey player; centre; 731 goals, third all-time.

DIONNE sisters, medicine. Corbeil, Ont., 1934. Annette, Emilie (d. 1954), Yvonne (d. 2001), Cecile and Marie (d. 1970), identical quintuplets born to poor rural family, became tourist attraction through government exploitation.

DMYTRYK, Edward, visual arts. Grand Forks, BC, 1908-99. Film director; film noir specialist. One of Hollywood Ten during McCarthy era. *Detour.*

DOBBS, Kildare Robert Eric, literary arts. India, 1923. Short story writer, essayist. *Coastal Canada; Historic Canada.*

DOER, Gary, politics. Winnipeg, Man., 1948. NDP premier of Manitoba, elected in 1999.

DOHERTY, Denny, performing arts. Halifax, NS, 1941. Pop singer; founding member, The Mamas and the Papas.

DONKIN, Eric Albert, performing arts. Eng., 1930–98. Classical actor who played 26 seasons at Ontario's Stratford Festival.

DOOHAN, James Montgomery, performing arts. Vancouver, BC, 1920. Actor; played Scotty (Lt. Commander Montgomery "Scotty" Scott) in *Star Trek* series.

DOSANJH, Ujjah, politics. India, 1947. NDP premier of BC 2000–01.

DOUGHTY, Arthur George (Sir), archivist. Eng., 1860–1936. Established Public Archives of Canada.

DOUGLAS, James (Sir), politics. British Guiana, 1803–77. Administrator; governor of BC, 1858–64.

DOUGLAS, Robert John Wilson, science. Southampton, Ont., 1920. Geologist; famous for geographical survey of structure of Rockies and foothills of southern Alberta.

DOUGLAS, Thomas Clement (Tommy), politics. Scot., 1904–86. Eloquent socialist; Sask. premier, 1944–61; NDP federal leader, 1961–71.

DRABINSKY, Garth Howard, performing arts. Toronto, Ont., 1948. Impresario; Cineplex founder, theatrical producer. *Show Boat.*

DRAPEAU, Jean, politics. Montreal, Que., 1916–99. Montreal mayor for 29 years; brought city Expo 67, 1976 Olympics, Montreal Expos.

DRESSLER, Marie (b. Leila von Koerber), performing arts. Cobourg, Ont., 1869–1934. Actress; oversize film star. *Min and Bill.*

DRYDEN, Kenneth Wayne, sports. Hamilton, Ont., 1947. Hockey goaltender; six-time all-star for Montreal; also lawyer and writer. *The Game.*

DUCKWORTH, Henry Edmison, science. Brandon, Man., 1915. With associates constructed highy accurate mass spectrometers for determination of atomic masses.

DUDEK, Louis, literary arts. Montreal, Que., 1918–2001. Poet, professor and literary critic, Dudek co-founded with Irving Layton and Raymond Souster Contact Press, which published major Canadian poets in the 1950s and '60s. *Surface of Time.*

DUGUID, Don, sports. Winnipeg, Man., 1935. Curler; Canadian and world champion, 1970, 1971.

DUMONT, Fernand, politics. Montmorency, Que., 1927–97. Quebec sovereigntist named deputy minister of cultural development for PQ in 1976; drafter of Bill 101, French Language Charter.

DUMONT, Gabriel, military. Red River, Sask., 1837–1906. Métis leader; guerrilla leader in NW Rebellion.

DUNBAR, Isobel Moira, Member of the Arctic section of the Defense Research Board; specialized in the study of sea ice and its relationship to climate. *Arctic Canada from the Air.* Scotland, 1918.

DUNNING, George, performing arts. Toronto, Ont., 1920. Animator and director; creator of Beatles *Yellow Submarine* film animation.

DUPLESSIS, Maurice Le Noblet, politics. Trois-Rivières, Que., 1890–1959. Powerful premier of Quebec, 1936–39, 1944–59.

DURBIN, Deanna (b. Edna Mae Durbin), performing arts. Winnipeg, Man., 1921. Actress; singer; teenage movie star. *3 Smart Girls.*

DURELLE, Yvon, sports. Baie Ste Anne, Que., 1929. Canadian middleweight boxing title 1953; light heavyweight 1953–54; British empire light heavyweight champion 1957.

DURHAM, John George Lambton, first Earl of, politics. Eng., 1792–1840. Statesman; "Radical Jack" urged union of English and French Canada.

DURNAN, William Arnold (Bill), sports. Toronto, Ont., 1915–72. Hockey goaltender; six-time Vezina Trophy winner for Montreal Canadiens.

DUTOIT, Charles Edouard, performing arts. Switz., 1936. Conductor of Montreal Symphony Orchestra.

DWAN, Allan, visual arts. Toronto, Ont., 1885–1981. Film director from silent era, made over 200 Hollywood films. *Sands of Iwo Jima.*

EATON, Cyrus Stephen, business. Pugwash, NS, 1883–1979. Financier; promoter of international peace.

EATON, Fredrik Stefan, business. Toronto, Ont., 1938. Retailer; former chairman, T. Eaton Co.

EATON, Timothy, business. Ire., 1834–1907. Retailer; innovative founder of T. Eaton Co. in 1867.

EDWARDS, Henrietta, public service. Montreal, Que., 1849–1931. In 1875 published first women's magazine in Canada, *Women's Work in Canada*; with Lady Aberdeen co-established the National Council of Women and the Victoria Order of Nurses.

EDWARDS, Robert Chambers (Bob), media. Scot., 1864–1922. Journalist; published satirical *Calgary Eye Opener.*

EGGLETON, Arthur C., politics. Toronto, Ont., 1943. Liberal MP, minister of national defense; mayor of Toronto 1980–91 (Toronto's longest-serving mayor).

EGOYAN, Atom, visual arts. Egypt, 1960. Film director; guitarist; playwright. *The Sweet Hereafter.*

EISLER, Lloyd, sports. Seaforth, Ont., 1963. Figure skater; with Isabelle Brasseur won world pairs title, 1993; Olympic bronze medals.

ELDER, Jim, sports. Toronto, Ont., 1934. Equestrian; team gold medal, 1968 Olympics.

ELGAARD, Ray, sports. Edmonton, Alta, 1959. Football player; Sask. Roughriders star wide receiver.

ELGIN, James Bruce, eighth Earl of, politics. Eng., 1811–63. Governor general, 1847–54.

EMERY, Victor, sports. Montreal, Que., 1933. Bobsledder; piloted 1964 Olympic gold medal team.

EMSLIE, Robert Daniel, sports. Guelph, Ont., 1859–1943. Major league baseball pitcher; won 32 games for Baltimore Orioles in 1884; umpire in National League, strove to improve working conditions and umpires' image.

ENGEL, Howard, literary arts. Toronto, Ont., 1931. Mystery writer. *Murder Sees the Light.*

ENGEL, Marian, literary arts. Toronto, Ont., 1933–85. Novelist. *Bear.*

ERASMUS, Georges Henry, politics. Ft Rae, NWT, 1948. Dene leader; former head, Assembly of First Nations.

ERICKSON, Arthur Charles, visual arts. Vancouver, BC, 1924. Architect; Simon Fraser University (Burnaby, BC).

ESPOSITO, Phillip Anthony (Phil), sports. Sault Ste Marie, Ont., 1942. Hockey player; Boston centre; 717 goals, fourth all-time.

ESTEY, Willard Zebedee "Bud", law. Saskatoon, Sask., 1919. Supreme Court justice, 1977–88; headed several royal commissions.

ETROG, Sorel, visual arts. Romania, 1933. Monumental sculptor; designer. "Ritual Head."

EVANGELISTA, Linda, media. St Catharines, Ont., 1965. International top model.

EVANS, Gil, performing arts. Toronto, Ont., 1912–88. Composer, arranger, pianist. Played free jazz, rock and funk. Gil Evans Orchestra.

EVANS, James, education. Eng., 1801–46. English Methodist missionary, invented Cree syllabic writing system. *Cree Syllabic Hymn Book.*

EVANSHEN, Terrance Anthony (Terry), sports. Montreal, Que., 1944. Football player; outstanding CFL receiver.

EYTON, Trevor, business. Quebec City, Que., 1934. Executive; president, Brascan Ltd; many corporate boards.

F

FACKENHEIM, Emil Ludwig, literary arts. Germany, 1916. Philosopher; works on religion and the Holocaust. *Quest for Past and Future.*

FAIRCLOUGH, Ellen Louks, politics. Hamilton, Ont., 1905. First woman Cabinet minister (1957).

FAIRFIELD, Robert, visual arts. St Catharines, Ont., 1918–95. Designed Stratford Festival Theatre, Ont.; Ontario pavilion at Expo 67.

FAIRLEY, Barker, visual arts. Eng., 1887–1986. Critic; essential Goethe scholar; portrait painter.

FAITH, Percy, performing arts. Toronto, Ont., 1908–76. Bandleader; top music arranger. "Canadian Sunset."

FALK, Gathie, visual arts. Alexander, Man., 1928. Multimedia artist, specializes in performance art, watercolour, drawings. Work shown at National Gallery of Canada.

FALONEY, Bernie, sports. USA, 1932. Football player; long-time star QB for Edmonton, Hamilton.

FARQUHARSON, Ray, Doctor who discovered Farquharson phenomenon, a hormone-related theory in secretion activity; his 1958 Farquharson Report led to the formation of the Medical Research Council in 1960. Claude, Ont., 1897–1965.

FAVREAU, Marc, performing arts. Montreal, Que., 1929. Actor; author, noted for role as the hapless, naïve clown Sol, performed on TV and in theatre. *Sol et Gobelet.*

FAVRO, Murray, visual arts. Huntsville, Ont., 1940. Artist noted for his "projected reconstruction"; he has projected slide images on life-size objects, also introduced invention themes into his work. *Windmill Electric Generator; Perpectual Motion Machine.*

FEINBERG, Abraham (Rabbi) (b. Abraham Nisselevicz, aka Anthony Frome), politics. USA, 1899–1986. Peace activist; champion of radical causes.

FEORE, Colm, USA, Actor; performing arts. Roles in Stratford Festival (Ont.); *Thirty-two Short Films about Glenn Gould.*

FERGUSON, Don, performing arts. Montreal, Que., 1946. Actor, writer, director of CHC documentaries; on team of CBC's *Royal Canadian Air Farce.* Impersonates Lucien Bouchard, Preston Manning.

FERGUSON, Ivan Graeme, invention. Toronto, Ont., 1929. Inventor; developed IMAX and OMNIMAX film systems.

FERGUSON, James Francis, performing arts. Ire., 1940–97. Founder, with George Millar, of the Irish Rovers, a singing group that popularized Irish pub music from the sixties on; appeared on CBC television.

FERGUSON, Max "Rawhide", media. Eng., 1924. Broadcaster; popular host of CBC Radio's *Rawhide.*

FERGUSON, Maynard, performing arts. Verdun, Que., 1928. Jazz trumpeter; versatile stylist made 50 albums.

FERRON, Jacques, literary arts/politics. Louiseville, Que., 1921–85. Playwright, *Contes du pays incertain*; Rhinoceros Party founder.

FESSENDEN, Reginald Aubrey, invention. Milton-Est, Canada E, 1866–1932. Inventor; transmitted world's first radio broadcast (1906).

FIELDING, Joy, literary arts. Toronto, Ont., 1945. Novelist, journalist, scriptwriter. *Tell Me No Stories.*

FILION, Herve, sports. Angers, Que., 1940. Harness driver; all-time leader in victories; 12,000+.

FILMON, Gary Albert, politics. Winnipeg, Man., 1942. PC Manitoba premier, 1988–1999.

FINDLEY, Timothy, literary arts. Toronto, Ont., 1930. Novelist; versatile writer. *The Wars.*

FITZ-JONES, Philip Chester, science. Vancouver, BC, 1920. Researched structure and chemical nature of bacterial spores.

FITZGERALD, Lionel LeMoine, visual arts. Winnipeg, Man., 1890–1956. Impressionist turned to abstracts. "Doc Snider's House."

FLAVELLE, Joseph Wesley (Sir), business. Peterborough, Ont., 1858–1939. Financier; executive for Canada Packers, Bank of Commerce, National Trust.

FLEMING, Sandford (Sir), invention. Scot., 1827–1915. Engineer; developed standard time; designed Canada's first postage stamp; built railways.

FOLEY, Dave, performing arts. Toronto, Ont., 1963. Actor; role of Dave Nelson in TV series *News Radio;* member of comedy troupe Kids in the Hall.

FOLLOWS, Megan, performing arts. Toronto, Ont., 1969. Actor who portrayed Anne of Green Gables in CBC TV series. *Silver Bullet.*

FONYO, Stephen Charles (Steve), sports. Montreal, Que., 1965. Handicapped runner; "Journey for Lives" raised funds for cancer research, 1985.

FORBES, Kenneth, visual arts. Toronto, Ont., 1892–1980. War artist, portrait painter (John Diefenbaker); works displayed in Canadian War Museum.

FORD, Glenn (b. Gwyllyn Samuel Newton Ford), performing arts. Quebec City, Que., 1916. Noted American actor of the 1940s and 1950s. *Gilda, Teahouse of the August Moon.*

FORRESTER, Helen, literary arts. Eng., 1919. Novelist. Wrote semiautobiographical Liverpool series: *Twopence to Cross the Mersey; Liverpool Miss; By the Waters of Liverpool; Lime Street at Two.*

FORRESTER, Maureen, performing arts. Monteal, Que., 1930. Operatic contralto; Canada's prima diva.

FORSEY, Eugene Alfred, politics. Grand Bank, Nfld, 1904–91. Intellectual; commentator on public affairs; social radical; strong federalist.

FORTIER, L. Yves, politics. Quebec City, Que., 1935. Former Canadian ambassador to the United Nations.

FOSTER, David Walter, performing arts. Victoria, BC, 1949. Musician; produced many major acts (Chicago, Barbra Streisand); 12 Grammy awards.

FOSTER, George Eulas (Sir), politics. Carleton, NB, 1847–1931. Statesman; central in Cdn political life; acting PM during Borden's illness (1920).

FOTHERINGHAM, Allan, media. Hearne, Sask., 1932. Journalist; popular political columnist.

FOWKE, Edith Margaret, literary arts. Lumsden, Sask., 1913–96. Music ethnologist, published traditional Canadian folksongs. *Penguin Book of Canadian Folksongs; Sally Go Round the Sun.*

FOX, Michael James (J.), performing arts. Edmonton Alta, 1961. Actor; diminutive leading man. *Back to the Future.*

FOX, Terrance Stanley (Terry), sports. Winnipeg, Man., 1958–81. Began "Marathon of Hope" cross-Canada run to raise funds for cancer research; Lou Marsh Trophy as Canada's top athlete, 1980.

FRANCA, Celia (b. Celia Franks), performing arts. Eng., 1921. Choreographer; founder of National Ballet of Canada.

FRANCK, Albert Jacques, visual arts. Holland, 1899–1973. Painter especially noted for his depiction of old houses and back lanes in the old city of Toronto.

FRANCKS, Don Harvey, performing arts. Burnaby, BC, 1932. Veteran actor, jazz musician, appeared in revue *Spring Thaw.* Also TV and film roles. *The Man From U.N.C.L.E.; Finian's Rainbow.*

FRANKLIN, John (Sir), exploration and discovery. Eng., 1786–1847. Bold, doomed Arctic explorer.

FRANKLIN, Ursula Martius, Physicist and educator; specialist in field of archeometry, which relates materials analysis with archeology; advocate for Science for Peace. Germany, 1921.

FRANKS, Wilbur Rounding, invention. Weston, Ont., 1901–86. Inventor; devised pressure suit for airplane pilots.

FRAPPIER, Armand, science. Valleyfield, Que., 1904–91. Influential microbiologist.

FRASER, Anna, sports. Ottawa, Ont., 1963. Free-style skier; World Cup Aerial Champion (1986).

FRASER, Brendan, performing arts. USA, 1968. Comedic actor who has appeared in films *George of the Jungle; Airheads;* and *Dudley Do-Right.*

FRASER, John Anderson, literary arts. Montreal, Que., 1944. Author; former editor of *Saturday Night* magazine; master of Massey College, Toronto. *The Chinese: A Portrait of a People.*

FRASER, Simon, exploration and discovery. USA, 1776–1862. First white man to explore Fraser River.

FRASER, Sylvia Lois, literary arts. Hamilton, Ont., 1935. Novelist. *Pandora; Berlin Solstice; My Father's House; The Emperor's Virgin.*

FRECHETTE, Sylvie, sports. Laval, Que., 1967. Received post-event gold medal in synchronized swimming; 1992 Olympics.

FREEDMAN, Harry, Composer of chamber, symphonic, instrumental music; also wrote scores for stage and film (*The Pyx*). *Encounter.* Poland, 1922.

FRENCH, David, literary arts. Coley's Point, Nfld, 1939. Playwright. *Salt-Water Moon; Jitters; Leaving Home.*

FREUND, Kurt, medicine. Czech., 1914–96. Psychiatrist; noted researcher into human sexuality.

FROBISHER, Martin (Sir), exploration and discovery. Eng., 1539–94. Mariner; discovered Frobisher Bay.

FRONTENAC ET PALLUAU, (Louis de Buade) Comte de, politics. France, 1622–98. Gov. gen, New France, 1672–82, 1689–98.

FROST, Leslie Miscampbell, politics. Orillia, Ont., 1895–1973. PC premier of Ontario, 1949–61.

FRUM, Barbara Ruth, media. USA, 1937–92. Broadcaster; interviewer. *As It Happens; The Journal.*

FRUM, David, literary arts. Toronto, Ont., 1960. Journalist of "new right."

FRYE, Herman Northrop, literary arts. Sherbrooke, Que., 1912–91. Canada's most influential literary critic. *Anatomy of Criticism.*

FULFORD, Robert Marshall Blount, media. Ottawa, Ont., 1932. Journalist; former editor, *Saturday Night*; columnist.

FULTON, E. Davie, politics. Kamloops, BC, 1916–2000. Justice minister in John Diefenbaker's government, beginning 1957; became BC Supreme Court judge 1973–81.

FUNG, Donna Lori, sports. Vancouver, BC, 1963. Rhythmic gymnast; gold medal, 1984 Olympics.

FURST, Judith, performing arts. New Westminster, BC, 1943. Opera singer; internationally renowned diva.

G

GABEREAU, Vicki Frances, media. Vancouver, BC, 1946. Broadcaster, author. Host of CBC Radio's *Gabereau,* 1988–97. Host of TV talk show on Baton Broadcasting.

GABRIEL, Tony, sports. Hamilton, Ont., 1948. Football player; CFL tight end; held record 138 straight games with receptions until 1995.

GAGNON, André, performing arts. Saint-Pacôme-de-Kamouraska, Que., 1942. Pianist; composer. "Le Saint-Laurent."

GAGNON, André Phillipe, performing arts. Loretteville, Que., 1961. Comedian, impressionist, noted for one-man shows.

GALBRAITH, John Kenneth, business/literary arts. Iona Station, Ont., 1908. Economist; author; influential intellectual. *The Affluent Society.*

GALLANT, Mavis Leslie, literary arts. Montreal, Que., 1922. Author of more than 100 short stories. "A Fairly Good Time."

GALLEY, Harry A., invention. Montreal, Que., 1903–95. Inco employee; designer of first mass-produced stainless steel sink.

GALLIVAN, Danny, sports. Montreal, Que., 1917–93. Hockey announcer; voice of the Montreal Canadiens.

GALT, Alexander Tilloch, politics. Eng., 1817–93. Railway promoter; proposed union of all British colonies.

GARBER, Victor, performing arts. London, Ont., 1949. Character actor in Hollywood, formerly led folk band The Sugar Shoppe. Roles include Jesus in *Godspell*; also appeared in films *Titanic* and *First Wives Club*.

GARNEAU, François Xavier, literary arts. Quebec City, Que., 1809–66. Writer; early historian. *Histoire du Canada*.

GARNEAU, Hector de Saint Denys, literary arts. Montreal, Que., 1912–43. Poet. "Regards et jeux dans l'espace."

GARNEAU, Marc, science. Quebec City, Que., 1949. First Canadian astronaut (1984) to achieve liftoff.

GARNER, Hugh, literary arts. Eng., 1913–79. Working class novelist. *Cabbagetown*.

GASCON, Jean, performing arts. Montreal, Que., 1921–88. Actor; director; influential man of the theatre; headed Stratford Festival, Natl Arts Centre.

GAYFORD, Thomas Franklin, sports. Toronto, Ont., 1928. Equestrian; won gold medal Prix des Nations in 1968 Olympics.

GEDGE, Pauline, literary arts. New Zealand, 1945. Novelist. *Scroll of Saqqara; The Twelfth Transforming; The Covenant*.

GEHRY, Frank, visual arts. Toronto, Ont., 1929. Internationally recognized architect. Guggenheim Museum in Bilbao, Spain; Art and Teaching Museum, University of Minnesota.

GELBER, Arthur Ellis, public service. Toronto, Ont., 1915–98. Philanthropist who was prominent on arts boards, including National Arts Centre, National Ballet of Canada and the Ontario Arts Council.

GELINAS, Gratien, performing arts. St Tite, Que., 1909–99. Actor; director; playwright; crucial to modern Quebec theatre.

GEOFFRION, Joseph André Bernard "Boom Boom", sports. Montreal, Que., 1931. Hockey player; right-winger, Montreal Canadiens (1950–64), noted for strength and speed.

GEORGE, Dan (Teswahno), performing arts. Burrard Reserve, BC, 1899–1981. Actor; helped redefine image of Aboriginal peoples in media. *Little Big Man.*

GERUSSI, Bruno, performing arts. Medicine Hat, Alta, 1928–95. Actor; regular on *The Beachcombers.*

GESNER, Abraham, invention. Cornwallis, NS, 1797–1864. Inventor of kerosene oil.

GETTY, Donald Ross, politics/sports. Montreal, Que., 1933. Edmonton Eskimos quarterback; PC premier of Alberta, 1985–92.

GHIZ, Joseph Atallah, politics. Charlettetown, PEI, 1945–97. Liberal premier of PEI 1986–93. Avid supporter of Meech Lake Accord and Charlottetown Accord.

GIAUQUE, William Francis, science. Niagara Falls, Ont., 1895–1982. Chemist who won 1949 Nobel Prize in chemistry for studies of properties of substances at temperatures near absolute zero.

GIBSON, George "Mooney", sports. London, Ont., 1880–1967. Baseball player; pro catcher, 1905–18.

GIBSON, Graeme C., literary arts. London, Ont., 1934. Novelist. *Five Legs; Perpetual Motion.*

GIBSON, William, literary arts. USA, 1948. Science fiction writer, pioneered "Cyberpunk" paradigm; novel *Neuromancer* won Hugo and Nebula awards; wrote screenplay for *Johnny Mnemonic.*

GILLIS, Margie, performing arts. Montreal, Que., 1953. Dancer, choreographer; depicts social and political themes; an internationally acclaimed soloist, she has toured with Les Grands Ballet Canadiens, and introduced modern dance to China after the revolution. *Mercy.*

GILMOUR, Clyde, media. Calgary, Alta, 1912–97. Journalist; arts radio broadcaster. *Gilmour's Albums.*

GIMBY, Bobbie (b. Robert Stead), performing arts. Cabri, Sask., 1918–98. Trumpeter, songwriter. Appeared in CBC radio series *The Happy Gang.* Composed "CA-NA-DA" in 1967 for centennial celebrations.

GISBORNE, Frederick Newton, invention. Eng., 1824–92. Inventor; developed undersea telegraph cable (1852).

GIVENS, Philip, politics. Toronto, Ont., 1922–95. Mayor of Toronto 1964–66; responsible for acquisition of Henry Moore's *The Archer* sculpture at Toronto's New City Hall.

GOLDSMITH, Robert, literary arts. St Andrews, NB, 1794–1861. First Canadian-born poet to write in English: *The Rising Village* described Acadian experience.

GOMEZ, Avelino, sports. Cuba, 1928–80. Jockey; over 4,000 career wins, including four Queen's Plates.

GOODERHAM, William, business. England, 1790–1881. With nephew James built Canada West's largest distillery, in 1859; Gooderham and Worts eventually had interests in distilleries, railways, transportation and retailing.

GOODMAN, Henry George, business. USA, 1907–97. Philanthropist, volunteer and lawyer who helped initiate and served as president of the Jewish Children's Aid Society in Toronto.

GOODYEAR, Scott, sports. Toronto, Ont., 1959. Indy car driver; winner of Canadian Racing Drivers Association Driver of the Year award; first Canadian to win oval race.

GORDON, Charles William, literary arts. Glengarry Cty, Canada W, 1860–1937. Presbyterian minister who wrote western-style novels, *The Sky Pilot, The Prospector*, as well as *Glengarry School Days.*

GORDON, Donald, business. Scot., 1901–69. Executive; controversial head of CNR, 1950–66.

GORDON, Walter Lockhart, politics. Toronto, Ont., 1906–87. Economic nationalist; inspired creation of Committee for an Independent Canada.

GORMAN, Charles, sports. Saint John, NB, 1897–1940. Speed skater; held seven world records.

GOTLIEB, Allan Ezra, politics. Winnipeg, Man., 1928. Career public servant; Canadian ambassador to US 1981–89.

GOTLIEB, Phyllis Fay, literary arts. Toronto, Ont., 1926. Poet, science fiction writer. *Heart of Red Iron; The Kingdom of the Cats.*

GOTLIEB, Sondra, literary arts. Winnipeg, Man., 1936. Newspaper columnist with *Washington Post, Globe and Mail.* Writer: *"Wife Of": An Irreverent Account of Life in Washington; True Confections.*

GOUGEON, Hélène Carroll, media. Ottawa, Ont., 1924–2000. Veteran journalist on radio, TV and in print; culinary expertise led to her *The Original Canadian Cookbook.* Also wrote for *Weekend; Toronto Star; Ottawa Journal.*

GOUIN, Jean-Lomer (Sir), politics. Canada E, 1861–1929. Liberal premier of Quebec, 1905–20.

GOULD, Glenn Herbert, performing arts. Toronto, Ont., 1932–82. Classical pianist; *Goldberg Variations* stand out in brilliant, eccentric career.

GOULET, Robert Gerard, performing arts. USA, 1933. Singer/actor, noted for romantic male leads. *South Pacific; Camelot.*

GOUZENKO, Igor Sergeievich, military. USSR, 1919–82. Spy; defector exposed Soviet espionage network.

GOVIER, Katherine Mary, literary arts. Edmonton, Alta, 1948. Novelist, short story writer. *Random Descent; Angel Walk.*

GOWAN, Elsie Park, literary arts. Scot., 1905–99. Internationally recognized playwright for radio and stage. *Beeches from Bond Street; The Building of Canada.*

GOWDY, Barbara, literary arts. Windsor, Ont., 1950. Editor, writer. *Through the Green Valley; We So Seldom Look on Love.*

GOY, Luba, performing arts. Germany, 1946. Comedian on *Royal Canadian Air Farce*; impersonations include Sheila Copps, Pamela Wallin.

GRANT, Charles, law. Toronto, Ont., 1902–80. Activist; fought anti-Semitism, racism, bigotry.

GRANT, George Parkin, literary arts. Toronto, Ont., 1918–88. Philosopher; influential pessimistic thinker and nationalist. *Lament for a Nation.*

GRAY, George R., sports. Canada W, 1865–1933. Shot putter; world record holder during 1880s.

GRAY, Herbert Eser, politics. Windsor, Ont., 1931. Liberal Party stalwart: has served as government leader; solicitor general; deputy prime minister for Jean Chrétien 1997–.

GRAY, James Henry, literary arts. Whitemouth, Man., 1906–98. Social historian whose works reflected Western Canadian society. *The Winter Years,* a story about the Depression; *The Boy From Winnipeg.*

GREEN, Tom, performing arts. Pembroke, Ont., 1971. Satirical "shock" comedian, stages outrageous publicity stunts. *The Tom Green Show.*

GREENE, Graham, performing arts. Six Nations Reserve, Ont., 1952. Film/TV actor. *Dances with Wolves.*

GREENE, Lorne Hyman, performing arts. Ottawa, Ont., 1915–87. Actor; Ben Cartwright on TV's *Bonanza* for 14 years.

GREENE, Nancy Catherine, sports. Ottawa, Ont., 1943. Skier; World Cup winner, 1967, 1968; gold and silver slalom medals.

GREENOUGH, Gail, sports. Edmonton, Alta, 1960. Equestrian; 1986 world champion, individual show jumping.

GREENSPAN, Edward Leonard, law. Niagara Falls, Ont., 1944. Distinguished criminal lawyer.

GRENFELL, Wilfred Thomason (Sir), medicine. Eng., 1865–1940. Medical missionary; builder of hospitals in Nfld.

GRETZKY, Wayne, sports. Brantford, Ont., 1961. Hockey player; all-time leading NHL scorer.

GREY, Deborah C., politics. Vancouver, BC, 1952. Canadian Alliance MP; deputy parliamentary leader; co-founder of Reform Party.

GREY OWL (b. Archibald Stansfield Belaney), literary arts. Eng., 1888–1938. Writer; conservationist who identified with Aboriginal peoples. *Pilgrims of the Wild.*

GRIERSON, John, visual arts. Scot., 1898–1972. Documentarist; creator of National Film Board.

GRIFFITH, Linda, performing arts. Toronto, Ont., 1953. Film, TV and stage actress. *Maggie and Pierre.*

GRIMES, Roger D., politics. Grand Falls, Nfld, 1950. Liberal premier of Nova Scotia 2001–; formerly minister of education.

GROSS, Paul, performing arts. Calgary, Alta, 1959. Actor, playwright; starred in TV series *Due South.*

GROSSMAN, Daniel Williams, performing arts. USA, 1942. Founder of the Danny Groosman Dance Co.; specializes in contemporary dance, set to jazz, rock music. *Higher; Nobody's Business.*

GROSSMAN, Lawrence S. (Larry), politics. Toronto, Ont., 1943–97. High-profile minister in Bill Davis's Ontario PC government, ran unsuccessfully as Tory leader against David Peterson in 1975.

GROULX, Lionel Adolphe, religion. Vaudreuil, Que., 1878–1967. Historian; Quebec religious nationalist.

GROVE, Frederick Philip, literary arts. Prussia, 1879–1948. Writer. *In Search of Myself.*

GUERIN, Gertrude Ettershank (Klaw Law We Leth), politics. Mission Reserve, N. Vancouver, BC. A Musqueam chief, considered to be the first native woman to hold such a high-ranking position.

GUILLET, James Edwin Dr., invention. Toronto, Ont., 1927. Inventor of biodegradable plastics.

GUNHOUSE, Joyce, business. Toronto, Ont., 1961. With partner Judith Cornish designs Comrags fashion design label.

GUSTAFSON, Ralph Barker, literary arts. Lime Ridge, Que., 1909–95. Founder of League of Canadian Poets. Governor General's Award, 1974. *Fire and Stone.*

GWYN, Sandra (Alexandra) Jean Fraser, literary arts. St John's, Nfld, 1935–2000. Governor General's Award, 1984. *The Private Capital; Tapestry of War.*

GWYNNE, Horace "Lefty", sports. Toronto, Ont., 1912. Boxer; bantamweight gold medal, 1932 Olympics.

GZOWSKI, Casimir Stanislaus (Sir), exploration and discovery. Russia, 1813–98. Engineer; built roads, bridges, and railroads.

GZOWSKI, Peter, media. Toronto, Ont., 1934. Broadcaster; author; long-time radio host. *Morningside.*

H

HACKNER, Allan, sports. Nipigon, Ont., 1954. Curler; Canadian and world champion, 1982, 1985.

HADFIELD, Chris Austin, science. Sarnia, Ont., 1959. Astronaut, first Canadian mission specialist on space shuttle, 1996.

HAILEY, Arthur, literary arts. Eng., 1920. Writer; produced string of best-sellers. *Airport.*

HAIM, Corey, performing arts. Toronto, Ont., 1972. Actor, producer. *Demolition High; Life 101.*

HALDER, Walter (Wally), sports. Toronto, Ont., 1925–94. Leading goal scorer on Canada's gold medallist team at 1948 Olympic Winter Games.

HALIBURTON, Thomas Chandler, literary arts. Windsor, NS, 1796–1865. Writer; social satirist. *The Clockmaker.*

HALL, Emmett Matthew, public service. Saint-Columban, Que., 1898–1995. Chief Justice of Saskatchewan; co-author of Ontario's 1966 Hall-Dennis education report.

HALL, Glenn Henry, sports. Humboldt, Sask., 1931. Hockey goaltender; 11-time all-star; record 502 consecutive games.

HALL, Monty, performing arts. Winnipeg, Man., 1925. Long-time TV host of *Let's Make a Deal* show.

HALPERT, Herbert, Newfoundland folklorist and academic; author of *Folktales of Newfoundland; Christmas Mumming in Newfoundland: Folklore and History.* USA, 1911–2000.

HAMEL, Theophile, visual arts. Ste-Foy, LC, 1817–70. Painted life-like official portraits.

HAMILTON, Barbara, performing arts. Toronto, Ont., 1926–96. Veteran screen and stage actor. *Anne of Green Gables; Crazy for You.*

HAMM, John F., politics. New Glasgow, NS, 1938. PC premier of Nova Scotia, 1999–.

HAMPSON, Sharon, performing arts. Toronto, Ont., 1943. Member of children's musical entertainment group Sharon, Lois and Bram; live on TV. *The Elephant Show.*

HANLAN, Edward (Ned), sports. Toronto, Ont., 1855–1908. World champion oarsman, 1880–84.

HANSEN, Rick, sports. Port Alberni, BC, 1957. Wheelchair athlete; "Man in Motion" tour raised $20M for medical research.

HANSON, Melvin "Fritzie", sports. USA, 1912. Football player; led Winnipeg to first western Grey Cup (1935).

HARCOURT, Michael Franklin, politics. Edmonton, Alta, 1943. NDP Premier of BC 1991–96.

HARDY, Hagood, performing arts. USA, 1937–97. Pop/jazz pianist and composer; Juno award-winner. "The Homecoming"; scores for *Anne of Green Gables, Road to Avonlea.*

HARE, Frederick Kenneth, science. Eng., 1919. Environmentalist; expert on climate change, greenhouse effect.

HARNOY, Ofra, performing arts. Israel, 1965. International virtuoso cellist.

HARPER, Elijah, politics. Red Sucker L, Man. MLA in Manitoba legislature who blocked passage of Meech Lake Accord.

HARPER, J. Russell, visual arts. Caledonia, Ont., 1914–83. Art historian; pioneered study of art history.

HARRINGTON, Michael Francis, performing arts. St John's, Nfld, 1916–99. Supporter of an independent Newfoundland prior to 1949 confederation, Harrington hosted popular 1940s Newfoundland radio program *The Barrelman;* co-edited complete National Convention debates.

HARRINGTON, Rex Howard, performing arts. Peterborough, Ont., 1962. Internationally recognized ballet dancer; principal with National Ballet of Canada.

HARRINGTON, Richard, Photographer whose stark portraits of a starving Inuit population in the late 1940s brought world attention to the grim situation caused partly by the disappearance of the caribou. *The Inuit: Life as It Was; Richard Harrington's Yukon.* Germany, 1911.

HARRIS, Lawren Stewart, visual arts. Brantford, Ont., 1885–1970. Founder of Group of Seven; noted for stark landscapes, *Above Lake Superior.*

HARRIS, Micheal Deane, politics. Toronto, Ont., 1945. PC premier of Ontario 1995–.

HARRIS, Mike, sports. Georgetown, Ont., 1967. Skip of the silver-medal-winning curling team during the 1998 winter Olympics in Nagano, Japan.

HARRIS, Wayne, sports. USA, 1938. Football player; outstanding Calgary Stampeders linebacker.

HARRON, Donald (Don), performing arts. Toronto, Ont., 1924. Actor; comedian; host of *Morningside* 1977–82; also noted for portraying farmer Charlie Farquharson.

HART, Corey Mitchell, performing arts. Montreal, Que., 1962. Pop singer; teen heartthrob. *Boy in the Box.*

HART, Evelyn Anne, performing arts. Toronto, Ont., 1956. Prima ballerina, Royal Winnipeg Ballet.

HARTMAN, Grace, business. Toronto, Ont., 1918. Labour leader; first woman to head Canadian Union of Public Employees (1975–83).

HARVEY, Douglas N. (Doug), sports. Montreal, Que., 1924–90. Hockey player; Montreal Canadiens defenceman; won seven Norris Trophies.

HARWOOD, Vanessa Clare, performing arts. Eng., 1947. National Ballet soloist.

HATFIELD, Richard Bennett, politics. Woodstock, NB, 1931–91. PC premier of NB, 1970–87.

HAWKINS, Ronald "Rompin' Ronnie", performing arts. USA, 1935. Pop/country singer; pioneer of Canadian rock. "Mary Lou."

HAWLEY, Sanford Desmond (Sandy), sports. Oshawa, Ont., 1949. Jockey; winner of more than 6,000 races.

HAYDEN, Melissa (b. Mildred Herman), performing arts. Toronto, Ont., 1923. Virtuoso with New York City Ballet.

HEALEY, Jeff, performing arts. Toronto, Ont., 1966. Blind vocalist and guitarist, rock, blues music; Jeff Healey Trio. "Angel Eyes"; "See the Light."

HEARNE, Samuel, exploration and discovery. Eng., 1745–92. Explorer; *A Journey from Prince of Wales's Fort in Hudson's Bay to the Northern Ocean* is one of the great travel narratives.

HEATH, John Geoffrey "Jeff", sports. Ft William, Ont., 1915–75. Baseball player; hit .293 in 14-year career.

HEBB, Donald Olding, science. Chester, NS, 1904–85. Psychologist; developmental work showed importance of environmental stimulation.

HEBERT, Anne, literary arts. Ste-Catherine-de-Fossambault, Que., 1916-2000. Novelist. *Kamouraska.*

HEBERT, Louis-Philippe, visual arts. Megantic, Que., 1850–1917. Commemorative sculptor of many public monuments. *Queen Victoria.*

HEDDLE, Kathleen, sports. Vancouver, BC, 1965. With Marnie McBean won women's double sculls rowing medals: two golds in 1992 at Barcelona Olympics; one gold, one bronze in 1996 Olympics in Atlanta.

HEES, George Harris, politics. Toronto, Ont., 1910–96. PC cabinet minister for John Diefenbaker and Brian Mulroney.

HEGGTVEIT, Anne, sports. Ottawa, Ont., 1939. Skier; Canada's first Olympic gold medal in skiing; women's slalom, 1960.

HELLSTROM, Sheila Anne (Brig-Gen.), military. Bridgewater, NS, 1935. Soldier; first Cdn woman general.

HELWIG, David Gordon, literary arts. Toronto, Ont., 1938. Poet; novelist. "Figures in a Landscape."

HENLEY, Garney, sports. USA, 1935. Football player; Hamilton star CFL's most versatile player.

HENNING, Douglas, performing arts. Ft Garry, Man., 1947-2000. Magician; co-founder, Natural Law Party.

HENRY, Martha, performing arts. USA, 1938. TV/film actress; Stratford regular. *The Wars.*

HENSON, Josiah, politics. USA, 1789–1883. Black leader; escaped slave; model for *Uncle Tom's Cabin.*

HENSTRIDGE, Natasha, performing arts. Springdale, Nfld. 1974. Model turned actress; appeared in *Species* movie series; also films *Dog Park* and *The Whole Nine Yards.*

HEPBURN, Doug, sports. Vancouver, BC, 1926. Weight lifter; world heavyweight title, 1953.

HEPBURN, Mitchell Frederick, politics. St Thomas, Ont., 1896–1953. Liberal Ontario premier, 1934–42.

HEPPNER, Ben, performing arts. Murrayville, BC, 1956. Tenor opera singer, Metropolitan debut in 1991.

HERBERT, Paul, performing arts. Thetford Mines, Que., 1924. Actor; screenwriter; director.

HERIOT, George, visual arts. Scot., 1759–1839. Watercolourist. *Lake St Charles Near Quebec.*

HEROUX, Denis, visual arts. Montreal, Que., 1940. Film producer. *Atlantic City.*

HERZBERG, Gerhard, medicine. Germany, 1904–99. Physicist; molecular analyst; Nobel Prize, chemistry, 1971.

HEWITT, Angela Mary, performing arts. Internationally renowned classical pianist; Bach specialist. Winner of 1985 International Bach Competition in Toronto, Ont. Ottawa, Ont., 1958.

HEWITT, Foster William, sports. Toronto, Ont., 1903–85. Hockey announcer; voice of Toronto Maple Leafs.

HIBBERT, Curtis, sports. Mississauga, Ont., 1966. Gymnast; won five gold medals in 1990 Commonwealth Games.

HIGHWAY, Tomson, literary arts. Brovchet, Man., 1951. Playwright. *Dry Lips Oughta Move to Kapuskasing.*

HILL, Arthur, performing arts. Melfort, Sask., 1922. Stage and film performer. *The Ugly American.*

HILL, Dan Jr, performing arts. Toronto, Ont., 1954. Ballad singer and composer. "Sometimes When We Touch."

HILL, Daniel Grafton Sr, politics. USA, 1923. Reformer; human rights; black history activist and writer.

HILL, James Jerome, business. Rockwood, Ont., 1838–1916. In 1890 consolidated vast railway holdings into the Great Northern Railway Co., also was integral in the building of the Canadian Pacific Railway.

HILLER, Arthur Garfin, visual arts. Edmonton, Alta, 1923. Filmmaker/director. *Love Story.*

HILLIARD, Anna Marion, medicine. Morrisburg, Ont., 1902-58. In 1947 helped develop the Pap test to detect cervical cancer; facilitated its initiation at Women's College Hospital in Toronto in 1948. Wrote *A Woman Doctor Looks at Love and Life.*

HILLIER, James, invention. Brantford, Ont., 1915. Inventor; pioneered electron microscopes.

HIRSCH, John Stephen, performing arts. Hungary, 1930–89. Stage director; founded Manitoba Theatre Centre; headed Stratford Festival, CBC TV drama.

HITSCHMANOVA, Lotta, politics. Czech., 1909–80. Activist; founding director, Unitarian Service Committee of Canada development agency.

HNATYSHYN, Ramon John, politics. Saskatoon, Sask., 1934. Governor general of Canada 1990–95.

HODGINS, Jack Stanley, literary arts. Comox, BC, 1938. Novelist. *The Resurrection of Joseph Bourne.*

HODGSON, George Ritchie, sports. Montreal, Que., 1893–1983. Swimmer; first Canadian Olympic gold medals in swimming; 400 m, 1500 m freestyle in 1912.

HOFFMAN, Abigail (Abbie), sports. Toronto, Ont., 1947. Sports feminist; director of Sport Canada.

HOFFMEISTER, Bertram Meryl, military. Vancouver, BC, 1907-99. Canadian general in WWII, considered brilliant battle strategist, later chairman of lumber conglomerate MacMillan Bloedel.

HOGG-PRIESTLY, Helen Battles, science. USA, 1905–93. Astronomer; star clusters expert; asteroid named for her.

HOHL, Elmer, sports. Wellesley, Ont., 1919–87. Horseshoe pitcher; world champion, 1965–87.

HOLGATE, Edwin, visual arts. Allandale, Ont., 1892–1977. Group of Seven artist, noted for portraiture; member of Royal Canadian Academy of Arts.

HOLLINGSHEAD, Gregory Albert Frank, literary arts. Toronto, Ont., 1947. Governor General's Award for fiction, 1995, *The Roaring Girl.*

HOMME, Robert, performing arts. USA, 1919–2000. Portrayed the Friendly Giant on long-running CBC children's program of same name.

HOOD, Hugh John Blagdon, literary arts. Toronto, Ont., 1928. Novelist; essayist. *The Swing in the Garden.*

HORTON, Miles Gilbert "Tim", sports. Cochrane, Ont., 1930–74. Toronto Maple Leaf hockey player, five Stanley Cup wins; founder of national doughnut chain.

HOSPITAL, Janette Turner, literary arts. Australia, 1942. Winner of the Seal first Novel Award, 1982, *The Ivory Swing. Isobars.*

HOUSSER, Yvonne McKague, visual arts. Toronto, Ont., 1898–1996. Group of Seven-influenced paintings: National Art Gallery; Art Gallery of Ontario; McMichael Gallery.

HOUSTON, Heather, sports. Thunder Bay, Ont., 1959. Curler; skip of 1989 world championship team; Canadian championships 1988, 1989.

HOUSTON, James Archibald, literary/visual arts. Toronto, Ont., 1921. In the 1950s became a major buyer and supporter of Inuit art. *White Dawn; Confessions of an Igloo Dweller.*

HOWARD, Russ, sports. Penetanguishene, Ont., 1955. Curler; Canadian and world champion, 1987, 1993.

HOWE, Clarence Decatur (C.D.), business/politics. USA, 1886–1960. Foremost grain elevator builder of his day, Howe was a Liberal minister of transport; helped create Trans-Canada Airlines, forerunner of Air Canada.

HOWE, Gordon (Gordie), sports. Floral, Sask., 1928. Hockey player; Detroit Red Wings great; 801 NHL goals.

HOWE, Joseph, politics. Halifax, NS, 1804–73. Led fight against Nova Scotia entry into Confederation; later joined cabinet.

HUBEL, David Hunter, science. Windsor, Ont., 1926. Winner of 1981 Nobel Prize in medicine and physiology for research in processing the visual system.

HUGGINS, Charles Brenton, science. Halifax, NS, 1901. Won Nobel Prize for medicine in 1966 for discoveries concerning hormonal treatment of prostate cancer.

HULL, Robert Marvin, sports. Pte Anne, Ont., 1939. Hockey player; "Golden Jet," left winger for Chicago and Winnipeg; 610 NHL goals.

HUMPHREY, John Peters, public service. Hampton, NB, 1905–95. Principal author of the Universal Declaration of Human Rights; founder of the Canadian Human Rights Foundation and Amnesty International (Can.).

HUNGERFORD, George William, sports. Vancouver, BC, 1944. Rower; gold medal, coxless pairs, 1964 Olympics.

HUNTER, Thomas James (Tommy), performing arts. London, Ont., 1937. Country singer; *Tommy Hunter Show* on CBC, 1965–92.

HUNTSMAN, Archibald Gowanlock, science. Tintern, Ont., 1883–1973. Biologist; pioneered fisheries science.

HUOT, Juliette, Tétraultville, Que., performing arts.

HURTIG, Melvyn (Mel), literary arts. Edmonton, Alta, 1932. Publisher; Canadian nationalist. *The Canadian Encyclopedia.*

HUSTON, Walter (b. Walter Houghston), performing arts. Toronto, Ont., 1884–1960. Actor. *Treasure of the Sierra Madre.*

HUTCHISON, William Bruce, literary arts. Prescott, Ont., 1901–92. Political historian; biographer of W. L. Mackenzie King, *The Incredible Canadian.*

HUTT, William Ian deWitt, performing arts. Toronto, Ont., 1920. Stage actor; distinguished Stratford leading player.

HYLAND, Francis, performing arts. Regina, Sask., c. 1932. Actor with Stratford Festival, Ont.

I

IBERVILLE, Pierre Le Moyne, Sieur d', military. Montreal, Que., 1661–1706. soldier; daring, often cruel, adventurer.

IDE, Thomas Ranald (Ran), media. Ottawa, Ont., 1919–96. Appointed in 1966 to set up TVOntario, an innovative education network.

IGALI, Baraladei Daniel, Won gold medal in 2000 Sydney Olympics in freestyle wrestling. Nigeria, 1974.

IGNATIEFF, George, politics. Russia, 1913–89. Diplomat; expert in East-West relations; UN ambassador.

IGNATIEFF, Michael, literary arts/media. Toronto, Ont., 1947. Writer; broadcaster. *The Russian Album.*

IMLACH, George "Punch", sports. Toronto, Ont., 1918–87. Hockey coach and manager; during 11 seasons with Toronto Maple Leafs won four Stanley Cups.

INNIS, Harold Adams, politics. Otterville, Ont., 1894–1952. Political economist; communications theorist. *Empire and Communications.*

IRELAND, John, performing arts. Vancouver, BC, 1914. Actor; often played a heavy. *Red River.*

IRONSIDE, Michael, performing arts. Toronto, Ont., 1950. Character actor, specializes in heavies and thugs; has appeared in films *Top Gun; Highlander II.* Also on TV's *ER* series.

IRVIN, Dick Sr, sports. Limestone Ridge, Ont., 1892–1957. Hockey executive; innovative coach/mgr of Montreal Canadiens, Toronto Maple Leafs.

IRVING, Kenneth Colin (K.C.), business. Buctouche, NB, 1899–1992. Industrialist; founder of NB business empire, from oil to broadcasting.

IRWIN, Mary (b. May Campbell), performing arts. Whitby, Ont., 1862–1938. Broadway, vaudeville star; famous for first screen kiss in film *The Kiss,* in 1896. Sang "After the Ball."

ISELER, Elmer Walter, performing arts. Port Colbourne, Ont., 1927–98. Choral conductor who founded Festival Singers of Canada; from 1964 to 1997 conductor of the Toronto Mendelssohn Choir; also founded the Elmer Iseler Singers.

ISRAEL, Werner, science. Germany, 1931. Physicist; pioneered study of black holes, gravitation.

ISSAJENKO, Angella (Taylor), sports. Jamaica, 1958. Sprinter; many medals in 100 m races.

J

JACKS, Terry, performing arts. Winnipeg, Man., 1944. Singer; founding member, the Poppy Family.

JACKSON, Alexander Young (A.Y.), visual arts. Montreal, Que., 1882–1974. Painter; landscape artist; member, Group of Seven. *Barns.*

JACKSON, Donald, sports. Oshawa, Ont., 1940. Figure skater; men's world champion, 1962.

JACKSON, Roger, sports. Toronto, Ont., 1942. Rower; gold medal, coxless pairs, 1964 Olympics.

JACKSON, Russell Stanley (Russ), sports. Hamilton, Ont., 1936. Football player; Ottawa quarterback; 3-time Schenley Award winner as CFL top player.

JACKSON, Tom, performing arts. Winnipeg, Man. Native actor and singer, has appeared on CBC's *North of 60; Medicine River; The Diviners.*

JACOBI, Lou, performing arts. Toronto, Ont., 1913. Character actor; has appeared in *Spring Thaw* revue; on Broadway; and in film (*Irma la Douce*).

JACOBS, "Indian" Jack, sports. USA, 1920–74. Football player; fiery quarterback for Winnipeg Blue Bombers; helped popularize CFL.

JACOBS, Jane, literary arts. USA, 1916. Urban critic; major urban thinker. *Systems of Survival.*

JAMES, Colin, performing arts. Regina, Sask., 1964. Songwriter, guitarist; plays blues, pop, swing. *Hook, Line & Single; Colin James.*

JAMES, Gerry, sports. Regina, Sask., 1934. Football/hockey player; rare pro double; Winnipeg Blue Bombers, Toronto Maple Leafs.

JANES, Percy Maxwell, literary arts. St John's, Nfld, 1922–99. Newfoundland writer whose gritty works depicted the reality of life on the island. *House of Hate.*

JARVIS, Judy, performing arts. Ottawa, Ont., 1946-86. Dancer, founder of the Judy Jarvis Dance and Theatre Co.; innovative teacher and choreographer and instrumental in development of Canadian contemporary dance. *Bird; Three Women.*

JELINEK, Otto John, sports/politics. Czech., 1940. PC minister; with sister Maria won world pairs figure skating title (1972).

JENKINS, Ferguson Arthur, sports. Chatham, Ont., 1943. Baseball pitcher; only Canadian in Hall of Fame, 284 career wins.

JENNESS, Diamond, literary arts. New Zealand, 1886–1969. Anthropolgist; author; expert on native Canadians. *The People of the Twilight.*

JENNINGS, Peter Charles, media. Toronto, Ont., 1938. Broadcaster; anchorman, *ABC Evening News.*

JEROME, Harry Winston, sports. Prince Albert, Sask., 1940–82. Sprinter; one-time world record holder in 100 m.

JEWISON, Norman Frederick, visual arts. Toronto, Ont., 1926. Film director; founded Canadian Film Centre in Toronto. *In the Heat of the Night.*

JOHANSSON, Herman Smith "Chief Jackrabbit", sports. Norway, 1875–1986. Skier; popularizer of cross-country skiing.

JOHNS, Harold Elford (Dr), medicine. China, 1915. Physician; developed cobalt bomb for treating cancer.

JOHNSON, Ben, sports. Jamaica, 1961. Sprinter; stripped of 100 m world record time gold medal in 1988 Olympics for using banned drug.

JOHNSON, Daniel, politics. Montreal, Que., 1944. Liberal opposition leader in Quebec 1994–98.

JOHNSON, Edward, performing arts. Guelph, Ont., 1878–1959. Opera singer, performed at Metropolitan Opera in New York; later chairman of board of Royal Conservatory of Music in Toronto.

JOHNSON, Emily Pauline "Tekahionwake", literary arts. Six Nations Reserve, UC, 1861–1913. Her poetry celebrated Canada and her native heritage. "Flint and Feather."

JOHNSTON, Francis Hans (Franz), visual arts. Toronto, Ont., 1888–1949. Early Group of Seven member. *Batchawana Falls.*

JOHNSTON, Lynn, visual arts. Collingwood, Ont., 1947. Cartoonist; creator, "For Better or For Worse."

JOHNSTON, Rita Margaret, politics. Melville, Sask., 1935. First woman premier in Canada (BC) in 1991, succeeded Bill Vander Zalm.

JOLIAT, Aurele, sports. Ottawa, Ont., 1908–86. Hockey player; left winger for Montreal Canadiens.

JOLLIET, Louis, exploration and discovery. Quebec City, Que., 1645–1700. Co-discoverer of the Mississippi R.

JONAS, George, literary arts. Hungary, 1935. Poet, writer, scriptwriter. Script for CBC's *The Scales of Justice; Vengeance; By Persons Unknown: The Strange Death of Christine Demeter.*

JONES KONIHOWSKI, Diane, sports. Vancouver, BC, 1951. Canadian pentathlon record holder.

JORY, Victor, performing arts. Yukon, 1902–82. Actor; Hollywood villain. *Huckleberry Finn.*

JUCKES, Gordon, sports. Watrous, Sask., 1914–95. Hockey and Sports Hall of Fame member, established national team program.

JULIEN, Pauline, performing arts. Trois-Rivières, Que., 1928–98. Quebec singer, political activist, separatist and feminist, Julien embodied the spirit of Quebec through songs of her own composition as well as Kurt Weill, Bertolt Brecht and Gilles Vigneault.

JULIETTE (b. Juliette Augustina Sysak), performing arts. Winnipeg, Man., 1927. Singer; early TV star; own show, 1954–66.

JUNEAU, Pierre, business. Verdun, Que., 1922. Broadcast executive; headed CRTC, 1968–75.

JUTRA, Claude, visual arts. Montreal, Que., 1930–87. Film director. *Mon Oncle Antoine.*

K

KAIN, Karen, performing arts. Hamilton, Ont., 1951. Prima ballerina, National Ballet of Canada.

KALVAK, Helen, visual arts. Victoria I., NWT, 1901–84. Inuit artist; over 300 prints portray the life of the Copper Inuit, frequent spiritual themes. *Kidnapper.*

KANE, Lori, sports. Charlottetown, PEI, 1964. Golfer: member of Canadian Inernational Team 1989–92; member of Commonwealth Team in 1991; 1992 Canadian World Amateur Team; 1997, Canadian Athlete of the Year.

KANE, Paul, visual arts. Ire., 1810–71. Painter of the Canadian West and native peoples.

KARPIS, Alvin (b. Albin Karpowicz). Montreal, Que., 1908–79. Barker Gang member; US Public Enemy No. 1.

KARSH, Yousuf, visual arts. Armenia, 1908. Photographer; portraitist of the famous, e.g., Churchill.

KEDROVA, Lila Howard, performing arts. Russia, 1920–2000. Actress noted for role as Madame Hortense in film *Zorba the Greek,* also appeared in *High Wind in Jamaica.*

KEELER, Ruby (b. Ethel Keeler), performing arts. Halifax, NS, 1909–93. Actress; dancer. *42nd Street.*

KEITH, Vicki, sports. Winnipeg, Man., 1961. Swam all five Great Lakes in 1988.

KELESI, Helen Mersi, sports. Victoria, BC, 1969. Tennis player; Canadian women's championship 1987–90.

KELLY, Leonard "Red", sports. Simcoe, Ont., 1927. Hockey player; star defenceman with Detroit and Toronto; two-time Liberal MP.

KELLY, Milton Terrence (M.T.), literary arts. Toronto, Ont., 1947. Poet, playwright, novelist. *A Dream Like Mine.*

KELSO, John Joseph, politics. Ire., 1864–1935. Reformer; founded Toronto Humane Society, Children's Aid.

KENOJUAK Ashevak, visual arts. Baffin Island, NWT, 1927. Artist noted for bird graphics.

KEON, David Michael, sports. Noranda, Que., 1940. Hockey player with Toronto Maple Leafs 1960–75. Team Canada member 1977. Winner of Conn Smythe trophy, 1967.

KHANJIAN, Arsinée, performing arts. Lebanon, 1958. Film and theatre actress, wife of film director Atom Egoyan. *Next of Kin; Exotica.*

KHORANA, Har Gobind, science. India, 1922. Chemist; Nobel Prize in medicine (1968) for DNA research.

KIDD, Bruce, sports. Ottawa, Ont., 1943. Runner; many wins at various distances; outstanding athlete in Canada, 1961 and 1962.

KIDDER, Margot, performing arts. Yellowknife, NWT, 1948. Actress; Hollywood star. *Superman.*

KIERANS, Eric William, politics. Montreal, Que., 1914. Economist; outspoken nationalist.

KILBOURN, William, literary arts. Toronto, Ont., 1926–95. Writer; historian; biographer of C.D. Howe.

KILLAM, Isaac Walton, business. Yarmouth, NS, 1885–1955. Industrialist; built business empire; known for philanthropy.

KING, Allan Winton, visual arts. Vancouver, BC, 1930. Filmmaker; documentarist. *Warrendale.*

KING, Thomas, literary arts. USA, 1943. Aboriginal writer, novelist. Creator of "Dead Dog Café" on CBC radio programs *Morningside* and *This Morning. Medicine River.*

KING, William Lyon Mackenzie, politics. Kitchener, Ont., 1874–1950. Prime minister of Canada during WWII.

KINSELLA, William Patrick (W. P.), literary arts. Edmonton, Alta, 1935. Writer; known for poetic baseball fiction. *Shoeless Joe.*

KIRKE, David (Sir), exploration and discovery. France, 1597–1654. First governor of Nfld, 1637.

KLEIN, Abraham Moses, literary arts. Ukraine, 1909–72. Poet of Jewish themes. "The Rocking Chair."

KLEIN, George John, invention. Hamilton, Ont., 1904–92. Productive inventor: wind tunnels, gearing systems, Canadarm gear design.

KLEIN, Ralph Philip, politics. Calgary, Alta, 1942. PC premier of Alberta, 1992–.

KNOTT, Elsie Marie, politics. Curve Lake, Ont., 1922–95. First native woman in Canada to be elected chief, at Ojibwa reserve near Peterborough, Ont.

KNOWLES, Stanley Howard, politics. USA, 1908–97. A founder of the New Democratic Party; represented Winnipeg North Centre riding 1942–81. Admired for his support of old-age pensions; president of Canadian Labour Congress 1958–62.

KNUDSON, George, sports. Winnipeg, Man., 1937–89. Golfer; Canada's top pro; 12 PGA tour victories.

KOFFLER, Murray Bernard, business. Toronto, Ont., 1924. Entrepreneur; made Shopper's Drug Mart Canada's largest pharmacy chain.

KOFFMAN, Morris (Moe), performing arts. Toronto, Ont., 1928–2001. Jazz flautist. "Swinging Shepherd Blues."

KOGAWA, Joy Nozomi, literary arts. Vancouver, BC, 1935. Writer. *Obasan; Itsuka.*

KOTCHEFF, William Theodore (Ted), visual arts. Toronto, Ont., 1931. Film director. *The Apprenticeship of Duddy Kravitz.*

KRAATZ, Victor, sports. Germany, 1971. Ice dancing; with Shae-Lynn Bourne won Canadian title, 1993–96; third in World Championships, 1996.

KRALL, Diana, performing arts. Nanaimo, BC, 1964. Sultry jazz vocalist. *When I Look Into Your Eyes.*

KREINER, Kathy, sports. Timmins, Ont., 1957. Skier; gold medal, giant slalom, 1976 Olympics.

KREVER, Horace, law. Montreal, Que., 1929. Judge who led Royal Commission of Inquiry on the Blood System in Canada, 1997–97.

KRIEGHOFF, Cornelius David, visual arts. Holland, 1815–72. Known for paintings of Quebec life. *The Habitant Farm.*

KROL, Joseph "Joe King", sports. Hamilton, Ont., 1919. Football player; Toronto Argos star; top athlete, 1946.

KUDELKA, James, performing arts. Newmarket, Ont., 1955. Artistic director for the National Ballet of Canada; also choreographer, dancer. Critically acclaimed work with classical and modern influences. *Spring Awakening.*

KUERTI, Anton Emil, performing arts. Austria, 1938. Leading pianist; composer; Beethoven specialist.

KURELEK, William (Wasyl), visual arts. Whitfield, Alta, 1927–77. Symbolist religious painter.

KUWABARA, Bruce, visual arts. Hamilton, Ont., 1949. Partner with Toronto-based architecture firm Kuwabara Payne McKenna Blumberg; award-winning designer of Kitchener, Ont., City Hall; City Hall in Richmond, BC.

LA SALLE, Rene Robert Cavelier, Sieur de, exploration and discovery. France, 1643–87. Became commandant of Fort Frontenac in present-day Kingston, Ont., 1673.

LA VERENDRYE, Pierre Gaultier de Varennes, Sieur de, exploration and discovery. Trois-Rivières, Que., 1685–1749. Explorer of W Canada.

LABATT, John Kinder, business. Ireland, 1803–66. In 1855 became owner of a small brewery in London, Ont., the origin of the giant brewery empire.

LAFLEUR, Guy Damien, sports. Thurso, Que., 1951. Hockey player; Canadiens star right winger; 560 goals.

LAFONTAINE, Louis Hippolyte (Sir), politics. Boucher-ville, LC, 1807–64. In effect, Canada's first PM, 1848–51.

LALONDE, Donny, sports. Kitchener, Ont., 1960. Boxer; WBC light heavyweight champion (1987–88).

LALONDE, Edouard Charles, sports. Cornwall, Ont., 1887–1970. In 1950 named as one of Canada's outstanding lacrosse players of the half-century; played NHL Montreal Canadiens, scoring 124 goals in 98 games 1913–18.

LALONDE, Marc, politics. Ile-Perrot, Que., 1929. Pierre Trudeau's principle secretary 1968–72; held various port-folios until retirement in 1984.

LAMBERT, Natalie, sports. Montreal, Que., 1963. Speed skater; short track title, 500 m, 1993.

LAMBERTS, Heath, performing arts. Toronto, Ont., 1941. Actor at Stratford Festival, Ont. *Glengarry Glen Ross; Cyrano de Bergerac.*

LAMER, Antonio, law. Montreal, Que., 1933. Chief justice of the Supreme Court 1990-99.

LAMPMAN, Archibald, literary arts. Morpeth, Canada W, 1861–99. Nature poet. "Lyrics of Earth."

LANCASTER, Ron, sports. USA, 1938. Football player; coach; quarterback set 30 CFL records.

LANCTOT, Françoise, performing arts. Montreal, Que., 1947. Actress, film director; winner of Etrog for *La vrai nature du Bernadette. The Apprenticeship of Duddy Kravitz.*

LANDRY, G. Yves, business. Thetford Mines, Que., 1938–98. Died while chairman, president and CEO of Chrysler Canada; co-chairman of Automotive Advisory Committee to the Minister of Industry Canada.

LANDRY, Jean-Bernard, Saint-Jacques, Montcalm Co, Que., politics.

LANG, Katherine Dawn (k.d.), performing arts. Consort, Alta, 1961. Country-torch singer; vegetarian activist. *Shadowlands.*

LANGFORD, Sam, sports. Weymouth Falls, NS, 1886–1956. Boxer; great fighter; denied title shot.

LANOIS, Daniel, performing arts. Hamilton, Ont., 1953. Singer; producer of Peter Gabriel's "Sledgehammer" and with Brian Eno U2's *Joshua Tree.*

LANTOS, Robert, visual arts. Hungary, 1949. Film producer; CEO, Alliance Communications. *Black Robe.*

LAPIERRE, Laurier L., media. Megantic, Que., 1929. TV personality, author; co-host, *This Hour Has Seven Days.*

LASKIN, Bora, law. Ft William, Ont., 1912–84. Chief justice of Canada, 1973–84.

LASTMAN, Melvin Douglas (Mel), politics. Toronto, Ont., 1933. Elected mayor of the amalgamated City of Toronto in 1997; formerly long-time mayor of North York, a satellite "city" of the former Metropolitan Toronto.

LAU, Evelyn, literary arts. Vancouver, BC, 1971. Poet, novelist, short story writer, used own experiences to portray the lives of street kids. *Runaway: Diary of a Street Kid; You Are Not Who You Claim; Oedipal Dreams.*

LAUMANN, Silken, sports. Toronto, Ont., 1964. Rower; braved broken leg for bronze medal in 1992 Olympics; Athlete of the Year 1991, 1992.

LAURE, Carole (b. Carol Champagne), performing arts. Montreal, Que., 1949. Actress; screen star. *Maria Chapdelaine.*

LAURENCE, Jean Margaret, literary arts. Neepawa, Man., 1926–87. Writer; created fictional setting of Manawaka. *The Diviners.*

LAURENDEAU, Joseph-Edmond-André, politics. Montreal, Que., 1912–68. Co-chairman of Royal Commission on Bilingualism and Biculturalism 1963–68; editor of Montreal's *Le Devoir* 1958–68.

LAURIER, Wilfrid (Sir), politics. St-Lin, Canada E, 1841–1919. Canada's first French-speaking prime minister.

LAURIN, Camille, politics. Charlemagne, Que., 1922–99. Drafted Bill 101, Quebec's French Language Charter; joined Quebec National Assembly in 1970, member of Parti Québécois.

LAVAL, François de, religion. France, 1623–1708. First bishop of Quebec (1674–88).

LAVALLEE, Calixa, performing arts. Verchères, Canada E, 1842–1891. Composer of "O Canada."

LAW, Andrew Bonar, politics. Rexton, NB, 1858–1923. Prime Minister of Britain 1922–23; signed Treaty of Versailles on behalf of Great Britain in 1919.

LAWRENCE, Florence, performing arts. Hamilton, Ont., 1890–1938. Film and vaudeville actress; first to use publicity stunt to launch career. *Daniel Boone; Resurrection.*

LAYTON, Irving Peter, literary arts. Romania, 1912. Prolific, flamboyant poet. "A Red Carpet for the Sun."

LE CAINE, Hugh, performing arts/science. Port Arthur, Ont., 1914–77. Physicist; composer; designed the sackbut, the first musical synthesizer.

LEACOCK, Stephen Butler, literary arts. Eng., 1869–1944. Humorist. *Sunshine Sketches of a Little Town.*

LEBLANC, Romeo, politics. Memramcook, NB, 1927. Governor-General of Canada 1994–99; former Liberal MP.

LEBLOND, Charles Philippe, science. France, 1910. Anatomist; pioneer in cell biology.

LECLERC, Felix, performing arts. La Tuque, Que., 1914–88. Singer/songwriter; influential chansonnier and Quebec nationalist.

LEE, Dennis Beynon, literary arts. Toronto, Ont., 1939. Poet, children's writer. *Alligator Pie; Garbage Delight.*

LEE, Geddy, performing arts. Toronto, Ont., 1953. Singer/songwriter; lead singer for Rush. *Moving Pictures.*

LEE-GARTNER, Kerrin, sports. Trail, BC, 1966. Skier; gold medal, women's downhill, 1992 Olympics.

LEGER, Gabrielle Carmel, politics. Montreal, Que., 1916–98. Wife of the late governor general Jules Leger; acted for her husband when he suffered a stroke shortly after taking office.

LEGER, Jules, politics. St-Anicet, Que., 1913–80. Canada's governor general, 1974–79.

LEGER, Paul-Emile, religion. Valleyfield, Que., 1904–91. Cardinal; eloquent, compassionate religious leader; became missionary in Africa.

LEMELIN, Roger, literary arts. Quebec City, Que., 1919–92. Writer; creator of the popular Plouffe family.

LEMIEUX, Jean-Paul, visual arts. Quebec City, Que., 1904–90. Landscape painter. *Le Visiteur du Soir; Lazare.*

LEMIEUX, Mario, sports. Montreal, Que., 1965. Hockey player; Pittsburgh Penguins centre, one of two players to average two points per game.

LEMIEUX, Raymond Urgel, medicine. La Biche, Alta, 1920. Scientist with National Research Council, solved riddle of synthesis of sucrose; pioneer in blood-typing serum.

LENNOX, Edward James, visual arts. Toronto, Ont., 1854–1933. Architect of "Richardson Romanesque" style. Toronto's Old City Hall, Casa Loma; powerhouse at Niagara Falls, Ont.

LEONARD, Stanley, sports. Vancouver, BC, 1915. Golfer; won many Canadian titles; three US tour wins.

LEPAGE, Robert, performing arts. Quebec City, Que., 1957. Actor, screenwriter, director; former artistic director of Ottawa's National Arts Centre; Théâtre français. *Secret War Tour.*

LESAGE, Jean, politics. Montreal, Que., 1912–80. Liberal premier of Quebec, 1960–66.

LETHEREN, Carol Anne, sports. Toronto, Ont., 1942–2001. Chief executive of Canadian Olympic Association.

LEVESQUE, Georges-Henri, politics. Roberval, Que., 1902–2000. Dominican priest, founded Faculty of Social Sciences at Laval University; major figure in Quebec's Quiet Revolution.

LEVESQUE, Jean-Louis, business. Nouvelle, Que., 1911. Financier; co-founder of Levesque Beaubien Inc., Quebec's largest brokerage house.

LEVESQUE, René, politics. New Carlisle, Que., 1922–87. Led Parti Québécois; Quebec premier 1976–85.

LEVY, Eugene, performing arts. Hamilton, Ont., 1946. Actor; comedian; *SCTV* regular (Earl Camembert, Bobby Bitman).

LEWIS, David, politics. Russia, 1909–81. Federal NDP leader, 1971–75; eloquent speaker.

LEWIS, Lennox, sports. Eng., 1965. Boxer; super heavyweight gold medal, 1988 Olympics.

LEWIS, Stephen Henry, politics. Ottawa, Ont., 1937. Ont. NDP leader; Cdn UN ambassador.

LEWIS, Wilfrid Bennett, science. Eng., 1908–87. Physicist; prime role in developing CANDU reactor.

LEYRAC, Monique, performing arts. Montreal, Que., 1928. Actress; popular Quebec chanteuse.

LIGHTFOOT, Gordon Meredith, performing arts. Orillia, Ont., 1938. Singer/songwriter; popular vocalist with many hits. "Canadian Railroad Trilogy."

LILIENSTEIN, Lois, performing arts. USA, 1936. Member of children's musical entertainment group Sharon, Lois and Bram; live and on TV. *The Elephant Show.*

LILLIE, Beatrice Gladys, performing arts. Toronto, Ont., 1894–1989. Stage comedienne. *Auntie Mame.*

LINDER, Cec, performing arts. Poland, 1921–92. Television, stage and film character actor. *Goldfinger; A Touch of Class; The Edge of Night.*

LINDROS, Eric, sports. London, Ont., 1973. Hockey player; centre for Philadelphia Flyers; winner of Hart Trophy, 1995.

LINDSAY, Robert Blake Theodore (Ted), sports. Renfrew, Ont., 1925. Hockey player; left winger 17 seasons with Detroit and Chicago.

LINKLETTER, Art (b. Arthur Brown), performing arts. Moose Jaw, Sask., 1912. Radio/TV host. *People Are Funny.*

LISMER, Arthur, visual arts. Eng., 1885–1969. Painter; Group of Seven founding member. *September Gale.*

LITTLE, Jean, literary arts. Taiwan, 1932. Popular writer of children's literature, poetry; blends themes of alienation and troubled relationships. *From Anna; Mama's Going to Buy You a Mockingbird; His Banner Over Me.*

LITTLE, Richard Carruthers (Rich), performing arts. Ottawa, Ont., 1938. Impersonator; night club and television performer.

LIVESAY, Dorothy, literary arts. Winnipeg, Man., 1909–96. Poet; sensitive feminist writer. *Poems for People.*

LOATES, Glen Martin, visual arts. Toronto, Ont., 1945. Wildlife artist; painter and naturalist.

LOCKHART, Gene, performing arts. London, Ont., 1891–1957. Character actor appeared in *Miracle on 34th Street, Carousel,* and on Broadway. Father of actress June Lockhart.

LOGAN, William Edmond (Sir), science. Montreal, Que., 1798–1875. Geologist; first head of Geological Survey of Canada; first to map Laurentian Shield.

LOMBARDI, Johnny, business. Toronto, Ont., 1915. Pioneer broadcaster whose CHIN Radio in Toronto, Ont., became first multicultural broadcasting voice in Ontario.

LOMBARDO, Gaetano Alberto "Guy", performing arts. London, Ont., 1902–77. Bandleader; his Royal Canadians most popular band in N America; 300 million records sold. Also won International World Cup in speed boating in 1946; US champion 1946–49; Canadian title in 1955, 1956.

LONGBOAT, Thomas Charles, sports. Brantford, Ont., 1887–1949. Runner; set record in 1907 Boston Marathon.

LONGDEN, John (Johnny), sports. Eng., 1910. Jockey; first N American with 4,000 winners (career: 6,032).

LORD, Bernard, politics. Moncton, NB, 1965. PC premier of NB, elected in 1999.

LORTIE, Louis, performing arts. Montreal, Que., 1959. Pianist; five-time winner of Canadian Music Competition, 1968–72, 1990 Juno for Best Classical Album.

LOUGHEED, Edgar Peter, politics. Calgary, Alta, 1928. PC premier of Alberta, 1971–85; played strong role in federal politics.

LOVELL, Jocelyn, sports. Eng., 1950. Canada's leading cyclist 1970–83; winner of 1000 m silver medal in 1978 world championships; paralysed in training accident 1983.

LOWRY, (Clarence) Malcolm, literary arts. Eng., 1909–57. British novelist whose powerful novels reflected his turbulent life; lived in BC 1937–54. *Under the Volcano.*

LUBA (b. Luba Kowalchyk), performing arts. Montreal, Que., 1958. Pop singer-songwriter. "Between the Earth and Sky"; "All or Nothing."

LUND, Alan, performing arts. Toronto, Ont., 1927–92. Dancer/choreographer. With wife Blanche Harris performed as an Astaire/Rogers-style dancing team; Stratford Festival, Charlettetown Festival.

LUNDSTROM, Linda, business. Red Lake, Ont., 1951. Founder of fashion business with boutiques across North America; her signature LaParka has long been her Canadian culture statement, as are her all-Canadian made clothes.

M

MacDONALD, Flora Isabel, politics. Sydney, NS, 1926. First woman to hold senior cabinet post; external affairs in Clark govt (1979).

MacDONALD, James Edward Hervey (J.E.H.), visual arts. Eng., 1874–1932. Landscape painter; Group of Seven founder. *Mist Fantasy.*

MacDONALD, James Williamson Galloway (Jock), visual arts. Scot., 1897–1960. Early abstract painter; member, Painters Eleven.

MACDONALD, John Alexander (Sir), politics. Scot., 1815–91. Canada's first official prime minister.

MacDOUGALL, Fraser, media. Stratford, Ont., 1907–2000. Longtime journalism figure; Ottawa bureau chief for Canadian Press; active on Ontario Press Council; chairman of Michener journalism awards.

MacEACHEN, Allan Joseph, politics. Inverness, NS, 1921. Liberal MP, portfolios in finance, external affairs; deputy MP in Trudeau government.

MacEWEN, Gwendolyn, literary arts. Toronto, Ont., 1941–87. Poet. *The Shadow-Maker.*

MacGILL, Elizabeth "Elsie" Muriel Gregory, science. Vancouver, BC, 1905–80. Designer of Maple Leaf Trainer aircraft during WWII; designed winterized version of Hawker Hurricane fighter plane.

MacGREGOR, Roy, literary arts. Whitney, Ont., 1948. Novelist, columnist. *Home Game: Hockey and Life in Canada; The Last Season.*

MacGUIGAN, Mark Rudolph, politics. Charlettetown, PEI, 1931–98. Liberal politician who served with Pierre Trudeau, ran unsuccessfully for leader in 1984, later appointed judge of the Federal Court of Appeal. Founding member of the Canadian Civil Liberties Association.

MacISAAC, Ashley, performing arts. Antigonish, NS, 1975. Eclectic musician who blends pop music with traditional Celtic sound. *How Are You Today?; Fine Thank You Very Much.*

MACKENZIE, Alexander, politics. Scot., 1822–1892. Canada's second prime minister.

MacKENZIE, Alexander (Sir), exploration and discovery. Scot., 1764–1820. Charted MacKenzie R. (1789); crossed from L. Athabasca to Pacific Ocean (1793).

MacKENZIE, Maj.-Gen. Lewis W., military. Truro, NS, 1940. Soldier; led UN soldiers from 33 nations (incl. Canada) in opening Sarajevo airport for delivery of humanitarian aid during Bosnian civil war.

MacKENZIE, William Lyon, politics. Scot., 1795–1861. Led 1837 rebellion for reform in Upper Canada; Toronto's first mayor.

MacLEAN, John Angus, politics. Lewes, PEI, 1914–2000. Premier PEI 1979-81; instigator of equalization payments for troubled Atlantic fisheries.

MACLEAN, John Bayne, media. Crieff, Ont., 1862–1950. Founder of *Maclean's* magazine in 1905; also of *Financial Post, Chatelaine.*

MacLEAN, Steven Glenwood, science. Ottawa, Ont., 1954. Laser physicist who trained with NASA's astronaut program, specializes with NASA's robotics branch.

MacLENNAN, John Hugh, literary arts. Glace Bay, NS, 1907–90. Respected Canadian novelist. *The Watch That Ends the Night.*

MacLEOD, Alistair, literary arts. North Battleford, Sask., 1936. Short story writer, novelist; his Cape Breton saga, *No Great Mischief,* winner of Trillium Book Award. *Island: The Collected Stories.*

MacLEOD, John James Rickard, medicine. Scot., 1876–1935. Medical researcher, co-winner with Drs. Banting and Best of Nobel Prize in 1923 for discovery of insulin.

MacMILLAN, Ernest Campbell (Sir), performing arts. Mimico, Ont., 1893–1973. Renowned conductor, composer, arranger; championed Canadian works.

MacMILLAN, Harvey Reginald (H.R.), business. Newmarket, Ont., 1885–1976: Industrialist; established forerunner of logging giant MacMillan Bloedel.

MacNAUGHTON, Andrew George Latta, military. Moosomin, NWT, 1887–1966. Soldier; led Cdn army in WWII; endorsed Dieppe raid; diplomat; UN Atomic Energy Assn.

MacNEIL, Rita, performing arts. Big Pond, NS, 1944. Cape Breton country singer; star of CBC's *Rita MacNeil Show.*

MacNEIL, Robert Breckenridge Ware, media. Toronto, Ont., 1932. TV host, newscaster, reporter, co-hosted public television series in USA, *MacNeil-Lehrer Newshour.*

MacNUTT, Walter, performing arts. Charlettetown, PEI, 1910–96. Composer of orchestral, chamber, choral, vocal, and keyboard music; noted for compositions for Anglo-Catholic service.

MACPHAIL, Agnes Campbell, politics. Proton Twp, Ont., 1890–1954. Only woman MP in 1921 (first women's vote); founded Elizabeth Fry Society.

MacPHERSON, Cluny, invention. St John's, Nfld, 1879–1966. Invented the gas helmet.

MacPHERSON, Duncan, visual arts. Toronto, Ont., 1925–93. Long-time *Toronto Star* cartoonist.

MAGEE, Helen Gagan, journalism. Toronto, Ont., 1908–98. Author and food writer for the Toronto *Globe and Mail* and former *Telegram.*

MAGNUSSEN, Karen Diane, sports. North Vancouver, BC, 1952. Figure skater; world champion, 1973.

MAHOVLICH, Francis William, sports. Timmins, Ont., 1938. Toronto Maple Leaf hockey player, 1957–68; winner of Calder Trophy, 1958.

MAILLET, Antonine, literary arts. Buctouche, NB, 1929. Novelist of Acadian life. Winner of France's *La Prix Goncourt. La Sagouine.*

MAISONNEUVE, Paul de Chomedey, Sieur de, politics. France, 1612–76. Founder of Montreal, 1642.

MAITLAND, (Herbert) Alan, performing arts. Lilburn, Ont., 1920–99. Long-running CBC radio host noted for his rich, resonant voice; appeared on *Maitland Manor, Read to Me* and most notably, *As It Happens,* with co-hosts Barbara Frum and Michael Enright, among others, from 1974–93.

MAK, Tak Wah, medicine. China, 1946. Research led him to discover the T-cell receptor, crucial to understanding the human immune system.

MANDEL, Howie, performing arts. Toronto, Ont., 1955. Manic comic and TV actor. *St Elsewhere.*

MANGUEL, Alberto Adrian, literary arts. Argentina, 1948. Critic, anthologist, novelist. *News from a Foreign Country; The Oxford Book of Canadian Ghost Stories.*

MANLEY, Elizabeth, sports. Belleville, Ont., 1965. Figure skater; silver medal, 1988 Olympics.

MANLEY, John, politics. Ottawa, Ont., 1950. Liberal MP; minister of foreign affairs; former minister of industry.

MANNING, Ernest Charles, politics. Carnduff, Sask., 1908–96. Alberta's Social Credit premier 1943–68; father of Reform Party leader Preston Manning.

MANNING, Ernest Preston, politics. Edmonton, Alta, 1942. Led Reform Party to breakthrough in 1993 federal election; leader to 2000.

MANNING, Thomas Henry, exploration and discovery. Eng., 1911–98. Mapmaker who charted vast territories of the Arctic; also biologist and naturalist focusing on Arctic environment.

MANSBRIDGE, Peter, media. Eng., 1948. Broadcaster; anchorman, CBC national news.

MANSOURI, Lotfallah (Lotfi), performing arts. Iran, 1929. Former general director of Canadian Opera Company; creator of "surtitles", English translations of opera house librettos screened above stage.

MARCHAND, Leonard Stephen, politics. Vernon, BC, 1933. Native politician; first native federal cabinet minister.

MARCHILDON, Philip Edward, sports. Penetanguishene, Ont., 1913. Began career with Philadelphia Athletics in 1940; won 68 major league games before retirement in 1950.

MARCUS, Egerton, sports. Guyana, 1919–65. Boxer; silver medalist, middleweight category in 1988 Olympics.

MARCUS, Rudolph A., science. Montreal, Que., 1923. Winner of 1992 Nobel Prize in chemistry for work on electron transfer reactions in chemical systems.

MARGISON, Richard, performing arts. Victoria, BC, 1953. Tenor opera singer whose repertoire includes Verdi, Puccini and Bizet; international reputation.

MARIE-VICTORIN, Frère, science. Kingsley Falls, Que., 1885–1944. Distinguished botanist, author of *Croquis laurentiens; Les filicinée de Québec.*

MARK, J. Carson, science. Lindsay, Ont., 1913–97. Head of theoretical division of Los Alamos Scientific Library, influence in creation of hydrogen bomb.

MARQUETTE, Jacques, exploration and discovery. France, 1637–75. Jesuit priest explored North America with Louis Jolliet; served at Sault Ste Marie, 1666.

MARSHALL, Amanda, performing arts. Toronto, Ont., 1964. Singer, songwriter with powerful voice. "Birmingham."

MARSHALL, Donald, law. Sydney, NS, 1953. Acquitted of murder after serving 11 years in prison.

MARSHALL, Lois Catherine, performing arts. Toronto, Ont., 1924–97. Soprano, career began with Sir Ernest MacMillan's Bach's *St Matthew's Passion* with Mendelssohn Choir and Toronto Symphony; Toronto Arts Award for Music, 1989.

MARSHALL, Phyllis, performing arts. Barrie, Ont., 1921–96. Jazz singer; pioneer among black Canadian performers; performed with Cab Calloway, Percy Faith; 1949–52 on CBC radio's *Blues for Friday.*

MARTIN, Andrea, performing arts. USA, 1947. Stage, television and film actor particularly well known for comic roles in *SCTV* series.

MARTIN, Clara Brett, law. Toronto, Ont., 1874–1923. First woman lawyer in British Empire.

MARTIN, Paul Edgar Philippe, politics. Windsor, Ont., 1938. Liberal minister of finance.

MARTIN, Paul Joseph James, politics. Ottawa, Ont., 1903–92. Long-time Liberal cabinet minister.

MARTINI, Paul, sports. Weston, Ont., 1960. Figure skater; world pairs champion (with Barbara Underhill), 1984.

MASON, Roger Burford, literary arts. Eng., 1943–98. Editor and writer, short stories: *The Beaver Picture & Other Stories;* biography of John Evans, who devised a Cree alphabet (*Travels in the Shining Island*); and a biography of artist Franz Johnson.

MASSE, Marcel, politics. St-Jean-de-Matha, Que., 1936. Leader of Union Nationale 1966–70; later minister of communications; national defense in PC federal government.

MASSEY, Charles Vincent, politics. Toronto, Ont., 1887–1967. First Canadian-born governor general, 1952–59.

MASSEY, Hart Almerrin, business. Haldemand Twp, Ont., 1823–96. Capitalist; developed Massey-Ferguson Ltd.

MASSEY, Raymond Hart, performing arts. Toronto, Ont., 1896–1983. Craggy-faced actor often played Lincoln. *Dr. Kildare.*

MASSON, Henri Leopold, visual arts. Belgium, 1907–96. Paintings of city and landscapes in the 1940s; National Gallery.

MAXWELL, Lois (b. Lois Ruth Hooker), performing arts. Kitchener, Ont., 1927. Actress, columnist. Played character Moneypenny in James Bond movie series from 1963–83. Former columnist for Toronto *Sun.*

MAYER, Louis B. (Burt) (b. Eliezer Mayer), performing arts. Russia, 1885–1957. Grew up in Saint John, NB; with Samuel Goldwyn formed MGM movie studio in 1924; co-founded the Academy of Motion Picture Arts and Sciences in 1927.

McBEAN, Marnie, sports. Toronto, Ont., 1968. With Kathleen Heddle won women's double sculls rowing medals: two gold in 1992 Barcelona Olympics; one gold, one bronze in 1996 Olympics in Atlanta.

McBRIDE, Robert Bruce (Bob), performing arts. Toronto, Ont., 1946–98. Juno–award-winning lead singer of the 1970s rock band Lighthouse.

McCAIN, H. Harrison, business. Florenceville, NB, 1927. Industrialist; turned potato-processing plant into international firm.

McCARTHY, Doris, visual arts. Calgary, Alta, 1910. Artist, calligrapher, more than 90 solo exhibitions.

McCLELLAND, John Gordon (Jack), literary arts. Toronto, Ont., 1922. Publisher; his McClelland & Stewart nurtured Canadian writing; over 5,000 Canadian titles.

McCLUNG, Nellie Letitia, law. Chatsworth, Ont., 1873–1951. Reformer; fought for women's suffrage.

McCONNELL, Robert Murray Gordon, performing arts. London, Ont., 1935. Jazz musician; founded Boss Brass, major big band.

McCRAE, John, literary arts. Guelph, Ont., 1872–1918. Poet; physician who wrote "In Flanders Field."

McCULLOCH, Bruce Ian, performing arts. Edmonton, Alta, 1961. Versatile comedic actor, director, writer.

McCURDY, Edward Potts, performing arts. USA, 1919–2000. Folk singer, played in Ontario's Mariposa Folk Festival; noted for his huge repertoire of folk music that reflected the cultural history of Canada, specializing in Maritimes music.

McCURDY, Howard Douglas, politics. London, Ont., 1932. Black activist; also biologist.

McCURDY, John Alexander Douglas, exploration and discovery. Baddeck, NS, 1886–1961. Pilot; first airplane flight in British Empire in Silver Dart (1909).

McDERMOTT, Dennis, business. Eng., 1922. Labour leader; former president, Canadian Labour Congress.

McDONALD, Bruce, performing arts. Kingston, Ont., 1959. Film director. *Roadkill; Highway 61; Dance Me Outside.*

McDOUGALL, Barbara Jean, politics. Toronto, Ont., 1937. PC external affairs minister 1991–93; political commentator and journalist.

McELCHERAN, William, visual arts. Hamilton, Ont., 1927–99. Internationally renowned sculptor; designer of ACTRA's Nellie award; famous for bronze "Everyman" sculptures depicting burly businessmen in striking poses.

McEWEN, Jean Albert, visual arts. Montreal, Que., 1923–99. "Nonfigurative" artist inspired by Riopelle, French Impressionists and American abstract artists.

McFARLANE, Leslie (F. W. Dixon), literary arts. Ottawa, Ont., 1903–77 Author of *Hardy Boys* adventure series.

McFARLENE, Todd, literary arts. Calgary, Alta, 1961. Creator of cult comic book *Spawn;* the first issue in 1992 was best-selling independent comic at 1.7 million copies sold.

McGARRIGLE, Anna and Kate, performing arts. Montreal, Que., 1944, 1946. Songwriters/ singers. Unique duo sings folk, own compositions. "Love Over and Over."

McGEE, Thomas D'Arcy, politics. Ire., 1825–68. Eloquent proponent of Confederation; assassinated 1868.

McGIBBON, Pauline Emily, politics. Sarnia, Ont., 1910. Cda's first woman lieutenant-governor (Ont., 1974).

McINTOSH, John, invention. USA, 1777–1845. Inventor; breeder of McIntosh apple.

McKELLAR, Don, performing arts. Filmmaker, screenwriter, actor. *Thirty Two Short Films About Glenn Gould; Last Night.* Toronto, Ont., 1963.

McKENNA, Frank Joseph, politics. Apolaqui, NB, 1948. Liberal premier of NB 1987–97.

McKENNA, Patrick Ivan Peter, performing arts. Hamilton, Ont., 1960. Comic actor played Harold on *Red Green Show.* Also on drama series *Traders.*

McKENNITT, Loreena, performing arts. Morden, Man., 1957. Singer; harpist; Celtic music repertoire.

McKENZIE, Robert Tait, visual arts. Almonte, Ont., 1867–1938. Sculptor, orthopedic surgeon; designer of war memorials, sculptures.

McKINNEY, Louise, politics. Frankville, Ont., 1868–1931. First woman in Commonwealth to serve as an MLA (Alberta, 1917), the first year women could vote and run for office.

McKINNON, Catherine, performing arts. Saint John, NB, 1944. Singer, actress. Appeared in CBC's *Don Messer's Jubilee; Spring Thaw* revue; *The Catherine McKinnon Show;* Charlottetown Festival. Married to actor/humorist Don Harron.

McKOY, Mark, sports. Guyana, 1961. Hurdler; gold medal, 110 m hurdles, 1992 Olympics.

McLACHLAN, Beverly, public service. Pincher Creek, Alta, 1943. Former BC Chief Justice of Supreme Court; in January 2000 became Chief Justice of Supreme Court of Canada.

McLACHLAN, Sara, performing arts. Halifax, NS, 1968. Singer-songwriter of pop music. *Surfacing.*

McLAREN, Norman, visual arts. Scot., 1914–87. Filmmaker; innovative NFB animator. *Pas de deux.*

McLARNIN, Jimmy, sports. Ire., 1907. Boxer; world welterweight champion, 1933–35.

McLAUCHLAN, Murray Edward, performing arts. Scot., 1948. Country performer; *Swingin' on a Star,* CBC Radio (1990); seven-time Juno award winner.

McLAUGHLIN, Audrey, politics. Dutton, Ont., 1936. NDP national leader 1989–95. First woman to lead a national party.

McLAUGHLIN, Robert Samuel (Col.), business. Enniskillen, Ont., 1871–1972. Industrialist; founded firm that became General Motors of Canada.

McLEAN, Stuart, media. Montreal, Que., 1948. Broadcaster on CBC's *Morningside; Vinyl Café;* author of *Welcome Home: Travels in Small Town Canada.*

McLUHAN, Herbert Marshall, media. Edmonton, Alta, 1911–80. Media theorist; developed theory about "hot" and "cool" media. *The Gutenburg Galaxy.*

McMURTRY, Roland Roy, politics. Toronto, Ont., 1932. Chief Justice of Ontario Court of Justice.

McNAUGHTON, Andrew George Latta, military. Moosomin, NWT, 1887–1966. Army officer, scientist, as chief of general staff of Armed Forces 1929–35 began modernization of nonpermanent militia; 1935–39 president of National Research Council of Canada.

McNAUGHTON, Duncan Anderson, sports. Cornwall, Ont., 1910. High jumper; 1932 Olympic high jump gold medal.

McPHERSON, Aimee Semple, religion. Ingersoll, Ont., 1890–1944. Controversial evangelist.

McPHERSON, Donald, sports. Windsor, Ont., 1945. World professional champion figure skater, 1965.

McTAGGART, David, environment. Vancouver, BC, 1932–2001. Co-founder of environmental protectionist organization Greenpeace International. McTaggart came to prominence when protesting French nuclear testing in 1972 in Polynesia; the French rammed his boat and testing was postponed.

MEAGHER, Blanche Margaret, public service. Halifax, NS, 1911–99. Canada's first woman ambassador beginning in 1942, Meagher was posted in various locations: Mexico, Israel, Sweden, Uganda and London.

MEHTA, Deepa, Award-winning film director, producer and screenwriter. *Sam and Me; Camilla; Fire.* India, 1950.

MEIGHEN, Arthur, politics. Anderson, Ont., 1874–1960. Succeeded Sir Robert Borden as prime minister of Canada.

MEILLEUR, Marie Louise Febronie Chasse, Kamouraska, Que., 1880–1998. Recognized in 1997 as the world's oldest person, lived in rural Ontario for most of her life.

MERCER, Ruby, performing arts. USA, 1906–99. Former opera singer who debuted at New York's Metropolitan Opera in 1936, Mercer was instrumental in the development of Canadian opera; founder of *Opera Canada* magazine, Canadian Children's Opera Chorus and host of CBC radio's *Opera Time* and *Opera in Stereo.*

MERCREDI, Ovide William, politics. Grand Rapids, Man., 1946. National chief of the Assembly of First Nations, 1991–2000.

MERRIL, Judith, literary arts. USA, 1923–97. Science fiction writer, novelist, editor, short story writer, critic. *Survival Ship and Other Stories; Daughters of the Earth and Other Stories.*

MESSER, Donald Charles Frederick (Don), performing arts. Tweedside, NB, 1909–73. Bandleader; popular maker of traditional fiddle and dance music. *Don Messer's Jubilee.*

METCALF, John Wesley, literary arts. Eng., 1938. Essayist; short story writer. *Going Down Slow; Private Parts: A Memoir; Adult Entertainment.*

MICHAELS, Lorne (b. Lorne Lipowitz), media. Toronto, Ont., 1945. TV producer; founding producer, *Saturday Night Live.*

MICHENER, Daniel Roland, politics. Lacombe, Alta, 1900–91. Governor general of Canada, 1967–74.

MIKITA, Stan (b. Stanislaus Gvoth), sports. Czech., 1940. Hockey player; centre with Chicago Blackhawks (1959–80); first Czech to play in NHL.

MILLAR, Ian D., sports. Halifax, NS, 1947. Eight-time Canadian show-jumping champian, Cdn Athlete of the Year, 1987, 1989.

MILLAR, Margaret, literary arts. Kitchener, Ont., 1915. Thriller writer. *Beast in View.*

MILLS, Frank, performing arts. Montreal, Que., 1942. Pianist, composer; early career was member of pop group The Bells; solo career on TV and the concert stage. "Love Me Love Me Love"; "Music Box Dancer."

MILNE, David Brown, visual arts. Paisley, Ont., 1882–1953. Versatile painter. *Raspberry Jam.*

MILNER, Brenda, science. Eng., 1915. Neuropsychologist; ground-breaking brain researcher.

MINER, John Thomas (Jack), science. USA, 1865–1944. Conservationist; pioneered bird sanctuaries, migratory banding.

MIRVISH, Edwin (Ed) (b. Yehudi Mirvish), business. USA, 1914. Entrepreneur; retailer (Honest Ed's) and theatre owner.

MISTRY, Rohinton, literary arts. India, 1952. Novelist, short story writer. *Such a Long Journey; A Fine Balance.*

MITCHELL, Joni (b. Roberta Joan Anderson), performing arts. Ft Macleod, Alta, 1943. Singer/songwriter; influential lyricist. *Court and Spark.*

MITCHELL, Ray, sports. Peace River, Alta, 1931. Bowler; winner of 1972 Canadian and world 10-pin championship.

MITCHELL, William Ormond (W.O.), literary arts. Weyburn, Sask., 1914–98. Prairie novelist. *Who Has Seen the Wind?*

MOLSON, John, business. Eng., 1764–1836. Founded Molson brewery; built railroads.

MONTCALM DE SAINT VERAN, Louis Joseph de Montcalm Grozon, military. France, 1712–59. Soldier; French commander in Seven Years War; died on Plains of Abraham.

MONTGOMERY, Lucy Maud, literary arts. Clifton, PEI, 1874–1942. Writer; creator of *Anne of Green Gables.*

MONTGOMERY, Robert Douglas, performing arts. Bradford, Ont., 1908–66. Movie actor, played Laurie in 1933 version of *Little Women* opposite Katharine Hepburn.

MOODIE, Susanna, literary arts. Eng., 1803–85. Writer; pioneer author of *Roughing It in the Bush.*

MOORE, Brian, literary arts. N Ire., 1921–99. Prolific novelist; winner of two Governor General's Awards. *The Luck of Ginger Coffey; Black Robe.*

MOORE, Dora Mavor, performing arts. Scotland, 1888–1979. Actress appeared in Canada and US; founded Village Players in 1938 in Toronto, Ont.; toured schools. *Spring Thaw.*

MOORE, Gregory William, sports. Vancouver, BC, 1975–99. Four time winner of Championship Auto Racing Teams (CART) circuit; died in Marlboro 500 race in California.

MOORE, James Mavor, literary arts. Toronto, Ont., 1919. TV producer; librettist; columnist; critic.

MOORES, Frank Duff, politics. Carbonear, Nfld, 1933. PC premier of Newfoundland, 1972–79.

MORANIS, Rick, performing arts. Toronto, Ont., 1953. Comedian; actor; *SCTV* regular. *Ghostbusters.*

MORAWETZ, Oskar, performing arts. Czech., 1917. Composer. *From the Diary of Anne Frank.*

MORENZ, Howarth Williams (Howie), sports. Mitchell, Ont., 1902–37. Hockey player; centre; Canada's player of half century (CP), 1950; died of on-ice injuries.

MORGAN, Henry, business. Scotland, 1819–93. In 1852 Morgan founded a dry goods store in Montreal, which by 1950 became the national chain Henry Morgan & Co.; merged with Hudson's Bay Company in 1960.

MORGAN, John, performing arts. Wales. Comedian who appears on CBC's *Royal Canadian Air Farce,* roles include Jock McBile and Mike from Canmore.

MORGENTALER, Henry, medicine. Poland, 1923. Physician; challenge of abortion laws led to Supreme Court ruling them unconstitutional.

MORISSETTE, Alanis Nadine, performing arts. Ottawa, Ont., 1974. Singer-songwriter. Juno award winner 1996 for *Jagged Little Pill* (Best Album) and Female Vocalist of the Year; Grammy Award winner, 1996.

MORIYAMA, Raymond, visual arts. Vancouver, BC, 1929. Architect; Ontario Science Centre.

MORRICE, James Wilson (J.W.), visual arts. Montreal, Que., 1864–1924. Artist; early modernist. *The Ice Bridge.*

MORRIS, Alwyn, sports. Montreal, Que., 1957. With Hugh Fisher won gold medal in 1000 m and bronze in 500 m kayak doubles at 1984 Olympics.

MORRIS, Joseph (Joe), politics. Eng., 1913–96. Former president of Canadian Labour Congress; chairman of International Labour Organization.

MORRISON, Bram, performing arts. Toronto, Ont., 1940. Member of children's musical entertainment group Sharon, Lois and Bram; live and on TV. *The Elephant Show.*

MORRISSEAU, Norval, visual arts. Sand Point Reserve, Ont., 1932. Ojibway artist originated pictographic style.

MORSE, Barry, performing arts. Eng., 1918. Stage/film/TV actor; regular on *The Fugitive.*

MORTON, William Lewis (W.L.), literary arts. Gladstone, Man., 1908–80. Historian. *Manitoba: A History.*

MOSS, Carrie-Anne, performing arts. Vancouver, BC, 1967. Model turned actress who has appeared in *Dark Justice* TV series, as well as *Matrix; Models Inc.,* and *F/X The Series.*

MOWAT, Claire Angel, literary arts. Toronto, Ont., 1933. Graphic artist, fiction writer, wife of writer Farley Mowat. *The Girl From Away; The Outport People; The French Isles.*

MOWAT, Farley McGill, literary arts. Belleville, Ont., 1921. Controversial, popular naturalist writer. *A Whale for the Killing.*

MOWAT, Oliver (Sir), politics. Kingston, UC, 1820–1903. Ontario premier, 1872–96; lieutenant-governor, 1897–1903.

MUKHERJEE, Bharati, literary arts. India, 1940. Novelist, *The Middleman and Other Stories; Jasmine.*

MULRONEY, Brian Martin, politics. Baie Comeau, Que., 1939. Prime minister of Canada 1984–93.

MUNDELL, Robert, business. Kingston, Ont., 1932. Winner of 1999 Nobel Prize for economics for 1960s study of exchange rates and their relationship to monetary policy.

MUNK, Peter, business. Hungary, 1927. Capitalist; CEO, American Barrick Resources gold mining company.

MUNRO, Alice, literary arts. Wingham, Ont., 1931. Short story writer. Winner of 1998 Giller prize. *Lives of Girls and Women.*

MUNSCH, Robert, literary arts. USA, 1945. Children's writer. *The Paper Bag Princess; Love You Forever.*

MURPHY, Emily Cowan, law. Cookstown, Ont., 1868–1933. Legal reformer; first woman magistrate in British Empire; fought for women's rights.

MURPHY, Rex, media. Carbonear, Nfld, 1947. CBC news journalist with acerbic style. *Cross Country Checkup.*

MURRAY, Anne, performing arts. Springhill, NS, 1945. Singer; Canada's most successful performer; many Junos and Grammys. "Snowbird."

MURRAY, George Henry, politics. Grand Narrows, NS, 1861–1929. Lib. premier of NS, 1896–1923.

MURRAY, John Wilson, law. Scot., 1840–1906. Detective; pioneered scientific crime detection.

MURRAY, Margaret Teresa "Ma", media. USA, 1888–1982. Journalist; pungent editorialist in own magazines.

MURRAY, Robert George Everitt, science. Eng., 1919. With Philip Fitz-Jones, researched structure and chemical nature of bacterial tissues.

MUSGRAVE, Susan, literary arts. USA, 1951. Poet, novelist, children's writer. *The Embalmer's Art: Poems; The Charcoal Burners.*

MUSTARD, James Fraser, medicine. Toronto, Ont., 1927. Physician; medical humanitarian; found connection between aspirin and blood clotting.

MUSTARD, William, medicine. Clinton, Ont., 1914–87. Physician; beloved children's surgeon developed operations for blue babies, polio cripples.

MYERS, Barton, visual arts. USA, 1934. Architect. Seagram Museum in Waterloo, Ont.; U of Toronto's Woodsworth College; UCLA Northwest Commons and Housing; Housing Union Building, U of Alta.

MYERS, Mike, performing arts. Toronto, Ont., 1963. Comic actor has appeared in movies *Austin Powers; It's a Dog's Life; Wayne's World,* also appeared on *Saturday Night Live.*

MYLES, Alannah, performing arts. Toronto, Ont., 1958. Pop singer/composer of hard rock, ballads. "Lover of Mine"; *Black Velvet; Al-Lan-Nah.*

NAISMITH, James A., sports. Almonte, Ont., 1861–1939. Physician; invented basketball in 1891.

NAKAMURA, Kazio, visual arts. Vancouver, BC, 1926. Japanese-Canadian artist who was interned during World War II; a member of Painters Eleven group, he represents the chaos of the universe through abstracts, landscapes and surreal images.

NAMARO, James (Jimmy), performing arts. USA, 1913–98. A member of the CBC's *Happy Gang,* the longest-running program on the radio network; also led his own jazz band.

NANOGAK, Agnes, visual arts. Baillie I., NWT, 1925. Inuit artist whose prints depict Inuit myths and legends, operating out of Holman I. Artist co-op. Illustrated *Tales from the Igloo.*

NASH, Cyril Knowlton, media. Toronto, Ont., 1927. Broadcaster; former anchorman, CBC national news.

NATTRASS, Susan Marie, sports. Medicine Hat, Alta, 1950. Shooter; six women's world trapshooting titles.

NAULT, Fernand (b. Fernand-Noel Boissonneault), performing arts. Montreal, Que., 1921. Dancer; choreographer, Les Grands Ballets Canadiens.

NELLIGAN, Emile, literary arts. Montreal, Que., 1879–1941. Romantic poet. "Romance du Vin."

NELLIGAN, Kate, performing arts. London, Ont., 1951. Actor; appears on both stage and film. *Eleni.*

NEMETZ, Nathaniel "Sonny", law. Winnipeg, Man., 1913–97. Chief Justice of British Columbia 1979–88, leading judicial administrator in BC.

NEVILLE, John, performing arts. Eng., 1925. Actor, director. Stratford Festival, Ont.; director of Stratford's The Young Company.

NEWMAN, Peter Charles, media. Austria, 1929. Journalist; popular historian. *The Canadian Establishment, Maclean's* editor, 1971–82.

NEWTON, Margaret, science. Montreal, Que., 1887–1971. Plant pathologist; first scientist to research rust in wheat.

NICHOL, Barrie Phillip (bp), literary arts. Vancouver, BC, 1944–88. Concrete and sound poet, novelist. *Journeying and Returns; Love: A Book of Remembrance.*

NICHOL, Dave, business. Chatham, Ont., 1940. Made Loblaws stores market leader with President's Choice label.

NICHOLAS, Cynthia (Cindy), sports. Toronto, Ont., 1957. Marathon swimmer; first woman to swim English Channel both ways.

NICOL, Eric, media. Kingston, Ont., 1919. Humour columnist. "Girdle Me a Globe."

NIELSEN, Erik Hersholt, politics. Regina, Sask., 1924. PC MP elected in Yukon 1957, served as deputy prime minister in Mulroney government.

NIELSEN, Leslie, performing arts. Regina, Sask., 1926. Deadpan film/TV comedian. *Naked Gun.*

NORQUAY, John, politics. St Andrews, Man., 1841–89. Manitoba premier of mixed European and native ancestry, 1878–87.

NORTHCOTT, Ronald Charles, sports. Innisfail, Alta, 1935. Curler; skipped three Brier and world champion rinks.

NOTMAN, William, Innovative Montreal-based portrait photographer who sent his studio photographers across Canada and the US to record social landscape, recording the growth and character of the continent. Scotland, 1826-91.

NOWLAN, Alden, literary arts. Windsor, NS, 1933–83. Poet. "Bread, Wine and Salt."

O'BRIEN, Mary, public service. Scot., 1926–98. Midwife, philosopher; founding member of the Feminist Party of Canada, wrote *The Politics of Reproduction; Reproducing the World.*

O'HARA, Catherine, performing arts. Toronto, Ont., 1954. Actor; comedian; *SCTV* regular (Lola Heatherton).

O'NEILL, James Edward "Tip", sports. Canada W, 1859–1918. Baseball player; batted .326 in 10-year career.

OAKS, Sir Harry, business. USA, 1874–1943. Oaks made his fortune through hold mine near Swastika, Ont., became North America's second largest gold mine; retired to the Bahamas, victim of unsolved murder.

ODJIG, Daphne, visual arts. Manitoulin Island, Ont., 1919. Blends western and native styles. *The Indian in Transition.*

OKALIK, Paul, politics. Pangnirtung, NWT, 1964. First premier of 19-member Legislative Assembly for Nunavit in the Eastern Arctic, created in 1999.

OLCOTT, Sidney, performing arts. Toronto, Ont., 1873–1949. Director of Hollywood silent films, pioneered locations shots, westerns. *Ben Hur.*

OLIPHANT, Betty, performing arts. Eng., 1918. Founded National Ballet School.

ONDAATJE, Christopher, business/literary arts. Sri Lanka, 1933. Financier; author. *Leopard in the Afternoon.*

ONDAATJE, Michael, literary arts. Sri Lanka, 1943. Poet; editor; novelist. *The English Patient* (Booker Prize).

OONARK, Jessie, visual arts. Back River, NWT, 1906–85. Inuit artist who employed brilliant colours to depict both traditional images and Christian themes in her drawings and wall hangings.

ORBINSKI, James, medicine. England, 1960. President, International Council, for Doctors Without Borders; accepted 1999 Nobel Peace Prize on behalf of the international organization.

ORONHYATEKHA (Peter Martin), business. Six Nations Reserve, Ont., 1841–1907. First native Canadian to receive a degree from a Canadian university; founder of the Independent Order of Foresters, a fraternal life insurance organization.

ORR, Robert Gordon (Bobby), sports. Parry Sound, Ont., 1948. Hockey player; spectacular offensive defenceman; won eight consecutive Norris trophies.

ORSER, Brian Ernest, sports. Belleville, Ont., 1961. Figure skater; 1987 world champion, twice Olympic silver medallist (1984, 1988).

ORTON, George W., sports. Strathroy, Ont., 1873–1958. Runner; Canada's first Olympic gold medallist, winning for USA in 1900 (2500 m steeplechase).

OSGOODE, William, First chief justice of Upper Canada; played key role in development of Canadian legislation. England, 1754–1824.

OSLER, William (Sir), medicine. Bond Head, UC, 1849–1919. Physician; renowned medical educator; author of authoritative textbooks.

OSTANEK, Walter, performing arts. Duparket, Que., 1935. "King of Polka"; popular piano accordionist with more than 60 polka recordings.

OTTENBRITE, Anne, sports. Whitby, Ont., 1966. Swimmer; gold medal, 200 m, 1984 Olympics.

OUIMET, Joseph Alphonse, media. Montreal, Que., 1908–88. TV executive; designed first Canadian TV receiver; CBC president, 1958–67.

P

PACE, Kate, sports. North Bay, Ont., 1969. Skier; World Cup downhill champion, 1993.

PACHTER, Charles, visual arts. Toronto, Ont., 1942. Painter famous for flag series; 1973 acrylic sketch titled *Queen on Moose.*

PAGE, Patricia Kathleen, (P.K.), literary arts. Eng., 1916. Poet; novelist; artist. "The Metal and the Flower."

PANNETON, Philippe (Ringuet), literary arts. Trois-Rivières, Que., 1895–1960. Man of letters; acclaimed Quebec writer. *Trente Arpents.*

PAPINEAU, Louis Joseph, politics. Montreal, Que., 1786–1871. Led political reform movement in Lower Canada.

PARIS, Erna, literary arts. Toronto, Ont., 1938. Writer. *The Garden and the Gun; End of Days.*

PARIZEAU, Jacques, politics. Montreal, Que., 1930. Leader, Parti Québécois 1987–95.

PARKER, Jackie, sports. USA, 1932. Football player; coach; Edmonton Eskimos star quarterback; named CFL outstanding player three times.

PARKER, Jon Kimura, performing arts. Vancouver, BC, 1959. Concert pianist, performed for Queen, prime ministers, and at Carnegie Hall.

PARKIN, John Burnett, visual arts. Toronto, Ont., 1911-75. Partnered with John Cresswell Parkin (no relation) to build major public buildings, including hospitals, schools, airports. Largest firm in Canada in the 1950s and '60s. Union Station (Ottawa), IBM head office (Toronto).

PARROT, Jean-Claude, business. Montreal, Que., 1936. Labour leader; leader of militant postal union.

PARRY, Sir William Edward, Parry's explorations into the Arctic led to the discovery of the North Pole and the charting of the Northwest Passage. England, 1790–1855.

PARTRIDGE, Edward Alexander, business. Canada W, 1862–1931. Farm reformer; visionary in grain industry fought monopolies, started growers' cooperative.

PASSAGLIA, Lui, sports. Vancouver, BC, 1954. Football player; kicker with BC Lions; CFL's all-time scoring leader.

PATRICK, Lester, sports. Drummondville, Que., 1883–1960. Hockey executive; NHL builder.

PATTISON, James Allen, business. Saskatoon, Sask., 1928. Industrialist; developed car dealership into business empire; chairman, Expo 86.

PAUL, Robert, sports. Toronto, Ont., 1937. Figure skater; with Barbara Wagner, won four pairs titles, 1960 Olympic gold.

PAYETTE, Julie, science. Montreal, Que., 1963. Astronaut and mission specialist on crew of STS-96 Atlantis, a 10-day logistics and resupply mission that launched in May 1999.

PAYETTE, Lise, media/politics. Montreal, Que., 1931. Broadcaster, writer, politician; her radio show with Radio-Canada, *Place Aux Femmes*, aired in the 1960s; Parti Québécois MNA1976-80.

PEAKER, Charles, performing arts. Eng., 1899–1978. Organist, choirmaster, writer. Foremost concert organist in Canada. Edited *Organ Music of Canada.*

PEARSON, Lester Bowles, politics. Newtonbrook, Ont., 1897–1972. Prime minister of Canada 1963–1968; awarded Nobel Peace Prize in 1957.

PECKFORD, Alfred Brian, politics. Whitbourne, Nfld, 1942. PC premier of Nfld, 1979–89.

PEEL, Paul, visual arts. London, Ont., 1860–92. Painter famous for *After the Bath*, which depicts two children warming themselves before a fireplace. *The Tired Model; Good News, Toronto.*

PELADEAU, Pierre, media. Outremont, Que., 1925–97. Publisher; head of newspaper giant Quebecor.

PELLAN, Alfred, visual arts. Quebec City, Que., 1906–88. Painter; cubist and surrealist artist.

PELLATT, Henry Mill (Sir), military. Kingston, Canada W, 1860–1939. Soldier; builder of eccentric Toronto mansion, Casa Loma.

PELLETIER, Gerard, politics. Victoriaville, Que., 1919–97. Chief editor for *La Presse* (1961–65); federal deputy minister for Montreal riding of Hochelaga 1965–75. Later ambassador for Canada in Paris and for United Nations.

PENFIELD, Wilder Groves Dr, medicine. USA, 1891–1976. Neurologist; writer; pioneered mapping of brain functions; founded Montreal Neurological Inst.

PENNELL, Nicholas, performing arts. Eng., 1938–95. Former actor at Stratford Festival; starred in British TV series *The Forsyte Saga.*

PENNER, Fredrick Ralph, performing arts. Winnipeg, Man., 1946. Popular children's entertainer; host of CBC TV's *Fred Penner's Place;* former national spokesperson for UNICEF. *Moonlight Express.*

PENTLAND, Barbara Lally, performing arts. Winnipeg, Man., 1912–2000. Celebrated avant-garde composer; noted for anti-tonal style. *Concerto for Piano and String Orchestra.*

PEPIN, Jean-Luc, politics. Drummondville, Que., 1924–95. Longtime Liberal cabinet minister; served on Anti-Inflation Board, co-chairman of 1977 unity task force.

PEPIN, Marcel, politics. Montreal, Que., 1926–2000. Became president of Confederation of National Trade unions in 1965; responsible for uniting public service unions in Quebec and instigator of illegal Common Front Strike of 1972; later head of World Confederation of Labour.

PERCIVAL, Lloyd, sports. Toronto, Ont., 1913–1974. Sports enthusiast; in 1941 founded CBC Radio Sports College; founder of Fitness Institute and coach to many successful athletes.

PERCY, Karen, sports. Edmonton, Alta, 1966. Skier; won two bronze medals, 1988 Olympics.

PERRAULT, Pierre, visual arts. Montreal, Que., 1927. Filmmaker; realist director. *L'Acadie, L'Acadie.*

PETERSON, Eric, performing arts. Indian Head, Sask., 1946. Actor. *Billy Bishop Goes to War;* CBC's *Street Legal* series.

PETERSON, Oscar Emmanuel, performing arts. Montreal, Que., 1925. Jazz pianist; "Canadiana Suite"; over 90 albums.

PETRIE, Daniel, performing arts. Glace Bay, NS, 1920. Film director, won Genie award for *Bay Boy; A Raisin in the Sun.*

PETTIGREW, Pierre, politics. Quebec City, Que., 1951. Liberal MP; minister of international trade; strong federalist voice against Quebec separatism.

PEZER, Vera, sports. Melfort, Sask., 1939. Curler; Canadian women's champion, 1971–73.

PFLUG, Christiane, visual arts. Germany, 1936–72. Painter of melancholy landscapes and domestic scenes. *Cottingham School After the Rain; Kitchen Door with Esther.*

PHILLIPS, Robin, performing arts. Eng., 1942. Director, Stratford Festival, 1975–80, 1986–87.

PICKFORD, Mary (b. Gladys Smith), performing arts. Toronto, Ont., 1893–1979. Actress; "America's Sweetheart" was early movie star. *Sparrows.*

PIDGEON, Walter, performing arts. E Saint John, NB, 1897–1984. Leading man. *Mrs. Miniver.*

PINSENT, Gordon Edward, performing arts. Grand Falls, Nfld, 1930. Versatile actor. *The Rowdyman; Due South.*

PITSEOLAK Ashoona, visual arts. NWT, 1904–83. Artist of Inuit myth and legend.

PITSEOLAK, Peter, visual arts. NWT, 1902–73. Photographer; recorded passing of traditional Inuit life.

PLAMONDON, Antoine, visual arts. Lorette, Que., 1804–95. Portraitist and religious painter.

PLAMONDON, Luc, performing arts. St Raymond-de-Portneuf, Que., 1945. Lyricist; wrote rock opera *Starmania;* collaborated with Britain's Tim Rice; has written songs for Celine Dion.

PLANTE, Jacques, sports. Mt Carmel, Que., 1929–86. Hockey goaltender; seven-time Vezina winner; originated face mask.

PLAUT, Gunther, religion. Germany, 1912. Rabbi (Toronto's Holy Blossom Temple); author; advocate of modern secular Judaism. Wrote *The Torah: A Modern Commentary; The Man Who Would Be Messiah,* a novel.

PLUMMER, Arthur Christopher Orme, performing arts. Toronto, Ont., 1929. Stage and film star. *Murder By Decree.*

POCKINGTON, Peter H., business. Regina, Sask., 1941. Entrepreneur; owner of Edmonton Oilers.

POCOCK, Nancy Meek, philanthropy. USA, 1911–98. Quaker and pacifist, an antiwar and refugee advocate; won the Medal of Friendship from Socialist Republic of Vietnam.

PODBORSKI, Steve, sports. Toronto, Ont., 1957. Skier; world downhill champion, 1982.

POITRAS, Jean-Claude, business. Montreal, Que., 1949. Designer of couture-quality fashion under own label; founder of Fashion Societé Design collections.

POLANYI, John Charles, science. Germany, 1929. Chemist; Nobel Prize (1986) for work on infrared chemiluminescence.

POLLEY, Sarah, performing arts. Toronto, Ont., 1979. Actress; *The Road to Avonlea; The Sweet Hereafter.*

POLLOCK, Sam, sports. Montreal, Que., 1925. Hockey executive; built Montreal Canadiens dynasty.

POLLOCK, Sharon, literary arts. Fredericton, NB, 1936. Playwright; writer of conscience. *Blood Relations.*

PONTIAC, military. USA, 1720?–69. Ottawa Indian chief who formed alliance with various Indian federations to attack English, including a fort at Point Pelee, Ont.; in 1765 key signer of peace treaties with the English.

PORTER, Anna Maria, literary arts. Hungary. Publisher, author. CEO and director of Key Porter Books; mystery writer. *The Bookfair Murders; Mortal Sins.*

POST, Sandra, sports. Oakville, Ont., 1943. Golfer; Canada's first woman touring professional.

POTTS, Jerry (b. Ky-yo-Kosi), military. USA, 1840–96. Native scout; Blackfoot became NWMP special constable.

POTVIN, Dennis, sports. Ottawa, Ont., 1953. Hockey player; as defenceman with New York Islanders (1973–88) all-time leader in goals and assists.

POWELL, Marion, medicine. Toronto, Ont., 1923–97. Former president of Planned Parenthood in Toronto; a pioneer in introducing birth control information in the 1960s.

PRATLEY, Gerald Arthur, performing arts. England, 1923. Film critic; founder of Ontario Film Institute in 1968; CBC's first film critic 1948–75. *Pratley at the Movies.*

PRATT, Edwin James (E.J.), literary arts. Western Bay, Nfld, 1883–1964. Leading pre-WWII poet. "Newfoundland Verse."

PRATT, John Christopher, visual arts. St John's, Nfld, 1935. Artist; developed style of "conceptual realism."

PRATT, Mary, visual arts. Fredericton, NB, 1935. Artist; her paintings portray kitchen imagery and domestic themes. Illustrated Cynthia Wine's *Across the Table: An Indulgent Look at Food in Canada.*

PREVOST, André, performing arts. Hawkesbury, Ont., 1934–2001. Quebec-based composer whose humanistic works included *Terre des Hommes (Man and His World)*; *Cantate pour cordes*; and *Chorégraphie*, which was inspired by the 1972 assassination of Olympic athletes in Munich.

PRIESTLEY, Jason Bradford, performing arts. Vancouver, BC, 1969. Popular actor noted for his brooding looks. *Beverly Hills, 90210.*

PURDY, Alfred Wellington, literary arts. Wooler, Ont., 1918–2000. Working-class poet. "The Cariboo Horses."

Q

QUARRINGTON, Paul Lewis, literary arts. Toronto, Ont., 1953. Governor General's Award for Fiction, 1990. *Home Game; Whale Music.*

QUILICO, Louis, performing arts. Montreal, Que., 1925–2000. Operatic baritone; appeared with most major companies.

R

RADDAL, Thomas Head, literary arts. Eng., 1903–94. Governor General's Award winning historical novelist. *The Pied Piper of Dipper Creek and Other Tales; His Majesty's Yankees.*

RADISSON, Pierre Esprit, exploration and discovery. France, 1636–1710. Explorer; fur trader; important in early history of Hudson's Bay Co as guide and advisor.

RAE, John, Explorer who found evidence of Sir John Franklin's fated expedition in the Canadian north; surveyor for the Hudson's Bay Company, charting northern regions and western Canada. Orkney, 1813–1893.

RAE, Robert Keith (Bob), politics. Ottawa, Ont., 1948. NDP premier of Ontario 1990–95.

RAFFI (b. Raffi Cavoukian), performing arts. Egypt, 1948. Singer. *Baby Beluga.*

RAIN, Douglas, Actor; has played more than 30 seasons with Ontario's Stratford Festival; voice of Hal the Computer in the films *2001* and *2002*. Winnipeg, Man., 1928.

RANKIN, John Morris, performing arts. Mabou, NS, 1959–2000. Head of musical group The Rankin Family, later The Rankins, Cape Breton musicians instrumental in popular revival of East Coast Celtic tradition.

RASKY, Harry, performing arts. Toronto, Ont., 1928. Filmmaker; noted documentarist. *The Dispossessed: The War Against the Indians.*

RASMINSKY, Louis, business. Montreal, Que., 1908–98. Governor, Bank of Canada, 1961–72.

RAYNER, Gordon, visual arts. Toronto, Ont., 1935. Realist, abstract painter, landscapes and cityscapes; northern Ontario landscapes. *Magnetawan No. 2.*

READ, Ken, sports. 1955. Skier; winner of five World Cup downhill victories (1975–80).

REANEY, James Crerar, literary arts. Easthope, Ont., 1926. Playwright; poet; critic. "A Suit of Nettles."

REBICK, Judy, politics. USA, 1945. Former head, Natl Action Committee on Status of Women.

REED, George Robert, sports. USA, 1939. Football player; running back with Sask. Roughriders; 44 CFL records.

REEVES, Keanu, performing arts. Lebanon, 1965. Actor. *Bill and Ted's Excellent Adventure; My Own Private Idaho.*

REGAN, Gerald Augustine, politics. Windsor, NS, 1928. Liberal premier of NS, 1970–78.

REICHMANN, Paul, business. Austria, 1930. Developer; philanthropist; with brothers Albert and Ralph, built Olympia & York into world's largest real estate developers in 1980s.

REID, Daphne Kate, performing arts. Eng., 1930–93. Primarily stage actress; Stratford mainstay.

REID, Fiona, politics. Eng., 1951. Dramatic and comedic actor. CBC's *King of Kensington* series; Stratford Festival, Ont.

REID, William Ronald (Bill), visual arts. Victoria, BC, 1920–98. Noted artist who promoted Northwest Coast native carving; also a sculptor whose works appear in major galleries and buildings.

REITMAN, Ivan, visual arts. Czech., 1946. Film director; producer; went from exploitation movies to blockbusters. *Ghostbusters.*

RENO, Ginette, performing arts. Montreal, Que., 1946. Popular chanteuse of sentimental ballads. "Tu vivras toujours dans mon Coeur"; "A ma manière."

REYNOLDS, John McCombe "Mac", visual arts. Toronto, Ont., 1916–99. Internationally renowned sculptor, painter and social historian for CBC.

RICCI, Nino Pio, literary arts. Leamington, Ont., 1959. Novelist, recipient of Governor General's Award for Fiction, 1990, for *Lives of the Saints.*

RICHARD, Joseph Henry Maurice "Rocket", sports. Montreal, Que., 1921–2000. Hockey player; legendary right winger; hockey's first 50-goal, 500-goal scorer.

RICHARDS, David Adams, literary arts. Author of fiction, stage and screen plays, and poetry; co-winner of 2000 Giller Prize for *Mercy Among the Children.* Newcastle, NB, 1950.

RICHARDSON, Ernie, sports. Stoughton, Sask., 1931. Curler; skipped four Brier and world title rinks.

RICHARDSON, James Armstrong, business. Kingston, Ont., 1885–1939. Financier; founded family grain business and investment house.

RICHLER, Mordecai, literary arts. Montreal, Que., 1931–2001. Novelist; essayist; acerbic comic writer. *St Urbain's Horseman.*

RIDOUT, Godfrey, performing arts. Toronto, Ont., 1918–94. Composer of chamber, symphonic and religious choral works.

RIEL, Louis, politics. St Boniface, Man., 1844–85. Métis leader; led North West Rebellion, 1870 and 1885; hanged for treason; rehabilitated and recognized as a founder of Manitoba in 1992.

RIOPELLE, Jean-Paul, visual arts. Montreal, Que., 1923. Acclaimed painter, sculptor. *Autrich.*

RITCHIE, Charles Stewart Almon, politics. Halifax, NS, 1906–95. Diplomat post–WWII; author of a number of books. *The Siren Years.*

RITTER, Erika, literary arts. Regina, Sask., 1948. Playwright, essayist, broadcaster. Her plays are a light-hearted look at serious women's issues. *The Visitor From Charleston; Automatic Pilot; Urban Scrawl.*

ROBARTS, John Parmenter, politics. Banff, Alta, 1917–82. PC premier of Ontario, 1961–71.

ROBERSTON, Jaime Robbie, performing arts. Toronto, Ont., 1944. Singer, songwriter, played with Ronnie Hawkins and the Band; wrote scores for films including *Raging Bull; King of Comedy.*

ROBERTS, Charles George Douglas (Sir), literary arts. Douglas, NB, 1860–1943. Poet; animal story writer. *Eyes of the Wilderness.*

ROBERTSON, Heather Margaret, literary arts. Winnipeg, Man., 1942. Novelist, critic. *More Than a Rose: Prime Ministers, Wives and Other Women.*

ROBERTSON, John Ross, business. Toronto, Ont., 1841–1918. Financier; publisher and philanthropist.

ROBERTSON, Lloyd, media. Stratford, Ont., 1934. Broadcaster; chief anchor, CTV news.

ROBICHAUD, Louis Joseph, politics. St-Antoine, NB, 1925. Liberal premier of NB, 1960–70.

ROBILLARD, Lucienne, politics. Montreal, Que., 1945. Liberal MP active in Quebec referendum debate; president of treasury board; formerly minister of citizenship and immigration.

ROBINETTE, John Josiah (J.J.), law. Toronto, Ont., 1906–96. Lawyer; prominent in criminal and constitutional law.

ROBINSON, Svend J., politics. USA, 1952. NDP MP, British Columbia; social activist, gay rights.

ROBLIN, Dufferin (Duff), politics. Winnipeg, Man., 1917. PC premier of Manitoba, 1958–67.

ROBLIN, Rodmond Palen (Sir), politics. Sophiasburg, Canada W, 1853–1937. PC premier of Manitoba, 1900–15.

ROCK, Allan Michael, politics. Ottawa, Ont., 1947. Liberal MP made minister of justice and attorney general in 1993, introduced major changes in Young Offender's Act and gun control legislation, minister of health in Chrétien government.

RODRIGUEZ, Sue, public service. Winnipeg, Man., 1959–94. Lou Gehrig's disease victim who championed right to die.

ROGERS, Edward S. (Ted), business. Toronto, Ont., 1933. Cable TV executive; runs Canada's largest cable system; 1994 take-over of Maclean Hunter.

ROGERS, Edward Samuel, invention. Toronto, Ont., 1900–39. Radio inventor; perfected alternating current radio tube, revolutionizing the industry.

ROGERS, Shelagh, media. Ottawa, Ont., 1956. CBC radio personality. Host of CBC's *This Morning; Take Five with Shelagh Rogers.*

ROGERS, Stan, performing arts. Hamilton, Ont., 1949–83. Folk singer/songwriter. "Between the Breaks."

ROHMER, Richard, literary arts. Hamilton, Ont., 1924. Writer. *Triad, Red Arctic, Death by Deficit.*

ROLPH, John, medicine. Eng., 1793–1870. Physician; ran medical school; constitutional reformer.

ROMAN, Stephen Boleslav, business. Slovakia, 1921–88. Industrialist; founded Denison Mines Ltd.

ROMANOW, Roy John, politics. Saskatoon, Sask., 1939. NDP premier of Sask 1991–2001.

RONALD, William (b. William Smith), visual arts. Stratford, Ont., 1926–98. Abstract artist; host, *As It Happens.*

ROOKE, Leon, literary arts. USA, 1934. Short story writer, novelist, playwright. *Krokodile; Shakespeare's Dog; How I Saved the Province; A Bit of White Cloth.*

ROSE, Fred (b. Fred Rosenburg), politics. Poland, 1907–83. Only Canadian Communist MP (1945); jailed as spy.

ROSENFELD, Fanny "Bobbie", sports. Russia, 1905–69. Track star; Canada's female athlete of half century.

ROSS, Anne Glass, medicine. Ukraine, 1911–98. Executive director of Winnipeg's Mount Carmel community health clinic, the first of its kind in Canada; birth control advocate. *Pregnant and Alone; Clinic with a Heart.*

ROSS, James Sinclair, literary arts. Shellbrook, Sask., 1908–96. Novelist. *As for Me and My House.*

ROSS, Sir James Clark, With Sir William Edward Parry searched for North Pole; discovered magnetic pole on Boothia Peninsula in 1831. England, 1800–1862.

ROTHSTEIN, Aser, science. Vancouver, BC, 1918. Physiologist; introduced radioisotopes in biology.

ROULEAU, Joseph, performing arts. Matane, Que., 1929. Operatic bass; internationally famous singer.

ROUX, Jean-Louis, performing arts/politics. Montreal, Que., 1923. Actor, playwright with successful career was rejected as deputy lieutenant governor of Quebec in 1997 due to youthful support of Nazi regime during WWII; appointed head of Canada Council in 1998.

ROY, Gabrielle, literary arts. St Boniface, Man., 1909–83. Popular novelist. *The Tin Flute.*

ROY, Patrick, sports. Quebec City, Que., 1965. Hockey player with Montreal Canadiens; Colorado Avalanche; youngest ever to win Conn Smythe trophy; in 1989–92 considered to be one of best goalies in the world.

ROZEMA, Patricia, politics. Kingston, Ont., 1958. Filmmaker; *I've Heard the Mermaids Singing, White Room.*

RUBENSTEIN, Louis, sports. Montreal, Que., 1861–1931. Canadian figure skating champion 1883–89; in 1890 won unofficial world title in Russia; also cyclist, bowler.

RUBES, Jan, performing arts. Czech., 1920. Singer; actor; operatic bass; TV host; film actor.

RUBINEK, Saul, performing arts. Toronto, Ont., 1948. Versatile character player. *The Quarrel.*

RUBINSKY, Yuri, business. Lebanon, 1952–96. Founder of Banff Publishing Workshop; co-director of SoftQuad Inc.; software designer.

RULE, Jane Vance, literary arts. USA, 1931. Novelist, short story writer. *Desert of the Heart; After the Fire; Contract With the World.*

RUSSELL, Loris Shano, science. USA, 1904. Paleontologist; suggested dinosaurs might be warm-blooded.

RUTHERFORD, Ann, performing arts. Toronto, Ont., 1917. Actress who appeared as Andy Hardy's girlfriend, Polly Benedict, in 12 Hardy films. *Secret Life of Walter Mitty.*

RUTHERFORD, Ernest (Rutherford of Nelson), science. NZ, 1871–1937. Physicist; much of his seminal work done at McGill University.

RYAN, Pat, sports. Winnipeg, Man., 1955. Curler; skip of world championship team in 1989; Canadian championship 1988, 1989.

RYAN, Thomas F. (Tommy), business. Guelph, Ont., 1872–1961. Entrepreneur; invented five-pin bowling (1909).

RYBCZYNSKI, Witold, literary arts/visual arts. Scot., 1943. Architect; critic; writer. *Paper Heroes.*

RYERSON, Adolphus Egerton, politics. Norfolk County, UC, 1803–82..Leading figure in 19th century politics and education.

RYGA, George, literary arts. Deep Creek, Alta, 1932–87. Playwright, novelist. *Ecstasy of Rita Joe; Night Desk.*

S

SABIA, Laura Louise, public service. Pembroke, Ont., 1916–96. Headed Royal Commission on the Status of Women in 1960s; became president of National Action Commitee on the Status of Women 1973.

SAFDIE, Moshe, visual arts. Israel, 1938. Architect; Habitat, National Gallery of Canada.

SAFER, Morley, media. Toronto, Ont., 1931. Broadcaster; co-host, *60 Minutes* since 1971.

SAHL, Mort, performing arts. Montreal, Que., 1926. Comedian; delivered political satire in monologues.

SAINTE-MARIE, Buffy, performing arts. Craven, Sask., 1941. Native singer. "Soldier Blue."

SALABERRY, Charles Michel D'Irumberry de, military. Beauport, Que., 1778–1829. Soldier; repelled American force in Battle of Chateauguay (1813).

SALTZMAN, Harry, performing arts. Saint John, NB, 1915–94. Co-producer of James Bond films. *The Man With the Golden Gun; The Ipcress File.*

SALUTIN, Rick, literary arts. Toronto, Ont., 1942. Playwright; columnist; leftist commentator. *Marginal Notes; Challenges to the Mainstream; Globe and Mail* columnist.

SARLOS, Andrew, business. Hungary, 1931–97. Financial trader with Toronto Stock Exchange. Realized $22 million profit from Hiram-Walker-Consumer's Gas merger.

SARRAZIN, Michael, performing arts. Quebec City, Que., 1940. Leading man. *They Shoot Horses, Don't They?*

SAUL, John Ralston, literary arts. Ottawa, Ont., 1947. Novelist, essayist. *The Paradise Eater; Voltaire's Bastards: The Dictatorship of Reason in the West.*

SAUNDERS, Charles Edward (Sir), science. London, Ont., 1867–1937. Agriculturalist; introduced Marquis wheat to W Canada.

SAUVE, Jeanne Mathilde, politics. Prud'homme, Sask., 1922–93. Governor general, 1984–89.

SAWCHUK, Terrence Gordon, sports. Winnipeg, Man., 1929–70. Hockey goaltender; all-time shutouts leader (103).

SAWYER, Robert, literary arts. Ottawa, Ont., 1960. Science fiction writer, winner of US Nebula award, awards in Japan, France, Spain. *Flashforward; Factoring Humanity.*

SCHAEFER, Carl Fellman, visual arts. Hanover, Ont., 1903–95. Painter of rural Ontario landscapes, director of Ontario College of Art.

SCHAFER, Raymond Murray, performing arts. Sarnia, Ont., 1933. Composer of contemporary music, first recipient of Glenn Gould Award in 1987.

SCHALLY, Andrew Victor, science. Poland, 1926. Winner of 1977 Noble Prize in medicine and physiology, for research into understanding peptide hormones in the brain.

SCHAWLOW, Arthur, science. USA, 1921–99. Canadian educated scientist, winner of 1964 Nobel Prize with Charles Hand Townes, co-patented the laser.

SCHLESINGER, Joe, media. Austria, 1928. Journalist; long-time CBC foreign correspondent.

SCHMIRLER, Sandra Marie, sports. Biggar, Sask., 1963-2000. Skip of the gold-medal-winning curling team at the 1998 Winter Olympics in Nagano, Japan.

SCHNARRE, Monika, performing arts. Toronto, Ont., 1971. Won 1986 Face of the 1980s modeling award; acting career includes role on *The Bold and the Beautiful.*

SCHOLES, Myron, economics. Timmins, Ont., 1941. Stanford University-based co-winner (with Harvard academic Robert Merton) of Nobel Prize for economics, for developing a mathematical formula for estimating values in the worldwide market of derivatives, known as the Black-Scholes formula.

SCHREYER, Edward Richard, politics. Beausejour, Man., 1935. NDP premier of Man., 1969–77; governor general of Canada, 1979–84.

SCOTT, Barbara Ann, sports. Ottawa, Ont., 1928. Figure skater; women's world champion, 1947–48; Olympic gold medal, 1948.

SCOTT, Duncan Campbell, literary arts. Ottawa, Ont., 1862–1947. Poet. "New World Lyrics and Ballads."

SCOTT, Francis (Frank) Reginald, literary arts. Quebec City, Que., 1899–1985. Poet. "Collected Poems."

SCOTT, Jack, performing arts. Windsor, Ont., 1936. Singer; 1950s rockabilly star. "My True Love."

SCRIVEN, Joseph Medlicott, religion. Ire., 1919–86. Hymn writer; wrote "What a Friend We Have in Jesus."

SEAGRAM, Joseph Emm, business. Fishers Mills, Ont., 1841–1919. Founder of world's largest distillery for spirits and wine-making; active as race horse owner; PC MP in Waterloo, Ont.

SECORD, Laura, military. USA, 1775–1868. Heroine; warned British of American attack (1813).

SEGAL, Hugh, politics. Montreal, Que., 1950. Back-room PC advisor to Robert Stanfield, William Davis and Brian Mulroney.

SELKIRK, George, sports. Huntsville, Ont., 1899–1987. Baseball player; outfielder on several NY Yankee champions; replaced Babe Ruth in 1934.

SELKIRK, Thomas Douglas, fifth Earl of, exploration and discovery. Scot., 1771–1820. Colonizer; established Red River settlement in Manitoba.

SELYE, Hans, medicine. Austria, 1907–82. Endocrinologist; author; pioneer in stress research. *The Stress of Life.*

SENNETT, Mack (b. Mikail Sinnott), visual arts. Danville, Que., 1880–1960. Producer; silent comedy pioneer; Keystone Kops.

SERVICE, Robert William, literary arts. Eng., 1874–1958. Poet of the Yukon, "Songs of a Sourdough."

SETON, Ernest Thompson, literary arts. Eng., 1860–1946. Naturalist; writer. *Wild Animals I Have Known.*

SHADBOLT, John Leonard (Jack), visual arts. Eng., 1909–98. BC artist noted for nature and native Canadian influenced work.

SHANNON, Kathleen, performing arts. Vancouver, BC, 1935–98. Founder of National Film Board's Studio D in 1974, which provided female filmmakers an opportunity to create documentaries with a feminist perspective. *If You Love This Planet; Not a Love Story.*

SHARP, Mitchell, politics. Winnipeg, Man., 1911. From 1942 to 1978 Liberal Party luminary; personal adviser to prime minister Jean Chrétien.

SHARPE, Isadore Nataniel, business. Toronto, Ont., 1931. Opened first Four Seasons Hotel in Toronto in 1961 on Jarvis Street, now a worldwide chain of luxury hotels.

SHATNER, William, performing arts. Montreal, Que., 1931. Actor; Capt. Kirk on TV/movies *Star Trek.*

SHAVER, Helen, performing arts. St Thomas, Ont., 1951. Actress appeared in *The Amityville Horror; Bethune: the Making of a Hero.*

SHEARER, Douglas, performing arts. Westmount, Que., 1899–1971. Sound recording technician, 40 years with MGM; won 12 Academy Awards; brother of actress Norma Shearer. *The Great Caruso; The Big House.*

SHEARER, Norma, performing arts. Edmonton, Alta, 1900–83. Actress; Hollywood star. *Romeo and Juliet.*

SHEBIB, Donald, visual arts. Toronto, Ont., 1939. Acclaimed filmmaker: *Goin' Down the Road; Heartaches.*

SHIELDS, Carol, literary arts. USA, 1935. Writer; won 1993 Booker and Pulitzer prizes for *The Stone Diaries.*

SHORE, Eddie, sports. Ft Qu'Apelle, Sask., 1902–85. Hockey player; Boston defenceman; four-time Hart Trophy winner.

SHORT, Martin, performing arts. Toronto, Ont., 1951. Comedian; TV/film star; *SCTV*'s Ed Grimley. *3 Amigos.*

SHULMAN, Morton (Dr), business/medicine. Toronto, Ont., 1925–2000. Investor; physician; author; stock promoter; introduced anti-Parkinson's disease drug into Canada.

SHUSTER, Frank, performing arts. Toronto, Ont., 1918. Comedian; straighter half of Wayne & Shuster team.

SHUSTER, Joe, visual arts. Toronto, Ont., 1914–92. Cartoonist; co-creator of Superman.

SIBERRY, Jane, performing arts. Ottawa, Ont., 1955. Singer, songwriter, guitarist. Contemporary folk style. *Jane Siberry; No Borders Here.*

SIFTON, Clifford (Sir), politics. Arva, Canada W, 1861–1929. Promoted immigration to settle western Canada.

SILVERHEELS, Harold Jay Smith, performing arts. Six Nations Reserve, Ont., 1919–80. Actor; played Tonto in Lone Ranger.

SIMARD, Réné, performing arts. Chicoutimi, Que., 1961. Quebec pop singer began as boy soprano turned international pop star. *The Rene Simard Show* on CBC.

SIMCOE, Elizabeth Posthuma, Wife of John Graves Simcoe, first governor of Upper Canada; her diary and watercolours of Upper Canada provide a unique picture of contemporary life in the colony. England, 1766–1850.

SIMCOE, John Graves, politics. Eng., 1752–1806. Upper Canada's first lieutenant-governor, 1792–96.

SIMPSON, Allan John, public service. Ottawa, Ont., 1939–98. Co-founder of Canadians with Disabilities and the Canadian Association of Independent Living Centres; created first Pan-Am Wheelchair Games and Canadian Wheelchair Sports Association. Lobbied to have disabled included in Charter of Rights and Freedoms.

SIMPSON, Sir George, business. Scot., 1787–1860. Financier; governor, Hudson's Bay Co., 1820–60.

SINCLAIR, Gordon Allan, media. Toronto, Ont., 1900–84. Journalist; feisty commentator; long-time Front Page Challenge panelist.

SITTLER, Darryl Glen, sports. St Jacob's, Ont., 1950. Hockey player; with Toronto Maple Leafs set NHL record 10 points in one game.

SKVORECKY, Josef, literary arts. Czech., 1924. Intellectual writer; novelist; critic. *The Engineer of Human Souls.*

SLADE, Bernard (b. Bernard Slade Newbound), performing arts. St Catharines, Ont., 1930. Sitcom pilot writer for *The Flying Nun; The Partridge Family; Bridget loves Bernie.* Wrote screenplay for *Same Time Next Year.*

SLOCUM, Joshua, literary arts. Wilmot Twp, NS, 1844–1909. Sailor; wrote classic *Sailing Alone Around the World.*

SMALLWOOD, Joseph Roberts (Joey), politics. Gambo, Nfld, 1900–92. Led Newfoundland into Confederation, 1949; premier 1949–72.

SMART, Elizabeth, literary arts. Ottawa, Ont., 1913–86. Novelist. *By Grand Central Station I Sat Down and Wept.*

SMELLIE, Elizabeth Lawrie, medicine. Port Arthur, Ont., 1884–1968. Nurse; builder, Victorian Order of Nurses.

SMITH, Alexis, performing arts. Penticton, BC, 1921–93. Film and television actress appeared in *Marcus Welby; Rhapsody in Blue; Of Human Bondage.*

SMITH, Byron, exploration and discovery. Winnipeg, Manitoba, 1960. Leader of AGF Everest 2000 expedition, reached summit May 21, 2000, with team members Tim Rippel and Brad Wrobleski.

SMITH, Donald Graham, sports. Edmonton, Alta, 1958. Swimmer; six gold medals, 1978 Commonwealth Games.

SMITH, Lois Irene, performing arts. Vancouver, BC, 1929. National Ballet's first prima ballerina.

SMITH, Michael, science. Eng., 1932–2000. Biochemist; 1993–2000 Nobel Prize winner in chemistry.

SMITH, Michael, sports. Kenora, Ont., 1967. Decathlete; silver medal, 1991 world championships.

SMITH, Stephen Richard (Steve), performing arts. Toronto, Ont., 1945. Comedian who stars in *Red Green Show*, also plays stand-up comedy.

SMITH, Wilfred Cantwell, literary arts. Toronto, Ont., 1916–2000. Founder of McGill University's Islamic Institute; co-founder of Harvard's Center for Study of World Religions. *Islam in Modern History*.

SMITS, Sonja, performing arts. Sudbury, Ont., 1958. Star of CBC series *Street Legal*; CBC's *The Diviners*. Appeared in stage production of *Nothing Sacred*.

SMYTH, Constantine Falkland Cary (Conn), sports. Toronto, Ont., 1895–1980. Hockey executive; owner of Toronto Maple Leafs, 1930–61.

SNIDERMAN, Sam, business. Toronto, Ont., 1920. Retailer; established Sam the Record Man; 130 stores.

SNOW, Clarence Eugene "Hank", performing arts. Liverpool, NS, 1914–2000. Country music singer. "I'm Movin' On."

SNOW, Michael James Aleck, visual arts. Toronto, Ont., 1929. Painter; sculptor; filmmaker; photographer.

SOBEY, Frank, business. Lyons Brook, NS, 1902–85. Industrialist; turned family grocery business into a major industry.

SOMERS, Harry Stewart, performing arts. Toronto, Ont., 1925–99. Composer of opera, orchestral, vocal and ballet music, acclaimed for operas *Louis Riel* and *The Fool*; commissioned by Yehudi Menuhin to write *Music for Solo Violin*.

SOPINKA, John, law/sports. Broderick, Sask., 1933–97. Supreme Court justice; former CFL player.

SOUSTER, Raymond Holmes, literary arts. Toronto, Ont., 1921. Poet; editor. "The Colour of the Times."

SOUTHAM, William, media. Montreal, Que., 1843–1932. Publisher; founded Southam newspaper dynasty.

SPICER, Keith, media. Toronto, Ont., 1934. Civil servant; chairman, Canadian Radio-Television and Telecommunications Commission.

SPOHR, Arnold, performing arts. Rhein, Sask., 1927. Ballet teacher; led Royal Winnipeg Ballet to world fame.

ST LAURENT, Louis Stephen, politics. Compton, Que., 1882–1973. Prime minister of Canada 1948–57; one of the architects of NATO.

STAEBLER, Edna, media. Kitchener, Ont., 1906. Journalist, cookbook writer, specializing in Mennonite cuisine. *Food That Really Schmecks; Whatever Happened to Maggie?*

STANFIELD, Robert Lorne, politics. Truro, NS, 1914. PC premier of NS, 1956–67; as federal PC leader, lost three elections to Trudeau.

STANLEY, George Frances Gillman, literary arts. Westmount, Que., 1907. Historian; proposed basic design of Maple Leaf flag in 1965.

STAROWICZ, Marc, Longtime CBC luminary; producer of radio and television documentaries and current affairs programming. *Witness; Life & Times; The Journal; As It Happens*; and *Canada: A People's History*. England, 1946.

STARYK, Steven, performing arts. Toronto, Ont., 1932. Violinist; virtuoso performer and teacher.

STEACIE, Edgar William Richard, science. Montreal, Que., 1900–62. Chemist; authority on free radical kinetics.

STEELE, Samuel Benfield (Sir), military. Purbrook, Canada W, 1849–1919. NWMP and WWI officer.

STEFANSSON, Vilhjalmur, exploration and discovery. Arnes, Man., 1879–1962. Controversial Arctic explorer. Wrote *My Life with the Eskimo; The Friendly Arctic*.

STEINBERG, David (b. Duddy Steinberg), performing arts. St Boniface, Man., 1942. Stand-up comic; talk show host.

STEINBERG, Samuel, business. Hungary, 1905–78. Retailer; turned family grocery into supermarket empire.

STEPHENSON, William Samuel (Sir), military. Winnipeg, Man., 1896–1989. Spy; "Intrepid," head of British counterespionage during WWII; invented wirephotos.

STERN, Bonnie Susan, business. Toronto, Ont., 1947. Food commentator and cookbook editor; founder of Bonnie Stern Cooking Schools; host of WTN TV show *Bonnie Stern Entertains*. Author of *Bonnie Stern Cooks; Simply Heart Smart Cooking*.

STEWART, Walter Douglas, literary arts. Toronto, Ont., 1931. Journalist, editor, social commentator; noted for acerbic wit. Author of *Shrug: Trudeau in Power; Towers of Gold, Feet of Clay*; and *True Blue*, a history of United Empire Loyalists.

STOJKO, Elvis, sports. Newmarket, Ont., 1972. Figure skater; silver medal, 1994 Olympics; world champion, 1995.

STOWE, Emily Howard, medicine. Norwich, UC, 1831–1903. Physician; first Canadian woman to practice medicine; had to obtain degree in US.

STRACHAN, John, religion. Scot., 1778–1867. Anglican bishop; strove to keep Upper Canada British.

STRATAS, Teresa (b. Anastasia Stratakis), performing arts. Toronto, Ont., 1938. Opera soprano; diva with strong stage presence.

STRATHCONA, Donald Alexander Smith (Sir), first Baron, politics. Scot., 1820–1914. Politician, businessman, diplomat; drove the Last Spike.

STRATTON, Dorothy (b. Dorothy Ruth Hoogstratten), performing arts. Vancouver, BC, 1960–80. *Playboy* model; murdered by estranged husband. Her story was told in film *Star 80*, starring Mariel Hemingway.

STREIT, Marlene Stewart, sports. Cereal, Alta, 1934. Golfer; won many international titles. Canadian Athlete of the Year, 1951, 1956.

STRONACH, Frank, business. Austria, 1954. Industrialist; chairman, Magna Intl; built machine company into global enterprise.

STRONG, Lori, sports. Toronto, Ont., 1972. Gymnast; winner of four gold medals at 1990 Commonwealth Games.

STRONG, Maurice Frederick, business. Oak Lake, Man., 1929. Headed Canadian International Development Agency; secretary-general of UN Conference in the Human Environment; head of Petro-Canada and Ontario Hydro; Canadian Ambassador to the UN.

SULLIVAN, Kevin Roderick, performing arts. Toronto, Ont., 1955. Producer; made *Anne of Green Gables*; launched popular *Road to Avonlea* TV series.

SUNG, Alfred (b. Sung Wang Moon), business. Toronto, Ont., 1948. Fashion designer; top designer of the 1980s.

SURIN, Bruny, sports. Haiti, 1967. Sprinter; world 100 m outdoor champion, 1993.

SUTHERLAND, Donald, performing arts. Saint John, NB, 1934. Versatile actor of Hollywood and Canadian films. *Murder by Decree; Don't Look Now*.

SUTHERLAND, Kiefer, performing arts. Eng., 1964. Actor. *Bay Boy, Flatliners, Stand By Me.*

SUZUKI, David Takayoshi, media/science. Vancouver, BC, 1936. Geneticist; promoter of environmental causes; columnist; host of CBC's *The Nature of Things.*

SWAN, Anna Haining, performing arts. Mill Brook, NS, 1846–88. Giantess, at 7 ft. 6 in., 352 lbs; was P.T. Barnum star.

SWAN, Susan, literary arts. Midland, Ont., 1945. Novelist. *Women of the World; The Last of the Golden Girls.*

SYDOR, Alison, sports. Vancouver, BC, 1966. Champion mountain biker; won 1996 Olympics silver award, three-time World MTB champion, 1994, 1995, 1996.

SZNAJDER, Andrew, sports. Toronto, Ont., 1968. Four-time Canadian singles tennis champ.

TALBOT, Thomas, Personal secretary to Lieutenant Governor of Upper Canada John Graves Simcoe; fostered creation of Talbot Trail, the first transport artery to be built across southwestern Ontario. Ireland, 1771–1853.

TALON, Jean-Baptiste, politics. France, 1625–94. Governor; as intendant, sought to diversify economy of New France with minerals, timber, farming.

TANNER, Elaine, sports. Vancouver, BC, 1951. Canada's best woman swimmer by age 15; world records in individual medley and butterfly; won silver and bronze medals in 1968 Olympics.

TASCHEREAU, Louis-Alexandre, politics. Quebec City, Que., 1867–1952. Liberal premier of Quebec, 1920–36; anti-nationalist leader.

TAUBE, Henry, science. Neudorf, Sask., 1915. Nobel Prize winner in 1983 in chemistry for research into electron transfer reactions, especially in metal complexes.

TAYLOR, Edward Plunket (E.P.), business. Ottawa, Ont., 1901–89. Industrialist; founded Argus Corp; notable horseman.

TAYLOR, Fred "Cyclone", sports. Tara, Ont., 1883–1979. Hockey's first great star.

TAYLOR, Kenneth Douglas, politics. Calgary, Alta, 1934. Diplomat; engineering freedom for six US hostages in Iran made him an instant celebrity in 1980.

TAYLOR, Richard Edward, science. Medicine Hat, Alta, 1929. Physicist; nuclear accelerator pioneer; 1990 Nobel Prize in physics.

TAYLOR, Ronald, medicine/sports. Toronto, Ont., 1937. Major league relief pitcher (1962–72) and sports medicine pioneer.

TECUMSEH, military. USA, 1768–1813. Chief of Shawnee Indians, ally of Britain and Canada during the War of 1812.

TEMPLETON, Charles Bradley, media. Toronto, Ont., 1915–2001. Author, broadcaster, playwright, evangelist, journalist; wrote controversial *Act of God.*

TENNANT, Veronica, performing arts. Eng., 1947. Prima ballerina, National Ballet of Canada.

TEWKSBURY, Mark, sports. Calgary, Alta, 1968. Swimmer; gold medal, 100 m backstroke, 1992 Olympics.

THERIAULT, Yves, literary arts. Quebec City, Que., 1915–83. Novelist, dramatist. *Contes pour un homme seul; Agaguk.*

THICKE, Alan (b. Alan Jeffery), performing arts. Kirkland Lake, Ont., 1948. Actor and talk show host, host of TV game show *Pictionary,* formerly host of talk show *Thicke of the Night.*

THIRSK, Robert Brent (Bob), science. New Westminster, BC, 1953. In 1996 flew a 17-day journey on space shuttle Columbia, conducting experiments on space sickness and researching other areas.

THOM, Linda, sports. Hamilton, Ont., 1943. Shooter; gold medal, women's sports pistol, 1984 Olympics.

THOM, Ronald James, visual arts. Penticton, BC, 1923. Architect; Shaw Festival Theatre, Toronto Zoo.

THOMAS, Dave, performing arts. Toronto, Ont., 1953. Comedic actor noted for roles on *SCTV,* portrayed with Rick Moranis one of the McKenzie Brothers in *Strange Brew.*

THOMPSON, David, exploration and discovery. Eng., 1770–1857. Charted Columbia River.

THOMPSON, John Sparrow David (Sir), politics. Halifax, NS, 1845–94. Canada's fourth prime minister, 1892–94; largely responsible for establishment of the Criminal Code.

THOMSON, Andrew, science. Dobbinton, Ont., 1893–1974. Co-founder of World Meteorological Organization; established weather-forecasting centres across Canada.

THOMSON, David Kenneth Roy, business. Toronto, Ont., 1923. Businessman; art collector; chairman, Thomson Newspapers Ltd.

THOMSON, Roy Herbert (R. H.), performing arts. Toronto, Ont., 1947. Stage and television actor. *Charlie Grant's War; Cry from the Heart; Ticket to Heaven.*

THOMSON, Roy (Lord Thomson of Fleet), media. Toronto, Ont., 1894–1976. Publisher; owned major newspapers in English-speaking world.

THOMSON, Thomas John (Tom), visual arts. Claremont, Ont., 1877–1917. Influential painter. *Autumn Foliage.*

THORBURN, Clifford Charles Devlin, sports. Victoria, BC, 1948. Snooker player; world champion, 1980.

TILLY, Jennifer, performing arts. USA, 1959. Actress, appeared in Woody Allen's *Bullets Over Broadway.*

TILLY, Margaret (Meg), performing arts. Texada Is., BC, 1960. Actress whose winsome face appeared in *The Body Snatchers; The Big Chill.*

TIMMINS, Noah Anthony, business. Mattawa, Ont., 1867–1936. Mining operator; developed N America's largest gold mine; town named for him.

TINTNER, Georg, performing arts. Vienna, 1917–99. Conductor of Nova Scotia Symphony Orchestra 1987–94; noted for recordings of Anton Bruckner.

TOBIN, Brian Vincent, politics. Stephenville, Nfld, 1954. Began "cod war" with Spain while serving as Liberal Minister of Fisheries and Oceans, 1995; premier of Nfld, 1996–2001.

TORGOV, Morley Edward, literary arts. Sault Ste Marie, Ont., 1927. Story writer. *The Abramsky Variations; The Outside Chance of Maximilian Glick.*

TORY, Henry Marshall, educator. Pt Shoreham, NS, 1864–1947. University founder: UBC, Carleton.

TOTH, Jerry (Jaroslav), performing arts. Windsor, Ont., 1929–99. Saxophonist, clarinetist, arranger, conductor and producer, Toth was responsible for the *Hockey Night in Canada* theme on CBC, as well as many other network productions: *Wayne and Shuster; Parade*. Member of Boss Brass ensemble for 20 years.

TOWN, Harold Barling, visual arts. Toronto, Ont., 1924–90. Influential painter, sculptor, writer.

TOWNSEND, Eleanor, performing arts. Goderich, Ont., 1944–98. Fiddling champion who was first woman to win North American Fiddle Championship at Shelburne, Ont.; member of both Canada's and US Fiddling Halls of Fame.

TRACY, Paul, sports. Scarborough, Ont., 1968. Auto racer; winner of three Indy titles in 1993.

TRAILL, Catharine Parr, literary arts. Eng., 1802–99. Writer. *The Backwoods of Canada.*

TRAVERS, Mary (La Bolduc), performing arts. Newport, Que., 1894–1941. Singer, songwriter, fiddler whose songs in colloquial French about common people's concerns were widely recorded and hugely popular.

TREBEK, Alex, performing arts. Sudbury, Ont., 1940. TV host of *Jeopardy* quiz show.

TREMBLAY, Jean-Claude, sports. Bagotville, Ont., 1939–94. Star defenceman for Montreal Canadiens in 1960s.

TREMBLAY, Michel, literary arts. Montreal, Que., 1942. Playwright; novelist. *Le Vrai Monde.*

TROIANO, Dominic, performing arts. Italy, 1946. Rock guitarist collaborted with the Mandalas, The Guess Who; wrote for CBC TV. *Night Heat; Diamonds.*

TROUT, Jennie Kidd, First woman in Canada licensed to practice medicine; established Ontario Medical College for Women in Kingston, Ont. Scotland, 1841–1921.

TRUDEAU, Pierre Elliott, politics. Montreal, Que., 1919–2000. Prime minister of Canada 1968–79, 1980–84.

TRYGGVASON, Bjarni V., science. Iceland, 1945. Astronaut who flew aboard the Discovery in 1997 for 11 days to test Canadian-made equipment at zero gravity.

TSUI, Dr Lap-Chee, science. China, 1950. Geneticist; identified gene carrying cystic fibrosis.

TUBMAN, Harriet Ross (b. Araminta Ross), Former slave who was instrumental in freeing slaves via the Underground Railroad; escaped persecution in St. Catharine's, Ont. USA, 1820–1913.

TUPPER, Charles (Sir), politics. Amherst, NS, 1821–1915. Appointed as Canada's sixth prime minister, 1896.

TURCOTTE, Ron, sports. Drummond, NB, 1941. Jockey; long-time leading jockey rode Secretariat to Triple Crown (1973).

TURNBULL, Wallace, invention. Saint John, NB, 1870–1954. Inventor of variable pitch propeller in 1927, contributed to improved flying safety.

TURNER, John Napier, politics. Eng., 1929. Prime minister of Canada June 1984–July 1984.

TUROFSKY, Riki, performing arts. Toronto, Ont., 1944. Debuted in 1972 at New York City Opera in *Carmen*; host of CBC's *Summer Festival* in 1978; *Festival Today* in 1984.

TWAIN, Shania (b. Eileen Regina Edwards), performing arts. Windsor, Ont., 1965. Winner of Country Music of the Year Award (US) 1995. *The Woman in Me.*

TYRRELL, Joseph Burr, science. Weston, Canada W, 1858–1957. Geologist; discovered S Alberta dinosaur beds.

TYSON, Ian Dawson, performing arts. Victoria, BC, 1933. Singer/songwriter; half of Ian and Sylvia. "Four Strong Winds."

TYSON, Sylvia Fricker, performing arts. Chatham, Ont., 1940. Singer; half of Ian and Sylvia. "You Were on My Mind."

UNDERHILL, Barbara Ann, sports. Pembroke, Ont., 1963. Figure skater; world pairs champion (with Paul Martini), 1984.

UNGER, James, visual arts. Eng., 1937. Cartoonist; creator of popular "Herman" cartoon strip.

URQUHART, Jane, literary arts. Little Long Lac, Que., 1949. Novelist, short story writer. *Away; The Underpainter; The Whirlpool.*

VAILLANCOURT, Armand J. R., visual arts. Black L., Que., 1932. Sculpts in aid of social activism.

VALDY, (b. Vladimir Horsdal), performing arts. Ottawa, Ont., 1946. Country-folk singer-songwriter, guitarist. "Rock and Roll Song"; *Valdy; Notes from Places.*

VALLIERES, Pierre, politics. Montreal, Que., 1938–98. Journalist and former leader of Front de Libération de Québec (FLQ); author of *White Niggers of America,* which compared Québécois with American Blacks; fell out with FLQ after murder of labour minister Pierre Laporte.

VAN HERK, Aritha, literary arts. Wetaskiwin, Alta, 1954. Novelist. *Judith; No Fixed Address; Places Far from Ellesmere.*

VAN HORNE, William Cornelius (Sir), business. USA, 1843–1915. Driving force behind Canadian Pacific Railroad.

VAN VOGT, Alfred Elton (A.E.), literary arts. Winnipeg, Man., 1912. Writer; science fiction standout. *Slan.*

VANCOUVER, George, exploration and discovery. Eng., 1757–98. Navigator; surveyor of BC coastline.

VANDER ZALM, William Nick, politics. Holland, 1934. Social Credit premier of BC 1986–91, proponent of free trade.

VANDERBURG, Helen, sports. Calgary, Alta, 1959. Synchronized swimmer; dominated sport in 1979.

VANDERHAEGHE, Guy Clarence, literary arts. Esterhazy, Sask., 1951. Novelist, won 1982 Governor General's Award for *Man Descending. My Present Age; Homesick.*

VANIER, Georges Phileas, politics. Montreal, Que., 1888–1967. Governor general, 1959–67.

VANIER, Jean, public service. Switz., 1928. Spiritual leader; man of great moral conviction established homes for handicapped around the world.

VANNELLI, Gino, performing arts. Montreal, Que., 1954. Pop singer. *Brother to Brother; Nightwalker.*

VARLEY, Frederick Horsman, visual arts. Eng., 1881–1969. Member, Group of Seven. *Vera.*

VEREGIN, Peter Vasilevich, religion. Russia, 1859–1924. Charismatic Doukhobor leader.

VERNON, John, performing arts. Montreal, Que., 1931. TV and film actor. *Wojeck.*

VEZINA, Georges, sports. Chicoutimi, Que., 1887–1926. Hockey goalie; NHL trophy named for him.

VICKERS, Jonathan Stewart (Jon), performing arts. Prince Albert, Sask., 1926. Tenor; operatic star; Wagner specialist.

VICKREY, William, economics. Victoria, BC, 1914–96. Winner of Nobel Prize in economics in 1996. Worked with United Nations on tax issues in African countries.

VIGNEAULT, Gilles, performing arts. Natashquan, Que., 1928. Beloved poet and cultural icon of Québécois. "Mon Pays."

VILLENEUVE, Gilles, sports. St-Jean, Que., 1950–82. Auto racer; won six Grand Prix titles.

VILLENEUVE, Jacques, sports. St-Jean, Que., 1971. Winner of Indianapolis 500 in 1995; Lou Marsh trophy for Canadian Athlete of the Year, 1995.

VINCENT, Anthony Gustave, public service. Eng., 1939. Canadian ambassador to Peru when, in December 1996, Tupac Amaru guerrillas stormed Japanese ambassador's residence in Lima, taking 575 hostages. Vincent attempted negotiations with leader Nestor Cerpa; the remaining hostages were freed when troops stormed residence in April 1997.

W

WAGNER, Barbara Aileen, sports. Toronto, Ont., 1938. Figure skater; with Robert Paul, won four pairs titles and 1960 Olympic gold.

WALDO, Carolyn, sports. Montreal, Que., 1964. Synchronized swimmer; two gold medals, 1988 Olympics.

WALKER, Larry, sports. Maple Ridge, BC, 1966. Baseball player; star outfielder for Montreal Expos, Colorado Rockies. NL MVP, 1997. NL batting champion, 1998.

WALLIN, Pamela, media. Wadena, Sask., 1953. Longtime CBC journalist and independent news magazine host. *Pamela Wallin.*

WALLS, Earl, sports. Puce, Ont., 1928–96. Canadian heavyweight boxing champion, 1952.

WALSH, Richard "Hock", performing arts. Co-founder in 1969 with brother Donnie of Downchild Blues Band; inspiration for Dan Aykroyd and John Belushi in movie *The Blues Brothers.* Toronto, Ont., 1948–2000. Co-founder in 1969 with brother Donnie of Downchild Blues Band; inspiration for Dan Aykroyd and John Belushi in movie *The Blues Brothers.*

WALTERS, Angus, exploration and discovery. Lunenburg, NS, 1882–1968. *Bluenose* captain; skipper of celebrated schooner.

WALTERS, Eric, literary arts. Toronto, Ont., 1957. Popular writer of young people's adventure books. *Tiger by the Tail; Trapped in Ice.*

WARD, Maxwell William, business. Edmonton, Alta, 1921. Capitalist; charter flights pioneer; founded Wardair.

WARNER, Jack L., performing arts. London, Ont., 1892–1978. Head of production at Warner Brothers in 1927; launched talkies with *The Jazz Singer*, starring Al Jolson.

WATKINS, Melville Henry, business. Toronto, Ont., 1932. Economist; founded left-wing Waffle Movement.

WATSON, Hilda Pauline, politics. Kuest, Sask., 1922–96. Leader of the Yukon Territorial Progressive Conservatives, 1978. First woman to lead a political party in Canada.

WATSON, Homer Ransford, visual arts. Doon, Canada W, 1855–1936. Landscape painter. *The Pioneer Mill.*

WATSON, John, literary arts. Scot., 1847–1939. Philosopher; metaphysician. "Kant and His English Critics."

WATSON, Ken, sports. Minnedosa, Man., 1904–86. Curler; three-time Brier winner; curling teacher.

WATSON, Patrick, media. Toronto, Ont., 1929. TV host; actor; writer; producer.

WATSON, Sheila Doherty, literary arts. New Westminster, BC, 1909–98. Author of *Double Hook*, considered to be the first modern Canadian novel; also *Deep Hollow Creek.* Described experiences as schoolteacher in central BC in the 1930s.

WATSON, William "Whipper Billy", sports. Toronto, Ont., 1917–1990. Wrestler; twice world pro champion.

WAXMAN, Albert Samuel (Al), performing arts. Toronto, Ont., 1935–2001 Movie and TV performer. King of Kensington.

WAYNE, John Louis (Johnny), performing arts. Toronto, Ont., 1918–90. Comedian; wilder half of Wayne and Shuster comedy team.

WEBSTER, Donald Colin "Ben", invention. Montreal, Que., 1928–97. Founder of high-tech Helix Investments (Canada), credited with introduction of the fastening material Velcro.

WEBSTER, John Edgar (Jack), media. Scot., 1918–99. Broadcaster; journalist on Vancouver *Sun.* Noted for outspoken opinions.

WEINZWEIG, John Jacob, performing arts. Toronto, Ont., 1913. Influential composer using 12-tone technique. "Red Ear of Corn."

WEIR, Michael Richard, sports. Sarnia, Ont., 1970. Winner of 2000 World Golf Championship and American Express Championship; 1999 PGA Air Canada Championship.

WEIR, Robert Stanley, literary arts. Hamilton, Ont., 1856–1926. Jurist; author; wrote English lyrics of National Anthem, "O Canada."

WELLS, Clyde Kirby, politics. Buchans Junction, Nfld, 1937. Newfoundland premier 1989–96.

WELSH, Kenneth, politics. Edmonton, Alta, 1942. Versatile actor noted for roles in *Empire Inc.; And Then You Die; The Tar Sands.*

WESTON, Hilary M., politics. Ire., 1942. Appointed lieutenant governor of Ontario in 1997, wife of grocery magnate Galen Weston.

WESTON, W. Galen Gordon, business. Eng., 1940. Industrialist; Canadian head for George Weston Ltd.

WESTON, Willard Garfield, business. Toronto, Ont., 1893–1978. Industrialist; pioneer in food retailing.

WHEELER, Anne, visual arts. Edmonton, Alta, 1946. Filmmaker. *A Change of Heart; Bye Bye Blues.*

WHEELER, Lucille, sports. Montreal, Que., 1935. Skier; first N American to win world title, downhill and slalom (1958).

WHITE, Bob, business. Ire., 1935. Labour leader; first head of Canadian Auto Workers' Union.

WHITFIELD, Simon, sports. Victoria, BC, 1975. Gold medallist for triathlon in 2000 Sydney Olympics; 1998, 1999 Canadian champion.

WHITTON, Charlotte Elizabeth, politics. Renfrew, Ont., 1896–1975. Reformer; outspoken Ottawa mayor.

WIEBE, Rudy Henry, literary arts. Speedwell, Sask., 1934. Mennonite novelist. *Temptations of Big Bear.*

WILLAN, James Healey, performing arts. Eng., 1880–1968. Classical composer and musician. "O Lord, Our Governour" sung at Queen Elizabeth II's coronation in Westminster Abbey.

WILLIAMS, Daffyd (Dave) Rhys, science. Saskatoon, Sask., 1954. Astronaut, flew on 16-day Spacelab flight aboard Space Shuttle Columbia in 1998; coordinator of Canadian Astronaut Program Space Unit Life Simulation (CAPSULS) project.

WILLIAMS, Percy Alfred, sports. Vancouver, BC, 1908–82. Sprinter; Olympic gold in 100 m and 200 m, 1928.

WILSON, Bertha, law. Scot., 1923. First woman named to Supreme Court of Canada (1982).

WILSON, Cairine Reay, politics. Montreal, Que., 1885–1962. Canada's first woman senator, 1930 (Lib.).

WILSON, Daniel (Sir), educator. Scot., 1816–92. Darwinian opposed idea of natural selection; energetic administrator, author, scholar.

WILSON, Ethel Davis, literary arts. S Africa, 1888–1980. BC novelist. *Swamp Angel.*

WILSON, John Tuzo, science. Ottawa, Ont., 1908–93. Geophysicist; pioneered plate tectonics theory.

WILSON, Lois Miriam, religion. Winnipeg, Man., 1927. First woman president of Canadian Council of Churches, in 1976; first woman Moderator of United Church of Canada in 1980. Peace advocate and active in antipoverty initiatives.

WILSON, Michael Holcombe, politics. Toronto, Ont., 1937. PC minister of industry, science and technology; international trade; finance minister (1984–91).

WISEMAN, Adele, literary arts. Winnipeg, Man., 1928–92. Novelist, poet. *The Sacrifice; Crackpot.*

WISEMAN, Joseph, performing arts. Montreal, Que., 1918. Actor; title role in James Bond movie, *Dr. No.*

WOLFE, James, military. Eng., 1727–59. Soldier; took Quebec for British; died on Plains of Abraham.

WONG, Celia Jan, media. Montreal, Que., 1952. *Globe and Mail* correspondant in China, 1988–94. *Red China Blues.*

WOOD, Elizabeth Wyn, visual arts. Orillia, Ont., 1903–66. Sculptor; fountains and panels for Rainbow Bridge Gardens, monument to King George VI, Niagara Falls.

WOODCOCK, George, literary arts. Winnipeg, Man., 1912–95. Historian; journalist; activist. *Anarchism.*

WOODSWORTH, James Shaver, politics. Etobicoke, Ont., 1874–1942. Founder Cooperative Commonwealth Federation (later NDP).

WRAY, Fay, performing arts. Medicine Hat, Alta, 1910. Famous as screaming heroine in *King Kong.*

WRIGHT, Eric Stanley, literary arts. Eng., 1929. Mystery writer. *A Sensitive Case; Final Cut.*

WRIGHT, Michelle, performing arts. Merlin, Ont., 1960. Sultry country songstress. "Now and Then."

YANOFSKY, Abe (b. Daniel Abraham), sports. Poland, 1925–2000. First chess grandmaster in Commonwealth; child prodigy in 1939 Chess Olympics in Buenos Aires; active in Winnipeg city council.

YANOVSKY, Zal, performing arts. Toronto, Ont., 1944. Singer; member of folk-rock group, Lovin' Spoonful.

YOST, Elwy, performing arts. Toronto, Ont., 1925. Affable and knowledgeable host of TVOntario's popular *Saturday Night at the Movies.*

YOUNG, Neil Percival, performing arts. Toronto, Ont., 1945. Singer/songwriter; seminal rocker. *After the Gold Rush.*

YOUNG, Scott Alexander, literary arts. Glenboro, Man., 1918. Novelist, short story writer, children's writer, biographer. *The Boys of Saturday Night; Power Play.*

YOUVILLE, Marie Marguerite d', religion. Varennes, Que., 1701–71. First Canadian to be beatified by Pope; founded Grey Nuns.

Z

ZEIDLER, Eberhard Heinrich, visual arts. Germany, 1936. Award-winning architect of Toronto Eaton Centre, Toronto's Queen's Quay Terminal, Ontario Place.

ZNAIMER, Moses, business. Toronto, Ont., 1942. TV executive; founder of CITY-TV, Much Music.

ZOLF, Larry, media. Winnipeg, Man., 1934. Broadcaster; journalist; writer. CBC's *Fifth Estate.*

ZUCKERMAN, Mortimer, business. Montreal, Que., 1937. Financier; developer, magazine publisher.

BASEBALL

American League Final Standings, 2001

Eastern Division

TEAM	W	L	%	GB
Y-NY Yankees	95	65	.594	–
Boston	82	79	.509	13½
Toronto	80	82	.494	16
Baltimore	63	98	.391	32½
Tampa Bay	62	100	.383	34

Central Division

TEAM	W	L	%	GB
Y-Cleveland	91	71	.562	–
Minnesota	85	77	.525	6
Chi White Sox	83	79	.512	8
Detroit	66	96	.407	25
Kansas City	65	97	.401	26

Western Division

TEAM	W	L	%	GB
Y-Seattle	116	46	.716	–
X-Oakland	102	60	.630	14
Anaheim	75	87	.463	41
Texas	73	89	.451	43

Source: *Canadian Press*

X — Wild Card Y — Division Title.

American League Leaders, 2001

Batting

Batting Average

Suzuki, Sea	.350
Ja. Giambi, Oak	.342
Alomar, Clev	.336
Boone, Sea	.331
Catalanotto, Tex	.330
Gonzalez, Clev	.325
A. Rodriguez, Tex.	.318
Stewart, Tor	.316
Jeter, NY	.311
Conine, Balt	.311

On-Base Percentage

Ja. Giambi, Oak	.477
Martinez, Sea	.423
Thome, Clev	.416
Alomar, Clev	.415
Delgado, Tor	.408
Ramirez, Bos	.405
Olerud, Sea	.401
A. Rodriguez, Tex.	.399
B. Williams, NY	.395
Catalanotto, Tex	.391

Runs

A. Rodriguez, Tex.	133
Suzuki, Sea	127
Boone, Sea.	118
Alomar, Clev.	113
Jeter, NY	110
Ja. Giambi, Oak	109
Damon, Oak	108
Tejada, Oak	107
Beltran, KC.	106
Durham, Chi.	104

Hits

Suzuki, Sea	242
Boone, Sea.	206
Stewart, Tor	202
A. Rodriguez, Tex.	201
Anderson, Ana	194
Alomar, Clev.	193
Jeter, NY	191
Beltran, KC	189
Ordonez, Chi	181
2 tied	178

Runs Batted In

Boone, Sea.	141
Gonzalez, Clev	140
A. Rodriguez, Tex.	135
Ramirez, Bos	125
Thome, Clev	124
Anderson, Ana	123
Palmeiro, Tex.	123
Ja. Giambi, Oak	120
Martinez, Sea	116
Chavez, Oak	114

Doubles

Ja. Giambi, Oak	47
Sweeney, KC	46
Stewart, Tor	44
Chavez, Oak	43
Durham, Chi.	42
Martinez, Sea	40
Ordonez, Chi	40
Anderson, Ana	39
Mientkiewicz, Minn	39
3 tied	38

Triples

Guzman, Minn	14
Alomar, Clev.	12
Beltran, KC.	12
Cedeno, Det	11
Durham, Chi.	10
McLemore, Sea	9
Suzuki, Sea	8
Vizquel, Clev.	8
4 tied	7

Home Runs

A. Rodriguez, Tex.	52
Thome, Clev.	49
Palmeiro, Tex.	47
Glaus, Ana.	41
Ramirez, Bos	41
Delgado, Tor	39
Ja. Giambi, Oak	38
Boone, Sea.	37
Gonzalez, Clev	35
2 tied	34

Slugging Average

Ja. Giambi, Oak	.660
Thome, Clev.	.624
A. Rodriguez, Tex.	.622
Ramirez, Bos	.609
Gonzalez, Clev	.590
Boone, Sea.	.578
Palmeiro, Tex.	.563
Martinez, Sea	.543
Burks, Clev.	.542
Sweeney, KC	.542

Stolen Bases

Suzuki, Sea	56
Cedeno, Det	55
Soriano, NY	43
McLemore, Sea	39
Knoblauch, NY	38
Cameron, Sea.	34
Cruz, Tor	32
Beltran, KC.	31
Rivas, Minn	31
Tyner, TB	31

Walks

Ja. Giambi, Oak	129
Delgado, Tor	111
Thome, Clev	111
Glaus, Ana	107
Palmeiro, Tex.	101
Salmon, Ana.	96
Olerud, Sea	94
Martinez, Sea	93
Grieve, TB	87
Ramirez, Bos	81

Total Bases

A. Rodriguez, Tex.	393
Boone, Sea.	360
Ja. Giambi, Oak	343
Palmeiro, Tex.	338
Thome, Clev.	328
Ramirez, Bos	322
Anderson, Ana	321
Beltran, KC.	317
Ordonez, Chi	316
Suzuki, Sea	316 ▶

Pitching

Wins – Losses			Earned Run Average	
Mulder, Oak	21	8	Garcia, Sea	3.05
Clemens, NY	20	3	Mussina, NY	3.15
Moyer, Sea	20	6	Mays, Minn	3.16
Garcia, Sea	18	6	Buehrle, Chi	3.29
Hudson, Oak	18	9	Hudson, Oak	3.37
Abbott, Sea	17	4	Moyer, Sea	3.43
Sabathia, Clev	17	5	Mulder, Oak	3.45
Zito, Oak	17	8	Zito, Oak	3.49
Mussina, NY	17	11	Clemens, NY	3.51
Mays, Minn	17	13	Lidle, Oak	3.59

Strikeouts		Saves		Shutouts	
Nomo, Bos	220	M. Rivera, NY	50	Mulder, Oak	4
Mussina, NY	214	Sasaki, Sea	45	Garcia, Sea	3
Clemens, NY	213	Foulke, Chi	42	Mussina, NY	3
Zito, Oak	205	Percival, Ana	39	Buehrle, Chi	2
Colon, Clev	201	Koch, Tor	36	Carpenter, Tor	2
Hudson, Oak	181	Isringhausen, Oak	34	Mays, Minn	2
Sabathia, Clev	171	Wickman, Clev	32	Nomo, Bos	2
Pettitte, NY	164	Hawkins, Minn	28	Radke, Minn	2
Garcia, Sea	163	Hernandez, KC	28	Zito, Oak	2
Martinez, Bos	163	Zimmerman, Tex	28	11 tied	1

Innings Pitched		Games		Complete Games	
Garcia, Sea	238.2	Quantrill, Tor	80	Sparks, Det	8
Hudson, Oak	235.0	Stanton, NY	76	Mulder, Oak	6
Mays, Minn	233.2	Grimsley, KC	73	Radke, Minn	6
Sparks, Det	232.0	Foulke, Chi	72	Weaver, Det	5
Mulder, Oak	229.1	Borbon, Tor	71	Buehrle, Chi	4
Weaver, Det	229.1	Rhodes, Sea	71	Garcia, Sea	4
Mussina, NY	228.2	M. Rivera, NY	71	Mays, Minn	4
Radke, Minn	226.0	4 tied	70	Mussina, NY	4
Colon, Clev	222.1			4 tied	3
Buehrle, Chi	221.1				

Source: *Canadian Press*

National League Final Standings, 2001

Eastern Division					Central Division					Western Division				
TEAM	W	L	%	GB	TEAM	W	L	%	GB	TEAM	W	L	%	GB
Y-Atlanta	88	74	.543	-	Y-Houston	93	69	.574	-	Y-Arizona	92	70	.568	-
Philadelphia	86	76	.531	2	X-St Louis	93	69	.574	-	San Francisco	90	72	.556	2
NY Mets	82	80	.506	6	Chicago	88	74	.543	5	Los Angeles	86	76	.531	6
Florida	76	86	.469	12	Milwaukee	68	94	.420	25	San Diego	79	83	.488	13
Montreal	68	94	.420	20	Cincinnati	66	96	.407	27	Colorado	73	89	.451	19
					Pittsburgh	62	100	.383	31					

Source: *Canadian Press*

X — Wild Card Y — Division Title.

National League Leaders, 2001

Batting

Batting Average		On-Base Percentage		Runs	
L. Walker, Col	.350	Bonds, SF	.515	Sosa, Chi	146
Helton, Col	.336	L. Walker, Col	.449	Helton, Col	132
Alou, Hou	.331	Sosa, Chi	.437	Bonds, SF	129
Berkman, Hou	.331	Helton, Col	.432	Gonzalez, Ari	128
C. Jones, Atl	.330	Berkman, Hou	.430	Bagwell, Hou	126
Pujols, Hou	.329	Gonzalez, Ari	.429	Floyd, Fla	123
Bonds, SF	.328	C. Jones, Atl	.427	Green, LA	121
Sosa, Chi	.328	Sheffield, LA	.417	Abreu, Phil	118
Pierre, Col	.327	Edmonds, StL	.410	Biggio, Hou	118
Gonzalez, Ari	.325	Giles, Pitt	.404	Giles, Pitt	116

Hits

Aurilia, SF.	206
Pierre, Col	202
Gonzalez, Ari	198
Helton, Col	197
Pujols, StL	194
Berkman, Hou	191
Vina, StL	191
C. Jones, Atl.	189
Sosa, Chi	189
2 tied	184

Runs Batted In

Sosa, Chi	160
Helton, Col	146
Gonzalez, Ari	142
Bonds, SF.	137
Bagwell, Hou	130
Pujols, StL	130
Berkman, Hou	126
Nevin, SD.	126
Green, LA.	125
Sexson, Mil	125

Doubles

Berkman, Hou	55
Helton, Col	54
Kent, SF.	49
Abreu, Phil	48
Pujols, StL	47
Guerrero, Mtl	45
Floyd, Fla	44
Bagwell, Hou	43
Young, Chi	43
Cabrera, Mtl	41

Triples

Rollins, Phil	12
Pierre, Col	11
Uribe, Col	11
Castillo, Fla.	10
Perez, Col.	8
Tucker, Cin–Chi	8
Vina, StL	8
Giles, Pitt	7
Gonzalez, Ari	7
Ochoa, Cin–Col	7

Home Runs

Bonds, SF.	73
Sosa, Chi	64
Gonzalez, Ari	57
Green, LA.	49
Helton, Col.	49
Sexson, Mil	45
Nevin, SD.	41
Bagwell, Hou	39
C. Jones, Atl.	38
L. Walker, Col.	38

Slugging Average

Bonds, SF.	.863
Sosa, Chi	.737
Gonzalez, Ari	.688
Helton, Col.	.685
L. Walker, Col.	.662
Berkman, Hou	.620
Pujols, StL	.610
C. Jones, Atl.	.605
Green, LA.	.598
Giles, Pitt	.590

Stolen Bases

Pierre, Col	46
Rollins, Phil	46
Guerrero, Mtl	37
Abreu, Phil.	36
Castillo, Fla.	33
Young, Chi	31
Glanville, Phil.	28
Womack, StL	28
Henderson, SD.	25
Reese, Cin	25

Walks

Bonds, SF.	177
Sosa, Chi	116
Abreu, Phil	106
Bagwell, Hou	106
Gonzalez, Ari	100
Helton, Col	98
C. Jones, Atl.	98
Sheffield, LA.	94
Edmonds, StL	93
Berkman, Hou	92

Total Bases

Sosa, Chi	425
Gonzalez, Ari	419
Bonds, SF.	411
Helton, Col	402
Green, LA.	370
Aurilia, SF.	364
Pujols, StL	360
Berkman, Hou	358
C. Jones, Atl.	346
Bagwell, Hou	341

Pitching

Wins – Losses

Schilling, Ari.	22	6
Morris, StL.	22	8
Johnson, Ari.	21	6
Lieber, Chi	20	6
Ortiz, SF.	17	9
Maddux, Atl	17	11
Glavine, Atl.	16	7
Miller, Hou	16	8
Kile, StL	16	11
Vazquez, Mtl.	16	11

Earned Run Average

Johnson, Ari.	2.49
Schilling, Ari.	2.98
Burkett, Atl	3.04
Maddux, Atl	3.05
Kile, StL	3.09
Morris, StL.	3.16
Ortiz, SF.	3.29
Leiter, NY.	3.31
Wood, Chi	3.36
Miller, Hou	3.40

Strikeouts

Johnson, Ari.	372
Schilling, Ari.	293
Park, LA.	218
Wood, Chi	217
Vazquez, Mtl.	208
Burkett, Atl.	187
Morris, StL.	185
Miller, Hou.	183
Person, Phil.	183
Kile, StL	179

Saves

Nen, SF.	45
Benitez, NY.	43
Hoffman, SD.	43
Shaw, LA.	43
Mesa, Phil.	42
Wagner, Hou.	39
Graves, Cin.	32
Alfonseca, Fla.	28
Gordon, Chi	27
Williams, Pitt–Hou	22

Shutouts

Maddux, Atl.	3
Vazquez, Mtl.	3
Johnson, Ari.	2
Lopez, Ari.	2
Ritchie, Pitt	2
Wolf, Phil.	2
27 tied	1

Innings Pitched

Schilling, Ari.	256.2
Johnson, Ari.	249.2
Park, LA.	234.0
Maddux, Atl	233.0
Lieber, Chi	232.1
Kile, StL	227.1
Hernandez, SF.	226.2
Vazquez, Mtl.	223.2
Williams, SD–StL	220.0
2 tied	219.1

Games

Kline, StL	89
Lloyd, Mtl.	84
Fassero, Chi	82
King, Mil.	82
Rodriguez, SF.	80
Weathers, Mil–Chi	80
Nen, SF.	79
Sullivan, Cin.	79
Kim, Ari	78
2 tied	77

Complete Games

Schilling, Ari.	6
Lieber, Chi	5
Vazquez, Mtl.	5
Astacio, Col–Hou	4
Ritchie, Pitt	4
Wolf, Phil.	4
7 tied	3

Source: *Canadian Press*

Major League Pennant Winners, 1960–2000

	National League					American League			
	Winner	Won	Lost	%		Winner	Won	Lost	%
1960	Pittsburgh	95	59	.617	1960	New York	97	57	.630
1961	Cincinnati	93	61	.604	1961	New York	109	53	.673
1962	San Francisco	103	62	.624	1962	New York	96	66	.593
1963	Los Angeles	99	63	.611	1963	New York	104	57	.646
1964	St. Louis	93	69	.574	1964	New York	99	63	.611
1965	Los Angeles	97	65	.599	1965	Minnesota	102	60	.630
1966	Los Angeles	95	67	.586	1966	Baltimore	97	63	.606
1967	St. Louis	101	60	.627	1967	Boston	92	70	.568
1968	St. Louis	97	65	.599	1968	Detroit	103	59	.636
1969	New York	100	62	.617	1969	Baltimore	109	53	.673
1970	Cincinnati	102	60	.630	1970	Baltimore	108	54	.667
1971	Pittsburgh	97	65	.599	1971	Baltimore	101	57	.639
1972	Cincinnati	95	59	.617	1972	Oakland	93	62	.600
1973	New York	82	79	.509	1973	Oakland	94	68	.580
1974	Los Angeles	102	60	.630	1974	Oakland	90	72	.556
1975	Cincinnati	108	54	.667	1975	Boston	95	65	.594
1976	Cincinnati	102	60	.630	1976	New York	97	62	.610
1977	Los Angeles	98	64	.605	1977	New York	100	62	.617
1978	Los Angeles	95	67	.586	1978	New York	100	63	.613
1979	Pittsburgh	98	64	.605	1979	Baltimore	102	57	.642
1980	Philadelphia	91	71	.562	1980	Kansas City	97	65	.599
1981	Los Angeles	63	47	.573	1981	New York	59	48	.551
1982	St. Louis	92	70	.568	1982	Milwaukee	95	67	.586
1983	Philadelphia	90	72	.556	1983	Baltimore	98	64	.605
1984	San Diego	92	70	.568	1984	Detroit	104	58	.642
1985	St. Louis	101	61	.623	1985	Kansas City	91	71	.562
1986	New York	108	54	.667	1986	Boston	95	66	.590
1987	St. Louis	95	67	.586	1987	Minnesota	85	77	.525
1988	Los Angeles	94	67	.584	1988	Oakland	104	58	.642
1989	San Francisco	92	70	.568	1989	Oakland	99	63	.611
1990	Cincinnati	91	71	.562	1990	Oakland	103	59	.636
1991	Atlanta	94	68	.580	1991	Minnesota	95	67	.586
1992	Atlanta	98	64	.605	1992	**Toronto**	**96**	**66**	**.593**
1993	Philadelphia	97	65	.599	1993	**Toronto**	**95**	**67**	**.586**
1994[1]	no winner				1994[1]	no winner			
1995	Atlanta	90	54	.625	1995	Cleveland	100	44	.694
1996	Atlanta	96	66	.593	1996	New York	92	70	.569
1997	Florida	92	70	.568	1997	Cleveland	86	75	.534
1998	San Diego	98	64	.605	1998	New York	114	48	.704
1999	Atlanta	103	59	.639	1999	New York	98	64	.605
2000	New York	94	68	.580	2000	New York	87	74	.540

Source: *Canadian Press*   (1) Players strike Aug. 12, 1994; owners suspended season, Sept. 14, 1994.

World Series Results, 1961–2000

	Champion	Final Opponent	Series Result
1961	New York Yankees, AL	Cincinnati Reds, NL	4–1
1962	New York Yankees, AL	San Francisco Giants, NL	4–3
1963	Los Angeles Dodgers, NL	New York Yankees, AL	4–0
1964	St. Louis Cardinals, NL	New York Yankees, AL	4–3
1965	Los Angeles Dodgers, NL	Minnesota Twins, AL	4–3
1966	Baltimore Orioles, AL	Los Angeles Dodgers, NL	4–0
1967	St. Louis Cardinals, NL	Boston Red Sox, AL	4–3
1968	Detroit Tigers, AL	St. Louis Cardinals, NL	4–3
1969	New York Mets, NL	Baltimore Orioles, AL	4–1
1970	Baltimore Orioles, AL	Cincinnati Reds, NL	4–1
1971	Pittsburgh Pirates, NL	Baltimore Orioles, AL	4–3
1972	Oakland Athletics, AL	Cincinnati Reds, NL	4–3
1973	Oakland Athletics, AL	New York Mets, NL	4–3
1974	Oakland Athletics, AL	Los Angeles Dodgers, NL	4–1
1975	Cincinnati Reds, NL	Boston Red Sox, AL	4–3
1976	Cincinnati Reds, NL	New York Yankees, AL	4–0
1977	New York Yankees, AL	Los Angeles Dodgers, NL	4–2
1978	New York Yankees, AL	Los Angeles Dodgers, NL	4–2
1979	Pittsburgh Pirates, NL	Baltimore Orioles, AL	4–3
1980	Philadelphia Phillies, NL	Kansas City Royals, AL	4–2
1981	Los Angeles Dodgers, NL	New York Yankees, AL	4–2
1982	St. Louis Cardinals, NL	Milwaukee Brewers, AL	4–3
1983	Baltimore Orioles, AL	Philadelphia Phillies, NL	4–1
1984	Detroit Tigers, AL	San Diego Padres, NL	4–1
1985	Kansas City Royals, AL	St. Louis Cardinals, NL	4–3
1986	New York Mets, NL	Boston Red Sox, AL	4–3
1987	Minnesota Twins, AL	St. Louis Cardinals, NL	4–3
1988	Los Angeles Dodgers, NL	Oakland Athletics, AL	4–1
1989	Oakland Athletics, AL	San Francisco Giants, NL	4–0
1990	Cincinnati Reds, NL	Oakland Athletics, AL	4–0
1991	Minnesota Twins, AL	Atlanta Braves, NL	4–3
1992	**Toronto Blue Jays, AL**	Atlanta Braves, NL	4–2
1993	**Toronto Blue Jays, AL**	Philadelphia Phillies, NL	4–2
1994	No World Series: season suspended Sept. 15, 1994		
1995	Atlanta Braves, NL	Cleveland Indians, AL	4–2
1996	New York, AL	Atlanta, NL	4–2
1997	Florida, NL	Cleveland, AL	4–3
1998	New York Yankees, AL	San Diego, NL	4–0
1999	New York Yankees, AL	Atlanta Braves, NL	4–0
2000	New York Yankees, AL	New York Mets, NL	4–1

Source: *Canadian Press*

World Series MVPs, 1961–2000

1961	Whitey Ford, NY (AL)	**1975**	Pete Rose, Cin	**1987**	Frank Viola, Min
1962	Ralph Terry, NY (AL)	**1976**	Johnny Bench, Cin	**1988**	Orel Hershiser, LA
1963	Sandy Koufax, LA	**1977**	Reggie Jackson, NY (AL)	**1989**	Dave Stewart, Oak
1964	Bob Gibson, StL	**1978**	Bucky Dent, NY (AL)	**1990**	Jose Rijo, Cin
1965	Sandy Koufax, LA	**1979**	Willie Stargell, Pgh	**1991**	Jack Morris, Min
1966	Frank Robinson, Bal	**1980**	Mike Schmidt, Pha	**1992**	**Pat Borders, Tor**
1967	Bob Gibson, StL	**1981**	Ron Cey, LA[1]	**1993**	**Paul Molitor, Tor**
1968	Mickey Lolich, Det	**1981**	Pedro Guerrero, LA[1]	**1994**	No award
1969	Donn Clendenon, NY (NL)	**1981**	Steve Yeager, LA[1]	**1995**	Tom Glavine, Atl
1970	Brooks Robinson, Bal	**1982**	Darrell Porter, StL	**1996**	John Wetteland, NY
1971	Roberto Clemente, Pgh	**1983**	Rick Dempsey, Bal	**1997**	Livan Hernandez, Fla
1972	Gene Tenace, Oak	**1984**	Alan Trammell, Det	**1998**	Scott Brosius, NY
1973	Reggie Jackson, Oak	**1985**	Bret Saberhagen, KC	**1999**	Mariano Rivera, NY
1974	Rollie Fingers, Oak	**1986**	Ray Knight, NY (NL)	**2000**	Mariano Rivera, NY

Source: *Canadian Press*   (1) Joint winners.

Cy Young Award Winners, 1961–2000

	Player, Club
1961[1]	Whitey Ford, New York Yankees
1962[1]	Don Drysdale, Los Angeles Dodgers
1963[1]	Sandy Koufax, Los Angeles Dodgers
1964[1]	Dean Chance, California Angels
1965[1]	Sandy Koufax, Los Angeles Dodgers
1966[1]	Sandy Koufax, Los Angeles Dodgers
1967 (NL)	Mike McCormick, San Francisco Giants
(AL)	Jim Lonborg, Boston Red Sox
1968 (NL)	Bob Gibson, St. Louis Cardinals
(AL)	Dennis McLain, Detroit Tigers
1969 (NL)	Tom Seaver, New York Mets
(AL)	Dennis McLain, Detroit Tigers
(AL)	Mike Cuellar, Baltimore Orioles
1970 (NL)	Bob Gibson, St. Louis Cardinals
(AL)	Jim Perry, Minnesota Twins
1971 (NL)	Ferguson Jenkins, Chicago Cubs
(AL)	Vida Blue, Oakland A's
1972 (NL)	Steve Carlton, Philadelphia Phillies
(AL)	Gaylord Perry, Cleveland Indians
1973 (NL)	Tom Seaver, New York Mets
(AL)	Jim Palmer, Baltimore Orioles
1974 (NL)	Mike Marshall, Los Angeles Dodgers
(AL)	Jim (Catfish) Hunter, Oakland A's
1975 (NL)	Tom Seaver, New York Mets
(AL)	Jim Palmer, Baltimore Orioles
1976 (NL)	Randy Jones, San Diego Padres
(AL)	Jim Palmer, Baltimore Orioles
1977 (NL)	Steve Carlton, Philadelphia Phillies
(AL)	Sparky Lyle, New York Yankees
1978 (NL)	Gaylord Perry, San Diego Padres
(AL)	Ron Guidry, New York Yankees
1979 (NL)	Bruce Sutter, Chicago Cubs
(AL)	Mike Flanagan, Baltimore Orioles
1980 (NL)	Steve Carlton, Philadelphia Phillies
(AL)	Steve Stone, Baltimore Orioles
1981 (NL)	Fernando Valenzuela, Los Angeles Dodgers
(AL)	Rollie Fingers, Milwaukee Brewers
1982 (NL)	Steve Carlton, Philadelphia Phillies
(AL)	Pete Vuckovich, Milwaukee Brewers

	Player, Club
1983 (NL)	John Denny, Philadelphia Phillies
(AL)	LaMarr Hoyt, Chicago White Sox
1984 (NL)	Rick Sutcliffe, Chicago Cubs
(AL)	Willie Hernandez, Detroit Tigers
1985 (NL)	Dwight Gooden, New York Mets
(AL)	Bret Saberhagen, Kansas City Royals
1986 (NL)	Mike Scott, Houston Astros
(AL)	Roger Clemens, Boston Red Sox
1987 (NL)	Steve Bedrosian, Philadelphia Phillies
(AL)	Roger Clemens, Boston Red Sox
1988 (NL)	Orel Hershiser, Los Angeles Dodgers
(AL)	Frank Viola, Minnesota Twins
1989 (NL)	Mark Davis, San Diego Padres
(AL)	Bret Saberhagen, Kansas City Royals
1990 (NL)	Doug Drabek, Pittsburgh Pirates
(AL)	Bob Welch, Oakland A's
1991 (NL)	Tom Glavine, Atlanta Braves
(AL)	Roger Clemens, Boston Red Sox
1992 (NL)	Greg Maddux, Chicago Cubs
(AL)	Dennis Eckersley, Oakland A's
1993 (NL)	Greg Maddux, Atlanta Braves
(AL)	Jack McDowell, Chicago White Sox
1994 (NL)	Greg Maddux, Atlanta Braves
(AL)	David Cone, Kansas City Royals
1995 (NL)	Greg Maddux, Atlanta Braves
(AL)	Randy Johnson, Seattle Mariner
1996 (NL)	John Smoltz, Atlanta Braves
(AL)	**Pat Hentgen, Toronto Blue Jays**
1997 (NL)	**Pedro Martinez, Montreal Expos**
(AL)	**Roger Clemens, Toronto Blue Jays**
1998 (NL)	Tom Glavine, Atlanta Braves
(AL)	**Roger Clemens, Toronto Blue Jays**
1999 (NL)	Randy Johnson, Arizona
(AL)	Pedro Martinez, Boston
2000 (NL)	Randy Johnson, Arizona
(AL)	Pedro Martinez, Boston

Source: *Canadian Press*

(1) One award, 1960–66.

Most Valuable Player, 1961–2000

	National League	American League
1961	Frank Robinson, Cincinnati Reds	Roger Maris, New York Yankees
1962	Maury Wills, Los Angeles Dodgers	Mickey Mantle, New York Yankees
1963	Sandy Koufax, Los Angeles Dodgers	Elston Howard, New York Yankees
1964	Ken Boyer, St. Louis Cardinals	Brooks Robinson, Baltimore Orioles
1965	Willie Mays, San Francisco Giants	Zoilo Versalles, Minnesota Twins
1966	Roberto Clemente, Pittsburgh Pirates	Frank Robinson, Baltimore Orioles
1967	Orlando Cepeda, St. Louis Cardinals	Carl Yastrzemski, Boston Red Sox
1968	Bob Gibson, St. Louis Cardinals	Denny McLain, Detroit Tigers
1969	Willie McCovey, San Francisco Giants	Harmon Killebrew, Minnesota Twins
1971	Joe Torre, St. Louis Cardinals	Vida Blue, Oakland Athletics
1972	Johnny Bench, Cincinnati Reds	Dick Allen, Chicago White Sox
1975	Joe Morgan, Cincinnati Reds	Fred Lynn, Boston Red Sox
1976	Joe Morgan, Cincinnati Reds	Thurman Munson, New York Yankees
1979	Keith Hernandez, St. Louis Cardinals; Willie Stargell, Pittsburgh Pirates	Don Baylor, California Angels
1980	Mike Schmidt, Philadelphia Phillies	George Brett, Kansas City Royals
1981	Mike Schmidt, Philadelphia Phillies	Rollie Fingers, Milwaukee Brewers
1982	Dale Murphy, Atlanta Braves	Robin Yount, Milwaukee Brewers
1983	Dale Murphy, Atlanta Braves	Cal Ripken, Jr., Baltimore Orioles
1984	Ryne Sandberg, Chicago Cubs	Willie Hernandez, Detroit Tigers
1985	Willie McGee, St. Louis Cardinals	Don Mattingly, New York Yankees
1986	Mike Schmidt, Philadelphia Phillies	Roger Clemens, Boston Red Sox
1987	André Dawson, Chicago Cubs	**George Bell, Toronto Blue Jays**
1988	Kirk Gibson, Los Angeles Dodgers	Jose Canseco, Oakland Athletics
1989	Kevin Mitchell, San Francisco Giants	Robin Yount, Milwaukee Brewers
1990	Barry Bonds, Pittsburgh Pirates	Rickey Henderson, Oakland Athletics
1991	Terry Pendleton, Atlanta Braves	Cal Ripken, Jr., Baltimore Orioles
1992	Barry Bonds, Pittsburgh Pirates	Dennis Eckersley, Oakland A's
1993	Barry Bonds, San Francisco Giants	Frank Thomas, Chicago White Sox
1994	Jeff Bagwell, Houston Astras	Frank Thomas, Chicago White Sox
1995	Barry Larkin, Cincinnati Reds	Mo Vaughn, Boston Red Sox
1996	Ken Caminiti, San Diego Padres	Juan Gonzalez, Texas Rangers
1997	Larry Walker, Colorado Rockies	Ken Griffey Jr., Seattle Mariners
1998	Sammy Sosa, Chicago Cubs	Juan Gonzalez, Texas Rangers
1999	Chipper Jones, Atlanta Braves	Ivan Rodriguez, Texas Rangers
2000	Jeff Kent, San Francisco	Jason Giambi, Oakland A's

Source: *Canadian Press*

All-time Single Season Home Run Record

*D*uring the 2001 season, San Francisco Giants left-fielder Barry Bonds was on the fastest home run pace in baseball history. As of September 27, Bonds was closing in on Mark McGwire's 1998 record of 70 with 67 homers. "He's totally blown away what I did, even if the year ended today," said McGwire. Bonds, a left-handed power-hitter, made his MLB debut in 1986 but hasn't won a World Series yet. "Breaking the record wouldn't necessarily mean that much to me... What I really want is a world championship for the Giants and the ring that goes with it for myself." Bonds ended the season with 73 home runs and 177 walks.

Batting Champions, 1962–2001

	National League				American League	
	Player, Club	**%**			**Player, Club**	**%**
1962	Tommy Davis, Los Angeles	.346		1962	Pete Runnels, Boston	.326
1963	Tommy Davis, Los Angeles	.326		1963	Carl Yastrzemski, Boston	.321
1964	Roberto Clemente, Pittsburgh	.339		1964	Tony Oliva, Minnesota	.323
1965	Roberto Clemente, Pittsburgh	.329		1965	Tony Oliva, Minnesota	.321
1966	Matty Alou, Pittsburgh	.342		1966	Frank Robinson, Baltimore	.316
1967	Roberto Clemente, Pittsburgh	.357		1967	Carl Yastrzemski, Boston	.326
1968	Pete Rose, Cincinnati	.335		1968	Carl Yastrzemski, Boston	.301
1969	Pete Rose, Cincinnati	.348		1969	Rod Carew, Minnesota	.332
1970	Rico Carty, Atlanta	.366		1970	Alex Johnson, California	.329
1971	Joe Torre, St. Louis	.363		1971	Tony Oliva, Minnesota	.337
1972	Billy Williams, Chicago	.333		1972	Rod Carew, Minnesota	.318
1973	Pete Rose, Cincinnati	.338		1973	Rod Carew, Minnesota	.350
1974	Ralph Garr, Atlanta	.353		1974	Rod Carew, Minnesota	.364
1975	Bill Madlock, Chicago	.354		1975	Rod Carew, Minnesota	.359
1976	Bill Madlock, Chicago	.339		1976	George Brett, Kansas City	.333
1977	Dave Parker, Pittsburgh	.338		1977	Rod Carew, Minnesota	.388
1978	Dave Parker, Pittsburgh	.334		1978	Rod Carew, Minnesota	.333
1979	Keith Hernandez, St. Louis	.344		1979	Fred Lynn, Boston	.333
1980	Bill Buckner, Chicago	.324		1980	George Brett, Kansas City	.390
1981	Bill Madlock, Pittsburgh[1]	.341		1981	Carney Lansford, Boston	.336
1982	**Al Oliver, Montreal**	**.331**		1982	Willie Wilson, Kansas City	.332
1983	Bill Madlock, Pittsburgh	.323		1983	Wade Boggs, Boston	.361
1984	Tony Gwynn, San Diego	.351		1984	Don Mattingly, New York	.343
1985	Willie McGee, St. Louis	.353		1985	Wade Boggs, Boston	.368
1986	**Tim Raines, Montreal**	**.334**		1986	Wade Boggs, Boston	.357
1987	Tony Gwynn, San Diego	.370		1987	Wade Boggs, Boston	.363
1988	Tony Gwynn, San Diego	.313		1988	Wade Boggs, Boston	.366
1989	Tony Gwynn, San Diego	.336		1989	Kirby Puckett, Minnesota	.339
1990	Willie McGee, St. Louis	.335		1990	George Brett, Kansas City	.329
1991	Terry Pendleton, Atlanta	.319		1991	Julio Franco, Texas	.341
1992	Gary Sheffield, San Diego	.330		1992	Edgar Martinez, Seattle	.343
1993	Andres Galarraga, Colorado	.370		1993	**John Olerud, Toronto**	**.363**
1994	Tony Gwynn, San Diego[1]	.394		1994	Paul O'Neill, New York[1]	.359
1995	Tony Gwynn, San Diego	.368		1995	Edgar Martinez, Seattle	.356
1996	Tony Gwynn, San Diego	.353		1996	Alex Rodriguez, Seattle	.358
1997	Tony Gwynn, San Diego	.372		1997	Frank Thomas, Chicago	.347
1998	Larry Walker, Colorado	.363		1998	Bernie Williams, New York	.339
1999	Larry Walker, Colorado	.379		1999	Nomar Garciaparra, Boston	**.357**
2000	Todd Helton, Colorado	.372		2000	Nomar Garciaparra, Boston	.372
2001	Larry Walker, Colorado	.350		2001	Ichiro Suzuki, Seattle	.350

Source: *Canadian Press*   (1) Strike abbreviated season.

Home Run Seasons

HR	Player, Team	Year	HR	Player, Team	Year	HR	Player, Team	Year
73	Barry Bonds, SF	2001	57	Luis Gonzalez, Ari	2001	52	Alex Rodriguez,Tex	2001
70	Mark McGwire, StL	1998	56	Hack Wilson, Chi Cubs	1930	51	Ralph Kiner, Pit	1947
66	Sammy Sosa, Chi Cubs	1998	56	Ken Griffey Jr., Sea	1998	51	Johnny Mize,	
65	Mark McGwire, StL	1999	56	Ken Griffey Jr., Sea	1997		NY Giants	1947
64	Sammy Sosa, Chi Cubs	2001	54	Babe Ruth, NYY	1920	51	Willie Mays, NY Giants	1955
63	Sammy Sosa, Chi Cubs	1999	54	Babe Ruth, NYY	1928	51	Cecil Fielder, Det	1990
61	Roger Maris, NYY	1961	54	Ralph Kiner, Pit	1949	50	Jimmie Foxx, Bos	1938
60	Babe Ruth, NYY	1927	54	Mickey Mantle, NYY	1961	50	Albert Belle, Cle	1995
59	Babe Ruth, NYY	1921	52	Mickey Mantle, NYY	1956	50	Brady Anderson, Bal	1996
58	Jimmie Foxx, Phi Athletics	1932	52	Willie Mays, SF	1965	50	Greg Vaughn, SD	1998
58	Hank Greenberg, Det	1938	52	George Foster, Cin	1977			
58	Mark McGwire, Oak/ StL	1997	52	Mark McGwire, Oak	1996			

Source: *Canadian Press*

Individual Earned Run Average Leaders, 1961–2001

National League

	Player, Team	ERA
1961	Warren Spahn, Mil	3.02
1962	Sandy Koufax, LA	2.54
1963	Sandy Koufax, LA	1.88
1964	Sandy Koufax, LA	1.74
1965	Sandy Koufax, LA	2.04
1966	Sandy Koufax, LA	1.73
1967	Phil Niekro, Atl	1.87
1968	Bob Gibson, StL	1.12
1969	Juan Marichal, SF	2.10
1970	Tom Seaver, NY	2.81
1971	Tom Seaver, NY	1.76
1972	Steve Carlton, Pha	1.97
1973	Tom Seaver, NY	2.08
1974	Buzz Capra, Atl	2.28
1975	Randy Jones, SD	2.24
1976	John Denny, StL	2.52
1977	John Candelaria, Pgh	2.34
1978	Craig Swan, NY	2.43
1979	J.R. Richard, Hou	2.71
1980	Don Sutton, LA	2.21
1981	Nolan Ryan, Hou	1.69[1]
1982	Steve Rogers, Mtl	2.40
1983	Atlee Hammaker, SF	2.25
1984	Alejandro Pena, LA	2.48
1985	Dwight Gooden, NY	1.53
1986	Mike Scott, Hou	2.22
1987	Nolan Ryan, Hou	2.76
1988	Joe Magrane, StL	2.18
1989	Scott Garrelts, SF	2.28
1990	Danny Darwin, Hou	2.21
1991	Dennis Martinez, Mtl	2.39
1992	Bill Swift, SF	2.08
1993	Greg Maddux, Atl	2.36
1994	Greg Maddux, Atl	1.56[1]
1995	Greg Maddux, Atl	1.63
1996	Kevin Brown, Fla	1.89
1997	Pedro Martinez, Mtl	1.90
1998	Greg Maddux, Atl	2.22
1999	Randy Johnson, Ari	2.48
2000	Kevin Brown, LA	2.58
2001	Randy Johnson, Ari	2.49

American League

	Player, Team	ERA
1961	Dick Donovan, Wash	2.40
1962	Hank Aguirre, Det	2.21
1963	Gary Peters, Chi	2.33
1964	Dean Chance, LA	1.65
1965	Sam McDowell, Cle	2.18
1966	Gary Peters, Chi	1.98
1967	Joel Horlen, Chi	2.06
1968	Luis Tiant, Cle	1.60
1969	Dick Bosman, Wash	2.19
1970	Diego Segui, Oak	2.56
1971	Vida Blue, Oak	1.82
1972	Luis Tiant, Bos	1.91
1973	Jim Palmer, Bal	2.40
1974	Catfish Hunter, Oak	2.49
1975	Jim Palmer, Bal	2.09
1976	Mark Fidrych, Det	2.34
1977	Frank Tanana, Cal	2.54
1978	Ron Guidry, NY	1.74
1979	Ron Guidry, NY	2.78
1980	Rudy May, NY	2.47
1981	Steve McCatty, Oak	2.32[1]
1982	Rick Sutcliffe, Cle	2.96
1983	Rick Honeycutt, Tex	2.42
1984	Mike Boddicker, Bal	2.79
1985	Dave Stieb, Tor	2.48
1986	Roger Clemens, Bos	2.48
1987	Jimmy Key, Tor	2.76
1988	Allan Anderson, Min	2.45
1989	Bret Saberhagen, KC	2.16
1990	Roger Clemens, Bos	1.93
1991	Roger Clemens, Bos	2.62
1992	Roger Clemens, Bos	2.41
1993	Kevin Appier, KC	2.56
1994	Steve Ontiveras, Oak	2.65[1]
1995	Randy Johnson, Sea	2.48
1996	Juan Guzman, Tor	2.93
1997	Roger Clemens, Tor	2.05
1998	Roger Clemens, Tor	2.65
1999	Pedro Martinez, Bos	2.07
2000	Pedro Martinez, Bos	1.74
2001	Freddy Garcia, Sea	3.05

(1) Strike abbreviated season.

Directory of Selected Baseball Organizations in Canada

Canadian Federation of Amateur Baseball
1600 James Naismith Dr.
Gloucester, Ont.
K1B 5N4
Tel: (613) 748-5606
Fax: (613) 748-5706

Major League Baseball
350 Park Ave.
New York, NY 10022
Tel: (212) 339-7800
www.majorleague
baseball.com

Montreal Expos Baseball Club
P.O. Box 500, Station M
Montreal, Que
H1V 3P2
Tel: (514) 253-3434
Fax: (514) 253-8282
www.montrealexpos.com

Toronto Blue Jays
The Skydome
300 The Esplanade West,
Suite 3200
Toronto, Ont.
M5V 3B3
Tel: (416) 341-1000
www.bluejays.ca

Canadian Players in Major League Baseball, 2001

Batter	AVG	OBA	AB	R	H	2B	3B	HR	RBI	BB	SO	SB	CS	E
Rob Ducey, Montreal	.233	.374	73	10	17	3	0	3	12	16	25	0	1	0
Corey Koskie, Minnesota	.276	.362	.562	100	155	37	2	26	103	68	118	27	6	15
Matt Stairs, Chicago (NL)	.250	.358	340	48	85	21	0	17	61	52	76	2	3	4
Larry Walker, Colorado	.350	.449	497	107	174	35	3	38	123	82	103	14	5	4

Pitchers	W	L	ERA	G	GS	SV	IP	H	R	ER	HR	BB	SO
Rheal Cormier, Philadelphia	5	6	4.21	60	0	1	51.1	49	26	24	5	17	37
Ryan Dempster, Florida	15	12	4.94	34	34	0	211.1	218	123	116	21	112	171
Eric Gagne, Los Angeles	6	7	4.75	33	24	0	151.2	144	90	80	24	46	130
Aaron Myette, Texas	4	5	7.14	19	15	0	80.2	94	65	64	12	37	67
Paul Quantrill, Toronto	11	2	3.04	80	0	2	83.0	86	29	28	6	12	58
Chris Reitsma, Cincinnati	7	15	5.29	36	29	0	182.0	209	121	107	23	49	96
Jeff Zimmerman, Texas	4	4	2.40	66	0	28	71.1	48	19	19	10	16	72

Source: *Canadian Press*

Career Records of Some Canadian Major League Players of the Past

Player	Years	G	AB	R	H	HR	RBI	AVG	OBP	SLG	BB	SO	SB	CS
Tip O'Neill . . . 1922-23	1054	4255	880	1386	52	757	.326	.392	.458	421	146	161	—
Pop Smith . . . 1880-91	1110	4230	642	939	24	358	.300	.287	.313	325	345	169	—
Doc Mille 1910-14	557	1717	184	507	12	235	.295	.343	.390	121	149	64	—
Jeff Heath . . . 1936-49	1383	4937	777	1447	194	887	.293	.370	.509	593	670	56	47
Goody Rosen . 1937-46	551	1916	310	557	22	197	.291	.364	.398	218	166	12	—
George Selkirk 1934-42	846	2790	503	810	108	576	.290	.400	.483	486	319	49	32
Terry Puhl . . . 1977-91	1531	4855	676	1361	62	435	.280	.349	.388	505	507	217	99
Bill Phillips . . . 1879-88	1038	4255	562	1130	17	534	.266	.299	.374	178	215	39	—

Pitcher	Years	W	L	IP	ERA	G	GS	CG	SV	H	ER	BB	K
Fergie Jenkins 1965-83	284	226	4500.2	3.34	664	594	267	7	4142	1669	997	3192
Kirk McCaskill 1985-96	106	108	1729.0	4.12	380	242	30	7	1748	791	665	1003
Reggie Cleveland . . 1969-81	105	106	1809.0	4.02	428	203	57	25	1843	807	543	930
John Hiller 1965-80	87	76	1242.0	2.83	545	43	13	125	1040	391	535	1036
Phil Marchildon . . . 1940-50	68	75	1214.1	3.93	185	162	82	2	1084	530	684	481
Dick Fowler 1941-52	66	79	1303.0	4.11	221	170	75	4	1367	595	578	382
Claude Raymond . . 1959-71	46	53	721.0	3.66	449	7	2	83	711	293	225	497
Ron Taylor 1962-72	45	43	800.0	3.93	491	17	3	72	794	349	209	464

Source: *Sportspic.com*

G = Games played. AB = At bats. R = Runs. H = Hits. 2B = Doubles. 3B = Triples. HR = Home runs. RBI = Runs batted in. BA = Batting average. OBA = On-base percentage. SA = Slugging average.

W = Wins. L = Losses. % = Percentage. G = Games pitched. SHO = Shutouts. SV = Saves. IP = Innings pitched. H = Hits allowed. BB = Walks. SO = Strikeouts. ERA = Earned run average.

(1) Marchildon was in the Canadian Armed Forces in 1943–44.

Montreal Expos Year-By-Year Record, 1969–2001

	Won	Lost	%	Pos.	Home Attendance	Manager		Won	Lost	%	Pos.	Home Attendance	Manager
1969...	52	110	.321	6th	1 212 608	Gene Mauch	**1986**...	78	83	.484	4th	1 128 981	Buck Rodgers
1970...	73	89	.451	6th	1 424 683	Gene Mauch	**1987**...	91	71	.562	3rd	1 850 324	Buck Rodgers
1971...	71	90	.441	5th	1 290 963	Gene Mauch	**1988**...	81	81	.500	3rd	1 478 659	Buck Rodgers
1972...	70	86	.449	5th	1 142 145	Gene Mauch	**1989**...	81	81	.500	4th	1 783 533	Buck Rodgers
1973...	79	83	.488	4th	1 246 863	Gene Mauch	**1990**...	85	77	.525	3rd	1 421 388	Buck Rodgers
1974...	79	82	.491	4th	1 019 134	Gene Mauch	**1991**...	70	91	.441	6th	978 045	Buck Rodgers/
1975...	75	87	.463	5th	908 292	Gene Mauch							Tom Runnells
1976...	55	107	.340	6th	646 704	K. Kuehl/C. Fox	**1992**...	87	75	.537	2nd	1 731 566	Tom Runnells/
1977...	75	87	.463	5th	1 433 757	Dick Williams							Felipe Alou
1978...	76	86	.469	4th	1 427 007	Dick Williams	**1993**...	94	68	.580	2nd	1 641 437	Felipe Alou
1979...	95	65	.594	2nd	2 102 173	Dick Williams	**1994**...	74	40	.649	1st(a)	1 276 250	Felipe Alou
1980...	90	72	.556	2nd	2 208 175	Dick Williams	**1995**...	66	78	.458	5th	1 309 618	Felipe Alou
1981...	60	48	.556	—	1 534 564	Dick Williams/	**1996**...	88	74	.543	2nd	1 618 573	Felipe Alou
						Jim Fanning	**1997**...	78	84	.481	4th	1 175 000	Felipe Alou
1982...	86	76	.531	3rd	2 318 292	Jim Fanning	**1998**...	65	97	.401	4th	914 909	Felipe Alou
1983...	82	80	.506	3rd	2 320 651	Bill Virdon	**1999**...	68	94	.420	4th	773 277	Felipe Alou
1984...	78	83	.484	5th	1 606 531	Bill Virdon/	**2000**...	67	95	.414	4th	926 427	Felipe Alou
						Jim Fanning	**2001**...	68	94	.420	5th	642 745	Felipe Alou/
1985...	84	77	.522	3rd	1 502 494	Buck Rodgers							Jeff Torborg

Source: *Canadian Press*   (a) Eastern Division: first year with three divisions.

Montreal Expos Individual Statistics, 2001

Batters

	Avg	OBA	AB	R	H	2B	3B	HR	RBI	BB	SO	SB	CS	E
Mateo	.333	.333	9	1	3	1	0	0	0	0	1	0	0	2
Vidro	.319	.371	486	82	155	34	1	15	59	31	49	4	1	9
Schneider	.317	.396	41	4	13	3	0	1	6	6	3	0	0	0
Raines	.308	.433	78	13	24	8	1	0	4	18	6	1	0	0
Guerrero	.307	.377	599	107	184	45	4	34	108	60	88	37	16	12
Mordecai	.280	.330	254	28	71	17	2	3	32	19	53	2	2	3
Cabrera	.276	.324	626	64	173	41	6	14	96	43	54	19	7	11
Jones	.260	.278	77	8	20	5	0	0	2	2	11	3	0	1
Tatis	.255	.339	145	20	37	9	0	2	11	16	43	0	0	9
Barrett	.250	.289	472	42	118	33	2	6	38	25	54	2	1	7
Pride	.250	.345	76	8	19	3	1	1	9	9	22	3	2	0
Stevens	.245	.338	542	77	133	35	1	25	95	74	157	2	1	19
Smith	.242	.326	194	28	47	13	1	6	18	23	38	0	2	0
Blum	.236	.313	453	57	107	25	0	9	50	43	94	9	5	8
Ducey	.233	.374	73	10	17	3	0	3	12	16	25	0	1	0
Bradley	.223	.287	220	19	49	16	3	1	19	19	62	7	4	2
Knorr	.220	.287	91	13	20	2	0	3	10	8	22	0	0	2
Bergeron	.211	.275	375	53	79	11	4	3	16	28	87	10	7	1
Wilkerson	.205	.304	117	11	24	7	2	1	5	17	41	2	1	2
Minor	.158	.234	95	10	15	2	0	2	13	9	31	0	1	2
Seguignol	.140	.185	50	0	7	2	0	0	5	2	17	0	0	2
Tracy	.109	.190	55	4	6	1	0	2	8	6	26	0	0	0
De La Rosa	.000	.000	1	0	0	0	0	0	0	0	0	0	0	0
Martinez	.000	.000	1	0	0	0	0	0	0	0	0	0	0	0

Source: *Canadian Press*

AVG = Batting average; OBA = On base average; AB = Times at bat; R = Runs; H = Hits; 2B = Doubles; 3B = Triples; HR = Home runs; RBI = Runs batted in; BB = Walks; SO = strikeouts; SB = Stolen bases; CS = Caught stealing; E = Errors.

Pitchers

	W	L	ERA	G	GS	SV	IP	H	R	ER	HR	BB	SO
Strickland	2	6	3.21	77	0	9	81.1	67	36	29	9	41	85
Vazquez	16	11	3.42	32	32	0	223.2	197	92	85	24	44	208
Stewart	3	1	3.78	62	0	3	47.2	43	20	20	5	13	39
Armas	9	14	4.03	34	34	0	196.2	180	101	88	18	91	176
Cubillan	0	0	4.10	29	0	0	26.1	31	13	12	1	12	19
Urbina	2	1	4.24	45	0	15	46.2	42	24	22	8	21	57
Lloyd	9	5	4.35	84	0	1	70.1	74	38	34	6	21	44
Johnson	0	0	4.76	10	0	0	11.1	13	6	6	3	4	10
Ohka	1	4	4.77	10	10	0	54.2	65	30	29	8	10	31
Yoshii	4	7	4.78	42	11	0	113.0	127	65	60	18	26	63
Eischen	0	1	4.85	24	0	0	29.2	29	17	16	4	16	19
Irabu	0	2	4.86	3	3	0	16.2	22	9	9	3	3	18
Munoz	0	4	5.14	15	7	0	42.0	53	25	24	6	21	21
Blank	2	2	5.16	5	4	0	22.2	23	14	13	5	13	11
Mota	1	3	5.26	53	0	0	49.2	51	30	29	9	18	31
Thurman	9	11	5.33	28	26	0	147.0	172	90	87	21	50	96
Reames	4	8	5.59	41	13	0	95.0	101	68	59	16	48	86
Mattes	3	3	6.00	8	8	0	45.0	51	33	30	9	21	26
Pavano	1	6	6.33	8	8	0	42.2	59	33	30	7	16	36
Peters	2	4	7.55	13	6	0	31.0	47	26	26	7	15	14
Scanlan	0	0	7.86	18	0	0	26.1	37	23	23	0	14	5
Telford	0	1	10.29	8	0	0	7.0	14	12	8	2	5	5
Lira	0	0	12.60	4	0	0	5.0	11	7	7	1	2	3

Source: *Canadian Press*
W = Games won; L = Games lost; ERA = Earned run average; G = Games played in; GS = Games started; SV = Saves; IP = Innings pitched; H = Hits allowed; R = Runs allowed; ER = Earned runs; HR = Home runs allowed; BB = Walks allowed; SO = Strikeouts.

Montreal Expos Team Records up to 2001 Season

Batting

Single Season

Batting Average: Vladimir Guerrero, 2000, .345
At Bats: Warren Cromartie, 1979, 659
Games: Rusty Staub, 1971, 162; Ken Singleton, 1973, 162;
Warren Cromartie, 1980, 162
Hits: Al Oliver, 1982, 204
Runs: Tim Raines, 1983, 133
Singles: Tim Raines, 1986, 140
Doubles: Mark Grudzielanek, 1997, 54
Triples: Rodney Scott, 1980, 13; Tim Raines, 1985, 13; Mitch Webster, 1986, 13
Home Runs: Vladimir Guerrero, 2000, 44
Runs Batted In: Vladimir Guerrero, 1999, 131
Total Bases: Andre Dawson, 1983, 341
Slugging Average: Moises Alou, 1994, .592 (106g); Andre Dawson, 1981, .553
On-Base Average: Tim Raines, 1987, .431
Stolen Bases: Ron LeFlore, 1980, 97
Strikeouts: Andres Galarraga, 1990, 169
Walks: Ken Singleton, 1973, 123
Hit By Pitch: Ron Hunt, 1971, 50
Hitting Streak: Vladimir Guerrero, 1999, 31
Pinch Hits: Jose Morales, 1976, 25

Career Leaders

Batting Average: Al Oliver, .315
At Bats: Tim Wallach, 6 529
Games: Tim Wallach, 1 767

Hits: Tim Wallach, 1 694
Runs: Tim Raines, 934
Singles: Tim Raines, 1,148
Doubles: Tim Wallach, 360
Triples: Tim Raines, 81
Home Runs: Andre Dawson, 225
Runs Batted In: Tim Wallach, 905
Total Bases: Tim Wallach, 2,728

Stolen Bases: Tim Raines, 634
Strikeouts: Tim Wallach, 1,008
Walks: Tim Raines, 775

Pitching

Single Season

Games: Mike Marshall, 1973, 92
Games Started: Steve Rogers, 1977, 40
Complete Games: Bill Stoneman, 1971, 20
Innings Pitched: Steve Rogers, 1977, 302
Wins: Ross Grimsley, 1978, 20
Losses: Steve Rogers, 1974, 22
Saves: John Wetteland, 1993, 43
Earned Run Average: Ugueth Urbina, 1998, 1.30
Strikeouts: Pedro Martinez, 1997, 305

Career Leaders

Games: Tim Burke, 425
Games Started: Steve Rogers, 393
Complete Games: Steve Rogers, 129
Innings Pitched: Steve Rogers, 2 839
Wins: Steve Rogers, 158
Losses: Steve Rogers, 152
Saves: Jeff Reardon, 152
Earned Run Average: Dennis Martinez, 2.93

Source: *Canadian Press*

Montreal Expos Player of the Year, 1969–2000

1969 Rusty Staub	**1978** Ross Grimsley	**1986** Tim Raines	**1995** David Segui
1970 Carl Morton	**1979** Larry Parrish	**1987** Tim Wallach	**1996** Hank Rodriguez
1971 Ron Hunt	**1980** Gary Carter	**1988** Andres Galarraga	**1997** Pedro Martinez
1972 Mike Marshall	**1981** Andre Dawson	**1989** Tim Wallach	**1998** Vladimir Guerrero
1973 Mike Marshall	**1982** Al Oliver	**1990** Tim Wallach	**1999** Vladimir Guerrero
1974 Willie Davis	**1983** Andre Dawson;	**1991** Dennis Martinez	**2000** Vladimir Guerrero
1975 Gary Carter	Tim Raines (tie)	**1992** Larry Walker	
1976 Woodie Fryman	**1984** Gary Carter	**1993** Marquis Grissom	
1977 Gary Carter	**1985** Tim Raines	**1994** Moises Alou	

Directory of Sports Organizations

A number of Canadian amateur sports organizations can be reached at 1600 James Naismith Drive, Gloucester, Ont. K1B 5N4. These include:

Other sports organizations include:

Basketball Canada
Tel: (613) 748-5607
www.cdnsport.cu/basketball

Canadian Amateur Boxing Assn
Tel: (613) 748-5611
Fax: (613) 748-5740
www.boxing.ca/cuba.html

Canadian Amateur Diving Assn
Tel: (613) 748-5631

Canadian Amateur Hockey Association
Tel: (613) 748-5613
Fax: (613) 748-5709

Canadian Curling Association
Tel: (613) 748-5628
Fax: (613) 748-5713
www.curling.ca

Canadian Cycling Assn
Tel: (613) 748-5629
Fax: (613) 748-5692
www.canadian-cycling.com

Canadian Federation of Amateur Baseball
Tel: (613) 748-5606
Fax: (613) 748-5706

Canadian Figure Skating Association
Tel: (613) 748-5635
Fax: (613) 748-5718
www.cfsa.ca

Canadian Interuniversity Athletic Union
Tel: (613) 748-5619
Fax: (613) 748-5764
www.ciau.ca

Canadian Soccer Association
Tel: (613) 748-5667
Fax: (613) 745-1938

Canadian Track and Field Assn
Tel: (613) 748-5678
Fax: (613) 748-5645

Canadian Volleyball Assn
Tel: (613) 748-5681

Football Canada
Tel: (613) 748-5636
Fax: (613) 748-5702

Rowing Canada
Tel: (613) 748-5656
Fax: (613) 748-5712

Softball Canada
Tel: (613) 748-5668

Swimming Canada
Tel: (613) 748-5673
Fax: (613) 748-5715
www.swimming.ca

Canadian Automobile Sports Clubs
Tel: (905) 667-9500
Fax: (905) 667-9555
www3.sympatico.ca/case.or

Canadian Trotting Assn
2150 Meadowvale Blvd.
Mississauga, Ont.
L5N 6R6
Tel: (905) 858-3060
Fax: (905) 858-3111

Royal Canadian Golf Association
1333 Dorval Dr.
Oakville, Ont.
L6J 4Z3
Tel: (416) 849-9700
Fax: (416) 845-7040
www.rcga.org

Toronto Blue Jays Year-By-Year Record, 1977–2001

	Won	Lost	%	Pos.	Home Attendance	Manager		Won	Lost	%	Pos.	Home Attendance	Manager
1977 ..	54	107	.335	7th	1 701 052	Roy Hartsfield	**1989** ..	89	73	.549	1st	3 375 573	Williams/
1978 ..	59	102	.366	7th	1 562 585	Roy Hartsfield							Cito Gaston
1979 ..	53	109	.327	7th	1 431 651	Roy Hartsfield	**1990** ..	86	76	.531	2nd	3 885 284	Cito Gaston
1980 ..	67	95	.414	7th	1 400 327	Bob Mattick	**1991** ..	91	71	.562	1st	4 001 526	Cito Gaston
1981 ..	37	69	.349	—	755 083	Bob Mattick	**1992** ..	96	66	.593	1st	4 028 318	Cito Gaston
1st half	16	42	.276	7th			**1993** ..	95	67	.586	1st	4 057 947	Cito Gaston
2nd half	21	27	.438	7th	—		**1994** ..	55	60	.476	3rd[2]	2 907 933	Cito Gaston
1982 ..	78	84	.481	6th[1]	1 275 978	Bobby Cox	**1995** ..	56	88	.389	5th	2 826 483	Cito Gaston
1983 ..	89	73	.549	4th	1 930 415	Bobby Cox	**1996** ..	74	88	.457	4th	2 559 563	Cito Gaston
1984 ..	89	73	.549	2nd	2 110 009	Bobby Cox	**1997** ..	76	86	.469	5th	2 589 297	Cito Gaston[3]
1985 ..	99	62	.615	1st	2 468 925	Bobby Cox	**1998** ..	88	74	.543	3rd	2 454 303	Tim Johnson
1986 ..	86	76	.531	4th	2 455 477	Jimy Williams	**1999** ..	84	78	.518	3rd	2 163 473	Jim Fregosi
1987 ..	96	66	.593	2nd	2 778 459	Jimy Williams	**2000** ..	83	78	.516	3rd	1 819 886	Jim Fregosi
1988 ..	87	75	.537	3rd	2 595 175	Jimy Williams	**2001** ..	80	82	.494	3rd	1 915 438	Buck Martinez

Source: *Canadian Press*

(1) Tied. (2) Eastern Division: first year with three divisions (3) Gaston was fired with five games remaining in the 1997 season.

Toronto Blue Jays Individual Statistics, 2001

Batters

	AVG	OBA	AB	R	H	2B	3B	HR	RBI	BB	SO	SB	CS	E
Stewart	.316	.371	640	103	202	44	7	12	60	46	72	27	10	5
Wells	.312	.350	96	14	30	8	0	1	6	5	15	5	0	2
Bush	.306	.336	271	32	83	11	1	3	27	8	50	13	4	4
Fernandez	.305	.323	59	5	18	4	0	1	12	1	8	0	1	0
Delgado	.279	.408	574	102	160	31	1	39	102	111	136	3	0	9
Latham	.274	.369	73	12	20	3	1	2	10	10	28	4	1	0
Fullmer	.274	.326	522	71	143	31	2	18	83	38	88	5	2	0
Cruz	.274	.326	577	92	158	38	4	34	88	45	138	32	5	3
Freel	.273	.333	22	1	6	1	0	0	3	1	4	2	1	1
Izturis	.269	.279	134	19	36	6	2	2	9	2	15	8	1	3
F. Lopez	.260	.304	177	21	46	5	4	5	23	12	39	4	3	9
Gonzalez	.253	.303	636	79	161	25	5	17	76	43	149	18	11	10
Mondesi	.252	.342	572	88	144	26	4	27	84	73	128	30	11	8
Frye	.246	.305	175	24	43	6	1	2	15	12	18	2	1	1
L. Lopez	.244	.291	119	10	29	4	0	3	10	8	16	0	0	5
Fletcher	.226	.274	416	36	94	20	0	11	56	24	43	0	1	4
Castillo	.198	.255	131	9	26	4	0	1	4	7	30	1	1	4
Woodward	.190	.203	63	9	12	3	2	2	5	1	14	0	1	8
Simmons	.178	.239	107	8	19	5	0	2	8	8	26	1	0	0
Phelps	.000	.143	12	3	0	0	0	0	1	2	5	1	0	0
Thompson	—	—	0	0	0	0	0	0	0	0	0	0	0	0

Source: *Canadian Press*

AVG = batting average; OBA = on base average; AB = times at bat; R = runs; H = hits; 2B = doubles; 3B = triples; HR = home runs; RBI = runs batted in; BB = walks; SO = strikeouts; SB = stolen bases; CS = caught stealing; E = errors.

▶

Pitchers

	W	L	ERA	G	GS	SV	IP	H	R	ER	HR	BB	SO
▶ Bowles............	0	0	0.00	2	0	0	3.2	4	0	0	0	1	4
Frascatore..........	1	0	2.20	12	0	0	16.1	16	4	4	4	4	9
Quantrill...........	11	2	3.04	80	0	2	83.0	86	29	28	6	12	58
Halladay...........	5	3	3.16	17	16	0	105.1	97	41	37	3	25	96
File..............	5	3	3.27	60	0	0	74.1	57	28	27	6	29	38
Eyre.............	1	2	3.45	17	0	2	15.2	15	6	6	1	7	16
Escobar...........	6	8	3.50	59	11	0	126.0	93	51	49	8	52	121
Plesac............	4	5	3.57	62	0	1	45.1	34	18	18	4	24	68
Borbon	2	4	3.71	71	0	0	53.1	48	24	22	8	12	45
DeWitt............	0	2	3.79	16	0	0	19.0	22	8	8	2	10	13
Carpenter..........	11	11	4.09	34	34	0	215.2	229	112	98	29	75	157
Lyon	5	4	4.29	11	11	0	63.0	63	31	30	6	15	35
Coco	1	0	4.40	7	1	0	14.1	12	8	7	0	6	9
Parris............	4	6	4.60	19	19	0	105.2	126	60	54	18	41	49
Koch	2	5	4.80	69	0	36	69.1	69	39	37	7	33	55
Loaiza	11	11	5.02	36	30	0	190.0	239	113	106	27	40	110
Hamilton	5	8	5.89	22	22	0	122.1	170	88	80	17	38	82
Painter............	0	1	7.85	10	0	0	18.1	27	17	16	4	11	14
Beirne	0	0	12.86	5	0	0	7.0	13	10	10	1	6	5

Source: *Canadian Press*

W = Games won; L = Games lost; ERA = Earned run average; G = Games played in; GS = Games started; SV = Saves; IP = Innings pitched; H = Hits allowed; R = Runs allowed; ER = Earned runs; HR = Home runs allowed; BB = Walks allowed; SO = Strikeouts.

Toronto Blue Jays Team Records up to 2001 Season

Batting

Single Season

Batting Average: John Olerud, 1993, .363

At Bats: Tony Fernandez, 1986, 687

Games: Tony Fernandez, 1986, 163

Hits: Tony Fernandez, 1986, 213

Runs: Shawn Green, 1999, 134

Singles: Tony Fernandez, 1986, 161

Doubles: Carlos Delgado, 2000, 57

Triples: Tony Fernandez, 1990, 17

Home Runs: George Bell, 1987, 47

Runs Batted In: Carlos Delgado, 2000, 137

Total Bases: Carlos Delgado, 2000, 378

Slugging Average: Carlos Delgado, 2000, .664

On-Base Average: John Olerud, 1993, .473

Stolen Bases: Dave Collins, 1984, 60

Strikeouts: José Canseco, 1998, 159

Walks: Carlos Delgado, 2000, 123

Hit By Pitch: Charlie O'Brien, 1996, 17

Hitting Streak: Shawn Green ,1999, 28

Career Leaders

Batting Average: Roberto Alomar, .310

At Bats: Tony Fernandez, 5,335

Games: Tony Fernandez, 1,450

Hits: Tony Fernandez, 1,583

Runs: Lloyd Moseby, 768

Singles: Tony Fernandez, 1,035

Doubles: Tony Fernandez, 291

Triples: Tony Fernandez, 72

Home Runs: Carlos Delgado, 229

Runs Batted In: George Bell, 740

Total Bases: George Bell, 2,201

Slugging Average: Carlos Delgado, .557

On-Base Average: John Olarud, .395

Stolen Bases: Lloyd Moseby, 255

Strikeouts: Lloyd Moseby, 1,015

Walks: Lloyd Moseby/Carlos Delgado, 547

Hit By Pitch: Lloyd Moseby, 50

▶

Pitching

Single Season	Career Leaders
Games: Mark Eichhorn, 1987, 89	**Games:** Duane Ward, 452
Games Started: Jim Clancy, 1982, 40	**Games Started:** Dave Stieb, 408
Complete Games: Dave Stieb, 1982, 19	**Complete Games:** Dave Stieb, 103
Innings Pitched: Dave Stieb, 1982, 288.1	**Innings Pitched:** Dave Stieb, 2 872.1
Wins: Jack Morris, 1992, 21	
Roger Clemens, 1997, 21	**Wins:** Dave Stieb, 175
Losses: Jerry Garvin, 1977, 18; Phil Huffman, 1979, 18	**Losses:** Jim Clancy, 140
Saves: Duane Ward, 1993, 45	**Saves:** Tom Henke, 217
Earned Run Average: Mark Eichhorn, 1986, 1.72	**Earned Run Average:** Tom Henke, 2.48
Shutouts: Dave Stieb, 1982, 5	**Shutouts:** Dave Stieb, 30
Strikeouts: Roger Clemens, 1997, 292	**Strikeouts:** Dave Stieb, 1 658
Walks: Jim Clancy, 1980, 128	**Walks:** Dave Stieb, 1 020
Home Runs Allowed: Woody Williams, 1998, 36	**Home Runs Allowed:** Dave Stieb, 224
Hit Batsmen: Dave Stieb, 1986, 15	**Hit Batsmen:** Dave Stieb, 129

Source: *Canadian Press*

Toronto Blue Jays Player of the Year, 1977–2000

1977	Bob Bailor	1985	Jesse Barfield	1993	Paul Molitor
1978	Bob Bailor	1986	Jesse Barfield	1994	Joe Carter
1979	Alfredo Griffin	1987	George Bell	1995	Roberto Alomar
1980	John Mayberry	1988	Fred McGriff	1996	Ed Sprague
1981	Dave Stieb	1989	George Bell	1997	Carlos Delgado
1982	Damaso Garcia	1990	Kelly Gruber	1998	Carlos Delgado
1983	Lloyd Moseby	1991	Roberto Alomar	1999	Shawn Green
1984	Dave Collins	1992	Roberto Alomar	2000	Carlos Delgado

Want to Surf for Sports Info?

Football

Canadian Football League
www.cfl.ca
All you need to know about the CFL

National Football League
www.nfl.com
All the information you want on the NFL

Canadian Junior Football League
www.cjfl.ca
Scores, standings and stats

Hockey
Canadian Hockey League
www.canoe.ca/CHL/
Info on Canadian junior hockey
with links to various leagues

Ontario Hockey League
www.ontariohockeyleague.com
Scores, standings, game recaps
and news

American Hockey League
www.theahl.com
Stats, rosters and team info

The Hockey News
www.thn.com
News and stats

*Hockey Future: The Hockey Propects
Resource*
www.hockeysfuture.com
Learn about the stars of tomorrow today

National Basketball Association, 2000–2001

Final Regular Season Standings

Eastern Conference

■ Atlantic Division

	W	L	%	GB
a-Philadelphia (1)	56	26	.683	0.0
x-Miami (3)	50	32	.610	6.0
x-New York (4)	48	34	.585	8.0
x-Orlando (7)	43	39	.524	13.0
Boston	36	46	.439	20.0
New Jersey	26	56	.317	30.0
Washington	19	63	.232	37.0

■ Central Division

	W	L	%	GB
c-Milwaukee (2)	52	30	.634	0.0
x-Toronto (5)	**47**	**35**	**.573**	**5.0**
x-Charlotte (6)	46	36	.561	6.0
x-Indiana (8)	41	41	.500	11.0
Detroit	32	50	.390	20.0
Cleveland	30	52	.366	22.0
Atlanta	25	57	.305	27.0
Chicago	15	67	.183	37.0

Western Conference

■ Midwest Division

	W	L	%	GB
m-San Antonio (1)	58	24	.707	0.0
x-Utah (4)	53	29	.646	5.0
x-Dallas (5)	53	29	.646	5.0
x-Minnesota (8)	47	35	.573	11.0
Houston	45	37	.549	13.0
Denver	40	42	.488	18.0
Vancouver	**23**	**59**	**.280**	**35.0**

■ Pacific Division

	W	L	%	GB
p-L.A. Lakers (2)	56	26	.683	0.0
x-Sacramento (3)	55	27	.671	1.0
x-Phoenix (6)	51	31	.622	5.0
x-Portland (7)	50	32	.610	6.0
Seattle	44	38	.537	12.0
L.A. Clippers	31	51	.378	25.0
Golden State	17	65	.207	39.0

a-Clinched Atlantic Division Title   c-Clinched Central Division Title   p-Clinched Pacific Division Title   m-Clinched Midwest Division Title   x-Clinched Playoff Berth

Source: *NBA*

NBA Playoff Results, 2000–2001

QUARTERFINAL — Toronto defeated New York 3-2

Knicks 92	Raptors 85
Raptors 94	Knicks 74
Knicks 97	Raptors 89
Raptors 100	Knicks 93
Raptors 93	Knicks 89

Philadelphia defeated Indiana 3-1
Milwaukee defeated Orlando 3-1
Charlotte defeated Miami 3-0

SEMIFINAL — Philadelphia defeated Toronto 4-3

Raptors 96	Sixers 93
Sixers 97	Raptors 92
Raptors 102	Sixers 78
Sixers 84	Raptors 79
Sixers 122	Raptors 88
Raptors 101	Sixers 89
Sixers 88	Raptors 87

Milwaukee defeated Charlotte 4-3

EASTERN CONFERENCE FINAL

Philadelphia defeated Milwaukee 4-3

Source: *NBA*

QUARTERFINAL

San Antonio defeated Minnesota 3-1
Los Angeles Lakers defeated Portland 3-0
Sacramento defeated Phoenix 3-1
Dallas defeated Utah 3-2

SEMIFINAL

San Antonio defeated Dallas 4-1
Los Angeles Lakers defeated Sacramento 4-0

WESTERN CONFERENCE FINAL

Los Angeles Lakers defeated San Antonio 4-0

FINAL
Los Angeles Lakers defeated Philadelphia 4-1

Individual Statistical Leaders, 2000–2001

(Final Regular Season)

■ Scoring

	GP	PTS	AVG
Iverson, PHI	71	2207	31.1
Stackhouse, DET	80	2380	29.8
O'Neal, LAL	74	2125	28.7
Bryant, LAL	68	1938	28.5
Carter, TOR	75	2070	27.6
Webber, SAC	70	1898	27.1
McGrady, ORL	77	2065	26.8
Pierce, BOS	82	2071	25.3
Jamison, GSW	82	2044	25.9
Marbury, NJN	67	1598	23.9

■ Field Goal Percentage

	FGM	FGA	%
Rogers, HOU	75	110	.682
Outlaw, ORL	226	368	.614
Spencer, NYK	12	20	.600
MacCulloch, PHI	109	185	.589
Fortson, GSW	29	50	.580
Cato, HOU	64	111	.577
O'Neal, LAL	813	1422	.572
Reid, ORL	82	145	.566
Bowen, DEN	80	144	.556
DeClercq, ORL	107	193	.554

■ Rebounds Per Game

	GP	REB	AVG
Fortson, GSW	6	98	16.3
Mutombo, PHI	75	1014	13.5
Wallace, DET	80	1052	13.2
O'Neal, LAL	74	940	12.7
Duncan, SAS	82	997	12.2
McDyess, DEN	70	845	12.1
Camby, NYK	63	723	11.5
Garnett, MIN	81	921	11.4
Webber, SAC	70	776	11.1
Marion, PHO	79	847	10.7

■ Free Throw Percentage

	FTM	FTA	%
Fuller, MIA	8	8	1.000
Kerr, SAS	14	15	.933
Del Negro, PHO	41	44	.932
Miller, IND	323	348	.928
David, DET	12	13	.923
Houston, NYK	279	307	.909
Penberthy, LAL	28	31	.903
Christie, SAC	280	312	.897
Edney, IND	35	39	.897
Nash, DAL	231	258	.895

■ Assists Per Game

	GP	AST	AVG
Kidd, PHO	77	753	9.8
Stockton, UTH	82	713	8.7
Van Exel, DEN	71	600	8.4
Bibby, VAN	82	685	8.4
Payton, SEA	79	642	8.1
Miller, CLE	82	657	8.0
Jackson, NYK	83	661	8.0
Cassell, MIL	76	580	7.6
Marbury, NJN	67	506	7.6
Brandon, MIN	78	583	7.5

■ 3-Point Field Goal Percentage

	3FG	3FGA	%
Barry, SEA	109	229	.476
Allen, MIA	202	467	.433
Garrity, ORL	97	224	.433
Lewis, SEA	123	285	.432
Porter, SAS	87	205	.424
Russell, UTH	95	230	.413
Thomas, MIL	107	260	.412
Hoiberg, CHI	103	250	.412
Carter, TOR	162	397	.408
Miller, ORL	148	364	.407

■ Steals Per Game

	GP	STL	AVG
Iverson, PHI	71	178	2.5
Blaylock, GSW	60	163	2.4
Christie, SAC	81	183	2.3
Kidd, PHO	77	166	2.2
Davis, CHA	82	170	2.1
Brandon, MIN	78	161	2.1
Artest, CHI	76	152	2.0
Fisher, LAL	20	39	2.0
Hughes, GSW	50	96	1.9
Knight, ATL	53	101	1.9

■ Blocked Shots Per Game

	GP	BLK	AVG
Ratliff, ATL	50	187	3.7
O'Neal, IND	81	228	2.8
Bradley, DAL	82	228	2.8
O'Neal, LAL	74	204	2.8
Mutombo, PHI	75	202	2.7
Foyle, GSW	58	155	2.7
LaFrentz, DEN	78	205	2.6
Roboinson, SAS	80	197	2.5
Mourning, MIA	13	31	2.4
Duncan, SAS	82	192	2.3

All-Time NBA Statistical Leaders

(as of the end of the 2000–2001 season)

Most Points, career
Kareem Abdul-Jabbar	38 387
x-Karl Malone	32 909
Wilt Chamberlain	31 419
Michael Jordan	29 277
Moses Malone	27 409
Elvin Hayes	27 313
Oscar Robertson	26 710
Dominique Wilkins	26 668
x-Hakeem Olajuwon	26 511
John Havlicek	26 395

Most Rebounds, career
Wilt Chamberlain	23 924
Bill Russell	21 620
Kareem Abdul-Jabbar	17 440
Elvin Hayes	16 279
Moses Malone	16 212
Robert Parish	14 715
Nate Thurmond	14 464
Walt Bellamy	14 241
Wes Unseld	13 769
x-Hakeem Olajuwon	13 387

Most Assists , career
x-John Stockton	14 503
Magic Johnson	10 141
Oscar Robertson	9 887
x-Mark Jackson	9 235
Isiah Thomas	9 061
Maurice Cheeks	7 392
Len Wilkens	7 215
x-Rod Strickland	7 035
Bob Cousy	6 955
x-Terry Porter	6 953

Most Blocks, career
x-Hakeem Olajuwon	3 741
Kareem Abdul-Jabbar	3 189
Mark Eaton	3 064
x-Patrick Ewing	2 849
x-David Robinson	2 706
x-Dikembe Mutombo	2 642
Tree Rollins	2 542
Robert Parish	2 361
Manute Bol	2 086
George Johnson	2 082

Source: insidehoops.com

x-active

Jordan Returns

Michael Jordan held many invitation-only pickup games with NBA players in Chicago over the summer of 2001, and during six months of play he suffered back spasms, knee tendonitis and two cracked ribs from a run-in with Chicago Bull Ron Artest. (That injury sidelined him for about a month.) Despite the injuries, Jordan signed a two-year deal with the Washington Wizards. At a post-signing press conference, Jordan said he was inspired by the successful return of the NHL's Mario Lemieux.

The Wizards won 19 games the previous season, and have not won a playoff game in 13 years. Jordan has never missed the playoffs in 13 seasons as a player. In order return, he had to sell his ownership shares with the NBA Wizards and the NHL Capitals. NBC, TBS and TNT have changed their schedules to air Wizard games since Jordan's announcement.

Jordan first retired in October 1993 after three titles with the Bulls. He played minor league baseball for a season with the Chicago White Sox before returning to the Bulls in March 1995. The team earned three more titles before he retired a second time in January 1999.

Jordan is donating his first year salary (US$1 million) to the victims of September 11, 2001. His season debut was slated for Madison Square Gardens on October 30, against the Knicks. Jordan's first home game was November 3 with visiting fast guy Allen Iverson. On December 16, Jordan matches Vince Carter, another North Carolina native, in Toronto. The Bulls visit January 4, when Jordan takes on Ron Artest. But Jordan doesn't trek to Chicago until January 19 and March 1. Two-time defending Lakers meet Jordan February 12, when Kobe Bryant learns if he truly is the next Michael Jordan. Foe Scottie Pipen plays Jordan February 27 in Washington, and Bryon Russell of the Utah Jazz takes him on March 21. The last game April 16 might be a playoff determiner for the Knicks or the Wizards.

"I am disappointed... that he turned down my standing invitation to play for the champs— the Lakers," said LA coach Phil Jackson.

Toronto Raptors Individual Statistics 2000–2001

Player Averages

	G	MIN	PPG	RPG	APG	OFF	DEF	TOT	AST	STL	BLK	TO	PF
Carter	75	2979	27.6	5.6	3.9	176	240	416	291	114	82	167	205
Davis	78	2729	13.7	10.1	1.4	274	513	787	106	22	151	135	230
Williams	82	2394	9.8	2.6	5.0	50	162	212	407	123	26	103	171
Oakley	78	2767	9.6	9.5	3.4	142	599	741	264	76	48	139	258
Peterson	80	1809	9.3	3.2	1.3	112	147	259	105	63	20	78	164
Clark	81	1720	7.9	5.4	0.9	136	298	434	72	32	154	90	244
Williams	59	1182	6.3	6.5	0.8	133	249	382	45	57	20	63	124
Curry	71	956	6.0	1.2	1.1	16	69	85	75	27	8	39	66
Murray	51	588	5.0	1.6	0.5	22	59	81	23	12	7	26	53
Childs	77	1859	4.7	2.6	4.6	24	178	202	355	59	15	156	242
Montross	54	649	2.2	3.2	0.4	52	121	173	19	11	26	41	115
Ndiaye	3	10	1.3	0.7	0.0	1	1	2	0	0	0	0	3
Stewart	26	123	1.3	1.1	0.1	16	13	29	2	4	3	5	19

Player Totals

TEAM	FG M-A	PCT	3PT M-A	PCT	FT M-A	PCT	PTS	HI
Carter	762-1656	.460	162-397	.408	384-502	.765	2070	48
Davis	375-866	.433	0-1	.000	319-423	.754	1069	31
Williams	330-767	.430	33-108	.306	109-145	.752	802	23
Oakley	305-786	.388	11-49	.224	127-152	.836	748	23
Peterson	290-673	.431	63-165	.382	104-145	.717	747	29
Clark	249-519	.480	0-1	.000	142-240	.592	640	23
Williams	136-294	.463	0-3	.000	100-135	.741	372	15
Curry	162-382	.424	62-145	.428	43-51	.843	429	23
Murray	94-248	.379	36-103	.350	33-42	.786	257	20
Childs	135-335	.403	31-106	.302	60-71	.845	362	17
Montross	56-183	.406	0	.000	8-31	.258	120	13
Ndiaye	1-4	.250	0	.000	2-2	1.000	4	2
Stewart	11-34	.324	0	.000	11-18	.611	33	6

Source: *Canadian Press*

3PT M-A = three-point field goal-attempts; APG = assists per game; AST = assists; BLK = block; DEF = defensive rebounds; FG M-A = field goals made-attempts; FT M-A = free throw made-attempts; G = games played; MIN = minutes; OFF = offensive rebounds; PCT = percentage; PF = personal fouls; PPG = points per game; PTS = points; RPG = rebounds per game; STL = steals; TO = turnovers; TOT = total.

Vince and Hakeem Team-up for the Raptors

*N**BA celebrity Vince Carter signed a six-year contract extension with the Toronto Raptors, in time for the 2001 season. Carter, the most prolific player in Raptors history, will earn more than $85 million over the length of the deal. In his first three seasons with Toronto he averaged 24.6 points a game. General manager Glen Grunwald has also signed Houston Rockets Hakeem Olajuwon. Olajuwon snubbed the Rockets' three-year, $10.2-million proposal and their final offer of $13 million to accept a three-year contract at $16.7 million with Toronto. In 17 seasons he averaged 22.5 points, 11.4 rebounds, is the NBA's career blocked shots leader with 3,740 and a 14-time All-Star. He also has two NBA championship rings from 1994 and 1995. Grunwald isn't anxious over a blood clot that threatened Olajuwon's career last season. Antonio Davis re-signed for five-years as did Guard Alvin Williams and Jerome Williams, making Toronto a favourite for the Eastern Conference.*

Vancouver Grizzlies 2000–2001 Statistics

PLAYER AVERAGES

TEAM	G	MIN	PPG	RPG	APG	OFF	DEF	TOT	AST	STL	BLK	TO	PF
Abdur-rahim	81	3241	20.5	9.1	3.1	175	560	735	250	90	77	232	238
Dickerson	70	2618	16.3	3.3	3.3	70	159	229	233	62	27	162	207
Bibby	82	3190	15.9	3.7	8.4	47	257	304	685	107	12	248	148
Reeves	75	1832	8.3	6.0	1.1	132	320	452	80	43	54	90	243
Jones	71	1415	6.5	1.8	3.2	16	108	124	224	36	1	76	58
Abdul-rauf	41	486	6.5	0.6	1.9	5	20	25	76	9	1	26	50
Long	66	1507	6.0	4.2	1.3	76	198	274	83	72	15	62	160
Strickland	50	830	5.2	2.6	1.9	18	110	128	95	44	2	48	88
Swift	80	1312	4.9	3.6	0.4	109	175	284	28	62	82	64	160
Massenburg	52	823	4.5	4.0	0.2	75	135	210	9	10	28	48	122
Austin	52	845	4.4	4.3	1.1	50	172	222	58	20	23	54	94
Edwards	46	634	3.5	1.8	1.1	23	59	82	52	29	8	37	46
Price	6	30	2.2	0.7	0.8	1	3	4	5	2	0	4	8
West	15	171	1.9	1.0	0.9	4	11	15	14	3	4	4	21

PLAYER TOTALS

TEAM	FG M-A	PCT	3PT M-A	PCT	FT M-A	PCT	PTS	HI
Abdur-rahim	604-1280	.472	12-64	.188	443-531	.834	1663	38
Dickerson	425-1020	.417	86-230	.374	206-270	.763	1142	32
Bibby	525-1157	.454	108-285	.379	143-188	.761	1301	37
Reeves	254-552	.460	1-4	.250	113-142	.796	622	31
Jones	170-416	.409	84-231	.364	37-52	.712	461	25
Abdul-rauf	120-246	.488	4-14	.286	22-29	.759	266	25
Long	140-139	.439	4-15	.267	112-157	.713	396	16
Strickland	81-627	.303	30-95	.316	68-79	.861	260	15
Swift	153-339	.451	0-4	.000	85-141	.603	391	17
Massenburg	92-199	.462	0-0	.000	49-70	.700	233	14
Austin	96-270	.356	6-24	.250	28-40	.700	226	15
Edwards	56-170	.329	5-19	.263	43-53	.811	160	13
Price	3-11	.273	1-4	.250	6-7	.857	13	5
West	11-38	.289	0-2	.000	6-7	.857	28	6

Source: *sports.yahoo.com*

NBA Franchise Moves

1951: Tri-Cities Blackhawks become Milwaukee Hawks
1955: Milwaukee Hawks to St. Louis
1957: Rochester Royals to Cincinnati
1958: Fort Wayne Pistons to Detroit
1960: Minneapolis Lakers to Los Angeles
1962: Philadelphia Warriors to San Francisco
1963: Chicago Zephyrs become Baltimore Bullets
1963: Syracuse Nationals become the Philadelphia 76ers
1968: St. Louis Hawks to Atlanta

1971: San Diego Rockets to Houston
1971: San Francisco Warriors to Oakland
1972: Cincinnati Royals become the Kansas City-Omaha Kings
1973: Baltimore Bullets to Washington
1977: New York Nets to New Jersey
1978: Buffalo Braves become the San Diego Clippers
1979: New Orleans Jazz to Utah
1984: San Diego Clippers to Los Angeles
1985: Kansas City Kings to Sacramento
2001: Vancouver Grizzlies to Memphis

Source: *ESPN*

Canadian Men's Results at the 2001 COPABA Tournament

The Confederation of Panamerican Basketball Associations (COPABA) is a confederation of 40 national basketball federations that includes representatives from North America, South America, Central America and the Caribbean. The organization promotes and directs the sport of basketball in the Americas. Its primary function, however, is to conduct qualification tournaments for the Olympic Games and world championship competitions.

On August 26, 2000, the Canadian men's basketball team defeated Puerto Rico 102-95 to capture third place at the COPABA Tournament of the Americas in Neuquen, Argentina. In the game, Steve Nash (Victoria, BC) led Canada with 22 points and 11 assists while Kevin Jobity (Toronto, ON) finished with 21 (8-10 from the floor). With the win, Canada qualified for the 2002 World Championships in Indianapolis.

Round One Results

Aug 16	**Canada 108**, U.S. Virgin Islands 97	
Aug 17	Puerto Rico 101, **Canada 98**	
Aug 19	**Canada 89**, Panama 82	
Aug 20	**Canada 104**, Mexico 92	

Semifinal

Aug 25	Argentina 97, **Canada 76**

Round Two Results

Aug 21	**Canada 108**, Venezuela 100
Aug 22	**Canada 101**, Uruguay 77
Aug 23	Argentina 85, **Canada 76**
Aug 24	Brazil 78, **Canada 69**

Medal Round Result

Aug 26	**Canada 102**, Puerto Rico 95

Canadian Men's Roster for 2001 COPABA Tournament

Name	School/Club	HT	Hometown	POS
Daniels, David	MZT Skopje 2000, Macedonia	5' 10"	Fort St. John, B.C.	G
Guarasci, Peter	Cordivari Roseto, Italy	6' 9"	Niagara Falls, ON	F
Hamilton, Sherman	Germany	6' 1"	Malton, ON	G
Jobity, Kevin	Israel	6' 10"	Toronto, ON	F
Karangwa, Prosper	Siena College	6' 7"	Montreal, P.Q.	G/F
Kwiatkowski, Andrew	University of Western Ontario	6' 8"	Cambridge, ON	F
MacCulloch, Todd	New Jersey Nets	7"	Winnipeg, MB	C
Meeks, Michael	Unics Kazan, Russia	6' 9"	Brampton, ON	F
Nash, Steve	Dallas Mavericks	6' 3"	Victoria, BC	G
Robinson, Jerome	Bradley University	6' 3"	Mississauga, ON	G
Swords, Shawn	Besançon, France	6' 3"	Ottawa, ON	G
Walker, Dean	Central Connecticut	6' 5"	Toronto, ON	G

Canadian Women Finish Fourth

*S*eptember 14, 2001 the Canadian senior women's basketball team lost to Argentina at the COPABA Tournament of the Americas. In the first quarter, Teresa Kleindienst got a three-pointer at the 8:00 minute mark. In the second, Carolyn Ganes entered at 3:42 when Michelle Hendry picked up her third foul. Isabelle Grenier hit a three-pointer 41 seconds before break and Canada led 27-22. In the third quarter Grenier and Stacey Dales shot three-pointers. Dales picked up her fourth foul with 22 seconds left. Canada led 40-34. In the fourth quarter Grenier hit three pointers but it was 48-45 at the 4:00 minute mark. Dianne Norman made a rebound. The score was 50-48 Canada. Argentina recovered a jumpball and hit a three-pointer with two seconds left, winning 51-50. Grenier was the only Canadian to score in double figures. She finished with 15 points shooting 100% (5-5) from beyond the three-point line. Brazil won gold, Cuba silver and Argentina bronze.

Source: eteamz.com, Inc.

FOOTBALL

Canadian Football League

(2000 Regular Season Standings)

Team	W	L	T	OTL	F	A	PTS	Team	W	L	T	OTL	F	A	PTS
East Division								**West Division**							
Montreal	12	6	0	0	594	379	24	Calgary	12	5	1	0	604	495	25
Hamilton	9	9	0	2	470	446	20	Edmonton	10	7	0	1	527	520	21
Winnipeg	7	10	1	1	539	596	16	British Columbia ..	8	10	0	1	513	529	17
Toronto	7	10	1	0	390	562	15	Saskatchewan	5	12	1	0	516	626	11

Divisional Semi-finals:
Winnipeg 22, Hamilton 20
British Columbia 34, Edmonton 32

Divisional Finals:
Montreal 35, Winnipeg 24
British Columbia 37, Calgary 23

Grey Cup:
British Columbia 28, Montreal 26

Source: *Canadian Football League*

Canadian Football League All-Stars, 2000

(voted by Football Reporters of Canada)

Offence

Quarterback: Dave Dickenson, Calgary
Running Back: Sean Millington, B.C.
Running Back: Mike Pringle, Montreal
Slotback: Derrell Mitchell, Toronto
Slotback: Milt Stegall, Winnipeg
Wide Receiver: Travis Moore, Calgary
Wide Receiver: Curtis Marsh, Saskatchewan
Centre: Bryan Chiu, Montreal
Guard: Andrew Greene, Saskatchewan
Guard: Pierre Vercheval, Montreal
Tackle: Bruce Beaton, Edmonton
Tackle: Christopher Perez, B.C.
Punter: Noel Prefontaine, Toronto
Defensive Back: Eddie Davis, Calgary
Kicker: Lui Passaglia, B.C.
Special Teams: Albert Johnson, Winnipeg

Defence

Defensive Tackle: Demetrious Maxie, Saskatchewan
Defensive Tackle: Joe Fleming,
Defensive End: Shont'e Peoples, Calgary
Defensive End: Joe Montford, Hamilton
Linebacker: Alondra Johnson, Calgary
Linebacker: Terry Ray, Edmonton
Linebacker: George White, Saskatchewan
Cornerback: Marvin Coleman, Calgary
Cornerback: Davis Sanchez, Montreal
Halfback: Gerald Vaughn, Hamilton
Halfback: Barron Miles, Montreal
Safety: Greg Frers, Calgary
Defensive Back: Eddie Davis, Calgary
Defensive Back: Barron Miles, Montreal

Source: *Canadian Football League*

The Grey Cup, 1909–2000

The Grey Cup was donated in 1909 by Governor General Earl Grey for the "Rugby Football Championship of Canada." Since 1954, only teams in the Canadian Football League have challenged for the trophy, with the winners of the East and West divisions meeting in the championship game.

1909	U. of Toronto 26, Parkdale 6
1910	U. of Toronto 16, Ham. Tigers 7
1911	U. of Toronto 14, Toronto 7
1912	Ham. Alerts 11, Toronto 4
1913	Ham. Tigers 44, Parkdale 2
1914	Toronto 14, U. of Toronto 2
1915	Ham. Tigers 13, Tor. R.A.A. 7
1916–19	No games held.
1920	U. of Toronto 16, Toronto 3
1921	Toronto 23, Edmonton 0
1922	Queen's U. 13, Edmonton 1
1923	Queen's U. 54, Regina 0
1924	Queen's U. 11, Balmy Beach 3
1925	Ott. Senators 24, Winnipeg 1
1926	Ott. Senators 10, U. of Toronto 7
1927	Balmy Beach 9, Ham. Tigers 6
1928	Ham. Tigers 30, Regina 0
1929	Ham. Tigers 14, Regina 3
1930	Balmy Beach 11, Regina 6
1931	Mtl. A.A.A. 22, Regina 0
1932	Ham. Tigers 25, Regina 6
1933	Toronto 4, Sarnia 3
1934	Sarnia 20, Regina 12
1935	Winnipeg 18, Ham. Tigers 12
1936	Sarnia 26, Ott. R.R. 20
1937	Toronto 4, Winnipeg 3
1938	Toronto 30, Winnipeg 7
1939	Winnipeg 8, Ottawa 7
1940[1]	Ottawa 12, Balmy Beach 5
	Ottawa 8, Balmy Beach 2
1941	Winnipeg 18, Ottawa 16
1942	Tor. R.C.A.F. 8, Win. R.C.A.F. 5
1943	Ham. F. Wild 23, Win. R.C.A.F. 14
1944	Mtl. St. H.D. Navy 7, Ham. F. Wild 6
1945	Toronto 35, Winnipeg 0
1946	Toronto 28, Winnipeg 6
1947	Toronto 10, Winnipeg 9
1948	Calgary 12, Ottawa 7
1949	Mtl. Als. 28, Calgary 15
1950	Toronto 13, Winnipeg 0
1951	Ottawa 21, Saskatchewan 14
1952	Toronto 21, Edmonton 11
1953	Hamilton 12, Winnipeg 6
1954	Edmonton 26, Montreal 25
1955	Edmonton 34, Montreal 19
1956	Edmonton 50, Montreal 27
1957	Hamilton 32, Winnipeg 7
1958	Winnipeg 35, Hamilton 28
1959	Winnipeg 21, Hamilton 7
1960	Ottawa 16, Edmonton 6
1961	Winnipeg 21, Hamilton 14
1962	Winnipeg 28, Hamilton 27
1963	Hamilton 21, BC 10
1964	BC 34, Hamilton 24
1965	Hamilton 22, Winnipeg 16
1966	Saskatchewan 29, Ottawa 14
1967	Hamilton 24, Saskatchewan 1
1968	Ottawa 24, Calgary 21
1969	Ottawa 29, Saskatchewan 11
1970	Montreal 23, Calgary 10
1971	Calgary 14, Toronto 11
1972	Hamilton 13, Saskatchewan 10
1973	Ottawa 22, Edmonton 18
1974	Montreal 20, Edmonton 7
1975	Edmonton 9, Montreal 8
1976	Ottawa 23, Saskatchewan 20
1977	Montreal 41, Edmonton 6
1978	Edmonton 20, Montreal 13
1979	Edmonton 17, Montreal 9
1980	Edmonton 48, Hamilton 10
1981	Edmonton 26, Ottawa 23
1982	Edmonton 32, Toronto 16
1983	Toronto 18, BC 17
1984	Winnipeg 47, Hamilton 17
1985	BC 37, Hamilton 24
1986	Hamilton 39, Edmonton 15
1987	Edmonton 38, Toronto 36
1988	Winnipeg 22, BC 21
1989	Saskatchewan 43, Hamilton 40
1990	Winnipeg 50, Edmonton 11
1991	Toronto 36, Calgary 21
1992	Calgary 24, Winnipeg 10
1993	Edmonton 33, Winnipeg 23
1994	BC 26, Baltimore 23
1995	Baltimore 37, Calgary 20
1996	Toronto 43, Edmonton 37
1997	Toronto 47, Saskatchewan 23
1998	Calgary 26, Hamilton 24
1999	Hamilton 32, Calgary 21
2000	BC 28, Montreal 26

Source: *Canadian Press*

(1) A 2-game total point series.

All-Time Leading CFL Players

(up to the end of the 2000 season)

Games Played

All-Time Leaders — Games Played

Lui Passaglia (B.C.) 1976–00 408
Bob Cameron (Winnipeg) 1980–00. 358
Miles Gorrell (Five Teams) 1978–96 321
Ron Lancaster (Two Teams) 1960–78. 288

All-Time Leaders — Consecutive Games Played

Bob Cameron (Winnipeg) 1980–00. 353
Dave Cutler (Edmonton) 1969–84. 253
Leo Groenewegen (Three teams) 1987–00 252
Roger Aldag (Saskatchewan) 1976–91 250

All-Time Leaders — Seasons Played

Lui Passaglia (B.C.) 1976–00 25
Eddie Emerson (Ottawa) 1911–37 22
Bob Cameron (Winnipeg) 1980–00. 21
Ron Lancaster (Two Teams) 1960–1978. 21
Miles Gorrell (Five Teams) 1978–96 19
Hank Ilesic (Two Teams) 1977–93, 1995–98 19

All-Time Leaders — Consecutive Seasons Played

Lui Passaglia (B.C.) 1976–00 25
Bob Cameron (Winnipeg) 1980–00. 21
Miles Gorrell (Five teams) 1978–97 19
Ron Lancaster (Two Teams) 1960–78. 19

Scoring

All-Time Leaders — Scoring

	PTS
Lui Passaglia (B.C.)	3985
Mark McLoughlin (Calgary)	2517
Paul Osbaldiston (Three Teams)	2510
Dave Ridgway (Saskatchewan)	2374
Dave Cutler (Edmonton)	2237

Most Points — One Season

	PTS
Lance Chomyc (Toronto) 1991	236
Roman Anderson (San Antonio) 1995	235
Paul Osbaldiston (Hamilton) 1989	233
Dave Ridgway (Saskatchewan) 1990	233
Carlos Huerta (Baltimore) 1995	228

All-Time Leaders — Touchdowns

	Number of TDs
George Reed (Saskatchewan)	137
Allen Pitts (Calgary)	117
Brian Kelly (Edmonton)	97
Dick Shatto (Toronto)	91
Tom Scott (Three Teams)	91

Most Touchdowns — One Season

	Number of TDs
Cory Philpot (B.C.) 1995	22
Allen Pitts (Calgary) 1994	21
Pat Abbruzzi (Montreal) 1956	20
Darrell K. Smith (Toronto) 1990	20
Blake Marshall (Edmonton) 1991	20
Jon Volpe (B.C.) 1991	20

Most Touchdowns — One Game

	Number of TDs
Bob McNamara (Winnipeg) Oct 13, 1956	6
Eddie James (Winnipeg) Sept 28, 1932	
Ernie Pitts (Winnipeg) Aug 29, 1959	5
Fred Burket (Saskatchewan) Oct 26, 1959	
Earl Lunsford (Calgary) Sept 2, 1962	
Martin Patton (Shreveport) Aug 5, 1995	
Eric Blount (Edmonton) Sept 15, 1995	

Most Points — One Game

	PTS
Bob McNamara (Winnipeg) Oct 13, 1965	36
Ernie Pitts (Winnipeg) Aug 29, 1959	
Fred Burket (Saskatchewan) Oct 26, 1959	
Earl Lunsford (Calgary) Sept 2, 1962	30
Martin Patton (Shreveport) Aug 5, 1995	
Eric Blount (Edmonton) Sept 15, 1995	

FOCUS ON...

The Roots of North American Football

In Canada

The first recorded game of football in Canada was played at University College, University of Toronto, on November 9, 1861 between the "Mulock" team and the "Smith" team. This original University College Football Club (UCFC) played games largely amongst themselves, as there were no other clubs playing by the same rules.

Football in the mid-19th Century was a chaotic game, with wide variance in the rules from place to place and club to club. In 1876, a number of clubs tried to adopt the Scottish Football Association rules, but this effort foundered; in 1877, the UCFC adopted the Rugby Football Union laws as introduced by student J.H. Mayne Campbell. However, "Canadian Rugby" evolved along indigenous lines, influenced by both British and American developments.

In 1882, the open formation and three-man "heelback" scrimmage (similar to Rugby League) replaced the eight-man scrum. In 1899, U of T Varsity captain John Thrift Meldrum Burnside proposed a series of rules changes for the Mulock Cup intramural competition: the throw in from touch was abolished; the requirement to advance 10 yards in 3 downs was established; the opposing scrimmagers were required to stand clear of each other and the ball; the number of players was reduced to 12 a side; and the three-man heelback scrimmage was replaced by a single man using the snapback, with 6 men along the line of scrimmage. The Canadian Rugby Union adopted the "Burnside Rules" for all club play in 1906, thus paving the way for the evolution of the modern game of Canadian Football.

Meanwhile, in the United States

The seed that sprouted the 32-team National Football League was planted Nov. 6, 1869, when Rutgers and Princeton played a college soccer game. The game used modified London Football Association rules. During the next seven years, rugby gained favor over soccer with the major eastern schools, and modern football began to develop from rugby. According to the *NFL Record & Fact Book,* the first rules for American football were written during the Massasoit convention in 1876. At this time Walter Camp, who would become known as the father of American football, first became involved with the game.

The Pittsburgh Athletic Club signed one of its players (probably halfback Grant Dilbert) to the first known pro-football contract in 1893. Three years later, the Allegheny Athletic Association team fielded the first completely professional team for its abbreviated two-game schedule. In 1899, Chris O'Brien formed the Morgan Athletic Club on the south side of Chicago. The team later became known as the Normals, then the Racine Cardinals, the Chicago Cardinals, the St. Louis Cardinals, the Phoenix Cardinals and, in 1994, the Arizona Cardinals. The team is the oldest continuing operation in pro football.

The Philadelphia Athletics and Philadelphia Phillies—professional baseball teams—joined the Pittsburgh Stars in the first attempt to form a pro football league: the National Football League. The Athletics defeated Kanaweoia AC 39-0 on Nov. 21, 1902, in the first night football game. In another first, New York and Syracuse played Dec. 28 at Madison Square Garden—the first indoor football game.

Rugby in Canada

*T*raditional rugby, however, is a fast-growing sport in Canada and the Canadian men's team enjoys an enviable reputation as the 12th ranked team in the world. In May 2001, Canada played host to the VISA Pan Am Rugby Championship in Kingston, Hamilton, and Markham, Ontario. The Canadians finished second in the tournament, behind South American power Argentina.

Canada's next challenge was the 2001 Pacific Rim Tournament. The tournament was restructured for 2001, with USA and **Canada** playing once for a spot in the semifinals. **Canada's 19-10** victory sent them to the July 4-8 semifinals in Tokyo. Samoa dispatched Japan 47-8 in the first semi and Fiji defeated **Canada 52-23** in the second semifinal. Japan upset **Canada 39-7** for third overall.

CFL Outstanding Player Awards[1]

Outstanding Player

1980 Deiter Brock, Wpg	1987 Tom Clements, Wpg	1994 Doug Flutie, Cal
1981 Deiter Brock, Wpg	1988 David Williams, BC	1995 Mike Pringle, Bal
1982 Condredge Holloway, Tor	1989 Tracy Ham, Edm	1996 Doug Flutie, Tor
1983 Warren Moon, Edm	1990 Mike Clemons, Tor	1997 Doug Flutie, Tor
1984 Willard Reaves, Wpg	1991 Doug Flutie, BC	1998 Mike Pringle, Mtl
1985 Mervyn Fernandez, BC	1992 Doug Flutie, Cal	1999 Danny McManus, Ham
1986 James Murphy, Wpg	1993 Doug Flutie, Cal	2000 Dave Dickenson, Cal

Outstanding Canadian

1980 Gerry Dattilio, Mtl	1987 Scott Flagel, Wpg	1994 Gerald Wilcox, Wpg
1981 Joe Poplawski, Wpg	1988 Ray Elgaard, Sask	1995 Dave Sapunjis, Cal
1982 Rocky DiPietro, Ham	1989 Rocky DiPietro, Ham	1996 Leroy Blugh, Edm
1983 Paul Bennett, Wpg	1990 Ray Elgaard, Sask	1997 Sean Millington, BC
1984 Nick Arakgi, Mtl	1991 Blake Marshall, Edm	1998 Mike Morreale, Ham
1985 Paul Bennett, Ham	1992 Ray Elgaard, Sask	1999 Mike O'Shea, Tor
1986 Joe Poplawski, Wpg	1993 Dave Sapunjis, Cal	2000 Sean Millington, BC

Outstanding Defensive Player

1980 Dan Kepley, Edm	1987 Gregg Stumon, BC	1994 Willie Pless, Edm
1981 Dan Kepley, Edm	1988 Grover Covington, Ham	1995 Willie Pless, Edm
1982 James Parker, Edm	1989 Danny Bass, Edm	1996 Willie Pless, Edm
1983 Greg Marshall, Ott	1990 Greg Battle, Wpg	1997 Willie Pless, Edm
1984 James Parker, BC	1991 Greg Battle, Wpg	1998 Joe Montford, Ham
1985 Tyrone Jones, Wpg	1992 Willie Pless, Edm	1999 Calvin Tiggle, Ham
1986 James Parker, BC	1993 Jearld Baylis, Sask	2000 Jon Montford, Ham

Outstanding Offensive Lineman

1980 Mike Wilson, Edm	1987 Chris Walby, Wpg	1994 Shar Pourdanesh, Bal
1981 Larry Butler, Wpg	1988 Roger Aldag, Sask	1995 Mike Withycombe, Bal
1982 Rudy Phillips, Ott	1989 Rod Connop, Edm	1996 Mike Kiselak, Tor
1983 Rudy Phillips, Ott	1990 Jim Mills, BC	1997 Mike Kiselak, Tor
1984 John Bonk, Wpg	1991 Jim Mills, BC	1998 Fred Childress, Cal
1985 Nick Bastaja, Wpg	1992 Rob Smith, Ott	1999 Uzooma Okeke, Mtl
1986 Roger Aldag, Sask	1993 Chris Walby, Wpg	2000 Pierre Vercheval, Mtl

Outstanding Rookie

1980 William Miller, Wpg	1987 Gill Fenerty, Tor	1994 Matt Goodwin, Bal
1981 Vince Goldsmith, Sask	1988 Orville Lee, Ott	1995 Shalon Baker, Edm
1982 Chris Isaac, Ott	1989 Stephen Jordan, Ham	1996 Kelvin Anderson, Cal
1983 Johnny Shepherd, Ham	1990 Reggie Barnes, Ott	1997 Derrell Mitchell, Tor
1984 Dwaine Wilson, Mtl	1991 Jon Volpe, BC	1998 Steve Muhammad, BC
1985 Michael Gray, BC	1992 Mike Richardson, Wpg	1999 Pat LaCoste, BC
1986 Harold Hallman, Cal	1993 Michael O'Shea, Ham	2000 Albert Johnson III, Wpg

Source: *Canadian Football League*

(1) Winners are chosen by a vote of the Football Reporters of Canada; prior to 1989 they were known as the Schenley Awards.

Canadian Football Hall of Fame

(only players listed (year of election))

Player, Year Elected, Team(s)

Ah You, Junior (1997) Mtl
Atchison, Ron, (1978) Sask
Bailey, Byron (1975) BC
Baker, Bitt (1994) Sask/BC
Barrow, John (1976) Ham
Bass, Danny (2000) Tor/Cgy/Edm
Batstone, Harry (1963) Tor/Queen's
Beach, Ormond (1963) Sarnia
Benecick, Al (1996) Sask
Box, Ab (1965) Balmy Beach/Tor
Breen, Joseph (1963) U of Toronto/Tor
Bright, Johnny (1970) Edm/Cal
Brock, Ralph Dieter (1995) Wpg/Ham
Brown, Tom (1984) BC
Burden, Willie (2001) Cal
Campbell, Jerry "Soupy" (1996) Cal/Ott
Casey, Tom (1964) Wpg
Charlton, Ken (1992) Ott/Sask
Clements, Tom (1994) Ott/Sask/Ham/Wpg
Clark, Bill (1996) Sask
Coffey, Tommy Joe (1977) Edm/Cal
Conacher, Lionel (1963) Tor
Copeland, Royal (1988) Tor
Corrigal, Jim (1990) Tor
Covington, Grover (2000) Ham
Cox, Ernest (1963) Ham
Craig, Ross (1964) Ham
Cronin, Carl (1967) Wpg
Cutler, Dave (1998) Edm
Cutler, Wes (1968) Tor
Dalla Riva, Peter (1993) Mtl
Dipietro, Rocky (1997) Ham
Dixon, George (1974) Mtl
Eliowitz, Abe (1969) Ott/Mtl
Emerson, Eddie (1963) Ott
Etcheverry, Sam (1969) Mtl
Evanshen, Terry (1984) Mtl/Cal/Ham/Tor
Faloney, Bernie (1974) Edm/Ham
Fear, Cap (1967) Tor/Mtl/Ham
Fennell, Dave (1990) Edm
Ferraro, John (196)6 Ham/Mtl
Fieldgate, Norm (1979) BC
Fleming, Willie (1982) BC
Frank, Bill (2001) BC/Tor/Wpg
Gabriel, Tony (1984) Ham/Ott
Gaines, Geve (1994) Mtl/Ott
Gall, Hugh (1963) U of Toronto
Golab, Tony (1964) Ott

Player, Year Elected, Team(s)

Grant, Tom (1995) Ham/Wpg
Gray, Herb (1983) Wpg
Griffing, Dean (1965) Sask/Cal
Hanson, Fritz (1963) Wpg
Harris, Dickie (1998) Mtl
Harris, Wayne (1976) Cal
Harrison, Herman (1993) Cal
Helton, John (1985) Cal/Wpg
Henley, Garney (1979) Ham
Hinton, Tom (1991) BC
Holloway, Condredge (1998) O/Tor/BC
Huffman, Dick (1987) Wpg/Cal
Isbister, Bob (1965) Ham
Jackson, Russ (1973) Ott
Jacobs, Jack (1963) Wpg
James, Eddie (1963) Wpg/Reg
James, Gerry (1981) Wpg
Kabat, Greg (1966) Wpg
Kapp, Joe (1984) Cal/BC
Keeling, Jerry (1989) Cal/Ott/Ham
Kelly, Brian (1991) Edm
Kelly, Ellison (1992) Edm/Ham
Kepley, Dan (1996) Edm
Krol, Joe (1963) Tor/Ham
Kwong, Normie (1969) Cal/Edm
Lawson, Smirle (1963) U. of Toronto
Leadlay, Frank (1963) Queen's/Ham
Lear, Les (1974) Wpg/Cal
Lewis, Leo (1973) Wpg
Lunsford, Earl (1983) Cal
Luster, Marv (1990) Mtl/Tor
Luzzi, Don (1985) Cal
McCance, Chester (1976) Wpg/Mtl
McGill, Frank (1965) Mtl
McQuarters, Ed (1988) Sask
Miles, Rollie (1980) Edm
Moon, Warren (2001) Edm
Morris, Frank (1983) Tor/Edm
Morris, Ted (1964) Tor
Mosca, Angelo (1987) Ham
Murphy, James (2000) Wpg
Nelson, Roger (1985) Edm
Neumann, Peter (1979) Ham
O'Quinn, Red (1981) Mtl
Pajaczkowski, Tony (1988) Cal/Mtl
Parker, Jackie (1971) Edm/Tor/BC
Parker, James (2001) Edm/BC/Tor

Player, Year Elected, Team(s)

Patterson, Hal (1971) Mtl/Ham
Perry, Gordon (1970) Mtl
Perry, Norman (1963) Sarnia
Ploen, Ken (1975) Wpg
Poplawski, Joe (1998) Wpg
Quilty, Silver (1966) U. of Ottawa
Raimy, Dave (2000) Wpg/Tor
Rebholz, Russ (1963) Wpg
Reed, George (1979) Sask
Reeve, Ted (1963) Tor
Rigney, Frank (1984) Wpg
Robinson, Larry (1998) Cal
Rodden, Michael (1964) Queen's/Tor
Rowe, Paul (1964) Cal
Ruby, Martin (1974) Sask
Russel, Jeff (1963) Ott
Scott, Tom (1998) Wpg/Edm
Scott, Vince (1982) Ham
Shatto, Dick (1975) Tor
Simpson, Benjamin (1963) Ham
Simpson, Bob (1976) Ott
Sprague, David (1963) Ham/Ott
Stevenson, Art (1969) Wpg
Stewart, Ron (1977) Ott
Stirling, Bummer (1966) Sarnia
Sutherin, Don (1992) Ham/Ott
Symons, Bill (1997) BC/Tor
Thelen, Dave (1989) Ott/Tor
Timmis, Brian (1963) Ham/Ott
Tinsley, Buddy (1982) Wpg
Tommy, Andrew (1989) Ott/Tor
Trawick, Herb (1975) Mtl
Tubman, Joe (1968) Ott
Tucker, Whit (1993) Ott
Urness, Ted (1989) Sask
Vaughn, Kaye (1978) Ott
Wagner, Virgil (1980) Mtl
Welch, Huck (1964) Ham/Mtl
Wilkinson, Tom (1987) Edm
Wilson, Al (1997) BC
Wylie, Harvey (1980) Cal
Young, Jim (1991) BC
Zock, William (1984) Tor/Edm

Source: *Canadian Football League*

2001 CFL Hall Of Fame Inductees

■ **Willie Burden (Player):**

Willie Burden played his entire eight-year CFL career with the Calgary Stampeders in the running back position. Burden played 103 games as a Stampeder, but it was during the 1975 season that he was really outstanding. He was named to the Western All-Star team, the CFL All-Star team and was the recipient of the Schenley Most Outstanding Player Award. Burden was also the recipient of the Eddie James Memorial Trophy, and Jeff Nicklin Memorial Awards. Burden played with the Calgary Stampeders from 1974 to 1981. As a tribute to his dedication to the game and his ability as a player, the Calgary Stampeders retired his number (10) in 1982 and he was named to the Stampeder Wall of Fame in 1992.

■ **Sid Forster (Builder):**

Sid Forster devoted his life to football at the amateur level. He became a legend in Sudbury where he spent 28 seasons as head coach of the Sudbury Spartans of the Northern Football Conference, leading his team to the Northern Football Conference Championships twelve times. Forster was also involved in high school football and was instrumental in forming the Joe MacDonald Youth Football League in Sudbury in 1993. Sid Forster served in the executive capacity for the Northern Football Conference as President in 1977, Past President in 1978, Secretary in 1989 and 1990 and was the NFC delegate to Football Ontario from 1978 to 1983. Forster has received many awards and honours recognizing the significant contributions he made to amateur football.

■ **Bill Frank (Player):**

Bill Frank began his CFL career with the B.C. Lions in 1962 where he played the offensive and defensive tackle positions. He remained with the team until 1964. After a brief stint with the Dallas Cowboys of the NFL, Frank joined the Toronto Argonauts in 1965 where he was selected for the CFL All-Star team in three straight years. At the beginning of the 1969 season, he was in Western Canada again with the Winnipeg Blue Bombers where his tremendous strength on the Bomber front line earned him the position of offensive captain and the nickname "Head Hog." Bill Frank was CFL All-Star seven times, Eastern All-Star three times and Western All-Star four times. He also won many other awards and honours recognizing his achievements during his fifteen year CFL career.

■ **Warren Moon (Player):**

Schenley Award winner Warren Moon spent his entire CFL career with the Edmonton Eskimos, from 1978 to 1983. In 1980, he became the team's starting quarterback and led the team to it's third straight Grey Cup victory. He led the team to the Grey Cup game for three years in a row, where the team won two of three games. Warren Moon was named to the CFL All-Star team, the Western All-Star team and won the Schenley Most Outstanding Player Award in 1983. It is fitting that Moon finished his career in the CFL in 1983 as the League's leading passer with 380 completions of 664 attempts for 5,648 yards and 31 touchdowns.

■ **James Parker (Player):**

James Parker joined the CFL with the Edmonton Eskimos in 1980 as a defensive end and went straight to the Grey Cup his first season. He led the League in sacks in 1981 and 1982 and was named to the Western All-Star team and CFL All-Star teams both years. He moved to the B.C. Lions in the 1984 season and became the League sack leader with an average of 26.5 sacks in a single season which is still an all-time CFL record today. In addition, Parker remains third in the league record books with a career total of 139.5 regular-season quarterback sacks. James Parker finished his CFL career as a member of the Toronto Argonauts where he played the 1990 season and one game in the 1991 season.

These five individuals were formally inducted into the Canadian Football Hall of Fame during the Induction Weekend festivities in Hamilton, Ontario from September 20th to September 22nd, 2001.

Source: *Canadian Football League*

Canadian Football Hall of Fame

*I*nterested in Canadian football? Visit www.footballhof.com, *the CFL's official website. When it's up and running, you'll be able to kick a virtual field goal, check out the Heritage Zone or participate in one of their student education programs. The programs help kids build language skills or explore social studies as they discover the star players and tour exhibits. The CFL Hall of Fame itself is located at 58 Jackson Street West, Hamilton, Ontario and is open year round Tuesday to Saturday, 9:30 a.m. till 4:30 p.m. It's closed Statutory holidays and long weekends. For information call (905) 528-7566.*

NFL Final Standings, 2000

American Football Conference

■ Eastern Division	W	L	T	PF	PA
Miami	11	5	0	323	226
Indianapolis	10	6	0	429	326
New York Jets	9	7	0	321	321
Buffalo	8	8	0	315	350
New England	5	11	0	276	338

■ Central Division	W	L	T	PF	PA
Tennessee	13	3	0	343	191
Baltimore	12	4	0	333	165
Pittsburgh	9	7	0	321	255
Jacksonville	7	9	0	367	327
Cincinnati	4	12	0	185	359
Cleveland	3	13	0	161	419

■ Western Division	W	L	T	PF	PA
Oakland	12	4	0	479	299
Denver	11	5	0	485	369
Kansas City	7	9	0	355	354
Seattle	6	10	0	320	405
San Diego	1	15	0	269	440

National Football Conference

■ Eastern Division	W	L	T	PF	PA
NY Giants	12	4	0	328	246
Philadelphia	11	5	0	351	245
Washington	8	8	0	281	269
Dallas	5	11	0	294	361
Arizona	3	13	0	210	443

■ Central Division	W	L	T	PF	PA
Minnesota	11	5	0	397	371
Tampa Bay	10	6	0	388	269
Detroit	9	7	0	307	307
Green Bay	9	7	0	353	323
Chicago	5	11	0	216	355

■ Western Division	W	L	T	PF	PA
St. Louis	10	6	0	540	471
New Orleans	10	6	0	354	305
Carolina	7	9	0	310	310
San Francisco	6	10	0	388	422
Atlanta	4	12	0	252	413

Playoffs

■ **Wild Cards**
Miami Dolphins 23, Indianapolis Colts 17 (OT)
New Orleans Saints 31, St. Louis Rams 28
Baltimore Ravens 21, Denver Broncos 3
Philadelphia Eagles 21, Tampa Bay Buccaneers 3

■ **Conference Championship**
New York Giants 41, Minnesota 0
Baltimore 16, Oakland 3

■ **Divisional Playoffs**
Minnesota Vikings 34, New Orleans Saints 16
Oakland Raiders 27, Miami Dolphins 0
Baltimore Ravens 24, Tennessee Titans 10
New York Giants 20, Philadelphia Eagles 10

■ **SUPER BOWL XXXV at Raymond James Stadium, Tampa**
Sunday, Jan. 28, 2001
Baltimore 34, New York Giants 7

Source: *National Football League*

It's the Texans in 2002

*I*n October 2000, the NFL picked Houston over Los Angeles for its next expansion team. The offer, the richest ever for a franchise, came from Houston businessman Bob McNair and includes the US$700 million franchise price, plus a US$310 million retractable roof stadium.

The Houston Texans will begin play in 2002 in the AFC, where the old Oilers played before moving to Tennessee after the 1996 season. NFL owners also voted to adjust the league alignment to eight divisions of four teams each.

The vote to award Houston the NFL's 32nd franchise was 29-0. Arizona and St. Louis abstained because of questions over the proposed alignment. Failure to come up with a suitable stadium doomed Los Angeles, the nation's second-largest TV market.

Not only will the 31 present NFL owners split Houston's US$700 million franchise fee, they also raised the figure on their teams' values. The Washington Redskins sold for US$800 million earlier in 2000, but that price included the stadium, so the franchise price works out around to US$600 million. Jerry Jones paid US$180 million for the Dallas Cowboys in 1989, at the time considered an astronomical price for a team. In early 2000, Rupert Murdoch failed in his attempt to buy the Manchester United soccer team for US$1 billion—this would have made Manchester the most expensive team in the world.

Source: *Associated Press*

National Football League Individual Statistics by Top Ten, 2000

■ PASSING	ATT.	COMP.	COMP%	YDS	YDS/ATT.	TD	TD%	LONG	INT.	RATING
K. Warner, STL	499	325	65.1	4353	8.7	41	8.2	75t	13	109.2
S. Beuerlein, CAR	571	343	60.1	4436	7.8	36	6.3	88t	15	94.6
J. George, MIN	329	191	58.1	2816	8.6	23	7.0	80t	12	94.2
P.Manning, IND	533	331	62.1	4135	7.8	26	4.9	80t	15	90.7
B. Johnson,WAS	519	316	60.9	4005	7.7	24	4.6	65t	13	90.0
R. Gannon, OAK	515	304	59.0	3840	7.5	24	4.7	50	14	86.5
R. Lucas, NYJ	272	161	59.2	1678	6.2	14	5.1	56t	6	85.1
C. Batch, DET	270	151	55.9	1957	7.3	13	4.8	74t	7	84.1
G. Frerotte, DET	288	175	60.8	2117	7.4	9	3.1	77t	7	83.6
C. Chandler, ATL	307	174	56.7	2339	7.6	16	5.2	60t	11	83.5

■ RECEIVING	YDS	REC.	YDS/REC.	LONG	TD
M. Harrison, IND	1663	115	14.5	57t	12
J. Smith, JAC	1636	116	14.1	62	6
R. Moss, MIN	1413	80	17.7	67t	11
M. Robinson, CHI	1400	84	16.7	80t	9
T. Brown, OAK	1344	90	14.9	47	6
G. Crowell, DET	1338	81	16.5	77t	7
M. Muhammad, CAR	1253	96	13.1	60t	8
C. Carter, MIN	1241	90	13.8	68	13
M. Westbrook, WAS	1191	65	18.3	65	9
A. Toomer, NYG	1183	79	15.0	80	6

■ RUSHING	ATT.	YDS	YDS/ATT.	LONG	TD
E. James, IND	369	1553	4.2	72	13
C. Martin, NYJ	367	1464	4.0	50	5
S. Davis, WAS	290	1405	4.8	76t	17
E. Smith, DAL	329	1397	4.2	63t	11
M. Faulk, STL	253	1381	5.5	58	7
E. George, TEN	320	1304	4.1	40	9
D. Staley, PHI	325	1273	3.9	29	4
C. Garner, SFO	241	1229	5.1	53	4
R. Watters, SEA	325	1210	3.7	45	5
C. Dillon, CIN	263	1200	4.6	50	5

Source: *NFL*

Early NFL Trivia

In 1935, the NFL adopted Bert Bell's proposal to hold an annual draft of college players, to begin in '36, with teams selecting in an inverse order of finish. Jay Berwanger of the University of Chicago was the first player ever selected, by Philadelphia. In 1938, the Pro Bowl, a game between the NFL champions and a team of pro all-stars, was established. The New York Giants defeated the Pro All-Stars 13-10 in the Pro Bowl played Jan. 15, 1939, at Wrigley Field in Los Angeles. Also in '39, an NFL game was first televised when NBC broadcast the Brooklyn-Philadelphia game from Ebbetts Field to the approximately 1,000 sets then in New York. On Dec. 8, 1940, Red Barber broadcast the first NFL championship carried on network radio.

Super Bowl Results, 1980–2001

Date	Results	MVP
Jan. 20, 1980	Pittsburgh 31, L.A. Rams 19	Terry Bradshaw, Pittsburgh
Jan. 25, 1981	Oakland 27, Philadelphia 10	Jim Plunkett, Oakland
Jan. 24, 1982	San Francisco 26, Cincinnati 21	Joe Montana, San Francisco
Jan. 30, 1983	Washington 27, Miami 17	John Riggins, Washington
Jan. 22, 1984	L.A. Raiders 38, Washington 9	Marcus Allen, L.A. Raiders
Jan. 20, 1985	San Francisco 38, Miami 16	Joe Montana, San Francisco
Jan. 26, 1986	Chicago 46, New England 10	Richard Dent, Chicago
Jan. 25, 1987	N.Y. Giants 39, Denver 20	Phil Simms, N.Y. Giants
Jan. 31, 1988	Washington 42, Denver 10	Doug Williams, Washington
Jan. 22, 1989	San Francisco 20, Cincinnati 16	Jerry Rice, San Francisco
Jan. 28, 1990	San Francisco 55, Denver 10	Joe Montana, San Francisco
Jan. 27, 1991	N.Y. Giants 20, Buffalo 19	Ottis Anderson, N.Y. Giants
Jan. 26, 1992	Washington 37, Buffalo 24	Mark Rypien, Washington
Jan. 31, 1993	Dallas 52, Buffalo 17	Troy Aikman, Dallas
Jan. 30, 1994	Dallas 30, Buffalo 13	Emmitt Smith, Dallas
Jan. 29, 1995	San Francisco 49, San Diego 26	Steve Young, San Francisco
Jan. 28, 1996	Dallas 27, Pittsburgh 17	Larry Brown, Dallas
Jan. 26, 1997	Green Bay 35, New England 21	Desmond Howard, Green Bay
Jan. 25, 1998	Denver 31, Green Bay 24	Terrell Davis, Denver
Jan. 31, 1999	Denver 34, Atlanta 19	John Elway, Denver
Jan. 30, 2000	St. Louis 23, Tennessee 16	Kurt Warren, St. Louis
Jan. 28, 2001	Baltimore 34, New York Giants 7	Ray Lewis, Baltimore

Jesse James Palmer–Rising Young Gun

*J*esse James Palmer's father, Bill James, was a quarterback with the Ottawa Rough Riders. Weaned on the game, Jesse was in grade school when he first revealed his dream to become an NFL quarterback. Today the 22-year-old Palmer is closer to his NFL dream than any Canadian-born and raised quarterback before him. When the NFC champion New York Giants opened the 2001 NFL season against the Denver Broncos, the Nepean, Ontario native was the team's third-string quarterback.

"If you really want to make it in pro sports, especially football, you really have to stay on that path," he said in a recent interview at the Giants training camp in Albany. "I've managed to stay focussed and dedicated with a good work ethic and just kept pushing."

At 6-foot-1, 219 pounds, he has a powerful presence in the pocket and the ability to rifle the ball 60 yards downfield while standing flat-footed. His path to the NFL, however, was not easy. When he wasn't being heavily recruited south of the border, Palmer put his own highlight package together and circulated it to major U.S. colleges. When one got in the hands of Gators' coach Steve Spurrier, he couldn't get him to the Florida campus fast enough. So began a bumpy ride in Gainesville. Palmer started midway through his freshman season but as a junior was being platooned. In his final season last year, Palmer lost his starting job to Rex Grossman.

Palmer was confident he would be playing pro football somewhere and after the Sugar Bowl, where the Gators lost to the Miami Hurricanes, he changed focus and began preparing for the two college all-star games. He was strong in the Senior Bowl and scouts noticed him. The Giants liked what they saw and on draft day, Palmer was selected late in the fourth round by the New York club.

The Rocket Dies — May 27, 2000

Maurice Richard—the Rocket—was born August 4, 1921 in Montreal, and learned how to skate on the Rivieres de Prairies near Laval.

Early in his hockey career, critics focused on Richard's tendency towards injury—a broken wrist while at the Canadiens Seniors' training camp in 1940, and a fractured ankle during his first season with the NHL Canadiens in 1942–43. But no one disputed that there was something different about this wartime athlete.

"I first saw him in 1942," reminisced teammate Ken Reardon, who later became the vice-president of the Canadiens. "I see this guy skating at me with wild, bloody hair the way he had it then, eyes just outside of the nut house. 'I'll take this guy,' I said to myself. He went around me like a hoop around a barrel."

In 1944, Richard scored 23 of his 32 regular season goals in 22 games. The Canadiens had a 38-5-7 season with a 22-0-3 home record. On March 23, he gave the greatest individual performance in NHL playoff history. Richard scored a 5–1 victory over the Toronto Maple Leafs, and went on to score 12 goals in nine playoff games. It was his first Stanley Cup with the Canadiens. On March 18, 1945, Richard became the first player in NHL history to score 50 goals in a season. The 1944–45 season only consisted of 50 games. By 1947, he was named the NHL's most valuable player.

The intense loyalty of Canadiens fans to their hero led to the infamous "Richard Riot" in 1955. (Some claimed it was also emblematic of the French-English tensions in Montreal at the time, with NHL President Clarence Campbell representing the Anglo elite and Richard was the French Canadian hero.) Richard was involved in a fight with Hal Laycoe of the Boston Bruins in a March game that escalated into a stick attack on Laycoe; during attempts to subdue Richard, the Rocket landed two punches on a linesman. The assault led to his suspension from the final three games of the season and from the playoffs. The sentence meant that Richard would not win a scoring title, and that the Canadiens would not win the Cup. Against counsel, NHL President Clarence Campbell attended the St. Patrick's Day game in Montreal against Detroit, the day after the Rocket's sentence was announced. The fans threw eggs and tomatoes in his direction. One fan slapped his face. Someone let off a tear gas bomb, and the patrons ran screaming from the arena, fearing fire. A forfeit was ruled in favour of the Red Wings. Crowds in the street broke windows in a five-block area, flipped cars, set fires and looted stores on rue St. Catherine. 41 were arrested.

Richard led his team to five consecutive Stanley Cups between 1956–60; retiring in 1960. The CBC announced the news nationally in a half-hour telecast. Best known as captain of the Canadiens, he played 18 years in the NHL, with 978 career games. His 544 regular season goals are the most in Canadiens' history. He had 421 assists, was an all-star 14 times, made 15 post-season appearances, won eight Stanley cup rings, and set 16 NHL records. (He also spent more than 21 hours in the penalty box.) His record of six overtime playoff goals remains untouched.

On March 11, 1996, during the final game at the historic Montreal Forum, Richard received a standing ovation that lasted more than 11 minutes. He hadn't played in 36 years, but the crowd–approximately 75% of whom had not seen him play — loved him nevertheless as an icon.

Richard was a referee for the Legends of Hockey games in the Oldtimers' Hockey Tour. At each game a tribute was given to him as he skated across the ice, with both teams kneeling in respect. Richard fought cancer for more than two years, before he died at age 79.

Guy LaFleur, former Canadien, remembered Richard fondly, "We all wanted to wear (his) No. 9 when we were kids–not just me. This man played a role in my career through the pride he displayed each time he wore the sweater of the Montreal Canadiens."

National Hockey League, 2000–2001

Final Standings

Eastern Conference

■ Atlantic Division

	W	L	T	GF	GA	PTS
New Jersey	48	19	12	295	195	111
Philadelphia	43	25	11	240	207	100
Pittsburgh	42	28	9	281	256	100
NY Rangers	33	43	5	250	290	72
NY Islanders	21	51	7	185	268	52

■ Northeast Division

	W	L	T	GF	GA	PTS
Ottawa	48	21	9	274	205	109
Buffalo	46	30	5	218	184	98
Toronto	37	29	11	232	207	90
Boston	36	30	8	227	249	88
Montreal	28	40	8	206	232	70

■ Southeast Division

	W	L	T	GF	GA	PTS
Washington	41	27	10	233	211	96
Carolina	38	32	9	212	225	88
Florida	22	38	13	200	246	66
Atlanta	23	45	12	211	289	60
Tampa Bay	24	47	6	201	280	59

Western Conference

■ Central Division

	W	L	T	GF	GA	PTS
Detroit	49	20	9	253	202	111
St. Louis	43	22	12	249	195	103
Nashville	34	36	9	186	200	80
Chicago	29	40	8	210	246	71
Columbus	28	39	9	190	233	71

■ Northwest Division

	W	L	T	GF	GA	PTS
Colorado	52	16	10	270	192	118
Edmonton	39	28	12	243	222	93
Vancouver	36	28	11	239	238	90
Calgary	27	36	15	197	210	73
Minnesota	25	39	13	168	210	68

■ Pacific Division

	W	L	T	GF	GA	PTS
Dallas	48	24	8	241	187	106
San Jose	40	27	12	217	192	95
Los Angeles	38	28	13	252	228	92
Phoenix	35	27	17	214	212	90
Anaheim	25	41	11	188	245	66

Source: *The Hockey Nut*
Note: A team scoring a goal in overtime is credited with two points and a victory in the W column; the team giving up a goal in overtime gets one point and the game is counted in the RT (Regulation Tie) and the loss column.

Berard Returns

Bryan Berard had a stellar junior hockey career. The left-shooting defenseman started playing his pro career in 1996-7 with the New York Islanders and won the Calder Trophy during his first season. In 1998, he played with the US Olympic team at Nagano, Japan. His game performance dropped in his second season and halfway through his third the Islanders traded him to Toronto. Here he advanced with the Leafs to his first Eastern Conference finals. During the next season, on March 11, 2000, during a 4-2 win over the Senators, a high-stick from Ottawa's Marian Hossa sliced Bryan's right eye. Hossa received a double minor penalty for the accident. Bryan underwent four hours of surgery in New York, where doctors re-attracted his retina. The damage was so bad they considered removing his eye. In February 2001, Bryan announced his retirement.

NHL by-law 12.7 requires that all players have at least 20/400 vision. As a result of the accident, Berard's is 20/600. He has undergone seven eye operations since the injury. Thinking Bryan had retired, the Leafs didn't give a qualifying offer for the current season, making him a free agent. During early September 2001, he competed at the US Olympic Orientation Camp in Colorado Springs and he looked good. The Leafs and other teams wooed him, but the Rangers were the eventual winners. He underwent a physical and an eye exam before signing a seven-day contingency contract. With a special contact lens Bryan meets regulations and has been approved to play by the NHL. He played his first preseason game Saturday, September 29, 2001. Bryan has agreed to a four-year deal worth at least US$11 million. His first year's salary of UD$2 million will go to his insurance company, which gave him a US$6.5 million payout when he retired.

NHL Playoff Results 2000–2001

■ **CONFERENCE QUARTER-FINALS**

Eastern Conference – 1

Matchup	Result
Carolina at New Jersey	New Jersey, 5-1
Carolina at New Jersey	New Jersey, 2-0
New Jersey at Carolina	New Jersey, 4-0
New Jersey at Carolina	Carolina, 3-2 (OT)
Carolina at New Jersey	Carolina, 3-2
New Jersey at Carolina	New Jersey, 5-1
New Jersey Wins Series, 4-2	

Eastern Conference – 2

Matchup	Result
Toronto at Ottawa	Toronto, 1-0
Toronto at Ottawa	Toronto, 3-0
Ottawa at Toronto	Toronto, 3-2 (OT)
Ottawa at Toronto	Toronto, 3-1
Toronto Wins Series, 4-0	

Eastern Conference – 3

Matchup	Result
Pittsburgh at Washington	Washington, 1-0
Pittsburgh at Washington	Pittsburgh, 2-1
Washington at Pittsburgh	Pittsburgh, 3-0
Washington at Pittsburgh	Washington, 4-3 (OT)
Pittsburgh at Washington	Pittsburgh, 2-1
Washington at Pittsburgh	Pittsburgh, 4-3 (OT)
Pittsburg Wins Series, 4-2	

Eastern Conference – 4

Matchup	Result
Buffalo at Philadelphia	Buffalo, 2-1
Buffalo at Philadelphia	Buffalo, 4-3 (OT)
Philadelphia at Buffalo	Philadelphia, 3-2
Philadelphia at Buffalo	Buffalo, 4-3 (OT)
Buffalo at Philadelphia	Philadelphia, 3-1
Philadelphia at Buffalo	Buffalo, 8-0
Buffalo Wins Series, 4-2	

Western Conference – 1

Matchup	Result
Vancouver at Colorado	Colorado, 5-4
Vancouver at Colorado	Colorado, 2-1
Colorado at Vancouver	Colorado, 4-3 (OT)
Colorado at Vancouver	Colorado, 5-1
Colorado Wins Series, 4-0	

Western Conference – 2

Matchup	Result
Los Angeles at Detroit	Detroit, 5-3
Los Angeles at Detroit	Detroit, 4-0
Detroit at Los Angeles	Los Angeles, 2-1
Detroit at Los Angeles	Los Angeles, 4-3 (OT)
Los Angeles at Detroit	Los Angeles, 3-2
Detroit at Los Angeles	Los Angeles, 3-2 (OT)
Los Angeles Wins Series, 4-2	

Western Conference – 3

Matchup	Result
Edmonton at Dallas	Dallas, 2-1 (OT)
Edmonton at Dallas	Edmonton, 4-3
Dallas at Edmonton	Dallas, 3-2 (OT)
Dallas at Edmonton	Edmonton, 2-1 (OT)
Edmonton at Dallas	Dallas, 4-3 (OT)
Dallas at Edmonton	Dallas, 3-1
Dallas Wins Series, 4-2	

Western Conference – 4

Matchup	Result
San Jose at St. Louis	St. Louis, 3-1
San Jose at St. Louis	San Jose, 1-0
St. Louis at San Jose	St. Louis, 6-3
St. Louis at San Jose	San Jose, 3-2
San Jose at St. Louis	St. Louis, 3-2 (OT)
St. Louis at San Jose	St. Louis, 2-1
St. Louis Wins Series, 4-2	

■ **CONFERENCE SEMI-FINALS**

Eastern Conference – 1

Matchup	Result
Toronto at New Jersey	Toronto, 2-0
Toronto at New Jersey	New Jersey, 6-5 (OT)
New Jersey at Toronto	New Jersey, 3-2 (OT)
New Jersey at Toronto	Toronto, 3-1
Toronto at New Jersey	Toronto, 3-2
New Jersey at Toronto	New Jersey, 4-2
Toronto at New Jersey	New Jersey, 5-1
New Jersey Wins Series, 4-3	

Western Conference – 1

Matchup	Result
Los Angeles at Colorado	Los Angeles, 4-3 (OT)
Los Angeles at Colorado	Colorado, 2-0
Colorado at Los Angeles	Colorado, 4-3
Colorado at Los Angeles	Colorado, 3-0
Los Angeles at Colorado	Los Angeles, 1-0
Colorado at Los Angeles	Los Angeles, 1-0 (2OT)
Los Angeles at Colorado	Colorado, 5-1
Colorado Wins Series, 4-3	

▶

▶ CONFERENCE SEMI-FINALS (continued)

Eastern Conference – 2

Matchup	Result
Pittsburgh at Buffalo	Pittsburgh, 3-0
Pittsburgh at Buffalo	Pittsburgh, 3-1
Buffalo at Pittsburgh	Buffalo, 4-1
Buffalo at Pittsburgh	Buffalo, 5-2
Pittsburgh at Buffalo	Buffalo, 3-2 (OT)
Buffalo at Pittsburgh	Pittsburgh, 3-2 (OT)
Pittsburgh at Buffalo	Pittsburgh, 3-2 (OT)
Pittsburgh Wins Series, 4-3	

Western Conference – 2

Matchup	Result
St. Louis at Dallas	St. Louis, 4-2
St. Louis at Dallas	St. Louis, 2-1
Dallas at St. Louis	St. Louis, 3-2 (2OT)
Dallas at St. Louis	St. Louis, 4-1
St. Louis Wins Series, 4-0	

■ CONFERENCE FINALS

Eastern

Matchup	Result
Pittsburgh at New Jersey	New Jersey, 3-1
Pittsburgh at New Jersey	Pittsburgh, 4-2
New Jersey at Pittsburgh	New Jersey, 3-0
New Jersey at Pittsburgh	New Jersey, 5-0
Pittsburgh at New Jersey	New Jersey, 4-2
New Jersey Wins Series, 4-1	

Western

Matchup	Result
St. Louis at Colorado	Colorado, 4-1
St. Louis at Colorado	Colorado, 4-2
Colorado at St. Louis	St. Louis, 4-3, 2OT
Colorado at St. Louis	Colorado, 4-3, OT
St. Louis at Colorado	Colorado, 2-1, OT
Colorado Wins Series, 4-1	

STANLEY CUP FINAL

Matchup	Result
New Jersey at Colorado	Colorado, 5-0
New Jersey at Colorado	New Jersey, 2-1
Colorado at New Jersey	Colorado, 3-1
Colorado at New Jersey	New Jersey, 3-2
New Jersey at Colorado	New Jersey, 4-1
Colorado at New Jersey	Colorado, 4-0
New Jersey at Colorado	Colorado, 3-1
Colorado Wins Series, 4-3	

Source: *CBS Sportsline.com Inc.*

The Yukon Quest

*I*n the Bull's Eye Saloon in Fairbanks, Alaska, historian Roger Williams and mushers Leroy Shank, Ron Rosser and Willie Libb founded the Yukon Quest International Sled Dog Race: a race that traces the 1898 gold rush route that prospectors took to the Alaskan interior. The annual event was first held in 1984.

The contestants race for US$125,000 that's split amongst 15 finishing teams. The winner earns US$30,000. Mushers start the 1,000 mile trek with eight to fourteen dogs, and must finish with at least six—and the same sled. Dogs wear booties, and mushers wear mukluks. There are vets at checkpoints, and pro handlers take over on the dangerous descents—it's riskier than the Iditarod trail. Despite the rules and vet programme, the Quest remains the toughest dogsled race in the world. While trail-breaking machines pack down the route ahead of teams, who follow reflective markers through 20, 50-mile runs (marked by checkpoints, cabins and campsites) and use of GPS is allowed, it is a true distance race with no supplies flown in and no caches along the trail. Mushers work, eat, and sleep with their canines. It takes 10 to 13 days to finish the trek. The 2002 race starts in Fairbanks on February 9th. Visit www.yukonquest.org to find out more.

Lemieux Returns

October 5, 1965: Mario Lemieux arrives for his first breath. October 11, 1984: Mario Lemieux arrives for his first shift in the National Hockey League, steals the puck from Boston defenseman Ray Bourque and beats goalie Pete Peeters with the first shot he takes. October 3, 2001: Super Mario again skates with his Pittsburgh Penguins on opening night in Pittsburgh, this time against the Colorado Avalanche.

Pen fans didn't need to worry that Mario is merely Mister October, of course. In his time with the Penguins, he was a great playoff asset in winning back-to-back Stanley Cups in 1990–91 and 1991–92. The numbers he attained and the trophies he's collected are astounding in themselves: two Stanley Cups, a Calder Trophy as top rookie in 1984–85, three Hart Trophies as the league MVP, two Conn Smythe trophies as the playoff MVP, and six scoring titles.

What makes the Lemieux story so interesting is the number of times he can come back and perform. In the 1991–92 playoffs, Mario suffered a broken left hand—he returned five games later, won the Conn Smythe trophy as the playoff MVP, and carried the Pens to their second straight Stanley Cup. In the 1992–93 season, he underwent radiation treatment to try to contain his Hodgkins disease, and he returned to shine in the playoffs one month

later. He took the entire 1994–95 season off because of radiation aftereffects, and returned for another Hart Trophy in the 1995–96 season. His back problems and the "clutch and grab" style of play that became dominant in the NHL led him to retire at the age of 31. In retirement, his former team filed for bankruptcy, imperiling millions of deferred dollars owed to him. Lemieux successfully led a group to buy the Penguins in time for the 1999–00 season. In the 2000–01 season, after a three-year absence, he returned to the ice after his retired number 66 is lowered from the Igloo rafters and where his son Austin sees him play for the first time. Austin was excited to see his father, one of the greatest players of all time, skate alongside one of today's best players Jaromir Jagr. 66 was a force with 68 in the playoffs, and the Penguins advanced to the Eastern Conference finals against the New Jersey Devils. Lemieux seemed to be an even better player last year, and was spotted behind his own net to carry out his defensive responsibilities. Lemieux, 66, will return for the 2001–02 season, but Jagr, 68, has been traded for players that will likely help the Penguins after Lemieux has retired for good. Only time will tell how Lemieux will fare without Jagr alongside, but do not be surprised if he makes as great a comeback as he has done each other time.

■ Mario Lemieux Profile
Born: Montreal, October 5, 1965
Arrived: Selected by the Pittsburgh Penguins in the 1st round (1st overall) of the 1984 NHL Entry Draft
Position: Center

Regular Season / **Post-season**

YR	Team	GP	G	A	PTS	PIM	+/-	SHOTS	PCT	GP	G	A	PTS	PIM
84–85	Pit	73	43	57	100	54	–35	209	20.6	—	—	—	—	—
85–86	Pit	79	48	93	141	43	–6	276	17.6	—	—	—	—	—
86–87	Pit	63	54	53	107	57	13	267	20.2	—	—	—	—	—
87–88	Pit	77	70	98	168	92	23	382	18.3	—	—	—	—	—
88–89	Pit	76	85	114	199	100	41	313	27.2	11	12	7	19	16
89–90	Pit	59	45	78	123	78	–18	226	19.9	—	—	—	—	—
90–91	Pit	26	19	26	45	30	8	89	21.3	23	16	28	44	16
91–92	Pit	64	44	87	131	94	27	249	17.7	15	16	18	34	2
92–93	Pit	60	69	91	160	38	55	286	24.1	11	8	10	18	10
93–94	Pit	22	17	20	37	32	–2	92	18.5	6	4	3	7	2
95–96	Pit	70	69	92	161	54	10	338	20.4	18	11	16	27	33
96–97	Pit	76	50	72	122	65	27	327	15.3	5	3	3	6	4
00–01	Pit	43	35	41	76	18	15	171	20.5	18	6	11	17	4
Totals		**788**	**648**	**922**	**1570**	**755**	**158**	**3225**	**20.1**	**107**	**76**	**96**	**172**	**87**

Stanley Cup Champions, 1926–2001

The Stanley Cup, the oldest trophy competed for by professional athletes in North America, was donated by Frederick Arthur, Lord Stanley of Preston, in 1893. Originally presented to the amateur hockey champions of Canada, it has been awarded to the top professional team since 1910 and, since 1926, has been competed for only by NHL teams.

Year	Champion	Final Opponent	Series Result	Winning Coach	Winning Manager
1926	Montreal Maroons	Victoria	3-1	Eddie Gerard	Eddie Gerard
1927	Ottawa Senators	Boston	2-0	Dave Gill	Dave Gill
1928	New York Rangers	Montreal	3-2	Lester Patrick	Lester Patrick
1929	Boston Bruins	New York	2-0	Cy Denneny	Art Ross
1930	Montreal Canadiens	Boston	2-0	Cecil Hart	Cecil Hart
1931	Montreal Canadiens	Chicago	3-2	Cecil Hart	Cecil Hart
1932	Toronto Maple Leafs	New York	3-0	Dick Irvin	Conn Smythe
1933	New York Rangers	Toronto	3-1	Lester Patrick	Lester Patrick
1934	Chicago Black Hawks	Detroit	3-1	Tommy Gorman	Tommy Gorman
1935	Montreal Maroons	Toronto	3-0	Tommy Gorman	Tommy Gorman
1936	Detroit Red Wings	Toronto	4-0	Jack Adams	Jack Adams
1937	Detroit Red Wings	New York	3-2	Jack Adams	Jack Adams
1938	Chicago Black Hawks	Toronto	4-1	Bill Stewart	Bill Stewart
1939	Boston Bruins	Toronto	4-1	Art Ross	Art Ross
1940	New York Rangers	Toronto	4-2	Frank Boucher	Lester Patrick
1941	Boston Bruins	Detroit	4-0	Cooney Weiland	Art Ross
1942	Toronto Maple Leafs	Detroit	4-3	Hap Day	Conn Smythe
1943	Detroit Red Wings	Boston	4-0	Jack Adams	Jack Adams
1944	Montreal Canadiens	Chicago	4-0	Dick Irvin	Tommy Gorman
1945	Toronto Maple Leafs	Detroit	4-3	Hap Day	Conn Smythe
1946	Montreal Canadiens	Boston	4-1	Dick Irvin	Tommy Gorman
1947	Toronto Maple Leafs	Montreal	4-2	Hap Day	Conn Smythe
1948	Toronto Maple Leafs	Detroit	4-0	Hap Day	Conn Smythe
1949	Toronto Maple Leafs	Detroit	4-0	Hap Day	Conn Smythe
1950	Detroit Red Wings	New York	4-3	Tommy Ivan	Jack Adams
1951	Toronto Maple Leafs	Montreal	4-1	Joe Primeau	Conn Smythe
1952	Detroit Red Wings	Montreal	4-0	Tommy Ivan	Jack Adams
1953	Montreal Canadiens	Boston	4-1	Dick Irvin	Frank Selke
1954	Detroit Red Wings	Montreal	4-3	Tommy Ivan	Jack Adams
1955	Detroit Red Wings	Montreal	4-3	Jimmy Skinner	Jack Adams
1956	Montreal Canadiens	Detroit	4-1	Toe Blake	Frank Selke
1957	Montreal Canadiens	Boston	4-1	Toe Blake	Frank Selke
1958	Montreal Canadiens	Boston	4-2	Toe Blake	Frank Selke
1959	Montreal Canadiens	Toronto	4-1	Toe Blake	Frank Selke
1960	Montreal Canadiens	Toronto	4-0	Toe Blake	Frank Selke
1961	Chicago Black Hawks	Detroit	4-2	Rudy Pilous	Tommy Ivan
1962	Toronto Maple Leafs	Chicago	4-2	Punch Imlach	Punch Imlach
1963	Toronto Maple Leafs	Detroit	4-1	Punch Imlach	Punch Imlach
1964	Toronto Maple Leafs	Detroit	4-3	Punch Imlach	Punch Imlach
1965	Montreal Canadiens	Chicago	4-3	Toe Blake	Sam Pollock

▶

Year	Champion	Final Opponent	Series Result	Winning Coach	Winning Manager
1966	Montreal Canadiens	Detroit	4-2	Toe Blake	Sam Pollock
1967	Toronto Maple Leafs	Montreal	4-2	Punch Imlach	Punch Imlach
1968	Montreal Canadiens	St. Louis	4-0	Toe Blake	Sam Pollock
1969	Montreal Canadiens	St. Louis	4-0	Claude Ruel	Sam Pollock
1970	Boston Bruins	St. Louis	4-0	Harry Sinden	Milt Schmidt
1971	Montreal Canadiens	Chicago	4-3	Al MacNeil	Sam Pollock
1972	Boston Bruins	New York	4-2	Tom Johnson	Milt Schmidt
1973	Montreal Canadiens	Chicago	4-2	Scotty Bowman	Sam Pollock
1974	Philadelphia Flyers	Boston	4-2	Fred Shero	Keith Allen
1975	Philadelphia Flyers	Buffalo	4-2	Fred Shero	Keith Allen
1976	Montreal Canadiens	Philadelphia	4-0	Scotty Bowman	Sam Pollock
1977	Montreal Canadiens	Boston	4-0	Scotty Bowman	Sam Pollock
1978	Montreal Canadiens	Boston	4-2	Scotty Bowman	Sam Pollock
1979	Montreal Canadiens	New York	4-1	Scotty Bowman	Irving Grundman
1980	N.Y. Islanders	Philadelphia	4-2	Al Arbour	Bill Torrey
1981	N.Y. Islanders	Minnesota	4-1	Al Arbour	Bill Torrey
1982	N.Y. Islanders	Vancouver	4-0	Al Arbour	Bill Torrey
1983	N.Y. Islanders	Edmonton	4-0	Al Arbour	Bill Torrey
1984	Edmonton Oilers	New York	4-1	Glen Sather	Glen Sather
1985	Edmonton Oilers	Philadelphia	4-1	Glen Sather	Glen Sather
1986	Montreal Canadiens	Calgary	4-1	Jean Perron	Serge Savard
1987	Edmonton Oilers	Philadelphia	4-3	Glen Sather	Glen Sather
1988	Edmonton Oilers	Boston	4-0	Glen Sather	Glen Sather
1989	Calgary Flames	Montreal	4-2	Terry Crisp	Cliff Fletcher
1990	Edmonton Oilers	Boston	4-1	John Muckler	Glen Sather
1991	Pittsburgh Penguins	Minnesota	4-2	Bob Johnson	Craig Patrick
1992	Pittsburgh Penguins	Chicago	4-0	Scotty Bowman	Craig Patrick
1993	Montreal Canadiens	Los Angeles	4-1	Jacques Demers	Serge Savard
1994	New York Rangers	Vancouver	4-3	Mike Keenan	Neil Smith
1995	New Jersey Devils	Detroit	4-0	Jacques Lemaire	Lou Lamoriello
1996	Colorado Avalanche	Florida	4-0	Marc Crawford	Pierre Lacroix
1997	Detroit Red Wings	Philadelphia	4-0	Scotty Bowman	Scotty Bowman
1998	Detroit Red Wings	Washington	4-0	Scotty Bowman	Ken Holland
1999	Dallas Stars	Buffalo	4-2	Ken Hitchcock	Bob Gainey
2000	New Jersey Devils	Dallas	4-2	Larry Robinson	Lou Lamoriello
2001	Colorado Avalanche	New Jersey	4-3	Bob Harley	Pierre Lacroix

Source: *National Hockey League*

Ray Bourque Retires from the NHL

Star defenseman Ray Bourque, age 40, announced his retirement at the Denver Pepsi Center 17 days after his team won the 2000-2001 Stanley Cup. On June 9th The Colorado Avalanche was victorious in Denver, with a Game 7 win over the New Jersey Devils. Since the announcement, the Avalanche have made plans to retire Bourque's No. 77 jersey, and Harry Sinden, general manager of Bourque's former team, the Boston Bruins, likewise plans to hang Bourque's number in the rafters of the Fleet Center, with other famous jerseys.

Bourque spent 15 months with the Colorado Avalanche. With 1,800 games played during a 22-year career, he is recognised as the highest-scoring defenseman in NHL history, a 19-time All-Star player, and five-time winner of the Norris Trophy as the league's best defenseman.

Though Bourque may always be a Bruin in his heart, it was Colorado that took on the mission to have him on a cup-winning team before he hung up his skates. Sinden sent Bourque to Colorado after he'd asked to be traded in March 2000. Bruins fans were supportive of the trade, expressing gratitude and respect towards Bourque's 20-year run in Boston.

Originally from St. Laurent, in Montreal, Quebec, Bourque was confident he would play in the NHL. His career began in September 1979 when he headed off to his first training camp with the Boston Bruins. Since then Bourque has become an international role model to young players who are as shy and quiet as he was. They too can hope to make it into the big league, and just may become future Hockey Hall of Fame inductees.

In 2004, Ray Bourque will become an eligible inductee for the Hockey Hall of Fame. He may be the first inductee from the Colorado Avalanche, and he'll join 40 Boston Bruins previously inducted into the Hockey Hall of Fame.

■ Ray Bourque Profile

Born: Montreal, December 28, 1960
Arrived: Boston's 1st choice, 8th overall 1979 draft
Position: Captain of the Bruins from 1988–89 until traded in March 2000.

| | | **Regular Season** | | | | | | | | **Post-season** | | | | |
YR	Team	GP	G	A	PTS	PIM	+/−	SHOTS	PCT	GP	G	A	PTS	PIM
79–80	Bos	80	17	48	65	73	52	185	9.2	10	2	9	11	27
80–81	Bos	67	27	29	56	96	29	207	13.0	3	0	1	1	2
81–82	Bos	65	17	49	66	51	22	211	8.1	9	1	5	6	16
82–83	Bos	65	22	51	73	20	49	205	10.7	17	8	15	23	10
83–84	Bos	78	31	65	96	57	51	340	9.1	3	0	2	2	0
84–85	Bos	73	20	66	86	53	30	333	6.0	5	0	3	3	4
85–86	Bos	74	19	58	77	68	17	289	6.6	3	0	0	0	0
86–87	Bos	78	23	72	95	36	44	334	6.9	4	1	2	3	0
87–88	Bos	78	17	64	81	72	34	344	4.9	23	3	18	21	26
88–89	Bos	60	18	43	61	52	20	243	7.4	10	0	4	4	6
89–90	Bos	76	19	65	84	50	31	310	6.1	17	5	12	17	16
90–91	Bos	76	21	73	94	75	33	323	6.5	19	7	18	25	12
91–92	Bos	80	21	60	81	56	11	334	6.3	12	3	6	9	12
92–93	Bos	78	19	63	82	40	38	330	5.8	4	1	0	1	2
93–94	Bos	72	20	71	91	58	26	386	5.2	13	2	8	10	0
94–95	Bos	46	12	31	43	20	3	210	5.7	5	0	3	3	0
95–96	Bos	82	20	62	82	58	31	390	5.1	5	1	6	7	2
96–97	Bos	62	19	31	50	18	−11	230	8.3	—	—	—	—	—
97–98	Bos	82	13	35	48	80	2	264	4.9	6	1	4	5	2
98–99	Bos	81	10	47	57	34	−7	262	3.8	12	1	9	10	14
99–00	Bos	65	10	28	38	20	−11	217	4.6	—	—	—	—	—
...	Col	14	8	6	14	6	9	43	18.6	13	1	8	9	8
Season		79	18	34	52	26	−2	260	6.9	13	1	8	9	8
00–01	Col	80	7	52	59	48	25	216	3.2	21	4	6	10	12
Totals		1612	410	1169	1579	1141	528	6206	6.6	214	41	139	180	171

GP — games played; G — goals; A — assists; Pts — points; PIM — penalties in minutes; +/− — plus/minus stats showing the number of even-strength and short-handed goals scored by a player's team, minus those scored against while he is on the ice; Shots — shots on goal; Pct — scoring percentage

NHL Scoring Leaders, 2000–2001

Regular Season

Player	GP	G	A	P	+/–	PIM	SPCT	S
Jaromir Jagr, PIT	81	52	69	121	19	42	16.4	317
Joe Sakic, COL	82	54	64	118	45	30	16.3	332
Patrik Elias, NJD	82	40	56	96	45	51	18.2	220
Alexei Kovalev, PIT	79	44	51	95	12	96	14.3	307
Jason Allison, BOS	82	36	59	95	-8	85	19.5	185
Martin Straka, PIT	82	27	68	95	19	38	14.6	185
Pavel Bure, FLA	82	59	33	92	-2	58	15.4	384
Doug Weight, EDM	82	25	65	90	12	91	13.3	188
Zigmund Palffy, LOS	73	38	51	89	22	20	17.5	217
Peter Forsberg, COL	73	27	62	89	23	54	15.2	178
Alexei Yashin, OTT	82	40	48	88	10	30	15.2	263
Luc Robitaille, LOS	82	37	51	88	10	66	15.7	235
Bill Guerin, BOS	85	40	45	85	7	140	13.8	289
Mike Modano, DAL	81	33	51	84	26	52	15.9	208
Alexander Mogilny, NJD	75	43	40	83	10	43	17.9	240
Pierre Turgeon, STL	79	30	52	82	14	37	17.5	171
Adam Oates, WAS	81	13	69	82	-9	28	18.1	72
Peter Bondra, WAS	82	45	36	81	8	60	14.8	305
Petr Sykora, NJD	73	35	46	81	36	32	14.1	249
Robert Lang, PIT	82	32	48	80	20	28	18.1	177

Playoffs

Player	GP	G	A	P	+/–	PIM	SPCT	S
Joe Sakic, COL	21	13	13	26	6	6	16.5	79
Patrik Elias, NJD	25	9	14	23	11	10	15.5	58
Milan Hejduk, COL	23	7	16	23	8	6	13.7	51
Petr Sykora, NJD	25	10	12	22	11	12	14.1	71
Alex Tanguay, COL	23	6	15	21	13	8	16.2	37
Rob Blake, COL	23	6	13	19	6	16	7.2	83
Brian Rafalski, NJD	25	7	11	18	10	7	14.9	47
Mario Lemieux, PIT	18	6	11	17	4	4	15.4	39
Chris Drury, COL	23	11	5	16	5	4	17.7	62
Bobby Holik, NJD	25	6	10	16	1	37	9.1	66
Alexander Mogilny, NJD	25	5	11	16	3	8	6.6	76
Jason Arnott, NJD	23	8	7	15	8	16	19.0	42
Pierre Turgeon, STL	15	5	10	15	8	2	16.7	30
Scott Gomez, NJD	25	5	9	14	7	24	7.1	70
Peter Forsberg, COL	11	4	10	14	5	6	17.4	23
Mats Sundin, TOR	11	6	7	13	5	12	14.3	42
Scott Young, STL	15	6	7	13	9	2	11.5	52
Martin Straka, PIT	18	5	8	13	-1	8	10.6	47
Miroslav Satan, BUF	13	3	10	13	4	8	7.5	40
Jaromir Jagr, PIT	16	2	10	12	3	18	5.3	38
Gary Roberts, TOR	11	2	9	11	5	0	13.3	15

Source: *The Hockey Nut* and *CBS SportsLine.com*

GP = Games played; G = Goals; A = Assists; Pts = Points; +/– = Plus/minus statistic, which shows the number of even-strength and shorthanded goals scored by a player's team, minus those scored against, while he is on the ice; PIM = Penalties in minutes; SPCT = Shots on goal percentage; S = Shots on goal.

NHL All Time Individual Scoring Leaders

(at the end of the 2000 – 2001 season)

	Seasons	Goals	Assists	PTS
1. Wayne Gretzky, Edm/LA/StL/NYR	20	894	1963	2857
2. Gordie Howe, Det/Hfd	26	801	1049	1850
3. **Mark Messier, Edm/NYR/Vcr**	22	627	1087	1714
4. Marcel Dionne, Det/LA/NYR	18	731	1040	1771
5. **Ron Francis, Hfd/Pitt/Car**	20	487	1137	1624
6. **Steve Yzerman, Det**	17	645	969	1614
7. Phil Esposito, Chi/Bos/NYR	18	717	873	1590
8. **Ray Bourque, Bos/Col**	22	410	1169	1579
9. **Mario Lemieux, Pitt**	14	648	922	1570
10. Paul Coffey, Edm/Pitt/La/Det/Hfd/Pha/Chi/Car . . .	21	396	1135	1531
11. Stan Mikita, Chi	22	541	926	1467
12. Bryan Trottier, NYI/Pitt	21	524	901	1425
13. Dale Hawerchuk, Wpg/Buf/StL/Pha	16	518	891	1409
14. Jari Kurri, Edm/LA/NYR/Ana/Col	17	601	797	1398
15. Johnny Bucyk, Det/Bos	23	556	813	1369
16. Guy Lafleur, Mtl/NYR/Que	17	560	793	1353
17. **Doug Gilmour, StL/Cgy/Tor/NJ/Chi/Buf**	18	429	914	1343
18. Denis Savard, Chi/Mtl/TB	18	473	865	1338
19. Mike Gartner, Wsh/Min/NYR/Tor/Phx	19	708	627	1335
20. Gilbert Perreault, Buf	17	512	814	1326

Source: *Stats Hockey*　　　　　　　　　　　　　　　　　　　　Active players are in bold.

Directory of Selected Hockey Organizations

Hockey Hall of Fame
BCE Place
30 Yonge St.
Toronto, Ont.
M5E 1X8
Tel: (416) 360-7735
Fax: (416) 360-1501
http://www.hhof.com

National Hockey League
1251 Avenue of the Americas
New York, NY
10020
Tel: (212) 789-2000
http://www.nhl.com

National Hockey League
Players' Association
777 Bay St., Suite 2400
Toronto, Ont.
M5G 2C8
Tel: (416) 313-2300
Fax: (416) 313-2301
http://www.nhlpa.com

Sources: *Hockey Hall of Fame, NHL, NHLPA*

Hockey Hall of Fame Museum

*I*nterested in learning about ice hockey? Visit the Hockey Hall of Fame Museum online through *a virtual tour or in person to experience their latest acquisitions. Tours last about three hours. Educational programs exist for junior, intermediate and senior students. Outreach programs such as* Shut Out, Shutdown, *and the* Legends of Hockey Mobile Exhibit *are also available. The Hockey Hall of Fame is in Toronto's BCE Place at 30 Yonge Street. It's open every day except Christmas, New Year's Day and Induction Day. See their website at* http://www.hhof.com *or call (416) 360-7735 for daily hours.*

Regular Season NHL Scoring Champions, 1960–2001

Season	Player, Team	GP	G	A	PTS	Season	Player, Team	GP	G	A	PTS
1959–60	Bobby Hull, Chi.	70	39	42	81	1980–81	Wayne Gretzky, Edm.	80	55	109	164
1960–61	Bernie Geoffrion, Mtl	64	50	45	95	1981–82	Wayne Gretzky, Edm.	80	92	120	212
1961–62	Bobby Hull, Chi.	70	50	34	84	1982–83	Wayne Gretzky, Edm.	80	71	125	196
1962–63	Gordie Howe, Det	70	38	48	86	1983–84	Wayne Gretzky, Edm.	74	87	118	205
1963–64	Stan Mikita, Chi	70	39	50	89	1984–85	Wayne Gretzky, Edm.	80	73	135	208
1964–65	Stan Mikita, Chi	70	28	59	87	1985–86	Wayne Gretzky, Edm.	80	52	163	215
1965–66	Bobby Hull, Chi.	65	54	43	97	1986–87	Wayne Gretzky, Edm.	79	62	121	183
1966–67	Stan Mikita, Chi	70	35	62	97	1987–88	Mario Lemieux, Pitt	77	70	98	168
1967–68	Stan Mikita, Chi	72	40	47	87	1988–89	Mario Lemieux, Pitt	76	85	114	199
1968–69	Phil Esposito, Bos.	74	49	77	126	1989–90	Wayne Gretzky, L.A.	73	40	102	142
1969–70	Bobby Orr, Bos	76	33	87	120	1990–91	Wayne Gretzky, L.A.	78	41	122	163
1970–71	Phil Esposito, Bos.	78	76	76	152	1991–92	Mario Lemieux, Pitt	64	44	87	131
1971–72	Phil Esposito, Bos.	76	66	67	133	1992–93	Mario Lemieux, Pitt	60	69	91	160
1972–73	Phil Esposito, Bos.	78	55	75	130	1993–94	Wayne Gretzky, L.A.	81	38	92	130
1973–74	Phil Esposito, Bos.	78	68	77	145	1994–95	Jaromir Jagr[1], Pitt.	48[2]	32	38	70
1974–75	Bobby Orr, Bos	80	46	89	135	1995–96	Mario Lemieux, Pitt	70	69	92	161
1975–76	Guy Lafleur, Mtl	80	56	69	125	1996–97	Mario Lemieux, Pitt	76	50	72	122
1976–77	Guy Lafleur, Mtl .	80	56	80	136	1997–98	Jaromir Jagr, Pitt	77	35	67	102
1977–78	Guy Lafleur, Mtl	78	60	72	132	1998–99	Jaromir Jagr, Pitt	81	44	83	127
1978–79	Bryan Trottier, NYI	76	47	87	134	1999–00	Jaromir Jagr, Pitt	63	42	54	96
1979–80	Marcel Dionne, L.A.	80	53	84	137	2000–01	Jaromir Jagr, Pitt	81	52	69	121

Source: *StatsHockey.com*
1 Jagr tied with Lindros (Phi); awarded title based on most goals scored. 2 Season shortened to 48 games due to owner/player dispute.

NHL $5-Million Dollar Club for the 2000–2001 Season

(as of October 1, 2001; all figures in US dollars)

Player	Club	Salary	Player	Club	Salary
Jaromir Jagr	WAS	$10,033,333	Patrick Roy	COL	$7,500,000
Peter Forsberg	COL	$10,000,000	Nicklas Lidstrom	DET	$7,250,000
Paul Kariya	ANA	$10,000,000	Michael Modano	DAL	$7,000,000
Joe Sakic	COL	$9,832,727	Brendan Shanahan	DET	$6,500,000
Robert Blake	COL	$9,285,194	Curtis Joseph	TOR	$6,150,000
Pavel Bure	FLA	$9,000,000	Theoren Fleury	NYRA	$6,000,000
Dominik Hasek	DET	$9,000,000	Douglas Gilmour	BUF	$6,000,000
John LeClair	PHIL	$9,000,000	Pierre Turgeon	DAL	$6,000,000
Doug Weight	STL	$9,000,000	Mike Richter	NYRA	$5,600,000
Jeremy Roenick	PHIL	$8,500,000	Alexander Mogilny	TOR	$5,500,000
Teemu Selanne	SANJ	$8,000,000	Chris Chelios	DET	$5,500,000
Steve Yzerman	DET	$8,000,000	Ray Bourque	COL	$5,500,000
Brian Leetch	NYRA	$7,680,000	Ed Belfour	DAL	$5,500,000

Source: *National Hockey League Players' Association*

2001 NHL DRAFT – First Round Selections

Pick, Team, Player, Position, Last Team (league)

1 **Atlanta:** Ilya Kovalchuk, C, Spartak (Russia, Div. 1)
2 **Ottawa (from Islanders):** Jason Spezza, F, Windsor (OHL)
3 **Tampa Bay:** Alexander Svitov, C, Avangard, Omsk (Russia SR.)
4 **Florida:** Stephen Weiss, C, Plymouth (OHL)
5 **Anaheim:** Stanislav Chistov, F, Omsk (Russia)
6 **Minnesota:** Mikko Koivu, C, Tps (Finland)
7 **Montreal:** Mike Komisarek, D, University of Michigan (CCHA)
8 **Columbus:** Pascal Leclaire, G, Halifax (QMJHL)
9 **Chicago:** Tuomo Ruutu, C, Jokerit (Finland, Div. 1)
10 **Rangers:** Dan Blackburn, G, Kootenay (WHL)
11 **Phoenix** (from Calgary): Fredrik Sjöström, RW, Frolunda (Sweden)
12 **Nashville:** Dan Hamhuis, D, Prince George (WHL)
13 **Edmonton** (from Boston): Ales Hemsky, RW, Hull (QMJHL)
14 **Calgary** (from Phoenix): Chuck Kobasew, RW, Boston College (HE)
15 **Carolina:** Igor Knyazev, D, Spartak (Russia, JR)
16 **Vancouver:** R.J. Umberger, C, Ohio State (CCHA)
17 **Toronto:** Carlo Colaiacovo, D, Erie (OHL)

18 **Los Angeles:** Jens Karlsson, RW, Froludna (Sweden)
19 **Boston** (from Edmonton): Shaone Morrisonn, D, Kamloops (WHL)
20 **San Jose:** Marcel Goc, C, Schwenningen (Germany)
21 **Pittsburgh:** Colby Armstrong, RW, Red Deer (WHL)
22 **Buffalo:** Jiri Novotny, C, Budejovice (Czech Republic)
23 **Ottawa** (from Philadelphia): Tim Gleason, D, Windsor (OHL)
24 **Florida** (from Devils through St. Louis): Lukas Krajicek, D, Petersborough (OHL)
25 **Montreal** (from Washington): Alexander Perezhogin, C, Omsk (Russia)
26 **Dallas:** Jason Bacashihua, G, Chicago (NAHL)
27 **Philadelphia** (from Ottawa): Jeff Woywitka, D, Red Deer (WHL)
28 **Devils:** Adrian Foster, LW, Saskatoon (WHL)
29 **Chicago** (from Detroit): Adam Munro, G, Erie (OHL)
30 **Los Angeles** (from Colorado): David Steckel, C, Ohio State (CCHA)

Sources: *North Jersey Media Group Inc.* and *NHL.com Network*

NHL All-Star Teams, 1996–2001

First Team	Second Team	First Team	Second Team
1996		**1999**	
Jim Carey, Wash, G	Chris Osgood, Det, G	Dominik Hasek, Buf, G	Bryon Dafoe, Bos, G
Chris Chelios, Chi, D	Brian Leetch, NYR, D	Al MacInnis, StL, D	Raymond Bourque, Bos, D
Raymond Bourque, Bos, D	Konstantinov, Det, D	Nicklas Lidstrom, Det, D	Eric Desjardins, Pha, D
Mario Lemieux, Pitt, C	Eric Lindros, Phil, C	Peter Forsberg, Col, C	Alexei Yashin, Ott, C
Jaromir Jagr, Pitt, RW	Alexander Mogilny, Van, RW	Jaromir Jagr, Pitt, RW	Teemu Selanne, Ana, RW
Paul Kariya, Ana, LW	John LeClair, Phil, LW	Paul Kariya, Ana, LW	John LeClair, Phil, LW
1997		**2000**	
Dominik Hasek, Buf, G	Martin Brodeur, NJ, G	Olaf Kolzig, Was, G	Roman Turek, StL, G
Sandis Ozolinsh, Col, D	Chris Chelios, Chi, D	Chris Pronger, StL, D	Rob Blake, LA, D
Brian Leetch, NYR, D	Scott Stevens, NJ, D	Nicklas Lidstrom, Det, D	Eric Desjardins, Phil, D
Mario Lemieux, Pitt, C	Wayne Gretzky, NYR, C	Steve Yzerman, Det, C	Mike Modano, Dal, C
Teemu Selanne, Ana, RW	Jaromir Jagr, Pitt, RW	Jaromir Jagr, Pitt, RW	Pavel Bure, Fla, RW
Paul Kariiya, Ana, LW	John LeClair, Phil, LW	Brendan Shanahan, Det, LW	Paul Kariya, Ana, LW
1998		**2001**	
Dominik Hasek, Buf, G	Martin Brodeur, NJ, G	Dominik Hasek, Det, G	Roman Cechmanek, Phil, G
Rob Blake, LA, D	Raymond Bourque, Bos, D	Ray Bourque, Col, D	Rob Blake, Col, D
Nicklas Lidstrom, Det, D	Chris Pronger, StL, D	Nicklas Lidstrom, Det, D	Scott Stevens, NJD, D
Peter Forsberg, Col, C	Wayne Gretzky, NYR, C	Joe Sakic, Col, C	Mario Lemieux, Pitt. C
Jaromir Jagr, Pitt, RW	Teemu Selanne, Ana, RW	Jaromir Jagr, Wash, RW	Pavel Bure, Fla, RW
John LeClair, Phi, LW	Keith Tkachuk, Pho, LW	Patrik Elias, NJD, LW	Luc Robitaille, Det, LW

Source: *National Hockey League*   As selected by members of the Professional Hockey Writers' Association.

NHL All-Star Voting Results, 2001

Name	NHL Team	Votes
Wings		
Theoren Fleury (Can)	NY Rangers	152,785
Paul Kariya (Can)	Anaheim	151,893
Brett Hull (US)	Dallas	134,241
Brendan Shanahan (Can)	Detroit*	115,208
Adam Deadmarsh (US)	Colorado	97,391
Owen Nolan (Can)	San Jose	93,133
Luc Robitaille (Can)	Los Angeles	83,312
John LeClair (US)	Philadelphia	71,269
Bill Guerin (US)	Boston	65,897
Keith Tkachuk (US)	Phoenix	62,539
Tony Amonte (US)	Chicago	58,978
Jeff Friesen (Can)	San Jose	50,663
Mark Recchi (Can)	Philadelphia	45,628
Jeff O'Neill (Can)	Carolina	37,032
Ray Whitney (Can)	Florida	22,714
Jarome Iginla (Can)	Calgary	21,096
Centres		
Joe Sakic (Can)	Colorado	126,073
Mike Modano (US)	Dallas	72,810
Steve Yzerman (Can)	Detroit	64,379
Vincent Damphousse (Can)	San Jose	43,319
Mark Messier (Can)	NY Rangers	41,091
Ron Francis (Can)	Carolina	40,588
Scott Gomez (US)	New Jersey	37,840
Jason Allison (Can)	Boston	34,082
Pierre Turgeon (Can)	St. Louis	33,558
Chris Drury (US)	Colorado	29,666
Vincent Lecavalier (Can)	Tampa Bay	28,720
Jeremy Roenick (US)	Phoenix	28,148
Doug Weight (US)	Edmonton	27,826
Joe Nieuwendyk (Can)	Dallas	19,993
Adam Oates (Can)	Washington	18,416
Keith Primeau (Can)	Philadelphia	17,789

Name	NHL Team	Votes
Defensemen		
Ray Bourque (Can)	Colorado	215,903
Chris Pronger (Can)	St. Louis	176,667
Rob Blake (Can)	Los Angeles	104,025
Adam Foote (Can)	Colorado	103,059
Scott Stevens (Can)	New Jersey	102,457
Brian Leetch (US)	NY Rangers	96,387
Al MacInnis (Can)	St. Louis	90,410
Derian Hatcher (US)	Dallas	83,385
Chris Chelios (US)	Detroit	62,804
Darryl Sydor (Can)	Dallas	58,786
Scott Niedermayer (Can)	New Jersey	55,798
Eric Desjardins (Can)	Philadelphia	40,213
Jason Woolley (Can)	Buffalo	32,766
Wade Redden (Can)	Ottawa	29,784
Kyle McLaren (Can)	Boston	18,817
Phil Housley (US)	Calgary	18,025
Goaltenders		
Patrick Roy (Can)	Colorado	174,963
Curtis Joseph (Can)	Toronto	116,319
Martin Brodeur (Can)	New Jersey	97,186
Ed Belfour (Can)	Dallas	93,942
Mike Dunham (US)	Nashville	54,163
Ron Tugnutt (Can)	Columbus	45,133
Mike Richter (US)	NY Rangers	26,097
Chris Osgood (Can)	Detroit	25,570
Brian Boucher (US)	Philadelphia	22,890
Guy Hebert (US)	Anaheim	18,051
Byron Dafoe (Can)	Boston	15,818
Jeff Hackett (Can)	Montreal	6,958

Source: *Canoe Partnership Limited*

Longest and Highest Paying Contract in NHL History

A lexie Yashin, the Ottawa Senators captain who sat out a year in a contract dispute that saw him forced to play out his original deal, signed a contract with the New York Islanders in September 2001 that will pay him US$87.5 million over ten years. NHL salaries are on an upward draft: compare that to a five-year US$50.5 million contract Joe Sakic has signed with Colorado, and a two-year US$20.7 million contract Jaromir Jagr signed with Washington. Yashin's number will be 79, since his former number (19) is being retired to honour Bryan Trottier.

NHL Individual Award Winners, 1981–2001

Hart Trophy (Most Valuable Player)[1]

1981 Wayne Gretzky, Edm	**1988** Mario Lemieux, Pitt	**1995** Eric Lindros, Phil
1982 Wayne Gretzky, Edm	**1989** Wayne Gretzky, LA	**1996** Mario Lemieux, Pitt
1983 Wayne Gretzky, Edm	**1990** Mark Messier, Edm	**1997** Dominik Hasek, Buf
1984 Wayne Gretzky, Edm	**1991** Brett Hull, StL	**1998** Dominik Hasek, Buf
1985 Wayne Gretzky, Edm	**1992** Mark Messier, NYR	**1999** Jaromir Jagr, Pitt
1986 Wayne Gretzky, Edm	**1993** Mario Lemieux, Pitt	**2000** Chris Pranger, StL
1987 Wayne Gretzky, Edm	**1994** Sergei Fedorov, Det	**2001** Joe Sakic, Col

Calder Trophy (Best Rookie)[1]

1981 Peter Stastny, Que	**1988** Joe Nieuwendyk, Cal	**1995** Peter Forsberg, Que
1982 Dale Hawerchuck, Wpg	**1989** Brian Leetch, NYR	**1996** Daniel Alfredsson, Ott
1983 Steve Larmer, Chi	**1990** Sergei Makarov, Cal	**1997** Bryan Berard, NYI
1984 Tom Barrasso, Buf	**1991** Ed Belfour, Chi	**1998** Sergei Samsonov, Bos
1985 Mario Lemieux, Pitt	**1992** Pavel Bure, Vcr	**1999** Chris Drury, Col
1986 Gary Suter, Cal	**1993** Teemu Selanne, Wpg	**2000** Scott Gomez, NJ
1987 Luc Robitaille, LA	**1994** Martin Brodeur, NJ	**2001** Evgeni Nabokov, SJ

James Norris Trophy (Best Defenceman)[1]

1981 Randy Carlyle, Pitt	**1988** Raymond Bourque, Bos	**1995** Paul Coffey, Det
1982 Doug Wilson, Chi	**1989** Chris Chelios, Mtl	**1996** Chris Chelios, Chi
1983 Rod Langway, Wash	**1990** Raymond Bourque, Bos	**1997** Brian Leetch, NYR
1984 Rod Langway, Wash	**1991** Raymond Bourque, Bos	**1998** Rob Blake, LA
1985 Paul Coffey, Edm	**1992** Brian Leetch, NYR	**1999** Al MacInnis, StL
1986 Paul Coffey, Edm	**1993** Chris Chelios, Chi	**2000** Chris Pranger, StL
1987 Raymond Bourque, Bos	**1994** Raymond Bourque, Bos	**2001** Nicklas Lindstrom, Det

Veniza Trophy (Best Goalkeeper)[2]

1981 Richard Sevigny, Mtl	**1987** Ron Hextall, Phil	**1995** Dominik Hasek, Buf
Denis Herron, Mtl	**1988** Grant Fuhr, Edm	**1996** Jim Carey, Wash
Michel Larocque, Mtl	**1989** Patrick Roy, Mtl	**1997** Dominik Hasek, Buf
1982 Bill Smith, NYI	**1990** Patrick Roy, Mtl	**1998** Dominik Hasek, Buf
1983 Pete Peeters, Bos	**1991** Ed Belfour, Chi	**1999** Dominik Hasek, Buf
1984 Tom Barrasso, Buf	**1992** Patrick Roy, Mtl	**2000** Olaf Kolzig, Wash
1985 Pelle Lindbergh, Phil	**1993** Ed Belfour, Chi	**2001** Dominik Hasek, Buf
1986 John Vanbiesbrouck, NYR	**1994** Dominik Hasek, Buf	

Lady Byng Trophy (Most Sportsmanlike)[1]

1981 Rick Kehoe, Pitt	**1988** Mats Naslund, Mtl	**1995** Ron Francis, Pitt
1982 Rick Middleton, Bos	**1989** Joe Mullen, Cal	**1996** Paul Kariya, Ana
1983 Mike Bossy, NYI	**1990** Brett Hull, StL	**1997** Paul Kariya, Ana
1984 Mike Bossy, NYI	**1991** Wayne Gretzky, LA	**1998** Ron Francis, Pitt
1985 Jari Kurri, Edm	**1992** Wayne Gretzky, LA	**1999** Wayne Gretzky, NYR
1986 Mike Bossy, NYI	**1993** Pierre Turgeon, NYI	**2000** Pavol Demitra, StL
1987 Joe Mullen, Cal	**1994** Wayne Gretzky, LA	**2001** Joe Sakic, Col

▶

(1) As selected at the end of the regular season by members of the Professional Hockey Writers' Association in the NHL cities. (2) Since the 1981–82 season, Vezina Trophy winners have been selected by general managers of the NHL clubs. In earlier seasons the trophy was awarded to the goalkeeper(s) of the team allowing the fewest goals during the regular season.

▶

Conn Smythe Trophy (Most Valuable in Playoffs)[3]

1981 Butch Goring, NYI	1988 Wayne Gretzky, Edm	1995 Claude Lemieux, NJ
1982 Mike Bossy, NYI	1989 Al MacInnis, Cal	1996 Joe Sakic, Col
1983 Bill Smith, NYI	1990 Bill Ranford, Edm	1997 Mike Vernon, Det
1984 Mark Messier, Edm	1991 Mario Lemieux, Pitt	1998 Steve Yzerman, Det
1985 Wayne Gretzky, Edm	1992 Mario Lemieux, Pitt	1999 Joe Nieuwendyk, Dal
1986 Patrick Roy, Mtl	1993 Patrick Roy, Mtl	2000 Scott Stevens, NJ
1987 Ron Hextall, Phil	1994 Brian Leetch, NYR	2001 Patrick Roy, Col

Frank J. Selke Trophy (Best Defensive Forward)[1]

1981 Bob Gainey, Mtl	1988 Guy Carbonneau, Mtl	1995 Ron Francis, Det
1982 Steve Kasper, Bos	1989 Guy Carbonneau, Mtl	1996 Sergei Fedorov, Det
1983 Bobby Clarke, Phil	1990 Rick Meagher, StL	1997 Mike Peca, Buf
1984 Doug Jarvis, Wash	1991 Dirk Graham, Chi	1998 Jere Lehtinen, Dal
1985 Craig Ramsay, Buf	1992 Guy Carbonneau, Mtl	1999 Jere Lehtinen, Dal
1986 Troy Murray, Chi	1993 Doug Gilmour, Tor	2000 Steve Yzerman, Det
1987 Dave Poulin, Phil	1994 Sergei Fedorov, Det	2001 John Madden, NJ

Jack Adams Trophy (Coach of the Year)

1981 Red Berenson, StL	1988 Jacques Demers, Det	1995 Marc Crawford, Que
1982 Tom Watt, Wpg	1989 Pat Burns, Det	1996 Scotty Bowman, Det
1983 Orval Tessier, Chi	1990 Bob Murdoch, Wpg	1997 Ted Nolan, Buf
1984 Bryan Murray, Wash	1991 Brian Sutter, StL	1998 Pat Burns, Bos
1985 Mike Keenan, Phil	1992 Pat Quinn, Van	1999 Jacques Martin, Ott
1986 Glen Sather, Edm	1993 Pat Burns, Tor	2000 Joel Quenneville, StL
1987 Jacques Demers, Det	1994 Jacques Lemaire, NJ	2001 Bill Barber, Phil

Source: *HickokSports.com*

(3) As selected by members of the Professional Hockey Writers' Association at the end of the last game of the Stanley Cup finals.

Top NHL Draft Picks Since 1980

Player, Team Selected by, Position, Junior Team	Player, Team Selected by, Position, Junior Team
1980 Doug Wickenheiser, Montreal, C, Regina (WHL)	1992 Roman Hamrlik, Tampa Bay, D, ZPS Zlin (Czech)
1981 Dale Hawerchuk, Winnipeg, C, Cornwall (QMJHL)	1993 Alexandre Daigle, Ottawa, C, Victoriaville (QMJHL)
1982 Gord Kluzak, Boston, D, Billings (WHL)	1994 Ed Jovanovski, Florida, D, Windsor (OHL)
1983 Brian Lawton, Minnesota, C, Mount St. Charles HS	1995 Bryan Berard, Ottawa, D, Detroit (OHL)
1984 Mario Lemieux, Pittsburgh, C, Laval (QMJHL)	1996 Chris Phillips, Ottawa, D, Prince Albert (WHL)
1985 Wendel Clark, Toronto, LW-D, Saskatoon (WHL)	1997 Joe Thornton, Boston, C, Sault Ste. Marie (OHL)
1986 Joe Murphy, Detroit, C, Michigan State	1998 Vincent Lecavalier, Tampa Bay, C, Rimouski (QMJHL)
1987 Pierre Turgeon, Buffalo, C, Granby (QMJHL)	
1988 Mike Modano, Minnesota, C, Prince Albert (WHL)	
1989 Mats Sundin, Quebec, RW, Nacka (Sweden)	1999 Patrik Stefan, Atlanta, C, Long Beach (IHL)
1990 Owen Nolan, Quebec, RW, Cornwall (OHL)	2000 Rick DiPietro, N.Y. Islanders, G, Boston University
1991 Eric Lindros, Quebec, C, Oshawa (OHL)	2001 Ilya Kovalchuk, Atlanta, C, Spartak (Russia, Div. 1)

Source: *The Sports Network Inc.*

Men's World Hockey Championships, 2001

(Hanover and Cologne, Germany, April 28–May 15, 2001)

STANDINGS

(Top four in each group advance to quarter-finals)

Group E Team	W	L	T	GF	GA	PTS	Group F Team	W	L	T	GF	GA	PTS
Czech Republic	4	0	1	24	8	9	Finland	4	1	0	23	12	8
Canada	3	1	1	19	11	7	Sweden	3	1	1	25	8	7
Russia	3	2	0	16	11	6	USA	3	1	1	15	10	7
Germany	1	2	2	10	12	4	Slovakia	2	3	0	12	12	4
Switzerland	1	4	0	13	15	2	Ukraine	1	4	0	7	21	2
Italy	1	4	0	5	30	2	Austria	1	4	0	4	23	2

Semifinals	Czech Republic 3, Sweden 2 (SO)
	Finland 3, USA 1
Third Place	Sweden 3, USA 2
Championship	Czech Republic 3, Finland 2 (OT)

Source: *International Ice Hockey Federation*

IIHF Women's World Hockey Championship, 2001

(Minnesota, USA, April 2–8, 2001)

STANDINGS

Pool A	GP	W	L	T	GF	GA	PTS	Pool B	GP	W	L	T	GF	GA	PTS
Canada	3	3	0	0	29	1	6	USA	3	3	0	0	35	0	6
Russia	3	2	1	0	12	7	4	Finland	3	2	1	0	12	17	4
Sweden	3	1	2	0	3	17	2	China	3	0	2	1	6	20	1
Kazakstan	3	0	3	0	3	22	0	Germany	3	0	2	1	2	18	1

5th/6th place – Germany 1, China 0
7th/8th place – Sweden 3, Kazakstan 1
Semifinals – Canada 8, Finland 0
USA 6, Russia 1
Bronze Medal – Russia 2, Finland 1
Gold Medal – Canada 3, U.S. 2

Source: *International Ice Hockey Federation*

2001 World Junior Hockey Championship

(Czech Republic, December 25, 2000 to January 4, 2001)

Final Round Robin Standings

Group A	GP	W	L	T	GF	GA	PTS	Group B	GP	W	L	T	GF	GA	PTS
Czech Republic	4	4	0	0	20	4	8	Finland	4	3	0	1	13	5	7
United States	4	3	1	0	21	8	6	Russia	4	2	1	1	19	8	5
Sweden	4	2	2	0	13	8	4	Canada	4	2	1	1	20	9	5
Slovakia	4	1	3	0	10	15	2	Switzerland	4	1	2	1	12	15	3
Kazakhstan	4	0	4	0	4	33	0	Belarus	4	0	4	0	2	29	0

7th place Russia 4 – Slovakia 3
5th place USA 4 – Switzerland 0
Bronze **Canada 2** – Sweden 1 (OT)
Gold Czech Rep 2 – Finland 1

Source: *The Sports Network Inc.*

World Hockey Championships, 1981–2001
Team Canada's Leading Scorers

		GP	G	A	PTS			GP	G	A	PTS
1981	Dennis Maruk	8	5	3	8	1992	Steve Thomas	6	2	2	4
1982	Wayne Gretzky	10	6	8	14	1993	Eric Lindros	8	11	6	17
1983	Michel Goulet	10	1	8	9	1994	Paul Kariya	8	5	7	12
1984	Marcel Dionne	10	6	3	9	1995	Andrew McKim	8	6	7	13
1985	Mario Lemieux	9	4	6	10	1996	Yanic Perrault	8	6	3	9
1986	Brent Sutter	8	4	7	11	1997	Travis Green	11	3	5	8
1987	Tony Tanti	10	6	2	8	1998	Ray Whitney	6	4	2	6
1989[1]	Brian Bellows	10	8	7	15	1999	Corey Stillman	10	4	4	8
1990	Steve Yzerman	10	9	10	19	2000	Todd Bertuzzi	9	5	4	9
1991	Joe Sakic	10	6	5	11	2001	Brad Richards	7	3	3	6

Source: *International Ice Hockey Federation*   (1) No championship held in 1988.

World Hockey Championships
First All-Star Teams since 1991

(forwards, defence, goalie)

1991 Valeri Kamensky (Urs), Thomas Rundquist (Swe), Jari Kurri (Fin), Alexei Kasatonov (Urs), Sean Burke (Cda), Viacheslav Fetisov (Urs)

1992 Mats Sundin (Swe), Petr Hrbek (Tch), Jarkko Varvio (Fin), Frantisek Musil (Tch), Markus Ketterer (Fin); Timo Jutila (Fin)

1993 Ulf Dahlen (Swe), Eric Lindros (Cda), Mikael Renberg (Swe), Ilya Byakin (Rus), Petr Briza (Cze), Dave Manson (Cda)

1994 Paul Kariya (Cda), Saku Koivu (Fin), Jari Kurri (Fin), Magnus Svensson (Swe), Timo Jutila (Fin), Bill Ranford (Cda)

1995 Ville Peltonen (Fin), Saku Koivu (Fin), Jere Lehtinen (Fin), Tommy Sjodin (Swe), Timo Jutila (Fin), Roman Turek (Cze)

1996 Robert Reichel (Cze), Otakar Vejvoda (Cze), Paul Kariya (Cda), Michal Sykora (Cze), Alexei Zhitnik (Rus), Roman Turek (Cze)

1997 Vladimir Vujtek (Cze), Michael Nylander (Swe), Martin Prochazka (Cze), Rob Blake (Cda), Teppo Numminen (Fin), Tommy Salo (Swe)

1998 Peter Forsberg (Swe), Mats Sundin (Swe), Ville Peltonen (Fin), Frantisek Kucera (Cze), Jere Karalahti (Fin), Tommmy Salo (Swe)

1999 Martin Rucinsky, (Cze), Saku Koivu (Fin), Teemu Selanne (Fin), Jere Karalahti (Fin), Pavel Kubina (Cze), Tommy Salo (Swe)

2000 Jiri Dopita (Cze), Miroslav Satan (Slv), Tomas Vlasak (Cze), Michal Sykora (Cze), Petteri Nummelin (Fin), Roman Cechmanek (Cze).

2001 Radek Dvorak (Cze), Robert Reichel (Cze), Martin Rucinsky (Cze), Pavel Kubina (Cze), Jaroslav Spacek (Cze), Milan Hnilicka (Cze).

Source: *International Ice Hockey Federation*

World Junior Hockey Medal Winners, 1981–2001

1981	Sweden, Finland, Soviet Union
1982	**Canada**, Czechoslovakia, Finland
1983	Soviet Union, Czechoslovakia, **Canada**
1984	Soviet Union, Finland, Czechoslovakia
1985	**Canada**, Czechoslovakia, Soviet Union
1986	Soviet Union, **Canada**, United States
1987	Finland, Czechoslovakia, Sweden
1988	**Canada**, Soviet Union, Finland
1989	Soviet Union, Sweden, Czechoslovakia
1990	**Canada**, Soviet Union, Czechoslovakia
1991	**Canada**, Soviet Union, Czechoslovakia
1992	C.I.S., Sweden, United States
1993	**Canada**, Sweden, Czech-Slovak
1994	**Canada**, Sweden, Russia
1995	**Canada**, Russia, Sweden
1996	**Canada**, Sweden, Russia
1997	**Canada**, United States, Russia
1998	Finland, Russia, Switzerland
1999	Russia, **Canada**, Slovakia
2000	Czech Republic, Russia, **Canada**
2001	Czech Republic, Finland, **Canada**

Source: *The Sports Network Inc.*

Memorial Cup Winners, 1961–2001

(Canadian Junior Hockey Champions)

1961	St. Michael's Majors	1983	Portland Winter Hawks
1962	Hamilton Red Wings	1984	Ottawa 67's
1963	Edmonton Oil Kings	1985	Prince Albert Raiders
1964	Toronto Marlboros	1986	Guelph Platers
1965	Niagara Falls Flyers	1987	Medicine Hat Tigers
1966	Edmonton Oil Kings	1988	Medicine Hat Tigers
1967	Toronto Marlboros	1989	Swift Current Broncos
1968	Niagara Falls Flyers	1990	Oshawa Generals
1969	Montreal Jr. Canadiens	1991	Spokane Chiefs
1970	Montreal Jr. Canadiens	1992	Kamloops Blazers
1971	Quebec Ramparts	1993	Sault Ste. Marie Greyhounds
1972	Cornwall Royals	1994	Kamloops Blazers
1973	Toronto Marlboros	1995	Kamloops Blazers
1974	Regina Pats	1996	Granby Predateurs
1975	Toronto Marlboros	1997	Hull Olympiques
1976	Hamilton Fincups	1998	Portland Winterhawks
1977	New Westminster Bruins	1999	Ottawa 67s
1978	New Westminster Bruins	2000	Rimouski Oceanic
1979	Peterborough Petes	2001	Red Deer Rebels
1980	Cornwall Royals		
1981	Cornwall Royals		
1982	Kitchener Rangers		

Source: *Canoe Limited Partnership*

2001 Memorial Cup

Team Standings

Team	W	L	T	GF	GA	PTS
Val d'Or Foreurs	3	2	0	25	18	6
Red Deer Rebels	3	1	0	17	16	6
Regina Pats	2	3	0	17	17	4
Ottawa 67s	1	3	0	8	16	2

Semi-Final, May 26:
    Val d'Or Foreurs 5, Regina Pats 4 (OT)
Final, May 27:
    Red Deer Rebels 6, Val d'Or Foreurs 5 (OT)

Source: *Canoe Limited Partnership*

MasterCard Memorial Cup Awards

HAP EMMS MEMORIAL TROPHY
Outstanding Goaltender

1991	Felix Potvin, Chicoutimi
1992	Corey Hirsch, Kamloops
1993	Kevin Hodson, Sault Ste. Marie
1994	Eric Fichaud, Chicoutimi
1995	Jason Saal, Detroit
1996	Frederic Deschenes, Granby
1997	Christian Bronsard, Hull
1998	Chris Madden, Guelph
1999	Cory Campbell, Belleville
2000	Sebastien Caron, Rimouski
2001	Maxime Daigneault, Val d'Or

STAFFORD SMYTHE MEMORIAL TROPHY
Memorial Cup MVP

1991	Pat Falloon, Spokane
1992	Scott Niedermayer, Kamloops
1993	Ralph Intranuovo, S.S. Marie
1994	Darcy Tucker, Kamloops
1995	Shane Doan, Kamloops
1996	Cameron Mann, Peterborough
1997	Christian Dube, Hull
1998	Chris Madden, Guelph
1999	Nick Boynton, Ottawa
2000	Brad Richards, Rimouski
2001	Kyle Wanvig, Red Deer

ED CHYNOWETH TROPHY
Memorial Cup Top Scorer

1996	Philippe Audet, Granby
1997	Christian Dube, Hull
1998	Andrej Podkonicky, Portland
1999	Justin Davis, Ottawa
2000	Ramzi Abid, Halifax
2001	Simon Gamache, Val d'Or

GEORGE PARSONS TROPHY
Sportsmanship

1996	Mike Williams, Peterborough
1997	Radsoslav Suchy, Chicoutimi
1998	Manny Malhotra, Guelph
1999	Brian Campbell, Ottawa
2000	Brandon Reid, Halifax
2001	Brandon Reid, Val d'Or

Source: *Canoe Limited Partnership*

Memorial Cup All-Stars, 1991–2001

1991 *Goal:* Félix Potvin, Chicoutimi. *Defence:* Patrice Brisebois, Drummondville; Brad Tiley, Sault Ste. Marie. *Forwards:* Pat Falloon, Spokane; Ray Whitney, Spokane; Brent Thurston, Spokane.

1992 *Goal:* Corey Hirsch, Kamloops. *Defence:* Scott Niedermayer, Kamloops; Drew Bannister, S.S. Marie. *Forwards:* Colin Miller, Sault Ste. Marie; Mike Mathers, Kamloops; Turner Stevenson, Seattle.

1993 *Goal:* Kevin Hodson, Sault Ste. Marie. *Defence:* Michael Gaul, Laval; Drew Bannister, S.S. Marie. *Forwards:* Ralph Intranuovo, S.S. Marie; Chad Penney, Sault Ste. Marie; Martin Lapointe, Laval.

1994 *Goal:* Eric Fichaud, Chicoutimi. *Defence:* Aaron Keller, Kamloops; Nolan Baumgartner, Kamloops. *Forwards:* Darcy Tucker, Kamloops; Alain Côté, Laval; Rod Stevens, Kamloops.

1995 *Goal:* Jason Saal, Detroit. *Defence:* Nolan Baumgartner, Kamloops; Bryan McCabe, Brandon. *Forwards:* Darcy Tucker, Kamloops; Sean Haggerty, Detroit; Shane Doan, Kamloops.

1996 *Goal:* Frédéric Deschenes, Granby. *Defence:* Wade Redden, Brandon; Jason Doig, Granby. *Forwards:* Xavier Delisle, Granby; Philippe Audet, Granby; Cameron Mann, Peterborough.

1997 *Goal:* Christian Bronsard, Hull. *Defence:* Chris Phillips, Lethbridge; Jan Snopek, Oshawa. *Forwards:* Christian Dube, Hull; Byron Ritchie, Lethbridge; Martin Menard, Hull.

1998 *Goal:* Chris Madden, Guelph. *Defence:* Brad Ference, Spokane; Francis Lessard, Val d'Or. *Forwards:* Andrej Podkonicky, Portland; Manny Malhotra, Guelph; Marian Hossa, Portland.

1999 *Goal:* Cory Campbell, Belleville. *Defence:* Matt Kinch, Calgary; Nick Boynton, Ottawa. *Forwards:* Pavel Brendl, Calgary; Glenn Crawford, Belleville; Joe Talbot, Ottawa.

2000 *Goal:* Sebastien Caron, Rimouski. *Defence:* Eric Reitz, Barrie; Michel Periard, Rimouski. *Forwards:* Brad Richards, Rimouski; Juraj Kolnik, Rimouski; Sheldon Keefe, Barrie.

2001 *Goal:* Maxime Daigneault, Val d'Or. *Defence:* Paul Elliott, Regina; Chris Lyness, Val d'Or (tie); Ross Lupaschuk, Red Deer (tie). *Forwards:* Brett Lysak, Regina; Simon Gamache, Val d'Or; Kyle Wanvig, Red Deer.

Source: *Canoe Limited Partnership*

OLYMPICS

Summer Olympics

Location	Date of Competition	Competitors		Nations Repre- sented	Unofficial Winners
		Men	Women		
1896 Athens, Greece	Apr. 6–15	311	0	13	United States
1900 Paris, France	May 20–Oct. 28	1 319	11	22	United States
1904 St. Louis, United States	July 1–Nov. 23	681	6	12	United States
1906[1] Athens, Greece	Apr. 22–May 2	877	7	20	United States
1908 London, England	Apr. 27–Oct. 31	1 999	36	23	United States
1912 Stockholm, Sweden	May 5–July 22	2 490	57	28	United States
1916 Cancelled because of World War I					
1920 Antwerp, Belgium	Apr. 20–Sept. 12	2 543	64	29	United States
1924 Paris, France	May 4–July 27	2 956	136	44	United States
1928 Amsterdam, Netherlands	May 17–Aug. 12	2 724	290	46	United States
1932 Los Angeles, United States	July 30–Aug. 14	1 281	127	37	United States
1936 Berlin, Germany	Aug. 1–16	3 738	328	49	Germany
1940 Cancelled because of World War II					
1944 Cancelled because of World War II					
1948 London, England	July 29–Aug. 14	3 714	385	59	United States
1952 Helsinki, Finland	July 19–Aug.3	4 407	518	69	United States
1956 Melbourne, Australia[2]	Nov. 22–Dec. 8	2 958	384	67	USSR
1960 Rome, Italy	Aug. 25–Sept. 11	4 738	610	83	USSR
1964 Tokyo, Japan	Oct. 10–24	4 457	683	93	United States
1968 Mexico City, Mexico	Oct. 12–27	4 750	781	112	United States
1972 Munich, West Germany	Aug. 26–Sept. 10	5 848	1 299	122	USSR
1976 Montreal, Canada	July 17–Aug. 1	4 834	1 251	92[3]	USSR
1980 Moscow, USSR	July 19–Aug. 3	4 265	1 088	81	USSR
1984 Los Angeles, United States	July 28–Aug. 12	5 458	1 620	141	United States
1988 Seoul, South Korea	Sept. 17–Oct. 2	7 105	2 476	160	USSR
1992 Barcelona, Spain	July 25–Aug. 9	7 555	3 008	172	Unified Team
1996 Atlanta, United States	July 19–Aug. 4	7 000	3 800	197	United States
2000 Sydney, Australia	Sept. 16–Oct. 1	6 582	4 069	199	United States
2004 Athens, Greece	Aug. 13–29				
2008 Beijing, China					

Source: *Canadian Olympic Association, International Olympic Committee*

(n.a.) not available.
(1) 1906 Games were not recognized by the International Olympic Committee.
(2) The equestrian events were held in Stockholm, Sweden, June 10–17, 1956.
(3) Most sources list this figure as 88. Cameroon, Egypt, Morocco and Tunisia all boycotted the 1976 Olympics; however, their athletes had already competed before the boycott was officially announced.

Canada's Olympic Gold Medalists, 1920–2000

■ Winter Olympic Games

1920 Winnipeg Falcons, Ice Hockey (Although the Olympic Winter Games did not begin until 1924, ice hockey was an official event at the 1920 Olympic Games.)

1924 Toronto Granites, Ice Hockey

1928 University of Toronto Graduates, Ice Hockey

1932 Winnipeg Hockey Team, Ice Hockey

1948 Barbara Ann **Scott,** Women's Figure Skating; **RCAF Flyers,** Ice Hockey

1952 Edmonton Mercurys, Ice Hockey

1960 Anne **Heggtveit,** Alpine Skiing, Women's Slalom; Barbara **Wagner** & Robert **Paul,** Pairs Figure Skating

1964 Vic **Emery,** John **Emery,** Douglas **Anakin** & Peter **Kirby,** Four-Man Bobsled

1968 Nancy **Greene,** Alpine Skiing, Women's Giant Slalom

1976 Kathy **Kreiner,** Alpine Skiing, Women's Giant Slalom

1984 Gaetan **Boucher,** Speed Skating, Men's 1 000 m; Gaetan **Boucher,** Speed Skating, Men's 1 500 m

1992 Kerrin **Lee-Gartner,** Alpine Skiing, Women's Downhill; Sylvie **Daigle,** Nathalie **Lambert,** Annie **Perreault,** Angela **Cutrone,** Speed Skating, Women's Short Track Relay; Philippe **Laroche,** Freestyle Skiing, Men's Aerials (demonstration)

1994 Jean-Luc **Brassard,** Freestyle Skiing, Men's Alpine; Myriam **Bedard,** Biathlon, Women's 7.5 km Sprint; Myriam **Bedard,** Biathlon, Women's 15 km

1998 Pierre **Lueders** and Dave **MacEachern,** Bobsled (Two-man); Sandra **Schmirler,** Jan **Betker,** Joan **McCusker,** Marcia **Gudereit** and Atina **Ford,** Curling (Women); Ross **Rebagliati,** Snowboarding (Giant Slalom); Catriona **Le May Doan,** Speed Skating, Long Track (500 metres); Annie **Perreault,** Speed Skating, Short Track (500 metres); Eric **Bedard,** Derrick **Campbell,** Francois **Drolet,** and Marc **Gagnon,** Speed Skating, Short Track (5,000-metre relay).

■ Summer Olympic Games

1900 George **Orton,** 2 500 Steeplechase (Although a Canadian citizen, he represented the University of Pennsylvania; Canada did not officially appear at the Olympics until 1904.)

1904 Étienne **Desmarteau,** 56-pound Weight Throw; George **Lyon,** Golf; **The Galt Association Football Club,** Football (Soccer); **The Winnipeg Shamrocks Lacrosse Club,** Lacrosse 190; William **Sherring,** Marathon (The 1906 Games are not officially recognized by the I.O.C.)

1908 Walter **Ewing,** Trapshooting; Robert **Kerr,** Men's 200 m Run; **The All Canadas,** Lacrosse

1912 George **Goulding,** 10 000 m Walk; George **Hodgson,** Swimming, Men's 400 m Freestyle; George **Hodgson,** Swimming, Men's 1 500 m Freestyle

1920 Albert **Schneider,** Boxing, Welterweight; Earl **Thomson,** Men's 110 m Hurdles

1928 Ethel **Catherwood,** Women's High Jump; Percy **Williams,** Men's 100 m Run; Percy **Williams,** Men's 200 m Run; Women's Relay Team (Fanny **Rosenfeld,** Ethel **Smith,** Florence **Bell** & Myrtle **Cook),** Women's 4 x 100 m Relay

1932 Horace **Gwynne,** Boxing, Bantamweight; Duncan ▶

▶ **McNaughton,** Men's High Jump

1936 Francis **Amyot,** Canoeing, Canadian Singles 1 000 m

1952 George **Genereux,** Trapshooting

1956 Gerald **Ouellette,** Small-Bore Rifle (Prone); University of British Columbia Team (Archibald **McKinnon,** Lorne **Loomer,** Walter **D'Hondt** & Donald **Arnold,** Rowing, Four-Oared Shell without Coxswain

1964 George **Hungerford** & Roger **Jackson,** Rowing, Pair-Oared Shell without Coxswain

1968 Equestrian Team (James **Elder,** James **Day** & Thomas **Gayford**), Grand Prix (Jumping)

1984 Alex **Baumann,** Swimming, Men's 200 m Individual Medley; Alex **Baumann,** Swimming, Men's 400 m Individual Medley; Sylvie **Bernier,** Women's Spring-board Diving; Larry **Cain,** Canoeing, Canadian Singles 500 m; Victor **Davis,** Swimming, 200 m Breaststroke; Hugh **Fisher** & Alwyn **Morris,** Canoeing, Kayak Pairs 1 000 m; Lori **Fung,** Rhythmic Gymnastics, All-Around; Anne **Otten-brite,** Swimming, Women's 200 m Breast-stroke; Linda **Thom,** Women's Sport Pistol; National Team (Patrick **Turner,** Kevin **Neufeld,** Mark **Evans,** Grant **Main,** Paul **Steele,** J. Michael **Evans,** Dean **Crawford,** Blair **Horn** & Brian **McMahon**), Eight-Oared Shell with Coxswain

1988 Lennox **Lewis,** Boxing, Super heavyweight; Carolyn **Waldo,** Synchronized Swimming, Solo; Carolyn **Waldo** & Michelle **Cameron,** Synchronized Swimming, Duet

1992 Marnie **McBean** and Kathleen **Heddle,** Rowing, Women's Pairs; Mark **McKoy,** Track, Men's 110 m Hurdles; Mark **Tewksbury,** Swimming, Men's 100 m Backstroke; Women's Fours, Rowing (Kirsten **Barnes,** Brenda **Taylor,** Jessica **Monroe,** Kay **Worthington**); Men's Eights,

Rowing (John **Wallace,** Bruce **Robertson,** Michael **Forgeron,** Darren **Barber,** Robert **Marland,** Michael **Rascher,** Andy **Crosby,** Derek **Porter,** Terry **Paul**); Women's Eights, Rowing (Kirsten **Barnes,** Brenda **Taylor,** Megan **Delehanty,** Shannon **Crawford,** Marnie **McBean,** Kay **Worthington,** Jessica **Monroe,** Kathleen **Heddle,** Lesley **Thompson**); Sylvie **Frechette,** synchronized swimming

1996 Donovan **Bailey,** Track, Men's 100m; Donovan **Bailey,** Bruny Surin, Glenroy **Gilbert,** Robert **Esmie,** Carlton **Chambers,** Men's 4x100 Relay; Marnie **McBean** and Kathleen **Heddle,** Rowing, Women's Double Sculls.

2000 GOLD: Daniel **Igali,** Freestyle Wrestling, 69-kg; Sebastien **Lareau** and Daniel **Nestor,** Tennis, Men's Doubles; Simon **Whitfield,** Men's Triathlon.

SILVER: Caroline **Brunet,** Kayak, Singles 500m; Nicolas **Gill,** Judo, 100-kg; Emilie **Heymans** and Anne **Montminy,** Diving, 10m Synchronized Platform.

BRONZE: Dominique **Bosshart,** Taekwondo, +67-kg; Karen **Cockburn,** Trampoline, Women's; Steve **Giles,** Canoeing, Singles 1 000 m; Anne **Montminy,** Diving, 10 m Platform; Rowing, Women's Eight (Buffy **Alexander,** Laryssa **Biesenthal,** Heather **Davis,** Alison **Korn,** Theresa **Luke,** Heather **McDermid,** Emma **Robinson,** Lesley **Thompson,** Dorota **Urbaniak**); Synchronized Swimming, Women's Team (Lyne **Beaumont,** Claire **Carver-Dias,** Erin **Chan,** Jessica **Chase,** Catherine **Garceau,** Fanny **Letourneau,** Kirstin **Normand,** Jacinthe **Taillon,** Reidun **Tatham**); Curtis **Myden,** Swimming, Men's 400m Individual Medley; Mathieu **Turgeon,** Trampoline, Men's.

Source: *Canadian Press*

Winter Olympics

Year	Location	Date of Competition	Competitors Men	Competitors Women	Nations Represented	Unofficial Winners
1924	Chamonix, France	Jan. 25–Feb. 4	281	13	16	Norway
1928	St. Moritz, Switzerland	Feb. 11–19	468	27	25	Norway
1932	Lake Placid, United States	Feb. 4–15	274	32	17	United States
1936	Garmisch-Partenkirchen, Germany	Feb. 6–16	675	80	28	Norway
1940	Cancelled because of World War II					
1944	Cancelled because of World War II					
1948	St. Moritz, Switzerland	Jan. 30–Feb. 8	636	77	28	Sweden
1952	Oslo, Norway	Feb. 14–25	623	109	30	Norway
1956	Cortina d'Ampezzo, Italy	Jan. 26–Feb. 5	686	132	32	U.S.S.R.
1960	Squaw Valley, United States	Feb. 18–28	521	144	30	U.S.S.R.
1964	Innsbruck, Austria	Jan. 29–Feb. 9	986	200	36	U.S.S.R.
1968	Grenoble, France	Feb. 6–18	1 081	212	37	Norway
1972	Sapporo, Japan	Feb. 3–13	1 015	217	35	U.S.S.R.
1976	Innsbruck, Austria	Feb. 4–15	900	228	37	U.S.S.R.
1980	Lake Placid, United States	Feb. 14–23	833	234	37	East Germany
1984	Sarajevo, Yugoslavia	Feb. 7–19	1 180	409	49	U.S.S.R.
1988	Calgary, Canada	Feb. 13–28	1 128	317	57	U.S.S.R.
1992	Albertville, France	Feb. 8–23	1 545	602	64	Germany
1994	Lillehammer, Norway	Feb. 12–27	1 216	521	67	Norway
1998	Nagano, Japan	Feb. 7–22	1 488	814	72	Germany
2002	Salt Lake City	Feb. 8–24				
2006	Torino, Italy	Feb. 11–26				

Source: *International Olympic Committee, Canadian Olympic Association*

1998 Winter Olympics Medal Standings by Country

Country	Gold	Silver	Bronze	Total
Germany	12	9	8	29
Norway	10	10	5	25
Russia	9	6	3	18
Austria	3	5	9	17
Canada	6	5	4	15
United States	6	3	4	13
Finland	2	4	6	12
Netherlands	5	4	2	11
Japan	5	1	4	10
Italy	2	6	2	10
France	2	1	5	8
China	0	6	2	8

Country	Gold	Silver	Bronze	Total
Switzerland	2	2	3	7
Korea	3	1	2	6
Czech Republic	1	1	1	3
Sweden	0	2	1	3
Belarus	0	0	2	2
Kazakhstan	0	0	2	2
Bulgaria	1	0	0	1
Denmark	0	1	0	1
Ukraine	0	1	0	1
Britain	0	0	1	1
Australia	0	0	1	1
Belgium	0	0	1	1

Source: *(CP)*

Medal Winners, 1998 Winter Olympics

(Nagano, Japan)

■ Alpine Skiing

Men's Downhill

Gold	Jean-Luc Cretier	France
Silver	Lasse Kjus	Norway
Bronze	Hannes Trinkl	Austria

Men's Slalom

Gold	Hans-Petter Buraas	Norway
Silver	Ole Christian Furuseth	Norway
Bronze	Thomas Sykora	Austria

Men's Giant Slalom

Gold	Hermann Maier	Austria
Silver	Stefan Eberharter	Austria
Bronze	Michael von Gruenigen	Switzerland

Men's Super Giant Slalom

Gold	Hermann Maier	Austria
Silver	Didier Cuche	Swtizerland
Silver	Hans Knauss	Austria

Men's Combined

Gold	Mario Reiter	Austria
Silver	Lasse Kjus	Norway
Bronze	Christian Mayer	Austria

Women's Downhill

Gold	Katja Seizinger	Germany
Silver	Pernilla Wiberg	Sweden
Bronze	Florence Masnada	France

Women's Slalom

Gold	Hilde Gerg	Germany
Silver	Deborah Compagnoni	Italy
Bronze	Zali Steggall	Australia

Women's Giant Slalom

Gold	Deborah Compagnoni	Italy
Silver	Alexandra Meissnitzer	Austria
Bronze	Katja Seizinger	Germany

Women's Super Giant Slalom

Gold	Picabo Street	U.S.
Silver	Mechaela Dorfmeister	Austria
Bronze	Alexandra Meissnitzer	Austria

Women's Combined

Gold	Katja Seizinger	Germany
Silver	Martina Ertl	Germany
Bronze	Hilde Gerg	Germany

■ Biathlon

Men's 10 K

Gold	Ole Einar Bjoerndalen	Norway
Silver	Frode Andresen	Norway
Bronze	Ville Raikkonen	Finland

Men's 20 K

Gold	Halvard Hanevold	Norway
Silver	Pier Alberto Carrara	Italy
Bronze	Aleksei Aidarov	Belarus

Men's 4x7.5 K Relay

Gold	Germany
Silver	Norway
Bronze	Russia

Women's 7.5 k

Gold	Galina Koukleva	Russia
Silver	Ursula Disl	Germany
Bronze	Katrin Apel	Germany

Women's 15 k

Gold	Yekaterina Dafovska	Bulgaria
Silver	Yelena Petrova	Ukraine
Bronze	Ursula Disl	Germany

Women's 4x7.5 K Relay

Gold	Germany
Silver	Russia
Bronze	Norway

■ Bobsled

Two-man

Gold	**Lueders-MacEachern**	**Canada**
Gold	Huber-Tartaglia	Italy
Bronze	Langen-Zimmermann	Germany
	Bronze	

Four-man

Gold	Germany
Silver	Switzerland
Bronze	France
	Britain

■ Cross-Country Skiing

Men's 10 K

Gold	Bjoern Daehlie	Norway
Silver	Markus Gandler	Austria
Bronze	Mika Myllylae	Finland

Women's 5 K

Gold	Larissa Lazutina	Russia
Silver	Katerina Neumannova	Czech Rep.
Bronze	Bente Martinsen	Norway

Men 15 K

Gold	Thomas Alsgaard	Norway
Silver	Bjoern Daehlie	Norway
Bronze	Vladimir Smirnov	Kazakhstan

Men's 30 K

Gold	Mika Myllylae	Finland
Silver	Erling Jevne	Norway
Bronze	Silvio Fauner	Italy

50 K freestyle

Gold	Bjorn Daehlie	Norway
Silver	Niklas Jonsson	Sweden
Bronze	Christian Hoffmann	Austria

Men's 4x10 K Relay

Gold	Norway
Silver	Italy
Bronze	Finland

Women's 10 K

Gold	Larissa Lazutina	Russia
Silver	Olga Danilova	Russia
Bronze	Katerina Neumanova	Czech Rep.

Women's 15 K

Gold	Olga Danilova	Russia
Silver	Larissa Lazutina	Russia
Bronze	Anita Moen-Guidon	Norway

Women's 30 K

Gold	Julija Tchepalova	Russia
Silver	Stefania Belmondo	Italy
Bronze	Larissa Lazutina	Russia

Women's 4x5 K Relay

Gold	Russia
Silver	Norway
Bronze	Italy

■ Curling

Men		**Women**	
Gold	Switzerland	**Gold**	**Canada**
Silver	**Canada**	Silver	Denmark
Bronze	Norway	Bronze	Sweden

■ Figure Skating

Pairs

Gold	Kazakova-Dmitriev	Russia
Silver	Berezhnaya-Sikharulidze	Russia
Bronze	Wotzel-Steuer	Germany

Men's Singles

Gold	Ilia Kulik	Russia
Silver	**Elvis Stojko**	**Canada**
Bronze	Philippe Candeloro	France

Dance

Gold	Grishuk-Platov	Russia
Silver	Krylova-Ovsyannikov	Russia
Bronze	Anissina-Peizerat	France

Women's Singles

Gold	Tara Lipinski	U.S.
Silver	Michelle Kwan	U.S.
Bronze	Lu Chen	China

■ Freestyle Skiing

Men's Aerials

Gold	Eric Bergoust	U.S.
Silver	Sebastien Foucras	France
Bronze	Dmitri Dashchinsky	Belarus

Men's Moguls

Gold	Jonny Moseley	U.S.
Silver	Janne Lahtela	Finland
Bronze	Sami Mustonen	Finland

Women's Aerials

Gold	Nikki Stone	U.S.
Silver	Nannan Xu	China
Bronze	Colette Brand	Swtzerland

Women's Moguls

Gold	Tae Satoya	Japan
Silver	Tatjana Mittermayer	Germany
Bronze	Kari Traa	Norway

■ Hockey

Men		**Women**	
Gold	Czech Republic	Gold	U.S.
Silver	Russia	**Silver**	**Canada**
Bronze	Finland	Bronze	Finland

■ Luge

Men's Doubles

Gold	Krausse-Behrendt	Germany
Silver	Thorpe-Sheer	U.S.
Bronze	Grimmette-Martin	U.S.

Men's Singles			Women's Singles		
Gold	Georg Hackl	Germany	Gold	Silke Kraushaar	Germany
Silver	Armin Zoeggeler	Italy	Silver	Barbara Niedernhuber	Germany
Bronze	Jens Mueller	Germany	Bronze	Angelika Neuner	Austria

■ Nordic Combined (ski jump and cross country)

Individual			Team		
Gold	Bjarte Engen Vik	Norway	Gold	Norway	
Silver	Samppa Jajunen	Finland	Silver	Finland	
Bronze	Valerij Stoljarov	Russia	Bronze	France	

■ Ski Jumping

90 metre hill			120 metre hill		
Gold	Jani Soininen	Finland	Gold	Kazuyoshi Funaki	Japan
Silver	Kazuyoshi Funaki	Japan	Silver	Jani Soininen	Finland
Bronze	Andreas Widhoelzl	Austria	Bronze	Masahiko Harada	Japan

Team 120 metre hill	
Gold	Japan
Silver	Germany
Bronze	Austria

■ Snowboarding

Men's Giant Slalom			Women's Giant Slalom		
Gold	**Ross Rebagliati**	**Canada**	Gold	Karine Ruby	France
Silver	Thomas Prugger	Italy	Silver	Heidi Renoth	Germany
Bronze	Ueli Kestenholz	Switzerland	Bronze	Brigitte Koeck	Austria
Men's Halfpipe			**Women's Halfpipe**		
Gold	Gian Simmen	Switzerland	Gold	Nicola Thost	Germany
Silver	Daniel Franck	Norway	Silver	Stine Brun Kjeldaas	Norway
Bronze	Russ Powers	U.S.	Bronze	Shannon Dunn	U.S.

■ Speed Skating

Men's 500 metres			Women's 500 metres		
Gold	Hiroyasu Shimizu	Japan	**Gold**	**Catriona Lemay-Doan**	
Silver	**Jeremy Wotherspoon**	**Canada**	**Silver**	**Susan Auch**	
Bronze	**Kevin Overland**	**Canada**	Bronze	Tomomi Okazaki	
Men's 1,000 metres			Women's 1,000 metres		
Gold	Ids Postma	Netherlands	Gold	Marianne Timmer	Netherlands
Silver	Jan Bos	Netherlands	Silver	Chris Witty	U.S.
Bronze	Hiroyasu Shimizu	Japan	**Bronze**	**Catriona Lemay-Doan**	**Canada**
Men's 1,500 metres			Women's 1,500 metres		
Gold	Aadne Sondral	Norway	Gold	Marianne Timmer	Netherlands
Silver	Ids Postma	Netherlands	Silver	Gunda Niemann-Stirnemann	Germany
Bronze	Rintje Ritsma	Netherlands	Bronze	Chris Witty	U.S.
Men's 5,000 metres			Women's 3,000 metres		
Gold	Gianni Romme	Netherlands	Gold	Gunda Niemann-Stirnemann	Germany
Silver	Rintje Ritsma	Netherlands	Silver	Claudia Pechstein	Germany
Bronze	Bart Veldkamp	Belgium	Bronze	Anna Friesinger	Germany

Men's 10,000 metres		
Gold	Gianni Romme	Netherlands
Silver	Bob De Jong	Netherlands
Bronze	Rintje Ritsma	Netherlands

Women's 5,000 metres		
Gold	Claudia Pechstein	Germany
Silver	Gunda Niemann-Stirnemann	Germany
Bronze	Lyudmila Prokasheva	Kaskhstan

■ Short Track

Men's 1,000 metres		
Gold	Kim Dong-Sung	Korea
Silver	Jiajun Li	China
Bronze	**Eric Bedard**	**Canada**

Women's 1,000 metres		
Gold	Chun Lee-kyung	Korea
Silver	Yang Yang	China
Bronze	Won Hye-kyung	Korea

Men's 500 metres		
Gold	Takafumi Nishitani	Japan
Silver	Yulong An	China
Bronze	Hitoshi Uematsu	Japan

Women's 500 metres		
Gold	**Annie Perreault**	**Canada**
Silver	Yang Yang	China
Bronze	Chun Lee-Kyung	Korea

Men's 5,000-metre Relay	
Gold	**Canada**
Silver	Korea
Bronze	China

Women's 3,000-metre Relay	
Gold	Korea
Silver	China
Bronze	**Canada**

Canadian medal winners at the 1998 Winter Olympics

(Nagano, Japan)

■ Gold (6)

Bobsled (two-man)
Pierre Lueders, Edmonton, and Dave MacEachern, Charlottetown

Curling (women)
Skip – Sandra Schmirler; Third – Jan Betker; Second – Joan McCusker; Lead – Marcia Gudereit and spare Atina Ford, all Regina

Snowboarding (giant slalom)
Ross Rebagliati, Whistler, B.C.

Speed Skating, long track (500 metres)
Catriona Le May Doan, Saskatoon

Speed Skating, short track (500 metres)
Annie Perreault, Rock Forest, Que.

Speed Skating, short track (5,000-metre relay)
Eric Bedard, Ste-Thecle, Que.; Derrick Campbell, Cambridge, Ont.; Francois Drolet, Quebec City; Marc Gagnon, Chicoutimi, Que.

■ Silver (5)

Curling (Men)
Skip – Mike Harris; Third – Richard Hart; Second – Collin Mitchell; Lead – George Karrys and spare Paul Savage, all Toronto.

Figure Skating (men's singles)
Elvis Stojko, Richmond Hill, Ont.

Hockey (women)
Women's team.

Speed Skating, long track (500 metres)
Jeremy Wotherspoon, Red Deer, Alta.

Speed Skating, long track (500 metres)
Susan Auch, Winnipeg.

■ Bronze (4)

Speed Skating, long track (500 metres)
Kevin Overland, Kitchener, Ont.

Speed Skating, long track (1,000 metres)
Catriona Le May Doan, Saskatoon

Speed Skating, short track (1,000 metres)
Eric Bedard, Ste-Thecle, Que.

Speed Skating, short track (3,000-metre relay)
Chritine Boudrias, Montreal; Isabelle Charest, Montreal; Annie Perreault, Rock Forrest, Que., and Tania Vicent, Laval, Que.

Source: *Canadian Olympic Association*

Guide to Salt Lake 2002 – XIX Olympic Winter Games

(Events — February 8-24)

Sport	Men's events	Women's events
■ **Bobsleigh**	Two-man runs Four-man runs	Two-woman runs
■ **Curling**	10-team tournament	10-team tournament
■ **Hockey**	14-team tournament	8-team tournament*
■ **Luge**	Single Double*	Single
■ **Skating Events**		
Figure skating	Single Mixed pairs Mixed ice dancing	Single Mixed pairs Mixed ice dancing
Short track speed skating	500 m 1000 m 1500 m* 5000 m relay	500 m 1000 m 1500 m* 3000 m relay
Speed skating	500 m 1000 m 1500 m 5000 m 10,000 m	500 m 1000 m 1500 m 3000 m 5000 m
■ **Ski Events**		
Alpine ski	Downhill Super-G Giant Slalom Slalom Combined	Downhill Super-G Giant Slalom Slalom Combined
Biathlon	10 km sprint 12.5 km pursuit 20 km individual 4 x 7.5 km relay	7.5 km sprint 10 km pursuit 15 km individual 4 x 7.5 km relay
Cross-country ski	1.5 km sprint* 15 km classic* 20 km combined pursuit* 30 km classic* 4 x 10 km relay	1.5 km sprint* 10 km classic* 10 km combined pursuit* 15 km freestyle* 4 x 5 km relay
Freestyle ski	Moguls Aerials	Moguls Aerials
Nordic ski combined	Individual – 90 m x 15 km Sprint – 120 m x 7.5 km Team – 90 m / 4 x 5 km relay	
Ski jump	90 m individual 120 m individual 120 m team	
■ **Skeleton***	Single	Single*
■ **Snowboard**	Halfpipe Parallel giant slalom*	Halfpipe Parallel giant slalom*

*different than previous Olympic schedules or original to Salt Lake games

■ Bobsleigh

Bobsleigh, once referred to as the "Formula One race on ice", debuted at the 1924 Olympic Winter Games in Chamonix. It has been contested at every Game since, with the exception of Squaw Valley in 1960.

The competition consists of three events: two-man, four-man and two-woman. Women are competing for the first time at Salt Lake.

A gravitational force, otherwise known as the g-force, holds the sled and athletes on the wall of a banked turn. This force is so powerful, it makes the athletes feel like they weigh more than five times their actual weight.

Germany and Switzerland have traditionally dominated the Olympic sport.

Schedule

2-man runs (1 & 2)	men	Feb. 16
2-man runs (3 & 4 – final)	men	Feb. 17
2-woman runs (final)	women	Feb. 19
4-man runs (1 & 2)	men	Feb. 22
4-man runs (3 & 4 – final)	men	Feb. 23

■ Curling

Curling was invented in Scotland during the 16th century. Games were played on frozen ponds, lochs and marshes where stones were taken from river bottoms. British troops brought curling to North America during the mid-1700s, and the first curling club was established in Montreal during 1807.

At Salt Lake both men's and women's tournaments will consist of 10 teams.

Canada, Denmark and Switzerland showed the strongest earning of points at the 1998 inaugural games.

Schedule

Semi-finals	women	Feb. 20
Semi-finals	men	Feb. 20
Bronze and gold medals	women	Feb. 21
Bronze and gold medals	men	Feb. 22

■ Ice Hockey

Both men's and women's hockey tournaments are Olympic events. The men's tournament is made of 14 teams and consists of a preliminary, final and playoff round. The women's tournament is made of eight teams and consists of a preliminary and playoff round. In both men's and women's tournaments, the winner is determined by a gold-medal game.

Rules of Olympic ice hockey are different than those from NHL. The International Ice Hockey Federation (IIHF) governs over Olympic ice hockey rules of play.

Canada and the Russian federation have been the two dominant teams in ice hockey history. The US team won the first women's gold in 1998, with Canada earning a silver medal.

Schedule

Canada vs. Kazakhstan (preliminary)	women	Feb. 11
Russia vs. Canada (preliminary)	women	Feb. 13
Canada vs. Sweden (final)	men	Feb. 15
Canada vs. Sweden (preliminary)	women	Feb. 16
Canada vs. Qualifier 2 (final)	men	Feb. 17
Czech Republic vs. Canada (final)	men	Feb. 18
Semi-final	women	Feb. 19
Quarterfinal	men	Feb. 20
Bronze & gold medals	women	Feb. 21
Semi-finals (game 32)	men	Feb. 22
Bronze medal	men	Feb. 23
Gold medal	men	Feb. 24

■ Luge

Luge speeds at the Utah track are considered the world's fastest, with sliders exceeding speeds of 144 km/hr. The track has 17 curves and is 1316 metres in length. Luge athletes must be at least 15 years of age to compete.

Lugers race in a face-up prone position. They steer with their calves by pressing against the outside of the front-runners. In the doubles event, the larger of the two lies on top for a more aerodynamic fit. Races can be won or lost by a thousandth of a second. Though the doubles event is a mixed-gender competition, there has not been a mixed-gender team in the Olympics yet.

Lugers from Germany, Austria, Italy and the Russian federation are traditionally the most successful athletes in this sport.

Schedule

Singles 1 & 2	men	Feb. 10
Singles 3 & 4 (final)	men	Feb. 11
Singles 1 & 2	women	Feb. 12
Singles 3 &4 (final)	women	Feb. 13
Doubles	men	Feb. 15

■ Skating Events

Figure skating: Olympic figure skating consists of four medal disciplines: ladies' singles, men's singles, pairs, and ice dancing.

A separate panel of nine judges evaluate each figure skating discipline. Marks are awarded from a scale of 0-6. Decimals to one tenth are used to further separate performances.

The Russian federation does exceedingly well in Olympic figure skating competitions.

Composition

Singles

Short program	2 minutes 40 seconds
Free skate (men)	4 minutes 30 seconds
Free skate (women)	4 minutes

Pairs

Short program	2 minutes 40 seconds
Free skate	4 minutes 30 seconds

Ice Dancing

Compulsory	-
Original	2 minutes
Free	4 minutes

Schedule

Pairs

Short program	Feb. 9
Free program	Feb. 11

Singles

Men's short program	Feb. 12
Men's free program	Feb. 14

Dance

Compulsory	Feb. 15
Original	Feb. 17
Free	Feb. 18

Singles

Women's short program	Feb. 19
Women's free program	Feb. 21
Exhibition	Feb. 22

Short track speed skating: Short track speed skating includes eight separate men's and women's events. Generally four skaters race side by side counter-clockwise in a series of elimination rounds. The first two of each heat to cross the finish line advance to the next round. Time is secondary, with records having been set in non-medal heats.

The Salt Lake games are hosting a men's and women's 1500 metre event. Instead of four skaters per heat, the 1500 metre races six. All heats, quarterfinals, semi-finals and the final are contested in one day, so great stamina and strategy are required from the racers.

Short track speed skating was first introduced in the Olympics as a demonstration sport at Calgary in 1988.

Schedule

1500 m (final)	women	Feb. 13
500 m	women	Feb. 16
1000 m (final)	men	Feb. 16
1500 m (final)	men	Feb. 20
3000 m relay (final)	women	Feb. 20
500 m	men	Feb. 23
1000 m (final)	women	Feb. 23
5000 m relay (final)	men	Feb. 23

Speed skating: It is believed that skates were invented about 3,000 years ago in Scandinavia. Although the sport of speed skating originates from the Netherlands, the first known competition was held in England. It was a 15-metre race in 1763.

Speed skating, otherwise known as long track speed skating, has been part of the Olympic Games since 1924. There are 100 speed skating events being held at Salt Lake. They are equally divided to represent both men's and women's events.

Schedule

5000 m	men	Feb. 9
3000 m	women	Feb. 10
500 m	men	Feb. 11 & 12
500 m	women	Feb. 13 & 14
1000 m	men	Feb. 16
1000 m	women	Feb. 17
1500 m	men	Feb. 19
1500 m	women	Feb. 20
10000 m	men	Feb. 22
5000 m	women	Feb. 23

■ Skeleton

Skeleton is the world's first sliding sport—it is a head-first version of the luge. It originates from St. Moritz, Switzerland during the 1800s. Back then, the winner's trophy was a bottle of champagne. Salt Lake has brought the skeleton back to the Olympics after a 54-year absence. It is the first time women have participated in the Olympic event. All drivers must be at least 18 years of age to race.

A skeleton sled is approximately 1 m long and 40 cm wide. It weights from 32 - 52 kg . The sleds are made of fibreglass or steel. An audio and visual signal authorises the start of the race. The driver has 30 seconds to commence racing. He or she accelerates by pushing the sled. Any other help at the start is prohibited.

An athlete races in a prone position on the sled. They are allowed two runs, and an aggregate total becomes their score. The driver is permitted to leave the sled in order to push or move it, but he or she must be on the sled when passing the finish line for the run to be considered valid.

Traditionally the USA has faired well in this sport.

Schedule

Skeleton	men	Feb. 20
Skeleton	women	Feb. 20

■ Ski Events

Alpine Skiing: There are five different alpine races: downhill, super-G, giant slalom, slalom, and combined. Salt Lake will be holding the entire combined event on a single day at the same venue. This is a first in Olympic history.

The combined event is made up of one downhill race and two slalom runs. The times are added together and the winner is the athlete with the fastest total time. These runs are contested independently of the regular downhill and slalom events. The combined courses are also shorter than the regular competitions.

Austria, Switzerland and France have been the strongest contenders in the alpine skiing events.

Schedule

Downhill	men	Feb. 10
Downhill	women	Feb. 11
Combined (downhill and slalom - final)	men	Feb. 13
Combined (downhill and slalom - final)	women	Feb. 14
Super-G	men	Feb. 16
Super-G	women	Feb. 17
Slalom (final)	women	Feb. 20
Giant slalom (final)	men	Feb. 21
Giant slalom (final)	women	Feb. 22
Slalom (final)	men	Feb. 23

Biathlon: Biathlon is the combined sport of cross-country skiing and rifle shooting. Though the biathlon has been an Olympic sport since 1924, pursuit events are making their debut in 2002 at Salt Lake. There are four different biathlon events: individual, sprint, pursuit, and relay.

In the pursuit, competitors start at intervals based upon their sprint finish. Men race 12.5 kilometres and women race 10 kilometres. They are allowed to ski freestyle, which is faster than the more rigid classical style. Competitors make four stops. At each stop they must hit five targets with five bullets. Skis are not to be removed while shooting at targets. If they miss a hit, a penalty lap of 150 metres is assigned. The penalty must be skied immediately after a miss. The first person to cross the finish line is the winner.

The Nordic nations and the Russian federation have historically dominated biathlon events.

Schedule

15 km individual	women	Feb. 11
20 km individual	men	Feb. 11
7.5 km sprint	women	Feb. 13
10 km sprint	men	Feb. 13
10 km pursuit	women	Feb. 16
12.5 km pursuit	men	Feb. 16
4 x 7.5 km relay	women	Feb. 18
4 x 7.5 km relay	men	Feb. 20

Cross-country skiing: Much has changed within this event during the 2002 season.

The men and women's 1.5 km sprint is being contested for the first time in Salt Lake. It is the shortest cross-country event. Any style is allowed. The sprints are different in that they are contested in a series of elimination rounds. The winner of the final round is the gold medallist.

The women's 10 km and men's 15 cm classic has been brought back since the 1988 Olympics. It is an individual start race.

Combined pursuits are two separate races that are now being held during the same day. The first race is a classic with an individual start. The second race is a freestyle with a pursuit start (the winner of the classic starts first). The two races are no longer separate medal events.

The women's 15 km and the men's 30 km races have been changed into freestyle events. They will be mass start races. Likewise the women's 30 km and the men's 50 km races have been changed into classic races. They will be individual starts.

The Russian federation and Norway have historically done well in these events.

Schedule

10 km classic	women	Feb. 10
15 km classic	men	Feb. 10
Pursuit	men	Feb. 14
Pursuit	women	Feb. 15
4 x 10 km relay	men	Feb. 17
1.5 km sprint	men and women	Feb. 19
4 x 5 km relay	women	Feb 21
50 km classic	men	Feb. 23
30 km classic	women	Feb. 24

Freestyle Skiing: Freestyle skiing originated in the USA during the 1960s. It was introduced to the Olympics as a demonstration event at the 1988 Calgary Olympics.

The moguls competition consists of a 27-degree slope with bumps up to 1.2 metres in height and two jumps. Skiers wear colourful kneepads to attract attention to their skiing expertise. Points are awarded by judges for speed, accuracy of turns, aggressiveness, style, and dynamic movement. Skis are not to leave the snow surface unless at predetermined jumps.

In the aerial competition skiers perform combinations of flips and twists off jumps that are as high as four metres, with takeoffs as steep as 70-degrees. They drop from a height equal to a three or four story building, and land in an area that has a 37-degree gradient, covered in soft, churned snow to absorb impact. Points are awarded for turns, air, speed, form and landing.

Schedule

Freestyle moguls	women	Feb. 9
Freestyle moguls	men	Feb. 12
Freestyle aerials	women	Feb. 18
Freestyle aerials	men	Feb. 19

Nordic Combined: This event combines ski jumping and cross-country skiing. It has been part of every Olympic Winter Game since 1924. The sprint event makes its debut at the Salt Lake City Games.

The Nordic combined sprint is made up of a ski jump competition from the large hill and a 7.5 km cross-country race (freestyle). The jump measures 120 metres. The winner of the jump starts the race, with the others staggered behind. The first person to cross the finish line wins.

Females are not prohibited from competing in nordic combination events; however, a woman has yet to compete in the Olympic sport.

Norway, Finland and Germany have dominated the nordic combined events in the past.

Schedule

K90 individual jumps	men	Feb. 9
15 km individual	men	Feb. 10
Team K90 jump	men	Feb. 14
Team 4 x 5 km relay	men	Feb. 15
Sprint K120 jump	men	Feb. 21
Sprint 7.5 km	men	Feb. 22

Ski Jumping: This sport has been part of the Winter Games since 1924. Though women are not prohibited from competing in ski jump events, they have never competed in the Olympic sport.

Jumpers receive both distance and style points to determine ranking. For style, each of the five judges award a maximum of 20 points. The highest and lowest of these five scores are dropped, and the remaining three totalled. Distance points are calculated by awarding 60 points for a landing at the critical 'K' point.

Skiers previously kept their skis parallel, but discovered that making a V provides extra lift. Today's skiers use this form. J. Bokloeg of Sweden discovered the technique accidentally during the 1988-89 World Cup season. The shape of his legs forced his skis apart, forming a

V. Other skiers imitated him and learned that by doing so they could increase their distance by three to five metres on the normal hill and five to 15 metres on the large hill.

Norway and Finland have excelled at ski jumping in the past.

Schedule

K90 individual	men	Feb. 10
K120 individual	men	Feb. 13
K120 team	men	Feb 18

■ Snowboarding

Snowboarding has been an Olympic sport since the 1998 Nagano Games. The two traditional giant slaloms of Nagano have been replaced by a parallel giant slalom in the alpine event at Salt Lake.

The parallel giant slalom begins with qualifying, where each competitor takes one run down the course. The top 16 athletes advance into the first-round match-ups. From this heat onward, snowboarders compete side by side down two parallel courses. After the first run, athletes switch sides to race again. The winner is the boarder with the best total time. Eight athletes advance to compete in the quarterfinals, and four in the semi-finals. The two best total times from the semi-finals race for the gold medal.

The halfpipe is performed in a half-cylinder-shaped course dug deep into the hill. Applying speed gained on the slope, boarders come up over the lip of the wall to jump, rotate and perform other mid-air acrobatics. The object is to demonstrate difficult moves in perfect form. Five judges award up to 10 points for their area of expertise: standard manoeuvres, rotations, amplitude, and overall impression.

The US snowboarding team did quite well during the 1998 snowboarding competitions.

Schedule

Halfpipe	women	Feb. 10
Halfpipe	men	Feb. 11
Parallel giant slalom (qualification)	men and women	Feb. 14
Parallel giant slalom (final)	men and women	Feb. 15

Salt Lake Information on the Web

To get the latest information on ticket availability, visitor information, events (including the arts festival), athletes' bios or results, visit www.slc2002.org

Source: *Salt Lake Organizing Committee for the Olympic Winter Games of 2002*

Canadian Curling Champions

Men

Skip, Province	Skip, Province	Skip, Province
1927 Murray Macneill, NS	**1954** Matt Baldwin, Alta	**1978** Ed Lukowich, Alta
1928 Gordon Hudson, Man.	**1955** Garnet Campbell, Sask.	**1979** Barry Fry, Man.
1929 Gordon Hudson, Man.	**1956** Billy Walsh, Man.	**1980** Rick Folk, Sask.
1930 Howard Wood, Man.	**1957** Matt Baldwin, Alta	**1981** Kerry Burtnyk, Man.
1931 Bob Gourley, Man.	**1958** Matt Baldwin, Alta	**1982** Al Hackner, N. Ont.
1932 Jim Congalton, Man.	**1959** Ernie Richardson, Sask.	**1983** Ed Werenich, Ont.
1933 Cliff Manahan, Alta	**1960** Ernie Richardson, Sask.	**1984** Mike Riley, Man.
1934 Leo Johnson, Man.	**1961** Hec Gervais, Alta	**1985** Al Hackner, N. Ont.
1935 Gordon Campbell, Ont.	**1962** Ernie Richardson, Sask.	**1986** Ed Lukowich, Alta
1936 Ken Watson, Man.	**1963** Ernie Richardson, Sask.	**1987** Russ Howard, Ont.
1937 Cliff Manahan, Alta	**1964** Lyall Dagg, BC	**1988** Pat Ryan, Alta
1938 Ab Gowanlock, Man.	**1965** Terry Braunstein, Man.	**1989** Pat Ryan, Alta
1939 Bert Hall, Ont.	**1966** Ron Northcott, Alta	**1990** Ed Werenich, Ont.
1940 Howard Wood, Man.	**1967** Alf Phillips, Jr., Ont.	**1991** Kevin Martin, Alta
1941 Howard Palmer, Alta	**1968** Ron Northcott, Alta	**1992** Vic Peters, Man.
1942 Ken Watson, Man.	**1969** Ron Northcott, Alta	**1993** Russ Howard, Ont.
1946 Billy Rose, Alta	**1970** Don Duguid, Man.	**1994** Rick Folk, BC
1947 Jimmy Welsh, Man.	**1971** Don Duguid, Man.	**1995** Kerry Burtnyk, Man
1948 Frenchy D'Amour, BC	**1972** Orest Meleschuk, Man.	**1996** Jeff Stoughton, Man
1949 Ken Watson, Man.	**1973** Harvey Mazinke, Sask.	**1997** Kevin Martin, Alta
1950 Tom Ramsay, N. Ont.	**1974** Hector Gervais, Alta	**1998** Wayne Middaugh, Ont.
1951 Don Oyler, NS	**1975** Bill Tetley, N. Ont.	**1999** Jeff Stoughton, Man.
1952 Billy Walsh, Man.	**1976** Jack MacDuff, Nfld.	**2000** Greg McAuley, BC
1953 Ab Gowanlock, Man.	**1977** Jim Ursel, Que.	**2001** Randy Ferbey, Alta

Women

Skip, Province	Skip, Province	Skip, Province
1961 Joyce McKee, Sask.	**1975** Lee Tobin, Que.	**1989** Heather Houston, Ont.
1962 Ina Hansen, BC	**1976** Lindsay Davie, BC	**1990** Alison Goring, Ont.
1963 Mabel DeWare, NB	**1977** Myrna McQuarrie, Alta.	**1991** Julie Sutton, BC
1964 Ina Hansen, BC	**1978** Cathy Pidzarko, Man.	**1992** Connie Laliberte, Man.
1965 Peggy Casselman, Man.	**1979** Lindsay Sparkes, BC	**1993** Sandra Peterson, Sask.
1966 Gail Lee, Alta.	**1980** Marj Mitchell, Sask.	**1994** Sandra Peterson, Sask
1967 Betty Duguid, Man.	**1981** Susan Seitz, Alta.	**1995** Connie Laliberte, Man.
1968 Hazel Jamieson, Alta.	**1982** Colleen Jones, NS	**1996** Marilyn Bodogh, Ont.
1969 Joyce McKee, Sask.	**1983** Penny LaRocque, NS	**1997** Sandra Schmirler, Sask.
1970 Dorenda Schoenhais, Sask.	**1984** Connie Laliberte, Man.	**1998** Cathy Borst, Alta.
1971 Vera Pezer, Sask.	**1985** Linda Moore, BC	**1999** Colleen Jones, NS
1972 Vera Pezer, Sask.	**1986** Marilyn Darte, Ont.	**2000** Kelly Law, BC
1973 Vera Pezer, Sask.	**1987** Pat Sanders, BC	**2001** Colleen Jones, NS
1974 Emily Farnham, Sask.	**1988** Heather Houston, Ont.	

Source: *Canadian Press*

IAFF Track and Field Results

(Edmonton, August 5-11, 2001)

100 Metre

	Women				Men		
	Athlete	Country	Mark m/s		Athlete	Country	Mark m/s
1	Zhanna Pintusevich-Block	UKR	10.82	1	Maurice Greene	USA	9.82
2	Marion Jones	USA	10.85	2	Tim Montgomery	USA	9.85
3	Ekaterini Thanou	GRE	10.91	3	Bernard Williams	USA	9.94

200 Metre

	Women				Men		
	Athlete	Country	Mark m/s		Athlete	Country	Mark m/s
1	Marion Jones	USA	22.39	1	Konstadinos Kederis	GRE	20.04
2	Debbie Ferguson	BAH	22.52	2	Christopher Williams	JAM	20.20
3	Kelli White	USA	22.56	3	Kim Collins	SKN	20.20

400 Metre

	Women				Men		
	Athlete	Country	Mark m/s		Athlete	Country	Mark m/s
1	Thiam Amy Mbacke	SEN	49.86	1	Avard Moncur	BAH	44.64
2	Lorraine Fenton	JAM	49.88	2	Ingo Schultz Ingo	GER	44.87
3	Ana Guevara	MEX	49.97	3	Gregory Haughton	JAM	44.98

800 Metre

	Women				Men		
	Athlete	Country	Mark m/s		Athlete	Country	Mark m/s
1	Maria de Lourdes Mutola	MOZ	1:57.17	1	Andre Bucher	SUI	1:43.70
2	Stephanie Graf	AUT	1:57.20	2	Wilfred Bungei	KEN	1:44.55
3	Letitia Vriesde	SUR	1:57.35	3	Pawel Czapiewski	POL	1:44.55

1500 Metre

	Women				Men		
	Athlete	Country	Mark m/s		Athlete	Country	Mark m/s
1	Gabriela Szabo	ROM	4:00.57	1	Hicham El Guerrouj	MAR	3:30
2	Violeta Szekely	ROM	4:01.70	2	Bernard Lagat	KEN	3:31.10
3	Natalya Gorelova	RUS	4:02.40	3	Driss Maazouzi	FRA	3:31.54

5000 Metre

	Women				Men		
	Athlete	Country	Mark m/s		Athlete	Country	Mark m/s
1	Olga Yegorova	RUS	15:03.39	1	Richard Limo	KEN	13:00.77
2	Marta Domínguez	ESP	15:06.59	2	Ali Saïdi-Sief	ALG	13:02.16
3	Ayelech Worku	ETH	15:10.17	3	Million Wolde	ETH	13:03.47

10000 Metre

	Women				Men		
	Athlete	Country	Mark m/s		Athlete	Country	Mark m/s
1	Derartu Tulu	ETH	31:48.81	1	Charles Kamathi	KEN	27:53.25
2	Berhane Adere	ETH	31:48.85	2	Assefa Mezgebu	ETH	27:53.97
3	Gete Wami	ETH	31:49.98	3	Haile Gebrselassie	ETH	27:54.41

▶ **Marathon**

Steeplechase

Women			Men			Men's 300 Metres Steeplechase		
	Country	Mark m/s		Country	Mark m/s	Athlete	Country	Mark m/s
1	Japan	7:22:36	1	Ethiopia	6:43:32	Reuben Kosgei	KEN	8:15.16
2	Russia	7:26:00	2	Japan	6:48:36	Ali Ezzine	MAR	8:16.21
3	Romania	7:29:44	3	Italy	6:51:56	Bernard Barmasai	KEN	8:16.59

Hurdles

Women's 100 Metres Hurdles			Men's 110 Metres Hurdles		
Athlete	Country	Mark m/s	Athlete	Country	Mark m/s
1 Anjanette Kirkland	USA	12.42	Allen Johnson	USA	13.04
2 Gail Devers	USA	12.54	Anier García	CUB	13.07
3 Olga Shishigina	KAZ	12.58	Dudley Dorival	HAI	13.25

Hurdles – 400 Metres

Women			Men		
Athlete	Country	Mark m/s	Athlete	Country	Mark m/s
1 Nezha Bidouane	MAR	53.34	Felix Sánchez	DOM	47.49
2 Yuliya Nosova	RUS	54.27	Fabrizio Mori	ITA	47.54
3 Daimí Pernía	CUB	54.51	Dai Tamesue	JPN	47.89

High Jump

Women			Men		
Athlete	Country	Mark m/s	Athlete	Country	Mark m/s
1 Hestrie Cloete	RSA	2.00	Martin Buss	GER	2.36
2 Inha Babakova	UKR	2.00	Vyacheslav Voronin	RUS	2.33
3 Kajsa Bergqvist	SWE	1.97	Yaroslav Rybakov	RUS	2.33

Pole Vault

Women			Men		
Athlete	Country	Mark m/s	Athlete	Country	Mark m/s
1 Stacy Dragila	USA	4.75	Dmitri Markov	AUS	6.05
2 Svetlana Feofanova	RUS	4.75	Aleksandr Averbukh	ISR	5.85
3 Monika Pyrek	POL	4.55	Nick Hysong	USA	5.85

Long Jump

Women			Men		
Athlete	Country	Mark m/s	Athlete	Country	Mark m/s
1 Fiona May	ITA	7.02	Iván Pedroso	CUB	8.40
2 Tatyana Kotova	RUS	7.01	Savante Stringfellow	USA	8.24
3 Niurka Montalvo	ESP	6.88	Carlos Calado	POR	8.21

Triple Jump

Women			Men		
Athlete	Country	Mark m/s	Athlete	Country	Mark m/s
1 Tatyana Lebedeva	RUS	15.25	Jonathan Edwards	GBR	17.92
2 Etone Françoise Mbango	CMR	14.60	Christian Olsson	SWE	17.47
3 Tereza Marinova	BUL	14.58	Igor Spasovkhodskiy	RUS	17.44

Shot Put

Women			Men		
Athlete	Country	Mark m/s	Athlete	Country	Mark m/s
1 Yanina Korolchik	BLR	20.61	John Godina	USA	21.87
2 Nadine Kleinert-Schmitt	GER	19.86	Adam Nelson	USA	21.24
3 Vita Pavlysh	UKR	19.41	Arsi Harju	FIN	20.93

▶

Discus Throw

Women				Men			
	Athlete	Country	Mark m/s		Athlete	Country	Mark m/s
1	Natalya Sadova	RUS	68.57	1	Lars Riedel	GER	69.72
2	Ellina Zvereva	BLR	67.10	2	Virgilijus Alekna	LTU	69.40
3	Nicoleta Grasu	ROM	66.24	3	Michael Möllenbeck	GER	67.61

Hammer Throw

Women				Men			
	Athlete	Country	Mark m/s		Athlete	Country	Mark m/s
1	Yipsi Moreno	CUB	70.65	1	Szymon Ziólkowski	POL	83.38
2	Olga Kuzenkova	RUS	70.61	2	Koji Murofushi	JPN	82.92
3	Bronwyn Eagles	AUS	68.87	3	Ilya Konovalov	RUS	80.27

Javelin Throw

Women				Men			
	Athlete	Country	Mark m/s		Athlete	Country	Mark m/s
1	Osleidys Menéndez	CUB	69.53	1	Jan Zelezny	CZE	92.80
2	Miréla Manjani-Tzelíli	GRE	65.78	2	Aki Parviainen	FIN	91.31
3	Sonia Bisset	CUB	64.69	3	Konstadinós Gatsioúdis	GRE	89.95

20 Kilometre Walk

Women				Men			
	Athlete	Country	Mark		Athlete	Country	Mark
1	Olimpiada Ivanova	RUS	1:27:48	1	Roman Rasskazov	RUS	1:20:31
2	Valentina Tsybulskaya	BLR	1:28:49	2	Ilya Markov	RUS	1:20:33
3	Elisabetta Perrone	ITA	1:28:56	3	Viktor Burayev	RUS	1:20:36

50 Kilometre Walk

Men			
	Athlete	Country	Mark
1	Robert Korzeniowski	POL	3:42:08
2	Jesús Angel García	ESP	3:43:07
3	Edgar Hernandez	MEX	3:46:12

4 x 100 Metres

Women			Men		
	Team	Mark m/s		Team	Mark m/s
1	USA	41.71	1	United States	37.96
2	Germany	42.32	2	South Africa	38.47
3	France	42.39	3	Trinidad Tobago	38.58

4 x 400 Metres

Women			Men		
	Team	Mark m/s		Team	Mark m/s
1	Jamaica	3:20.65	1	USA	2:57.54
2	Germany	3:21.97	2	Bahamas	2:58.19
3	Russia	3:24.92	3	Jamaica	2:58.39

Amputees

Women's 100 Metres				Men's 200 Metres			
	Athlete	Country	Mark m/s		Athlete	Country	Mark m/s
1	Amy Winters	AUS	12.72	1	Neil Fuller	AUS	23.32
2	Catherine Bader-Bille	GER	13.75	2	Marcus Ehm	GER	23.74
3	Meaghan Starr	AUS	13.76	3	Dominique Andre	FRA	24.26

Blind

Women's 200 Metres				Men's 100 Metres			
	Athlete	Country	Mark m/s		Athlete	Country	Mark m/s
1	Adria Rocha Santos	BRA	25.76	1	Lorenzo Ricci	ITA	11.71
2	Purificacion Santamarta	ESP	26.83	2	Julio Requena	ESP	11.79
3	Maria Jose Alves	BRA	26.86	3	Koji Saito	JPN	11.83

▶

▶ **Wheelchair**

	Women's 800 Metre				Men's 1500 Metre		
	Athlete	Country	Mark m/s		Athlete	Country	Mark m/s
1	Louise Sauvage	AUS	1:56.86	1	Aaron Gordian	MEX	3:08.04
2	Ariadne Hernandez	MEX	1:56.99	2	**Jeff Adams**	**CAN**	**3:08.13**
3	Wakako Tsuchido	JPN	1:57.35	3	Saul Mendoza	MEX	3:08.16

Heptathlon and Decathlon

	Women's Heptathlon				Men's Decathlon		
	Athlete	Country	Mark m/s		Athlete	Country	Mark m/s
1	Yelena Prokhorova	RUS	6694	1	Tomás Dvořák	CZE	8902
2	Natalya Sazanovich	BLR	6539	2	Erki Nool	EST	8815
3	Shelia Burrell	USA	6472	3	Dean Macey	GBR	8603

Source: *International Association of Athletics Federations*

Men's ATP Rankings, 2001

(as of September 30, 2001)

Rank	Country	Rank	Country
1. Gustavo Kuerten	Brazil	6. Yevgeny Kafelnikov	Russia
2. Andre Agassi	USA	7. Sebastien Grosjean	France
3. Lleyton Hewitt	Australia	8. Pete Sampras	USA
4. Patrick Rafter	Australia	9. Tim Henman	Great Britain
5. Juan Carlos Ferrero	Spain	10. Roger Federer	Switzerland

Source: *Association of Tennis Professionals*

Women's Tennis Association—2001 Grand Slam Events

Event	Date	Winner	Event	Date	Winner
Australian Open	Jan. 16-28	Jennifer Capriati	Wimbledon	June 25-July 8	Venus Williams
French Open	May 28-June 10	Jennifer Capriati	U.S. Open	Aug 27-Sept 9	Venus Williams

Source: *Women's Tennis Association*

Women's Tennis Association Rankings, 2001

(as of September 30, 2001)

Rank	Country	Rank	Country
1. Martina Hingis	Switzerland	6. Amelie Mauresmo	France
2. Jennifer Capriati	USA	7. Serena Williams	USA
3. Lindsay Davenport	USA	8. Justine Henin	Belgium
4. Venus Williams	USA	9. Monica Seles	USA
5. Kim Clijsters	Belgium	10. Nathalie Tauziat	France

Source: *Women's Tennis Association*

Royal Canadian Henley Regatta — Efficiency Trophy Final Standings

(St. Catharines, Ontario)

Standing	Club Name	Sweep Oar Y = 1; N = 2	Eff'y %	Poss Points	Actual Points	# of Finals
1st	University of Victoria	1	85.77	260	223	14
2nd	Boston RC	1	77.17	92	71	5
3rd	Mobjack RA	1	75.00	60	45	3
4th	Victoria City RC	1	63.72	215	137	12
5th	Waiariki RC	1	60.74	135	82	7
6th	New York AC	1	54.69	245	134	9
7th	Brockville RC	1	54.44	90	49	5
8th	Brock University RC	1	54.40	250	136	14
9th	Riverside BC	1	53.23	434	231	25
10th	West Side RC	1	52.32	302	158	15
11th	Thames River Sculls	1	51.40	107	55	5
12th	University of British Columbia	1	46.13	271	125	16
13th	Camp Randall	1	45.52	145	66	9
14th	St. Catharines RC	1	43.76	553	242	32
15th	Fedemex RC	1	43.48	138	60	9
16th	Western RC	1	43.08	195	84	14
17th	North Country RC	1	40.87	115	47	5
18th	Community RC	1	40.58	138	56	8
19th	Penn AC	1	40.00	140	56	7
20th	Kingston RC	1	38.10	63	24	5
21st	Don RC	1	37.71	175	66	12
22nd	Montreal RC	1	36.80	125	46	9
23rd	Hanlan BC	1	36.67	90	33	5
24th	Nereid BC	1	35.60	250	89	14
25th	Niskayuna HS	1	35.56	45	16	3
26th	South Niagara RC	1	33.00	100	33	7
27th	Ottawa RC	1	32.12	330	106	20
28th	Potomac BC	1	30.86	162	50	9
29th	Argonaut RC	1	25.00	40	10	3
30th	Wyandott BC	1	25.00	80	20	4
31st	Leander BC	1	24.62	65	16	3
32nd	Steel City RC	1	23.33	30	7	2
33rd	Saratoga RA	1	22.22	45	10	2
34th	Burnt Hills RA	1	20.00	25	5	1

Source: *Royal Canadian Henley Regatta — Canadian Henley Rowing Corporation*

2001 National Lacrosse League Final Standings

TEAM	GP	WON	LOST	PCT	GF	GA	GFA	GAA
**Toronto Rock	14	11	3	0.786	168	125	12.0	8.9
*Philadelphia Wings	14	10	4	0.714	205	177	14.6	12.6
*Rochester Knighthawks	14	10	4	0.714	198	159	14.1	11.4
*Washington Power	14	9	5	0.643	226	204	16.1	14.6
Buffalo Bandits	14	8	6	0.571	248	218	17.7	15.6
New York Saints	14	6	8	0.429	179	181	12.8	12.9
Albany Attack	14	5	9	0.357	152	169	10.9	12.1
Columbus Landsharks	14	3	11	0.214	134	201	9.6	14.4
Ottawa Rebel	14	1	13	0.071	144	220	10.3	15.7

Source: *Toronto Rock*   *Clinched Playoff Berth **Clinched Regular Season Title

Semi-Finals:
April 21,**Toronto Rock 10** Washington Power 9
April 20, Philadelphia Wings 12, Rochester Knighthawks 11

Championship Game:
Fri. April 27, Philadelphia Wings 9 **Toronto Rock 8**
Game MVP: Dallas Eliuk, Philadelphia

Toronto Rock 2001 Regular Season Statistics

#	Player	GP	G	AST	PTS	PPG	SHG	GW	SH	SON	PIM	FW	FL	LB
7	Doyle, Colin	14	26	33	59	9	0	1	143	96	28	0	0	55
93	Squire, Kim	13	26	30	56	8	1	2	184	135	31	1	0	72
9	Toth, Kaleb	14	23	22	45	6	0	0	133	95	10	0	0	81
8	Stroup, Dan	14	19	19	38	8	1	2	137	94	0	0	0	87
17	Toll, Steve	14	15	20	35	2	3	1	80	69	6	83	97	128
25	Gill, Chris	14	19	15	34	5	0	0	115	83	0	0	0	57
32	Veltman, Jim	14	9	23	32	0	0	3	41	37	13	1	0	161
33	Millin, Ken	14	7	10	17	1	0	0	59	44	12	73	91	49
2	Coyle, Pat	14	4	10	14	0	0	0	20	17	65	0	0	104
10	Langdale, Chris	14	5	9	14	0	0	0	49	35	18	0	0	35
67	O'Connor, Ryan	7	4	5	9	1	1	0	28	22	6	0	0	11
29	Watson, Bob	14	0	7	7	0	0	0	0	0	2	0	0	105
11	Clark, Glenn	7	5	2	7	0	1	0	20	13	16	0	0	67
34	Squire, Rodd	4	2	4	6	0	0	1	11	7	4	0	0	19
43	Taylor, Jamie	2	1	1	2	0	0	0	10	7	4	1	2	4
97	Bullen, Terry	11	1	1	2	0	0	0	4	3	18	0	0	54
14	Harrison, Dean	3	1	0	1	0	0	0	10	7	2	0	1	8
6	Ladouceur, Dan	13	1	0	1	0	0	1	2	2	60	0	0	20
23	Gelsvik, Craig	14	0	2	2	0	0	0	8	5	51	0	0	42
44	Cosmo, Anthony	5	0	0	0	0	0	0	0	0	0	0	0	29
76	Maynard, Niall	10	0	0	0	0	0	0	0	0	13	0	0	14
	BENCH	14						10						
	TOTALS	14	168	213	381	40	7	11	1054	771	369	159	191	1202
	Opponent Totals	14	125	161	286	28	5	3	894	609	377	191	159	1055

#	Goaltenders	GPI	W	L	MIN	SV	GA	AVG
44	Cosmo, Anthony	4	1	1	132:17	69	19	8.62
29	Watson, Bob	13	10	2	715:28	415	106	8.89
	TOTALS	14	11	3	849:23	484	125	8.83
	Opponent Totals	14	3	11	849:23	603	168	11.87

Source: *Toronto Rock*

Lacrosse—The Mann Cup, 1910–2001

The Mann Cup was presented by the late Sir Donald Mann, builder of the Canadian Northern Railway, for the Senior Amateur Championship of Canada and was originally a challenge cup.

1910	Young Torontos, Toronto, Ont.
1911	Vancouver Athletic Club, Vancouver, BC
1912	Vancouver Athletic Club, Vancouver, BC
1913	Vancouver Athletic Club, Vancouver, BC
1914	Vancouver Athletic Club, Vancouver, BC
1915	Salmonbellies, New Westminster, BC
1916	Salmonbellies, New Westminster, BC
1917	Salmonbellies, New Westminster, BC
1918	Coughlans, Vancouver, BC
1919	Foundation Club, Vancouver, BC
1920–1925	Salmonbellies, New Westminster, BC
1926	Westonmen, Weston, Ont.
1927	Salmonbellies, New Westminster, BC
1928	Emmets, Ottawa, Ont.
1929	Generals, Oshawa, Ont.
1930	Excelsiors, Brampton, Ont.
1931	Excelsiors, Brampton, Ont.
1932	Mountaineers, Mimico, Ont.
1933	Tigers, Hamilton, Ont.
1934	Terriers, Orillia, Ont.
1935	Terriers, Orillia, Ont.
1936	Terriers, Orillia, Ont.
1937	Salmonbellies, New Westminster, BC
1938	Athletics, St. Catharines, Ont.
1939	Adanacs, New Westminster, BC
1940	Athletics, St. Catharines, Ont.
1941	Athletics, St. Catharines, Ont.
1942	Combines, Mimico/Brampton, Ont.
1943	Salmonbellies, New Westminster, BC
1944	Athletics, St. Catharines, Ont.
1945	Burrards, Vancouver, BC
1946	Athletics, St. Catharines, Ont.
1947	Adanacs, New Westminster, BC
1948	Tigers, Hamilton, Ont.
1949	Burrards, Vancouver, BC
1950	Crescents, Owen Sound, Ont.
1951	Timbermen, Peterborough, Ont.
1952	Timbermen, Peterborough, Ont.
1953	Timbermen, Peterborough, Ont.
1954	Timbermen, Peterborough, Ont.
1955	Shamrocks, Victoria, BC
1956	Timbermen, Nanaimo, BC
1957	Shamrocks, Victoria, BC
1958	Salmonberries, New Westminster, BC
1959	O'Keefes, New Westminster, BC
1960	Sailors, Port Credit, Ont.
1961	Burrards, Vancouver, BC
1962	O'Keefes, New Westminster, BC
1963	Carlings, Vancouver, BC
1964	Carlings, Vancouver, BC
1965	Salmonbellies, New Westminster, BC
1966	Lakers, Peterborough, Ont.
1967	Carlings, Vancouver, BC
1968	Redmed, Brooklin, Ont.
1969	Redmen, Brooklin, Ont.
1970	Salmonbellies, New Westminster, BC
1971	Warriors, Brantford, Ont.
1972	Salmonbellies, New Westminster, BC
1973	Lakers, Peterborough, Ont.
1974	Salmonbellies, New Westminster, BC
1975	Burrards, Vancouver, BC
1976	Salmonbellies, New Westminster, BC
1977	Burrards, Vancouver, BC
1978	Red Oaks, Peterborough, Ont.
1979	Shamrocks, Victoria, BC
1980	Excelsiors, Brampton, Ont.
1981	Salmonbellies, New Westminster, BC
1982	Lakers, Peterborough, Ont.
1983	Payless, Victoria, BC
1984	Lakers, Peterborough, Ont.
1985	Redmen, Brooklin, Ont.
1986	Salmonbellies, New Westminster, BC
1987	Redmen, Brooklin, Ont.
1988	Redmen, Brooklin, Ont.
1989	Salmonbellies, New Westminster, BC
1990	Redmen, Brooklin, Ont.
1991	Salmonbellies, New Westminster, BC
1992	Excelsiors, Brampton, Ont.
1993	Excelsiors, Brampton, Ont.
1994	Chiefs, Six Nations, Ont.
1995	Chiefs, Six Nations, Ont.
1996	Chiefs, Six Nations, Ont.
1997	Shamrocks, Victoria, BC
1998	Excelsiors, Brampton, Ont.
1999	Shamrocks, Victoria, BC
2000	Redmen, Brooklin, Ont.
2001	Adanacs, Coquitlam, BC

Source: *Canadian Lacrosse Association*

Figure Skating Champions, 1956–2001

	Canadian Champions		World Champions	
	Men	**Women**	**Men**	**Women**
1956	Charles Snelling	Carole Jane Pachl	Hayes Jenkins, US	Carol Heiss, US
1957	Charles Snelling	Carole Jane Pachl	Dave Jenkins, US	Carol Heiss, US
1958	Charles Snelling	Margaret Crosland	Dave Jenkins, US	Carol Heiss, US
1959	Donald Jackson	Margaret Crosland	Dave Jenkins, US	Carol Heiss, US
1960	Donald Jackson	Wendy Griner	Alain Giletti, France	Carol Heiss, US
1961	Donald Jackson	Wendy Griner	—[1]	—[1]
1962	Donald Jackson	Wendy Griner	Don Jackson, Canada	Sjoukje Dijkstra, Neth.
1963	Donald McPherson	Wendy Griner	Don McPherson, Canada	Sjoukje Dijkstra, Neth.
1964	Charles Snelling	Petra Burka	Manfred Schnelldorfer, W. Germany	Sjoukje Dijkstra, Neth.
1965	Donald Knight	Petra Burka	Alain Calmat, France	Petra Burka, Canada
1966	Donald Knight	Petra Burka	Emmerich Danzer, Austria	Peggy Fleming, US
1967	Donald Knight	Valerie Jones	Emmerich Danzer, Austria	Peggy Fleming, US
1968	Jay Humphry	Karen Magnussen	Emmerich Danzer, Austria	Peggy Fleming, US
1969	Jay Humphry	Linda Carbonetto	Tim Wood, US	Gabriele Seyfert, E. Germany
1970	David McGillivray	Karen Magnussen	Tim Wood, US	Gabriele Seyfert, E. Germany
1971	Toller Cranston	Karen Magnussen	Ondrej Nepela, Czech.	Beatrix Schuba, Austria
1972	Toller Cranston	Karen Magnussen	Ondrej Nepela, Czech.	Beatrix Schuba, Austria
1973	Toller Cranston	Karen Magnussen	Ondrej Nepela, Czech.	Karen Magnussen, Canada
1974	Toller Cranston	Lynn Nightingale	Jan Hoffman, E. Germany	Christine Errath, E. Germany
1975	Toller Cranston	Lynn Nightingale	Sergei Volkov, USSR	Dianne de Leeuw, Neth.-US
1976	Toller Cranston	Lynn Nightingale	John Curry, Gr. Brit.	Dorothy Hamill, US
1977	Ron Shaver	Lynn Nightingale	Vladimir Kovalev, USSR	Linda Fratianne, US
1978	Brian Pockar	Heather Kemkaran	Charles Tickner, US	Anett Poetzsch, E. Germany
1979	Brian Pockar	Janet Morrisey	Vladimir Kovalev, USSR	Linda Fratianne, US
1980	Brian Pockar	Heather Kemkaran	Jan Hoffmann, E. Germany	Anett Poetzsch, E. Germany
1981	Brian Orser	Tracey Wainman	Scott Hamilton, US	Denise Biellmann, Switzerland
1982	Brian Orser	Kay Thomson	Scott Hamilton, US	Elaine Zayak, US
1983	Brian Orser	Kay Thomson	Scott Hamilton, US	Rosalyn Sumners, US
1984	Brian Orser	Kay Thomson	Scott Hamilton, US	Katarina Witt, E. Germany
1985	Brian Orser	Elizabeth Manley	Alexandre Fadeev, USSR	Katarina Witt, E. Germany
1986	Brian Orser	Tracey Wainman	Brian Boitano, US	Debi Thomas, US
1987	Brian Orser	Elizabeth Manley	Brian Orser, Canada	Katarina Witt, E. Germany
1988	Brian Orser	Elizabeth Manley	Brian Boitano, US	Katarina Witt, E. Germany
1989	Kurt Browning	Karen Preston	Kurt Browning, Canada	Midori Ito, Japan
1990	Kurt Browning	Lisa Sargeant	Kurt Browning, Canada	Jill Trenary, US
1991	Kurt Browning	Josée Chouinard	Kurt Browning, Canada	Kristi Yamaguchi, US
1992	Michael Slipchuk	Karen Preston	Victor Petrenko, Russia	Kristi Yameguchi, US
1993	Kurt Browning	Josée Chouinard	Kurt Browning, Canada	Oksana Baiul, Ukraine
1994	Elvis Stojko	Josée Chouinard	Elvis Stojko, Canada	Yuka Sato, Japan
1995	Sebastien Britten	Netty Kim	Elvis Stojko, Canada	Lu Chen, China
1996	Elvis Stojko	Jennifer Robinson	Todd Eldredge, US	Michelle Kwan, US
1997	Elvis Stojko	Susan Humphreys	Elvis Stojko, Canada	Tara Lapinski, US
1998	Elvis Stojko	Angela Derochie	Alexei Yagudin, Russia	Michelle Kwan, US
1999	Elvis Stojko	Jennifer Robinson	Alexei Yagudin, Russia	Maria Butyrskaya, Russia
2000	Elvis Stojko	Jennifer Robinson	Alexei Yagudin, Russia	Michelle Kwan, US
2001	Emmanuel Sandhu	Jennifer Robinson	Eugeni Plushenko, Russia	Michelle Kwan, US

Source: *Canadian Figure Skating Association*

(1) The 1961 world championships were cancelled after an air crash killed the entire US team travelling to the competition.

Canadian Open Golf Tournament, 1981–2001

	Winner	Score		Winner	Score
1981	Peter Oosterhuis	280	**1992**	Greg Norman	280
1982	Bruce Lietzke	277	**1993**	David Frost	279
1983	John Cook	277	**1994**	Nick Price	275
1984	Greg Norman	278	**1995**	Mark O'Meara	274
1985	Curtis Strange	279	**1996**	Dudley Hart	202[1]
1986	Bob Murphy	280	**1997**	Steve Jones	275
1987	Curtis Strange	276	**1998**	Billy Andrade	275
1988	Ken Green	275	**1999**	Hal Sutton	275
1989	Steve Jones	271	**2000**	Tiger Woods	266
1990	Wayne Levi	278	**2001**	Scott Verplank	266
1991	Nick Price	273			

Source: *Canadian Press*   (1) Held to 54 holes by bad weather.

Women's British Open[1]

	Winner	Score		Winner	Score		Winner	Score
1981	Debbie Massey	295	**1988**	Corinne Dibnah[2]	295	**1995**	Karrie Webb	278
1982	Marta Figueras-Dotti	296	**1989**	Jane Geddes	274	**1996**	Emilee Klein	277
1983	Not Held		**1990**	Helen Alfredsson[2]	288	**1997**	Karrie Webb	269
1984	Ayako Okamoto	289	**1991**	Penny Grice-Whittaker	284	**1998**	Sherri Steinhauer	292
1985	Betsy King	300	**1992**	Patty Sheehan[3]	207	**1999**	Sherri Steinhauer	283
1986	Laura Davies	283	**1993**	Karen Lunn	275	**2000**	Sophie Gustafson	282
1987	Alison Nicholas	296	**1994**	Liselotte Neumann	280	**2001**	Se Ri Pak	277

Source: *The Ladies Professional Golf Association*   (1) Previously called Ladies British Open Championship (1976–1986).
(2) Won in playoff. (3) Rain shortened.

Lorie Kane has another great year

*L*orie Kane, 37, has been golfing since she was five. She grew up in PEI, studied at Acadia University and lives in Charlottetown. In 1991 she became the Mexican Amateur Champion. She turned professional in 1993, and won the du Maurier Ltd. Series in 1994 and 1995. Her LPGA rookie year was 1995. That year in Titusville, Florida she met Danny Sharpe, and he became her caddy. He and Anne Chouinard make up her teaching team.

In 1997 she won her first Bobbie Rosenfeld Award, which is awarded to Canada's female athlete of the year. In 1998 she won a Heather Farr Player Award. She had 13 top-ten finishes in 1999 and passed a $1 million career earnings mark. She tied with Sherri Steinhauer for the most events played in 2000 (30 starts). She won three events within 10 weeks—the Mizuno Classic, the Albany Golf Classic, and the Michelob Light Classic, where pros sprayed her with beer at the 18th hole. She won the 2000 William and Mousie Powell Award, and in December her second Bobbie Rosenfeld Award. In 2001 she won the Takefuji LPGA Classic. By August 2001, she was approaching a US$3 million career earnings mark. As of October 1, 2001, she was the fourth highest money-earning player in the LPGA tour for the season, and had the fourth highest rounds under par average (57/82). Liberal Shawn Murphy described Lorie succinctly during his House of Commons speech that year by recognising and saluting her as "Canada's premier female golfer."

Professional Golfers Association (PGA), 2001

Major Tournaments	Date	Leaders
The Masters	April 2-8	Tiger Woods
US Open Championship	June 14-17	Retief Goosen
British Open Championship	July 16-22	David Duval
PGA Championship	Aug. 13-19	David Toms

Source: *PGA of America*

2001 PGA Tour Money Leaders

(as of October, 2001)[1]

		Events	Winnings (US$)			Events	Winnings (US$)
1.	Tiger Woods	17	5 517 777	9.	Davis Love III	16	2 360 263
2.	Phil Mickelson	23	4 404 883	10.	David Duvall	17	2 255 294
3.	Vijay Singh	23	3 151 100	11.	Joe Durant	22	2 245 017
4.	Scott Hoch	21	2 794 319	12.	Robert Allenby	25	2 088 232
5.	David Toms	23	2 677 267	13.	Ernie Ells	17	1 951 456
6.	Sergio Garcia	16	2 513 635	14.	Mark Calcavecchia	21	1 893 576
7.	Scott Verplank	23	2 435 700	15.	Brad Faxon	24	1 860 932
8.	Jim Furyk	20	2 374 067	16.	Frank Lickliter II	24	1 833 311

Source: *GolfWeb/SportsLine.com*   (1) Not yet over — ends December 16th.

Ladies Professional Golf Association (LPGA), 2001

Major Tournaments	Date	Leaders
Nabisco Dinah Shore	Mar. 19-25	Annika Sorenstam
LPGA Championship	June 21-24	Karrie Webb
US Open Championship	June 14-17	Karrie Webb
British Open	Aug. 2-5	Se Ri Pak

Source: *USA Today*

2001 LPGA Tour Money Leaders and Canadians

(as of October, 2001)

		Events	Winnings (US$)			Events	Winnings (US$)
1.	Annika Sorenstam	22	1 666 306	9.	Rosie Jones	21	715 010
2.	Se Ri Pak	19	1 451 509	10.	Catriona Matthew	25	689 873
3.	Karrie Webb	20	1 223 904	11.	Wendy Ward	24	656 344
4.	**Lorie Kane**	**23**	**825 634**	12.	Rachel Teske	24	652 353
5.	Maria Hjorth	25	783 363	13.	Emilee Klein	28	552 380
6.	Dottie Pepper	21	741 332	14.	Sophie Gustafson	21	527 242
7.	Mi Hyun Kim	28	732 363	15.	Michele Redman	23	484 266
8.	Laura Diaz	25	715 816	16.	Janice Moodie	24	468 901

Source: *Ladies Professional Golf Association*

The Queen's Plate, 1970–2001

The Queen's Plate, first run in 1860, is North America's oldest annual sports event. The race for 3-year-olds foaled in Canada, is run at Toronto's Woodbine Race Track in late June or July.

	Winner	Jockey	Time		Winner	Jockey	Time
1970	Almoner	Sandy Hawley	2:04.4	1978	Regal Embrace	Sandy Hawley	2:02
1986	Golden Choice	Vince Bracciale	2:07.1	1994	Basqueian	Jack Laron	2:03.4
1971	Kennedy Road	Sandy Hawley	2:03	1979	Steady Growth	Brian Swatuk	2:06.3
1987	Market Control	Ken Skinner	2:03.2	1995	Regal Discovery	Todd Kabel	2:03.4
1972	Victoria Song	Robin Platts	2:03.1	1980	Driving Home	Bill Parsons	2:04.1
1988	Regal Intention	Jack Lauzon	2:06.1	1996	Victor Cooley	Emke Ramsammy	2:03.8
1973	Royal Chocolate	Ted Colangelo	2:08	1981	Fiddle Dancer Boy	David Clark	2:04.4
1989	With Approval	Don Seymour	2:03	1997	Awesome Again	A.E. Smith	2:04
1974	Amber Herod	Robin Platts	2:09.1	1982	Son of Briartic	John-Paul Souter	2:04.3
1990	Izvestia	Don Seymour	2:01.4	1998	Archer's Bay	Kent Desormeaux	2:02.1
1975	L'Enjoleur	Sandy Hawley	2:02.3	1983	Bompago	Larry Attard	2:04.1
1991	Dance Smartly	Pal Day	2:03.2	1999	Woodcarver	Mickey Walls	2:03
1976	Norcliffe	Jeffrey Fell	2:05	1984	Key to the Moon	Robin Platts	2:03.4
1992	Alydeed	Craig Perret	2:04.6	2000	Scatter the Gold	Todd Kabel	1:56.0
1977	Sound Reason	Robin Platts	2:06.3	1985	La Lorgnette	David Clark	2:04.3
1993	Peteski	Craig Perret	2:04.2	2001	Dancethruthedawn	Gary Boulanger	2:03.8

Source: *Woodbine Entertainment Group*

Thoroughbred Racing

Thoroughbred racing's coveted Triple Crown has only been won 11 times: Sir Barton (1919); Gallant Fax (1930); Omaha (1935); War Admiral (1937); Whirlaway (1941); Count Fleet (1943); Assault (1946); Citation (1948); Secretariat (1973); Seattle Slew (1977) and Affirmed (1978). The challenge will be taken up anew in 2002: The Kentucky Derby will be held at Churchill Downs on May 4, 2002; The Preakness Stakes will be held at Pimlico on May 18, 2002; and The Belmont Stakes will be held at Belmont Park on June 8, 2002.

Triple Crown	Date	Winner
Kentucky Derby	May 5, 2001	Monarchos
Preakness Stakes	May 19, 2001	Point Given
Belmont Stakes	June 9, 2001	Point Given

Source: *ESPN Network*

Harness Racing

	Date	Winner	Driver	Time
North American Cup	June 23, 2001	Bettor's Delight	Mike LaChance	1:50.0
Canadian Trotting Classic	June 23, 2001	SJ's Cavier	Robert Blanton Jr.	1:55.2
Maple Leaf Trot	Aug 25, 2001	Plesac	Doug Brown	1:53.4
The Metro Pace	Sept 1, 2001	Mach Three	Mike LaChance	1:51.4
The Canadian Pacing Derby	Sept 15, 2001	Gallo Blue Chip	Daniel Dube	1:49.4

Source: *Woodbine Entertainment Group*

Prince of Wales Stakes, 1961–2001

	Winner	Jockey	Time[1]		Winner	Jockey	Time[1]
1961	Song of Even	Jim Fitzsimmons	2:29.0	**1980**	Allan Blue	Joe Belowus	2:34.4
1962	King Gorm	Hugo Dittfach	2:21.1	**1981**	Cadet Corps	Robin Platts	2:34.4
1963	Canebora	Hugo Dittfach	2:30.3	**1982**	Runaway Groom	Robin Platts	2:38.2
1964	Canadillis	Avelino Gomez	2:35.0	**1983**	Archdeacon	Vince Bracciale	2:32.0
1965	Good Old Mort	S. McComb	2:22.4	**1984**	Val Dansant	John LeBlanc	2:48.3
1966	He's A Smoothie	Hugo Dittfach	2:19.0	**1985**	Imperial Choice	Irwin Driedger	2:34.3
1967	Battling	Hugo Dittfach	2:21.0	**1986**	Golden Choice	Vince Bracciale	2:44.2
1968	Rouletabille	Richard Grubb	2:18.3	**1987**	Coryphee	Brian Swatuk	2:39.3
1969	Sharp-Eyed Quillo	H. Gustines	2:16.3	**1988**	Regal Classic	Sandy Hawley	2:00.1
1970	Almoner	Sandy Hawley	2:19.4	**1989**	With Approval	Don Seymour	1:56.4
1971	New Pro	Jim Kelly	2:15.1	**1990**	Izvestia	Don Seymour	1:56.2
1972	Presidial	John LeBlanc	2:16.3	**1991**	Dance Smartly	Pal Day	1:56.3
1973	Tara Road	Sandy Hawley	2:16.4	**1992**	Benburb	Larry Attard	1:57.2
1974	Rushton's Corsair	Jim Kelly	2:23.2	**1993**	Peteski	Dave Penna	1:34.4
1975	L'Enjoleur	Sandy Hawley	2:32.2	**1994**	Bruce's Mill	Craig Perret	1:53.4
1976	Norcliffe	Jeff Fell	2:30.1	**1995**	Kiridashi	Larry Attard	1:55.0
1977	Dance in Time	Gary Stahlbaum	2:31.4	**1996**	Stephanotis	Mickey Walls	1:55.2
1978	Overskate	Robin Platts	2:34.2	**1997**	Cryptocloser	W. Martinez	1:56
1979	Mass Rally	George Ho Sang	2:33.2	**1998**[2]	Archer's Bay	Robert Landry	1:55.1
				1999	Gandria	Constant Montpellier	1:56.4
				2000	Scatter the Gold	Todd Kabel	1:56.0
				2001	Fantastic Light	Frankie Dettori	2:04.4

Source: *Ontario Jockey Club*   (1) Fractions of a second are in fifths. (2) Held July 25, 1999.

Breeders Stakes, 1961–2001

	Winner	Jockey	Time[1]		Winner	Jockey	Time[1]
1961	Song of Even	Jim Fitzsimmons	2:31.3	**1981**	Social Wizard	George Ho Sang	2:48.4
1962	Crafty Lace	Ron Turcotte	2:52	**1982**	Runaway Groom	Robin Platts	2:32.1
1963	Canebora	Manuel Ycaza	2:32.1	**1983**	Kingsbridge	Robin Platts	2:32.2
1964	Artic Hills	R. Armstrong	2:33.3	**1984**	Bounding Away	David Clark	2:32.3
1965	Good Old Mort	P. Kallai	2:43	**1985**	Crowning Honors	Brian Swatuk	2:50
1966	Titled Hero	Avelino Gomez	2:31.2	**1986**	Carotene	Richard Dos Ramos	2:32.3
1967	Pine Point	Avelino Gomez	2:32.1	**1987**	Hangin On a Star	Dave Penna	2:30
1968	No Parando	John LeBlanc	2:30	**1988**	King's Deputy	Sandy Hawley	2:30.3
1969	Grey Whiz	John LeBlanc	2:29	**1989**	With Approval	Don Seymour	2:29
1970	Mary of Scotland	Richard Grubb	2:38.2	**1990**	Izvestia	Don Seymour	2:33.2
1971	Belle Geste	Noel Turcotte	2:28	**1991**	Dance Smartly	Pal Day	2:31.2
1972	Nice Dancer	Sandy Hawley	2:35.4	**1992**	Blitzer	Don Seymour	2:35.3
1973	Come In Dad	Wayne Green	2:33.3	**1993**	Peteski	Craig Perret	2:30.4
1974	Haymaker's Jig	Robin Platts	2:30.4	**1994**	Basquein	Jack Lauzon	2:47.4
1975	Momigi	Gary Melanson	2:38.1	**1995**	Charlie's Dewan	Craig Perret	2:26.4
1976	Tiny Tinker	Sandy Hawley	2:31.1	**1996**	Chief Bearheart	Mickey Walls	2:28.3
1977	Dance in Time	Gary Stahlbaum	3:01.3	**1997**	John The Magician	Steven Bahen	2:35
1978	Overskate	Robin Platts	2:29.2	**1998**[2]	Pinafore Park	Robert Landry	2:30.1
1979	Bridle Path	Sandy Hawley	2:29.3	**1999**	Free Vacation	Laurie Gulas	2:28.4
1980	Ben Fab	Gary Stahlbaum	2:31.3	**2000**	Lodge Hill	Todd Pletcher	2:28
				2001	Sweetest Thing	James McAleney	2:29.9

Source: *Ontario Jockey Club*   (1) Fractions of a second are in fifths. (2) August 15, 1999.

Auto Racing—1991–2001

Molson Indy

	Toronto				Vancouver		
1991	Michael Andretti	1997	Mark Blundell	1991	Michael Andretti	1997	Alex Zanardi
1992	Michael Andretti	1998	Alex Zanardi	1992	Michael Andretti	1998	Dario Franchitti
1993	**Paul Tracy[1]**	1999	Dario Franchitti	1993	Al Unser Jr.	1999	Juan Montoya
1994	Michael Andretti			1994	Al Unser Jr.		
1995	Michael Andretti	2000	Michael Andretti	1995	Al Unser Jr.	2000	**Paul Tracy[1]**
1996	Adrian Fernandez	2001	Michael Andretti	1996	Michael Andretti	2001	Roberto Moreno

Source: *Canadian Press*

(1) Canadian.

Championship Auto Racing Teams (CART) 2001

(as of October 1, 2001)

	Date	Winner
Tecate Telmex Monterrey Grand Prix	March 11	Cristiano da Matta
Toyota Grand Prix of Long Beach	April 8	Helio Castroneves
Firestone Firehawk 600	April 29	Postponed (safety concern)
Lehigh Valley Grand Prix	May 6	R-Scott Dixon
Firestone Firehawk 500	May 18	Kenny Brack
Miller Lite 225	June 3	Kenny Brack
Tenneco Automotive Grand Prix of Detroit	June 17	Helio Castroneves
Freightliner/G.I. Joe's 200	June 24	Max Papis
Marconi Grand Prix of Cleveland	July 1	Dario Franchitti
Molson Indy	July 15	Michael Andretti
Harrah's 500	July 22	**Patrick Carpentier**
Target Grand Prix	July 29	Kenny Brack
Miller Lite 200	August 12	Helio Castroneves
Motorola 220	August 19	Bruno Junqueira
Molson Indy Vancouver	September 2	Roberto Moreno
German 500	September 15	Kenny Brack
Rockingham 500	September 22	Gil de Ferran

Source: *CART Inc.*

Formula One, 2001

(as of October 1, 2001)

	Date	Winner	Team
Grand Prix of Australia	March 4	Michael Schumacher	Ferrari
Malaysian Grand Prix	March 18	Michael Schumacher	Ferrari
Brazilian Grand Prix	April 1	David Coulthard	McLaren
San Marino Grand Prix	April 15	Ralf Schumacher	Williams
Spanish Grand Prix	April 29	Michael Schumacher	Ferrari
Grand Prix of Austria	May 13	David Coulthard	McLaren
Grand Prix of Monaco	May 27	Michael Schumacher	Ferrari
Canadian Grand Prix	June 10	Ralf Schumacher	Williams
European Grand Prix	June 24	Michael Schumacher	Ferrari
French Grand Prix	July 1	Michael Schumacher	Ferrari
British Grand Prix	July 15	Mika Hakkinen	McLaren
German Grand Prix	July 29	Ralf Schumacher	Williams
Hungarian Grand Prix	Aug 19	Michael Schumacher	Williams
Belgium Grand Prix	Sept 2	Michael Schumacher	Ferrari
Italian Grand Prix	Sept 16	Juan Pablo Montoga	Williams
American Grand Prix	Sept 30	Mika Hakkinen	McLaren

Source: *Formula1.com Ltd.*

Tour de France: Winners, 1982–2001

1982	Bernard Hinault, France	1992	Miguel Indurain, Spain
1983	Laurent Fignon, France	1993	Miguel Indurain, Spain
1984	Laurent Fignon, France	1994	Miguel Indurain, Spain
1985	Bernard Hinault, France	1995	Miguel Indurain, Spain
1986	Greg LeMond, United States	1996	Bjarne Riis, Denmark
1987	Stephen Roche, Ireland	1997	Jan Ullrich, Germany
1988	Pedro Delgado, Spain	1998	Marco Pantani, Italy
1989	Greg LeMond, United States	1999	Lance Armstrong, United States
1990	Greg LeMond, United States	2000	Lance Armstrong, United States
1991	Miguel Indurain, Spain	2001	Lance Armstrong, United States

Source: *sports.excite.com*

2001 UCI[1] World Rankings of Top Canadian Cyclists

■ Road Elite Men

Place	Name	Age	UCI Points
315	Wohlberg, Eric	36	160
317	Fraser, Gord	33	159
338	Barry, Michea	26	148
488	Green, Roland	27	87

■ Road Elite Women

Place	Name	Age	UCI Points
8	Bessette, Lyne	26	340
27	Jeanson, Geneviève	19	158
50	Espeseth, Sandy	38	82
103	Palmer, Sue	34	29

■ Mountain Bike Cross-country — Individual Men

Place	Name	Age	UCI Points
4	Green, Roland	26	1032
15	Hesjedal, Ryder	20	683
22	Kabush, Geoff	23	606
28	Mcgrath, Seamus	24	517
53	Tourville, Eric	27	339
58	Sheppard, Chris	28	307
62	Hestler, Andreas	30	294
83	Toulouse, Mathieu		231
95	Wedge, Peter	28	215
101	Hurley, Bill	33	204

■ Mountain Bike Cross-country — Individual Women

Place	Name	Age	UCI Points
5	Sydor, Alison	34	999
7	Redden, Chrissy	35	941
22	Premont, Marie-Helene	23	494
25	Sinclair, Trish	32	443
26	Tomlinson, Leslie	41	441
65	Bisaro, Kiara	25	207
68	Townsend, Claire	26	204
93	Yew, Ann	26	162
98	Robichaud, Linda	34	159

■ Mountain Bike Downhill — Individual Men

Place	Name	Age	UCI Points
44	Shandro, Andrew	30	283
67	Watson, David	24	166
78	Cseff, Eric	23	150
87	Porter, Trevor	29	128

■ Mountain Bike Downhill — Individual Women

Place	Name	Age	UCI Points
38	Meade, Tera	26	241
40	Allen, Sylvie	28	228
43	Blancher, Lorraine	25	224
62	Haley, Barb	30	134
63	Watanabe, Karey	33	131
69	Boon, Cassandra	22	105
70	Huard, Kin	21	102
71	Gambin, Cecile	32	100
73	Walton, Anne	33	98

Source: *Canadian Cycling Association*

(1) Union cycliste Internationale.

The CONCACAF[1] Gold Cup 2000

The Gold Cup in 2000 was the fifth edition of the soccer tournament to decide the regional champion of the North America, Central America and the Caribbean areas. The tournament ran from February 12-27, 2000 in the USA with matches being played in Miami, San Diego and Los Angeles. There were three guest teams from outside the region in the 2000 tournament: Peru, South Korea and Colombia. They joined nine other teams from the region to form four groups of three in the first round.

■ History

USA and Mexico have dominated the tournament as the two strongest teams of the region and entered the 2000 tournament as favourites. The previous results in the final are:

YEAR	WINNER	LOSER	SCORE
1991	USA	Honduras	0-0, 4-3 on penalties
1993	Mexico	USA	4-0
1996	Mexico	Brazil	2-0
1998	Mexico	USA	1-0

■ Tournament

After the group stage the four first-placed teams played the four second-placed teams in the quarterfinals. Jamaica, World Cup 1998 qualifiers, was knocked out after losing to both Honduras and Colombia. Surprisingly, all the group winners lost, with three-time-champion Mexico beaten by a golden goal by Canada. Colombia won 3-2 on penalties against the USA, the other favourite, and Peru won 5-3 against Honduras in one of the most exciting games of the tournament. The four teams in the semi-finals were surprising and the winners of the matches were Colombia and Canada. In the final, Canada stopped a guest team from winning for the first time with a 2-0 victory.

Group Stage

■ Group A

Feb 12	Colombia 1, Jamaica 0
Feb 14	Honduras 2, Jamaica 0
Feb 16	Honduras 2, Colombia 0

■ Group B

Feb 12	USA 3, Haiti 0
Feb 14	Haiti 1, Peru 1
Feb 16	USA 1, Peru 0

■ Group C

Feb 13	Mexico 4 T & T 0
Feb 15	T & T 4 Guatemala 2
Feb 17	Guatemala 1, Mexico 1

■ Group D

Feb 13	**Costa Rica 2, Canada 2**
Feb 15	**Canada 0, South Korea 0**
Feb 17	South Korea 2, Costa Rica 2

■ Quarter Finals

Feb 19	USA 2, Colombia 2 (2-3 PENALTIES)
Feb 19	Peru 5, Honduras 3
Feb 20	Costa Rica 1 T & T 2
Feb 20	**Mexico 1, Canada 2**

■ Semi Finals

Feb 23	Colombia 2, Peru 1
Feb 24	**Canada 1 T&T 0**

Final (Los Angeles)

Feb 27	**Canada 2, Colombia 0**

■ Top Goalscorer

4 - Carlo Corazzin - Canada
3 - Carlos Pavon - Honduras
2 - Juan Francisco Palencia - Mexico

2 - Roberto Palacios - Peru
2 - Arnold Dwarika - T & T
2 - Cobi Jones - USA

Source: *Street's Soccer Site. Street's Soccer Site was created by Robert Street, and it shows information about the potential stars of the future, the 2000 Olympics, English football and various other statistics, features and soccer news from around the world.*

(1) Confederation of North, Central American and Caribbean Association Football.

FIFA's[1] Confederations' Cup 2001

(Host Nations: Korea, Japan)

As a result of winning the Gold Cup (CONCA-CAF Championship) in February 2000, Canada took part in the Confederations Cup in Japan and Korea in May and June 2001.

Teams

France	World Champions, FIFA World Cup 1998
Brazil	Champions of CONMEBOL, Copa America 1999
Mexico	Defending Champions, FIFA Confederations Cup 1999
Canada	**Champions of CONCACAF, Gold Cup 2000**
Cameroon	Champions of CAF, African Nations Cup 2000
Australia	Champions of OFC, Oceania Nations Cup 2000
Japan	Co-Hosts Nation and Champions of AFC, Asian Cup 2000,
South Korea	Co-Hosts Nation AFC, Asian Cup 2000

■ Group A (Korea)

May 30	France 5, South Korea 0
May 30	Australia 2, Mexico 0
June 1	Australia 1, France 0
June 1	South Korea 2, Mexico 1
June 3	France 4, Mexico 0
June 3	South Korea 1, Australia 0

■ Group B (Japan)

May 31	Brazil 2, Cameroon 0
May 31	**Japan 3, Canada 0**
June 2	**Brazil 0, Canada 0**
June 4	**Cameroon 2, Canada** 0
June 6	Japan 2, Cameroon 0
June 6	Brazil 0, Japan 0

	P	W	D	L	GF	GA	GDif	Pts
France	3	2	0	1	9	1	+8	6
Australia	3	2	0	1	3	1	+2	6
South Korea	3	2	0	1	3	6	-3	6
Mexico	3	0	0	3	1	8	-7	0

	P	W	D	L	GF	GA	GDif	Pts
Japan	3	2	1	0	5	0	+5	7
Brazil	3	1	2	0	2	0	+2	5
Cameroon	3	1	0	2	2	4	-2	3
Canada	**3**	**0**	**1**	**2**	**0**	**5**	**-5**	**1**

Semifinal (Yokohama, Japan)
June 7   Japan 1, Australia 0

Semifinal (Suwon, Korea)
June 7   France 2, Brazil 1

3rd Place (Ulsan, Korea)
June 9   Australia 1, Brazil 0

FINAL (Yokohama, Japan)
June 10   France 1, Japan 0

P = Played. W = Wins. D = Draw. L = Losses.
GF = Goals for. GA = Goals against. GDif = Goal differential.
Pts = Points.

(1) Federation Internationale de Football Association.

Canada's March to the 2003 World Cup

The International Cricket Council (ICC) Trophy

The 2001 ICC Trophy, held in June and July in Toronto, saw the Netherlands crowned champions, surprising runners-up Namibia. Both teams had already earned places for the 2003 World Cup in South Africa. Host **Canada** secured World Cup qualification by beating Scotland in the third place play-off.

Two Canadians Make "Team of the Tournament"

Joe Harris: Joe Harris's inclusion in the team could have been made simply for his effort in leading Canada to the sacred ground of a World Cup berth for the first time in 24 years. But, in reality, his place was sealed by a series of excellent contributions with the bat and a spell of 2-28 that helped to turn the World Cup Qualifying Final against Scotland decisively in his team's favour.

Matches	Runs (Ave)	Best Batting	Wkts (Ave)	Best Bowling	Ct/St
10	329 @ 41.12	79 v USA	2 @ 23.00	2-28 v Sco	1/-

Sanjay Thuraisingam: Particularly to local audiences, pace bowler Sanjay Thuraisingam will always be best remembered for his effort in one match—the winner-take-all World Cup Qualifying Final against Scotland—in the tournament. In truth, though, his decisive five-wicket haul in that contest came on the heels of a series of consistent performances. Before being rested in the team's closing Super League game, the new ball bowler had snared 14 wickets at low cost with a blend of accuracy, impeccable length and subtle variations of pace. His "Man of the Match" winning role in Canada's most important fixture in 22 years only served to confirm his impact.

Matches	Runs (Ave)	Best Batting	Wkts (Ave)	Best Bowling	Ct/St
9	25 @ 4.16	8 v UAE	19 @ 15.00	5-25 v Sco	3/-

■ Canada's Round Robin Results

Toronto, June 28, 2001	**Canada** v Singapore	S'pore 169 (49.3) **Can** 171/1 (34.2)	Canada won by 9 wickets
Toronto, June 30, 2001	**Canada** v Scotland	Scot 201/8 (50) **Can** 189 (49)	Scotland won by 12 runs
Toronto, July 2, 2001	**Canada** v Netherlands	Can 95 (32) NL 98/4 (34.4)	Netherlands won by 6 wickets
Toronto, July 3, 2001	**Canada** v United Arab Emirates	UAE 228/7 (50) **Can** 229/8 (49.4)	Canada won by 2 wickets
Toronto, July 5, 2001	**Canada** v Fiji	**Can** 315/4 (50) Fiji 136 (42.4)	Canada won by 179 runs

■ Super League Stage

Toronto, July 9, 2001	**Canada** v Namibia	**Can** 189 (48) Namib 190/8 (49.3)	Namibia won by 2 wickets
Toronto, July 10, 2001	**Canada** v Denmark	**Can** 161 (47) Dnmrk 136 (47.4)	Canada won by 25 runs
Toronto, July 12, 2001	**Canada** v United States of America	Can 265 (50) USA 144 (38.4)	Canada won by 121 runs
Toronto, July 13, 2001	**Canada** v Ireland	Can 217 (49.5) Ireland 218 (44.4)	Ireland won by 7 wickets

■ World Cup Qualifying Final

Toronto, July 17, 2001	**Canada** v Scotland	Scot 176/9 (50) **Can** 177/5 (39.5)	Canada won by 5 wickets

Source: *Canadian Cricket Association*

Canadian Sports Hall of Fame

(living members as of October 1, 2001)[1]

Anakin, Douglas, bobsled
Arnold, Don, rowing
Athans, George, Jr., water skiing
Aubut, Marcel, hockey builder
Balding, Al, golf
Baldwin, Matt, curling
Bassett-Seguso, Carling, tennis[2]
Baumann, Alex, swimming
Bédard, Myriam, biathlon
Bedard, Robert, tennis
Béliveau, Jean, hockey
Bell, Marilyn, marathon swimming
Bernier, Sylvie, diving
Betger, Jan, curling
Boldt, Arnie, field high jump
Boucher, Gaetan, speed skating
Bower, Johnny, hockey
Box, Ab, football
Boys, Bev, diving
Brasseur, Isabelle, figure skating
Brooks, Lela, speed skating
Brouillard, Lou, boxing
Browning, Kurt, figure skating
Burka, Ellen, figure skating builder
Burka, Petra, figure skating
Burka, Sylvia, speed skating
Cain, Larry, canoeing
Cameron, Michelle, synchro swimming
Carnegie, Herb, hockey[2]
Chuvalo, George, boxing
Cliff, Leslie, swimming
Clifford, Betsy, skiing
Cowan, Gary, golf
Cranston, Toller, figure skating
Crothers, Bill, track mid-distance
D'hondt, Walter, rowing
Dafoe, Frances, figure skating
Day, James, equestrian
Dexter, Glen, yachting
Dionne, Marcel, hockey
Dojack, Paul, football builder
Drake, Clare, hockey builder
Drayton, Jerome, marathon running
Dryden, Ken, hockey
Duguid, Don, curling
Dunnell, Milt, sports broadcaster
Durrelle, Yvon, boxing

Eisler, Lloyd, figure skating
Elder, James, equestrian
Emery, Dr. John, bobsled
Emery, Victor, bobsled
Esaw, Johnny, all-around builder
Esposito, Phil, hockey
Filion, Hervé, harness racing
Fisher, Hugh, canoeing
Fogh, Hans, yachting
Fortier, Sylvie, synchro swimming
Frechette, Sylvie, synchro swimming
Gabriel, Tony, football
Gainey, Bob, hockey
Galbraith, Sheldon, figure skating builder
Gate, George, swimming builder
Gaudaur, Jake, Jr., football builder
Gayford, Tom, equestrian
Geoffrion, Bernard "Boom Boom," hockey
Golab, Tony, football
Graham, Laurie, skiing
Greene, Nancy, skiing
Grenier, Jean, speed skating builder
Gretzky, Wayne, hockey
Gudereit, Marcia, curling
Hall, Glenn, hockey
Hartman, Barney, skeet shooting
Hawley, Sandy, horse racing
Heddle, Kathleen, rowing
Heggtveit, Anne, skiing
Henderson, Paul, hockey
Hepburn, Doug, weightlifting
Hildebrand, Ike, lacrosse
Hiller, John, baseball
Howe, Gordie, hockey
Hull, Bobby, hockey
Hungerford, George W., rowing
Hunter, Bill, builder[2]
Huot, Jules, golf
Hutton, Ralph, swimming
Jackson, Donald, figure skating
Jackson, Dr. Roger, rowing
Jackson, Russ, football
Jelinek, Maria, figure skating
Jelinek, Otto, figure skating
Jenkins, Ferguson, baseball
Josenhans, Andreas, yachting
Kelly, Leonard (Red), hockey

▶

▶ **Kidd**, Bruce, track mid-distance
Kirby, Peter, bobsled
Kreiner, Kathy, skiing
Krol, Joe, football
Kwong, Norm, football
Lafleur, Guy, hockey
Lancaster, Ron, football
Laumann, Silken, rowing
Lee-Gartner, Kerrin, skiing
Lemieux, Mario, hockey
Leonard, Stan, golf
Lessard, Lucille, archery
Lidstone, Dorothy, archery
Loney, Don, football builder
Longden, Johnny, horse racing
Loomer, Lorne, rowing
Lovell, Jocelyn, cycling
Luftspring, Sammy, boxing
MacDonald, Irene, diving
MacDonald, Noel, basketball
MacMillan, Sandy, yachting
Magnussen, Karen, figure skating
Mahovlich, Frank, hockey
Mara, George, multi-sport builder
Martini, Paul, figure skating
McBean, Marnie, rowing
McCusker, Joan, curling
McLarnin, Jimmy, boxing
McPherson, Donald, figure skating
Miles, John C., marathon swimming
Millar, Ian, equestrian
Mitchell, Ray, bowling
Morris, Alwyn, canoeing
Muir, Debbie, synchro swim builder
Nattrass, Susan, trap shooting
Nicholas, Cindy, marathon swimming
Northcott, Ron, curling
O'Donnell, Bill, harness racing
Orr, Robert (Bobby), hockey
Orser, Brian, figure skating
Ottenbrite, Anne, swimming
Parker, Jackie, football
Pashby, Dr. Tom, multi-sport builder[1]
Paul, Robert, figure skating
Peden, Doug, multi-sport
Percy, Karen, skiing
Perry, Gordon, football

Podborski, Steve, skiing
Pollock, Sam, hockey builder
Post, Sandra, golf
Potvin, Denis, hockey[2]
Presley, Gerald, bobsled
Primrose, John, trap shooting
Ramage, Pat, skiing builder
Read, Ken, skiing
Reed, George, football
Richard, Henri, hockey
Richardson, Arnold, curling
Richardson, Ernie, curling
Richardson, Garnet, curling
Richardson, Wes, curling
Robertson, Bruce, swimming
Rogers, Doug, judo
Saunders, Claude, rowing builder
Schmidt, Milt, hockey
Scott, Barbara Ann, figure skating
Shedd, Marjory, badminton
Smith, Graham, swimming
Sorensen, Gerry, skiing
Steen, Dave, decathlon
Stewart, Marlene, golf
Stewart, Ron, football
Storey, R.A. (Red), all-around
Stukus, Annis, football builder
Tanner, Elaine, swimming
Taylor, Ron, baseball
Tewksbury, Mark, swimming
Thom, Linda, pistol shooting
Thompson, James, speedboating builder
Thorburn, Cliff, snooker[2]
Townsend, Cathy, bowling
Turcotte, Ron, horse racing
Underhill, Barbara, figure skating
Van Vliet, Maury, builder
Vanderburg, Helen, synchro swimming
Wagner, Barbara, figure skating
Waldo, Carolyn, synchro swimming
Waples, Keith, harness racing
Weslock, Nick, golf
Wheeler, Lucille, skiing
Whitaker, Brig. Gen. Denis, equestrian builder
Wilson, Bruce, soccer
Worrall, Jim, builder
Young, Michael, bobsled

Source: *Canadian Sports Hall of Fame*
(1) For a complete listing of all members, visit http://home.inforamp.net/~cshof.
(2) New members in 2001.

QUICK REFERENCE

Temperature Equivalents

(Celsius and Fahrenheit)

°C	°F	°C	°F	°C	°F	°C	°F	°C	°F
-50	-58	-30	-22	-10	14	10	50	30	86
-49	-56.2	-29	-20.2	-9	15.8	11	51.8	31	87.8
-48	-54.4	-28	-18.4	-8	17.6	12	53.6	32	89.6
-47	-52.6	-27	-16.6	-7	19.4	13	55.4	33	91.4
-46	-50.8	-26	-14.8	-6	21.2	14	57.2	34	93.2
-45	-49	-25	-13	-5	23	15	59	35	95
-44	-47.2	-24	-11.2	-4	24.8	16	60.8	36	96.8
-43	-45.4	-23	-9.4	-3	26.6	17	62.6	37	98.6
-42	-43.6	-22	-7.6	-2	28.4	18	64.4	38	100.4
-41	-41.8	-21	-5.8	-1	30.2	19	66.2	39	102.2
-40	-40	-20	-4	0	32	20	68	40	104
-39	-38.2	-19	-2.2	1	33.8	21	69.8	41	105.8
-38	-36.4	-18	-0.4	2	35.6	22	71.6	42	107.6
-37	-34.6	-17	1.4	3	37.4	23	73.4	43	109.4
-36	-32.8	-16	3.2	4	39.2	24	75.2	44	111.2
-35	-31	-15	5	5	41	25	77	45	113
-34	-29.2	-14	6.8	6	42.8	26	78.8	50	122
-33	-27.4	-13	8.6	7	44.6	27	80.6	100	212
-32	-25.6	-12	10.4	8	46.4	28	82.4	150	302
-31	-23.8	-11	12.2	9	48.2	29	84.2	200	392

Household Measures, Metric Equivalents

Volume

Imperial	Metric	Imperial	Metric	Imperial	Metric
1/4 tsp	1 mL	1/4 cup	50 mL	4 cups	1 L
1/2 tsp	2 mL	1/3 cup	75 mL	5 cups	1.25 L
3/4 tsp	4 mL	1/2 cup	125 mL	6 cups	1.5 L
1 tsp	5 mL	2/3 cup	150 mL	7 cups	1.75 L
2 tsp	10 mL	3/4 cup	175 mL	8 cups	2 L
1 tbsp (3 tsp)	15 mL	1 cup	250 mL		

Weight

Imperial	Metric	Imperial	Metric	Imperial	Metric
1 oz	25 g	1/2 lb.	250 g	1 3/4 lb.	875 g
2 oz	50 g	2/3 lb.	350 g	2.2 lb	1 kg
3 oz	75 g	3/4 lb.	375 g	3 lb.	1.5 kg
1/4 lb.	125 g	1 lb.	500 g	5 lb.	2.2 kg
1/3 lb.	175 g	1 1/2 lb.	750 g	10 lb.	4.5 kg

Oven Temperatures

Imperial (°F)	Metric (°C)	Imperial (°F)	Metric (°C)	Imperial (°F)	Metric (°C)
250	120	350	180	450	230
275	135	375	190	475	245
300	150	400	200	500	260
325	160	425	220		

Canadian Imperial and Metric Measures

Name	Abbrev.	Equivalent in Related Units	Metric Equivalent
■ Length			
inch	in.	—	2.54 cm
foot	ft.	12 in.	30.48 cm
yard	yd.	3 ft.; 36 in.	0.91 m
mile	mi.	1 760 yd.; 5 280 ft.	1.609 km
■ Mass (Weight)			
grain	gr.	—	0.06 g
dram	dr.	27.343 gr.	1.77 g
ounce	oz.	16 dr.	28.35 g
pound	lb.	16 oz.	0.453 kg
hundredweight			
(short)	cwt.	100 lb.	45.36 kg
(long)	cwt.	112 lb.	50.80 kg
ton (short)	—	2 000 lb.	0.907 t
ton (long)	—	2 240 lb.	1.016 t
■ Volume and Capacity			
fluid dram	fl. dr.	0.22 cu. in.	3.55 cm^3
fluid ounce	fl. oz.	8 fl. dr.; 1.7 cu. in.	28.41 cm^3
pint	pt.	20 fl. oz.; 34.7 cu. in.	568.3 cm^3
quart	qt.	2 pt.; 69.4 cu. in.	1.14 dm^3
gallon	gal.	4 qt.; 277 cu. in.	4.55 dm^3
peck	pk.	2 gal.; 555 cu. in.	9.09 dm^3
bushel	bu.	4 pk.; 2 219 cu. in.	36.37 dm^3
barrel (oil)	bbl	35 gal.	0.159 m^3
cubic foot	ft.^{3}	1 728 in.^{3}	0.028 m^3
cubic yard	yd.^{3}	27 ft.^{3}	0.765 m^3
■ Area			
square foot	ft.^{2}	144 sq. in.	0.09 m^2
square yard	yd.^{2}	9 sq. ft.	0.836 m^2
acre	—	4 840 sq. yd.	4 047 m^2
square mile	sq. mi.	640 acres	2.590 km^2

Source: *Gage Canadian Dictionary*

Roman Numerals

I	1	VII	7	XX	20	C	100	$\overline{V}$	5 000
II	2	VIII	8	XXX	30	CC	200	$\overline{X}$	10 000
III	3	IX	9	XL	40	CD	400	$\overline{L}$	50 000
IV	4	X	10	L	50	D	500	$\overline{C}$	100 000
V	5	XI	11	LX	60	CM	900	$\overline{D}$	500 000
VI	6	XIX	19	XC	90	M	1 000	$\overline{M}$	1 000 000

Canada's Food Guide To Healthy Eating[1]

Canada's Food Guide, revised in November of 1992, recognizes that the amount of food each Canadian needs every day from the four food groups and other foods depends on age, body size, activity level, whether the individual is male or female, and if the individual is pregnant or breast-feeding. That's why the Food Guide gives a range of possible servings for each food group—young children can choose the lower number of recommended servings from a particular group, while male teenagers can go to the higher number. Most other people can choose servings somewhere in between.

Canada's Food Guide recommends, every day:

■ 5 to 12 servings from the grain products group. An example of one serving would be one slice of bread; 30 g of cold cereal or 175 mL of hot cereal. Two servings would be a bagel, pita or bun; or 250 mL of rice or pasta.

■ 5 to 10 servings of vegetables and fruit.

One serving would be one medium size vegetable or fruit; 125 mL of fresh, frozen or canned vegetables or fruit; 250 mL of salad; or 125 mL of juice.

■ 2 to 3 servings of meat or alternatives. One serving would be 50-100 g of meat, poultry or fish; 1-2 eggs; 125-250 mL of beans; 100 g of tofu; or 30 mL of peanut butter.

■ Recommended servings of milk products vary according to age: 2-3 servings for children aged 4-9; 3-4 servings for young people aged 10-16; 2-4 servings for adults; and 3-4 servings for pregnant or breast-feeding women. Examples of one serving would be 250 mL of milk, 50 g of cheese or 175 g of yogurt.

Taste and enjoyment can also come from other foods and beverages that are not part of the four food groups. Some of these foods are higher in fat or calories, so it is recommended that these foods be used in moderation. The important things to remember are: enjoy a variety of foods from each group every day and choose lower-fat foods more often.

Source: *Health and Welfare Canada*

(1) For people four years and over.

Functions of Nutrients

Calcium aids in the formation and maintenance of strong bones and teeth; promotes healthy nerve function and normal blood clotting.

Carbohydrate supplies energy; assists in the utilization of fats.

Fat supplies energy; aids in the absorption of fat-soluble vitamins.

Fibre provides undigestible bulk, which encourages the normal elimination of body wastes.

Folacin (folic acid) aids red blood cell formation.

Iodine aids in function of the thyroid gland.

Iron combines with protein to form hemoglobin, the red blood cell constituent that transports oxygen and carbon dioxide.

Magnesium aids in formation and maintenance of strong bones and teeth; aids in energy metabolism and tissue formation.

Phosphorus aids in formation and maintenance of strong bones and teeth.

Protein builds and repairs body tissues; builds antibodies, the blood components that fight infection.

Riboflavin (vitamin B_2) maintains healthy skin and eyes; maintains a normal nervous system; releases energy to body cells during metabolism.

Thiamin (vitamin B_1) releases energy from carbohydrate; aids normal growth and appetite.

Vitamin A aids normal bone and tooth development; promotes good night vision; maintains the health of skin and membranes.

Vitamin B_{12} (cobalamin) aids in red blood cell formation; maintains healthy nerve and gastrointestinal tissues.

Vitamin C (ascorbic acid) maintains healthy teeth and gums; maintains strong vessel walls.

Vitamin E (tocopherol) protects the fat in body tissues from oxidation.

Zinc aids in energy and metabolism and tissue formation.

Source: *Canada's Food Guide Handbook*

Health   Santé
Canada   Canadá

CANADA'S
Food Guide
TO HEALTHY EATING
**FOR PEOPLE FOUR YEARS
AND OVER**

Enjoy a variety
of foods from each
group every day.

Choose lower-
fat foods
more often.

2%

SKIM

Grain Products
Choose whole grain
and enriched
products more often.

Vegetables and Fruit
Choose dark green and
orange vegetables and
orange fruit more often.

Milk Products
Choose lower-fat milk
products more often.

Meat and Alternatives
Choose leaner meats,
poultry and fish, as well
as dried peas, beans
and lentils more often.

Canada

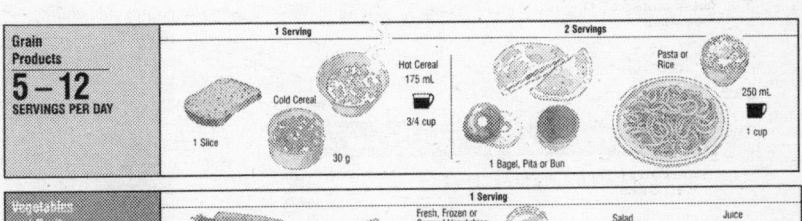

Grain Products
5 – 12
SERVINGS PER DAY

1 Serving — 1 Slice — Cold Cereal 30 g — Hot Cereal 175 mL 3/4 cup

2 Servings — 1 Bagel, Pita or Bun — Pasta or Rice 250 mL 1 cup

Vegetables and Fruit
5 – 10
SERVINGS PER DAY

1 Serving — 1 Medium Size Vegetable or Fruit — Fresh, Frozen or Canned Vegetables or Fruit 125 mL 1/2 cup — Salad 250 mL 1 cup — Juice 125 mL 1/2 cup

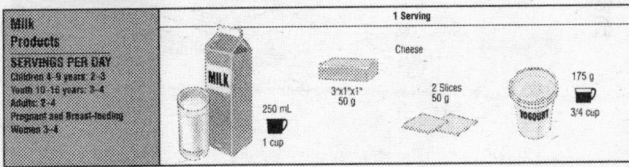

Milk Products
SERVINGS PER DAY
Children 4-9 years: 2-3
Youth 10-16 years: 3-4
Adults: 2-4
Pregnant and Breast-feeding Women 3-4

1 Serving — MILK 250 mL 1 cup — Cheese 3"x1"x1" 50 g — 2 Slices 50 g — 175 g 3/4 cup

Other Foods

Taste and enjoyment can also come from other foods and beverages that are not part of the 4 food groups. Some of these foods are higher in fat or Calories, so use these foods in moderation.

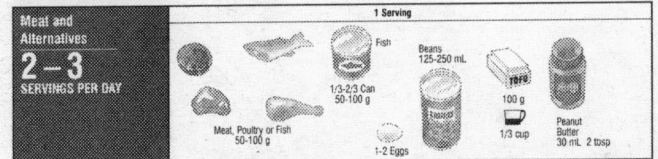

Meat and Alternatives
2 – 3
SERVINGS PER DAY

1 Serving — Meat, Poultry or Fish 50-100 g — Fish 1/3-2/3 Can 50-100 g — Beans 125-250 mL — 1-2 Eggs — TOFU 100 g 1/3 cup — Peanut Butter 30 mL 2 tbsp

Different People Need Different Amounts of Food

The amount of food you need every day from the 4 food groups and other foods depends on your age, body size, activity level, whether you are male or female and if you are pregnant or breast-feeding. That's why the Food Guide gives a lower and higher number of servings for each food group. For example, young children can choose the lower number of servings, while male teenagers can go to the higher number. Most other people can choose servings somewhere in between.

Consult *Canada's Physical Activity Guide to Healthy Active Living* to help you build physical activity into your daily life.

Enjoy eating well, being active and feeling good about yourself. That's VITALIT

© Minister of Public Works and Government Services Canada, 1997
Cat. No. H39-252/1992E   ISBN 0-662-19648-1
No changes permitted. Reprint permission not required.

In 1997, Federal, Provincial and Territorial Ministers responsible for fitness, active living, recreation and sport recognized physical inactivity as a serious health issue and set a target to reduce inactivity by 10 percent by 2003. In response, Health Canada and partners launched "Canada's Physical Activity Guide to Healthy Active Living" in 1998, our first-ever set of national guidelines designed to help Canadians improve their health through regular physical activity. In 1999, "Canada's Physical Activity Guide for Older Adults" was launched. To order free copies of both Guides, call toll free 1-888-334-9769, or visit the Guide's Web site (http://www.paguide.com).

CANADA'S
Physical Activity Guide
to Healthy Active Living

Physical activity improves health.

Every little bit counts, but more is even better – everyone can do it!

Get active your way – build physical activity into your daily life...

* at home
* at school
* at work
* at play
* on the way

...that's active living!

Increase Endurance Activities

Increase Flexibility Activities

Increase Strength Activities

Reduce Sitting for long periods

Health Canada   Santé Canada

Canadian Society for Exercise Physiology

Choose a variety of activities from these three groups:

Endurance

4-7 days a week
Continuous activities for your heart, lungs and circulatory system.

Flexibility

4-7 days a week
Gentle reaching, bending and stretching activities to keep your muscles relaxed and joints mobile.

Strength

2-4 days a week
Activities against resistance to strengthen muscles and bones and improve posture.

Starting slowly is very safe for most people. Not sure? Consult your health professional.

For a copy of the *Guide Handbook* and more information:
1-888-334-9769, or
www.paguide.com

Eating well is also important. Follow *Canada's Food Guide to Healthy Eating* to make wise food choices.

Get Active Your Way, Every Day—For Life!

Scientists say accumulate 60 minutes of physical activity every day to stay healthy or improve your health. As you progress to moderate activities you can cut down to 30 minutes, 4 days a week. Add-up your activities in periods of at least 10 minutes each. Start slowly... and build up.

Time needed depends on effort

Very Light Effort	Light Effort 60 minutes	Moderate Effort 30-60 minutes	Vigorous Effort 20-30 minutes	Maximum Effort
• Strolling • Dusting	• Light walking • Volleyball • Easy gardening • Stretching	• Brisk walking • Biking • Raking leaves • Swimming • Dancing • Water aerobics	• Aerobics • Jogging • Hockey • Basketball • Fast swimming • Fast dancing	• Sprinting • Racing

Range needed to stay healthy

You Can Do It – Getting started is easier than you think

Physical activity doesn't have to be very hard. Build physical activities into your daily routine.

* Walk whenever you can – get off the bus early, use the stairs instead of the elevator.
* Reduce inactivity for long periods, like watching TV.
* Get up from the couch and stretch and bend for a few minutes every hour.
* Play actively with your kids.
* Choose to walk, wheel or cycle for short trips.

* Start with a 10 minute walk – gradually increase the time.
* Find out about walking and cycling paths nearby and use them.
* Observe a physical activity class to see if you want to try it.
* Try one class to start – you don't have to make a long-term commitment.
* Do the activities you are doing now, more often.

Benefits of regular activity:

* better health
* improved fitness
* better posture and balance
* better self-esteem
* weight control
* stronger muscles and bones
* feeling more energetic
* relaxation and reduced stress
* continued independent living in later life

Health risks of inactivity:

* premature death
* heart disease
* obesity
* high blood pressure
* adult-onset diabetes
* osteoporosis
* stroke
* depression
* colon cancer

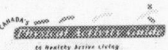

Laundry Care Symbols

The Canadian Care Labelling Program is a voluntary one that provides consumer information on the care of textiles, usually clothing. It uses five basic symbols, illustrated in the conventional "traffic light" colours. The program takes into consideration the fabric's colourfastness (i.e. whether the dye will bleed into the water and other clothing); whether it will shrink or stretch; how bleach will affect the garment; and how it may be ironed safely.

This labelling program does not apply to upholstered furniture, mattresses, carpets, leather, fur, or yarn.

The basic symbols represent washing, bleaching, drying, ironing and drycleaning, and the colours represent stop/do not (red), be careful (yellow), and go ahead (green). The red/crossed out symbol is only used when the procedure would damage the article.

Symbol	Red — Stop	Yellow — Be careful	Green — Go ahead
Washing	Do not wash	Hand wash in cool water; Machine wash in cool water at a gentle setting—reduced agitation (30°C); Machine wash in lukewarm water at a gentle setting—reduced agitation (40°C); Machine wash in warm water at a gentle setting—reduced agitation (50°C)	Machine wash in warm water at a normal setting (50°C); Machine wash in hot water at a normal setting (70°C)
Bleaching	Do not use chlorine bleach	Use chlorine bleach with care	
Drying		Dry flat; Tumble dry at low temperature	Tumble dry at medium to high temperature; Hang to dry; Drip dry
Ironing	Do not iron	Iron at low setting (110°C); Iron at medium setting (150°C)	Iron at high setting (200°C)
Dry Cleaning	Do not dry clean	Dry clean—with caution	Dry clean

Product Safety Symbols

Health Canada has devised a set of safety symbols for containers of household chemicals and other materials. These symbols indicate possible hazards associated with various products such as cleaning liquids and powders, paint thinners, drain cleaners, windshield washer fluids and polishes, as well as some glues and treatments for household surfaces such as brick and metal, and garden chemicals.

The symbols indicate the type of danger and are contained in a frame that indicates the degree of danger—the more sides the frame has, the more dangerous the product is. In addition to the symbols, the labels on most of these containers include a safety warning. Learn the symbols opposite and handle the materials with care, especially if children live in the home or visit often.

Follow these steps to Safety:

- Teach children that the symbols mean Danger! Do Not Touch!
- Chemical product containers, even if sealed or empty, are not toys. Never let children play with them.
- If there is anything in the label instructions that you don't understand, ask for help. Make sure the symbols and labels on containers are not removed or covered up.
- Keep household chemicals in their original containers. Never mix them together. Some mixtures can produce harmful gases.
- Close the cap on the container tightly, even if you set it down for just a moment. Make sure that child-resistant containers are working.
- Keep all chemical products out of sight and out of reach of children.

Corrosive: the product can burn skin or eyes, and if swallowed, will damage the throat and stomach.

Explosive: the container can explode if heated or punctured. Flying pieces of metal or plastic from the container can cause serious injury, especially to the eyes.

Flammable: the product or its vapous will catch fire easily if it is near heat, flames or sparks

Poison: if the product is swallowed, licked or even, in some cases inhaled, it can cause sickness or death

If someone is injured:

- Call your doctor or the Poison Control Centre immediately.
- Give the information from the label to the person answering.
- Take the container with you when you go for help.

CANADIAN IDENTITY

Canadian identification includes birth certificates, Social Insurance Numbers and health cards at a minimum, plus passports. These documents are necessary to prove identity (including citizenship) or establish eligibility for social benefits.

■ Birth certificate

A birth certificate is the document that initially establishes legal identity. Individuals should be registered at birth; the Canadian certificate that is issued is necessary to obtain health cards, SINs and passports. Foreign birth certificates are also the starting point for establishing identity or eligibility in Canada.

If you need to register a birth or replace a lost Canadian birth certificate, contact the Vital Statistics department of your provincial government.

■ Social Insurance Number (SIN)

Social Insurance Numbers are issued by Human Resources Development Canada. The nine-digit number identifies you for taxation, premiums (and payments) for pensions and employment insurance. The SIN is also used as a form of identification when applying for jobs or gaining admittance to an academic program.

How do you get a SIN? Apply for one in person at a Human Resources Centre (check the blue pages in your local telephone book for the office nearest you) or by mail. You can obtain the form by downloading it from HRDC's web site (http://www.hrdc-drhc.gc.ca).

You must fully complete the application with your name, date of birth, place of birth and your mother's and father's birth names. You must also provide the original (or a certified copy) of the document(s) that prove your identity and your status in Canada. If you are a Canadian citizen born in Canada, you may use your birth certificate or passport; in Quebec and Newfoundland, a baptismal certificate is also acceptable. If you are a Canadian citizen born outside the country, a Certificate of Canadian Citizenship or a valid passport is required. A Permanent Resident can use a Canadian Immigration Record and Visa or Record of Landing, a Confirmation of Landing Document, a Canada Travel Document, a Canadian Certificate of Identity, a foreign passport stamped "Permanent Resident" by Canada Immigration or a Returning Resident Permit.

If the name you currently use is different from the name on the original documents, you must also supply evidence that your name was legally changed either by marriage/divorce or by law.

If the card is lost or stolen, notify the local HRDC office immediately. The staff will advise you of the steps needed to protect yourself from SIN fraud. (This usually takes the form of someone else applying for government benefits under your name. SIN fraud is also defined as: knowingly applying for more than one SIN; using someone else's number to obtain financial benefits or establish an identity; loaning or selling a SIN or card to another party; or manufacturing a SIN card.)

■ Canadian Passports

The best of proof of citizenship when you are travelling outside Canada is a valid passport. It is the only proof that is accepted in all countries. While passports are not officially required for entry into the US, many Canadians have been stopped for failure to have photo identification and proof of citizenship. In the aftermath of the September 11, 2001 terrorist bombings, the possession of valid and trusted identification will become even more important. Passports can be useful when cashing travellers' cheques or completing legal transactions in the US, and a passport is essential if the US is only one stop in a multi-destination tour.

Any Canadian citizen may obtain a passport. The passport is good for five years; it cannot be renewed or extended. Make sure that you will be back home before the expiry date. (Some countries will not allow entry unless the passport is valid long after you plan to return home.) Many countries require a visa in addition to a valid passport. Always check with your travel agent, the Department of Foreign Affairs or that country's representative (listed in "Nations of the World") before you leave home, to ensure you have all of the required documentation.

How do you get a passport? Application forms are available at post offices and passport offices (there are 28 of them across the country). The form requires basic information about birth, citizenship, marital status and residence, in addition to two copies of a passport photo, which must conform to specific requirements relating to size and type of shot. (Passport photos can be obtained at many photo supply stores as well as other outlets. They can be in black and white or colour. Family snapshots are not suitable.)

The completed form must be witnessed by a "guarantor": someone who has known you for at least two years and can attest to the truth of the information submitted. A guarantor must come from a recognized profession such as engineering, medicine or clergy or be in a senior administrative position in an academic or financial institution.

A passport is a valuable document—traffic in stolen passports is brisk and they can be used to assist in illegal activities. To ensure your passport is safe, consider locking it up when away from home—many hotels offer safe places for valuables. Carry a photocopy with you as a back-up document. If you carry your passport with you, check for it and other valuables at least once a day. You have a better chance of retracing your steps to find a misplaced passport (or reporting a stolen credit card before too much damage is done to your credit line) if it has been missing for less than 24 hours.

While it is your responsibility to protect your passport and other valuables during your trip, the nearest Canadian diplomatic or consular mission can help if your passport is lost or stolen. The loss must also be reported to the local police. (The same applies if your passport is lost or stolen at home. The police must be notified as well as the nearest passport office.)

Canada's Department of Foreign Affairs and International Trade (DFAIT) maintains a network of 250 offices, embassies, high commissions, consulates, honorary consuls and development offices in over 180 countries.

(Australian diplomatic officers provide services where Canada does not have a presence.) For a list of Canadian representation abroad, consult the country-by-country listings in "Nations of the World." The offices are also listed in a government booklet entitled *Bon Voyage, But....*

Should you become ill, incapacitated or a victim of crime (or arrested), consular staff can provide assistance. In addition, emergency services can be obtained by calling (613) 996-8885 at any time. (Collect calls will be accepted.)

■ Pre-trip Planning

Make sure that you have **proper identification** before you go away, plus any required **visas**. Take out-of-country **medical insurance** and enough medication or other medical appliances you may require; it may be difficult to replace them—"common" items can be hard to find in some places.

Check to see if any **Travel Advisories** have been issued for travellers abroad. Call 1-800-575-2500 or visit the government's web site at http://www.voyage.gc.ca. Choose your preferred language, then select "Country Travel Reports." Travel advisories can cover anything from the local political situation to an outbreak of Yellow Fever.

The events of September 11, 2001 have resulted in increased security checks of both travellers and belongings. If you are travelling by air or crossing into the US, give yourself extra time to clear security checks. Ensure that you can answer detailed questions about your belongings and provide quick access to everything. There will be random, thorough checks. No sharp objects of any kind will be allowed in aircraft cabins and casual joking about threats will be taken seriously. In addition, Foreign Affairs suggests that, if at all possible, detailed travel plan information should be left with family or friends in Canada.

Planning to Work Abroad?

*A*s the Department of Foreign Affairs and International Trade notes, all countries have prohibitions concerning foreigners working without special permission. The permission to work abroad is usually in the form of a **work visa** that must be obtained before entering the country. Most countries will not grant permission for a foreigner to work if that person entered the country as a tourist or on some other basis.

The DFAIT brochure "Working Abroad: Unravelling the Maze" provides advice and guidance about the preparations that are necessary.

Canadian Postal Rates

(as of April 21, 2001)

Within Canada		
Lettermail and postcards (letter size max. 245 mm x 150 mm x 5 mm)	0-29 g	$0.47[1]
	30-50 g	$0.75[1]
Non-standard and oversize items (max. 380 mm x 270 mm x 20 mm)	0-100 g	$0.94
	101-200 g	$1.55
	201-500 g	$2.05
Registered mail		$4.00 plus applicable postage

To the USA		
Lettermail and postcards (airmail) (letter size max. 245 mm x 150 mm x 5 mm)	0-30 g	$0.60
	31-50 g	$0.85
Non-standard and oversize items (max. 38 mm x 270 mm x 20 mm)	0-100 g	$1.30
	101-200 g	$2.45
	201-500 g	$4.20
Registered mail		$4.00 plus applicable postage

Note: GST is applicable to all postal charges. Other services for parcels, bulk mailings or expedited delivery are also available.
(1) Surcharges apply if mail is not coded. Postal rates for uncoded letter 0–29g: $0.60; 30–50g: $0.86.

■ What's the best way to address an envelope?

A wide variety of packages and styles of address make it through Canada Post's system, however there are ways to ensure that your mail is handled most efficiently. While the computerized systems can read a range of addresses—including handwriting—the system's preferred style is as follows:

Line 1: name of the recipient
Line 2: title, floor number, attention line
Line 3: If business, company name
Line 4: unit number (if applicable) –
street number and name
If post office box, information should appear above municipality name
Line 5: municipality, province   postal code

While the system can read upper and lower case, upper case is preferred, with an aligned left margin. Address lines should be less than 40 characters long. The first three elements of the postal code should be separated from the final three by a space, never a hyphen.

The return address should be formatted the same way, in the upper left corner (or on the back at the top). If on the front, it should be clearly separated from the destination address and preferably be smaller than the destination address.

Characters should be larger than 2 mm and smaller than 5 mm (10 to 12 point).

When addressing mail to the United States, the US Postal Service prefers the use of the two-character state symbol rather than having the name of the state spelled out. The ZIP code should come two spaces after the state code and appear on the same line. The final line should be USA. When addressing international mail, the name of the country should be spelled out in full (GREAT BRITAIN) and should appear on the last line of the address, below any other municipality, city name or code information.

■ Province and Territory Symbols

The two-character symbols have been designated by Canada Post in order to make mailing more efficient. The codes for Canada's ten provinces and three territories are:

Newfoundland	NF
Prince Edward Island	PE
Nova Scotia	NS
New Brunswick	NB
Quebec	QC
Ontario	ON
Manitoba	MB
Saskatchewan	SK
Alberta	AB
British Columbia	BC
Yukon Territory	YT
Northwest Territories	NT
Nunavut	NT

Source: *Canada Post*

October 1, 2000–September 30, 2001

AALIYAH (b. Aaliyah Haughton), 22. Budding R & B singer whose "If Your Girl Only Knew" went double platinum in 1996. Her acting career including a starring role in the film *The Queen of the Damned*. Died in a plane crash in the Bahamas. August 25, 2001.

ADAMS, Douglas Noel, 49. British author of *The Hitchhiker's Guide to the Galaxy*, a satirical, humorous tale about interplanetary travel; the *Guide* started out as a BBC radio show, was published in book format, and became the subject of a television series. May 11, 2001.

ALLEN, Steve, 78. Star of the original *Tonight Show* and later of the *Steve Allen Show*, Allen was a noted comic, performer, songwriter and author. In 1956 he starred in the film *The Benny Goodman Story;* from 1976-79 he was moderator on the series *Meeting of Minds*. October 30, 2000.

ASPIN, Tony, 31. PEI sculptor whose massive *Canadian Tree* project was displayed at the Confederation Centre of the Arts in Charlottetown, and toured across Canada. The "tree" was decorated with nationalistic artefacts, many of which were donated by well-known contributors, such as Peter Gzowski and Margaret Atwood. August 17, 2001.

ATKINS, Chester Burton (Chet), 77. An American guitarist and record producer who transformed country music in Nashville during the 1950s, Atkins was noted for his versatility in genres that included religious, jazz and classical music. He is credited with launching the careers of Dolly Parton, Waylon Jennings and Charlie Pride, among other notables. June 30, 2001.

BANDARANAIKE, Sirimavo, 84. World's first woman prime minister, Bandaranaike became prime minister of Sri Lanka in 1960, ruling to 1965, and was reelected in 1970, holding the position until 1980. October 10, 2000.

BARNARD, Christian Neethling, 78. Pioneer South African heart surgeon who performed the first heart transplant in 1967 in Cape Town, transferring the heart of a woman into a man. A fervent critic of the apartheid system in South Africa, he also made inroads by allowing black and white nurses to work alongside him, and by replacing the heart of a black man with one from a white woman. September 2, 2001.

BERLIN, Boris, 94. Teacher to many of Canada's leading pianists, Berlin was associated with Toronto's Royal Conservatory of Music since 1928. Author and co-author of widely used pedagogical texts. *The Modern Piano Student; Basics of Ear Training*. March 24, 2001.

BESRE, Jean, 64. Québécois stage and television performer and screenwriter, Besré was hugely popular for his role in Quebec's long-running television series *Jamais deux sans toi;* he appeared in children's television series, on stage (*Hamlet, Tartuffe*) and in the television series *La P'tite Semaine*. March 14, 2001.

BIRENDRA, King of Nepal, 55. Popular Nepalese king was murdered, along with his wife, Queen Aiswarya, and six family members, by his son, Crown Prince Dipendra, who later committed suicide; the killings were thought to be the result of a family quarrel. June 1, 2001.

BLACKBURN, Clyde Robert, 74. Veteran newspaper journalist whose work appeared in the *Ottawa Citizen*, the *Toronto Telegram* and the *Toronto Sun*; specialized as a television columnist. November 26, 2000.

BORGE, Victor (b. Borge Rosenbaum), 91. Danish-born pianist and conductor, Borge was beloved for his *Comedy in Music* show, which he performed both live and on television. His humorous and irreverent approach to the great composers led him to perform routines such as imagined renditions of Happy Birthday by Bach and Beethoven. Borge always treated the audience to his accomplished talent as a classical pianist after the laughter died down. December 23, 2000.

BRAUN, Victor, 65. Baritone opera singer who debuted in 1957 with the Canadian Opera Company, later performed at the New York Metropolitan Opera, Covent Garden and other international venues. Noted for his solid classical and modern repertoire; recorded the works of Schubert, Wagner and Schumann. January 6, 2001.

BREWER, Carl, 62. A talented NHL defenceman, Brewer played on three Stanley Cup wins with the Toronto Maple Leafs and was four times on the all-stars team; he was also instrumental in the downfall of Alan Eagleson, formerly the head of the NHL Players' Association. August 25, 2001.

BROOKS, Gwendolyn, 83. American poet who was the first black woman to win the Pulitzer Prize, in 1950, for her second book, *Annie Allen*. Illinois' poet laureate since 1968, Brooks focused on cultural themes of black society in America. December 3, 2000.

BROWER, David, 88. The Sierra Club's executive director from 1952-69, Brower, an environmental activist, influenced the club's growth from its hiking club roots to become a major voice in the environmental movement. Later headed Friends of the Earth and the League of Conservation Voters. November 5, 2000.

BRYDSON, George D., 94. Gentlemanly golf pro, winner of 1944 Canadian Professional Golfers Association championship and the 1944 Ontario Open; also played professional hockey and briefly with the Toronto Argonauts football team. February 4, 2001.

BUCHWOLD, Sidney, 84. Mayor of Saskatoon, Sask., for three terms, Buchwold was a pioneer in municipal projects and urban renewal; he was appointed to the Senate in 1971 and led a senate committee in 1990 that surveyed Canadians' opinions of the GST, of which he was a fervent critic. June 27, 2001.

CALLAWAY, Ely, 82. His company, Callaway Golf Co., introduced the oversized driver known as the Big Bertha, and made long, high and straight drives possible for both average golfers and the pros. July 5, 2001.

COCA, Imogene, 92. Comedian who played with Sid Caesar on NBC's hugely popular and highly innovative television program, *Your Show of Shows*, in the early 1950s. Best known for her zany expressions comic ability, she also had a successful singing and dancing career. June 2, 2001.

COLEMAN, Jim, 89. Nationally acclaimed sportswriter who was filing copy until his death. Coleman wrote columns for newspapers from Vancouver to Toronto during his long career. He wrote his first assignments with *The Winnipeg Tribune* in 1931 and ended his days at *The Province* in Vancouver. January 13, 2001.

COMO, Pierino (Perry), 88. Easy-listening crooner who hosted the popular *Perry Como Show* from 1948-63 on NBC; during a career that began in the mid 1930s, he sold more than 100 million records. "Let the Stars Get in Your Eyes." May 12, 2001.

COOMBS, Ernie, 73. Beloved children's entertainer, Coombs started out on CBC's *Butternut Square* in 1964; in 1967 he hosted the CBC children's show *Mr. Dressup*, (which ran until 1996) with fellow hosts, puppets Casey and Finnegan. Coombs's gentle manner endeared him to generations of Canadian children. September 18, 2001.

CORBEIL, Carole, 48. A journalist at the *Globe and Mail* and the *Toronto Star,* Corbeil's first novel, *Voice-Over,* a story of two sisters who experience French and English life in Canada, won the City of Toronto Book Award and was a Canadian bestseller. Also wrote *In the Wings.* October 5, 2000.

CUCCIONE, Michael, 16. Actor who appeared in TV series *Baywatch,* played in rock band 2gether, a spinoff from the Vancouver-based TV series. He co-authored *There Are Survivors: The Michael Cuccione Story,* and raised funds for research into Hodgkin's disease, to which he succumbed. January 13, 2001.

D'ALLEMAGNE, André, 71. Co-founder, in 1960, of the Rassemblement pour l'indépendance nationale, a Quebec political party that evolved into the Parti Québécois in 1968 under the leadership of René Lévesque. Wrote *Colonialism in Quebec.* February 1, 2001.

DANCE, Helen Oakley, 88. As a record producer and jazz and blues journalist, Toronto-born Dance, with her husband Stanley Dance, acted as personal assistant to jazz greats such as Duke Ellington; also active in the American civil rights movement. May 27, 2001.

DAUDELIN, Charles, 81. Artist and sculptor whose spiritually themed works are exhibited in

Canada and in Europe. He designed the awards for the France-Canada and Jutra prizes. April 2, 2001.

DEKKER, Paul, 70. Former CFL star with the Hamilton Tiger-Cats was ranked as one of the best tight ends in the league. In the 1961 Grey Cup final against Winnipeg, Dekker made a record 90-yard catch-and-run touchdown. May 8, 2001.

DEWAR, Donald, 63. In May 1999 Labour Party leader Dewar was elected as Scotland's First Minister after the country achieved devolution from Westminster, a step leading to greater autonomy for the country; died suddenly while in office. October 11, 2000.

De WOLF, Harry, 97. The most decorated officer in Canada, Vice-Admiral de Wolf was at the helm of the HMSC *Haida* during the Allied invasion of Normandy. December 18, 2000.

DIONNE, Yvonne, 67. One of the famous Dionne quintuplets, Yvonne is survived by her sisters Annette and Cecile. She lived a quiet life as a clerk until 1998, when she and her sisters sued the Ontario government for damages arising from the exploitative and abusive upbringing they suffered while under the government's guardianship in the 1930s; they received $4 million after much legal wrangling. June 23, 2001.

DONAHUE, Troy (b. Merle Johnson), 65. Blond, blue-eyed heartthrob of the 1950s and '60s, Donahue was active in "beach" movies, often partnered with Sandra Dee and Connie Stevens, and later in television (*Hawaiian Eye, Surfside Six*). *A Summer Place; Palm Springs Weekend; Rome Adventure; Godfather II.* September 3, 2001.

DUDEK, Louis, 83. Celebrated poet and author who, with Irving Layton and Raymond Souster, co-founded Contact Press, which published noted Canadian poets in the 1950s and '60s. *The Theory of the Image in Modern Poetry; Cross Section.* March 22, 2001.

DYER, Kenneth, 80(?). During the 1962 Cuban crisis, Rear Admiral Dyer sent Canadian warships to aid the U.S. blockade of Cuba, although the government of Prime Minister John Diefenbaker had yet to make an official decision regarding Canada's position in the situation. October 9, 2000.

EPSTEIN, William, 88. In the late 1940s, Epstein became permanent chief of the Middle East section at the United Nations, following his role as adviser to Arab-Israeli peace talks in 1946. He was a long-standing proponent of disarmament policies at the UN. *The Last Chance: Nuclear Proliferation and Arms Control.* February 9, 2001.

EVANS, Dale (b. Frances Octavia Smith), 88. The "Queen of the West" performed in more than 35 movies with husband Roy Rogers; beginning with *The Cowboy and the Senorita,* the two went on to star in the 1950s television series *The Roy Rogers Show,* later *The Roy Rogers and Dale Evans Show.* With Rogers, she co-wrote more than 400 songs, including their signature ballad, "Happy Trails to You." February 7, 2001.

FARNSWORTH, Richard, 80. Former Hollywood stunt man who later broke into acting, often playing crusty cowboys, Farnsworth was the oldest man to receive an Oscar nomination for his last movie, *The Straight Story* (1999). He was celebrated for his leading role in *The Grey Fox.* October 6, 2000.

FRANCIS, Arlene (b. Arlene Francis Kazanjian), 93. US actress, best known for her appearance on CBS's long-running game show *What's My Line* for the show's entire duration, from 1950-75; she also appeared on radio, on Broadway and in movies. May 31, 2001.

FREIDMAN, Dr. Meyer, 90. American cardiologist who, with Dr. Ray Rosenman, developed the theory of Type A behaviour, which they identified as a cause of heart attacks. *Type A Behavior and Your Heart.* April 27, 2001.

GRAHAM, Katharine, 84. Pulitzer Prize winner (for her memoir *Personal History*) and publisher of the *Washington Post* from 1969-79, Graham was noted for her pioneering role as a female journalist, her acerbic wit, and her support of the *Washington Post's* revelation of the Watergate scandal in 1973, which ultimately ended the career of president Richard Nixon. July 17, 2001.

GWYNNE, Horace (Lefty), 88. Canadian boxing champion who won the gold medal in the bantam weight division of the 1932 Los Angeles Summer Olympics. April 2001.

HALPERT, Herbert, 89. Newfoundland folklorist, founder of Memorial University's Folklore and Language Archive and their Department of Folklore, Halpert wrote *Folktales of Newfoundland* and *Christmas Mumming in Newfoundland: Essays in Anthropology, Folklore and History.* December 29, 2000.

HANNA William, 90. Co-creator (with Joseph Barbera) of cartoon characters Tom and Jerry, Huckleberry Hound, Fred Flintstone and Yogi Bear. March 22, 2001.

HARMAN, Jack, 73. Sculptor and expert in bronze casting, Harman was especially noted for his Peacekeeping Monument and for his depiction of the Queen on horseback, both in Ottawa; also his *Spirit of the Republic* in Victoria, BC, which commemorates Canadian contributions to the Spanish Civil War; and his statue of Olympic gold medallist Harry Jerome in Vancouver. January 3, 2001.

HARRIS, Billy, 66. Centre with the Toronto Maple Leafs when they won the Stanley Cup in 1962, 1963 and 1964. Traded to Detroit, Harris went on to play for a number of teams and went on to coach national teams in Europe. Served as spokesman for the Leukemia Research Fund of Canada. September 19, 2001.

HEARST, Randolph Apperson, 85. Heir to the newspaper empire founded by his father, William Randolph Hearst, and father of Patricia Hearst, whose 1974 kidnapping by the radical Symbionese Liberation Army made front-page news. December 18, 2000.

HERBERT, John (b. John Herbert Brundage), 74. Innovative gay playwright and sometimes drag queen, Herbert received both accolades and shocked criticism with his 1964 play *Fortune and Men's Eyes,* which described the plight of gay prisoners in penal institutions. June 22, 2001.

HEWLETT, William Redington, 87. Co-founder in 1938, with David Packard, of Hewlett-Packard, a company that not only was a pioneer in the electronics field, but was innovative in employee relations, introducing profit-sharing schemes. January 12, 2001.

HIMEL, Irving, 86. Toronto lawyer who championed the rights of minorities within the law; he was a founding member of the Canadian Civil Liberties Association. With fellow lawyer Kew Dock Yip, Himel successfully lobbied the government to repeal the Chinese Immigration Act in 1947; his efforts also saw the removal of discriminatory clauses against Jews from real estate deeds. July 16, 2001.

HOOKER, John Lee, 83. American blues singer enjoyed a 70-year career, influencing rock and roll and R & B singers with his distinctive "boogie" style. "Boom Boom"; "Boogie Chillen." June 21, 2001.

HOW, Harry, 80. Served for six years as Attorney General of Nova Scotia during the 1980s under a PC government; also became chief judge of the provincial court in 1983; remembered for his charisma and compassion. February 1, 2001.

HOWARD, Bob, 69. President of Skate Canada in 1987 and 1988, Howard presided during the Calgary Olympics, a promising competition for Canadian figure skating competitors; credited for encouraging athletic and marketing aspects of figure skating. March 18, 2001.

HOWARD, Wilbur, 88. In 1941 Howard became the first black to be ordained a United Church minister. After working with church-sponsored youth groups and on Christian education in Manitoba, Howard received his own parish in Ottawa 20 years after his ordination, and served as moderator of the United Church 1974-77. April 17, 2001.

HOYLE, Fred, 86. British astrophysicist, invented term Big Bang theory, his derisive description for a cosmic-origins concept he disagreed with; he believed that the universe is a static entity. August 20, 2001.

HUOT, Juliette, 89. Hugely popular Quebec actress on radio, television, stage and film, Huot played roles that celebrated the French-Canadian matriarch. In addition to her own televised cooking show, Huot appeared in the film *Les Plouffes* and the TV series *Jamais deux sans toi.* March 16, 2001.

INGRID, Queen Mother of Denmark, 90. Daughter of Sweden's King Gustaf VI Adolf, Ingrid married King Frederick IX of Denmark in 1935; mother of Queen Margrethe of Denmark. As Queen Mother to Europe's oldest royal family, Ingrid was credited with her businesslike approach to her work and her far-reaching philanthropy. November 7, 2000.

INGSTAD, Helge, 101. Norwegian explorer who traced Viking settlement to Newfoundland's L'Anse aux Meadows, verifying that the site, Lief Ericson's Vinland, was founded 500 years before Columbus arrived. *Westward to Vinland.* March 29, 2001.

KABILA, Laurent Desiré, 62. Kabila declared himself president of the Congo (formerly Zaire) in 1997, ousting former president Mobutu Sese Seko. He spurned Western attempts to stabilize the government and attempted to control all facets of the country, not only politically but in economics and policy-making as well. His death by assassination leaves the country still at war with six other African nations. January 17, 2001.

KAEL, Pauline, 82. Long-time film critic (from 1968-91) for the *New Yorker* magazine and author of several books on the subject, Kael combined her love for movies with an intellectual approach to criticism, celebrating especially American movies made between the late 1960s to the late '70s. *I Lost It at the Movies; Kiss Kiss Bang Bang.* September 3, 2001.

KETCHAM, Hank, 81. American cartoonist who created *Dennis the Menace,* the comic strip featuring a mischievous little boy with long-suffering parents, his bossy friend Margaret and grumpy neighbour, Mr. Wilson; the strip ran for more than 50 years. June 1, 2001.

KIAM, Victor Kermit, 74. Hugely successful owner of Remington Products Co., Kiam became internationally famous for his "I liked the shaver so much, I bought the company" slogan. May 27, 2001.

KOFFMAN, Morris (Moe), 72. One of Canada's leading jazz musicians, Koffman played saxophone, flute, clarinet and piccolo, incorporating jazz, swing and classical music in his repertoire; he performed regularly at Toronto's George's Spaghetti House, and on television, film and radio. With Oscar Peterson was first inductee in Canadian Jazz and Blues Hall of Fame. *Back to Bach;* "Swingin' Shepherd Blues." March 28, 2001.

KOSSAR, Leon, 72. Founder of Caravan festival in Toronto in 1968, one of Canada's first such celebrations, at the advent of the federal Liberal Party's multicultural agenda. At its height, Caravan boasted 50 pavilions across Toronto representing various countries, where attendees could enjoy the nations' food and culture. August 4, 2001.

KRAMER, Stanley Earl, 87. Independent American producer and director who focused on significant twentieth-century themes including racism, nuclear holocaust and war crimes. *Guess Who's Coming to Dinner; Judgment at Nuremberg; Inherit the Wind; High Noon;* and *On the Beach.* February 19, 2001.

KRAY, Reggie, 66. With twin brother Ronnie and brother Charlie, Kray terrorized East London with a violent extortion racket in the 1960s; subject of the film *The Kray Brothers.* October 1, 2000.

LEMMON, John Uhler (Jack), 76. Veteran American actor, specialized in roles that portrayed decent "everyman" characters in both comedy and drama; during a career that began in 1954 he appeared in at least 100 movies, including *Some Like it Hot; Days of Wine and Roses; The Odd Couple;* and *Glengarry Glen Ross.* June 27, 2001.

LETHEREN, Carol Anne, 58. The first woman to head the Canadian Olympic Association, Letheren encouraged the government to support elite athletic training to ensure Canada's Olympic success. During her successful and sometimes controversial career she ordered Ben Johnson to return his gold medal when he failed drug testing in the 1988 Seoul Olympics; she was responsible for refining the internal structure of the COA. February 2, 2001.

LEWIS, John Aaron, 80. American musician who in 1952 founded the Modern Jazz Quartet; Lewis, musical director and pianist for the innovative group, brought jazz to classical status by taking it out of nightclubs and into the concert hall. March 29, 2001.

LINDBERGH, Anne Morrow, 94. Wife of famed aviator Charles A. Lindbergh and a successful aviator herself, she joined her husband on several ground-breaking flights, among them, to Latin America and Asia. She made news when her infant son was kidnapped and murdered in 1932, and became a literary success with her book *Gift From the Sea*. February 7, 2001.

LOWNDES, Joan, 86. Art critic for the *Vancouver Province* and later the *Vancouver Sun*, Lowndes was credited with bringing West Coast artists, including Jack Shadbolt, Eric Metcalfe and Gathie Falk, to national prominence. June 20, 2001.

LUDLUM, Robert, 73. One of the world's most widely read writers, Ludlum published 22 books, which were noted for their high suspense; more than 200 million copies were sold throughout his career. *The Bourne Identity; The Scarlatti Inheritance*. March 12, 2001.

MAAS, Peter, 72. Hugely popular American nonfiction crime writer; Maas's extensive research led to the success of books such as *Serpico*, a police thriller, and *The Valachi Papers*, which detailed the inner workings of organized crime. August 23, 2001.

MacDONALD, Carol-Ann Duthie, 63. In 1953 champion water skier MacDonald won the U.S. Open, the Canadian Open, the Mexican Open and the World Junior Championship, and appeared in Toronto's CNE Aquarama show, which her parents produced. August 21, 2001.

MacMILLAN, Norma, 79. Vancouver native who began as a stage actress with the Totem Theatre company and went on to become the voice of Casper the Friendly Ghost and Goo. March 16, 2001.

MALTBY, David Barker, 38. Photographer and social activist; Maltby's arresting photographs, many of which documented occupations of public buildings, the homeless and political protests, appeared in Toronto's *Globe and Mail, NOW* magazine and in Toronto galleries. May 17, 2001.

MANARIN, Sofie, 17. Top Canadian cross-country skier was killed during a cycling training session on a highway in Sudbury. Manarin had put in the best North American performance when she placed 28th in the women's 15-km event in world junior championships in February. June 3, 2001.

MARTIN, Goldwyn Arthur, 87. Considered one of Canada's top criminal lawyers, Martin, who practised law from 1940-73, was noted for his innovative methods of cross-examination and skill in the use of expert witnesses. A highly respected Ontario Court of Appeal judge, he was also instrumental in the development of Ontario's legal aid system. February 26, 2001.

MAWSON, Michael, 54. First principal of the Stratford Festival Conservatory for Classical Theatre Training in Ontario. October 24, 2000.

MAXWELL, Joan, 70. A leading mezzo-soprano opera singer whose career ended abruptly after an injury, Maxwell sang with the Canadian Opera Company, the Winnipeg Symphony Orchestra and Winnipeg Philharmonic Choir. She hosted CBC television's *Moods in Music*. December 17, 2000.

McTAGGART, David Fraser, 68. Chairman of Greenpeace International from 1979-91, McTaggart is credited with developing the organization's worldwide reputation. He first made headlines in 1972 when he protested French nuclear testing by sailing into the test field and prompting the French navy to ram his boat. Died in a car crash in Italy, where he had retired. March 23, 2001.

METCALFE, Sam, 61. Inuit carver whose studies in linguistics led to his collaboration on an Inuktituk-English dictionary; he later joined the linguistics division of Indian and Northern Affairs. He became a contributor to CBC Radio and represented aboriginal concerns in the mining development in Voisey's Bay, Labrador. October 11, 2000.

MOLGAT, Gildas, 74. Leader of Liberal opposition in Manitoba legislature 1961-68; senator, and two-term speaker of the Senate. February 28, 2001.

MONTGOMERY, George, 84. Rugged American actor best remembered for his role in the late 1950s TV series *Cimarron City*. He was active in movies, starring in *The Cisco Kid and the Lady; Riders of the Purple Sage;* and *Wild Wind*. December 12, 2000.

NICHOL, Marjorie Elizabeth Kenyon Fellowes, 72. Founder of Vancouver's Equinox Gallery, which launched the careers of West

Coast artists such as Bill Reid and Gathie Falk. Nichol is credited with bringing the works of international artists to the city, as well, including Andy Warhol, David Hockney and Roy Lichenstein. December 3, 2000.

NURENBERGER, Meyer Joshua, 90. Founder of the *Canadian Jewish News* and later the *Jewish Times,* Nurenberger was internationally recognized for his journalistic acumen, advising prime minister John Diefenbaker on Middle East policy. August 11, 2001.

O'CONNOR, Carroll, 76. American actor best known for his role as the irascible, prejudiced, blue-collar Archie Bunker in the long-running television comedy *All in the Family* from 1971-79. The series tackled issues ranging from racial prejudice, women's rights and anti-war sentiments. Also starred in TV drama series *In the Heat of the Night* from 1987-94. June 21, 2001.

PHILLIPS, John Edmund Andrew, 65. Co-founder and songwriter of the Mamas and the Papas, the hugely popular pop group of the late '60s, with his wife Michelle Phillips, Cass Elliot and Dennie Doherty. "I Saw Her Again Last Night"; "Monday, Monday"; "California Dreamin'." March 18, 2001.

POWLESS, Gaylord, 54. Member of both the Canadian and Ontario lacrosse halls of fame, Powless, of Mohawk birth, scored 376 goals and 624 assists in his career, playing with the Oshawa Green Gaels; his skills were compared to those of Wayne Gretzky's. August 28, 2001.

PREBBLE, John, 85. Journalist, novelist and historian, Prebble is best known for his trilogy on Scottish history, which detailed the Battles of Culloden and Glencoe, and the Highland Clearances. January 30, 2001.

PREVOST, André, 66. Quebec composer whose *Terre des Hommes (Man and His World)* opened Expo 67 in Montreal. His prolific work was influenced by a variety of genres. He wrote *Cantate pour cordes* for Yehudi Menuhin, and his work was commissioned by the Toronto and Montreal Symphony orchestras. Among his works: *Fantasme,* which was dedicated to John F. Kennedy after his assassination; and *Chorégraphie,* inspired by the 1972 assassination of Olympic athletes in Munich. January 27, 2001.

PROUDFOOT, Jim, 67. Acclaimed sportswriter was inducted into both the hockey and Canadian football halls of fame. His 49-year career at the *Toronto Star* had him travelling the world to cover every sport played. April 1, 2001.

QUINN, Anthony (b. Rudolph Oaxaca), 86. Veteran American actor whose ability to portray earthy characters of various nationalities led to huge screen success. Best known for his role as the macho, lusty Zorba in the 1954 film *Zorba the Greek,* he also appeared in *Viva Zapata!; Lust for Life;* and *The Passage.* June 3, 2001.

RABIN, Leah, 72. Widow of assassinated Israeli leader Yitzhak Rabin, she continued to crusade for Israeli-Arab peace, earning her the respect of world leaders, and the scorn of those who opposed her. November 12, 2000.

RAFKIN, Alan, 73. An Emmy Award-winning director, Rafkin was the name behind television's most beloved sitcoms, among them, *The Dick Van Dyke Show, The Mary Tyler Moore Show, Andy Griffith, Laverne & Shirley* and *Suddenly Susan.* August 6, 2001.

RAMONE, Joey (b. Jeffrey Hyman), 49. Lead singer of the punk rock group the Ramones, an American band that performed from 1974-96 and enjoyed international success, especially in Europe. "Teenage Lobotomy." April 15, 2001.

REAGAN, Maureen Elizabeth, 60. Daughter of former US president Ronald Reagan and Jane Wyman, Reagan became a spokesperson for the Alzheimer's Association after her father was stricken with the disease in the early 1990s. *First Father, First Daughter: A Memoir.* August 8, 2001.

RICHLER, Mordecai, 70. Acclaimed novelist and children's writer, Mordecai Richler was known for his acerbic wit and outspoken opinions; he was a vociferous critic of excessive nationalism, focusing on the Quebec separatist movement. His Montreal Jewish roots were echoed in his work. Among his bestselling books: *The Apprenticeship of Duddy Kravitz; St. Urbain's Horseman; Barney's Version* and the children's books *Jacob Two-Two Meets the Hooded Fang* and *Jacob-Two-Two and the Dinosaur.* July 3, 2001.

ROBARDS, Jason, 78. Robards was a crusty, silver-haired American actor who performed on stage and in film. Noted for his roles in Eugene O'Neill plays, including *The Iceman Cometh* and *Long Day's Journey into Night,* he also starred in the films *All the President's Men* and *Julia,* for which he won consecutive Oscars, and performed at Ontario's Stratford Festival in 1958. December 26, 2000.

ROWZEE, Edwin Ralph, 92. US-born inventor of synthesized rubber, originally for use by Allied forces in World War Two; founder of Polymer Corp. in Sarnia, Ont. February 14, 2001.

RUNCIE, Robert, 78. Archbishop of Canterbury 1980-91, Runcie was a strong critic of then prime minister Margaret Thatcher, arguing that her government policies hurt the unemployed and the poor. Although he was conservative in issues such as women's ordination in the Anglican Church, he is credited with advancing Jewish-Christian relations. July 11, 2001.

RUNCIMAN, Alexander "Mac" McInnes, 86. Runciman was president of the United Grain Growers from 1961-81 and was instrumental in changing the Crow rate, which regulated the freight rates for farmers to ship grain. He was first chairman of the Canada Grain Council. December 6, 2000.

SCRIBNER, Ronald Haldane, 58. One of Canada's first, and later leading, rock music agents, Scribner headed Bigland Agency, which had an impressive client roster, including The Guess Who, Bobby Curtola, David Clayton Thomas and Domenic Troiano. He later became a sales rep for Marsh & Co., a real estate firm that specialized in entertainment venues. October 29, 2000.

SECOMBE, Sir Harry Donald, 79. With Peter Sellers and Spike Milligan, Sir Harry Secombe hosted the satirical, absurd and extremely popular British comedy radio program *The Goon Show* in the 1950s and went on to appear in film and on television. April 11, 2001.

SHERPA, Babu Chhiri, 35. A sherpa mountaineer who in 2000 set the world record for the fastest ascent of Mount Everest, in 16 hours, 56 minutes; also the first person to survive camping at the mountain's summit without the aid of bottled oxygen. Died in a mountaineering accident on Everest. April 29, 2001.

SHOCTOR, Joseph, 78. Edmonton-based instigator of the city's Citadel Theatre, Shoctor promoted the city's theatrical productions on Broadway. Also responsible for returning Edmonton Eskimos to the CFL in 1949. April 19, 2001.

SHULL, Clifford G., 85. Physicist at the Massachusetts Institute of Technology, he shared the 1994 Nobel Prize with Canadian Bertram Brockhouse for research into neutron scattering. March 31, 2001.

SMITH, Michael, 68. Winner of the 1993 Nobel Prize for Chemistry, Smith, a biochemist, pioneered work in the field of genetic engineering, specifically in site-directed mutagenesis. Noted for his philanthropy, Smith was the recipient of many awards, and taught at the University of British Columbia. October 4, 2000.

SMITH, Scott, 45. Smith was bass player for the Canadian hard rock band Loverboy, which initially formed in Vancouver in the 1980s; the group had a recent revival. Scott died during a boating accident in San Francisco. "Turn Me Loose." November 30, 2000.

SOTHERN, Ann (b. Harriette Lake), 92. American movie actress who went on to portray the first working woman on American sitcom television in her roles on *Private Secretary* and the *Ann Sothern Show,* during the 1950s. March 15, 2001.

STARGELL, Willie, 61. Slugger with the Pittsburgh Pirates had a career total of 475 homers and two World Series titles. Stargell was inducted into baseball's Hall of Fame in 1988. April 9, 2001.

STERN, Isaac, 81. A virtuoso classical violinist, Stern, who was born in the Ukraine and arrived in the US as an infant, was mentor to many of the world's top musicians. His long association with Carnegie Hall in New York City was evident when he helped save the venerable building from demolition in the late 1920s. Stern was active in Israel-US cultural matters. September 22, 2001.

TEMPLETON, Charles Bradley, 85. A longtime Canadian celebrity, Templeton enjoyed a versatile career: as an evangelist who was billed with Billy Graham; a newspaperman with the *Toronto Star;* a playwright and public affairs director with CTV; a magazine editor (*Maclean's*); and a novelist and writer of nonfiction. *The Kidnapping of the President; Act of God; Farewell to God.* June 7, 2001.

THIEU, Nguyen van, 78. President of South Vietnam from 1965 to 1975, when Saigon fell to the Communist forces of North Vietnam. In the early years of his presidency he brought a measure of stability to the war-torn country, but he was unable to ward off Communist forces, despite US military support. September 29, 2001.

VON KUSTER, Clifford, 79. Head of the Faculty of Music at the University of Western Ontario, von Kuster presided over a music school that was at one time the largest in Canada and became a major force in music education in the country. November 5, 2000.

WALSTON, Ray, 86. Veteran American actor, starred in 1960s TV series *My Favorite Martian* with Bill Bixby; played the devil in the movie *Damn Yankees,* as well as a variety of supporting roles on Broadway and in movies. January 1, 2001.

WAUGH, Auberon Alexander, 61. British novelist and acidic political columnist for *Private Eye,* the *Spectator* and the *New Statesman;* son of novelist Evelyn Waugh. January 16, 2001.

WAXMAN, Albert Samuel (Al), 65. Beloved Canadian actor best known for his lead role in the CBC TV series *King of Kensington* (1975-80), Waxman also starred in the American television drama *Cagney & Lacey.* Starting out in CBC radio dramas, he made his film debut in *The War Lover* with Steve McQueen. He recently played Willy Loman in *Death of a Salesman* on stage, and portrayed a prison warden in the film *The Hurricane,* the saga of wrongfully accused Hurricane Carter. Waxman died shortly after elective heart bypass surgery. January 17, 2001.

WELLS, Thomas Leonard, 70. Silver-haired Ontario PC cabinet minister best known for his education portfolio in the 1970s, when teacher unrest led to confrontations; he also became minister of health in 1969 and was instrumental in the creation of the medicare system. October 11, 2000.

WELTY, Eudora, 92. Pulitzer Prize winning author of short stories and newspaper articles began her long career during the Depression. Won the Pulitzer in 1972 for *The Optimist's Daughter.* July 23, 2001.

WHERRY, Don, 66. Versatile percussionist who appeared with the Toronto Symphony, the Bolshoi Ballet, and who performed with R. Murray Shafer, Anne Murray and Seiji Ozawa among others; he co-founded Sound Symposium, an international music festival, and was a member of the music groups Black Auks, Fusion and the Scrungeons. July 28, 2001.

WHITAKER, Denis, 86. Brigadier General who was one of Canada's most decorated officers and a two-time winner of the Distinguished Service Order. He led the Royal Hamilton Infantry during the battle at Dieppe battle during World War Two. May 30, 2001.

WOODS, Donald, 67. South African editor of the *Daily Dispatch,* whose support of anti-apartheid activist Steve Biko, who was murdered while in police custody, was the background for the 1987 film *Cry Freedom.* Forced into exile in Britain, he continued to speak against the apartheid movement. August 19, 2001.

WRIGHT, Laurali Rose (L.R.) "Bunny", 61. An award-winning novelist, Wright specialized in crime novels. Her fictional Staff Sergeant Karl Alberg was a recurring character in novels that evoked the unique character of British Columbia's coast. *The Suspect; A Chill Rain.* February 25, 2001.

YIP, Kew Dock, 94. The first Asian to become a lawyer in Canada, Yip, with lawyer Irving Himel, who died in July 2001, was instrumental in the government's 1947 repeal of the Chinese Immigration Act, and was responsible for bringing together families who had been separated as a result of the Act. While practising law in Toronto, Yip also was a firm advocate of ESL and heritage language classes, served briefly as a school trustee, and worked toward eliminating racist elements from immigration laws. July 9, 2001.

NOTE: Names in boldface indicate Canadian-born.

NEWS EVENTS OF 2000–2001

October 1, 2000 to September 30, 2001

(See also Obituaries pages 809–17.)

October 2000

INTERNATIONAL

Albania: Governing Socialists were re-elected (Oct. 15). **Australia**: Mid-month, officials announced that the hole in the Earth's ozone layer now stretched over a populated area in southern Chile; residents there had been exposed to very high levels of UV radiation for two days on Sept. 9 and 10. **Burundi**: Civil war continued as two rebel Hutu groups refused to accept the peace accord mediated by Nelson Mandela. **China**: About 150 coal miners were killed in a poisonous gas explosion (Oct. 7). On Oct. 12, Gao Xingjian became the first Chinese writer to win the Nobel Prize for literature. **Denmark**: 53.1 percent of referendum voters rejected the euro as its common currency, joining the UK and Sweden in their decision to stay out of the next step in economic integration in the EU. **Eritrea**: The first UN military observers took up their posts on the border between Ethiopia and Eritrea as 4,000 troops began deployment to implement the cease-fire. **France**: Two weeks in mid-October saw over 90 attacks on Jewish targets; the violence was blamed on disadvantaged French-Arabs inspired by the *intifadah*. **India**: More than 1,000 people were killed in Bangladesh after monsoon rains combined with water released from reservoirs to overwhelm West Bengal state. **Indonesia**: Former President Suharto was declared unfit to stand trial on corruption charges; subsequent protest riots left one dead and dozens injured. **Israel**: Violence escalated throughout the month after Ariel Sharon visited the disputed Temple Mount holy site at the end of September and a 12-year-old Palestinian boy, caught in crossfire, died on September 30. On Oct. 12, Palestinians murdered and mutilated two Israeli soldiers who had entered the West Bank city of Ramallah. Prime Minister Ehud Barak ordered a military retaliation. **Italy**: Floods and mudslides hit the Italian and Swiss Alps, killing at least 35 people (Oct. 23). **Korea, South**: South Korean President Kim Dae-jung won the Nobel Peace Prize for efforts toward reconciliation with North Korea (Oct. 13). **Nepal**: On Oct. 7, Davo Karnicar of Slovenia became the first person to ski non-stop down Mount Everest. It took the 38-year-old four days to reach the summit and five hours to ski back to base camp. **Serbia and Montenegro**: On Oct. 6, Slobodan Milosevic conceded defeat in Yugoslavia's Sept. 24 presidential election, after mass protests by thousands of citizens. Opposition supporters had blocked roads, staged mass strikes, burned the Parliament buildings and taken control of the government TV station to force Milosevic to turn over power to Vojislav Kostunica. **Spain**: Basque separatists, members of ETA, killed Jose Luis Ruiz Casado, a local councilor for Prime Minister Jose Maria Aznar's Popular Party, which governs Spain. **Taipei**: A Singapore Airlines Boeing 747 jumbo jet took the wrong runway during a severe storm on Oct. 31 and slammed into parked construction equipment while trying to take off, killing 81 of 179 people on board. **Taiwan**: Typhoon Xangsane killed 89 as it tore through the island (Oct. 31). **United Kingdom**: Britain announced a multi-million-dollar compensation package for the families of victims of mad-cow disease; a report had criticized the government's handling of the crisis in the mid-1990s. The European Convention on Human Rights was incorporated into the country's judicial system, setting out specific rights relating to privacy, family life, free expression and fair trial, after hundreds of years of negative rights that allowed any activity not expressly forbidden. **United**

States: The US health authorities approved the "morning after pill" for sale. Hackers broke into Microsoft Corp.'s computer network and gained access to blueprints for the company's latest software (Oct. 27). The hacker had high-level access for 12 days. **Yemen**: A terrorist bomb exploded, smashing a hole in the *USS Cole* that was in the harbour at Aden, Yemen, killing 17 sailors and injuring 38 (Oct. 12). **Zimbabwe**: A 30 percent rise in food costs sparked rioting in Harare; the country's economic crisis spelled further unemployment in a country where over 50 percent have no work (Oct. 18).

CANADA

Canadian wrestler Daniel Igali won an Olympic gold medal at the summer games in Sydney, Australia. Canada won three gold, three silver and eight bronze medals (Oct. 1). The state funeral for former Prime Minister Pierre Trudeau at Notre Dame Basilica in Montreal drew world dignitaries and thousands of onlookers (Oct. 3). NHL player Marty McSorley was found guilty of assault with a weapon in a February attack on Donald Brashear of the Vancouver Canucks (Oct. 6). Maurice ("Mom") Boucher, 47, leader of the Quebec Hell's Angels biker gang, was arrested Oct. 10 after the Quebec Court of Appeal quashed a not-guilty verdict issued in a double murder trial two years ago in Montreal. He was accused of ordering the ambush murders of two prison guards in 1997. Boucher had been a central figure in a bloody gang war between the Angels and its rival, Rock Machine, that has claimed 155 lives over six years. On Oct. 16, Newfoundland premier Brian Tobin announced he would step down to run for the Liberals in the upcoming federal election. Prime Minister Jean Chretien called a federal election for Nov. 27 (Oct. 22). RCMP charged a Vancouver businessman and a millworker from Kamloops with first-degree murder in connection with the 1985 bombing of an Air India jetliner that killed 329 people (Oct. 27). The two men were powerful behind-the-scenes players among Indo-Canadians, often opposing moderates in favour of fundamentalist candidates in a range of offices.

November 2000

INTERNATIONAL

Angola: Forty-eight people were killed when a Russian-built Antonov plane crashed in flames in northeastern Angola (Nov. 1). Two weeks later, 39 died when another Antonov plane crashed near the Angolan capital. **Argentina:** A 36-hour general strike by half of the country's 14 million workers brought the country to a standstill. The strike was held to protest austerity measures designed to win an aid package from the International Monetary Fund (Nov. 23-4). **Austria**: 155 people died in a mountain tunnel near Kaprun when a cable car filled with skiers and snowboarders caught fire; only 12 passengers managed to escape the blaze (Nov. 11). **Cambodia**: The worst flooding in 70 years caused 333 deaths and displaced 3.4 million people, many of whom were in need of emergency food aid (Oct-Nov.). **China:** Mary Robinson, the UN High Commissioner for Human Rights, signed a memorandum of understanding with the Chinese government that allowed for technical cooperation with the UN agency on human rights issues (Oct. 5). **Colombia**: Colombia's National Liberation Army (ELN) guerrilla group released the last 16 victims of a dramatic mass kidnapping that had been staged on the outskirts of Cali. The ELN had abducted 55 people from roadside restaurants and a country home on Sept. 17. Three of the victims died in captivity and 36 were handed over to Red Cross officials in the days immediately following their abduction. **Ethiopia**: A coffin carrying Ethiopia's late emperor, Haile Selassie, was laid in its final resting place in Addis Ababa on Nov. 5, 25 years after his death. He ruled Ethiopia for 44 years before being overthrown in 1974. **Fiji**: Eight people were killed and at least 22 wounded when a small group of special-forces soldiers staged an abortive mutiny at Fijian Military Forces headquarters (Nov. 13). Nine of the rebels were facing court martial for their alleged involvement in the May 19, 2000 coup attempt led by George Speight. **France**: A court in France ordered US-based Internet company Yahoo to block French users' access to its auctions of Nazi memorabilia. The decision, which complied with France's anti-hate laws, raised questions about whether a country can censor Internet content originating abroad. Yahoo insisted the ruling violated US constitutional rights to free speech. **Haiti**: Jean-Bertrand Aristide was returned to office with 92 percent of the vote in a Nov. 26 election. The election was boycotted by political opponents. **India**: Rajkumar, 72, beloved Indian movie star kidnapped by the bandit Veerappan, was released in Bangalore, India after 109 days in jungle captivity (Nov. 15). Veerappan has been accused of 120 murders but has eluded capture for 30 years, and is regarded as a hero among Tamil separatists. The bandit took a US$2.17 million ransom raised by two Indian state governments and retreated to his hideout, forgoing his demand for the release of government prisoners. **Indonesia**: More than 85 people were killed in late November when torrential rain triggered flooding and landslides on Sumatra. The same storms killed another 70 people in Thailand and Malaysia. **Israel**: The death toll in four weeks of violence rose to 137 when a suicide bomber blew himself up near a border checkpoint with Israel during the first week of November. **Ivory Coast**: Laurent Gbagbo was sworn in as the newly elected president after street demonstrations forced military dictator General Robert Guei from office. Guei had attempted to nullify the results of the election after his apparent loss at the ballot box. **Kenya**: At least 110 people died in Nairobia after drinking moonshine brewed with methanol (Nov. 20). Officials feared that many of the 400 survivors would lose their eyesight. **Mozambique**: An estimated 70 Mozambican prisoners died, possibly of suffocation, when they were jammed into a small cell in an overcrowded prison 1,600 km north of the capital Maputo. **Netherlands**: Dutch parliament passed legislation allowing euthanasia and physician-assisted suicide (Nov. 28). **Peru**: Under attack for election

fraud in a vote held six months earlier, President Alberto Fujimori faxed his resignation to the country's congress from Japan; the resignation was rejected as the congress declared him unfit to hold office and dismissed him (Nov. 20). Congressman Valentin Paniagua was named as interim president. **Philippines**: Typhoon Bebinca killed 24 when it hit the island of Luzon on Nov. 3. President Joseph Estrada was impeached by the House of Representatives on charges of corruption, bribery, graft and betrayal of public trust, among others (Nov. 13). **Russia**: After 15 years as world champion, Russian chess master Garry Kasparov lost the title on Nov. 2 to former pupil Vladimir Kramnik, 25. Kramnik, nicknamed Supernerd, won US$1.3 million for his victory. **Serbia and Montenegro:** The US, Germany, France and Britain restored diplomatic ties with the country in the wake of the establishment of the elected government of Vojislav Kostunica. **Tonga**: The government signed an agreement with Autogen of Australia that allows the company to study the genes of the country's small, isolated population. Volunteers will provide DNA samples, and the culture's well-documented lineages are expected to help researchers identify specific genes linked to certain chronic and life-threatening conditions. The government will retain ownership of the samples and receive a share of the profits from the research. **United Kingdom**: Eva Morris, the world's oldest woman, died Nov. 2, just six days before her 115th birthday. Morris attributed her longevity to her consumption of whiskey and boiled onions. **United States**: Bill Shepherd, Yuri Gidzenko and Sergei Krikalev become the first crew of the space station *Alpha* on Nov. 2. The US presidential election on Nov. 7 was a virtual tie, with a recount called in Florida to determine the winner. Vice-president Al Gore had a slight edge in the popular vote, but the winner of Florida's electoral college votes would have enough support to become president. The problem was compounded by voter difficulties with ballots in Palm Beach county, where confused voters claimed to have accidentally voted for the wrong candidate. Bush was certified as election winner on Nov. 26 with 537-vote margin over Gore in Florida, but legal battles continued. In the largest ever settlement in a racial discrimination case, beverage giant Coca-Cola agreed to pay $193 million to settle claims of racial bias against black workers (Nov. 17). The employees filed suit last year alleging that they were discriminated against in matters of pay, promotion and performance evaluations. Three Los Angeles Police Department anti-gang officers were convicted of conspiracy to obstruct justice by planting evidence and framing gang members, casting doubt on hundreds of convictions. The affair first came to light last year when another officer was caught stealing US$1 million worth of cocaine from an evidence room. One worker died and nine were rescued, after the scaffolding they were using while painting the Ambassador Bridge between Detroit and Windsor collapsed (Nov. 15).

CANADA

Two 14-year-olds died on "Take Our Kids to Work Day" when the utility vehicle they were driving crashed into a parked truck at the John Deere plant in Welland, Ont. (Nov. 2). Author Margaret Atwood won the Booker Prize, a prestigious British literary award, for her novel *The Blind Assassin* (Nov. 7). Health officials removed gasoline-sniffing children from a Labrador community after Innu leaders asked for help in dealing with substance abuse problems (Nov. 21). NASDAQ, the US-based tech-oriented stock exchange, launched NASDAQ Canada in Montreal, to create a direct link to Canadian investors (Nov. 21). Police in Vancouver arrested Lai Changxing, the man allegedly at the centre of China's biggest corruption scandal. His Xiamen-based Yuanhua group is believed to have smuggled $10 billion worth of crude oil, cars and other goods into China. (He later claimed refugee status in a bid to avoid extradition.) Liberal Prime Minister Jean Chretien won his third consecutive majority government on Nov. 27; his party

took 172 seats out of a possible 301. The Canadian Alliance, led by Stockwell Day, showed few gains in Ontario, but won enough seats to become the Official Opposition. On Nov. 27 an inquest into the deaths of 12 babies at Winnipeg Health Sciences Centre blamed mismanagement, surgical error and inexperienced doctors.

December 2000

INTERNATIONAL

Chile: Former Chilean dictator Augusto Pinochet was arrested Dec. 8 and ordered to stand trial in Santiago on charges of kidnapping and murder. Pinochet returned to Chile in March 2000 after more than a year under house arrest in Britain. **China:** A dance-hall fire in Luoyang killed 309 people on Christmas day. (In mid-January police arrested four welders who were working at the hall and were suspected of accidentally causing the blaze.) **France:** The 15 members of the European Union met in Nice to hammer out a deal that allowed for the expansion of the union with former east-bloc countries (Dec. 7-9). As many as 15 more countries could join the EU by 2010. Police fired tear gas and stun grenades at about 4,000 demonstrators who tried to disrupt the meeting. **Ghana:** John Agyekum Kufuor won run-off elections against John Atta-Mills, ending Jerry Rawlings's 19 years in power (Dec. 27). Rawlings, the former fighter pilot, seized power twice and led a harsh military regime before turning to democracy. He was constitutionally barred from running again. (He stepped down as president on Jan. 7.) **Iraq:** In defiance of world sanctions, oil exports were halted unless buyers agreed to a US$.50/barrel surcharge to be paid directly to Iraqi bank accounts. **Israel:** Prime Minister Ehud Barak announced his resignation in a surprise move to force the country to choose among options in negotiating a Mid-East peace settlement (Dec. 10). **Japan:** Construction firm Kajima Corp. agreed to pay Chinese labourers forced to work as slaves at its Hanaoka mine during World War II. Of the

986 workers brought from China to work at the site, more than 400 had died by the end of 1945. While not admitting legal responsibility, the firm set up a US$4.6 million fund for survivors and their families. **Korea, North:** A series of natural disasters severely cut food production in previous seasons and the UN World Food Program asked for 800,000 tons of food to help starving people (Dec. 7); more than two million people reportedly had already perished. **Mexico:** Popcatepetl erupted on Dec. 18, sending 40,000 people in search of safer ground. Residents were last evacuated in 1994. **Pakistan:** The military government, which had ruled the country since the ouster of former Prime Minister Nawaz Sharif from power in a non-violent coup, released Sharif from jail in December and exiled him to Saudi Arabia. Sharif had been serving a life sentence on terrorism and hijacking charges relating to a 1999 coup, when he attempted to prevent a plane carrying General Pervez Musharraf from returning to Pakistan. Musharraf's subsequent seizure of power, which he initially insisted was only a temporary measure, was welcomed by many Pakistanis who had grown frustrated with continued government corruption. **Philippines:** Five bombs exploded in Manila as residents prepared to celebrate the new year. The explosions targeted transportation links. **Serbia and Montenegro:** The coalition led by President Kostunica took more than two-thirds of the 250 seats in the Serbian parliament in an election that gave them 64 percent of the vote. On other fronts, the country's stability was hampered by power shortages caused by a crumbling infrastructure and incursions from Albanian rebels. **Sweden:** In an audacious pre-Christmas heist, thieves stole a Rembrandt self-portrait and two paintings by Renoir from Stockholm's National Museum, later demanding US$1 million each in ransom for their return (Dec. 23). **Turkey:** The country's faltering economy was patched with an emergency US$7.5 billion loan from the IMF. The country's line of credit had been cut off, and interest rates had soared to 2000 percent in an effort to stop the outflow of cash. **Uganda:** Dr. Matthew Lukwiya, one of the leaders of the fight against the Ebola virus, died Dec. 4, the first doctor killed by the disease. Several nurses and hundreds of patients were killed by the outbreak. **Ukraine:** Engineers at Ukraine's Chernobyl nuclear power plant, the site of the world's worst nuclear accident, shut down its last remaining reactor (Dec. 15). In 1986, an explosion at the plant spewed radioactive dust over Ukraine, Belarus, Russia and other regions of Europe. Illnesses related to exposure to radiation have killed thousands of people. **United Kingdom:** The peace process in Northern Ireland continued to falter as the first sectarian murders in 18 months marred preparations for the Dec. 12 visit of US Pres. Bill Clinton. Passengers aboard a British Airways jumbo jet screamed in terror when a man burst into the cockpit and sent the plane into a steep dive during a night flight from London to Nairobi (Dec. 28). Several passengers subdued and bound the 27-year-old Kenyan intruder as he attacked the pilot. The co-pilot regained control of the plane after a harrowing 3,000-foot descent. **United States:** Benjamin Harrison Holcomb, the world's oldest man, died at 111 in Oklahoma on Dec. 4. On Dec. 12, a split (5-4) US Supreme Court overturned a ballot recount ordered by the Florida court and the next day George W. Bush was declared President-elect of the US, 36 days after the polls closed. US Federal Trade Commission approved the $202 billion merger of Time Warner and America Online (Dec. 14). At the United Nations, Russia and the US demanded an arms embargo and other sanctions against Afghanistan in a bid to force the country to close its terrorist training camps and surrender Osama bin Laden. Retail chain Montgomery Ward & Co., a century-old company, announced it would cease to operate, shutting down 250 stores and ending employment for 28,000 workers (Dec. 28).

CANADA

Astronaut Marc Garneau, 51, embarked on his third mission when the space shuttle *Endeavour* lifted off from Cape Canaveral, Fla. (Dec. 1). Garneau was part of a five-member crew responsible for delivering, assembling and activating the first of four towers of solar panels that will provide power for the international space station, *Alpha*. Garneau used the CANADARM to remove the $600-million, 16-ton tower from the *Endeavour's* cargo bay. Seagram Co. was voted out of existence on Dec. 5 in a merger between the 76-year-old Canadian company and French conglomerate Vivendi. In another merger, Shaw Communications Inc. announced plans to purchase Moffat Communications of Winnipeg and consolidate the cable industry leader's hold on the western Canadian market. Protesters against Quebec's Bill 170, which would amalgamate Montreal's suburbs into a megacity, rallied on Dec. 10 to try to stop the disappearance of 8 of the 28 municipalities and the removal of the right to tax from the 26 new boroughs. On Dec. 11, an Alberta judge ruled that a law that prohibits the cultivation of marijuana is unconstitutional because it doesn't allow for medical use of the drug. Justice Darlene Acton threw out a charge of cultivating marijuana against Grant Krieger, who grew and used pot to alleviate the symptoms of his multiple sclerosis. Canadian Alliance Leader Stockwell Day settled out of court with an Alberta lawyer suing him over comments about the lawyer's defence of a man accused of possessing child pornography (Dec. 21). The settlement of the defamation suit, filed by Red Deer lawyer Lorne Goddard, came one day after the latest in a series of legal rulings against Day's defence team.

January 2001

INTERNATIONAL

Belgium: Norwegian and EU officials announced a temporary moratorium on cod fishing, during the spawning season, in about 20 percent of the North Sea. This move, plus another to cut the allowable catch by 40 percent, was aimed at a long-term recovery of the dwindling cod stocks. **China:** The country continued its fledgling space program, successfully launching its second unmanned spacecraft; animals and other life forms were sent into orbit as scientists tested instrument panels and monitored the functioning of life support systems. On Jan. 23, five Falun Gong supporters set themselves on fire in Tiananmen Square in Beijing, killing one woman. The government responded by increasing security in the area. **Congo:** On Jan. 17, President Laurent Kabila died of wounds sustained in a gun battle with one of his own bodyguards at the presidential palace in Kinshasa on the previous day. Kabila, who had deposed longtime dictator Mobuto Sese Seko in 1997, was replaced by his son Joseph. **Ecuador:** An oil tanker ran aground near the Galapagos Islands; the 1,200 sq. km oil slick which resulted threatened the wildlife sanctuary. Favourable winds and currents minimized the damage however, the government announced that shipping regulations for the area surrounding the Galapagos would be reviewed. **El Salvador:** An earthquake registering 7.6 on the Richter scale shook Santa Tecia, 12 km outside of San Salvador on Jan. 13, killing nearly 700, destroying 91,000 homes and causing $1.5 billion in damage. Post-quake landslides added to the damage, with critics charging that unregulated construction practices had stripped the hillsides of protective vegetation that could have lessened the dangers. **Germany:** 244 women, the first allowed into combat units in the country's armed forces, reported for basic training the first week in January. **India:** At least 10,000 monkeys overran government offices in New Delhi; by Jan. 13, they were threatening workers, stealing equipment and destroying documents. A massive earthquake measuring 7.9 on the Richter scale hit the northern state of Gujarat, killing 15,000, injuring 60,000 and leaving 600,000 homeless (Jan. 26). **Iraq:** On the eve of the 10th anniversary of the Gulf War, the country signed a free-trade agreement with Egypt in a bid to end its continuing isolation. **Netherlands:** A dozen people were killed when a fire broke out in a café northeast of Amsterdam shortly after midnight on New Year's Eve. On Jan. 30, a Scottish court sitting in Camp Zeist, Netherlands, convicted a Libyan intelligence officer of murder and sentenced him to life in prison for the 1998 bombing of Pan Am Flight 103 over Lockerbie, Scotland, which killed 270. A second man was acquitted. **Nigeria:** A 17-year-old Nigerian was given 180 lashes for having premarital sex, even though she testified that her father had forced her to have sex with three of his friends (Jan. 27). The young woman had given birth to a baby girl three weeks before the flogging. She was married in an attempt to prevent punishment, but a judge ruled that her current marital status was immaterial. **Norway:** Government officials announced the resumption of the export of whale products, seeking to find a market for 500 tons of blubber in storage and angering conservationists who oppose commercial whaling (Jan. 22). **Philippines:** Gloria Macapagal Arroyo became president of the Philippines on Jan. 20, replacing Joseph Estrada, who was forced out over charges of corruption and massive street demonstrations. The change in leadership became possible when the country's Supreme Court declared the presidency vacant after Estrada failed to resign by the agreed-upon deadline. **Russia:** Bitter cold was blamed for 113 deaths in northeastern Asia in mid-January. Temperatures in Siberia hit minus 50 degrees C for more than two weeks. **Thailand:** The 12-year-old Htoo twins, alleged leaders of the Karen rebel group known as God's Army, surrendered to Thai authorities in exchange for sanctuary after a year of hiding in the mountains and some successful raids that gave them legend status among their supporters (Jan. 16). The Karen people have been fighting for a homeland in Thai-Myanmar territory for over 50 years. **Turkey:** A ship loaded with illegal immigrants foundered off the coast of Turkey on

New Year's Day and sank, killing 50. **United States:** California communities around San Francisco and Los Angeles spent a half-day with rotating 90-minute power blackouts after the deregulated electrical system left the state short of power (Jan. 18). George W. Bush was sworn in as the 43rd president on Jan. 20. Emergency purchases from BC Hydro bridged the energy gap for the short term. President Bush refused to put ratification of the international criminal court treaty before the US Senate, insisting that the accord was flawed.

CANADA

Despite a last-minute rush to meet the Jan. 1 deadline, hundreds of thousands of gun owners didn't register their guns and now possessed their weapons illegally, leaving them unable to buy ammunition and facing fines. Gun owners must register all firearms by 2003. On Jan. 2, residents of Banff were shaken by three separate cougar attacks, one fatal. The daylight attacks were unusual for the normally shy, nocturnal animals. Wardens moved herds of elk—the cougar's prey—farther from the town site. Quebec Premier Lucien Bouchard announced his resignation as premier and his decision to leave public life on Jan. 11, setting the stage for a change in the province's leadership in the spring. Two gay couples, one male and one female, were married Jan. 14 in a Toronto church service as part of a campaign to change Canada's ban on same-sex marriages. In a rare settlement, the Correctional Service of Canada agreed to pay $215,000 to a sexual-assault victim—only hours before her civil suit against the prison system was due to begin. The woman was attacked in 1998 by James Armbruster, a career criminal with more than 60 convictions. He was serving time for armed robbery and sexual assault with a weapon when he was granted day parole and transferred to an Abbotsford, BC, halfway house. A stowaway who tried to sneak into the US on the undercarriage of a Buffalo-bound bus died after he became entangled in the vehicle's driveshaft. Andrew

Mazanembi Mutizira, 36, was spotted during a routine customs inspection on the US side of the Peace Bridge. Mutizira, who had a valid US visa, came to Canada on Jan. 2 to meet relatives flying to Toronto from Zimbabwe. US officials had revoked his visa when they caught him trying to cross the border from Windsor, Ont., to Detroit with the Zimbabweans hiding under a blanket in the backseat of his car. Mutizira then drove to Niagara Falls, Ont., where he hid under the bus. Lorne Calvert was elected leader of the NDP in Saskatchewan and the province's premier at a Jan. 27 leadership convention held in Saskatoon. Russian diplomat Andrey Knyazev returned to Moscow after a car he was driving while drunk struck and killed Catherine MacLean as she walked along a sidewalk in Ottawa (Jan. 27). Knyazev claimed diplomatic immunity. Russia said he would face charges under its legal system.

February 2001

INTERNATIONAL

Antarctica: British researchers announced that the middle of the ice sheet in West Antarctic had thinned by 10 m between 1992 and 1999. They raised concerns that if such a melt rate continued on the Pine Island Glacier, ocean levels would rise considerably and threaten the existence of coastal cities around the world. **Brazil:** More than 20,000 prisoners staged co-ordinated riots in prisons in Sao Paulo state which killed 16 people. A prison gang known as the First Commano of the Capital organized the action to protest the transfer of its leaders to another prison (Feb. 18). **El Salvador:** At least 280 people were killed, more than 2,400 injured and around 123,000 left homeless, after an earthquake struck, the second to strike the country in four weeks (Feb. 16). Measuring 6.6, the new quake was smaller than January's, but due to its land-based epicenter, caused more damage. **France:** Up to 1,500 people, mainly Kurds, were on a ship that ran aground off the coast of southern France (Feb. 23). The Cambodian-registered *East Sea* appeared to

have been deliberately run on to Boulouris beach near Saint Raphael. The boat had left Greece eight days earlier and had stopped in Turkey. The vessel's human cargo included 300 children under age 10 and was assumed to be transporting potential illegal migrants. **Germany:** Former German Chancellor Helmut Kohl agreed to pay a $143,000 fine to settle a criminal investigation over illegal campaign finance contributions. Kohl had been under investigation for 13 months after admitting he had received $1 million in campaign contributions he did not report as required by law. Kohl still refused to name the donors, continuing a political scandal that hobbled his political party, the Christian Democratic Union. **Guinea:** The southern part of the country was overwhelmed by refugees from wars in neighbouring Sierra Leone and Liberia; 250,000 people fled the various conflicts and required aid. The country itself was under attack by antigovernment rebels, which made the delivery of aid to the area nearly impossible. **Indonesia:** Over 7,000 Madurese immigrants fled the island of Borneo for Java after members of the indigenous Dayak tribe killed 469 of them during a week of violence (Feb. 24). **Iraq:** US and British jets bombed nearly 20 radar sites near Baghdad (Feb. 16); the attacks came as the country worked with Chinese technicians to improve its air defences. **Israel:** Ariel Sharon defeated Ehud Barak in an election to become Prime Minister as voters chose the hardliner in the hope of gaining some security against the Palestinian uprisings (Feb. 6). **Saudi Arabia:** Canadian Bill Sampson and two other men–a Briton and a Belgian–were arrested in connection with two bombings in Riyadh in November, 2000. The men appeared on Saudi TV on Feb. 4 and explained how they carried out the attacks, which killed one Briton and injured four others. The men could face death by public beheading if sentenced according to Shari'a law. Sampson was working in Riyadh for a Saudi government agency. **Thailand:** Thailand's new parliament formally elected telecommunications tycoon

Thaksin Shinawatra as the country's 23rd Prime Minister by a vote of 340 to 127, with 33 abstentions. Thaksin gained an overwhelming majority in the 500-member lower house when his Thai Rak Thai Party dominated national elections on Jan. 6. **United Kingdom**: An outbreak of foot-and-mouth disease first spotted in a slaughterhouse in Essex on February 19th led to the destruction of thousands of head of cattle and sheep, a ban on exports and travel restrictions that crippled the tourist industry at the beginning of its season. **United States**: Nine people were killed when a US nuclear submarine collided with a Japanese fishing vessel off the coast of Hawaii (Feb. 9). The Pearl Harbor-based USS *Greeneville* was on routine patrol when it surfaced rapidly under the *Ehime Maru*, which sank within minutes. Two teachers and 13 students from a fisheries school were on the fishing boat. A California court ruled that Napster, the popular Internet service used to swap music, must stop helping its users with illegal exchanges of copyrighted material. Napster eventually shut down while it tried to develop safeguards that would prevent users from breaking the law. The Senate voted to pay US$582 million of the nearly US$1 billion that it owed the United Nations in dues. The decision came after membership dues were cut by the UN; Washington will now pay 22 percent of the organization's administration costs instead of 25 percent. FBI agent Robert Philip Hanssen was arrested Feb. 18 and charged with spying for Russia since 1985. He was accused of handing over highly classified documents and betraying American intelligence sources and electronic surveillance methods in exchange for an estimated $2.1 million in cash and diamonds. (In July Hanssen pleaded guilty to several charges. Sentencing was scheduled for January, 2002.) On Feb. 28, a 6.8 magnitude earthquake rattled Seattle and the Pacific northwest; the epicentre was near Olympia, WA, but tremors were felt as far away as Salt Lake City and Vancouver. Damage, at $3 billion, was considered to be modest.

CANADA

Ottawa banned the importation of Brazilian beef on Feb. 2 as a precaution against mad cow disease. Brazil claimed there was no danger of the disease and said the move was a political one, part of a long-running trade battle. Roger Grimes became premier of Newfoundland on Feb. 13, replacing Brian Tobin, who had resigned to run in the November federal election. The Supreme Court of Canada ruled unanimously against extradition to countries that have capital punishment, unless there is assurance that detainees will not be executed if convicted of a crime carrying the death penalty. The ruling came in the case of two young Vancouver men, Glen Sebastian Burns and Atif Ahmad Rafay, wanted in Washington state for the brutal 1994 murders of Rafay's mother, father and sister. (In March, Washington state said the two would not face the death penalty. They were extradited and pleaded not guilty.) On Feb. 24, 13-month-old Erika Nordby of Edmonton wandered into sub-zero temperatures wearing only a diaper. By the time her mother found her, she was frozen almost solid and her heart had stopped beating for nearly two hours. Erika's body temperature when she arrived at hospital was 16 degrees C—about half of what is considered normal; she was revived in hospital and staff speculated that she would suffer only minor damage to her fingers and toes.

March 2001

INTERNATIONAL

Afghanistan: Ignoring international protests by governments, religious leaders and archaeologists, Taliban forces destroyed statues, including ancient works of art, that the hard-line government said violate the tenets of Islam, which forbids the worship of images. Two huge fifth-century depictions of Buddha, carved into a mountainside in Bamiyan, west of Kabul, were among the works destroyed (Mar. 10). **Brazil**: Three explosions rocked the biggest offshore oil platform in the world, killing 10 workers (Mar. 16). More than 160 people were rescued from the Petrobras rig, which sank about 200 km north of Rio de Janeiro, near Campos (Mar. 20). **China**: More than 40 schoolchildren, some as young as eight, were killed when an explosion ripped through their primary school, demolishing several classrooms. The school had used the children to assemble fireworks to help raise money (Mar. 6). **Congo, Democratic Republic:** The UN brokered a deal to withdraw multinational forces from the DRC and for rebel combat to cease within two weeks; UN personnel would be sent in to monitor the process (Mar. 15). **Ecuador**: Nearly five months after their abduction, seven foreign oil workers were freed in a jungle region of Ecuador. The men—four Americans, a New Zealander, a Chilean and an Argentine, were taken from an oilfield owned by Repsol YPF, a Spanish-Argentine company. Their employers paid a $13 million ransom before they were set free (Mar. 1). **France:** The first case of foot-and-mouth disease was confirmed in central France on Mar. 12. New cases were also reported in Argentina, Saudi Arabia and the UAE. **Hungary:** Flooding along the Tizla River killed seven and forced the evacuation of 30,000 in Hungary, Romania and Ukraine. **Kuwait**: Three 227-kg bombs killed five American servicemen and one New Zealander when a US fighter jet missed its target in a training exercise (Mar. 12). The F-18 navy plane dropped its load on an observation post and parked cars more than two kilometres from its intended target. **Mozambique**: The centre of the island nation was hard hit by heavy rains and floods in late March, just a year after the worst flooding in the country's history. 25,000 people were displaced by the crisis. **Portugal**: At least 70 people plummeted to their deaths when a bridge over the Douro River collapsed, sending a tour bus and three cars into the water (Mar. 3). Minister of Public Works Jorge Coelho resigned after the disaster, accepting political responsibility. **Russia**: Space station *Mir* returned to the Earth's atmosphere and burned up over the South Pacific. A final thrust was given Mar. 22; the debris landed in the Pacific Ocean on Mar. 23. **Saudi Arabia**: Thirty-five people were trampled to death during a symbolic ritual in which pilgrims throw stones at pillars representing Satan, part of the annual pilgrimage Muslims take to retrace the footsteps of the prophet Muhammad (Mar. 5). In Medina, Saudi commandos stormed a Russian airliner hijacked by Chechen rebels, freeing more than 100 passengers and crew (Mar. 16). Three people were killed in the rescue operation, which was authorized after hijackers threatened to blow up the plane. Three hijackers had seized control of the Moscow-bound Tuplov 154 jet as it left Istanbul airport, issuing a list of demands including an end to Russia's military campaign in Chechnya. **Uganda**: Ugandan President Yoweri Museveni won re-election with 69 per cent of the vote against 28 per cent for his main rival, Kizza Besigye (Mar. 12). **United Kingdom**: The farming industry continued to suffer through mass killings of herds and the discovery of foot-and-mouth disease on a pig farm. **United States**: President George W. Bush angered environmentalists when he dropped plans to support legislation that would require power plants to reduce emissions of carbon dioxide, the chief greenhouse gas implicated in global warming. Shortly after, he let the world know that the US would no longer support the Kyoto Agreement to reduce greenhouse gas emissions.

CANADA

Bernard Landry was acclaimed as premier of Quebec on March 8, replacing Lucien Bouchard. Landry did not face a leadership race for the top job as leader of the Parti Quebecois. Karla Homolka was at risk to kill again and should serve her entire prison sentence for her role in the sex slayings of two Ontario teenagers, the National Parole Board ruled. Homolka will remain behind bars until July 2005. Three teens died while playing on an ice floe in the small

Newfoundland community of Pouch Cove, 18 km north of St. John's (Mar. 8). The youths were jumping from slab to slab when a wave swept two of them into the frigid water. A third fell in while attempting to rescue his friends, and all three slipped under the ice. A fourth teen managed to escape. Alberta Premier Ralph Klein won his third term in the March 12 election, capturing 74 seats, 11 more than in 1997; the Liberals won seven seats and the NDP two. Hundreds of tractors and other farm vehicles headed for downtown Ottawa as part of a Canada-wide protest to back demands for more financial support for farmers. The federal government unveiled a $500-million aid package, but farmers—hurt by low commodity prices and a series of poor harvests due to drought-like conditions—said it was not nearly enough to keep them going. The National Day of Action across Canada was held on March 14. The British Columbia Supreme Court ruled that parents are liable if their teenage children's party guests drink too much and drive. A family in Enderby, BC, was ordered to pay part of the $2.5 million in damages awarded to a teenage boy who was seriously injured in a 1998 car crash after leaving a party (Mar. 15). Canada's softwood lumber deal with the US expired on Mar. 31; US companies immediately began asking Washington to establish antidumping and countervailing duties against Canadian products.

APRIL 2001

INTERNATIONAL

Algeria: The death of a Berber high school student while in police custody touched off two months of riots that spread beyond Berber territory to disaffected youth enraged by joblessness and police brutality (Apr. 18). **China:** A US spy plane was forced to land in China Apr. 1 after colliding with a Chinese fighter plane; the Chinese pilot was killed when his plane crashed. The crew was held for 11 days until the Chinese accepted a carefully worded US letter of apology. The US agreed to pay $35,000 to cover the cost of feeding and caring for the crew. (The plane was sent home, in pieces, in July.) **Peru:** The April 8th presidential election gave Alejandro Toledo the lead, but his failure to get 50 percent of the vote meant there would be a run-off vote later in the year. **Japan:** Reformer Junichiro Koizumi was elected Prime Minister of Japan; his first cabinet included more women and younger politicians than the government had seen in decades. Koizumi became the country's 11th prime minister in 13 years (Apr. 27). **Philippines:** Former Philippines president Joseph Estrada was charged Apr. 16th with two counts of corruption in office. He was forced out of office in January. **Russia:** Sixty-year-old California millionaire Dennis Tito, the world's first space tourist, spent six days at the international space station *Alpha* (Apr. 28). He paid Russia US $20 million for the trip. **Serbia and Montenegro:** Commandos stormed the retreat of ousted president Slobodan Milosevic and arrested him after a two-day standoff. He was charged with stealing money from the government (Apr. 1). **Sudan:** Sudan's deputy defence minister and 13 other high-ranking military officers were killed after their plane crashed while taking off in southern Sudan (Apr. 4). **United Kingdom:** A Dutch truck driver was sentenced to 14 years in prison for manslaughter after 58 Chinese immigrants slowly suffocated to death during a six-hour ride in the back of his truck on June 19, 2000. **United States:** Ahmed Ressam, an Algerian and former Montreal resident was found guilty of nine criminal offences—the most serious being conspiracy to commit terrorist acts by bringing explosives into the US to disrupt millennium celebrations (Apr. 6). He faced 130 years in prison, but sentencing was delayed until September while he testified against a co-conspirator. Two days of violent protests, fires and looting rocked Cincinnati following the April 7th killing of an unarmed black man by police, the fifth African-American killed by Cincinnati police in seven months. The protests subsided Apr. 11 after a night of fires and looting.

CANADA

Newfoundland was hit by major snowstorm on Apr. 2 during a strike by provincial workers; as a result the roads were not cleared. The blizzard capped a winter that set the all-time record for snowfall. Health minister Allan Rock appointed former Saskatchewan premier Roy Romanow to investigate the Canadian health care system and consider the role of private health care. A VIA train derailed in Stewiacke, NS, injuring 24, when a switch lock was set incorrectly (Apr. 12). A teen was later charged with mischief. Astronaut Chris Hadfield became the first Canadian to walk in space as he deployed the new CANADARM2 during a Space Shuttle mission to space station *Alpha* (Apr. 19). The Summit of the Americas was held in Quebec City from April 20-22. More than 30,000 demonstrators marched and attempted to disrupt the meeting of national leaders from North, Central and South America. Several hundred were arrested following battles with police, and thousands were tear-gassed as they tried to break through a chain link fence that surrounded the area. Edmonton Alliance MP Rahim Jaffer apologized to Parliament, his party, his constituents and his parents after admitting that his executive assistant had impersonated him over the phone during a 40-minute interview on a Vancouver radio show and that Jaffer had lied to cover it up. Vancouver Liberal Hedy Fry, the Secretary of State for Multiculturalism, apologized twice in Parliament after stating in a speech on racism that there were Ku Klux Klan-style cross-burnings on the lawns of Prince George, BC. No evidence of such events was found. Ontario Chief Justice Patrick LeSage approved a no-fault settlement in a class-action suit that arose from the tainted water tragedy in Walkerton, Ont. In May 2000, seven people died and 2,300 became ill from the town's contaminated tap water supply. Under the settlement, all of the town's 5,000 residents plus visitors, who got sick, received at least $2,000. Those who became ill, lost loved ones or experienced economic losses could apply for further compensation. After 14 years in provincial politics, New Brunswick Liberal leader Camille Theriault, 46, quit as party leader and resigned his seat in the legislature. Theriault was premier from May 1998, to June 1999. More than 2,000 police officers swooped down on Hell's Angels and other motorcycle gangs in Quebec, Ontario and British Columbia, arresting as many as 130 people (Mar. 28). Police also laid 13 new charges of first-degree murder against Angels' national president Maurice (Mom) Boucher, who was already in custody in Quebec facing murder charges for the 1997 deaths of two prison guards. Thirty-six Chinese migrants were found aboard a cargo ship docked in Vancouver. The migrants, who had spent 15 days in containers, were believed to be headed for California.

May 2001

INTERNATIONAL

Afghanistan: The Taliban government ordered all non-Muslims to wear a yellow piece of cloth to identify themselves; officials insisted that the ruling was in order to protect the minority from harassment by the religious police. **Chile:** Twenty-six prisoners burned to death in a crowded jail in Iquique, 1,800 kilometres north of Santiago. Prisoners said the fire started by accident, but authorities said the prisoners were protesting crowded conditions. **China:** A landslide caused by severe rain caused the collapse of a nine-storey building, killing 75 people in Chongqing (May 1). **Ghana:** 126 people were killed in a stampede at a packed soccer game between two of Ghana's leading teams (May 10). Police had fired tear gas into the crowd after fans hurled debris onto the field. **Korea, North:** The European Commission decided to establish diplomatic relations with North Korea to facilitate European efforts to secure reconciliation on the Korean peninsula and boost support for "economic reform and easing of the acute food and health problems" in North Korea. **Italy:** Silvio Berlusconi won re-election as president despite reports of corruption (May 14). **Nepal**: Two Americans reached the peak of Mount Everest on May 24, becoming the first blind climber and the oldest man to step onto the roof of the world. The blind climber, Erik Weihenmayer, 32, of Golden, Colo., and Sherman Bull, a 64-year-old physician from New Canaan, Conn., reached the summit of the world's tallest mountain only minutes apart, climbing with different groups. **Pakistan**: Temperatures that soared to 122 degrees F killed at least 36 people during a lengthy heatwave that lasted for much of the month. **Philippines**: Muslim militiamen, Abu Sayyaf guerrillas who want an independent homeland, seized three Americans and 17 Filipino hostages from a tourist resort. They freed some hostages, reportedly for large ransom payments, but seized more captives and beheaded five, including one American. **Russia:** Siberia's Yakutia region suffered a week of serious flooding that displaced 42,000 people and did $6 billion in damage along the shores of the Lena River. By May 21, Russian bombers were blasting ice blocks in an effort to improve the water flow. **Spain**: Parties backing independence for the troubled Basque region won the most seats in a key election on May 13, but voters rejected a party linked to violent separatism. **United States**: Alfred Taubman, 76, former chairman of Sotheby's Holdings Inc., and Sir Anthony Tennant, 71, former chairman of Christie's International, were arrested on charges that their auction houses colluded to fix commission rates and overcharged sellers by $400 million over six years. The Journal of the American Medical Association published a study involving 1,417 women in the US and Canada and the world's first contraceptive patch (May 9). The study revealed that the patch was as safe and effective as the pill and easier to use. The May 16 execution of convicted Oklahoma bomber Timothy McVeigh was delayed when the FBI revealed new evidence that had not been presented at his trial. Republican senator James Jeffords resigned from his party to sit as an independent, robbing the Republicans of control of the Senate and handing it to the Democrats (May 24).

CANADA

American George Gillett closed a deal to buy 80 per cent of the Montreal Canadiens from Molson Inc. for $275 million (May 7). (The deal was approved by the National Hockey League in June and became final in July.) Toronto Liberal MP Tom Wappel ignited a firestorm of controversy when it was revealed that he had refused to help an elderly, handicapped constituent because the man had not voted for him (May 9). The MP issued an apology on May 10. On May 15, eight Alliance MPs left the party and formed a rebel faction. Throughout the month, speculation was high concerning who else might abandon the party over the continuing debate concerning leader Stockwell Day's performance. Ottawa announced that the last underground coal mine in Cape Breton would be shut down by the fall, citing unprofitability; 500 jobs will disappear, along with a 280-year tradition (May 16). Liberal leader Gordon Campbell became Premier of British Columbia after his party defeated the NDP led by Ujjal Dosanjh in a May 16 vote. The NDP was reduced to just two seats, not enough to be an official opposition party. Campbell moved quickly to cut taxes, end photo radar and replace many unpopular NDP laws. The CANADARM2, recently installed at the International Space Station, froze on May 17 during a rigorous testing procedure. It took staff at the arm's manufacturer 40 days to repair the problem, which was a computer malfunction. Nova Scotia passed legislation giving gay couples registered with the Department of Vital Statistics some of the rights formerly reserved for married heterosexual couples. Alistair MacLeod won the world's richest literary prize—the annual $172,000 International IMPAC Dublin Literary Award—for his debut novel, *No Great Mischief*.

JUNE 2001

INTERNATIONAL

Argentina: Carlos Menem, 70, the President of Argentina from 1989 to 1999, was arrested on charges of leading a conspiracy to smuggle 6,500 tons of arms to Croatia and Ecuador while in office (June 7). **China**: A fire at a kindergarten dormitory in Nanching killed 13 children, the oldest just four years old. The blaze started when a burning coil of mosquito repellent set fire to bedding. Typhoon Chebi killed at least 75 people when it hit China's southeastern coast, after leaving nine dead in Taiwan. Another 85 people were killed in coastal Fujian province (June 23-24). **Ecuador**: Torrential rains set off an avalanche of rock and mud that slammed down on a group of stranded motorists in the Andes, killing 36 (June 12). **India**: A four-day curfew was imposed after rioters burned Manipur state government buildings to protest a cease-fire deal with separatist rebels. A three-day strike preceded the rioting, in which 16 protesters were killed by police as police tried to prevent a mob from burning the official residence of the state's top official (June 18). The legislature building, political party offices and a dozen politicians' homes were torched. **Ireland**: The worst riots in Belfast in three years injured 39 police as they clashed with demonstrators (June 21). **Israel**: A suicide bomber slipped in among Israelis at a beachfront night spot in Tel Aviv and detonated his belt of explosives, blasting ball bearings, nails and screws through the crowd (June 1). Eighteen were killed and 115 injured. Over 520 people were reported killed in violence that had been escalating since September 2000. **Japan**: A man brandishing a knife burst into an elementary school in Ikeda, 400 km west of Tokyo, killing eight children and slashing 15 others. The 37-year-old man was subdued by a vice-principal and a teacher, who was slightly injured (June 8). **Macedonia**: Ethnic Albanian rebels, fighting for independence in the Kosovo border region, advanced within mortar distance of the capital's airport as NATO and the country's government tried to find a workable cease-fire and a means of disarming the rebel forces. **Nepal**: On June 1, Nepalese Crown Prince Dipendra shot and killed his parents and nine other family members before turning the gun on himself. He was reportedly outraged by his family's disapprovel of his choice of a bride. The prince, though in a coma, was enthroned as king, only to die on June 4th. Gyanendra, younger brother of the late King Birendra and a less ardent supporter of democracy than his brother, went from regent to king after Dipendra's death. **Pakistan**: Pakistan's military ruler Gen. Pervez Musharraf dismissed the president and took the post himself, consolidating power ahead of a summit with the prime minister of nuclear rival India (June 20). Musharraf promised to return the country to democracy by 2002. **Peru**: More than 70 people were killed when a massive earthquake hit Arequipa, Peru's second-largest city (June 23). Fugitive Peruvian spymaster Vladimir Montesinos, accused of amassing a fortune from arms dealing and drug trafficking, was captured in Caracas. **Rwanda**: Four people, including two Catholic nuns, were sentenced to prison terms of 12 to 20 years for their roles in the 1994 Hutu extermination of the Tutsi in Rwanda. The nuns turned over as many as 7,000 people seeking refuge in their convent to the Hutu militia. **Serbia and Montenegro**: Slobodan Milosevic was extradited to The Hague on June 28 to stand trial before the war crimes tribunal on charges of crimes against humanity for the deaths of Kosovo Albanians in 1999. **United Kingdom:** Labour Prime Minister Tony Blair's government was re-elected in a landslide, with 413 seats in Parliament, compared to 166 for the Conservatives (June 7). A judge granted Jon Venables and Robert Thompson, the convicted killers of two-year-old James Bulger, anonymity when they were released from prison on parole (June 22). The decision banned the media from disclosing any information about their new identities or location.

Venables and Thompson were 10 when they abducted Bulger from a Liverpool shopping mall in 1993 before beating him to death. **United States**: In New York, at the United Nations, Kofi Annan won election to a second five-year term at the helm of the United Nations with support from every corner of the globe (June 29). Convicted Oklahoma City bomber Timothy McVeigh was executed on June 11 by lethal injection. McVeigh admitted setting the bomb that killed 168 people in the Oklahoma City federal building in 1995. Napster, the formerly free online music service, announced a for-pay download venture in conjunction with AOL Time Warner Inc., Bertelsmann AG and EMI Group. Since the shutdown of Napster's free service, a number of free alternative services have proliferated on the Internet. Microsoft won a key legal battle when a US court overturned an order to break-up the company, saying the judge may have appeared to be biased. It ordered another hearing on remedies for its anti-competitive behaviour. The US National Academy of Sciences released a report confirming that global warming is a serious problem, only weeks after US President Bush rejected the Kyoto Protocol, designed to deal with the problem.

CANADA

Rei Fujii, 23, was charged with two counts of murder after police found the body of Fujii's 15-month-old son, Domenic Brown, in her empty Calgary apartment on June 5. Police believe the body of his three-month-old sister, Gemini, was wrapped in a garbage bag and dumped in the Bow River, but her body was not found. The CRTC ruled that cable companies would be allowed to buy specialty TV channels, paving the way for further convergence in Canada's media. Members of Parliament voted to fast-track a new pay package for themselves, which included a 20 percent raise but an end to their tax-free expense allowance (June 5). Liberals and Bloc Quebecois members voted for the hike, along with some Alliance and Conservative

members. All NDP members opposed it. Under the new package, backbenchers will get $131,000 a year and cabinet ministers $194,000. The prime minister will receive $262,000. In British Columbia, 11,000 health care workers held an illegal two-day walkout in a bid to get a collective agreement (June 18). Calgary-based Gulf Canada Resources Ltd. agreed to be taken over by Conoco Inc. of Houston for $9.8 billion. The Ontario government became the first provincial government to offer tax credits to families with children in private or independent religious schools (June 27). The credit will be phased in over five years. On June 27, Nova Scotia's Bill 68, which took away the right to strike from many health-care workers and allowed the provincial cabinet to set contract terms, passed, after two weeks of heated debate. The total of Alliance defections reached 11 on June 27, putting the rebel group one member shy of qualifying for party status on their own. The Supreme Court of Canada ruled that municipalities have the right to ban pesticide use on public and private property. The court stated that the Montreal suburb of Hudson was within its rights when it became the first Canadian municipality to outlaw the use of pesticides on lawns in 1991 (June 29). Ontario Premier Mike Harris testified before the Walkerton inquiry that he was never warned of risks to human health posed by funding cuts to the Environment Ministry (June 29). Contaminated drinking water in Walkerton killed seven people and made 2,000 sick in the spring of 2000.

July 2001

INTERNATIONAL

Belgium: The competition division of the European Commission in Brussels, which claims jurisdiction over any merger between firms with a combined $4.3 billion in sales globally and more than $215 million of its business in Europe, refused to approve the merger of Honeywell International and General Electric (July 3). **Brazil**: More than

100 inmates escaped from a maximum-security prison in Sao Paulo by tunnelling into the city sewers. Many were quickly recaptured. Most of the escaped convicts were members of the First Capital Command, an organized crime group working within Brazil's prison system. **Burundi**: President Pierre Buyoya sealed a power-sharing deal aimed at ending the country's eight-year civil war just hours after Tutsi soldiers opposed to the deal staged a mutiny and kidnapped the army chief. The mutineers later surrendered. **Chile**: An appeals court ruled that Gen. Augusto Pinochet could not be tried on human rights charges because of the 85-year-old former dictator's deteriorating mental health. The trial against Pinochet, dictator of the South American country from 1973 to 1990, concerned the murder of political opponents after a coup in 1973. **China**: Fourteen imprisoned followers of the banned Falun Gong sect committed suicide in a north China labor camp, making ropes from sheets and hanging themselves from bunk beds. More than 100 miners were killed when a powerful blast ripped through an illegally operated coal pit in the southeastern province of Jiangsu. Citizens celebrated in Tiananmen Square when the IOC announced that Beijing would be the site of the 2008 Summer Olympic Games (July 13). **Germany**: Negotiators from 178 nations meeting in Bonn reached a deal to salvage a treaty on combatting global warming, following marathon negotiations (July 26). **India**: The man charged with shooting India's "Bandit Queen," Phoolan Devi, said he killed the outlaw-turned-politician in revenge for a massacre of 21 upper caste men two decades ago. Devi, 38, was gunned down in New Delhi outside her home as she arrived for a lunch break from Parliament. **Indonesia**: Legislators voted to dismiss popular President Abdurrahman Wahid and swear in his estranged Vice-President, Megawati Sukarnoputri. Wahid at first refused to step down, but eventually left for medical treatment in the US (July 26). **Israel**: As violence continued to escalate, an Israeli heli-copter destroyed the party office of Palestinian President Yasser Arafat. Witnesses claimed that two missiles were fired. **Italy**: An anti-globalization demonstration got violent at a G8 meeting in Genoa and protester Carlo Giuliani, 23, was shot dead by police during a violent assault on a vehicle carrying several police officers (July 20). Mount Etna, which had been giving off warning signs for weeks, began to spew gas, lava and ash, forcing residents of Catania, at the foot of the mountain, to evacuate and destroying ski-lift pylons at a nearby resort (July 28). **Jamaica**: Twenty-seven people were killed and 40 wounded in the violence that began July 7 during a police weapons sweep in a neighbourhood considered a stronghold of government opposition groups. Police said snipers fired first, launching the battle. The military moved in two days later to calm the situation. Five more people were killed later in the month in the same area. **Macedonia**: The Macedonian government announced a cease-fire with ethnic Albanian rebels whose four-month insurgency had threatened political stability however, a NATO-inspired peace deal sparked riots as forces attempted to move 300 Albanian fighters to an ethnic Albanian area in the north. **Pakistan**: Torrential downpours killed 200 people in Pakistan and caused millions of dollars worth of damage. Most of the deaths were caused by mudslides, flash floods and collapsing houses in the North West Frontier Province, the capital Islamabad and the adjacent city of Rawalpindi. **Philippines**: Typhoon Utor battered the northern Philippines, killing at least 120 people. The storm also killed 60 people in Taiwan and 30 in China (July 4-5). **Taiwan**: Typhoon Toraji left at 61 people dead and at month's end 150 were still missing in the rock and mudslides and flash floods (July 30). The same day, a 4.9 earthquake rattled the area. **United Kingdom**: Protestant leader David Trimble resigned after the IRA once again failed to turn over its weapons by the set date (July 1). 120 police officers in northern England were injured by mobs of white and South Asian

youths armed with bats, rocks and firebombs (July 22). Several buildings were looted and torched. The violence was largely blamed on agitation by right-wing groups. A newly modified British Airways Concorde roared across the Atlantic on the first supersonic test flight since the fleet was grounded last year after a crash near Paris. Belfast rioters injured 110 police officers after members of the Orange Order paraded past a Catholic neighbourhood (July 13). **United States**: Doctors in Kentucky implanted the first self-contained artificial heart in a human, 59-year-old Robert Tools (July 2). The surgery was performed by Dr. Laman Gray and Dr. Robert Dowling, who trained by implanting the grapefruit-sized device in calves. A shark attacked an eight-year-old boy at Pensacola Beach, Fla., tearing off his right arm; firefighters managed to retrieve the arm and surgeons reattached it (July 6). On July 12, the jury began deliberations in the trial of Ahmed Ressam, accused in an alleged terrorist plot involving a bombing at the Los Angeles airport. A freight train derailed in a Baltimore tunnel and caught fire, forcing the city to shut down major highways and cancel events; the train was carrying hazardous materials and residents were urged to stay indoors (July 19). It took five days to clear the wreckage. The US rejected an agreement to enforce the 1972 biological weapons convention, citing national security concerns. In a separate conference, US negotiators threatened to leave the table at a UN conference on small arms, claiming it would interfere in their citizens' right to bear arms. **Uganda**: Over 200 suspected witches were hacked to death in villages in rebel-held northeastern Congo in killings that began in mid-June.

CANADA

Responding to Nova Scotia's Bill 68, healthcare workers threatened to walk off the job almost immediately; nurses were in a legal position to strike on July 10 and 1,450 of them signed letters of resignation. In the face of the protest, Premier Hamm agreed to send the dispute to binding arbitration (July 6). Alliance MP Deborah Grey resigned from the party's executive in the ongoing dispute over Stockwell Day's leadership (July 13). Nortel Networks announced the biggest quarterly loss in Canadian corporate history as it lost US$19.4 billion in its second quarter (July 20). MPs from the Canadian Alliance and the Conservative party held two days of meetings in Halifax; on July 27, the group issued a pledge to work more closely together. In British Columbia, 11,000 health care workers held an illegal two-day walkout in a bid to get a collective agreement. The strike defied a provincial labour board ruling and a legislated return-to-work order in June after the workers staged rotating walkouts. Threats of large fines forced the union to call off the strike. Seven children, removed from their Aylmer, Ont. home by local Children's Aid authorities in a clash over spanking and medical care, were reunited with their Christian fundamentalist parents. On July 30, United Grain Growers and Agricore announced a merger to create a new company, Agricore United. The new company will control close to 40 percent of western Canadian grain.

August 2001

INTERNATIONAL

Australia: More than 430 refugees, mostly Afghans, were taken away from Christmas Island, Australia, by a warship on their way to New Zealand and Nauru and eventual resettlement. Four crew members of an Indonesian ferry were charged with trying to smuggle the refugees into the country. A Norwegian cargo ship rescued the refugees when the ferry began sinking, but the group was forced to remain aboard the rescue vessel for a week until an agreement was worked out on where to send them. **Fiji**: Laisenia Qarase, who had been installed by the military as caretaker prime minister, was elected to the post in late August. But former prime minister, Labour Party leader Mahendra Chaudhry said his party would exercise its constitutional right to take almost half the posts in the cabinet. Qarase's Fijian United Party won 31 seats and Labour 27. **Iraq**: An unmanned US reconnaissance aircraft was shot at over southern Iraq (July 26). **Ireland**: The Irish Republican Army withdrew its agreement on a method for disarming, rebuffing Britain's efforts to create more negotiating time to preserve Northern Ireland's power-sharing government. **Israel**: An Israeli missile killed two Hamas officials in a strike against a Hamas office in Nablus. A suicide bomber killed 15 in a downtown Jerusalem restaurant and Israel retaliated by bombing a West Bank security post. On Aug. 14, Israeli tanks went deep into the West Bank territory in a sortie against Palestinian fighters. **Japan:** Prime Minister Junichiro Koizumi faced criticism at home and abroad after he visited a controversial shrine that included 14 war criminals along with a tribute to the country's 2.5 million dead (Aug. 5). **Macedonia**: Rival political leaders signed a landmark peace accord aimed at ending six months of bloody conflict and clearing the way for NATO troops to disarm ethnic-Albanian rebels. The deal gave ethnic-Albanians a larger share of power in the police ranks, parliament and education. It also paved the way for NATO to send in 3,500 troops to disarm the rebels. **Malaysia**: Police arrested 10 members of the Malaysian Mujahideen Group as *jihad*-style violence began to infiltrate the Muslim-Christian battles (Aug. 4). **Portugal**: An Air Transat plane en route to Lisbon from Toronto ran out of fuel in mid-flight due to a mechanical problem. The pilot managed to glide the plane for 180 km and land safely, without power, in the Azores (Aug. 24). **Ukraine**: Forty-seven miners were trapped in a mine by a gas explosion at Zasyadko mine near the eastern city of Donetsk. **United States**: The Federal Bureau of Investigation arrested eight people allegedly involved in a scheme to defraud the McDonald's Corp. of $13 million by rigging several of the fast food company's promotional games since 1995. Under the scheme—involving friends and family

members—insiders won the top prizes in games by obtaining key game pieces. The US Coast Guard said the Russian-operated oil tanker *Virgo* collided with the American fishing boat *Starbound* on Aug. 5, killing three of the four men on board. Canadian authorities seized the 180-metre ship when it arrived at the refinery near Come-By-Chance, Nfld., on Aug. 7. The ship was freed after Primorsk Shipping Corp., which manages the MT *Virgo*, agreed to post a US$23-million bond to cover potential damages. President Bush announced approval for federal funding for limited medical research on stem cells extracted from human embryos, adding he had come down in favour of funding because of the potential for new cures for chronic diseases.

CANADA

The World Championships in Athletics opened in Edmonton on Aug. 3 for a 10-day span of competition. Health care turmoil continued in British Columbia as nurses walked off their jobs in illegal strike action, a day after the provincial government moved to legislate a contract (Aug. 7). Workers at 34 nursing homes in New Brunswick went on strike to back contract demands. All but four homes reached an agreement after one day, and the final three settled after four days. The provincial premiers, in a rare show of solidarity, demanded $7-billion from Ottawa to shore up their health-care systems or cuts would be made to service (Aug. 3). The US commerce department levied a 19.3 percent duty on Canadian softwood lumber from all provinces outside Atlantic Canada; the duty was made retroactive to mid-May and was projected to cost Canadian producers $4 billion a year (Aug. 10). On Aug. 11, a malfunction on the Welland Canal damaged a freighter in transit; the disabled ship and subsequent fire shut down the busy shipping route for two days. Conrad Black announced he was selling his remaining half interest in the *National Post* newspaper to the Asper family's CanWest Global, which bought half the paper when he purchased several

Hollinger papers from Black (Aug. 24). An arbitrator appointed by the Nova Scotia government in the health care workers' dispute agreed with the pay hike proposed by the union representing Nova Scotia's registered nurses, but sided with the province in lesser increases for other health workers (Aug. 14). By Aug. 28, 10 birds in Southern Ontario were found to be carrying the West Nile virus, which can be fatal in humans. No human cases were reported in Canada. The disease is spread by mosquitoes. The hot dry summer continued to affect most of the country, with prairie farmers waiting in vain for rain and getting a swarm of grasshoppers instead in many regions; a heat emergency was declared in Toronto; yet another smog alert was in effect for southern Ontario; and Nova Scotia was forced to ban campfires. On Aug. 30, Foreign Affairs Minister John Manley announced that he would not be attending the UN's controversial conference on racism; junior minister Hedy Fry would attend. On Aug. 31, fishermen in Burnt Church, NB replaced lobster traps that had been seized the day before by fisheries officials, as the month-long battle over rights in Miramichi Bay neared a climax.

September 2001

INTERNATIONAL

Afghanistan: Spokesmen for the Taliban government claimed to have shot down a US spy plane as tensions in the region mounted after the terrorist bombings in the US (Sept. 22). As the threat of military action grew, thousands of Afghan citizens fled to the border with Pakistan to avoid the conflict and a humanitarian crisis loomed for those who were displaced. **Belarus:** President Alexander Lukashenko, Belarus' authoritarian president, swept to another five-year term on promises to merge with Russia and stand up to the West, but international monitors denounced the election as unfair. **Egypt:** A 15-year-old boy was sentenced Sept. 18 to three years in prison for practising homosexuality, the first verdict in the mass Egyptian gay trial. The

youth, who was found guilty of homosexuality and debauchery, was ordered to serve his sentence in a prison for young offenders. **France:** A surgical team in New York performed a gallbladder operation on a patient in Strasbourg, France, by sending high-speed signals to robots. Dr. Jacques Marescaux of France's Research Institute Against Cancers of the Digestive Tract was in New York for the Sept. 7 operation, watching the patient, a 68-year-old woman, on a screen and using tools hooked up to sensors. The patient had no complications and was released from hospital two days later. A huge accidental explosion at a chemical fertilizer plant in Toulouse killed 45 people and injured hundreds (Sept. 21). Windows were blown out for kilometres around and a nearby sports stadium sustained extensive structural damage. **Indonesia:** At least 40 people were killed Sept. 2 when a passenger train slammed into a locomotive in the town of Cirebon on Indonesia's main island of Java. **Japan:** The first case of mad cow disease in Japan, or anywhere in Asia, was discovered in one cow east of Tokyo. Contaminated feed was believed to be the cause of the disease. **Macedonia:** The Macedonian parliament gave preliminary approval to changes in the country's constitution that would entrench Albanian language rights and guarantee Albanians a role in the national police force. While this was no guarantee that the measures would pass, the leader of Macedonia's ethnic-Albanian rebels declared Sept. 27 that his group had formally disbanded, just hours after NATO wrapped up its mission collecting arms from the guerrillas. The rebel move came as NATO promised that a new 1,000-strong force would deploy quickly to help provide security in still-tense Macedonia. The rebels handed over the final batch of a total of 3,875 rifles, mortars, howitzers and a tank. **Poland:** A leftist party with roots in Poland's former communist regime won a majority in parliamentary elections. Solidarity—the party that led Poland out of communism 12 years ago but splintered to a remnant of its former self under a string of defections, infighting and corruption scandals—failed to get any seats (Sept. 23). **South Africa**: A United Nations conference on racism held in Durban was the centre of racist allegations as several countries, but not Canada, withdrew over a resolution equating Zionism with racism against Arabs. **Switzerland**: A Swiss man went on a shooting rampage during a session at a state legislature in Zug on Sept. 27, spraying an assault rifle at random and setting off an explosive. Fourteen people were killed, including the gunman. The man had a grievance against local officials and was dressed as a policeman. **Taiwan:** Typhoon Nari killed 85 people and dumped four months' worth of rain in just over two days (Sept. 18-19). Millions of dollars of damage was done and the capital's mass rapid transit system was shut down indefinitely after flooding. **United Kingdom**: Protestant demonstrators screamed and threw stones as young Roman Catholic schoolgirls walked through their Belfast neighbourhood in the Ardoyne area to get to school. The Protestant cause was condemned worldwide as the photos were flashed around the world. On Sept. 5, the third day of protest, a pipe bomb exploded outside the entrance to the primary school; police and soldiers brought in to protect the children and their parents were injured. On Sept. 22, Northern Ireland's regional assembly was reinstated after a 24-hour shut down designed to save the body from collapse. The assembly was also suspended for 24 hours six weeks earlier after a crisis sparked by the resignation of assembly leader David Trimble. Under the laws that created the power-sharing Northern Ireland Assembly, it must be suspended and power handed back to London if it goes more than six weeks without a leader. **United States**: On Sept. 1, a shark attacked a 10-year-old boy at Virginia Beach, Va. Two days later, a couple were attacked while wading in the surf off North Carolina's Outer Banks, killing the man and critically injuring his girlfriend, who lost her left foot. Hewlett-Packard Co. announced it would buy fellow computer maker Compaq Computer Corp. for an estimated US$25 billion, a deal meant to bolster the two companies that had been saddled with sagging profits and massive job cuts.

September 11: The US suffers the worst terrorist attack in its history, with total casualties estimated at 6,500.

Chronology:

7:59 a.m. American Airlines Flight 11 (92 passengers) left Logan International Airport (Boston) for Los Angeles.

8:01 a.m. United Airlines Flight 93 (45 passengers) left Newark International Airport for San Francisco.

8:10 a.m. American Airlines Flight 77 (64 passengers) left Dulles International Airport (Washington) for Los Angeles.

8:14 a.m. United Airlines Flight 175 (65 passengers) left Logan International Airport (Boston) for Los Angeles.

8:48 a.m. American Airlines Flight 11 crashed into the World Trade Centre, north tower, and exploded.

9:06 a.m. United Airlines Flight 175 crashed into the World Trade Centre, south tower, and exploded.

9:17 a.m. US FAA shut down all airports in the New York City area.

9:21 a.m. Port Authority of New York shut down all bridges and tunnels in the New York area.

9:43 a.m. American Airlines Flight 77 crashed into the Pentagon, causing one side of the building to collapse.

9:45 a.m. US FAA stopped all takeoffs in the US and closed US airspace. International flights were directed to land at the closest destination available.

9:50 a.m. The north tower of the World Trade Centre collapsed.

10:10 a.m. United Airlines Flight 93 crashed near Shanksville, Pa., 130 km southeast of Pittsburgh.

10:29 a.m. The south tower of the World Trade Centre collapsed.

11:30 a.m. US government buildings across

the country were evacuated; UN was closed down; US financial markets were closed and lower Manhattan was evacuated.

In the days that followed the attacks, 7,000 FBI agents were assigned to the investigation and the US administration moved quickly to build a global alliance to combat the terrorist threat. Suspects were detained in Canada, the UK, Germany, and Middle Eastern and African countries as efforts were made to identify supporters of the suicide bombers and uncover the network that fueled their activities. The US and its allies focussed much of their attention on the Taliban regime in Afghanistan and their "guest" Osama bin Laden, a terrorist supporter already implicated in the bombing of the US embassies in Africa and the attack on the USS *Cole*. US demands that the Taliban surrender bin Laden were met with some resistance from the regime, which demanded proof before they would undertake such action. On Friday, September 14, a day of mourning was marked in many countries around the world as citizens expressed their condolences to the people of the US.

In the wake of the attacks, the U.S. stock market fell, wiping out a trillion dollars off the value of major companies. Hundreds of thousands of airline and travel industry workers were laid off, as air travel was reduced and the US pledged funds to keep the major airlines in business and to prime the faltering economy.

On Sept. 15, five people died when a group of barges smashed a 73 m section out of a bridge leading to South Padre Island, Tex., and their vehicles plunged into the water over 25 m below. On Sept. 24, a tornado tore through an area from Culpeper, VA to Laurel, skirting the US capital, left three dead and caused millions of dollars in damage as it downed trees and power lines and shut down the University of Maryland.

CANADA

On Sept. 5, the Saskatchewan government assured the province's hunters that they would not be prosecuted for hunting without their firearm registration if they could prove

they had applied for one. The backlog in registrations had many concerned over the coming season. On Sept. 7, nearly 50 new channels, including The Documentary Channel and Country Canada, were offered to viewers who receive digital TV through set-top boxes or satellite dishes. On Sept. 11, three of the Alliance dissidents returned to the party caucus and the remaining eight formed a coalition with the Conservatives in the House of Commons. Hundreds of flights denied entry into US airspace were grounded in Canada after the terrorist attacks; thousands of travellers were put up in various Canadian communities, from Gander to Vancouver, as space was found in hotels, motels, school gyms and private homes. In the wake of the Sept. 11 attacks in the US, stricter surveillance made it tougher to cross the Canada-U.S. border and delayed shipments, forcing thousands of layoffs in the Ontario auto industry. The ban on air traffic in Canada was lifted on the afternoon of Sept. 12; however, it took days for air traffic to return to normal schedules. On Sept. 14, 100,000 gathered on Parliament Hill to pay their respects to the victims of the US terrorist attacks, while thousands more across the country observed a minute in silence. Tropical storm Gabrielle pounded the eastern coast of Newfoundland with lashing rain and hurricane force winds of 111 kilometres an hour (Sept. 19). The damage prompted the provincial government to apply for assistance from the federal disaster relief fund. On Sept. 24, the group of 20 in the rightwing coalition were given permission by the House speaker to sit and work together however, they were denied party status because they were not serving "under the same banner." General Motors announced that it would close its assembly plant in Broisbriand, Que. in the fall of 2002, eliminating 1,200 jobs and the auto industry in that province (Sept. 25). The plant made Firebirds and Camaros, two products that would be phased-out by 2002. On Sept. 26, Ottawa announced it would freeze the assets of any group the US identified as having terrorist links.

Index

N

2001

JANUARY
S	M	T	W	T	F	S
	[1]	2	3	4	5	6
7	8	9	10	11	12	13
14	15	16	17	18	19	20
21	22	23	24	25	26	27
28	29	30	31			

FEBRUARY
S	M	T	W	T	F	S
				1	2	3
4	5	6	7	8	9	10
11	12	13	14	15	16	17
18	19	20	21	22	23	24
25	26	27	28			

MARCH
S	M	T	W	T	F	S
				1	2	3
4	5	6	7	8	9	10
11	12	13	14	15	16	17
18	19	20	21	22	23	24
25	26	27	28	29	30	31

APRIL
S	M	T	W	T	F	S
1	2	3	4	5	6	7
8	9	10	11	12	[13]	14
15	16	17	18	19	20	21
22	23	24	25	26	27	28
29	30					

MAY
S	M	T	W	T	F	S
		1	2	3	4	5
6	7	8	9	10	11	12
13	14	15	16	17	18	19
20	[21]	22	23	24	25	26
27	28	29	30	31		

JUNE
S	M	T	W	T	F	S
					1	2
3	4	5	6	7	8	9
10	11	12	13	14	15	16
17	18	19	20	21	22	23
24	25	26	27	28	29	30

JULY
S	M	T	W	T	F	S
[1]	2	3	4	5	6	7
8	9	10	11	12	13	14
15	16	17	18	19	20	21
22	23	24	25	26	27	28
29	30	31				

AUGUST
S	M	T	W	T	F	S
			1	2	3	4
5	6	7	8	9	10	11
12	13	14	15	16	17	18
19	20	21	22	23	24	25
26	27	28	29	30	31	

SEPTEMBER
S	M	T	W	T	F	S
						1
2	[3]	4	5	6	7	8
9	10	11	12	13	14	15
16	17	18	19	20	21	22
23	24	25	26	27	28	29
30						

OCTOBER
S	M	T	W	T	F	S
	1	2	3	4	5	6
7	[8]	9	10	11	12	13
14	15	16	17	18	19	20
21	22	23	24	25	26	27
28	29	30	31			

NOVEMBER
S	M	T	W	T	F	S
				1	2	3
4	5	6	7	8	9	10
11	12	13	14	15	16	17
18	19	20	21	22	23	24
25	26	27	28	29	30	

DECEMBER
S	M	T	W	T	F	S
						1
2	3	4	5	6	7	8
9	10	11	12	13	14	15
16	17	18	19	20	21	22
23	24	[25]	[26]	27	28	29
30	31					

2003

JANUARY
S	M	T	W	T	F	S
			[1]	2	3	4
5	6	7	8	9	10	11
12	13	14	15	16	17	18
19	20	21	22	23	24	25
26	27	28	29	30	31	

FEBRUARY
S	M	T	W	T	F	S
						1
2	3	4	5	6	7	8
9	10	11	12	13	14	15
16	17	18	19	20	21	22
23	24	25	26	27	28	

MARCH
S	M	T	W	T	F	S
						1
2	3	4	5	6	7	8
9	10	11	12	13	14	15
16	17	18	19	20	21	22
23	24	25	26	27	28	29
30	31					

APRIL
S	M	T	W	T	F	S
		1	2	3	4	5
6	7	8	9	10	11	12
13	14	15	16	17	[18]	19
20	21	22	23	24	25	26
27	28	29	30			

MAY
S	M	T	W	T	F	S
				1	2	3
4	5	6	7	8	9	10
11	12	13	14	15	16	17
18	[19]	20	21	22	23	24
25	26	27	28	29	30	31

JUNE
S	M	T	W	T	F	S
1	2	3	4	5	6	7
8	9	10	11	12	13	14
15	16	17	18	19	20	21
22	23	24	25	26	27	28
29	30					

JULY
S	M	T	W	T	F	S
		[1]	2	3	4	5
6	7	8	9	10	11	12
13	14	15	16	17	18	19
20	21	22	23	24	25	26
27	28	29	30	31		

AUGUST
S	M	T	W	T	F	S
					1	2
3	4	5	6	7	8	9
10	11	12	13	14	15	16
17	18	19	20	21	22	23
24	25	26	27	28	29	30
31						

SEPTEMBER
S	M	T	W	T	F	S
	[1]	2	3	4	5	6
7	8	9	10	11	12	13
14	15	16	17	18	19	20
21	22	23	24	25	26	27
28	29	30				

OCTOBER
S	M	T	W	T	F	S
			1	2	3	4
5	6	7	8	9	10	11
12	[13]	14	15	16	17	18
19	20	21	22	23	24	25
26	27	28	29	30	31	

NOVEMBER
S	M	T	W	T	F	S
						1
2	3	4	5	6	7	8
9	10	11	12	13	14	15
16	17	18	19	20	21	22
23	24	25	26	27	28	29
30						

DECEMBER
S	M	T	W	T	F	S
	1	2	3	4	5	6
7	8	9	10	11	12	13
14	15	16	17	18	19	20
21	22	23	24	[25]	[26]	27
28	29	30	31			

2002 CALENDAR AND HOLIDAYS

JANUARY
S	M	T	W	T	F	S
		1	2	3	4	5
6	7	8	9	10	11	12
13	14	15	16	17	18	19
20	21	22	23	24	25	26
27	28	29	30	31		

FEBRUARY
S	M	T	W	T	F	S
					1	2
3	4	5	6	7	8	9
10	11	12	13	14	15	16
17	18	19	20	21	22	23
24	25	26	27	28		

MARCH
S	M	T	W	T	F	S
					1	2
3	4	5	6	7	8	9
10	11	12	13	14	15	16
17	18	19	20	21	22	23
24	25	26	27	28	29	30
31						

APRIL
S	M	T	W	T	F	S
	1	2	3	4	5	6
7	8	9	10	11	12	13
14	15	16	17	18	19	20
21	22	23	24	25	26	27
28	29	30				

MAY
S	M	T	W	T	F	S
			1	2	3	4
5	6	7	8	9	10	11
12	13	14	15	16	17	18
19	20	21	22	23	24	25
26	27	28	29	30	31	

JUNE
S	M	T	W	T	F	S
						1
2	3	4	5	6	7	8
9	10	11	12	13	14	15
16	17	18	19	20	21	22
23	24	25	26	27	28	29
30						

JULY
S	M	T	W	T	F	S
	1	2	3	4	5	6
7	8	9	10	11	12	13
14	15	16	17	18	19	20
21	22	23	24	25	26	27
28	29	30	31			

AUGUST
S	M	T	W	T	F	S
				1	2	3
4	5	6	7	8	9	10
11	12	13	14	15	16	17
18	19	20	21	22	23	24
25	26	27	28	29	30	31

SEPTEMBER
S	M	T	W	T	F	S
1	2	3	4	5	6	7
8	9	10	11	12	13	14
15	16	17	18	19	20	21
22	23	24	25	26	27	28
29	30					

OCTOBER
S	M	T	W	T	F	S
		1	2	3	4	5
6	7	8	9	10	11	12
13	14	15	16	17	18	19
20	21	22	23	24	25	26
27	28	29	30	31		

NOVEMBER
S	M	T	W	T	F	S
					1	2
3	4	5	6	7	8	9
10	11	12	13	14	15	16
17	18	19	20	21	22	23
24	25	26	27	28	29	30

DECEMBER
S	M	T	W	T	F	S
1	2	3	4	5	6	7
8	9	10	11	12	13	14
15	16	17	18	19	20	21
22	23	24	25	26	27	28
29	30	31				

New Year's Day (January 1), Good Friday (March 29), Victoria Day (May 20), Canada Day (July 1), Labour Day (September 2), Thanksgiving (October 14), Christmas Day and Boxing Day (December 25 and 26).

Other Holidays and Holy Days

Government and bank holidays: April 1 (Easter Monday), November 11 (Remembrance Day).
Islamic Holy Days: These are subject to the sighting of the moon. The key days are: Nuzulul Qur'an; Eidul Fitri; Eidul Adha; Islamic New Year; Ashoora; Maulid Nabi; Isra'and Miraj; First Day of Ramadhan.

Jewish Holy Days: Purim—February 26; Passover—March 28–29; Pesach—April 3–4; Shavuot—May 17–18; Rosh Hashanah—September 7–8; Yom Kippur—September 16; Sukkot—September 21–22; Simchat Torah—September 28–29; Hanukkah—November 30–December 7.
Chinese New Year—February 12, 2002.